GW01239703

The Foundations of Continuous Time Finance

The International Library of Critical Writings in Financial Economics

Series Editor: Richard Roll
Allstate Professor of Economics
The Anderson School at UCLA, USA

This major series presents by field outstanding selections of the most important articles across the entire spectrum of financial economics – one of the fastest growing areas in business schools and economics departments. Each collection has been prepared by a leading specialist who has written an authoritative introduction to the literature.

1. The Theory of Corporate Finance (Volumes I and II)
   Michael J. Brennan
2. Futures Markets (Volumes I, II and III)
   A.G. Malliaris
3. Market Efficiency: Stock Market Behaviour in Theory and Practice (Volumes I and II)
   Andrew W. Lo
4. Microstructure: The Organization of Trading and Short Term Price Behavior (Volumes I and II)
   Hans R. Stoll
5. The Debt Market (Volumes I, II and III)
   Stephen A. Ross
6. Options Markets (Volumes I, II and III)
   George M. Constantinides and A.G. Malliaris
7. Empirical Corporate Finance (Volumes I, II, III and IV)
   Michael J. Brennan
8. The Foundations of Continuous Time Finance
   Stephen M. Schaefer

Future titles will include:

Behavioral Finance
Harold M. Shefrin

International Securities
George C. Philippatos and Gregory D. Koutmos

Emerging Markets

Asset Pricing Theory and Tests
Robert Grauer

Financial Forecasting

International Capital Markets

Wherever possible, the articles in these volumes have been reproduced as originally published using facsimile reproduction, inclusive of footnotes and pagination to facilitate ease of reference.

For a list of all Edward Elgar published titles visit our site on the World Wide Web at http://www.e-elgar.co.uk

The Foundations of Continuous Time Finance

Edited by

Stephen M. Schaefer

Tokai Bank Professor of Finance,
London Business School, UK

THE INTERNATIONAL LIBRARY OF CRITICAL WRITINGS IN FINANCIAL ECONOMICS

An Elgar Reference Collection
Cheltenham, UK • Northampton, MA, USA

© Stephen M. Schaefer 2001. For copyright of individual articles, please refer to the Acknowledgements.

All rights reserved. No part of this publication may be reproduced, stored in a retrieval system, or transmitted in any form or by any means, electronic, mechanical, photocopying, recording, or otherwise without the prior permission of the publisher.

Published by
Edward Elgar Publishing Limited
Glensanda House
Montpellier Parade
Cheltenham
Glos GL50 1UA
UK

Edward Elgar Publishing, Inc.
136 West Street
Suite 202
Northampton
Massachusetts 01060
USA

A catalogue record for this book is available from the British Library.

Library of Congress Cataloguing in Publication Data

The foundations of continuous time finance / edited by Stephen M. Schaefer.
p. cm. — (The International library of critical writings in financial economics ; 8)
Includes bibliographical references and index.
1. Finance—Mathematical models. 2. Investments—Mathematical models. 3. Portfolio management—Mathematical models. 4. Options (Finance)—Mathematical models. 5. Finance, Public—Mathematical models. I. Schaefer, Stephen M. II. Series.

HG173 .F68 2001
332.6'01'5118—dc21 00–065409

ISBN 1 85898 750 4

Printed and bound in Great Britain by MPG Books Ltd, Bodmin, Cornwall

Contents

Acknowledgements

The editor and publishers wish to thank the authors and the following publishers who have kindly given permission for the use of copyright material.

Academic Press, Inc. for articles: Robert C. Merton (1971), 'Optimum Consumption and Portfolio Rules in a Continuous-Time Model', *Journal of Economic Theory*, **3** (3), September, 373–413; J. Michael Harrison and David M. Kreps (1979), 'Martingales and Arbitrage in Multiperiod Securities Markets', *Journal of Economic Theory*, **20** (3), June, 381–408; John C. Cox and Chi-fu Huang (1989), 'Optimal Consumption and Portfolio Policies when Asset Prices Follow a Diffusion Process', *Journal of Economic Theory*, **49** (1), 33–83.

Applied Probability Trust for article: Hélyette Geman, Nicole El Karoui and Jean-Charles Rochet (1995), 'Changes of Numéraire, Changes of Probability Measure and Option Pricing', *Journal of Applied Probability*, **32**, 443–58.

Blackwell Publishers, Inc. for articles: Fischer Black and John C. Cox (1976), 'Valuing Corporate Securities: Some Effects of Bond Indenture Provisions', *Journal of Finance*, **31** (2), May, 351–67; William Margrabe (1978), 'The Value of an Option to Exchange One Asset for Another', *Journal of Finance*, **33** (1), March, 177–86; M. Barry Goldman, Howard B. Sosin and Mary Ann Gatto (1979), 'Path Dependent Options: "Buy at the Low, Sell at the High"', *Journal of Finance*, **34** (5), December, 1111–127; Farshid Jamshidian (1993), 'Option and Futures Evaluation with Deterministic Volatilities', *Mathematical Finance*, **3** (2), April, 149–59; Hayne E. Leland (1994), 'Corporate Debt Value, Bond Covenants, and Optimal Capital Structure', *Journal of Finance*, **49** (4), September, 1213–252.

Econometric Society for articles: Robert C. Merton (1973), 'An Intertemporal Capital Asset Pricing Model', *Econometrica*, **41** (5), September, 867–87; John C. Cox, Jonathan E. Ingersoll, Jr. and Stephen A. Ross (1985), 'An Intertemporal General Equilibrium Model of Asset Prices', *Econometrica*, **53** (2), March, 363–84; John C. Cox, Jonathan E. Ingersoll, Jr. and Stephen A. Ross (1985), 'A Theory of the Term Structure of Interest Rates', *Econometrica*, **53** (2), March, 385–407; Darrell Duffie and Chi-fu Huang (1985), 'Implementing Arrow-Debreu Equilibria by Continuous Trading of a Few Long-Lived Securities', *Econometrica*, **53** (6), November, 1337–56.

Elsevier Science Ltd for articles: Robert C. Merton (1977), 'On the Pricing of Contingent Claims and the Modigliani-Miller Theorem', *Journal of Financial Economics*, **5** (2), November, 241–9; Richard Roll (1977), 'An Analytic Valuation Formula for Unprotected American Call Options on Stocks with Known Dividends', *Journal of Financial Economics*, **5** (2), November, 251–8; Douglas T. Breeden (1979), 'An Intertemporal Asset Pricing Model with Stochastic Consumption and Investment Opportunities', *Journal of Financial Economics*, **7** (3), September,

265–96; Douglas T. Breeden (1986), 'Consumption, Production, Inflation and Interest Rates: A Synthesis', *Journal of Financial Economics*, **16** (1), May, 3–39; John C. Cox and Chi-fu Huang (1991), 'A Variational Problem Arising in Financial Economics', *Journal of Mathematical Economics*, **20** (5), 465–87.

Institute for Operations Research and the Management Sciences for article: M.H.A. Davis and A.R. Norman (1990), 'Portfolio Selection with Transaction Costs', *Mathematics of Operations Research*, **15** (4), November, 676–713.

MIT Press Journals for article: Robert C. Merton (1969), 'Lifetime Portfolio Selection Under Uncertainty: The Continuous-Time Case', *Review of Economics and Statistics*, **51** (3), August, 247–57.

Oxford University Press for article: Hua He and Hayne Leland (1993), 'On Equilibrium Asset Price Processes', *Review of Financial Studies*, **6** (3), 593–617.

Prentice-Hall, Inc. for excerpt: Robert C. Merton (1982), 'On the Mathematics and Economics Assumptions of Continuous-Time Models', in William F. Sharpe and Cathryn M. Cootner (eds), *Financial Economics: Essays in Honor of Paul Cootner*, 19–51.

Review of Economic Studies Ltd for article: Lucien Foldes (1978), 'Optimal Saving and Risk in Continuous Time', *Review of Economic Studies*, **45** (1), February, 39–65.

University of Chicago Press for articles: J. Michael Harrison, Richard Pitbladdo and Stephen M. Schaefer (1984), 'Continuous Price Processes in Frictionless Markets Have Infinite Variation', *Journal of Business*, **57** (3), July, 353–65; Michael J. Brennan and Eduardo S. Schwartz (1985), 'Evaluating Natural Resource Investments', *Journal of Business*, **58** (2), April, 135–57.

Every effort has been made to trace all the copyright holders but if any have been inadvertently overlooked the publishers will be pleased to make the necessary arrangement at the first opportunity.

In addition the publishers wish to thank the Library of the London School of Economics and Political Science, the Marshall Library of Economics, Cambridge University, B & N Microfilm, London and the Library of Indiana University at Bloomington, USA for their assistance in obtaining these articles.

Foreword

Continuous-time methods have played a major role in twentieth-century science, where they are the foundations of theories ranging from acoustics to zymosis. As Professor Schaefer notes in his introduction, one of their earliest applications was in finance, by Bachelier in 1900. There was, however, a rather long hiatus in finance until they were resurrected in the 1970s by Merton and others working on financial derivatives.

Indeed, as Schaefer emphasizes, it seems doubtful that the derivatives market could have progressed to its current state of refinement without continuous-time mathematics. He states, ". . . particularly in the context of derivative pricing, the distinction between discrete and continuous trading opportunities is critical." Continuous trading allows one to form a hypothetically perfect replicating hedge portfolio for a derivative. Combining the hedge portfolio with the derivative in the proper proportions produces a riskless investment position and, more important, a differential equation whose solution is the derivative's value.

This was certainly not obvious to scholars before the early 1970s, which explains why the Nobel Committee properly honored Merton and Scholes for their discoveries.

Continuous-time methods are now applied to virtually all areas of finance, but aside from derivatives they have had the greatest influence on intertemporal portfolio selection. They are commonly used also in theories of the term structure of interest rates and, more recently, in capital budgeting.

Professor Schaefer has selected twenty-five of the most influential continuous-time papers and divided them into five subject categories. There are four papers on the continuous-time model in finance. There are six papers on intertemporal portfolio selection. Five papers have been included under the category of equilibrium models. Six papers are about derivative pricing and there are four papers in the category of term structure and other applications.

Moreover, the first section contains two papers on the mathematical fundamentals of continuous-time. These are required reading for the novice for they help explain certain anti-intuitive attributes of continuous processes such as "infinite variation." Infinite variation implies that a continuous trader would run up an infinite bill for trading costs, which makes it obvious that these models cannot be taken literally. They exist only in the idealized imagination, but that suffices to make them highly useful constructs. As is often the case in science, the elegance and simplicity of abstract theory provides insight that would not be perceived in the blizzard of reality.

Richard Roll

Foreword

Introduction[1]

Stephen M. Schaefer
Tokai Bank Professor of Finance, London Business School

1. Introduction to the Collection

In the standard continuous-time framework agents observe prices and have the opportunity to make decisions, for example on portfolio composition, at each point in time. This is to be contrasted with a discrete-time framework where agents are assumed to be able to observe prices and make decisions only at discrete points in time, e.g., every day, every week or, more generally, at times $t_1, t_2, t_3 \ldots$ etc. In itself this distinction may seem rather fine and, perhaps, of no great importance; in fact, it often changes things a great deal.

The use of continuous-time methods has turned out to be critical to some of the most important developments in financial economics and, in particular, to two major areas: (i) the dynamic analysis of portfolio choice and equilibrium asset pricing and (ii) derivative pricing. The number of important papers that use these methods is very large and many of those that could not be accommodated here are contained in companion volumes in this series, particularly those devoted to futures, options and bonds.[2] The aim of this volume is to bring together first, the key papers that have shaped those areas where continuous-time methods have had a decisive influence, and second, the papers which illustrate the main methodological innovations of the approach.

At the risk of over-simplifying, there are two main aspects to the contribution of continuous-time methods to financial economics. First, in intertemporal portfolio selection and asset pricing, it turns out that many results are either much more easily obtained, or emerge in a simpler and more elegant form, in a continuous-time rather than a discrete-time setting. Second, and more profoundly, in the theory of derivative pricing developed by Black and Scholes (1973) and Merton (1973), continuous trading opportunities result in a form of market completeness that, under certain conditions, allows the relation between assets prices – e.g., an option and the underlying stock – to be derived using no-arbitrage arguments alone. Corresponding results in a discrete-time setting arise only when prices follow certain restrictive, and rather unrealistic, processes.

Uncertainty, or risk, is an essential ingredient of the majority of interesting problems in modern finance and this is certainly true of the main areas where continuous-time methods have been used. The problem of choosing a portfolio or pricing an option when future asset prices are known precisely is neither realistic nor very interesting. Therefore, in the continuous-time framework, when agents make their decisions continuously, prices must be modeled in such a way that some uncertainty about even the immediate future is preserved. The development of a stochastic model of prices that has these features has been key to many of the most important results.

The first such model was developed by Bachelier (1900) in an extraordinary PhD thesis at the Sorbonne in Paris. Bachelier was the first to develop the mathematics of the process that later became known as Brownian motion and on which much of modern finance depends. At an intuitive level, Brownian motion can be considered as the continuous-time limit of a discrete-time random walk, a process whose increments have zero mean and are independently and identically distributed over time:

$$\begin{aligned} x_{t+1} &= x_t + \tilde{u}_{t+1}, \\ Var(\tilde{u}_{t+1}) &= \sigma^2, \\ E(x_{t+k} - x_t) &= 0, \\ Var(x_{t+k} - x_t) &= k\sigma^2. \end{aligned} \tag{1}$$

In (1) x_t is the level of the random walk at time t and $\tilde{u}_{t+1}$ is an *iid* random variate with zero mean and variance σ^2.

Brownian motion itself is a process in continuous-time that has properties analogous to those described in equation (1) and, in addition, has increments that are normally distributed over any period. A *standard Brownian motion*, denoted $B(t)$, is a Brownian motion scaled to have a variance of one per unit time. Thus, denoting the increase in the value of $B(t)$ across an interval of length dt as dB, a standard Brownian motion satisfies:

$$\begin{aligned} E(dB) &= 0, \\ E(dB^2) &= dt, \\ E(B_{t+s} - B_t) &= 0, \\ Var(B_{t+s} - B_t) &= s. \end{aligned} \tag{2}$$

Bachelier proposed Brownian motion itself as a model of stock prices but this has the unattractive feature the price may become negative. Fortunately, this problem is relatively easily solved by using Brownian motion to model the innovation in *proportional*, rather than *arithmetic*, price changes.[3]

$$\frac{dP}{P} = \mu_p dt + \sigma_p dB. \tag{3}$$

In (3) P represents an asset price, μ_p and σ_p are, respectively, the expected value and local standard deviation of the asset's rate of return and, as before, dB represents an increment of standard Brownian motion. This process – *geometric* Brownian motion – is one of the cornerstones of continuous-time finance. It represents a simple and yet plausible model of the evolution of asset prices and is a standard assumption in analyses of portfolio selection, asset pricing and derivative pricing.

It is important to understand clearly the time sequence of information arrival, portfolio formation and change in price in the continuous-time model, and it is useful briefly to discuss these issues by analogy with the discrete-time counterpart to equation (3):

$$\frac{P_{t+\Delta t} - P_t}{P_t} = m_p \Delta t + s_p \tilde{u}_{t+1}. \tag{4}$$

In equation (4) m_p and s_p are the mean and standard deviation of the asset's rate of return over the time interval, Δt and $\tilde{u}_{t+1}$ is as defined above. In the discrete-time case, if an agent chooses a portfolio at time t, he can base his choice only on the information available at that time. This includes the history of prices up to and including P_t itself but, self evidently, it does not include $P_{t+\Delta t}$, the price at the *end* of the period for which we are currently making a decision. We would all like to decide which stocks to hold on Tuesday based on what prices *will actually be* on Wednesday but, of course, this is not possible.

This natural restriction, that when prices evolve over an interval of time decisions can be based only on prices up to the beginning of that interval and not on prices at the end, naturally applies in the continuous-time case also and so, at least for these purposes, the discrete-time process (4) provides entirely reliable intuition on how the continuous-time model works.

In much of the analysis of portfolio selection and equilibrium asset pricing the analogy between the discrete and continuous-time cases works very well. Here the distinctive contribution of the continuous-time treatment is often one of tractability: results are obtained more easily and in a more elegant form. In terms of economics, however, the analysis of portfolio selection and equilibrium asset pricing in the discrete and the continuous cases are largely the same.

However, the similarity between the two cases does not extend so easily to derivative pricing. Here, when agents have the opportunity to trade more and more frequently and prices are Brownian in character, e.g., when they are described by equation (3), the market becomes, in the limiting case of continuous trading, *complete*. Completeness, in this context, means that essentially all claims, e.g., call and put options, on an asset may be *replicated* by a trading strategy that combines the asset with borrowing or lending. The possibility of replication means that, to avoid the opportunity for pure arbitrage, the price of these claims must be equal to the cost of the replicating portfolio. If prices follow geometric Brownian motion but agents cannot trade continuously such replication is infeasible. Thus, particularly in the context of derivative pricing, the distinction between discrete and continuous trading opportunities is critical.

The papers selected for this volume fall into two categories. The first includes those that either have made major contributions to the development of the approach or provide a particularly clear and insightful exposition of an area. The second category includes those papers that illustrate key application areas.

The book is divided into five parts each containing between four and six papers. Part I deals with foundational issues of the continuous-time model: the relation between continuous-time and discrete-time models, properties of the continuous-time price process and the analysis of replicating trading strategies.

Part II deals with the important problem of how agents allocate their resources over time between saving and consumption and how they choose their portfolios. The papers in Part III then analyze the pricing implications of the portfolio models of the previous section. This section includes the seminal papers on the Intertemporal Capital Asset Pricing Model (ICAPM) and the Consumption Capital Asset Pricing Model (CCAPM). Parts IV and V are devoted to contingent claims applications of the continuous-time model. Part IV deals with option pricing and Part V with other applications including the term structure of interest rates, credit risky debt and real options. The papers within each section are in chronological order unless the relation between the papers suggests otherwise.

2. The Continuous-time Model in Finance

The phrase "the continuous-time model" refers to a setting in which time is measured along the continuum, prices are defined at each point in time and where, in most cases, agents are free to trade at each point in time. This setting provides the foundation for the analysis in substantially all of the papers in this volume and the four papers in Part I provide important insights into the properties of this model.

The first two papers are concerned with the properties of the prices modeled as functions of Brownian motion.[4] **Merton (1982)**[5] provides a masterly introduction to the continuous-time model assuming nothing more than familiarity with the standard tools of probability and elementary calculus. Merton's paper is particularly helpful since it develops the continuous-time case as the limit of a discrete-time process and thus allows the simple intuition of the latter to be maintained. Using the same tools he also develops Itô's lemma and demonstrates the continuity of Brownian price paths.

An important property of Brownian motion is that, although continuous, it has *infinite variation*. Intuitively, what this means is that if we plot Brownian motion against time, the position of the process (as measured on the "*y*" axis) travels an infinite distance in any finite time interval. This property is important for a number of reasons. For example, in models of portfolio selection and derivative pricing this property is inherited by variables other than asset prices, such as the quantity held of different assets. Continuous-time models therefore often have the disturbing feature that they imply an infinite volume of trading in any finite period.

Harrison, Pitbladdo and Schaefer (1984) shed light on the relation between two important properties of Brownian motion: infinite variation and path continuity. In their paper they show that, in a frictionless market, any model of prices in which prices are continuous must have infinite variation to avoid arbitrage.[6] The intuition is that, without infinite variation, prices are "too smooth"; as a result it becomes possible to exploit short-term "trends" in the data and so make arbitrage profits. To eliminate the possibility of arbitrage we could turn to models in which prices experience "jumps" and price paths are therefore no longer continuous.[7] Within the class of price processes with continuous sample paths, however, only those with infinite variation are viable and this effectively limits the choice to Brownian motion and its close relations.

The key discovery in the Black-Scholes-Merton [BSM] model of derivative pricing[8] was that the value of a broad class of contracts, such as options, may be replicated with dynamically managed portfolios containing the asset on which the option was written and riskless borrowing or lending. The price of an option could therefore be calculated as the cost of the replicating portfolio; if this were not the case arbitrage profits could be made either by buying the option and selling the replicating portfolio or the reverse.

Valuation through replication was, in itself, not new; after all the familiar present value formula for riskless cash flows is nothing more than the cost of replicating the cash flows in the bond market. The same technique – valuation through replication – had also previously been applied to risky assets, for example to the valuation of forward contracts and to the valuation of levered equity in the famous Modigliani and Miller (1958) paper on capital structure. What was revolutionary in the BSM approach was the use of replication to value assets where the relation between the cash flows on one asset (the "derivative") and the price of the other (the underlying "stock") was *non-linear*. In all previous applications of the replication approach the relation between these two quantities had been linear and this had the important simplifying consequence that the composition of the replicating portfolio remained the same through time and was easy to compute. In the BSM model, the value of the option – at maturity, for example – is a nonlinear function of the price of the underlying stock and this means the option value cannot be replicated with a portfolio that stays constant over time and contains just the underlying stock and riskless borrowing or lending. In fact, in the BSM model, replication is achieved using a dynamic portfolio strategy in which the quantity of the stock held is a function of the stock price at that time.

The idea that the ability to trade a long-lived asset increases the variety of achievable cash flow patterns goes back at least to Arrow (1952). But BSM made this idea much more precise and showed that, for at least some types of assets, exact replication could be achieved.

In a famous paper **Harrison and Kreps (1979)** set out to identify exactly which types of contingent claims may be replicated (or are *spanned*) in a given market. In a discrete-time, discrete-state model, it is well known, and simple to show, that the absence of arbitrage is equivalent to (a) the existence of a vector of state-prices which values the cash flows on each asset at its market price or, equivalently, (b) the existence of a risk-neutral probability distribution under which the current price is equal to the expectation of the future price discounted at the riskless interest rate. The latter result says that, under this probability distribution, (suitably scaled) prices follow a martingale. In the discrete-time case if, in addition, the vector of state prices (or risk-neutral probabilities) is unique, then the market is complete. An important contribution of Harrison and Kreps's paper is to demonstrate that exactly equivalent conditions also hold in the continuous-time, continuous-space model. Their paper also introduces some language – *self-financing portfolios*, *simple trading strategies*, *equivalent martingale measure* etc. – which has become standard for analyses in this area and demonstrates the importance of martingale methods in the analysis of contingent claims.

Harrison and Kreps's results imply that the market in the Brownian continuous-time model is complete in the sense that (almost) all claims can be priced by no-arbitrage. They also show that this condition – again, analogous to the discrete-time case – is equivalent to the existence of a unique probability measure under which prices follow a martingale.

Duffie and Huang (1985) analyze these issues further and demonstrate the role of trading strategies in long-lived securities in achieving equilibrium. Specifically, they show that an Arrow-Debreu equilibrium, which might typically require the existence of an infinite number of securities, may be achieved through trading a small number of securities; in fact, just two in an example using Brownian motion.

3. Intertemporal Portfolio Selection

The theory of portfolio selection, developed by Markowitz (1952, 1959), deals with the allocation of wealth over a number of risky assets. The original theory was static in the sense that it dealt just with two periods: the current period, when the portfolio allocation is made, and one future period when the proceeds from the portfolio are consumed. It did not address either how agents should divide their wealth between consumption and investment or how the task of portfolio selection might change when agents know they will have the opportunity to rebalance their portfolios in the future. Extending portfolio selection to a dynamic setting, allowing agents to decide at each point in time both how much to save and how to allocate those savings over risky assets was, at the end of the 1960s, an unsolved problem of great importance.

The two papers by **Merton (1969, 1971)** provide a thorough solution to this problem. **Merton (1969)** is the first treatment of the consumption–portfolio investment problem in continuous-time and deals primarily with the two-asset case. Under the assumption of constant relative or constant absolute risk aversion, the paper demonstrates the use of dynamic programming in solving for optimal saving and portfolio allocation decisions. **Merton (1971)** extends the analysis to more general utility functions and, under the assumption that prices follow geometric Brownian motion, proves a two-fund separation theorem that is analogous to the familiar result in the two-period case. Merton also derives the optimal consumption and portfolio rules for the HARA class of utility functions.[9]

The framework pioneered by Merton in these papers set the stage for at least a generation of researchers working on dynamic portfolio theory and asset pricing. Evidence of Merton's influence is clearly seen in many important papers that have followed. See, for example, **Cox and Huang (1989)**, **Breeden (1979)** and **Cox, Ingersoll and Ross (1985a)** in this volume.

Merton uses dynamic stochastic programming to obtain solutions to the dynamic portfolio problems and, here, market completeness – critical to the analysis of contingent claims – plays essentially no role. Thus, in Merton's analysis, agents attempt to maximize the expected value of lifetime consumption and final bequest subject to an intertemporal budget constraint in which the link between wealth at two points in time is determined by the rate of consumption, the rates of return on assets and the portfolio allocation. In a complete market, however, we may consider that a claim on consumption at any date t and in each state of the world is traded. This means that an agent may directly choose her optimal consumption plan subject to a constraint that the value (or cost) of the plan, computed using the implicit Arrow-Debreu prices, does not exceed the agent's time zero resources. This is the approach introduced by **Cox and Huang (1989, 1991)** and it has the advantage of converting what is a dynamic control problem into a static problem where the agent optimizes consumption over all possible states. The Cox-Huang approach also has the significant advantage over dynamic programming that it is much easier to include non-negativity constraints on consumption and wealth.

Following the seminal paper by **Harrison and Kreps (1979)** the use of martingale methods in the analysis of derivative pricing has become widespread. Their application to dynamic consumption–investment problems, with one notable exception, came later and starts with **Cox and Huang (1989, 1991)** and Karatzas, Lehoczky and Shreve (1987). The "notable exception" is **Foldes (1978)**, a paper that predates even **Harrison and Kreps (1979)**. Foldes tackles the single asset case and characterizes the optimal consumption–investment plan in terms of martingale conditions.

To this point all the papers in this section assume that markets are frictionless in the sense that assets may be bought and sold without cost. The problem of including transaction costs in dynamic portfolio theory is an important one and has been studied by a number of scholars over the years. The problem is significant, not least because of the infinite variation property of Brownian motion.[10] Apart from the fact that portfolio policies derived in the frictionless model might in any case be sub-optimal in the presence of transaction costs, infinite variation means that such policies will often give rise to infinite transaction costs in the presence of a (finite) proportional transaction cost.

Davis and Norman (1990) study optimal portfolio policy in the presence of proportional costs. The paper provides a particularly thorough treatment of a problem which sounds much simpler than it is: that of solving for optimal consumption and investment in a market with one risky and one riskless asset where transaction costs are proportional to the quantity traded.

4. Equilibrium Models

Given his pioneering role in the development of continuous-time portfolio selection, it is no surprise to find that the seminal contribution in intertemporal capital asset pricing is, once again, provided by **Merton (1973)**. Apart from the fact that agents plan their consumption–investment decisions over time, the main difference between the problem addressed by this paper and the classical (Markowitz) portfolio problem is that here the opportunity set – i.e., asset expected returns and risks – evolves over time stochastically. As a result, agents' asset demand functions are not simply mean-variance efficient portfolios, as in the static problem, but include a component which hedges their expected lifetime utility against unfavorable changes in the opportunity set.

In Merton's model the equilibrium risk premium is expressed as the sum of a number of terms, each of which is associated with a state variable. **Breeden (1979)**, in a brilliant re-interpretation of Merton's model, points out that all the components of the risk premium in Merton's model may be collapsed into one term that is proportional to the covariance between the asset's rate of return and aggregate consumption. With hindsight, this remarkable result is also highly intuitive. In general – and in Merton's model in particular – the risk premium on an asset is proportional to the covariance between its rate of return and the marginal utility of wealth, as measured by the first derivative of the indirect utility function. With time additive preferences, the latter is simply equal to the marginal utility of consumption and, using Itô's lemma, it is easily shown that the covariance between asset returns and the marginal utility of consumption is proportional to the covariance of returns with consumption itself.

While the economy studied in **Cox, Ingersoll and Ross (1985a)** [CIRa] is similar to that described in **Merton (1973)** and **Breeden (1979)**, the paper has a number of important distinguishing features. First, in Merton/Breeden the distinction between a "firm" and an "asset" is slight, while in CIRa a stochastic production possibilities frontier is explicitly modeled and firms make optimal investment decisions. Second, in their Theorem 3 CIRa derive a "fundamental valuation equation", satisfied by all contingent claims in the economy. This equation is, in effect, the Black-Scholes-Merton valuation equation for the case where the underlying state variables are not asset prices. In this equation the drift term associated with each state variable must be adjusted by the corresponding risk premium and CIRa are able to do this using their results on equilibrium risk premia.

In a companion paper, included in Part V, **Cox, Ingersoll and Ross (1985b)**, derive the implications of their model for the term structure of interest rates. This paper includes the derivation of the now famous "CIR" term structure model. Using a framework that is similar but in some respects more general than **Cox, Ingersoll and Ross (1985a)**, **Breeden (1986)** also focuses on the term structure and, in particular, on the interaction between production and asset prices. While exploiting the analytical tractability of the continuous-time setting, Breeden's paper is also notable for the fact that the first part of the paper is conducted in discrete time. This provides a useful opportunity to study the similarities and differences between the continuous and discrete-time approaches.

5. Derivative Pricing

Derivative pricing has turned out possibly to be an even more fruitful area for the continuous-time framework than dynamic portfolio theory and equilibrium asset pricing. The literature on this topic is simply enormous.[11] The small number of papers in this section could not, and are not intended to cover the field. Instead, the papers here have been chosen because they represent key developments in methodology or entirely new areas of application.

The single most important achievement of the BSM approach was to show that, under their assumptions, a wide variety of contingent claims can be replicated. To put the point in a slightly different way, consider a market where, in addition to riskless borrowing and lending, an option (say) and the underlying stock are traded. Then, in the BSM framework, one of the assets or riskless borrowing/lending is *redundant* in the sense that it may be replicated using the other two.

In their original paper, Black and Scholes (1973) combine an option with the underlying asset to replicate the riskless asset. This has the drawback that it involves assuming some properties of the relation between the option price, the underlying asset and time to maturity. These assumptions turn out to be correct but the alternative proof given by **Merton (1977)** manages to finesse this problem. Instead of using the option as part of the portfolio that replicates riskless lending, Merton combines the underlying stock and riskless borrowing or lending to replicate the option. It is a very elegant – "look no hands" – solution to the problem.

Closed-form solutions, such as the formulae for European calls and puts given by Black and Scholes (1973), are generally not available for American options which give the holder the right to exercise before maturity. The American call option on a dividend paying stock proves to be an exception for which **Roll (1977)** derives a closed-form solution. Roll points out that, on the ex-dividend date, the value of the option is that of a call option written on a call option, a so-called *compound option*. Using this insight and drawing on earlier work by Geske (1976), Roll derives a formula for the option value.

An important generalization of conventional options is analysed in **Margrabe (1978)**. This paper deals with the value of a contract in which the holder receives the underlying asset in exchange for one unit of another *risky* asset, rather than a fixed sum, as in the case of a conventional call.[12] Margrabe's insight was to realize that, by changing the numeraire and expressing cash flows in terms of the price of the asset that is given up, this contract and the standard call option become isomorphic. This same idea has been formalized and extended by others (for example, **Geman, El Karoui and Rochet (1995)**) and has proved a powerful method for simplifying a number of apparently complicated valuation problems.

The option to exchange one asset for another, considered by **Margrabe (1978)**, represents one important generalization of the BSM framework to derivatives other than conventional puts and calls. Over the years a wide range of ever more imaginative *exotic* options has been developed and analyzed. Among the first were *lookback options* that are the subject of the paper by **Goldman, Sosin and Gatto (1979)**. The holder of a lookback call, for example, has the right to buy the underlying asset at the lowest price the stock achieves over the period of the contract; a lookback put gives the right to sell at the maximum price. Goldman, Sosin and Gatto's key insight in valuing a lookback option is that, even though the option value at some time between inception and maturity depends on the minimum or maximum price achieved so far, this quantity is itself locally deterministic. Consequently the replicating portfolio does not have to hedge local changes in the minimum or maximum price.

The range of replicable contracts is undoubtedly much wider than imagined in the earliest days of option pricing theory and, in recent years, a great deal of effort has been devoted to the analysis of contracts where interest rate uncertainty is important. **Jamshidian (1993)** makes an important contribution to this field and analyses a range of option contracts where the underlying "asset" is a forward or futures contract. His paper shows that closed form solutions may often be obtained when certain covariances – e.g., between a futures price and the price of a zero coupon bond – are deterministic.

The concept of risk-neutral valuation, described briefly in Section 2, has proved to be one of the most fruitful in the whole of the literature on derivative pricing. Introduced in the early work of Cox and Ross (1976a, 1976b) it was refined by **Harrison and Kreps (1979)** who showed that it could be interpreted as the result of using as a numeraire the value of a continuously compounded money-market account. The relation between change of probability measure and change of numeraire is important and this is the focus of the paper by **Geman, El Karoui and Rochet (1995)** who show that a wide range of option pricing problems may be solved through a judicious choice of numeraire.

6. Term Structure and Other Applications

Writing in 1973, Merton could say: "...options are specialized and relatively unimportant financial securities...".[13] At the time this was certainly an accurate statement and the important applications of the newly developed BSM theory appeared to lie elsewhere. In their 1973 paper, Black and Scholes pointed out the option characteristics that are present in the equity and debt securities of firms with limited liability and, at the time, this seemed to be the area in which option pricing theory would have the greatest impact.

The scale of the development of both exchange traded and over-the-counter (OTC) options markets which has taken place in the intervening years was at the time entirely unforeseen. Yet, with the benefit of hindsight, it is clearly in these markets that the BSM approach has been applied to the greatest effect. The application of the theory to the valuation of corporate liabilities and, in particular, to corporate debt, has taken much longer. There are number of reasons for this but one is that the contractual provisions of corporate debt, in practice, are relatively complicated; much more complicated than simple call and put options.

Black and Cox (1976) make an important and early contribution to this area in their analysis of the valuation of corporate debt in the presence of bond indentures. Their starting point is the original Black and Scholes (1973) paper which pointed out that, when a firm has a single zero-coupon bond outstanding, the value of the bond is the value of a corresponding riskless bond minus the value of a put on the assets of the firm. The Black and Scholes analysis, however, assumes that the lenders have no rights to intervene before the maturity of the bond even when the value of the firm falls to a very low level. In contrast, Black and Cox introduce the idea of a "reorganization boundary" – defined in terms of the value of the firm – where the lenders assume greater control rights. This idea has been taken up again in recent years in papers such as Longstaff and Schwartz (1995) and Saa-Requejo and Santa-Clara (1997).

Leland (1994) uses a similar framework to analyze the relation between the firm's optimal capital structure decision and the value of its debt. Under the assumption that the firm's debt is perpetual, Leland is able to derive a closed form solution for the value of the debt. One of the important contributions of Leland's paper is to model the decision by shareholders to declare bankruptcy. In the model equity holders have an incentive to issue debt because they capture the benefits of the tax deductibility of interest. On the other hand, because it is assumed that equity holders have to put their hands in their own pockets to pay the coupons on the debt, there is a point where the value of the firm is so low that avoiding default by continuing to pay the coupon is no longer worthwhile.

The continuous time framework has also contributed in a very major way to the development of the theory of term structure. The three companion volumes on *The Debt Market*[14] provide an excellent picture of the current state of development of term structure theory and related areas; **Cox, Ingersoll and Ross (1985b)** [CIRb] is an excellent example of this work.

CIRb is a specialization of their companion paper CIRa in Part III of this volume. The paper deals with the case where there is a single state variable, Y, driving production possibilities and where the dynamics of the state variable are such that dY has a drift which is linear in Y and a variance which is proportional to Y. These assumptions are sufficient to identify the dynamics of the short-term interest rate, the risk premium associated with the state variable and, from these, the prices of both bonds and bond options.

The final paper in this section is devoted to the traditional area of capital budgeting. The problem considered in **Brennan and Schwartz (1985)** is that of valuing natural resource investments but, as they point out, the potential area of application for their approach is much broader. A famous proposition of Hotelling (1931) states that the value of a gold mine is equal to the quantity of gold in the ground, evaluated at the current spot price, minus the present value of the extraction costs.[15] However, when the future gold price is uncertain this value is likely to be an under-estimate if the owners of the goldmine have the opportunity to abandon the mine in the event that the spot gold price in the future becomes sufficiently low. In effect the mine represents an *option* to extract the gold and the difference in valuation, between approaches of Hotelling and Brennan and Schwartz, reflects the value of the flexibility that the owners have over future operations. The importance of such "real options" has become increasingly widely recognized over the years, not only in the context of the extraction of natural resources but in any circumstances where future cash flows are subject to substantial uncertainty and where the owners have some flexibility in terms of their future management. Common examples are the possibilities of abandoning a project or making follow-on investments.

7. Conclusion

There is no doubt that the contribution of continuous-time methods to the development of financial economics has been immense. Without this apparatus it is difficult to see how the great progress in dynamic consumption–investment theory, inter-temporal asset pricing and derivative pricing could have been achieved. At the same time, while admitting that these methods do involve some technical apparatus, the "barriers to entry" for those new to the field have been lowered with the publication of a number of new and excellent textbooks.[16] Interested readers should also consult the outstanding recent survey article by Sundaresan (2000).

The papers included in this volume represent some of the high points of financial economics. Tyros and experts alike will find wisdom, insight and beauty in the pages that follow.

Notes

1. I am grateful to Andrea Berardi and Rajiv Guha for helpful comments. The idiosyncrasies and errors are my own.
2. See Malliaris (1997), Constantinides and Malliaris (forthcoming) and Ross (2000).
3. Geometric Brownian motion was introduced by Samuelson (1965).
4. For a description of Brownian motion and related processes see, e.g., Karatzas and Shreve (1991).
5. References to papers contained in this volume are given in **boldface**.
6. See Section 3 for the consequences of infinite variation for transactions costs.
7. See, e.g., Merton (1976), Amin (1993), Bates (1996).
8. Black and Scholes (1973) and Merton (1973). Scholes and Merton shared the Nobel Prize in economics for their work on derivative pricing in 1997. Fischer Black, who would undoubtedly have shared the prize had he lived, died in 1995.
9. These are utility functions displaying hyperbolic absolute risk aversion (HARA) or, more simply, linear risk tolerance.
10. See Part II.
11. See, for example, the three-volume work *Options Markets* in this series, Constantinides and Malliaris (forthcoming).
12. This is Margrabe's generalization for a call; the terms for a put are exactly parallel.
13. Merton (1973), p. 141.
14. Stephen Ross (2000).
15. Gold is a useful example because it is also a "financial asset" in the sense that it has a convenience yield of almost zero.
16. See, e.g., Baxter and Rennie (1996), and Björk (1998), Duffie (1996), Duffie (1988), Merton (1990) and Neftci (1996).

References

Amin, Kaushik (1993), 'Jump Diffusion Option Valuation in Discrete Time', *Journal of Finance*, **48**, 1833–63.

Arrow, K. (1952), 'Le rôle des valeurs boursières pour la repartition la meilleure des risques', *Econometrie*, Colloques Internationale du Centre National de la Recherche Scientifique, **40**, 41–8; translated in *Review of Economic Studies*, **31** (1964), 91–6.

Bachelier, L. (1900), 'Theorie de la speculation', *Ann. Sci Ecole Norm Sup.*, **17**, 21–86.

Bates, David (1996), 'Jumps and Stochastic Volatility: Exchange Rate Processes Implicit in Deutche Mark Options', *Review of Financial Studies*, **9**, 69–107.

Baxter, M.W. and A.J.O. Rennie (1996), *Financial Calculus*, Cambridge: Cambridge University Press.

Black, Fischer and Myron Scholes (1973), 'The Pricing of Options and Corporate Liabilities', *Journal of Political Economy*, **81**, 637–54.

Björk, Tomas (1998), *Arbitrage Theory in Continuous Time*, Oxford: Oxford University Press.

Constantinides, George M. and A.G. Malliaris (forthcoming), *Options Markets*, The International Library of Critical Writings in Financial Economics, Cheltenham, UK and Northampton, MA, USA: Edward Elgar.

Cox, John C. and Stephen A. Ross (1976a), 'A Survey of Some New Results in Financial Options Pricing Theory', *Journal of Finance*, **31**, 382–402.

Cox, John C. and Stephen A. Ross (1976b), 'The Valuation of Options for Alternative Stochastic Processes', *Journal of Financial Economics*, **3**, 145–66.

Duffie, Darrell (1988), 'Securities Markets: Stochastic Models', Boston: Academic Press.

Duffie, Darrell (1996), *Dynamic Asset Pricing Theory*, Princeton, New Jersey: Princeton University Press.

Geske, R. (1976), The Valuation of Compound Options, Working Paper (University of California, Berkeley, CA). Later published as 'The Valuation of Compound Options', *Journal of Financial Economics*, **7** (1979), 63–81.

Hotelling, Harold (1931), 'The Economics of Exhaustible Resources', *Journal of Political Economy*, **39** (April), 137–75.

Karatzas, Ioannis and Steve E. Shreve (1991), *Brownian Motion and Stochastic Calculus*, Second Edition, Graduate Texts in Mathematics, 113, New York, Heidelberg & Berlin: Springer Verlag.

Karatzas, Ioannis, J.P. Lehoczky and S.E. Shreve (1987), 'Optimal Portfolio and Consumption Decisions for a Small Investor on a Finite Horizon', *SIAM Journal of Control and Optimization*, **25**, 1157–86.

Longstaff, Francis and Eduardo Schwartz (1995), 'A Simple Approach to Valuing Risky Fixed and Floating Rate Debt', *Journal of Finance*, **50**, 789–819.

Malliaris, A.G. (1997), *Futures Markets*, The International Library of Critical Writings in Financial Economics, Cheltenham, UK and Northampton, MA, USA: Edward Elgar

Markowitz, Harry (1952), 'Portfolio Selection', *Journal of Finance*, **7**, 77–91.

Markowitz, Harry (1959), *Portfolio Selection: Efficient Diversification of Investment*, New York: John Wiley and Sons.

Merton, Robert C. (1973), 'Theory of Rational Option Pricing', *Bell Journal of Economics*, **4**, 141–83.

Merton, Robert C. (1976), 'Option Pricing when Underlying Stock Returns are Discontinuous', *Journal of Financial Economics*, **3**, 125–44.

Merton, Robert C. (1990), *Continuous-Time Finance*, Oxford: Basil Blackwell.

Modigliani, Franco and Merton H. Miller (1958), 'The Cost of Capital, Corporation Finance and the Theory of Investment', *American Economic Review*, **48**, 261–97.

Neftci, Salih N. (1996), *Mathematics of Financial Derivatives*, New York: Academic Press.

Ross, Stephen A. (2000), *The Debt Market*, The International Library of Critical Writings in Financial Economics, Cheltenham, UK and Northampton, MA, USA: Edward Elgar.

Saa-Requejo, J. and P. Santa-Clara (1997), 'Bond Pricing with Default Risk', Working Paper, UCLA.

Samuelson, P.A. (1965), 'Rational Theory of Warrant Pricing', *Industrial Management Review*, **6** (Spring), 13–31.

Sundaresan, Suresh M. (2000), 'Continuous-Time Methods in Finance: A Review and an Assessment', *Journal of Finance*, **55** (4).

Part I
The Continuous Time Model in Finance

[1]

ON THE MATHEMATICS AND ECONOMICS ASSUMPTIONS OF CONTINUOUS-TIME MODELS

ROBERT C. MERTON*
Massachusetts Institute of Technology

I. INTRODUCTION

The mathematical tools required for the formal manipulations used in continuous-time uncertainty analysis are somewhat specialized and, therefore, may not be familiar. For example, the sample paths for stochastic variables generated by diffusion processes, while continuous, are almost nowhere differentiable in the usual sense; therefore, a more general type of differential equation is required to express the dynamics of such processes. While there is substantial mathematic literature on these generalized stochastic equations,[1] the derivations, although elegant, are often cryptic and difficult to follow. Moreover, these derivations provide little insight into the relationships between the formal mathematical assumptions and the corresponding economic assumptions. This paper attempts to bridge the gap by using only elementary probability theory and the calculus to derive the basic theorems required for continuous-time analysis and, as part of the derivations, to make explicit the economic assumptions implicitly

**Aid from the National Science Foundation is gratefully acknowledged.*

[1]See Arnold (1974), Cox and Miller (1968), Itô and McKean (1964), McKean (1969), and McShane (1974) for the general mathematics associated with diffusion processes and stochastic differential equations. Kushner (1967) presents the optimal control and stability analysis for dynamics described by these processes.

imbedded in the mathematical assumptions. The latter is especially important because the way in which the economic assumptions are frequently stated in the substantive economics literature can make them appear to be more restrictive than they really are. While the general approach is to keep the assumptions as weak as possible, assumptions which are more restrictive than necessary are made in those places where the "trade-off" between the losses in generality and the reduction in mathematical complexity appears to be favorable. To motivate the study of continuous-time analysis, we begin with a brief review of the role that it has played in the development of financial economics during the last decade.

The substantive contributions of continuous-time analysis to financial economic theory are discussed at length in an earlier paper where special emphasis was placed on the contributions to the theories of intertemporal portfolio selection and the pricing of corporate liabilities.[2] Therefore, only the most cryptic description of these contributions is made here. By assuming that trading takes place continuously in time and that the underlying stochastic variables follow diffusion-type motions with continuous sample paths, a set of behavioral equations for intertemporal portfolio selection can be derived which are both simpler and richer than those derived from the usual discrete-trading model assumptions. Using these same assumptions, Black and Scholes (1973) derived a formula for pricing options which provided the foundation for a unified theory of corporate liability evaluation.

Of course, continuous trading like any other continuous revision process is an abstraction from physical reality. However, if the length of time between revisions is very short (or indeterminately small), then the continuous-trading solution will be a reasonable approximation to the discrete-trading solution. Whether or not the length of time between revisions is short enough for the continuous solution to provide a good approximation must be decided on a case-by-case basis by making a relative comparison with other time scales in the problem. The analysis in this paper is presented in the context of a securities market where, in fact, the length of time between observed transactions ranges from at most a few days to less than a minute.

However, the continuous analysis can provide a good approximation even if the length of time between revisions is not this short. For example, in the analysis of long-run economic growth in a neoclassical capital model, it is the practice to neglect "short-run" business cycle fluctuations and to assume a full-employment economy. Moreover, the exogeneous factors usually assumed to affect the time path of the economy in such models are either demographic or technological changes. Since major changes in either generally take place over

[2]Merton (1975b). See Merton (1981) for further discussion. Merton (1971) and (1973b) studies the intertemporal portfolio selection problem with continuous trading. In a seminal paper, Black and Scholes (1973) use the continuous-trading assumption to derive a pricing formula for options and corporate liabilities. Smith (1976) provides an excellent survey article on this approach to the pricing of corporate liabilities.

rather long periods of time, the length of time between revisions in the capital stock, while hardly instantaneous, may well be quite short relative to the scale of the exogeneous factors.[3]

The application of continuous-time analysis in the empirical study of financial economic data is, by comparison, more recent and less developed. However, it shows promise of providing new approaches to resolving some of the major issues in the empirical study of speculative price time series as outlined in Cootner (1964, pp. 79–83 and 189–197) and Fama (1970).

It was the standard practice in early studies to assume that the logarithm of the ratio of successive prices had a Gaussian distribution with time-homogeneous independent increments and stationary parameters. However, the sample characteristics of the time series were frequently inconsistent with these assumed population properties. One of the more important inconsistencies was that the empirical distributions of price changes were often too "peaked" to be consistent with the Gaussian distribution. That is, the frequency of extreme observations is too high to be consistent with samples from a normal distribution.

Attempts to resolve these discrepancies proceeded along one of two paths. The first, pioneered by Mandelbrot (1963a; 1963b) and Fama (1963; 1965a), maintains the independent increments and stationarity assumptions but replaces the Gaussian assumption with a more general stable (Pareto-Levy) distribution assumption. Although non-Gaussian members of the stable family frequently fit the tails of the empirical distributions better than the Gaussian, there is little empirical evidence to support adoption of the stable Paretian hypothesis over that of any leptokurtotic distribution. Moreover, as discussed in Cootner (1964, pp. 333–37), the infinite variance property of the non-Gaussian stable distributions implies that most of our statistical tools which are based upon finite-moment assumptions (for example, least squares) are useless. It also implies that even the first-moment or expected value of the *arithmetic* price change does not exist.

The considerable theoretical and empirical difficulties with the stable Paretian hypothesis led Cootner (1964) and others to consider the alternative path of finite-moment processes whose distributions are nonstationary. It is in this approach where the continuous-time analysis shows promise. The general continuous-time framework, which requires that the underlying process be a mixture of diffusion and Poisson-directed processes, can accomodate a wide range of specific hypotheses including the "reflecting barrier" model proposed by Cootner (1964, pp. 231–52). Rosenberg (1972) shows that a Gaussian model with a changing (and forecastable) variance rate appears to "explain" the observed fat tail characteristics of stock market returns. Rosenfeld (1980) has developed statistical techniques for estimating the parameters of continuous-time processes

[3]See Bourgnignon (1974) and Merton (1975a) for neoclassical growth models under uncertainty that use diffusion processes.

and has applied them in constructing a likelihood test for choosing between a diffusion process with a changing variance rate and a mixed diffusion and Poisson-directed process. As discussed in Merton (1976; 1980), if the parameters are slowly varying functions of time, then it is possible to exploit the different "time scales" of the component parts of continuous-time processes to identify and estimate these parameters.

Of course, considerably more research is required before a judgement can be made as to the success of this approach. However, the extensive mathematics literature on the distributional characteristics of these processes together with their finite-moment properties make the development of hypothesis tests considerably easier for these processes than for the stable Pareto-Levy processes.[4]

With this as a background, we now turn to the formal development of the mathematics and economics assumptions of continuous-time models.

Let h denote the trading horizon which is the *minimum* length of time between which successive transactions by investors can be made in the securities market. In an intertemporal analysis, h is the length of time between successive market openings and is, of course, part of the specification of the structure of markets in the economy. While this structure will depend upon the trade-off between the costs of operating the market and its benefits, this time scale is not determined by the individual investor and is the same for all investors in the economy. If $X(t)$ denotes the price of a security at time t, then the change in the price of the security between time $t = 0$ and time $T \equiv nh > 0$, can be written as

$$X(T) - X(0) = \sum_{1}^{n} X(k) - X(k-1) \tag{1}$$

where n is the number of trading intervals between time 0 and T and $[X(k) - X(k-1)]$, which is a shorthand for $\{X(kh) - X[(k-1)h]\}$, is the change in price over the kth trading interval, $k = 1, 2, \ldots, n$.

The continuous-trading assumption implies that the trading interval h is equal to the continuous-time infinitesimal dt, and as is usual for differential calculus, all terms of higher order than dt will be neglected. To derive the economic implications of continuous-trading, it is necessary to derive the mathematical properties of the time series of price changes in this environment. Specifically, the limiting distributional properties are derived for both the price change over a single trading interval and the change over a fixed, finite time interval T as the length of the trading interval becomes very small and the number of trading intervals in $[0, T]$, n, becomes very large. In interpreting this limit analysis it may be helpful to think of the process as a sequence of market structures where

[4]Samuelson (1967) derived a few theorems about the portfolio selection behavior of risk-averse investors facing stable Pareto–Levy-distributed investments. However, to my knowledge, no one has derived any such behavioral equations when the investments are distributed log-stable. This is, of course, the distributional assumption made in those empirical studies with logarithmic returns distributed stable. This lack of theory makes the development of testable model specifications under the stable Paretian hypothesis quite difficult.

in each stage of the sequence, the institutionally imposed length of the trading interval is reduced from the previous stage. So, for example, the limiting mathematical analysis shows how the distribution of a given security's price change over one year will change as a result of changing the trading intervals from monthly to weekly. As I have emphasized elsewhere,[5] it is unreasonable to assume that the equilibrium distribution of returns on a security over a specified time period (for example, one year) will be invariant to the trading interval for that security because investors' optimal demand functions will depend upon how frequently they can revise their portfolios. Therefore, it should be pointed out that nowhere in the analysis presented here is it assumed that the distribution of $X(T) - X(0)$ is invariant to h.

Define the conditional expectation operator "E_t" to be the expectation operator conditional, on knowing all relevant information revealed as of time t or before. Define the random variables, $\epsilon(k)$, by

$$\epsilon(k) \equiv X(k) - X(k-1) - E_{k-1}[X(k) - X(k-1)], k = 1, \ldots, n \qquad \textbf{(2)}$$

where "time k" is used as a shorthand for "time kh." By construction, $E_{k-1}(\epsilon_k) = 0$, and $\epsilon(k)$ is the *unanticipated* price change in the security between $k - 1$ and k, conditional on being at time $k - 1$. Moreover, by the properties of conditional expectation, it follows that $E_{k-j}[\epsilon(k)] = 0$ for $j = 1, \ldots, k$. Hence the partial sums $S_n \equiv \sum_1^n \epsilon(k)$, form a *martingale*.[6] As will be seen, the mathematical analysis to follow depends heavily on the properties of martingales. The theory of martingales is usually associated in the financial economics literature with the "efficient markets hypothesis" of Fama and Samuelson.[7] Therefore, the reader may be tempted to connect the martingale property of the unanticipated returns derived here with an implicit assumption that "securities are priced correctly." However, the martingale property of the unanticipated returns here is purely a result of construction, and therefore imposes no such economic assumption. However, two economic assumptions that will be imposed are:

ASSUMPTION (A.1): For each finite time interval $[0,T]$, there exists a number $A_1 > 0$, independent of the number of trading intervals, n, such that Var $(S_n) \geq A_1$ where Var $(S_n) \equiv E_0\left(\left[\sum_1^n \epsilon(k)\right]^2\right)$.

ASSUMPTION (A.2): For each finite time interval $[0, T]$, there exists a number $A_2 < \infty$, independent of n, such that $\text{Var}(S_n) \leq A_2$.

Assumption (A.1) ensures that the uncertainty associated with the unanti-

[5]See Merton (1975b).

[6]For a formal definition of the martingale and discussions of its properties, see Feller (1966, Volume II, pp. 210–15; 234–38).

[7]See Fama (1965b) and (1970) and Samuelson (1965) and (1973). Also Cootner (1964).

cipated price changes is not "washed out" or eliminated even in the limit of continuous trading. That is, even as $h \to dt$, the "end-of-period" price at time k will be uncertain relative to time $(k - 1)$. This assumption is essential for the continuous-trading model to capture this fundamental property of common stock price behavior.

Assumption (A.2) ensures that the uncertainty associated with the unanticipated price changes over a finite period of time is not so great that the variance becomes unbounded. It rules out the possibility that the very act of allowing more frequent trading will induce sufficient price instability so as to cause the limiting variance of $X(T) - X(0)$ to become unbounded, and it also rules out the Pareto-Levy stable distributions with infinite variances.

Define $V(k) \equiv E_0[\epsilon(k)]^2$, $k = 1, 2, \ldots, n$, to be the variance of the dollar return on the security between time $(k - 1)$ and k based upon information available as of time zero, and define $V \equiv \underset{k}{\text{Max}}\{V(k)\}$.

ASSUMPTION (A.3): There exists a number, A_3, $1 \geq A_3 > 0$, independent of n, such that for $k = 1, \ldots, n$, $V(k)/V \geq A_3$.

Assumption (A.3) is closely related to (A.1) and, in effect, rules out the possibility that all the uncertainty in the unanticipated price changes over $[0, T]$ is concentrated in a few of the many trading periods. In other words, there is significant price uncertainty in virtually all trading periods.[8] So, for example (A.3) rules out a lottery ticket where the drawing will take place at time T. In that case, the price of the lottery ticket will just appreciate at the riskless rate of interest until the final moment when the drawing is made. Hence, for every n, $V(k) = 0$ for $k = 1, 2, \ldots, n - 1$ and $V(n) = \sigma^2 \cdot n$ where σ^2 is the variance of the dollar payoffs in the lottery.

At this point, I make a brief digression to define some mathematical symbols that will be used throughout the analysis. Let $\psi(h)$ and $\lambda(h)$ be functions of h. Define the *asymptotic order symbols*, $O[\lambda(h)]$ and $o[\lambda(h)]$, by $\psi(h) = O[\lambda(h)]$ if limit $[\psi(h)/\lambda(h)]$ is bounded as $h \to 0$ and by $\psi(h) = o[\lambda(h)]$ if limit $[\psi(h)/\lambda(h)] = 0$ as $h \to 0$. So, for example, if $\psi(h) = c\sqrt{h}\, e^h$, then $\psi(h) = O(h^\gamma)$ for any value of $\gamma \leq 1/2$. To see this, note that $[\psi(h)/h^\gamma]$ equals $ch^{1/2-\gamma} e^h$, and the limit of this expression as h goes to zero is bounded for $\gamma \leq 1/2$. Moreover, $\psi(h) = o(h^\gamma)$ for $\gamma < 1/2$ because the limit of $[\psi(h)/h^\gamma]$ as h goes to zero is zero for $\gamma \leq 1/2$. If $\psi(h) = O[\lambda(h)]$ and $\psi(h) \neq o(\lambda(h))$, then $\psi(h) \sim \lambda(h)$ where the symbol "$\sim$" means "is asymptotically proportional to" as $h \to 0$. In the above example, $\psi(h) \sim \sqrt{h}$. In essence, the asymptotic order symbols, $O(\ )$, $o(\ )$, and $\sim$, are used to describe the behavior of the function ψ relative to the function $\lambda(h)$ for values of h close to zero.

[8]Actually, the analysis will go through even if Assumption (E.3) is weakened to allow $V(k) = 0$ in some of the trading intervals provided that the number of such intervals has an upper bound independent of n. However, since virtually all "real-world" financial securities with uncertain returns exhibit some price uncertainty over even very small time intervals, the assumption as stated in the text should cover most empirically relevant cases.

PROPOSITION (P.1): If assumptions (A.1), (A.2), and (A.3) hold, then $V(k) \sim h$, $k = 1, \ldots, n$. That is, $V(k) = O(h)$ and $V(k) \neq o(h)$, and $V(k)$ is asymptotically proportional to h where the proportionality factor is positive.

Proof: $\mathrm{Var}(S_n) = E_0\left\{\sum_1^n \sum_1^n \epsilon(k)\epsilon(j)\right\} = \sum_1^n \sum_1^n E_0[\epsilon(k)\epsilon(j)]$. Consider a typical term in the double sum $E_0[\epsilon(k)\epsilon(j)]$. Suppose $k \neq j$. Choose $k > j$. Then, $E_0[\epsilon(k)\epsilon(j)] = E_0\{\epsilon(j)E_j[\epsilon(k)]\}$. But, by construction, $E_j[\epsilon(k)] = 0$, $j < k$. Hence, $E_0[\epsilon(k)\epsilon(j)] = 0$ for $k \neq j$. Therefore, $\mathrm{Var}(S_n) = \sum_1^n V(k)$. From (A.3) and (A.2), $nV\ A_3 \leqq \sum_1^n V(k) \leq A_2$, and therefore, $V(k) \leqq A_2 h/A_3 T$ where $0 < (A_2/A_3) < \infty$. Hence, $V(k) = O(h)$. From (A.3) and (A.1), $V(k) \geqq (A_1 A_3)h/T$ where $(A_1 A_3) > 0$. Hence, $V(k) \neq o(h)$.

Armed with Proposition (P.1), we now turn to a detailed examination of the return distribution over a single trading interval. For some trading interval $[k - 1, k]$, suppose that $\epsilon(k)$ can take on any one of m distinct values denoted by $\epsilon_j(k)$, $j = 1, \ldots, m$ where m is finite. Whenever there is no ambiguity about the epoch of time k, we will denote $\epsilon_j(k)$ by simply ϵ_j. Suppose further that there exists a number $M < \infty$, independent of n, such that $\epsilon_j^2 \leq M$. While the assumption of a discrete distribution of bounded range for $\epsilon(k)$ clearly restricts the class of admissible distributions, this assumption enormously simplifies the formal mathematical arguments without imposing any significant economic restrictions.[9] If $P_j(k) \equiv \mathrm{prob}\{\epsilon(k) = \epsilon(k) |$ information available as of time zero$\}$, then from Proposition (P.1) it follows that

$$\sum_1^m P_j \epsilon_j^2 = O(h), \tag{3}$$

and because m is finite, it follows from (3) that

$$P_j \epsilon_j^2 = O(h), \qquad j = 1, \ldots, m \tag{4}$$

Any event j such that $p_j \epsilon_j^2 = o(h)$ will asymptotically contribute a negligible amount to the variance of (1) because $V(k) \neq o(h)$. Because m is finite, it follows that there exist at least two events such that $p_j \epsilon_j^2 \neq o(h)$, and from (4), $p_j \epsilon_j^2 \sim h$ for such events. Moreover, these events will determine the asymptotic characteristics of the distributions as one goes to the limit of continuous time. Hence, without loss of generality, it is assumed that $p_j \epsilon_j^2 \neq o(h)$, $j = 1, \ldots, m$, and therefore, $p_j \epsilon_j^2 \sim h$, $j = 1, 2, \ldots, m$.

ASSUMPTION (A.4): For $j = 1, 2, \ldots, m$, p_j and ϵ_j are sufficiently "well-behaved" functions of h that there exists numbers q_j and r_j such that $p_j \sim h^{q_j}$ and $\epsilon_j \sim h^{r_j}$.

[9]The class can be expanded to include continuous distributions with bounded ranges and most well-behaved continuous distributions with unbounded ranges (for example, the normal distribution). However, to do so, the mathematical analysis required to prove the results derived in the text would be both longer and more complex. Because this additional mathematical complexity would provide little, if any, additional insights into the economic assumptions, to have included this larger class would have been at cross purposes with the paper's objectives.

While (A.4) is a convenient assumption for expositional purposes, it is stronger then is necessary. For example, if $p_j \sim h \log(1/h)$ in a neighborhood of $h = 0$, then (A.4) would not be satisfied. However, the results to be derived would still obtain if p_j behaved in this fashion.

From (E.4), we have that $p_j\epsilon_j^2 \sim h^{q_j - 2r_j}$. But, $p_j\epsilon_j^2 \sim h$. Hence, it follows that the values taken on by q_j and r_j cannot be arbitrary, and indeed, must satisfy

$$q_j + 2r_j = 1, \qquad j = 1, 2, \ldots, m \tag{5}$$

Because we are interested in the properties of these functions in a neighborhood of $h = 0$ and $h << 1$, those events with large values for r_j will have smaller-in-magnitude outcomes than those events with small values for r_j. Similarly, those events with large values for q_j are less likely to occur than those events with small values for q_j. Equation (5) defines the relationship between these two numbers that must be satisfied for each event j. In essence, Equation (5) says that "the larger the magnitude of the outcome, the smaller the likelihood that the event will occur." Because $p_j \leq 1$ and ϵ_j^2 is bounded, both q_j and r_j must be nonnegative, and therefore, from (5), it follows that $0 \leq q_j \leq 1$ and $0 \leq r_j \leq 1/2$, $j = 1, 2, \ldots, m$.

As will be shown, those outcomes located at the extremes of the permissible range for r_j will determine the asymptotic distributional properties of $\epsilon(k)$. It will, therefore, be useful to partition its outcomes into three types: a "Type I" outcome is one such that $r_j = 1/2$; a "Type II" outcome is one such that $0 < r_j < 1/2$; and a "Type III" outcome is one such that $r_j = 0$.

Let J denote the set of events j such that the outcomes ϵ_j are of Type I. It follows from (5) that for $j\epsilon J$, $q_j = 0$, and therefore, $p_j = o(1)$. Moreover, for all events $j\epsilon J^c$ (that is, events with Types II or III outcomes), $p_j = o(1)$, and because m is finite, $\Sigma p_j = o(1)$, $j\epsilon J^c$. Hence, because $\Sigma_1^m p_j = 1$, the set J cannot be empty and, indeed, virtually all the probability mass for $\epsilon(k)$ will be on events contained in J. In other words, for small trading intervals h, virtually all observations of $\epsilon(k)$ will be Type I outcomes, and therefore an apt name for J^c might be "the set of rare events." This finding suggests a natural hierarchy for analysis: First, the asymptotic properties for $\epsilon(k)$ are derived for the case where all outcomes are of Type I. Second, the properties are derived for the case where outcomes can be Type I and Type II. Finally, they are derived for the general case where outcomes can be Type I, Type II, and Type III.

II. CONTINUOUS SAMPLE PATH PROCESSES WITH "NO RARE EVENTS"

In this section, it is assumed that all possible outcomes for $\epsilon(k)$, $k = 1, \ldots, n$ are of Type I, and therefore, J^c is empty—that is, there are no rare events, and each possible outcome ϵ_j, $j = 1, \ldots, m$, can occur with finite probability.

Define the conditional expected dollar return per unit time on the security, α_k, by

$$\alpha_k \equiv E_{k-1}[X(k) - X(k-1)]/h, \qquad k = 1, \ldots, n. \tag{6}$$

ASSUMPTION (A.5): For every h, it is assumed that α_k exists, $k = 1, \ldots, n$ and that there exists a number $\alpha < \infty$, independent of h, such that $|\alpha_k| \leq \alpha$.

Assumption (A.5) simply ensures that for all securities with a finite price the expected rate of return per unit time over the trading horizon is finite, no matter how short that horizon is. Note: It is not assumed that α_k is a constant over time, and indeed, α_k may itself be a random variable relative to information available as of times earlier than $(k - 1)$. From (2) and (6), we can write the dollar return on the security between $(k - 1)$ and k as

$$X(k) - X(k-1) = \alpha_k h + \epsilon(k), \qquad k = 1, \ldots, n. \tag{7}$$

As discussed in the Introduction, an important assumption usually made in continuous-trading models is that the sample paths for security prices are continuous over time. The discrete-time analog to continuity of the sample path is that in short intervals of time, prices cannot fluctuate greatly. Because Type I outcomes are $o(\sqrt{h})$, it may come as no surprise that this continuity assumption will be satisfied when all possible outcomes are of this type.

PROPOSITION (P.2): If, for $k = 1, \ldots, n$, all possible outcomes for $\epsilon(k)$ are Type I outcomes, then the continuous-time sample path for the price of the security will be continuous.

Proof: Let $Q_k(\delta)$ be the probability that $|X(k) - X(k-1)| \geq \delta$ conditional on knowing all information available as of time $(k - 1)$. A necessary and sufficient condition[10] for continuity of the sample path for X is that for every $\delta > 0$, $Q_k(\delta) = o(h)$. Define $\bar{u} = \underset{\{j\}}{\text{Max}}|\epsilon_j|/\sqrt{h}$. By hypothesis all outcomes for $\epsilon(k)$ are Type I, and therefore $\bar{u} = O(1)$. For each number $\delta > 0$, define the function $h^\dagger(\delta)$ as the solution to the equation $\delta = \alpha h^\dagger + \bar{u}\sqrt{h^\dagger}$. Because α and $\bar{u}$ are $o(1)$, $h^\dagger > 0$ for every $\delta > 0$. Clearly, for all $h < h^\dagger(\delta)$ and every possible outcome, $X(k)$, $|X(k) - X(k-1)| < \delta$. Therefore, for every h, $0 \leq h < h^\dagger$, $Q_k(\delta) \equiv 0$, and hence limit $[Q_k(\delta)/h] = 0$ as $h \to 0$.

As illustrated in Figure 1, while the sample path for $X(t)$ is continuous, it is almost nowhere differentiable. Consider the change in X between k and $(k - 1)$ when the realization for $\epsilon(k) = \epsilon_j$. It follows that $[X(k) - X(k-1)]/h = \alpha_k + \epsilon_j/h$. But ϵ_j is asymptotically proportional to $\sqrt{h}$, and hence $[X(k) - X(k-1)]/h = O(1/\sqrt{h})$ which diverges as $h \to 0$. Thus, the usual calculus

[10]This condition is called the "Lindeberg condition." See Feller (1966, Volume II, pp. 321 and 491) for a discussion.

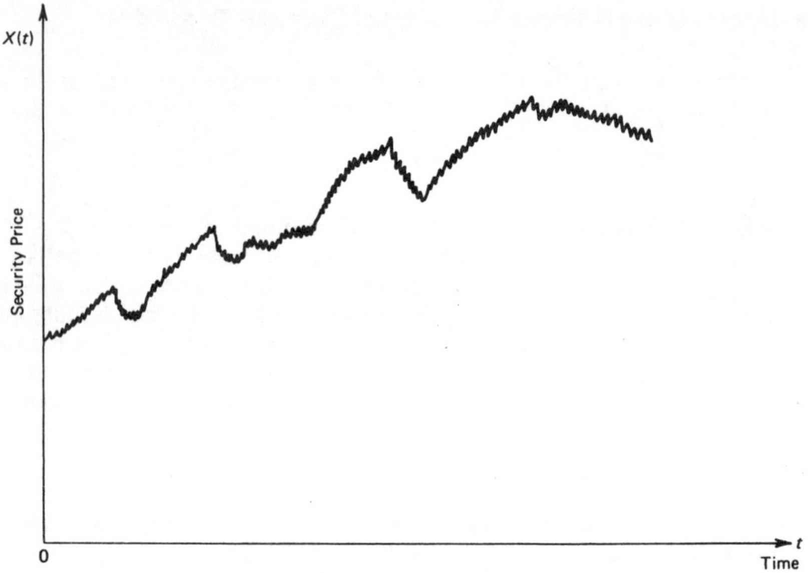

Figure 1 Continuous-Time Sample Path for Security Price "Type I" Outcomes

and standard theory of differential equations cannot be used to describe the dynamics of stock price movements. However, there exists a generalized calculus and corresponding theory of stochastic differential equations which can be used instead.

In preparation for the derivation of this generalized calculus, it will be useful to establish certain moment properties for $X(k) - X(k-1)$. Define the conditional variance per unit time of the dollar return on the security, σ_k^2, by

$$\sigma_k^2 \equiv E_{k-1}[\epsilon^2(k)]/h, \qquad k = 1, \ldots, n. \tag{8}$$

Because for every outcome ϵ_j, $\epsilon_j^2 = O(h)$, it follows that $\sigma_k^2 = O(1)$. Moreover, from (A.1) and (A.3), it follows that $\sigma_k^2 > 0$ for all h. Because α_k is bounded, it follows that

$$E_{k-1}\{[X(k) - X(k-1)]^2\} = \sigma_k^2 h + o(h), \qquad k = 1, \ldots, n. \tag{9}$$

Hence, to order h, the conditional second central and noncentral moments of $X(k) - X(k-1)$ are the same. Note: It is not assumed that σ_k^2 is constant through time, and indeed it can be a random variable when viewed from times earlier than $(k-1)$.

Consider now the Nth unconditional absolute moment of $\epsilon(k)$, $2 < N < \infty$. Using the same definition for $\bar{u}$ given in the proof of Proposition (P.2), we have that $k = 1, 2, \ldots, n$

$$
\begin{aligned}
E_o\{|\epsilon(k)|^N\} &= \Sigma_1^m p_j |\epsilon_j|^N \\
&\leqq \Sigma_1^m p_j (\bar{u})^N h^{N/2} \\
&\leqq \bar{u}^N h^{N/2} = o(h) \qquad \text{for } N > 2.
\end{aligned}
\tag{10}
$$

Thus, all the absolute moments of $\epsilon(k)$ higher than the second are asymptotically insignificant by comparison with the first two moments. Similarly, we have that

$$
\begin{aligned}
E_o\{|X(k) - X(k-1)|^N\} &\leqq (\alpha h + \bar{u}\sqrt{h})^N \\
&= \bar{u}^N h^{N/2} + o(h^{N/2}).
\end{aligned}
\tag{11}
$$

Hence, to order $h^{N/2}$, the unconditional Nth central and noncentral absolute moments of $X(k) - X(k-1)$ are the same.

Since the order relationships among the moments derived in (10) and (11) depend only upon the $\{\epsilon_j\} = O(\sqrt{h})$ and the boundedness of α_k and not upon the probabilities of specific outcomes (p_j), it follows immediately that the order relationships among the conditional moments will be the same as for the unconditional moments. Therefore,

$$E_{k-1}\{|\epsilon(k)|^N\} = o(h) \qquad \text{for } N > 2 \tag{12}$$

and

$$E_{k-1}\{|X(k) - X(k-1)|^N\} = E_{k-1}\{|\epsilon(k)|^N\} + o(h^{N/2}). \tag{13}$$

Define the random variable $u(k)$, $k = 1, \ldots, n$, by

$$u(k) \equiv \epsilon(k)/\sqrt{\sigma_k^2 h} \tag{14}$$

where by construction, $u_j \equiv \epsilon_j/\sqrt{\sigma_k^2 h} = O(1)$, $j = 1, \ldots, m$; $E_{k-1}[u(k)] = 0$; $E_{k-1}[u^2(k)] = 1$; and $E_{k-1}[|u(k)|^N] = O(1)$, $N > 2$. We can rewrite (7) as

$$X(k) - X(k-1) = \alpha_k h + \sigma_k u(k)\sqrt{h}, \qquad k = 1, \ldots, n. \tag{15}$$

Hence, whenever the unanticipated price changes of a security have only Type I outcomes, the dynamics for the price change can be written as a stochastic difference equation in the form of equation (15) where all the explicit random variables on the right hand side are $O(1)$ and are, therefore, neither degenerate nor explosive in the limit as $h \to 0$. Moreover, as of time $(k - 1)$, the only random variable is $u(k)$, and in this case (15) is called a conditional stochastic difference equation.

The form of (15) makes explicit an important property frequently observed in security returns: namely, because α_k, σ_k, and $u(k)$ are all $O(1)$, the realized return on a security over a very short trading interval will be completely dominated by its unanticipated component, $\sigma_k u(k)\sqrt{h}$. For example, it is not uncommon to find stocks with annual standard deviations of their percentage returns of between 15 and 20 percent. This would imply that price changes of the order of 1 percent in a trading day are not uncommon. However, as appears to be the case empirically, if the expected annual rate of return on a stock is of the same order as its annual standard deviation, say 15 percent, then the expected rate of return per trading day would be of the order of 1/20 of 1 percent which is negligible by comparison with the standard deviation. Of course, this point was implicitly made in the earlier discussion of moments when it was shown that to order h, the second central and noncentral moments of $X(k) - X(k-1)$ were the same. However, it does not follow that in choosing an optimal portfolio, even with continuous trading, the investor should neglect differences in the expected returns among stocks. As is well known, it is the moments of the returns which matter, and, as was already shown, the first and second moments of the returns are of the same order of magnitude: namely h.

Having established many of the essential asymptotic properties for $X(k) - X(k-1)$, we now derive the distributional characteristics of random variables which are themselves functions of security prices. These distributional characteristics are especially important to the theories of portfolio selection and contingent claims pricing. One example of such a contingent claim is a common stock call option that gives its owner the right to purchase a specified number of shares of stock at a specified price on or before a specified date. Clearly, the price of the option will be a function of the underlying stock's price.

Let $F(t)$ be a random variable given by the rule that $F(t) = f[X, t]$ if $X(t) = X$, where f is a C^2 function with bounded third partial derivatives.[11] Following the convention established for $X(t)$, we use the shorthand "$F(k)$" for "$F(kh)$" and "$f[X(k), k]$" for "$f[X(kh), kh]$." Suppose we are at time $(k-1)$ and, therefore, know the values of $X(k-1)$, α_k, σ_k^2, and $\{p_j'\}$ where p_j' is defined to be the conditional probability that $u(k) = u_j$, $j = 1, \ldots, m$, conditional on information available as of time $(k-1)$. Denote by X the known value of $X(k-1)$. Define the numbers $\{X_j\}$ by

$$X_j \equiv X + \alpha_k h + \sigma_k u_j \sqrt{h}, \qquad j = 1, \ldots, m. \tag{16}$$

For each value X_j, we can use Taylor's Theorem to write $f[X_j, k]$ as

$$\begin{aligned} f[X_j, k] &= f[X, k-1] + f_1[X, k-1](\alpha_k h + \sigma_k u_j \sqrt{h}) + f_2[X, k-1]h \\ &\quad + \frac{1}{2} f_{11}[X, k-1](\alpha_k h + \sigma_k u_j \sqrt{h})^2 + R_j, \qquad j = 1, \ldots, m \end{aligned} \tag{17}$$

where subscripts on f denote partial derivatives, and R_j is defined by

$$\begin{aligned} R_j \equiv{}& \frac{1}{2} f_{22}[X, k-1]h^2 + f_{12}[X, k-1](\alpha_k h + \sigma_k u_j \sqrt{h})h + \frac{1}{6} f_{111}[\eta_j, \zeta_n](X_j - X)^3 \\ &+ \frac{1}{2} f_{112}[\eta_j, \zeta_j](X_j - X)^2 h + \frac{1}{2} f_{122}[\eta_j, \zeta_j][X_j - X]h^2 + \frac{1}{6} f_{222}[\eta_j, \zeta_j]h^3 \end{aligned} \tag{18}$$

[11]The assumption that f has bounded third derivatives is not essential to the analysis, but is simply made for analytical convenience. Actually, all that is required is that the third derivatives be bounded in a small neighborhood of $X(t) = X$.

where $\eta_j \equiv X + \theta_j(X_j - X)$ and $\zeta_j \equiv (k - 1) + \upsilon_j$ for some θ_j, υ_j such that $0 \leq \theta_j \leq 1$ and $0 \leq \upsilon_j \leq 1$. Because all third partial derivatives of f are bounded and $u_j = O(1)$, $j = 1, \ldots, m$, we have by substitution for X_j from (16) into (18), that, for each and every j,

$$|R_j| = O(h\sqrt{h}) = o(h), \qquad j = 1, \ldots, m. \tag{19}$$

Noting that $[\alpha_k h + \sigma_k u_j \sqrt{h}]^2 = \sigma_k^2 u_j^2 h + o(h)$, we can rewrite (17) as

$$\begin{aligned} f[X_j, k] &= f[X, k-1] + f_1[X, k-1](\alpha_k h + \sigma_k u_j \sqrt{h}) + f_2[X, k-1]h \\ &\quad + \frac{1}{2} f_{11}[X, k-1]\sigma_k^2 u_j^2 h + o(h), \qquad j = 1, \ldots, m. \end{aligned} \tag{20}$$

Since (20) holds for each and every j, we can describe the dynamics for $F(k)$ in the form of a (approximate) conditional stochastic difference equation by

$$\begin{aligned} F(k) - F(k-1) &= \{f_1[X(k-1), k-1]\alpha_k + f_2[X(k-1), k-1] \\ &\quad + \frac{1}{2} f_{11}[X(k-1), k-1]\sigma_k^2 u^2(k)\}h \\ &\quad + f_1[X(k-1), k-1]\sigma_k u(k)\sqrt{h} + o(h), \\ &\qquad\qquad k = 1, \ldots, n \end{aligned} \tag{21}$$

where (21) is conditional on knowing $X(k-1)$, α_k, and σ_k.

Formally applying the conditional expectation operator E_{k-1} to both sides of (21) leads to the same result as the rigorous operation of multiplying both sides of (20) by p_j' and then summing from $j = 1, \ldots, m$. Noting that the derivatives of f on the right hand side of (21) are evaluated at $X(k-1)$ and are, therefore, nonstochastic relative to time $(k-1)$, we have that, for $k = 1, \ldots, n$,

$$\begin{aligned} E_{k-1}[F(k) - F(k-1)] &= \{f_1[X(k-1), k-1]\alpha_k + f_2[X(k-1), k-1] \\ &\quad + \frac{1}{2} f_{11}[X(k-1), k-1]\sigma_k^2\}h + o(h). \end{aligned} \tag{22}$$

Define $\mu_k \equiv E_{k-1}[F(k) - F(k-1)]/h$ to be the conditional expected change in F per unit time, and from (22), we have that, $k = 1, \ldots, n$,

$$\begin{aligned} \mu_k &= \{f_1[X(k-1), k-1]\alpha_k + f_2[X(k-1), k-1] \\ &\quad + \frac{1}{2} f_{11}[X(k-1), k-1]\sigma_k^2\} + o(1). \end{aligned} \tag{23}$$

Like α_k, $\mu_k = O(1)$, and to that order, it is completely determined by knowing $X(k-1)$ and only the first two moments for the change in X.

Substituting from (23), we can rewrite (21) as

$$\begin{aligned} F(k) - F(k-1) &= \mu_k h + \frac{1}{2} f_{11}[X(k-1), k-1]\sigma_k^2(u^2(k) - 1)h \\ &\quad + f_1[X(k-1), k-1]\sigma_k u(k)\sqrt{h} + o(h). \end{aligned} \tag{24}$$

Inspection of (24) shows that to order h, the conditional stochastic difference equation for $F(k) - F(k-1)$ is essentially of the same form as equation (15) for $X(k) - X(k-1)$ except for the additional $O(h)$ stochastic component. In an analogous fashion to the discussion of equation (15), it is clear that the realized change in F over a very short time interval is completely dominated by the $f_1[X(k-1), k-1]\sigma_k u(k)\sqrt{h}$ component of the unanticipated change. Indeed, from (24), we can write the conditional moments for $F(k) - F(k-1)$ as

$$E_{k-1}\{[F(k) - F(k-1)]^2\} = [f_1[X(k-1), k-1]\sigma_k]^2 h + o(h) \tag{25}$$

and

$$E_{k-1}\{[F(k) - F(k-1)]^N\} = O(h^{N/2}) = o(h), \qquad N > 2. \tag{26}$$

Hence, the order relationship for the conditional moments of $F(k) - F(k-1)$ is the same as for the conditional moments of $X(k) - X(k-1)$, and the $O(h)$ stochastic component makes a negligible contribution to the moments of $F(k) - F(k-1)$.

Indeed, not only is the order relationship of the own moments for the changes in F and X the same, but the comoments between them of contemporaneous changes have the same order relationship. Namely, from (15) and (24), we have that

$$E_{k-1}\{[F(k) - F(k-1)][X(k) - X(k-1)]\} = [f_1[X(k-1), k-1]\sigma_k^2]h + o(h) \tag{27}$$

and

$$E_{k-1}\{[F(k) - F(k-1)]^N[X(k) - X(k-1)]^{N-j}\} = O(h^{N/2}) = o(h), \tag{28}$$

$$j = 1, \ldots, N, \; N > 2.$$

Although (27) and (28) are the noncentral comoments, the difference between the central and noncentral comoments will be $o(h)$, and, therefore, the two can be used interchangeably. For example, the covariance between the change in F and X will differ from the right hand side of (27) by $-\mu_k\alpha_k h^2 = o(h)$.

Finally, we have the rather powerful result that, to order h, the contemporaneous changes in F and X are perfectly correlated. Thus, if ρ_k is defined to be the conditional correlation coefficient per unit time between contemporaneous changes in F and X, then, from (25) and (27)

$$\begin{aligned} \rho_k &= 1 + o(1) \quad \text{if} \quad f_1[X(k-1), k-1] > 0 \\ &= -1 + o(1) \quad \text{if} \quad f_1[X(k-1), k-1] < 0 \end{aligned} \tag{29}$$

Hence, even if F is a nonlinear function of X, in the limit of continuous time, their instantaneous, contemporaneous changes will be perfectly correlated.

Having demonstrated that the $O(h)$ stochastic term contributes a negligible amount to the variation in F over a very short time interval, we now study its contribution to the change in F over a finite, and not necessarily small, time interval. Define the random variable $G(t)$ by

$$G(k) - G(k-1) \equiv F(k) - F(k-1) - \mu_k h - f_1[X(k-1), k-1]\sigma_k u(k)\sqrt{h}, \qquad k = 1, \ldots, n. \tag{30}$$

Hence, $G(k) - G(k-1)$ is the random variable error from approximating $F(k) - F(k-1)$ by $\mu_k h + f_1\sigma_k u(k)\sqrt{h}$. If we define $y(k) \equiv f_{11}[X(k-1), k-1]\sigma_k^2[u^2(k) - 1]/2$, then from (24) we can rewrite (30) as

$$G(k) - G(k-1) = y(k)h + o(h), \qquad k = 1, \ldots, n. \tag{31}$$

By construction, $E_{k-1}[y(k)] = 0$, and therefore, $E_{k-j}[y(k)] = 0$, $j = 1, \ldots, k$. Therefore, the partial sums $\Sigma_1^n y(k)$ form a martingale. Because $E_0(\Sigma_1^n y^2(k)/k^2) < \infty$ as $n \to \infty$, it follows from the Law of Large Numbers for martingales[12] that

$$\lim[h\Sigma_1^n y(k)] = T \lim\left[\frac{1}{n}\Sigma_1^n y(k)\right] \to 0 \text{ as } n \to \infty. \tag{32}$$

From (31), we have that, for fixed $T(\equiv nh) > 0$,

$$\begin{aligned} G(T) - G(0) &= h\Sigma_1^n y(k) + \Sigma_1^n o(h) \\ &= h\Sigma_1^n y(k) + O(h). \end{aligned} \tag{33}$$

Taking the limit of (33) as $n \to \infty$ $(h \to 0)$, we have from (32), that $[G(T) - G(0)] \to 0$. That is, the cumulative error of the approximation goes to zero with probability one.

Hence, for $T > 0$, we have from (30) that in the limit of continuous time (as $h \to 0$)

$$F(T) - F(0) = \Sigma_1^n F(k) - F(k-1) = \Sigma_1^n \mu_k h + \Sigma_1^n f_1[X(k-1), k-1]\sigma_k u(k)\sqrt{h} \tag{34}$$

with probability one. Hence, in the limit of continuous time, the $O(h)$ stochastic term in (24) will have a negligible effect on the change in F over a finite time interval.

It is natural to interpret the limiting sums in (34) as integrals. For each k, $k = 1, \ldots, n$, define $t \equiv kh$. By the usual limiting arguments for Riemann integration, we have that

$$\lim_{n \to \infty}\left[\Sigma_1^n \mu_k h\right] = \int_0^T \mu(t)dt \tag{35}$$

where $\mu(t)$ is the continuous time limit of μ_k and is called the instantaneous conditional expected change in F per unit time, conditional on information available at time t. Of course, because of the $\sqrt{h}$ coefficient, the second sum

[12]For a statement and proof of the Law of Large Numbers for Martingales, see Feller (1966, Volume II, Theorem 2, p. 238).

will not satisfy the usual Riemann integral conditions. However, we can proceed formally and define the stochastic integral as the limiting sum given by

$$\lim_{n\to\infty}\left[\Sigma_1^n f_1[X(k-1), k-1]\sigma_k u(k)\sqrt{h}\right] \equiv \int_0^T f_1[X(t), t]\sigma(t)u(t)\sqrt{dt} \qquad \textbf{(36)}$$

where the formalism "$\sqrt{dt}$" is used to distinguish this integral from the usual Riemann integral in (35). Hence, we have from (34) that change in F between O and T can be written

$$F(T) - F(0) = \int_0^T \mu(t)dt + \int_0^T f_1[X(t), t]\sigma(t)u(t)\sqrt{dt} \qquad \textbf{(37)}$$

where equality in (37) is understood to hold with probability one.

Given this stochastic integral representation for the change in F over a finite time interval, we proceed formally to define the stochastic differential for F by

$$dF(t) = \mu(t)dt + f_1[X(t), t]\sigma(t)u(t)\sqrt{dt} \qquad \textbf{(38)}$$

where the differential form dF is used rather than the usual time derivative notation, dF/dt, to underscore the previously discussed result that the sample paths are almost nowhere differentiable in the usual sense.

In an analogous fashion to the difference equations (15) and (24), (38) can be interpreted as a conditional stochastic differential equation, conditional on information available as of time t which includes $\mu(t)$, $X(t)$, and $\sigma(t)$, but not, of course, $u(t)$ which is the source of the random change in F from $F(t)$ to $F(t + dt)$. Taking the formal limit of (24) as $h \to dt$ and neglecting terms of order $o(dt)$, it appears that (38) has left out an $O(dt)$ term: namely, $\frac{1}{2} f_{11}[X(t), t]\sigma^2(t)[u^2(t) - 1]dt$. However, as has been shown, the contribution of this $O(dt)$ stochastic term to the moments of dF over the infinitesimal interval dt is $o(dt)$, and over finite intervals it disappears by the Law of Large Numbers. Hence, with probability one, the distribution implied by the process described in (38) is indistinguishable from the one implied by including the extra $O(dt)$ stochastic term. While $\mu(t)dt$ is of the same order as the neglected $O(dt)$ stochastic term, it cannot be neglected over the infinitesimal interval because it *is* the first moment for the change in F which is of the same order as the second moment. It cannot be neglected over the finite interval $[0, T]$ because, unlike the $O(dt)$ stochastic term, the partial sums of $\mu_k dt$ do not form a martingale, and the Law of Large Numbers does not apply.

The corresponding stochastic integral and differential representation for the dynamics of $X(t)$ itself can be written down immediately from (37) and (38) by simply choosing $f[X, t] = X$. Namely, from (37),

$$X(T) - X(0) = \int_0^T \alpha(t)dt + \int_0^T \sigma(t)u(t)\sqrt{dt} \qquad \textbf{(39)}$$

and $$dX(t) = \alpha(t)dt + \sigma(t)u(t)\sqrt{dt} \tag{40}$$

where in this case the neglected $O(dt)$ stochastic term is identically zero because $f_{11} \equiv 0$.

Throughout this analysis, the only restrictions on the distribution for $u(t)$ were: (1) $E\{u(t)\} = 0$; (2) $E\{u^2(t)\} = 1$; (3) $u(t) = O(1)$; and (4) the distribution for $u(t)$ is discrete. Restrictions (1) and (2) are purely by construction, and (3) and (4) can be weakened to allow most well-behaved continuous distributions including ones with unbounded domain. In particular, it was not assumed that the $\{u(t)\}$ were either identically distributed or serially independent. However, to develop the analysis further requires an additional economic assumption:

ASSUMPTION (A.6): The stochastic process for $X(t)$ is a Markov process.[13] In other words, the conditional probability distribution for future values of X, conditional on being at time t, depends only on the current value of X and the inclusion of further information available as of that date will not alter this conditional probability.

While this assumption may appear to be quite restrictive, many processes that are formally not Markov can be transformed into the Markov format by the method of "expansion of the states,"[14] and therefore Assumption (A.6) could be weakened to say that the conditional probabilities for X depend upon only a finite amount of past information. From (A.6), we can write the conditional probability density for $X(T) = X$ at time T, conditional on $X(t) = x$ as

$$p[x, t] \equiv p[x, t; X, T] = \text{prob}\{X(T) = X|X(t) = x\}, t < T, \tag{41}$$

where suppression of the explicit arguments "X" and "T" will be understood to mean holding these two values fixed. Hence, for fixed X and T, $p[X(t), t]$ (viewed from dates earlier than t) is a random variable which is itself a function of the security price at time t. Therefore, provided that p is a well-behaved function of x and t, it will satisfy all the properties previously derived for $F(t)$. In particular, in the limit of continuous trading, dp will satisfy (38) where $\mu(t)$ is the conditional expected change per unit time in p. However, p is a probability density, and therefore, its *expected* change is zero. Taking the limit of (23) as $h \to 0$ and applying the condition that $\mu(t) = 0$, we have that

$$0 = \frac{1}{2}\sigma^2(x, t)p_{11}[x, t] + \alpha(x, t)p_1[x, t] + p_2[x, t] \tag{42}$$

where the subscripts on p denote partial derivatives. Moreover, by the Markov assumption (E.5), $\alpha(t)$ and $\sigma^2(t)$ are, at most, functions of $x(t)$ and t. Hence, we

[13]See Feller (1966, Volume II, Chapter X, pp. 311–43) for a formal definition and a discussion of the properties of Markov processes. The Markov assumption is almost universal among substantive models of stock price returns.

[14]See Cox and Miller (1968, pp. 16–18) for a brief discussion and further references on this method.

make this dependence explicit by rewriting these functions as $\alpha(x, t)$ and $\sigma^2(x, t)$ respectively. Inspection of (42) shows that it is a linear partial differential equation of the parabolic type and is sometimes called the "Kolmogorov backward equation."[15] Therefore, subject to boundary conditions, (42) completely specifies the transition probability densities for the security price. Hence, in the limit of continuous trading, knowledge of the two functions, $\sigma^2(x, t)$ and $\alpha(x, t)$, is sufficient to determine the probability distribution for the change in a security's price between any two dates.

It follows, therefore, that the only characteristics of the distributions for the $\{u(t)\}$ that affect the asymptotic distribution for the security price are the first and second moments, and, by construction, they are constant through time. That is, except for the scaling requirement on the first two moments, the distributional characteristics of the $\{u(t)\}$ can be chosen almost arbitrarily without having any effect upon the asymptotic distribution for the price of the security. Hence, in the limit of continuous trading, nothing of economic content is lost by assuming that the $\{u(t)\}$ are independent and identically distributed, and, therefore, for the rest of this section we make this assumption. *Warning:* This assumption *does not* imply that changes in $X(t)$ or $F(t)$ have these properties. Indeed, if either $\alpha(t)$ or $\sigma^2(t)$ is a function of $X(t)$, then changes in $X(t)$ will be neither independent nor identically distributed.

Define $Z(t)$ to be a random variable whose change in value over time is described by a stochastic difference equation like (15) but with $\alpha_k \equiv 0$ and $\sigma_k \equiv 1$, $k = 1, \ldots, n$. In other words, the conditional expected change in $Z(t)$ per unit time is zero and the conditional variance of that change per unit time is one. Therefore,

$$\begin{aligned} Z(T) - Z(0) &= \Sigma_1^n Z(k) - Z(k-1) \\ &= \sqrt{h}\,\Sigma_1^n u(k) \\ &= \sqrt{T}\left\{\Sigma_1^n u(k)/\sqrt{n}\right\} \end{aligned} \qquad \textbf{(43)}$$

The $\{u(k)\}$ are independent and identically distributed with a zero mean and unit variance. Therefore, by the Central Limit Theorem,[16] in the limit of continuous trading, $\{\Sigma_1^n u(k)/\sqrt{n}\}$ will have a standard normal distribution. It follows from (43) that, asymptotically, $Z(T) - Z(0)$ will be normally distributed with a zero mean and a variance equal to T for all $T > 0$. Indeed, the solution to (42) with $\sigma^2 = 1$ and $\alpha = 0$ is

$$p[x, t; X, T] = \exp[-(X - x)^2/2(T - t)]/\sqrt{2\pi(T - t)} \qquad \textbf{(44)}$$

which is a normal density function.

Since the distributional choice for $\{u(t)\}$ can be made almost arbitrarily and the limiting distribution for $Z(T) - Z(0)$ is gaussian for all finite T, it is natural

[15]See Cox and Miller (1968, p. 215).

[16]See Feller (1966, Volume II, Theorem 1, p. 488).

and convenient to assume that the $\{u(t)\}$ are standard normally distributed. In an analogous fashion to (40), we can write the stochastic differential equation representation for $Z(t)$ as

$$dZ(t) = u(t)\sqrt{dt} \tag{45}$$

In the case where the $u(t)$ are independent and distributed standard normal, the dZ process described in (45) is called a Weiner or Brownian motion process,[17] and we shall reserve the notation "dZ" to denote such a process throughout this paper.

Since this distributional choice for $u(t)$ does not affect the limiting distribution for X without loss of generality, we can rewrite the stochastic integral and differential representation for the dynamics of $X(t)$, equations (39) and (40), as

$$X(T) - X(0) = \int_0^T \alpha[X(t), t]dt + \int_0^T \sigma[X(t), t]dZ(t) \tag{46}$$

and

$$dX(t) = \alpha[X(t), t]dt + \sigma[X(t), t]dZ(t). \tag{47}$$

The class of continuous-time Markov processes whose dynamics can be written in the form of (46) and (47) are called Itô processes, and are a special case of a more general class of stochastic processes called Strong diffusion processes.

It follows immediately from (37) and (38) that if the dynamics of $X(t)$ can be described by an Itô process, then the dynamics of well-behaved functions of $X(t)$ will also be described by an Itô process. This relationship between the dynamics of $X(t)$ and $F(t)$ is formalized in the following lemma:

ITÔ'S LEMMA[18]: Let $f(X, t)$ be a C^2 function defined on $RX[0, \infty]$ and take the stochastic integral defined by (46), then the time-dependent random variable $F \equiv f$ is a stochastic integral and its stochastic differential is

$$dF = f_1[X, t]dX + f_2[X, t]dt + \frac{1}{2}f_{11}[X, t](dX)^2$$

where the product of the differentials is defined by the multiplication rules: $(dZ)^2 = dt$; $dZdt = 0$; and $(dt)^2 = 0$.

The proof of Itô's Lemma follows from (23), (35), (37), and (38). Itô's Lemma provides the differentiation rule for the generalized stochastic calculus, and as such is analogous to the Fundamental Theorem of the Calculus for standard time derivatives.

With the derivation of Itô's Lemma, the formal mathematical analysis of this section is complete and a summary is in order. Suppose that the economic

[17]See McKean (1969) for an excellent, rigorous discussion of Weiner processes. Cox and Miller (1968, Chapter 5) provides a less formal approach.

[18]For a rigorous proof of Itô's Lemma, see McKean (1969, p. 32). For its application in economics, see Merton (1971), (1973a), and (1975a).

structure to be analyzed is such that assumptions (A.1) to (A.5) obtain and unanticipated security price changes can have only "Type I" outcomes (that is, there are no "rare events"). Then, in continuous-trading models of that structure, security price dynamics can always be described by Itô processes with no loss of generality. Indeed, possibly because the integral of a Weiner process is normally distributed, it is not uncommon in the financial economics literature to find the price dynamics assumption stated as "the change in the security price over short intervals of time, $X(t + h) - X(t)$, is approximately normally distributed" instead of stating the formal equation (47). If it is appropriately interpreted, there is no harm in stating the price dynamics assumption in this fashion. However, it can be misleading in at least two ways.

First, stating the assumption in this fashion carries with it the implication that the $\{u(t)\}$ are independent and identically distributed standard normal. Hence, one might be led to the belief that the normality assumption is essential to the analysis rather than merely a convenience. For example, the derived continuous-trading dynamics are equally valid if $u(t)$ had a binomial distribution provided that the parameters of that distribution are chosen so as to satisfy $E\{u(t)\} = 0$ and $E\{u^2(t)\} = 1$.[19] While in the sequence-of-market structure analysis, the corresponding sequence of distribution functions for $X(t + h) - X(t)$ will depend upon the distribution of the $\{u(t)\}$, the limit distribution of that sequence does not. Moreover, independent of the distribution of $u(t)$, the continuous-trading solutions will provide a uniformly valid approximation [of $o(h)$] to the discrete-trading solutions. Therefore, the normality assumption for the $\{u(t)\}$ imposes no further restrictions on the process beyond those of (A.1) to (A.6).

Second, because $X(T) - X(0) = \Sigma_1^n X(k) - X(k - 1)$, stating the assumption in this fashion might lead one to believe that the distribution for the security price change over a finite interval, $[0, T]$ will be (approximately) normally distributed, and this is clearly not implied by equation (47). For example, if $\alpha(X, t) = aX$ and $\sigma(X, t) = bX$, with a and b constant, then by solving equation (42), $X(T)$ can be shown to have a log-normal distribution with $E_0\{X(T)\} = X(0)\exp[aT]$ and $\text{Var}\{\log[X(T)]\} = b^2T$ for all $T > 0$, and the normal and log-normal distributions are not the same. Indeed, a normal distribution for $X(T) - X(0)$ implies a positive probability that $X(T)$ can be negative while a log-normal distribution implies that $X(T)$ can never be negative.

Along these lines, a less misleading way to state the assumed price dynamics would be: "For very short trading intervals, one may treat the change in the security price over a trading interval 'as if' it were normally distributed." However, this simply restates the conditions summarized by (13) and (26): Namely, for short trading intervals, only the first two moments "matter."

The substantive benefits from using continuous-time models with Itô process

[19]The binomial distribution which satisfies these conditions must have $u_1 = 1$ with probability 1/2 and $u_2 = -1$ with probability 1/2. Hence, in this special case, $u^2(t) = 1$ with probability one, and therefore, the $O(h)$ stochastic term analyzed in equations (24), (30), (31), (32), and (33) will be zero even for finite h.

price dynamics have been amply demonstrated in the financial economics literature, and, therefore, only a few brief remarks will be made here. For example, in solving the intertemporal portfolio selection problem, the optimal portfolio demand functions will depend only upon the first two moments of the security return distributions. Not only does this vastly reduce the amount of information about the returns distributions required to choose an optimal portfolio, but it also guarantees that the first-order conditions are linear in the demand functions, and, therefore, explicit solutions for these functions can be obtained by simple matrix inversion.

The analysis of corporate liability and option pricing is also simplified by using Itô's Lemma which provides a direct method for deriving the dynamics and transition probabilities for functions of security prices. Moreover, while the analysis presented here is for scalar processes, it can easily be generalized to vector processes.[20]

Of course, all the results derived in this section were based upon the assumption that changes in the security price are all "Type I" outcomes. As discussed in the introductory section, this class of processes is only a subset of the set of processes which satisfy economic assumptions (A.1) to (A.6). Hence, to complete the study of the mathematics of continuous-trading models, we now provide a companion analysis of those processes which allow for the possibility of "rare events."

III. CONTINUOUS SAMPLE PATH PROCESSES WITH "RARE EVENTS"

In this section, it is assumed that the outcomes for $\epsilon(k)$, $k = 1, \ldots, n$ can be either of Type I or Type II, but not Type III. Thus, we allow for the possibility of rare events with Type II outcomes although, as was shown in section I, virtually all observations of $\epsilon(k)$ will be Type I outcomes.

The format of the analysis presented here is essentially the same as in the previous section. Indeed, the principal conclusion of this analysis will be that in the limit of continuous trading, the distributional properties of security returns are indistinguishable from those of section II. In other words, rare events with Type II outcomes "do not matter."

To show this, we begin by proving that, in the limit of continuous trading, the sample paths for security prices are continuous over time. For each time period k, define $r \equiv \min\{r_j\}$ where the lead order term for ϵ_j is h^{r_j}, $j = 1, \ldots, m$. Because all outcomes are either Type I or Type II, $r > 0$, and $|\epsilon_j| = O(h^r)$, $j = 1, \ldots, m$.

[20]See McKean (1969, p. 44) for the proof of Itô's Lemma for vector processes. Also see Cox and Miller (1968, pp. 246–48).

PROPOSITION (P.3): If, for $k = 1, \ldots, n$, all possible outcomes for $\epsilon(k)$ are either Type I or Type II outcomes, then the continuous-time sample path for the price of the security will be continuous.

Proof: Let $Q_k(\delta)$ be the probability that $|X(k) - X(k-1)| \geqq \delta$ conditional on knowing all information available as of time $(k-1)$. As in the proof of (P.2), a necessary and sufficient condition for continuity of the sample path for X is that for every $\delta > 0$, $Q_k(\delta) = o(h)$. Define $\bar{u} \equiv \underset{\{j\}}{\text{Max}} |\epsilon_j| h^{-r}$. By the definition of r, $\bar{u} = o(1)$. For each number $\delta > 0$, define the function $h^{\dagger}(\delta)$ as the solution to the equation $\delta = \alpha h^{\dagger} + \bar{u}(h^{\dagger})^r$ where by Assumption (E.4), α is $O(1)$. Because $r > 0$ and α and $\bar{u}$ are both $O(1)$, there exists a solution $h^{\dagger} > 0$ for every $\delta > 0$. Therefore, for all $h < h^{\dagger}(\delta)$ and every possible outcome $X(k)$, $|X(k) - X(k-1)| < \delta$. Hence, for every h, $0 \leq h < h^{\dagger}$, $Q_k(\delta) \equiv 0$, and limit $[Q_k(\delta)/h] = 0$ as $h \to 0$.

Having established the continuity of the sample path, we now show that the moment properties for $X(k) - X(k-1)$ are the same as in section II. From Assumption (E.4), $E_{k-1}[X(k) - X(k-1)]$ is asymptotically proportional to h, and, therefore, so is $E_0[X(k) - X(k-1)]$. Therefore, from Proposition (P.1) and equation (5), the unconditional variance of $[X(k) - X(k-1)]$ is asympotically proportional to h. The Nth unconditional absolute moment of $\epsilon(k)$, $2 < N < \infty$ can be written as

$$
\begin{aligned}
E_0\{|\epsilon(k)|^N\} &= \Sigma_1^m p_j |\epsilon_j|^N \\
&= O(\Sigma_1^m h^{(N-2)r_j + 1}, \text{ from equation (5)} \\
&= O(h^{(N-2)r + 1}) \\
&= o(h) \qquad \text{for } N > 2,
\end{aligned}
\tag{48}
$$

because $r > 0$. Thus, all the absolute moments of $\epsilon(k)$ higher than the second are asymptotically insignificant by comparison with the first two moments. Moreover, by Assumption (A.4), these same order relationships will obtain for both the central and noncentral moments of $X(k) - X(k-1)$.

Provided that the order relationships between the unconditional and conditional probabilities remain the same, the conditional moments of $X(k) - X(k-1)$ have the same order properties as the unconditional moments: Namely,

$$
E_{k-1}\{[X(k) - X(k-1)]^2\} = \sigma_k^2 h + o(h), k = 1, \ldots, n \tag{49}
$$

where σ_k^2 is the conditional variance per unit time defined in (8) and $\sigma_k^2 > 0$ and $O(1)$, and

$$
E_{k-1}\{|X(k) - X(k-1)|^N\} = o(h) \qquad \text{for } N > 2. \tag{50}
$$

Hence, the moment relationships for $X(k) - X(k-1)$ are identical to those derived in section II where only Type I outcomes were allowed.

To complete the analysis, we examine the distributional characteristics of random variables which are functions of security prices. Let $F(t)$ be a random variable given by the rule that $F(t) = f(X)$ if $X(t) = X$. The reader will note that unlike the parallel analysis in section II, the explicit dependence of f on t has been eliminated. This is done solely to keep both the notation and analysis relatively simple. However, including the explicit time dependence would not have changed either the method of derivation or the conclusions.

Define K to be the smallest integer such that $Kr \geqq 1$. Because $r > 0$, K is finite. If f is a C^2 function with a bounded $(K + 1)$st order derivative, then from Taylor's Theorem and (49) and (50), we have that

$$E_{k-1}\{F(k) - F(k-1)\} = \{f^{(1)}[X(k-1)]\alpha_k + \frac{1}{2}f^{(2)}[X(k-1)]\sigma_k^2\}h + o(h), \quad \textbf{(51)}$$

where $f^{(i)}[\ ]$ denotes the ith derivative of f. Note that (51) is identical to the corresponding equation (22) in section II when f is not an explicit function of time. Moreover, it is straightforward to show that the conditional moments for $F(k) - F(k-1)$ here are the same as derived in equations (25) and (26) of section II: Namely,

$$E_{k-1}\{[F(k) - F(k-1)]^2\} = [f^{(1)}[X(k-1)\sigma_k]^2 h + o(h) \quad \textbf{(52)}$$

and

$$E_{k-1}\{[F(k) - F(k-1)]^N\} = o(h) \qquad \text{for } N > 2. \quad \textbf{(53)}$$

Hence, the order relationship for the conditional moments of $F(k) - F(k-1)$ is the same as for the conditional moments of $X(k) - X(k-1)$. Therefore, over short intervals of time, the unanticipated part of the change in F here will be dominated by the $f^{(1)}[X(k-1)]\epsilon(k)$ term in the same fashion that it dominated the change in F in section II.

Having studied the change in F over a very short time interval, we now examine the stochastic properties for the change in F over a finite, and not necessarily small, time interval. For each k, $k = 1, \ldots, n$, define the random variables $\{y_j(k)\}$ by

$$y_j(k) \equiv f^{(j)}[X(k-1)]\{[X(k) - X(k-1)]^j - E_{k-1}[X(k) - X(k-1)]^j\}/j!, \quad \textbf{(54)}$$
$$j = 2, \ldots, K.$$

Further define the random variable $G(t)$ by

$$G(k) - G(k-1) \equiv F(k) - F(k-1) - E_{k-1}\{F(k) - F(k-1)\}$$
$$- f^{(1)}[X(k-1)]\epsilon(k), \; k = 1, \ldots, n \quad \textbf{(55)}$$

which by Taylor's Theorem can be rewritten as

$$G(k) - G(k-1) = \Sigma_{j=2}^{K} y_j(k) + R_{K+1} \quad \textbf{(56)}$$

where R_{K+1} is defined by

$$R_{K+1} \equiv f^{(K+1)}[\theta X(k-1) + (1-\theta)X(k)]\{[X(k) - X(k-1)]^{K+1} - E_{k-1}[X(k) - X(k-1)]^{K+1}\}/(K+1)! \tag{57}$$

for some θ, $0 \leq \theta \leq 1$. But $f^{(K+1)}$ is bounded and $[\alpha_k h + \epsilon(k)]^{K+1} = O(h^{r(K+1)})$ for every possible outcome for $\epsilon(k)$. Hence, because $rK \geq 1$, $R_{K+1} = o(h)$. Therefore, we can rewrite (56) as

$$G(k) - G(k-1) = \Sigma_{j=2}^{K} y_j(k) + o(h), k = 1, \ldots, n. \tag{58}$$

From (58), we can write the unconditional variance of $G(k) - G(k-1)$ as

$$\begin{aligned} \text{Var}[G(k) - G(k-1)] &= E_0\{\Sigma_2^K \Sigma_2^K y_j(k) y_i(k)\} + o(h) \\ &\leqq \Sigma_2^K \Sigma_2^K M_i M_j E_o |\{[X(k) - X(k-1)]^i \\ &\quad - E_{k-1}[X(k) - X(k-1)]^i\} \end{aligned} \tag{59}$$

$$\{[X(k) - X(k-1)]^j - E_{k-1}[X(k) - X(k-1)]^j\}|/k!j! + o(h)$$

where M_i is the least upper bound on $|f^{(i)}|$, $i = 2, \ldots, K$. From (48) and (59), we have, therefore, that

$$\begin{aligned} \text{Var}[G(k) - G(k-1)] &= O(h^{2r+1}) + o(h) \\ &= o(h) \end{aligned} \tag{60}$$

because $r > 0$. For the finite time interval $[0, T]$, we have that

$$\begin{aligned} G(T) - G(0) &= \Sigma_{k=1}^{n} G(k) - G(k-1) \\ &= \Sigma_1^n \Sigma_2^K y_j(k) + o(1). \end{aligned} \tag{61}$$

$\Sigma_1^n \Sigma_2^K y_j(k)$ form a martingale, and therefore the unconditional variance of $G(T) - G(0)$ can be written as

$$\text{Var}[G(T) - G(0)] = \Sigma_1^n \text{Var}[G(k) - G(k-1)] + o(1). \tag{62}$$

But, from (60) and (62), it follows that

$$\begin{aligned} \text{Var}[G(T) - G(0)] &= O(h^{2r}) + o(h) + o(1) \\ &= o(1), \end{aligned} \tag{63}$$

and, therefore, in the limit of continuous-trading as $h \to 0$, the variance of $G(T) - G(0)$ goes to zero for every finite time interval $[0, T]$.

Hence, for $T > 0$, we have from (51), (52), (53), and (63), that in the limit as $h \to 0$

$$F(T) - F(0) = \Sigma_1^n F(k) - F(k-1) = \Sigma_1^N \mu_k h + \Sigma_1^n f^{(1)}[X(k-1)]\epsilon(k) \tag{64}$$

with probability one where μ_k is the conditional expected change in F per unit time defined in (23). In a similar fashion to the analysis in section II, we can formally express the limiting sum in (64) as the sum of two integrals: Namely,

$$F(T) - F(0) = \int_0^T \mu(t)dt + \int_0^T f^{(1)}[X(t)]\epsilon(t) \quad \textbf{(65)}$$

where (65) is understood to hold with probability one. As in (38) of section II, we can formally define the stochastic differential for F by

$$dF(t) = \mu(t)dt + f^{(1)}[X(t)]\epsilon(t). \quad \textbf{(66)}$$

Moreover, if the Markov assumption (E.6) obtains, then the limiting transition probabilities for X will satisfy equation (42). Finally, although it is not the case that $[\epsilon(t)]^2 = O(h)$, with probability one, the formal differentiation rules provided by Itô's Lemma still apply. Hence, in the limit of continuous trading, processes with Type I and Type II outcomes are indistinguishable from processes with Type I outcomes only.

IV. DISCONTINUOUS SAMPLE PATH PROCESSES WITH "RARE EVENTS"

In this concluding section, the general case is analyzed where the outcomes for $\epsilon(k)$, $k = 1, \ldots, n$ can be Type I, Type II, or Type III. As was true for the processes in section III, virtually all observations of $\epsilon(k)$ will be Type I outcomes. However, unlike the findings in section III, the possibility of rare events with Type III outcomes "does matter." While the Type III outcomes with their probabilities proportional to h are the "rarest" of the admissible outcomes, the magnitudes of these outcomes are also the largest. Indeed, because these outcomes are $O(1)$, it follows that X can have nonlocal changes in value, even over an infinitesimal time interval, and, therefore, the resulting sample path for X will be discontinuous. The analysis demonstrating this and other important properties can be simplified by neglecting the Type II outcomes, and in the light of the conclusions reached in section III, this simplification can be made with no loss in generality.

PROPOSITION (P.4): If, for $k = 1, \ldots, n$, at least one possible outcome for $\epsilon(k)$ is a Type III outcome, then the continuous-time sample path for the price of the security will not be continuous.

Proof: Let $Q_k(\delta)$ be the probability that $|X(k) - X(k-1)| \geqq \delta$ conditional on knowing all information available as of time $(k - 1)$. As in the proofs of (P.2) and (P.3), a necessary and sufficient condition for continuity of the sample path for X is that for every $\delta > 0$, $Q_k(\delta) = o(h)$. By renumbering, if necessary, for each k, suppose event j denotes a Type III outcome for $\epsilon(k)$ where $\epsilon(k) = \epsilon_j$ and

ϵ_j is $O(1)$. If p_j is the conditional probability as of time $(k-1)$ that event j occurs, then from (5), p_j can be written as $\lambda_j h$ where $\lambda_j = O(1)$. Pick a number θ such that $0 < \theta < 1$. Define $h^\dagger$ by $h^\dagger = \infty$ if $\alpha_k \epsilon_j \geq 0$ and $h^\dagger = (\theta - 1)\epsilon_j/\alpha_k$ if $\alpha_k \epsilon_j < 0$. Note: $h^\dagger > 0$, independent of h. Define $\delta^\dagger \equiv \theta|\epsilon_j|$. Note: $\delta^\dagger > 0$, independent of h. For all h such that $0 < h \leq h^\dagger$, it follows that if $\epsilon(k) = \epsilon_j$, then $|X(k) - X(k-1)| > \delta^\dagger$. Hence, for $0 < h \leq h^\dagger$ and any δ such that $0 < \delta \leq \delta^\dagger$, $|X(k) - X(k-1)| > \delta$ if $\epsilon(k) = \epsilon_j$, and therefore $Q_k(\delta) \geq \lambda_j h = o(h)$ because $\lambda_j = O(1)$. Hence, the sample path is not continuous.

As illustrated in Figure 2, a typical sample path will contain mostly local or continuous changes with infrequent, nonlocal changes or "jumps" corresponding to the relatively rare Type III outcomes.

These fundamental discontinuities in the sample path manifest themselves in the moment properties of $X(k) - X(k-1)$. Like the processes in sections II and III, the first and second unconditional moments of $X(k) - X(k-1)$ are asymptotically proportional to h. However, unlike the processes in those sections, the Nth unconditional absolute moments, $2 < N < \infty$, are asymptotically proportional to h as well. That is,

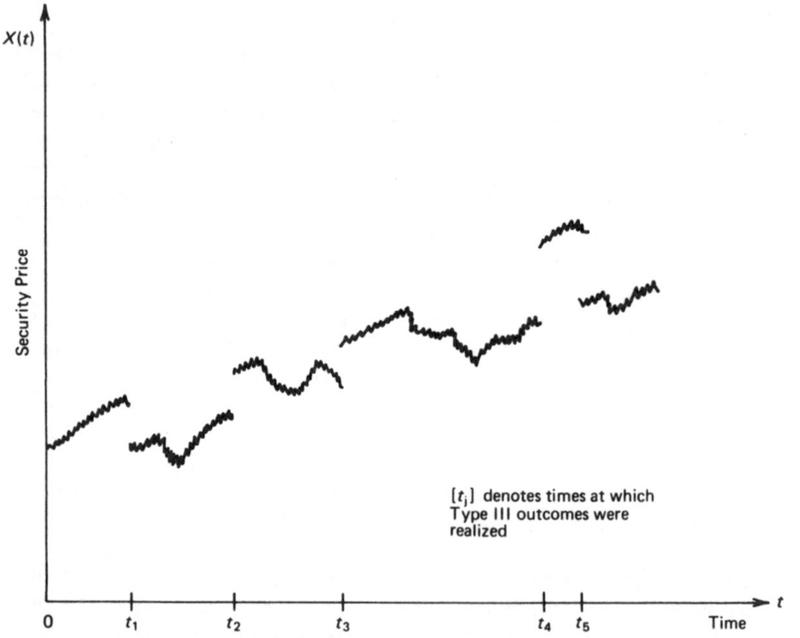

Figure 2 Continuous-Time Sample Path for Security Price "Type I" and "Type III" Outcomes

$$
\begin{aligned}
E_0\{|\epsilon(k)|^N\} &= \Sigma_1^m p_j |\epsilon_j|^N \\
&= O[(\Sigma_1^m h^{(N-2)r_j+1})] \text{ from equation (5)} \\
&= O(h), \qquad N > 2
\end{aligned}
\tag{67}
$$

because $r_j = 0$ for all Type III outcomes. Hence, all the absolute moments of $X(k) - X(k-1)$ are of the same order of magnitude, and therefore none of the moments can be neglected even in the limit of continuous trading. However, the contributions of the Type I outcomes for $\epsilon(k)$ to the moments higher than the second will be shown to be asymptotically insignificant. To show this along with the other results, it is useful to formally partition the outcomes for $\epsilon(k)$ into its Type I and Type III components.

Define the conditional random variable $u(k)$ by $u(k) \equiv \epsilon(k)/\sqrt{h}$ conditional on $\epsilon(k)$ having a Type I outcome. Similarly, define the conditional random variable $y(k)$ by $y(k) \equiv \epsilon(k)$ conditional on $\epsilon(k)$ having a Type III outcome. If $\lambda(k)h$ denotes the conditional probability as of time $(k-1)$ that $\epsilon(k)$ has a Type III outcome, then, as of time $(k-1)$, we can rewrite $\epsilon(k)$ as

$$
\begin{aligned}
\epsilon(k) &= u(k)\sqrt{h} &&\text{with probability } 1 - \lambda(k)h \\
&= y(k) &&\text{with probability } \lambda(k)h,
\end{aligned}
\tag{68}
$$

and, by construction, $u(k)$, $y(k)$, and $\lambda(k)$ are all $O(1)$.

If E_{k-1}^y denotes the conditional expectation as of time $(k-1)$ over the distribution function for $y(k)$ and E_{k-1}^u denotes the corresponding conditional expectation over the distribution for $u(k)$, then $\bar{y}(k) \equiv E_{k-1}^y[y(k)] = E_{k-1}\{\epsilon(k)|\text{ Type III outcome}\}$ and $\bar{u}(k)\sqrt{h} \equiv \sqrt{h}\,E_{k-1}^u[u(k)] = E_{k-1}\{\epsilon(k)|\text{ Type I outcome}\}$. Because $E_{k-1}[\epsilon(k)] = 0$, it follows immediately from the properties of conditional expectation that

$$
\begin{aligned}
\bar{u}(k) &= -\lambda(k)\bar{y}(k)\sqrt{h}/[1 - \lambda(k)h] \\
&= -\lambda\bar{y}\sqrt{h} + o(h)
\end{aligned}
\tag{69}
$$

where we surpress the explicit dependence of u, y, and λ on k whenever there is no ambiguity about the time.

If σ_k^2 is the conditional variance per unit time for $\epsilon(k)$, then $E_{k-1}[\epsilon^2(k)] = \sigma_k^2 h$, and it follows that

$$
\begin{aligned}
\sigma_u^2 &= [\sigma_k^2 - \lambda\sigma_y^2]/(1 - \lambda h) \\
&= \sigma_k^2 - \lambda\sigma_y^2 + O(h)
\end{aligned}
\tag{70}
$$

where σ_u^2 is the conditional variance of $u(k)$ and σ_y^2 is the conditional variance of $y(k)$. Note: σ_k^2, σ_u^2, and σ_y^2 are all $O(1)$. Further, for $N > 2$, it follows that

$$
E_{k-1}[\epsilon^N(k)] = \lambda(k)E_{k-1}^y[y^N(k)]h + o(h). \tag{71}
$$

Thus, while both the Type I and Type III contribute significantly to the mean and variance of $\epsilon(k)$, the contributions of the Type I outcomes to the higher moments of $\epsilon(k)$ are asymptotically insignificant.

As was done in the earlier sections, we complete the analysis by examining the distributional characteristics of random variables which are functions of security prices. As in section II, let $F(t)$ be a random variable given by the rule that $F(t) = f[X, t]$ if $X(t) = X$, where f is a C^2 function with bounded third partial derivatives.

For a given outcome $y(k) = y$, we have by Taylor's Theorem that

$$\begin{aligned} f[X(k-1) + \alpha_k h + y, k] = f[X(k-1) + y, k-1] & \\ + f_1[X(k-1) + y, k-1]\alpha_k h & \\ + f_2[X(k-1) + y, k-1]h + o(h) & \end{aligned} \tag{72}$$

where, as in section II, subscripts on f denote partial derivatives.

Similarly, for a given outcome $u(k) = u$, we have that

$$\begin{aligned} f[X(k-1) + \alpha_k h + u\sqrt{h}, k] = f[X(k-1), k-1] & \\ + f_1[X(k-1)\, k-1]\,[\alpha_k h + u\sqrt{h}] & \\ + f_2[X(k-1), k-1]h & \\ + \frac{1}{2} f_{11}[X(k-1), k-1]u^2 h + o(h). & \end{aligned} \tag{73}$$

By the properties of conditional expectation, it follows that

$$\begin{aligned} E_{k-1}[F(k) - F(k-1)] = \lambda(k)hE^y_{k-1}[F(k) - F(k-1)] & \\ + (1 - \lambda(k)h)E^u_{k-1}[F(k) - F(k-1)]. & \end{aligned} \tag{74}$$

Substituting from (72) and (73) into (74) and eliminating explicit representation of terms that are $o(h)$, we can rewrite (74) as

$$\begin{aligned} E_{k-1}[F(k) - F(k-1)] = \Big(& \frac{1}{2} f_{11}[X(k-1), k-1]\sigma_u^2 \\ & + f_1[X(k-1), k-1](\alpha_k - \lambda\overline{y}) \\ & + f_2[X(k-1), k-1] + \lambda E^y_{k-1}\{f[X(k-1) \\ & + y(k), k-1] \\ & - f[X(k-1), k-1]\}\Big)h + o(h). \end{aligned} \tag{75}$$

If in a corresponding fashion to equation (23), we define the conditional expected change in F per unit time to be $\mu_k \equiv E_{k-1}[F(k) - F(k-1)]/h$, then by dividing (75) by h and taking the limit as $h \rightarrow 0$, we can write the instantaneous conditional expected change in F per unit time, $\mu(t)$, as

$$\mu(t) = \frac{1}{2}f_{11}[X(t), t]\sigma_u^2(t) + f_1[X(t), t][\alpha(t) - \lambda(t)\bar{y}(t)] + f_2[X(t), t] + \lambda(t)E_t^y\{f[X(t) + y(t), t] - f[X(t), t]\}. \tag{76}$$

Note: In the special case when $\lambda(t) = 0$ and there are no Type III outcomes, the expression for $\mu(t)$ in (76) reduces to the corresponding limiting form of (23) derived in section II.

In a similar fashion, the higher conditional moments for the change in F can be written as

$$E_{k-1}\{[F(k) - F(k-1)^2\} = \Big[\lambda E_{k-1}^y\{[f[X(k-1) + y(k), k-1] - f[X(k-1), k-1]\}^2 + f_1^2[X(k-1), k-1]\sigma_u^2\Big]h + o(h) \tag{77}$$

and for $N > 2$,

$$E_{k-1}\{[F(k) - F(k-1)]^N\} = \lambda E_{k-1}^y\{f[X(k-1) + y(k), k-1] - f[X(k-1), k-1]\}^N h + o(h). \tag{78}$$

As was the case for the moments of $X(k) - X(k-1)$, all the moments of $F(k) - F(k-1)$ are of the same order of magnitude, and only the Type III outcomes contribute significantly to the moments higher than the second. Hence, in the limit of continuous trading, the only characteristics of $u(k)$ which matter are its first two moments.

If we now reintroduce Assumption (E.5) that the stochastic process for $X(t)$ is Markov, then $\lambda(k) = \lambda[X(k-1), k-1]$; $\alpha_k = \alpha_k[X(k-1), k-1]$; $\sigma_u^2(k) = \sigma_u^2[X(k-1), k-1]$; and $g_k(y)$, the conditional density function for $y(k)$, can be written as $g[y(k); X(k-1), k-1]$. As defined in (41) of section II, let $p[x, t]$ denote the conditional probability density for $X(T) = X$ at time T, conditional on $X(t) = x$. For fixed X and T, $p[X(t), t]$ is a random variable which is a function of the security price at time t. Hence, in the limit of continuous trading, the instantaneous expected change in p per unit time will satisfy (76). However, because p is a probability density, its expected change is zero. Substituting the condition that $\mu(t) = 0$ into (76), we have that p must satisfy

$$0 = \frac{1}{2}\sigma_u^2 p_{11}[x, t] + (\alpha - \lambda\bar{y})p_1[x, t] + p_2[x, t] + \lambda\int p[x + y, t]g(y; x, t)dy \tag{79}$$

which is a linear partial differential-difference equation for the transition probabilities $p[x, t]$. Hence, knowledge of the functions σ_u^2, α, λ, and g is sufficient to determine the probability distribution for the change in X between any two dates. Moreover, from (79), it can be shown that the asymptotic distribution for $X(t)$ is identical to that of a stochastic process driven by a linear superposition of a continuous-sample-path diffusion process and a "Poisson-directed" process.[21] That is, let $Q(t+h) - Q(t)$ be a Poisson-distributed random variable with characteristic parameter $\lambda[X(t), t]h$. Define formally the differential $dQ(t)$ to be the limit of $Q(t + h) - Q(t)$ as $h \rightarrow dt$. It follows from the Poisson density function, therefore, that

$$\begin{aligned} dQ(t) &= 0 \quad \text{with probability} \quad 1 - \lambda[X(t), t]dt + o(dt) \\ &= 1 \quad \text{with probability} \quad \lambda[X(t), t]dt + o(dt) \\ &= N \quad \text{with probability} \quad o(dt), N = 2, \ldots. \end{aligned} \tag{80}$$

Define the random variable $X_1(t)$ by the process $dX_1(t) = y(t)dQ(t)$ where $y(t)$ is a $O(1)$ random variable with probability density $g(y; X(t), t)$. Then, dX_1 is an example of a "Poisson-directed" process. Note: The instantaneous expected change in dX_1 is $\lambda\bar{y}(t)dt$. Define a second random variable $X_2(t)$ by the process $dX_2(t) = \alpha\, dt + \sigma' dZ$ where dZ is a Weiner process as defined by (45) in section II. From (47) in section II, dX_2 is a diffusion process with a continuous sample path. If the function α' is chosen such that $\alpha' \equiv \alpha[X(t), t] - \lambda[X(t), t]\bar{y}(t)$ and $\sigma' \equiv \sigma_u[X(t), t]$, then from (79), the limiting process for the change in X, $dX(t)$, will be identical to the process described by $dX_1(t) + dX_2(t)$.

Hence, with no loss in generality, we can always describe the continuous-trading dynamics for $X(t)$ by the stochastic differential equation

$$dX(t) = \{\alpha[X(t), t] - \lambda[X(t), t]\bar{y}(t)\}dt + \sigma[X(t), t]dZ(t) + y(t)dQ(t) \tag{81}$$

where α is the instantaneous expected change in X per unit time; σ^2 is the instantaneous variance of the change in X, conditional on the change being a Type I outcome; λ is the probability per unit time that the change in X is a Type III outcome; and $y(t)$ is the random variable outcome for the change in X, conditional on the change being a Type III outcome. As was discussed in section II, the stochastic differential representation in (81) is actually defined by a stochastic integral, $X(T) - X(0) = \int_0^t dX(t)$. Of course, if $\lambda \equiv 0$ and only Type I outcomes can occur, then (81) reduces to (47) in section II.

In a similar fashion, it can be shown that stochastic differential representation for F can be written as

$$\begin{aligned} dF(t) = &\left\{\frac{1}{2}\sigma^2 f_{11}[X(t), t] + [\alpha - \lambda\bar{y}]f_1[X(t), t] + f_2[X(t), t]\right\}dt \\ &+ \sigma f_1[X(t), t]dZ(t) + \left\{f[X(t) + y(t), t] - f[X(t), t]\right\}dQ(t) \end{aligned} \tag{82}$$

Thus, if the dynamics of $X(t)$ can be described by a superposition of diffusion- and Poisson-directed processes, then the dynamics of well-behaved functions of $X(t)$ can be described in the same way. Hence, (82) provides the transformation rule corresponding to Itô's Lemma for pure diffusion processes.

[21]See Cox and Miller (1968, pp. 237–246) for the formal analysis of "mixed" processes of this type where it is shown that such processes will have transition probabilities which satisfy (79). For "jump" processes alone, see Feller (1966, Volume II, pp. 316–20).

In summary, if the economic structure to be analyzed is such that assumptions (E.1) to (E.5) obtain, then in continuous-trading models security price dynamics can always be described by a "mixture" of continuous-sample-path diffusion processes and Poisson-directed processes with no loss in generality. The diffusion process component describes the frequent local changes in prices and is, indeed, sufficient in structures where the magnitudes of the state variables cannot change "radically" in a short period of time. The Poisson-directed process component is used to capture those rare events when the state variables have nonlocal changes and security prices "jump."[22]

While the introduction of a "jump" component provides a significant complication to the analysis over a pure diffusion process, the analysis of the general continuous-trading model is still much simpler than for its discrete-trading counterpart. As (79) demonstrates, the transition probabilities are completely specified by only the four functions: α, σ, λ, and g. Not only does this simplify the structural analysis, but it makes the testing of these model structures empirically feasible. Indeed, because for a given magnitude of change, each of the components has a different "time scale," it should be possible to design tests such that these various functions can be identified. For example, by using time series data with very short time intervals between observations, one could identify any "nonlocal" price movement between observations, as a "jump," and hence, calculate an estimate of λ. Similarly, the squares of local price movements between observations could be used to estimate σ^2. Finally, armed with λ and σ^2, the price movements over relatively long time periods could be used to estimate α and $\bar{y}$.

[22]For examples of Poisson-directed processes in intertemporal portfolio selection, see Merton (1971, pp. 395–401). For studies of the impact on corporate liabilities pricing theory when the underlying state variables have "jump" components, see Cox and Ross (1976) and Merton (1976).

Bibliography

Arnold, L., *Stochastic Differential Equations: Theory and Applications.* New York: John Wiley, 1974.

Black, F., and **M. Scholes,** "The Pricing of Options and Corporate Liabilities," *Journal of Political Economy,* 81 (1973), 637–54.

Bourgnignon, F., "A Particular Class of Continuous-Time Stochastic Growth Models," *Journal of Economic Theory,* 9 (October 1974).

Cootner, P. H. ed., *The Random Character of Stock Market Prices.* Cambridge, Mass.: M.I.T. Press, 1964.

Cox, D. A., and **H. D. Miller,** *The Theory of Stochastic Processes.* New York: John Wiley, 1968.

Cox, J., and **S. Ross,** "The Valuation of Options for Alternative Stochastic Processes," *Journal of Financial Economics,* 3 (1976), 145–66.

Fama, E., "Mandelbrot and the Stable Paretian Hypothesis," *Journal of Business,* 36 (1963), 420–29.

———, "Portfolio Analysis in a Stable Paretian Market," *Management Science,* II, no. 3 (1965a), 404–19.

———, "The Behavior of Stock Market Prices," *Journal of Business,* 38 (1965b), 34–105.

———, "Efficient Capital Markets: A Review of Theory and Empirical Work," *Journal of Finance,* 25 (1970), 383-417.

Feller, W., *An Introduction to Probability Theory and Its Applications.* New York: John Wiley, 1966.

Itô, K. and **H. P. McKean, Jr.,** *Diffusion Processes and Their Sample Paths.* New York: Academic Press, 1964.

Kushner, H., *Stochastic Stability and Control.* New York: Academic Press, 1967.

Mandelbrot, B., "New Methods in Statistical Economics," *Journal of Political Economy,* 61 (1963a).

———, "The Variation of Certain Speculative Prices," *Journal of Business,* 36 (1963b), 394-419.

McKean, H. P., Jr., *Stochastic Integrals.* New York: Academic Press, 1969.

McShane, E. J., *Stochastic Calculus and Stochastic Models.* New York: Academic Press, 1974.

Merton, R. C., "Optimum Consumption and Portfolio Rules in a Continuous-Time Model," *Journal of Economic Theory,* 3 (1971), 373-413.

———, "Theory of Rational Option Pricing," *Bell Journal of Economics and Management Science,* 4 (1973a), 141–83.

———, "An Intertemporal Capital Asset Pricing Model," *Econometrica,* 41 (1973b), 867-87.

———, "An Asymptotic Theory of Growth Under Uncertainty," *Review of Economic Studies,* XLII (1975a), 373–93.

———, "Theory of Finance from the Perspective of Continuous Time," *Journal of Financial and Quantitative Analysis,* 10 (1975b), 659–74.

———, "Option Pricing When Underlying Stock Returns Are Discontinuous," *Journal of Financial Economics,* 3 (1976), 125-44.

———, "On Estimating the Expected Return on the Market: An Exploratory Investigation," *Journal of Financial Economics,* 8 (1980), 323–61.

———, "On the Microeconomic Theory of Investment Under Uncertainty," in *Handbook of Mathematical Economics,* Vol. II, K. Arrow and M. Intriligator, eds., Amsterdam: North-Holland, 1981.

Rosenberg, B., "The Behavior of Random Variables with Nonstationary Variance and the Distribution of Security Prices," Graduate School of Business Administration Working Paper #11, University of California, Berkeley (December 1972).

Rosenfeld, E., *Stochastic Processes of Common Stock Returns: An Empirical Examination,* Ph.D. Dissertation, Sloan School of Management, M.I.T., 1980.

Samuelson, P. A., "Proof that Properly Anticipated Prices Fluctuate Randomly," *Industrial Management Review,* 6 (1965), 41–49.

———, "Efficient Portfolio Selection for Pareto Levy Investments," *Journal of Financial and Quantitative Analysis* (1967), 107–22.

———, "Proof that Properly Discounted Percent Values of Assets Vibrate Randomly," *Bell Journal of Economics and Management Science,* 4 (1973), 369–74.

Smith, C. W., "Option Pricing: A Review," *Journal of Financial Economics,* 3 (1976), 3–52.

[2]

J. Michael Harrison
Richard Pitbladdo
Stanford University

Stephen M. Schaefer
London Business School

Continuous Price Processes in Frictionless Markets Have Infinite Variation

The "continuous time model" in finance makes assumptions both about the characteristics of the market (absence of frictions, continuous trading opportunities, and so forth) and about the stochastic process that governs prices. Usually, these assumptions are introduced as if they were independent, that is, as if the characteristics of the market did not constrain the choice of stochastic process. In this paper we ask the following question: If trading is continuous and frictionless, what classes of stochastic process may be chosen that also admit equilibrium? We restrict our attention to processes whose sample paths are continuous. Our conclusion is given by the title of the paper.

I. Introduction

The "continuous time model" is central to much of financial economics, forming the basis of option-pricing theory (Black and Scholes 1973; Merton 1973*b*) and a number of intertemporal valuation models (Merton 1973*a*; Breeden 1979). The continuous time model involves two sets of assumptions. The first concerns the characteristics of the market (absence of frictions, continuous trading opportunities, and so forth); the second concerns the stochastic process governing prices. These assumptions are usually introduced as if they were independent; that is, as if the characteristics of the market did not constrain the nature of the stochastic process. In this paper we ask the following question: If trading is continuous and frictionless, what classes of stochastic processes may be chosen to describe prices which also admit equilibrium? Attention will be restricted to processes whose sample paths are continuous.

The most frequently employed continuous processes are diffusions, all intimately related to Brownian motion. Among the characteristics of such processes is that their sample paths display unbounded variation. (Variation, to be defined rigorously in Sec. III, represents the cumulative upward and downward displacement of the function in question.) This property makes the as-

(*Journal of Business*, 1984, vol. 57, no. 3)
© 1984 by The University of Chicago. All rights reserved.
0021-9398/84/5703-0004$01.50

sumption of zero transaction costs quite critical in some cases. Consider the hedging strategy dictated by the usual derivation of the Black-Scholes option-pricing formula. If proportional transaction costs were positive rather than zero—no matter how small—then the total transaction costs would be infinite over any finite interval.

This observation motivates the following related question: Is it possible to represent prices with a process that has sample paths with bounded variation? We show that a continuous stochastic price process whose sample paths have bounded variation must necessarily admit arbitrage opportunities. The intuition behind this result is that continuous, bounded variation price processes are "too smooth," resulting in significant positive correlation between successive small increments. An investor who can trade continuously and without cost would be able to spot the direction in which prices are moving and exploit this in trading. Thus, if arbitrage opportunities are not present, prices must have unbounded variation.

The effect of our analysis is to rule out certain stochastic processes as equilibrium price models, because they are too smooth. Is this result obvious? To argue that it is not, we identify three levels of increasing smoothness for continuous functions: (*a*) finite variation, (*b*) absolute continuity, and (*c*) absolute continuity with a continuous density. If a price process has paths that are smooth in the sense of *b*, this means that the rate of price change is well defined for each security and each time point, and *c* means that furthermore that rate varies continuously with time. It really is obvious that *c* implies arbitrage opportunities unless all securities are identical, and most economists familiar with continuous time models would say that *b* is obviously too smooth as well. So the contribution of this paper is to rule out processes whose paths fall in category *a* but not *b*. In Section VII we give an example which illustrates this distinction.

The paper is organized as follows. In Section II we give an heuristic account of the portfolio policies that lead to arbitrage when prices have bounded variation. Sections III–VI provide a rigorous version of this argument. Finally, Section VII contains the example and our conclusions.

II. The Heuristic Argument

Consider a market in which K securities are traded. For each security k we denote by X_k the associated price process, $X_k(t)$, representing the price of one share of security k and time t. Units are chosen so that $X_k(0) = 1$, and it is assumed throughout that X_k is continuous, strictly positive, and has finite variation with certainty ($k = 1, \ldots, K$). When discussing trading strategies, we denote by $S_k(t)$ the number of shares of security k held at time t and by $V(t)$ the total dollar value of the portfolio held at time t. That is,

$$V(t) = \sum_{k=1}^{K} X_k(t)S_k(t), \quad t \geq 0. \tag{1}$$

As indicated above, one might attempt arbitrage profits by buying the "hot" stocks and selling the cold ones. As it happens, one need not be so sophisticated; it is enough to buy those securities that have performed better *since time zero* and sell those that have performed worse since time zero. Roughly, the argument goes as follows.

Let p be a fixed real number. Consider a portfolio with an initial investment of one dollar and no net investment thereafter, which is continuously adjusted so that the dollar value of holdings of security k at time t is proportional to $[X_k(t)]^p$. In symbols, this last property is expressed by

$$\frac{X_k(t)S_k(t)}{V(t)} = \frac{[X_k(t)]^p}{\sum_{j=1}^{K}[X_j(t)]^p}. \tag{2}$$

For high values of p, (2) says that relatively larger amounts of the higher priced securities are held, and vice versa for low values of p. If $p = 1$, then (2) describes the buy-and-hold strategy where $S_k(t) = 1/K$ for all k and t. If $p = 0$, (2) describes the continuous-dollar-equalization strategy, where one equalizes the dollar value of holdings in each security at each point in time.

Now, just exactly how does one adjust one's portfolio over time to achieve (2)? Obviously, (2) gives

$$S_k(t) = \frac{V(t)\,[X_k(t)]^{p-1}}{\Sigma[X_j(t)]^p}, \tag{3}$$

but it remains to express V in terms not involving $S_1, \ldots, S_K$. In differential terms, the zero net new investment requirement is expressed as

$$dV(t) = \Sigma\, S_k(t)dX_k(t), \tag{4}$$

this saying that all changes in portfolio value are due to capital gains. Now (3) and (4) together give, for the case $p \neq 0$,

$$\begin{aligned} dV(t) &= \frac{V(t)\Sigma[X_k(t)]^{p-1}dX_k(t)}{\Sigma[X_k(t)]^p} \\ &= \frac{V(t)\Sigma\,\frac{1}{p}\,d[X_k(t)]^p}{\Sigma[X_k(t)]^p}. \end{aligned} \tag{5}$$

That is,

$$\frac{dV(t)}{V(t)} = \frac{1}{p} \frac{d\,\Sigma[X_k(t)]^p}{\Sigma[X_k(t)]^p}. \tag{6}$$

or

$$d \log V(t) = \frac{1}{p} d \log \Sigma[X_k(t)]^p. \tag{7}$$

Using the fact that $V(0) = X_k(0) = 1$, we deduce from (7) that

$$V(t) = \left\{\frac{1}{K} \sum_{k=1}^{K} [X_k(t)]^p\right\}^{1/p}. \tag{8}$$

Thus $V(t)$ is the pth order *power mean* of the prices $X_1(t), \ldots, X_K(t)$, provided that the heuristics have not led us astray (as they would have in the case of diffusions). Hereafter this pth order power mean will be denoted by $V^p(t)$ rather than $V(t)$, and trading strategy (3) will be called the p-strategy. A similar set of calculations suggest that in the case $p = 0$,

$$V^0(t) = \left\{\prod_{k=1}^{K} X_k(t)\right\}^{1/K},$$

the geometric mean. Note that execution of these strategies requires only knowledge of past and present prices.

Together, (3) and (8) spell out in explicit terms a trading strategy that yields at time t a portfolio with market value $V^p(t)$. How does this strategy constitute an arbitrage opportunity? The following property of power means is proved by Hardy, Littlewood, and Polya (1959); it is an easy consequence of Jensen's inequality.

Proposition 1: If $-\infty < p < q < \infty$, then $V^p(t) \leqslant V^q(t)$, with equality only when $X_1(t) = \ldots = X_K(t)$.

To make arbitrage profits, buy $1/K$ shares of each security at time zero and manage this portfolio according to the q-strategy, and sell $1/K$ shares of each security at time zero and manage these short positions according to the p-strategy. This yields a profit of $V^q(t) - V^p(t)$ at time t with no investment.

In what sense is the preceding argument heuristic? Expressed in mathematical terms, the answer is that we have not justified the progression from (5) to (8) rigorously. To put this in economic terms, we have not really shown that the p-strategy requires zero net new investment after time zero. In the language of Harrison and Kreps (1979), we have not shown that the p-strategy is "self-financing." The usual condition given to justify manipulations like (5)–(8) is differentiability of the price process. In the sections to follow, it will be shown that this justification extends to the more general case under consideration and hence that the p-strategy really *is* self-financing.

Of course, it makes sense to take q very large and p very negative. Examining the limiting values, we see that

$$\lim_{q\to\infty}\left(\frac{1}{K}\sum X_k(t)^q\right)^{1/q} = \max_{k=1,\ldots,K}\{X_k(t)\}$$

and

$$\lim_{p\to-\infty}\left(\frac{1}{K}\sum X_k(t)^p\right)^{1/p} = \min_{k=1,\ldots,K}\{X_k(t)\},$$

(the convergence is not uniform). Furthermore, as $q \to \infty$, the associated strategy comes closer to holding only the highest-priced security (equal division when there is more than one security at the maximum). The fact that $V^q(t) \to \max_k X_k(t)$ as $q \to \infty$ lends credibility to such a strategy of "going with the leader," provided the price process is smooth enough to justify the heuristics. (In the case where the X_k are diffusions, the described strategy has such a pervasive set of discontinuities that it is not readily approximated by simple strategies. In trying to go with the leader in a realistic way, one cannot keep up when the lead changes hands.)

Our analysis is an extension of earlier work by Hodges and Schaefer (1974), who used the strategies described above to argue that geometric stock price indices (e.g., the Valueline Index) were misleading because the conditions under which a geometric price index represents a feasible portfolio strategy also lead to arbitrage opportunities. Hodges and Schaefer were able to demonstrate the connection between continuous dollar equalization and the geometric mean only in the case where price paths are differentiable.

III. Notation and Definitions

Let f be a real-valued function on $[0, \infty)$. Consider an interval $[a, b]$, $0 \leq a \leq b \leq \infty$ and a finite partition $P = (x_1, x_2, \ldots, x_n)$ of $[a, b]$, where $a \leq x_1 < x_2 < \ldots < x_n \leq b$. Now define $v_f(P) = \Sigma_{i=2}^n |f(x_i) - f(x_{i-1})|$. Further define $V_f[a, b] = \sup\{v_f(P): P \text{ is a finite partition of } [a, b]\}$. If $V_f[a, b] < \infty$ we say that f has bounded variation over $[a, b]$, or that $f \in BV[a, b]$, and $V_f[a, b]$ is called the total variation of f over $[a, b]$. If $V_f[a, b] < \infty$ for all such choices of $[a, b]$, then we say that $f \in BV[0, \infty)$. The proof of the following proposition may be found in Royden (1963, p. 100).

Proposition 2: $f \in BV[a, b]$ if and only if f is the difference of two increasing functions on $[a, b]$.

The decomposition given in Royden also shows that if $f \in BV[a, b]$ is continuous, it is the difference between two continuous increasing functions whose sum is $V_f[a, t]$, $t \in (a, b)$. Thus we have the following:

PROPOSITION 3: If $f \in BV[a, b]$ is continuous, then $V_f[a, t]$ is continuous in t on $[a, b]$. It is also easy to see that if $f \in BV[a, c]$ and $a < b < c$, then $V_f[a, b] + V_f[b, c] = V_f[a, c]$.

IV. Riemann-Stieltjes Integrals

We claimed earlier that continuous price processes whose sample paths have bounded variation admit arbitrage opportunities. The proof hinges on the valuation of certain Riemann-Stieltjes integrals. These integrals have the form $\int_0^T f(t)dg(t)$, $0 \leq T < \infty$, where f and g are real-valued functions on $[0, \infty)$. In this section we record some properties of Riemann-Stieltjes integration that will be needed later. For a definition of the Riemann-Stieltjes integral, see Bartle (1976, pp. 212–14).

PROPOSITION 4: If f is continuous and $g \in BV[0, T]$, the f is integrable with respect to g on $[0, T]$.

Remark. This is proved in Bartle (1976, theorem 30.2) for the case where g is monotone. But if proposition 2 above and the bilinearity property are used, the extension follows easily. (The bilinearity property, theorem 29.5 of Bartle [1976], says that the integral is linear in both f and g).

The next two results are not found in standard introductions to Riemann-Stieltjes integration. Nevertheless, we do not claim originality.

PROPOSITION 5 (chain rule): Let f and g be continuous on $[0, \infty)$ with $g \in BV[0, \infty)$. If $\phi: \mathbf{R} \to \mathbf{R}$ is continuously differentiable, then

$$\int_0^T f(t)d\phi[g(t)] = \int_0^T f(t)\phi'[g(t)]dg(t), \quad 0 < T < \infty.$$

(Implicit here is the statement that both integrals exist.)

PROOF: See Appendix A.

PROPOSITION 6 (change of variables): Let h be continuous on $[0, \infty)$ and let $g \in BV\,[0, \infty)$ be continuous. Then

$$\int_0^t h[g(u)]dg(u) = \int_{g(0)}^{g(t)} h(v)dv.$$

Remark. This result is usually stated for the case where g is monotone, but the direct method of proof used for that case does not extend to our case.

PROOF: See Appendix B.

V. Formal Verification

We now formally verify that V^p satisfies (4). This amounts to a rigorous justification of the progression from (5) to (8) in Section II. As in Section II, assume $p > 0$ and define

$$S_k(t) = V^p(t)\,\frac{[X_k(t)]^{p-1}}{\Sigma_j[X_j(t)]^p},$$

where $V^p(t) = \{(1/K)\,\Sigma_k[X_k(t)]^p\}^{1/p}$ and $X_1, \ldots, X_K$ are stochastic processes whose sample paths are continuous and strictly positive and have bounded variation.

PROPOSITION 7: $V^p(t) = V^p(0) + \Sigma_k \int_0^t S_k(u)dX_k(u)$.

COROLLARY: $\Sigma_k \int_0^t X_k(u)dS_k(u) = 0$.

PROOF: The corollary follows from the proposition by integration by parts (see Bartle 1976, p. 219). If $p \neq 0$, then

$$\begin{aligned}
\sum_{k=1}^{K}\int_0^t S_k(u)dX_k(u) &= \sum_{k=1}^{K}\int_0^t \left(\frac{1}{K}\right)^{1/p} \{\Sigma_j[X_j(u)]^p\}^{1/p-1}[X_k(u)]^{p-1}dX_k(u) \\
&= \Sigma_k \int_0^t \left(\frac{1}{K}\right)^{1/p} \{\Sigma_j[X_j(u)]^{p}\}^{1/p-1} d\left\{\frac{1}{p}[X_k(u)]^p\right\} \\
&= \left(\frac{1}{K}\right)^{1/p} \int_0^t \frac{1}{p}\{\Sigma_j[X_j(u)]^p\}^{1/p-1} d\{\Sigma_k[X_k(u)]^p\} \\
&= \left(\frac{1}{K}\right)^{1/p} \int_{\Sigma_k[X_k(0)]^p}^{\Sigma_k[X_k(t)]^p} \frac{1}{p}\, v^{1/p-1}dv \\
&= \left(\frac{1}{K}\right)^{1/p} \left(\{\Sigma_k[X_k(t)]^p\}^{1/p} - \{\Sigma_k[X_k(0)]^p\}^{1/p}\right) \\
&= V^p(t) - V^p(0).
\end{aligned}$$

The first equality is by substitution, the second from proposition 5, the third from the bilinearity property, and the fourth from proposition 6. The case $p = 0$ is similar and is left to the reader. Q.E.D.

Proposition 7 and its corollary provide two articulations of the self-financing character of the trading strategy $S_1, \ldots, S_K$. The second term on the right-hand side of the proposition represents the investor's total earnings (or capital gains) up to time t, so the proposition states that all changes in the market value of the portfolio are due to capital gains or losses, as opposed to cash withdrawal (through liquidation) or the infusion of new funds. The corollary states the same thing in simpler terms. Its left-hand side represents the net cost of transactions (cumulative cost of purchases minus cumulative revenue from sales) between times zero and t, and this is found to be zero. To paraphrase, the increment of revenue generated by the sale of securities over any period is exactly balanced by the cost of security purchases over that same period.

The preceding statements are valid only if the definition of the Riemann-Stieltjes integral is such that $\Sigma_k \int_0^t S_k(u)dX_k(u)$ is the correct expression for capital gains over $[0, T]$, and that $\Sigma_k \int_0^t X_k(u)dS_k(u)$ is the correct expression for the net cost of transactions over $[0, T]$. This is the subject of the next section.

VI. Approximating Simple Strategies

There are two ways to justify the use of Riemann-Stieltjes integrals. The first approach will be sketched. The second approach is technically more difficult and thus will be examined rigorously.

Fix a time $T > 0$, let N be a large fixed integer and let $t_n = nT/N$ for $n = 0, 1, \ldots, N$. Consider a trading strategy which at time $t_0 = 0$ buys $1/K$ units of each security and holds them until time t_1, at which time the portfolio is liquidated and $S_k(t_1)$ units of each security are purchased. Similarly, at each time t_i, the portfolio is liquidated and $S_k(t_i)$ units of each security are purchased. Holdings in this strategy are the same as $S_k(t)$ at each time t_i, and are close to $S_k(t)$ in each interval $[t_i, t_{i+1})$ by virtue of the continuity of S_k. The described strategy is not self-financing, but the net cost of transactions over $[0, t]$ for such a strategy is seen to be an approximating sum for $\Sigma_k \int_0^t X_k(u)dS_k(u)$, and the capital gains from such a strategy is seen to be an approximating sum for $\Sigma_k \int_0^t S_k(u)dX_k(u)$. The details of this argument are straightforward and are left to the reader.

Thus the use of Riemann-Stieltjes theory is justified by showing that simple strategies "close" to S_k are "nearly" self-financing. Alternatively, one might approximate S_k by a simple strategy which is self-financing and of which the value at time T is close to $V^P(T)$.

Fix a time $T > 0$. Let N be a large fixed integer and let $t_n = nT/N$ for $n = 0, 1, \ldots, N$. Consider a trading strategy which initially buys $1/K$ shares of each security $k = 1, 2, \ldots, K$ and thereafter trades only at times t_n. At those times the portfolio is adjusted so that the dollar value of holdings of each security k is proportional to $[X_k(t_n)]^p$, much like the continually adjusted strategy S^p. No net infusion of funds takes place at these times. Thus it is seen that (employing the obvious notation)

$$S_{Nk}(t_n) = V_N^p(t_n)\frac{[X_k(t_n)]^{p-1}}{\Sigma_j[X_j(t_n)]^p},$$

where $V_N^p(t_n) = \Sigma_k S_{Nk}(t_{n-1})X_k(t_n)$.

The following fact is elementary and the proof is left to the reader.

PROPOSITION 8: Let f be integrable with respect to g. Then

$$\left|\int_0^t f(u)dg(u)\right| \leq \sup_{0 \leq u \leq t}|f(u)|V_g[0, t].$$

PROPOSITION 9: For each sample path (for which $X_1, \ldots, X_K$ are continuous and have bounded variation), $\lim_{N\to\infty} V_N^p(T) = V^p(T)$.

PROOF: Let $\delta = \inf_{0<t<T} V^p(t)'' > 0$. Given $\epsilon > 0$, let N be large enough so that $|S_k(t_n) - S_k(\xi)| < \epsilon$ for all $\xi \in [t_n, t_{n+1}]$ and $V_{X_k}[t_n, t_{n+1}] < \delta/K$, $k = 1, 2, \ldots, K$ and $n = 0, 1, \ldots, N$. This is possible by the uniform continuity of the functions S_k and of $V_{X_k}[0, \cdot]$ (see proposition 3). Note that

$$\frac{S_k(t_n)}{V^p(t_n)} = \frac{S_{Nk}(t_n)}{V_N^p(t_n)}$$

for $n = 0, 1, \ldots, N$, so that

$$\begin{aligned}\sum_{k=1}^{K} S_k(t_n)X_k(t_{n+1}) &= \frac{V^p(t_n)}{V_N^p(t_n)} \sum_{k=1}^{K} S_{Nk}(t_n)X_k(t_{n+1}) \\ &= V^p(t_n)\frac{V_N^p(t_{n+1})}{V_N^p(t_n)}.\end{aligned}$$

Thus we have

$$\begin{aligned}&\left|V^p(t_{n+1}) - V^p(t_n)\frac{V_N^p(t_{n+1})}{V_N^p(t_n)}\right| \\ &= \left|V^p(t_{n+1}) - \sum_{k=1}^{K} S_k(t_n)X_k(t_{n+1})\right| \\ &= \left|V^p(t_{n+1}) - V^p(t_n) - \sum_{k=1}^{K} S_k(t_n)\,[X_k(t_{n+1}) - X_k(t_n)]\right| \\ &= \left|V^p(t_{n+1}) - V^p(t_n) - \sum_{k=1}^{K} \int_{t_n}^{t_{n+1}} S_k(t_n)dX_k(u)\right| \\ &= \left|\sum_{k=1}^{K} \int_{t_n}^{t_{n+1}} [S_k(u) - S_k(t_n)]dX_k(u)\right| \\ &\leqslant \epsilon \sum_{k=1}^{K} V_{X_k}[t_n, t_{n+1}].\end{aligned}$$

The last inequality is by proposition 8. Dividing the left-hand side of the inequality above by $V^p(t_{n+1})$ and the right-hand side by δ $[\leqslant V^p(t_{n+1})]$, we have

$$\left|1 - \frac{V^p(t_n)}{V^p(t_{n+1})}\,\frac{V_N^p(t_{n+1})}{V_N^p(t_n)}\right| \leqslant \frac{\epsilon}{\delta} \sum_{k=1}^{K} V_{X_k}[t_n, t_{n+1}],$$

or

$$1 - \frac{\epsilon}{\delta}\sum_{k=1}^{K} V_{X_k}[t_n, t_{n+1}] \leqslant \frac{V^p(t_n)}{V^p(t_{n+1})}\,\frac{V_N^p(t_{n+1})}{V_N^p(t_n)} \leqslant 1 + \frac{\epsilon}{\delta}\sum_{k=1}^{K} V_{X_k}[t_n, t_{n+1}].$$

Since $V_{X_k}(t_n, t_{n+1}) < \delta/K$, we may take the logarithm of each term:

$$\log\left[1 - \frac{\epsilon}{\delta}\sum_{k=1}^{K} V_{X_k}[t_n, t_{n+1}]\right] \leqslant \log\left[\frac{V_N^p(t_{n+1})}{V^p(t_{n+1})}\right] - \log\left[\frac{V_N^p(t_n)}{V^p(t_n)}\right] \leqslant \log\left[1 + \frac{\epsilon}{\delta}\sum_{k=1}^{K} V_{X_k}[t_n, t_{n+1}]\right],$$

Summing up,

$$\sum_{n=0}^{N-1}\log\left[1 - \frac{\epsilon}{\delta}\sum_{k=1}^{K} V_{X_k}[t_n, t_{n+1}]\right] \leqslant \log\left[\frac{V_N^p(T)}{V^p(T)}\right] \leqslant \sum_{n=0}^{N-1}\log\left[1 + \frac{\epsilon}{\delta}\sum_{k=1}^{K} V_{X_k}[t_n, t_{n+1}]\right].$$

Now by the mean value theorem we know that for some $\xi \in \{-\epsilon/\delta\ \Sigma_{k=1}^{K} V_{X_k}[t_n, t_{n+1}], 0\}$,

$$\log\left(1 - \frac{\epsilon}{\delta}\sum_{k=1}^{K} V_{X_k}[t_n, t_{n+1}]\right) = \frac{-1}{1+\xi}\,\frac{\epsilon}{\delta}\sum_{k=1}^{K} V_{X_k}[t_n, t_{n+1}].$$

Also, for some $\eta \in [0, \epsilon/\delta\ \Sigma_{k=1}^{K} V_{X_k}[t_n, t_{n+1}]]$

$$\log\left(1 + \frac{\epsilon}{\delta}\sum_{k=1}^{K} V_{X_k}[t_n, t_{n+1}]\right) = \frac{1}{1+\eta}\,\frac{\epsilon}{\delta}\sum_{k=1}^{K} V_{X_k}[t_n, t_{n+1}].$$

Now $\epsilon/\delta\ \Sigma_{k=1}^{K} V_{X_k}(t_n, t_{n+1}) \leqslant \epsilon$, so that $\xi \geqslant -\epsilon$, and

$$\frac{-1}{1-\epsilon}\,\frac{\epsilon}{\delta}\sum_{k=1}^{K} V_{X_k}[0, T] = \frac{-1}{1-\epsilon}\,\frac{\epsilon}{\delta}\sum_{n=0}^{N-1}\sum_{k=1}^{K} V_{X_k}[t_n, t_{n+1}]$$
$$\leqslant \log V_N^p(T) - \log V^p(T) \leqslant \frac{\epsilon}{\delta}\sum_{n=0}^{N-1}\sum_{k=1}^{K} V_{X_k}\,[t_n, t_{n+1}]$$
$$\leqslant \frac{\epsilon}{\delta}\sum_{k=1}^{K} V_{X_k}[0, T].$$

Since the first and last terms are arbitrarily small by taking ϵ small, the same holds true for the middle term. Q.E.D.

VII. Concluding Remarks

We set out to show that in a frictionless market with continuous trading, if equilibrium prices are continuous, they must have unbounded variation with positive probability. The proof involved showing that without unbounded variation, arbitrage opportunities are present. Thus we have provided a link between the characteristics of the market (absence of frictions, continuous trading, etc.) and the characteristics of admissible price processes.

Section I raised the question whether our result is obvious. We argued that while absolute continuity in prices obviously gives rise to arbitrage opportunities unless all securities are identical, the same is not true for price processes that have finite variation but are not absolutely continuous. We conclude with an example of such a process.

Let X and Y be two independent Brownian motions with $X(0) = Y(0) = 0$, and define $Z(t) = \sup_{0 \leq s \leq t} X(s) - \sup_{0 \leq s \leq t} Y(s)$, $t \geq 0$. Each sample path of Z is the difference of two continuous increasing functions, so each is continuous and has finite variation on finite intervals. It is well known, however, that the maximum process of a Brownian motion increases only on a set of time points having zero Lebesque measure; increases in the maximum process are very jerky. Thus Z is flat except on a set of measure zero, and it is meaningless to talk about the rate of increase or rate of decrease for Z. The derivative of Z exists and equals zero at almost all time points, and yet Z is not constant.

Consider a market with one stock and one bond. Assume that the bond price process is constant (the riskless interest rate is zero) and the stock price at time t is $\exp[Z(t)]$. It is important that investors cannot see X and Y; they have knowledge of the past and present stock prices only. Do arbitrage opportunities exist in this market? We have shown in this paper that they do, but it is not a priori obvious. In particular, one cannot earn arbitrage profits by holding stock only when the stock price is rising, because the stock price is almost always constant.

Appendix A

Proof of Proposition 5

PROOF: Existence of the second integral is by proposition 4. Let M bound $|f|$ on $[0, T]$, and let $\epsilon > 0$ be given. Let P_ϵ be a partition such that if $P = (0, x_1, \ldots, x_n)$ is any refinement of P_ϵ, and if $\xi_i \in [x_{i-1}, x_i]$ and $\nu_i \in [x_{i-1}, x_i]$, then

$$\left| \sum_{i=1}^{n} f(\xi_i)\phi'[g(\xi_i)][g(x_i) - g(x_{i-1})] - \int_0^T f(t)\phi'[g(t)]dg(t) \right| < \epsilon,$$

and

$$|\phi'[g(\nu_i)] - \phi'[g(\xi_i)]| < \epsilon \quad i = 1, 2, \ldots, n.$$

The first inequality is possible from the definition of the integral, and the second arises from the (uniform) continuity of $\phi'[g(\cdot)]$ on $[0, T]$.

Now for any such partition P there exists $\eta_i \in (x_{i-1}, x_i)$ such that $\phi[g(x_i)] - \phi[g(x_{i-1})] = \phi'[g(\eta_i)][g(x_i) - g(x_{i-1})]$. This follows from the mean value and intermediate value theorems. Thus,

$$\left|\sum_{i=1}^{n} f(\xi_i)\{\phi[g(x_i)] - \phi[g(x_{i-1})]\} - \int_0^T f(t)\phi'[g(t)]dg(t)\right|$$

$$= \left|\sum_{i=1}^{n} f(\xi_i)\,\phi'(\eta_i)[g(x_i) - g(x_{i-1})]' - \int_0^T f(t)\phi'[g(t)]dg(t)\right|$$

$$\leqslant \left|\sum_{i=1}^{n} f(\xi_i)(\phi'[g(\eta_i)] - \phi'[g(\xi_i)][g(x_i) - g(x_{i-1})]\right|$$

$$+ \left|\sum_{i=1}^{n} f(\xi_i)\phi'[g(\xi_i)][g(x_i) - g(x_{i-1})] - \int_0^T f(t)\phi'[g(t)]dg(t)\right|.$$

Now the first term of the expression above is less than or equal to $M\epsilon\, \Sigma_{i=1}^{n}\, |g(x_i) - g(i=1)| \leqslant M\epsilon V_g[0, T]$, so that

$$\left|\sum_{i=1}^{n} f(\xi_i)\{\phi[g(x_i)] - \phi[g(x_{i-1})]\} - \int_0^T f(t)\phi'[g(t)]dg(t)\right|$$

$$\leqslant (M \cdot V_g[0, T] + 1)\epsilon.$$

Thus the first integral exists and equals the second. Q.E.D.

Appendix B

Proof of Proposition 6

PROOF: Let $H(y) = \int_{g(0)}^{y} h(v)dv$. Then

$$\int_0^t h[g(u)]dg(u) = \int_0^t H'[g(u)]dg(u) = \int_0^t dH[g(u)]$$

$$= H[g(t)] - H[g(0)] = \int_{g(0)}^{g(t)} h(v)dv.$$

The first equality is by the fundamental theorem of calculus, and the second equality follows from proposition 5. Q.E.D.

References

Bartle, R. G. 1976. *Elements of Real Analysis*. 2d ed. New York: Wiley.

Black, F., and Scholes, M. 1973. The pricing of options and corporate liabilities. *Journal of Political Economy* 81:637–54.

Breeden, D. T. 1979. An intertemporal asset pricing model with stochastic consumption and investment opportunities. *Journal of Financial Economics* 7:265–96.

Hardy, G. H.; Littlewood, J. E.; and Polya, G. 1959. *Inequalities*. 2d ed. Cambridge: Cambridge University Press.

Harrison, J. M., and Kreps, D. M. 1979. Martingales and arbitrage in multiperiod securities markets. *Journal of Economic Theory* 20:381–408.
Hodges, S. D., and Schaefer, S. M. 1974. On the interpretation of the geometric mean: A comment. *Journal of Financial and Quantitative Analysis* 9:497–504.
Merton, R. C., 1973*a*. An intertemporal capital asset pricing model. *Econometrica* 41:867–88.
Merton, R. C. 1973*b*. Theory of rational option pricing. *Bell Journal of Economics and Management Science* 4:141–83.
Royden, E. 1963. *Real Analysis*. 2d ed. New York: Macmillan.

[3]

JOURNAL OF ECONOMIC THEORY **20**, 381–408 (1979)

Martingales and Arbitrage in Multiperiod Securities Markets

J. MICHAEL HARRISON AND DAVID M. KREPS

Graduate School of Business, Stanford University, Stanford, California 94305

Received May 24, 1978; revised February 9, 1979

1. INTRODUCTION AND SUMMARY

We consider in this paper some foundational issues that arise in conjunction with the arbitrage theory of option pricing. In this theory, initiated by Black and Scholes [4], one takes as given the price dynamics of certain securities (such as stocks and bonds). From these, one tries to determine the prices of other contingent claims (such as options written on a stock) through arbitrage considerations alone. That is, one seeks to show that there exists a single price for a specified contingent claim which, together with the given securities prices, will not permit arbitrage profits.

This paper contains a fairly general theory of contingent claim valuation along these lines. We begin in Section 2 with a general theory of arbitrage in a two-date economy with uncertainty. The dates are indexed $t = 0, T$. A probability space (Ω, F, P) if given, where points $\omega \in \Omega$ represent states of the world. The probability measure P can be interpreted for now as a set of unanimously held subjective probability assessments concerning the state of the world. There is a single consumption good, the numeraire, and agents are interested in certain consumption at date zero and state contingent consumption at date T. Thus we consider consumption bundles of the form $(r, x) \in R \times X$, where R is the real line and X is a space of random variables on (Ω, F). Here (r, x) represents r units of consumption at date zero and $x(\omega)$ units of consumption at date T if the state is ω.

Agents are specified by their preferences over $R \times X$, these being interpreted as preferences for *net trade vectors*. More explicitly, an agent's preferences are given by a complete and transitive binary relation $\succsim$ on $R \times X$ that is assumed to be convex, continuous and strictly increasing, in a sense to be made precise.

A *price system* for this economy is a pair (M, π) where M is a subspace of X and π is a linear functional on M. The interpretation is that agents can purchase any bundle $(r, m) \in R \times M$ at a price (in units of date zero consumption) of $r + \pi(m)$. In taking M to be a subspace and π a linear functional, we are assuming frictionless markets (no transaction costs and unrestricted

0022-0531/79/030381–28$02.00/0
Copyright © 1979 by Academic Press, Inc.

short sales). A price system (M, π) is said to be *viable* if there exists an agent (represented by $\gtrsim$) and a bundle $(r^*, m^*) \in R \times M$ such that

$$r^* + \pi(m^*) \leqslant 0 \text{ and } (r^*, m^*) \gtrsim (r, m) \text{ for all } (r, m) \in R \times M \text{ such that } r + \pi(m) \leqslant 0. \tag{1.1}$$

Since (r, m) is a net trade vector, the condition $r + \pi(m) \leqslant 0$ is the agent's budget constraint. Thus (1.1) is a necessary and sufficient condition for (M, π) to be viable *as a model of an economic equilibrium*. An equivalent condition is established in Theorem 1. A price system (M, π) is shown to be viable if and only if there exists a continuous and strictly positive extension of π to all of X.

Given a viable price system (M, π) and a contingent claim $x \in X$, what price in date zero consumption might x command? If x sold for price p, agents could purchase any claim of the form $m + \lambda x$ at a price of $\pi(m) + \lambda p$ (for $m \in M$ and λ real). It is natural, therefore, to say that price p for x *is consistent with* (M, π) if this augmented price system is viable. Claim x is said to be *priced by arbitrage* if there is a unique price for x that is consistent with (M, π). In this case, the unique consistent price is called the *arbitrage value* of x. As a corollary to Theorem 1, we find that x is priced by arbitrage if and only if it has the same value under every continuous and strictly positive linear extension of π to all of X, in which case that common value is the arbitrage value of the claim.

In Section 3 these general concepts are adapted to models of multiperiod securities markets. Given (Ω, F, P) and T as before, a *securities market model* consists of a set $\mathbf{T} \subseteq [0, T]$ of *trading dates*, an *information structure* represented by an increasing family of sub-σ-algebras, and a vector stochastic process $Z = \{Z(t); t \in \mathbf{T}\}$ that gives the prices of a finite collection of traded securities for every date $t \in \mathbf{T}$ and state $\omega \in \Omega$. We assume that one of these securities is a riskless bond and that the rate of return to this bond is zero. (This entails no significant loss of generality, as we discuss in Section 7.)

We next consider how agents can use the traded securities to transfer consumption between dates zero and T. We require (somewhat arbitrarily) that agents employ only what we call *simple trading strategies*. The key restriction is that an agent may change the contents of his portfolio of securities at only a finite number N of prespecified trading dates, although N may be arbitrarily large (if $\mathbf{T}$ is infinite). A simple trading strategy is said to be *self-financing* if the cost of any security purchase after date zero is exactly equal to the revenue generated by a simultaneous sale of some other securities, and if any sale is similarly matched by some purchase. As these trading strategies neither require nor generate funds between dates zero and T, they represent the means available to agents for transfering consumption between dates zero and T. They give rise to a space of implicitly marketed claims M

and prices π for these claims, to which the results of Section 2 can be applied. Thus we say that a securities market model is viable if the corresponding price system (M, π) is viable, that a contingent claim's price is determined by arbitrage from a viable securities market model if its price is determined from the corresponding (M, π), and so on.

For a securities market model as above, an *equivalent martingale measure* is a probability measure P^* on (Ω, F) having three properties. The first is technical. The second is that P and P^* are equivalent, meaning that $P^*(B) > 0$ if and only if $P(B) > 0$. The third property is that the price process Z becomes a (vector) martingale when P is replaced by P^*. Thus the conversion from P to P^* represents a redistribution of probability mass that causes every security to earn (in expected value) at the riskless rate zero without changing the set of events that receive positive probability. Let (M, π) be the price system corresponding to a given securities market model. Theorem 2 establishes a one-to-one correspondence between equivalent martingale measures P^* and those continuous and strictly positive linear functionals ψ which extend π to all of X. This correspondence is given by

$$\psi(x) = E^*(x) \text{ for } x \in X, \text{ and } P^*(B) = \psi(1_B) \text{ for } B \in F,$$

where E^* is the expectation operator associated with P^*. When combined with earlier results, this yields the following. A securities market model is viable if and only if there exists at least one equivalent martingale measure for it. For a viable securities market model, the price of a contingent claim x is determined by arbitrage if and only if x has the same expectation under every equivalent martingale measure, in which case the arbitrage value of x is that common expectation.

To illustrate these propositions, we apply them in Section 4 to the case where both Ω and $\mathbf{T}$ are finite. In Section 5 we consider the much more complex case where $\mathbf{T} = [0, T]$ and Z is a vector diffusion process. With mild regularity assumptions, it is shown (Theorem 3) that there exists a unique equivalent martingale measure. Thus the model is viable, and the price of every contingent claim (depending on the complete price history in an arbitrary way) is determined by arbitrage. The conversion to the equivalent martingale measure is accomplished by simply zeroing out the drift in the original model. Thus, in principle, all arbitrage values can be computed.

The theory developed in Section 3 is profoundly affected by our restriction to simple trading strategies. This restriction is made for technical reasons and cannot be completely justified on economic grounds. In Section 6 we discuss various alternative approaches that might be taken, and we illustrate the pitfalls that must be avoided if one is to model directly continuous trading (or otherwise expand the class of trading strategies permitted to agents).

Extensions of our theory are discussed in Section 7. We indicate how to apply our results when there is not a riskless security with rate of interest zero, when contingent claims may pay off at multiple and/or varying dates, and when one wishes to value an option (such as an American put) where the holder has some discretion as to the time and/or amount of payoff. Also, we discuss a technical matter concerning the topology in which agents' preferences are assumed to be continuous.

Section 8 contains some miscellaneous concluding remarks. For the most part, comments on connections with the extant literature are reserved for this section.

2. Viability and Arbitrage

As outlined in Section 1, a probability space (Ω, F, P) and two dates ($t = 0$ and $t = T$) are fixed. For the space X of contingent claims to consumption at date T, we shall take the space of F-measurable random variables that are square integrable. That is, we take $X = L^2(\Omega, F, P)$. This restriction of attention to square integrable contingent claims is made for expositional and mathematical ease. It is not necessary for most of the development that follows, and extensions are discussed in Section 7.

Agents are characterized by their preferences on the space of net trades, $R \times X$. Such preferences are represented mathematically by complete and transitive binary relations $\succsim$ on $R \times X$. (In the usual fashion, $\succ$ denotes strict preference defined from $\succsim$.) The preferences of agents in this economy are assumed to satisfy three requirements. First, they are convex.

$$\text{For all } (r, x) \in R \times X, \text{ the set } \{(r', x') \in R \times X : (r', x') \succsim (r, x)\} \text{ is convex.} \tag{2.1}$$

Second, they are continuous in the following sense. Let τ be the product topology on $R \times X$ derived from the Euclidean topology on R and the L^2 norm topology on X.

$$\begin{aligned}&\text{For all } (r, x) \in R \times X, \text{ the sets } \{(r', x') \in R \times X : (r', x') \succsim (r, x)\} \\ &\quad \text{and } \{(r', x') \in R \times X : (r, x) \succsim (r', x')\} \text{ are } \tau \text{ closed.}\end{aligned} \tag{2.2}$$

Third, they are strictly increasing in the following sense. Let X^+ be the set of contingent claims x satisfying $P(x \geqslant 0) = 1$ and $P(x > 0) > 0$.

$$\begin{aligned}&\text{For all } (r, x) \in R \times X, r' \in (0, \infty) \text{ and } x' \in X^+, (r + r', x) \succ (r, x) \\ &\quad \text{and } (r, x + x') \succ (r, x).\end{aligned} \tag{2.3}$$

In words, if we start with a net trade (r, x) and add to it either a positive amount of time zero consumption or a claim $x \in X^+$ (which does not decrease time T consumption and may increase it), then the resulting net trade vector is strictly preferred to the original. The set of complete and transitive binary relations $\gtrsim$ on $R \times X$ that satisfy (2.1), (2.2) and (2.3) is denoted **A**. Thus **A** represents the class of conceivable agents.

To illustrate the role of the probability measure P in our theory, we consider the following special case. Suppose that there exists a probability measure Q on (Ω, F) and a function $u : R \times R \to R$ such that $\gtrsim$ is given by

$$(r, x) \gtrsim (r', x') \text{ if } \int u(r, x(\omega))\, Q(d\omega) \geqslant \int u(r', x'(\omega))\, Q(d\omega).$$

(This assumes that u and Q are sufficiently well behaved so that all integrals of the indicated form exist and are finite.) For $\gtrsim$ to be in **A** it is sufficient that u be concave and strictly increasing and grow in absolute value at no more than quadratic rate, that Q and P have the same null sets, and that dQ/dP be bounded. This example shows that P plays three roles. It determines the space X of contingent claims, it determines the continuity requirement for $\gtrsim \in \mathbf{A}$, and through its null sets it plays a role in the requirement that $\gtrsim \in \mathbf{A}$ be strictly increasing.

A *price system* is a subspace M of X and a linear functional π on M. The interpretation is that in this economy, agents are able to buy and sell some contingent claims at a cost in date zero consumption. The markets in which this can be done are frictionless, meaning that there are no transaction costs and no restrictions on short selling. Thus M represents the subspace of marketed contingent claims (which will be smaller than X if markets are incomplete), and π gives the prices for claims $m \in M$ in units of date zero consumption.

Given a price system (M, π), is it *viable* as a model of economic equilibrium for agents from the class **A**? Formally, a price system (M, π) is said to be viable if there exists some $\gtrsim \in \mathbf{A}$ and $(r^*, m^*) \in R \times M$ such that

$$r^* + \pi(m^*) \leqslant 0 \text{ and } (r^*, m^*) \gtrsim (r, m) \text{ for all } (r, m) \in R \times M \text{ such that } r + \pi(m) \leqslant 0. \tag{2.4}$$

This says that there is some agent from the class **A** who, when choosing a best net trade subject to his budget constraint $r + \pi(m) \leqslant 0$, is able to find an optimal trade. The necessity of this condition is clear. It is also sufficient in the following sense. Given an agent $\gtrsim \in \mathbf{A}$ and $(r^*, m^*) \in R \times M$ satisfying (2.4), define a relation $\gtrsim'$ on $R \times X$ by

$$(r, x) \gtrsim' (r', x') \text{ if } (r + r^*, x + m^*) \gtrsim (r' + r^*, x' + m^*).$$

Then $\gtrsim' \in \mathbf{A}$, and an agent with preferences $\gtrsim'$ weakly prefers $(0, 0)$ to every net trade $(r, m) \in R \times M$ such that $r + \pi(m) \leqslant 0$. Thus (M, π) is an equilibrium price system for an economy populated by agents from the class

A. In an economy where all agents have preferences $\gtrsim'$, at prices π every agent is content to remain at his endowment point.

The following theorem characterizes viable price systems in terms of continuous (in the L^2 norm topology) linear functionals on X. Such a linear functional ψ is said to be strictly positive if $\psi(x) > 0$ for all $x \in X^+$. Let Ψ denote the set of all continuous and strictly positive linear functionals on X.

THEOREM 1. *A price system (M, π) is viable if and only if there exists an extension of π to all of X that lies in Ψ.*

(We use the notation $\psi \mid M$ to denote the restriction of ψ to the subspace M, and thus the condition can be rephrased as follows. There exists $\psi \in \Psi$ such that $\psi \mid M = \pi$.)

Proof. Suppose (M, π) are such that there exists $\psi \in \Psi$ satisfying $\psi \mid M = \pi$. Then define $\gtrsim$ on $R \times X$ by

$$(r, x) \gtrsim (r', x') \text{ if } r + \psi(x) \geqslant r' + \psi(x').$$

It is easy to see that the relation $\gtrsim$ so defined is in **A** and that this $\gtrsim$ and the choice $(r^*, m^*) = (0, 0)$ satisfy (2.4). Thus (M, π) is viable.

Suppose (M, π) is viable. Let $\gtrsim \in$ **A** and (r^*, m^*) be such that (2.4) holds. Previous discussion shows that $(r^*, m^*) = (0, 0)$ may be assumed without loss of generality. Define

$$G = \{(r, x) \in R \times X : (r, x) \succ (0, 0)\}$$

and

$$H = \{(r, m) \in R \times M : r + \pi(m) \leqslant 0\}.$$

The sets G and H are disjoint because of (2.4), both are convex (G because preferences are convex) and G is open (because preferences are continuous). Thus there exists a nontrivial continuous linear functional ϕ on $R \times M$ such that $\phi(r, x) \geqslant 0$ for $(r, x) \in G$ and $\phi(r, x) \leqslant 0$ for $(r, x) \in H$. This is one version of the separating hyperplane theorem; see Holmes [11, p. 63].

We claim that $\phi(1, 0) > 0$. To see this, note that there is some (r', x') such that $\phi(r', x') > 0$ because ϕ is nontrivial. Since $\gtrsim \in$ **A**, we have $(1, 0) \succ (0, 0)$. Thus by continuity of $\gtrsim$, there exists $\lambda > 0$ sufficiently small so that $(1 - \lambda r', -\lambda x') \succ (0, 0)$. Therefore

$$\phi(1 - \lambda r', -\lambda x') = \phi(1, 0) - \lambda\phi(r', x') \geqslant 0,$$

and $\phi(1, 0) \geqslant \lambda\phi(r', x') > 0$. Renormalize ϕ so that $\phi(1, 0) = 1$, and write $\phi(r, x) = r + \psi(x)$, where ψ is a continuous linear functional on X.

We claim that ψ is strictly positive. For $x \in X^+$, we have $(0, x) \succ (0, 0)$, thus there exists $\lambda > 0$ such that $(-\lambda, x) \succ (0, 0)$. This implies $\psi(x) - \lambda \geqslant 0$ or $\psi(x) \geqslant \lambda > 0$.

We claim that $\psi \mid M = \pi$. For $m \in M$, note that $(-\pi(m), m)$ and $(\pi(m), -m)$ are both in H, and thus $0 = \phi(\pi(m), -m) = \pi(m) - \psi(m)$, or $\pi(m) = \psi(m)$. This completes the proof.

This equivalent characterization of viability has a partial equilibrium-general equilibrium flavor to it. Imagine an economy where markets exist for all claims $x \in X$, one portion of that economy being the market where claims $m \in M$ can be bought and sold at prices π. Then these prices must be part of a general equilibrium system of prices ψ for all of X. And as agents come from the class **A**, these general equilibrium prices must be continuous and strictly positive.

Suppose a viable price system (M, π) is given. At what prices might some other claim $x \notin M$ sell for? If x sold at a price p, agents would be able to purchase any claim $m + \lambda x \in span(M \cup \{x\})$ at a price $\pi(m) + \lambda p$. Writing M' for $span\,(M \cup \{x\})$ and π' for the linear functional $\pi'(m + \lambda x) = \pi(m) + \lambda p$, it is natural to say that price p for x *is consistent with the price system* (M, π) if (M', π') is viable. Immediately from Theorem 1 we have the following corollary.

COROLLARY 1. *If a price system (M, π) is viable, then for all $x \in X$ there exists some price that is consistent with (M, π). Moreover, for viable (M, π), the set of prices for x consistent with (M, π) is the set $\{\psi(x) : \psi \in \Psi$ and $\psi \mid M = \pi\}$.*

When there is a single price for a claim x consistent with (M, π), we say that the price of x is *determined by arbitrage* from (M, π), and this unique price for x is called the *arbitrage value* of x (determined from (M, π)).

COROLLARY 2. *If a price system (M, π) is viable, then the price of $x \in X$ is determined by arbitrage if and only if the set $\{\psi(x) : \psi \in \Psi$ and $\psi \mid M = \pi\}$ is singleton, in which case that single element is the arbitrage value of x.*

Given a viable price system (M, π), let $\hat{M}$ be the set of all contingent claims whose prices are determined by arbitrage. Let $\hat{\pi}(x)$ denote the arbitrage value of claim $x \in \hat{M}$. If X is finite dimensional (which will be the case if Ω is finite), it can be shown that $\hat{M} = M$. If X is infinite dimensional (which will typically be the case if Ω is infinite), it follows from Corollary 2 that $\hat{M}$ contains at least the τ closure of M, and it may contain other claims as well. Because our primary interest here is in multiperiod securities markets, we shall not further develop the general concepts of viability and arbitrage that have been advanced. A great deal more can be said, however, and the interested reader is directed to [12].

3. Securities Market Models

As stated earlier, the additional primitive objects required for our securities market model are a set of trading dates, an information structure, and a price process. The trading dates are a set $\mathbf{T} \subseteq [0, T]$ with $0, T \in \mathbf{T}$. Interpret $\mathbf{T}$ as a collection of points in time at which certain (as yet unspecified) securities can be traded. The terms *discrete time* and *continuous time* refer to the cases where $\mathbf{T}$ is finite and where $\mathbf{T} = [0, T]$, respectively.

The information structure is given by an increasing family of sub-σ-algebras $\{F_t \,;\, t \in \mathbf{T}\}$. We assume for convenience that F_0 is the trivial σ-algebra $\{\varnothing, \Omega\}$ and that $F_T = F$. Interpret F_t as the class of all events B such that agents will be able to tell at time t whether the true state of the world is in B. In other words, F_t represents the information available at time t. The price process is a $(K + 1)$-dimensional stochastic process $Z = \{Z(t);\, t \in \mathbf{T}\}$ which is adapted to $\{F_t\}$. The components of $Z(t)$ are denoted $Z_k(t)$ for $k = 0, 1,..., K$. Interpret $K + 1$ as the number of securities traded in this market, with $Z_k(t, \omega)$ representing the price of security k at time t if the state is ω. The assumption that Z is adapted to $\{F_t\}$ simply means that among the information available at time t are the prices then prevailing for all traded securities. We assume for now that these securities do not generate any revenue such as dividends. Also, we assume that $Z_0(t, \omega) = 1$ for all t and ω. The latter assumption means that security zero is a riskless asset (a bond) with interest rate zero. This seems highly restrictive but is not, as we shall discuss in Section 7. Finally, we assume that $E(Z_k^2(t)) < \infty$ for all $t \in \mathbf{T}$ and $k = 1,..., K$.

Hereafter we refer to the probability space (Ω, F, P), the set of trading dates $\mathbf{T}$, the information structure $\{F_t\}$, and the price process Z together as a *securities market model.*

For a concrete example, fix some $T > 0$, set $\mathbf{T} = [0, T]$ and let (Ω, F, P) be a probability space on which is defined a standard (zero drift and unit variance) Brownian Motion $\{W(t);\, 0 \leqslant t \leqslant T\}$. Let F_t be the σ-algebra generated by $\{W(u);\, 0 \leqslant u \leqslant t\}$ and assume $F = F_T$. Define $Z_0(t) \equiv 1$ and $Z_1(t, \omega) = \exp\{\sigma W(t, \omega) + \mu t\}$ for constants $\sigma > 0$ and μ. This is the price model of Black and Scholes [4], where Z_0 and Z_1 are the bond price process and stock price process respectively. (We are specializing the Black-Scholes model by taking the riskless interest rate to be zero, but this distinction is a trivial one.)

By trading in the primitive securities whose prices are given by Z, what trades can an agent affect between consumption at time zero and at time T? To answer this question, we must further specify in our model the trading strategies that an agent is capable of employing. We might, for example, allow agents to trade in discrete lumps only, or continuously in rates, or both. Throughout this paper, we shall assume that agents are able to employ only *simple trading strategies*. Formally, a simple strategy is a $(K + 1)$-dimensional process $\theta = \{\theta(t);\ t \in \mathbf{T}\}$ that satisfies three conditions. First, $\theta(t)$ is measurable with respect to F_t for each $t \in \mathbf{T}$. Second, the product $\theta_k(t)\, Z_k(t)$ is an element of X for each $t \in \mathbf{T}$ and $k = 0, 1,..., K$. Third, there exists a finite integer N and a sequence of dates $0 = t_0 < \cdots < t_N = T$ such that $t_n \in \mathbf{T}$ and $\theta(t, \omega)$ is constant over the interval $t_{n-1} \leqslant t < t_n$ for every state ω $(n = 1,..., N)$.

Interpret such a θ as a dynamic rule for holding the $K + 1$ securities, with $\theta_k(t, \omega)$ representing the amount (in shares) of security k held at time t if the state is ω. Our first condition on θ says that the portfolio held at time t may depend on the state only through information available at that time. Our second condition is technical in nature, guaranteeing that the amounts of the various securities bought and sold at trading dates t_n do not vary too wildly as functions of ω. This is needed in the sequel in order to take certain conditional expectations.

Our third requirement for a simple strategy says that an agent may trade at only a finite number of dates (although that finite number can be arbitrarily large), and that the trading dates must be specified in advance. This represents a relatively restrictive view of agents' capabilities in the continuous time case, and we will make no attempt to defend the restriction economically. But as we shall discuss in Section 6, great care must be taken if one is to admit any larger class of trading strategies in a continuous time model. For the moment, we can only beg the reader's indulgence.

Let θ be a simple strategy with trading at dates $t_0, t_1,..., t_N$. The vector product $\theta(t) \cdot Z(t)$ represents the value of the portfolio at date t (a random variable). The value before trading at date t_n is $\theta(t_{n-1}) \cdot Z(t_n)$, and the value after trading is $\theta(t_n) \cdot Z(t_n)$. Call θ a *self-financing* simple strategy if $\theta(t_{n-1}) \cdot Z(t_n) = \theta(t_n) \cdot Z(t_n)$ for $n = 1,..., N$. Implicit in our terminology is an assumption of frictionless trading. Self-financing simple strategies are those which neither require nor generate funds between dates zero and T. Thus they represent the ways in which consumption can be shifted between dates zero and T.

A self-financing simple strategy θ will be called a *simple free lunch* if $\theta(0) \cdot Z(0) \leqslant 0$ and $\theta(T) \cdot Z(T) \in X^+$. Such an item, when and if it exists, represents an opportunity to make arbitrage profits. It allows an agent to increase (or at least not decrease) consumption at date zero, and increase (with positive probability) consumption at date T. Simple free lunches are thus inconsistent with an economic equilibrium for agents from our class $\mathbf{A}$.

A claim $x \in X$ is said to be *marketed* at date zero if there exists a self-financing simple strategy θ such that $\theta(T) \cdot Z(T) = x$ almost surely. In this case we say that θ *generates* x and that $\theta(0) \cdot Z(0)$ is the (implicit) *price* of x. Again the interpretation is straightforward. At a cost of $\theta(0) \cdot Z(0)$ units of consumption at date zero, an agent can buy the portfolio $\theta(0)$. Then at times $t_1, t_2,..., t_N$ he can costlessly change his holdings so as to conform to the strategy θ. At time T he holds a portfolio worth $\theta(T, \omega) \cdot Z(T, \omega) = x(\omega)$ units of time T consumption in state ω.

If the prices of marketed claims are to be well defined, we must ensure that if two self-financing simple strategies θ and θ' both generate a claim x, then $\theta(0) \cdot Z(0) = \theta'(0) \cdot Z(0)$. This need not be true in general, but it clearly will be true if no simple free luches exist. Assuming this is the case, let M be the set of marketed claims, and let $\pi : M \to R$ give the prices of claims $m \in M$. Clearly, if there are no simple free lunches, then π is a linear functional on M, which is a subspace of X. For a security market model that admits no simple free lunches, we call (M, π) the price system corresponding to the model. We say that a security market model is *viable* if it admits no simple free lunches and if the corresponding (M, π) is viable. Given a viable security market model, we say that the price of claim x is determined by arbitrage from the model and that the arbitrage value of x is p, if these statements are true of the corresponding price system (M, π). We define $\hat{M}$ and $\hat{\pi}$ as in Section 2.

For a given security market model, we wish to know whether it is viable and if it is, to identify $\hat{M}$ and $\hat{\pi}$. Given that the model admits no simple free lunches, we therefore seek to identify those linear functionals $\psi \in \Psi$ such that $\psi \mid M = \pi$ for the corresponding price system (M, π). In the remainder of this section we develop a probabilistic characterization of such functionals, which allows arbitrage questions to be recast in purely probabilistic terms. As will be seen later in our treatment of diffusion models, a powerful and well developed body of mathematical theory can then be brought to bear on the issues at hand.

An *equivalent martingale measure* is a probability measure P^* on (Ω, F) which has the following three properties. First, P and P^* are equivalent in the probabilistic sense, meaning that $P(B) = 0$ if and only if $P^*(B) = 0$ for $B \in F$. (Briefly, the *null sets* of P and P^* coincide.) Second, the Radon-Nikodym derivative $\rho = dP^*/dP$ satisfies $E(\rho^2) < \infty$, or $\rho \in L^2(\Omega, F, P)$. Finally, the process Z is a martingale over the fields $\{F_t\}$ with respect to P^*. That is, denoting by $E^*(\cdot)$ the expectation operator associated with P^*, we have $E^*(Z_k(u) | F_t) = Z_k(t)$ for all $k = 0, 1, \ldots, K$ and $u, t \in \mathbf{T}$ with $t \leqslant u$. The utility of this somewhat abstruse concept is established by the following result.

THEOREM 2. *Suppose the security price model admits no simple free lunches. Then there is a one-to-one correspondence between equivalent martingale measures P^* and linear functionals $\psi \in \Psi$ such that $\psi \mid M = \pi$. This correspondence is given by*

$$P^*(B) = \psi(1_B) \text{ and } \psi(x) = E^*(x). \tag{3.1}$$

Remark 1. If the primitive price model admits simple free lunches, then there cannot exist any equivalent martingale measures. (This will be established as part of Corollary 2.) Also, in such circumstances, π is not well defined. Thus the supposition in Theorem 2 is in a sense unnecessary.

Remark 2. In the proof to follow, note that the strict positivity of ψ corresponds to the equivalence of P and P^*, the continuity of ψ corresponds to $E(\rho^2) < \infty$, and the extension property $\psi \mid M = \pi$ corresponds to the martingale property of P^*.

Proof. Recall that a linear functional ψ on X is continuous if and only if $\psi(x) = E(\rho x)$ for some $\rho \in L^2(\Omega, F, P)$. This is the Riesz Representation Theorem for L^2 spaces.

First, let P^* be an equivalent martingale measure. Set $\rho = dP^*/dP$ and define ψ from P^* by (3.1). Since $\rho \in L^2(\Omega, F, P)$ we have that ψ is continuous. Since P and P^* are equivalent, ρ is strictly positive. Thus ψ is strictly positive, and we have $\psi \in \Psi$. It remains to show that $\psi \mid M = \pi$. Take $m \in M$ and let θ be the simple self-financing strategy that generates m. Let $0 = t_0 < t_1 < \cdots < t_N = T$ be the dates at which the value of θ may change. Then for $n = 1, 2, \ldots, N$

$$E^*(\theta(t_n) \cdot Z(t_n) | F_{t_{n-1}}) = E^*(\theta(t_{n-1}) \cdot Z(t_n) | F_{t_{n-1}})$$

because θ is self-financing

$$= \theta(t_{n-1}) \cdot E^*(Z(t_n) | F_{t_{n-1}}) = \theta(t_{n-1}) \cdot Z(t_{n-1}),$$

because Z is a martingale with respect to P^*. Iterating this equality yields

$$E^*(\theta(T) \cdot Z(T)) = \theta(0) \cdot Z(0),$$

which, since $m = \theta(T) \cdot Z(T)$ and $\pi(m) = \theta(0) \cdot Z(0)$, is $E^*(m) = \psi(m) = \pi(m)$.

Conversely, let $\psi \in \Psi$ be such that $\psi \mid M = \pi$. Define P^* from ψ by (3.1). If $P(B) = 0$, then 1_B is identified as 0 in X and so $P^*(B) = \psi(1_B) = 0$. If $P(B) > 0$, then $1_B \in X^+$ and $0 < \psi(1_B) = P^*(B)$. Thus P and P^* are equivalent. Since ψ is continuous, $\psi(x) = E(\rho x)$ for some $\rho \in L^2(\Omega, F, P)$. Thus $P^*(B) = E(\rho 1_B)$, P^* is a σ-additive measure, and $dP^*/dP = \rho$ is square integrable. Because $1_\Omega \in M$ and $\psi(1_\Omega) = 1$, it follows that $P^*(\Omega) = 1$ and hence P^* is a probability measure. It remains to show that $\{Z_k(t), F_t; t \in \mathbf{T}\}$ is a martingale under P^* for each k. For $k = 0$, this is obvious. Fix $k > 0$, t and $u \in \mathbf{T}$ such that $t \leqslant u$, and $B \in F_t$. Consider the simple self-financing trading strategy θ defined by

$$\theta_k(s, \omega) = \begin{cases} 1 & \text{for } s \in [t, u) \text{ and } \omega \in B \\ 0 & \text{otherwise} \end{cases}$$

$$\theta_0(s, \omega) = \begin{cases} -Z_k(t, \omega) & \text{for } s \in [t, u) \text{ and } \omega \in B \\ Z_k(u, \omega) - Z_k(t, \omega) & \text{for } s \in [u, T] \text{ and } \omega \in B \\ 0 & \text{otherwise} \end{cases}$$

$$\theta_j(s, \omega) = 0 \qquad \text{for all } j \neq 0, k.$$

This looks more complicated than it is. It represents the strategy of buying one share of k at time t if in the event B and then selling at time u, using security zero so that all transactions (including the original purchase, if $t = 0$) are costless. This trading strategy yields at date T a portfolio worth

$$\theta(T) \cdot Z(T) = (Z_k(u) - Z_k(t)) \cdot 1_B,$$

so this claim is marketed and has price zero. It follows from $\psi \mid M = \pi$ that $\psi((Z_k(u) - Z_k(t)) \cdot 1_B) = 0$. In terms of $E^*(\cdot)$ this is

$$E^*((Z_k(u) - Z_k(t)) \cdot 1_B) = 0 \text{ or } E^*(Z_k(u) \cdot 1_B) = E^*(Z_k(t) \cdot 1_B).$$

This is true for all $B \in F_t$ and thus $Z_k(t)$ is a version of $E^*(Z_k(u) | F_t)$, completing the proof.

From this correspondence and from our earlier results, we obtain the following proposition, which is the starting point for analysis of examples.

COROLLARY. (a) *The security market model is viable if and only if there exists at least one equivalent martingale measure.* (b) *Assume that the security market model is viable. Let* $\mathbf{P}$ *denote the (nonempty) set of equivalent martingale measures. Then* $x \in \hat{M}$ *if and only if* $E^*(x)$ *is constant over all* $P^* \in \mathbf{P}$*, in which case this constant is* $\hat{\pi}(x)$. (c) *The security market model is viable and every claim* $x \in X$ *is priced by arbitrage if and only if there exists a unique equivalent martingale measure.*

Proof. In part (a) we need to show that if there exists an equivalent martingale measure P^*, then no simple free lunches exist. Suppose that θ is a simple self-financing strategy with $\theta(T) \cdot Z(T) \in X^+$. Since P^* is equivalent to P, $P^*(\theta(T) \cdot Z(T) \geqslant 0) = 1$ and $P^*(\theta(T) \cdot Z(T) > 0) > 0$. Thus $E^*(\theta(T) \cdot Z(T)) > 0$. By the argument of Theorem 2, $\theta(0) \cdot Z(0) = E^*(\theta(T) \cdot Z(T))$. Thus $\theta(0) \cdot Z(0) > 0$ if $\theta(T) \cdot Z(T) \in X^+$, and no simple free lunches exist. With this, (a) and (b) follow directly from previous results, and (c) is a direct consequence of (a) and (b).

4. THE FINITE CASE

To illustrate our results, we first consider models where both Ω and $\mathbf{T}$ are finite. In such models, the space X consists of *all* F-measurable functions from Ω to R, the model is viable if and only if there are no simple free lunches, and a claim's price is determined by arbitrage if and only if it is marketed. (The proofs of these statements are left to the reader.)

Consider the numerical example portrayed in Figure 1. There are nine states of the world, denoted $\omega_1, \ldots, \omega_9$, and the trading dates are $\mathbf{T} = \{0, 1, 2\}$. We take F_1 to be the field generated by the partition with cells $B_1 = \{\omega_1, \omega_2, \omega_3\}$, $B_2 = \{\omega_4, \omega_5, \omega_6\}$, and $B_3 = \{\omega_7, \omega_8, \omega_9\}$, and $F_2 = F$ to be the field generated by the total partition of Ω. In other words, investors know at time $t = 1$ which of the events B_j has occurred, and they know at time $t = 2$ the state of the world. There are three securities. Of course, $Z_0(t) \equiv 1$. The prices $Z_1(t)$ and $Z_2(t)$ are given in Figure 1 as the nodes of the tree, $Z_1(t)$ being the upper number and $Z_2(t)$ the lower. Thus $Z_1(0, \omega_1) = 10$, $Z_1(1, \omega_1) = 11$, and $Z_1(2, \omega_1) = 14$. We shall not specify the original probability measure P on Ω except to say that $P(\omega_i) > 0$ for all i. (The specific probabilities are irrelevant for our purposes.)

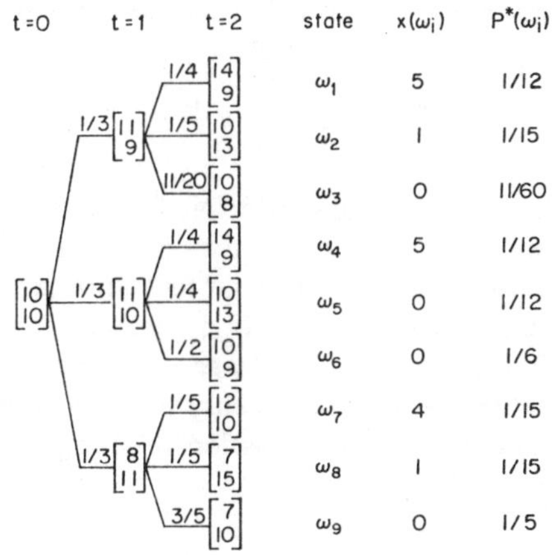

FIG. 1. A Finite Example

We wish to know whether this model is viable and, if so, which claims are priced by arbitrage. To be concrete, we define the contingent claim

$$x = \{2Z_1(2) + Z_2(2) - [14 + 2 \min_{0 \leqslant t \leqslant 2} \min(Z_1(t), Z_2(t))]\}^+.$$

This claim represents the right to buy, at the terminal date $t = 2$, two shares of security 1 plus one share of security 2 at a price of 14 plus twice the lowest price achieved by either of the risky securities on any of the three trading dates. The value of the claim $x(\omega_i)$ is shown for each state of the world ω_i in Figure 1. We have chosen this rather silly example to emphasize that claims may depend on the complete price histories of the primitive securities.

Notice, for example, that the terminal securities prices are identical in states ω_2 and ω_5, but x yields different payoffs in these two states.

We now determine the set $\mathbf{P}$ of all equivalent martingale measures. First, if $P^* \in \mathbf{P}$, then $E^*(Z_1(1)) = 10$ and $E^*(Z_2(1)) = 10$. Writing p for $P^*(B_1)$ and q for $P^*(B_2)$, this means that $11p + 11q + 8(1 - p - q) = 10$ and $9p + 10q + 11(1 - p - q) = 10$, which yields $p = q = 1/3$. These probabilities are recorded in Figure 1 on the appropriate branches of the tree. Next, it must be that $E^*(Z_1(2)| B_1) = 11$ and $E^*(Z_2(2)| B_1) = 9$. Calculating as above, we find that this implies $P^*(\omega_1 \mid B_1) = 1/4$, $P^*(\omega_2 \mid B_1) = 1/5$, and $P^*(\omega_3 \mid B_1) = 11/20$. The conditional probabilities are recorded on the appropriate branches of the tree in Figure 1, together with the corresponding conditional probabilities for various terminal states given B_2 and B_3, which are computed similarly. Since each of these branch probabilities is unique, there is a unique equivalent martingale measure P^*, which is recorded in the last column of Figure 1. This implies that the model is viable, that all claims are priced by arbitrage, and in particular that the arbitrage value of x is

$$\hat{\pi}(x) = E^*(x) = \sum_{i=1}^{9} x(\omega_i)\, P^*(\omega_i) = 1.2333.$$

Our example illustrates a general principle for finite models. Suppose that at each trading date t there are no more than $K + 1$ price vectors that can result at the next trading date, given the information available at time t. *If* the model is viable, then (barring certain degeneracies) all contingent claims are priced by arbitrage and their arbitrage values can be calculated with a simple recursive technique. This fact is easy to prove directly (and the argument is widely known). For an exposition of this point when $K = 1$, see Sharpe [19, Chap. 14].

5. The Case of Diffusions

We consider in this section the special case where $\mathbf{T} = [0, T]$ and Z is a vector diffusion process. For notational ease, we shall first specify a K-dimensional diffusion $Y = \{Y(t); 0 \leqslant t \leqslant T\}$ and then construct the price process Z by setting $Z_k(t) = Y_k(t)$ for $k = 1,\ldots, K$ and $Z_0(t) \equiv 1$.

We assume that there is defined on the basic probability space (Ω, F, P) a K-dimensional standard Brownian Motion $W = \{W(t); 0 \leqslant t \leqslant T\}$. The component processes $W_1(t),\ldots, W_K(t)$ are independent one-dimensional Brownian Motions with zero drift and unit variance and $W_k(0) = 0$. Let $F_t = F\{W(s); 0 \leqslant s \leqslant t\}$ for $0 \leqslant t \leqslant T$. Recall that we take $F = F_T$. Let

$$\sigma(x, t) : R^K \times [0, T] \to R^{K \times K} \text{ and } \mu(x, t) : R^K \times [0, T] \to R^K$$

be given functions, continuous in x and t. We assume that the $K \times K$ matrix $\sigma(x, t)$ is nonsingular for each x and t, so that there is a unique function $\alpha(x, t)$ satisfying

$$\sigma(x, t) \cdot \alpha(x, t) + \mu(x, t) = 0 \text{ for } x \in R^K, t \in [0, T]. \tag{5.1}$$

Here $\alpha(x, t)$ and $\mu(x, t)$ should be envisioned as column vectors. Let Y be a process adapted to $\{F_t\}$ and satisfying the (Ito) stochastic integral equation

$$Y_k(t) = Y_k(0) + \sum_{j=1}^{K} \int_0^t \sigma_{kj}(Y(s), s)\, dW_j(s) + \int_0^t \mu_k(Y(s), s)\, ds \tag{5.2}$$

for $k = 1,..., K$ and $0 \leqslant t \leqslant T$, where $Y(0)$ is a constant K-vector. See Gihman and Skorohod [9] for basic definitions relating to the Ito integral and stochastic integral equations. In the usual way, we express (5.2) more compactly as

$$Y(t) = Y(0) + \int_0^t \sigma(Y(s), s)\, dW + \int_0^t \mu(Y(s), s)\, ds. \tag{5.3}$$

We now define the price process Z in terms of Y as explained above. As our final assumption, we suppose the existence of a continuous K-dimensional process $Y^* = \{Y^*(t); 0 \leqslant t \leqslant T\}$ which *uniquely* (up to an equivalence) satisfies

$$Y^*(t) = Y(0) + \int_0^t \sigma(Y^*(s), s)\, dW, \; 0 \leqslant t \leqslant T. \tag{5.4}$$

This requires some further regularity (beyond simple continuity) for the function $\sigma(\cdot, \cdot)$. See Gihman and Skorohod [9, p. 40] for sufficient conditions. We define a $(K + 1)$-dimensional process Z^* by setting $Z_k^*(t) = Y_k^*(t)$ for $k \geqslant 1$ and $Z_0^*(t) \equiv 1$. Before presenting our main result, we state a preliminary proposition which is very important for subsequent interpretations. For this proposition, let $C[0, T]$ be the space of continuous functions from $[0, T]$ to R^K, endowed with the topology of uniform convergence. When we say that $f: C[0, T] \to R$ is a measurable functional, we mean measurable with respect to the Borel σ-field of $C[0, T]$.

PROPOSITION 1. *For $0 \leqslant t \leqslant T$, the σ-field F_t is generated by $\{Z(s); 0 \leqslant s \leqslant t\}$. Thus every contingent claim x has the form $x = f(Z)$ for some measurable functional $f: C[0, T] \to R$.*

The proof is deferred until later in this section. Proposition 1 shows that, in allowing investors to form portfolios based on the information structure $\{F_t\}$, we are giving them access *only* to past and present price information at each time t. Also, with our convention $F = F_T$, every contingent claim can be expressed as a function of the vector price history over the interval $[0, T]$. Claims may depend on prices in very complicated ways, however.

The following is our main result. For a column vector γ, we adopt the notation γ^2 for $\gamma_1^2 + \cdots + \gamma_K^2$.

THEOREM 3. *The set* $\mathbf{P}$ *of equivalent martingale measures is non-empty if and only if*

(a) $\int_0^T \alpha^2(Y(t), t)\, dt < \infty$ *a.s.*,

(b) $E(\rho^2) < \infty$, *where* $\rho = \exp(\int_0^T \alpha(Y(t), t)\, dW(t) - \frac{1}{2} \int_0^T \alpha^2(Y(t), t)\, dt)$

and

(c) Y^* *is a martingale over* $\{F_t\}$.

In this case, there is a unique $P^* \in \mathbf{P}$, *its Radon-Nikodym derivative is* $dP^*/dP = \rho$, *and the distribution of* Z *on* (Ω, F, P^*) *coincides with the distribution of* Z^* *on* (Ω, F, P).

Remark. A well-known sufficient condition for (c) is

$$\sum_{i=1}^{K} \sum_{j=1}^{K} E\left[\int_0^T \{\sigma_{ij}(Y^*(t), t)\}^2\, dt\right] < \infty.$$

See, for example, Ash and Gardner [2, p. 215].

COROLLARY. *The securities market model is viable if and only if* (a)-(c) *hold. In this case, each contingent claim* $x \in X$ *is priced by arbitrage, with arbitrage value* $\hat{\pi}(x) = E(f(Z^*)) = E^*(f(Z))$, *where* $x = f(Z)$ *as in Proposition* 1.

Proof of Proposition 1. For the first statement, we must show that F_t equals the σ-field G_t generated by $\{Y(s); 0 \leq s \leq t\}$. Let

$$V(t) = Y(t) - Y(0) - \int_0^t \mu(Y(s), s)\, ds = \int_0^t \sigma(Y(s), s)\, dW(s)$$

for $0 \leq t \leq T$. Observe that V is adapted to $\{G_t\}$. Fix $t > 0$ and define

$$W_N(t) = \sum_{n=0}^{2^N-1} \{\sigma(Y(t_n), t_n)\}^{-1} \cdot [V(t_{n+1}) - V(t_n)]$$

for integer N, where $t_n = nt/2^N$. (Recall that σ is assumed nonsingular.) Clearly $W_N(t)$ is G_t-measurable. Using the continuity of μ and σ, it is easy to show that $W_N(t) \to W(t)$ a.s. as $N \to \infty$, so $W(t)$ is G_t-measurable. Thus $F_t \subseteq G_t$. It was assumed at the outset that Y is adapted to $\{F_t\}$, so $G_t \subseteq F_t$, and the first statement is proved. The second statement (regarding measurability) is standard and will not be proved. See, for example, Chung [5, p. 299].

Proof of Theorem 3. We denote by Φ the set of K-dimensional processes $\phi = \{\phi(t); 0 \leqslant t \leqslant T\}$ such that $\phi_k(t, \omega)$ is jointly measurable in t and ω for each component $k = 1,..., K$, ϕ is adapted to the Brownian fields $\{F_t\}$, and $\int_0^T \phi^2(t)\,dt < \infty$ a.s. Elements of ϕ will be called non-anticipating functions. The stochastic integral $\int \phi(s)\,dB(s)$ is defined for integrands $\phi \in \Phi$. Let P^* be an equivalent martingale measure with $dP^* = \zeta dP$. Thus ζ is strictly positive and square integrable by definition, and the process $\{\zeta(t); 0 \leqslant t \leqslant T\}$ defined by $\zeta(t) = E(\zeta \mid F_t)$ is a strictly positive martingale over the Brownian fields $\{F_t\}$, with $\zeta(T) = \zeta$ and $E(\zeta(t)) = E(\zeta) = 1$ for all t. Also, using Jensen's inequality, it is easy to show that $\zeta(t)$ is square integrable for each t. It is shown in Section 4 of Kunita and Watanabe [13] that any such martingale can be represented in the form

$$\zeta(t) = 1 + \int_0^t \gamma(s)\,dW(s),\ 0 \leqslant t \leqslant T, \tag{5.5}$$

where $\gamma \in \Phi$ further satisfies $\int_0^T E(\gamma^2(t))\,dt < \infty$. Observe that $\zeta(\cdot)$ is almost surely continuous by (5.5), and from this it follows that the sample path $\zeta_k(\cdot, \omega)$ of the kth component process is bounded away from zero for almost every ω. Define a K-dimensional non-anticipating function ϕ by setting $\phi_k(t) = \gamma_k(t)/\zeta(t)$ for $k = 1,..., K$. It then follows from Ito's Lemma and (5.5) that

$$\ln(\zeta(t)) = \int_0^t \phi(s)\,dW(s) - \tfrac{1}{2}\int_0^t \phi^2(s)\,ds,\ 0 \leqslant t \leqslant T.$$

In particular, we have

$$\zeta = \exp\left\{\int_0^T \phi(s)\,dW(s) - \tfrac{1}{2}\int_0^T \phi^2(s)\,ds\right\}. \tag{5.6}$$

In these manipulations, we have not used the fact that P^* is (by assumption) an equivalent *martingale* measure. Using the results of Kunita and Watanabe, it has simply been shown that any strictly positive and square integrable random variable ζ can be represented in the form (5.6).

Having achieved this representation for the Radon–Nikodym derivative ζ, we can use the powerful theorem of Girsanov [10] to show that the non-anticipating function $\phi(t)$ in (5.6) must in fact be $\alpha(Y(t), t)$. Let

$$W^*(t) = W(t) - \int_0^t \phi(s)\,ds,\ 0 \leqslant t \leqslant T.$$

Girsanov's Fundamental Theorem 1 says that W^* is a K-dimensional standard Brownian Motion on (Ω, F, P^*) where $dP^* = \zeta dP$ and that Y satisfies the stochastic integral equation

$$Y(t) = Y(0) + \int_0^t \sigma(Y(s), s)\, dW^*(s) + \int_0^t \mu^*(s)\, ds, \tag{5.7}$$

on (Ω, F, P^*), where $\mu^*(t) = \mu(Y(t), t) + \sigma(Y(t), t)\,\phi(t)$. Suppose for the moment that $\sigma(x, t)$ is a bounded function. Then the stochastic integral on the right side of (5.7) is a martingale on (Ω, F, P^*). Since Y is by assumption a martingale on (Ω, F, P^*), the absolutely continuous component $\int \mu^*(s)\, ds$ must also be a martingale and this is true if and only if $\mu^*(t) \equiv 0$ for almost every t. Note well, it is in this argument that we use the assumption that P^* is an equivalent *martingale* measure. For the case of general σ the same conclusion can be reached by a stopping argument, using the fact that $\sigma(\cdot, \cdot)$ is bounded on bounded sets. Let $b > 0$ be large and let τ be the first time t such that $Y_k(t) = \pm b$ for some k, with $\tau = T$ if no such t exists. If Y is a martingale on (Ω, F, P^*), then the stopped process $Y(t \wedge \tau)$ is as well, and from this one can easily argue that $\mu^*(t) \equiv 0$ for $0 \leqslant t \leqslant \tau$. But $\tau \to T$ a.s. as $b \to \infty$, so it follows that $\mu^*(t) \equiv 0$ for all t. Details of these arguments are left to the reader. Finally, observe that $\mu^*(t) = 0$ if and only if $\phi(t) = \alpha(Y(t), t)$ a.s.

We have now established that ζ can be the Radon-Nikodym derivative of an equivalent martingale measure P^* only if ζ satisfies (5.6) with $\phi(t) = \alpha(Y(t), t)$ for all t, which is equivalent to the requirement $\zeta = \rho$. Thus $\mathbf{P}$ is non-empty only if ρ is well defined and square integrable. This means that conditions (a) and (b) of Theorem 3 are *necessary* for $\mathbf{P}$ to be nonempty.

Suppose now that (a) and (b) hold. It is well known that this implies $E(\rho) = 1$, cf. Gihman and Skorohod [9, p. 82], so ρ is a legitimate Radon-Nikodym derivative. With $dP^* = \rho dP$, we argue exactly as above to establish that

$$Y(t) = Y(0) + \int_0^t \sigma(Y(s), s)\, dW^*(s),\ 0 \leqslant t \leqslant T, \tag{5.8}$$

on (Ω, F, P^*). Since Y^* uniquely satisfies (5.4) on (Ω, F, P) by assumption, we conclude that Y uniquely satisfies (5.8) on (Ω, F, P^*) and that its distribution coincides with that of Y^* on (Ω, F, P). Thus, given (a) and (b) a necessary and sufficient condition for P^* to be an equivalent martingale measure is (c). This concludes the proof of Theorem 3. The corollary follows from Theorem 2 and its corollary.

Girsanov [10] uses the term diffusion in a broader sense than is usual, allowing the parameter functions σ and μ to depend on both past and present values of the vector process Y. Theorem 3 can easily be extended to this larger class of processes, but one then needs quite a lot of measure theoretic notation to make a rigorous statement of the result. (This is required to make precise the notion of a parameter value which depends on the complete process Y in a non-anticipating way.) It also is harder to state the continuity requirement for σ, but the proof need hardly be changed at all.

6. Other Trading Strategies

We can not defend on economic grounds our restriction to simple trading strategies, but we can offer some comments on the consequences of relaxing it. If a larger class of trading strategies is allowed, it is necessary to say what constitutes a self-financing strategy within that larger class. Assuming this is possible, the analysis in Section 3 up to the introduction of equivalent martingale measures would not change at all. One asks whether free lunches exist and, if not, one defines the set of marketed claims (denote it M') and the associated price functional (denote it π'). The security market model is viable if and only if there exists some $\psi \in \Psi$ such that $\psi \mid M' = \pi'$, and assuming the model is viable, a claim x is priced by arbitrage if and only if $\psi(x)$ is constant as ψ ranges over the set $\{\psi \in \Psi : \psi \mid M' = \pi'\}$. What may no longer hold is the one-to-one correspondence between this set of functionals ψ and equivalent martingale measures. Assuming no free lunches exist with the larger class of admissible trading strategies, we have $M \subseteq M'$ and $\pi' \mid M = \pi$. Therefore any $\psi \in \Psi$ such that $\psi \mid M' = \pi'$ satisfies $\psi \mid M = \pi$ and gives an equivalent martingale measure (by the usual correspondence). But it may be that an equivalent martingale measure gives rise to a $\psi \in \Psi$ such that $\psi \mid M' \neq \pi'$. Thus a claim will be priced by arbitrage if it has constant expectation under all equivalent martingale measures, and its arbitrage value will be that constant, but the converse may fail to hold. Of course, if it is true that

$$\psi \mid M' = \pi' \text{ for all } \psi \in \Psi \text{ such that } \psi \mid M = \pi, \tag{6.1}$$

then the converse does hold. Condition (6.1) simply says that the one-to-one correspondence between equivalent martingale measures and $\{\psi \in \Psi: \Psi \mid M' = \pi'\}$ does (fortuitously) hold.

Consider, for example, the Black-Scholes model. Enlarge the set of admissible trading strategies by allowing $t_1, t_2, \ldots, t_{N-1}$ to be stopping times relative to $\{F_t\}$. One can show that this enlargment does not cause free lunches to appear and that (6.1) holds. Thus, with this enlarged class of trading strategies, the Black-Scholes model is viable and all claims are priced by arbitrage.

To see how things may go awry when the set of admissible trading strategies is expanded, consider again the Black-Scholes model, and now suppose the total number of trades N is allowed to be state dependent (random). Formally, there are non-random times $0 = t_0 < t_1 < \cdots < T$ and an integer valued random variable N such that $\theta(\cdot)$ changes value only at times $t_1, \ldots, t_N$. So that trading strategies do not anticipate the future, we add the requirement that $\{N \geqslant n\} \in F_{t_n}$ for all n. Call such trading strategies *almost simple*. Then define almost simple self-financing strategies and almost simple free lunches in the obvious way. The punchline is that almost simple free lunches exist. In fact there exists an almost simple self-financing trading strategy θ such that

$$\theta(0) \cdot Z(0) = 0 \text{ and } \theta(T) \cdot Z(T) \geqslant 1 \text{ a.s.} \tag{6.2}$$

This means that if agents can employ almost simple trading strategies, the Black-Scholes model is a nonsensical model of an economic equilibrium. It is worth noting that this is not due to some peculiar property of Brownian Motion. The same statement is true for the jump process model of Cox and Ross [6].

The trading strategy that accomplishes (6.2) is not very complicated. It amounts to the well known doubling strategy by which one is sure to win at roulette: Bet on red, and keep doubling your bets until red comes out. To effect this strategy, you must be able to bet a countable number of times, although you will only bet finitely many times in any particular state. If we take $t_n = T - T/2^N$, this gives us a countable number of times to bet. To effect this strategy you also must be able to keep doubling. You will only need a finite amount of wealth for any particular state ω, but this amount cannot be bounded in ω. In the Black-Scholes model of frictionless markets, short sales of the bond give you the necessary funds. (This may seem to the reader an abuse of the frictionless markets assumption. Certainly, this free lunch is exorcised if there is an upper limit on the amount any agent can borrow. It would be interesting to see an alternate development of this general problem that proceeds with this sort of constraint on trading strategies.)

In the seminal papers of Black and Scholes [4] and Merton [14] on option pricing for diffusion models, and in the large literature that has followed, investors are allowed to trade continuously. This continuous trading is modeled by means of Ito integrals. Denoting by $\theta(t)$ the investor's portfolio at time t, it is assumed that $\theta(t)$ is a smooth function of t and the vector of current security prices $Z(t)$. Since Z is an Ito process, the same is true of θ, and it follows that a typical trading strategy θ is of unbounded variation in every finite interval. With such a strategy, an agent not only executes an infinite number of transactions (trades continuously), but also buys and sells infinite *quantities* of stock and bond in every time interval. Defining the value process $V(t) = \theta(t) \cdot Z(t)$ as before, the definition of the Ito integral suggests that self-financing trading strategies should be defined by the restriction

$$V(t) = V(0) + \int_0^t \theta(u)\, dZ(u), \quad 0 \leqslant t \leqslant T.$$

This restriction is implicit in the original treatment of Black and Scholes [4] and is explicitly displayed in Merton [15]. With these definitions, do free lunches exist? If not, is the security market model viable for some reasonable class of agents? We intend to discuss these questions in a future paper.

7. Extensions

In this section we discuss a number of extensions of the model analyzed in Sections 2 through 5. We do not give rigorous treatments owing to the amount of space that would be required. We hope that the reader will see how to make our informal arguments exact.

We have assumed throughout that one of the primitive securities is riskless and has rate of interest zero. This may seem a very restrictive assumption, but in fact it is not. We must assume that *one* of the securities always has strictly positive price, but if this mild assumption is met, we can use the price of that security as the numeraire. Of course, in the security market model with prices so normalized, the security which is used as numeraire is riskless and has interest rate zero.

A formal statement of this runs as follows. Fix a security market model in which no security is riskless with rate of interest zero but in which one of the $K + 1$ securities, say security zero, has $Z_0(t, \omega) > 0$ for all t and ω. Now construct a new securities market model with the same probability space (Ω, F, P), trading dates $\mathbf{T}$, information structure $\{F_t\}$, but with price process $\{Z'(t)\}$ defined by

$$Z_k'(t, \omega) = Z_k(t, \omega)/Z_0(t, \omega).$$

Obviously, $Z_0'(t, \omega) \equiv 1$. Roughly, the original model is viable if and only if the primed model is, and claim x in the original model is priced by arbitrage if and only if claim $x' = x/Z_0(T)$ is priced by arbitrage in the primed model. Moreover, if x and x' are priced by arbitrage in their respective models, their arbitrage values are related by $\hat{\pi}'(x') = \hat{\pi}(x)/Z_0(0)$. This is so (roughly) because θ is a simple self-financing trading strategy in the original model if and only if it is as well in the primed model. To see this, note that if θ trades at times $t_0, t_1, \ldots, t_N$, then

$$\theta(t_{n-1}) \cdot Z(t_n) = \theta(t_n) \cdot Z(t_n) \text{ if and only if } \theta(t_{n-1}) \cdot Z'(t_n) = \theta(t_n) \cdot Z'(t_n).$$

Thus, $m \in M$ if and only if $m' = m/Z_0(T) \in M'$, and $\pi'(m') = \pi(m)/Z_0(0)$.

To make this correspondence exact, a bit of care must be taken. Passing from the original to the primed model involves only a change in units. Thus this transition should be economically neutral. The transition should not change the space of contingent claims, nor should it change the topology in which agents' preferences are assumed to be continuous. That is, it should be the case that $x \in X$ if and only if $x' \in X'$ and $x_n \to x$ in X if and only if $x'_n \to x'$ in X'. If $Z_0(T)$ is not bounded above and away from zero, this means that we cannot take $X' = L^2(\Omega, F, P)$ and the topology on X' to be the L^2-norm topology. Rather,

$$x' \in X' \qquad \text{if } E((x' Z_0(T))^2) < \infty,$$

and

$$x'_n \to x' \qquad \text{if } E(\{(x'_n - x)\, Z_0(T)\}^2) \to 0.$$

Thus to be an equivalent martingale measure in the primed model, P^* must satisfy $E(\{(dP^*/dP)\, Z_0(T)\}^2) < \infty$ instead of $E(\{dP^*/dP\}^2) < \infty$. Of course, when $Z_0(T)$ does live in a bounded subinterval of $(0, \infty)$, this complication can be ignored: X' is $L^2(\Omega, F, P)$, the topology on X' is the L^2 norm topology, and thus $dP^*/dP \in L^2$ is the proper continuity requirement for an equivalent martingale measure.

To see this applied, consider the model actually posited by Black and Scholes [4]. There are two securities, a bond with interest rate r, so that $Z_0(t) = \exp(rt)$, and a stock whose price dynamics are given by

$$dZ_1(t) = \mu Z_1(t)\, dt + \sigma Z_1(t)\, dW(t),$$

where μ and σ are constants. The fields $\{F_t\}$ are those generated by the Brownian motion W. Moving to the primed model, we obtain $Z'_0(t) = 1$ and $Z'_1(t) = Z_1(t)\exp(-rt)$. Thus,

$$dZ'_1(t) = (\mu - r)\, Z'_1(t)\, dt + \sigma Z'_1(t)\, dW(t).$$

Applying the results of Section 5, we know that this model is viable and that all claims are priced by arbitrage. To find the arbitrage value of a particular claim, say $x = (Z_1(T) - a)^+$, transfer to the primed model, where $x' = (Z'_1(T)\exp(rT) - a)^+/\exp(rT)$. Then

$$\hat{\pi}'(x') = E(e^{-rT}(Z_1^*(T)\, e^{rT} - a)^+)$$

where $dZ_1^* = Z_1^*\, dW$. Letting $dZ_1{}^0 = rZ_1{}^0\, dt + \sigma Z_1{}^0\, dW$, this is

$$\hat{\pi}(x) = \hat{\pi}'(x')/Z_0(0) = \hat{\pi}'(x') = E(e^{-rT}(Z_1{}^0(T) - a)^+),$$

which is the Black-Scholes formula. The reader is invited to apply this transformation to Merton's model with a stochastic interest rate [14]. There is no problem in passing to the primed model, but the results in Section 5 do not allow us to claim that, say, European call options can be priced by arbitrage.

Our analysis has been conducted for a world where agents consume only at dates zero and T. In the usual fashion, this can be thought of as a partial equilibrium analysis of the tradeoff between consumption at these two dates, where consumption at other dates is held fixed. But to consider claims that may pay at dates before T, including claims that may pay dividends and claims that expire at random dates, it is useful to extend our analysis to include consumption at all dates. To provide details for this would take many pages, so we leave the task to the reader. But as long as units are chosen so that there is a riskless security with rate of interest zero, the basic results that we have given hold up. Roughly, the reason is as follows. Represent a contingent claim by a function $x : \Omega \times \mathbf{T} \to R$ where $x(\omega, t)$ is the *total* amount paid by the claim in the time interval $(0, t]$ if the state is ω. For example, if the claim pays at a rate $d(\omega, t)$ until some random time τ and then pays a lump sum $l(\omega, \tau)$, we would have

$$x(\omega, t) = \int_0^{t\wedge\tau} d(\omega, s)\, ds + l(\omega, \tau) \cdot 1_{\{\tau \leqslant t\}} .$$

Consider any claim x so represented and another claim x' where $x'(\omega, t) = 0$ for all $t < T$ and $x'(\omega, T) = x(\omega, T)$. That is, x' pays nothing until time T, at which point it pays the *total* amount paid out by x from 0 until T. Assuming the model is viable, the price of x is determined by arbitrage if and only if that of x' is, and their arbitrage values are equal. This is because if an agent possesses the claim x, he can invest payoffs that accrue before time T in the riskless security. As the riskless rate of interest is zero, this yields a claim that pays $x(\omega, T)$ at date T, which is exactly the claim x'. On the other hand, if an agent possesses x', he can borrow using the riskless security to produce the pattern of returns x and, at date T, x' will provide precisely enough funds to cover his debts. Thus the claims x and x' are worth the same amount. The theory we have developed tells us whether claims x' have their prices determined by arbitrage and, if so, what are their arbitrage values. Therefore this theory answers these questions for claims such as x. One can similarly answer questions about viability by considering only claims such as x'.

Dividends paid by the primitive securities can be dealt with similarly. Again we leave the details to the reader, but note that there are a number of ways to proceed. Dividends can be "instantaneously" reinvested, either in the security which issues them or in the riskless security. Alternatively, cumulative dividends may be subtracted from the claim being valued.

Consider options next. Options are financial instruments where the bearer has some discretion as to the form or timing of the payouts. We model an option as a collection of claims $\{x_\alpha\, ; \alpha \in \mathscr{A}\}$, where the bearer has the right to specify at the outset which claim x_α he will take. For example, American puts are such collections, where $\alpha \in \mathscr{A}$ indexes all stopping times relative to $\{F_t\}$. (We will return to this example momentarily.) For a viable security market model, let **P** denote the set of equivalent martingale measures. Then for any choice of α, the claim x_α is worth no less than $\inf_{P^* \in \mathbf{P}} E^*(x_\alpha)$ and no more than $\sup_{P^* \in \mathbf{P}} E^*(x_\alpha)$. Thus the option is worth *at least*

$$\sup_{\alpha \in \mathscr{A}} \inf_{P^* \in \mathbf{P}} E^*(x_\alpha),$$

and *at most*

$$\sup_{\alpha \in \mathscr{A}} \sup_{P^* \in \mathbf{P}} E^*(x_\alpha).$$

When these two numbers are equal, the option's price is determined by arbitrage, the common number being the arbitrage value. When **P** is a singleton, the two numbers are obviously equal, and the value of the option is $\sup_{\alpha \in \mathscr{A}} E^*(x_\alpha)$, where $E^*(\cdot)$ denotes expectation with respect to the single equivalent martingale measure. Note that in such cases, the choice of which strategy α to elect is independent of the bearer's attitude towards risk.

An example illustrates the three extensions given above. Consider the Black-Scholes model described above (with r possibly different from zero) and the problem of valuing an American put with exercise price a and expiration date T. If the put is exercised using the stopping rule τ, it generates $(a - Z_1(\tau))^+$ at time τ. If $Z_1(\tau) > a$, rule τ is interpreted to imply that the put is never exercised. First we transfer to a model with zero rate of interest, getting Z' as above. In the primed model, the option exercised using τ generates $(a \exp(-r\tau) - Z_1'(\tau))^+$ at time τ. This is equivalent to the claim which generates $(a \exp(-r\tau) - Z_1'(\tau))^+$ at time T by the second extension. This claim has arbitrage value

$$E(\{ae^{-r\tau} - Z_1^*(\tau)\}^+),$$

where $dZ_1^* = \sigma Z_1^* \, dW$, according to Section 5. Thus the put option has arbitrage value

$$\sup_\tau E(\{ae^{-r\tau} - Z_1^*(\tau)\}^+),$$

where the supremum is over all stopping times τ with $0 \leqslant \tau \leqslant T$. (This is the arbitrage value in both the original and the primed model, as $Z_0(0) = 1$.) The valuation of this put is reduced to an optimal stopping problem, to which one may apply the methods of potential theory.

It is quite simple to extend beyond our restriction of X to square integrable claims and our use of the L^2 norm topology. In Section 2, we only used the facts that X is a real linear space of F-measurable random variable on Ω and that the topology on X is linear, Hausdorff and locally convex. (Also, it is necessary that if $x \in X$ and x' is a random variable such that $P(x = x') = 1$, then x' is *identified* with x as one element of X.) For any real linear space of F-measurable random variables on Ω topologized in a manner that meets these requirements, Theorem 1 is proven exactly as above. See [12] for further extensions and refinements of this.

In establishing the correspondence between $\psi \in \Psi$ such that $\psi \mid M = \pi$ and equivalent martingale measures (Theorem 2), we made use of the Riesz Representation Theorem. That is, ψ is a continuous linear functional on X if and only if $\psi(x) = E(\rho x)$ for some $\rho \in L^2(\Omega, F, P)$. This told us that given a continuous linear functional ψ, defining $P^*(B) = \psi(1_B)$ created a (σ-additive) measure absolutely continuous with respect to P and satisfying $dP^*/dP \in L^2$. Conversely, given a probability measure P^* absolutely continuous with respect to P and satisfying $dP^*/dP \in L^2$, defining $\psi(x) = E^*(x)$ for $x \in X$ creates a continuous linear functional on X. Suppose therefore, that we fix $p \in [1, \infty]$ and take $X = L^p(\Omega, F, P)$, topologized so that ψ is a continuous linear functional on X if and only if $\psi(x) = E(\rho x)$ for some $\rho \in L^q(\Omega, F, P)$, where $q^{-1} + p^{-1} = 1$. For example, if $p < \infty$, the topology on X can be the standard L^p norm topology. If $p = \infty$, the topology on X can be the L^1-Mackey topology. We would need to assume that $Z_k(t) \in X$ for all k and t, and we would need to change the definition of an equivalent martingale measure to read that $dP^*/dP \in L^q$. (In order to take needed conditional expectations, we would also need to require of a simple trading strategy θ that $\theta_k(t)\, Z_k(t) \in X$ for all k and t.) With these changes, the development could proceed exactly as in Section 3.

In applying this to the case of diffusions, difficulties do arise. Our use of Kunita and Watanabe [13] does require require that $\rho \in L^2$. So we only know conditions under which there is a unique equivalent martingale measure P^* such that $dP^*/dP \in L^2$. If, using the terminology of the above paragraph, we chose a $p < 2$, then the requirement would change to $dP^*/dP \in L^q$ where $q > 2$. This is more stringent than $dP^*/dP \in L^2$, so the conditions given in Theorem 3 establish that there is at *most* a single equivalent martingale measure. If that measure does satisfy $dP^*/dP \in L^q$, then the model is viable and all claims are priced by arbitrage. If that measure does not satisfy $dP^*/dP \in L^q$, then the model is not viable. For example, consider the Black-Scholes model for $\mu + \sigma^2/2 \neq 0$. The Radon-Nikodym derivative dP^*/dP can be explicitly computed, and it does not satisfy $dP^*/dP \in L^\infty$. Thus if $p = 1$, the Black-Scholes model is not a viable model of economic equilibrium.

On the other hand, if $p > 2$, then the requirement becomes $dP^*/dP \in L^q$ for $q < 2$. This is less stringent. Although Theorem 3 establishes the viability of a class of models (for $p > 2$), it does not show that the price of every contingent claim is determined by arbitrage. To do that, we would need to sharpen the Kunita–Watanabe result, and we can only conjecture that this is possible.

8. Concluding Remarks

The basic question addressed in this paper is the following. What contingent claims are "spanned" by a given set of marketed securities? To the best of our knowledge, this question first appears in the Economics literature in the classic paper by Arrow [1]. Other, more recent references include Friesen [7], Ross [16], Stiglitz [20], and the *Bell Journal* Symposium on the Optimality of Capital Markets [3]. The papers of Garman [8], Ross [17], and Rubinstein [18] all contain arguments similar in spirit to ours, using linear functionals to value claims whose price is determined by arbitrage.

Except for the papers of Black and Scholes [4] and Merton [14], the greatest single stimulus for the work reported here was the paper by Cox and Ross [6]. Cox and Ross provide the following key observation. If a claim is priced by arbitrage in a world with one stock and one bond, then its value can be found by first modifying the model so that the stock earns at the riskless rate, and then computing the expected value of the claim. They analyze two examples, and in each case they determine the correct modification by the following procedure. First, using the technique of Black and Scholes, they derive an analytical expression (differential or differential-difference equation) that the value of the claim must satisfy. Having observed that one model parameter does *not* appear in this relationship, they then adjust the value of that parameter (only) so that the stock earns at the riskless rate. Their first example is the diffusion model of Black and Scholes, where the free parameter is the drift rate of the stock price process. In their second example, the stock price pricess Y satisfies

$$Y(t) = Y(0) + \int_0^t aY(s)\,dN(s) - \int_0^t bY(s)\,ds, \tag{8.1}$$

where $N = \{N(t); 0 \leqslant t \leqslant T\}$ is a Poisson process with jump rate λ, and a and b are specified positive constants. It is found that the free parameter is λ, and that $\lambda^* = b/a$ causes Y to earn at the riskless rate (zero).

For the Black-Scholes model, we have displayed in Section 6 the Radon–Nikodym derivative of the *unique* equivalent martingale measure P^* under which the stock earns at the riskless rate. Substitution of P^* for P is equivalent to the drift rate adjustment of Cox and Ross. For the jump process model (8.1), there also exists a unique equivalent martingale measure P^*, and substitution of P^* for P accomplishes the jump rate adjustment of Cox and Ross (without affecting the parameters a and b). Furthermore, it is possible to explicitly compute the Radon–Nikodym derivative of P^* with respect to P. We leave to the reader the (relatively difficulty) task of computing dP^*/dP and proving that P^* is in fact the unique equivalent martingale measure.

The careful reader may be troubled by this comparison of Cox and Ross with our results, because Cox and Ross state that arbitrage is independent of preferences, whereas in our treatment arbitrage is crucially tied up with a particular class of agents, the class **A**. It is clear how these two positions are reconciled. When Cox and Ross construct the preferences of the risk neutral agent who gives the arbitrage value of claims, they are constructing an equivalent martingale measure. In both their examples, the preferences/measure constructed preserve the null sets of the original measure and are continuous in the sense we require. That is, their risk neutral agent is a member of our class **A**, as he must be.

ACKNOWLEDGMENTS

Conversations with Paul Milgrom stimulated a substantial revision of this paper, including a reformulation of the problem under discussion. We are pleased to acknowledge his very significant contributions. We also benefited from conversations with James Hoag, Krishna Ramaswamy, William Sharpe, Robert Wilson, and especially George Feiger and Bertrand Jacquillat. This work was supported by a grant from the Atlantic Richfield Foundation to the Graduate School of Business, Stanford University, by National Science Foundation Grant SOC77-07741 A01 at the Institute for Mathematical Studies in the Social Sciences, Stanford University, by the Mellon Foundation, by the Churchill Foundation, and by the Social Science Research Council of the U.K.

REFERENCES

1. K. ARROW, The role of securities in the optimal allocation of risk-bearing, *Rev. Econ. Stud.* **31** (1964), 91–96.
2. R. ASH AND M. GARDNER, "Topics in Stochastic Processes," Academic Press, New York, 1975.
3. *Bell J. Econ. Manag. Sci.*, Symposium on the Optimality of Competitive Capital Markets, **5** (1974); H. LELAND, Production theory and the stock market, 125–144; R. MERTON AND M. SUBRAHMANYAM, The optimality of a competitive stock market, 145–170; S. EKERN AND R. WILSON, On the theory of the firm in an economy with incomplete markets, 171–180; R. RADNER, A note on unanimity of stockholders' preferences among alternative production plans: A reformulation of the Ekern–Wilson model, 181–186.
4. F. BLACK AND M. SCHOLES, The pricing of options and corporate liabilities, *J. Polit. Econ.* **81** (1973), 637–659.
5. K. CHUNG, "A Course in Probability Theory," 2nd ed. Academic Press, New York, 1974.
6. J. COX AND S. ROSS, The valuation of options for alternative stochastic processes, *J. Financial Econ.* **3** (1976), 145–166.
7. P. FRIESEN, A Reinterpretation of the Equilibrium Theory of Arrow and Debreu in Terms of Financial Markets, Stanford University Institute for Mathematical Studies in the Social Sciences Technical Report No. 126, 1974.
8. M. GARMAN, A General Theory of Asset Valuation under Diffusion State Processes, University of California, Berkeley, Research Program in Finance Working Paper No. 50, 1976.

9. I. Gihman and A. Skorohod, "Stochastic Differential Equations," Springer-Verlag, New York, 1972.
10. I. Girsanov, On transforming a certain class of stochastic processes by absolutely continuous substitution of measures, *Theor. Probability Appl.* **5** (1960), 285–301.
11. R. Holmes, "Geometric Functional Analysis and Its Applications," Springer-Verlag, New York, 1975.
12. D. Kreps, Arbitrage and Equilibrium in Economics with Infinitely Many Commodities, Economic Theory Discussion Paper, Cambridge University, 1979.
13. H. Kunita and S. Watanabe, On square integrable martingales, *Nagoya Math. J.* **30** (1967), 209–245.
14. R. Merton, Theory of rational option pricing, *Bell J. Econ. Manag. Sci.* **4** (1973), 141–183.
15. R. Merton, On the pricing of contingent claims and the Modigliani–Miller theorem, *J. Financial Econ.* **5** (1977), 241–249.
16. S. Ross, The arbitrage theory of capital asset pricing, *J. Econ. Theor.* **13** (1976), 341–360.
17. S. Ross, A simple approach to the valuation of risky streams, *J. Business* **51** (1978), 453–475.
18. M. Rubinstein, The valuation of uncertain income streams and the pricing of options, *Bell J. Econ.* **2** (1976), 407–425.
19. W. Sharpe, "Investments," Prentice-Hall, Englewood Cliffs, N.J., 1978.
20. J. Stiglitz, On the optimality of the stock market allocation of investment, *Quart. J. Econ.* **86** (1972), 25–60.

[4]

Econometrica, Vol. 53, No. 6 (November, 1985)

IMPLEMENTING ARROW-DEBREU EQUILIBRIA BY CONTINUOUS TRADING OF FEW LONG-LIVED SECURITIES

BY DARRELL DUFFIE AND CHI-FU HUANG[1]

A two-period (0 and T) Arrow-Debreu economy is set up with a general model of uncertainty. We suppose that an equilibrium exists for this economy. The Arrow-Debreu economy is placed in a Radner (dynamic) setting; agents may trade claims at any time during $[0, T]$. Under appropriate conditions it is possible to implement the original Arrow-Debreu equilibrium, which may have an infinite-dimensional commodity space, in a Radner equilibrium with only a finite number of securities. This is done by opening the "right" set of security markets, a set which effectively completes markets for the Radner economy.

1. INTRODUCTION

FIGURE 1 DEPICTS A SIMPLE event tree information structure. Let's momentarily consider an exchange economy with endowments of and preferences for random time T consumption, depending on the state $\omega \in \Omega$ chosen by nature from the final five nodes of this event tree. A competitive equilibrium will exist under standard assumptions (Debreu [**5**, Chapter **7**]), including markets for securities whose time T consumption payoff vectors span R^5. This entails at least five security markets, while intuition suggests that, with the ability to learn information and trade during $[0, T]$, only three securities which are always available for trading, or *long-lived securities* [**13**], might be enough to effectively complete markets. This is the maximum number of branches leaving any node in the tree. The reasoning is given by Kreps [**13**] and in alternative more general form later in this paper. An early precurser to this work is Arrow [**1**], which showed the spanning effectiveness of financial securities when trade can occur twice in a two-period model.

One major purpose of this paper is to verify this intuition for a very general class of information structures, including those which cannot be represented by event trees, such as the filtration generated by continuous-time "state-variable" stochastic processes. In some cases, where an Arrow-Debreu style equilibrium would call for an infinite number of securities, we show how a continuous trading Radner [**20**] *equilibrium of plans, prices and price expectations* can implement the same Arrow-Debreu consumption allocations with only a finite number of long-lived securities. It is misleading, of course, to use the number of security markets alone as a measure of the efficiency of the market structure; the number of transactions which must be performed to achieve a given allocation must also be considered. Largely for want of a reasonable model to study this tradeoff, we have not addressed the issue of the efficiency of market structure.

A comparison of Event Trees A of Figure 1 and B of Figure 2, which are intended to correspond to the same two-period Arrow-Debreu economy, obviates the role of the information structure in determining the number of long-lived

[1] We would like to thank David Kreps, John Cox, Michael Harrison, and David Luenberger for helpful comments. We are also grateful to Larry Jones, Donald Brown, and David Kreps for pointing out an error in the earlier version of this paper. That and any remaining errors are our own.

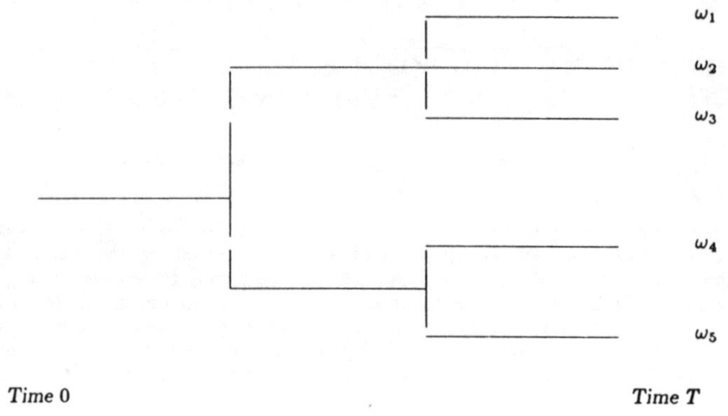

$\Omega = \{\omega_1, \ldots, \omega_5\}$

FIGURE 1.

securities required to dynamically "span" the consumption space, or the *spanning number.* We later give this term a more precise meaning. Since all uncertainty is resolved at once in Event Tree *B*, the spanning number is five, instead of three for Event Tree *A*. Intuitively speaking, the maximum number of "dimensions of uncertainty" which could be resolved at any one time is the key determining property. This vague notion actually takes a precise form as the *martingale multiplicity* of the information structure, defined in the Appendix. A key result of this paper is that the spanning number is the martingale multiplicity plus one. The "plus one" is no mystery; in addition to spanning uncertainty, agents must have the ability to transfer purchasing power across time.

The notion that certain securities are redundant because their payoffs can be replicated by trading other securities over time, yielding arbitrage pricing relationships among securities, was dramatized in the Black–Scholes [**2**] option pricing

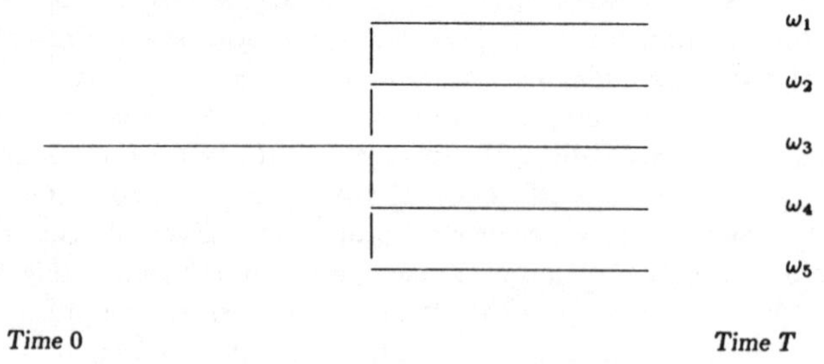

$\Omega = \{\omega_1, \ldots, \omega_5\}$

FIGURE 2.

formula.[2] Provided the equilibrium price process for one security happens to be a geometric Brownian Motion, and for another is a (deterministic) exponential of time, then any contingent claim whose payoff depends (measurably) on the path taken by the underlying Brownian Motion, such as a call option on the risky security, is redundant and priced by arbitrage. This discovery curiously preceded its simpler logical antecedents, such as the corresponding results for event tree information structures. Only in the past few years have the implications of the spanning properties of price processes (e.g., [**13**]), the connection between martingale theory and equilibrium price processes (e.g., [**8**]), and the mathematical machinery for continuous security trading [**9**] been formalized.

In all of the above mentioned literature the takeoff point is a given set of security price processes, implicitly imbedded in a Radner equilibrium. Our second major goal is to begin more primitively with a given Arrow-Debreu equilibrium, one in which trading over time is not of concern since markets are complete at time zero. From that point we construct the consumption payoffs and price processes for a set of long-lived securities in such a way that agents may be allocated trading strategies allowing them to consume their original Arrow-Debreu allocations within a Radner style equilibrium. In short, we implement a given Arrow-Debreu equilibrium by continuous trading of a set of long-lived securities which is typically much smaller in number than the dimension of the consumption space. Merton [**19**; p. 666] recently predicted that results such as ours would appear.

The paper unfolds in the following order. First we describe the economy (Section 2) and an Arrow-Debreu equilibrium for it (Section 3). Section 4 provides a constructive proof of a Radner equilibrium which implements a given Arrow-Debreu equilibrium under stated conditions, based on a martingale representation technique. Section 5 characterizes the spanning number in terms of martingale multiplicity. Section 6 discusses the continuous trading machinery, some generalizations, and two examples of the model. Section 7 adds concluding remarks.

2. THE ECONOMY

Uncertainty in our economy is modeled as a complete probability space $(\Omega, \mathscr{F}, P)$. The set Ω constitutes all possible states of the world which could exist at a terminal date $T>0$. The *tribe* $\mathscr{F}$ is the σ-algebra of measurable subsets of Ω, or events, of which agents can make probability assessments based on the probability measure P. Events are revealed over time according to a *filtration*, $\boldsymbol{F}=\{\mathscr{F}_t, t\in[0,T]\}$, a right-continuous increasing family of sub-tribes of $\mathscr{F}$, where $\mathscr{F}_T=\mathscr{F}$ and $\mathscr{F}_0$ is almost trivial (the tribe generated by Ω and all of the P-null sets). We can interpret this by thinking of $\mathscr{F}_t$ as the set of all events which could occur at or before time t. The assumption that $\boldsymbol{F}$ is increasing, or $\mathscr{F}_t\subset\mathscr{F}_s$ for $s>t$, means simply that agents do not forget that an event has occurred once it

[2] Merton [**18**] is also seminal in this regard. Similar results were obtained by Cox and Ross [**3**] for other models of uncertainty.

is revealed. The above descriptions of $\mathcal{F}_0$ and $\mathcal{F}_T$ means that no information is known at time 0, and all uncertainty is resolved at time T.

Each agent in the economy is characterized by the following properties: (i) a known endowment of a perishable consumption good at time zero, (ii) a random, that is, state-dependent, endowment of the consumption good at time T, and (iii) preferences over consumption pairs (r, x), where r is time zero consumption and x is a random variable describing time T consumption, $x(\omega)$ in state $\omega \in \Omega$.

We will only consider consumption claims with finite variance. The consumption space is thus formalized as $V = R \times L^2(P)$, where $L^2(P)$ is the space of (equivalence classes) of square-integrable random-variables on $(\Omega, \mathcal{F}, P)$, with the usual product topology on V given by the Euclidean and L^2 norms.

The agents, finite in number, are indexed by $i = 1, \ldots, I$. The preferences of agent i are modeled as a complete transitive binary relation, or *preference order*, $\succcurlyeq_i$ on $V_i \subset V$, the ith agent's consumption set.

The whole economy can then be summarized in the usual way by the collection

$$\mathscr{E} = (V_i, \hat{v}_i, \succcurlyeq_i; i = 1, \ldots, I),$$

where $\hat{v}_i = (\hat{r}_i, \hat{x}_i) \in V_i$ is the ith agent's endowment. It is not important for this paper whether or not one assumes positive consumption or endowments.

3. ARROW-DEBREU EQUILIBRIUM

An Arrow-Debreu equilibrium for $\mathscr{E}$ is a nonzero linear (price) functional $\Psi: V \to R$ and a set of allocations $(v_i^* \in V_i; i = 1, \ldots, I)$ satisfying, for all i,

$$\Psi(v_i^*) \leqslant \Psi(\hat{v}_i),$$

$$v \succ_i v_i^* \quad \Rightarrow \quad \Psi(v) > \Psi(v_i^*) \quad \forall v \in V_i, \tag{3.1}$$

$$\sum_{i=1}^{I} v_i^* = \sum_{i=i}^{I} \hat{v}_i.$$

We will assume that at least one agent i has strictly monotonic preferences. Specifically, if $v \in V_i$ and $v' \geqslant v$ (in the obvious product order on V), then $v' \in V_i$ and $v' \succ_i v$ provided $v \neq v'$. This ensures that in equilibrium Ψ is a strictly positive linear functional. Since V is a Hilbert lattice **[21]**, this then implies that Ψ is a continuous linear functional on V, which can therefore be represented by some element (a, ξ) of V itself in the form:

$$\Psi(r, x) = ar + \int_\Omega x(\omega)\xi(\omega)\, dP(\omega) \quad \forall (r, x) \in V.$$

Without loss of generality we can normalize Ψ by a constant so that the positive random variable ξ has unit expectation, in order to construct the probability measure Q on $(\Omega, \mathcal{F})$ by the relation

$$Q(B) = \int_B 1_B(\omega)\xi(\omega)\, dP(\omega) \quad \forall B \in \mathcal{F}.$$

Equivalently, ξ is the Radon-Nikodym derivative dQ/dP. This leaves the simple representation

$$(3.2)\qquad \Psi(r, x) = ar + E^*(x) \quad \forall (r, x) \in V,$$

where E^* denotes expectation under Q. Thus the equilibrium price of any random consumption claim $x \in L^2(P)$ is simply its expected consumption payoff under Q. For this reason we call Q an *equilibrium price measure.*

For tractability we will want any random variable which has finite variance under P to have finite variance under Q, and *vice versa.* A necessary and sufficient condition is that P and Q are *uniformly absolutely continuous*, denoted $Q \approx P$ (Halmos [**7**, p. 100]), or equivalently, that the Radon-Nikodym derivative dQ/dP is bounded above and below away from zero. Sufficient conditions for this can be given when preferences can be represented by von-Neumann-Morgenstern utility functions, in terms of bounds on marginal utility for time T consumption. We do not pursue this here since we are taking ξ as a primitive, rather than deriving it from preferences.[3]

A second regularity condition which comes into play is the separability[4] of $\mathcal{F}$ under P. This assumption should not be viewed as too restrictive. One can, for example, construct Brownian Motion on a separable probability space. Given $Q \approx P$ it is then easy to show the separability of $\mathcal{F}$ under Q by making use of the upper essential bound on dQ/dP.

Since uniform absolute continuity of two measures implies their equivalence (that is, they give probability zero to the same events), we can use the symbol a.s. for "almost surely" indiscriminately in this paper.

4. RADNER EQUILIBRIUM

A *long-lived security* is a consumption claim (to some element of $L^2(P)$) available for trade throughout $[0, T]$. A *price process* for a long-lived security is a semimartingale[5] on our given probability space adapted to the given information structure $\mathbf{F}$. In general the number of units of a long-lived security which are held by an agent over time defines some stochastic process θ. We will say θ is an *admissible* trading process for a long-lived security with price process S if it meets the following regularity conditions:

(i) *predictability*, defined in the Appendix and denoted $\theta \in \mathcal{P}$;

(ii) *square-integrability*, or $\theta \in L^2_P[S] \equiv \{\phi \in \mathcal{P}: E(\int_0^T \phi_t^2\, d[S]_t) < \infty\}$, where $[S]$ denotes the quadratic variation process for S (Jacod [**11**]); and

[3] Work subsequent to this paper shows extremely general continuity assumptions which yield these bounds [**6**].

[4] A tribe $\mathcal{F}$ is said to be separable under P if there exists a countable number of elements $B_1, B_2, \ldots$ in $\mathcal{F}$ such that, for any $B \in \mathcal{F}$ and $\varepsilon > 0$ there exists B_n in the sequence with $P\{B \Delta B_n\} < \varepsilon$, where Δ denotes symmetric difference.

[5] See Jacod [**11**], for example, for the definition of a semimartingale. This is not at all a severe restriction on price processes if one is to obtain a meaningful model of gains and losses from security trades.

(iii) the *gains process* $\int \theta\, dS$ is well defined as a stochastic integral. We will be dealing with price processes in this paper for which square-integrability (ii) is sufficient for this condition. Memin [**16**] gives a full set of sufficient conditions in the general case.

The stochastic integral $\int_0^t \theta(s)\, dS(s)$ is a model of the gains or losses realized up to and including time t by trading a security with price process S using the trading process θ. Interpreted as a Stieltjes integral this model is obvious, but the integral is generally well defined only as a stochastic integral. This model, formalized by Harrison and Pliska [**9**], is discussed further in Section 6, as are the other regularity conditions on θ.

Taking $S=(S_1,\ldots,S_N)$, $N\leqslant\infty$, as the set of all long-lived security price processes, any corresponding set of admissible trading processes $\theta=(\theta_1,\ldots,\theta_N)$ must also meet the accounting identity:

$$(4.1)\qquad \theta(t)^{\top}S(t)=\theta(0)^{\top}S(0)+\int_0^t \theta(s)^{\top}\, dS(s)\quad \forall t\in[0,T]\qquad \text{a.s.,}$$

meaning that the current value of a portfolio must be its initial value plus any gains or losses incurred from trading. The symbol $^{\top}$ denotes the obvious shorthand notation for summation from 1 to N. We'll adopt the notation $\Theta(S)$ for the space of trading strategies $\theta=(\theta_1,\ldots,\theta_N)$ meeting the regularity conditions (i)-(ii)-(iii) for each long-lived security and satisfying the "self-financing"restriction (4.1).

A *Radner equilibrium* for $\mathscr{E}$ is comprised of:

(1) a set of long-lived securities claiming $d=(d_1,\ldots,d_N)$, $d_n\in L^2(P)$, $1\leqslant n\leqslant N\leqslant\infty$, with corresponding price processes $S=(S_1,\ldots,S_N)$;

(2) a set of trading strategies $\theta^i\in\Theta(S)$, one for each agent $i=1,\ldots,I$; and

(3) a price $a\in R_+$ for time zero consumption;

all of these satisfying:

(4) budget constrained optimality: for each agent i,

$$\left(\hat{r}_i-\frac{\theta^i(0)^{\top}S(0)}{a},\ \hat{x}_i+\theta^i(T)^{\top}d\right)$$

is $\succcurlyeq_i$-maximal in the budget set:

$$\left\{\left(\hat{r}_i-\frac{\theta(0)^{\top}S(0)}{a},\ \hat{x}_i+\theta(T)^{\top}d\right)\in V_i\colon \theta\in\Theta(S)\right\},$$

and

(5) market clearing:

$$\sum_{i=1}^{I}\theta^i(t)=0\quad \forall t\in[0,T].$$

The space of square-integrable martingales under Q, denoted $\mathscr{M}_Q^2$; its multiplicity, denoted $M(\mathscr{M}_Q^2)$; and a corresponding orthogonal 2-basis of martingales, $m=(m_1,\ldots,m_N)$, where $N=M(\mathscr{M}_Q^2)\leqslant\infty$; are all defined in the Appendix. The central concept is that any of the martingales associated with the given information structure can be represented as the sum of $M(\mathcal{M}_Q^2)$ stochastic integrals against the fixed 2-basis of martingales m, in the manner given by the following theorem. This result is a direct consequence of the definition of martingale multiplicity. The content of the result lies with specific examples in which martingale multiplicity is characterized. Details, beyond those in the Appendix, may be found in the fourth chapter of Jacod [**11**]. Kunita and Watanabe [**14**] as well as Davis and Varaiya [**4**] also include the essentials.

THEOREM 4.1: *For any $X \in \mathcal{M}_Q^2$ there exists $\theta = (\theta_1, \ldots, \theta_N)$, where $\theta_n \in L_Q^2[m_n]$ for all n, such that*

$$X_t = \int_0^t \theta(s)^\top \, dm(s) \quad \forall t \in [0, T] \quad \text{a.s.}$$

We should remark that when $Q \approx P$, the spaces $L_Q^2[m_n]$ and $L_P^2[m_n]$ are identical because of the bounds implied on dQ/dP. We also use the fact that a martingale under Q is a semimartingale under P given the equivalence of P and Q. Thus any element of $\mathcal{M}_Q^2$ is a valid price process. This can be checked in Jacod [**11**, Chapter 7], along with the existence of $\int \theta_n \, dm_n$ as a stochastic integral under P whenever $\theta_n \in L_P^2[m_n]$.

Now we have the main result.

THEOREM 4.2: *Suppose $(\Psi, v_i^*, i = 1, \ldots, I)$ is an Arrow-Debreu equilibrium for $\mathscr{E}$, where without loss of generality Ψ has the representation (a, Q) given by relation* (3.2). *Provided $Q \approx P$ and $\mathscr{F}$ is separable under P, there is a Radner equilibrium for $\mathscr{E}$ achieving the Arrow-Debreu equilibrium allocations.*

PROOF: The proof takes four steps:

(1) Specify a set of long-lived securities.

(2) Announce a price for time zero consumption and price processes for the long-lived securities.

(3) Allocate a trading strategy to each agent which generates that agent's Arrow-Debreu allocation and which, collectively, clears markets.

(4) Prove that no agent has any incentive to deviate from the allocated trading strategy.

STEP 1: Select the following elements of $L^2(P)$ as the claims of the available long-lived securities:

$$d_0 = 1_\Omega,$$

$$d_n = m_n(T), \quad 1 \le n \le N = M(\mathcal{M}_Q^2),$$

where 1_Ω is the random variable whose value is identically 1 (the indicator function on Ω), and $m = (m_1, \ldots, m_N)$ is an orthogonal 2-basis for $\mathcal{M}_Q^2$. Since $Q \approx P$, the final values of the martingales, $m_n(T)$, are elements of $L^2(P)$.

STEP 2: For $0 \leq n \leq N$ let $S_n(t)$, the price of d_n at time t, be announced as $E^*[d_n | \mathcal{F}_t]$. In other words, each long-lived security's current price is the conditional expectation under Q of its consumption value. For convenience we actually take RCLL[6] versions of these price processes. There is obviously some forethought here, for the result is $S_0 \equiv 1$ and $S_n = m_n$, $1 \leq n \leq N$, implying that the last N price processes are themselves an orthogonal 2-basis for $\mathcal{M}_Q^2$, suggesting their ability to "span" (in the sense of Theorem 4.1) all consumption claims not actually available for trading. The first security serves as a "store-of-value", since its price is constant. We also announce the positive scalar a given in the statement of the theorem as the price of time zero consumption.

STEP 3: For any agent i, for $1 \leq i \leq I-1$, let $e_i = x_i^* - \hat{x}_i$. Then the process

$$X_i(t) = E^*(e_i | \mathcal{F}_t) - E^*(e_i), \quad t \in [0, T], \tag{4.2}$$

is an element of $\mathcal{M}_Q^2$, given $Q \approx P$, which can be reconstructed via Theorem 4.1 as

$$X_i(t) = \sum_{n=1}^{N} \int_0^t \theta_n^i(s)\, dS_n(s), \quad \forall t \in [0, T] \quad \text{a.s.}, \tag{4.3}$$

for some $\theta_n^i \in L_P^2[S_n]$, $1 \leq n \leq N$.

In order to meet the accounting restriction (4.1), we set the following trading process for the "store-of-value" security:

$$\theta_0^i(t) = E^*(e_i) + \sum_{n=1}^{N} \int_0^t \theta_n^i(s)\, dS_n(s) - \theta_n^i(t) S_n(t), \quad t \in [0, T]. \tag{4.4}$$

Of course $\int \theta_0^i\, dS_0 \equiv 0$ since $S_0 \equiv 1$. A technical argument showing $\theta_0^i \in \mathcal{P}$ is given as Appendix Lemma A.1, which then implies $\theta_0^i \in L_P^2[S_0]$.

Substituting (4.4) into (4.3), noting that $m_n(0) = 0\ \forall n$, we then have

$$\theta^i(t)^{\mathsf{T}} S(t) = \theta^i(0)^{\mathsf{T}} S(0) + \int_0^t \theta^i(s)^{\mathsf{T}} dS(s) \quad \forall t \in [0, T], \quad \text{a.s.}, \tag{4.5}$$

confirming (4.1). This yields the final requirement for claiming the trading strategy is admissible, or $\theta^i = (\theta_0^i, \ldots, \theta_N^i) \in \Theta(S)$. Evaluating (4.5) at times T and 0, using the definitions of e_i and X_i yields:

$$\theta^i(T)^{\mathsf{T}} d + \hat{x}_i = \theta^i(T)^{\mathsf{T}} S(T) + \hat{x}_i = x_i^* \quad \text{a.s.}$$

and

$$\theta^i(0)^{\mathsf{T}} S(0) = E^*(x_i^* - \hat{x}_i) = \Psi(0, x_i^*) - \Psi(0, \hat{x}_i) = (\hat{r}_i - r_i^*)a,$$

the last line making use of the budget constraint on the Arrow-Debreu allocation for agent i. Thus by adopting the trading strategy θ^i, and faced with the time-zero consumption price of a, agent i can consume precisely $(r_i^*, x_i^*) = v_i^*$.

The above construction applies for agents 1 through $I-1$. For the last agent, agent I, let $\theta^I = -\sum_{i=1}^{I-1} \theta^i$. By the Kunita-Watanabe inequality [**14**], $\Theta(S)$ is a

[6] An *RCLL* process is one whose sample paths are right continuous with left limits almost surely.

linear space, so $\theta^I \in \Theta(S)$. Market clearing is obviously met by construction. To complete this step it remains to show that θ^I generates the consumption allocation $(r_i^*, x_i^*) = v_i^*$, but this is immediate from the linearity of stochastic integrals and market clearing in the Arrow-Debreu equilibrium.

STEP 4: We proceed by contradiction. Suppose some agent j can obtain a strictly preferred allocation $(r, x) >_j (r_j^*, x_j^*)$ by adopting a different trading strategy $\theta \in \Theta(S)$. Then the Arrow-Debreu price of (r, x) must be strictly higher than that of (r_j^*, x_j^*), or

$$ar + E^*(x) > ar_j^* + E^*(x_j^*).$$

Substituting the Radner budget constraint for r and x,

$$a\hat{r}_j - \theta(0)^\top S(0) + E^*\left[\hat{x}_j + \theta(0)^\top S(0) + \int_0^T \theta(t)^\top \, dS(t)\right] > ar_j^* + E^*(x_j^*),$$

or

$$a\hat{r}_j + E^*(\hat{x}_j) > ar_j^* + E^*(x_j^*). \tag{4.6}$$

The last line uses the fact that $E^*[\int_0^T \theta(t)^\top \, dS(t)] = 0$ since $\int \theta^\top \, dS$ is a Q-martingale for any $\theta \in \Theta(S)$, from the fact that $\int \phi \, dS_n \in \mathcal{M}_Q^2 \; \forall \phi \in L_Q^2[S_n]$ **[11**, Chapter 4]. But (4.6) contradicts the Arrow-Debreu budget-constrained optimality of (r_j^*, x_j^*). This establishes the theorem. *Q.E.D.*

Of course, under the standard weak conditions ensuring that an Arrow-Debreu equilibrium allocation is Pareto optimal, the resulting Radner equilibrium allocation of this theorem is also Pareto optimal as it implements the Arrow-Debreu allocation.

5. THE SPANNING NUMBER OF RADNER EQUILIBRIA

The key idea of the last proof is that an appropriately selected and priced set of long-lived securities "spans" the entire final period consumption space in the sense that any $x \in L^2(P)$ can be represented in the form

$$E^*[x \mid \mathcal{F}_t] = \theta(t)^\top S(t) = \theta(0)^\top S(0) + \int_0^t \theta(s)^\top \, dS(s) \quad \forall t \in [0, T] \quad \text{a.s.,} \tag{5.1}$$

where $S = (S_0, \ldots, S_N)$ is the set of $(N+1)$ security price processes constructed in the proof and $\theta \in \Theta(S)$ is an appropriate trading strategy. In particular, $E^*[x \mid \mathcal{F}_T] = x$ a.s. As examples in the following section will show, this number of securities, $N+1$, or the multiplicity of $\mathcal{M}_Q^2$ plus one, can be considerably smaller than the dimension of $L^2(P)$. But is this the "smallest number" which will serve this purpose, or the "spanning number" in some sense? To be more precise, we will prove the following result, still assuming $Q \approx P$ and the separability of $\mathcal{F}$.

PROPOSITION 5.1: *Suppose long-lived security prices for $\mathscr{E}$ are square-integrable martingales under Q, the equilibrium price measure for $\mathscr{E}$. Then the minimum number of long-lived securities which completes markets in the sense of* (5.1) *is* $M(\mathcal{M}_Q^2)+1$.

PROOF: That $M(\mathcal{M}_Q^2)+1$ is a sufficient number is given by construction in the proof of Theorem 4.2. The remainder of the proof is devoted to showing that at least this number is required.

If $M(\mathcal{M}_Q^2)=\infty$ we are done. Otherwise, suppose $S=(S_1,\ldots,S_K)$, $K<\infty$, is a set of square-integrable Q-martingale security price processes with the representation property (5.1). By the definition of multiplicity it follows that $K\geqslant M(\mathcal{M}_Q^2)$. It remains to show that $K=M(\mathcal{M}_Q^2)$ implies a contradiction, which we now pursue.

Let $x=k+\mathbf{1}^\top S(T)\in L^2(P)$, where k is any real constant and $\mathbf{1}$ is a K-dimensional vector of ones. If S has the representation property (5.1) there exists some $\theta\in\Theta(S)$ satisfying (5.1) for this particular x. Furthermore, since S is a vector of Q-martingales,

$$E^*[x|\mathscr{F}_t]=k+\mathbf{1}^\top S(t)=k+\mathbf{1}^\top S(0)+\int_0^t \mathbf{1}^\top\, dS(s)\quad \forall t\in[0,T]\quad \text{a.s.} \tag{5.2}$$

Since $\theta(0)^\top S(0)=E^*(x)=k+\mathbf{1}^\top S(0)$, equating the right hand sides of (5.1) and (5.2) yields

$$\int_0^t \theta(s)^\top\, dS(s)=\int_0^t \mathbf{1}^\top\, dS(s)\quad \forall t\in[0,T]\quad \text{a.s.}$$

Appendix Lemma A.2 then implies

$$Q\{\exists t\in[0,T]\colon \theta(t)=1\}>0.$$

Since $Q\approx P$, the above event also has strictly positive P-probability, and equating the second members of (5.1) and (5.2) yields

$$P\{\exists t\in[0,T]\colon \mathbf{1}^\top S(t)=\mathbf{1}^\top S(t)+k\}>0,$$

an obvious absurdity if $k\neq 0$. *Q.E.D.*

The reader will likely have raised two points by now. First, having shown that the "spanning number" is $M(\mathcal{M}_Q^2)+1$ when long-lived securities are square-integrable martingales under Q, what do we know about the spanning number in general? From the work of Harrison and Kreps [**8**], we see that a "viable" Radner equilibrium *must* be of the form of security price processes which are martingales under *some* probability measure. Their framework, somewhat less general than ours, was extended in Huang [**10**] to a setting much like our own. Readers may wish to confirm that the same result can be proved in the same manner for the present setting. We have chosen to announce prices as martingales under Q, rather than some other probability measure, as this follows from the natural selection of a numeraire claiming one unit of consumption in every state, the security claiming d_0 in Theorem 4.2. Other numeraires could be chosen; if a random numeraire is selected then in equilibrium security prices will be martingales under some other probability measure, say $\hat{P}$, and the spanning number will be $M(\mathcal{M}^2_{\hat{P}})+1$, if the appropriate regularity conditions are adhered to. Does this number differ from $M(\mathcal{M}^2_Q)+1$; that is, can the martingale multiplicity for the same information structure change under substitution of probability measures? Within the class of equivalent probability measures, those giving zero probability to the same events, this seems unlikely. It is certainly not true for event trees. We put off a direct assault on this question to a subsequent paper. We will show later, however, that if the information is generated by a Standard Brownian Motion, then $M(\mathcal{M}^2_{\hat{P}})=M(\mathcal{M}^2_Q)$.

The second point which ought to have been raised is the number of securities required to implement an Arrow-Debreu equilibrium in a Radner style model, *dropping the requirement for complete markets.* For example, with only two agents, a single security which pays the difference between the endowment and the Arrow-Debreu allocation of one of the agents will obviously allow the two to trade to equilibrium at time zero. This is not a very robust regime of markets, of course. By fixing such agent-specific securities, any perturbation of agents' endowments or preferences which preserves Arrow-Debreu prices will generally preclude an efficient Radner equilibrium. Agents will generally be unable to reach their perturbed Arrow-Debreu allocations without a new set of long-lived securities. A set of long-lived securities which completes markets in the dynamic sense of relation (5.1) is constrastingly robust, although the selection still depends endogenously on Arrow-Debreu prices. It remains a formidable challenge to show how markets can be completed by selecting the claims of long-lived securities entirely on the basis of the exogenous information structure $\boldsymbol{F}$. (As an aside, however, this is easily done for event trees. From this proof of the Proposition it is apparent that a selection of consumption payoffs for long-lived securities can be designed which (generically) completes markets for any Arrow-Debreu equilibrium prices.) There are no economic grounds, of course, precluding the selection of security markets from being an endogenous part of the equilibrium. One would in fact expect this to be the case, an interesting problem for future theoretical and empirical research.

Nothing precludes the fact that some of the martingale price processes in our model may take negative values, even if a positive constant (which is innocuous) is added. For a "spanning" set of positive price processes, one could split each of the original spanning martingales into its positive and negative parts, for a set of $2M(\mathcal{M}^2_Q)+1$ price processes in all. The existence of the required stochastic integrals follows easily.

6. DISCUSSION

In this section we discuss some definitional issues, generalizations of the model, and some specific examples.

6.1. *The Gains Process and Admissible Trading Strategies*

Why is $L_P^2[S]$ an appropriate restriction on trading strategies for a security with price process S? Why is the stochastic integral $\int \theta \, dS$, for $\theta \in L_P^2[S]$, then the appropriate definition of gains from such a strategy? These are questions raised earlier by Harrison and Pliska [**9**].

Following Harrison and Pliska [**9**], we will say that a predictable trading strategy is *simple*, denoted $\theta \in \Lambda$, if there is a partition $\{0 = t_0, t_1, \ldots, t_{n-1}, t_n = T\}$ of $[0, T]$ and bounded random variables $\{h_0, \ldots, h_{n-1}\}$, where h_i is measurable with respect to $\mathscr{F}_{t_i}$, satisfying

$$\theta(t) = h_i, \quad t \in (t_i, t_{i+1}].$$

A simple trading strategy θ, roughly speaking, is one which is piecewise constant and for which $\theta(t)$ can be determined by information available up to, *but not including*, time t. The latter restriction is the basic content of *predictability*. This is not an unreasonable abstraction of "real" trading strategies. The gains process $\int \theta \, dS$, for $\theta \in \Lambda$, is furthermore defined path by path as a Stieltjes integral. That is, the gains at time t_i are

$$\int_0^{t_i} \theta(s) \, dS(s) = \sum_{j=0}^{i-1} \theta(t_j)[S(t_{j+1}) - S(t_j)],$$

simply the sum of profits and losses realized at discrete points in time.

We will give the space $\mathscr{M}_Q^2$ the norm

$$\|m\|_{\mathscr{M}_Q^2} = [E^*([m]_T)]^{1/2} \quad \forall m \in \mathscr{M}_Q^2,$$

and give $L_P^2[S]$ the semi-norm

$$\|\theta\|_{L_P^2[S]} = \left[E\left(\int_0^T \theta^2(t) \, d[S]_t \right) \right]^{1/2}.$$

PROPOSITION 6.1: *For every trading strategy $\theta \in L_P^2[S]$ there exists a sequence (θ_n) of simple trading strategies converging to θ in $L_P^2[S]$ (in the given semi-norm). For any such sequence, the corresponding gains processes $\int \theta_n \, dS$ converge to $\int \theta \, dS$ in $\mathscr{M}_Q^2$ in the given norm.*

PROOF: This is the way Ito originally extended the definition of stochastic integrals. His theorem uses the fact that Λ is dense in $L_Q^2[S]$ and shows that $\theta \mapsto \int \theta \, dS$, $\theta \in \Lambda$, extends uniquely to an isometry of $L_Q^2[S]$ in $\mathscr{M}_Q^2$. These facts can be checked, for instance, in Jacod [**11**, Chapter 4]. Since dQ/dP is assumed to be bounded above and below away from zero, the semi-norms $\|\cdot\|_{L_P[S]}$ and $\|\cdot\|_{L_Q^2[S]}$ are equivalent, and the result is proved. *Q.E.D.*

Interpreting this result: for any admissible strategy $\theta \in \Theta(S)$ there is a sequence of simple trading strategies converging (as agents are able to trade more and more frequently) to θ, with the corresponding gains processes converging to that generated by θ. The sequence of simple trading strategies can also be chosen to be self-financing (4.1) by using the same construction shown in the proof of Theorem 4.2 for the "store-of-value" strategy. A store-of-value security, one whose price is identically one for instance, is again called for. The minimal requirements for a "store-of-value" security price process have not been fully explored.

In what way have we limited agents by restricting them to $L^2_P[S]$ trading strategies? It is known, for instance, that by removing this constraint the so-called "suicide" and "doubling" strategies may become feasible, as discussed by Harrison and Pliska [**9**] and Kreps [**12**]. A suicide strategy makes nothing out of something almost surely, which no one would want to do anyway. A doubling strategy, however, generates a "free lunch," which shouldn't happen in equilibrium. More precisely, an equilibrium can't happen if doubling strategies are allowed. There are no doubling strategies in $L^2_P[S]$ since these strategies only generate martingales (under Q). There is also some comfort in knowing that, since $L^2_P[S]$ is a complete space, there is no sequence of simple or even general $L^2_P[S]$ strategies which converges to a doubling strategy in the sense of Proposition 6.1.

6.2. *Some Generalizations*

There is of course no difficulty in having heterogeneous probability assessments, provided all agents' subjective probability measures on $(\Omega, \mathscr{F})$ are uniformly absolutely continuous. This preserves the topologies on the consumption and strategy spaces across agents.

As a second generalization we could allow the consumption space to be $R \times L^q(P)$ for any $q \in [1, \infty)$, relaxing from $q = 2$. The allowable trading strategies should be generalized to $L^q_P[\underline{S}]$, as defined by Jacod [**11**, (4.59)], since there is then no guarantee of an orthogonal q-basis for $\mathscr{M}^2_Q$. It is a straightforward task to carry out all of the proofs in this paper under both of these generalizations. All interesting models of uncertainty we are aware of, however, are for $q = 2$.

It is also easy, but cumbersome, to extend our results to an economy with production and with a finite number of different consumption goods.

6.3. *Example: Economies on Event Trees*

If the information structure $\boldsymbol{F}$ is such that $\mathscr{F}_t$ contains only a finite number of events at each time t, then it can be represented in the form of an event tree, as in Figure 1.

For finite horizon problems, the terminal nodes of the tree can be treated as the elements of Ω. They are equal in number with the contingent claims forming a complete regime of Arrow-Debreu "simple securities." Yet, as the following proposition demonstrates, a complete markets Radner equilibrium can be established with far fewer securities, except in degenerate cases. Since integrability is not a consideration when Ω is finite, we characterize martingale multiplicity directly in terms of the "finite" filtration $\mathbf{F}$, limiting consideration to probability measures under which each $\omega \in \Omega$ has strictly positive probability.

PROPOSITION 6.2: *The multiplicity of a finite filtration* $\mathbf{F}$, *under any of a set of equivalent probability measures, is the maximum number of branches leaving any node of the corresponding event tree, minus one.*

The proof, given in the Appendix, presents an algorithm for constructing an orthogonal martingale basis. Just as in Section 4, a complete markets Radner equilibrium can be constructed from any given Arrow-Debreu equilibrium provided there are markets for long-lived securities paying the terminal values of such a Q-martingale basis in time T consumption, and one store-of-value security paying one unit of consumption at time T in each state $\omega \in \Omega$.

By drawing simple examples of event trees, however, it soon becomes apparent that many other choices for the spanning securities will work. This is consistent with Kreps [**13**]. His Proposition 2 effectively states that a necessary and sufficient condition for a complete markets Radner economy is that at any node of the event tree the following condition is met: The dimension of the span of the vectors of "branch-contingent" prices of the available long-lived securities must be the number of branches leaving that node. Kreps goes on to state that the number of long-lived securities required for implementing an Arrow-Debreu equilibrium in this manner must be at least K, the maximum number of branches leaving any node, consistent with our "spanning number" (the martingale multiplicity plus one), as demonstrated by the previous proposition. Kreps also obtains the genericity result: except for a "sparse" set of long-lived securities, a set of measure zero in a sense given in the Kreps article, *any* selection of K or more long-lived security price processes admits a complete markets Radner economy. (The economy needn't be in equilibrium of course.) This result seems exceedingly difficult to extend to a general continuous-time model.

One should beware of taking the "limit by compression" of finite filtrations and expecting the spanning number to be preserved. For example, we have seen statements in the finance literature to the following effect: "In the Black-Scholes option pricing model it is to be expected that continuous trading on *two* securities can replicate any claim since Brownian Motion is the limit of a normalized sequence of coin-toss random walks, each of which has only two outcomes at any toss." If this logic is correct it hides some unexplained reasoning. For example, two simultaneous independent coin-toss random walks generate a martingale space of multiplicity *three* (four branches at each node, minus one), whereas the corresponding Brownian Motion limits (Williams [**22**, Chapter 1]) generate a martingale space of multiplicity *two.* Somehow one dimension of "local uncertainty" is lost in the limiting procedure.

6.4. *A Brownian Motion Example*

This subsection illustrates an infinite dimensional consumption space whose economy (under regularity conditions) has a complete markets Radner equilibrium including only two securities!

Suppose uncertainty is characterized, and information is revealed, by a Standard Brownian Motion, W. To be precise, each $\omega \in \Omega$ corresponds to a particular sample path chosen for W from the continuous functions on $[0, T]$, denoted $C[0, T]$, according to the Wiener probability measure P on $\mathcal{F}$, the completed Borel tribe on $C[0, T]$. The probability space, then, is the completed Wiener triple $(\Omega, \mathcal{F}, P)$ and the filtration is the family $\boldsymbol{F} = \{\mathcal{F}_t, t \in [0, T]\}$, where $\mathcal{F}_t$ is the completion of the Borel tribe on $C[0, t]$. For conciseness, we'll call $(\Omega, \boldsymbol{F}, P)$ the completed filtered Wiener triple. More details on this construction are given in the first chapter of Williams [**22**].

To construct a complete markets Radner equilibrium from a given Arrow-Debreu equilibrium, as in Section 4, we need an orthogonal 2-basis for $\mathcal{M}^2_Q$, where Q is an equilibrium price measure for the Arrow-Debreu economy. In this case we can actually show that a particular Standard Brownian Motion on $(\Omega, \boldsymbol{F}, Q)$ is just such a 2-basis!

It is a well known result (e.g. [**14**]) that the underlying Brownian Motion W is a 2-basis for $\mathcal{M}^2_P$. Assuming $Q \approx P$, the process

$$Z(t) = E\left[\frac{dQ}{dP}\,\middle|\,\mathcal{F}_t\right], \quad t \in [0, T],$$

is a square-integrable martingale on $(\Omega, \boldsymbol{F}, P)$, with $E[Z(T)] = 1$. Then, by Theorem 4.1, there exists some $\rho \in L^2_P[W]$ giving the representation:

$$Z(t) = 1 + \int_0^t \rho(s)\, dW(s) \quad \forall t \in [0, T] \quad \text{a.s.}$$

It follows from Ito's Lemma that, defining the process $\eta(t) = \rho(t)/Z(t)$, we have the alternative representation:

$$Z(t) = \exp\left\{\int_0^t \eta(s)\, dW(s) - \tfrac{1}{2}\int_0^t \eta^2(s)\, ds\right\} \quad \forall t \in [0, T] \quad \text{a.s.}$$

From this, the new process

$$W^*(t) = W(t) - \int_0^t \eta(s)\, ds, \quad t \in [0, T], \tag{6.1}$$

defines a Standard Brownian Motion on $(\Omega, \boldsymbol{F}, Q)$ by Girsanov's Fundamental Theorem (Lipster and Shiryayev [**15**, p. 232]). It remains to show that W^* is itself a 2-basis for $\mathcal{M}^2_Q$, but this is immediate from Theorem 5.18 of Liptser and Shiryayev [**15**], using the uniform absolute continuity of P and Q. This construction is summarized as follows.

PROPOSITION 6.3: *Suppose W is the Standard Brownian Motion underlying the filtered Wiener triple (Ω, F, P) and $Q \approx P$. Then W^* defined by* (6.1) *is a Standard Brownian Motion under Q which is a 2-basis for $\mathcal{M}_Q^2$. In particular, $M(\mathcal{M}_P^2) = M(\mathcal{M}_Q^2) = 1$.*

By a slightly more subtle argument, we could have reached the same conclusion under the weaker assumption that P and Q are merely equivalent, but $Q \approx P$ is needed for other reasons in Theorem 4.1.

In short, by marketing just two long-lived securities, one paying $W^*(T)$ in time T consumption, the other paying one unit of time T consumption with certainty, and announcing their price processes as $W^*(t)$ and 1 (for all t), a complete markets Radner equilibrium is achieved.

This example can be extended to filtrations generated by vector diffusion processes. Under well known conditions (e.g. [**8**]) a vector diffusion generates the same filtration as the underlying vector of independent Brownian Motions. An orthogonal 2-basis for $\mathcal{M}_P^2$ is then simply these Brownian Motions themselves [**14**]. By generalizing the result quoted from Lipster and Shiryayev [**15**, Theorem 5.18], one can then demonstrate a vector of equally many Brownian Motions under Q which form a martingale basis for $\mathcal{M}_Q^2$ in the sense of Theorem 4.1. Since the manipulations are rather involved, and because the results raise some provocative issues concerning the "inter-temporal capital asset pricing models" (e.g., [**17**]) which are also based on diffusion uncertainty, we put off this development to a subsequent paper. It is also known that the filtration generated by a Poisson process corresponds to a martingale multiplicity of one [**11**].

7. CONCLUDING REMARKS

We are working on several extensions and improvements suggested by the results of this paper.

The first major step will be to demonstrate the existence of continuous trading Radner equilibria "from scratch," that is, taking endowments and preferences as agent primitives and proving the existence of an equilibrium such as that demonstrated in Theorem 4.2. In particular, the existence of an Arrow-Debreu equilibrium and the condition $Q \approx P$ must be proven from exogenous assumptions, rather than assumed. A full-blown Radner economy is also being examined, one with consumption occurring over time rather than at the two points 0 and T.

The Brownian Motion example of Section 6.4, as suggested there, is being extended to the case in which uncertainty and information are characterized by a vector of diffusion "state-variable" processes. This will allow us to tie in with, and provide a critical evaluation of, the inter-temporal capital asset pricing models popular in the financial economics literature.

We left off in Section 5 by characterizing the spanning number in terms of (endogenous) Arrow-Debreu prices through the equilibrium price measure Q. Our next efforts will be directed at showing that, subject to regularity conditions, martingale multiplicity is invariant under substitution of equivalent probability measures. In that case the spanning number can be stated to be the exogenously given number, $M(\mathcal{M}_P^2)+1$.

Stanford University
and
Massachusetts Institute of Technology

Manuscript received December 1983; final revision received January, 1985.

APPENDIX

MARTINGALE MULTIPLICITY

What follows is a heavily condensed treatment, taken mainly from the fourth chapter of Jacod [**11**].

A square-integrable martingale on the filtered probability space (Ω, F, P) is an F-adapted[7] process $X=\{X_t;\ t\in[0,T]\}$ with the properties: (i) $E[X(t)^2]<\infty$ for all $t\in[0,T]$, and (ii) $E[X(t)\mid \mathcal{F}_s]=X(s)$ a.s. for all $t\geq s$.

We will also assume without loss of generality for this paper that each martingale is an RCLL process. The first property (i) is *square-integrability*, the second (ii) is *martingale*, meaning roughly that the expected future value of X given current information is always the current value of X.

The space of square-integrable martingales on (Ω, F, P) which are null at zero (or $X(0)=0$) is denoted $\mathcal{M}_P^2$. The spaces $\mathcal{M}_P^2$ and $L^2(P)$ are in one to one correspondence via the relationship, between some $X\in\mathcal{M}_P^2$ and $x\in L^2(P)$:

$$X(t)=E[x|\mathcal{F}_t],\quad t\in[0,T],$$

where all RCLL versions of the conditional expectation process are indistinguishable and therefore identified.

An F-adapted process is termed *predictable* if it is measurable with respect to the tribe $\mathcal{P}$ on $\Omega\times[0,T]$ generated by the left-continuous F-adapted processes. At an intuitive level, θ is a predictable process if the value of $\theta(t)$ can be determined from information available up to, *but not including*, time t, for each $t\in[0,T]$.

Two martingales X and Y are said to be *orthogonal* if the product XY is a martingale. From this point we'll assume that $\mathcal{F}$ is a separable tribe under P. In that case the path breaking work of Kunita and Watanabe [**14**] shows the existence of an orthogonal 2-*basis* for $\mathcal{M}_P^2$, defined as a minimal set of mutually orthogonal elements of $\mathcal{M}_P^2$ with the representation property stated in Theorem 4.1. By "minimal," we mean that no fewer elements of $\mathcal{M}_P^2$ have this property. The number of elements of a 2-basis, whether countably infinite or some positive integer, is called the *multiplicity* of $\mathcal{M}_P^2$, denoted $M(\mathcal{M}_P^2)$.

The following lemma makes a technical argument used in the proof of Theorem 4.2.

LEMMA A.1: *Suppose the process X is defined by*

$$X(t)=\sum_{n=1}^{N}\left[\int_0^t \theta_n(s)\,dS_n(s)-\theta_n(t)S_n(t)\right],\quad t\in[0,T],$$

where $\int\theta_n\,dS_n$ is the stochastic integral of a predictable process θ_n with respect to a semi-martingale S_n, for $1\leq n\leq N<\infty$. Then X is predictable.

PROOF: For any left-limits process Z, let $Z(t-)$ denote the left limit of Z at $t\in[0,T]$, and denote the "jump" of Z at t by $\Delta Z(t)=Z(t)-Z(t-)$, where we have used the convention that $Z(0-)=Z(0)$. Then we can write

$$X(t)=\sum_{n=1}^{N}\left[\int_0^{t-}\theta_n(s)\,dS_n(s)-\theta_n(t)S_n(t)+\theta_n(t)\,\Delta S_n(t)\right]$$

[7] A stochastic process $X=\{X_t;\ t\in[0,T]\}$ is adapted to a filtration $F=\{\mathcal{F}_t;\ t\in[0,T]\}$ if X_t is measurable with respect to $\mathcal{F}_t$ for all $t\in[0,T]$.

since

$$\Delta\left(\int_0^t \theta_n(s)\, dS_n(s)\right) = \theta_n(t)\, \Delta S_n(t)$$

by the definition of a stochastic integral. Then, using

$$\theta_n(t)S_n(t) = \theta_n(t)[S_n(t-) + \Delta S_n(t)],$$

we have

$$X(t) = \sum_{n=1}^{N}\left[\int_0^{t-} \theta_n(s)\, dS_n(s) - \theta_n(t)S_n(t-)\right], \quad t \in [0, T].$$

Since $\int_0^{t-} \theta_n\, dS_n$ and $S_n(t-)$ are left-continuous processes, and therefore predictable, and $\theta_n(t)$ is predictable, we know X is predictable because sums and products of measurable functions are measurable. *Q.E.D.*

For any two elements X and Y of $\mathcal{M}_P^2$, let $\langle X, Y\rangle$ denote the unique predictable process with the property that $XY - \langle X, Y\rangle$ is a martingale and $\langle X, Y\rangle_0 = 0$.

LEMMA A.2: *Suppose* $(m_1, \ldots, m_N)$ *constitute a finite set of elements of* $\mathcal{M}_Q^2$ *with the representation property given in the statement of Theorem* 4.1, *where* $N = M(\mathcal{M}_Q^2)$. *If* θ_n *and* ϕ_n *are elements of* $L_Q^2[m_n]$, *for* $1 \leq n \leq N$, *satisfying (with the obvious shorthand)*

$$\text{(a.1)} \qquad \int_0^t \theta^\top dm = \int_0^t \phi^\top dm \quad \forall t \in [0, T] \quad \text{a.s.,}$$

then

$$Q\{\exists t \in [0, T]: \theta(t) = \phi(t)\} > 0.$$

PROOF: Jacod [11] shows the existence of a predictable positive semi-definite $N \times N$ matrix valued process c and an increasing predictable process C with the property, for any α_n and β_n in $L_Q^2[m_n]$, $1 \leq n \leq N$,

$$\text{(a.2)} \qquad \left\langle \int \alpha^\top dm, \int \beta^\top dm \right\rangle_t = \int_0^t \alpha(s)^\top c(s)\beta(s)\, dC(s) \quad \forall t \in [0, T] \quad \text{a.s.}$$

The process C also defines a Doléans measure (also denoted C) on $(\Omega \times [0, T], \mathcal{P})$ according to

$$C(B) = \int_\Omega \int_{[0,T]} 1_B(\omega, s)\, dC(\omega, s)\, dQ(\omega) \quad \forall B \in \mathcal{P}.$$

By (4.43) of Jacod [11], the matrix process c reaches full rank, and is thus positive definite, on some set $B^* \in \mathcal{P}$ of strictly positive C-measure. But, by (a.1) and (a.2),

$$\text{(a.3)} \qquad \int_0^t [\theta(\omega, s) - \phi(\omega, s)]^\top c(\omega, s)[\theta(\omega, s) - \phi(\omega, s)]\, dC(\omega, s) = 0 \quad \forall t \in [0, T] \quad \text{a.s.}$$

Ignoring without loss of generality the Q-null set on which (a.3) does not hold, this implies that $\theta(\omega, t) = \phi(\omega, t)$ for all time points of increase of C on B^*, which have strictly positive Q-probability since the projection of B^* on Ω must have strictly positive Q-measure for B^* to have strictly positive C-measure. *Q.E.D.*

PROOF OF PROPOSITION 6.2—MULTIPLICITY OF AN EVENT TREE: Let N denote the maximum number of branches leaving any node of the event tree, minus one. The proposition will be proved by constructing an orthogonal martingale basis on this filtration consisting of the N processes $m_1, \ldots, m_N$.

Any martingale on a finite filtration is characterized entirely by its right-continuous jumps at each node in the corresponding event tree. Denote the jump of m_j at a generic node with L departing branches by the vector $\delta_j = (\delta_{j1}, \ldots, \delta_{jL})$. That is, $\delta_j \in R^L$ represents the random variable which takes the real number δ_{jl} if branch l is the realized event at this node. Let $p = (p_1, \ldots, p_L) \in R^L$ denote the vector of conditional branching probabilities at this node.

The processes $m_1, \ldots, m_n$ are then mutually orthogonal martingales if they satisfy the following two conditions at each node:

(i) $p^\top \delta_j = 0$, $j = 1, \ldots, N$ (zero mean jumps, the martingale property), and

(ii) $\delta_j^\top [p] \delta_k = 0$, $\forall_j \neq k$, where $[p]$ denotes the diagonal matrix whose lth diagonal element is p_l (mutually uncorrelated jumps, implying mutually orthogonal martingales).

We construct the processes $m_1, \ldots, m_N$ by designing their jumps at each node of the event tree, in any order, taking $m_j(0) = 0 \; \forall j$. At a given node (with L branches), it is simple to choose nonzero vectors $\delta_1, \ldots, \delta_{L-1}$ in R^L satisfying

$$\text{(a.4)} \qquad \Delta_j [p] \delta_j = 0, \quad 1 \leq j \leq L-1,$$

where Δ_j is the $j \times L$ matrix whose first row is a vector of ones and whose kth row is, for $k \geq 2$, $\delta_{k-1}^\top$. This cannot be done for $j \geq L$ since $\Delta_L [p]^{1/2}$ is a full rank $L \times L$ matrix (its rows are nonzero and mutually orthogonal). Instead, let $\delta_L, \ldots, \delta_N$ each be zero vectors. One can quickly verify that this construction meets the conditions (i)-(ii) for $m_1, \ldots, m_N$ to be mutually orthogonal martingales. They are nontrivial since there is at least one node with $N+1$ branches, by definition of N. They form a basis (in the sense of Theorem 4.1) for all martingales since at each node the subspace $\{\delta \in R^L : \delta^\top p = 0\}$ has linearly independent spanning vectors $\delta_1, \ldots, \delta_{L-1}$. That is, the jump of any given martingale at this node is a linear combination of the jumps of the first $L-1$ martingales of the set $\{m_1, \ldots, m_N\}$. At least N martingales are needed for a martingale basis since at some node this subspace has dimension N, by definition of N. *Q.E.D.*

EXAMPLE: A MARKOV CHAIN: As a simple example, consider a finite state-space Markov chain information structure. Transition probabilities are given by the matrix

$$\Pi = (\pi_{\alpha\beta}) \quad 1 \leq \alpha \leq n; 1 \leq \beta \leq n;$$

where $\pi_{\alpha\beta}$ denotes the one-step transition probability from state α to state β. Let π^α denote the αth row of Π and $\delta_j^\alpha \in R^n$ denote the vector of jumps of the process m_j at any node corresponding to state α, for $1 \leq j \leq n-1$. We will assume at least one row of Π has no zero elements. Then the multiplicity of the space of martingales on this Markov chain is $n-1$, and the processes $m_1, \ldots, m_{n-1}$ form an orthogonal martingale basis provided, for $\alpha = 1, \ldots, n$,

$$\pi^{\alpha\top} \delta_j^\alpha = 0, \quad 1 \leq j \leq n-1,$$

and

$$\delta_j^{\alpha\top} [\pi^\alpha] \delta_k^\alpha = 0, \quad j \neq k,$$

corresponding to conditions (i)-(ii) above, and $\delta_j^\alpha \neq 0$ for all α and all j.

If, for instance,

$$\Pi = \begin{pmatrix} 0.3 & 0.3 & 0.4 \\ 0.3 & 0.3 & 0.4 \\ 0.3 & 0.3 & 0.4 \end{pmatrix},$$

then the two martingales m_1 and m_2 are an orthogonal martingale basis, where, at any node, m_1 jumps +2 if state 1 follows, jumps +2 if state 2 follows, and jumps −3 if state 3 follows, or $\delta_1 = (2, 2, -3)$; and similarly m_2 is characterized by jumps $\delta_2 = (1, -1, 0)$. To be even more explicit, if state 2 occurs at time 1, state 3 at time 2, and the chain terminates at time 2.5, the sample path for m_1 is

$$m_1(t) = 0, \quad 0 \leq t < 1,$$

$$m_1(t) = 2, \quad 1 \leq t < 2,$$

$$m_1(t) = -1, \quad 2 \leq t \leq 2.5.$$

REFERENCES

[1] ARROW, K.: "Le rôle des valeurs boursières pour la repartition la meillure des risques," *Econometrie*, 40(1952), 41-48; translated in *Review of Economic Studies*, 31(1964), 91-96.

[2] BLACK, F., AND M. SCHOLES: "The Pricing of Options and Corporate Liabilities," *Journal of Political Economy*, 81(1973), 637–654.

[3] COX, J., AND S. ROSS: "The Valuation of Options for Alternative Stochastic Processes," *Journal of Financial Economics*, 3(1976), 145–166.

[4] DAVIS, M. H., AND P. VARAIYA: "The Multiplicity of an Increasing Family of σ-Fields," *The Annals of Probability*, 2(1974), 958–963.

[5] DEBREU, G.: *Theory of Value*. Cowles Foundation Monograph 17. New Haven: Yale University Press, 1959.

[6] DUFFIE, J. D.: "Advances in General Equilibrium Theory," Ph.D. Dissertation, Stanford University, 1984.

[7] HALMOS, P.: *Measure Theory*. Princeton: Van Nostrand, 1950.

[8] HARRISON, J., AND D. KREPS: "Martingales and Arbitrage in Multiperiod Securities Markets," *Journal of Economic Theory*, 20(1979), 381–408.

[9] HARRISON, J., AND S. PLISKA: "Martingales and Stochastic Integrals in the Theory of Continuous Trading," *Stochastic Processes and Their Applications*, 11(1981), 215–260.

[10] HUANG, C.: "Information Structure and Equilibrium Asset Prices," *Journal of Economic Theory*, 35(1985), 33–71.

[11] JACOD, J.; *Calcul Stochastique et Problémes de Martingales, Lecture Notes in Mathematics, No. 714*. Berlin: Springer-Verlag, 1979.

[12] KREPS, D.: "Three Essays on Capital Markets," Technical Report 298, Institute for Mathematical Studies in The Social Sciences, Stanford University, 1979.

[13] ———: "Multiperiod Securities and the Efficient Allocation of Risk: A Comment on the Black-Scholes Option Pricing Model," *The Economics of Uncertainty and Information*, ed. by J. McCall. Chicago: University of Chicago Press, 1982.

[14] KUNITA, H., AND S. WATANABE: "On Square-Integrable Martingales," *Nagoya Mathematics Journal*, 30(1967), 209–245.

[15] LIPTSER, R., AND A. SHIRYAYEV: *Statistics of Random Processes I: General Theory*. New York: Springer-Verlag, 1977.

[16] MEMIN, JEAN: "Espaces de semi Martingales et Changement de Probabilité," *Zeitschrift für Wahrscheinlichkeitstheorie*, 52(1980), 9–39.

[17] MERTON, R.: "An Intertemporal Capital Asset Pricing Model," *Econometrica*, 41(1973), 867–888.

[18] ———: "The Theory of Rational Option Pricing," *Bell Journal of Economics and Management Science*, 4(1973), 141–183.

[19] ———: "On the Microeconomic Theory of Investment Under Uncertainty," in *Handbook of Mathematical Economics, Vol. II*, ed. by K. Arrow and M. Intriligator. Amsterdam: North-Holland Publishing Company, 1982.

[20] RADNER, R.: "Existence of Equilibrium of Plans, Prices and Price Expectations in a Sequence of Markets," *Econometrica*, 40(1972), 289–303.

[21] SCHAEFER, H. H.: *Banach Lattices and Positive Operators*. New York: Springer-Verlag, 1974.

[22] WILLIAMS, D.: *Diffusions, Markov Processes, and Martingales, Vol. 1*. New York: Wiley, 1979.

Part II
Intertemporal Portfolio Selection

[5]

LIFETIME PORTFOLIO SELECTION UNDER UNCERTAINTY: THE CONTINUOUS-TIME CASE

Robert C. Merton *

I Introduction

MOST models of portfolio selection have been one-period models. I examine the combined problem of optimal portfolio selection and consumption rules for an individual in a continuous-time model where his income is generated by returns on assets and these returns or instantaneous "growth rates" are stochastic. P. A. Samuelson has developed a similar model in discrete-time for more general probability distributions in a companion paper [8].

I derive the optimality equations for a multi-asset problem when the rate of returns are generated by a Wiener Brownian-motion process. A particular case examined in detail is the two-asset model with constant relative risk-aversion or iso-elastic marginal utility. An explicit solution is also found for the case of constant absolute risk-aversion. The general technique employed can be used to examine a wide class of intertemporal economic problems under uncertainty.

In addition to the Samuelson paper [8], there is the multi-period analysis of Tobin [9]. Phelps [6] has a model used to determine the optimal consumption rule for a multi-period example where income is partly generated by an asset with an uncertain return. Mirrless [5] has developed a continuous-time optimal consumption model of the neoclassical type with technical progress a random variable.

II Dynamics of the Model: The Budget Equation

In the usual continuous-time model under certainty, the budget equation is a differential equation. However, when uncertainty is introduced by a random variable, the budget equation must be generalized to become a stochastic differential equation. To see the meaning of such an equation, it is easiest to work out the discrete-time version and then pass to the limit of continuous time.

Define

$W(t)$ = total wealth at time t

$X_i(t)$ = price of the ith asset at time t, $(i = 1, \ldots, m)$

$C(t)$ = consumption per unit time at time t

$w_i(t)$ = proportion of total wealth in the ith asset at time t, $(i = 1, \ldots, m)$

Note

$$\left(\sum_{i=1}^{m} w_i(t) \underset{t}{\equiv} 1 \right)$$

The budget equation can be written as

$$W(t) = \left[\sum_{i=1}^{m} w_i(t_0) \frac{X_i(t)}{X_i(t_0)} \right] \cdot \left[W(t_0) - C(t_0)h \right] \tag{1}$$

where $t \equiv t_0 + h$ and the time interval between periods is h. By subtracting $W(t_0)$ from both sides and using $\sum_{i=1}^{m} w_i(t_0) = 1$, we can rewrite (1) as,

$$\begin{aligned} W(t) - W(t_0) &= \left[\sum_{i=1}^{m} w_i(t_0) \left(\frac{X_i(t) - X_i(t_0)}{X_i(t_0)} \right) \right] \cdot \left[W(t_0) - C(t_0)h \right] - C(t_0)h \\ &= \left[\sum_{i=1}^{m} w_i(t_0) \left(e^{g_i(t_0)h} - 1 \right) \right] \cdot \left[W(t_0) - C(t_0)h \right] - C(t_0)h \end{aligned} \tag{2}$$

where

$$g_i(t_0)h \equiv \log \left[X_i(t)/X_i(t_0) \right],$$

the rate of return per unit time on the ith asset. The $g_i(t)$ are assumed to be generated by a stochastic process.

In discrete time, I make the further assumption that $g_i(t)$ is determined as follows,

$$g_i(t)h = (\alpha_i - \sigma_i^2/2)h + \triangle Y_i \tag{3}$$

where α_i, the "expected" rate of return, is con-

* This work was done during the tenure of a National Defense Education Act Fellowship. Aid from the National Science Foundation is gratefully acknowledged. I am indebted to Paul A. Samuelson for many discussions and his helpful suggestions. I wish to thank Stanley Fischer, Massachusetts Institute of Technology, for his comments on section 7 and John S. Flemming for his criticism of an earlier version.

stant; and $Y_i(t)$ is generated by a Gaussian random-walk as expressed by the stochastic difference equation,

$$Y_i(t) - Y_i(t_0) \equiv \Delta Y_i = \sigma_i Z_i(t)\sqrt{h} \qquad (4)$$

where each $Z_i(t)$ is an independent variate with a standard normal distribution for every t, σ_i^2 is the variance per unit time of the process Y_i, and the mean of the increment ΔY_i is zero.

Substituting for $g_i(t)$ from (3), we can re-write (2) as,

$$W(t) - W(t_0) = \sum_1^m w_i(t_0)\left(e^{(a_i-\sigma_i^2/2(h+\Delta Y)} - 1\right)(W(t_0) - C(t_0)h) - C(t_0)h. \qquad (5)$$

Before passing in the limit to continuous time, there are two implications of (5) which will be useful later in the paper.

$$E(t_0)\;[W(t) - W(t_0)] = \left\{\sum_1^m w_i(t_0)a_iW(t_0) - C(t_0)\right\} h + 0(h^2) \qquad (6)$$

and

$$E(t_0)[(W(t)-W(t_0))^2] = \sum_{i=1}^m\sum_{j=1}^m w_i(t_0)w_j(t_0)\cdot E(t_0)\,(\Delta Y_i\Delta Y_j)\cdot W^2(t_0) + 0(h^2) \qquad (7)$$

where $E(t_0)$ is the conditional expectation operator (conditional on the knowledge of $W(t_0)$), and $0(\cdot)$ is the usual asymptotic order symbol meaning "the same order as."

The limit of the process described in (4) as $h \to 0$ (continuous time) can be expressed by the formalism of the stochastic differential equation,[1]

$$dY_i = \sigma_i Z_i(t)\sqrt{dt} \qquad (4')$$

and $Y_i(t)$ is said to be generated by a Wiener process.

By applying the same limit process to the discrete-time budget equation, we write (5) as

$$dW = \left[\sum_1^m w_i(t)a_iW(t) - C(t)\right]dt + \sum_1^m w_i(t)\sigma_iZ_i(t)W(t)\sqrt{dt}. \qquad (5')$$

The stochastic differential equation (5′) is the generalization of the continuous-time budget equation under uncertainty.

[1] See K. Itô [4], for a rigorous discussion of stochastic differential equations.

A more familiar equation would be the *averaged* budget equation derived as follows: From (5), we have

$$E(t_0)\left[\frac{W(t) - W(t_0)}{h}\right] = \sum_1^m w_i(t_0)a_i[W(t_0) - C(t_0)h] - C(t_0) + 0(h). \qquad (8)$$

Now, take the limit as $h \to 0$, so that (8) becomes the following expression for the defined "mean rate of change of wealth":

$$\overset{\circ}{W}(t_0) \underset{\text{def.}}{\equiv} \lim_{h\to 0} E(t_0)\left[\frac{W(t) - W(t_0)}{h}\right] = \sum_1^m w_i(t_0)a_iW(t_0) - C(t_0). \qquad (8')$$

III The Two-Asset Model

For simplicity, I first derive the optimal equations and properties for the two-asset model and then, in section 8, display the general equations and results for the m-asset case.

Define

$w_1(t) \equiv w(t)$ = proportion invested in the risky asset

$w_2(t) = 1 - w(t)$ = proportion invested in the sure asset

$g_1(t) = g(t)$ = return on the risky asset (Var $g_1 > 0$)

$g_2(t) = r$ = return on the sure asset (Var $g_2 = 0$)

Then, for $g(t)h = (a - \sigma^2/2)\;h + \Delta Y$, equations (5), (6), (7), and (8′) can be written as,

$$W(t) - W(t_0) = [w(t_0)(e^{(a-\sigma^2/2(h+\Delta Y)} - 1) + (1 - w(t_0))(e^{rh} - 1)]\cdot(W(t_0) - C(t_0)h - C(t_0)h. \qquad (9)$$

$$E(t_0)\;[W(t) - W(t_0)] = \left\{[w(t_0)(a-r) + r]W(t_0) - C(t_0)\right\} h + 0(h^2). \qquad (10)$$

$$E(t_0)\;[(W(t) - W(t_0))^2] = w^2(t_0)\,W^2(t_0)\,E(t_0)[(\Delta Y)^2] + 0(h^2) = w^2(t_0)W^2(t_0)\sigma^2h + 0(h^2). \qquad (11)$$

$$dW = [(w(t)(a-r) + r)W(t) - C(t)]dt + w(t)\sigma Z(t)W(t)\sqrt{dt}. \qquad (12)$$

$$\overset{\circ}{W}(t) = [w(t)(a-r) + r]W(t) - C(t). \qquad (13)$$

The problem of choosing optimal portfolio selection and consumption rules is formulated as follows,

$$\operatorname{Max} E\left\{\int_0^t e^{-\rho t} U[C(t)]\, dt + B[W(T),T]\right\} \tag{14}$$

subject to: the budget constraint (12),

$C(t) \geqq 0;\ W(t) > 0;\ W(0) = W_0 > 0$

and where $U(C)$ is assumed to be a strictly concave utility function (i.e., $U'(C) > 0$; $U''(C) < 0$); where $g(t)$ is a random variable generated by the previously described Wiener process. $B[W(T),T]$ is to be a specified "bequest valuation function" (also referred to in production growth models as the "scrap function," and usually assumed to be concave in $W(T)$). "E" in (14) is short for $E(0)$, the conditional expectation operator, given $W(0) = W_0$ as known.

To derive the optimality equations, I restate (14) in a dynamic programming form so that the Bellman principle of optimality[2] can be applied. To do this, define,

$$I[W(t),t] \equiv \underset{\{C(s),w(s)\}}{\operatorname{Max}} E(t) \left[\int_t^T e^{-\rho s} U[C(s)]ds + B[W(T),T]\right] \tag{15}$$

where (15) is subject to the same constraints as (14). Therefore,

$$I[W(T),T] = B[W(T),T]. \tag{15'}$$

In general, from definition (15),

$$I[W(t_0),t_0] = \underset{\{C(s),w(s)\}}{\operatorname{Max}} E(t_0) \left[\int_{t_0}^t e^{-\rho s} U[C(s)]ds + I[W(t),t]\right] \tag{16}$$

and, in particular, (14) can be rewritten as

$$I(W_0,0) = \underset{\{C(s),w(s)\}}{\operatorname{Max}} E\left[\int_0^t e^{-\rho s} U[C(s)]ds + I[W(t),t]\right]. \tag{14'}$$

If $t \equiv t_0 + h$ and the third partial derivatives of $I[W(t_0),t_0]$ are bounded, then by Taylor's theorem and the mean value theorem for integrals, (16) can be rewritten as

$$I[W(t_0,t_0] = \underset{\{C,w\}}{\operatorname{Max}} E(t_0) \left\{ e^{-\rho \bar{t}} U[C(t)] + I[W(t_0),t_0] + \frac{\partial I[W(t_0),t_0]}{\partial t} + \frac{\partial I[W(t_0),t_0]}{\partial W}[W(t) - W(t_0)] + \frac{1}{2}\frac{\partial^2 I[W(t_0),t_0]}{\partial W^2} \cdot [W(t) - W(t_0)]^2 + 0(h^2) \right\}$$

where $\bar{t} \in [t_0,t]$. (17)

In (17), take the $E(t_0)$ operator onto each term and, noting that $I[W(t_0),t_0] = E(t_0) I[W(t_0),t_0]$, subtract $I[W(t_0)t_0]$ from both sides. Substitute from equations (10) and (11) for $E(t_0)[W(t) - W(t_0)]$ and $E(t_0)[(W(t) - W(t_0))^2]$, and then divide the equation by h. Take the limit of the resultant equation as $h \to 0$ and (17) becomes a continuous-time version of the Bellman-Dreyfus fundamental equation of optimality, (17′).

$$0 = \underset{\{C(t),w(t)\}}{\operatorname{Max}} \left[e^{-\rho t} U[C(t)] + \frac{\partial I_t}{\partial t} + \frac{\partial I_t}{\partial W}[(w(t)(a-r) + r)W(t) - C(t)] + 1/2 \frac{\partial^2 I_t}{\partial W^2} \sigma^2 w^2(t) W^2(t)] \right] \tag{17'}$$

where I_t is short for $I[W(t),t]$ and the subscript on t_0 has been dropped to reflect that (17′) holds for any $t \in [0,T]$.

If we define $\phi(w,C;W;t) \equiv \left\{ e^{-\rho t} U(C) + \frac{\partial I_t}{\partial t} + \frac{\partial I_t}{\partial W}[(w(t)(a-r) + r)W(t) - C(t)] + 1/2 \frac{\partial^2 I_t}{\partial W^2} \sigma^2 w^2(t) W^2(t) \right\}$,[3] then (17′) can be written in the more compact form,

$$\underset{\{C,w\}}{\operatorname{Max}}\ \phi(w,C;W,t) = 0. \tag{17''}$$

The first-order conditions for a regular interior maximum to (17″) are,

$$\phi_C[w^*,C^*;W,:t] = 0 = e^{-\rho t} U'(C) - \partial I_t/\partial W \tag{18}$$

and

$$\phi_w[w^*;C^*;W;t] = 0 = (a-r)\frac{\partial I_t}{\partial W} + \frac{\partial^2 I_t}{\partial W^2} wW\sigma^2. \tag{19}$$

A set of sufficient conditions for a regular interior maximum is

$$\phi_{ww} < 0;\ \phi_{CC} < 0;\ \det\begin{bmatrix}\phi_{ww} & \phi_{wC}\\ \phi_{Cw} & \phi_{CC}\end{bmatrix} > 0.$$

$\phi_{wC} = \phi_{Cw} = 0$, and if $I[W(t),t]$ were strictly concave in W, then

$$\phi_{CC} = U''(c) < 0, \text{ by the strict concavity of } U \tag{20}$$

and

[2] The basic derivation of the optimality equations in this section follows that of S. E. Dreyfus [2], Chapter VII.

[3] $\phi(w,C:W:t)$ is short for the rigorous $\phi[w,C;\ \partial I_t/\partial t;\ \partial I_t/\partial W;\ \partial^2 I_t/\partial W^2;\ I_t : W;t]$.

$$\phi_{ww} = W(t)\sigma^2 \frac{\partial^2 I_t}{\partial W^2} < 0^4, \text{ by the strict concavity of } I_t, \tag{21}$$

and the sufficient conditions would be satisfied. Thus a candidate for an optimal solution which causes $I[W(t),t]$ to be strictly concave will be any solution of the conditions (17′)–(21).

The optimality conditions can be re-written as a set of two algebraic and one partial differential equation to be solved for $w^*(t)$, $C^*(t)$, and $I[W(t),t]$.

$$(*)\left\{\begin{array}{lr} \phi[w^*,C^*;W;t] = 0 & (17'') \\ \phi_C[w^*;C^*;W;t] = 0 & (18) \\ \phi_w[w^*,C^*;W;t] = 0 & (19) \\ \text{subject to the boundary condition} & \\ I[W(T),T] = B[W(T),T] \text{ and} & \\ \text{the solution being a feasible solu-} & \\ \text{tion to (14).} & \end{array}\right.$$

IV Constant Relative Risk Aversion

The system (*) of a nonlinear partial differential equation coupled with two algebraic equations is difficult to solve in general. However, if the utility function is assumed to be of the form yielding constant relative risk-aversion (i.e., iso-elastic marginal utility), then (*) can be solved explicitly. Therefore, let $U(C) = C^\gamma/\gamma$, $\gamma < 1$ and $\gamma \neq 0$ or $U(C) = \log C$ (the limiting form for $\gamma = 0$) where $-U''(C)C/U'(C) = 1 - \gamma \equiv \delta$ is Pratt's [7] measure of relative risk aversion. Then, system (*) can be written in this particular case as

$$(*')\left\{\begin{array}{lr} 0 = \left[\frac{(1-\gamma)}{\gamma}\frac{\partial I_t}{\partial W}\right]^{\gamma/\gamma-1} e^{-\rho t/1-\gamma} + \frac{\partial I_t}{\partial t} + \frac{\partial I_t}{\partial W} rW - \frac{(\alpha-r)^2}{2\sigma^2}\frac{[\partial I_t/\partial W]^2}{\partial^2 I_t/\partial W^2} & (17'') \\ C^*(t) = \left[e^{\rho t}\frac{\partial I_t}{\partial W}\right]^{1/\gamma-1} & (18) \\ w^*(t) = \frac{-(\alpha-r)\,\partial I_t/\partial W}{\sigma^2 W\,\partial^2 I_t/\partial W^2} & (19) \\ \text{subject to } I[W(T),T] = \epsilon^{1-\gamma} e^{-\rho T} [W(T)]^\gamma/\gamma, \text{ for } 0 < \epsilon << 1 & \end{array}\right.$$

where a strategically-simplifying assumption has been made as to the particular form of the bequest valuation function, $B[W(T),T]$.[5]

To solve (17″) of (*′), take as a trial solution,

$$\bar{I}_t[W(t),t] = \frac{b(t)}{\gamma} e^{-\rho t} [W(t)]^\gamma. \tag{22}$$

By substitution of the trial solution into (17″), a necessary condition that $\bar{I}_t[W(t),t]$ be a solution to (17″) is found to be that $b(t)$ must satisfy the following ordinary differential equation,

$$\dot{b}(t) = \mu b(t) - (1-\gamma)\,[b(t)]^{-\gamma/1-\gamma} \tag{23}$$

subject to $b(T) = \epsilon^{1-\gamma}$, and where $\mu \equiv \rho - \gamma[(\alpha - r)^2/2\sigma^2(1 - \gamma) + r]$. The resulting decision rules for consumption and portfolio selection, $C^*(t)$ and $w^*(t)$, are from equations (18) and (19) of (*′), then

$$C^*(t) = [b(t)]^{1/\gamma-1} W(t) \tag{24}$$

and

$$w^*(t) = \frac{(\alpha-r)}{\sigma^2(1-\gamma)}. \tag{25}$$

The solution to (23) is

$$b(t) = \{[1 + (\nu\epsilon - 1)\,e^{\nu(t-T)}]/\nu\}^{1-\gamma} \tag{26}$$

where $\nu \equiv \mu/(1 - \gamma)$.

A sufficient condition for $I[W(t),t]$ to be a solution to (*′) is that $I[W(t),t]$ satisfy

A. $\bar{I}[W(t),t]$ be real (feasibility)

B. $\frac{\partial^2 \bar{I}_t}{\partial W^2} < 0$ (concavity for a maximum)

C. $C^*(t) \geqq 0$ (feasibility)

The condition that A, B, and C are satisfied in the iso-elastic case is that

$$[1 + (\nu\epsilon - 1)\,e^{\nu(t-T)}]/\nu > 0,\ 0 \leqq t \leqq T \tag{27}$$

which is satisfied for all values of ν when $T < \infty$.

Because (27) holds, the optimal consumption and portfolio selection rules are,[6]

[4] By the substitution of the results of (18) into (19) at (C^*,w^*), we have the condition $w^*(t)(\alpha - r) > 0$ if and only if $\frac{\partial^2 I_t}{\partial W^2} < 0$.

The paper considers only interior optimal solutions. The problem could have been formulated in the more general Kuhn-Tucker form in which case the equalities of (18) and (19) would be replaced with inequalities.

[5] The form of the bequest valuation function (the boundary condition), as is usual for partial differential equations, can cause major changes in the solution to (*). The particular form of the function chosen in (*′) is used as a proxy for the "no-bequest" condition ($\epsilon = 0$). A slightly more general form which can be used without altering the resulting solution substantively is $B[W(T),T] = e^{-\rho t}G(T)[W(T)]^\gamma/\gamma$ for arbitrary $G(T)$. If B is not of the iso-elastic family, systematic effects of age will appear in the optimal decision-making.

[6] Although not derived explicitly here, the special case ($\gamma = 0$) of Bernoulli logarithmic utility has (29) with $\gamma = 0$ as a solution, and the limiting form of (28), namely

$$C^*(t) = \left[\frac{\rho}{1 + (\rho\epsilon - 1)e^{\rho(t-T)}}\right] W(t).$$

$$C^*(t) = [\nu/(1+(\nu\epsilon-1)\,e^{\nu(t-T)})]\,W(t), \quad \text{for } \nu \neq 0$$
$$= [1/(T-t+\epsilon)]\,W(t), \quad \text{for } \nu = 0 \tag{28}$$

and

$$w^*(t) = \frac{(a-r)}{\sigma^2(1-\gamma)} \equiv w^*, \text{ a constant independent of } W \text{ or } t. \tag{29}$$

V Dynamic Behavior and the Bequest Valuation Function

The purpose behind the choice of the particular bequest valuation function in (*′) was primarily mathematical. The economic motive is that the "true" function for no bequests is $B[W(T),T] = 0$ (i.e., $\epsilon = 0$). From (28), $C^*(t)$ will have a pole at $t = T$ when $\epsilon = 0$. So, to examine the dynamic behavior of $C^*(t)$ and to determine whether the pole is a mathematical "error" or an implicit part of the economic requirements of the problem, the parameter ϵ was introduced.
From figure 1, $(C^*/W)_{t=T} \to \infty$ as $\epsilon \to 0$. However, one must not interpret this as an infinite

FIGURE 1. —

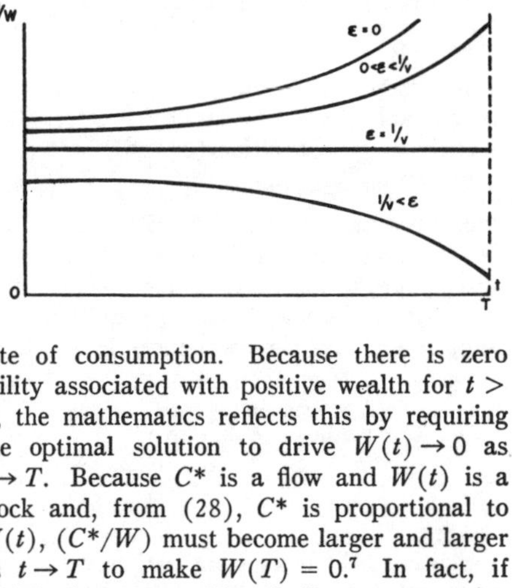

rate of consumption. Because there is zero utility associated with positive wealth for $t > T$, the mathematics reflects this by requiring the optimal solution to drive $W(t) \to 0$ as $t \to T$. Because C^* is a flow and $W(t)$ is a stock and, from (28), C^* is proportional to $W(t)$, (C^*/W) must become larger and larger as $t \to T$ to make $W(T) = 0$.[7] In fact, if $W(T)-) > 0$, an "impulse" of consumption would be required to make $W(T) = 0$. Thus, equation (28) is valid for $\epsilon = 0$.

[7] The problem described is essentially one of exponential decay. If $W(t) = W_0 e^{-f(t)}$, $f(t) > 0$, finite for all t, and $W_0 > 0$, then it will take an infinite length of time for $W(t) = 0$. However, if $f(t) \to \infty$ as $t \to T$, then $W(t) \to 0$ as $t \to T$.

To examine some of the dynamic properties of $C^*(t)$, let $\epsilon = 0$, and define $V(t) \equiv [C^*(t)/W(t)]$, the instantaneous marginal (in this case, also average) propensity to consume out of wealth. Then, from (28),

$$\dot{V}(t) = [V(t)]^2\, e^{\nu(t-T)} \tag{30}$$

and, as observed in figure 1 (for $\epsilon = 0$), $V(t)$ is an increasing function of time. In a generalization of the half-life calculation of radioactive decay, define τ as that $t \in [0,T]$ such that $V(\tau) = nV(0)$ (i.e., τ is the length of time required for $V(t)$ to grow to n times its initial size). Then, from (28),

$$\tau = \log\left[e^{\nu T}\left(1-\frac{1}{n}\right)+\frac{1}{n}\right]\Big/\nu; \quad \text{for } \nu \neq 0$$
$$= \frac{(n-1)}{(n)}\,T \quad , \text{ for } \nu = 0. \tag{31}$$

To examine the dynamic behavior of $W(t)$ under the optimal decision rules, it only makes sense to discuss the expected or "averaged" behavior because $W(t)$ is a function of a random variable. To do this, we consider equation (13), the averaged budget equation, and evaluate it at the optimal (w^*,C^*) to form

$$\frac{\overset{\circ}{W}(t)}{W(t)} = a_* - V(t) \tag{13′}$$

where $a_* = \left[\dfrac{(a-r)^2}{\sigma^2(1-\gamma)} + r\right]$, and, in section VII, a_* will be shown to be the expected return on the optimal portfolio.

By differentiating (13′) and using (30), we get

$$\frac{d}{dt}\left[\frac{\overset{\circ}{W}}{W}\right] = -\dot{V}(t) < 0 \tag{32}$$

which implies that for all finite-horizon optimal paths, the expected rate of growth of wealth is a diminishing function of time. Therefore, if $a_* < V(0)$, the individual will dis-invest (i.e., he will *plan* to consume more than his expected income, $a_*W(t)$). If $a_* > V(0)$, he will plan to increase his wealth for $0 < t < \bar{t}$, and then, dis-invest at an expected rate $a_* < V(t)$ for $\bar{t} < t < T$ where $\bar{t}$ is defined as the solution to

$$\bar{t} = T + \frac{1}{\nu}\log\left[\frac{a_*-\nu}{a_*}\right]. \tag{33}$$

Further, $\partial\bar{t}/\partial a_* > 0$ which implies that the length of time for which the individual is a net saver increases with increasing expected returns on the portfolio. Thus, in the case $\alpha_* > V(0)$, we find the familiar result of "hump saving."[8]

VI Infinite Time Horizon

Although the infinite time horizon case ($T = \infty$) yields essentially the same substantive results as in the finite time horizon case, it is worth examining separately because the optimality equations are easier to solve than for finite time. Therefore, for solving more complicated problems of this type, the infinite time horizon problem should be examined first.

The equation of optimality is, from section III,

$$0 = \underset{\{C,w\}}{\text{Max}} \left[e^{-\rho t} U(C) + \frac{\partial I_t}{\partial t} + \frac{\partial I_t}{\partial W} [(w(t)(\alpha - r) + r)W(t) - C(t)] + 1/2 \frac{\partial^2 I_t}{\partial W^2} \sigma^2 w^2(t) W^2(t) \right]. \tag{17'}$$

However (17') can be greatly simplified by eliminating its explicit time-dependence. Define

$$\begin{aligned} J[W(t),t] &\equiv e^{\rho t} I[W(t),t] \\ &= \underset{\{C,w\}}{\text{Max}}\ E(t) \textstyle\int_t^\infty e^{-\rho(s-t)} U[C] ds \\ &= \underset{\{C,w\}}{\text{Max}}\ E \textstyle\int_0^\infty e^{-\rho v} U[C] dv, \end{aligned}$$

independent of explicit time. (34)

Thus, write $J[W(t),t] = J[W]$ to reflect this independence. Substituting $J[W]$, dividing by $e^{-\rho t}$, and dropping all t subscripts, we can rewrite (17') as,

$$0 = \underset{\{C,w\}}{\text{Max}} [U(C) - \rho J + J'(W) \cdot \{(w(t)(\alpha - r) + r)W - C\} + 1/2\, J''(W) \sigma^2 w^2 W^2]. \tag{35}$$

Note: when (35) is evaluated at the optimum (C^*, w^*), it becomes an *ordinary* differential equation instead of the usual partial differential equation of (17'). For the iso-elastic case, (35) can be written as

$$0 = \frac{(1-\gamma)}{\gamma} [J'(W)]^{-\gamma/1-\gamma} - \rho J(W) - \frac{(\alpha - r)^2}{2\sigma^2} \frac{[J'(W)]^2}{J''(W)} + rWJ'(W) \tag{36}$$

where the functional equations for C^* and w^* have been substituted in equation (36).

The first-order conditions corresponding to (18) and (19) are

$$0 = U'(C) - J'(W) \tag{37}$$

and

$$0 = (\alpha - r)J'(W) + J'' w W \sigma^2 \tag{38}$$

and assuming that $\lim_{T\to\infty} B[W(T),T] = 0$, the boundary condition becomes the transversality condition,

$$\lim_{t\to\infty} E[I[W(t),t]] = 0 \tag{39}$$

or

$$\lim_{t\to\infty} E[e^{-\rho t} J[W(t)]] = 0$$

which is a condition for convergence of the integral in (14). A solution to (14) must satisfy (39) plus conditions A, B, and C of section IV. Conditions A, B, and C will be satisfied in the iso-elastic case if

$$V^* \equiv \nu = \frac{\rho}{1-\gamma} - \gamma \left[\frac{(\alpha - r)^2}{2\sigma^2 (1-\gamma)^2} + \frac{r}{1-\gamma} \right] > 0 \tag{40}$$

holds where (40) is the limit of condition (27) in section IV, as $T \to \infty$ and $V^* = C^*(t)/W(t)$ when $T = \infty$. Condition (39) will hold if $\rho > \gamma \overset{\circ}{W}/W$ where, as defined in (13), $\overset{\circ}{W}(t)$ is the stochastic time derivative of $W(t)$ and $\overset{\circ}{W}(t)/W(t)$ is the "expected" net growth of wealth after allowing for consumption. That (39) is satisfied can be rewritten as a condition on the subjective rate of time preference, ρ, as follows:

for $\gamma < 0$ (bounded utility), $\rho > 0$

$\gamma = 0$ (Bernoulli log case), $\rho > 0$

$0 < \gamma < 1$ (unbounded utility), $\rho > \gamma \left[\frac{(\alpha - r)^2 (2-\gamma)}{2\sigma^2 (1-\gamma)} + r \right].$ (41)

Condition (41) is a generalization of the usual assumption required in deterministic optimal consumption growth models when the production function is linear: namely, that $\rho > \text{Max}[0, \gamma\beta]$ where β = yield on capital.[9] If a "di-

[8] "Hump saving" has been widely discussed in the literature. (See J. De V. Graaff [3] for such a discussion.) Usually "hump saving" is discussed in the context of work and retirement periods. Clearly, such a phenomenon can occur without these assumptions as the example in this paper shows.

[9] If one takes the limit as $\sigma_*^2 \to 0$ (where σ_*^2 is the variance of the composite portfolio) of condition (41), then

minishing-returns," strictly-concave "production" function for wealth were introduced, then a positive ρ would suffice.

If condition (41) is satisfied, then condition (40) is satisfied. Therefore, if it is assumed that ρ satisfies (41), then the rest of the derivation is the same as for the finite horizon case and the optimal decision rules are,

$$C_\infty^*(t) = \left\{ \frac{\rho}{1-\gamma} - \gamma\left[\frac{(a-r)^2}{2\sigma^2(1-\gamma)^2} + \frac{r}{1-\gamma}\right]\right\} W(t) \qquad (42)$$

and

$$w_\infty^*(t) = \frac{(a-r)}{\sigma^2(1-\gamma)}. \qquad (43)$$

The ordinary differential equation (35), $J'' = f(J,J')$, has "extraneous" solutions other than the one that generates (42) and (43). However, these solutions are ruled out by the transversality condition, (39), and conditions A, B, and C of section IV. As was expected, $\lim_{T\to\infty} C^*(t) = C_\infty^*(t)$ and $\lim_{T\to\infty} w^*(t) = w_\infty^*(t)$.

The main purpose of this section was to show that the partial differential equation (17′) can be reduced in the case of infinite time horizon to an ordinary differential equation.

VII Economic Interpretation of the Optimal Decision Rules for Portfolio Selection and Consumption

An important result is the confirmation of the theorem proved by Samuelson [8], for the discrete-time case, stating that, for iso-elastic marginal utility, the portfolio-selection decision is independent of the consumption decision. Further, for the special case of Bernoulli logarithmic utility ($\gamma = 0$), the separation goes both ways, i.e., the consumption decision is independent of the financial parameters and is only dependent upon the level of wealth. This is a result of two assumptions: (1) constant relative risk-aversion (iso-elastic marginal utility) which implies that one's attitude toward financial risk is independent of one's wealth level, and (2) the stochastic process which generates the price changes (independent increments assumption of the Wiener process). With these two assumptions, the only feedbacks of the system, the price change and the resulting level of wealth, have zero relevance for the portfolio decision and hence, it is constant.

The optimal proportion in the risky asset,[10] w^*, can be rewritten in terms of Pratt's relative risk-aversion measure, δ, as

$$w^* = \frac{(a-r)}{\sigma^2\delta}. \qquad (29')$$

The qualitative results that $\partial w^*/\partial a > 0$, $\partial w^*/\partial r < 0$, $\partial w^*/\partial \sigma^2 < 0$, and $\partial w^*/\partial \delta < 0$ are intuitively clear and need no discussion. However, because the optimal portfolio selection rule is constant, one can define the optimum composite portfolio and it will have a constant mean and variance. Namely,

$$a_* = E[w^*(a+\Delta Y) + (1-w^*)r] = w^*a + (1-w^*)r = \frac{(a-r)^2}{\sigma^2\delta} + r \qquad (44)$$

$$\sigma_*^2 = \text{Var}\,[w^*(a+\Delta Y) + (1-w^*)r] = w^{*2}\sigma^2 = \frac{(a-r)^2}{\sigma^2\delta^2}. \qquad (45)$$

After having determined the optimal w^*, one can now think of the original problem as having been reduced to a simple Phelps-Ramsey problem, in which we seek an optimal consumption rule given that income is generated by the uncertain yield of an (composite) asset.

Thus, the problem becomes a continuous-time analog of the one examined by Phelps [6] in discrete time. Therefore, for consistency, $C_\infty^*(t)$ should be expressible in terms of a_*, σ_*^2, δ, ρ, and $W(t)$ only. To show that this is, in fact, the result, (42) can be rewritten as,[11]

(41) becomes the condition that $\rho > \max[0, \gamma a^*]$ where a^* is the yield on the composite portfolio. Thus, the deterministic case is the limiting form of (41).

[10] Note: no restriction on borrowing or going short was imposed on the problem, and therefore, w^* can be greater than one or less than zero. Thus, if $a < r$, the risk-averter will short some of the risky asset, and if $a > r + \sigma^2\delta$, he will borrow funds to invest in the risky asset. If one wished to restrict $w^* \epsilon [0,1]$, then such a constraint could be introduced and handled by the usual Kuhn-Tucker methods with resulting inequalities.

[11] Because this section is concerned with the qualitative changes in the solution with respect to shifts in the parameters, the more-simple form of the infinite-time horizon case is examined. The essential difference between $C_\infty^*(t)$ and $C^*(t)$ is the explicit time dependence of $C^*(t)$ which was discussed in section V. For simplicity, the "∞" on subscript $C_\infty^*(t)$ will be deleted for the rest of this section.

$$C^*(t) = \left[\frac{\rho}{\delta} + (\delta-1)\left(\frac{a_*}{\delta} - \frac{\sigma_*^2}{2}\right)\right]W(t)$$
$$= V\,W(t) \qquad (46)$$

where V = the marginal propensity to consume out of wealth.

The tools of comparative statics are used to examine the effect of shifts in the mean and variance on consumption behavior in this model. The comparison is between two economies with different investment opportunities, but with the individuals in both economies having the same utility function.

If θ is a financial parameter, then define $\left[\frac{\partial C^*}{\partial \theta}\right]_{\bar{I}_0}$, the partial derivative of consumption with respect to θ, $I_0[W_0]$ being held fixed, as the intertemporal generalization of the Hicks-Slutsky "substitution" effect, $\left[\frac{\partial C^*}{\partial \theta}\right]_{\bar{U}}$ for static models. $[\partial C^*/\partial\theta - (\partial C^*/\partial\theta)_{I_0}]$ will be defined as the intertemporal "income" or "wealth" effect. Then, from equation (22) with I_0 held fixed, one derives by total differentiation,

$$0 = -\frac{1}{\delta-1}\,\frac{\partial b(0)}{\partial\theta}\,W_0 + b(0)\left(\frac{\partial W_0}{\partial\theta}\right)_{\bar{I}_0}. \qquad (47)$$

From equations (24) and (46), $b(0) = V^{-\delta}$, and so solving for $(\partial W_0/\partial\theta)_{I_0}$ in (47), we can write it as

$$\left(\frac{\partial W_0}{\partial\theta}\right)_{\bar{I}_0} = \frac{-\delta W_0}{(\delta-1)V}\,\frac{\partial V}{\partial\theta}. \qquad (48)$$

Consider the case where $\theta = a_*$, then from (46),

$$\frac{\partial V}{\partial a_*} = \frac{(\delta-1)}{\delta} \qquad (49)$$

and from (48),

$$\left(\frac{\partial C^*}{\partial a_*}\right)_{\bar{I}_0} = -\frac{W_0}{V}. \qquad (50)$$

Thus, we can derive the substitution effect of an increase in the mean of the composite portfolio as follows,

$$\left(\frac{\partial C^*}{\partial a_*}\right)_{\bar{I}_0} = \left[\frac{\partial V}{\partial a_*}W_0 + V\frac{\partial W_0}{\partial a_*}\right]_{\bar{I}_0}$$
$$= -\frac{W_0}{\delta} < 0. \qquad (51)$$

Because $\partial C^*/\partial a_* = (\partial V/\partial a_*)W_0 = [(\delta-1)/\delta]W_0$, then the income or wealth effect is

$$\left[\frac{\partial C^*}{\partial a_*} - \left(\frac{\partial C^*}{\partial a_*}\right)_{\bar{I}_0}\right] = W_0 > 0. \qquad (52)$$

Therefore, by combining the effects of (51) and (52), one can see that individuals with low relative risk-aversion ($0 < \delta < 1$) will choose to consume less now and save more to take advantage of the higher yield available (i.e., the substitution effect dominates the income effect). For high risk-averters ($\delta > 1$), the reverse is true and the income effect dominates the substitution effect. In the borderline case of Bernoulli logarithmic utility ($\delta = 1$), the income and substitution effect just offset one another.[12]

In a similar fashion, consider the case of $\theta = -\sigma_*^2$,[13] then from, (46) and (48), we derive

$$\left(\frac{\partial W_0}{\partial(-\sigma_*^2)}\right)_{\bar{I}_0} = \frac{-\delta W_0}{2V} \qquad (53)$$

and

$$\left(\frac{\partial C^*}{\partial(-\sigma_*^2)}\right)_{\bar{I}_0} = \frac{-W_0}{2} < 0, \text{ the substitution effect.} \qquad (54)$$

Further, $\partial C^*/\partial(-\sigma_*^2) = (\delta-1)W_0/2$, and so

$$\left[\frac{\partial C^*}{\partial(-\sigma_*^2)} - \left(\frac{\partial C^*}{\partial(-\sigma_*^2)}\right)_{\bar{I}_0}\right]$$
$$= \frac{\delta}{2}W_0 > 0, \text{ the income effect.} \qquad (55)$$

To compare the relative effect on consumption behavior of an upward shift in the mean versus a downward shift in variance, we examine the elasticities. Define the elasticity of consumption with respect to the mean as

$$E_1 \equiv a_*\frac{\partial C^*}{\partial a_*}/C^* = a_*(\delta-1)/\delta V \qquad (56)$$

and similarly, the elasticity of consumption with respect to the variance as,

$$E_2 \equiv \sigma_*^2\frac{\partial C^*}{\partial \sigma_*^2}/C^* = -\sigma_*^2(\delta-1)/2V \qquad (57)$$

For graphical simplicity, we plot $e_1 \equiv [VE_1/a_*]$ and $e_2 \equiv -[VE_2/a_*]$ and define $k \equiv$

[12] Many writers have independently discovered that Bernoulli utility is a borderline case in various comparative-static situations. See, for example, Phelps [6] and Arrow [1].

[13] Because increased variance for a fixed mean usually (always for normal variates) decreases the desirability of investment for the risk-averter, it provides a more symmetric discussion to consider the effect of a decrease in variance.

FIGURE 2.—

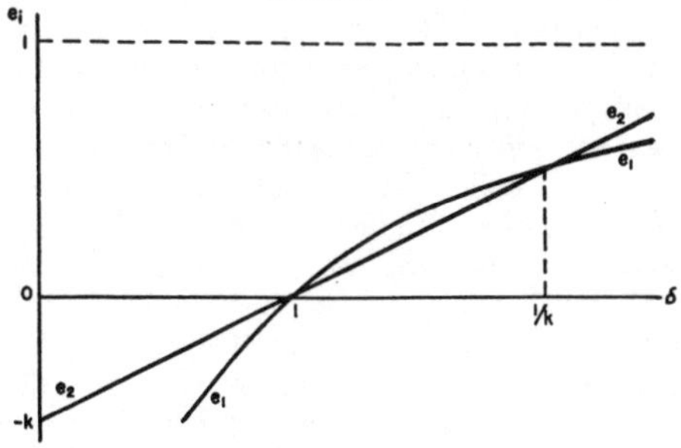

$\sigma_*^2/2a_*$. e_1 and e_2 are equal at $\delta = 1, 1/k$. The particular case drawn is for $k < 1$.

For relatively high variance ($k > 1$), the high risk averter ($\delta > 1$) will always increase present consumption more with a decrease in variance than for the same percentage increase in mean. Because a high risk-averter prefers a steadier flow of consumption at a lower level than a more erratic flow at a higher level, it makes sense that a decrease in variance would have a greater effect than an increase in mean. On the other hand, for relatively low variance ($k < 1$), a low risk averter ($0 < \delta < 1$) will always decrease his present consumption more with an increase in the mean than for the same percentage decrease in variance because such an individual (although a risk-averter) will prefer to accept a more erratic flow of consumption in return for a higher level of consumption. Of course, these qualitative results will vary depending upon the size of k. If the riskiness of the returns is very small (i.e., $k << 1$), then the high risk-averter will increase his present consumption more with an upward shift in mean. Similarly, if the risk-level is very high (i.e., $k >> 1$) the low risk averter will change his consumption more with decreases in variance.

The results of this analysis can be summed up as follows: Because all individuals in this model are risk-averters, when risk is a dominant factor ($k >> 1$), a decrease in risk will have the larger effect on their consumption decisions. When risk is unimportant (i.e., $k << 1$), they all react stronger to an increase in the mean yield. For all degrees of relative riskiness, the low risk-averter will give up some present consumption to attain an expected higher future consumption while the high risk averter will always choose to increase the amount of present consumption.

VIII Extension to Many Assets

The model presented in section IV, can be extended to the m-asset case with little difficulty. For simplicity, the solution is derived in the infinite time horizon case, but the result is similar for finite time. Assume the mth asset to be the only certain asset with an instantaneous rate of return $a_m = r$.[14] Using the general equations derived in section II, and substituting for $w_m(t) = 1 - \sum_{i=1}^{n} w_i(t)$ where $n \equiv m - 1$, equations (6) and (7) can be written as,

$$E(t_0)\ [W(t) - W(t_0)] = [w'(t_0)(a - \hat{r}) + r]\, W(t_0)h - C(t_0)h + 0(h^2) \tag{6}$$

and

$$E(t_0)\ [(W(t) - W(t_0))^2] = w'(t_0)\,\Omega\, w(t_0)\, W^2(t_0)h + 0(h^2) \tag{7}$$

where

$w'(t_0) \equiv [w_1(t_0), \ldots, w_n(t_0)]$, a n-vector

$a' \equiv [a_1, \ldots, a_n]$

$\hat{r}' \equiv [r, \ldots, r]$ a n-vector

$\Omega \equiv [\sigma_{ij}]$, the $n \times n$ variance-covariance matrix of the risky assets

Ω is symmetric and positive definite.

Then, the general form of (35) for m-assets is, in matrix notation,

$$0 = \underset{\{C,w\}}{\text{Max}}\ [U(C) - \rho J(W) + J'(W)\{[w'(a-\hat{r}) + r]\, W - C\} + \frac{1}{2} J''(W)\, w'\,\Omega\, wW^2] \tag{58}$$

and instead of two, there will be m first-order conditions corresponding to a maximization of (35) with respect to $w_1, \ldots, w_n$ and C. The optimal decision rules corresponding to (42) and (43) in the two-asset case, are

$$C_\infty^*(t) = \left\{ \frac{\rho}{1-\gamma} - \gamma \left[\frac{(a-\hat{r})'\Omega^{-1}(a-\hat{r})}{2\,(1-\gamma)^2} + \frac{r}{1-\gamma} \right] \right\} W(t) \tag{59}$$

[14] Clearly, if there were more than one certain asset, the one with the highest rate of return would dominate the others.

and

$$w_\infty^*(t) = \frac{1}{(1-\gamma)} \Omega^{-1} (\alpha - \hat{r}) \tag{60}$$

where $w_\infty^{*\prime}(t) = [w_1^*(t), \ldots, w_n^*(t)]$.

IX Constant Absolute Risk Aversion

System (*) of section III, can be solved explicitly for a second special class of utility functions of the form yielding constant absolute risk-aversion. Let $U(C) = -e^{-\eta C}/\eta$, $\eta > 0$, where $-U''(C)/U'(C) = \eta$ is Pratt's [17] measure of absolute risk-aversion. For convenience, I return to the two-asset case and infinite-time horizon form of system (*) which can be written in this case as,

$$(*'') \begin{cases} 0 = \dfrac{-J'(W)}{\eta} - \rho J(W) + J'(W) r W + \dfrac{J'(W)}{\eta} \log [J'(W)] - \dfrac{(\alpha - r)^2}{2\sigma^2} \dfrac{[J'(W)]^2}{J''(W)} & (17'') \\ C^*(t) = -\dfrac{1}{\eta} \log [J'(W)] & (18) \\ w^*(t) = -J'(W)(\alpha - r)/\sigma^2 W J''(W) \\ \text{subject to } \lim_{t \to \infty} E[e^{-\rho t} J(W(t))] = 0 & (19) \end{cases}$$

where $J(W) \equiv e^{\rho t} I[W(t), t]$ as defined in section VI.

To solve (17″) of (*″), take as a trial solution,

$$\bar{J}(W) = \frac{-p}{q} e^{-qW}. \tag{61}$$

By substitution of the trial solution into (17″), a necessary condition that $\bar{J}(W)$ be a solution to (17″) is found to be that p and q must satisfy the following two algebraic equations:

$$q = \eta r \tag{62}$$

and

$$p = e^{\left(\frac{r - \rho - (\alpha - r)^2/2\sigma^2}{r} \right)} \tag{63}$$

The resulting optimal decision rules for portfolio selection and consumption are,

$$C^*(t) = rW(t) + \left[\frac{\rho - r + (\alpha - r)^2/2\sigma^2}{\eta r} \right] \tag{64}$$

and

$$w^*(t) = \frac{(\alpha - r)}{\eta r \sigma^2 W(t)}. \tag{65}$$

Comparing equations (64) and (65) with their counterparts for the constant relative risk-aversion case, (42) and (43), one finds that consumption is no longer a constant proportion of wealth (i.e., marginal propensity to consume does not equal the average propensity) although it is still linear in wealth. Instead of the proportion of wealth invested in the risky asset being constant (i.e., $w^*(t)$ a constant), the total dollar value of wealth invested in the risky asset is kept constant (i.e., $w^*(t)W(t)$ a constant). As one becomes wealthier, the proportion of his wealth invested in the risky asset falls, and asymptotically, as $W \to \infty$, one invests all his wealth in the certain asset and consumes all his (certain) income. Although one can do the same type of comparative statics for this utility function as was done in section VII for the case of constant relative risk-aversion, it will not be done in this paper for the sake of brevity and because I find this special form of the utility function behaviorially less plausible than constant relative risk aversion. It is interesting to note that the substitution effect in this case, $\left[\dfrac{\partial C}{\partial \theta} \right]_{\bar{I}_0}$, is zero except when $r = \theta$.

X Other Extensions of the Model

The requirements for the general class of probability distributions which could be acceptable in this model are,

(1) the stochastic process must be Markovian.

(2) the first two moments of the distribution must be $O(\Delta t)$ and the higher-order moments $o(\Delta t)$ where $o(\cdot)$ is the order symbol meaning "smaller order than."

So, for example, the simple Wiener process postulated in this model could be generalized to include $\alpha_i = \alpha_i(X_1, \ldots, X_m, W, t)$ and $\sigma_i = \sigma_i(X_1, \ldots, X_m, W, t)$, where X_i is the price of the ith asset. In this case, there will be $(m+1)$ state variables and (17′) will be generated from the general Taylor series expansion of $I[X_2], \ldots, X_m, W, t]$ for many variables. A particular example would be if the ith asset is a bond which fluctuates in price for $t < t_i$, but will be called at a fixed price at time $t = t_i$. Then $\alpha_i = \alpha_i(X_i, t)$ and $\sigma_i = \sigma_i(X_i, t) > 0$ when $t < t_i$ and $\sigma_i = 0$ for $t > t_i$.

A more general production function of a neoclassical type could be introduced to replace the simple linear one of this model. Mirrlees [5] has examined this case in the context of a growth model with Harrod-neutral technical progress a random variable. His equations (19) and (20) correspond to my equations (35) and (37) with the obvious proper substitutions for variables.

Thus, the technique employed for this model can be extended to a wide class of economic models. However, because the optimality equations involve a partial differential equation, computational solution of even a slightly generalized model may be quite difficult.

REFERENCES

[1] Arrow, K. J., "Aspects of the Theory of Risk-Bearing," Helsinki, Finland, Yrjö Jahnssonin Säätio, 1965.

[2] Dreyfus, S. E., *Dynamic Programming and the Calculus of Variations* (New York: Academic Press, 1965).

[3] Graaff, J. De V., "Mr. Harrod on Hump Saving," *Economica* (Feb. 1950), 81–90.

[4] Itô, K., "On Stochastic Differential Equations," *Memoirs, American Mathematical Society*, No. 4 (1965), 1–51.

[5] Mirrlees, J. A., "Optimum Accumulation Under Uncertainty," Dec. 1965, unpublished

[6] Phelps, E. S., "The Accumulation of Risky Capital: A Sequential Utility Analysis," *Econometrica*, 30 (1962), 729–743.

[7] Pratt, J., "Risk Aversion in the Small and in the Large," *Econometrica*, 32 (Jan. 1964), 122–136.

[8] Samuelson, P. A., "Lifetime Portfolio Selection by Dynamic Stochastic Programming," this REVIEW, L (Aug. 1969).

[9] Tobin, J., "The Theory of Portfolio Selection," *The Theory of Interest Rates*, F. H. Hahn and F. P. R. Brechling, (ed.) (London: MacMillan Co., 1965).

[6]

JOURNAL OF ECONOMIC THEORY 3, 373–413 (1971)

Optimum Consumption and Portfolio Rules in a Continuous-Time Model*

ROBERT C. MERTON

Sloan School of Management, Massachusetts Institute of Technology, Cambridge, Massachusetts 02139

Received September 30, 1970

1. INTRODUCTION

A common hypothesis about the behavior of (limited liability) asset prices in perfect markets is the random walk of returns or (in its continous-time form) the "geometric Brownian motion" hypothesis which implies that asset prices are stationary and log-normally distributed. A number of investigators of the behavior of stock and commodity prices have questioned the accuracy of the hypothesis.[1] In particular, Cootner [2] and others have criticized the independent increments assumption, and Osborne [2] has examined the assumption of stationariness. Mandelbrot [2] and Fama [2] argue that stock and commodity price changes follow a stable-Paretian distribution with infinite second moments. The nonacademic literature on the stock market is also filled with theories of stock price patterns and trading rules to "beat the market," rules often called "technical analysis" or "charting," and that presupposes a departure from random price changes.

In an earlier paper [12], I examined the continuous-time consumption-portfolio problem for an individual whose income is generated by capital gains on investments in assets with prices assumed to satisfy the "geometric Brownian motion" hypothesis; i.e., I studied Max $E\int_0^T U(C, t)\,dt$

* I would like to thank P. A. Samuelson, R. M. Solow, P. A. Diamond, J. A. Mirrlees, J. A. Flemming, and D. T. Scheffman for their helpful discussions. Of course, all errors are mine. Aid from the National Science Foundation is gratefully acknowledged. An earlier version of the paper was presented at the second World Congress of the Econometric Society, Cambridge, England.

[1] For a number of interesting papers on the subject, see Cootner [2]. An excellent survey article is "Efficient Capital Markets: A Review of Theory and Empirical Work," by E. Fama, *Journal of Finance*, May, 1970.

where U is the instantaneous utility function, C is consumption, and E is the expectation operator. Under the additional assumption of a constant relative or constant absolute risk-aversion utility function, explicit solutions for the optimal consumption and portfolio rules were derived. The changes in these optimal rules with respect to shifts in various parameters such as expected return, interest rates, and risk were examined by the technique of comparative statics.

The present paper extends these results for more general utility functions, price behavior assumptions, and for income generated also from non-capital gains sources. It is shown that if the "geometric Brownian motion" hypothesis is accepted, then a general "Separation" or "mutual fund" theorem can be proved such that, in this model, the classical Tobin mean-variance rules hold without the objectionable assumptions of quadratic utility or of normality of distributions for prices. Hence, when asset prices are generated by a geometric Brownian motion, one can work with the two-asset case without loss of generality. If the further assumption is made that the utility function of the individual is a member of the family of utility functions called the "HARA" family, explicit solutions for the optimal consumption and portfolio rules are derived and a number of theorems proved. In the last parts of the paper, the effects on the consumption and portfolio rules of alternative asset price dynamics, in which changes are neither stationary nor independent, are examined along with the effects of introducing wage income, uncertainty of life expectancy, and the possibility of default on (formerly) "risk-free" assets.

2. A Digression on Itô Processes

To apply the dynamic programming technique in a continuous-time model, the state variable dynamics must be expressible as Markov stochastic processes defined over time intervals of length h, no matter how small h is. Such processes are referred to as infinitely divisible in time. The two processes of this type[2] are: functions of Gauss–Wiener Brownian motions which are continuous in the "space" variables and functions of Poisson processes which are discrete in the space variables. Because neither of these processes is differentiable in the usual sense, a more general type of differential equation must be developed to express the dynamics of such processes. A particular class of continuous-time

[2] I ignore those infinitely divisible processes with infinite moments which include those members of the stable Paretian family other than the normal.

Markov processes of the first type called Itô Processes are defined as the solution to the stochastic differential equation[3]

$$dP = f(P, t)\, dt + g(P, t)\, dz, \tag{1}$$

where P, f, and g are n vectors and $z(t)$ is an n vector of standard normal random variables. Then $dz(t)$ is called a multidimensional Wiener process (or Brownian motion).[4]

The fundamental tool for formal manipulation and solution of stochastic processes of the Itô type is Itô's Lemma stated as follows[5]

LEMMA. *Let $F(P_1, \ldots, P_n, t)$ be a C^2 function defined on $R^n X[0, \infty)$ and take the stochastic integrals*

$$P_i(t) = P_i(0) + \int_0^t f_i(P, s)\, ds + \int_0^t g_i(P, s)\, dz_i, \qquad i = 1, \ldots, n;$$

then the time-dependent random variable $Y \equiv F$ is a stochastic integral and its stochastic differential is

$$dY = \sum_1^n \frac{\partial F}{\partial P_i} dP_i + \frac{\partial F}{\partial t} dt + \frac{1}{2} \sum_1^n \sum_1^n \frac{\partial^2 F}{\partial P_i \partial P_j} dP_i\, dP_j,$$

where the product of the differentials $dP_i\, dP_j$ are defined by the multiplication rule

$$dz_i\, dz_j = \rho_{ij}\, dt, \qquad i, j = 1, \ldots, n,$$
$$dz_i\, dt = 0, \qquad i = 1, \ldots, n,$$

[3] Itô Processes are a special case of a more general class of stochastic processes called Strong diffusion processes (see Kushner [9, p. 22]). (1) is a short-hand expression for the stochastic integral

$$P(t) = P(0) + \int_0^t f(P, s)\, ds + \int_0^t g(P, s)\, dz,$$

where $P(t)$ is the solution to (1) with probability one.

A rigorous discussion of the meaning of a solution to equations like (1) is not presented here. Only those theorems needed for formal manipulation and solution of stochastic differential equations are in the text and these without proof. For a complete discussion of Itô Processes, see the seminal paper of Itô [7], Itô and McKean [8], and McKean [11]. For a short description and some proofs, see Kushner [9, pp. 12–18]. For an heuristic discussion of continuous-time Markov processes in general, see Cox and Miller [3, Chap. 5].

[4] dz is often referred to in the literature as "Gaussian White Noise." There are some regularity conditions imposed on the functions f and g. It is assumed throughout the paper that such conditions are satisfied. For the details, see [9] or [11].

[5] See McKean [11, pp. 32–35 and 44] for proofs of the Lemma in one and n dimensions.

where ρ_{ij} is the instantaneous correlation coefficient between the Wiener processes dz_i and dz_j .[6]

Armed with Itô's Lemma, we are now able to formally differentiate most smooth functions of Brownian motions (and hence integrate stochastic differential equations of the Itô type).[7]

Before proceeding to the discussion of asset price behavior, another concept useful for working with Itô Processes is the differential generator (or weak infinitesimal operator) of the stochastic process $P(t)$. Define the function $\mathring{G}(P, t)$ by

$$\mathring{G}(P, t) \equiv \lim_{h \to 0} E_t \left[\frac{G(P(t+h), t+h) - G(P(t), t)}{h} \right], \qquad (2)$$

when the limit exists and where "E_t" is the conditional expectation operator, conditional on knowing $P(t)$. If the $P_i(t)$ are generated by Itô Processes, then the differential generator of P, $\mathscr{L}_P$, is defined by

$$\mathscr{L}_P \equiv \sum_1^n f_i \frac{\partial}{\partial P_i} + \frac{\partial}{\partial t} + \frac{1}{2} \sum_1^n \sum_1^n a_{ij} \frac{\partial^2}{\partial P_i \, \partial P_j},$$

where $f = (f_1 ,..., f_n)$, $g = (g_1 ,..., g_n)$, and $a_{ij} \equiv g_i g_j \rho_{ij}$. Further, it can be shown that

$$\mathring{G}(P, t) = \mathscr{L}_P[G(P, t)]. \qquad (4)$$

$\mathring{G}$ can be interpreted as the "average" or expected time rate of change of

[6] This multiplication rule has given rise to the formalism of writing the Wiener process differentials as $dz_i = \mathscr{S}_i \sqrt{dt}$ where the $\mathscr{S}_i$ are standard normal variates (*e.g.*, see [3]).

[7] Warning: derivatives (and integrals) of functions of Brownian motions are similar to, but different from, the rules for deterministic differentials and integrals. For example, if

$$P(t) = P(0)\, e^{\int_0^t dz - \frac{1}{2}t} = P(0)\, e^{z(t) - z(0) - \frac{1}{2}t},$$

then $dP = Pdz$. Hence

$$\int_0^t \frac{dP}{P} = \int_0^t dz \neq \log (P(t)/P(0)).$$

Stratonovich [15] has developed a symmetric definition of stochastic differential equations which formally follows the ordinary rules of differentiation and integration. However, this alternative to the Itô formalism will not be discussed here.

the function $G(P, t)$ and as such is the natural generalization of the ordinary time derivative for deterministic functions.[8]

3. Asset Price Dynamics and the Budget Equation

Throughout the paper, it is assumed that all assets are of the limited liability type, that there exist continuously-trading perfect markets with no transactions costs for all assets, and that the prices per share, $\{P_i(t)\}$, are generated by Itô Processes, i.e.,

$$\frac{dP_i}{P_i} = \alpha_i(P, t)\, dt + \sigma_i(P, t)\, dz_i\,, \tag{5}$$

where α_i is the instantaneous conditional expected percentage change in price per unit time and σ_i^2 is the instantaneous conditional variance per unit time. In the particular case where the "geometric Brownian motion hypothesis is assumed to hold for asset prices, α_i and σ_i will be constants. For this case, prices will be stationarily and log-normally distributed and it will be shown that this assumption about asset prices simplifies the continuous-time model in the same way that the assumption of normality of prices simplifies the static one-period portfolio model.

To derive the correct budget equation, it is necessary to examine the discrete-time formulation of the model and then to take limits carefully to obtain the continuous-time form. Consider a period model with periods of length h, where all income is generated by capital gains, and wealth, $W(t)$ and $P_i(t)$ are known at the *beginning* of period t. Let the decision variables be indexed such that the indices coincide with the period in which the decisions are implemented. Namely, let

$N_i(t) \equiv$ number of shares of asset i purchased during period t, i.e., between t and $t + h$

and (6)

$C(t) \equiv$ amount of consumption per unit time during period t.

[8] A heuristic method for finding the differential generator is to take the conditional expectation of dG (found by Itô's Lemma) and "divide" by dt. The result of this operation will be $\mathscr{L}_P[G]$, i.e., formally,

$$\frac{1}{dt} E_t(dG) = \mathring{G} = \mathscr{L}_P[G].$$

The "$\mathscr{L}_P$" operator is often called a Dynkin operator and is often written as "D_P".

The model assumes that the individual "comes into" period t with wealth invested in assets so that

$$W(t) = \sum_1^n N_i(t-h)\, P_i(t). \tag{7}$$

Notice that it is $N_i(t-h)$ because $N_i(t-h)$ is the number of shares purchased for the portfolio in period $(t-h)$ and it is $P_i(t)$ because $P_i(t)$ is the *current* value of a share of the i-th asset. The amount of consumption for the period, $C(t)\,h$, and the new portfolio, $N_i(t)$, are simultaneously chosen, and if it is assumed that all trades are made at (known) current prices, then we have that

$$-C(t)\,h = \sum_1^n [N_i(t) - N_i(t-h)]\, P_i(t). \tag{8}$$

The "dice" are rolled and a new set of prices is determined, $P_i(t+h)$, and the value of the portfolio is now $\sum_1^n N_i(t)\, P_i(t+h)$. So the individual "comes into" period $(t+h)$ with wealth $W(t+h) = \sum_1^n N_i(t)\, P_i(t+h)$ and the process continues.

Incrementing (7) and (8) by h to eliminate backward differences, we have that

$$\begin{aligned} -C(t+h)\,h &= \sum_1^n [N_i(t+h) - N_i(t)]\, P_i(t+h) \\ &= \sum_1^n [N_i(t+h) - N_i(t)][P_i(t+h) - P_i(t)] \\ &\quad + \sum_1^n [N_i(t+h) - N_i(t)]\, P_i(t) \end{aligned} \tag{9}$$

and

$$W(t+h) = \sum_1^n N_i(t)\, P_i(t+h). \tag{10}$$

Taking the limits as $h \to 0$,[9] we arrive at the continuous version of (9) and (10),

$$-C(t)\,dt = \sum_1^n dN_i(t)\, dP_i(t) + \sum_1^n dN_i(t)\, P_i(t) \tag{9'}$$

[9] We use here the result that Itô Processes are right-continuous [9, p. 15] and hence $P_i(t)$ and $W(t)$ are right-continuous. It is assumed that $C(t)$ is a right-continuous function, and, throughout the paper, the choice of $C(t)$ is restricted to this class of functions.

and

$$W(t) = \sum_1^n N_i(t)\, P_i(t). \tag{10'}$$

Using Itô's Lemma, we differentiate (10′) to get

$$dW = \sum_1^n N_i\, dP_i + \sum_1^n dN_i P_i + \sum_1^n dN_i\, dP_i\,. \tag{11}$$

The last two terms, $\sum_1^n dN_i P_i + \sum_1^n dN_i\, dP_i$, are the net value of additions to wealth from sources other than capital gains.[10] Hence, if $dy(t) =$ (possibly stochastic) instantaneous flow of noncapital gains (wage) income, then we have that

$$dy - C(t)\, dt = \sum_1^n dN_i P_i + \sum_1^n dN_i\, dP_i\,. \tag{12}$$

From (11) and (12), the budget or accumulation equation is written as

$$dW = \sum_1^n N_i(t)\, dP_i + dy - C(t)\, dt. \tag{13}$$

It is advantageous to eliminate $N_i(t)$ from (13) by defining a new variable, $w_i(t) \equiv N_i(t)\, P_i(t)/W(t)$, the percentage of wealth invested in the i-th asset at time t. Substituting for dP_i/P_i from (5), we can write (13) as

$$dW = \sum_1^n w_i W \alpha_i\, dt - C\, dt + dy + \sum_1^n w_i W \sigma_i\, dz_i\,, \tag{14}$$

where, by definition, $\sum_1^n w_i \underset{t}{\equiv} 1$.[11]

Until Section 7, it will be assumed that $dy \equiv 0$, i.e., all income is derived from capital gains on assets. If one of the n-assets is "risk-free"

[10] This result follows directly from the discrete-time argument used to derive (9′) where $-C(t)\, dt$ is replaced by a general $dv(t)$ where $dv(t)$ is the instantaneous flow of funds from all noncapital gains sources.

It was necessary to derive (12) by starting with the discrete-time formulation because it is not obvious from the continuous version directly whether $dy - C(t)\, dt$ equals $\sum_1^n dN_i P_i + \sum_1^n dN_i\, dP_i$ or just $\sum_1^n dN_i P_i$.

[11] There are no other restrictions on the individual w_i because borrowing and short-selling are allowed.

(by convention, the n-th asset), then $\sigma_n = 0$, the instantaneous rate of return, α_n, will be called r, and (14) is rewritten as

$$dW = \sum_1^m w_i(\alpha_i - r)\, W\, dt + (rW - C)\, dt + dy + \sum_1^m W_i \sigma_i\, dz_i\,, \quad (14')$$

where $m \equiv n - 1$ and the $w_1, \ldots, w_m$ are unconstrained by virtue of the fact that the relation $w_n = 1 - \sum_1^m w_i$ will ensure that the identity constraint in (14) is satisfied.

4. Optimal Portfolio and Consumption Rules: The Equations of Optimality

The problem of choosing optimal portfolio and consumption rules for an individual who lives T years is formulated as follows:

$$\max E_0 \left[\int_0^T U(C(t), t)\, dt + B(W(T), T) \right] \quad (15)$$

subject to: $W(0) = W_0$; the budget constraint (14), which in the case of a "risk-free" asset becomes (14'); and where the utility function (during life) U is assumed to be strictly concave in C and the "bequest" function B is assumed also to be concave in W.[12]

To derive the optimal rules, the technique of stochastic dynamic programming is used. Define

$$J(W, P, t) \equiv \max_{\{C, w\}} E_t \left[\int_t^T U(C, s)\, ds + B(W(T), T) \right], \quad (16)$$

where as before, "E_t" is the conditional expectation operator, conditional on $W(t) = W$ and $P_i(t) = P_i$. Define

$$\phi(w, C; W, P, t) \equiv U(C, t) + \mathscr{L}[J], \quad (17)$$

[12] Where there is no "risk-free" asset, it is assumed that no asset can be expressed as a linear combination of the other assets, implying that the $n \times n$ variance-covariance matrix of returns, $\Omega = [\sigma_{ij}]$, where $\sigma_{ij} \equiv \rho_{ij}\sigma_i\sigma_j$, is nonsingular. In the case when there is a "risk-free" asset, the same assumption is made about the "reduced" $m \times m$ variance-covariance matrix.

given $w_i(t) = w_i$, $C(t) = C$, $W(t) = W$, and $P_i(t) = P_i$.[13] From the theory of stochastic dynamic programming, the following theorem provides the method for deriving the optimal rules, C^* and w^*.

THEOREM I.[14] *If the $P_i(t)$ are generated by a strong diffusion process, U is strictly concave in C, and B is concave in W, then there exists a set of optimal rules (controls), w^* and C^*, satisfying $\sum_1^n w_i^* = 1$ and $J(W, P, T) = B(W, T)$ and these controls satisfy*

$$0 = \phi(C^*, w^*; W, P, t) \geqslant \phi(C, w; W, P, t)$$

for $t \in [0, T]$.

From Theorem I, we have that

$$0 = \max_{\{C,w\}}\{\phi(C, w; W, P, t)\} \tag{18}$$

In the usual fashion of maximization under constraint, we define the Lagrangian, $L \equiv \phi + \lambda[1 - \sum_1^n w_i]$ where λ is the multiplier and find the extreme points from the first-order conditions

$$0 = L_C(C^*, w^*) = U_C(C^*, t) - J_W, \tag{19}$$

$$\begin{aligned} 0 = L_{w_k}(C^*, w^*) &= -\lambda + J_W \alpha_k W + J_{WW} \sum_1^n \sigma_{kj} w_j^* W^2 \\ &\quad + \sum_1^n J_{jW} \sigma_{kj} P_j W, \qquad k = 1,\dots, n, \end{aligned} \tag{20}$$

$$0 = L_\lambda(C^*, w^*) = 1 - \sum_1^n w_i^*, \tag{21}$$

[13] "$\mathscr{L}$" is short for the rigorous $\mathscr{L}_{P,W}^{w,C}$, the Dynkin operator over the variables P and W for a given set of controls w and C.

$$\begin{aligned} \mathscr{L} &\equiv \frac{\partial}{\partial t} + \left[\sum_1^n w_i \alpha_i W - C\right] \frac{\partial}{\partial W} + \sum_1^n \alpha_i P_i \frac{\partial}{\partial P_i} \\ &\quad + \frac{1}{2} \sum_1^n \sum_1^n \sigma_{ij} w_i w_j W^2 \frac{\partial^2}{\partial W^2} + \frac{1}{2} \sum_1^n \sum_1^n P_i P_j \sigma_{ij} \frac{\partial^2}{\partial P_i \partial P_j} \\ &\quad + \sum_1^n \sum_1^n P_i W w_j \sigma_{ij} \frac{\partial^2}{\partial P_i \partial W}. \end{aligned}$$

[14] For an heuristic proof of this theorem and the derivation of the stochastic Bellman equation, see Dreyfus [4] and Merton [12]. For a rigorous proof and discussion of weaker conditions, see Kushner [9, Chap. IV, especially Theorem 7].

where the notation for partial derivatives is $J_W \equiv \partial J/\partial W$, $J_t \equiv \partial J/\partial t$, $U_C \equiv \partial U/\partial C$, $J_i \equiv \partial J/\partial P_i$, $J_{ij} \equiv \partial^2 J/\partial P_i\, \partial P_j$, and $J_{jW} \equiv \partial^2 J/\partial P_j\, \partial W$.

Because $L_{CC} = \phi_{CC} = U_{CC} < 0$, $L_{Cw_k} = \phi_{Cw_k} = 0$, $L_{w_k w_k} = \sigma_k{}^2 W^2 J_{WW}$, $L_{w_k w_j} = 0$, $k \neq j$, a sufficient condition for a unique interior maximum is that $J_{WW} < 0$ (i.e., that J be strictly concave in W). That assumed, as an immediate consequence of differentiating (19) totally with respect to W, we have

$$\frac{\partial C^*}{\partial W} > 0. \tag{22}$$

To solve explicitly for C^* and w^*, we solve the $n + 2$ nondynamic implicit equations, (19)–(21), for C^*, and w^*, and λ as functions of J_W, J_{WW}, J_{jW}, W, P, and t. Then, C^* and w^* are substituted in (18) which now becomes a second-order partial differential equation for J, subject to the boundary condition $J(W, P, T) = B(W, T)$. Having (in principle at least) solved this equation for J, we then substitute back into (19)–(21) to derive the optimal rules as functions of W, P, and t. Define the inverse function $G \equiv [U_C]^{-1}$. Then, from (19),

$$C^* = G(J_W, t). \tag{23}$$

To solve for the w_i^*, note that (20) is a linear system in w_i^* and hence can be solved explicitly. Define

$$\begin{aligned} \Omega &\equiv [\sigma_{ij}], \qquad \text{the } n \times n \text{ variance-covariance matrix,} \\ [v_{ij}] &\equiv \Omega^{-1}, \text{[15]} \\ \Gamma &\equiv \sum_1^n \sum_1^n v_{ij}. \end{aligned} \tag{24}$$

Eliminating λ from (20), the solution for w_k^* can be written as

$$w_k^* = h_k(P, t) + m(P, W, t)\, g_k(P, t) + f_k(P, W, t), \qquad k = 1, \ldots, n, \tag{25}$$

where $\sum_1^n h_k \equiv 1$, $\sum_1^n g_k \equiv 0$, and $\sum_1^n f_k \equiv 0$.[16]

[15] Ω^{-1} exists by the assumption on Ω in footnote 12.

[16]
$$h_k(P, t) \equiv \sum_1^n v_{kj}/\Gamma; \; m(P, W, t) \equiv -Jw/WJww;$$
$$g_k(P, t) \equiv \frac{1}{\Gamma} \sum_1^n v_{kl} \left(\Gamma \alpha_l - \sum_1^n \sum_1^n v_{ij} \alpha_j \right); f_k(P, W, t)$$
$$\equiv \left[\Gamma J_{kw} P_k - \sum_1^n J_{iw} P_i \sum_1^n v_{kj} \right] \Big/ \Gamma W Jww.$$

Substituting for w^* and C^* in (18), we arrive at the fundamental partial differential equation for J as a function of W, P, and t,

$$\begin{aligned}0 &= U[G,t] + J_t + J_W\left[\frac{\sum_1^n \sum_1^n v_{kj}\alpha_k W}{\Gamma} - G\right] \\ &+ \sum_1^n J_i\alpha_i P_i + \frac{1}{2}\sum_1^n\sum_1^n J_{ij}\sigma_{ij}P_iP_j + \frac{W}{\Gamma}\sum_1^n J_{jW}P_j \\ &- \frac{J_W}{\Gamma J_{WW}}\left(\sum_1^n \Gamma J_{kW}P_k\alpha_k - \sum_1^n J_{jW}P_j \sum_1^n\sum_1^n v_{kl}\alpha_l\right) \\ &+ \frac{J_{WW}W^2}{2\Gamma} - \frac{1}{2\Gamma J_{WW}}\left[\sum_1^n\sum_1^n J_{jW}J_{mW}P_jP_m\sigma_{mj}\Gamma - \left(\sum_1^n J_{iW}P_i\right)^2\right] \\ &- \frac{J_W^2}{2\Gamma J_{WW}}\left[\sum_1^n\sum_1^n v_{kl}\alpha_k\alpha_l\Gamma - \left(\sum_1^n\sum_1^n v_{kl}\alpha_k\right)^2\right] \qquad (26)\end{aligned}$$

subject to the boundary condition $J(W, P, T) = B(W, T)$. If (26) were solved, the solution J could be substituted into (23) and (25) to obtain C^* and w^* as functions of W, P, and t.

For the case where one of the assets is "risk-free," the equations are somewhat simplified because the problem can be solved directly as an unconstrained maximum by eliminating w_n as was done in (14'). In this case, the optimal proportions in the risky assets are

$$w_k^* = -\frac{J_W}{J_{WW}W}\sum_1^m v_{kj}(\alpha_{j-r}) - \frac{J_{kW}P_k}{J_{WW}W}, \qquad k = 1,\dots,m. \qquad (27)$$

The partial differential equation for J corresponding to (26) becomes

$$\begin{aligned}0 &= U[G,T] + J_t + J_W[rW - G] + \sum_1^m J_i\alpha_i P_i \\ &+ \frac{1}{2}\sum_1^m\sum_1^m J_{ij}\sigma_{ij}P_iP_j - \frac{J_W}{J_{WW}}\sum_1^m J_{jW}P_j(\alpha_j - r) \\ &+ \frac{J_W^2}{2J_{WW}}\sum_1^m\sum_1^m v_{ij}(\alpha_i - r)(\alpha_j - r) - \frac{1}{2J_{WW}}\sum_1^m\sum_1^m J_{iW}J_{jW}\sigma_{ij}P_iP_i \qquad (28)\end{aligned}$$

subject to the boundary condition $J(W, P, T) = B(W, T)$.

Although (28) is a simplified version of (26), neither (26) nor (28) lend themselves to easy solution. The complexities of (26) and (28) are caused by the basic nonlinearity of the equations and the large number of state variables. Although there is little that can be done about the nonlinearities, in some cases, it may be possible to reduce the number of state variables.

5. Log-Normality of Prices and the Continuous-Time Analog to Tobin–Markowitz Mean-Variance Analysis

When, for $k = 1,\ldots, n$, α_k and σ_k are constants, the asset prices have stationary, log-normal distributions. In this case, J will be a function of W and t only and not P. Then (26) reduces to

$$0 = U[G, t] + J_t + J_W \left[\frac{\sum_1^n \sum_1^n v_{kj}\alpha_k}{\Gamma} W - G\right] + \frac{J_{WW} W^2}{2\Gamma} - \frac{J_W^2}{2\Gamma J_{WW}} \left[\sum_1^n \sum_1^n v_{kl}\alpha_k\alpha_l \Gamma - \left(\sum_1^n \sum_1^n v_{kl}\alpha_k\right)^2\right]. \tag{29}$$

From (25), the optimal portfolio rule becomes

$$w_k{}^* = h_k + m(W, t)\, g_k, \tag{30}$$

where $\sum_1^n h_k \equiv 1$ and $\sum_1^n g_k \equiv 0$ and h_k and g_k are constants.

From (30), the following "separation" or "mutual fund" theorem can be proved.

Theorem II.[17] *Given n assets with prices P_i whose changes are log-normally distributed, then* (1) *there exist a unique* (*up to a nonsingular transformation*) *pair of "mutual funds" constructed from linear combinations of these assets such that, independent of preferences* (*i.e., the form of the utility function*), *wealth distribution, or time horizon, individuals will be indifferent between choosing from a linear combination of these two funds or a linear combination of the original n assets.* (2) *If P_f is the price per share of either fund, then P_f is log-normally distributed. Further,* (3) *if δ_k = percentage of one mutual fund's value held in the k-th asset and if λ_k = percentage of the other mutual fund's value held in the k-th asset, then one can find that*

$$\delta_k = h_k + \frac{(1-\eta)}{\nu} g_k, \qquad k = 1,\ldots, n,$$

[17] See Cass and Stiglitz [1] for a general discussion of Separation theorems. The only degenerate case is when all the assets are identically distributed (i.e., symmetry) in which case, only one mutual fund is needed.

and

$$\lambda_k = h_k - \frac{\eta}{\nu} g_k, \qquad k = 1,..., n,$$

where ν, η *are arbitrary constants* ($\nu \neq 0$).

Proof. (1) (30) is a parametric representation of a line in the hyperplane defined by $\sum_1^n w_k{}^* = 1$.[18] Hence, there exist two linearly independent vectors (namely, the vectors of asset proportions held by the two mutual funds) which form a basis for all optimal portfolios chosen by the individuals. Therefore, each individual would be indifferent between choosing a linear combination of the mutual fund shares or a linear combination of the original n assets.

(2) Let $V \equiv N_f P_f =$ the total value of (either) fund where $N_f =$ number of shares of the fund outstanding. Let $N_k =$ number of shares of asset k held by the fund and $\mu_k \equiv N_k P_k / V =$ percentage of total value invested in the k-th asset. Then $V = \sum_1^n N_k P_k$ and

$$\begin{aligned} dV &= \sum_1^n N_k\, dP_k + \sum_1^n P_k\, dN_k + \sum dP_k\, dN_k \\ &= N_f\, dP_f + P_f\, dN_f + dP_f\, dN_f . \end{aligned} \tag{31}$$

But

$$\begin{aligned} \sum_1^n P_k\, dN_k + \sum_1^n dP_k\, dN_k &= \text{net inflow of funds from non-capital-gain sources} \\ &= \text{net value of new shares issued} \\ &= P_f\, dN_f + dN_f\, dP_f . \end{aligned} \tag{32}$$

From (31) and (32), we have that

$$N_f\, dP_f = \sum_1^n N_k\, dP_k . \tag{33}$$

By the definition of V and μ_k, (33) can be rewritten as

$$\begin{aligned} \frac{dP_f}{P_f} &= \sum_1^n \mu_k \frac{dP_k}{P_k} \\ &= \sum_1^n \mu_k \alpha_k\, dt + \sum_1^n \mu_k \sigma_k\, dz_k . \end{aligned} \tag{34}$$

[18] See [1, p. 15].

By Itô's Lemma and (34), we have that

$$P_f(t) = P_f(0) \exp\left[\left(\sum_1^n \mu_k\alpha_k - \tfrac{1}{2}\sum_1^n\sum_1^n \mu_k\mu_j\sigma_{kj}\right) t + \sum_1^n \mu_k\sigma_k \int_0^t dz_k\right]. \quad (35)$$

So, $P_f(t)$ is log-normally distributed.

(3) Let $a(W, t; U) \equiv$ percentage of wealth invested in the first mutual fund by an individual with utility function U and wealth W at time t. Then, $(1 - a)$ must equal the percentage of wealth invested in the second mutual fund. Because the individual is indifferent between these asset holdings or an optimal portfolio chosen from the original n assets, it must be that

$$w_k^* = h_k + m(W, t)\, g_k = a\delta_k + (1 - a)\,\lambda_k, \qquad k = 1,\ldots, n. \quad (36)$$

All the solutions to the linear system (36) for all W, t, and U are of the form

$$\begin{aligned} \delta_k &= h_k + \frac{(1-\eta)}{\nu} g_k, \qquad && k = 1,\ldots, n, \\ \lambda_k &= h_k - \frac{\eta}{\nu} g_k, && k = 1,\ldots, n, \\ a &= \nu m(W, t) + \eta, && \nu \neq 0. \end{aligned} \quad (37)$$

Note that

$$\sum_1^n \delta_k = \sum_1^n \left(h_k + \frac{(1-\eta)}{\nu} g_k\right) \equiv 1$$

and

$$\sum_1^n \lambda_k = \sum_1^n \left(h_k - \frac{\eta}{\nu} g_k\right) \equiv 1. \qquad \text{Q.E.D.}$$

For the case when one of the assets is "risk-free," there is a corollary to Theorem II. Namely,

COROLLARY. *If one of the assets is "risk-free," then the proportions of each asset held by the mutual funds are*

$$\delta_k = \frac{\eta}{\nu} \sum_1^m v_{kj}(\alpha_j - r), \qquad \lambda_k = \frac{(\eta - 1)}{\nu} \sum_1^m v_{kj}(\alpha_j - r),$$

$$\delta_n = 1 - \sum_1^m \delta_k, \qquad \lambda_n = 1 - \sum_1^m \lambda_k.$$

Proof. By the assumption of log-normal prices, (27) reduces to

$$w_k{}^* = m(W, t) \sum_1^m v_{kj}(\alpha_j - r), \qquad k = 1,..., m, \tag{38}$$

and

$$w_n{}^* = 1 - \sum_1^m w_k{}^* = 1 - m(W, t) \sum_1^m \sum_1^m v_{kj}(\alpha_j - r). \tag{39}$$

By the same argument used in the proof of Theorem II, (38) and (39) define a line in the hyperplane defined by $\sum_1^n w_i{}^* = 1$ and by the same technique used in Theorem II, we derive the fund proportions stated in the corollary with $a(W, t; u) = \nu m(W, t) + \eta$, where ν, η are arbitrary constants ($\nu \neq 0$). Q.E.D.

Thus, if we have an economy where all asset prices are log-normally distributed, the investment decision can be divided into two parts by the establishment of two financial intermediaries (mutual funds) to hold all individual securities and to issue shares of their own for purchase by individual investors. The separation is complete because the "instructions" given the fund managers, namely, to hold proportions δ_k and λ_k of the k-th security, $k = 1,..., n$, depend only on the price distribution parameters and are independent of individual preferences, wealth distribution, or age distribution.

The similarity of this result to that of the classical Tobin–Markowitz analysis is clearest when we choose one of the funds to be the risk-free asset (i.e., set $\eta = 1$), and the other fund to hold only risky assets (which is possible by setting $\nu = \sum_1^m \sum_1^m v_{ij}(\alpha_j - r)$, provided that the double sum is not zero). Consider the investment rule given to the "risky" fund's manager when there exists a "risk-free" asset (money) with zero return ($r = 0$). It is easy to show that the δ_k proportions prescribed in the corollary are derived by finding the locus of points in the (instantaneous) mean-standard deviation space of composite returns which minimize variance for a given mean (i.e., the efficient risky-asset frontier), and then by finding the point where a line drawn from the origin is tangent to the locus. This point determines the δ_k as illustrated in Fig. 1.

Given the α^*, the δ_k are determined. So the log-normal assumption in the continuous-time model is sufficient to allow the same analysis as in the static mean-variance model but without the objectionable assumptions of quadratic utility or normality of the distribution of absolute price changes. (Log-normality of price changes is much less objectionable, since this does invoke "limited liability" and, by the central limit theorem

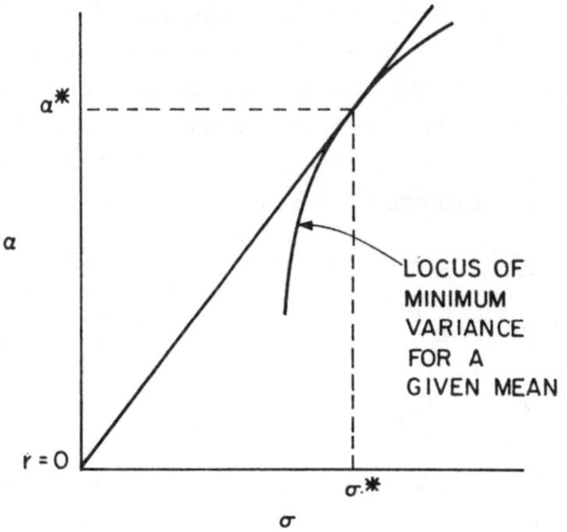

FIG. 1. Determination of the optimal combination of risky assets.

is the only regular solution to any continuous-space, infinitely-divisible process in time.)

An immediate advantage for the present analysis is that whenever log-normality of prices is assumed, we can work, without loss of generality, with just two assets, one "risk-free" and one risky with its price log-normally distributed. The risky asset can always be thought of as a composite asset with price $P(t)$ defined by the process

$$\frac{dP}{P} = \alpha\, dt + \sigma\, dz, \tag{40}$$

where

$$\alpha \equiv \sum_1^m \sum_1^m v_{kj}(\alpha_j - r)\, \alpha_k \Big/ \sum_1^m \sum_1^m v_{ij}(\alpha_j - r),$$

$$\sigma^2 \equiv \sum_1^m \sum_1^m \delta_k \delta_j \sigma_{kj}\,, \tag{41}$$

$$dz \equiv \sum_1^m \delta_k \sigma_k\, dz_k / \sigma.$$

6. Explicit Solutions for a Particular Class of Utility Functions

On the assumption of log-normality of prices, some characteristics of the asset demand functions were shown. If a further assumption about the preferences of the individual is made, then Eq. (28) can be solved in closed form, and the optimal consumption and portfolio rules derived explicitly. Assume that the utility function for the individual, $U(C, t)$, can be written as $U(C, t) = e^{-\rho t}V(C)$, where V is a member of the family of utility functions whose measure of absolute risk aversion is positive and hyperbolic in consumption, i.e.,

$$A(C) \equiv -V''/V' = 1\Big/\left(\frac{C}{1-\gamma} + \eta/\beta\right) > 0,$$

subject to the restrictions:

$$\gamma \neq 1; \quad \beta > 0; \quad \left(\frac{\beta C}{1-\gamma} + \eta\right) > 0; \quad \eta = 1 \text{ if } \gamma = -\infty. \tag{42}$$

All members of the HARA (hyperbolic absolute risk-aversion) family can be expressed as

$$V(C) = \frac{(1-\gamma)}{\gamma}\left(\frac{\beta C}{1-\gamma} + \eta\right)^{\gamma}. \tag{43}$$

This family is rich, in the sense that by suitable adjustment of the parameters, one can have a utility function with absolute or relative risk aversion increasing, decreasing, or constant.[19]

[19]

TABLE I

Properties of HARA Utility Functions

$A(C) = \dfrac{1}{\dfrac{C}{1-\gamma} + \dfrac{\eta}{\beta}} > 0$	(implies $\eta > 0$ for $\gamma > 1$)
$A'(C) = \dfrac{-1}{(1-\gamma)\left(\dfrac{C}{1-\gamma} + \dfrac{\eta}{\beta}\right)^2}$	< 0 for $-\infty < \gamma < 1$ > 0 for $1 < \gamma < \infty$ $= 0$ for $\gamma = +\infty$
Relative risk aversion $R(C) \equiv -V''C/V' = A(C)C$	
$R'(C) = \dfrac{\eta/\beta}{\left(\dfrac{C}{1-\gamma} + \dfrac{\eta}{\beta}\right)^2}$	> 0 for $\eta > 0$ $(-\infty \leqslant \gamma \leqslant \infty, \gamma \neq 1)$ $= 0$ for $\eta = 0$ < 0 for $\eta < 0$ $(-\infty < \gamma < 1)$

Note that included as members of the HARA family are the widely used isoelastic (constant relative risk aversion), exponential (constant absolute risk aversion), and quadratic utility functions. As is well known for the quadratic case, the members of the HARA family with $\gamma > 1$ are only defined for a restricted range of consumption, namely $0 < C < (\gamma - 1)\eta/\beta$. [1, 5, 6, 10, 12, 13, 16] discuss the properties of various members of the HARA family in a portfolio context. Although this is not done here, the HARA definition can be generalized to include the cases when γ, β, and η are functions of time subject to the restrictions in (42).

Without loss of generality, assume that there are two assets, one "risk-free" asset with return r and the other, a "risky" asset whose price is log-normally distributed satisfying (40). From (28), the optimality equation for J is

$$0 = \frac{(1-\gamma)^2}{\gamma} e^{-\rho t} \left[\frac{e^{\rho t} J_W}{\beta}\right]^{\frac{\gamma}{\gamma-1}} + J_t + [(1-\gamma)\,\eta/\beta + rW]\,J_W - \frac{J_W^2}{J_{WW}} \frac{(\alpha - r)^2}{\alpha\sigma^2}. \tag{44}$$

subject to $J(W, T) = 0$.[20] The equations for the optimal consumption and portfolio rules are

$$C^*(t) = \frac{(1-\gamma)}{\beta}\left[\frac{e^{\rho t} J_W}{\beta}\right]^{\frac{1}{\gamma-1}} - \frac{(1-\gamma)\,\eta}{\beta} \tag{45}$$

and

$$w^*(t) = -\frac{J_W}{J_{WW} W} \frac{(\alpha - r)}{\sigma^2}, \tag{46}$$

where $w^*(t)$ is the optimal proportion of wealth invested in the risky asset at time t. A solution[21] to (44) is

$$J(W, t) = \delta\beta^{+\gamma} e^{-\rho t}\left[\frac{\delta(1 - e^{-\left(\frac{\rho-\gamma\nu}{\delta}\right)(T-t)})}{\rho - \gamma\nu}\right]^{\delta}\left[\frac{W}{\delta} + \frac{\eta}{\beta r}(1 - e^{-r(T-t)})\right]^{\gamma}, \tag{47}$$

where $\delta \equiv 1 - \gamma$ and $\nu \equiv r + (\alpha - r)^2/2\delta\sigma^2$.

From (45)–(47), the optimal consumption and portfolio rules can be written in explicit form as

$$C^*(t) = \frac{[\rho - \gamma\nu]\left[W(t) + \frac{\delta\eta}{\beta r}(1 - e^{r(t-T)})\right]}{\delta\left(1 - \exp\left[\frac{(\rho - \gamma\nu)}{\delta}(t - T)\right]\right)} - \frac{\delta\eta}{\beta} \tag{48}$$

and

$$w^*(t)\,W(t) = \frac{(\alpha - r)}{\delta\sigma^2} W(t) + \frac{\eta(\alpha - r)}{\beta r\sigma^2}(1 - e^{r(t-T)}). \tag{49}$$

[20] It is assumed for simplicity that the individual has a zero bequest function, i.e., $B \equiv 0$. If $B(W, T) = H(T)(aW + b)^{\gamma}$, the basic functional form for J in (47) will be the same. Otherwise, systematic effects of age will be involved in the solution.

[21] By Theorem I, there is no need to be concerned with uniqueness although, in this case, the solution is unique.

The manifest characteristic of (48) and (49) is that the demand functions are linear in wealth. It will be shown that the HARA family is the only class of concave utility functions which imply linear solutions. For notation purposes, define $I(X, t) \subset \text{HARA}(X)$ if $-I_{XX}/I_X = 1/(\alpha X + \beta) > 0$, where α and β are, at most, functions of time and I is a strictly concave function of X.

THEOREM III. *Given the model specified in this section, then* $C^* = aW + b$ *and* $w^*W = gW + h$ *where a, b, g, and h are, at most, functions of time if and only if* $U(C, t) \subset \text{HARA}(C)$.

Proof. "If" part is proved directly by (48) and (49). "Only if" part: Suppose $w^*W = gW + h$ and $C^* = aW + b$. From (19), we have that $U_C(C^*, t) = J_W(W, t)$. Differentiating this expression totally with respect to W, we have that $U_{CC}\, dC^*/dW = J_{WW}$ or $aU_{CC} = J_{WW}$ and hence

$$\frac{-U_{CC}a}{U_C} = \frac{-J_{WW}}{J_W}. \tag{50}$$

From (46), $w^*W = gW + h = -J_W(\alpha - r)/J_{WW}\sigma^2$ or

$$-J_{WW}/J_W = 1\Big/\Big[\Big(\frac{\sigma^2 g}{(\alpha - r)}\Big) W + \frac{\sigma^2 h}{(\alpha - r)}\Big]. \tag{51}$$

So, from (50) and (51), we have that U must satisfy

$$-U_{CC}/U_C = 1/(a'C^* + b'), \tag{52}$$

where $a' \equiv \sigma^2 g/(\alpha - r)$ and $b' \equiv (a\sigma^2 h - b\sigma^2 g)/(\alpha - r)$. Hence $U \subset \text{HARA}(C)$. Q.E.D.

As an immediate result of Theorem III, a second theorem can be proved.

THEOREM IV. *Given the model specified in this section,* $J(W, t) \subset \text{HARA}(W)$ *if and only if* $U \subset \text{HARA}(C)$.

Proof. "If" part is proved directly by (47). "Only if" part: suppose $J(W, t) \subset \text{HARA}(W)$. Then, from (46), w^*W is a linear function of W. If (28) is differentiated totally with respect to wealth and given the specific price behavior assumptions of this section, we have that C^* must satisfy

$$C^* = rW + \frac{J_{tW}}{J_{WW}} + \frac{rJ_W}{J_{WW}} - w^*W\frac{d(w^*W)}{dW} - \frac{J_{WWW}}{2J_{WW}}\Big(\frac{J_W}{J_{WW}}\Big)^2 \frac{(\alpha - r)^2}{\sigma^2}. \tag{53}$$

But if $J \subset \mathrm{HARA}(W)$, then (53) implies that C^* is linear in wealth. Hence, by Theorem III, $U \subset \mathrm{HARA}(C)$. Q.E.D.

Given (48) and (49), the stochastic process which generates wealth when the optimal rules are applied, can be derived. From the budget equation (14′), we have that

$$\begin{aligned} dW &= [(w^*(\alpha - r) + r)\, W - C^*]\, dt + \sigma w^* W\, dz \\ &= \left\{\left[\frac{(\alpha - r)^2}{\sigma^2 \delta} - \frac{\mu}{1 - e^{\mu(t-T)}}\right] dt + \frac{(\alpha - r)}{\sigma\delta}\, dz\right\} X(t) \\ &\quad + r\left[W + \frac{\delta\eta}{\beta r}\right] dt, \end{aligned} \tag{54}$$

where $X(t) \equiv W(t) + \delta\eta/\beta r(1 - e^{r(t-T)})$ for $0 \leqslant t \leqslant T$ and $\mu \equiv (\rho - \gamma\nu)/\delta$. By Itô's Lemma, $X(t)$ is the solution to

$$\frac{dX}{X} = \left[\delta - \frac{\mu}{(1 - e^{\mu(t-T)})}\right] dt + \frac{(\alpha - r)}{\sigma\delta}\, dz. \tag{55}$$

Again using Itô's Lemma, integrating (55) we have that

$$\begin{aligned} X(t) = X(0) \exp &\left\{\left[\delta - \mu - \frac{(\alpha - r)^2}{2\sigma^2\delta^2}\right] t + \frac{(\alpha - r)}{\sigma\delta} \int_0^t dz\right\} \\ &\times (1 - e^{\mu(t-T)})/(1 - e^{-\mu T}) \end{aligned} \tag{56}$$

and, hence, $X(t)$ is log-normally distributed. Therefore,

$$W(t) = X(t) - \frac{\delta\eta}{\beta r}(1 - e^{r(t-T)})$$

is a "displaced" or "three-parameter" log-normally distributed random variable. By Itô's Lemma, solution (56) to (55) holds with probability one and because $W(t)$ is a continuous process, we have with probability one that

$$\lim_{t \to T} W(t) = 0. \tag{57}$$

From (48), with probability one,

$$\lim_{t \to T} C^*(t) = 0. \tag{58}$$

Further, from (48), $C^* + \delta\eta/\beta$ is proportional to $X(t)$ and from the definition of $U(C^*, t)$, $U(C^*, t)$ is a log-normally distributed random variable.[22] The following theorem shows that this result holds only if $U(C, t) \subset \text{HARA}(C)$.

THEOREM V. *Given the model specified in this section and the time-dependent random variable* $Y(t) \equiv U(C^*, t)$, *then* Y *is log-normally distributed if and only if* $U(C, t) \subset \text{HARA}(C)$.

Proof. "If" part: it was previously shown that if $U \subset \text{HARA}(C)$, then Y is log-normally distributed. "Only if" part: let $C^* \equiv g(W, t)$ and $w^*W \equiv f(W, t)$. By Itô's Lemma,

$$\begin{aligned} dY &= U_C\, dC^* + U_t\, dt + \tfrac{1}{2}U_{CC}(dC^*)^2, \\ dC^* &= g_W\, dW + g_t\, dt + \tfrac{1}{2}g_{WW}(dW)^2, \\ dW &= [f(\alpha - r) + rW - g]\, dt + \sigma f\, dz. \end{aligned} \tag{59}$$

Because $(dW)^2 = \sigma^2 f^2\, dt$, we have that

$$dC^* = [g_W f(\alpha - r) + g_W rW - gg_W + \tfrac{1}{2}g_{WW}\sigma^2 f^2 + g_t]\, dt + \sigma f g_W\, dz \tag{60}$$

and

$$\begin{aligned} dY = \{&U_C[g_W f(\alpha - r) + rg_W W - gg_W + \tfrac{1}{2}g_{WW}\sigma^2 f^2 + g_t] + U_t \\ &+ \tfrac{1}{2}U_{CC}\sigma^2 f^2 g_W^2\}\, dt + \sigma f g_W U_C\, dz. \end{aligned} \tag{61}$$

A necessary condition for Y to be log-normal is that Y satisfy

$$\frac{dY}{Y} = F(Y)\, dt + b\, dz, \tag{62}$$

where b is, at most, a function of time. If Y is log-normal, from (61) and (62), we have that

$$b(t) = \sigma f g_W U_C / U. \tag{63}$$

From the first-order conditions, f and g must satisfy

$$U_{CC} g_W = J_{WW}, \qquad f = -J_W(\alpha - r)/\sigma^2 J_{WW}. \tag{64}$$

22 $$U = \frac{(1-\gamma)}{\gamma} e^{-\rho t} \left[\frac{\beta C}{1-\gamma} + \eta\right]^{\gamma}$$

and products and powers of log-normal variates are log normal with one exception: the logarithmic utility function ($\gamma = 0$) is a singular case where $U(C^*, t) = \log C^*$ is normally distributed.

But (63) and (64) imply that

$$bU/\sigma U_C = fg_W = 1 - (\alpha - r)\, U_C/\sigma^2 U_{CC} \tag{65}$$

or

$$-U_{CC}/U_C = \eta(t)\, U_C/U, \tag{66}$$

where $\eta(t) \equiv (\alpha - r)/\sigma b(t)$. Integrating (66), we have that

$$U = [(\eta + 1)(C + \mu)\, \zeta(t)]^{\frac{1}{\eta+1}}, \tag{67}$$

where $\zeta(t)$ and μ are, at most, functions of time and, hence, $U \subset \text{HARA}(C)$.
Q.E.D.

For the case when asset prices satisfy the "geometric" Brownian motion hypothesis and the individual's utility function is a member of the HARA family, the consumption-portfolio problem is completely solved. From (48) and (49), one could examine the effects of shifts in various parameters on the consumption and portfolio rules by the methods of comparative statics as was done for the isoelastic case in [12].

7. Noncapital Gains Income: Wages

In the previous sections, it was assumed that all income was generated by capital gains. If a (certain) wage income flow, $dy = Y(t)\, dt$, is introduced, the optimality equation (18) becomes

$$0 = \max_{\{C, w\}}[U(C, t) + \mathscr{P}(J)], \tag{68}$$

where the operator $\mathscr{P}$ is defined by $\mathscr{P} \equiv \mathscr{L} + Y(t)\, \partial/\partial W$. This new complication causes no particular computational difficulties. If a new control variable, $\tilde{C}(t)$, and new utility function, $V(\tilde{C}, t)$ are defined by $\tilde{C}(t) \equiv C(t) - Y(t)$ and $V(\tilde{C}, t) \equiv U(\tilde{C}(t) + Y(t), t)$, then (68) can be rewritten as

$$0 = \max_{\{\tilde{C}, w\}}[V(\tilde{C}, t) + \mathscr{L}[J]], \tag{69}$$

which is the same equation as the optimality equation (18) when there is no wage income and where consumption has been re-defined as consumption in excess of wage income.

In particular, if $Y(t) \equiv Y$, a constant, and $U \subset \text{HARA}(C)$, then the optimal consumption and portfolio rules corresponding to (48) and (49) are

$$C^*(t) = \frac{[\rho - \gamma\nu]\left[W + \frac{Y(1 - e^{r(t-T)})}{r} + \frac{\delta\eta}{\beta r}(1 - e^{r(t-T)})\right]}{\delta(1 - \exp[(\rho - \gamma\nu)(t - T)/\delta])} - \frac{\delta\eta}{\beta} \tag{70}$$

and

$$w^*W = \frac{(\alpha - r)}{\delta\sigma^2}\left(W + \frac{Y(1 - e^{r(t-T)})}{r}\right) + \frac{(\alpha - r)\,\eta}{\beta r\sigma^2}(1 - e^{r(t-T)}). \tag{71}$$

Comparing (70) and (71) with (48) and (49), one finds that, in computing the optimal decision rules, the individual capitalizes the lifetime flow of wage income at the market (risk-free) rate of interest and then treats the capitalized value as an addition to the current stock of wealth.[23]

The introduction of a stochastic wage income will cause increased computational difficulties although the basic analysis is the same as for the no-wage income case. For a solution to a particular example of a stochastic wage problem, see example two of Section 8.

8. Poisson Processes

The previous analyses always assumed that the underlying stochastic processes were smooth functions of Brownian motions and, therefore, continuous in both the time and state spaces. Although such processes are reasonable models for price behavior of many types of liquid assets, they are rather poor models for the description of other types. The Poisson process is a continuous-time process which allows discrete (or discontinuous) changes in the variables. The simplest independent Poisson process defines the probability of an event occuring during a time interval of length h (where h is as small as you like) as follows:

$$\begin{aligned} &\text{prob}\{\text{the event does not occur in the time interval } (t, t+h)\} \\ &\qquad = 1 - \lambda h + O(h), \\ &\text{prob}\{\text{the event occurs once in the time interval } (t, t+h)\} \\ &\qquad = \lambda h + O(h), \\ &\text{prob}\{\text{the event occurs more than once in the time interval} \\ &\qquad (t, t+h)\} = O(h), \end{aligned} \tag{72}$$

[23] As Hakansson [6] has pointed out, (70) and (71) are consistent with the Friedman Permanent Income and the Modigliani Life-Cycle hypotheses. However, in general, this result will not hold.

where $O(h)$ is the asymptotic order symbol defined by

$$\psi(h) \text{ is } O(h) \qquad \text{if } \lim_{h\to 0}(\psi(h)/h) = 0 \tag{73}$$

and $\lambda =$ the mean number of occurrences per unit time.

Given the Poisson process, the "event" can be defined in a number of interesting ways. To illustrate the degree of latitude, three examples of applications of Poisson processes in the consumption-portfolio choice problem are presented below. Before examining these examples, it is first necessary to develop some of the mathematical properties of Poisson processes. There is a theory of stochastic differential equations for Poisson processes similar to the one for Brownian motion discussed in Section 2. Let $q(t)$ be an independent Poisson process with probability structure as described in (72). Let the event be that a state variable $x(t)$ has a jump in amplitude of size $\mathscr{S}$ where $\mathscr{S}$ is a random variable whose probability measure has compact support. Then, a Poisson differential equation for $x(t)$ can be written as

$$dx = f(x, t)\,dt + g(x, t)\,dq \tag{74}$$

and the corresponding differential generator, $\mathscr{L}_x$, is defined by

$$\mathscr{L}_x[h(x, t)] \equiv h_t + f(x, t)\,h_x + E_t\{\lambda[h(x + \mathscr{S}g, t) - h(x, t)]\}, \tag{75}$$

where "E_t" is the conditional expectation over the random variable $\mathscr{S}$, conditional on knowing $x(t) = x$, and where $h(x, t)$ is a C^1 function of x and t.[24] Further, Theorem I holds for Poisson processes.[25]

Returning to the consumption-portfolio problem, consider first the two-asset case. Assume that one asset is a common stock whose price is log-normally distributed and that the other asset is a "risky" bond which pays an instantaneous rate of interest r when not in default but, in the event of default, the price of the bond becomes zero.[26]

From (74), the process which generates the bond's price can be written as

$$dP = rP\,dt - P\,dq, \tag{76}$$

[24] For a short discussion of Poisson differential equations and a proof of (75) as well as other references, see Kushner [9, pp. 18–22].

[25] See Dreyfus [4, p. 225] and Kushner [9, Chap. IV].

[26] That the price of the bond is zero in the event of default is an extreme assumption made only to illustrate how a default can be treated in the analysis. One could made the more reasonable assumption that the price in the event of default is a random variable. The degree of computational difficulty caused by this more reasonable assumption will depend on the choice of distribution for the random variable as well as the utility function of the individual.

where dq is as previously defined and $\mathscr{S} \equiv 1$ with probability one. Substituting the explicit price dynamics into (14′), the budget equation becomes

$$dW = \{wW(\alpha - r) + rW - C\}\, dt + w\sigma W\, dz - (1 - w)\, W\, dq. \quad (77)$$

From (75), (77), and Theorem I, we have that the optimality equation can be written as

$$\begin{aligned} 0 = {} & U(C^*, t) + J_t(W, t) + \lambda[J(w^* W, t) - J(W, t)] \\ & + J_W(W, t)[(w^*(\alpha - r) + r)\, W - C^*] + \tfrac{1}{2} J_{WW}(W, t)\, \sigma^2 w^{*2} W^2, \quad (78) \end{aligned}$$

where C^* and w^* are determined by the implicit equations

$$0 = U_C(C^*, t) - J_W(W, t) \quad (79)$$

and

$$0 = \lambda J_W(w^* W, t) + J_W(W, t)(\alpha - r) + J_{WW}(W, t)\, \sigma^2 w^* W. \quad (80)$$

To see the effect of default on the portfolio and consumption decisions, consider the particular case when $U(C, t) \equiv C^\gamma/\gamma$, for $\gamma < 1$. The solutions to (79) and (80) are

$$C^*(t) = AW(t)/(1 - \gamma)(1 - \exp[A(t - T)/1 - \gamma]), \quad (79')$$

where

$$A \equiv -\gamma \left[\frac{(\alpha - r)^2}{2\sigma^2(1 - \gamma)} + r\right] + \lambda \left[1 - \frac{(2 - \gamma)}{\gamma}\, w^{*\gamma} - \frac{\gamma(\alpha - r)}{2\sigma^2(1 - \gamma)}\, w^{*\gamma - 1}\right]$$

and

$$w^* = \frac{(\alpha - r)}{\sigma^2(1 - \gamma)} + \frac{\lambda}{\sigma^2(1 - \gamma)}\, (w^*)^{\gamma - 1}. \quad (80')$$ [27]

As might be expected, the demand for the common stock is an increasing function of λ and, for $\lambda > 0$, $w^* > 0$ holds for all values of α, r, or σ^2.

For the second example, consider an individual who receives a wage, $Y(t)$, which is incremented by a constant amount ϵ at random points in time. Suppose that the event of a wage increase is a Poisson process with parameter λ. Then, the dynamics of the wage-rate state variable are described by

$$dY = \epsilon\, dq, \qquad \text{with } \mathscr{S} \equiv 1 \text{ with probability one.} \quad (81)$$

[27] Note that (79′) and (80′) with $\lambda = 0$ reduce to the solutions (48) and (49) when $\eta = \rho = 0$ and $\beta = 1 - \gamma$.

Suppose further that the individual's utility function is of the form $U(C, t) \equiv e^{-\rho t}V(C)$ and that his time horizon is infinite (i.e., $T = \infty$).[28] Then, for the two-asset case of Section 6, the optimality equation can be written as

$$\begin{aligned} 0 = {} & V(C^*) - \rho I(W, Y) + \lambda[I(W, Y + \epsilon) - I(W, Y)] \\ & + I_W(W, Y)[(w^*(\alpha - r) + r) W + Y - C^*] \\ & + \tfrac{1}{2} I_{WW}(W, Y)\, \sigma^2 w^{*2} W^2, \end{aligned} \tag{83}$$

where $I(W,Y) \equiv e^{\rho t}J(W, Y, t)$. If it is further assumed that $V(C) = -e^{-\eta C}/\eta$, then the optimal consumption and portfolio rules, derived from (83), are

$$C^*(t) = r\left[W(t) + \frac{Y(t)}{r} + \frac{\lambda}{r^2}\left(\frac{1 - e^{-\eta\epsilon}}{\eta}\right)\right] + \frac{1}{\eta r}\left[\rho - r + \frac{(\alpha - r)^2}{2\sigma^2}\right] \tag{84}$$

and

$$w^*(t)\, W(t) = \frac{(\alpha - r)}{\eta \sigma^2 r}. \tag{85}$$

In (84), $[W(t) + Y(t)/r + \lambda(1 - e^{-\eta\epsilon})/\eta r^2]$ is the general wealth term, equal to the sum of present wealth and capitalized future wage earnings. If $\lambda = 0$, then (84) reduces to (70) in Section 7, where the wage rate was fixed and known with certainty. When $\lambda > 0$, $\lambda(1 - e^{-\eta\epsilon})/\eta r^2$ is the capitalized value of (expected) future increments to the wage rate, *capitalized at a somewhat higher rate than the risk-free market rate reflecting the risk-aversion of the individual.*[29] Let $X(t)$ be the "Certainty-equivalent wage rate at time t" defined as the solution to

$$U[X(t)] = E_0 U[Y(t)]. \tag{86}$$

[28] I have shown elsewhere [12, p. 252] that if $U = e^{-\rho t}V(C)$ and U is bounded or ρ sufficiently large to ensure convergence of the integral and if the underlying stochastic processes are stationary, then the optimality equation (18) can be written, independent of explicit time, as

$$0 = \max_{\{C,w\}} [V(C) + \bar{\mathscr{L}}[I]], \tag{82}$$

where $\bar{\mathscr{L}} \equiv \mathscr{L} - \rho - \dfrac{\partial}{\partial t}$ and $I(W, P) \equiv e^{\rho t}J(W, P, t)$.

A solution to (82) is called the "stationary" solution to the consumption-portfolio problem. Because the time state variable is eliminated, solutions to (82) are computationally easier to find than for the finite-horizon case.

[29] The usual expected present discounted value of the increments to the wage flow is

$$E_t \int_t^\infty e^{-r(s-t)} [Y(s) - Y(t)]\, ds = \int_t^\infty \lambda\epsilon\, e^{-r(s-t)}(s - t)\, ds = \lambda\epsilon/r^2,$$

which is greater than $\lambda(1 - e^{-\eta\epsilon})/\eta r^2$ for $\epsilon > 0$.

For this example, $X(t)$ is calculated as follows:

$$\begin{aligned} -\frac{e^{-\eta X(t)}}{\eta} &= -\frac{1}{\eta} E_0 e^{-\eta Y(t)} \\ &= -\frac{1}{\eta} e^{-\eta Y(0)} \sum_{k=0}^{\infty} \frac{(\lambda t)^k}{k!} e^{-\lambda t} e^{-\eta k \epsilon} \\ &= -\frac{1}{\eta} e^{-\eta Y(0) - \lambda t + \lambda e^{-\eta \epsilon} t}. \end{aligned} \tag{87}$$

Solving for $X(t)$ from (87), we have that

$$X(t) = Y(0) + \lambda t(1 - e^{-\eta\epsilon})/\eta. \tag{88}$$

The capitalized value of the Certainty-equivalent wage income flow is

$$\begin{aligned} \int_0^\infty e^{-rs} X(s)\, ds &= \int_0^\infty Y(0)\, e^{-rs}\, ds + \int_0^\infty \frac{\lambda(1 - e^{-\eta\epsilon})}{\eta} s e^{-rs}\, ds \\ &= \frac{Y(0)}{r} + \frac{\lambda(1 - e^{-\eta\epsilon})}{\eta r^2}. \end{aligned} \tag{89}$$

Thus, for this example,[30] the individual, in computing the present value of future earnings, determines the Certainty-equivalent flow and then capitalizes this flow at the (certain) market rate of interest.

The third example of a Poisson process differs from the first two because the occurrence of the event does not involve an explicit change in a state variable. Consider an individual whose age of death is a random variable. Further assume that the event of death at each instant of time is an independent Poisson process with parameter λ. Then, the age of death, τ, is the first time that the event (of death) occurs and is an exponentially distributed random variable with parameter λ. The optimality criterion is to

$$\max E_0 \left\{ \int_0^\tau U(C, t)\, dt + B(W(\tau), \tau) \right\} \tag{90}$$

and the associated optimality equation is

$$0 = U(C^*, t) + \lambda[B(W, t) - J(W, t)] + \mathscr{L}[J]. \tag{91}$$

[30] The reader should not infer that this result holds in general. Although (86) is a common definition of Certainty-equivalent in one-period utility-of-wealth models, it is not satisfactory for dynamic consumption-portfolio models. The reason it works for this example is due to the particular relationship between the J and U functions when U is exponential.

To derive (91), an "artificial" state variable, $x(t)$, is constructed with $x(t) = 0$ while the individual is alive and $x(t) = 1$ in the event of death. Therefore, the stochastic process which generates x is defined by

$$dx = dq \quad \text{and} \quad \mathscr{S} \equiv 1 \text{ with probability one} \tag{92}$$

and τ is now defined by x as

$$\tau = \min\{t \mid t > 0 \text{ and } x(t) = 1\}. \tag{93}$$

The derived utility function, J, can be considered a function of the state variables W, x, and t subject to the boundary condition

$$J(W, x, t) = B(W, t) \quad \text{when} \quad x = 1. \tag{94}$$

In this form, example three is shown to be of the same type as examples one and two in that the occurrence of the Poisson event causes a state variable to be incremented, and (91) is of the same form as (78) and (83).

A comparison of (91) for the particular case when $B \equiv 0$ (no bequests) with (82) suggested the following theorem.[31]

THEOREM VI. *If τ is as defined in* (93) *and U is such that the integral $E_0[\int_0^\tau U(C, t)\, dt]$ is absolutely convergent, then the maximization of $E_0[\int_0^\tau U(C, t)\, dt]$ is equivalent to the maximization of $\mathscr{E}_0[\int_0^\infty e^{-\lambda t} U(C, t)\, dt]$ where "E_0" is the conditional expectation operator over all random variables including τ and "$\mathscr{E}_0$" is the conditional expectation operator over all random variables excluding τ.*

Proof. τ is distributed exponentially and is independent of the other random variables in the problem. Hence, we have that

$$\begin{aligned} E_0\left[\int_0^\tau U(C, t)\, dt\right] &= \int_0^\infty \lambda e^{-\lambda\tau}\, d\tau\, \mathscr{E}_0 \int_0^\tau U(C, t)\, dt \\ &= \int_0^\infty \int_0^\tau \lambda g(t)\, e^{-\lambda\tau}\, dt\, d\tau, \end{aligned} \tag{95}$$

where $g(t) \equiv \mathscr{E}_0[U(C, t)]$. Because the integral in (95) is absolutely con-

[31] I believe that a similar theorem has been proved by J. A. Mirrlees, but I have no reference. D. Cass and M. E. Yaari, in "Individual Saving, Aggregate Capital Accumulation, and Efficient Growth," in "Essays on the Theory of Optimal Economic Growth," ed., K. Shell, (M.I.T. Press 1967), prove a similar theorem on page 262.

vergent, the order of integration can be interchanged, i.e., $\mathscr{E}_0 \int_0^\tau U(C,t)\,dt = \int_0^\tau \mathscr{E}_0 U(C,t)\,dt$. By integration by parts, (95) can be rewritten as

$$\int_0^\infty \int_0^\tau e^{-\lambda\tau} g(t)\,dt\,d\tau = \int_0^\infty e^{-\lambda s} g(s)\,ds$$
$$= \mathscr{E}_0 \int_0^\infty e^{-\lambda t} U(C,t)\,dt. \qquad \text{Q.E.D.} \tag{96}$$

Thus, an individual who faces an exponentially-distributed uncertain age of death acts as if he will live forever, but with a subjective rate of time preference equal to his "force of mortality," i.e., to the reciprocal of his life expectancy.

9. Alternative Price Expectations to the Geometric Brownian Motion

The assumption of the geometric Brownian motion hypothesis is a rich one because it is a reasonably good model of observed stock price behavior and it allows the proof of a number of strong theorems about the optimal consumption-portfolio rules, as was illustrated in the previous sections. However, as mentioned in the Introduction, there have been some disagreements with the underlying assumptions required to accept this hypothesis. The geometric Brownian motion hypothesis best describes a stationary equilibrium economy where expectations about future returns have settled down, and as such, really describes a "long-run" equilibrium model for asset prices. Therefore, to explain "short-run" consumption and portfolio selection behavior one must introduce alternative models of price behavior which reflect the dynamic adjustment of expectations.

In this section, alternative price behavior mechanisms are postulated which attempt to capture in a simple fashion the effects of changing expectations, and then comparisons are made between the optimal decision rules derived under these mechanisms with the ones derived in the previous sections. The choices of mechanisms are not exhaustive nor are they necessarily representative of observed asset price behavior. Rather they have been chosen as representative examples of price adjustment mechanisms commonly used in economic and financial models.

Little can be said in general about the form of a solution to (28) when α_k and σ_k depend in an arbitrary manner on the price levels. If it is specified that the utility function is a member of the HARA family, i.e.,

$$U(C,t) = \frac{(1-\gamma)}{\gamma} F(t) \left(\frac{\beta C}{1-\gamma} + \eta\right)^\gamma \tag{97}$$

subject to the restrictions in (42), then (28) can be simplified because $J(W, P, t)$ is separable into a product of functions, one depending on W and t, and the other on P and t.[32] In particular, if we take $J(W, P, t)$ to be of the form

$$J(W, P, t) = \frac{(1-\gamma)}{\gamma} H(P, t) F(t) \left(\frac{W}{1-\gamma} + \frac{\eta}{\beta r}[1 - e^{r(t-T)}]\right)^{\gamma}, \quad (98)$$

substitute for J in (28), and divide out the common factor

$$F(t) \left(\frac{W}{1-\gamma} + \frac{\eta}{\beta r}\left[1 - e^{r(t-T)}\right]\right)^{\gamma},$$

then we derive a "reduced" equation for H,

$$\begin{aligned} 0 = {} & \frac{(1-\gamma)^2}{\gamma}\left(\frac{H}{\beta}\right)^{\frac{\gamma}{\gamma-1}} + \frac{(1-\gamma)}{\gamma}\left(\frac{\dot{F}}{F} + H_t\right) + (1-\gamma) rH \\ & + \frac{(1-\gamma)}{\gamma}\sum_1^m \alpha_i P_i H_i + \frac{(1-\gamma)}{2\gamma}\sum_1^m\sum_1^m \sigma_{ij} P_i P_j H_{ij} \\ & + \sum_1^m (\alpha_i - r) P_i H_i + \frac{H}{2}\sum_1^m\sum_1^m v_{ij}(\alpha_i - r)(\alpha_j - r) \\ & + \frac{1}{2H}\sum_1^m\sum_1^m \sigma_{ij} P_i P_j H_i H_j \end{aligned} \quad (99)$$

and the associated optimal consumption and portfolio rules are

$$C^*(t) = \frac{(1-\gamma)}{\beta}\left[\left(\frac{H}{\beta}\right)^{\frac{1}{\gamma-1}}\left(\frac{W}{1-\gamma} + \frac{\eta}{\beta r}[1 - e^{r(t-T)}]\right) - \eta\right] \quad (100)$$

and

$$w_k^*(t)\, W = \left[\sum_1^m v_{jk}(\alpha_j - r) + \frac{H_k P_k}{H}\right]\left(\frac{W}{1-\gamma} + \frac{\eta}{\beta r}[1 - e^{r(t-T)}]\right), \quad (101)$$

$$k = 1, \ldots, m.$$

Although (99) is still a formidable equation from a computational point of view, it is less complex than the general equation (28), and it is possible

[32] This separability property was noted in [1, 5, 6, 10, 12, and 13]. It is assumed throughout this section that the bequest function satisfies the conditions of footnote 20.

to obtain an explicit solution for particular assumptions about the dependence of α_k and σ_k on the prices. Notice that both consumption and the asset demands are linear functions of wealth.

For a particular member of the HARA family, namely the Bernoulli logarithmic utility ($\gamma = 0 = \eta$ and $\beta = 1 - \gamma = 1$) function, (28) can be solved in general. In this case, J will be of the form

$$J(W, P, t) = a(t) \log W + H(P, t) \quad \text{with} \quad H(P, T) = a(T) = 0, \tag{102}$$

with $a(t)$ independent of the α_k and σ_k (and hence, the P_k). For the case when $F(t) \equiv 1$, we find $a(t) = T - t$ and the optimal rules become

$$C^* = \frac{W}{T - t} \tag{103}$$

and

$$w_k^* = \sum_1^m v_{kj}(\alpha_j - r), \qquad k = 1,\dots, m. \tag{104}$$

For the log case, the optimal rules are identical to those derived when α_k and σ_k were constants, with the understanding that the α_k and σ_k are evaluated at current prices. Hence, although we can solve this case for general price mechanisms, it is not an interesting one because different assumptions about price behavior have no effect on the decision rules.

The first of the alternative price mechanisms considered is called the "asymptotic 'normal' price-level" hypothesis which assumes that there exists a "normal" price function, $\bar{P}(t)$, such that

$$\lim_{t\to\infty} E_T[P(t)/\bar{P}(t)] = 1, \qquad \text{for} \quad 0 \leqslant T < t < \infty, \tag{105}$$

i.e., independent of the current level of the asset price, the investor expects the "long-run" price to approach the normal price. A particular example which satisfies the hypothesis is that

$$\bar{P}(t) = \bar{P}(0)\, e^{\nu t} \tag{106}$$

and

$$\frac{dP}{P} = \beta[\phi + \nu t - \log(P(t)/P(0))]\, dt + \sigma\, dz, \tag{107}$$

where $\phi \equiv k + \nu/\beta + \sigma^2/4\beta$ and $k \equiv \log[\bar{P}(0)/P(0)]$.[33] For the purpose of analysis, it is more convenient to work with the variable

[33] In the notation used in previous sections, (107) corresponds to (5) with $\alpha(P, t) \equiv \beta[\phi + \nu t - \log(P(t)/P(0))]$. Note: "normal" does not mean "Gaussian" in the above use, but rather the normal long-run price of Alfred Marshall.

$Y(t) \equiv \log[P(t)/P(0)]$ rather than $P(t)$. Substituting for P in (107) by using Itô's Lemma, we can write the dynamics for Y as

$$dY = \beta[\mu + \nu t - Y]\, dt + \sigma\, dz, \tag{108}$$

where $\mu \equiv \phi - \sigma^2/2\beta$. Before examining the effects of this price mechanism on the optimal portfolio decisions, it is useful to investigate the price behavior implied by (106) and (107). (107) implies an exponentially-regressive price adjustment toward a normal price, adjusted for trend. By inspection of (108), Y is a normally-distributed random variable generated by a Markov process which is not stationary and does not have independent increments.[34] Therefore, from the definition of Y, $P(t)$ is log-normal and Markov. Using Itô's Lemma, one can solve (108) for $Y(t)$, conditional on knowing $Y(T)$, as

$$Y(t) - Y(T) = \left(k + \nu T - \frac{\sigma^2}{4\beta} - Y(T)\right)(1 - e^{-\beta\tau}) + \nu\tau + \sigma e^{-\beta t} \int_T^t e^{\beta s}\, dz, \tag{109}$$

where $\tau \equiv t - T > 0$. The instantaneous conditional variance of $Y(t)$ is

$$\operatorname{var}[Y(t) \mid Y(T)] = \frac{\sigma^2}{2\beta}(1 - e^{-2\beta\tau}). \tag{110}$$

Given the characteristics of $Y(t)$, it is straightforward to derive the price behavior. For example, the conditional expected price can be derived from (110) and written as

$$\begin{aligned} &E_T(P(t)/P(T)) \\ &\quad = E_T \exp[Y(t) - Y(T)] \\ &\quad = \exp\left[\left(k + \nu T - \frac{\sigma^2}{4\beta} - Y(T)\right)(1 - e^{-\beta\tau}) + \nu\tau + \frac{\sigma^2}{4\beta}(1 - e^{-2\beta\tau})\right]. \end{aligned} \tag{111}$$

It is easy to verify that (105) holds by applying the appropriate limit process to (111). Figure 2 illustrates the behavior of the conditional expectation mechanism over time.

For computational simplicity in deriving the optimal consumption and portfolio rules, the two-asset model is used with the individual having an infinite time horizon and a constant absolute risk-aversion utility

[34] Processes such as (108) are called Ornstein–Uhlenbeck processes and are discussed, for example, in [3, p. 225].

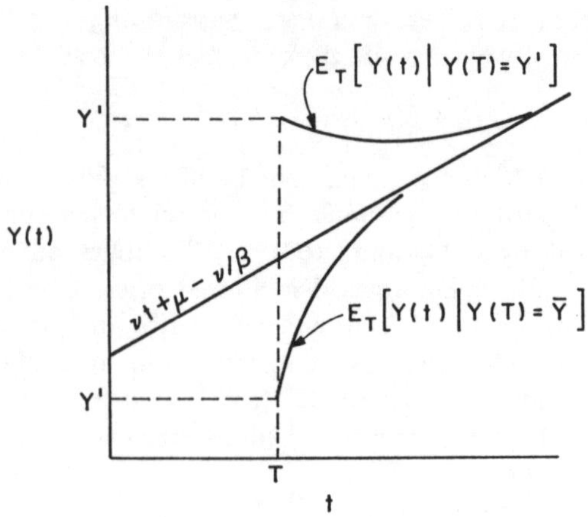

FIG. 2. The time-pattern of the expected value of the logarithm of price under the "normal" price-level hypothesis.

function, $U(C, t) = -e^{-\eta C}/\eta$. The fundamental optimality equation then is written as

$$0 = -e^{-\eta C^*}/\eta + J_t + J_W[w^*(\beta(\phi + \nu t - Y) - r) W + rW - C^*] + \tfrac{1}{2}J_{WW}w^{*2}W^2\sigma^2 + J_Y\beta(\mu + \nu t - Y) + \tfrac{1}{2}J_{YY}\sigma^2 + J_{YW}w^*W\sigma^2 \quad (112)$$

and the associated equations for the optimal rules are

$$w^*W = -J_W[\beta(\phi + \nu t - Y) - r]/J_{WW}\sigma^2 - J_{YW}/J_{WW} \quad (113)$$

and

$$C^* = -\log(J_W)/\eta. \quad (114)$$

Solving (112), (113), and (114), we write the optimal rules in explicit form as

$$w^*W = \frac{1}{\eta r\sigma^2}\left[\left(1 + \frac{\beta}{r}\right)(\alpha(P, t) - r) + \frac{\beta^2}{r^2}\left(\frac{\sigma^2}{2} + \nu - r\right)\right] \quad (115)$$

and

$$C^* = rW + \frac{\beta^2}{2\sigma^2\eta r}Y^2 - \frac{\beta}{\eta r\sigma^2}\left(\beta\nu t + \beta\phi - r + \beta\left(\nu + \frac{\sigma^2}{2} - r\right)\right)Y + a(t),^{35} \quad (116)$$

[35] $$a(t) \equiv \frac{1}{\eta}\left\{\frac{r}{2\sigma^2} - 1 + \frac{\beta}{\sigma^2}\left(\phi - 1 - \frac{\sigma^2}{2r}\right) + \frac{\beta^2}{r\sigma^2}\left[\left(1 - \frac{\sigma^2}{2r}\right)\left(\phi + \frac{\nu}{r} + \frac{\sigma^2}{2r} - 1\right) - \frac{\phi^2}{2} - \frac{\sigma^2}{2r}\right] + \frac{\beta\nu}{\sigma^2 r^2}\left(r + \beta - \beta\phi - \frac{\beta\sigma^2}{2r}\right) - \frac{\beta^2\nu^2}{2\sigma^2 r^3} + \frac{\beta\nu t}{r\sigma^2}\left[r + \beta - \beta\phi - \frac{\beta\sigma^2}{2r}\right] - \frac{\beta^2\nu^2 t^2}{2\sigma^2 r}\right\}.$$

where $\alpha(P, t)$ is the instantaneous expected rate of return defined explicitly in footnote 33. To provide a basis for comparison, the solutions when the geometric Brownian motion hypothesis is assumed are presented as[36]

$$w^*W = \frac{(\alpha - r)}{\eta r \sigma^2} \tag{117}$$

and

$$C^* = rW + \frac{1}{\eta r}\left[\frac{(\alpha - r)^2}{2\sigma^2} - r\right]. \tag{118}$$

To examine the effects of the alternative "normal price" hypothesis on the consumption-portfolio decisions, the (constant) α of (117) and (118) is chosen equal to $\alpha(P, t)$ of (115) and (116) so that, in both cases, the *instantaneous* expected return and variance are the same at the point of time of comparison. Comparing (115) with (117), we find that the proportion of wealth invested in the risky asset is always larger under the "normal price" hypothesis than under the geometric Brownian motion hypothesis.[37] In particular, notice that even if $\alpha < r$, unlike in the geometric Brownian motion case, a positive amount of the risky asset is held. Figures 3a and 3b illustrate the behavior of the optimal portfolio holdings.

The most striking feature of this analysis is that, despite the ability to make continuous portfolio adjustments, a person who believes that prices satisfy the "normal" price hypothesis will hold more of the risky asset than one who believes that prices satisfy the geometric Brownian motion hypothesis, even though they both have the same utility function and the same expectations about the instantaneous mean and variance.

The primary interest in examining these alternative price mechanisms is to see the effects on portfolio behavior, and so, little will be said about the effects on consumption other than to present the optimal rule.

The second alternative price mechanism assumes the same type of price-dynamics equation as was assumed for the geometric Brownian motion, namely,

$$\frac{dP}{P} = \alpha\, dt + \sigma\, dz. \tag{119}$$

However, instead of the instantaneous expected rate of return α being a

[36] For a derivation of (117) and (118), see [12, p. 256].

[37] It is assumed that $\nu + \sigma^2/2 > r$, i.e., the "long-run" rate of growth of the "normal" price is greater than the sure rate of interest so that something of the risky asset will be held in the short and long run.

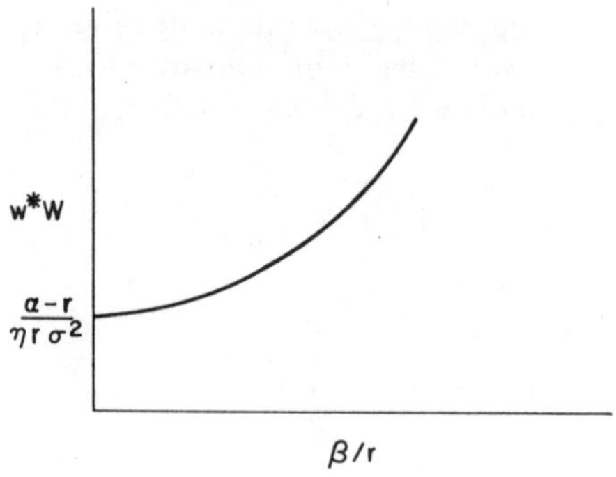

FIG. 3a. The demand for the risky asset as a function of the speed of adjustment

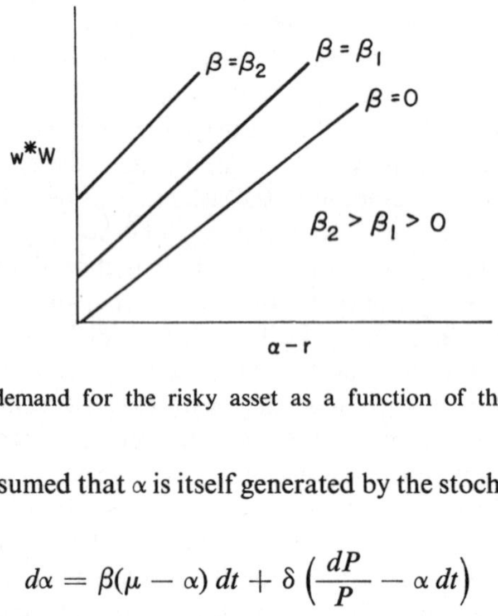

FIG. 3b. The demand for the risky asset as a function of the expected return.

constant, it is assumed that α is itself generated by the stochastic differential equation

$$\begin{aligned} d\alpha &= \beta(\mu - \alpha)\, dt + \delta\left(\frac{dP}{P} - \alpha\, dt\right) \\ &= \beta(\mu - \alpha)\, dt + \delta\sigma\, dz. \end{aligned} \tag{120}$$

The first term in (120) implies a long-run, regressive adjustment of the expected rate of return toward a "normal" rate of return, μ, where β is the speed of adjustment. The second term in (120) implies a short-run, extrapolative adjustment of the expected rate of return of the "error-learning" type, where δ is the speed of adjustment. I will call the assumption of a price mechanism described by (119) and (120) the "De Leeuw" hypothesis for Frank De Leeuw who first introduced this type mechanism to explain interest rate behavior.

To examine the price behavior implied by (119) and (120), we first derive the behavior of α, and then P. The equation for α, (120), is of the same type as (108) described previously. Hence, α is normally distributed and is generated by a Markov process. The solution of (120), conditional on knowing $\alpha(T)$ is

$$\alpha(t) - \alpha(T) = (\mu - \alpha(T))(1 - e^{-\beta\tau}) + \delta\sigma e^{-\beta t} \int_T^t e^{\beta s}\, dz, \tag{121}$$

where $\tau \equiv t - T > 0$. From (121), the conditional mean and variance of $\alpha(t) - \alpha(T)$ are

$$E_T(\alpha(t) - \alpha(T)) = (\mu - \alpha(T))(1 - e^{-\beta\tau}) \tag{122}$$

and

$$\operatorname{var}[\alpha(t) - \alpha(T) \mid \alpha(T)] = \frac{\delta^2\sigma^2}{2\beta}(1 - e^{-2\beta\tau}). \tag{123}$$

To derive the dynamics of P, note that, unlike α, P is not Markov although the joint process $[P, \alpha]$ is. Combining the results derived for $\alpha(t)$ with (119), we solve directly for the price, conditional on knowing $P(T)$ and $\alpha(T)$,

$$Y(t) - Y(T) = (\mu - \tfrac{1}{2}\sigma^2)\tau - \frac{(\mu - \alpha(T))}{\beta}(1 - e^{-\beta\tau}) + \sigma\delta \int_T^t \int_T^s e^{-\beta(s-s')}\, dz(s')\, ds + \sigma \int_T^t dz, \tag{124}$$

where $Y(t) \equiv \log[P(t)]$. From (124), the conditional mean and variance of $Y(t) - Y(T)$ are

$$E_T[Y(t) - Y(T)] = (\mu - \tfrac{1}{2}\sigma^2)\tau - \frac{(\mu - \alpha(T))}{\beta}(1 - e^{-\beta\tau}) \tag{125}$$

and

$$\operatorname{var}[Y(t) - Y(T) \mid Y(T)] = \sigma^2\tau + \frac{\sigma^2\delta^2}{2\beta^3}[\beta\tau - 2(1 - e^{-\beta\tau}) + \tfrac{1}{2}(1 - e^{-2\beta\tau})] + \frac{2\delta\sigma^2}{\beta^2}[\beta\tau - (1 - e^{-\beta\tau})]. \tag{126}$$

Since $P(t)$ is log-normal, it is straightforward to derive the moments for $P(t)$ from (124)–(126). Figure 4 illustrates the behavior of the expected price mechanism. The equilibrium or "long-run" (i.e., $\tau \to \infty$) distribution for $\alpha(t)$ is stationary gaussian with mean μ and variance $\delta^2\sigma^2/2\beta$, and the equilibrium distribution for $P(t)/P(T)$ is a stationary log-normal. Hence, the long-run behavior of prices under the De Leeuw hypothesis approaches the geometric Brownian motion.

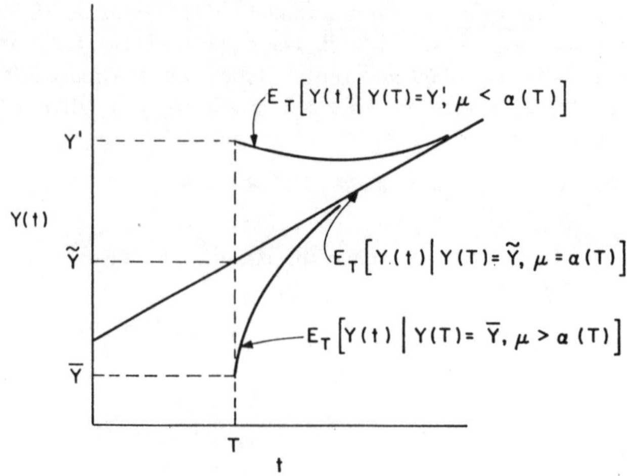

FIG. 4. The time-pattern of the expected value of the logarithm of price under the De Leeuw hypothesis.

Again, the two-asset model is used with the individual having an infinite time horizon and a constant absolute risk-aversion utility function, $U(C, t) = -e^{-\eta C}/\eta$. The fundamental optimality equation is written as

$$0 = -\frac{e^{-\eta C^*}}{\eta} + J_t + J_W[w^*(\alpha - r)\,W + rW - C^*]$$
$$+ \tfrac{1}{2}J_{WW}w^{*2}W^2\sigma^2 + J_\alpha\beta(\mu - \alpha) + \tfrac{1}{2}J_{\alpha\alpha}\delta^2\sigma^2 + J_{W\alpha}\delta\sigma^2 w^* W. \quad (127)$$

Notice that the state variables of the problem are W and α, which are both Markov, as is required for the dynamic programming technique. The optimal portfolio rule derived from (127) is,

$$w^*W = -\frac{J_W(\alpha - r)}{J_{WW}\sigma^2} - \frac{J_{W\alpha}\delta}{J_{WW}}. \quad (128)$$

The optimal consumption rule is the same as in (114). Solving (127) and (128), the explicit solution for the portfolio rule is

$$w^*W = \frac{1}{\eta r\sigma^2(r + 2\delta + 2\beta)}\left[(r + \delta + 2\beta)(\alpha - r) - \frac{\delta\beta(\mu - r)}{r + \delta + \beta}\right]. \quad (129)$$

Comparing (129) with (127) and assuming that $\mu > r$, we find that under the De Leeuw hypothesis, the individual will hold a smaller amount of the risky asset than under the geometric Brownian motion hypothesis. Note also that w^*W is a decreasing function of the long-run normal rate of return μ. The interpretation of this result is that as μ increases for a given α, the probability increases that future "α's" will be more favorable relative to the current α, and so there is a tendency to hold more of one's current wealth in the risk-free asset as a "reserve" for investment under more favorable conditions.

The last type of price mechanism examined differs from the previous two in that it is assumed that prices satisfy the geometric Brownian motion hypothesis. However, it is also assumed that the investor does not know the true value of the parameter α, but must estimate it from past data. Suppose P is generated by equation (119) with α and σ constants, and the investor has price data back to time $-\tau$. Then, the best estimator for α, $\hat{\alpha}(t)$, is

$$\hat{\alpha}(t) = \frac{1}{t+\tau} \int_{-\tau}^{t} \frac{dP}{P}, \tag{130}$$

where we assume, arbitrarily, that $\hat{\alpha}(-\tau) = 0$. From (130), we have that $E(\hat{\alpha}(t)) = \alpha$, and so, if we define the error term $\epsilon_t \equiv \alpha - \hat{\alpha}(t)$, then (119) can be re-written as

$$\frac{dP}{P} = \hat{\alpha}\, dt + \sigma\, d\hat{z}, \tag{131}$$

where $d\hat{z} \equiv dz + \epsilon_t\, dt/\sigma$. Further, by differentiating (130), we have the dynamics for $\hat{\alpha}$, namely

$$d\hat{\alpha} = \frac{\sigma}{t+\tau}\, d\hat{z}. \tag{132}$$

Comparing (131) and (132) with (119) and (120), we see that this "learning" model is equivalent to the special case of the De Leeuw hypothesis of pure extrapolation (i.e., $\beta = 0$), where the degree of extrapolation (δ) is decreasing over time. If the two-asset model is assumed with an investor who lives to time T with a constant absolute risk-aversion utility function, and if (for computational simplicity) the risk-free asset is money (i.e., $r = 0$), then the optimal portfolio rule is

$$w^* W = \frac{(t+\tau)}{\eta\sigma^2} \log\left(\frac{T+\tau}{t+\tau}\right) \hat{\alpha}(t) \tag{133}$$

and the optimal consumption rule is

$$\begin{aligned} C^* = \frac{W}{T-t} - \frac{1}{\eta}\Big[&\log(T+\tau) \\ &+ \frac{2}{T-t}(T - t - (T+\tau)\log(T+\tau) + (t+\tau)\log(t+\tau)) \\ &+ \frac{\hat{\alpha}^2}{2\sigma^2}\left[\frac{(t+\tau)^2}{(T-t)} \log\left(\frac{T+\tau}{t+\tau}\right) - \frac{(T-t)}{t+\tau}\right]\Big]. \end{aligned} \tag{134}$$

By differentiating (133) with respect to t, we find that w^*W is an increasing function of time for $t < \bar{t}$, reaches a maximum at $t = \bar{t}$, and then is a decreasing function of time for $\bar{t} < t < T$, where $\bar{t}$ is defined by

$$\bar{t} = [T + (1 - e)\,\tau]/e. \tag{135}$$

The reason for this behavior is that, early in life (i.e. for $t < \bar{t}$), the investor learns more about the price equation with each observation, and hence investment in the risky asset becomes more attractive. However, as he approaches the end of life (i.e., for $t > \bar{t}$), he is generally liquidating his portfolio to consume a larger fraction of his wealth, so that although investment in the risky asset is more favorable, the absolute dollar amount invested in the risky asset declines.

Consider the effect on (133) of increasing the number of available previous observations (i.e., increase τ). As expected, the dollar amount invested in the risky asset increases monotonically. Taking the limit of (133) as $\tau \to \infty$, we have that the optimal portfolio rule is

$$w^*W = \frac{(T - t)}{\eta\sigma^2}\,\alpha \qquad \text{as} \quad \tau \to \infty, \tag{136}$$

which is the optimal rule for the geometric Brownian motion case when α is known with certainty. Figure 5 illustrates graphically how the optimal rule changes with τ.

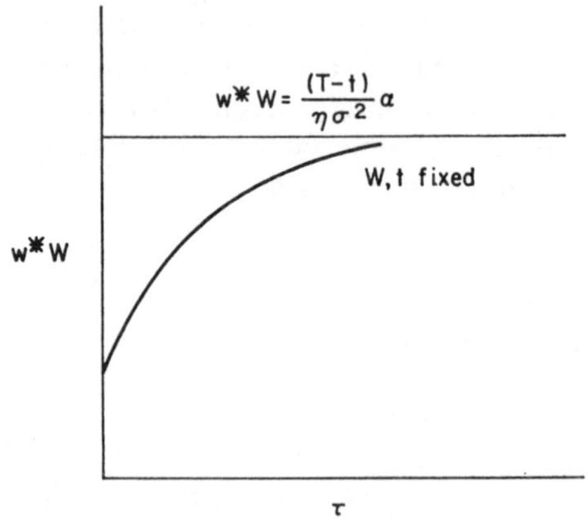

FIG. 5. The demand for the risky asset as a function of the number of previous price observations.

10. Conclusion

By the introduction of Itô's Lemma and the Fundamental Theorem of Stochastic Dynamic Programming (Theorem I), we have shown how to construct systematically and analyze optimal continuous-time dynamic models under uncertainty. The basic methods employed in studying the consumption-portfolio problem are applicable to a wide class of economic models of decision making under uncertainty.

A major advantage of the continuous-time model over its discrete time analog is that one need only consider two types of stochastic processes: functions of Brownian motions and Poisson processes. This result limits the number of parameters in the problem and allows one to take full advantage of the enormous amount of literature written about these processes. Although I have not done so here, it is straightforward to show that the limits of the discrete-time model solutions as the period spacing goes to zero are the solutions of the continuous-time model.[38]

A basic simplification gained by using the continuous-time model to analyze the consumption-portfolio problem is the justification of the Tobin–Markowitz portfolio efficiency conditions in the important case when asset price changes are stationarily and log-normally distributed. With earlier writers (Hakansson [6], Leland [10], Fischer [5], Samuelson [13], and Cass and Stiglitz [1]), we have shown that the assumption of the HARA utility function family simplifies the analysis and a number of strong theorems were proved about the optimal solutions. The introduction of stochastic wage income, risk of default, uncertainty about life expectancy, and alternative types of price dynamics serve to illustrate the power of the techniques as well as to provide insight into the effects of these complications on the optimal rules.

References

1. D. Cass and J. E. Stiglitz, The structure of investor perferences and asset Returns, and Separability in Portfolio Allocation: A Contribution to the Pure Theory of Mutual Funds," *J. Econ. Theory* **2** (1970), 122–160.
2. "The Random Character of Stock Market Prices," (P. Cootner, Ed.), Massachusetts Institute of Technology Press, Cambridge, Mass., 1964.
3. D. A. Cox and H. D. Miller, "The Theory of Stochastic Processes," John Wiley and Sons, New York, 1968.
4. S. E. Dreyfus, "Dynamic Programming and the Calculus of Variations," Academic Press, New York, 1965.

[38] For a general discussion of this result, see Samuelson [14].

5. S. Fischer, Essays on assets and contingent commodities, Ph.D. Dissertation, Department of Economics, Massachusetts Institute of Technology, August, 1969.
6. N. H. Hakansson, Optimal investment and consumption strategies under risk for a class of utility functions, *Econometrica* to appear.
7. K. Itô, On stochastic differential equations, *Mem. Amer. Math. Soc.* No. 4 1951.
8. K. Itô and H. P. McKean, Jr., "Diffusion Processes and Their Sample Paths, Academic Press, New York, 1964.
9. H. J. Kushner, "Stochastic Stability and Control," Academic Press, New York, 1967.
10. H. E. Leland, Dynamic portfolio theory, Ph.D. Dissertation Department of Economics, Harvard University, May, 1968.
11. H. P. McKean, Jr., "Stochastic Integrals," Academic Press, New York, 1969.
12. R. C. Merton, Lifetime portfolio selection under uncertainty: the continuous-time case, *Rev. Econ. Statist.* LI (August, 1969), 247–257.
13. P. A. Samuelson, Lifetime Portfolio Selection by Dynamic Stochastic Programming, *Rev. Econ. Statist.* LI (August 1969), 239–246.
14. P. A. Samuelson, The fundamental approximation theorem of portfolio analysis in terms of means, variances and higher moments, *Rev. Econ. Stud.* (October, 1970).
15. R. L. Stratonovich, "Conditional Markov Processes and Their Application to the Theory of Optimal Control," American Elsevier, New York, 1968.
16. F. Black, "Individual Investment and Consumption Strategies Under Uncertainty," Associates in Finance Financial Note No. 6C, September, 1970.

[7]

JOURNAL OF ECONOMIC THEORY **49**, 33–83 (1989)

Optimal Consumption and Portfolio Policies when Asset Prices Follow a Diffusion Process

JOHN C. COX AND CHI-FU HUANG*

Sloan School of Management, Massachusetts Institute of Technology, Cambridge, MA 02139

Received April 3, 1987; revised October 4, 1988

We consider a consumption–portfolio problem in continuous time under uncertainty. A martingale technique is employed to characterize optimal consumption–portfolio policies when there exist nonnegativity constraints on consumption and on final wealth. We also provide a way to compute and verify optimal policies. Our verification theorem for optimal policies involves a linear partial differential equation, unlike the nonlinear partial differential equation of dynamic programming. The relationship between our approach and dynamic programming is discussed. We demonstrate our technique by explicitly computing optimal policies in a series of examples. In particular, we solve the optimal consumption–portfolio problem for hyperbolic absolute risk aversion utility functions when the asset prices follow a geometric Brownian motion. The optimal policies in this case are no longer linear when nonnegativity constraints on consumption and on final wealth are included. By these examples, one can see that our approach is much easier than the dynamic programming approach. *Journal of Economic Literature* Classification Numbers: 022, 213, 522. © 1989 Academic Press, Inc.

1. INTRODUCTION

Optimal intertemporal consumption–portfolio policies in continuous time under uncertainty have traditionally been characterized by stochastic

* The authors thank Hua He, Hayne Leland, Robert Merton, Henri Pagès, Daniel Stroock, and Tong-sheng Sun for comments. Preliminary results of this paper were first reported at Carnegie-Mellon University in 1983, and summary results were given at the Institute of Mathematics and Its Applications at the University of Minnesota in the summer of 1986. The May 1986 version of this paper has been presented at Brown University, Cornell University, Massachusetts Institute of Technology, Northwestern University, the University of California at Berkeley, the University of Chicago, and the University of Pennsylvania. The current version has been presented at the Copenhagen Institute of Economics. We thank the seminar participants for their comments. We are grateful for the support of Batterymarch Financial Management, which provided fellowships for both authors at various times during the development of this paper. We are of course solely responsible for remaining errors.

0022-0531/89 $3.00

Copyright © 1989 by Academic Press, Inc.
All rights of reproduction in any form reserved.

dynamic programming. Merton [30] is the pioneering paper in this regard. To show the existence of a solution to the consumption–portfolio problem using dynamic programming, there are two approaches. The first is through application of the existence theorems in the theory of stochastic control. These existence theorems often require an admissible control to take its values in a compact set. This is unsatisfactory, since if we are modeling frictionless financial markets, any compactness assumption on the values of controls is arbitrary. Moreover, many of the existence theorems are limited to cases where the controls affect only the drift term of the controlled processes. This, unfortunately, rules out the portfolio problem under consideration.

The second approach is through construction: construct a control, usually by solving a nonlinear partial differential equation either analytically or numerically, and then use the verification theorem of dynamic programming to verify that it indeed is a solution. Merton's paper uses this second approach. It is in general difficult, however, to construct a solution. Moreover, when there are constraints on controls, such as the nonnegativity constraint on consumption, this approach becomes even more difficult.

Recently, a martingale representation technology has been used in place of the theory of stochastic control to show the existence of optimal consumption–portfolio policies without the requirement of compactness of the values of admissible controls; see Cox and Huang [6] and Pliska [32]. Notably, Cox and Huang show that, for a quite general class of utility functions, it suffices to check, for the existence of optimal controls, whether the parameters of a system of stochastic differential equations, derived completely from the price system, satisfy a local Lipschitz and a uniform growth condition. This approach takes care of the nonnegativity constraint on consumption in a simple and direct way.

The focus of this paper is on the explicit construction of optimal controls using the martingale technology, with the nonnegativity constraint on consumption being taken into account. We provide two characterization theorems of optimal policies (Theorems 2.1 and 2.2) and one verification theorem (Theorem 2.3). Theorem 2.3 is the counterpart of the verification theorem in dynamic programming. One advantage of our approach is that our verification theorem involves a *linear* partial differential equation, unlike the *nonlinear* partial differential equation appearing in dynamic programming. In many specific situations, optimal controls can even be directly computed without solving any partial differential equation. For example, we compute in closed form the optimal consumption–portfolio policies for hyperbolic absolute risk aversion (HARA) utility functions when the asset prices follow a geometric Brownian motion.

Besides Cox and Huang [6] and Pliska [32] mentioned above, other related work includes papers by Brennan and Solanki [4], Cox and Leland

[7], Duffie and Huang [9], Harrison and Kreps [17], Harrison and Pliska [18], Huang [22], and Kreps [26].[1]

Merton [31, Chap. 6] recently utilized the technology developed here to investigate an optimal consumption–portfolio problem with an infinite horizon in the geometric Brownian motion model of Merton [30]. He showed, for example, that in the region where an investor chooses to consume zero, his optimal portfolio policy is a constant-proportion, levered combination of the riskless security and the growth-optimal portfolio—the portfolio that maximizes the expected continuously compounded growth rate. Readers interested in applications of the techniques developed here should consult Merton [31].

The rest of this paper is organized as follows. Section 2 contains our general theory. We formulate a dynamic consumption–portfolio problem for an agent in continuous time with general diffusion price processes in Section 2.1. The agent's problem is to dynamically manage a portfolio of securities and withdraw funds out of it in order to maximize his expected utility of consumption over time and of final wealth, while facing a nonnegativity constraint on consumption as well as on final wealth. Section 2.2 contains the main results of Section 2. In Theorems 2.1 and 2.2, we give characterizations of optimal consumption–portfolio policies. We show in Theorem 2.3 how candidates for optimal policies can be constructed by solving a linear partial differential equation and how candidates can be verified to indeed be optimal. We discuss the relationship between our approach and dynamic programming in Section 2.3. We also demonstrate the connection between a solution with the nonnegativity constraint and a solution without the constraint.

In Section 3, we specialize the general model of Section 2 to a model originally considered by Merton [30], where securities price processes follow a geometric Brownian motion. In this case, optimal consumption–portfolio policies can be computed directly without solving any partial differential equation. Several examples of utility functions are considered. In particular, we solve the consumption and portfolio problem for the family of HARA utility functions. In the unconstrained case given in Merton [30], the optimal policies of HARA utility functions are linear in wealth; when nonnegativity constraints are included, this is no longer true. We also obtain some characterizations of optimal policies that are of independent interest.

Section 4 contains some concluding remarks.

[1] Karatzas, Lehoczky, and Shreve [25], done independently and concurrently with the May 1986 version of this paper, develops ideas similar to ours.

2. The General Case

In this section, a model of securities markets in continuous time with diffusion price processes will be formulated. We will consider the optimal consumption–portfolio policies of an agent while facing a nonnegativity constraint on consumption and on final wealth. The connection between our approach and dynamic programming will be demonstrated and the advantages of our approach will be pointed out. We will also discuss the relationship between a solution to the agent's problem with the non-negativity constraint and a solution to his problem without the constraint.

2.1. *The Formulation*

Taken as primitive are a complete probability space[2] $(\Omega, \mathscr{F}, P)$ and a time span $[0, T]$, where T is a strictly positive real number. Let there be an N-dimensional standard Brownian motion defined on the probability space, denoted by $w = \{w_n(t); t \in [0, T],\ n = 1, 2, ..., N\}$. Let $\mathbf{F} = \{\mathscr{F}_t; t \in [0, T]\}$ be the *filtration* generated by w. (A filtration is an increasing family of sub-sigma-fields of $\mathscr{F}$.) We will use $E[\cdot]$ to denote expectation under P.

We assume that $\mathscr{F}_0$ contains all the P-null sets and that $\mathscr{F}_T = \mathscr{F}$. Since for an N dimensional standard Brownian motion, $w(0) = 0$ a.s., $\mathscr{F}_0$ is almost trivial.[3]

A process $X = \{X(t); t \in [0, T]\}$ is said to be adapted to $\mathbf{F}$ if $X(t)$ is measurable with respect to $\mathscr{F}_t\ \forall t \in [0, T]$. In words, the value of X at time t cannot depend on the realizations of the Brownian motion strictly after time t.

We use $\mathscr{O}$ to denote the optional sigma-field and ν to denote the product measure on $\Omega \times [0, T]$ generated by P and the Lebesgue measure. (The optional sigma-field is the sigma-field on $\Omega \times [0, T]$ generated by $\mathbf{F}$-adapted right-continuous processes; see, e.g., Chung and Williams [5, p. 59].) A process measurable with respect to $\mathscr{O}$ is naturally adapted to $\mathbf{F}$ and is said to be an optional process. A pair of consumption rate process and final wealth (c, W) is said to be admissible if

$$(c, W) \in L^p_+(\nu) \times L^p_+(P) \equiv L^p_+(\Omega \times [0, T], \mathscr{O}, \nu) \times L^p_+(\Omega, \mathscr{F}, P)$$

for some $p > 1$, where $L^p_+(\nu)$ and $L^p_+(P)$ are the positive orthants of $L^p(\Omega \times [0, T], \mathscr{O}, \nu)$ and $L^p(\Omega, \mathscr{F}, P)$, respectively. As we mentioned above, since an optional process is adapted, all the consumption processes are adapted. Note that using the terminology of general equilibrium theory, we have taken the commodity space to be $L^p(\nu) \times L^p(P)$ and an agent's

[2] A probability space (Ω, F, P) is complete if any subset of a P-null set is contained in $\mathscr{F}$.

[3] A sigma-field is almost trivial if it contains only sets of probability zero or one.

consumption set to be $L^p_+(\nu) \times L^p_+(P)$. All the processes to appear will be adapted to **F**.

Consider a frictionless securities market with $N+1$ long-lived securities traded, indexed by $n = 0, 1, 2, ..., N$. Security $n \neq 0$ is risky and pays dividends at rate $\iota_n(t)$ and sells for $S_n(t)$ at time t. We will henceforth use $S(t)$ and $\iota(t)$ to denote $(S_1(t), ..., S_N(t))^{\mathsf{T}}$ and $(\iota_1(t), ..., \iota_N(t))^{\mathsf{T}}$, respectively, where ^{T} denotes "transpose." Security 0 is (locally) riskless, pays no dividends, and sells for $B(t) = B(0) \exp\{\int_0^t r(s)\, ds\}$ at time t, where $B(0)$ is a strictly positive real number. Assume further that $r(t) = r(S(t), t)$ with $r(x, t)$: $\Re^N \times [0, T] \to \Re_+$ continuous. Note that, since $r(t) \geqslant 0$, $B(t)$ is bounded below away from zero. Henceforth, we will refer to security 0 as the "bond."

We will use the following notation: If σ is a matrix or a column vector, then $|\sigma|^2$ denotes $\mathrm{tr}(\sigma\sigma^{\mathsf{T}})$ and tr denotes "trace."

The price processes for risky securities plus their accumulated dividends follow an Itô process satisfying

$$S(t) + \int_0^t \iota(S(s), s)\, ds = S(0) + \int_0^t \zeta(S(s), s)\, ds$$

$$+ \int_0^t \sigma(S(s), s)\, dw(s) \qquad \forall t \in [0, T], \qquad \text{a.s.,} \qquad (2.1)$$

where $\zeta(t)$ is an $N \times 1$ vector process and $\sigma(t)$ is an $N \times N$ matrix process. We assume that $\zeta(x, t)$ and $\sigma(x, t)$ are continuous in $x \in \Re^N$ and t, and $\sigma(x, t)$ is nonsingular for all $x \in \Re^N$ and t.

A trading strategy is an $(N+1)$-vector of processes, denoted generically by

$$\{\alpha(t), \theta(t) \equiv (\theta_1(t), ..., \theta_N(t))^{\mathsf{T}};\ t \in [0, T]\},$$

where $\alpha(t)$ and $\theta_n(t)$ are the number of shares of the 0th and the nth security held at time t, respectively. We will specify the set of admissible trading strategies more fully later. For now, an admissible trading strategy must satisfy the following conditions:

1. $$\int_0^T |\alpha(t) B(t) r(t) + \theta(t)^{\mathsf{T}} \zeta(t)|\, dt < \infty \qquad P-\text{a.s.,} \qquad (2.2)$$

2. $$\int_0^T |\theta(t)^{\mathsf{T}} \sigma(t)|^2\, dt < \infty \qquad P-\text{a.s.,} \qquad (2.3)$$

3. there exists a consumption-final wealth pair $(c, W) \in L^p_+(\nu) \times L^p_+(P)$ such that, $P-$a.s.,

$$\alpha(t)B(t)+\theta(t)^{\mathsf{T}}S(t)+\int_0^t c(s)\,ds$$

$$=\alpha(0)B(0)+\theta(0)^{\mathsf{T}}S(0)+\int_0^t (\alpha(s)B(s)r(s)+\theta(s)^{\mathsf{T}}\zeta(s))\,ds$$

$$+\int_0^t \theta(s)^{\mathsf{T}}\sigma(s)\,dw(s) \qquad \forall t\in[0,T], \tag{2.4}$$

4. $\alpha(T)B(T)+\theta(T)^{\mathsf{T}}S(T)=W \qquad P-\text{a.s.}$ (2.5)

Relations (2.2) and (2.3) ensure that the stochastic integrals of (2.4) are well-defined; see Liptser and Shiryayev [29, Chap. 4]. The left-hand side of (2.4) is the value of the portfolio at time t plus the accumulated withdrawals of consumption from time 0 to time t, while the right-hand side is equal to the initial value of the portfolio plus accumulated capital gains (losses) and dividends from trading from time 0 to time t. That the left-hand side is equal to the right-hand side is a natural budget constraint. Relation (2.5) simply says that the final wealth is equal to the final value of the portfolio. Note that since $W\in L^p_+(P)$ and thus $W\geqslant 0$ $P-$a.s., (2.5) also ensures that borrowing to consume without paying back is not admissible. The consumption–final wealth pair (c, W) of (2.4) and (2.5) will be said to be *financed* by the trading strategy (α, θ).

Trading strategies satisfying (2.2)–(2.3) include all the *simple trading strategies*—a trading strategy (α, θ) is simple if there exist a finite number of time points $0\leqslant t_0<t_1<\cdots<t_J=T$ and bounded random variables $\{x_{nj};\, n=0, 1, ..., N;\ j=0, 1, ..., J-1\}$ such that x_{nj} is measurable with respect to $\mathscr{F}_{t_j}$ and

$$\alpha(t)=x_{0j} \qquad P-\text{a.s.} \qquad \text{if} \quad t\in(t_j, t_{j+1}],$$
$$\theta_n(t)=x_{nj} \qquad P-\text{a.s.} \qquad \text{if} \quad t\in(t_j, t_{j+1}], \qquad \forall n=1, 2, ..., N.$$

Note that a simple trading strategy is a portfolio that changes its composition of assets at a finite number of nonstochastic time points. Simple trading strategies are among the strategies that can actually be implemented in the real world. Their inclusion in the set of admissible strategies is necessary for our model to be reasonable.

Now we will turn our attention momentarily to the price processes before completing our specification of the set of admissible trading strategies. Thus far, we have not put any restriction on the price processes other than certain continuity and nonsingularity conditions on their parameters. For our consumption–portfolio problem to be well-posed, we certainly do not want the price processes to allow something to be created from nothing when reasonable strategies are employed. Formally, a *free lunch* is a consumption–final wealth pair $(c, W) \in L^p_+(\nu) \times L^p_+(P)$ financed by an admissible trading strategy (α, θ) such that $\alpha(0)B(0)+\theta(0)^{\mathsf{T}}S(0)=0$ and either $c>0$ with a strictly positive ν-measure or $W>0$ with a strictly positive P-measure. In words, a free lunch is a consumption–final wealth pair that is nonnegative and nonzero and is financed by an admissible trading strategy with zero initial cost. Harrison and Kreps [17] and Huang [21] have shown that for free lunches not to be available for simple strategies it suffices that S is related to martingales after a change of unit and a change of probability, or equivalently, that there exists an *equivalent martingale measure.* An equivalent martingale measure Q is a probability measure on $(\Omega, \mathscr{F})$ equivalent to P such that the Radon–Nikodym derivative dQ/dP lies in $L^q(\Omega, \mathscr{F}, P)$ with $1/p+1/q=1$ and

$$G^*(t) \equiv S(t)/B(t) - S(0)/B(0) + \int_0^t \iota(s)/B(s)\,ds,$$

the accumulated capital gains plus accumulated dividends, in units of the bond, is a martingale under Q. The existence of an equivalent martingale measure can be ensured by some regularity conditions on the parameters of the price processes. Since this subject is treated elsewhere, we will simply assume that there exists an equivalent martingale measure and refer the reader to Cox and Huang [6, Proposition 2.1 and Section 4] for details.

Assumption 2.1. There exists an equivalent martingale measure denoted by Q.

Indeed, Cox and Huang [6, Proposition 2.1] shows that since $\sigma(x, t)$ is nonsingular for all x and t, Q must be the unique equivalent martingale measure. We will use $E[\cdot]$ to denote expectation under Q.

Remark 2.1. Probability measure Q is said to be equivalent to P if P and Q have the same measure zero sets. This definition is symmetric and thus we say P and Q are equivalent to each other. A necessary and sufficient condition for this is that the Radon–Nikodym derivative dQ/dP is strictly positive. If dQ/dP is merely positive, we say that Q is absolutely continuous with respect to P. Since P and Q are equivalent probability measures, all the *almost surely* statements to appear will be with respect to both. ▮

Remark 2.2. Harrison and Kreps [17] and Kreps [27] show that the existence of an equivalent martingale measure is not only a sufficient but also a necessary condition for free lunches not to be available for simple strategies *in the limit.* Interested readers should consult their work for details. We should also note that, in the setup of Harrison and Kreps [17], securities do not pay dividends and an individual maximizes his preferences for final wealth. Our model here is more general and uses results of Huang [21]. ∎

The unique martingale measure Q has an explicit expression. It follows from Harrison and Kreps [17, Theorem 3] and Huang [21, Theorem 4.1] that

$$dQ/dP = \exp\left\{\int_0^T \kappa(S(s), s)^\top \, dw(s) - \tfrac{1}{2}\int_0^T |\kappa(S(s), s)|^2 \, ds\right\}, \tag{2.6}$$

where

$$\kappa(S(t), t) \equiv -\sigma(S(t), t)^{-1}(\zeta(S(t), t) - r(S(t), t)S(t)). \tag{2.7}$$

For future use, we define a martingale under P:

$$\begin{aligned}\eta(t) &\equiv E[dQ/dP \mid \mathscr{F}_t] \quad \text{a.s.}\\ &= \exp\left\{\int_0^t \kappa(S(s), s)^\top \, dw(s) - \tfrac{1}{2}\int_0^t |\kappa(S(s), s)|^2 \, ds\right\} \quad \text{a.s.}\end{aligned} \tag{2.8}$$

Since dQ/dP is strictly positive, $\eta(t)$ is strictly positive. A P-martingale $\{X(t); t \in [0, T]\}$ is said to be an $L^p(P)$-martingale if

$$E[|X(t)|^p] < \infty \qquad \forall t \in [0, T].$$

By the fact that $dQ/dP \in L^q(P)$, $\{\eta(t); t \in [0, T]\}$ is an $L^q(P)$-martingale. We will demonstrate later that $\eta(\omega, t)B(0)/B(\omega, t)$ can be interpreted to be the price at time 0, per unit of P probability, of one unit of consumption at time t in state ω.

The following lemma will be useful later.

Lemma 2.1. *Under Q,*

$$w^*(t) \equiv w(t) - \int_0^t \kappa(S(s), s) \, ds \tag{2.9}$$

is a standard Brownian motion. We can write

$$G^*(t) = \int_0^t \sigma(S(s), s)/B(s) \, dw^*(s) \qquad \text{a.s.}, \tag{2.10}$$

which by assumption is a martingale under Q.

Proof. The first assertion follows from the Girsanov theorem; see, e.g., Liptser and Shiryayev [29, Chap. 6]. Next by Itô's lemma,

$$G^*(t) = \int_0^t [\zeta(S(s), s) - r(S(s), s) S(s)]/B(s)\, ds$$
$$+ \int_0^t \sigma(S(s), s)/B(s)\, dw(s).$$

The second assertion then follows from substituting w^* into the above relation and using the definition of κ in (2.7). ▮

The existence of an equivalent martingale measure ensures that there are no free lunches for simple strategies. However, free lunches financed by trading strategies satisfying (2.2)–(2.5) can still exist. For example, a doubling strategy, named after the strategy of doubling one's bet each time one loses at a roulette, can produce a free lunch, as was pointed out by Harrison and Kreps [17]. Therefore, either we allow only simple strategies or conditions in addition to (2.2)–(2.5) must be imposed to rule out free lunches for non-simple strategies. The former proves mathematically intractable since the set of consumption–final wealth pairs financed by simple strategies is not closed in $L^p(v) \times L^p(P)$ and the optimization problem is not well-posed. Moreover, the set of simple strategies is not "rich enough" in that it does not include strategies of practical interest such as those that replicate call options on securities.

There are two approaches for the latter. Both are motivated by the observation that for a doubling strategy to be implementable, it is necessary that an individual can borrow without bound and that there be no limit on the number of shares of risky securities held over time. The first approach is to put a nonnegative wealth constraint on trading strategies. Such a constraint certainly rules out doubling strategies, since it limits the amount of borrowing that one can make. Harrison and Kreps [17] conjectured that this constraint would also rule out all the free lunches. This conjecture was verified by Dybvig [10] in the model of Black and Scholes [2] and by Dybvig and Huang [11] in a model like ours. The second approach is to put a constraint on θ. Note that a bound on θ also constrains α through the budget constraint of (2.4) and (2.5). It turns out that a uniform bound on θ across states of nature is too strong—θ can be allowed to grow unbounded on sets of small Q-probability. Formally, the appropriate constraint is the following integrability condition on θ:

$$E^*\left[\left(\int_0^T |\theta(t)^\top \sigma(t)/B(t)|^2\, dt\right)^{p/2}\right] < \infty. \tag{2.11}$$

Duffie and Huang [9] used this kind of integrability constraint in their general equilibrium model. The two approaches discussed above are, however, shown to be equivalent for individuals with strictly increasing preferences by Dybvig and Huang [11]. They showed that any trading strategy that satisfies (2.2)–(2.5), and (2.11) must satisfy the nonnegative wealth constraint. The strategies satisfying (2.2)–(2.5) and the nonnegative wealth constraint but not (2.11) are suicidal strategies—strategies that essentially run a free lunch in reverse and throw money away. Any individual with strictly increasing preferences will certainly never employ a suicidal strategy. We note now that the following lemma shows that (2.11) is sufficient for (2.3).

LEMMA 2.2. *Let θ satisfy* (2.11). *Then θ satisfies* (2.3).

Proof. Let θ satisfy (2.11). Then it is necessary that

$$\int_0^T |\theta(t)\sigma(t)/B(t)|^2\, dt < \infty \qquad \text{a.s.}$$

Since $B(t)$ is a continuous process, a sample path is bounded on $[0, T]$ almost surely. Thus

$$\int_0^T |\theta(t)\sigma(t)|^2\, dt < \infty \qquad \text{a.s.,}$$

which is (2.3). ∎

Now we are ready to complete the specification of admissible trading strategies. A trading strategy (α, θ) is admissible if it satisfies (2.2), (2.4), (2.5), and (2.11). We will use $H(Q)$ to denote the space of admissible trading strategies, where Q signifies that the expectation of (2.11) is taken with respect to the unique equivalent martingale measure Q. One can verify that $H(Q)$ is a linear space by the linearity of the stochastic integral.

Now consider an agent with a time-additive utility function for consumption, $u(y, t)$, a utility function for final wealth, $V(y)$, and an initial wealth $W_0 > 0$. We assume that $u(y, t)$ and $V(y)$ are continuous, increasing, and strictly concave in y, and possibly unbounded from below at $y = 0$. The agent wants to solve the following problem:

$$\sup_{(c, W) \in L^p_+(\nu) \times L^p_+(P)} E\left[\int_0^T u(c(t), t)\, dt + V(W)\right]$$

$$\text{s.t.}\ (c, W) \text{ is financed by some } (\alpha, \theta) \in H(Q)$$

$$\text{with } \alpha(0) B(0) + \theta(0)^{\mathsf{T}} S(0) = W_0. \qquad (2.12)$$

Our task here is to provide ways to construct an optimal consumption–portfolio policy when one is known to exist, and to construct candidate policies to be verified to be optimal, when existence cannot be established on prior grounds.

We shall first record a mathematical result and a well-known property of the cost over time of a consumption–final wealth pair financed by some $(\alpha, \theta) \in H(Q)$.

LEMMA 2.3. *Let θ satisfy* (2.11). *Then*

$$\int_0^t \theta(s)^\top \sigma(s)/B(s)\, dw^*(s) \qquad t \in [0, T]$$

is an $L^p(Q)$-martingale.

Proof. See Jacod [23, Chap. IV]. ∎

LEMMA 2.4. *Let $(c, W) \in L^p_+(\nu) \times L^p_+(P)$ be financed by $(\alpha, \theta) \in H(Q)$. For all $t \in [0, T]$,*

$$E^*\left[\int_0^T c(s)/B(s)\, ds + W/B(T) \mid \mathscr{F}_t\right]$$

$$= \alpha(0) + \theta(0)^\top S(0)/B(0) + \int_0^t \theta(s)^\top \sigma(s)/B(s)\, dw^*(s)$$

$$= \alpha(t) + \theta(t)^\top S(t)/B(t) + \int_0^t c(s)/B(s)\, ds \qquad \textit{a.s.},$$

and as a consequence, the value of (c, W) at time t is

$$\alpha(t) B(t) + \theta(t)^\top S(t) = B(t) E^*\left[\int_t^T c(s)/B(s)\, ds + W/B(T) \mid \mathscr{F}_t\right] \quad \textit{a.s.} \quad (2.13)$$

Moreover, $\int_0^T c(s)/B(s)\, ds + W/B(T)$ is an element of $L^p(Q)$.

Proof. See, e.g., Cox and Huang [6, Proposition 2.2] for the first assertion. The second assertion follows from the first assertion and Lemma 2.3. ∎

With the aid of the following lemma, (2.13) has an intuitive interpretation in the context of Arrow–Debreu economies.

LEMMA 2.5. *Let g be an adapted process. Then*

$$E^*\left[\int_t^T g(s)\, ds \mid \mathscr{F}_t\right] = E\left[\int_t^T g(s)\eta(s)\, ds \mid \mathscr{F}_t\right] \Big/ \eta(t) \qquad \textit{a.s.}$$

whenever the integrals are well-defined. Thus for any $(c, W) \in L^p(\nu) \times L^p(P)$ *we can write*

$$B(t)E^*\left[\int_t^T c(s)/B(s)\,ds + W/B(T) \mid \mathscr{F}_t\right]$$

$$= B(t)E\left[\int_t^T c(s)\eta(s)/B(s)\,ds + W\eta(T)/B(T) \mid \mathscr{F}_t\right]\Big/\eta(t) \quad a.s. \qquad (2.14)$$

Proof. The first assertion follows from Dellacherie and Meyer [8, VI.57]. The second assertion follows since c and B are adapted processes. ∎

From Lemma 2.4, the left-hand side of (2.14) is the value at time t of (c, W). Thus, we can interpret $B(\omega, t)\eta(\omega, s)/(B(\omega, s)\eta(\omega, t))$ to be the time t price, per unit of P probability, of an Arrow–Debreu security that pays one unit of consumption in state ω at time $s \geq t$. That is, there exists an implicit system of Arrow–Debreu prices such that we can compute the value over time of a pair of $(c, W) \in L^p_+(\nu) \times L^p_+(P)$ financed by an admissible trading strategy. Note that since the equivalent martingale measure Q is unique and since $\eta(t)$ is constructed from Q, the system of implicit Arrow–Debreu prices is uniquely determined.

For future reference, we now cite several properties of a concave utility function. At every interior point of the domain of a concave function, the right-hand derivative and the left-hand derivative exist. At the left boundary of its domain, the right-hand derivative exists. The right-hand derivatives and the left-hand derivatives are decreasing functions and are equal to each other except possibly at a countable number of points. That is, a concave function is differentiable everywhere except possibly at a countable number of points and thus continuously differentiable at all but a countable number of points. (Note that for strictly concave functions, the *decreasing* relation above becomes a strict relation.) The right-hand derivative is a right-continuous function. Moreover, at every point, the left-hand derivative is greater than the right-hand derivative.

Now let $u_{y+}(y, t)$, $V'_+(y)$ and $u_{y-}(y, t)$, $V'_-(y)$ denote the right-hand derivatives and left-hand derivatives with respect to y, respectively, for $u(y, t)$ and for $V(y)$. Let $y < y'$, then $V'_-(y) \geq V'_+(y) > V'_-(y')$ by the strict concavity of V, and similarly for $u(y, t)$. We assume that

$$\lim_{y \to \infty} u_{y+}(y, t) = 0$$

and

$$\lim_{y \to \infty} V'_+(y) = 0.$$

Define *inverse functions* $\hat{f}(x^{-1}, t) = \inf\{y \in \mathfrak{R}_+ : u_{y+}(y, t) \leqslant x^{-1}\}$ and $V'^{-1}_+(x^{-1}) = \inf\{y \in \mathfrak{R}_+ : V'_+(y) \leqslant x^{-1}\}$. By the right-continuity of the right-hand derivatives, the infima are equal to minima.

Remark 2.3. Note that the assumption that utility functions are increasing and strictly concave implies that they are strictly increasing. ∎

We now state three sets of conditions that will be used in the next subsection. Conditions A and B concern properties of the price system, while Condition C concerns those of the utility functions. First define two processes

$$Z(t) = Z(0) + \int_0^t (r(S(s), s) + |\kappa(S(s), s)|^2) Z(s)\, ds - \int_0^t \kappa(S(s), s)^{\mathrm{T}} Z(s)\, dw(s) \qquad (2.15)$$

for some constant $Z(0) > 0$, and

$$Y(t) = \ln Z(0) + \int_0^t (r(S(s), s) + \tfrac{1}{2} |\kappa(S(s), s)|^2)\, ds - \int_0^t \kappa(S(s), s)^{\mathrm{T}} dw(s). \qquad (2.16)$$

Using Itô's lemma, it is easily verified that

$$Z(t) = Z(0) B(t)/(\eta(t) B(0)), \qquad (2.17)$$

and

$$Y(t) = \ln Z(t). \qquad (2.18)$$

Note that $(\ln Z(T) - \ln Z(0))/T$ is the realized continuously compounded growth rate from time 0 to time T of the growth-optimal portfolio—the portfolio that maximizes the expected continuously compounded growth rate.

We adopt the notation

$$D_y^m = \frac{\partial^m}{\partial y^m} = \frac{\partial^{m_1 + m_2 + \cdots + m_N}}{\partial y_1^{m_1} \cdots \partial y_N^{m_N}}; \qquad m = m_1 + \cdots + m_N$$

for positive integers $m_1, m_2, \ldots, m_N$. If $g: \mathfrak{R}^N \times [0, T] \mapsto \mathfrak{R}$ has partial derivatives with respect to its first N arguments, the vector $(\partial g/\partial y_1, \ldots, \partial g/\partial y_N)^{\mathrm{T}}$ is denoted by $D_y g$ or g_y.

Condition A. Write (2.1) and (2.16) compactly as follows:

$$\begin{pmatrix} S(t) \\ Y(t) \end{pmatrix} = \begin{pmatrix} S(0) \\ \ln Z(0) \end{pmatrix} + \int_0^t \hat{\zeta}(S(s), s)\, ds + \int_0^t \hat{\sigma}(S(s), s)\, dw(s)$$

$$\forall t \in [0, T], \quad \text{a.s.} \tag{2.19}$$

Suppose that there exist strictly positive constants K_1, K_2, K_3, and γ such that for all t

$$|\hat{\zeta}(x, t)| \leqslant K_1(1+|x|), \qquad |\hat{\sigma}(x, t)| \leqslant K_1(1+|x|) \qquad \forall x \in \mathfrak{R}^N, \tag{2.20}$$

$$\begin{aligned} &|\hat{\zeta}(x, t) - \hat{\zeta}(y, t)| \leqslant K_2\, |x-y|, \\ &|\hat{\sigma}(x, t) - \hat{\sigma}(y, t)| \leqslant K_2\, |x-y| \qquad \forall x, y \in \mathfrak{R}^N, \end{aligned} \tag{2.21}$$

that $D_y^m \hat{\zeta}(y, t)$ and $D_y^m \hat{\sigma}(y, t)$ exist for $m = 1, 2$ and are continuous in y and t, and that

$$|D_y^m \hat{\zeta}(y, t)| + |D_y^m \hat{\sigma}(y, t)| \leqslant K_3(1+|y|^\gamma) \tag{2.22}$$

for all $y \in \mathfrak{R}^N$.

Condition B. Consider the system of stochastic integral equations (2.1) and (2.15) under P and under the martingale measure Q:

$$\begin{aligned} \begin{pmatrix} S(t) \\ Z(t) \end{pmatrix} &= \begin{pmatrix} S(0) \\ Z(0) \end{pmatrix} + \int_0^t \zeta(S(s), Z(s), s)\, ds + \int_0^t \bar{\sigma}(S(s), Z(s), s)\, dw(s) \\ &= \begin{pmatrix} S(0) \\ Z(0) \end{pmatrix} + \int_0^t (\bar{\zeta}(S(s), Z(s), s) + \bar{\sigma}(S(s), Z(s), s)\kappa(S(s), s))\, ds \\ &\quad + \int_0^t \bar{\sigma}(S(s), Z(s), s)\, dw^*(s). \end{aligned} \tag{2.23}$$

Suppose that there exists a strictly positive constant K such that, for all $x \in \mathfrak{R}^{N+1}$,

$$\begin{aligned} |\bar{\zeta}(x, t) + \bar{\sigma}(x)\kappa(x, t)| \leqslant K(1+|x|), \qquad |\bar{\sigma}(x, t)| \leqslant K(1+|x|), \\ |\bar{\zeta}(x, t)| \leqslant K(1+|x|). \end{aligned} \tag{2.24}$$

Moreover, for any $M > 0$ there is a constant K_M such that for all $y, z \in \mathfrak{R}^{N+1}$ with $|y| \leqslant M$ and $|z| \leqslant M$ and $t \in [0, T]$

$$\begin{aligned} |\bar{\zeta}(y, t) + \bar{\sigma}(y, t)\kappa(y, t) - \bar{\zeta}(z, t) - \bar{\sigma}(z, t)\kappa(z, t)| &\leqslant K_M\, |y-z|, \\ |\bar{\sigma}(y, t) - \bar{\sigma}(z, t)| &\leqslant K_M\, |y-z|, \\ |\bar{\zeta}(y, t) - \bar{\zeta}(z, t)| &\leqslant K_M\, |y-z|. \end{aligned} \tag{2.25}$$

Note that (2.20) and (2.24) are linear growth conditions, (2.21) is a uniform Lipschitz condition, (2.25) is a local Lipschitz condition, and (2.22) is a polynomial growth condition.

Condition C. $e^{-x}\hat{f}(e^{-x}, t)$ and $e^{-x}V'^{-1}_{+}(e^{-x})$ are such that for $m \leqslant 2$, $D^m_x(e^{-x}\hat{f}(e^{-x}, t))$ and $D^m_x(e^{-x}V'^{-1}_{+}(e^{-x}))$ are continuous and satisfy a polynomial growth condition in that

$$|D^m_x(e^{-x}\hat{f}(e^{-x}, t))| \leqslant K(1+|x|^{\gamma}) \tag{2.26}$$

and

$$|D^m_x(e^{-x}V'^{-1}_{+}(e^{-x}))| \leqslant K(1+|x|^{\gamma}) \tag{2.27}$$

for some strictly positive constants K and γ.

The purpose of Conditions A and C is to guarantee that certain functionals of S and Y have two continuous derivatives. Here we remark that for $D^m_x(e^{-x}\hat{f}(e^{-x}, t))$ to exist and be continuous it is not necessary that $u(y, t)$ be continuously differentiable.

Condition B is to ensure that the moments of (Z, S) have certain nice properties under P and under Q. To have a feel of the restrictiveness of Condition C, we note that if $V(y) = y^{1-b}/(1-b)$ then $b \geqslant 1$. In many specific situations, differentiability will obtain under much weaker conditions. For example, in Section 3 of this paper, we consider a special case of the general model developed here. All the HARA utility functions give rise to the desired differentiability conditions.

2.2. *Main Results*

We will give explicit characterizations of an optimal consumption–portfolio policy under the assumption that the optimal consumption policy is also a solution to a corresponding static maximization problem. Assumption 2.2 is valid under quite mild regularity conditions, for which we refer the reader to Sections 2 and 4 of Cox and Huang [6].

Assume henceforth that

Assumption 2.2. There exists a solution to (2.12), denoted by (α, θ, c, W), if and only if (c, W) is a solution to

$$\sup_{(\hat{c}, \hat{W}) \in L^p_+(\nu) \times L^p_+(P)} E\left[\int_0^T u(\hat{c}, t)\, dt + V(\hat{W})\right]$$

$$\text{s.t. } B(0) E\left[\int_0^T \hat{c}(t)\eta(t)/B(t)\, dt + \hat{W}\eta(T)/B(T)\right] = W_0. \tag{2.28}$$

Remark 2.4. The idea behind Assumption 2.2 is as follows. The assumption that the martingale measure is unique, the integrability restriction on the trading strategies of (2.11), and some regularity conditions imply that any element of $L^p(\nu^*) \times L^p(Q)$ is financed by an admissible trading strategy, where ν^* is the product measure generated by Q and the Lebesgue measure. In such case, as long as the solution to (2.28) lies in $L^p(\nu^*) \times L^p(Q)$, Assumption 2.2 will be valid. ∎

It follows from the Lagrangian theory (see, e.g., Holmes [20] and Rockafellar [33]) that if (c, W) is a solution to (2.28), there exists a strictly positive real number λ such that

$$u_{c+}(c(\omega,t),t)\begin{cases}\leqslant \lambda\eta(\omega,t)B(0)/B(\omega,t)\leqslant u_{c-}(c(\omega,t),t) \\ \quad\text{for}\quad \nu-\text{a.e. }(\omega,t)\quad\text{such that } c(\omega,t)>0, \\ \leqslant \lambda\eta(\omega,t)B(0)/B(\omega,t) \\ \quad\text{for}\quad \nu-\text{a.e. }(\omega,t)\quad\text{such that } c(\omega,t)=0;\end{cases}$$
$$V'_{+}(W(\omega))\begin{cases}\leqslant \lambda\eta(\omega,T)B(0)/B(\omega,T)\leqslant V'_{-}(W(\omega)) \\ \quad\text{for}\quad P-\text{a.e. }\omega\quad\text{such that } W(\omega)>0, \\ \leqslant \lambda\eta(\omega,T)B(0)/B(\omega,T) \\ \quad\text{for}\quad P-\text{a.e. }\omega\quad\text{such that } W(\omega)=0.\end{cases} \tag{2.29}$$

Now let $\{Z(t); t\in[0,T]\}$ be defined as in (2.15) with the initial condition $Z(0)=1/\lambda$. Then the above first order conditions become

$$u_{c+}(c(\omega,t),t)\begin{cases}\leqslant Z(\omega,t)^{-1}\leqslant u_{c-}(c(\omega,t),t) \\ \quad\text{for}\quad \nu-\text{a.e. }(\omega,t)\quad\text{such that } c(\omega,t)>0, \\ \leqslant Z(\omega,t)^{-1} \\ \quad\text{for}\quad \nu-\text{a.e. }(\omega,t)\quad\text{such that } c(\omega,t)=0;\end{cases}$$
$$V'_{+}(W(\omega))\begin{cases}\leqslant Z(\omega,T)^{-1}\leqslant V'_{-}(W(\omega)) \\ \quad\text{for}\quad P-\text{a.e. }\omega\quad\text{such that } W(\omega)>0, \\ \leqslant Z(\omega,T)^{-1} \\ \quad\text{for}\quad P-\text{a.e. }\omega\quad\text{such that } W(\omega)=0;\end{cases} \tag{2.30}$$

where we have used (2.17). Thus we have

$$\begin{aligned} c(t)&=\hat{f}(Z(t)^{-1},t)=\hat{f}(e^{-Y(t)},t) \qquad \nu-\text{a.e.} \\ W&=V'^{-1}_{+}(Z(T)^{-1})=V'^{-1}_{+}(e^{-Y(T)}) \qquad \text{a.s.,}\end{aligned} \tag{2.31}$$

where we have used the fact that $Y(t)=\ln Z(t)$.

Here is our first main result:

THEOREM 2.1. *Suppose that there exists a solution to* (2.28) *with a*

Lagrangian multiplier $\lambda > 0$ and that Conditions A *and* C *are satisfied. Let $Z(0) = 1/\lambda$ and define the function*

$$F(Z(t), S(t), t) = Z(t)E\left[\int_t^T Z(s)^{-1}\hat{f}(Z(s)^{-1}, s)\,ds + V_+'^{-1}(Z(T)^{-1})Z(T)^{-1} \mid Z(t), S(t)\right]. \tag{2.32}$$

Then $D_y^m F(y, t)$ and $F_t(y, t)$ exist and are continuous for $m \leqslant 2$, and together with F satisfy the linear partial differential equation

$$\mathscr{L}F + F_t = F_Z Z\kappa^{\mathsf{T}}\kappa - F_S^{\mathsf{T}}\sigma\kappa + rF - \hat{f}(Z^{-1}, t) \tag{2.33}$$

with boundary conditions

$$\begin{aligned} F(Z, S, T) &= V_+'^{-1}(Z^{-1}), \\ F(Z(0), S(0), 0) &= W_0, \end{aligned} \tag{2.34}$$

where $\mathscr{L}$ is the differential generator of (Z, S) under P and $\mathscr{L}F = \frac{1}{2}\mathrm{tr}(F_{SS}\sigma\sigma^{\mathsf{T}}) + \frac{1}{2}F_{ZZ}Z^2\kappa^{\mathsf{T}}\kappa + F_{SZ}^{\mathsf{T}}\sigma\kappa + F_S^{\mathsf{T}}(\zeta - i) + F_Z Z(r + |\kappa|^2)$. The optimal portfolio policy is

$$\begin{aligned} \theta(t) &= [F_S(Z(t), S(t), t) + (\sigma(S(t), t)\sigma(S(t), t)^{\mathsf{T}})^{-1} \\ &\quad \times [\zeta(S(t), t) - r(S(t), t)S(t)]Z(t)F_Z(Z(t), S(t), t)], \quad \nu - a.e. \\ \alpha(t) &= [F(Z(t), S(t), t) - \theta(t)^{\mathsf{T}} S(t)]/B(t) \quad \nu - a.e., \end{aligned} \tag{2.35}$$

and the optimal consumption–final wealth pair is specified in (2.31).

Proof. Let (c, W) be the solution to (2.28). Then (c, W) satisfies (2.31) and according to Assumption 2.1 is an optimal consumption–final wealth pair to (2.12). Our task now is to construct an optimal trading strategy that finances (c, W). We first claim that F defined in (2.32) gives the value over time of (c, W). Moreover, it has continuous $D_y^m F(y, t)$ and $F_t(y, t)$ for $m \leqslant 2$ under Conditions A and C. Note that under Condition A, (Y, S) is a diffusion process and thus possesses the strong Markov property. Moreover, since $Z(t) = e^{Y(t)}$, (Z, S) is also a diffusion process, as it has continuous sample paths and possesses the strong Markov property. By Lemma 2.4, the value of (c, W) at time t is

$$
\begin{aligned}
B(t)E^*&\left[\int_t^T \hat{f}(Z(s)^{-1}, s)/B(s)\,ds + V_+'^{-1}(Z(T)^{-1})/B(T) \mid \mathcal{F}_t\right] \\
&= \eta(t)^{-1}B(t)E\left[\int_t^T \hat{f}(Z(s)^{-1}, s)\eta(s)/B(s)\,ds \right.\\
&\quad \left. + V_+'^{-1}(Z(T)^{-1})\eta(T)/B(T) \mid \mathcal{F}_t\right] \\
&= Z(t)E\left[\int_t^T Z(s)^{-1}\hat{f}(Z(s)^{-1}, s)\,ds \right.\\
&\quad \left. + Z(T)^{-1}V_+'^{-1}(Z(T)^{-1}) \mid Z(t), S(t)\right] \\
&= F(Z(t), S(t), t),
\end{aligned}
$$

where the first equality follows from (2.14), the second equality follows from (2.17) and the above mentioned fact that (Z, S) has the strong Markov property, and the third equality follows from the definition of F. Immediately, we have $F(Z(0), S(0), 0) = W_0$ and $F(Z, S, T) = V_+'^{-1}(Z^{-1})$, which are the boundary conditions of (2.34).

Now we claim that $D_y^m F(y, t)$ and $F_t(y, t)$ exist and are continuous for $m \leqslant 2$. To see, this, we define another function

$$
\begin{aligned}
G(Y(t), S(t), t) \equiv e^{Y(t)}E&\left[\int_t^T e^{-Y(s)}\hat{f}(e^{-Y(s)}, s)\,ds \right.\\
&\left. + e^{-Y(T)}V_+'^{-1}(e^{-Y(T)}) \mid Y(t), S(t)\right], \qquad (2.36)
\end{aligned}
$$

where we have fixed a right-continuous version of the conditional expectation. It is easily seen that $G(Y(t), S(t), t) = F(Z(t), S(t), t)$. Conditions A and C and a multidimensional version of Remark 11.3 of Gihman and Skorohod [16, p. 77] show that $D_y^m G(y, t)$ and $G_t(y, t)$ exist and are continuous for $m \leqslant 2$. It then follows that $D_y^m F(y, t)$ and $F_t(y, t)$ exist and are continuous for $m \leqslant 2$. Moreover, one can verify that $F_Z = Z^{-1}G_Y$, $F_S = G_S$, $F_t = G_t$, $F_{ZZ} = Z^{-2}G_{YY} - Z^{-2}G_Y$, $F_{SS} = G_{SS}$, and $F_{ZS} = Z^{-1}G_{YS}$. We have thus proved our claim that $D_y^m F(y, t)$ and $F_t(y, t)$ are continuous for $m \leqslant 2$ under Conditions A and C.

Since $D_y^m F(y, t)$ and $F_t(y, t)$ are continuous for $m \leqslant 2$, Itô's lemma implies that

$$F(Z(t), S(t), t)/B(t) + \int_0^t \hat{f}(Z(s)^{-1}, s)/B(s)\, ds$$

$$= F(0)/B(0) + \int_0^t (F_S(s)^\top \sigma(s) - F_Z(s) Z(s) \kappa(s)^\top)/B(s)\, dw^*(s),$$

$$+ \int_0^t (\mathscr{L}F(s) + F_s(s) - F_Z(s) Z(s) \kappa(s)^\top \kappa(s)$$

$$+ F_S(s)^\top \sigma(s) \kappa(s) - r(s) F(s) + \hat{f}(Z(s)^{-1}, s))/B(s)\, ds, \qquad (2.37)$$

where $\mathscr{L}$ is the differential generator of Z and S under P. By Lemmas 2.3 and 2.4, the left-hand side of the above relation is a L^p martingale under Q. Now note that the integrand of the Itô integral on the right-hand side is a continuous function of $Z(t)$, $S(t)$, and t, and thus

$$\int_0^T |F_S(s)^\top \sigma(s) - F_Z(s) Z(s) \kappa(s)^\top|^2 / B^2(s)\, ds < \infty, \qquad \text{a.s.} \qquad (2.38)$$

Let

$$T_n \equiv \inf \left\{ t \in [0, T]: \int_0^t |F_S(s)^\top \sigma(s) - F_Z(s) Z(s) \kappa(s)^\top|^2 / B^2(s)\, ds \geqslant n \right\},$$

where we have used the convention that if the infimum does not exist, it is set to be T. By (2.38), we know that $T_n \to T$ a.s. as $n \to \infty$. On the stochastic interval $[0, T_n]$, the Itô integral on the right-hand side of (2.37) is a $L^p(Q)$ martingale by Lemma 2.3. It then follows that the second integral on the right-hand side of (2.37) must also be a martingale on $[0, T_n]$. Indeed, it is a martingale with absolutely continuous sample paths. It is known that any continuous martingale must be a constant or have unbounded variation sample paths (see Fisk [12]). Hence the integrand of the second integral on the right-hand side of (2.37) must vanish on $[0, T_n]$. Since the integrand of the Lebesgue integral of the right-hand side of (2.37) is continuous and $T_n \to T$ a.s., we have, a.s., $\forall t \in [0, T]$,

$$\mathscr{L}F + F_t = F_Z Z \kappa^\top \kappa - F_S^\top \sigma \kappa + rF - \hat{f}(Z^{-1}, t)$$

which is (2.33).

Now we are ready to provide ways to compute an optimal trading strategy. Let (α, θ) be an optimal trading strategy that finances (c, W). From Lemma 2.4 we know that

$$W/B(T) + \int_0^T \hat{f}(Z(s)^{-1}, s)/B(s)\, ds$$

$$= F(Z(0), S(0), 0)/B(0) + \int_0^T \theta(s)^\top \sigma(s)/B(s)\, dw^*(s) \qquad (2.39)$$

lies in $L^p(Q)$. We can thus subtract (2.37) evaluated at $t = T$ from (2.39) and take the expectation under Q of the pth power of the difference to get

$$E^*\left[\left(\int_0^T (\theta(t) - (F_S + (\sigma\sigma^\top)^{-1}(\zeta - rS)ZF_Z))^\top \sigma\sigma^\top \right.\right.$$

$$\left.\left. \times (\theta(t) - (F_S + (\sigma\sigma^\top)^{-1}(\zeta - rS)ZF_Z))/B^2(t)\,dt\right)^{p/2}\right] = 0.$$

By assumption, $\sigma\sigma^\top$ is positive definitive. We therefore have

$$\begin{aligned}\theta(t) = [&F_S(Z(t), S(t), t) + (\sigma(S(t), t)\sigma(S(t), t)^\top)^{-1} \\ &\times (\zeta(S(t), t) - r(S(t), t)S(t))Z(t)F_Z(Z(t), S(t), t)], \qquad \nu - \text{a.e.}\end{aligned}$$

The rest of the assertion follows immediately. ∎

Note that in Theorem 2.1 we used Condition A, which involves the process Y rather than Z. This is because the parameters of the process Z fail to satisfy a uniform Lipschitz condition which is needed for the differentiability of the function F. Thus we transformed Z into Y. Condition A together with Condition C then ensures that the G function has the desired derivatives and so does F.

Theorem 2.1 is most useful when it is used together with Cox and Huang [6], where sufficient conditions for the existence of an optimal policy are given. Then, provided that Conditions A and C are satisfied, the optimal policy can be computed by taking derivatives of the function F, which gives the value of the optimally invested wealth over time. However, Conditions A and C may not be satisfied in applications. From the proof of Theorem 2.1, it should be clear that the sole function of Conditions A and C is to ensure that F has the desired derivatives for Itô's lemma to apply. Thus, if we can verify that F has the desired derivatives through other means, say through direct computation, then the conclusion of Theorem 2.1 follows. Theorem 2.2 states this fact.

THEOREM 2.2. *Let F be defined as in Theorem* 2.1. *Suppose that there exists a solution to* (2.28) *with a Lagrangian multiplier $\lambda > 0$ or equivalently there exists $Z_0 > 0$ such that $F(Z_0, S(0), 0) = W_0$ and that* (2.31) *lies in $L^p(\nu) \times L^p(P)$ when $Z(0) = Z_0$. If $D_y^m F(y, t)$ and $F_t(y, t)$ exist and are continuous for $m \leqslant 2$, then the optimal policy is specified in* (2.31) *and* (2.35). *Moreover, F satisfies* (2.33) *and* (2.34).

Proof. Note that if there exists $Z_0 > 0$ such that $F(Z_0, S(0), 0) = W_0$ and (2.31) lies in $L^p(\nu) \times L^p(P)$ with $Z(0) = Z_0$, then there exists a solution to (2.28) by the Lagrangian theory and thus there is a solution to (2.12). The rest of the proof is then identical to that of Theorem 2.1. ∎

Note that, consistent with results using stochastic dynamic programming (see Breeden [3], for example), (2.35) indicates that the optimal risky asset portfolio is composed of two parts: N portfolios most highly correlated with "state variables" S and an instantaneous mean–variance efficient portfolio, which are the first term and the second term, respectively, on the right-hand side of the first equation of (2.35). The mean–variance efficient portfolio here is just the growth-optimal portfolio discussed earlier. The portfolio having the maximum correlation with respect to S_n is just S_n itself.

Theorems 2.1 and 2.2 are characterization theorems—if an optimal policy exists and if F has the desired derivatives, then the optimal policy can be computed by taking derivatives of F. In many instances, we can verify neither the existence of a solution to (2.28), by citing an existence theorem, nor the desired differentiability of F. However, we may be able to construct a candidate policy and then verify that it indeed is an optimal policy. This procedure is termed the *verification procedure*. The following theorem gives a verification procedure and will be termed the verification theorem, which is the counterpart of the verification theorem in dynamic programming with one distinct aspect—in dynamic programming, one works with processes under P, while we work here mostly with processes under the equivalent martingale measure Q.

THEOREM 2.3. *Let Condition B be satisfied. Suppose that there exist* $Z_0 > 0$ *and* $F\colon (0, \infty) \times \Re^N \times [0, T] \mapsto \Re_+$ *such that* $DF_y^m(y, t)$ *and* $F_t(y, t)$ *are continuous for* $m \leqslant z$ *and that* F *is a solution to the partial differential equation of* (2.33) *with boundary conditions* (2.34) *by taking* $Z(0) = Z_0$ *and* $F(Z, S, t) \to F(Z, S, T)$ *as* $t \to T$. *Suppose also that, for all* t,

$$|F(y, t)| \leqslant K(1 + |y|^{\gamma}) \qquad \forall y \in (0, \infty) \times \Re^N,$$

for some strictly positive constants K *and* γ, *and that there exist strictly positive constants* K_1 *and* γ_1 *such that*

$$|\hat{f}(x^{-1}, t)| \leqslant K_1(1 + |x|^{\gamma_1}), \qquad |V_+'^{-1}(x^{-1})| \leqslant K_1(1 + |x|^{\gamma_1})$$

for all $x \in (0, \infty)$. *Then there exists a solution to* (2.12) *with optimal policies described in* (2.31) *and* (2.35) *and with* $Z(0) = Z_0$.

Proof. Define Z according to (2.15) with $Z(0) = Z_0$. Let $F\colon (0, \infty) \times \Re^N \mapsto \Re$ be the solution to (2.33) with boundary conditions (2.34). Since F has continuous partial derivatives, Itô's lemma implies that (2.37) is valid. Substituting (2.33) into (2.37) and evaluating (2.37) at $t = T$ gives

$$F(Z(T), S(T), T)/B(T) + \int_0^T \hat{f}(Z(s)^{-1}, s)/B(s)\,ds$$

$$= F(0)/B(0) + \int_0^T (F_S(s)^\top \sigma(s) - F_Z(s)Z(s)\kappa(s)^\top)/B(s)\,dw^*(s). \quad (2.40)$$

Suppose for the time being that the Itô integral on the right-hand side of (2.40) is a martingale under Q. We take the expectation under Q of both sides of (2.40) and use the boundary conditions of (2.34) to get

$$E^*\left[V'^{-1}_+(Z(T)^{-1})/B(T) + \int_0^T \hat{f}(Z(t)^{-1}, t)/B(t)\,dt\right]$$
$$= F(Z(0), S(0), 0)/B(0) = W_0/B(0). \quad (2.41)$$

That is, $(\hat{f}(Z(t)^{-1}, t), V'^{-1}_+(Z(T)^{-1})$ exhausts the initial wealth (recall Lemma 2.4). If we can verify that $(\hat{f}(Z(t)^{-1}, t), V'^{-1}_+(Z(T)^{-1}))$ lies in $L^p(v) \times L^p(P)$ then we are done, since it will be a solution to (2.28) and a solution to (2.12) by Assumption 2.2. The optimal trading strategy is then (2.35) by Theorem 2.2.

We shall first show that $(\hat{f}(Z(t)^{-1}, t), V'^{-1}_+(Z(T)^{-1}))$ lies in $L^p(v) \times L^p(P)$. Under Condition B, we know that ζ and $\bar{\sigma}$ satisfy a linear growth and a local Lipschitz condition. Theorem 5.2.3 of Friedman [14] then implies that, for all strictly positive integers m, there exist constants L_m such that

$$E[|Z(t)|^{2m}] \leqslant (1 + |Z(0)|^{2m})e^{L_m t}.$$

This and the growth condition on $\hat{f}$ imply that

$$E[|\hat{f}(Z(t)^{-1}, t)|^p] < K_3 e^{Lt}$$

for some strictly positive constants K_3 and L. The Fubini theorem then implies that $\{\hat{f}(Z(t)^{-1}, t)\} \in L^p(v)$. Similar arguments show that $V'^{-1}_+(Z(T)^{-1}) \in L^p(P)$.

Next we want to show that (2.41) holds generally. First note that the linear growth condition and local Lipschitz condition on $\zeta + \bar{\sigma}\kappa$ and $\bar{\sigma}$ in Condition B imply that, for all strictly positive integers m, there exist constants L_m such that

$$E^*[|Z(t)|^{2m}] \leqslant (1 + |Z(0)|^{2m})e^{L_m t}. \quad (2.42)$$

This and the growth condition on $\hat{f}$ and V'^{-1}_+ immediately imply

$$E^*\left[V'^{-1}_+(Z(T)^{-1})/B(T) + \int_0^T \hat{f}(Z(t)^{-1}, t)/B(t)\,dt\right] < \infty.$$

For convenience, we will write $\psi(t) = (S(t), Z(t))$ and $\hat{\psi}(t) = (S(t), \ln Z(t))$. Now let

$$T_n \equiv \inf\{t \in [0, T]: |\hat{\psi}(t)| \geq n\},$$

where we have used the convention that if $\{t \in [0, 1]: |\hat{\psi}(t)| \geq n\}$ is empty, then $T_n = 1$. On the stochastic interval $[0, T_n]$, $|S(t)|$ and $|\ln Z(t)|$ are bounded by n. Since F_S, F_Z, σ, and κ are continuous functions of S, Z, and t, the integrand of the Itô integral on the right-hand side of (2.40) is bounded on $[0, T_n]$ and hence the Itô integral is a L^p-martingale under Q by Lemma 2.3. (Here we note that the stopping time is defined with respect to the process ψ rather than $\hat{\psi}$, since F_Z and F_S can become unbounded when Z approaches zero.) It follows that

$$E^*\left[F(Z(T_n), S(T_n), T_n)/B(T_n) + \int_0^{T_n} \hat{f}(Z(s)^{-1}, s)/B(s)\, ds\right]$$
$$= F(Z(0), S(0), 0)/B(0). \tag{2.43}$$

By the continuity of F_Z, F_S, κ, and B, we know that $T_n \to T$ a.s. Thus, as $n \to \infty$,

$$\int_0^{T_n} \hat{f}(Z(s)^{-1}, s)/B(s)\, ds \to \int_0^T \hat{f}(Z(s)^{-1}, s)/B(s)\, ds \qquad \text{a.s.}$$

The Lebesgue convergence theorem implies that, as $n \to \infty$,

$$E^*\left[\int_0^{T_n} \hat{f}(Z(s)^{-1}, s)/B(s)\, ds\right] \to E^*\left[\int_0^T \hat{f}(Z(s)^{-1}, s)/B(s)\, ds\right].$$

If we can show that

$$E^*[F(Z(T_n), S(T_n), T_n)/B(T_n)] \to E^*[F(Z(T), S(T), T)/B(T)]$$

as $n \to \infty$ then we are done, since we can let $n \to \infty$ in (2.43), and (2.41) follows. The arguments for this use Condition B and the growth condition on F and are contained in Theorem V.4.2 of Fleming and Rishel [13]. For the completeness of the proof, we will repeat their arguments. Note that we will be working with the process ψ in the rest of the proof.

Put

$$H(x) \equiv Q\{\sup_{0 \leq t \leq T} |\psi(t)| > x\}.$$

Condition B implies that there exists $x_0 > 0$ such that for all positive integers m there is an $M_1 > 0$ with

$$H(x) \leqslant M_1 x^{-2m} \qquad \forall x \geqslant x_0. \tag{2.44}$$

Now $F(Z(T_n), S(T_n), T_n) \to F(Z(T), S(T), T)$ a.s. since F is continuous in Z and S and by the hypothesis $F(Z, S, t) \to F(Z, S, T)$ as $t \to T$. For $R > 0$, let

$$\chi_R = \begin{cases} 1 & \text{if } \sup_{0 \leqslant t \leqslant T} |\psi(t)| \leqslant R; \\ 0 & \text{if } \sup_{0 \leqslant t \leqslant T} |\psi(t)| > R. \end{cases}$$

By the dominated convergence theorem

$$\lim_{n \to \infty} E^*[F(Z(T_n), S(T_n), T_n)\chi_R] \to E^*[F(Z(T), S(T), T)\chi_R]$$

for each $R > 0$. Since $F(Z, S, t)$ satisfies a polynomial growth condition

$$|F(y, t)| \leqslant K(1 + |y|^\gamma),$$

we can write

$$|F(Z(T_n), S(T_n), T_n)| \leqslant K(1 + \sup_{0 \leqslant t \leqslant T} |\psi(t)|^\gamma).$$

Take $2m > \gamma$ in (2.44). Then

$$\int^\infty x^{\gamma - 1} H(x)\, dx < \infty,$$

which implies that, upon integration by parts on (R, ∞),

$$\lim_{R \to \infty} \int_R^\infty (1 + x^\gamma)\, dH(x) = 0.$$

Thus

$$E^*[|F(Z(T_n), S(T_n), T_n)|\, (1 - \chi_R)] \leqslant -K \int_R^\infty (1 + x^\gamma)\, dH(x),$$

and the right-hand side tends to 0 as $R \to \infty$. This shows that

$$E^*[F(Z(T_n), S(T_n), T_n)] \to E^*[F(Z(T), S(T), T)]$$

as $n \to \infty$, which was to be proved. ∎

Note that, unlike the verification theorem in dynamic proramming, the verification procedure in Theorem 2.3 involves a linear partial differential equation. Note also that in deriving (2.43) we have made a logarithmic transformation of Z into Y. This is because Z is strictly positive with probability one and F_Z and F_S may be unbounded as Z approaches zero. There is no need to perform the same transformation on S since, by assumption, S takes its values in the whole of $\Re^N$. When some of the price processes are strictly positive with probability one, they can similarly be handled by a logarithmic transformation.

For the rest of this section, we will assume that there exists a solution to (2.28) and that Conditions A and C are satisfied.

We use $\{W(t); t \in [0, T]\}$ to denote the process of the optimally invested wealth:

$$W(t) = F(Z(t), S(t), t).$$

It is clear that $W(T) = W$ a.s. The following proposition shows that after the optimally invested wealth reaches zero, the optimal consumption–portfolio policies are zeros.

Define an optional time $\mathcal{T} = \inf\{t \in [0, T)\colon W(t) \leqslant 0\}$, the first time the optimally invested wealth reaches zero. As a convention, when the infimum does not exist, it is set to be T.

PROPOSITION 2.1. *On the stochastic interval* $[\mathcal{T}, T]$,

$$\begin{aligned} \theta(Z(t), S(t), t) &= 0 \qquad \nu - a.e. \\ \alpha(Z(t), S(t), t) &= 0 \qquad \nu - a.e. \\ c(t) &= 0 \qquad \nu - a.e. \\ W &= 0 \qquad a.s. \end{aligned}$$

Proof. From the definition of F, it is clear that it is equal to zero at $\mathcal{T}$ if and only if on $[\mathcal{T}, T]$ the optimal consumption and final wealth are zeros. Arguments similar to the second half of the proof of Theorem 2.1 prove the rest of the assertion. ∎

Note that if we consider the agent's problem in the context of the theory of stochastic control, given the setup of the securities markets, we would like the optimal controls such as (α, θ, c, W) to be feedback controls. That is, the optimal controls at each time t depend only upon time t, the values of $S(t)$, and the agent's optimally invested wealth at that time. In the above theorem, the optimal controls are functions of $S(t)$, $Z(t)$, and t. However, Z is determined in part by the agent's initial wealth through the initial condition $Z(0) = 1/\lambda$. The following proposition shows that given $S(t)$ and t, the agent's optimally invested wealth at time t is an invertible function of Z if $u(y, t)$ and $V(y)$ are differentiable in y. Hence, the optimal controls are indeed feedback controls.

PROPOSITION 2.2. *$F_Z \geqslant 0$. Furthermore, if $u(y, t)$ and $V(y)$ are differentiable in y, then $F_Z > 0$ if $F > 0$, and there exists a function $F^{-1}(W(t), S(t), t) = Z(t)$ if $W(t) > 0$. In addition, F^{-1}_{WW}, F^{-1}_{W}, F^{-1}_{SS}, F^{-1}_{S}, and F^{-1}_{t} exist and are continuous. Thus we have*

$$\theta(Z(t), S(t), t) = \begin{cases} \theta(F^{-1}(W(t), S(t), t), S(t), t) & \nu-a.e. \\ \quad \text{if } W(t) > 0; \\ 0 \quad \text{if } W(t) = 0; \end{cases}$$

$$\alpha(Z(t), S(t), t) = \begin{cases} \theta(F^{-1}(W(t), S(t), t), S(t), t) & \nu-a.e. \\ \quad \text{if } W(t) > 0; \\ 0 \quad \text{if } W(t) = 0; \end{cases} \tag{2.45}$$

$$c(t) = \begin{cases} \hat{f}(1/F^{-1}(W(t), S(t), t), t) & \nu-a.e. \\ \quad \text{if } W(t) > 0; \\ 0 \quad \text{if } W(t) = 0; \end{cases}$$

$$W = W(T) \quad a.s.$$

Proof. It follows from Friedman [14, Theorem 5.5.5] and the fact that $\partial Z(s)/\partial Z(t) = Z(s)/Z(t)$ if $s \geqslant t$ we have

$$F_Z(Z(t), S(t), t) = -E\left[\int_t^T \frac{\hat{f}'(Z(s)^{-1}, s)}{Z^2(s)}\, ds + \frac{V'^{-1\prime}_{+}(Z(T)^{-1})}{Z^2(T)} \,\middle|\, Z(t), S(t)\right],$$

where $\hat{f}'$ denotes the derivative of $\hat{f}$ with respect to its first argument, and where $V'^{-1\prime}_{+}$ denotes the derivative of V'^{-1}_{+}. Thus $F_Z \geqslant 0$, since $\hat{f}(y, t)$ and $V'^{-1}_{+}(y)$ are decreasing in y. Note that if $u(y, t)$ is differentiable in y then $\hat{f}$ is strictly decreasing when $\hat{f}(y, t) > 0$; and similarly V'^{-1}_{+} is strictly decreasing if V is differentiable and if $V'^{-1}_{+}(y) > 0$. If $F_Z = 0$, it must be that $F(Z(t), S(t), t) = 0$ and Proposition 2.1 gives the optimal consumption and portfolio policies. If $F(Z(t), S(t), t) > 0$ then $F_Z(Z(t), S(t), t) > 0$. Therefore, given $S(t)$ and t, $Z(t)$ is an invertible function of $W(t)$ if $W(t) > 0$. Let this function be denoted by $F^{-1}(W(t), S(t), t)$. The differentiability of F^{-1} follows from the implicit function theorem; see, e.g., Hestenes [19, p. 172]. The rest of the assertion then follows from Theorem 2.1 and substitution. ∎

Remark 2.5. For $F_Z > 0$ when $F > 0$, it is certainly not necessary that $u(y, t)$ and $V(y)$ be differentiable in y. In the special case of our current general model to be dealt with in Section 3, many utility functions that are concave and nonlinear yield $F_Z > 0$ for $F > 0$. ▮

When utility functions have a finite marginal utility at zero, the optimal consumption policy may involve zero consumption. The following proposition identifies the circumstances in which optimal consumption is zero.

PROPOSITION 2.3. *Suppose that* $u_{c+}(0, t) < \infty$. *Consumption at time* t *is zero only if* $W(t) \leqslant F(u_{c+}(0, t)^{-1}, S(t), t)$. *Suppose in addition that* $u(y, t)$ *and* $V(y)$ *are differentiable in* y. *Then an optimal policy has the property that consumption will be zero if and only if wealth is less than the stochastic boundary* $F(u_{c+}(0, t)^{-1}, S(t), t)$.

Proof. From (2.30) we know that $c(t) \leqslant 0$ if and only if $u_{c+}(0, t) \leqslant Z(t)^{-1}$. It then follows from Proposition 2.2 that $u_{c+}(0, t) \leqslant Z(t)^{-1}$ only if

$$F(u_{c+}(0, t)^{-1}, S(t), t) \geqslant F(Z(t), S(t), t) = W(t).$$

This is the first assertion. Next suppose that both $u(y, t)$ and $V(y)$ are differentiable. We want to show that if $W(t) \leqslant F(u_{c+}(0, t)^{-1}, S(t), t)$, then $c(t) = 0$. We take two cases. Case 1: $W(t) = 0$. Then Proposition 2.1 shows that $c(t) = 0$. Case 2: $W(t) > 0$. Proposition 2.1 also shows that when $W(t) > 0$, $F_Z > 0$. Thus $u_{c+}(0, t) \leqslant Z(t)^{-1}$ if and only if

$$F(u_{c+}(0, t)^{-1}, S(t), t) \geqslant F(Z(t), S(t), t) = W(t). \quad ▮$$

By inspection of (2.35) and (2.45), we easily see that, when $F_Z > 0$, the *feedback controls* are differentiable functions of $W(t)$ and $S(t)$ (recall that Condition A is imposed). In particular, the optimal consumption policy is twice continuously differentiable in $W(t)$ and $S(t)$, which follows directly from the assumption that $\hat{f}(y, t)$ is two times continuously differentiable with respect to y (see Condition C).

The following proposition gives a complete characterization of utility functions such that $\hat{f}(y, t)$ is twice continuously differentiable with respect to y, given that $u(y, t)$ is differentiable in y.

PROPOSITION 2.4. *Suppose that* $u(y, t)$ *is differentiable with respect to* y. $D_y^m \hat{f}(y, t)$ *exists and is continuous for* $m \leqslant 2$ *if and only if* $D_y^m u(y, t)$ *exists and is continuous for* $m \leqslant 3$, *and for* $u_{y+}(0, t) < \infty$,

$$\lim_{y \downarrow 0} -\frac{u_y(y, t)}{u_{yy}(y, t)} = 0 \tag{2.46}$$

and

$$\lim_{y\downarrow 0} -\frac{u_{yyy}(y,t)}{u_{yy}(y,t)}\left(\frac{u_y(y,t)}{u_{yy}(y,t)}\right)^2 = 0. \tag{2.47}$$

Similar conclusions also hold for $V(y)$.

Proof. On the interval $(0, \infty)$, u_y is continuous and strictly decreasing. Hence $D_y^m \hat{f}(y, t)$ exists and is continuous for $m \leqslant 2$ in $(0, u_y(0, t))$ if and only if $D_y^m u(y, t)$ exists and is continuous for $m \leqslant 3$. When $u_y(0, t) < \infty$, on $(u_y(0, t), \infty)$, $D_y^m \hat{f}(y, t)$ is equal to zero for $m \leqslant 2$. This implies (2.46) and (2.47).

The proof for $V(y)$ is identical. ∎

2.3. *Relation to Dynamic Programming*

Traditionally, the agent's optimal consumption–portfolio policy is computed by stochastic dynamic programming; see, e.g., Merton [30]. We will now demonstrate the connection between our approach and stochastic dynamic programming.

The usual formulation of the consumption–portfolio problem uses a consumption policy and a vector of dollar amounts invested in risky assets as the controls. The former is denoted by $c(W(t), S(t), t)$ and the latter will be called an *investment policy* and be denoted by $A(W(t), S(t), t)$. Given a pair of controls (c, A), the dynamic behavior of the agent's wealth is

$$W(t) = W(0) + \int_0^t [W(s)r(s) - c(s) + A(s)I_{S^{-1}}(t)(\zeta(s) - r(s)S(s))]\, ds$$

$$+ \int_0^t A(s)I_{S^{-1}}(s)\sigma(s)\, dw(s) \qquad \forall t \in [0, T] \quad \text{a.s.},$$

where $I_{S^{-1}}(t)$ is a diagonal matrix with diagonal elements $S_n(t)^{-1}$. Define

$$J(W(t), S(t), t) = \sup_{c, A} E\left[\int_t^T u(c(s), s)\, ds + V(W(T)) \mid W(t), S(t)\right]$$

subject to the constraints that the wealth follows the above dynamics, that consumption cannot be negative, and that

$$J(0, S(t), t) = \int_t^T u(0, s)\, ds + V(0). \tag{2.48}$$

The last constraint is basically a nonnegative wealth constraint that rules out free lunches.

The existence of a pair of optimal controls is a nontrivial problem. We will refer readers to, for example, Krylov [28] for an extensive treatment using the theory of stochastic controls. For a much easier approach specific to the consumption–portfolio problem, we refer readers to Cox and Huang [6] and the references therein.

We assume that there exists a pair of optimal controls (c, A) and that J has two continuous derivatives with respect to its first two arguments and a continuous derivative with respect to t. The Bellman equation is then

$$0 = \max_{\hat{c}(t), \hat{A}(t)} \{u(\hat{c}(t), t) + \mathscr{L}J(W(t), S(t), t) + J_t(W(t), S(t), t)\}, \quad (2.49)$$

where $\mathscr{L}$ is the differential generator of (W, S). The optimal controls satisfy the first order necessary conditions

$$\begin{aligned} u_{c+}(c(t), t) &\begin{cases} \leqslant J_W(t) \leqslant u_{c-}(c(t), t) & \text{if} \quad c(t) > 0; \\ \leqslant J_W(t) & \text{if} \quad c(t) = 0; \end{cases} \\ V'_+(W) &\begin{cases} \leqslant J_W(T) \leqslant V'_-(W) & \text{if} \quad W > 0; \\ \leqslant J_W(T) & \text{if} \quad W = 0; \end{cases} \end{aligned} \quad (2.50)$$

$$A(t) = I_S(t)\left[\left(-\frac{J_{WS}(t)}{J_{WW}(t)}\right) + (\sigma(t)\sigma(t)^{\mathsf{T}})^{-1} \times (\zeta(t) - r(t)S(t))\left(-\frac{J_W(t)}{J_{WW}(t)}\right)\right], \quad (2.51)$$

where $I_S(t)$ is a diagonal matrix with diagonal elements $S_n(t)$. Substituting (2.50) and (2.51) into (2.49), we have a nonlinear partial differential equation for J. To compute the optimal controls, we need to solve this nonlinear partial differential equation with two boundary conditions: (2.48) and $J(W, S, T) = V(W)$. Once we solve this partial differential equation, the optimal controls can be gotten by simply substituting the solution into (2.50) and (2.51). Note that in solving the nonlinear partial differential equation, the nonnegativity constraint on consumption usually makes this nontrivial problem even more difficult when $\hat{f}$ is not differentiable at the boundary; see, e.g., Karatzas, Lehoczky, Sethi, and Shreve [25] for a special case of our general model.

To see that dynamic programming is consistent with our approach, note that at each time t, the dynamic strategy corresponds to the allocation that would be chosen in a newly initiated static problem of the form of (2.12) and that $Z(t)^{-1}$ is the marginal utility of wealth. Hence

$$u_{c+}(c(\omega, t), t) \begin{cases} \leqslant Z(\omega, t)^{-1} \leqslant u_{c-}(c(\omega, t), t) \\ \qquad \text{for} \quad \nu - \text{a.e.} \quad (\omega, t) \text{ such that } c(\omega, t) > 0, \\ \leqslant Z(\omega, t)^{-1} \\ \qquad \text{for} \quad \nu - \text{a.e.} \quad (\omega, t) \text{ such that } c(\omega, t) = 0; \end{cases} \quad (2.52)$$

$$V'_+(W(\omega))\begin{cases}\leqslant Z(\omega,T)^{-1}\leqslant V'_+(W(\omega)) \\ \qquad \text{for } P-\text{a.e.} \quad \omega \text{ such that } W(\omega)>0, \\ \leqslant Z(\omega,T)^{-1} \\ \qquad \text{for } P-\text{a.e.} \quad \omega \text{ such that } W(\omega)=0;\end{cases}$$

$$J_W(t)=Z(t)^{-1}=1/F^{-1}(W(t),S(t),t) \qquad \nu-\text{a.e.} \tag{2.53}$$

and

$$J_{WW}(t)=-F_W^{-1}(t)/(F^{-1}(t))^2 \quad \text{and} \quad J_{WS}(t)=F_S^{-1}(t)/(F^{-1}(t))^2. \tag{2.54}$$

Recall that

$$Z(t)=F^{-1}(W(t),S(t),t) \qquad \nu-\text{a.e.}$$

Therefore,

$$F_Z F_W^{-1}=1 \tag{2.55}$$

and

$$F_Z F_S^{-1}+F_S=0. \tag{2.56}$$

Relations (2.55) and (2.56) imply that

$$-\frac{J_{WS}}{J_{WW}}=F_S$$

and

$$-\frac{J_W}{J_{WW}}=F^{-1}/F_W^{-1}=F_Z Z.$$

Hence, it follows from (2.51) that

$$A(t)=I_S(t)[F_S(t)+(\sigma(t)\sigma(t)^\top)^{-1}(\zeta(t)-r(t)S(t))F_Z(t)Z(t)] \\ \nu-\text{a.e.}. \tag{2.57}$$

Relations (2.52) and (2.57) are consistent with (2.30) and (2.35).

Although our approach and stochastic dynamic programming are essentially consistent, there are several advantages to our approach.

First, as mentioned above, the problem of the existence of optimal consumption–portfolio policies can be dealt with very easily using our approach. This issue has been extensively discussed in Cox and Huang [6], to which we refer interested readers.

Second, in the verification theorem of dynamic programming, one needs to solve a nonlinear partial differential equation. On the other hand, Theorems 2.3 and 2.4 require only the solution of a linear partial differential equation.

Third, our approach yields optimal policies without having to find the indirect utility function. The indirect utility function will be a by-product of our analysis even when it does not have the desired derivatives to satisfy Bellman's equation. To see this, we put

$$\hat{J}(Z(t), S(t), t) \equiv E\left[\int_t^T u(\hat{f}(Z(s)^{-1}, s), s)\, ds + V(V_+'^{-1}(Z(T)^{-1})) \mid Z(t), S(t)\right].$$

Once we have $F_Z > 0$, the indirect utility function is

$$J(W(t), S(t), t) = \begin{cases} \hat{J}(F^{-1}(W(t), S(t), t), S(t), t) & \text{if } W(t) > 0; \\ \int_t^T u(0, s)\, ds + V(0) & \text{if } W(t) = 0. \end{cases}$$

The indirect utility function J may not be twice continuously differentiable in $W(t)$ and $S(t)$ and continuously differentiable in t. In such an event, the optimal policies cannot be determined by solving a nonlinear partial differential equation.

2.4. *The Relationship Between the Constrained and the Unconstrained Solutions*

The optimization problem of (2.12) has nonnegativity constraints on consumption as well as on final wealth. For utility functions that exhibit infinite marginal utilities at zero consumption and at zero wealth, the nonnegativity constraints are not binding at the optimal solution. For problems for which the nonnegativity constraints are binding, there is an intuitive way to interpret the optimal solution. To illustrate this, we will consider utility functions that are defined on the whole of the real line. If the consumption–portfolio problems for these utility functions have optimal solutions without the nonnegativity constraint, it is possible to obtain the optimal constrained solutions in a simple and direct way. In effect, the market informs an agent that he or she can follow an unconstrained consumption–portfolio policy only if he or she simultaneously buys an insurance package that will pay off the negative consumption and wealth as they are incurred. An optimal constrained policy will be one that allocates the initial wealth between an unconstrained policy and the insurance package on the unconstrained policy and exhausts all the initial wealth.

Formally, consider an agent with a utility function for consumption $u: \Re \times [0, T] \mapsto \Re$ and a utility function for final wealth $V: \Re \mapsto \Re$. Assume that $u(y, t)$ and $V(y)$ are increasing and strictly concave in y. Consider the program

$$\sup_{(\hat{c}, \hat{W}) \in L^p(\nu) \times L^p(P)} \quad E\left[\int_0^T u(\hat{c}, t)\, dt + V(\hat{W})\right]$$

$$\text{s.t.} \quad B(0) E\left[\int_0^T \hat{c}(t)\eta(t)/B(t)\, dt + \hat{W}\eta(T)/B(T)\right] = W_\lambda(0). \qquad (2.58)$$

Note that there is no nonnegativity constraint on consumption and on final wealth in (2.58). If there exists a solution to (2.58), by the strict concavity of the utility functions, the solution is unique and is denoted by $(\hat{c}_\lambda, \hat{W}_\lambda)$. By the Lagrangian theory, there exists a unique $\lambda > 0$ such that

$$\begin{aligned} &u_{c+}(c_\lambda(t), t) \leqslant \lambda\eta(t) B(0)/B(t) \leqslant u_{c-}(c_\lambda(t), t) \qquad \nu-\text{a.e.} \\ &V'_+(W_\lambda) \leqslant \lambda\eta(T) B(0)/B(T) \leqslant V'_-(W_\lambda) \qquad \text{a.s.} \end{aligned} \qquad (2.59)$$

We will use the following notation. Let $(\hat{c}, \hat{W}) \in L^p(\nu) \times L^p(P)$. Then $\hat{c}^+ \equiv \{\max[\hat{c}(t), 0];\ t \in [0, T]\}$ and $\hat{W}^+ \equiv \max[\hat{W}, 0]$. Similarly, $\hat{c}^- \equiv \{\max[-c(t), 0];\ t \in [0, T]\}$ and $\hat{W}^- \equiv \max[-\hat{W}, 0]$. By definition, we have $\hat{c} = \hat{c}^+ - \hat{c}^-$ and $\hat{W} = \hat{W}^+ - \hat{W}^-$. Moreover, by the fact that $L^p(\nu)$ and $L^p(P)$ are lattices, we know $\hat{c}^+$, $\hat{c}^-$ are elements of $L^p(\nu)$ and $\hat{W}^+$ and $\hat{W}^-$ are elements of $L^p(P)$.

The following is the main result of this subsection:

THEOREM 2.4. *Suppose that* $W_0 > 0$, (c_λ, W_λ) *is the solution to* (2.58) *with an initial wealth* $W_\lambda(0) \in (0, W(0)]$, *and*

$$B(0) E\left[\int_0^T c_\lambda^-(t)\eta(t)/B(t)\, dt + W_\lambda^- \eta(T)/B(T)\right] = W_0 - W_\lambda(0). \qquad (2.60)$$

Then $(c_\lambda^+, W_\lambda^+)$ *is the solution to* (2.58) *with the additional nonnegativity constraints* $\hat{c} \geqslant 0$ *and* $\hat{W} \geqslant 0$ *and with an initial wealth* $W_0 > 0$. *Conversely, suppose that there exists a solution to* (2.58) *with the additional nonnegativity constraints on consumption and on final wealth. Denote this solution by* (c, W). *Let* λ *be the Lagrangian multiplier associated with* (c, W). *Suppose that there exists* $(c_\lambda, W_\lambda) \in L^p(\nu) \times L^p(P)$ *such that* (2.59) *holds. Then there exists* $W_\lambda(0) \in (0, W(0)]$ *such that* (c_λ, W_λ) *is a solution to* (2.58) *with* $(c_\lambda^+, W_\lambda^+) = (c, W)$ *and* (2.60).

Proof. By concavity of the utility functions and (2.59) we have

$$u_{c+}(c_\lambda^+(\omega, t), t) \begin{cases} \leqslant \lambda\eta(\omega, t) B(0)/B(\omega, t) \leqslant u_{c-}(c_\lambda^+(\omega, t), t) \\ \qquad \text{for} \quad \nu-\text{a.e.} \quad (\omega, t) \text{ such that } c_\lambda^+(\omega, t) > 0; \\ \leqslant \lambda\eta(\omega, t) B(0)/B(\omega, t) \\ \qquad \text{for} \quad \nu-\text{a.e.} \quad (\omega, t) \text{ such that } c_\lambda^+(\omega, t) = 0. \end{cases} \qquad (2.61)$$

$$V'_+(W_\lambda^+(\omega))\begin{cases}\leqslant \lambda\eta(\omega, T)B(0)/B(\omega, T)\leqslant V'_-(W) \\ \qquad \text{for} \quad P-\text{a.e.} \qquad \omega \text{ such that } W_\lambda^+(\omega)>0; \\ \leqslant \lambda\eta(\omega, T)B(0)/B(\omega, T) \\ \qquad \text{for} \quad P-\text{a.e.} \qquad \omega \text{ such that } W_\lambda^+(\omega)=0.\end{cases}$$

Next we claim that $(c_\lambda^+, W_\lambda^+)$ has an initial value W_0. To see this, we recall that $c_\lambda = c_\lambda^+ - c_\lambda^-$ and $W_\lambda = W_\lambda^+ - W_\lambda^-$. Therefore,

$$\begin{aligned} B(0)E&\left[\int_0^T c_\lambda^+(t)\eta(t)/B(t)\,dt + W_\lambda^+\eta(T)/B(T)\right] \\ &= B(0)E\left[\int_0^T (c_\lambda(t)+c_\lambda^-(t))\eta(t)/B(t)\,dt \right. \\ &\qquad \left. + (W_\lambda + W_\lambda^-)\eta(T)/B(T)\right] \\ &= W_\lambda(0) + W_0 - W_\lambda(0) = W_0, \end{aligned} \tag{2.62}$$

where the second equality follows from (2.60). Finally, $(c_\lambda^+, W_\lambda^+)\in L_+^p(\nu)\times L_+^p(P)$, the concavity of the utility functions, (2.61), and (2.62) imply that $(c_\lambda^+, W_\lambda^+)$ is the solution to (2.58) with the nonnegativity constraints and with an initial wealth W_0.

Conversely, let (c, W) be the solution to (2.58) with the additional nonnegativity constraints and let $\lambda>0$ be the Lagrangian multiplier associated with it. By the hypothesis, there exists $(c_\lambda, W_\lambda)\in L^p(\nu)\times L^p(P)$ such that (2.59) holds. By the definition of (c_λ, W_λ), it is obvious that $(c_\lambda^+, W_\lambda^+) = (c, W)$. Now define

$$W_\lambda(0)\equiv B(0)E\left[\int_0^T c_\lambda(t)\,\eta(t)/B(t)\,dt + W_\lambda\eta(T)/B(T)\right].$$

The rest of the assertion then follows from direct verification. ∎

The agent invests $W_\lambda(0)$ in the unconstrained policy and then spends $W_0 - W_\lambda(0)$ on an insurance package that pays $(c_\lambda^-, W_\lambda^-)$. The combination of the unconstrained policy and the insurance package gives precisely the constrained policy. Note that the insurance package can be thought of as consisting of a continuum of put options with zero exercise price. To see this, we observe that $c_\lambda^-(t) = \max[-c_\lambda(t), 0]$ is the payoff of a European put option written on the unconstrained consumption policy at time t with a zero exercise price and $W_\lambda^- = \max[-W_\lambda, 0]$ is the payoff of a European put option written on the unconstrained policy for final wealth with an exercise price zero. The price at time 0 for the former is $B(0)E[c_\lambda^-(t)\eta(t)/B(t)]$ and for the latter is $B(0)E[W_\lambda^-\eta(T)/B(T)]$.

Consider buying a continuum of these put options on consumption according to the Lebesgue measure on $[0, T]$ and the put option on the final wealth. The payoff of this package is just $(c_\lambda^-, W_\lambda^-)$ and its price at time 0 is

$$\begin{aligned}\int_0^T & B(0)E[c_\lambda^-(t)\eta(t)/B(t)]\,dt + B(0)E[W_\lambda^-\eta(T)/B(T)] \\ &= B(0)E\left[\int_0^T c_\lambda^-(t)\eta(t)/B(t)\,dt + W_\lambda^-\eta(T)/B(T)\right] \\ &= W_0 - W_\lambda(0),\end{aligned}$$

where the first equality follows from the Fubini Theorem.

Once we solve the static problem, then we can use the methodology developed in Section 2.2 to compute the optimal portfolio strategy. In many specific situations, the optimal consumption–portfolio policies for the unconstrained problem are well know. We can thus simply find the optimal allocation of the initial wealth between the unconstrained policy and its associated insurance package, and then compute the portfolio strategy for the insurance package. The optimal consumption policy is then the positive part of the unconstrained consumption policy and the optimal portfolio policy is the sum of the known portfolio policy for the unconstrained problem and the portfolio policy for the insurance policy. This procedure will be demonstrated in the next section in the context of the model of Merton [30].

3. A Special Case

We now specialize our general model of uncertainty developed in Section 2 to the model considered by Merton [30] and revisited recently by Karatzas, Lehoczky, Sethi, and Shreve [25]. We will employ the general method developed in the previous section in place of the dynamic programming used in Karatzas *et al.* and Merton. The optimal consumption–portfolio policies for a class of utility functions will be explicitly computed. For many of the HARA utility functions for which the nonnegativity constraints are binding, the optimal policies fail to be linear policies. Note that the fact that the optimal policies fail to be linear policies has been pointed out by Sethi and Taksar [35]. They, however, do not provide closed form solutions for the complete family of HARA utility functions.

3.1. *Formulation*

We take the model of uncertainty of Section 2 with the following specialization. Assume that risky security gain processes follow a geometric Brownian motion:

$$S(t)+\int_0^t \iota(S(s),s)\,ds = S(0)+\int_0^t I_S(s)\mu\,ds+\int_0^t I_S(s)\sigma\,d\omega(s)$$

$$\forall t\in[0,T], \qquad \text{a.s.,}$$

where μ is an $N\times 1$ vector of constants, σ is an $N\times N$ nonsingular matrix of constants, and $I_S(t)$ is a diagonal matrix with elements $S_n(t)$. Assume further that $r(t)=r$ is a constant.

Given $Z(0)>0$, the process Z becomes

$$\begin{aligned}
Z(t) &= Z(0)+\int_0^t (r+(\mu-r\mathbf{1})^{\mathsf T}(\sigma\sigma^{\mathsf T})^{-1}(\mu-r\mathbf{1}))Z(s)\,ds \\
&\quad +\int_0^t (\mu-r\mathbf{1})^{\mathsf T}\sigma^{-1\mathsf T}Z(s)\,dw(s) \\
&= Z(0)\exp\{(\mu-r\mathbf{1})^{\mathsf T}\sigma^{-1\mathsf T}w(t) \\
&\quad +(r+\tfrac{1}{2}(\mu-r\mathbf{1})^{\mathsf T}(\sigma\sigma^{\mathsf T})^{-1}(\mu-r\mathbf{1}))t\} \\
&= Z(0)\exp\{(r-\tfrac{1}{2}(\mu-r\mathbf{1})^{\mathsf T}(\sigma\sigma^{\mathsf T})^{-1}(\mu-r\mathbf{1}))t \\
&\quad +(\mu-r\mathbf{1})^{\mathsf T}\sigma^{-1\mathsf T}w^*(t)\},
\end{aligned}$$

where $\mathbf{1}$ is an N-vector of ones. Thus, $\ln Z(t)$ is normally distributed with mean

$$\ln Z(0)+(r+\tfrac{1}{2}(\mu-r\mathbf{1})^{\mathsf T}(\sigma\sigma^{\mathsf T})^{-1}(\mu-r\mathbf{1}))t$$

and variance

$$(\mu-r\mathbf{1})^{\mathsf T}(\sigma\sigma^{\mathsf T})^{-1}(\mu-r\mathbf{1})t$$

under P and is normally distributed with mean

$$\ln Z(0)+(r-\tfrac{1}{2}(\mu-r\mathbf{1})^{\mathsf T}(\sigma\sigma^{\mathsf T})^{-1}(\mu-r\mathbf{1}))t$$

and variance

$$(\mu-r\mathbf{1})^{\mathsf T}(\sigma\sigma^{\mathsf T})^{-1}(\mu-r\mathbf{1})t$$

under Q. To simplify notation, we note that

$$\frac{(\sigma\sigma^{\mathsf T})^{-1}(\mu-r\mathbf{1})}{(\mu-r\mathbf{1})^{\mathsf T}(\sigma\sigma^{\mathsf T})^{-1}\mathbf{1}}$$

is an N vector of constants that sum to one and therefore can be thought of as a vector of portfolio weights on the N risky securities. The mean $\hat{\mu}$ and the variance $\hat{\sigma}^2$ of the rate of return of this portfolio are

$$\hat{\mu} = \frac{(\mu - r\mathbf{1})^{\mathrm{T}}(\sigma\sigma^{\mathrm{T}})^{-1}\mu}{(\mu - r\mathbf{1})^{\mathrm{T}}(\sigma\sigma^{\mathrm{T}})^{-1}\mathbf{1}},$$

$$\hat{\sigma}^2 = \frac{(\mu - r\mathbf{1})^{\mathrm{T}}(\sigma\sigma^{\mathrm{T}})^{-1}(\mu - r\mathbf{1})}{[(\mu - r\mathbf{1})^{\mathrm{T}}(\sigma\sigma^{\mathrm{T}})^{-1}\mathbf{1}]^2}.$$

To avoid the degenerate case, we assume that $\hat{\mu} \neq r$. Now put

$$\rho^2 \equiv (\mu - r\mathbf{1})^{\mathrm{T}}(\sigma\sigma^{\mathrm{T}})^{-1}(\mu - r\mathbf{1}) = \frac{(\hat{\mu} - r)^2}{\hat{\sigma}^2}$$

and we can write the mean and variance of $\ln Z(t)$ under P as $\ln Z(0) + (r + \frac{1}{2}\rho^2)t$ and $\rho^2 t$; and under Q as $\ln Z(0) + (r - \frac{1}{2}\rho^2)t$ and $\rho^2 t$.

For this special case of uncertainty, we will be able to consider a class of utility functions that is larger than that specified in Condition C. We assume that the utility function for consumption is continuous, increasing, and concave. It is either defined on the positive real line with a value at zero level of consumption possibly equal to minus infinity or defined on the whole of the real line. The utility function for the final wealth has the same characteristics. Note that we do not require the utility functions to be strictly concave and thus an optimal consumption–portfolio policy may not be unique when it exists. As in Section 2, we use $u(y, t)$ and $V(y)$ to denote utility function for consumption at time t and the utility function for final wealth. We also assume that one of $u(y, t)$ and $V(y)$ is nonlinear. We still maintain that

$$\lim_{y \to \infty} u_{y+}(y, t) = 0$$

and

$$\lim_{y \to \infty} V'_{+}(y) = 0,$$

and define $\hat{f}(y, t)$ and $V'^{-1}_{+}(y)$ as in Section 2. We further assume that $u_t(y, t)$ is continuous in t.

3.2. *Explicit Formulas for Optimal Consumption and Portfolio Policies*

We will continue to impose Assumption 2.2. Note that since $u(y, t)$ and $V(y)$ may not be strictly increasing in y, satiation may be attained. In such event, investing completelv in the riskless security while withdrawing minimum satiation levels of consumption over time is an optimal consumption–portfolio policy. Note that whenever

$$W(t) \geqslant \int_t^T e^{-r(s-t)}\hat{f}(0, s)\, ds + e^{-r(T-t)} V_+'^{-1}(0)$$

satiation occurs at time t.

When satiation has not occurred, define

$$\begin{aligned} F(Z(t), t) &= E^*\left[\int_t^T e^{-r(s-t)}\hat{f}(Z(s)^{-1}, s)\, ds \right. \\ &\qquad \left. + e^{-r(T-t)} V_+'^{-1}(Z(T)^{-1}) \mid Z(t)\right] \\ &= \int_0^{T-t} e^{-rs} \frac{1}{\rho\sqrt{s}} \int_{-\infty}^{+\infty} \hat{f}(e^{-x}, t+s) \\ &\qquad \times n\left(\frac{x - \ln Z(t) - (r - \frac{1}{2}\rho^2)s}{\rho\sqrt{s}}\right) dx\, ds \\ &\qquad + e^{-r(T-t)} \frac{1}{\rho\sqrt{T-t}} \int_{-\infty}^{+\infty} V_+'^{-1}(e^{-x}) \\ &\qquad \times n\left(\frac{x - \ln Z(t) - (r - \frac{1}{2}\rho^2)(T-t)}{\rho\sqrt{T-t}}\right) dx, \end{aligned} \tag{3.1}$$

where

$$n(y) = \frac{1}{\sqrt{2\pi}} \exp\left\{-\frac{y^2}{2}\right\}$$

is the standard normal density function. This function is just the F defined in Theorem 2.1. In our present setup, F is independent of $S(t)$.

For future reference, we will use $N(\cdot)$ to denote the distribution function for a standard normal random variable.

The following proposition shows that the optimally invested wealth will never become zero before time T.

PROPOSITION 3.1. *Suppose that there exists a solution to* (2.28) *with a Lagrangian multiplier λ. The optimally invested wealth will never reach zero before time T.*

Proof. If the agent reaches satiation, then the assertion is obvious. Now suppose that satiation does not occur and thus $\lambda > 0$. Define Z by taking

$Z(0)$ to be $1/\lambda$. Since either $u(y, t)$ or $V(y)$ is nontrivial, nonlinear, and concave, and since the support of a normally distributed random variable is the whole real line, the right-hand side of (3.1) is strictly positive for all $Z(t)$ and all $t \in [0, T)$. When there is no satiation, $F(Z(t), t)$ is equal to the optimally invested wealth at time t, and the assertion follows. ▮

The following proposition shows that in this special case we are currently considering, there is a one-to-one correspondence between $W(t)$ and $Z(t)$, where $W(t) \equiv F(Z(t), t)$, when satiation has not occurred.

PROPOSITION 3.2. *Suppose that there exists a solution to* (2.28). *When satiation has not occurred,* $F(Z(t), t)$ *is strictly increasing in* $Z(t)$ *and thus* $Z(t) = F^{-1}(W(t), t)$ $\nu-a.e.$

Proof. When satiation has not occurred, an increase in $Z(t)$ implies an increase in the mean for $\ln Z(s)$, $s > t$, while the variance stays the same. The assertion then follows from the hypothesis that either $u(y, t)$ or $V(y)$ is nontrivial, nonlinear, and concave. ▮

The following proposition is a specialization of Proposition 2.3.

PROPOSITION 3.3. *Suppose that* $u(y, t)$ *is nontrivial, that* $u_{c+}(0, t) < \infty$, *and that satiation has not occurred. An optimal consumption policy has the property that consumption will be zero if and only if wealth is less than the nonstochastic time dependent boundary given by*

$$\underline{W}(t) = \int_0^{T-t} \frac{e^{-rs}}{\rho\sqrt{s}} \int_{-\infty}^{+\infty} \hat{f}(e^{-x}, t+s) \times n\left(\frac{x + \ln u'_{c+}(0, t) - (r - \frac{1}{2}\rho^2)s}{\rho\sqrt{s}}\right) dx\, ds$$
$$+ \frac{e^{-r(T-t)}}{\rho\sqrt{T-t}} \int_{-\infty}^{+\infty} V'^{-1}_{+}(e^{-x}) \times n\left(\frac{x + \ln u_{c+}(0, t) - (r - \frac{1}{2}\rho^2)(T-t)}{\rho\sqrt{T-t}}\right) dx.$$

Proof. Note that $c(t) = 0$ if and only if $u_{c+}(0, t) \leq Z(t)^{-1}$. The assertion then follows from Proposition 3.2. ▮

The following propostion gives a set of sufficient conditions for $D_y^m F(y, t)$ and $F_t(y, t)$ to exist and to be continuous.

PROPOSITION 3.4. *Suppose that* (3.1) *is finite for all* $Z(t)$. *Suppose further that for every subinterval* $[a, b]$ *of* $\mathfrak{R}$ *and for every subinterval* $[a', b')$ *of* $[0, T)$ *there exist functions* $G^m(x, s)$, $m = 1, 2$, *such that for all* $t \in [a', b')$

$$\frac{1}{\rho\sqrt{s}} \hat{f}(e^{-x}, s+t) \left| \frac{\partial^m}{\partial y^m} n\left(\frac{x - y - (r - \frac{1}{2}\rho^2)s}{\rho\sqrt{s}}\right) \right| \leqslant G^m(x, s)$$
$$\forall y \in (a, b) \forall s \in (0, T-t)$$

and

$$\int_0^{T-t} \int_{-\infty}^{+\infty} G^m(x, s)\, dx\, ds < \infty,$$

and $\forall t \in [0, T)$ *and for every subinterval* $[a, b]$ *of* $\mathfrak{R}$ *there exists function* $H(x, s)$ *such that* $\forall s \in (0, T-t)$, $y \in (a, b)$, *and* x

$$\left| \frac{1}{\rho\sqrt{s}} \hat{f}_t(e^{-x}, t+s) n\left(\frac{x - y - (r - \frac{1}{2}\rho^2)s}{\rho\sqrt{s}}\right) \right| \leqslant H(x, s)$$

and

$$\int_0^{T-t} \int_{-\infty}^{+\infty} H(x, s)\, dx\, ds < \infty.$$

Then $D_y^m F(y, t) m \leqslant 2$ *and* $F_t(y, t)$ *exist and are continuous. In particular,*

$$\begin{aligned} F_Z(Z(t), t) = & \int_0^{T-t} \frac{e^{-rs}}{\rho\sqrt{s}} \int_{-\infty}^{+\infty} \hat{f}(e^{-x}, t+s) \\ & \times \frac{\partial}{\partial Z(t)} n\left(\frac{x - \ln Z(t) - (r - \frac{1}{2}\rho^2)s}{\rho\sqrt{s}}\right) dx\, ds \\ & + \frac{e^{-r(T-t)}}{\rho\sqrt{T-t}} \int_{-\infty}^{+\infty} V_+'^{-1}(e^{-x}) \\ & \times \frac{\partial}{\partial Z(t)} n\left(\frac{x - \ln Z(t) - (r - \frac{1}{2}\rho^2)(T-t)}{\rho\sqrt{T-t}}\right) dx. \end{aligned}$$

Proof. The assertions follow from repeated application of the Lebesgue convergence theorem, the fact that $u_{y+}(y, t)$ is continuous in t for every y, and the fact that the normal distribution density function is an exponential function; see, e.g., Theorems 10.38 and 10.39 of Apostol [1]. ▮

Note that the conditions in Proposition 3.4 do not involve the differentiability of $\hat{f}(e^{-x}, t)$ with respct to x, in contrast to Theorem 2.1. They do involve differentiability with respect to t, however. The proposition below is a direct consequence of Theorem 2.2, with the difference that now there exists a possibility of satiation.

PROPOSITION 3.5. *Suppose that $D^m F(y, t)$ and F_t exist and are continuous for $m \leqslant 2$, and that differentiation of F can be carried out under the integral sign. If $W(0) < \int_0^T e^{-rt} \hat{f}(0, t)\, dt + e^{-rT} V_+'^{-1}(0)$ and if there exists $Z_0 > 0$ such that $F(Z_0, 0) = W(0)$ and (2.31) lies in $L^p(v) \times L^p(P)$ with $Z(0) = Z_0$, a solution to (2.12) exists. Defining Z by taking $Z(0) = Z_0$, an optimal consumption–portfolio policy and its corresponding indirect utility function, before satiation occurs, are*

$$c(W(t), t) = \hat{f}(e^{-\ln F^{-1}(W(t), t)}, t)$$

$$\begin{aligned}
A(W(t), t) = (\sigma\sigma^{\top})^{-1}(\mu - r\mathbf{1}) \Bigg[\int_0^{T-t} \frac{e^{-rs}}{(\rho^2 s)^{3/2}} \\
\times \left(\int_{-\infty}^{+\infty} \hat{f}(e^{-x}, t+s)(x - \ln F^{-1}(W(t), t) - (r - \tfrac{1}{2}\rho^2) s) \right. \\
\left. \times\, n\left(\frac{x - \ln F^{-1}(W(t), t) - (r - \frac{1}{2}\rho^2) s}{\rho\sqrt{s}} \right) dx \right) ds \\
+ \frac{e^{-r(T-t)}}{(\rho^2 (T-t))^{3/2}} \int_{-\infty}^{+\infty} V_+'^{-1}(e^{-x}) \\
\times (x - \ln F^{-1}(W(t), t) - (r - \tfrac{1}{2}\rho^2)(T-t)) \\
\times\, n\left(\frac{x - \ln F^{-1}(W(t), t) - (r - \frac{1}{2}\rho^2)(T-t)}{\rho\sqrt{T-t}} \right) dx \Bigg]
\end{aligned}$$

$$\begin{aligned}
J(W(t), t) = \int_0^{T-t} \frac{1}{\rho\sqrt{s}} \int_{-\infty}^{+\infty} u(\hat{f}(e^{-x}, t+s), t+s) \\
\times\, n\left(\frac{x - \ln F^{-1}(W(t), t) - (r + \frac{1}{2}\rho) s}{\rho\sqrt{s}} \right) dx\, ds \\
+ \frac{1}{\rho\sqrt{T-t}} \int_{-\infty}^{+\infty} V(V_+'^{-1}(e^{-x})) \\
\times\, n\left(\frac{x - \ln F^{-1}(W(t), t) - (r + \frac{1}{2}\rho)(T-t)}{\rho\sqrt{T-t}} \right) dx.
\end{aligned}$$

When $W(t) \geqslant \int_t^T e^{-r(s-t)} \hat{f}(0, s)\, ds + e^{-r(T-t)} V_+'^{-1}(0)$, there is satiation at t and therefore investing completely in the riskless security and consuming $c(s) = \hat{f}(0, s)$ at time $s \geqslant t$ is an optimal strategy.

Proof. The first assertion is a consequence of Theorem 2.2. The second assertion is obvious. ∎

Note that with exponential discounting, the utility function has the form $u(y, t)=e^{-\rho t}u(y)$. For this important special case, $\hat{f}(e^{-x}, t)=u_+'^{-1}(e^{-x+\rho t})$.

We will now illustrate our results with several examples. Using Proposition 3.5 or Cox and Huang [6], one can verify that Assumption 2.2 is valid and there exists an optimal consumption–portfolio policy for all the examples. We will demonstrate our proposed method by computing explicit optimal consumption–portfolio policies. In particular, Example 3.4 solves the optimal consumption–portfolio problem for the complete family of HARA utility functions while taking into account the nonnegativity constraints on consumption and on final wealth.

EXAMPLE 3.1. Let $u(y, t)=0$ and

$$V(y)=\begin{cases} y & \text{for } 0\leqslant y<\bar{y}, \\ \bar{y} & \text{for } y\geqslant \bar{y}. \end{cases}$$

In this case, $V_+'(y)$ equals 1 for $0\leqslant y<\bar{y}$ and equals 0 for $y>\bar{y}$. Hence, $V_+'^{-1}(e^{-x})=\bar{y}$ for $x>0$ and $V_+'^{-1}(e^{-x})=0$ for $x\leqslant 0$. Computation yields

$$F(Z(t), t)=\bar{y}e^{-r(T-t)}N\left(\frac{\ln Z(t)+(r-\frac{1}{2}\rho^2)(T-t)}{\rho\sqrt{T-t}}\right).$$

Note that if $W(0)>e^{-rT}\bar{y}$, there is no $Z(0)<\infty$ such that $F(Z(0), 0)=W(0)$. This is so, because by investing $W(0)$ completely in the riskless asset, the agent will reach satiation at time T with probability one and this riskless strategy is an optimal strategy. For $W(0)<e^{-rT}\bar{y}$, an optimal investment strategy and its corresponding indirect utility function, before satiation occurs, are

$$A(W(t), t)=\bar{y}e^{-r(T-t)}(\sigma\sigma^{\top})^{-1}(\mu-r\mathbf{1})\frac{1}{\rho\sqrt{T-t}}$$
$$\times n\left(\frac{\ln F^{-1}(W(t), t)+(r-\frac{1}{2}\rho^2)(T-t)}{\rho\sqrt{T-t}}\right)$$

$$J(W(t), t)=\bar{y}N\left(\frac{\ln F^{-1}(W(t), t)+(r+\frac{1}{2}\rho^2)(T-t)}{\rho\sqrt{T-t}}\right).$$

Note that for any given time t, the optimal amount invested in the risky assets is the largest when $F^{-1}(W(t), t)=e^{-(r-\rho^2/2)(T-t)}$, which occurs when $W(t)=\frac{1}{2}\bar{y}e^{-r(T-t)}$. ∎

EXAMPLE 3.2. Let $u(y, t)=0$ and $V(y)=-e^{-ay}/a$, where $a>0$ is the constant absolute risk aversion. Then $V_+'(y)=e^{-ay}$ and $V_+'^{-1}(e^{-x})=[x/a]^+$. Hence we have

$$
\begin{aligned}
F(Z(t), t) &= e^{-r(T-t)} \frac{1}{a\rho\sqrt{T-t}} \\
&\quad \times \int_0^{\infty} x\, n\left(\frac{x - \ln Z(t) - (r - \frac{1}{2}\rho^2)(T-t)}{\rho\sqrt{T-t}}\right) dx \\
&= e^{-r(T-t)} \frac{\rho\sqrt{T-t}}{a} \left[\left(\frac{\ln Z(t) + (r - \frac{1}{2}\rho^2)(T-t)}{\rho\sqrt{T-t}}\right)\right. \\
&\quad \times N\left(\frac{\ln Z(t) + (r - \frac{1}{2}\rho^2)(T-t)}{\rho\sqrt{T-t}}\right) \\
&\quad \left. + n\left(\frac{\ln Z(t) + (r - \frac{1}{2}\rho^2)(T-t)}{\rho\sqrt{T-t}}\right)\right] \\
A(W(t), t) &= e^{r(T-t)} \frac{1}{a} (\sigma\sigma^{\top})^{-1}(\mu - r\mathbf{1}) \\
&\quad \times N\left(\frac{\ln F^{-1}(W(t), t) + (r - \frac{1}{2}\rho^2)(T-t)}{\rho\sqrt{T-t}}\right).
\end{aligned}
$$

Note that the optimal amount invested in the risky assets is not independent of the wealth level. This is a consequence of the nonnegativity constraint. However, note that

$$
\lim_{W(t) \to \infty} A(W(t), t) = e^{-r(T-t)} \frac{1}{a} (\sigma\sigma^{\top})^{-1} (\mu - r\mathbf{1}),
$$

which is a constant policy. ∎

Recall from Section 2.4 that there exists a relationship between constrained solutions and unconstrained solutions. The following example illustrates this connection.

EXAMPLE 3.3. Consider the utility function for wealth of Example 3.2. First assume that there is no nonnegativity constraint. Then $V_+'^{-1}(e^{-x}) = x/a$. Since x is normally distributed, x/a lies in $L^p(P)$. Let

$$
\begin{aligned}
\hat{F}(Z_\lambda(t), t) &\equiv e^{-r(T-t)} \frac{1}{a\rho\sqrt{T-t}} \\
&\quad \times \int_{-\infty}^{+\infty} x\, n\left(\frac{x - \ln Z_\lambda(t) - (r - \frac{1}{2}\rho^2)(T-t)}{\rho\sqrt{T-t}}\right) dx \\
&= e^{-r(T-t)} \frac{1}{a\rho\sqrt{T-t}} \ln Z_\lambda(t) + (r - \tfrac{1}{2}\rho^2)(T-t),
\end{aligned}
$$

where Z_λ denotes the process Z with $Z(0)=1/\lambda$. $\hat{F}$ is the value, at time t, of the optimally invested wealth given that the initial wealth $W_\lambda(0)$ gives rise to the Lagrangian multiplier λ. Independent of the initial wealth, the optimal amounts invested in risky assets are

$$\hat{A}(W_\lambda(t), t)=e^{-r(T-t)}\frac{1}{a}(\sigma\sigma^{\mathsf{T}})(\mu-r\mathbf{1}).$$

Following this strategy, the final wealth will be

$$W_\lambda(T)=\frac{1}{a}[\ln Z_\lambda(0)+\{(r-\tfrac{1}{2}\rho^2)T-(\mu-r\mathbf{1})^{\mathsf{T}}\sigma^{-1\mathsf{T}}w^*(T)\}].$$

The value at t of the European put option, $p(Z_\lambda(t), t)$, written on $W_\lambda(T)$ is

$$\begin{aligned}
\hat{\hat{W}}_\lambda(t)=p(Z_\lambda(t), t)&=e^{-r(T-t)}\frac{1}{a\rho\sqrt{T-t}}\\
&\quad\times\int_{-\infty}^{0} x\, n\left(\frac{x-\ln Z_\lambda(t)-(r-\frac{1}{2}\rho^2)(T-t)}{\rho\sqrt{T-t}}\right)dx\\
&=e^{-r(T-t)}\frac{\rho\sqrt{T-t}}{a}\left[n\left(\frac{-\ln Z_\lambda(t)-(r-\frac{1}{2}\rho^2)(T-t)}{\rho\sqrt{T-t}}\right)\right.\\
&\quad-\frac{\ln Z_\lambda(t)+(r-\frac{1}{2}\rho^2)(T-t)}{\rho\sqrt{T-t}}\\
&\quad\left.\times N\left(\frac{-\ln Z_\lambda(t)-(r-\frac{1}{2}\rho^2)(T-t)}{\rho\sqrt{T-t}}\right)\right].
\end{aligned}$$

The investment strategy in the risky assets that replicates this put option is

$$\begin{aligned}
\hat{\hat{A}}(\hat{\hat{W}}_\lambda(t), t)&=-e^{-r(T-t)}\frac{1}{a}(\sigma\sigma^{\mathsf{T}})^{-1}(\mu-r\mathbf{1})\\
&\quad\times N\left(\frac{-\ln p^{-1}(\hat{\hat{W}}_\lambda(t), t)-(r-\frac{1}{2}\rho^2)(T-t)}{\rho\sqrt{T-t}}\right).
\end{aligned}$$

Now we want to find $Z_\lambda(0)$ so that

$$\hat{F}(Z_\lambda(0), 0)+p(Z_\lambda(0), 0)=W_0.$$

Note that $\hat{F}(t)+p(t)=F(t)$, where $F(t)$ is the value of the constrained policy at time t. Hence

$$1/\lambda=Z_\lambda(0)=F^{-1}(W_0, t),$$

which is what we anticipated. Now the process Z_λ is well defined and the optimal investment strategy for the constrained problem is

$$\begin{aligned} A(W(t), t) &= \hat{A}(W_\lambda(t), t) + \hat{\hat{A}}(\hat{W}_\lambda(t), t) \\ &= e^{-r(T-t)} \frac{1}{a} (\sigma\sigma^\top)^{-1}(\mu - r\mathbf{1}) \\ &\quad \times N\left(\frac{\ln F^{-1}(W(t), t) + (r - \frac{1}{2}\rho^2)(T-t)}{\rho\sqrt{T-t}}\right), \end{aligned}$$

which is identical to that of Example 3.2. ∎

Among many other results in his pioneering paper, Merton [30] derived optimal consumption and portfolio rules for hyperbolic absolute risk aversion (HARA) utility functions when securities prices follow a geometric Brownian motion and the interest rate is constant. However, as Merton noted, the solutions given for some members of the HARA family are not completely appropriate, since they allow the agent to incur negative wealth and may require negative consumption. One might hope that this difficuly could easily be remedied by setting consumption equal to zero whenever negative consumption would have been required and by following the disignated rules only as long as wealth remains positive. Unfortunately, this is not the case. The optimal solution with nonnegativity constraints on consumption and wealth will have a completely different form as evidenced already by Example 3.2. In the following example, we will derive explicit solutions that satisfy these constraints.

Example 3.4. Let

$$u(y, t) = e^{-\phi t}\left(\frac{1-\gamma}{\gamma}\right)\left(\frac{\beta y}{1-\gamma} + \xi\right)^\gamma$$

$$V(y) = u(y, T)$$

with $\beta > 0$, $\gamma \neq 0$ or 1. It is understood that if $\gamma > 1$, then $u(y, t) = 0$ for all $y \geqslant (\gamma - 1)\xi/\beta$. With $\gamma < 1$ and $\xi < 0$, the agent's problem is not completely specified because the utility function does not state the consequence of consuming less than $|\xi|\,(1-\gamma)/\beta$. Furthermore, for sufficiently low initial wealth,

$$W_0 < |\xi|\,(1-\gamma)(1 - e^{-rT})/\beta r,$$

there is no policy that can guarantee $c(t) \geqslant |\xi|\,(1-\gamma)/\beta$ for all t with probability one. Consequently, we only consider the case $\xi > 0$.

By evaluating the integrals of (3.1), we obtain the following results for the HARA functions:

$$F(Z(t),t)=\left(\frac{1-\gamma}{\beta}\right)\int_0^{T-t}\Bigg((\beta Z(t))^{1/(1-\gamma)}e^{-\delta s}$$

$$\times N\left(\frac{\ln(\beta Z(t))^{1/(1-\gamma)}-\ln\xi+(r-\delta+\frac{1}{2}\bar{\sigma}^2)s}{(\operatorname{sgn}(1-\gamma))\bar{\sigma}\sqrt{s}}\right)$$

$$-\xi e^{-rs}N\left(\frac{\ln(\beta Z(t))^{1/(1-\gamma)}-\ln\xi+(r-\delta-\frac{1}{2}\bar{\sigma}^2)s}{(\operatorname{sgn}(1-\gamma))\bar{\sigma}\sqrt{s}}\right)\Bigg)\,ds$$

$$+\left(\frac{1-\gamma}{\beta}\right)\Bigg[(\beta Z(t))^{1/(1-\gamma)}e^{-\delta(T-t)}$$

$$\times N\left(\frac{\ln(\beta Z(t))^{1/(1-\gamma)}-\ln\xi+(r-\delta+\frac{1}{2}\bar{\sigma}^2)(T-t)}{(\operatorname{sgn}(1-\gamma))\bar{\sigma}\sqrt{T-t}}\right)$$

$$-\xi e^{-r(T-t)}N\left(\frac{\ln(\beta Z(t))^{1/(1-\gamma)}-\ln\xi+(r-\delta-\frac{1}{2}\bar{\sigma}^2)(T-t)}{(\operatorname{sgn}(1-\gamma))\bar{\sigma}\sqrt{T-t}}\right)\Bigg],$$

where

$$\delta=\left(\frac{1}{1-\gamma}\right)\left(\phi-\gamma\left(r+\frac{\rho^2}{2(1-\gamma)}\right)\right)$$

and

$$\bar{\sigma}^2=\left(\frac{1}{1-\gamma}\right)^2\rho^2.$$

Using the properties of $n(\cdot)$ and $N(\cdot)$, it can be verified that $D_y^m F(y,t)$, $m\leqslant 2$, and $F_t(y,t)$ exist and are continuous. In particular, $F_Z(Z(t),t)$ can be computed by differentiating under the integral sign. When $\gamma>1$, satiation occurs at t if

$$W(t)\geqslant\frac{1-(1-r)e^{-rT-t}}{r}\frac{(\gamma-1)\xi}{\beta}.$$

When satiation has not occurred, an optimal policy and its corresponding indirect utility function are

$$c(W(t),t)=\left[\left(\frac{1-\gamma}{\beta}\right)((\beta F^{-1}(W(t),t))^{1/(1-\gamma)}-\xi)\right]^{+}$$

$$\begin{aligned}A(W(t),t)=&(\sigma\sigma^{\top})^{-1}(\mu-r\mathbf{1})\left(\frac{(\beta F^{-1}(W(t),t))^{1/(1-\gamma)}}{\beta}\right)\\&\times\left[\int_0^{T-t}e^{-\phi s}N\left(\frac{\begin{bmatrix}\ln(\beta F^{-1}(W(t),t))^{1/(1-\gamma)}\\ -\ln\xi+(r-\delta-\frac{1}{2}\bar{\sigma}^2)s\end{bmatrix}}{(\operatorname{sgn}(1-\gamma))\bar{\sigma}\sqrt{s}}\right)ds\right.\\&\left.+e^{-\phi(T-t)}N\left(\frac{\begin{bmatrix}\ln(\beta F^{-1}(W(t),t))^{1/(1-\gamma)}\\ -\ln\xi+(r-\delta-\frac{1}{2}\bar{\sigma}^2)(T-t)\end{bmatrix}}{(\operatorname{sgn}(1-\gamma))\bar{\sigma}\sqrt{T-t}}\right)\right]\end{aligned}$$

$$\begin{aligned}J(W(t),t)=&\left(\frac{1-\gamma}{\gamma}\right)e^{-\phi t}\left[\int_0^{T-t}\left((\beta F^{-1}(W(t),t))^{\gamma/(1-\gamma)}e^{-\delta s}\right.\right.\\&\times N\left(\frac{\begin{bmatrix}\ln(\beta F^{-1}(W(t),t))^{\gamma/(1-\gamma)}\\ -\ln\xi^{\gamma}+(\phi-\delta+\frac{1}{2}\gamma^2\bar{\sigma}^2)s\end{bmatrix}}{[\operatorname{sgn}((1-\gamma)\gamma)]\bar{\sigma}\sqrt{s}}\right)\\&\left.+\xi^{\gamma}e^{-\phi s}N\left(\frac{\begin{bmatrix}-\ln(\beta F^{-1}(W(t),t))^{\gamma/(1-\gamma)}\\ +\ln\xi^{\gamma}-(\phi-\delta-\frac{1}{2}\gamma^2\bar{\sigma}^2)s\end{bmatrix}}{[\operatorname{sgn}((1-\gamma)\gamma)]\bar{\sigma}\sqrt{s}}\right)\right)ds\\&+(\beta F^{-1}(W(t),t))^{\gamma/(1-\gamma)}e^{-\delta(T-t)}\\&\times N\left(\frac{\begin{bmatrix}\ln(\beta F^{-1}(W(t),t))^{\gamma/(1-\gamma)}\\ -\ln\xi^{\gamma}+(\phi-\delta+\frac{1}{2}\gamma^2\bar{\sigma}^2)(T-t)\end{bmatrix}}{[\operatorname{sgn}((1-\gamma)\gamma)]\bar{\sigma}\sqrt{T-t}}\right)\\&\left.+\xi^{\gamma}e^{-\phi(T-t)}N\left(\frac{\begin{bmatrix}-\ln(\beta F^{-1}(W(t),t))^{\gamma/(1-\gamma)}\\ +\ln\xi^{\gamma}-(\phi-\delta-\frac{1}{2}\gamma^2\bar{\sigma}^2)(T-t)\end{bmatrix}}{[\operatorname{sgn}((1-\gamma)\gamma)]\bar{\sigma}\sqrt{T-t}}\right)\right].\end{aligned}$$

As $W(t)$ becomes large, the optimal consumption and investment policies approach the linear functions of wealth given in Merton [30]. ▮

Remark 3.1. Example 3.4 can easily be generalized to allow the utility function for final wealth to be a HARA function having a different coefficient than that of the utility function for consumption. No substantial changes need to be made in the solution; only trivial changes in notation are required. ▮

For many utility functions, the optimal consumption policy will not be differentiable and may not even be continuous in wealth. A specific example is given below.

EXAMPLE 3.5. Let

$$u(y, t) = \begin{cases} y & \text{for } 0 \leqslant y < \bar{y}, \\ \bar{y} & \text{for } y \geqslant \bar{y}, \end{cases}$$

and let $V(y) = 0$. Suppose that satiation does not occur. We know that

$$\hat{f}(e^{-x}, t) = \begin{cases} \bar{y} & \text{for } x > 0, \\ 0 & \text{for } x \leqslant 0. \end{cases}$$

Direct computation yields

$$F(Z(t), t) = \bar{y} \int_0^{T-t} e^{-rs} N\left(\frac{\ln Z(t) + (r - \frac{1}{2}\rho^2)s}{\rho\sqrt{s}}\right) ds.$$

The optimal time t consumption is zero if and only if $Z(t) < 1$. By the strict monotonicity of $F(y, t)$ in y, we know $Z(t) < 1$ if and only if $F(Z(t), t) < F(1, t)$. Thus we have

$$c(t) = \begin{cases} 0 & \text{if } W(t) < F(1, t); \\ \bar{y} & \text{if } W(t) \geqslant F(1, t). \end{cases}$$

The optimal consumption is not a continuous function of the wealth and fails to be differentiable at a single point. ▮

We conclude this section by giving, in the two propositions below, necessary and sufficient conditions for the consumption policy prescribed by $\hat{f}$ to have certain derivatives.

PROPOSITION 3.6. *Suppose that the utility function for consumption has a possibly time dependent satiation level* $\bar{c}(t)$ *and yields an* F *such that* $D_y^m F(y, t)$ *and* F_t *exist and are continuous. Suppose also that satiation has not occurred. Let* y' *be a point of discontinuity of* $u_{c+}(c, t)$. *A necessary and sufficient condition for* $c(W(t), t)$ *to be a differentiable function of* $W(t)$ *and* t *is that for all* $t \in [0, T]$ *and for all* y'

(i) $u(y, t)$ *is strictly concave for all* $y < \bar{c}(t)$;

(ii) $u(y, t)$ *is twice differentiable with respect to* y *for all* $y < \bar{c}(t)$ *except at* y';

(iii) $\lim_{y \to y'} -\dfrac{u_y(y, t)}{u_{yy}(y, t)} = 0$;

(iv) *for* $u_{y+}(0, t) < \infty$, $\lim_{y \downarrow 0} -\dfrac{u_y(y, t)}{u_{yy}(y, t)} = 0$;

(v) *for* $\bar{c}(t) < \infty$, $\lim_{y \uparrow \bar{c}(t)} -\dfrac{u_y(y, t)}{u_{yy}(y, t)} = 0$.

$c(W(t), t)$ *is a continuously differentiable function of* $W(t)$ *and* t *if and only if, in addition,* $u(y, t)$ *is twice continuously differentiable with respect to* y *for all* $y < \bar{c}(t)$ *except at* y' *and continuously differentiable with respect to* t.

Proof. Suppose first that $\bar{c}(t) = \infty$. $c(W(t), t)$ is differentiable in $W(t)$ if and only if $\hat{f}(y, t)$ is differentiable in y. For every subinterval (a, b) on which $u_{y+}(y, t)$ is continuous, $\hat{f}(y, t)$ is differentiable if and only if $u_{y+}(y, t)$ is strictly decreasing and differentiable in y, which is (i) and (ii). On the interval $(u_{y+}(y', t), u_{y-}(y', t))$, $\hat{f}$ is flat. Hence $\hat{f}(y, t)$ is differentiable in y at y' if and only if (iii). When $u_{y+}(0, t) < \infty$, $\hat{f}$ is flat on the interval $(u_{y+}(0, t), \infty)$. Thus $\hat{f}(y, t)$ is differentiable at 0 if and only if (iv). Similar arguments prove (v). ∎

The following proposition gives circumstances in which c_{ww} exists and is continuous.

PROPOSITION 3.7. *Suppose that the utility function for consumption has a possibly time dependent satiation level* $\bar{c}(t)$ *and yields an* F *such that* $D_y^m F(y, t)$ *and* F_t *exist and are continuous. Suppose also that satiation has not occurred. Let* y' *be a point of discontinuity of* $u_{c+}(c, t)$ *and suppose that* $u(y, t)$ *is three times differentiable with respect to* y *except at* y'. *A necessary and sufficient condition for* $c(W(t), t)$ *to be twice differentiable with respect* *to $W(t)$ is that for all t and for all y',* (i)–(v) *of Proposition* 3.4 *are satisfied and*

$$\text{(vi)}\quad \lim_{y \to y'} \left(\frac{u_y(y,t)}{u_{yy}(y,t)}\right)^2 \left(\frac{u_{yyy}(y,t)}{u_{yy}(y,t)}\right) = 0;$$

$$\text{(vii)}\quad \textit{for } u_{y+}(0,t) < \infty, \lim_{y \downarrow 0} \left(\frac{u_y(y,t)}{u_{yy}(y,t)}\right)^2 \left(\frac{u_{yyy}(y,t)}{u_{yy}(y,t)}\right) = 0;$$

$$\text{(viii)}\quad \textit{for } \bar{c}(t) < \infty, \lim_{y \uparrow \bar{c}(t)} \left(\frac{u_y(y,t)}{u_{yy}(y,t)}\right)^2 \left(\frac{u_{yyy}(y,t)}{u_{yy}(y,t)}\right) = 0.$$

$c(W(t), t)$ is a twice continuously differentiable function of $W(t)$ if and only if, in addition, $u(y, t)$ is three times continuously differentiable with respect to y for all $y < \bar{c}(t)$ except at y'.

Proof. The arguments are similar to those of Propositions 2.4 and 3.6, so we omit them. ▮

4. Concluding Remarks

The focus of our paper is on the characterization and computation of optimal consumption-portfolio policies. It is a companion paper to Cox and Huang [6], which examines the existence of optimal policies. Several questions remain for future research. First, we have assumed that markets are dynamically complete, or equivalently, that there are as many linearly independent risky securities as the dimension of the uncertainty. It would be interesting to generalize our approach to situations where markets are not dynamically complete. Second, we have shown how nonnegativity constraints on consumption and final wealth can be easily accommodated using our approach. An important question is the extent to which constraints on trading strategies, such as restrictions on borrowing, can also be included. Finally, we have used only time-additive utility functions in our analysis. An issue for further study is the extension of the methods developed here to the case of non-time-additive utility functions.

References

1. T. Apostol, "Mathematical Analysis," 2nd ed., Addison–Wesley, Reading, MA, 1974.
2. F. Black and M. Scholes, The pricing of options and corporate liabilities. *J. Polit. Econ.* **81** (1973), 637–654.

3. D. Breeden, An intertemporal capital asset pricing model with stochastic investment opportunities. *J. Finan. Econ.* **7** (1979), 265–296.
4. M. Brennan and R. Solanski, Optimal portfolio insurance, *J. Finan. Quant. Anal.* **16** (1981), 279–300.
5. K. Chung and R. Williams, "Introduction to Stochastic Integration," Birkhäuser. Boston, MA, 1983.
6. J. Cox and C. Huang, A variational problem arising in financial economics, mimeo. Sloan School of Management, Massachusetts Institute of Technology, 1985.
7. J. Cox and H. Leland, Notes on intertemporal investment policies, mimeo, Graduate School of Business, Stanford University, 1982.
8. C. Dellacherie and P. Meyer, "Probabilities and Potential B: Theory of Martingales," North-Holland, New York, 1982.
9. D. Duffie and C. Huang, Implementing Arrow–Debreu equilibria by continuous trading of few long-lived securities, *Econometrica* **53** (1985), 1337–1356.
10. P. Dybvig, A positive wealth constraint precludes arbitrage in the Black-Scholes model. mimeo, Economics Department, Princeton University, 1980.
11. P. Dybvig and C. Huang, Nonnegative wealth, absence of arbitrage, and feasible consumption plans, to appear in *Review of Finan. Stud.*
12. D. Fisk, Quasi-martingales, *Trans. Amer. Math. Soc.* **120** (1965), 369–389.
13. W. Fleming and R. Rishel, "Deterministic and Stochastic Optimal Control," Springer-Verlag, New York/Berlin, 1975.
14. A. Friedman, "Stochastic Differential Equations and Applications," Vol. 1, Academic Press, New York, 1975.
15. I. Gihman and A. Skorohod, "Stochastic Differential Equations," Springer-Verlag. New York/Berlin, 1972.
16. I. Gihman and A. Skorohod, "Controlled Stochastic Processes," Springer-Verlag. New York/Berlin, 1979.
17. M. Harrison and D. Kreps, Martingales and multiperiod securities markets, *J. Econ. Theory* **20** (1979), 381–408.
18. M. Harrison and S. Pliska, Martingales and stochastic integrals in the theory of continuous trading, *Stochastic Process Appl.* **11** (1981), 215–260.
19. M. Hestenes, "Optimization Theory: The Finite Dimensional Case," Wiley, New York. 1975.
20. R. Holmes, "Geometric Functional Analysis and Its Applications," Springer-Verlag. New York/Berlin, 1975.
21. C. Huang, Information structures and viable price systems, *J. Math. Econ.* **14** (1985). 215–240.
22. C. Huang, An intertemporal general equilibrium asset pricing model: The case of diffusion information, *Econometrica* **55** (1987), 117–142.
23. J. Jacod, "Calcul Stochastique et Problèmes de Martingales," Lecture Notes in Mathematics, Vol. 714, Springer-Verlag, New York/Berlin, 1979.
24. I. Karatzas, J. Lehoczky, S. Sethi, and S. Shreve, Explicit solution of a general consumption/investment problem, *Math. Oper. Res.* **11** (1986), 613–636.
25. I. Karatzas, J. Lehoczky, and S. Shreve, Optimal portfolio and consumption decisions for a "small investor" on a finite horizon, *SIAM J. Control Optim.* **25** (1987), 1557–1586.
26. D. Kreps, Three essays on capital markets, Technical Report 298, Institute for Mathematical Studies in the Social Sciences, Stanford University, 1979.
27. D. Kreps, Arbitrage and equilibrium in economies with infinitely many commodities. *J. Math. Econ.* **8** (1981), 15–35.
28. N. Krylov, "Controlled Diffusion Processes," Springer-Verlag, New York/Berlin, 1980.

29. R. LIPTSER AND A. SHIRYAYEV, "Statistics of Random Processes I: General Theory," Springer-Verlag, New York/Berlin, 1977.
30. R. MERTON, Optimum consumption and portfolio rules in a continuous time model, *J. Econ. Theory* **3** (1971), 373–413.
31. R. MERTON, "Continuous-Time Finance," Blackwell, Oxford, 1989.
32. S. PLISKA, A stochastic calculus model of continuous trading: Optimal portfolios, *Math. Oper. Res.* **11** (1986), 371–382.
33. R. ROCKAFELLAR, Integral functionals, normal integrands, and measurable selections, *in* "Nonlinear Operators and the Calculus of Variations," J. Gossez *et al.*, Springer-Verlag, New York/Berlin, 1975.
34. H. ROYDEN, "Real Analysis," Macmillan Co., New York, 1968.
35. S. SETHI AND M. TAKSAR, A note on Merton's optimum consumption and portfolio rules in a continuous-time model, *J. Econ. Theory* **46** (1988), 395–401.

Journal of Mathematical Economics 20 (1991) 465–487. North-Holland

A variational problem arising in financial economics*

John C. Cox and Chi-fu Huang

Sloan School of Management, Massachusetts Institute of Technology, Cambridge, MA 02139, USA

Submitted November 1988, accepted August 1990

We provide sufficient conditions for a dynamic consumption–portfolio problem in continuous time to have a solution. When the price processes satisfy a regularity condition, all utility functions that are continuous, increasing, concave, and are dominated by a strictly concave power function admit a solution.

1. Introduction

The study of an individual's optimal consumption and portfolio decisions over time is a classical problem in financial economics. Traditionally, this *consumption–portfolio problem* has been analyzed using stochastic dynamic programming; for example, see Merton (1969, 1971). More recently, a number of authors have used a martingale representation technique instead; see Cox and Huang (1989), Karatzas, Lehoczky and Shreve (1987), and Pliska (1986).

Cox and Huang (1989) focuses on the explicit construction of optimal consumption–portfolio policies when they are known to exist. Pliska (1986) gives conditions to guarantee the existence of an optimal consumption–portfolio policy when there is no positivity constraint on consumption, while Karatzas, Lehoczky and Shreve (1987) work on the same problem with a positivity constraint.[1] However, neither Pliska nor Karatzas, Lehoczky and

*We would like to acknowledge helpful conversations with Sergiu Hart, Andreu Mas-Colell, and Ho-Mou Wu. We are especially grateful to a referee, Kerry Back, who provided many insightful comments and an almost line by line proof of a key proposition. The December 1985 version of this paper was presented at the Summer Workshop of the Institute of Mathematics and Its Applications at the University of Minnesota in May 1986. Later versions were presented at seminars at Brown University, Cornell University, Massachusetts Institute of Technology, Northwestern University, University of California at Berkeley, University of Chicago, and University of Pennsylvania. We appreciate the comments made at these seminars. We are also grateful for the financial support provided by Batterymarch Financial Management. We are of course solely responsible for any remaining errors.

[1]Throughout, we will use weak relations, that is, positive means non-negative, increasing means non-decreasing, and so forth.

0304-4068/91/$03.50 © 1991—Elsevier Science Publishers B.V. All rights reserved

Shreve give explicit and easily verifiable conditions on an investor's utility function and on parameters of the price processes for existence.

In this paper, we consider a model of a securities market with price processes that are somewhat more general than those considered by Karatzas, Lehoczky and Shreve. Explicit conditions on utility functions are then given to ensure the existence of a solution to the consumption–portfolio problem. These conditions make admissible any utility function that is continuous, increasing, and concave, and is dominated by a strictly concave power function. These conditions thus include most utility functions of economic interest.

The paper is organized as follows. In section 2 we formulate a model of a securities market and state the consumption–portfolio problem. Section 3 establishes the connection between the dynamic maximization problem formulated in section 2 and a static maximization problem of the Arrow–Debreu type. Section 4 provides sufficient conditions on utility functions as well as on (Arrow–Debreu) prices to guarantee a solution to the static problem. The results of sections 3 and 4 are then combined in section 5 to give sufficient conditions for the existence of a solution to the dynamic problem. Section 6 contains some concluding remarks.

2. The dynamic consumption–portfolio problem

We fix a complete probability space $(\Omega, \mathcal{F}, P)$ and a time span $[0, T]$, where T is a strictly positive real number.[2] An element of Ω, denoted by ω, is a state of nature, which is a complete description of the exogenous uncertain environment from time 0 to time T. The sigma-field $\mathcal{F}$ is the collection of events distinguishable at time T and P is a probability measure representing an individual's beliefs about the likelihood of distinguishable events.

There is defined on the probability space an N-dimensional standard Brownian motion denoted by $w = \{w_n(t); t \in [0, T], n = 1, 2, \ldots, N\}$. Let $\mathcal{F}_t$ be the smallest sigma-field containing all the P-measure zero sets with respect to which $\{w(s); 0 \leqq s \leqq t\}$ is measurable. The increasing family of sub-sigma-fields of $\mathcal{F}, \boldsymbol{F} \equiv \{\mathcal{F}_t; t \in [0, T]\}$, is usually termed the *filtration* generated by w. We assume that $\mathcal{F}_T = \mathcal{F}$, that is, the true state of nature will be revealed at time T by observing w from time 0 to time T. Since a standard Brownian motion starts at zero P–a.s., $\mathcal{F}_0$ contains only sets of probability zero or one. All the processes to appear will be adapted to $\boldsymbol{F}$ unless otherwise specified.[3]

[2]A probability space $(\Omega, \mathcal{F}, P)$ is said to be complete if $A \in \mathcal{F}$ and $P(A) = 0$ imply $A' \in \mathcal{F}$ for any $A' \subset A$.

[3]A process $X = \{X(t); t \in [0, T]\}$ is said to be *adapted* to $\boldsymbol{F}$ if X, as a mapping from $\Omega \times [0, T]$ to $\mathfrak{R}$, is measurable with respect to the product sigma-field generated by $\mathcal{F}$ and the Borel sigma-field of $[0, T]$ and if $X(t)$ is measurable with respect to $\mathcal{F}_t \, \forall t \in [0, T]$.

We will use the following notation: If g is a matrix, $|g|^2$ denotes $\mathrm{tr}(gg^{\mathrm{T}})$ and $|g|$ denotes $\sqrt{\mathrm{tr}(gg^{\mathrm{T}})}$, where ^{T} denotes transpose and 'tr' denotes trace.

Consider a frictionless securities market with $N+1$ long-lived traded securities indexed by $n=0,1,2,\ldots,N$. A long-lived security is a security available for trading throughout the period from time 0 to time T. Security $n\neq 0$ is risky and is characterized by a cumulated dividend process $D_n=\{D_n(t): t\in[0,T]\}$ and a price process $S_n=\{S_n(t); t\in[0,T]\}$, where $D_n(t)$ has right-continuous and bounded variation sample paths and denotes the cumulated dividends paid out by security n from time 0 to time t, and $S_n(t)$ denotes the ex-dividend price of security n at time t. We will henceforth denote $(S_1(t),\ldots,S_N(t))^{\mathrm{T}}$ and $(D_1(t),\ldots,D_N(t))^{\mathrm{T}}$ by $S(t)$ and $D(t)$, respectively. Since securities will be traded ex-dividend, we assume without loss of generality that $D_n(0)=0$. We will use $\Delta D(t)$ to denote $(D_1(t)-D_1(t-),\ldots,D_N(t)-D_N(t-))^{\mathrm{T}}$, where $D_n(t-)$ is the left-limit of D_n at t, which exists since D_n is of bounded variation. Security 0 is locally riskless, pays no dividends, and sells for $B(t)=B(0)\exp\{\int_0^t r(s)\,\mathrm{d}s\}$ at time t, where $B(0)$ is a strictly positive real number and where $r(t)$ is the instantaneous riskless interest rate at time t. We assume that $r(t)$ is positive. Henceforth the 0th security will be termed the 'bond'.

Assume that $S+D$ is an Itô process:

$$S(t)+D(t)=S(0)+\int_0^t \zeta(s)\,\mathrm{d}s+\int_0^t \sigma(s)\,\mathrm{d}w(s) \quad \forall t\in[0,T], \quad P\text{–a.s.}, \tag{1}$$

where ζ and σ are, respectively, an $N\times 1$ vector process and an $N\times N$ matrix process satisfying

$$\int_0^T |\zeta(t)|\,\mathrm{d}t<\infty \quad P\text{–a.s.}, \tag{2}$$

and

$$\int_0^T |\sigma(t)|^2\,\mathrm{d}t<\infty \quad P\text{–a.s.} \tag{3}$$

Note that (2) and (3) are sufficient for the Itô process of (1) to be well-defined. We will also assume throughout that $\sigma(\omega,t)$ is non-singular for almost all ω and t.

Now consider an agent with a time-additive utility function for consumption, $u(\cdot,t)$, a utility function for final wealth, $V(\cdot)$, and an initial wealth $W_0>0$. This agent wants to manage a portfolio of the risky securities and the bond, and withdraw funds out of the portfolio to maximize his expected utility of consumption over time and final wealth. Our task here is to find explicit conditions on the utility functions, u and V, and on the parameters of the price processes to guarantee the existence of a solution to the agent's problem.

For the agent's problem to be well-posed, however, we need to first specify the admissible objects of choices, that is, the admissible trading strategies on the securities, consumption processes, and final wealth. This is the subject to which we now turn.

We will use c to denote a consumption rate process with $c(t)$ denoting the consumption rate at time t and use W to denote a final wealth. We will say that a consumption–final wealth pair (c, W) is *admissible* if

$$(c, W) \in L^p_+(\nu) \times L^p_+(P) \equiv L^p_+(\Omega \times [0, T], \mathcal{O}, \nu) \times L^p_+(\Omega, \mathcal{F}, P),$$

where $1 \leqq p < \infty$, ν is the product measure generated by P and Lebesgue measure, $\mathcal{O}$ denotes the optional sigma-field,[4] and $L^p_+(\Omega \times [0, T], \mathcal{O}, \nu)$ and $L^p_+(\Omega, \mathcal{F}, P)$ denote the positive orthants of $L^p(\Omega \times [0, T], \mathcal{O}, \nu)$ and $L^p(\Omega, \mathcal{F}, P)$, respectively. The requirement that c and W be positive is natural since otherwise would make no economic sense.

A trading strategy is an $(N+1)$-vector of processes, denoted generically by

$$\{\alpha(t), \theta(t) \equiv (\theta_1(t), \ldots, \theta_N(t))^{\mathrm{T}}; t \in [0, T]\},$$

where $\alpha(t)$ and $\theta_n(t)$ are the number of shares of the 0th and the nth security held at time t, respectively, satisfying the following conditions:

1. $$\int_0^T |\alpha(t)B(t)r(t) + \theta(t)^{\mathrm{T}}\zeta(t)| \, \mathrm{d}t < \infty \quad P\text{–a.s.}, \tag{4}$$

2. $$\int_0^T |\theta(t)^{\mathrm{T}}\sigma(t)|^2 \, \mathrm{d}t < \infty \quad P\text{–a.s.}, \tag{5}$$

3. there exists a consumption–final wealth pair $(c, W) \in L^p_+(\nu) \times L^p_+(P)$ such that, P–a.s.,

$$\alpha(t)B(t) + \theta(t)^{\mathrm{T}}(S(t) + \Delta D(t)) + \int_0^t c(s) \, \mathrm{d}s$$

[4]The smallest sigma-field of subsets of $\Omega \times [0, T]$ with respect to which all the processes adapted to F having right-continuous sample paths are measurable as mappings from $\Omega \times [0, T]$ to $\Re$ is termed the *optional*-sigma field and is denoted by $\mathcal{O}$. It is known that any process measurable with respect to $\mathcal{O}$ is adapted to F; see Chung and Williams (1983, p. 56).

$$= \alpha(0)B(0) + \theta(0)^{\mathrm{T}} S(0) + \int_0^t (\alpha(s)B(s)r(s) + \theta(s)^{\mathrm{T}}\zeta(s))\,\mathrm{d}s$$

$$+ \int_0^t \theta(s)^{\mathrm{T}}\sigma(s)\,\mathrm{d}w(s) \quad \forall t \in [0, T], \tag{6}$$

4. $$\alpha(T)B(T) + \theta(T)^{\mathrm{T}}(S(T) + \Delta D(T)) = W \quad P\text{–a.s.} \tag{7}$$

Relations (4) and (5) ensure that the integrals of (6) are well-defined [see Liptser and Shiryayev (1977, ch. 4)] while relations (6) and (7) are budget constraints. The consumption–final wealth pair (c, W) of (6) and (7) will be said to be *financed* by the trading strategy (α, θ). Note that all the *simple processes*[5] that finance admissible consumption–final wealth pairs are trading strategies. Also, a trading strategy (α, θ) is associated with a wealth process

$$W(t) \equiv \alpha(t)B(t) + \theta(t)^{\mathrm{T}}(S(t) + \Delta D(t)),$$

which is the value at time t of the portfolio plus the dividends received.

So far, we have not put any restriction on the price processes other than certain regularity conditions on their parameters. For our consumption–portfolio problem to be well-specified, we certainly do not want the price processes to allow something to be created from nothing, that is, allow *free lunches*,[6] when an admissible trading strategy is employed. Harrison and Kreps (1979), Huang (1985), and Kreps (1981) have shown that for free lunches not to be available for simple strategies it suffices that S and D are related to martingales after a change of numeraire and a change of probability, or equivalently, there exists an *equivalent martingale measure*.[7] However, free lunches can still exist for other strategies that satisfy (4)–(7).[8] Dybvig (1980) and Harrison and Pliska (1981) have shown that the natural economic requirement that the agent's wealth over time be positive rules out all the free lunches. This is the approach we will take. With the positive wealth constraint, we can also weaken the requirement that there exists an equivalent martingale measure. It suffices that S and D are related to local

[5]A simple process is one that has bounded values and changes its values at a finite number of predetermined non-stochastic time points.

[6]For a formal definition of a free lunch see Kreps (1981).

[7]An equivalent martingale measure Q is a probability measure on $(\Omega, \mathscr{F})$ equivalent to P so that $S(t)/B(t) + \int_0^t [1/B(s)]\,\mathrm{d}D(s)$, prices plus cumulated dividends, in units of the bond, is a martingale under Q. Probability measure Q is said to be equivalent to P if they have the same measure zero sets. This definition is symmetric and thus we say P and Q are equivalent to each other. A necessary and sufficient condition for this is that the Radon–Nikodym derivative $\mathrm{d}Q/\mathrm{d}P$ is strictly positive.

[8]An example is the doubling strategy of Harrison and Kreps (1979).

martingales[9] after a change of numeraire and a change of probability. This is the subject to which we now turn.

The following assumption will be made throughout our analysis.

Assumption 2.1. There exists $\bar{K}<\infty$ such that $|\sigma(t)^{-1}(\zeta(t)-r(t)S(t))|\leqq \bar{K}$ ν–a.e.

Put

$$G^*(t)\equiv S(t)/B(t)-S(0)/B(0)+\int_0^t \frac{1}{B(s)}\,\mathrm{d}D(s),$$

which is prices plus cumulated dividends, in units of the bond. Itô's lemma implies that

$$G^*(t)=\int_0^t \frac{1}{B(s)}[\zeta(s)-r(s)S(s)]\,\mathrm{d}s+\int_0^t \frac{\sigma(s)}{B(s)}\,\mathrm{d}w(s).$$

Now put

$$\kappa(t)\equiv-\sigma(t)^{-1}[\zeta(t)-r(t)S(t)]$$

and

$$\eta(t)\equiv\exp\left\{\int_0^t \kappa(s)^{\mathrm{T}}\,\mathrm{d}w(s)-\tfrac{1}{2}\int_0^t|\kappa(s)|^2\,\mathrm{d}s\right\}. \tag{8}$$

By Assumption 2.1, η is well-defined. Putting

$$Q(A)\equiv\int_A \eta(\omega,T)P(\mathrm{d}\omega),\quad \forall A\in\mathscr{F},$$

the following proposition shows that Q is the unique probability measure equivalent to P and under which G^* is a local martingale.

Proposition 2.1. η is a martingale under P with $\mathrm{E}[\eta(T)]=1$ *and Q is the unique probability measure equivalent to P that makes G^* a local martingale. Moreover, we have*

[9] A process is a local martingale under the probability Q if it has right-continuous paths and there exists a sequence of optional times $T_n\uparrow\infty$ Q–a.s. so that the process $\{X(T_n\wedge t);t\in\mathfrak{R}_+\}$ is a martingale under Q.

$$G^*(t)=\int_0^t \frac{\sigma(s)}{B(s)}\,\mathrm{d}w^*(s) \quad t\in[0,T]\,P\text{–a.s.},$$

where

$$w^*(t)\equiv w(t)-\int_0^t \kappa(s)\,\mathrm{d}s, \quad t\in[0,T]$$

is a standard Brownian motion under Q.

Proof. See appendix.

Since P and Q are equivalent and thus have the same probability zero sets, we will use a.s. to denote *almost surely* with respect to both measures from now on.

A trading strategy (α,θ) is admissible if it satisfies (4)–(7) and $W(t)\geqq 0$ P–a.s. for all t, where $W(t)$ is the wealth process associated with (α,θ). Henceforth, we will use H to denote the space of admissible trading strategies. Given Proposition 2.1, arguments identical to Dybvig and Huang (1989, Theorem 2) show that there are no free lunches for trading strategies in H.

The problem facing an agent can now be stated formally in the following way:

$$\sup_{(\alpha,\theta)\in H} \mathrm{E}\left[\int_0^T u(c(t),t)\,\mathrm{d}t+V(W)\right]$$

$$\text{s.t.}\quad (c,W)\text{ is financed by }(\alpha,\theta)\text{ and lies in }L^p_+(\nu)\times L^p_+(P)$$

$$\text{with}\quad \alpha(0)B(0)+\theta(0)^{\mathrm{T}}S(0)\leqq W_0. \tag{9}$$

3. The correspondence between a dynamic problem and a static problem

It is well-known that the dynamic consumption–portfolio problem formulated in section 2 can be transformed into a static problem of the Arrow–Debreu type; see Harrison and Kreps (1979) and Huang (1985), for example. For completeness, we will outline this transformation.

Consider the static variational problem:

$$\sup_{(c,W)\in L^p_+(\nu)\times L^p_+(P)} \mathrm{E}\left[\int_0^T u(c(t),t)\,\mathrm{d}t+V(W)\right]$$

$$\text{s.t.} \quad B(0)\,\mathrm{E}\left[\int_0^T c(t)\eta(t)/B(t)\,\mathrm{d}t + W\eta(T)/B(T)\right] \leqq W_0. \tag{10}$$

The following proposition shows that (9) and (10) have the same feasible set.

Proposition 3.1. *(c, W) is feasible in* (9) *if and only if it is feasible in* (10).

Proof. Let (c, W) be feasible in (9). Then it lies in $L_+^p(\nu) \times L_+^p(P)$ and is financed by some $(\alpha, \theta) \in H$. Itô's lemma, (6), (7), and Proposition 2.1 imply

$$W(t)/B(t) + \int_0^t c(s)/B(s)\,\mathrm{d}s$$

$$= \alpha(0) + \theta(0)^{\mathrm{T}} S(0)/B(0) + \int_0^t \theta(s)^{\mathrm{T}} \sigma(s)/B(s)\,\mathrm{d}w^*(s).$$

The left-hand side is positive since $c \in L_+^p(\nu)$ and the trading strategy satisfies the positive wealth constraint. It is known that a local martingale bounded from below is a supermartingale (this is a simple application of Fatou's lemma). Thus the right-hand side is a supermartingale under Q since an Itô integral is a local martingale.[10] This implies

$$\mathrm{E}^*\left[W/B(T) + \int_0^T c(t)/B(t)\,\mathrm{d}t\right] \leqq W(0)/B(0).$$

Equivalently,

$$B(0)\mathrm{E}\left[W\eta(T)/B(T) + \int_0^T c(t)\eta(t)/B(t)\,\mathrm{d}t\right] \leqq W(0) \leqq W_0,$$

where we have used Dellacherie and Meyer (1982, VI.57). We have therefore shown that (c, W) is feasible in (10).

Conversely, let (c, W) be feasible in (10). Thus it satisfies the integral constraint. From the previous paragraph, we know that the integral constraint can be written as

[10]For the fact that an Itô integral is a local martingale, see, e.g., Liptser and Shiryayev (1977, section 4.2.10).

$$\mathrm{E}^*\left[W/B(T)+\int_0^T c(t)/B(t)\,\mathrm{d}t\right]\leqq W(0)/B(0).$$

Thus

$$W/B(T)+\int_0^T c(t)/B(t)\,\mathrm{d}t\in L^1(Q).$$

Define a martingale under Q:

$$x(t)=\mathrm{E}^*\left[W/B(T)+\int_0^T c(t)/B(t)\,\mathrm{d}t\,\middle|\,\mathscr{F}_t\right]\quad \text{a.s.}$$

$$=(\mathrm{E}[W\eta(T)/B(T)+\eta(T)\textstyle\int_0^T c(t)/B(t)\,\mathrm{d}t\,|\,\mathscr{F}_t]/\eta(t))\quad \text{a.s.,}$$

where we have fixed a right-continuous version of a conditional expectation, which exists as $\boldsymbol{F}$ is right-continuous, and the second equality follows from the conditional Bayes rule. Note that both the numerator and the denominator on the right-hand side of the second equality of the last relation are martingales under P. By the martingale representation theorem [see Clark (1970, 1971)] we know there exists an N-dimensional process ϕ with

$$\int_0^T |\phi(t)|^2\,\mathrm{d}t<\infty\quad \text{a.s.}$$

so that

$$x(t)=\frac{\mathrm{E}[W\eta(T)/B(T)+\eta(T)\int_0^T c(t)/B(t)\,\mathrm{d}t]+\int_0^t \phi(s)^{\mathrm{T}}\,\mathrm{d}w(s)}{1+\int_0^t \eta(s)\kappa(s)^{\mathrm{T}}\,\mathrm{d}w(s)}.$$

Itô's lemma then implies that a.s. for all t

$$x(t)=x(0)+\int_0^t \frac{1}{\eta(s)}(\phi(s)^{\mathrm{T}}-y(s)\kappa(s)^{\mathrm{T}})\,(\mathrm{d}w(s)-\kappa(s)\,\mathrm{d}s)$$

$$=x(0)+\int_0^t \frac{1}{\eta(s)}(\phi(s)^{\mathrm{T}}-y(s)\kappa(s)^{\mathrm{T}})\,\mathrm{d}w^*(s),$$

where $y(t)=\mathrm{E}[W\eta(T)/B(T)+\eta(T)\int_0^T c(t)/B(t)\,\mathrm{d}t\,|\,\mathscr{F}_t]$. Putting $\theta(t)^{\mathrm{T}}=(\phi(t)-y(t)\kappa(t))^{\mathrm{T}}B(t)\sigma(t)^{-1}/\eta(t)$,

$$W(t)=B(t)\left(x(t)-\int_0^t \frac{c(s)}{B(s)}\,\mathrm{d}s\right),$$

and

$$\alpha(t)=(W(t)-\theta(t)(S(t)+\Delta D(t))/B(t).$$

It is easily verified that $(\alpha,\theta)\in H$ and finances (c, W). Thus (c, W) is feasible in (9). □

The following corollary records an immediate implication of Proposition 3.1.

Corollary 3.1. *(c, W) is a solution to* (9) *if and only if it is a solution to* (10).

Thus to investigate whether there exists a solution to (9), it suffices to study (10).

4. A static variational problem

In this section we will study a class of static variational problems of the kind described in (10). For expositional purpose, we will first analyze in detail a problem in which there are only preferences for final wealth and no preferences for intermediate consumption. Later, we will generalize the results in this simpler case to the more general case with intermediate consumption. In the simpler case, the sufficient condition for existence involves whether the 'inverse' of the implicit Arrow–Debreu price system has a certain finite moment. In the more general case, however, one verifies whether the time integral of certain moment of the inverse of the Arrow–Debreu prices over time is finite.

4.1. A simple static variational problem

We are interested in finding a solution to the following problem:

$$(\mathrm{A}_1)\qquad \begin{aligned}&\sup_{x\in L^p_+(P)}\ \mathrm{E}[V(x)]\\ &\text{s.t.}\quad \phi(x)\equiv \mathrm{E}[x\xi]\leqq K_0,\end{aligned}$$

where $1\leqq p<\infty$, $\xi\in L^q_+(P)$ with $1/p+1/q=1$, $\xi>0$ a.s., and K_0 is a strictly positive constant. As usual, we will say that there exists a solution to (A_1) if the supremum is finite and is attained by some $x\in L^p_+(P)$. Henceforth, denote the value of (A_1) by $\mathrm{val}(K_0)$. Assume throughout that $V:\mathfrak{R}_+\mapsto\mathfrak{R}\cup\{-\infty\}$ is a continuous, concave, and increasing function which can be unbounded from below at zero. It is easily seen that $\mathrm{val}(K_0) > -\infty$ since $K_0 > 0$. As will be shown in the following two examples, however, when $L^p_+(\mathrm{P})$ is infinite dimensional, (A_1) may not have a solution. Consider the following two examples.

Take Ω to be $[0,1]$, $\mathcal{F}$ to be the Borel σ-field of $[0,1]$, and P to be Lebesgue measure on $[0,1]$. Suppose that $u(z) = z^{2/3}$ and

$$\phi(x) = \int_0^1 2\omega x(\omega)\,\mathrm{d}\omega \quad \forall x \in L^p(\Omega, \mathcal{F}, P).$$

Consider the sequence

$$x_n(\omega) = K_0 n^2 1_{[0,1/n]}(\omega), \quad n = 1, 2, \ldots,$$

where $1_{[0,1/n]}$ is the indicator function of $[0, 1/n]$. It is easily verified that $x_n \in L^p(P)$ for all $p \geqq 1$ and $\phi(x_n) = K_0 \, \forall n$. However,

$$\int_0^1 u(x_n(\omega))\,\mathrm{d}\omega = K_0^{2/3} n^{1/3} \to \infty \quad \text{as} \quad n \to \infty.$$

Note that in the above example, the utility function is strictly concave, increasing, and continuous. It has a zero derivative at infinity and an infinite right-hand derivative at zero – all very nice properties for a utility function can have. The problem arises because the commodities close to $\omega = 0$ are worth almost nothing. The agent would like to put all his money in the commodity indexed by $\omega = 0$, but his expected utility will be zero since the event $\{\omega = 0\}$ is of zero measure. Thus he tries to purchase commodities as close to $\omega = 0$ as possible. He achieves this by going along the sequence $(K_0 n^2 1_{[0,1/n]})_{n=1}^{\infty}$. However, the utility function grows too fast to infinity as the consumption increases to infinity and the expected utility explodes.

The following example, which is adapted from Aumann and Perles (1965), shows that the supremum may not be attained even if it is finite. Take Ω to be $[0,1]$, $\mathcal{F}$ the Borel sigma-field of $[0,1]$, and

$$P(A) = \int_A \frac{2}{3}(\omega + 1)\,\mathrm{d}\omega, \quad \forall A \in \mathcal{F}.$$

In addition, let $V(z) = z$ and

$$\phi(x)=\int_0^1 x(\omega)\frac{3}{2(\omega+1)}P(\mathrm{d}\omega)=\int_0^1 x(\omega)\,\mathrm{d}\omega.$$

Note that since prices for commodities, $3/2(\omega+1)$, are bounded above, $\phi(x)<\infty$ for all $x\in L^p(P)$ for all $p\geqq 1$. In this case, it is easily verified that $\int_0^1 V(x(\omega))P(\mathrm{d}\omega)<\frac{4}{3}K_0$, but its supremum over all budget feasible $x\in L^p_+(P)$ is equal to $\frac{4}{3}K_0$, which is not attained. In this case, the prices as captured by $3/2(\omega+1)$ are bounded from below; but the utility function is linear and again grows to infinity too fast. Hence the agent chooses to concentrate his wealth buying inexpensive commodities close to $\omega=1$ and the supremum is not attained.

Aumann and Perles (1965) studied a class of problems very similar to (A_1). Briefly, they considered conditions under which a given finite supremum is attained in the following program:

$$(A_2)\qquad \begin{aligned}&\sup_{x\in L^1_+(P^*)}\int_\Omega f(x(\omega),\omega)P^*(\mathrm{d}\omega)\\ &\text{s.t.}\quad \int_\Omega x(\omega)P^*(\mathrm{d}\omega)\leqq K_0,\end{aligned}$$

where P^* is a finite measure on $(\Omega,\mathscr{F})$ and $f(z,\omega)$ is increasing, concave, continuous in z, and bounded from below, for P^*-almost every ω. The program (A_2) differs from (A_1) in that f is state dependent and cannot be unbounded from below at zero, and the prices of commodities are unity. We will show below how the results of Aumann and Perles (1965) can be adapted to provide conditions for the attainment of a finite supremum. Before that, in the following proposition, we will first give conditions on the price ξ and on the utility function so that the supremum in (A_1) is always finite. It will be demonstrated later that for utility functions unbounded from above, these conditions also ensure the attainment of the supremum.

Proposition 4.1. Suppose that V is unbounded from above and there exist $\beta_1\geqq 0$, $\beta_2>0$ and $b\in(0,1)$ such that

$$V(z)\leqq\beta_1+\beta_2 z^{1-b}\quad\forall z\in\Re_+.$$

Then $\operatorname{val}(K_0)$ *is finite if* $\xi^{-1}\in L^{p/b}(P)$.

Proof. It is easily verified that there exists a solution to (A_1) when $V(z)=\beta_1+\beta_2 z^{1-b}$ if and only if $\xi^{-1}\in L^{p/b}(P)$. Let $\operatorname{val}_b(K_0)$ denote the supremum in this case. In the general case, let (x_n) be a sequence in $L^p_+(P)$ so that $\mathrm{E}[V(x_n)]\to\operatorname{val}(K_0)$. By the hypothesis, $V(z)\leqq\beta_1+\beta_2 z^{1-b}$. Thus,

$E[V(x_n)] \leqq \beta_1 + \beta_2 E[x_n^{1-b}] \leqq \text{val}_b(K_0) < \infty$ for all n. The assertion then follows by letting $n \to \infty$. □

Note that $\text{val}(K_0)$ for utility functions bounded from above is certainly finite independently of ξ.

Now we turn our attention to the attainment of $\text{val}(K_0)$. We show that a generalization of Aumann and Perles (1965) can be brought to bear on our problem by a change of unit. We first give a definition which generalizes that of Aumann and Perles to include functions possibly unbounded from below at zero.

Definition 4.1. Let $f: \mathfrak{R}_+ \times \Omega \mapsto \mathfrak{R} \cup \{-\infty\}$ be possibly unbounded from below at zero and be measurable with respect to the product σ-field $\mathscr{B}(\mathfrak{R}_+) \times \mathscr{F}$, where $\mathscr{B}(\mathfrak{R}_+)$ denotes the Borel sigma-field of $\mathfrak{R}_+$. Then $f(z, \omega) = o(z)$ as $z \to \infty$, $L^p(P)$-integrably in ω, if for each $\varepsilon > 0$ there exists $y \in L^p_+(P)$ such that, P–a.s., $f(z, \omega) \leqq \varepsilon z$ whenever $z \geqq y(\omega)$.

The following technical lemma gives an equivalent definition of $f(z, \omega) = o(z)$ as $z \to \infty$, $L^p(P)$-integrably in ω.

Lemma 4.1. Let $f: \mathfrak{R}_+ \times \Omega \to \mathfrak{R} \cup \{-\infty\}$ be possibly unbounded from below at zero and be measurable with respect to $\mathscr{B}(\mathfrak{R}_+) \times \mathscr{F}$. For all $\varepsilon > 0$, there exists $y \in L^p_+(P)$ such that, P–a.s., $f(z, \omega) \leqq \varepsilon z$ whenever $z \geqq y(\omega)$ if and only if for all $\varepsilon > 0$ and $a \geqq 0$, there exists $y \in L^p_+(P)$ such that, P–a.s., $f(z, \omega) \leqq \varepsilon(z - a)$ whenever $z \geqq y(\omega)$.

Proof. The proof for the sufficiency part is easy by taking $a = 0$. We now prove the necessity part. Let $\varepsilon > 0$ and $a > 0$ be given. By the hypothesis, $\exists y \in L^p_+(P)$ such that, P–a.s., $f(z, \omega) \leq (\varepsilon/2) z$ if $z \geq y(\omega)$. Putting

$$y^*(\omega) = \begin{cases} y(\omega) & \text{if} \quad y(\omega) > 2a \\ 2a & \text{if} \quad y(\omega) \leqq 2a, \end{cases}$$

we have, P–a.s., $f(z, \omega) \leqq \varepsilon(z - a)$ whenever $z \geqq y^*(\omega)$. It is easily seen that $y^* \in L^p_+(P)$ and the assertion was proved. □

The following proposition is a generalization of Aumann and Perles (1965, Proposition 2.2) to allow f to be possibly unbounded from below at zero.

Proposition 4.2. Let f of (A_2) be possibly unbounded from below at zero and $f(z, \omega) = o(z)$ as $z \to \infty$, $L^p(P^*)$-integrably in ω. Suppose that there exists

$\rho \in L^p_+(P^*)$ such that $\int_\Omega f(\rho(\omega),\omega)P^*(\mathrm{d}\omega) > -\infty$ and the supremum of (A_2) is finite. Then there exists a solution to (A_2).[11]

Proof. See appendix.

Before the first main result of this section, we record two technical lemmas.

Lemma 4.2. Suppose that V is unbounded from above and $V(z) \leqq \beta_1 + \beta_2 z^{1-b}$ for some $\beta_1 \geqq 0$, $\beta_2 > 0$ and $\xi^{-1} \in L^{p/b}(P)$ for some $b \in (0,1)$. Then $V(z)\xi(\omega)^{-1} = o(z)$, $L^p(P)$-integrably in ω.

Proof. Since utility functions are defined up to a positive linear transformation, we assume without loss of generality that $\beta_1 = 0$. We claim that given $\varepsilon > 0$, there exists $y \in L^p_+(P)$ such that

$$V(z) \leqq \varepsilon z \xi(\omega) \quad \forall z \geqq y(\omega),$$

for P-almost every $\omega \in \Omega$. Note that

$$V(z)/z \leqq \beta_2 z^{-b} \quad \forall z \in \Re_+ \backslash \{0\}.$$

Putting

$$y(\omega) \equiv (\varepsilon/\beta_2)^{-1/b} \xi(\omega)^{-1/b},$$

it is clear that $y > 0$ a.s. and $y \in L^p(P)$ since $\xi^{-1} \in L^{p/b}(P)$. For $z \geqq y(\omega)$ we have

$$V(z)/z \leqq \beta_2 z^{-b} \leqq \beta_2 y(\omega)^{-b} = \varepsilon \xi(\omega).$$

Hence,

$$V(z)\xi(\omega)^{-1} \leqq \varepsilon z, \quad \forall z \geqq y(\omega),$$

which was to be shown. □

The following is the counterpart of Lemma 4.2 for utility functions bounded from above.

Lemma 4.3. Suppose that V is bounded from above and $\xi^{-1} \in L^p(P)$. Then $V(z)\xi(\omega)^{-1} = o(z)$, $L^p(P)$-integrably in ω.

[11] In an earlier version we had a different argument for the case where V is unbounded from below. We thank Kerry Back for providing almost a line by line proof of this proposition.

Proof. Fix $\varepsilon>0$ and let $a>0$ be such that $V(z)\leqq a$ for all z. Let $y(\omega)=(a/\varepsilon)\xi(\omega)^{-1}$. Then $y\in L_+^p(P)$ and $V(z)\xi(\omega)^{-1}\leqq\varepsilon z$ if $z\geqq y(\omega)$. □

Here is our main theorem of this section.

Theorem 4.1. Suppose that V is unbounded from above, $V(z)\leqq\beta_1+\beta_2 z^{1-b}$ for all $z\in\Re_+$ for some $\beta_1\geqq 0$, $\beta_2>0$, and $\xi^{-1}\in L^{p/b}(P)$ for some $b\in(0,1)$. Then there exists a solution to (A_1). Moreover, if $\xi^{-1}\in L^{p'/b}(\hat{P})$ for some $p'\geqq 1$, where $\hat{P}$ is a finite measure absolutely continuous with respect to P, then every solution to (A_1) lies in $L^{p'}(\hat{P})$.

Proof. First we note that by Proposition 4.1, $\mathrm{val}(K_0)$ is finite. Thus our problem is to show that the supremum is attained.

Define a measure on $(\Omega,\mathscr{F})$:

$$P^*(A)\equiv\int_A \xi(\omega)P(\mathrm{d}\omega)\quad \forall A\in\mathscr{F}.$$

It is easily seen that P^* is equivalent to P since $\xi>0$ P–a.s. We first claim that $V(z)\xi(\omega)^{-1}=o(z)$, $L^1(P^*)$-integrably in ω. By the assumption and Lemma 4.2, for every $\varepsilon>0$ there exists $y\in L_+^p(P)$ such that $V(z)\xi(\omega)^{-1}\leqq\varepsilon z$ P–a.s. $\forall z\geqq y(\omega)$. Letting $\mathrm{E}^{P^*}[\cdot]$ denote the expectation with respect to P^*, Hölder's inequality implies that

$$\mathrm{E}^{P^*}[y]=\mathrm{E}[y\xi]\leqq(\mathrm{E}[y^p])^{1/p}(\mathrm{E}[\xi^q])^{1/q}<\infty,$$

where $1/p+1/q=1$ and the last inequality follows since $y\in L^p(P)$ and $\xi\in L^q(P)$. The assertion then follows since P^* and P have the same null sets.

Consider the program:

$$(\mathrm{A}_1^*)\qquad \sup_{x\in L_+^1(P^*)}\int_\Omega V(x(\omega))P(\mathrm{d}\omega)\quad \text{s.t.}\quad \int_\Omega x(\omega)\xi(\omega)P(\mathrm{d}\omega)\leqq K_0.$$

We first claim that the value of this program is finite. This can be seen using arguments of Proposition 4.1 and the facts that $\xi^{-1}\in L^p(P)$, $\xi\in L^q(P)$, and $L^p(P)\subset L^1(P^*)$.

The above program can be rewritten as follows:

$$\sup_{x\in L_+^1(P^*)}\int_\Omega V(x(\omega))\xi(\omega)^{-1}P^*(\mathrm{d}\omega)$$

$$\text{s.t.} \quad \int_{\Omega} x(\omega) P^*(\mathrm{d}\omega) \leqq K_0.$$

Thus, Proposition 4.2 insures that (A_1^*) has a solution.

Note that the consumption set in (A_1^*) is $L_+^1(P^*)$. Therefore, a solution to (A_1^*) may not be a solution to (A_1), since $L_+^p(P) \subset L_+^1(P^*)$ and the inclusion may be strict. Our task now is to show that, indeed, every solution to (A_1^*) lies in $L^p(P)$.

Let $x^* \in L_+^1(P^*)$ be a solution to (A_1^*). Since the Slater's condition [cf. Holmes (1975)] is obviously satisfied, it follows from the Saddle-Point Theorem and Rockafellar (1975) that there exists a positive constant ψ such that for all $x \in L_+^1(P^*)$, P^*–a.e.,

$$V(x^*(\omega))\xi(\omega)^{-1} - V(x(\omega))\xi(\omega)^{-1} \geqq \psi(x^*(\omega) - x(\omega)).$$

Note that since V is unbounded from above and concave, it must be strictly increasing and thus $\psi > 0$. Without loss of generality we can assume that $V(a) = 0$ for some $a \geqq 0$. Now take $x(\omega) = a \; \forall \omega \in \Omega$ in the above relation. We get $V(x^*(\omega))\xi(\omega)^{-1} \geqq \psi(x^*(\omega) - a)$ P^*–a.e. Since $V(z)\xi(\omega)^{-1} = o(z)$, $L^p(P)$-integrably in ω, and since P and P^* are equivalent, Lemma 4.1 implies that there must exist an $y \in L_+^p(P)$ such that

$$x^*(\omega) \leqq y(\omega) \quad \text{a.s.}$$

This implies that $x^* \in L_+^p(P)$.

Suppose in addition that $\xi^{-1} \in L^{p'/b}(\hat{P})$ for some $p' \geqq 1$ and $\hat{P}$ is a finite measure absolutely continuous with respect to P. Then $V(z)\xi(\omega)^{-1} = o(z)$, $L^{p'}(\hat{P})$-integrably in ω by Lemma 4.2. From previous discussions and the fact that $\hat{P}$ is absolutely continuous with respect to P we have

$$V(x^*(\omega))\xi(\omega)^{-1} \geqq \psi(x^*(\omega) - a) \quad \hat{P}\text{–a.e.}$$

Lemma 4.1 then implies that there exists $y \in L_+^{p'}(\hat{P})$ such that $x^* \leqq y$ and thus $x^* \in L_+^{p'}(\hat{P})$. □

Lemma 4.3 and arguments similar to those used in proving Theorem 4.1 prove the following:

Theorem 4.2. Suppose that V is bounded from above, and $\xi^{-1} \in L^p(P)$. Then there exists a solution to (A_1). Moreover, if satiation does not occur and $\xi^{-1} \in L^{p'/b}(\hat{P})$ for some $p' \geqq 1$, where $\hat{P}$ is a finite measure absolutely continuous with respect to P, then every solution to (A_1) lies in $L^{p'}(\hat{P})$. On the other hand, when satiation occurs there is a solution to (A_1) that is bounded.

Proof. Proofs of the first and the second assertions are identical to those for Theorem 4.1. Suppose now that satiation occurs. Let $z_0 = \inf\{z \geqq 0: V(z) \geqq V(z')\,\forall z' \geqq 0\}$. By continuity, the infimum is attained. Since satiation occurs, $z_0 < \infty$ and $\int_\Omega z_0 \xi(\omega) P(d\omega) \leqq K_0$. Thus $x(\omega) = z_0$ is a solution to (A_1) and is obviously bounded. □

4.2. Generalization

In this subsection, we will give sufficient conditions for there to exist a solution to the Arrow–Debreu style variational problem of (10). For brevity we will state only a generalization where both the utility function for consumption and the utility function for final wealth satisfy conditions of Theorem 4.1. The utility function for consumption and the utility function for final wealth, however, can satisfy different combinations of conditions of Theorems 4.1 and 4.2. We leave this exercise to interested readers.

In the following theorem, and throughout the rest of the paper, we will use λ to denote Lebesgue measure on $[0, T]$ and put $\xi(t) \equiv \eta(t)B(0)/B(t)$. Here is the generalization of Theorem 4.1:

Theorem 4.3. Suppose that $u(z,t): \Re_+ \times [0,T]$ is Borel measurable, and is continuous, concave, increasing, and unbounded from above in z for λ-almost every $t \in [0,T]$. Suppose further that there exist $b_1, b_2 \in (0,1)$, bounded functions $\beta_1(t)$, $\phi_1(t) \geqq 0$, $\beta_2(t)$, $\phi_2(t) > 0$, such that for λ–a.e. t,

$$u(z,t) \leqq \beta_1(t) + \beta_2(t) z^{1-b_1} \quad \text{and} \quad V(z) \leqq \phi_2(t) + \phi_2(t) z^{1-b_2} \quad \forall z \in \Re_+.$$

For there to exist a solution to (10), it is sufficient that, $\xi^{-1} \in L^{p/b_1}(v)$ and $\xi(T)^{-1} \in L^{p/b_2}(P)$. Moreover, if $\xi^{-1} \in L^{p'/b_1}(\hat{v})$ and $\xi(T)^{-1} \in L^{p'/b_2}(\hat{P})$ for some $p' \geqq 1$, where $\hat{P}$ is a finite measure absolutely continuous with respect to P and $\hat{v}$ is the product measure of $\hat{P}$ and Lebesgue measure, then every solution to (10) is an element of $L^{p'}_+(\hat{v}) \times L^{p'}_+(\hat{P})$.

Proof. See appendix.

5. Existence of a solution to the dynamic problem

Now we will give conditions under which there is a solution to (10) and thus is a solution to the dynamic problem of (9).

Theorem 5.1. Suppose that $u(z,t)$ and $V(z)$ satisfy conditions in Theorem 4.3, and there exists $p' > p$ such that

$$\mathrm{E}\left[\int_0^T |B(t)|^{p'/b_1}\,\mathrm{d}t\right] < \infty \quad \textit{and} \quad \mathrm{E}[|B(T)|^{p'/b_2}] < \infty.$$

Then there exists a solution to (9).

Proof. We show first that $\xi(t)^{-1} = B(t)\eta(t)^{-1}/B(0) \in L^{p/b_1}(v)$. Putting $\hat{p} = p'/p > 1$ and $1/\hat{p} + 1/\hat{q} = 1$, we have

$$\mathrm{E}\left[\int_0^T |B(t)\eta(t)^{-1}|^{p/b_1}\,\mathrm{d}t\right] \leqq \left(\mathrm{E}\left[\int_0^T (|B(t)|^{p/b_1})^{\hat{p}}\,\mathrm{d}t\right]\right)^{1/\hat{p}}$$

$$\times \left(\mathrm{E}\left[\int_0^T (|\eta(t)^{-1}|^{p/b_1})^{\hat{q}}\,\mathrm{d}t\right]\right)^{1/\hat{q}} < \infty,$$

where the first inequality follows from Hölder's inequality and the second from the assumption of this proposition and the second assertion of Proposition 2.1. Thus $B(t)\eta(t)^{-1}/B(0) \in L^{p/b_1}(v)$. Identical arguments show that $B(T)\eta(T)^{-1} \in L^{p/b_2}(P)$. It then follows from Theorem 4.1 that there exists a solution to (10). By Corollary 3.1, we conclude that there is a solution to (9). □

Theorem 5.1 utilizes Theorem 4.3, which is a generalization of one of various combinations of Theorems 4.1 and 4.2. We leave other possibilities to the reader.

6. Concluding remarks

Throughout our analysis we assumed that $|\kappa(t)|$ is uniformly bounded, but this is not necessary. In fact, it suffices that $\eta(T)$ has a unit expectation, $\eta(T)$ and $\eta(T)^{-1}$ have certain finite moments, and the time integrals of certain moments of $\eta(t)$ and $\eta(t)^{-1}$, respectively, are finite. For specific applications, these integral conditions can be verified through either direct computation or simulation. We refer the interested reader to Cox and Huang (1989) for details.

Although we have dealt with state-independent utility functions, our results generalize easily to certain state-dependent utility functions. For example, in the context of Theorem 4.1, if a state-dependent utility function $V(z,\omega)$ is bounded from above by $\beta_1 + \beta_2 z^{1-b}$ uniformly across ω, then there exists a solution to (A_1).

Appendix: Proofs

Proof of Proposition 2.1

By Assumption 2.1, κ is uniformly bounded. Thus $\mathrm{E}[\eta(t)]=1$ for all t and η is a martingale under P; see Liptser and Shiryayev (1977, Theorem 6.1). The fact that Q is a probability measure equivalent to P follows from $\mathrm{E}[\eta(T)]=1$ and $\eta(T)>0$ P–a.s.

Now, we want to show that $G^*(t)$ is a local martingale under Q. By the Girsanov theorem [see Liptser and Shiryayev (1977, ch. 6)], we know

$$w^*(t) \equiv w(t) - \int_0^t \kappa(S(s),s)\,\mathrm{d}s \quad \forall t \in [0,T]$$

is an N-dimensional standard Brownian motion under Q. Thus we can write

$$G^*(t) = \int_0^t \frac{\sigma(S(s),s)}{B(s)}\,\mathrm{d}w^*(s) \quad \forall t \in [0,T].$$

The right-hand side of the above relation is an Itô integral under Q and thus is a local martingale under Q.[12]

The uniqueness of Q follows from arguments similar to those of Theorem 3 of Harrison and Kreps (1979).

Proof of Proposition 4.2

We will first prove a technical lemma:

Lemma A.1. *Let $x_n, x \in L^1_+(P^*)$, and $x_n \to x$ in $L^1(P^*)$ and $x_n \to x$ P^*–a.e. as $n \to \infty$. Then*

$$\limsup \int_\Omega f(x_n(\omega),\omega)P^*(\mathrm{d}\omega) \leqq \int_\Omega f(x(\omega),\omega)P^*(\mathrm{d}\omega).$$

Proof. Fix $\psi \in L^1_+(P^*)$ be such that $\psi \geqq \{\rho, x+1\}$ and P^*–a.s., $f(z,\omega) \leqq z$ if $z \geqq \psi(\omega)$. Put $U_n = \{\omega : x_n(\omega) \leqq \psi(\omega)\}$. Then $1_{U_k} \to 1$ P^*–a.e. and $\lim f(x_n(\omega),\omega) = f(x(\omega),\omega)$ P^*–a.e. by the hypothesis that $x_n \to x$ P^*–a.e. and $f(z,\omega)$ is continuous in z, where 1_{U_n} is the indicator function of the set U_n. To simplify notation, we shall henceforth write $f(x(\omega),\omega)$ briefly as $f(x)$ and the integral $\int_\Omega f(x(\omega),\omega)P^*(\mathrm{d}\omega)$ as $\int_\Omega f(x)$. Note that $1_{U_n} f(x_n) \leqq 1_{U_n} f(\psi) \leqq \psi$. Fatou's lemma then implies that

[12] Note again that an Itô integral is a local martingale; see, e.g., Liptser and Shiryayev (1977, section 4.2.10).

$$\limsup \int_\Omega 1_{U_n} f(x_n) \leqq \int_\Omega f(x).$$

We are now left to show that

$$\limsup \int_{\Omega \setminus U_n} f(x_n) \leqq 0.$$

For this note that

$$\begin{aligned}\int_{\Omega\setminus U_n} f(x_n) &\leqq \int_{\Omega\setminus U_n} x_n \\ &\leqq \int_{\Omega\setminus U_n} x + \int_{\Omega\setminus U_n} |x_n - x| \\ &= \int_{\Omega\setminus U_n} x + \int_\Omega |x_n - x| - \int_{U_n} |x_n - x| \\ &\leqq \int_{\Omega\setminus U_n} x + \int_\Omega |x_n - x| \to 0.\end{aligned}$$

Thus the assertion is proved. □

Let val(y) denote the supremum in (A_2) when K_0 is replaced by some $y>0$. By the hypothesis we know that $-\infty < \text{val}(K_0) < +\infty$. Put $\alpha = \text{val}(K_0)$, $D = \{y \in \mathfrak{R}: y \leqq K_0, \text{val}(y) = \alpha\}$, and let $y_0 = \inf\{y: y \in D\}$. Let $\{b_k\}$ be a sequence of points of D such that $b_k \downarrow y_0$. For each k, val$(b_k) = \alpha$. Let $\{x_k\}$ be a sequence in $L^1_+(P^*)$ such that $\int_\Omega x_k \leqq b_k$ and $\int_\Omega f(x_k) \uparrow \alpha$. We want to show that $\{x_k\}$ has a weak cluster point.

Since $\{x_k\}$ is $L^1(P^*)$-norm bounded, it suffices to show for each decreasing sequence $\{S_m\}$ of $\mathscr{F}$ such that $S_m \downarrow \emptyset$ we have $\int_{S_m} x_k \to 0$ uniformly in k [Dunford and Schwartz (1957, Theorem IV.8.9)]. Fix throughout $\varepsilon > 0$.

If $y_0 = 0$ then $\int_{S_m} x_k \leqq \int_\Omega x_k \leqq \varepsilon$ for all m, if k is sufficiently large. Thus we may choose m_0 such that $\int_{S_m} x_k \leqq \varepsilon$ for all k and all $m \geqq m_0$. Suppose that $y_0 > 0$.

Assume without loss of generality that $\varepsilon/2 < y_0$. Let $b = y_0 - \varepsilon/4$. By the hypothesis, val$(b) < \alpha$ since $b < y_0$. Since $b_k \downarrow y_0$ and $\int_\Omega f(x_k) \uparrow \alpha$, $\exists k_0$ such that $b_k < y_0 + \varepsilon/4$ and $\int_\Omega f(x_k) > [\text{val}(b) + \alpha]/2$ if $k \geqq k_0$. Put $\gamma = (\alpha - \text{val}(b))/2$ and choose $\phi \in L^1_+(P^*)$, $\phi \geqq \rho$ such that $f(z,\omega) \leqq [\gamma/4K_0]z$ if $z \geqq \phi(\omega)$. Note that $f(\rho) \leqq f(\phi) \leqq [\gamma/4K_0]\phi$. Thus $f(\phi)$ is integrable. Fix m_0 such that

$$\int_{S_m} \phi < \varepsilon/4 \quad \text{and} \quad \int_{S_m} |f(\phi)| < \gamma/4 \quad \forall m \geqq m_0.$$

Define $T_{km}=\{\omega\in S_m: x_k(\omega)>\phi(\omega)\}$ and set

$$x_{km}(\omega)=\begin{cases}\phi(\omega) & \text{if } \omega\in T_{km}\\ x_k(\omega) & \text{otherwise.}\end{cases}$$

For $k\geqq k_0$ and $m\geqq m_0$,

$$\int_\Omega f(x_{km})=\int_\Omega f(x_k)+\int_{T_{km}} f(\phi)-\int_{T_{km}} f(x_k)$$

$$>\frac{\text{val}(b)+\alpha}{2}-\int_{S_m}|f(\phi)|-\frac{\gamma}{4K_0}\int_{T_{km}} x_k$$

$$>\frac{\text{val}(b)+\alpha}{2}-\frac{\gamma}{4}-\frac{\gamma}{4K_0}b_k$$

$$\geqq \text{val}(b)+\gamma/2,$$

where the second inequality follows from the fact that $b_k\leqq K_0$. Thus $\int_\Omega x_{km}>b$. Now note that

$$\int_\Omega x_{km}=\int_\Omega x_k-\int_{T_{km}} x_k+\int_{T_{km}}\phi$$

$$\leqq b_k+\varepsilon/4-\int_{T_{km}} x_k,$$

for $m\geqq m_0$ and $k\geqq k_0$. This implies that

$$\int_{T_{km}} x_k\leqq b_k+\varepsilon/4-b<y_0+\varepsilon/2-b=3\varepsilon/4$$

and thus

$$\int_{S_m} x_k=\int_{S_m\backslash T_{km}} x_k+\int_{T_{km}} x_k$$

$$\leqq\int_{S_m\backslash T_{km}}\phi+3\varepsilon/4$$

$$\leqq\varepsilon.$$

Since we can choose $m_1\geqq m_0$ such that $\int_{S_m} x_k\leqq\varepsilon$ for $k\leqq k_0$ and all $m\geqq m_1$, we have $\int_{S_m} x_k\leqq\varepsilon$ for all k whenever $m\geqq m_1$, as desired. Thus there exists a weak cluster point $\hat{x}$ of the sequence $\{x_k\}$. That is, there exists a subsequence of $\{x_k\}$, $\{x_{k'}\}$ such that $x_{k'} \to \hat{x}$ weakly. Then there is a sequence $\{y_k\}$, each of which is a (finite) convex combination of $x_{k'}$'s such that $y_k \to \hat{x}$ in $L^1(P^*)$; see Dunford and Schwartz (1957, Corollary V.3.14). Thus there exists a subsequence of $\{y_k\}$, denoted by $\{y_{k'}\}$, such that $y_{k'} \to \hat{x}$ a.e. So there exists a sequence $\{y_{k'}\}$ so that $y_{k'} \to \hat{x}$ a.e. and in $L^1(P^*)$. Lemma A.1 implies that

$$\limsup \int_\Omega f(y_{k'}) \leqq \int_\Omega f(\hat{x}).$$

By concavity and the fact that $\int_\Omega f(x_1) \leqq \int_\Omega f(x_k)$ for $k \geqq 1$, we know $\int_\Omega f(y_{k'}) \geqq \int_\Omega f(x_1)$ and hence $\int_\Omega f(\hat{x}) \geqq \int_\Omega f(x_1)$. But for each k', the sequence $\{x_{k'}, x_{k'+1}, \ldots\}$ converges weakly to $\hat{x}$, so we may conclude in the same way that $\int_\Omega f(\hat{x}) \geqq \int_\Omega f(x_{k'})$ for all k'. Hence

$$\int_\Omega f(\hat{x}) \geqq \limsup \int_\Omega f(x_{k'}) = \alpha.$$

Finally, since the set $\{x \in L^1(P^*): \int_\Omega x \leqq K_0\}$ is weakly closed, $\int_\Omega \hat{x} \leqq K_0$. We have thus shown that $\hat{x}$ is budget feasible and achieves the supremum, which was to be proved.

Proof of Theorem 4.3

Since $\beta_1(t)$, $\beta_2(t)$, $\phi_1(t)$, and $\phi_2(t)$ are bounded positive functions of time, there exist constants $\bar{\beta}_1$, $\bar{\beta}_2$, $\bar{\phi}_1$, and $\bar{\phi}_2$ such that, λ-a.e. t,

$$u(z,t) \leqq \bar{\beta}_1 + \bar{\beta}_2 z^{1-b_1} \quad \text{and} \quad V(z) \leqq \bar{\phi}_1 + \bar{\phi}_2 z^{1-b_2} \quad \forall z \in \Re_+.$$

Without loss of generality, assume $\bar{\beta}_1 = \bar{\phi}_1 = 0$. Let $\xi^{-1} \in L^{p/b_1}(\nu)$ and $\xi(T)^{-1} \in L^{p/b_2}(P)$ and fix $\varepsilon > 0$. Define

$$y(\omega,t) = \begin{cases} (\varepsilon/\bar{\beta}_2)^{-1/b_1} \xi(\omega,t)^{-1/b_1} & \forall t \in [0,T) \\ (\varepsilon/\bar{\phi}_2)^{-1/b_2} \xi(\omega,T)^{-1/b_2}, & t = T. \end{cases}$$

It is easily verified that $y \in L^p_+(P)$ and $u(z,t)\xi(\omega,t)^{-1} = o(z)$, $L^p(\nu)$-integrably in (t,ω) and $V(z)\xi(\omega,T)^{-1} = o(z)$, $L^p(P)$-integrably in ω. Putting $u(z,T) = V(z)$, the objective function of (10) is equivalent to

$$\mathrm{E}\left[\int_0^T u(c(t),t)\,\mathrm{d}\hat{\lambda}\right],$$

where $\hat{\lambda}$ is Lebesgue measure plus a point mass at T. Apply Proposition 4.2 by taking the 'state space' to be $\Omega \times [0, T]$ equipped with product measure $P \times \hat{\lambda}$ to conclude that there exists a solution to (10). The rest of the assertion is left for the reader. □

References

Aumann, R. and M. Perles, 1965, A variational problem arising in economics, Journal of Mathematical Analysis and Applications 11, 488–503.

Chung, K. and R. Williams, 1983, An introduction to stochastic integration (Birkhauser Inc., Boston, MA).

Clark, J., 1970, The representation of functionals of Brownian motion by stochastic integrals, Annals of Mathematical Statistics 41, 1282–1296.

Clark J., 1971, Erratum, Annals of Mathematical Statistics 42, 1778.

Cox, J. and C. Huang, 1985, A variational problem arising in financial economics with an application to a portfolio turnpike theorem, Working paper no. 1751-86 (Sloan School of Management, Massachusetts Institute of Technology, Cambridge, MA).

Cox, J. and C. Huang, 1989, Optimal consumption and portfolio policies when asset prices follow a diffusion process, Journal of Economic Theory 49, 33–83.

Dellacherie, C. and P. Meyer, 1982, Probabilities and potential B: Theory of martingales (North-Holland, New York).

Dunford, N. and J. Schwartz, 1957, Linear operators, Part I: General theory, (Wiley, New York).

Dybvig, P., 1980, A positive wealth constraint precludes arbitrage in the Black–Scholes model, Unpublished manuscript (Yale University, New Haven, CT).

Dybvig, P. and C. Huang, 1989, Nonnegative wealth, absence of arbitrage and feasible consumption plans, Review of Financial Studies 1, 377–401.

Harrison, M. and D. Kreps, 1979, Martingales and multiperiod securities markets, Journal of Economic Theory 20, 381–408.

Harrison, M. and S. Pliska, 1981, Martingales and stochastic integrals in the theory of continuous trading, Stochastic Processes and their Applications 11, 215–260.

Holmes, R., 1975, Geometric functional analysis and its applications (Springer-Verlag, New York).

Huang, C., 1985, Information structure and viable price systems, Journal of Mathematical Economics 14, 215–240.

Karatzas, I., J. Lehoczky and S. Shreve, 1987, Optimal portfolio and consumption decisions for a 'small investor' on a finite horizon, SIAM Journal of Control and Optimization 25, 1557–1586.

Kreps, D., 1981, Arbitrage and equilibrium in economies with infinitely many commodities, Journal of Mathematical Economics 8, 15–35.

Liptser, R. and A. Shiryayev, 1977, Statistics of random processes I: General theory (Springer-Verlag, New York).

Merton, R., 1969, Lifetime portfolio selection under uncertainty: The continuous-time case, Review of Economics and Statistics 1, 247–257.

Merton, R., 1971, Optimum consumption and portfolio rules in a continuous time model, Journal of Economic Theory 3, 373–413.

Pliska, S., 1986, A stochastic calculus model of continuous trading: Optimal portfolios, Mathematics of Operations Research 11, 371–382.

Rockafellar, R., 1975, Integral functionals, normal integrands and measurable selections, in: J. Gossez et al., eds., Nonlinear operators and the calculus of variations (Springer-Verlag, New York).

[9]

Optimal Saving and Risk in Continuous Time

LUCIEN FOLDES
London School of Economics

1. INTRODUCTION

This article presents a new analysis of the optimal planning of saving and consumption in continuous, unbounded time, when the return to capital, the utility of consumption and the saver's lifetime are subject to risk. The model studied is a one-commodity world with return proportional to capital and a welfare functional whose supremum is finite. The treatment of risk, within this simple framework, aims at generality. Thus in the main theory the only assumptions of substance made about the random processes representing the return to capital and the utility of a constant level of consumption are those needed to ensure that the supremum is finite and that an optimum exists. The use of stochastic differential equations is avoided, partly for simplicity and generality, partly to unify the risk and certainty versions of the theory. The saver's information structure is specified in a general, abstract way which allows for continual learning and adaptation of plans. Corresponding to this treatment of risks, the theory is concerned mainly with the existence and properties of optimal plans in general, as distinct from special types such as stationary or asymptotic solutions. The results fall under three main headings:

(i) Conditions for the existence of an optimum, proved by a new compactness argument (Section 3, Theorem 3);
(ii) Conditions characterizing an optimum, in particular martingale conditions for shadow prices and conditions on the value of capital at infinity, derived by methods modelled on the classical calculus of variations (Sections 1 and 4-6, Theorems 1 and 4-6);
(iii) Explicit solutions for an important class of special models, characterized by iso-elastic utility functions and processes with independent increments, which are shown to be equivalent in some respects to models of certainty (Section 1, Theorem 2).

The Introduction begins with an informal survey of concepts and problems, dealing successively with (A) formulation, (B) existence and (C) conditions of optimality. A preliminary statement of the model is built up which allows some results of general interest to be presented independently of the main theory; these comprise (D) a sufficiency theorem and (E) explicit solutions for the special models mentioned above. Formally, the theory starts again in Section 2 with a specification of the model as required for the existence proofs, which appear in Section 3. The remaining sections, which are independent of Section 3, derive necessary and sufficient conditions for optimality.

(A) *Formulation.* The special features of the present theory, within the fields of optimal growth and stochastic control, stem mainly from a combination of three elements: continuous time, a general treatment of risk, and the use of techniques designed to exploit special economic assumptions, such as concavity and monotonicity of utility and linearity of production. Of these, continuous time needs little apology, since many questions concerning the timing and continuity of change, which are particularly subtle and interesting in the case of risk, can be adequately considered only in this setting. Some technical comparisons with discrete time may be found in [9] and [10].

Generality in the treatment of risk requires an abstract (measure-theoretic) description of the structure of information. Let $\mathcal{T} = [0, \infty)$ represent time, Ω the set of elementary events or states of nature (i.e. possible histories of the environment over the whole of time), $\mathcal{A}$ a σ-algebra of subsets of Ω called events, and P a probability on $\mathcal{A}$; write " a.s. " for " almost surely " or " with P-probability one ". The information available at a fixed time t is defined by a sub σ-algebra $\mathcal{A}_t$ of events—called events at t—of which the planner knows at t whether or not they occur; it is assumed that $\mathcal{A}_t \subseteq \mathcal{A}_T$ for $t<T$, to represent learning without forgetting. The overall information structure is defined by the family $(\mathcal{A}_t\colon\ t \in T)$. A random variable $v = v(\omega)$ is called $\mathcal{A}_t$-measurable if its value is known at t—more precisely, if for each numerical interval I the event $\{\omega\colon\ v(\omega) \in I\}$ belongs to $\mathcal{A}_t$. A random process $z = z(\omega, t) = (z_t;\ t \in \mathcal{T})$, i.e. a family of random variables indexed by time, is called adapted to the family $(\mathcal{A}_t)$ if, for each t, the variable z_t is $\mathcal{A}_t$-measurable—in other words, if at each time its previous history is known. All processes considered below are adapted, though for two distinct reasons: observed processes such as the return to capital because the planner is supposed to observe them continuously, immediately and precisely; controlled processes such as consumption because at each time the current value can be chosen only on the basis of available information. It is not necessary to state explicitly all the sources of information which generate the family $(\mathcal{A}_t)$. (Some further assumptions concerning the probability space and measurability are stated in Section 2. At this stage, note that any process $z = z(\omega, t)$ considered is supposed to be measurable, i.e. to define a measurable function of the pair (ω, t); this ensures that sample functions are Lebesgue measurable and that various results concerning integrals hold.)

Let $e^{x(\omega, t)}$ denote the net return from investing one unit of capital during $[0, t]$ when the state is ω; the finite, adapted process $x = x(\omega, t) = (x_t)$ with $x_0 = 0$ is called the (logarithmic) returns or compound interest process. The sample derivative $\dot{x}(\omega, t)$, if it exists, defines the instantaneous rate of net return, output or interest. By analogy with the case of certainty, it seems reasonable at first sight to define a feasible consumption plan, or c-plan, as a non-negative, adapted process $c = c(\omega, t) = (c_t)$ such that a.s. the solution $k(\omega, .)$ of the ordinary differential equation

$$\dot{k}(\omega, t) - \dot{x}(\omega, t)k(\omega, t) = -c(\omega, t), \quad k(\omega, 0) = K>0, \qquad \text{...(1.1)}$$

is non-negative on $\mathcal{T}$; here K denotes initial capital, and the processes k, $\dot{k}$ are the capital and investment plans corresponding to c. But, as is well known, (1.1) is meaningless for natural choices of x, such as the Brownian motion process whose sample functions are not differentiable, and the Poisson process whose sample functions are discontinuous. To avoid this difficulty, (1.1) will be replaced by its integrated form

$$K - k(\omega, T)e^{-x(\omega, T)} = \int_0^T c(\omega, t)e^{-x(\omega, t)}dt, \qquad \text{...(1.2)}$$

which has meaning even if $\dot{x}$ does not exist. The conditions $c \geqq 0$, $k \geqq 0$ then show that a process c is a c-plan iff it is non-negative, adapted and satisfies

$$\int_0^\infty c(\omega, t)e^{-x(\omega, t)}dt \leqq K \qquad \text{a.s.} \qquad \text{...(1.3)}$$

This characterization will now be taken as the definition, without explicit reference to the processes $\dot{x}$, k or $\dot{k}$; of course, k can still be defined from c by way of (1.2), but if $\dot{x}$ does not exist, then neither does $\dot{k}$.

It is useful to introduce an alternative notation for plans. The equation

$$g(\omega, t) = c(\omega, t)e^{-x(\omega, t)} \quad \omega \in \Omega, \quad t \in \mathcal{T} \qquad \text{...(1.4)}$$

assigns to each c-plan a process g, called the consumption plan net of compound interest, reduced consumption plan, g-plan or simply plan (the term " discounted " is avoided here for fear of confusion). Also, the equation

$$G(\omega, T) = \int_0^T g(\omega, t)dt \quad \omega \in \Omega, \quad t \in \mathscr{T} \qquad ...(1.5)$$

defines a process G, or G-plan, representing cumulative reduced consumption. Clearly, a process g is a plan iff it is non-negative, adapted and satisfies

$$G(\omega, \infty) = \int_0^\infty g(\omega, t)dt \leqq K \qquad \text{a.s.}; \qquad ...(1.6)$$

note that the constraint, when written in this form, is the same for each state. By virtue of (1.5), (1.2) can now be rewritten as $ke^{-x} = K - G$, or again as $k = (K-G)e^x$; the first form defines the reduced capital plan, the second the capital plan in natural units. It is worth noting that, while natural capital can be accumulated, reduced capital can only be depleted because $G(\omega, .)$ is non-decreasing; thus G may be called the depletion plan corresponding to g. The problem of optimal saving as defined here can be interpreted, either in the usual way as a problem of optimal accumulation, or as the problem of optimal depletion of a known stock K.

The above method of dealing with the problem of the missing derivative, although natural enough, is not the one usually adopted. An alternative is to replace (1.1) by a linear Itô stochastic differential equation, say

$$dk(\omega, t) - k(\omega, t)[\alpha(t)dt + \sigma(t)dB(\omega, t)] = -c(\omega, t)dt, \quad k(0) = K, \qquad ...(1.7)$$

where $\sigma > 0$ and α are sure functions (perhaps just constants), $B(t)$ is standard Brownian motion and the process x is a stochastic integral $\int \alpha dt + \int \sigma dB(t)$, or equivalently $dx(t) = \alpha dt + \sigma dB(t)$. An approach of this kind has been adopted by R. A. Merton in a series of distinguished papers, (see [8] and references there listed). It allows a powerful theory, tailor-made for a certain class of problems, to be applied directly to economics, and it has yielded simple, explicit results in a number of important cases. However the formulation based on (1.2) above has greater generality, at least in the present linear theory, since the process x is not required to be a stochastic integral. (The Brownian integral used in (1.7) is by no means the only one which may be considered, but the class of processes which can be represented as stochastic integrals is in any case subject to some restrictions which we shall not need). It should also be mentioned that stochastic integrals and derivatives obey unusual rules, so that the interpretations of the risk and certainty versions of the model do not correspond precisely. At all events we can avoid them, and it turns out that our approach can also take account of random utility without appreciable extra effort.

Returning to our model, we denote by $\mathscr{G}$ the set of all g-plans, and henceforth regard this set as the domain of the welfare functional

$$\phi(g) = E\int_0^\infty u[c(\omega, t); \ \omega, t]q(t)dt \quad g = ce^{-x} \in \mathscr{G}. \qquad ...(1.8)$$

Detailed assumptions concerning utility are stated in Section 2; at this stage note that, for each fixed level of consumption γ, $u(\gamma; \ ., \ .)$ is supposed to be an adapted process, while for each (ω, t) the function $u(.; \ \omega, t)$ is increasing, concave and (when required) differentiable with derivative $u'(.; \ \omega, t)$. The discount function q is assumed to have the properties of a positive probability density on $\mathscr{T}$. Since u also depends directly on t, the distinction between u and q is somewhat arbitrary, and may be chosen as convenient to satisfy the conditions of the existence theorem below; thus q may, but need not, represent " impatience ". Now let ϕ^* be the supremum of ϕ on $\mathscr{G}$, which is assumed to be finite; a plan $g^* \in \mathscr{G}$ is called optimal if $\phi(g^*) = \phi^*$, and the problem of optimal saving is to select such a plan if one exists.

The planning horizon is taken as infinite unless the contrary is stated, but an exogenous random horizon is easily introduced; two variants of the model will occasionally be considered. The " horizon model " postulates a stopping time $\Delta = \Delta(\omega)$—say, the time of death of the last surviving heir or member of society whose welfare concerns today's planner—after which utility is identically zero and bequests are worthless. For realism, it should no doubt be assumed that Δ is a.s. finite or has finite expectation; the latter assumption, together with bounded utility, would ensure a finite value of ϕ^*. In the " independent horizon model ", which is discussed only in the present section, the time of death is treated as a $\mathscr{T}$-valued random variable defined on some probability space independent of the space of " events ", and $q(t)$ is taken to be proportional to the probability of survival beyond t; (explicitly, $q = A(1-Z)$ with $A>0$, where the distribution function Z of Δ is such that $Z(0+) = 0, Z(\infty) = 1, Z(t)>0$ for $t>0$ and $1-Z$ is integrable on $\mathscr{T}$). This variant differs essentially from the basic model only in its interpretation; in particular, $u(.; \ ., t)$ denotes utility at t conditional upon survival to that time, and the functional (1.8) represents expected lifetime utility in the ordinary sense rather than " discounted " expected utility.

(B) *Existence*. The model of Section 2 below differs from that just outlined mainly in one technicality concerning information. In existence proofs it is convenient to replace the requirement that a process $z = (z_t)$ be adapted, which involves a separate condition of measurability for each t, by a single condition on $z(\omega, t)$ considered as a function of state and time, namely that it be measurable with respect to a certain sub σ-algebra $\mathscr{H}$ of (ω, t)-sets. The programme then is to imbed the set of plans in a function space of $\mathscr{H}$-measurable functions in such a way that a compactness argument applies. Since in this approach the constraints on choice due to incomplete information are represented simply by the condition of measurability, which moreover is preserved under the usual passages to the limit, the specifically stochastic aspects of proof procedures tend to become quite secondary—although naturally the stochastic character of the problem influences the choice of assumptions. The main difficulty, in the case of risk as of certainty, is that for obvious formulations the set of feasible (g or c) plans is usually not compact and the functional ϕ is not upper semi-continuous.

The existence of an optimum for the present model of saving under risk has apparently not been proved hitherto. The most general compactness argument available seems to be that given by T. F. Bewley [6] for economies whose production set is contained in the space L_∞ of bounded functions. This could be applied to our model if only bounded g or c were admitted and certain conditions (shown by Bewley to be acceptable for non-negative functionals) were imposed on ϕ. The application could presumably be extended to the case of risk by the method sketched above; but in this case at least the assumptions seem unduly restrictive, mainly because one cannot in general expect a truly optimal g to be bounded by a constant for all (ω, t) unless special conditions are imposed on the processes x and $u(\gamma)$. Be that as it may, we shall present a new procedure, designed specifically for our model.

The function space to be used is the space $L_1 = L_1(\mathscr{H}, \mu)$ of $\mathscr{H}$-measurable functions integrable with respect to the product probability μ defined by $d\mu(\omega, t) = dP(\omega)q(t)dt$; (use of a probability measure, rather than the infinite measure m defined by $dm = dP(\omega)dt$, simplifies the conditions for weak compactness). A sequence (f_n) of functions in L_1 will be called *weakly precompact* if it contains a subsequence converging weakly to some limit in L_1; and, as usual, (f_n) will be said to *converge weakly* to f if $\int f_n h d\mu \to \int f h d\mu$ for every $h \in L_\infty$. In the space L_1 we imbed, not the g or c plans themselves, but the corresponding utility or U-plans; explicitly, given $g = ce^{-x} \in G$, the U-plan is the process U_c defined by

$$U_c(\omega, t) = u[c(\omega, t); \ \omega, t] \quad \omega \in \Omega, \quad t \in T. \qquad \ldots(1.9)$$

The functional (1.8) can now be written

$$\phi(g) = \int u[c(\omega, t); \omega, t]d\mu = \int U_c(\omega, t)d\mu \quad g = ce^{-x} \in \mathscr{G}, \qquad \text{...(1.10)}$$

and U_c belongs to L_1 if $\phi(g) > -\infty$.

A sequence (g_n) from $\mathscr{G}$, and corresponding (U_n), will be called *maximizing* if

$$\phi(g_n) = \int U_n d\mu \rightarrow \phi^*.$$

Suppose that a weakly precompact maximizing sequence (U_n) exists; it can be replaced by a weakly convergent subsequence, which clearly is still maximizing and has a weak limit U^* satisfying $\int U^* d\mu = \phi^*$. If it can be inferred that U^* is the U-plan corresponding to some $g^* \in \mathscr{G}$, then $\phi(g^*) = \phi^*$ and an optimum exists. The Existence Lemma of Section 3 shows that this inference is valid, so that the problem of proving existence is reduced to the search for conditions which ensure that there is one weakly precompact maximizing (U_n). The conditions given in Section 3 achieve this by restricting the range of u or by imposing conditions of integrability which involve u, x and q jointly. It is enough if u is bounded. The unbounded cases $u \leqq 0$ and $u \geqq 0$ require distinct additional assumptions, but the results are easily combined if u is unbounded in both directions (see Theorem 1).

(C) *Conditions of Optimality*. The derivation of necessary and sufficient conditions is modelled closely on the classical calculus of variations. A maximum of the concave functional ϕ on the convex set $\mathscr{G}$ is first characterized as a point g^* at which the directional derivative in each admissible " direction " δg (the classical first variation) is non-positive. Then this result is applied to particular δg to obtain necessary conditions of the " Euler " and " transversality " types which are jointly sufficient for optimality. This approach is not usually regarded as suitable for stochastic problems; but it works well in the present case if goods and time are measured in suitable units, and the variational conditions yield directly a precise characterization of the random processes defining shadow prices.

Given a reduced plan $g^* = c^*e^{-x}$ with $\phi(g^*) > -\infty$, the corresponding reduced shadow price process y, or y-plan, is defined by

$$y(\omega, t) = e^{x(\omega, t)}u'[c^*(\omega, t); \omega, t]q(t) \quad \omega \in \Omega, \quad t \in \mathscr{T}. \qquad \text{...(1.11)}$$

To interpret this definition, imagine a perfect forward market at zero time in contracts for ' dated contingent goods at (ω, t) ", one unit of such a contract being a promise to deliver one natural unit of goods at t iff history until then is consistent with ω. If the (positive) quantities $c^*(\omega, t)$ are to be bought, the prices of the contracts must be proportional—say, equal—to the numbers $u'[c^*(\omega, t); \omega, t]q(t)$, and (in abridged notation) the sum paid for a promise of c^* must be $c^*u'q$. If quantities and prices are now quoted in reduced, instead of natural, units the formula $c^*u'q = (c^*e^{-x})(e^x u'q) = g^*y$ shows that c^* is replaced by g^* and $u'q$ by y. In this sense it is appropriate to regard (1.11) as defining the shadow forward prices at zero time, or marginal utilities, of dated contingent goods quoted in reduced units.

Now let $g = g^* + \delta g \in \mathscr{G}$ be another reduced plan, and consider the function

$$f(\alpha) = \phi(g^* + \alpha\delta g) - \phi(g^*), \quad 0 \leqq \alpha \leqq 1.$$

The derivative $D\phi(g^*, \delta g)$ of ϕ at g^* in the direction δg may be defined as the ordinary one-sided derivative $f'(0+)$, and g^* is optimal iff $D\phi(g^*, \delta g) \leqq 0$ for all δg. Under slight restrictions (see Section 4) this derivative can be evaluated by substituting in (1.8) and differentiating under the integral sign to obtain

$$D\phi(g^*, \delta g) = E\int_0^\infty \delta c . u'(c^*)q dt = E\int_0^\infty \delta g(\omega, t)y(\omega, t)dt; \qquad \text{...(1.12)}$$

here y is defined from g^* by (1.11), and (1.12) gives the " shadow value " of the variation $\delta g = \delta c.e^{-x}$ from g^*. Since g^* is optimal iff (1.12) is non-positive for all $g = g^* + \delta g \in \mathscr{G}$, this means that an optimal plan is one which is " supported " by the prices y which defines—in other words, one which maximizes the total value $E \int gydt$ calculated at those prices (see Theorem 4).

Turning to the detailed conditions of optimality, it is assumed that for each (ω, t) the marginal utility $u'(.; \omega, t)$ is decreasing and that $u'(0; \omega, t) = \infty$, so that for an optimum $c^*>0$, $g^*>0$ and $G^*<K$ everywhere. As an indication of the kind of results which one might hope to obtain, consider for a moment the case of certainty. It can be shown, either by variational or by Lagrangean methods, that optimality implies (a) $\phi(g^*)>-\infty$, (b) $y(t) = \text{constant}>0$, and (c) $G^*(t)\rightarrow K$, or equivalently $y(t)[K-G^*(t)]\rightarrow 0$, as $t\rightarrow\infty$; these conditions are also sufficient. The preceding discussion shows that (b) may be regarded as a form of the principle of equi-marginal utility applied to inter-temporal choice: a more familiar, though less general form of this condition is obtained by writing

$$0 = (d/dt) \ln y(t) = \dot{x} + \dot{q} + u''\dot{c}/u'.$$

In the case of risk, (a) remains unchanged. As to (b), if plans are made at a time T for later t, the current value of $y(T)$ cannot in general be equated with actual future $y(t)$ since the state is uncertain; at best it can be equated with the conditional expectation $E^T y(t)$ relative to the information $\mathscr{A}_T$. This suggests as a possible condition of optimality that the process $y = (y_t)$ be a *martingale* relative to the family $(\mathscr{A}_t)$; to be precise, this means that y is adapted, that $Ey(t)$ is finite for each $t \in \mathscr{T}$, and that $y(T) = E^T y(t)$ a.s. for each pair $T<t$ from $\mathscr{T}$. Finally, it is not immediately clear whether (c) should be replaced by $G^*(t)\rightarrow K$ a.s., by $y(t)[K-G^*(t)]\rightarrow 0$ a.s., or by $E\{y(t)[K-G^*(t)]\}\rightarrow 0$; it turns out that the last is appropriate.

In discrete time, conditions (a), (b) and (c) are, under slight restrictions, necessary and sufficient for optimality (see [10] for a general proof and discussion of prior work). For the present continuous model, it is shown in (D) below that the conditions are sufficient (Theorem 1), but in general they are not necessary. More precisely, the conditions are still satisfied (see Theorem 6) if the given optimum is unconstrained, i.e. if (α) $g^*(\omega, t)>0$ everywhere and (β) for each $t \in \mathscr{T}$, the reduced capital $K-G^*(\omega, t)$ is a.s. bounded away from zero. The proof of the super-martingale inequality $y(T) \geqq E^T y(t)$ for $T<t$ does not rely on (β); but without some such condition the construction of variations needed to derive the opposite inequality can break down, for reasons which have no counterpart in the case of certainty or in discrete time. The difficulty is connected with the fact that, given fixed times $T<T+h<T'$ and an event $A \in \mathscr{A}_T$, there may be no feasible variation δg such that, for all $\omega \in A$, $\delta g(\omega, .)>0$ on $[T, T+h)$ and $\delta g(\omega, .) = 0$ on $[0, T)$ and $[T+h, T')$; this can happen even if $G^*(., T)$ is bounded away from K on Ω. It seems that conditions which guarantee *a priori* that an optimum satisfies (β), or a suitable alternative condition, are quite restrictive.

Better results can be obtained if the periods during which a variation δg is required to be respectively positive and negative are specified, not as fixed intervals, but as stochastic intervals which begin and end at random times defined by depletion levels. Explicitly, each level $k \in [0, K)$ determines a random time $\tau(\omega, k)$, defined as the finite solution of

$$G^*[\omega, \tau(\omega, k)] = k$$

if this exists and as infinity otherwise. Variations which start and stop at such times naturally yield properties of plans considered as functions of $\tau(k)$ rather than t, and it is useful to introduce a time change at the outset—time along each state ω being measured, not by the clock, but by the depletion level $G^*(\omega, t)$. This change of variable defines a transformation of the structure of information and of all processes (see Section 5). For example, the transform of a G-plan has the form $\hat{G}(\omega, k) = G[\omega, \tau(\omega, k)]$, while the transform of the shadow price process y corresponding to g^* is defined by $\hat{y}(\omega, k) = y[\omega, \tau(\omega, k)]$ for $\tau<\infty$ and $\hat{y} = 0$ otherwise. In particular, the graph of the optimal depletion level $\hat{G}^*(k) = G[\tau(k)]$ as a function of the depletion time k is, for each state ω, just a 45° line up to the level $k^+ = G(\infty)$ and thereafter is horizontal. Thus for each depletion time k the random variable $\hat{G}^*(., k)$ is bounded away from K, while for each state ω the sample derivative of $\hat{G}^*(\omega, .)$ is $\hat{g}^*(\omega, .) = 1$ for $k<k^+$. The construction of the required variations now becomes very easy; indeed, the difficulty encountered previously could be ascribed to the use of a measure of time extraneous to the economic process. It is found that the principle of equi-marginal utility holds for depletion times, in the sense that $\hat{y}(k) = E^k\hat{y}(i)$ a.s. for $k<i$, where E^k denotes conditional expectation relative to information at the depletion time k. More precisely, if g^* is optimal, then (a) $\phi(g^*)>-\infty$, (b) the process $\hat{y} = (\hat{y}_k)$ is a martingale relative to the transformed information structure and (c) $E\{\hat{y}(k)[K-\hat{G}^*(k)]\}\to 0$ as $k\to K$; these conditions are also sufficient (Theorem 5). In Section 6 this more general result is proved first, and the necessary conditions in clock time inferred from it; the construction of variations in clock time is thus avoided.

(D) *A Sufficiency Theorem.* The sufficiency argument in clock time is given immediately, followed by applications. The proofs given in the rest of this section, which do not rely on later theorems, should be clear enough from the discussion of the model under (A) and (C) above, but for precision the relevant definitions and assumptions may be " read in " from Section 2. None of the numbered assumptions introduced in later sections is required at this stage.

Theorem 1. *A reduced consumption plan* $g^* \in \mathscr{G}$ *is optimal if* (a) $\phi(g^*)>-\infty$, (b) *the corresponding reduced shadow price process* $y = (y_t;\ t \in \mathscr{T})$ *defined by* (1.11) *is a martingale relative to the information structure* $(\mathscr{A}_t;\ t \in T)$, *and* (c) *the expected capital value vanishes at infinity, i.e.*

$$\lim_{T\to\infty} E\{y(T)[K-G^*(T)]\} = 0. \qquad \text{...(1.13)}$$

Proof. For $g \in \mathscr{G}$ and $0 \leqq t \leqq T \leqq \infty$ we have

$$E\{y(T)g(t)\} = E\{E^t[y(T)g(t)]\} = E\{g(t)E^t y(T)\} = E\{g(t)y(t)\}; \qquad \text{...(1.14)}$$

the first equality holds by the definition of conditional expectation, the second because $g(t)$ is $\mathscr{A}_t$-measurable, [3, II.47], and the third because y is a martingale. Integrating over $[0, T]$ on both sides of (1.14), taking E outside the time integral and using (1.5) yields

$$E\{y(T)G(T)\} = E\int_0^T y(t)g(t)dt. \qquad \text{...(1.15)}$$

Next, if $\phi(g)>-\infty$, the concavity of u implies

$$\phi(g)-\phi(g^*) = E\int_0^\infty [u(c)-u(c^*)]qdt \leqq E\int_0^\infty (c-c^*)u'(c^*)qdt = E\int_0^\infty (g-g^*)ydt, \qquad \text{...(1.16)}$$

the right-hand side being defined as a double integral and finite because the left-hand side is finite. Returning to (1.15), g and G may be replaced respectively by g^* and G^*, then on subtracting by $g-g^*$ and $G-G^*$. On letting $T\to\infty$ in the resulting equation, the right-hand side tends to the last expression in (1.16), while on the left-hand side we have

$$E\{y(T)[G(T)-G^*(T)]\} \leqq E\{y(T)[K-G^*(T)]\}\to 0 \qquad \text{...(1.17)}$$

by (1.13). Consequently $\phi(g)-\phi(g^*) \leqq 0$ and obviously g^* is optimal. ||

(E) *Explicit Solutions and Certainty Equivalence for a Class of Models.* A class of models will now be discussed for which Theorem 1 yields an explicit solution in which the optimal g^* is a sure plan. Two types of models belonging to this class are defined by the following assumptions:

Assumption (i). For some $b>0$, $b \neq 1$:

$$u(\gamma;\ \omega, t) = \gamma^{1-b}/(1-b) \quad 0 \leqq \gamma \leqq \infty, \quad \omega \in \Omega, \quad t \in \mathscr{T}; \qquad \text{...(1.18)}$$

$$Ee^{(1-b)x(t)}q(t) < \infty \quad t \in \mathscr{T}; \qquad \text{...(1.19)}$$

$$\int_0^\infty [Ee^{(1-b)x(t)}q(t)]^{1/b}dt < \infty. \qquad \text{...(1.20)}$$

Also, for each pair $T<t$ from $\mathscr{T}$, the increment $x(t)-x(T)$ is independent of $\mathscr{A}_T$ (i.e. of information at T).

Assumption (ii).

$$u(\gamma;\ \omega, t) = \ln \gamma \quad 0 \leqq \gamma \leqq \infty, \quad \omega \in \Omega, \quad t \in \mathscr{T}; \qquad \text{...(1.21)}$$

$$\left| \int_0^\infty [Ex(t)+\ln q(t)]q(t)dt \right| < \infty. \qquad \text{...(1.22)}$$

Random utility can be introduced, without substantial change in the resulting theory, if in the above assumptions γ is replaced by γe^z and x by $x+z$, where $z = (z_t)$ is an adapted process; this extension is omitted for brevity. Condition (1.19) can be omitted, in view of (1.20), if suitable reservations concerning null sets are entered. Note also that the last part of Assumption (i) (which is not required under Assumption (ii)) implies that x is a process with independent increments; but the converse may not hold since the planner may have sources of information other than observations of returns.

A reduced plan $g \in \mathscr{G}$ is called *sure* if there is a (Lebesgue measurable) function $g_0(t)$ such that $g(\omega, t) = g_0(t)$ on $\mathscr{T}$, a.s. Examples of such plans are the functions

$$g(\omega, t) = g_0(t) = K\beta e^{-\beta t} \quad \beta>0; \qquad \text{...(1.23)}$$

also, given any $g \in \mathscr{G}$, a sure plan is defined by $g_0(t) = Eg(t)$. The set of sure g-plans is denoted by $\mathscr{G}_0$, and an element which maximizes ϕ on this set is called an optimal sure plan. In general such a plan is not optimal, but it seems plausible that under Assumption (i) or Assumption (ii) the optimal proportional rate of depletion $g^*(\omega, t)/[K-G^*(\omega, t)]$ at a given time t should depend neither on the previous history defined by ω nor on the absolute level of $G^*(\omega, t)$, hence that g^* should be a sure plan. This conjecture will be confirmed by constructing a sure g^* which satisfies the conditions of Theorem 1.

For brevity we take $K = 1$. Note first that $u'(\gamma) = \gamma^{-b}$, with $b \neq 1$ under Assumption (i) and $b = 1$ under Assumption (ii), so that for sure g^* with $c^* = g^*e^x$ the definition (1.11) reads

$$y(\omega, t) = g^*(t)^{-b}e^{(1-b)x(\omega, t)}q(t). \qquad \text{...(1.24)}$$

If the process y so defined is to be a martingale, $Ey(t)$ must have a finite constant value, say

$$\bar{y} = g^*(t)^{-b}Ee^{(1-b)x(t)}q(t). \qquad \text{...(1.25)}$$

To determine the appropriate value of $\bar{y}$, assume that (1.25) can be solved for $g^*(t)$, integrate the resulting equation on both sides over $\mathscr{T}$, and set $G^*(\infty) = K = 1$; this yields

$$g^*(t) = [Ee^{(1-b)x(t)}q(t)/\bar{y}]^{1/b}, \quad \bar{y}^{1/b} = \int_0^\infty [Ee^{(1-b)x(t)}q(t)]^{1/b}dt. \qquad \text{...(1.26)}$$

To check that this definition makes sense, note that for $b \neq 1$ the values of $Ee^{(1-b)x(t)}q(t)$ and therefore of $\bar{y}$ are positive (because x is finite and $q>0$), and by (1.19-20) these values are also finite. Thus $g^*(t)$ also is positive and finite, and clearly this function belongs to $\mathscr{G}_0$.

We verify the conditions of Theorem 1 first for $b \neq 1$. First, (1.8) and (1.18) yield

$\phi(g^*) = \bar{y}/(1-b)$, which by (1.26) and (1.20) is finite. Next, (1.24-25) may be combined as

$$y(\omega, t) = \bar{y}e^{(1-b)x(\omega,t)}/Ee^{(1-b)x(t)}. \qquad \text{...(1.27)}$$

The process y is adapted to $(\mathscr{A}_t)$ because x has this property. To verify the martingale equality, let $T<t$, write $\Delta x = x(t)-x(T)$, and note that Δx, hence $e^{(1-b)\Delta x}$, is independent of $\mathscr{A}_T$ and therefore also independent of $x(T)$ and $e^{(1-b)x(T)}$. Using (1.27) we obtain

$$E^T y(t).Ee^{(1-b)x(t)} = \bar{y}e^{(1-b)x(T)}E^T e^{(1-b)\Delta x} = y(T)Ee^{(1-b)x(T)}E^T e^{(1-b)\Delta x}$$

$$= y(T)Ee^{(1-b)x(T)}Ee^{(1-b)\Delta x} = y(T)Ee^{(1-b)x(t)} \quad \text{a.s.,} \qquad \text{...(1.28)}$$

and it follows that $E^T y(t) = y(T)$ a.s. Finally we have

$$E\{y(t)[K-G^*(t)]\} = \bar{y}[1-G^*(t)] \to 0,$$

so that all conditions of Theorem 1 hold and g^* is optimal.

For $b = 1$, (1.26) yields $\bar{y} = 1$ since q is a probability density, hence $g^*(t) = q(t)$. On substituting this solution together with (1.21) into (1.8), it is found that the condition for $\phi(g^*)$ to be finite is (1.22). Next, (1.24) shows that $y = 1$ identically, which is trivially a martingale; since $G^*(t) \to K$, the conditions of Theorem 1 all hold.

This result can be interpreted as a principle of certainty equivalence for the problem of optimal saving under risk. Explicitly, it has been shown that under Assumption (i) or Assumption (ii) the search for a maximum of ϕ on $\mathscr{G}$ may be confined to $\mathscr{G}_0$, i.e. that it is enough to choose a sure function $g_0(t) \geqq 0$ to maximize $\phi(g_0)$ subject to a single, non-random constraint $G_0(\infty) \leqq 1$; this is clearly equivalent to a problem of optimal depletion under certainty. Of course, the equivalence extends only to the planning of quantities expressed in reduced units; in the case of risk, the natural consumption plan $c^* = g^*e^x$ and the shadow price plan y will generally be random processes. It is also noteworthy that for $b = 1$ the proof of certainty equivalence does not require the assumption of independent increments. For $b \neq 1$ the function g^* defined by (1.26) is an optimal sure plan even without this assumption, but in general is not optimal. To sum up, we have

Theorem 2. *Under Assumption* (i) *or Assumption* (ii), *an optimal reduced consumption plan exists and is sure, and may be obtained as the solution of a problem of optimal depletion under certainty. For* $K = 1$, *the optimal plan and associated shadow prices are given explicitly by* (1.26) *and* (1.27).

Consider now the special case, under Assumption (i) or Assumption (ii), where x is Brownian motion with drift and discounting is exponential; let $Ex(t) = tM$, var $x(t) = t\sigma^2$ with $\sigma^2>0$, and $q(t) = \delta e^{-\delta t}$ with $\delta>0$. The results obtained are interesting both in their own right and as a guide in formulating the general theory. Starting with Assumption (ii), it is easily verified that the existence condition (1.22) holds for any M and δ. The optimal solution in reduced and natural units, with corresponding shadow prices, is given (in abridged notation) by

$$g^* = \delta e^{-\delta t},\ y = 1; \quad c^* = \delta e^{x(\omega,t)-\delta t},\ u'q = ye^{-x} = e^{-x}. \qquad \text{...(1.29)}$$

In the case of Assumption (i), the moment generating function of the normal distribution yields

$$Ee^{(1-b)x(t)} = e^{[(1-b)M+(1-b)^2\sigma^2/2]t}, \qquad \text{...(1.30)}$$

so that (1.19) holds automatically and (1.20) becomes

$$n \equiv [\delta-(1-b)M-(1-b)^2\sigma^2/2]/b>0. \qquad \text{...(1.31)}$$

The following plans and prices are found:

$$g^* = ne^{-nt},\ y = \bar{y}e^{(1-b)[x(\omega,t)-Mt-(1-b)\sigma^2 t/2]},\ \bar{y} = \delta/n\ ^b = Ey(t);$$
$$c^* = ne^{x(\omega,t)-nt};\quad u'q = ye^{-x(\omega,t)}. \quad ...(1.32)$$

Thus the logarithms of prices in natural and reduced units, and of consumption in natural units, are Brownian motions with drift. The sample functions of such processes are a.s. continuous on $\mathscr{T}$, hence bounded on finite intervals, but they are not bounded on $\mathscr{T}$, nor are they uniformly bounded on finite intervals; the processes c and y also have these properties, and in particular are not bounded functions of (ω, t). It is also of interest that $y(\omega, t)$ converges a.s. to a limiting variable $y(\omega, \infty)$ as $t \to \infty$, so that " prices at infinity " are defined; this follows from the theorem that a non-negative martingale with a.s. right continuous sample functions converges a.s. to a limiting variable [3, VI.6]. We shall show that $y(\infty) = 0$ a.s. in the present example, so that the martingale y is not closed on the right, i.e. the limiting variable cannot be adjoined without destroying the martingale property (see also below, Section 6, Remark (iii). Note further that (1.13) implies that a.s. either $G^*(\infty) = K$ or $y(\infty) = 0$, so that either the reduced capital is totally depleted at infinity or the shadow price vanishes; the present example shows that these possibilities are not mutually exclusive.

To prove the convergence, suppose first that $b<1$ and let Φ denote the normal distribution function; by (1.30) and (1.32) we have, for each real A,

$$P\{y(t) \leqq \bar{y}e^A\} = P\left\{\frac{x(t)-Mt}{\sigma\sqrt{t}} \leqq \frac{A}{(1-b)\sigma\sqrt{t}} + \frac{(1-b)}{2}\sigma\sqrt{t}\right\}$$
$$= \Phi\left[\frac{A}{(1-b)\sigma\sqrt{t}} + \frac{(1-b)}{2}\sigma\sqrt{t}\right]. \quad ...(1.33)$$

For $t \to \infty$ this tends to $\Phi(\infty) = 1$. If $b>1$, the inequality in the second expression is reversed, and in the third Φ is replaced by $1-\Phi$ which tends to $1-\Phi(-\infty) = 1$. In either case (1.33) tends to 1 for each A, so that $y(t) \to 0$ in probability; but $y(t)$ converges a.s. to some $y(\infty)$ by martingale convergence, so that $y(\infty) = 0$ a.s. ‖

In the independent horizon model, $q(t)/\delta = e^{-\delta t}$ is interpreted as the probability of survival beyond time t; the results should then be supplemented by the distribution function F of the bequest $1-G^*(\Delta)$, i.e. of the reduced capital at the time of death.. A simple calculation yields $F(k) = k^{\delta/n}$, $0 \leqq k \leqq K = 1$, with $\delta/n = 1$ if $b = 1$. The effects of changes in the parameters on the various formulae are easily worked out.

Another important example is obtained by choosing q as above and letting x be a Poisson process with parameter λ. For $b \neq 1$, write $\alpha = e^{1-b}-1$, and note that

$$Ee^{(1-b)x(t)} = e^{\alpha\lambda t}$$

by the formula for the Poisson moment generating function. The existence condition (1.20) is satisfied iff $\alpha\lambda<\delta$, and then the following results are obtained:

$$\bar{y}g^{*b} = e^{(\alpha\lambda-\delta)t},\ y = \bar{y}e^{(1-b)x-\alpha\lambda t},\ \bar{y}^{1/b} = b/(\delta-\alpha\lambda);\ y(\infty) = 0;\ F(k) = k^{\delta b/(\delta-\alpha\lambda)}; \quad ...(1.34)$$

the asymptotic result follows as above from the fact that

$$P\{[x(t)-\lambda t]/\lambda t \leqq A\} \to \Phi(A) \quad \text{as} \quad t \to \infty \quad \text{for each } A.$$

2. FORMAL DESCRIPTION OF THE MODEL

This section gives a formal specification of the model, which in some respects amends earlier statements. The properties stated here will usually hold throughout, additional assumptions being introduced in other sections; in particular, the formal description of time change is deferred to Section 5. Relevant references on the abstract theory of stochastic processes are [1] and [3].

Let $\mathcal{T} = [0, \infty)$. On the σ-algebra $\mathcal{B}$ of Lebesgue sets of $\mathcal{T}$ we consider two measures, the Lebesgue measure λ and a probability Q, called discount measure, with density $q(t)>0$ on $\mathcal{T}$. The sub σ-algebra of $\mathcal{B}$ generated by the Lebesgue sets of $[0, t]$ is denoted $\mathcal{B}_t$. The notation " a.a.t " means " almost all t " or " all t outside a null set " with respect to λ or Q. Next, let $(\Omega, \mathcal{A}, P)$ be a complete probability space; the special terminology of probability—events, random variables, expectations, etc., is reserved for this space and its subspaces. Random variables are finite or extended real-valued, $\mathcal{A}$-measurable functions. The notation " a.s. " means " almost surely " or " all ω outside a P-null set ". Now let $\mathcal{S} = \Omega \times \mathcal{T}$ (product set), $\Sigma = \mathcal{A} \times \mathcal{B}$ (product σ-algebra) and $\mu = P \times Q$, $m = P \times \lambda$ (product measures, not necessarily completed). Processes are denoted by symbols like z, $(z_t;\ t \in \mathcal{T})$ or (z_t) when regarded as families of random variables indexed by $\mathcal{T}$, by z, $z(.)$ or $z(., .)$ when regarded as functions of $s = (\omega, t) \in \mathcal{S}$, the two points of view being used interchangeably. Random variables are denoted by symbols like v, $v(.)$, z_t, $z(t)$ or $z(., t)$, particular values usually by $v(\omega)$, $z(\omega, t)$ or $z(s)$; but some liberties are taken. Recall that two processes z and $z+\delta z$ are called *indistinguishable* if $P\{\omega\colon \sup_t |\delta z(\omega, t)| \neq 0\} = 0$, and are *modifications* (of one another) if $P\{\omega\colon \delta z(\omega, t) \neq 0\} = 0$ for each $t \in \mathcal{T}$; indistinguishable processes are modifications, but the converse is false [1, p. 46]. Note that the terms " positive ", " negative ", " increasing " and " decreasing " have their strict meaning throughout.

The *structure of information* is represented by an ascending family $(\mathcal{A}_t;\ t \in \mathcal{T})$ of sub σ-algebras of $\mathcal{A}$, i.e. $t<T$ implies $\mathcal{A}_t \subseteq \mathcal{A}_T$; it is assumed that $\mathcal{A}_0$ is generated by the null sets of $\mathcal{A}$ and that $\mathcal{A} = \mathcal{A}_\infty$, the smallest σ-algebra containing all $\mathcal{A}_t$. As explained in Section 1, it is natural to require that any observed or controlled process (function) z be adapted to $(\mathcal{A}_t)$ and Σ-measurable; these conditions are adequate for Theorems 1, 2 and 4, but for the theory as a whole it is more convenient to replace them by a single, slightly stronger condition requiring z to be measurable with respect to a suitable sub σ-algebra $\mathcal{H}$ of Σ. We select for $\mathcal{H}$ the σ-algebra of progressive (or progressively measurable) sets; a set $H \in \Sigma$ is called *progressive* relative to $(\mathcal{A}_t)$ if, for each $t \in \mathcal{T}$, the subset

$$H^t = H \cap \{\Omega \times [0, t]\}$$

belongs to the product σ-algebra $\mathcal{A}_t \times \mathcal{B}_t$. This condition implies that for each $\omega \in \Omega$ the section $H_\omega = \{t\colon (\omega, t) \in H\}$ is a Lebesgue set and that for each $t \in \mathcal{T}$ the section

$$H_t = \{\omega\colon (\omega, t) \in H\}$$

is in $\mathcal{A}_t$. A process $z = (z_t)$ is called *progressive* or *$\mathcal{H}$-measurable* if the function $z(., .)$ is $\mathcal{H}$-measurable; then each sample function $z(\omega, .)$ is a Lebesgue function and, for each $t \in \mathcal{T}$, the variable $z(., t)$ is $\mathcal{A}_t$-measurable, so that the process is adapted, see [3, IV.30 *et seq.*]. (Since conversely an adapted, Σ-measurable process has a progressive modification, the choice between these conditions turns on a logical distinction without an empirical difference.) We shall work mainly with the measurable space $(\mathcal{S}, \mathcal{H})$ equipped with one of the measures μ or m. Obviously $(\mathcal{S}, \mathcal{H}, \mu)$ is a probability space. Since $d\mu(\omega, t) = q(t)dm(\omega, t)$ and $q>0$, the null sets are the same for either measure, and we write simply " a.e. " for " almost everywhere " or " all (ω, t) outside a null set of $\mathcal{H}$ ". A set $H \in \mathcal{H}$, being a product set, is null iff $P(H_t) = 0$ for a.a.t, or again iff $\lambda(H_\omega) = 0$ a.s. Two $\mathcal{H}$-measurable processes z and $z+\delta z$ will be called *similar* if they differ only on a null set of $\mathcal{H}$, in other words iff $P\{\omega\colon \delta z(\omega, t) \neq 0\} = 0$ for a.a.t., or again iff $\lambda\{t\colon \delta z(\omega, t) \neq 0\} = 0$ a.s.; $\mathcal{H}$-measurable modifications are obviously similar. In certain cases, processes (functions) will be regarded as " defined only up to null sets of $\mathcal{H}$ ", i.e. classes of similar processes will be identified; a class will then be said to possess given properties if one of its elements possesses them.

All integrals in this article are defined as ordinary integrals with respect to some measure, and all sample integrals are defined as Lebesgue integrals. For $\mathcal{H}$-measurable functions which are non-negative or (μ or m) integrable we usually pass among the various iterated and product integrals without special justification; for example

$$\int z d\mu = \int zqdm = \int (Ez)qdt = E\left\{\int zqdt\right\}.$$

We denote by $L_1 = L_1(\mathscr{H}, \mu)$ the space of (classes of similar) $\mathscr{H}$-measurable, μ-integrable functions on $\mathscr{S}$ with the norm $\int |z| d\mu$. Since plans are defined below as classes of $\mathscr{H}$-measurable processes, it is necessary to check that the sample integrals of such processes are still $\mathscr{H}$-measurable, and to determine the relation between integral processes which corresponds to similarity. Now, if z is an $\mathscr{H}$-measurable and a.e. non-negative or m-integrable process, the sample integral $Z(\omega, T) = \int_0^T z(\omega, t)dt$ is defined for $T \in [0, \infty]$ and is a.s. finite on this interval if z is m-integrable. The process $(Z_T;\ T \in \mathscr{T})$ has continuous sample functions and is therefore $\mathscr{H}$-measurable [3, IV.47], hence adapted. If z and $z+\delta z$ are similar and m-integrable, the condition $\lambda\{t\colon \delta z(\omega, t) \neq 0\} = 0$ is equivalent to $\delta Z(\omega, T) = 0$ for all $T \in \mathscr{T}$, or again to $\sup_T |\delta Z(\omega, T)| = 0$, whence it follows that $\mathscr{H}$-measurable processes are similar iff their integral processes are indistinguishable. Analogous remarks apply if m, λ and dt are replaced by μ, Q and $q(t)dt$.

A g-plan will be defined below as a class of similar processes, so that the corresponding c, U and y plans will also be such classes, while a G-plan will be a class of indistinguishable processes. Within classes there will also be a correspondence among individual processes g, c, U, y and G, and we shall always work with such a collection of corresponding processes; if one process is replaced by another element in its class, it will be implicit that corresponding replacements are made in the corresponding classes. A collection of corresponding classes will be said to possess given properties if there is a collection of corresponding processes belonging to the respective classes which possess these properties. Granted these conventions, we shall usually refer to classes or plans as processes or functions, and conversely.

Now let $K>0$. A *reduced consumption plan* or *g-plan* is by definition a process (function) which is $\mathscr{H}$-measurable, a.e. defined and non-negative, and satisfies a.s. the inequalities (1.6). The set of all g-plans is $\mathscr{G}$; this is a convex set of the vector space of $\mathscr{H}$-measurable (classes of) functions, and is not empty since it contains the sure plans (1.23). The process G defined on $\mathscr{S}$ by (1.5) is the *depletion plan* or *G-plan* corresponding to g, and $K-G$ is the *reduced capital plan*. Obviously the sample functions $G(\omega, .)$ are a.s. absolutely continuous and non-decreasing (increasing where g is positive) and satisfy

$$0 = G(0) \leqq G(t) \leqq G(\infty) \leqq K.$$

Thus the limit $G(., \infty)$ is defined a.s. as a random variable, and g may be chosen in its class of similar functions so that the a.s. limit $g(., \infty) = 0$ is also defined. Next, the *returns process* x is defined everywhere on $\mathscr{S}$ (not just a.e.) by a finite, $\mathscr{H}$-measurable function $x(\omega, t)$, with $x(\omega, 0) = 0$ for all ω. Given any $g \in \mathscr{G}$, the corresponding *natural consumption plan* or *c-plan* is defined by $ce^{-x} = g$—see (1.4); clearly c is $\mathscr{H}$-measurable, a.e. defined and non-negative, and the functions g and c determine one another.

The *utility function* $u = u(\gamma;\ \omega, t)$ is defined on $[0, \infty] \times \mathscr{S}$ and takes values in $[-\infty, \infty]$; it is continuous, concave and increasing in γ for each $(\omega, t) \in \mathscr{S}$ and $\mathscr{H}$-measurable in (ω, t) for each $\gamma \in [0, \infty]$. As usual, u may be chosen from a collection of functions which differ only as to scale and origin. In Section 3 only weak concavity is assumed, and marginal utility is not required. Thereafter, and in Sections 1 (D) and 1 (E), it is assumed that the marginal utility function $u'(\gamma;\ \omega, t) = \partial u(\gamma;\ \omega, t)/\partial\gamma$ is defined on $[0, \infty] \times \mathscr{S}$, takes values in $[0, \infty]$ and is continuous and non-increasing in γ for each (ω, t); it is easily shown that this function is $\mathscr{H}$-measurable in (ω, t) for each γ. Decreasing marginal utility is introduced when required. Note that, although the functions

u and u' are regarded as defined for $\gamma = \infty$, infinite consumption cannot actually occur in a feasible plan outside a null set of $\mathscr{H}$.

Each c-plan defines a utility plan or *U-plan* $U = U_c$ by (1.9). To show that this function is $\mathscr{H}$-measurable, we check that, for fixed $a \in [-\infty, \infty]$, the set $\{s\colon U(s) < a\}$ belongs to $\mathscr{H}$. Let $v(a;\ .)$ be the function from $\mathscr{S}$ to $[0, \infty]$ whose value at s is the solution γ of the equation $u(\gamma;\ s) = a$ if this exists; otherwise, $v(a;\ s) = \infty$ if $u(\infty;\ s) < a$, and $v(a;\ s) = 0$ if $u(0;\ s) > a$. For each γ we have $\{s\colon \gamma < v(a;\ s)\} = \{s\colon u(\gamma;\ s) < a\}$; this set is in $\mathscr{H}$ because $u(\gamma;\ .)$ is an $\mathscr{H}$-measurable function, and it follows that $v(a;\ .)$ has this property also. Finally, we have $\{s\colon U(s) < a\} = \{s\colon u[c(s);\ s] < a\} = \{s\colon c(s) < v(a;\ s)\}$, and since $c(.)$ and $v(a;\ .)$ are $\mathscr{H}$-measurable this set belongs to $\mathscr{H}$. ||

The function U is now regarded as defined a.e., and c and U determine one another because $u(.\,;\ s)$ is increasing. In the same way, if u' exists, c defines a *reduced shadow price process* or *y-plan* as in (1.11); this is $\mathscr{H}$-measurable, a.e. defined, and in turn determines c if $u'(.\,;\ s)$ is decreasing.

The welfare functional ϕ is defined on $\mathscr{G}$ by (1.8); it is always assumed or inferred from other conditions that the positive part of the double integral is finite for each $g \in \mathscr{G}$, and further that the supremum ϕ^* of the functional is finite. An element $g^* \in \mathscr{G}$ is called *optimal* if $\phi(g^*) = \phi^*$ and ϕ^* is finite.

In conclusion, recall that a random variable $v = v(\omega)$ is called a *stopping time* relative to $(\mathscr{A}_t)$ if it takes values in $[0, \infty]$ and if, for each $t \in \mathscr{T}$, the event $\{\omega\colon v(\omega) \leqq t\}$ is in $\mathscr{A}_t$. The σ-algebra of events prior to v is

$$\mathscr{A}_v = \{A \in \mathscr{A}\colon \forall t \in \mathscr{T}, A \cap \{v(\omega) \leqq t\} \in \mathscr{A}_t\}; \qquad ...(2.1)$$

conditional expectations relative to $\mathscr{A}_v$ will be written E^v, with analogous notation in other cases. The *horizon model* is specified by introducing the *time of death* Δ as a stopping time relative to $(\mathscr{A}_t)$, defining the *life interval* $\mathscr{S}^l = \{(\omega,\ t) \in \mathscr{S}\colon\ t < \Delta(\omega)\}$, and setting $u(.\,;\ \omega, t) = 0$ identically for $(\omega, t) \in \mathscr{S} - \mathscr{S}^l$. According to [1, III.18], stochastic intervals like $\mathscr{S}^l$ are $\mathscr{H}$-measurable. It is convenient to regard g-plans and corresponding processes G, c, U and y as defined in the usual way on the whole of $\mathscr{S}$, while identifying plans which agree on $\mathscr{S}^l$. The horizon model will be considered only when this is mentioned explicitly.

3. EXISTENCE OF AN OPTIMUM

The results obtained in this section rest on the following

Existence Lemma. *Let ϕ^* be finite, and suppose that there is a maximizing sequence (g_n) from $\mathscr{G}$ such that the corresponding sequence (U_n) defined by* (1.9) *is weakly precompact in $L_1(\mathscr{H}, \mu)$. Then there is a $g^* \in \mathscr{G}$ such that $\phi(g^*) = \phi^*$.*

Proof. Selecting a subsequence if necessary, it may be assumed that (U_n) converges weakly to some U^* in L_1 This means (see [2, p. 291]) that the norms $\int |U_n|\, d\mu$ are uniformly bounded and that

$$\int_H U^*(s)d\mu = \lim_{n\to\infty} \int_H U_n(s)d\mu \quad H \in \mathscr{H}; \qquad ...(3.1)$$

for $H = \mathscr{S}$, it follows from (1.10) that

$$\int U^* d\mu = \lim_{n\to\infty} \int U_n d\mu = \lim_{n\to\infty} \phi(g_n) = \phi^*. \qquad ...(3.2)$$

From this U^*, define a function c^* by $U^*(s) = u[c^*(s);\ s]$ and then a function $g^* = c^* e^{-x}$ (compare (1.9) and (1.4)). The proof will be complete when it is shown that $g^* \in \mathscr{G}$. (In particular, while $c^*(s) = g^*(s) = \infty$ cannot be ruled out *a priori*, it will follow from $g^* \in \mathscr{G}$ that this value can occur at most on a null set of $\mathscr{H}$.)

We first check that c^*, and hence g^*, is $\mathscr{H}$-measurable and non-negative. For each $\gamma>0$ we have $\{s: c^*(s) \leqq \gamma\} = \{s: U^*(s) \leqq u(\gamma; s)\}$, and since $U^*(.)$ and $u(\gamma; .)$ are $\mathscr{H}$-measurable the same is true of $c^*(.)$. Also, $c^*(s) \geqq 0$ a.e. because $U^*(s)$ belongs to the range of $u(.; s)$ a.e.; if not, select for H successively the sets $\{s: U^*(s)>u(\infty, s)\}$ and $\{s: U^*(s)<u(0; s)\}$ to obtain a contradiction from (3.1) and the definition of the U_n. It remains to show that g^* satisfies the constraints (1.6) a.s.

Since (U_n) converges weakly to U^*, there is a sequence (V_m) of convex combinations

$$V_m = \sum_{j=1}^{m} \beta_{jm} U_j, \quad \sum_{j=1}^{m} \beta_{jm} = 1 \quad m = 1, 2, \ldots, \qquad \ldots(3.3)$$

with all $\beta_{jm} \geqq 0$, converging to U^* in the norm of L_1 (see [2, p. 422]). Since μ is a probability measure the sequence (V_m) also converges in measure and, selecting a subsequence if necessary, converges a.e. to the same limit. Using the constants β_{jm}, we now define the convex combinations of consumption plans

$$\bar{c}_m = \sum_{j=1}^{m} \beta_{jm} c_j \quad m = 1, 2, \ldots; \qquad \ldots(3.4)$$

the corresponding $\bar{g}_m = \bar{c}_m e^{-x}$ belong to $\mathscr{G}$ since this set is convex. Since $u(.; s)$ is concave we have

$$V_m(s) = \sum_{j=1}^{m} \beta_{jm} u[c_j(s); s] \leqq u[\bar{c}_m(s); s] \quad m = 1, 2, \ldots \qquad \ldots(3.5)$$

a.e., and then $(V_m) \to U^*$ a.e. implies

$$U^*(s) \leqq \liminf_{m\to\infty} u[\bar{c}_m(s); s] \qquad \ldots(3.6)$$

a.e. Now $u(.; s)$ is for each s a continuous, increasing function, and its inverse has the same property; thus it follows from (3.6) and the definition of c^* that

$$c^*(s) \leqq \liminf_{m\to\infty} \bar{c}_m(s) \qquad \ldots(3.7)$$

a.e. By making changes on null sets if necessary, it can be assumed that the inequalities (3.7), $c^*(s) \geqq 0$ and $\bar{c}_m(s) \geqq 0$ hold for all $s \in \mathscr{S}$. It remains to multiply both sides of (3.7) by $e^{-x(s)}$, replace ce^{-x} by g and s by (ω, t), integrate with respect to Lebesgue measure on $\mathscr{T}$ for each ω separately, and (noting that the integrands are non-negative) apply Fatou's Lemma to obtain

$$0 \leqq \int_0^\infty g^*(\omega, t)dt \leqq \int_0^\infty \liminf_{m\to\infty} \bar{g}_m(\omega, t)dt \leqq \liminf_{m\to\infty} \int_0^\infty \bar{g}_m(\omega, t)dt \leqq K \qquad \ldots(3.8)$$

a.s.; the last inequality follows from (1.6) because $\bar{g}_m \in \mathscr{G}$ for each m. But (3.8) shows that $g^* \in \mathscr{G}$. ‖

In order to apply this Lemma, we recall some conditions for a set $\mathscr{F}$ of functions in $L_1(\mathscr{H}, \mu)$, where μ is a probability measure, to be weakly sequentially compact, i.e. such that every infinite sequence from $\mathscr{F}$ contains a subsequence converging weakly to some limit in L_1 (see [3, II.17-23], also [2, Chapter IV]). It is necessary and sufficient (a) that the functions $f \in \mathscr{F}$ be uniformly μ-integrable, i.e. that

$$\lim_{a\to\infty} \int |f| I\{|f|>a\} d\mu = 0 \quad \text{uniformly for } f \in \mathscr{F}, \qquad \ldots(3.9)$$

or equivalently (b) that for $f \in \mathscr{F}$ the norms $\int |f| \, d\mu$ be uniformly bounded and the indefinite integrals be uniformly continuous, i.e. that for every $\varepsilon>0$ there be a $\delta>0$ such that, for every $f \in \mathscr{F}$, the conditions $H \in \mathscr{H}$ and $\mu(H) < \delta$ imply $\int_H |f|\,d\mu < \varepsilon$. Clearly, it is sufficient if there is an f^0 in L_1 such that, for each $f \in \mathscr{F}$, $|f| \leqq |f^0|$ a.e., and *a fortiori* if all $|f|$ are uniformly bounded (by a constant). It is also sufficient if there exists a non-negative, increasing function ψ on $[0, \infty)$ satisfying $\psi(u)/u \to \infty$ as $u \to \infty$, such that

$$\sup\left\{\int \psi(|f(s)|)d\mu(s) \colon f \in \mathscr{F}\right\} < \infty;$$

we shall consider functions of the form $\psi(u) = u^{1+\varepsilon}$ with $\varepsilon > 0$.

It is immediate that an optimum exists if u is bounded on $[0, \infty] \times \mathscr{S}$, since then ϕ^* is finite and all U-plans are uniformly bounded. For unbounded functions, it is convenient first to consider the cases of u bounded below and u bounded above separately—or equivalently, since the scale and origin are arbitrary, the cases $u \leqq 0$ and $u \geqq 0$. Suppose that $u \leqq 0$; it will be shown that an optimum exists under

Assumption (iii). There is a plan $g_+ = c_+ e^{-x}$ in $\mathscr{G}$ such that $\phi(hg_+) > -\infty$ for each $h \in (0, 1]$, i.e.

$$\int u[hc_+(\omega, t); \omega, t]d\mu = \int U_{hc_+}(\omega, t)d\mu > -\infty \quad h \in (0, 1]. \qquad \text{...(3.10)}$$

Proof. Clearly $u \leqq 0$ and (3.10) imply that ϕ^* is finite. We assume that no maximizing sequence (g_n) defines a sequence (U_n) which is weakly precompact in L_1 and derive a contradiction. Let (g_n), (c_n), (U_n) be maximizing; we may choose a fixed $\eta > 0$ and assume that

$$\phi^* - \eta < \int U_n d\mu \leqq \phi^* \quad n = 1, 2, \dots. \qquad \text{...(3.11)}$$

To say that the sequence (U_n) of non-positive functions is not weakly precompact is to say (see (3.9)), that

$$\exists\varepsilon\forall\alpha\exists a\colon a \geqq \alpha \text{ and } \exists n\colon \int U_n I\{U_n < -a\}d\mu < -\varepsilon, \qquad \text{...(3.12)}$$

where ε, α and a are all positive. Let $\alpha = 1, 2, \dots$; since $a = a(\alpha)$ and $n = n(a, \alpha) = n(\alpha)$ we can index the sequence defined by (3.12) with α and write U_α and c_α in place of $U_{n(\alpha)}$ and $c_{n(\alpha)}$. Now $\alpha \leqq a$ implies $\{s\colon U_\alpha < -\alpha\} \supseteq \{s\colon U_\alpha < -a\}$, so that the integral of the non-positive function U_α over the former set is $\leqq$ the integral over the latter and is therefore $< -\varepsilon$. Consequently

$$\exists\varepsilon\forall\alpha\colon \int U_\alpha I\{U_\alpha < -\alpha\}d\mu < -\varepsilon \quad \alpha = 1, 2, \dots. \qquad \text{...(3.13)}$$

Since (U_α) is a subsequence of (U_n) it is still maximizing; by (3.11) and Markov's inequality,

$$\mu\{U_\alpha < -\alpha\} \leqq -\int U_\alpha d\mu/\alpha < (\eta - \phi^*)/\alpha. \qquad \text{...(3.14)}$$

Now let c_+ be the function appearing in Assumption (iii), and for a fixed $h \in (0, 1]$—to be determined later—let

$$\bar{c}_\alpha = (1-h)c_\alpha + hc_+ \quad \alpha = 1, 2, \dots. \qquad \text{...(3.15)}$$

The plans $\bar{g}_\alpha = \bar{c}_\alpha e^{-x}$ belong to $\mathscr{G}$, and the concavity of u implies

$$\bar{U}_\alpha \geqq (1-h)U_\alpha(s) + hU_+(s) \quad s \in \mathscr{S}, \qquad \text{...(3.16)}$$

where $\bar{U}_\alpha$ corresponds to $\bar{c}_\alpha$ and U_+ to c_+. Note also that $\bar{U}_\alpha(s) \geqq U_{hc+}(s)$ because $\bar{c}_\alpha(s) \geqq hc_+(s)$. It follows that

$$\phi(\bar{g}_\alpha) = \int \bar{U}_\alpha I\{U_\alpha \geqq -\alpha\}d\mu + \int \bar{U}_\alpha I\{U_\alpha < -\alpha\}d\mu$$

$$\geqq (1-h)\int U_\alpha I\{U_\alpha \geqq -\alpha\}d\mu + h\int U_+ I\{U_\alpha \geqq -\alpha\}d\mu + \int U_{hc_+} I\{U_\alpha < -\alpha\}d\mu. \quad \text{...(3.17)}$$

Now let $\alpha \to \infty$. Since U_+ and U_{hc+} are integrable by Assumption (iii) and $\mu\{U_\alpha < -\alpha\} \to 0$ by (3.14), the second term on the right-hand side tends to $h\int U_+ d\mu = h\phi(g_+)$, the third to zero. The first term is equal to $(1-h)\left[\phi(g_\alpha) - \int U_\alpha I\{U_\alpha < -\alpha\}d\mu\right]$; by (3.13) this exceeds $(1-h)[\phi(g_\alpha)+\varepsilon]$, which tends to $(1-h)(\phi^*+\varepsilon)$ because (U_α) is maximizing. On collecting terms, it follows from (3.17) that

$$\liminf_{\alpha\to\infty} \phi(\bar{g}_\alpha) \geqq (1-h)(\phi^*+\varepsilon) + h\phi(g_+) = \phi^*+\varepsilon - h[\phi^*+\varepsilon-\phi(g_+)]. \quad \text{...(3.18)}$$

For h sufficiently small, the right-hand side exceeds $\phi^*+\varepsilon/2$, a contradiction since $\phi(\bar{g}_\alpha) \leqq \phi^*$ for each α. ‖

This result seems to be adequate for all applications with $u \leqq 0$. To illustrate, suppose that there is some $b > 1$ such that

$$u(\gamma;\ \omega, t) \geqq -\gamma^{1-b} \quad \gamma \in [0, \infty], \quad (\omega, t) \in \mathscr{S}; \quad \text{...(3.19)}$$

then (3.10) is satisfied if there is some $g_+ = c_+ e^{-x} \in \mathscr{G}$ such that

$$\int c_+^{1-b} d\mu = \int_0^\infty E\{g_+(t)e^{x(t)}\}^{1-b} q(t)dt < \infty. \quad \text{...(3.20)}$$

It is often useful to try g_+ of the form (1.26); then $g_+(t)$, being sure, can be taken outside the expectation sign, and it is found that (3.20) holds if x is a process (not necessarily with independent increments) satisfying (1.20). It is a convenient feature of this criterion that $Ee^{(1-b)x(t)}$ is simply a value of the moment generating function of $x(t)$. In particular, the existence of an optimum under Assumption (i) with $b > 1$ is obtained again as a special case of the present result.

Suppose now that $u \geqq 0$. Referring to the discussion of weak compactness, it is clear that ϕ^* is finite and that an optimum exists under

Assumption (iv). There is an $\varepsilon > 0$ such that

$$\sup\left\{\int U_c^{1+\varepsilon} d\mu:\ g = ce^{-x} \in \mathscr{G}\right\} < \infty. \quad \text{...(3.21)}$$

The question arises whether it is permissible in some cases to set $\varepsilon = 0$, i.e. whether $\phi^* < \infty$ may be sufficient (as well as necessary) for existence. To illustrate this and related questions, consider utilities of the form $u(\gamma) = \gamma^{1-b}$ with $b \in (0, 1)$. Write

$$M(r, c) = \left(\int c^r d\mu\right)^{1/r},\ M^*(r) = \sup\{M(r, c):\ ce^{-x} \in \mathscr{G}\} \quad r \in (0, \infty), \quad \text{...(3.22)}$$

and let $r_c^+ = \sup\{r:\ M(r, c) < \infty\}$ and $r^+ = \sup\{r:\ M^*(r) < \infty\}$. According to well-known properties of moments, the function $M(., c)$ is non-decreasing, continuous on $(0, r_c^+)$ and left continuous at r_c^+, and its logarithm is a convex function (i.e. no chord has points below the graph). It follows that $M^*(.)$ has the corresponding properties (because left continuity and lower semi-continuity are equivalent for non-decreasing functions, convexity and lower semi-continuity are preserved on passing to the supremum, and a convex function is continuous on any open interval where it is finite); in particular, M^* does not decrease, and is continuous on (0, 1) if either $r^+ \geqq 1$ or M^* is continuous at r^+. Now, for fixed b, we have $\phi^* = [M^*(1-b)]^{1-b}$; (3.21) therefore shows that optima exist for all $b \in (0, 1)$ if $r^+ \geqq 1$, and if $r^+ \in (0, 1)$ they exist for $1-b<r^+$. On the other hand, $1-b>r^+$ implies $\phi^* = \infty$, and the same is true for $1-b = r^+$ if M^* is continuous at r^+. Thus, if M^* is continuous on (0, 1), optima exist iff $\phi^*<\infty$; for example, this condition is satisfied in the Brownian and Poisson cases. Also, whenever Assumption (i) holds with $b<1$, the existence criterion (1.20) is equivalent to $\phi^*<\infty$. It seems that little can be said in general about the continuity of M^* at r^+, or about the existence of an optimum in case $1-b = r^+$ and $M^*(r^+)<\infty$.

The preceding paragraph relates existence to finite supremum properties; a criterion will now be given which, although usually less sharp, infers existence from the data of the problem. It will be shown that an optimum exists under

Assumption (v). There is a $b \in [0, 1)$ such that (3.23) below holds. In addition, (3.24) holds if $b \neq 0$, while (3.25) holds if $b = 1$.

$$u(\gamma;\ \omega, t) \leqq \gamma^{1-b} \quad \gamma \in [0, \infty],\quad (\omega, t) \in \mathscr{S}; \qquad \text{...(3.23)}$$

$$\int_0^\infty E[e^{(1-b)x(\omega,t)}q(t)]^{1/b}dt = \int (e^x q)^{(1-b)/b}d\mu<\infty; \qquad \text{...(3.24)}$$

$$E \sup \{e^{x(\omega,t)}q(t):\ \text{a.a. } t \in \mathscr{T}\}<\infty. \qquad \text{...(3.25)}$$

Proof. For brevity we discuss only the case $b \neq 0$. Consider any $g \in \mathscr{G}$ and corresponding c and U; for each $H \in \mathscr{H}$ we have (in abridged notation):

$$0 \leqq \int_H U d\mu \leqq \int_H c^{1-b}d\mu = \int_H (g^{1-b})(e^{(1-b)x}q)dm$$

$$\leqq \left[\int_H g dm\right]^{1-b}\left[\int_H (e^{(1-b)x}q)^{1/b}dm\right]^b \leqq K^{1-b}\left[\int_H (e^x q)^{(1-b)/b}d\mu\right]^b; \qquad \text{...(3.26)}$$

this uses (3.23), (1.4), Hölder's inequality with exponents $1/(1-b)$ and $1/b$, (1.6) and the definition $d\mu = qdm$. For $H = \mathscr{S}$, (3.26) shows that all $\int U d\mu$ are uniformly bounded, so that ϕ^* is finite. Moreover, (3.24) implies that the last term in (3.26) tends to zero uniformly in H as $\mu(H)\to 0$, so that all U-plans are uniformly integrable. ||

Optima can exist even though Assumption (v) fails, and better results can in general be obtained for special problems. For example, the weakest possible condition for existence under Assumption (i) with $b<1$ is (1.20), and Hölder's inequality shows that (3.24) is at least as strong a requirement; indeed, for Brownian motion with exponential discounting, (3.24) reduces to

$$\delta-(1-b)M-(1-b)^2\sigma^2/2b>0, \qquad \text{...(3.27)}$$

which is actually stronger than the corresponding condition (1.31) obtained from (1.20).

The results for positive and negative utilities are easily combined if u is unbounded both above and below. Suppose, for example, that u satisfies both Assumption (iii) and Assumption (v). Then clearly ϕ^* is finite. Let (U_n) be maximizing, and denote by (U_n^+) and (U_n^-) the sequences of positive and negative parts. The proof following Assumption (v), with U replaced by U^+, shows that the numbers $\int U_n^+ d\mu$ are bounded by some constant N, and that there is a subsequence, again denoted by (U_n), such that (U_n^+) is weakly convergent.

Then the proof following Assumption (iii), practically without change, shows that (U_n^-) is weakly precompact. A slight modification of (3.14) is needed, namely

$$\mu\{U_\alpha < -\alpha\} \leqq \int U_\alpha^- d\mu/\alpha = \left[\int U_\alpha^+ d\mu - \phi(g_\alpha)\right]/\alpha \leqq (N+\eta-\phi^*)/\alpha. \quad ...(3.28)$$

It follows that an optimum exists. Similar remarks apply if Assumption (v) is replaced by Assumption (iv) with U^+ substituted for U; in this case the boundedness of the $\int U^+ d\mu$ follows from that of the $\int (U^+)^{1+\varepsilon} d\mu$.

If the sequence (U_n) is weakly precompact in L_1, then clearly $(Bf_n + A)$ with $B>0$ is weakly precompact also; the preceding argument therefore applies if there is one choice of scale and origin for the utility function such that it satisfies both Assumption (iii) and either Assumption (v) or the amended Assumption (iv). In fact, the argument holds without substantial change if the two assumptions are satisfied with different choices. To sum up, we have

Theorem 3. *An optimum exists if the utility function u is bounded; if it is non-positive and satisfies Assumption* (iii)*; if it is non-negative and satisfies Assumption* (iv) *or Assumption* (v)*; or if it is unbounded in both directions and satisfies* (*possibly with different choices of scale and origin*) *both Assumption* (iii) *and either Assumption* (iv), *with U replaced by* U^+, *or Assumption* (v).

Remark (i). In general an optimum need not be unique; but if decreasing marginal utility is assumed, a concavity argument proves uniqueness apart from a null set of $\mathscr{H}$.

Remark (ii). The changes required for the horizon model are straightforward. If one assumes finite expectation of life, say $E\Delta = 1$, the model can be simplified by absorbing q into u, treating the life interval $\mathscr{S}^l$ with progressive sets $\mathscr{H}^l$ and measure $m^l = P \times \lambda$ as a probability space, and carrying out the existence argument in $L_1(\mathscr{S}^l, \mathscr{H}^l, m^l)$.

4. OPTIMALITY AND DIRECTIONAL DERIVATIVES

The rest of this article deals with the conditions in which an element g^* of $\mathscr{G}$ is optimal. The special assumptions of Section 3 are dropped and different analytic methods used. We begin with conditions of optimality expressed in terms of directional derivatives of the functional ϕ on $\mathscr{G}$, regarded simply as a convex subset of the vector space of $\mathscr{H}$-measurable functions on $\mathscr{S}$. Since derivatives of functionals are usually defined under conditions which differ slightly from those considered here (see for example [5]) it is convenient to give a self-contained statement.

It is now assumed directly that $\phi^* < \infty$. Let g^* and $g = g^* + \delta g$ be arbitrary elements of $\mathscr{G}$, with $\phi(g^*) > -\infty$; the function δg is called an(admissible or feasible) *direction* or *variation* at g^*, and the *directional derivative* of ϕ at g^* in the direction δg is defined by

$$D\phi(g^*, \delta g) = \lim_{\alpha \downarrow 0} (1/\alpha)[\phi(g^*+\alpha\delta g) - \phi(g^*)] = \lim_{\alpha \downarrow 0} (1/\alpha) \int [u(c^*+\alpha\delta c) - u(c^*)] d\mu; \quad ...(4.1)$$

here $c^* = g^* e^x$, $\delta c = \delta g . e^x$, $u(c^*) = u[c^*(\omega, t); \omega, t]$, etc. This limit certainly exists, since $f(\alpha) = \phi(g^*+\alpha\delta g) - \phi(g^*)$ is an ordinary concave function of α on $[0, 1]$, and

$$f'(0+) = D\phi(g^*, \delta g);$$

at present, the possibilities $f(\alpha) = -\infty$ for some $\alpha \in (0, 1)$ and $f'(0+) = \pm\infty$ are not excluded.

It is easily shown that $g^* \in \mathscr{G}$ is an optimum iff $\phi(g^*) > -\infty$ and $D\phi(g^*, \delta g) \leqq 0$ for all $g = g^* + \delta g \in \mathscr{G}$. Indeed, if g^* is optimal, then $\phi(g^*)$ is finite by definition and

$$\phi(g^*) \geqq \phi(g^* + \delta g)$$

for any fixed δg; hence $[\phi(g^* + \alpha\delta g) - \phi(g^*)]/\alpha \leqq 0$ for each $\alpha \in (0, 1]$ and it only remains to go to the limit. Conversely, concavity implies $\phi(g^* + \delta g) - \phi(g^*) \leqq D\phi(g^*, \delta g)$, and the result follows.

Now suppose further that $\phi(g) > -\infty$; then (4.1) can be evaluated by differentiating under the integral sign to obtain (in abridged notation)

$$D\phi(g^*, \delta g) = \int \delta c . u'(c^*) d\mu > -\infty. \qquad \text{...(4.2)}$$

To prove this, restrict α to $(0, 1]$ and write $c_\alpha = c^* + \alpha\delta c = (1-\alpha)c^* + \alpha c$; for each (ω, t), $c_\alpha - c^*$ and $u(c_\alpha) - u(c^*)$ have the same sign as $c - c^*$ for all α. The concavity of u implies

$$u(c) - u(c^*) \leqq (1/\alpha)[u(c_\alpha) - u(c^*)] \uparrow (c - c^*) u'(c^*), \quad \alpha \downarrow 0. \qquad \text{...(4.3)}$$

Now consider the integrals $(1/\alpha) \int [u(c_\alpha) - u(c^*)] d\mu$, $\alpha \in (0, 1]$, separately on the domains $\{c \geqq c^*\}$ and $\{c < c^*\}$. It follows from (4.3) that on $\{c \geqq c^*\}$ the integrands are non-negative and ascend as $\alpha \downarrow 0$, while on $\{c < c^*\}$ they are non-positive and bounded below by the μ-integrable function $u(c) - u(c^*)$; the passage under the integral sign is therefore permissible in each case, and the integral of the negative part is finite. ||

It is convenient to rewrite (4.2), using the definition (1.11) of the reduced shadow price process y corresponding to g^*; since $\delta c . u'(c^*) d\mu = \delta g . e^x u'(c^*) q . dtdP = \delta g . y . dtdP$, we have

$$D\phi(g^*, \delta g) = E \int_0^\infty y(t) \delta g(t) dt > -\infty. \qquad \text{...(4.4)}$$

Suppose now that g^* is optimal; henceforth we adopt the following mild restriction (which in the usual models holds for all plans with finite welfare, not just for optima):

Assumption (vi). If g^* is optimal, there is an $\alpha_0 \in (0, 1)$ such that

$$\phi(g^* - \alpha g^*) > -\infty \quad \text{for} \quad \alpha \in [0, \alpha_0].$$

It can now be shown that (4.2) or (4.4) holds at an optimum for every feasible δg, even if $\phi(g) = -\infty$. The proof is the same as before, except for the argument showing that the convergence on $\{c < c^*\}$ is dominated. For this step, replace the inequality in (4.3) by

$$(1/\alpha_0)[u(c^* - \alpha_0 c^*) - u(c^*)] \leqq (1/\alpha)[u(c^* - \alpha c^*) - u(c^*)] \leqq (1/\alpha)[u(c_\alpha) - u(c^*)], \qquad \text{...(4.5)}$$

$0 < \alpha \leqq \alpha_0$, using concavity and the definition of c_α. These expressions are non-positive, and the first of them is integrable over $\{c < c^*\}$ because by Assumption (vi) and optimality it is integrable over $\mathscr{S}$. ||

As a special case of (4.4), let $g = 0$, $\delta g = -g^*$ with g^* optimal; this yields

$$D^* \equiv -D\phi(g^*, -g^*) = E \int_0^\infty y(t) g^*(t) dt < \infty, \qquad \text{...(4.6)}$$

and obviously $-D^* = \min\{D\phi(g^*, g - g^*) \colon g \in \mathscr{G}\}$. The theory below depends on Assumption (vi) only by way of (4.6).

This discussion is summed up in the simple but important

Theorem 4. *Let $g^* \in \mathscr{G}$ be such that $\phi(g^*) > -\infty$, and let y be defined from g^* as in (1.11). Then (a) for each $g = g^* + \delta g \in \mathscr{G}$ such that $\phi(g) > -\infty$ the value of the directional derivative $D\phi(g^*, \delta g)$ is given by (4.2) or (4.4), and g^* is optimal iff all these numbers are non-positive. Moreover, (b) if g^* is optimal and Assumption (vi) holds, the value of $D\phi(g^*, \delta g)$ is given by (4.4) for every $g \in \mathscr{G}$, all these numbers are non-positive and their minimum is the finite number $-D^*$ defined by (4.6).*

5. DEPLETION TIME

The derivation of detailed necessary conditions relies on a change in the time variable, which replaces " clock " time by the " depletion " time associated with an optimal plan. The idea is that the depletion time k is reached in the state ω when a portion $k = G^*(\omega, t)$ of the initial stock K of reduced capital has been used up; but allowance must be made for the possibility that some of the " later " depletion times are never reached historically in certain states, since in general it cannot be assumed that $G^*(\omega, \infty) = K$ a.s. In this section optimality as such plays no part, the time change being defined for an arbitrary positive g^*. We follow the theory of time change expounded in [1] or [3] with some modifications, adding a Lemma on the inversion of the time change. From now on we adopt

Assumption (vii). The family $(\mathscr{A}_t; t \in \mathscr{T})$ is right continuous, i.e. for each $T \in \mathscr{T}$, $\mathscr{A}_T = \inf(\mathscr{A}_t; t > T)$.

This condition—" the future starts now "—is not restrictive in particular cases.

Let $g^* \in \mathscr{G}$ be positive everywhere (not just a.e.) and let G^* and y correspond to g^*; the sample functions $G^*(\omega, .)$ are increasing, with $0 < G^*(\omega, t) < K$ if $0 < t < \infty$. Write $\mathscr{K} = [0, K)$, $k^+(\omega) = G^*(\omega, \infty)$, and for $\omega \in \Omega$ and $k \in \mathscr{K}$ define a function τ as follows: if $k < k^+(\omega)$, $\tau(\omega, k)$ is the finite solution of

$$G^*[\omega, \tau(\omega, k)] = k; \qquad \ldots(5.1)$$

otherwise $\tau = \infty$. For each ω, $\tau(\omega, .)$ is strictly increasing on $[0, k^+(\omega))$ with derivative

$$\tau'(\omega, k) = d\tau(\omega, k)/dk = 1/g^*[\omega, \tau(\omega, k)], \qquad \ldots(5.2)$$

and by convention we set $\tau' = 0$ on $[k^+, K)$. It can be checked that for each $k \in \mathscr{K}$ the variable $\tau_k = \tau(., k)$ is a stopping time relative to the family $(\mathscr{A}_t)$, and by (2.1) the σ-algebra of events prior to this time, called *events prior to the depletion time* k, is

$$\hat{\mathscr{A}}_k = \{A \in \mathscr{A} : \forall t \in \mathscr{T}, A \cap \{k \leq G^*(t)\} \in \mathscr{A}_t\}. \qquad \ldots(5.3)$$

The family $(\hat{\mathscr{A}}_k; k \in \mathscr{K})$ is ascending and right continuous [3, IV.40, 42]. We regard $\mathscr{K}$ with its Lebesgue sets $\hat{\mathscr{B}}$ and Lebesgue measure $\hat{\lambda}$ as a measure space, and as in Section 2 form the product $(\hat{\mathscr{P}}, \hat{\Sigma}, \hat{m}) = (\Omega \times \mathscr{K}, \mathscr{A} \times \hat{\mathscr{B}}, P \times \hat{\lambda})$ and define the concepts of $\hat{\mathscr{H}}$-measurable function or progressive process, similar processes, martingale, stopping time, etc., relative to $(\hat{\mathscr{A}}_k)$.

The *time change* (from clock time to depletion time) is by definition the family of stopping times $\tau = (\tau_k; k \in \mathscr{K})$ regarded as a stochastic process; the family $(\hat{\mathscr{A}}_k)$ is the *transformed information structure.* If $z = (z_t; t \in \mathscr{T})$ is an $\mathscr{H}$-measurable process such that the limit $z(\infty)$ exists a.s., the *transform of z under the time change* τ is the process $\hat{z} = (\hat{z}_k; k \in \mathscr{K})$ defined by

$$\hat{z}(\omega, k) = z[\omega, \tau(\omega, k)] \quad \omega \in \Omega, \quad k \in \mathscr{K}; \qquad \ldots(5.4)$$

for each ω, the function $\hat{z}(\omega, .)$ is constant and equal to $z(\omega, \infty)$ on $[k^+(\omega), K)$ if this interval is not empty. (More generally, the place of the limiting variable may be taken by an arbitrary " variable at infinity ", but then the notation $z(\infty)$ is best avoided.) Now $\hat{z}$ is $\hat{\mathscr{H}}$-measurable, [3, IV.57], hence adapted to $(\hat{\mathscr{A}}_k)$, and it is easily checked that an alteration of z on a null set of $\mathscr{H}$, leaving the variable at infinity unchanged, alters $\hat{z}$ only on a null set of $\mathscr{H}$; conversely, if two transforms differ only on a null set of $\mathscr{H}$, their inverse images differ only on a null set of $\mathscr{H}$. The conventions concerning null sets and classes of similar functions adopted in Section 2 can therefore be extended in a natural way.

The *inverse time change* (from depletion time to clock time) is by definition the process $G^* = (G_t^*;\ t \in \mathscr{T})$. Explicitly, (5.1) shows that $\tau[\omega, G^*(\omega, t)] = t$ for $(\omega, t) \in \mathscr{S}$, and for each $t \in \mathscr{T}$ the random variable $G_t^* = G^*(., t)$ is a stopping time relative to $(\hat{\mathscr{A}}_k)$ taking values in $\mathscr{K}$; the Lemma below shows that the events prior to this time coincide with the events at t, so that the transformation of the information structure is inverted by G^*. No special definition of the inverse transform of an $\mathscr{H}$-measurable process $\hat{z}$ will be needed, since we shall apply this operation only where $\hat{z}$ can be represented as the transform of some z.

Lemma. *The σ-algebra $\mathscr{F}_t$ of events prior to G_t^* coincides with $\mathscr{A}_t$.*

Proof. From (2.1) and (5.3) we obtain

$$\mathscr{F}_t = \{A \in \mathscr{A}\colon\ \forall k \in \mathscr{K},\quad \forall T \in \mathscr{T},\quad A \cap \{G^*(t) \leqq k \leqq G^*(T)\} \in \mathscr{A}_T\}. \qquad \text{...(5.5)}$$

Let $B(k, T) = \{\omega\colon\ G^*(t) \leq k \leq G^*(T)\}$; for $T \geqq t$, this event occurs if the sample path $G^*(\omega, .)$ crosses the level k during $[t, T]$, and it belongs to $\mathscr{A}_T$ because G^* is adapted and the family $(\mathscr{A}_t)$ is ascending. If $A \in \mathscr{A}_t$, then for $T \geqq t$ the set $A \cap B(k, T)$ is clearly in $\mathscr{A}_T$, while for $T < t$ the set is empty and hence in $\mathscr{A}_T$; if follows that $A \in \mathscr{F}_t$. To prove the converse, we assume that $A \in \mathscr{F}_t$ and show that $A \in \mathscr{A}_T$ for each $T > t$, whence the result will follow by Assumption (vii). It is clear from (5.5) that $A \in \mathscr{A}_T$ if Ω can be written as a countable union of sets $B(k_i, T)$; but this can certainly be done, for example by letting k_i be an enumeration of rationals in $[0, K)$ and noting that each sample path of G^*, being continuous and increasing, must cross some rational level during $[t, T]$. ‖

The theory of Section 6 depends essentially only on the first part of this proof.

The theory developed in Sections 2 and 4 can now be translated from (ω, t) to (ω, k) coordinates; we set out only a few points. The transforms of G and g plans are defined as in (5.4), with limiting variables $G(\infty)$ and $g(\infty) = 0$. For any $g \in \mathscr{G}$, $\hat{G}$ clearly has non-decreasing sample functions, with derivative on $[0, k^+)$ given by;

$$d\hat{G}(\omega, k)/dk = dG[\tau(k)]/dk = g[\tau(k)]\tau'(k) = \hat{g}(k)\tau'(k); \qquad \text{...(5.6)}$$

the derivative vanishes for $k > k^+$, and (5.6) extends to the whole of $[0, K)$ by the definition of τ, provided that the right-hand derivative is taken at $k = k^+$. In particular, the transform of G^* is simply

$$\hat{G}^*(\omega, k) = k \wedge k^+(\omega) \quad \omega \in \Omega, \quad k \in \mathscr{K}, \qquad \text{...(5.7)}$$

where $\wedge$ means " the lesser of ". A special definition is needed for the transform $\hat{y}$ of y; we set, for each $\omega \in \Omega$,

$$\hat{y}(\omega, k) = y[\omega, \tau(\omega, k)] \text{ for } k \in [0, k^+(\omega)); \quad \hat{y}(\omega, k) = 0 \text{ for } k \in [k^+(\omega), K). \qquad \text{...(5.8)}$$

(This corresponds to setting the variable at infinity equal to zero for ω such that $k^+(\omega) < K$; other values may be left unspecified. This definition will agree with that obtained from a true limiting variable in case g^* is optimal and y is a martingale (see below, Section 6, Remark (ii).) The " transforms " of other definitions from Section 2 are fairly straightforward; for example, " $g \in \mathscr{G}$ " becomes

$\hat{g}$ is an $\mathscr{H}$-measurable, a.e. defined and non-negative function on $\mathscr{S}$, which a.s. vanishes on $[k^+(\omega), K)$ and satisfies $\hat{G}(\omega, K) \leqq K$. ...(5.9)

The effect of the time change is to replace integrals with respect to λ or m by integrals with respect to $\hat{\lambda}$ or $\hat{m}$. For example, we have

$$\int_{\tau(i)}^{\tau(j)} y(t)dG(t) = \int_{\tau(i)}^{\tau(j)} y(t)g(t)dt = \int_i^j y[\tau(k)]g[\tau(k)]\tau'(k)dk = \int_i^j \hat{y}(k)d\hat{G}(k), \qquad \text{...(5.10)}$$

$0 \leqq i \leqq j \leqq K$; note that the intervals of integration $[i, j)$ and $[i \wedge k^+, j \wedge k^+)$ may be interchanged by virtue of either (5.6) or (5.8). For fixed ω, all terms in (5.10) are defined as Lebesgue integrals (the Stieltjes notation being used for symmetry and to facilitate reference to [1] and [3]); explicitly, the first equality in (5.10) represents a mere change of notation, the second follows from the ordinary rule for a change of variable $t = \tau(k)$, while the third results from (5.6). The remarks on the measurability of integrals in Section 2 apply with routine changes; thus (5.10) with $i = 0$ and variable (ω, j) defines a process which is $\hat{\mathscr{H}}$-measurable, hence adapted to $(\hat{\mathscr{A}}_k)$. Applying the preceding remarks to the formulae which feature in Theorem 4, (4.4) and (4.6) may be rewritten as

$$D\phi(g^*, \delta g) = E\int_0^\infty y(t)d\delta G(t) = E\int_0^K \hat{y}(k)\delta\hat{g}(k)\tau'(k)dk = E\int_0^K \hat{y}(k)d\delta\hat{G}(k) > -\infty \quad \text{...(5.11)}$$

$$D^* = E\int_0^\infty y(t)dG^*(t) = E\int_0^K \hat{y}(k)dk < \infty. \quad \text{...(5.12)}$$

6. MARTINGALE CONDITIONS FOR SHADOW PRICES

An optimum will now be characterized by means of the corresponding shadow prices, beginning with necessary conditions. Until the statement of Theorem 5, g^* with corresponding functions G^* and y will be an optimum and $g = g^* + \delta g \in \mathscr{G}$ with corresponding $G = G^* + \delta G$ another plan. We now adopt

Assumption (viii). For each $(\omega, t) \in \mathscr{S}$, $u'(.;\ \omega, t)$ is decreasing on $[0, \infty]$ and $u'(0;\ \omega, t) = \infty$.

It follows that optimality implies $g^* > 0$ a.e.; to see this, define g as in (1.23), and observe that $c^* = g^* e^x = 0$ on a set H of positive μ-measure implies $\int_H \delta c . u'(c^*) d\mu = \infty$, contrary to Theorem 4 (b). We choose $g^* > 0$ and $c^* > 0$ everywhere, and define the time change as in Section 5.

It will first be shown that the process $\hat{y}$, possibly altered on a null set of $\hat{\mathscr{H}}$, is a martingale relative to $(\hat{\mathscr{A}}_k)$. Fix $i \in \mathscr{K}$ and $A \in \hat{\mathscr{A}}_i$, then choose j, h, h' and ε such that

$$i < i+h \leqq j < j+h' \leqq K \quad \text{and} \quad 0 < \varepsilon < h.$$

Let

$$\delta\hat{g}(\omega, k) = \begin{cases} -\varepsilon\hat{g}^*(\omega, k)/h & k \in [i, i+h), \quad \omega \in A, \\ +\varepsilon\hat{g}^*(\omega, k)/h' & k \in [j, j+h'), \quad \omega \in A, \end{cases} \quad \text{...(6.1)}$$

and $\delta\hat{g} = 0$ otherwise. The effect of this variation is to accumulate additional reduced capital ε during $[i, i+h)$ and then consume it during $[j, j+h')$, stopping at k^+ if this is reached before the programme is completed; (bear in mind that $\hat{g}^* = 0$ for $k \geqq k^+$). It can be checked that $\hat{g}^* + \delta\hat{g}$ satisfies (5.9) and so is feasible; in particular, the measurability of $\delta\hat{g}$ follows from that of $\hat{g}^*$. Moreover, $\hat{g}^* - \delta\hat{g}$ also is feasible provided that $j + \varepsilon < K$ and $\varepsilon < h'$, so that by Theorem 4 (b) the expression for $D\phi(g^*, \delta g)$ given by (5.11) must vanish. On substituting into this formula and using (5.2) and (5.8) we obtain

$$0 = \int_A dP\left\{-(\varepsilon/h)\int_i^{i+h} \hat{y}(k)dk + (\varepsilon/h')\int_j^{j+h'} \hat{y}(k)dk\right\}. \quad \text{...(6.2)}$$

Now cancel ε, write $\hat{Y}(A, k) = \int_A \hat{y}(\omega, k)dP$, and rearrange as

$$(1/h)\int_i^{i+h} \hat{Y}(A, k)dk = (1/h')\int_j^{j+h} \hat{Y}(A, k)dk. \quad \text{...(6.3)}$$

Since this equality holds for all j, h and h' chosen as prescribed, it is clear that the left-hand side has a constant value for all $h < K - i$, say;

$$\hat{Y}^0(A, i) = (1/h) \int_i^{i+h} \hat{Y}(A, k) dk \quad 0 < h < K - i, \qquad \ldots(6.4)$$

and consequently that

$$\hat{Y}(A, k) = \hat{Y}^0(A, i) \quad \text{a.a.} \quad k \in [i, K). \qquad \ldots(6.5)$$

Also, $A \in \mathscr{A}_i$ implies $A \in \mathscr{A}_k$ for each $k \geq i$, and it follows from (6.3-4) that

$$\hat{Y}^0(A, i) = \hat{Y}^0(A, k) \quad A \in \mathscr{A}_i, \quad k \in [i, K). \qquad \ldots(6.6)$$

In particular, for $i = 0$ and $A = \Omega$ it is seen that $\hat{Y}^0(\Omega, k)$ is constant for all $k \in \mathscr{K}$, and by (6.5) this constant also equals $\hat{Y}(\Omega, k) = E\hat{y}(k)$ for a.a. $k \in \mathscr{K}$; (5.12) then shows that the constant is D^*/K. Clearly, this number is an upper bound for all values of $\hat{Y}^0(A, k)$.

The equalities (6.6) are of martingale type, but they relate to set functions rather than random variables and to $\hat{Y}^0$ rather than $\hat{Y}$; these points will be taken in turn. Fix i, and note that for a.a. $k > i$ the restriction to $\mathscr{A}_i$ of the set function $\hat{Y}(A, k)$ is a P-continuous, non-negative measure; the same is therefore true of $\hat{Y}^0(A, i)$, and this measure is bounded by D^*/K. The Radon-Nikodym Theorem [2, III.10.2] then shows that there is an $\mathscr{A}_i$-measurable, P-integrable, a.s. unique and non-negative random variable $\hat{y}^0(., i)$ such that

$$\hat{Y}^0(A, i) = \int_A \hat{y}^0(\omega, i) dP \quad A \in \mathscr{A}_i; \qquad \ldots(6.7)$$

in particular, $\hat{Y}^0(\Omega, i) = E\hat{y}^0(i) = D^*/K$ for all $i \in \mathscr{K}$. Now consider $\hat{y}^0 = (\hat{y}_k^0; k \in \mathscr{K})$ as a process. It is adapted to $(\mathscr{A}_k)$, the variables are P-integrable, and for each fixed i the relations (6.6) and (6.7) imply

$$\hat{y}^0(\omega, i) = E^i \hat{y}^0(\omega, k) \quad \text{a.s.} \qquad \ldots(6.8)$$

for each $k \geq i$; thus $\hat{y}^0$ is a martingale. By [3, VI.4] there is a modification of $\hat{y}^0$ whose sample functions are right continuous; being right continuous, this process is $\mathscr{H}$-measurable [3, IV.47], hence similar to $\hat{y}^0$, and it shares all the properties of $\hat{y}^0$ mentioned so far. We replace $\hat{y}^0$ by this modification without changing the notation.

It remains to verify that $\hat{y}^0 = \hat{y}$ a.e. Since the processes are non-negative and their $\hat{m}$-integrals over $\mathscr{P}$ both equal D^*, it will be enough to show that $\hat{y}^0 \geq \hat{y}$ a.e. Now, since the processes are $\hat{m}$-integrable, their sample functions are λ-integrable, except perhaps for ω in a P-null set N. For $\omega \in \Omega$, $i \in \mathscr{K}$ and $A \in \mathscr{A}_i$ let

$$\hat{y}_0(\omega, i) = \liminf_{h \downarrow 0} (1/h) \int_i^{i+h} \hat{y}(\omega, k) dk, \quad \hat{Y}_0(A, i) = \int_A \hat{y}_0(\omega, i) dP; \qquad \ldots(6.9)$$

note that $\hat{y}_0$ is $\mathscr{H}$-measurable (as the pointwise limit of such functions), hence adapted to $(\mathscr{A}_k)$. For $\omega \notin N$, $\hat{y}_0$ and $\hat{y}$ have the same λ-integrals on Lebesgue sets of $\mathscr{K}$, [4, p. 255, Theorems 4-5], so that on sets of $\mathscr{H}$ the processes have the same $\hat{m}$-integrals; thus $\hat{y}_0 = \hat{y}$ a.e. On the other hand, an application of Fatou's Lemma to (6.9) and use of (6.4) shows that $\hat{Y}_0(A, i) \leq \hat{Y}^0(A, i)$ for $A \in \mathscr{A}_i$, hence $\hat{y}_0(\omega, i) \leq \hat{y}^0(\omega, i)$ a.s. for each i, so that $\hat{y}_0 \leq \hat{y}^0$ a.e. and the result follows.

(Here is another proof of similarity, based on the abstract theory of processes. By (6.5-6) the $\hat{m}$-integrals of $\hat{y}^0$ and $\hat{y}$ agree on any set of the form $A \times (i, j]$ with $0 \leq i < j < K$ and $A \in \mathscr{A}_i$, hence *a fortiori* on any set of this form with $A \in \sup (\mathscr{A}_k; k \leq i)$. The latter sets, together with the sets $A \times \{0\}$, $A \in \mathscr{A}_0$ generate a σ-algebra $\mathscr{F}$, namely the σ-algebra of " predictable " sets relative to $(\mathscr{A}_k)$, [1, pp. 67-68 and p. 79]. Clearly the equality of integrals extends to $\mathscr{F}$, and the processes would be equal a.e. if they were known to be " predictable ", i.e. $\mathscr{F}$-measurable; but this may be assumed, since progressive processes have predictable modifications [1, pp. 102-103].)

We now replace $\hat{y}$ by $\hat{y}^0$, and henceforth denote the latter function by $\hat{y}$. Note that the equation $\hat{y}(\omega, .) = 0$ on $[k^+(\omega), K)$, which according to (5.8) holds for each ω such that $k^+(\omega)<K$, continues to hold a.s. despite the changes on null sets. (The reason is that $\hat{y}$ as now defined has a.s. right continuous sample functions; one of these functions cannot be positive at a point of $[k^+, K)$ without being positive on an interval of positive length, which can happen only with zero probability if the new $\hat{y}$ is similar to the old.) The inverse image under the time change of the new $\hat{y}$ is now denoted by y; it is similar to y as originally defined, and its sample functions are a.s. right continuous.

The remaining necessary condition is

$$\lim_{i\to K} E\{\hat{y}(i)[K-\hat{G}^*(i)]\} = 0, \qquad \text{...(6.10)}$$

i.e. the " expected capital value " vanishes as $i\to K$. To prove this, fix i and note that $\hat{G}^*(i) = i$ for $i \leqq k^+(\omega)$ by (5.7), while $\hat{y}(\omega, i) = 0$ a.s. for $i>k^+(\omega)$; thus

$$0 \leqq E\{\hat{y}(i)[K-\hat{G}^*(i)]\} = E\{\hat{y}(i)(K-i)\} = (K-i)E\hat{y}(i) = (K-i)D^*/K\to 0$$

as $i\to K$.

This proves the direct part of

Theorem 5. *If $g^* \in \mathscr{G}$ is optimal, then under Assumptions* (vi), (vii) *and* (viii) *it follows that* (a) $\phi(g^*)>-\infty$, (b) *the process $\hat{y} = (\hat{y}_k;\ k\in\mathscr{K})$, denoting reduced shadow prices transformed to depletion time, is a martingale relative to the transformed information structure $(\hat{\mathscr{A}}_k;\ k\in\mathscr{K})$, and* (c) *the expected capital value vanishes as depletion time approaches K (see* (6.10)). *These conditions are also sufficient, without the stated assumptions.*

The proof of sufficiency is like that given for Theorem 1, with (1.15) replaced by

$$E\{\hat{y}(i)\hat{G}(i)\} = E\int_0^i \hat{y}(k)d\hat{G}(k) \quad i\in\mathscr{K},\quad g\in\mathscr{G}; \qquad \text{...(6.11)}$$

this equation can either be proved directly as in Section 1, or obtained from a known theorem on the integration of martingales [3, VII.16]. Now choose g with $\phi(g)>-\infty$, replace $\hat{G}$ by $\delta\hat{G} = \hat{G}-\hat{G}^*$ in (6.11), and let $i\to K$; then (5.11) shows that the right-hand side tends to $D\phi(g^*, \delta g)$, while on the left-hand side we have

$$E\{\hat{y}(i)\delta\hat{G}(i)\} \leqq E\{\hat{y}(i)[K-\hat{G}^*(i)]\}\to 0$$

by (6.10). Thus $D\phi(g^*, \delta g) \leqq 0$ and the result follows from Theorem 4 (a). ||

Turning now to necessary conditions in clock time, a further assumption is needed if y is to be a martingale. In particular, it is enough if only unconstrained optima are considered; an element $g^* \in \mathscr{G}$ is called *unconstrained* if $g^*(\omega, t)>0$ a.e. and a.s.sup $G^*(\omega, t)<K$ for each $t\in\mathscr{T}$. We have

Theorem 6. *If $g^* \in \mathscr{G}$ is optimal and unconstrained, then under Assumptions* (vi), (vii) *and* (viii) *it follows that* (a) $\phi(g^*)>-\infty$, (b) *the reduced shadow price process $y = (y_t;\ t\in\mathscr{T})$ is a martingale relative to the information structure $(\mathscr{A}_t;\ t\in\mathscr{T})$, and* (c) *the expected capital value $E\{y(T)[K-G^*(T)]\}$ vanishes as $T\to\infty$ (see* (1.13)). *These conditions are also sufficient, without the stated assumptions, as Theorem* 1 *shows.*

Proof. We infer (b) from Theorem 5, making use of the theorem on optional stopping [3, VI.13-14]. Applied to the right continuous, non-negative (henceforth r.c.n.) martingale $\hat{y}$, this theorem states that, if v and v' are stopping times relative to $(\hat{\mathscr{A}}_k)$ such that

$$0 \leqq v \leqq v' \leqq K \quad \text{a.s.,}$$

the variables $\hat{y}(v)$ and $\hat{y}(v')$ are P-integrable and satisfy $\hat{y}(v) \geqq E^v\hat{y}(v')$ a.s.; if moreover there is a $j<K$ such that $v'<j$ a.s., or if the variables $(\hat{y}_k;\ k\in\mathscr{K})$ are uniformly P-integrable, the inequality becomes an equality. Now, for each $t\in\mathscr{T}$, $G^*(t)$ defines a stopping time

relative to $(\hat{\mathscr{A}}_k)$, and the Lemma in Section 5 shows that the σ-algebra of events prior to this time is $\mathscr{A}_t$; since $\hat{y}[G^*(t)] = y(t)$, we have $y(t) \geqq E^t y(T)$ a.s. for $t \leqq T$. The fixed depletion times $k \in \mathscr{K}$ are also stopping times, and $E\hat{y}(k) = D^*/K$ for each k; thus $G^*(t) \geqq 0$ implies $Ey(t) \leqq D^*/K$, and y is a (r.c.n.) super-martingale. On the other hand, the assumption that g^* is unconstrained implies that, for each $T \in \mathscr{T}$, there is a number $j(T) < K$ such that $G^*(T) < j(T)$ a.s.; this yields the equalities $y(t) = E^t y(T)$ a.s. and $Ey(t) = D^*/K$. Thus y is a martingale; this implies that (1.15) holds with $g = g^*$, and then (4.6) yields

$$E\{y(T)[K - G^*(T)]\} = D^* - E\{y(T)G^*(T)\} = D^* - E\int_0^T y(t)g^*(t)dt \to 0 \quad \text{as} \quad T \to \infty;$$

this proves assertion (c). ‖

Remark (i). The assumption that g^* is unconstrained can be replaced in Theorem 6 by the condition

$$\lim_{i \to K} Ey(T \wedge \tau_i) = Ey(T) \quad T \in \mathscr{T}, \qquad \ldots(6.12)$$

and conversely this condition implies that y is a martingale. Indeed, the proof of Theorem 6 shows that y is in any case a super-martingale, and so will be a martingale if $Ey(T)$ is constant on $\mathscr{T}$ [3, V.5]. Now $y(T \wedge \tau_i) = \hat{y}(G_T^* \wedge i)$, and for $i < K$ the variables

$$(G_T^* \wedge i;\ T \in \mathscr{T})$$

are stopping times relative to $(\hat{\mathscr{A}}_k)$ which are bounded above by i; optional stopping therefore yields $E\hat{y}(G_T^* \wedge i) = E\hat{y}(i) = D^*/K$, hence $Ey(T) = D^*/K$ if (6.12) holds. Conversely, if y is a martingale, then for $T < \infty$ the variables $(T \wedge \tau_i;\ i \in \mathscr{K})$ are stopping times relative to $(\mathscr{A}_t)$ which are bounded above by T, so that $Ey(T \wedge \tau_i) = Ey(T)$ for each $i \in \mathscr{K}$ and (6.12) holds.

This remark also shows that, even if (y_t) is not a martingale, it is a local martingale, i.e. a process adapted to $(\mathscr{A}_t)$ such that, for some sequence v_n of stopping times increasing a.s. to infinity, the process equal to $y(t \wedge v_n)$ when $v_n > 0$ and equal to zero otherwise is a martingale for each n; it suffices to take $v_n = \tau(k_n)$ with $0 < k_n \to K$. If Theorem 5 is restated in this terminology, it is seen to correspond to a result obtained in [7] by a method based on the Hahn–Banach Theorem, for a problem related to that considered here but involving a linear maximand and a quadratic constraint.

Remark (ii). According to Theorem 5, $\hat{y}$ is a r.c.n. martingale, hence converges a.s. to a limiting variable $\hat{y}(K)$ when $k \to K$ [3, VI.6], and Theorem 5 (c) shows that a.s. either $k^+ = K$ (total depletion) or $\hat{y}(K) = 0$ (vanishing price); moreover $\hat{y}(k^+) = \hat{y}(K)$ by right continuity. At the same time, the r.c.n. super-martingale y converges when $t \to \infty$, and one can write this left-hand limit as $y(\infty) = \hat{y}(k^+ - 0)$. However, it does not in general follow that $y(\infty) = 0$ when $k^+ < K$, since the left and right limits of $\hat{y}$ at k^+ could differ. This awkward distinction disappears when Theorem 6 applies, since then a.s. either $k^+ = K$ or $y(\infty) = 0$. Moreover, in this case the special definition (5.8) of the transform $\hat{y}$ reduces to the definition by means of a genuine limiting variable.

Remark (iii). In general, the martingales $\hat{y}$ and y which feature in Theorem 5 and Theorem 6 are not closed on the right (see the example in Section 1 (E)). In the special case where (say) y is a right closed martingale we have $y(t) = E^t y(\infty)$ a.s. for each $t \in \mathscr{T}$; then all shadow prices can be written as conditional expectations of " prices at infinity ", and the entire optimal solution is determined by the single random variable $y(\infty)$. Conditions for this result to hold can be obtained from the theorem that, for a right continuous martingale y, right closure is equivalent to uniform P-integrability of the variables (y_t) [8, V.19 and VI.6 (d)]; for example, the condition $E\{\sup_t y(\omega, t)\} < \infty$ is sufficient. It turns out that $\hat{y}$ is a right closed (r.c.n.) martingale iff y has this property. Suppose for instance that $\hat{y}$ is right closed; then, for any stopping time v relative to $(\hat{\mathscr{A}}_k)$, $\hat{y}(v) = E^v \hat{y}(K)$ a.s.

[1, V.7]. It is then found, as in the proof of Theorem 6, that $y(t) = \hat{y}[G^*(t)] = E^t\hat{y}(K)$ a.s. for each t, so that $Ey(t)$ is constant and y is a martingale. Now $G^*(\infty) = k^+$ is also a stopping time, and the σ-algebra of events prior to this time is $\mathscr{A}_\infty = \mathscr{A}$; hence

$$y(\infty) = \hat{y}(k^+ - 0) = E^\infty \hat{y}(K) = \hat{y}(K) \quad \text{a.s.}$$

It follows that $y(t) = E^t y(\infty)$ a.s., so that y is right closed. A similar argument shows that, if y is a right closed martingale, then $\hat{y}$ is right closed.

Remark (iv). A number of analytic properties of the processes $\hat{y}$ and y, concerning for example the continuity, boundedness and oscillation of sample functions, can be obtained from standard theorems on martingales in continuous time (see [3, VI]). It is of some economic interest that these properties of reduced shadow prices follow from optimality as such, without corresponding *a-priori* restrictions on the functions x, q, u and u' or on the class $\mathscr{G}$ of plans.

Remark (v). The theory of Sections 4-6 extends to the horizon model, subject to certain changes connected with the argument that an optimal g^* is positive. It is clear that Assumption (viii), on which this argument previously rested, must be amended to apply only when (ω, t) belongs to the life interval $\mathscr{S}^l$, since on $\mathscr{S} - \mathscr{S}^l$ we have $u'(.;\ \omega, t) = 0$ identically. It then follows as above that an optimal g^* is a.e. positive on $\mathscr{S}^l$. On $\mathscr{S} - \mathscr{S}^l$ the definition of g^* is arbitrary, subject to the constraints; to be specific, we set

$$g^*(\omega, t) = [K - G^*(\omega, \Delta(\omega)]e^{-[t-\Delta(\omega)]} \quad t \in [\Delta(\omega), \infty). \qquad \text{...(6.13)}$$

This definition ensures that $g^* > 0$ a.e. in case there is probability one that either $\Delta = \infty$ (infinite life) or $K - G^*(\Delta) > 0$ (positive bequest); it is of interest to state a condition which guarantees that an optimal plan has this property. The idea is that, if the time of death is even slightly uncertain while life remains, some resources will be kept to the end in order to avoid the risk of a terminal period without consumption. To make this precise, recall that a stopping time v relative to $(\mathscr{A}_t)$ is called *predictable* if there is a sequence (v_n) of stopping times such that $v_n \uparrow v$ a.s. and, for every n, $v_n < v$ on $\{\omega\colon\ v(\omega) > 0\}$; the sequence (v_n) is then said to *foretell* v. A stopping time V is called *totally inaccessible* if

$$P\{\omega\colon\ V(\omega) = v(\omega) < \infty\} = 0$$

for every predictable v [1, pp. 56-58]. Suppose that the time of death Δ is totally inaccessible. The time $\tau(K) = \sup\{t\colon\ G^*(t) < K\}$ is predictable because the sample functions of G^* are continuous, and since $\tau(K) < \infty$ implies $G^*[\tau(K)] = K$ we have

$$P\{\Delta = \tau(K) < \infty\} = 0.$$

Now $\tau(K) < \Delta$ means that there is a time $\tau < \Delta$ such that $G^*(\tau) = K$, i.e. capital is exhausted before death; this cannot happen with positive probability, since $g^* > 0$ a.e. on $\mathscr{S}^l$. It follows that a.s. either $\Delta = \infty$ or $\tau(K) > \Delta$, as required. With this assumption, the theory remains practically unchanged. If the assumption is dropped, it may (but need not) happen that the event $\{G^*(\Delta) = K \text{ and } \Delta < \infty\}$ has positive probability. For ω in this set, we have $g^*(\omega, .) = 0$ on $[\Delta(\omega), \infty)$, so that depletion time does not increase with clock time; this necessitates some minor changes in Section 5, after which Theorem 5 stands unchanged. Theorem 6 as stated is no longer of interest since g^* is constrained, but alternative martingale conditions in clock time can be obtained in some cases. In particular, an obvious modification of Theorem 6 applies if $\Delta = \text{constant} < \infty$; then, if $G^*(t)$ is a.s. bounded away from K for each $t \in [0, \Delta)$, the process $(y_t;\ t < \Delta)$ is a martingale, and $E\{y(t)[K - G^*(t)]\} \to 0$ as $t \to \Delta$.

First version received June 1975; *final version accepted June* 1976 (*Eds.*).

I am indebted for comments on an earlier draft to a Referee, to Dr J.-M. Bismut and to Dr A. J. Ostaszewski.

REFERENCES

[1] Dellacherie, C. *Capacités et processus stochastiques* (Springer, 1972).
[2] Dunford, N. and Schwartz, J. T. *Linear Operators I* (Interscience, 1957).
[3] Meyer, P.-A. *Probabilités et potentiel* (Hermann, 1966; English translation Blaisdell, 1969).
[4] Natanson, I. P. *Theory of Functions of a Real Variable I* (Ungar, 1955).
[5] Vainberg, M. M. *Variational Methods for the Study of Nonlinear Operators* (Holden-Day, 1964).
[6] Bewley, T. F. " Existence of Equilibria in Economies with Infinitely Many Commodities ", *Journal of Economic Theory*, **4** (1972), 514-540.
[7] Bismut, J.-M. " An Example of Optimal Stochastic Control with Constraints ", *SIAM Journal on Control*, **12** (1974), 401-417.
[8] Merton, R. C. " An Asymptotic Theory of Growth under Uncertainty ", *Review of Economic Studies*, **42** (1975), 375-394.
[9] Mirrlees, J. A. " Optimal Allocation under Uncertainty: the Case of Stationary Returns to Investment ", in Drèze, J. (ed.), *Allocation under Uncertainty: Equilibrium and Optimality* (Macmillan, 1974).
[10] Foldes, L. P. " Martingale Conditions for Optimal Saving: Discrete Time ", *Journal of Mathematical Economics*, **5** (1978) (to appear).

[10]

PORTFOLIO SELECTION WITH TRANSACTION COSTS*

M. H. A. DAVIS AND A. R. NORMAN†

In this paper, optimal consumption and investment decisions are studied for an investor who has available a bank account paying a fixed rate of interest and a stock whose price is a log-normal diffusion. This problem was solved by Merton and others when transactions between bank and stock are costless. Here we suppose that there are charges on all transactions equal to a fixed percentage of the amount transacted. It is shown that the optimal buying and selling policies are the local times of the two-dimensional process of bank and stock holdings at the boundaries of a wedge-shaped region which is determined by the solution of a nonlinear free boundary problem. An algorithm for solving the free boundary problem is given.

1. Introduction. This paper concerns the optimal investment and consumption decisions of an individual who has available just two investment instruments: a bank account paying a fixed interest rate r, and a risky asset ("stock") whose price is a geometric Brownian motion with expected rate of return α and rate of return variation σ^2. Thus the stock grows at a mean rate α, with white noise fluctuations. It is assumed that stock may be bought and sold in arbitrary amounts (not necessarily integral numbers of shares). The investor consumes at rate $c(t)$ from the bank account; all income is derived from capital gains and consumption is subject to the constraint that the investor must be solvent. i.e. have nonnegative net worth, at all times. The investor's objective is to maximize the utility of consumption as measured by the quantity

$$\mathbb{E}\int_0^\infty e^{-\delta t}u(c(t))\,dt. \tag{1.1}$$

Here $\mathbb{E}$ denotes expectation and $\delta > 0$ is the interest rate for discounting. In this paper the utility function $u(c)$ will always be equal to c^γ/γ for some $\gamma \in \Gamma := \{\gamma \in \mathbb{R}: \gamma < 1 \text{ and } \gamma \neq 0\}$ or $u(c) = \log c$ ("log" denotes the natural logarithm). These functions form a subset of the so-called HARA (hyperbolic absolute risk aversion) class.

In the absence of any transactions between stock and bank, the investor's holding $s_0(t)$ and $s_1(t)$ in bank and stock respectively, expressed in monetary terms, evolve according to the following equations, the second of which is an Ito stochastic

*Received July 27, 1987; revised April 24, 1989.
AMS 1980 subject classification. Primary: 93E20. Secondary: 90A16, 60H10.
IAOR 1973 subject classification. Main: Stochastic control. Cross references: Investment.
OR/MS Index 1978 subject classification. Primary: 200 Finance/portfolio. Secondary: 564 Probability/diffusion.
Key words. Portfolio selection, transaction costs, stochastic control, reflecting diffusions, free boundary problem, local time.
†Supported in part by an SERC Postgraduate Studentship.

0364-765X/90/1504/0676/$01.25
Copyright © 1990, The Institute of Management Sciences/Operations Research Society of America

differential equation driven by a standard Brownian motion $z(t)$.

$$ds_0(t) = (rs_0(t) - c(t))\,dt, \tag{1.2}$$

$$ds_1(t) = \alpha s_1(t)\,dt + \sigma s_1(s)\,dz(t). \tag{1.3}$$

The investor starts off with an initial endowment $s_0(0) = x$, $s_1(0) = y$. To complete the specification of the problem we need to state how funds are transferred from bank to stock and vice versa. In the original paper of R. C. Merton [18], and in almost all subsequent work in this area, it assumed that such transfers can be made instantly and costlessly. In this case we can re-parametrize the problem by introducing new variables $w(t) = s_0(t) + s_1(t)$ (the total wealth) and $\pi(t) = s_1(t)/w(t)$ (the fraction of total wealth held in stock). Adding (1.2) and (1.3) and using these variables gives us the basic wealth equation

$$dw(t) = [rw(t) + (\alpha - r)\pi(t)w(t) - c(t)]\,dt + \sigma\pi(t)w(t)\,dz(t), \tag{1.4}$$

$$w(0) = x + y.$$

Since transactions are free and instantaneous we can regard $\pi(t)$—as well as $c(t)$—as a *decision variable*. We now have a completely formulated stochastic control problem: choose nonanticipative processes $\pi(t), c(t)$ so as to maximize (1.1) subject to (1.4) and the constraint $w(t) \geqslant 0$ for all t.

It is a remarkable fact that this is one of the few nonlinear stochastic control problems that can be explicitly solved. It turns out, as we will show in §2 below, that for utility functions in the HARA class the optimal investment strategy is to keep a *constant fraction of total wealth in the risky asset*, and to *consume at a rate proportional to total wealth*, i.e. the optimal $\pi(t), c(t)$ are $\pi(t) = \pi^*$ and $c(t) = Cw(t)$ for some constants π^*, C. This means that, optimally, the investor acts in such a way that the portfolio holdings are always on the line $s_1 = [\pi^*/(1 - \pi^*)]s_0$ in the (s_0, s_1) plane; we shall refer to this as the "Merton line" (Figure 1).

In a recent paper by Karatzas, Lehoczky, Sethi and Shreve [12], the constraint $w(t) \geqslant 0$ is replaced by the stipulation that evolution of the wealth process terminates on bankruptcy (i.e. the first time at which $w(t) = 0$), at which point the investor is retired on a lump-sum pension P. It turns out that if P is not large enough then it is optimal to avoid bankruptcy altogether (this can always be done) and then the policy described above is optimal. All of these results hold under a basic well-posedness condition, namely

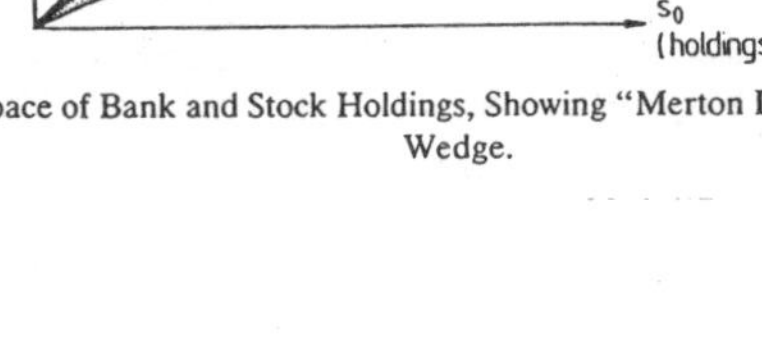

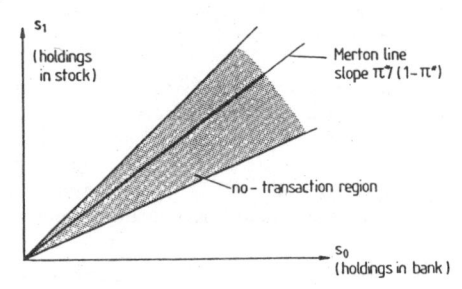

FIGURE 1. Space of Bank and Stock Holdings, Showing "Merton Line" and No-Transaction Wedge.

Condition A. $\delta > \gamma[r + (\alpha - r)^2/\sigma^2(1-\gamma)]$.

If this condition is violated then growth of discounted utility is possible and arbitrarily large utility may be obtained by policies of prolonged investment followed by massive consumption. The well-posedness condition for $u(c) = \log c$ is $\delta > 0$, which is just Condition A with $\gamma = 0$.

Any attempt to apply Merton's strategy in the face of transaction costs would result in immediate penury, since incessant trading is necessary to hold the portfolio on the Merton line. There must in such a case be some "no-transaction" region in (s_0, s_1) space inside which the portfolio is insufficiently far "out of line" to make trading worthwhile. In this paper we shall consider the case of proportional transaction costs:[1] the investor pays fractions λ and μ of the amount transacted, on purchase and sale of stock respectively. All such charges are paid from the bank account. In this case the bank and stock holdings must retain their separate identities rather than being merged into a single wealth process. The equations describing their evolution are

$$(1.5)\qquad \begin{aligned} ds_0(t) &= [rs_0(t) - c(t)]\,dt - (1+\lambda)\,dL_t + (1-\mu)\,dU_t,\\ ds_1(t) &= \alpha s_1(t)\,dt + \sigma s_1(t)\,dz(t) + dL_t - dU_t,\end{aligned}$$

where L_t, U_t represent cumulative purchase and sale of stock on the time interval $[0, t]$ respectively. This allows for instantaneous purchase or sale of finite amounts of stock as well as purchase and sale at a given rate and various other sorts of behaviour. One notices from (1.5) that purchase of dL units of stock requires a payment $(1+\lambda)\,dL$ from the bank, while sale of dU units of stock realizes only $(1-\mu)\,dU$ in cash. Obviously, it will never be optimal to buy and sell at the same time. If Condition A does not hold then arbitrarily high utility can be achieved as described above (the "prolonged investment" just has to be a little more prolonged). Under Condition A, we will show that *the no-transaction region is a wedge containing the Merton line* (Fig. 1); equivalently, the proportion of total wealth held in stock should be maintained between fractions π_1^* and π_2^*, which of course depend on λ and μ as well as the other constants in the problem. For example, when $\lambda = \mu = 0.015$ and $r = 0.07$, $\alpha = 0.12$, $\sigma = 0.4$, $\delta = 0.1$, and the utility function is $u(c) = -1/c$ we find that $\pi_1^* = 9.0\%$, $\pi_2^* = 19.8\%$ whereas the Merton proportion is $\pi^* = 15.6\%$ (see Figure 3 below). There is no closed-form expression for π_1^*, π_2^* but we state how to compute them. The optimal transaction policy is *minimal trading* to stay inside the wedge, preceded by an immediate transaction to the closest point in the wedge if the initial endowment is outside it. More technically, the optimally controlled process is a reflecting diffusion inside the wedge and the buying and selling policies (L_t, U_t) are the local times at the lower and upper boundaries respectively. Consumption takes place at a finite rate in the interior of the wedge (in which the process lies almost all of the time).

Our interest in this problem was aroused by the stimulating paper of Magill and Constantinides [17] on the same subject. This paper contains the fundamental insight that the no-transaction region is a wedge, but the argument is heuristic at best and no clear prescription as to how to compute the location of the boundaries, or what the controlled process should do when it reaches them, is given. The paper was in fact ahead of its time, in that an essential ingredient of any rigorous formulation, namely

[1] The case of fixed costs, where the investor pays a flat transaction fee regardless of the amount transacted, remains largely unexplored; this is a problem of *impulse control* [3]. There is some work in this direction by Duffie and Sun [7].

the theory of local time and reflecting diffusion, was unavailable to the authors, being at that time (1976) the exclusive property of a small band of pure mathematical votaries. Needless to say, Magill's and Constantinides' paper is far more valuable than many others of unimpeachable mathematical rectitude.

Stochastic control problems involving local time have received much attention in recent years. Early pioneering work of Bather and Chernoff was followed by the appearance of papers by Beneš, Shepp and Witsenhausen [2] and Harrison and Taylor [10] in which problems of "finite fuel" control and regulation of "Brownian storage systems" were solved rigorously, taking advantage of developments in stochastic calculus in the 1970s which made it possible to handle local times and reflecting diffusions in simple domains in a relatively straightforward way. The relevant theory can now be found in very compact form in Harrison's book [9]. All of these works, and the present paper, essentially concern free boundary problems, and indeed many of them are closely related to optimal stopping, as Karatzas and Shreve [14] have shown. This paper differs from all others we are aware of, however, in that our problem involves "continuous control" (i.e. consumption) as well as "singular control" (transactions). This leads to a free boundary problem for a *nonlinear* partial differential equation (PDE) as opposed to the linear PDEs which arise when singular control is the *only* control. The problem is for this reason substantially more delicate.

Three papers directly related to the present work are Constantinides [4], Duffie and Sun [7] and Taksar, Klass and Assaf [20]. Constantinides considers essentially the same problem as ours (or as the earlier paper of Magill and Constantinides [17]) and proposes an approximate solution based on making certain assumptions on the consumption process. Some further remarks on his results will be found in §7 below. Duffie and Sun [7] consider the case of fixed plus proportional transaction charges. Their results are quite different in character from ours. Taksar, Klass and Assaf [20], using the model (1.5) with $c \equiv 0$ (no consumption), study the problem of maximizing the long-run growth rate

$$\mathbb{E}\left\{\liminf_{t\to\infty}\frac{1}{t}\log(s_0(t)+s_1(t))\right\}.$$

In an ingenious analysis they reduce the problem to a 1-dimensional one and show that a "two-sided regulator" is optimal, which means that the process $(s_0(t), s_1(t))$ is, as in our case, optimally kept inside a wedge by reflection at the boundaries. The solution thus looks very similar to ours, but the details of the problem and the method of analysis are completely different. A study of the effects of transaction costs on *option pricing* is given by Leland [15].

The present paper is organized as follows. In §2 we give a self-contained treatment of the Merton (no transaction cost) problem. This is included because later on we need to use comparison arguments involving the Merton case, and also because no simple complete treatment seems to be readily available.[2] The transaction costs problem is formulated in §3, where we give informal arguments which indicate why the no-transaction region is wedge-shaped. We also show how the analytic problem may be reduced to a one-dimensional free boundary problem. In §4 we prove "verification theorems" which show that if the free boundary problem can be solved then a policy of minimal transaction to stay within the wedge defined by its solution is indeed optimal. Theorem 5.1 in §5 gives conditions under which the free boundary problem is solvable. In §6 we obtain a semimartingale representation of the evolution of the "value process". Apart from having some intrinsic interest, this is needed to

[2]The extra generality of the treatment in [12] necessitates more complicated arguments.

complete some technical argument in §4, and can be used to show that under the optimal policy the investor does not reach bankruptcy in finite time.

The main results of the paper are summarized in Theorem 7.1 in §7. This section also contains an algorithm for solving the free boundary problem together with numerical results, as well as concluding remarks. Finally, the Appendix contains a technical analysis of some differential equations arising in the solution of the free boundary problem.

A preliminary account of some of this work was given in Davis [5].

2. No transaction costs: the Merton problem. Throughout the paper $(\Omega, \mathfrak{F}, \mathbb{P})$ will denote a fixed complete probability space and $(\mathcal{F}_t)_{t\geqslant 0}$ a given filtration, i.e. a family of sub-σ-fields of $\mathfrak{F}$ such that (i) $\mathcal{F}_s \leqslant \mathcal{F}_t$ for $s \leqslant t$ and (ii) for each $t \geqslant 0$, $\mathcal{F}_t$ contains all null sets of $\mathfrak{F}$. The stochastic process[3] $(z_t)_{t\geqslant 0}$ will be a standard Brownian motion with respect to $(\mathcal{F}_t)$, i.e. (z_t) has almost all sample paths continuous, is adapted to $(\mathcal{F}_t)$, and for each $s, t \geqslant 0$ the increment $z_{t+s} - z_t$ is independent of $\mathcal{F}_t$ and is normally distributed with mean 0 and variance s.

In this section we study the "Merton problem" of choosing investment and consumption policies (π_t, c_t) so as to maximize utility when wealth evolves according to equation (1.4). Let $\mathfrak{U}$ denote the set of policies. A policy is a pair (c_t, π_t) of $\mathcal{F}_t$-adapted processes such that

(2.1) (i) $c(t,\omega) \geqslant 0$ and $\int_0^t c(s,\omega)\,ds < \infty$ for all (t,ω),

(ii) $|\pi(t,\omega)| \leqslant K$ for all (t,ω), where K is a constant which may vary from policy to policy, and

(iii) $w(t,\omega) \geqslant 0$ for all (t,ω), where (w_t) is the unique strong solution of the wealth equation

$$dw_t = (rw_t + (\alpha - r)\pi_t w_t - c_t)\,dt + w_t\pi_t\sigma\,dz_t, \tag{2.2}$$

$$w_0 = w.$$

Here $w \in \mathbb{R}_+$ is the initial endowment and α, r, σ are positive constants as described in §1. The existence of such a solution follows from standard theorems, which show that the map $t \to w_t(\omega)$ is continuous for almost all $\omega \in \Omega$. Let $\tau := \inf t\colon w_t = 0\}$. We note that $(c,\pi) \in \mathfrak{U}$ only if $c_t = 0$ a.s. for all $t \geqslant \tau$ and hence $w_t = 0$ for all $t \geqslant \tau$. The investment problem is to choose $(c,\pi) \in \mathfrak{U}$ so as to maximize

$$J_w(c,\pi) := \mathbb{E}_w \int_0^\infty e^{-\delta t} u(c_t)\,dt. \tag{2.3}$$

THEOREM 2.1. (a) *Suppose Condition* A *holds and that* $u(c) = c^\gamma/\gamma$, $\gamma \in \Gamma$. *Define*

$$C = \frac{1}{1-\gamma}\left[\delta - \gamma r - \frac{\gamma\beta^2}{2(1-\gamma)}\right] \tag{2.4}$$

[3]Throughout the paper we take the usual probabilist's license of denoting a random process such as (z_t) interchangeably as z_t, $z(t)$, $z_t(\omega)$ or $z(t,\omega)$. All exogenously defined processes are assumed to be measurable.

where $\beta := (\alpha - r)/\sigma$. *Then* $\sup_{(c,\pi)\in\mathfrak{U}} J_w(c,\pi) = v(w)$ *where*

$$v(w) = \frac{1}{\gamma} C^{\gamma-1} w^{\gamma}. \tag{2.5}$$

The optimal policy is

$$c_t^* = C w_t, \qquad \pi_t^* = \frac{\beta}{(1-\gamma)\sigma}. \tag{2.6}$$

(b) *Suppose* $u(c) = \log c$ *and that* $\delta > 0$. *Then*

$$\sup_{(c,\pi)\in\mathfrak{U}} J_w(c,\pi) = \frac{1}{\delta^2}\left[r + \frac{1}{2}\beta^2 - \delta\right] + \frac{1}{\delta}\log \delta w$$

and the optimal policy is $c_t^* = \delta w_t$, $\pi_t^* = \beta/\sigma$.

REMARK 2.2. As noted in §1, π^* is constant and c^* is proportional to current wealth. The condition $\delta > 0$ and the optimal policies (c^*, π^*) of case (b) are formally obtained from case (a) by setting $\gamma = 0$. We see from (2.6) that $\pi^* \in (0, 1)$ only when $r < \alpha < r + (1-\gamma)\sigma^2$. This is *hedging*: assets are split between stock and bank to reduce volatility. If $\alpha > r + (1-\gamma)\sigma^2$ then *leverage* is optimal: funds are borrowed from bank to invest in stock,[4] while if $\alpha < r$ then the converse—i.e. *shortselling*—is optimal. When $\alpha = r$, $\pi^* = 0$; in this case $v(w) = ((\delta - \gamma r)/(1-\gamma))^{\gamma-1}\gamma^{-1}w^{\gamma}$, which is just the utility of optimally consuming an initial endowment w in the bank.

PROOF. We will only prove part (a). Part (b) is proved by exactly the same arguments. The proof is an application of dynamic programming, cf. Chapter VI of Fleming and Rishel [8]. When c, π are constants the wealth process w_t given by (2.2) is a diffusion process with generator

$$A^{c,\pi}\tilde{v}(w) = [(r + (\alpha - r)\pi)w - c]\tilde{v}'(w) + \tfrac{1}{2}w^2\pi^2\sigma^2\tilde{v}''(w)$$

acting on C^2 functions $\tilde{v}$ ($\tilde{v}' = d\tilde{v}/dw$). The so-called *Bellman equation* of dynamic programming for maximizing (2.2) over control policies (c_t, π_t), to be solved for a function $\tilde{v}$, is

$$\max_{c,\pi}\left\{A^{c,\pi}\tilde{v} + \frac{1}{\gamma}c^{\gamma} - \delta\tilde{v}\right\} = 0. \tag{2.7}$$

The maxima are achieved at

$$c = (\tilde{v}')^{-1/(1-\gamma)}, \qquad \pi = \frac{-\beta\tilde{v}'}{w\sigma\tilde{v}''},$$

so that (2.7) is equivalent to

$$rw\tilde{v}' - \frac{\beta^2}{2}\frac{(\tilde{v}')^2}{\tilde{v}''} + \frac{1-\gamma}{\gamma}(\tilde{v}')^{-\gamma/(1-\gamma)} - \delta\tilde{v} = 0. \tag{2.8}$$

The justification for introducing this equation will be seen when we obtain the semimartingale decomposition of the process M_t defined below. (2.8) is satisfied by

[4]We are assuming that interest rates are the same on lending and borrowing.

$\bar{v} = v$ given by (2.5) and the maximizing π and c are equal to π^*, c^* given by (2.6). Condition (2.3) ensures that $c^*(t) \geqslant 0$.

Let $(c, \pi) \in \mathfrak{U}$ be an arbitrary policy. The solution of (2.2) is given by

$$(2.9)\quad w_t = \exp\left\{rt + \int_0^t \left((\alpha - r)\pi_u - \frac{1}{2}\sigma^2\pi_u^2\right) du + \sigma\int_0^t \pi_u\, Dz_u\right\}$$
$$\times\left\{w - \int_0^t c_s \exp\left[-\int_0^s \left((\alpha - r)\pi_u - \frac{1}{2}\sigma^2\pi_u^2\right) du - \sigma\int_0^s \pi_u\, dz_u\right] ds\right\}.$$

It follows from Hölder's inequality and the fact that π is bounded that w_t has finite moments of all orders, and it is also clear that $w_t \leqslant w_t^0$ where w_t^0 is the solution of (2.2) with the same π and $c_t \equiv 0$. Now define

$$(2.10)\qquad M_t := \frac{1}{\gamma}\int_0^t e^{-\delta s} c_s^\gamma\, ds + e^{-\delta t} v(w_t),$$

where v is defined by (2.5). By the Ito formula,

$$M_t - M_0 = \int_0^t e^{-\delta t}\left[A^{c,\pi}v + \frac{1}{\gamma}c^\gamma - \delta v\right] ds + \sigma C^{\gamma-1}\int_0^t e^{-\delta s}\pi_s w_s^\gamma\, dz_s.$$

It follows from the above argument that the second term on the right is a martingale, while the first term is, in view of (2.7), a decreasing process which is equal to zero when $(c, \pi) = (c^*, \pi^*)$. Thus M_t is a supermartingale, and is a martingale when $(c, \pi) = (c^*, \pi^*)$, so that

$$(2.11)\qquad v(w) = M_0 \geqslant \mathbb{E}_w M_t = \mathbb{E}_w \frac{1}{\gamma}\int_0^t e^{-\delta s} c_s^\gamma\, ds + \mathbb{E}_w e^{-\delta t} v(w_t).$$

By using the Ito formula and the wealth equation (2.2) we find that

$$(2.12)\qquad e^{-\delta t} w_t^\gamma = w_0^\gamma G_t \exp\left\{\int_0^t a(s)\, ds\right\},$$

where G_t is the exponential martingale (it *is* a martingale since π is bounded)

$$G_t = \exp\left\{\int_0^t \gamma\pi_s\sigma\, dz_s - \frac{1}{2}\int_0^t \gamma^2\pi_s^2\sigma^2\, ds\right\} \quad \text{and}$$

$$a(s) = \gamma\left[r + (\alpha - r)\pi_s - (c_s/w_s) - \tfrac{1}{2}(1 - \gamma)\pi_s^2\sigma^2\right] - \delta.$$

When $(c, \pi) = (c^*, \pi^*)$ we find that $a(s) = -C$ and hence from (2.12) that $\mathbb{E}_w e^{-\delta t} v(w_t) \to 0$ as $t \to \infty$. It now follows from (2.11) that $v(w) = J_w(c^*, \pi^*)$.

To complete the proof we have to consider the cases $0 < \gamma < 1$, $\gamma < 0$ separately. In the former,

$$(2.13)\qquad a(s) \leqslant -(1 - \gamma)C,$$

equality being achieved when $c_s = 0$ and $\pi_s = \pi^*$. This implies as above that $\mathbb{E}_w e^{-\delta t} v(w_t) \to 0$ as $t \to \infty$ and hence from (2.11) that, for any policy (c, π), $v(w) \geqslant J_w(c, \pi)$. Thus (c^*, π^*) is optimal.

Now take $\gamma < 0$. The preceding argument fails because there is no longer an *a priori* upper bound for $a(s)$. Instead, we proceed as follows. For $\epsilon > 0$ define

$$v_\epsilon(w) = \frac{1}{\gamma} C^{\gamma - 1}(w + \epsilon)^\gamma.$$

Then $v'_\epsilon(w) = v'(w + \epsilon)$ etc. and we see from (2.8) that v_ϵ satisfies

$$r(w+\epsilon)v'_\epsilon(w) - \frac{\beta^2}{2}\frac{(v'_\epsilon(w))^2}{v''_\epsilon(w)} + \frac{1-\gamma}{\gamma}(v'_\epsilon(w))^{-\gamma/(1-\gamma)} - \delta v_\epsilon(w) = 0.$$

Since $v'_\epsilon(w) > 0$ this shows that

$$rwv'_\epsilon - \frac{\beta^2}{2}\frac{(v'_\epsilon)^2}{v''_\epsilon} + \frac{1-\gamma}{\gamma}(v'_\epsilon)^{-\gamma/(1-\gamma)} - \delta v_\epsilon < 0,$$

i.e.

$$\max_{c,\pi}\left\{A^{c,\pi}v_\epsilon + \frac{1}{\gamma}c^\gamma - \delta v_\epsilon\right\} < 0.$$

Now v_ϵ is bounded on $\mathbb{R}_+$ with bounded first and second derivatives. We easily conclude, by introducing the process M_t as in (2.10) but with v_ϵ replacing v, that for any $(c, \pi) \in \mathfrak{U}$ and $w > 0$, $v_\epsilon(w) > J_w(c, \pi)$. Since $v_\epsilon(w) \downarrow v(w)$ as $\epsilon \downarrow 0$ this shows that $v(w) \geqslant \sup_{(c,\pi)\in\mathfrak{U}} J_w(c, \pi)$. But we know that $v(w) = J_w(c^*, \pi^*)$, so (c^*, π^*) is in fact optimal, as claimed.

COROLLARY 2.3. *Under the optimal policy (c^*, π^*) the wealth process $w(t)$ is given by*

$$w(t) = w(0)\exp\left(\frac{1}{(1-\gamma)}\left(r - \delta + \frac{\beta^2}{2}\left(\frac{2-\gamma}{1-\gamma}\right)\right)t\right)\exp\left(\frac{\beta}{(1-\gamma)}z_t - \frac{1}{2}\frac{\beta^2}{(1-\gamma)^2}t\right).$$

(This formula also applies when $u(c) = \log c$, setting $\gamma = 0$.) Using (2.5) we find that the evolution of *utility* is as follows:

$$v(w(t)) = v(w(0))\exp\left(\frac{\gamma}{(1-\gamma)}\left(r - \delta + \frac{\beta^2}{2(1-\gamma)}\right)t\right) \times\exp\left(\frac{\gamma\beta}{(1-\gamma)}z_t - \frac{1}{2}\frac{\gamma^2\beta^2}{(1-\gamma)^2}t\right) \tag{2.14}$$

(cf. Remark 6.3 below).

3. Transaction costs: preliminary discussion. Let us now consider the situation, outlined in §1, in which transaction charges are imposed equal to a constant fraction of the amount transacted, the fractions being λ and μ on purchase and sale respectively. The investor's holdings in bank and stock at time t are denoted $s_0(t), s_1(t)$ and these are constrained to lie in the closed solvency region

$$\mathscr{S}_{\lambda,\mu} = \{(x, y) \in \mathbb{R}^2 : x + (1-\mu)y \geqslant 0 \quad \text{and} \quad x + (1+\lambda)y \geqslant 0\}.$$

We denote by $\partial_\mu^+, \partial_\lambda^-$ the upper and lower boundaries of $\mathscr{S}_{\lambda,\mu}$ respectively (see

Figure 2 below). It is clear that the investor's net worth is zero on $\partial_\mu^+ \cup \partial_\lambda^-$. A *policy* for investment and consumption is any triple (c_t, L_t, U_t) of adapted processes such that (c_t) satisfies (2.1) and (L_t) and (U_t) are right-continuous and nondecreasing with $L_0 = U_0 = 0$. (L and U are the cumulative purchases and sales of stock respectively.) The investor's holdings $(s_0(t), s_1(t))$ starting with an endowment $(x, y) \in \mathscr{S}_{\lambda,\mu}$ evolve in the following way in response to a given policy (c, L, U):

$$\text{(3.1)}\quad ds_0(t) = (rs_0(t) - c(t))\,dt - (1+\lambda)\,dL_t + (1-\mu)\,dU_t, \qquad s_0(0) = x,$$

$$ds_1(t) = \alpha s_1(t)\,dt + \sigma s_1(t)\,dz_t + dL_t - dU_t, \qquad s_1(0) = y.$$

It follows from Doléans-Dade [6] that equations (3.1), have a unique strong solution at least up to the bankruptcy time $\tau = \inf\{t \geqslant 0\colon (s_0(t), s_1(t)) \notin \mathscr{S}_{\lambda,\mu}\}$.

An *admissible policy* is a policy (c, L, U) for which $\tau = \infty$ a.s. or, equivalently, for which $\mathbb{P}[(s_0(t), s_1(t)) \in \mathscr{S}_{\lambda,\mu}$ for all $t \geqslant 0] = 1$. We denote by $\mathfrak{U}$ the set of admissible policies. This set is clearly nonempty; indeed let (c, L, U) be any policy such that $(s_0(t), s_1(t))$ does not jump out of $\mathscr{S}_{\lambda,\mu}$ (i.e. it is never the case that $(s_0(t^-), s_1(t^-)) \in \mathscr{S}_{\lambda,\mu}$ but $(s_0(t), s_1(t)) \notin \mathscr{S}_{\lambda,\mu}$). Then an admissible policy $(\bar{c}, \bar{L}, \bar{U})$ can be constructed by terminating (c, L, U) at bankruptcy, i.e. setting $(\bar{c}(t)\bar{L}(t), \bar{U}(t)) = (c(t), L(t), U(t))$ for $t < \tau$,

$$\left.\begin{aligned} \Delta\bar{U}(\tau) &= s_1(\tau^-) \\ \Delta\bar{L}(\tau) &= 0 \end{aligned}\right\} \quad \text{if } (s_0(\tau^-), s_1(\tau^-)) \in {}^{+}_{\mu},$$

$$\left.\begin{aligned} \Delta\bar{U}(\tau) &= 0 \\ \Delta\bar{L}(\tau) &= s_1(\tau^-) \end{aligned}\right\} \quad \text{if } (s_0(\tau^-), s_1(\tau^-)) \in \partial_\lambda^-$$

and $\bar{L}(t) = \bar{L}(\tau)$, $\bar{U}(t) = \bar{U}(\tau)$, $c(t) = 0$ for $t \geqslant \tau$. Then $s_0(t) = s_1(t) = 0$ for $t \geqslant \tau$ under $(\bar{c}, \bar{L}, \bar{U})$.

The investor's objective is to maximize over $\mathfrak{U}$ the utility

$$J_{x,y}(c, L, U) = \mathbb{E}_{x,y} \int_0^\infty e^{-\delta t} u(c(t))\,dt.$$

Here $\mathbb{E}_{x,y}$ denotes the expectation given that the initial endowment is $s_0(0) = x$, $s_1(0) = y$. Define the value function v as:

$$\text{(3.2)}\qquad v(x, y) = \sup_{(c, L, U) \in \mathfrak{U}} J_{x,y}(c, L, U).$$

The following properties of v are easily established directly from the definition.

THEOREM 3.1. *Suppose* $u(c) = c^\gamma/\gamma$ *for* $\gamma \in \Gamma$, *or* $u(c) = \log c$. *Then*

(a) v *is concave.*

(b) v *has the homothetic property*: *for* $\rho > 0$

$$v(\rho x, \rho y) = \rho^\gamma v(x, y), \quad [u(c) = c^\gamma/\gamma],$$

$$v(\rho x, \rho y) = \frac{1}{\delta}\log\rho + v(x, y), \quad [u(c) = \log c].$$

PROOF. (a) This is easily established by considering convex combinations of initial states and control process and using the linearity of equations (3.1) and concavity of the utility function. This idea appears in [13].

(b) Denote by $\mathfrak{U}(x, y)$ the class of admissible policies starting at $(s_0(0), s_1(0)) = (x, y) \in \mathscr{S}_{\lambda,\mu}$. Then it is easily checked from equations (3.1) that for any $\rho > 0$.

$$\mathfrak{U}(\rho x, \rho y) = \{(\rho c, \rho L, \rho U) : (c, L, U) \in \mathfrak{U}(x, y)\}.$$

Thus

$$v(\rho x, \rho y) = \sup_{\mathfrak{U}(\rho x, \rho y)} \mathbb{E}_{\rho x, \rho y} \int_0^\infty e^{-\delta t} u(c_t)\, dt$$

$$= \sup_{\mathfrak{U}(x, y)} \mathbb{E}_{x, y} \int_0^\infty e^{-\delta t} u(\rho c_t)\, dt =: \hat{v}.$$

When $u(c) = c^\gamma/\gamma$ we have $u(\rho c) = \rho^\gamma u(c)$ so that $\hat{v} = \rho^\gamma v(x, y)$, whereas when $u(c) = \log c$ then $u(\rho c) = \log \rho + u(c)$ and $\hat{v} = (\log \rho)/\delta + v(x, y)$. This completes the proof.

In order to get some idea as to the nature of optimal policies, let us take $u(c) = c^\gamma/\gamma$ and consider a restricted class of policies in which L and U are constrained to be absolutely continuous with bounded derivatives, i.e.

$$L_t = \int_0^t l_s\, ds, \quad U_t = \int_0^t u_s\, ds, \qquad 0 \leqslant l_s, u_s \leqslant \kappa.$$

Equation (3.1) is then a vector SDE with controlled drift and the problem may be attacked in exactly the same way as in §2. The Bellman equation, to be solved for the value function $\tilde{v}$, is

$$\max_{c, l, u} \left\{ A^{c,l,u} \tilde{v}(x, y) + \frac{1}{\gamma} c^\gamma - \delta \tilde{v}(x, y) \right\} = 0,$$

where $A^{c,l,u}$ is the generator of (3.1) for fixed c, l, u. Written out in full this becomes

$$\text{(3.3)} \qquad \max_{c,l,u} \left\{ \frac{1}{2}\sigma^2 y^2 \tilde{v}_{yy} + rx\tilde{v}_x + \alpha y \tilde{v}_y + \frac{1}{\gamma} c^\gamma - c\tilde{v}_x \right.$$

$$\left. + \left[-(1+\lambda)\tilde{v}_x + \tilde{v}_y \right] l + \left[(1-\mu)\tilde{v}_x - \tilde{v}_y \right] u - \delta v \right\} = 0$$

where $\tilde{v}_x = \partial \tilde{v}/\partial x$, $\tilde{v}_y = \partial \tilde{v}/\partial y$. Note that both of these derivatives must be positive since extra wealth will provide increased utility. The maxima are achieved as follows:

$$c = (\tilde{v}_x)^{1/(\gamma - 1)},$$

$$l = \begin{cases} \kappa & \text{if} \quad \tilde{v}_y \geqslant (1+\lambda)\tilde{v}_x, \\ 0 & \text{if} \quad \tilde{v}_y < (1+\lambda)\tilde{v}_x, \end{cases}$$

$$u = \begin{cases} 0 & \text{if} \quad \tilde{v}_y > (1-\mu)\tilde{v}_x, \\ \kappa & \text{if} \quad \tilde{v}_y \leqslant (1-\mu)\tilde{v}_x. \end{cases}$$

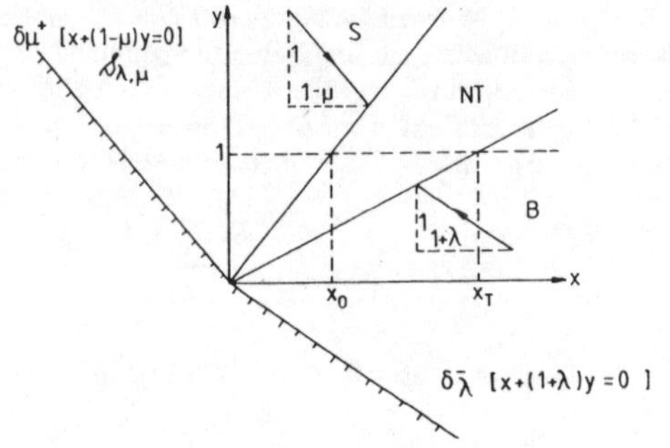

FIGURE 2. Bank/Stock Space Showing Directions of Finite Transactions and Solvency Region $\mathscr{S}_{\lambda,\mu}$.

This indicates that the optimal transaction policies are *bang-bang*: buying and selling either take place at maximum rate or not all all, and the solvency region $\mathscr{S}_{\lambda,\mu}$ splits into three regions, "buy" (B), "sell" (S) and "no transactions (NT). At the boundary between the B and NT regions, $\bar{v}_y = (1+\lambda)\bar{v}_x$ whereas at the boundary between NT and S, $\bar{v}_y = (1-\mu)\bar{v}_x$. We now have to consider what shape these boundaries are, and here we use the homothetic property (b) of Theorem 3.1. This property does not hold for the restricted problem we are presently considering, but will hold in the limit as $\kappa \to \infty$. Assuming that $\bar{v}$ is C^1 and homothetic, we find by direct calculation that for $\rho > 0$

$$\bar{v}_x(\rho x, \rho y) = \rho^{\gamma-1}\bar{v}_x(x,y), \quad \bar{v}_y(\rho x, \rho y) = \rho^{\gamma-1}\bar{v}_y(x,y).$$

It follows that *if* $\bar{v}_y(x,y) = (1+\lambda)\bar{v}_x(x,y)$ *or* $\bar{v}_y(x,y) = (1-\mu)\bar{v}_x(x,y)$ *for some* (x,y) *then the same is true at all points along the ray through* (x,y). This strongly suggests that the boundaries between the transaction and no-transaction (NT) regions are straight lines through the origin. In the transaction regions, transactions take place at maximum, i.e. infinite, speed, which implies that the investor will make an instantaneous finite transaction to the boundary of NT. These considerations suggest the picture shown in Fig. 2: the no-transaction region NT is a wedge, the regions above and below it being the sell (S) and buy (B) regions respectively. Note that a finite transaction in the S [B] region moves the portfolio down [up] a line of slope $-1/(1-\mu)$ [$-1/(1+\lambda)$].[5] After the initial transaction, all further transactions must take place at the boundaries, and this suggests a "local time" type of transaction policy. Meanwhile, consumption takes place at rate $v_x^{1/(\gamma-1)}$. In NT the value function $v(x,y)$ satisfies the Bellman equation (3.3) with $l = u = 0$:

$$\max_c \left\{ \frac{1}{2}\sigma^2 y^2 v_{yy} + (rx - c)v_x + \alpha y v_y + \frac{1}{\gamma}c^\gamma - \delta v \right\} = 0$$

i.e.

$$\frac{1}{2}\sigma^2 y^2 v_{yy} + rxv_x + \alpha y v_y + \left(\frac{1-\gamma}{\gamma}\right) v_x^{-\gamma/(-\gamma)} - \delta v = 0. \tag{3.4}$$

[5]The natural ranges of values for μ and λ are $[0,1]$ and $[0,\infty]$ respectively, these values corresponding to slopes of the finite transaction lines in S and B between $-45°$ and vertical (in S) or horizontal (in B).

To substantiate the conjectured solution just outlined we make essential use of the homothetic property of Theorem 3.1(b), by which the nonlinear partial differential equation (3.4) may be reduced to an equation in one variable. Indeed, define $\psi(x) := v(x,1)$. Then by the homothetic property $v(x,y) = y^\gamma \psi(x/y)$. If our conjectured optimal policy is correct then v is constant along lines of slope $(1-\mu)^{-1}$ in S and along lines of slope $(1+\lambda)^{-1}$ in B, and this implies by the homothetic property that

$$(3.5)\qquad \psi(x) = \frac{1}{\gamma}A(x+1-\mu)^\gamma, \qquad x \leqslant x_0,$$

$$\psi(x) = \frac{1}{\gamma}B(x+1+\lambda)^\gamma, \qquad x \geqslant x_T,$$

for some constants A, B, where x_0 and x_T are as shown in Figure 2. (The factor $1/\gamma$ in these expressions turns out to be notationally convenient.) Using the homothetic property again we find that, with $\psi' = d\psi/dx$,

$$(3.6)\qquad v_y(x,1) = \gamma\psi(x) - x\psi'(x), \qquad v_x(x,1) = \psi'(x),$$

$$v_{yy}(x,1) = -\gamma(1-\gamma)\psi(x) + 2(1-\gamma)x\psi'(x) + x^2\psi''(x),$$

and hence equation (3.4) reduces to

$$(3.7)\qquad \beta_3 x^2\psi''(x) + \beta_2 x\psi'(x) + \beta_1\psi(x) + \left(\frac{1-\gamma}{\gamma}\right)(\psi')^{-\gamma/(1-\gamma)} = 0, \qquad x \in [x_0, x_T], \quad \text{where}$$

$$(3.8)\qquad \beta_1 = -\tfrac{1}{2}\sigma^2\gamma(1-\gamma) + \alpha\gamma - \delta, \quad \beta_2 = \sigma^2(1-\gamma) + r - \alpha, \quad \beta_3 = \tfrac{1}{2}\sigma^2.$$

The key to solving this problem is thus to find constants x_0, x_T, A, B and a globally C^2 function ψ such that (3.5), (3.7) hold. The definitions of $\beta_1, \beta_2, \beta_3$ in (3.8) will be maintained throughout the paper.

4. A sufficiency theorem. In this section we will show that the existence of a C^2 function ψ satisfying (3.5) and (3.6) supplies a sufficient condition for optimality of a policy (c, L, U) such that the corresponding process $(s_0(t), s_1(t))$ is a reflecting diffusion in the wedge NT and L_t, U_t are the local times at the lower and upper boundaries respectively. We first verify in Theorem 4.1 that such reflecting diffusions are well-defined in arbitrary wedges in the positive orthant of $\mathbb{R}^2$. We then give the sufficiency theorems, Theorems 4.2 and 4.3. The existence of such a function ψ is demonstrated in §5.

THEOREM 4.1. *Take $0 < x_0 < x_T$ and let NT be the closed wedge shown in Figure 2, with upper and lower boundaries $\partial S, \partial B$ respectively. Let c: $NT \to \mathbb{R}^+$ be any Lipschitz continuous function and let $(x,y) \in NT$. Then there exist unique processes s_0, s_1 and continuous increasing processes L, U such that for $t < \tau = \inf\{t: (s_0(t), s_1(t)) = 0\}$*

$$(4.1)\qquad ds_0(t) = [rs_0(t) - c(s_0(t), s_1(t))]\,dt - (1+\lambda)\,dL_t + (1-\mu)\,dU_t, \qquad s_0(0) = x,$$

$$ds_1(t) = \alpha s_1(t)\,dt + \sigma s_1(t)\,dz_t - dU_t, \qquad s_1(0) = y,$$

$$L_t = \int_0^t I_{\{(s_0(\xi), s_1(\xi)) \in \partial B\}}\,dL_\xi, \quad U_t = \int_0^t I_{\{(s_0(\xi), s_1(\xi)) \in \partial S\}}\,dU_\xi.$$

The process $\bar{c}_t := c(s_0(t), s_1(t))$ satisfies condition (2.1)(i).

The proof will be omitted. Note that the directions of reflection are along the vectors $((1-\mu), -1)$ and $(-(1+\lambda), 1)$ at the upper and lower boundaries respectively. These coincide with the directions of finite transactions in S and B, as shown in Figure 2. The process (s_0, s_1) is a degenerate diffusion with coefficients which are not bounded away from zero, and with oblique reflection at a nonsmooth boundary. Because of this combination of factors, standard results on existence and uniqueness (e.g. Stroock and Varadhan [19]) do not apply. However, since one is only interested in the solution up to the first hitting time of the corner, the solution can be constructed piecewise, using a sequence of stopping times as in Varadhan and Williams [22], from diffusions reflecting off one or other of the two line boundaries. The technique also appears in Anderson and Orey [1]. The result may also be derived from Tanaka's theory of reflecting diffusions in convex regions [21].

For the sufficiency theorems which follow, we will only consider policies that do not involve shortselling (although borrowing is allowed). This class of policies is defined formally as

$$\mathfrak{U}' = \{(c, L, U) \in \mathfrak{U} : (s_0(t), s_1(t)) \in \mathcal{S}_\mu' \text{ for all } t \geq 0\} \tag{4.2}$$

where $\mathcal{S}_\mu' = \{(x, y) \in \mathbb{R}^2 : y \geq 0 \text{ and } (x + (1-\mu)y) \geq 0\}$. The results can be extended to cover policies which allow shortselling, but because of the way we have parametrized the problem a separate argument has to be introduced to show that shortselling is not optimal; it does not seem worth presenting this argument here. For some of the results it is necessary to restrict the admissible policies further to the slightly smaller class $\mathfrak{U}''$ defined as follows. For $\mu' > \mu$ let

$$\mathfrak{U}''(\mu') = \{(c, L, U) \in \mathfrak{U} : (s_0(t), s_1(t)) \in \mathcal{S}_{\mu'}' \text{ for all } t \geq 0\}.$$

Now define $\mathfrak{U}'' = \bigcup_{\mu' > \mu} \mathfrak{U}''(\mu')$. Using a policy in $\mathfrak{U}''$ means that the investor is always able to absorb a slight increase in the transaction costs. It seems certain that the results below remain true if $\mathfrak{U}''$ is replaced by $\mathfrak{U}'$, but our proof technique requires the smaller class.

Theorem 4.2, which we present next, covers the case $u(c) = c^\gamma/\gamma$ for $\gamma \in \Gamma$. The corresponding results for $u(c) = \log c$ are stated separately as Theorem 4.3.

THEOREM 4.2. *Take $\gamma \in \Gamma$ and assume that Condition A holds. Suppose there are constants A, B, x_0, x_T and a function $\psi: [-(1-\mu), \infty) \to \mathbb{R}$ such that*

$$0 < x_0 < x_T < \infty, \tag{4.3}$$

$$\psi \text{ is } C^2 \text{ and } \psi'(x) > 0 \quad \text{for all } x, \tag{4.4}$$

$$\psi(x) = \frac{1}{\gamma} A (x + 1 - \mu)^\gamma \quad \text{for } x \leq x_0, \tag{4.5}$$

$$\beta_3 x^2 \psi''(x) + \beta_2 x \psi'(x) + \beta_1 \psi(x) + \left(\frac{1-\gamma}{\gamma}\right)[\psi'(x)]^{-\gamma/(1-\gamma)} = 0 \quad \text{for } x \in [x_0, x_T], \tag{4.6}$$

$$\psi(x) = \frac{1}{\gamma} B (x + 1 + \lambda)^\lambda \quad \text{for } x \geq x_T. \tag{4.7}$$

Let NT denote the closed wedge $\{(x, y) \in \mathbb{R}_+^2 : x_T^{-1} \leq yx^{-1} \leq x_0^{-1}\}$ and let B and S

denote the regions below and above NT as shown in Figure 2. For $(x, y) \in NT \setminus \{(0,0)\}$ *define*

$$c^*(x, y) = y\left[\psi'\left(\frac{x}{y}\right)\right]^{-1/(1-\gamma)} \tag{4.8}$$

Let $\bar{c}_t^* = c^*(s_0(t), s_1(t))$ *where* (s_0, s_1, L^*, U^*) *is the solution of* (4.1) *with* $c := c^*$. *Then the policy* $(\bar{c}^*(t), L^*(t), U^*(t))$ *is optimal in the class* $\mathfrak{U}'$ *for any initial endowment* $(x, y) \in NT$ *when* $\gamma \in (0, 1)$. *When* $\gamma < 0$ *this policy is optimal in the class* $\mathfrak{U}''$. *In either case, if* $(x, y) \notin NT$ *then an immediate transaction to the closest point in NT followed by application of this policy is optimal in* $\mathfrak{U}', \mathfrak{U}''$ *respectively. The maximal expected utility is*

$$v(x, y) = y^\gamma \psi\left(\frac{x}{y}\right). \tag{4.9}$$

For the proof, we require the following lemma.

LEMMA 4.3. *Suppose* v *is defined as in* (4.9). *Then*

(i) v *is concave.*

(ii)
$$v(x, y) = \begin{cases} \dfrac{1}{\gamma}A(x + (1-\mu)y)^\gamma & \text{in } S, \\ \dfrac{1}{\gamma}B(x + (1+\lambda)y)^\gamma & \text{in } B. \end{cases}$$

(iii)
$$(1-\mu)v_x - v_y \leqslant 0 \quad \text{with equality in } S,$$
$$-(1+\lambda)v_x + v_y \leqslant 0 \quad \text{with equality in } B.$$

(iv) *Define*

$$Gv = \frac{1}{2}\sigma^2 y^2 v_{yy} + rxv_x + \alpha y v_y - \delta v + \frac{1-\gamma}{\gamma}(v_x)^{-\gamma/(1-\gamma)}. \tag{4.10}$$

Then

$$Gv = \max_c \left\{\frac{1}{2}\sigma^2 y^2 v_{yy} + (rx - c)v_x + \alpha y v_y + \frac{1}{\gamma}c^\gamma - \delta v\right\} \quad \text{and} \tag{4.11}$$

$$Gv = 0 \text{ in } NT \quad (\text{i.e. the Bellman equation is satisfied}), \tag{4.12}$$
$$Gv \leqslant 0 \quad \text{in } S \cup B.$$

PROOF. These properties can be verified directly from the construction of v.

PROOF OF THEOREM 4.2. Let (c, L, U) be a policy in $\mathfrak{U}'$ and let $(s_0(t), s_1(t))$ be the corresponding solution of (3.1) with initial point $(x, y) \in \mathscr{S}_\mu'$. For an arbitrary C^2 function χ let M_T^χ be the scalar process defined for $T \geqslant 0$ by

$$M_T^\chi := \int_0^T e^{-\delta t}\frac{1}{\gamma}c^\gamma(t)\,dt + e^{-\delta T}\chi(s_0(T), s_1(T)).$$

An application of the generalized Ito formula (Harrison [9, §4.7]) gives

$$(4.13)\quad M_T^\chi - M_0^\chi = \int_0^T e^{-\delta t}\left[\frac{1}{\gamma}c^\gamma(t) + (rs_0(t) - c(t))\chi_x + \alpha s_1(t)\chi_y + \frac{1}{2}\sigma^2 s_1^2(t)\chi_{yy} - \delta\chi\right] dt$$

$$+ \int_0^T e^{-\delta t}\left[-(1+\lambda)\chi_x + \chi_y\right] dL_t$$

$$+ \int_0^T e^{-\delta t}\left[(1-\mu)\chi_x - \chi_y\right] dU_T$$

$$+ \sum_{0 \leqslant t \leqslant T} e^{-\delta T}\left[\chi(s_0(t), s_1(t)) - \chi(s_0(t^-), s_1(t^-)) - \chi_x\,\Delta s_0(t) - \chi_y\,\Delta s_1(t)\right]$$

$$+ \int_0^T e^{-\delta t}\sigma\chi_y s_1(t)\, dz_t$$

$$=: I_1 + I_2 + I_3 + I_4 + I_5.$$

In this equation, χ, χ_x etc. are evaluated at $(s_0(t), s_1(t))$ unless noted otherwise.

Suppose first that $(c, L, U) = (c^*, L^*, U^*)$ as defined in the theorem statement and $(x, y) \in NT$, and let v be given by (4.9). The value of c^* is equal to $[v_x]^{-1/(1-\gamma)}$, the maximizing value obtained from the Bellman equation. Note from (4.8) that $c^*(\rho x, \rho y) = \rho c^*(x, y)$ for $\rho > 0$, and hence that $c_x^*(\rho x, \rho y) = c_x^*(x, y)$, $c_y^*(\rho x, \rho y) = c_y^*(x, y)$. It follows that c^* is Lipschitz continuous and that (4.1) has a unique solution $(s_0(t), s_1(t), L_t^*, U_t^*)$ when c is equal to c^*. Now consider (4.13) with $(c, L, U) = (c^*, L^*, U^*)$ and $\chi = v$. It follows from Lemma 4.3 that $I_1 = I_2 = I_3 = 0$, and I_4 vanishes since $(s_0(t), s_1(t))$ is continuous. Hence

$$(4.14)\quad v(x, y) = M_0^v = \int_0^T e^{-\delta t}\frac{1}{\gamma}c^\gamma(t)\, dt + e^{-\delta T}v(s_0(T), s_1(T)) - \int_0^T e^{-\delta T}\sigma v_y s_1(t)\, dz_t.$$

It is shown in Theorem 6.2 below that under (c^*, L^*, U^*) the value process $v(s_0(t), s_1(t))$ can be represented in the form

$$(4.15)\quad v(s_0(t), s_1(t)) = v(x, y)\exp\left(\int_0^t \left(\delta - g\left(\frac{s_0(u)}{s_1(u)}\right)\right) du\right)\tilde{G}(t)$$

where $\tilde{G}(t)$ is the Girsanov exponential

$$\tilde{G}(t) = \exp\left(\int_0^t \gamma\sigma(1-f)\, dz - \frac{1}{2}\int_0^t \gamma^2\sigma^2(1-f)^2\, du\right)$$

and f and g are bounded functions in NT with $g > 0$. It is also shown in Lemma 6.1

that in NT

$$yv_y(x,y) = \gamma\left(1 - f\left(\frac{x}{y}\right)\right)v(x,y). \tag{4.16}$$

Since f is bounded, $\mathbb{E}_{x,y}\tilde{G}^2(t) < \infty$ and it follows from (4.15) that the last term in (4.14) is a martingale. Thus

$$v(x,y) = \mathbb{E}_{x,y}\int_0^T e^{-\delta t}\frac{1}{\gamma}c^\gamma(t)\,dt + e^{-\delta T}\mathbb{E}_{x,y}[v(s_0(T), s_1(T))].$$

As $T \to \infty$, the last term converges to zero in view of (4.15) and this shows that, for $(x,y) \in NT$,

$$v(x,y) = J_{x,y}(c^*, L^*, U^*). \tag{4.17}$$

For $(x,y) \in \mathscr{S}'_\mu \setminus NT$ it is clear that $J_{x,y}(c^*, L^*, U^*) = J_{x',y'}(c^*, L^*, U^*)$ where (x', y') is the point on the boundary of the wedge to which the initial transaction is made. Since v is by construction constant on the line joining (x,y) to (x',y'), it follows that (4.17) holds throughout $\mathscr{S}'_\mu$.

We now show that $v(x,y) \geqslant J_{x,y}(c, L, U)$ for arbitrary (c, L, U). We need separate arguments for the two cases $0 < \gamma < 1$ and $\gamma < 0$.

Case (a): $0 < \gamma < 1$. Here we need the following lemma, whose proof is given later.

LEMMA 4.4. *Let v be defined by* (4.9) *with* $\gamma \in (0,1)$. *Then there is a constant K and for each $\epsilon > 0$ a constant K_ϵ such that*

$$0 \leqslant v(x,y) \leqslant K(x+y)^\gamma \quad \text{for all } (x,y) \in \mathscr{S}'_\mu, \tag{4.18}$$

$$0 \leqslant yv(x,y) \leqslant K_\epsilon(1 + x + y) \tag{4.19}$$

$$\text{for all } (x,y) \in \mathbb{R}^2_+ \cup \{(x,y) \in \mathscr{S}'_\mu : x + (1-\mu)y > \epsilon\}.$$

Let $(c, L, U) \in \mathfrak{U}'$ be an arbitrary policy and $(s_0(t), s_1(t))$ the corresponding solution of (3.1). If we define $\hat{w}_t := s_0(t) + s_1(t)$ and $\pi_t = s_1(t)/\hat{w}_t$ then (c_t, π_t) is an admissible policy for the Merton (no transaction costs) problem. From (3.1) we see that $\hat{w}_t$ satisfies

$$d\hat{w}_t = [(r + (\alpha - r)\pi_t)\hat{w}_t - c_t]\,dt + \sigma\hat{w}_t\pi_t\,dz_t - dA_t$$

where $A = \lambda L + \mu U$. By the Gronwall-Bellman lemma we conclude that $\hat{w}_t \leqslant w_t$ for all t, where w_t is the solution of the Merton wealth equation (2.1) with $w_0 = x + y$. Fix $\epsilon > 0$, define $v^\epsilon(x,y) = v(x+\epsilon, y)$, and consider equation (4.13) with $\chi := v^\epsilon$. From (4.19) we see that for any $T > 0$,

$$\mathbb{E}_{x,y}\int_0^T \left(v_y^\epsilon(s_0(t), s_1(t))s_1(t)\right)^2\Big]\,dt \leqslant K_\epsilon^2\int_0^T (1 + \epsilon + \hat{w}_t)^2\,dt$$

$$\leqslant K_\epsilon^2\mathbb{E}_{x,y}\int_0^T (1 + \epsilon + w_t)^2\,dt.$$

The last expression is finite as was shown in the proof of Theorem 2.1. Thus, the last term I_5 in (4.13) is a martingale. From part (iv) of Lemma 4.3 and since $v_x^\epsilon(x,y) =$

$v_x(x+\epsilon, y)$ etc. we find that

$$Gv^\epsilon(x,y) = Gv(x+\epsilon, y) - r\epsilon v_x(x+\epsilon, y).$$

In view of (4.6), (4.11) and (4.12) we see that for any $c \geqslant 0$ and $(x,y) \in \mathscr{S}_\mu'$,

$$\frac{1}{\gamma}c^\gamma + (rx-c)v_x^\epsilon + \alpha y v_y^\epsilon + \frac{1}{2}\alpha^2 y^2 v_{yy} - \delta v \leqslant 0.$$

Hence I_1 is a decreasing process. It follows from Lemma 4.3(iii) that I_2 and I_3 are decreasing while Lemma 4.3(i) implies that I_4 is decreasing. Thus $M_T^{v^\epsilon}$ is a supermartingale, i.e.

$$(4.20)\quad v^\epsilon(x,y) = M_0^{v^\epsilon} \geqslant \mathbb{E}_{x,y}\int_0^T e^{-\delta t}\frac{1}{\gamma}c^\gamma(t)\,dt + e^{-\delta T}\mathbb{E}_{x,y}v^\epsilon(s_0(T), s_1(T)).$$

Now using (4.18) we have

$$\begin{aligned} e^{-\delta T}\mathbb{E}_{x,y}v^\epsilon(s_0(t), s_1(t)) &\leqslant Ke^{-\delta T}\mathbb{E}_{x,y}(\epsilon + \hat{w}_T)^\gamma \\ &\leqslant Ke^{-\delta T}\mathbb{E}_{x,y}(\epsilon + w_T)^\gamma \\ &\leqslant Ke^{-\delta T}\mathbb{E}_{x,y}(K' + w_T^{\gamma'}) \end{aligned}$$

for some $K' > 0$, $\gamma' \in (\gamma, 1)$. It follows from (2.12), (2.13) that

$$\mathbb{E}_{x,y}\left[e^{-\delta T}w_T^{\gamma'}\right] \to 0 \quad \text{as } T \to \infty.$$

Thus taking the limit in (4.20) as $T \to \infty$ we obtain $v^\epsilon(x,y) \geqslant J_{x,y}(c, L, U)$. Now $v^\epsilon(x,y) \downarrow v(x,y)$ as $\epsilon \downarrow 0$, so that $v(x,y) \geqslant J_{x,y}(c, L, U)$. Thus (c^*, L^*, U^*) is optimal in the case $\gamma \in (0,1)$.

Case (b): $\gamma < 0$. The problem here is that the candidate value function $v(x,y)$ is unboundedly negative at low levels of wealth. We use an argument similar to the proof of Theorem 2.1, based on the following lemma, whose proof is again given at the end of this section.

LEMMA 4.5. *Let v be the function defined by* (4.9) *with $\gamma < 0$, and for $\theta, \epsilon > 0$ define $v^{\epsilon,\theta}(x,y) = v(x+\theta\epsilon, y+\epsilon)$. Fix $\mu' > \mu$. Then there exists $\theta > 0$ such that for all $\epsilon > 0$*

$$Gv^{\epsilon,\theta}(x,y) \leqslant 0 \quad \textit{for all } (x,y) \in \mathscr{S}_{\mu'}',$$

where G is defined by (4.10).

We note from Lemma 4.3(iv) that this result implies that for all $c \geqslant 0$,

$$(4.21)\quad \frac{1}{2}\sigma^2 y^2 v_{yy}^{\epsilon,\theta} + (rx-c)v_x^{\epsilon,\theta} + \alpha y v_y^\epsilon + \frac{1}{\gamma}c^\gamma - \delta v^{\epsilon,\theta} \leqslant 0, \qquad (x,y) \in \mathscr{S}_{\mu'}'.$$

We also note that for any $\epsilon, \theta > 0$, $v^{\epsilon,\theta}$ is bounded on $\mathscr{S}_{\mu'}'$ with bounded first and second partial derivatives. Now let (c, L, U) be an arbitrary policy in $\mathfrak{U}''$; then $(c, L, U) \in \mathfrak{U}''(\mu')$ for some $\mu' > \mu$. Consider the process M_T^χ of (4.13) with $\chi = v^{\epsilon,\theta}$. We conclude from (4.21) and Lemma 4.3 as before that $M_T^{v^{\epsilon,\theta}}$ is a supermartingale and hence that

$$v^{\epsilon}(x,y) \geqslant \mathbb{E}_{x,y}\left[\int_0^T e^{-\delta t}\frac{1}{\gamma}c^{\gamma}(t)\,dt\right] + \mathbb{E}_{x,y}\left[e^{-\delta T}v^{\epsilon,\theta}(s_0(T),s_1(T))\right].$$

The second term on the right converges to 0 as $T \to \infty$, while the bracket $[\dots]$ in the first term is monotone decreasing. It follows that

$$v^{\epsilon,\theta}(x,y) \geqslant \mathbb{E}_{x,y}\left[\int_0^\infty e^{-\delta t}\frac{1}{\gamma}c^{\gamma}(t)\,dt\right] = J_{x,y}(c,L,U).$$

Now $v^{\epsilon,\theta}(x,y)\downarrow v(x,y)$ as $\epsilon\downarrow 0$ and hence

$$v(x,y) \geqslant \sup_{(c,L,U)\in\mathfrak{U}''} J_{x,y}(c,L,U).$$

On the other hand we know that $v(x,y) = J_{x,y}(c^*,L^*,U^*)$ and it is clear that $(c^*,L^*,U^*) \in \mathfrak{U}''$ because the solution process is trapped inside the wedge NT after any initial transaction. Thus (c^*,L^*,U^*) is optimal in $\mathfrak{U}''$, as claimed.

PROOF OF LEMMA 4.4. Denote $S_+ = S \cap \mathbb{R}^2_+$ and $S_- = S \setminus S_+$, with similar definitions for B_+, B_- (note that $B_+ = B \cap \mathscr{S}_\mu'$). Elementary geometry shows that

$$y \leqslant \frac{1}{\mu}(x+y) \quad \text{for all } (x,y) \in \mathscr{S}_\mu'. \tag{4.22}$$

Using this, (4.18) is readily verified in $S \cup B_+$, while in NT,

$$v(x,y) = y^{\gamma}\psi\left(\frac{x}{y}\right) \leqslant M_0(x+y)^{\gamma}$$

where $M_0 = \mu^{-\gamma}\max_{\xi\in[x_0,x_T]}\psi(\xi)$. Thus (4.18) holds throughout S_μ'. In view of (4.9), in NT

$$yv_y(x,y) = \gamma y^{\gamma}\psi\left(\frac{x}{y}\right) - xy^{\gamma-1}\psi'\left(\frac{x}{y}\right) \leqslant \gamma M_0(x+y)^{\gamma}. \tag{4.23}$$

In B_+,

$$yv_y(x,y) = By(x+(1+\lambda)y)^{\gamma-1} \leqslant B(x+y)^{\gamma}, \tag{4.24}$$

and similarly in S_+,

$$yv_y(x,y) \leqslant A(1-\mu)^{\gamma-1}(x+y)^{\gamma}. \tag{4.25}$$

In S_- we note from (4.22) that when $(x+(1-\mu)y) > \epsilon$,

$$yv_y(x,y) = Ay(x+(1-\mu)y)^{\gamma-1} \leqslant \frac{A}{\mu\epsilon^{1-\gamma}}(x+y) \tag{4.26}$$

We can now choose K_ϵ such that $K_\epsilon(1+x+y)$ majorizes the right-hand sides of (4.23)–(4.26), thus establishing (4.19).

PROOF OF LEMMA 4.5. Take $\epsilon, \theta > 0$. We know from Lemma 4.3(iv) that

$$0 \geqslant Gv(x+\theta\epsilon, y+\epsilon)$$

$$= \tfrac{1}{2}\sigma^2(y+\epsilon)^2 v_{yy}(x+\theta\epsilon, y+\epsilon) + r(x+\theta\epsilon)v_x(x+\theta\epsilon, y+\epsilon)$$

$$+ \alpha(y+\epsilon)v_y(x+\theta\epsilon, y+\epsilon) + \frac{1-\gamma}{\gamma}(v_x)^{-\gamma/(1-\gamma)} - \delta v$$

$$= Gv^{\epsilon,\theta}(x,y) + \epsilon\rho(\epsilon) \quad \text{where} \quad \rho(\epsilon) := \tfrac{1}{2}\sigma^2(2y+\epsilon)v_{yy}^{\epsilon,\theta} + r\theta v_x^{\epsilon,\theta} + \alpha v_y^{\epsilon,\theta}.$$

We need to show that $\rho(\epsilon) \geqslant 0$ so that then $Gv^{\epsilon,\theta} \leqslant 0$. First, consider points (x, y) such that $(x+\theta\epsilon, y+\epsilon) \in NT$. Then, with $\xi := (x+\theta\epsilon)/(y+\epsilon)$, we have from (4.10)

$$v^{\epsilon,\theta}(x,y) = (y+\epsilon)^{\gamma}\psi(\xi),$$

$$v_x^{\epsilon,\theta}(x,y) = (y+\epsilon)^{\gamma-1}\psi'(\xi),$$

$$v_y^{\epsilon,\theta}(x,y) = (y+\epsilon)^{\gamma-1}(\gamma\psi(\xi) - \xi\psi'(\xi)),$$

$$v_{yy}^{\epsilon,\theta}(x,y) = (y+\epsilon)^{\gamma-2}(\xi^2\psi'' + 2(1-\gamma)\xi\psi' - \gamma(1-\gamma)\psi)$$

and hence

$$(4.27) \quad (y+\epsilon)^{2-\gamma}\rho(\epsilon) = r\theta\psi' + \tfrac{1}{2}\sigma^2\eta\xi^2\psi'' + \left[\sigma^2\eta(1-\gamma) - \alpha\right]\xi\psi' + \left[\alpha\gamma - \tfrac{1}{2}\sigma^2\eta\gamma(1-\gamma)\right]\psi$$

where $\eta := (2y+\epsilon)/(y+\epsilon)$. Now $\xi \in [x_0, x_T]$ and $\eta \in [1, 2]$, so that all the terms on the right of (4.27) are bounded. Since $\psi' > 0$ it follows that $\rho(\epsilon) > 0$ if θ is chosen sufficiently large. Note also that the minimum value of θ required does not depend on ϵ.

For $(x, y) \in S$ we have $v(x, y) = A(x + (1-\mu)y)^{\gamma}/\gamma$ and hence

$$\rho(\epsilon) = Ab^{\gamma-1}\left\{\frac{1}{2}\sigma^2(\gamma-1)(1-\mu)^2\frac{2y+\epsilon}{b} + r\theta + \alpha(1-\mu)\right\}$$

where $b := x + (1-\mu)y + (\theta + 1 - \mu)\epsilon$. In S_+ (i.e. when $x \geqslant 0$) we have

$$\frac{2y+\epsilon}{b} < \frac{2y+\epsilon}{(1-\mu)(y+\epsilon)} \leqslant \frac{2}{1-\mu},$$

so $\rho(\epsilon) \geqslant 0$ as long as

$$\theta > \frac{1-\mu}{\sigma}(\sigma^2(1-\gamma) - \alpha).$$

A similar calculation applies in B_+. The remaining case is $S'_- = S'_{\mu'} \cap \{x < 0\}$. Here we have $x + (1 - \mu')y \geqslant 0$ for some $\mu' > \mu$, so that

$$\frac{2y + \epsilon}{b} = \frac{2y + \epsilon}{x + (1 - \mu')y + (\mu' - \mu)y + (\theta + 1 - \mu)\epsilon}$$

$$\leqslant \frac{2y + \epsilon}{(\mu' - \mu)y + (1 - \mu)\epsilon}$$

$$= \frac{2y + \epsilon}{(\mu' - \mu)(y + \epsilon) + (1 - \mu')\epsilon} \leqslant \frac{2}{\mu' - \mu}.$$

Thus $\rho(\epsilon) > 0$ if

$$\theta > \frac{1 - \mu}{\sigma}\left(\sigma^2(1 - \gamma)\frac{(1 - \mu)}{\mu' - \mu} - \alpha\right),$$

the right-hand side being independent of ϵ. Thus for $\theta > \theta_0$, where θ_0 is a constant not depending on ϵ, we have $\rho(\epsilon) > 0$ throughout $S'_{\mu'}$. This completes the proof.

The following theorem covers the case $u(c) = \log c$. Its proof is similar to that of Theorem 4.2 and is omitted.

THEOREM 4.3. *Assume $\delta > 0$, let $\beta_1, \beta_2, \beta_3$ be defined as in* (3.8) *with $\gamma = 0$, and define $\beta_4 := (-\frac{1}{2}\sigma^2 + \alpha - \delta)/\delta$. Suppose that there are constants x_0, x_T, A, B and a function $\psi: [-(1 - \mu), \infty) \to \mathbb{R}$ such that*

$$0 < x_0 < x_T < \infty,$$

$$\psi \text{ is } C^2 \text{ and } \psi'(x) > 0 \quad \text{for all } x,$$

$$\psi(x) = \frac{1}{\delta}\log[A(x + (1 - \mu))] \quad \text{for } x \leqslant x_0,$$

$$\beta_1\psi(x) + \beta_2 x\psi'(x) + \beta_3 x^2\psi''(x) + \beta_4 - \log\psi'(x) = 0 \quad \text{for } x \in [x_0, x_T],$$

$$\psi(x) = \frac{1}{\delta}\log[B(x + 1 + \lambda)] \quad \text{for } x \geqslant x_T.$$

Let regions NT, B, S be defined as before and for $(x, y) \in NT \setminus \{(0, 0)\}$ define $c^*(x, y) = y[\psi'(x/y)]^{-1}$. Then with the utility function $u(c) = \log c$, the policy $(\tilde{c}^*(t) := c^*(s_0(t), s_1(t)), L_t^*, U_t^*)$, where (s_0, s_1, L^*, U^*) is the solution of (4.1) *with $c := c^*$, is optimal in the class $\mathfrak{U}''$ for any initial endowment $(x, y) \in NT$. If $(x, y) \notin NT$ then an initial transaction to the nearest point in NT followed by application of this policy is optimal. The maximum expected utility is*

$$v(x, y) = \frac{1}{\delta}\log y + \psi\left(\frac{x}{y}\right). \tag{4.28}$$

The existence of functions ψ satisfying the conditions of Theorems 4.2 and 4.3 is established in §5 below when $\alpha > r$. When $\alpha = r$, it is intuitive that we would invest only in the bank. Our final result in this section demonstrates that this is so.

THEOREM 4.4. *Suppose $\alpha = r$ and $\delta > \gamma r$. Then the optimal strategy in $\mathfrak{U}$ is to close out any position in stock and to consume optimally from bank.*

PROOF. [sketch] For $\gamma \in \Gamma$ and $(x, y) \in \mathscr{S}_{\mu,\lambda}$ define $w_1(x, y) = K(x + (1 - \mu)y)^\gamma$ and $w_2(x, y) = K(x + (1 + \lambda)y)^\gamma$ where $K := ((\delta - \gamma r)/(1 - \gamma))^{\gamma - 1}\gamma^{-1}$. In view of Remark 2.2, $w(x, y) := w_1(x, y) \wedge w_2(x, y)$ is the utility of the policy described in the theorem statement. Taking an arbitrary policy $(c, L, U) \in \mathfrak{U}$ and applying a supermartingale argument as in the proof of Theorem 4.2 successively to the functions w_1, w_2, we find that $J_{x,y}(c, L, U) \leqslant w_i(x, y)$, $i = 1, 2$ and hence that $J_{x,y}(c, L, U) \leqslant w(x, y)$. This approach sidesteps the nonsmoothness of w at $y = 0$. A similar argument handles the case $u(c) = \log c$, using the functions $w_1(x, y) = K' + \log[\delta(x + (1 - \mu)y)]/\delta$ and $w_2 = K' + \log[\delta(x + (1 + \lambda)y)]/\delta$, where $K' = (r - \delta)/\delta^2$.

5. Solution of the free boundary problem. In this section we give our main result, Theorem 5.1, concerning the existence of a solution to the free boundary problem. To prove this, we have to establish certain properties of the system of ordinary differential equations (5.11) below; this is done in the Appendix. We find that a technical condition, introduced in the Appendix as Condition B, is required. We are virtually certain that this condition is nugatory, i.e. is always satisfied, but we can prove this only in some cases. Further comments are given in the Appendix.

THEOREM 5.1. *Suppose that Conditions* A *and* B *hold, that* $\mu \in [0, 1[$, $\lambda \in [0, \infty[$, $\mu \vee \lambda > 0$, *and that*

$$0 < r < \alpha < r + (1 - \gamma)\sigma^2. \tag{5.1}$$

Then there is a C^2*-function* ψ: $(-(1 - \mu), \infty) \to \mathbb{R}$ *and there are positive constants* x_0, x_T, A, B *with* $0 < x_0 < x_T < \infty$ *satisfying*:

(a) *in case* $\gamma \in \Gamma$:

$$\psi(x) = \frac{1}{\gamma}A(x + 1 - \mu)^\gamma, \qquad x \leqslant x_0, \tag{5.2}$$

$$\beta_1\psi(x) + \beta_2 x\psi'(x) + \beta_3 x^2\psi''(x) + \left(\frac{1 - \gamma}{\gamma}\right)[\psi'(x)]^{-\gamma/(1-\gamma)} = 0, \qquad x \in [x_0, x_T], \tag{5.3}$$

$$\psi(x) = \frac{1}{\gamma}B(x + 1 + \lambda)^\gamma, \qquad x \geqslant x_T, \tag{5.4}$$

$$\gamma\psi(x)\psi''(x) + (1 - \gamma)(\psi'(x))^2 \leqslant 0 \quad \textit{with equality when } x \leqslant x_0 \textit{ or } x \geqslant x_T. \tag{5.5}$$

(b) *in case* $\gamma = 0$:

$$\psi(x) = \frac{1}{\delta}\log[A(x + 1 - \mu))], \qquad x \leqslant x_0, \tag{5.6}$$

$$\beta_1\psi(x) + \beta_2 x\psi'(x) + \beta_3 x^2\psi''(x) + \beta_4 - \log\psi'(x) = 0, \qquad x \in [x_0, x_T], \tag{5.7}$$

$$\psi(x) = \frac{1}{\delta}\log[B(x + 1 + \lambda)], \qquad x \geqslant x_T, \tag{5.8}$$

$$\frac{1}{\delta}\psi(x) + \psi'^2(x) \leqslant 0 \quad \textit{with equality for } x \leqslant x_0, x \geqslant x_T. \tag{5.9}$$

REMARK 5.2. Properties (5.5), (5.9) will be needed to prove that the functions v constructed in (4.9), (4.28) are concave. (5.1) is the same as the condition which ensures, in the Merton problem, that hedging, rather than leverage or shortselling, is optimal. See Remark 2.2.

Before proceeding to the proof, let us point out conceptually what is involved in solving the free boundary problem. At a given point x_0, (5.2) and (5.3) provide two different expressions for ψ''. Equating these, we find that there is a unique value of A, say $A(x_0)$, such that ψ'' is continuous at x_0. Similarly, continuity of ψ'' at x_T fixes $B(x_T)$. Now write $\zeta(x) = (\zeta^1(x), \zeta^2(x)) = (\psi(x), \psi'(x))$ and write the scalar second-order equation (5.3) as a 2-vector first-order equation in the form

$$\frac{d}{dx}\zeta(x) = f(x, \zeta(x)). \tag{5.10}$$

This can be solved, at least locally, from any initial vector ζ_0 at $x = x_0$; denote this solution $\zeta(x; \zeta_0, x_0)$. Now (5.2) implies that the initial vector ζ_0 is fixed once x_0 is given; indeed

$$\zeta_0 = \zeta_0(x_0) = \begin{bmatrix} \psi(x_0) \\ \psi'(x_0) \end{bmatrix} = \begin{bmatrix} \frac{1}{\gamma}A(x_0)(x_0 + 1 - \mu)^{\gamma} \\ A(x_0)(x_0 + 1 - \mu)^{\gamma - 1} \end{bmatrix}.$$

Thus for given x_0 the solution of (5.3) is $\zeta(x; \zeta_0(x_0), x_0)$. Similarly we see that (5.4) specifies the value $\zeta_T(x_T)$ of the terminal vector ζ_T. Thus the free boundary problem is solved if we can find x_0, x_T such that $\zeta_T(x_T) = \zeta(x_T; \zeta_0(x_0), x_0)$. Generically, there is no reason why this equation should be solvable, but the proof below shows that in fact such x_0, x_T exist under the specified conditions. As will be seen, the key to the proof is the introduction of nonlinear coordinate changes under which (5.10) takes a simpler form.

PROOF OF THEOREM 5.1. (a) For $f \in [0, 1]$ define quadratic functions $Q(f), R(f)$ by:

$$Q(f) := -\frac{1}{\gamma}\beta_1 - \beta_2 f + \beta_3(1 - \gamma)f^2,$$

$$R(f) := Q(f) + \beta_3(1 - f)f = -\frac{1}{\gamma}\beta_1 + (\beta_3 - \beta_2)f - \gamma\beta_3 f^2.$$

Notice that $Q(0) = R(0)$, $Q(1) = R(1)$. Now consider the following one-parameter family of initial vale problems $\{(x_0, f(\cdot), h(\cdot));\ 0 < x_0 < (1 - \mu)\beta_2/(\alpha - r)\}$, where x_0 is the starting value:

$$f'(x) = \frac{1}{\beta_3 x}[R(f(x)) - h(x)], \tag{5.11}$$

$$h'(x) = \frac{\gamma}{1 - \gamma}\frac{h(x)}{\beta_3 x f(x)}[h(x) - Q(f(x))], \qquad x \geqslant x_0,$$

$$f(x_0) = f_0 = \frac{x_0}{x_0 + 1 - \mu}, \qquad h(x_0) = h_0 = Q(f_0).$$

REMARK 5.3. The range of x_0 implies that $0 < f_0 < f_m = 1 - (\alpha - r)/(1-\gamma)\sigma^2$. Here f_m is the value of f at which $Q(f)$ achieves its minimum. Condition (5.1) ensures that $f_m \in (0,1)$ and we find that

$$Q(f_m) = \frac{\delta}{\gamma} - r - \frac{1}{2(1-\gamma)}\left(\frac{\alpha - r}{\sigma}\right)^2$$

so that Condition A ensures that $\gamma Q(f_m) > 0$.

It is shown in the Appendix that there exist x_0 and x_T and a solution $(f(\cdot), h(\cdot))$ to (5.11) such that

(5.12) (i) $$0 < x_0 < x_T,$$

(ii) $$f_0 = \frac{x_0}{x_0 + 1 - \mu}, \quad f(x_T) = \frac{x_T}{x_T + 1 + \lambda} =: f_T, \quad \text{say}.$$

(iii) $$h'(x_0) = h'(x_T) = 0, \quad h(x_0) = Q(f_0), \quad h(x_T) = Q(f_T),$$

(iv) $h(\cdot), f(\cdot)$ are increasing function on (x_0, x_T) with $\gamma h > 0$.

(v) $f(x) \in (0,1)$ for $x \in (x_0, x_T)$.

It is also shown that f_0 decreases and f_T increases with respect to λ for fixed μ. Next, define for $x \in [x_0, x_T]$

$$p(x) := \left[\frac{\gamma h(x)}{1-\gamma}\right]^{-(1-\gamma)/\gamma}, \quad q(x) := \frac{x(1-f(x))}{f(x)}.$$

In view of (5.12)(iv) above, $p(x)$ is decreasing on $[x_0, x_T]$. Elementary computations show that

$$p'(x) = -\frac{1}{\beta_3 x f(x)} p(x)[h(x) - Q(f(x))],$$

$$q'(x) = \frac{1}{\beta_3 f^2(x)}\left[\left(\frac{1-\gamma}{\gamma}\right)(p(x))^{-\gamma/(1-\gamma)} - Q(f(x))\right].$$

From (ii) above, we have that

(5.13) $$q(x_0) = 1 - \mu, \quad q(x_T) = 1 + \lambda.$$

Notice also that $p'/p = -fq'/x = -q'/x + q$; this implies that q is increasing on $[x_0, x_T]$. Now define

$$p(x)\,[q(x)] := \begin{cases} p(x_0)\,[q(x_0)], & x < x_0, \\ p(x_T)\,[q(x_T)], & x > x_T, \end{cases} \quad \text{and}$$

(5.14) $$\psi(x) := \frac{1}{\gamma} p^{\gamma}(x)[x + q(x)]^{\gamma}, \quad x \geqslant -(1-\mu).$$

For $x \in [x_0, x_T]$ we find, by using the above formulas for $p'(x)$ and $q'(x)$ and the relationship $x + q(x) = x/f(x)$, that

$$\psi'(x) = \frac{1}{x}\gamma\psi(x)f(x) \tag{5.15}$$

(and hence that $\psi'(x) > 0$ as (4.4) requires), and

$$\psi''(x) = \frac{\gamma\psi' f}{x} + \frac{\gamma\psi f'}{x} - \frac{\gamma\psi f}{x^2}$$

$$= \frac{\gamma^2\psi f^2}{x^2} + \frac{\gamma\psi}{x}\frac{1}{\beta_3 x}[R - h] - \frac{\gamma\psi f}{x^2}.$$

Also,

$$\left(\frac{1-\gamma}{\gamma}\right)[\psi']^{-\gamma/(1-\gamma)} = p^{-\gamma^2/(1-\gamma)}[x+q]^{\gamma}\left(\frac{1-\gamma}{\gamma}\right) = \gamma\psi p^{-\gamma/(1-\gamma)}\left(\frac{1-\gamma}{\gamma}\right)$$

$$= (1-\gamma)\psi p^{-\gamma/1-\gamma}$$

$$= (1-\gamma)\frac{\psi\gamma}{1-\gamma}h = \gamma\psi h.$$

Using these formulae it is easily verified that ψ satisfies (5.3). Putting $A = p^{\gamma}(x_0)$, $B = p^{\gamma}(x_T)$, we note that $\psi(\cdot)$ has the required form outside $[x_0, x_T]$. In view of (5.12)(iii), these continuations are in C^1, at least. Now, for x in $[x_0, x_T]$

$$\gamma\psi\psi'' + (1-\gamma)\psi'^2 = \gamma^3\frac{\psi^2 f^2}{x^2} + \frac{\gamma^2\psi^2}{\beta_3 x^2}[R-h] - \frac{\gamma^2\psi^2 f}{x^2} + (1-\gamma)\frac{\gamma^2\psi^2 f^2}{x^2}$$

$$= \frac{\gamma^2\psi^2}{\beta_3 x^2}[\beta_3\gamma f^2 + R - h - \beta_3 f + \beta_3(1-\gamma)f^2]$$

$$= \frac{\gamma^2\psi^2}{\beta_3 x^2}[-\beta_3(1-f)f + R - h]$$

$$= \frac{\gamma^2\psi^2}{\beta_3 x^2}[Q - h] \leqslant 0$$

with equality when $x = x_0$ or $x = x_T$, by (5.12(iii)) and the fact that h is increasing in (x_0, x_T). When $-(1-\mu) < x < x_0$,

$$\gamma\psi\psi'' + (1-\gamma)\psi'^2 = \gamma A^2(x + 1 - \mu)^{2\gamma-2}\frac{1}{\gamma}(\gamma - 1) + (1-\gamma)A^2(x+1-\mu)^{2\gamma-2}$$

$$= 0$$

and similarly when $x > x_T$. Then, since $\psi(x) > 0$ for all $x > -(1-\mu)$, it follows that $\psi''(\cdot)$ is continuous. Hence, the constructed function ψ is C^2, and satisfies (5.2)–(5.5).

(b) When $\gamma = 0$, the argument is similar. The corresponding initial value problems are:

$$(5.16) \quad f'(x) = \frac{1}{\beta_3 x}[R_1(f) - h],$$

$$h'(x) = \frac{\delta}{\beta_3 x f}[h - Q_1(f)], \qquad x \geqslant x_0 > 0, \quad \text{where}$$

$$Q_1(f) = -\delta\beta_4 - \delta \log \delta - \beta_2 f + \beta_3 f^2,$$

$$R_1(f) = Q_1(f) + \beta_3(1-f)f = -\delta\beta_4 - \delta \log \delta + (\beta_3 - \beta_2)f,$$

$$f(x_0) = f_0 := \frac{x_0}{x_0 + 1 - \mu}, \quad h(x_0) = h_0 = Q_1(f_0),$$

and $0 < x_0 < (1-\mu)\beta_2/(\alpha - r)$. In this case we define

$$q(x) := \frac{x(1-f(x))}{f(x)}, \quad p(x) := \exp\left(\frac{-h(x)}{\delta}\right).$$

Remarkably, the relation $p' = -pq'/(x+q)$ still holds; indeed, we find that

$$p' = \frac{-p}{\beta_3 x f}(h - Q_1),$$

$$q' = \frac{1-f}{f} - \frac{1}{\beta_3 f^2}(R_1 - h)$$

$$= \frac{1}{\beta_3 f^2}(\beta_3(1-f)f - R_1 + h)$$

$$= \frac{1}{\beta_3 f^2}(h - Q_1).$$

As before, we have $q(x_0) = 1 - \mu$, $q(x_T) = 1 + \lambda$, and we define $q(x) = q(x_0)$ for $x < x_0$, $q(x) = q(x_T)$ for $x \geqslant x_T$. Similarly, we define $p(x) = A = p(x_0)$ for $x \leqslant x_0$, $p(x) = p(x_T) = B$ for $x \geqslant x_T$. We can now verify in a similar manner to case (a) that

$$\psi(x) := \frac{1}{\delta}\log(p(x)(x + q(x)))$$

satisfies (5.6)–(5.11). This completes the proof.

6. A representation theorem for the value process. From the function introduced in the proof of Theorem 5.1, we can obtain useful representations of $yv_y(x, y)$ and $v(s_0^*(t), s_1^*(t))$, evolving under the optimal policy (c^*, L^*, U^*). These are needed to complete the proof of Theorem 4.2. They also, show that under the optimal policy, bankruptcy does not occur in finite time.

LEMMA 6.1.

$$(6.1)\ (i)\quad yv_y(x,y) = \gamma\left(1 - f\left(\frac{x}{y}\right)\right)v(x,y) \quad \textit{for } (x,y) \in NT \textit{ when } \gamma \in \Gamma$$

where f is given by (5.12)

$$(6.1')\ (ii)\quad yv_y(x,y) = \frac{1}{\delta}\left(1 - f\left(\frac{x}{y}\right)\right) \quad \textit{for } (x,y) \in NT \textit{ when } \gamma = 0$$

where f is given by (5.16).

PROOF. For case (i), express v_y in terms of ψ using (3.6) and obtain f from (5.14), together with the relations (5.15) and (5.16). An analogous procedure gives (6.1').

THEOREM 6.2. (a) *Let the conditions of Theorems* 4.2 *and* 5.1 *hold, let* (c^*, L^*, U^*) *be the policy described by Theorem* 4.2, *let* $s_0^*(t), s_1^*(t)$ *be the solution of equation* (4.1) *with starting point* (x, y), *and define* $\xi_t^* = s_0^*(t)/s_1^*(t)$. *Then, for* $u(c) = c^\gamma/\gamma$, $\gamma \in \Gamma$, *we have*

$$(6.2)\quad v(s_0^*(T), s_1^*(T)) = v(x,y)\exp\left[\int_0^T\left(\delta - \frac{\gamma}{1-\gamma}h(\xi_t^*)\right)dt\right]$$

$$\times\exp\left[\int_0^T \gamma\sigma(1 - f(\xi_t^*))\,dz(t) - \frac{1}{2}\int_0^T \gamma^2\sigma^2(-f(\xi_t^*))^2\,dt\right].$$

(b) *When* $u(c) = \log c$, *the corresponding result is*:

$$(6.2')\qquad v(s_0^*(t), s_1^*(T)) = v(x,y) + \int_0^T\left(-\log\delta - \frac{1}{\delta}h(\xi_t^*)\right)dt$$

$$+\frac{1}{2}\int_0^T \frac{\sigma}{\delta}(1 - f(\xi_t^*))\,dz(t).$$

REMARK 6.3. (6.2) and (6.2') are the counterparts in the transactions costs case of the expression for the wealth process in the Merton problem obtained in Corollary 2.3 above. Indeed, (6.2) reduces to (2.14) when $\lambda = \mu = 0$, because then $f(\xi_t^*) = f_m$, $h(\xi_t^*) = h_m$, where f_m and $h_m = Q(f_m)$ are as given in Remark 5.3 above. Substituting these values in (6.2), we obtain the Merton expression (2.14).

PROOF. First, observe that for any $(x, y) \in NT$, we have:

(a.i) When $u(c) = c^\gamma/\gamma$, $\gamma \in (0,1)$, then $v(x,y) \geqslant 0$ and $v(x,y) \neq 0 \Leftrightarrow (x,y)^T \neq (0,0)^T$.

(a.ii) When $u(c) = c^\gamma/\gamma$, $\gamma < 0$, then $v(x,y) < 0$ and $v(x,y) > -\infty \Leftrightarrow (x,y)^T \neq (0,0)^T$.

(b) $u(c) = \log c$, then $v(x,y)$ takes both positive and negative values, and $v(x,y) > -\infty \Leftrightarrow (x,y)^T \neq (0,0)^T$.

Suppose $\underline{s}^*(0) := (s_0^*(0), s_1^*(0)) = (x,y) \in NT\setminus\{0\}$ (without loss of generality). Let $\tau := \inf\{t\colon \underline{s}^*(t) = \underline{0}\}$. Then $\tau > 0$ a.s. by continuity of the wealth process.

(a) Applying the Ito differentiation formula to $\log[e^{-\delta(T\wedge\tau)}\gamma v(\underline{s}^*(T\wedge\tau))]$ yields:

$$(6.3)\qquad \log\left[e^{-\delta(T\wedge\tau)}\gamma v(\underline{s}^*(T\wedge\tau))\right] - \log\gamma v(\underline{s}^*(0))$$

$$= \int_0^{T\wedge\tau}\frac{1}{v}\left[-\delta v + rs_0^* v_x + \alpha s_1^* v_y + \frac{1}{2}\sigma^2 s_1^* v_{yy} - c^* v_x\right] dt$$

$$-\int_0^{T\wedge\tau}\frac{1}{2v^2}\sigma^2 s_1^{*2} v_y^2\, dt$$

$$+\int_0^{T\wedge\tau}\frac{1}{v}\left[\left(-(1+\lambda)v_x + v_y\right) dL^*(t) + \left((1-\mu)v_x - v_y\right) dU^*(t)\right]$$

$$+\int_0^{T\wedge\tau}\frac{1}{v} v_Y \sigma s_1^*\, dz(t)$$

$$= \int_0^{T\wedge\tau}\frac{1}{v}\left[Gv - \frac{1}{\gamma}(v_x)^{-\gamma/(1-\gamma)}\right] dt + \int_0^{T\wedge\tau}\frac{1}{v} v_y \sigma s_1^*\, dz(t)$$

$$-\int_0^{T\wedge\tau}\frac{1}{2v^2}\sigma^2 s_1^{*2} v_y^2\, dt,$$

since the boundary terms vanish, where

$$Gv = \frac{1}{2}\sigma^2 y^2 v_{yy} + rxv_x + \alpha y v_y - \delta v + \left(\frac{1-\gamma}{\gamma}\right)(v_x)^{-\gamma/(1-\gamma)}.$$

First, $Gv(\underline{s}^*) \equiv 0$. Next, recall from (4.9) that $v(x,y) = y^\gamma\psi(x/y)$. From (5.14), (5.15) we find that $(\gamma v)^{-1}(v_x)^{-\gamma/(1-\gamma)} = p^{-\gamma/(1-\gamma)}$, and from (6.1) that $yv_y/v = \gamma(1 - f(x/y))$. Thus (6.3) simplifies to

$$\log\left(\frac{e^{-\delta(T\wedge\tau)}\gamma v(\underline{s}^*(T\wedge\tau))}{\gamma v(\underline{s}^*(0))}\right) = \int_0^{T\wedge\tau}\left(-p^{-\gamma/(1-\gamma)} - \frac{1}{2}\gamma^2\sigma^2(1-f)^2\right) dt$$

$$+\int_0^{T\wedge\tau}\gamma\sigma(1-f)\, dz(t).$$

Put $h \equiv ((1-\gamma)/\gamma)p^{-\gamma/(1-\gamma)}$ and obtain the following, by exponentiation:

$$(6.4)\qquad \gamma v(s_0^*(T\wedge\tau), s_1^*(T\wedge\tau))$$

$$= \gamma v(x,y)\exp\left(\int_0^{T\wedge\tau}\left(\delta - \frac{\gamma}{1-\gamma}h(\xi_t^*)\right) dt\right)$$

$$\times\exp\left(\int_0^{T\wedge\tau}\gamma\sigma(1-f(\xi_t^*))\, dz(t) - \frac{1}{2}\int_0^{T\wedge\tau}\gamma^2\sigma^2(1-f(\xi_t^*))^2\, dt\right).$$

Since $f \in (0,1)$, $\int_0^t \gamma\sigma(1-f)\,dz$ is a time-changed Brownian motion, finite for all t almost surely. Also γh is bounded (away from zero). Write the right-hand side of (6.4) as $\gamma V(T\wedge\tau)$. Suppose $\tau < \infty$, on some set Δ of positive measure and choose a sample path in Δ.

If $0 < yv(x, y) < \infty$, then $0 < \lim_{t\to\tau} \gamma V(t \wedge \tau) < \infty$ since $V(t \wedge \tau)$ is a continuous process. On the other hand by definition of τ,

$$\lim_{t\to\tau} \gamma v(s_0^*(t \wedge \tau), s_1^*(t \wedge \tau)) = 0 \quad \text{or} \quad \infty$$

contradicting (6.4). Thus $\tau = \infty$, and $0 < yv(s_0^*(t), s_1^*(t)) < \infty$ for all $t \geqslant 0$ almost surely. So (6.4) is equivalent to (6.2).

(b) In the log case,

$$(6.3)' \quad v(\underline{s}^*(T \wedge \tau)) - v(\underline{s}^*(0)) = \int_0^{T\wedge\tau} [\log v_x + \delta v]\, dt + \int_0^{T\wedge\tau} v_y \sigma s_1^*\, dz(t).$$

Since v satisfies the Bellman equation, we find by introducing the functions p, q, f of §5 that the right-hand side of (6.3′) is equal to

$$\int_0^{T\wedge\tau} [-\log(\delta(s_0^* + q(\xi_t^*)s_1^*))]\, dt$$

$$+ \int_0^{T\wedge\tau} \log[p(\xi_t^*)(s_0^* + q(\xi_t^*)s_1^*)]\, dt + \int_0^{T\wedge\tau} \frac{\sigma}{\delta}(1-f)\, dz(t)$$

$$= \int_0^{T\wedge\tau} \log\left[\frac{1}{\delta} p(\xi_t^*)\right] dt + \int_0^{T\wedge\tau} \frac{1}{\delta}\sigma[1 - f(\xi_t^*)]\, dz(t)$$

$$= \int_0^{T\wedge\tau} \left[-\log \delta - \frac{1}{\delta} h(\xi_t^*)\right] dt + \int_0^{T\wedge\tau} \frac{1}{\delta}\sigma[1 - f(\xi_t^*)]\, dz(t)$$

where $h = -\delta \log p$. So

$$v(s_0^*(T \wedge \tau), s_1^*(T \wedge \tau)) = v(x, y) + \int_0^{T\wedge\tau} \left[-\log \delta - \frac{1}{\delta} h(\xi_t^*)\right] dt$$

$$+ \int_0^{T\wedge\tau} \frac{1}{\delta}\sigma[1 - f(\xi_t^*)]\, dz(t).$$

Again, the integrands are bounded. So the assumption that $\tau < \infty$ leads to a contradiction, as before. Thus $\tau = \infty$ and $v(s_0^*(t), s_1^*(t)) > -\infty$ for all t almost surely if $v(x, y) > -\infty$.

COROLLARY 6.4. *The optimal strategies do not lead to bankruptcy in finite time.*

7. Summary, numerical results and conclusions. Combining Theorems 4.2, 4.3 and 5.1 we can now state the main result of this paper.

THEOREM 7.1. *Suppose that* $\mu \in [0, 1[$, $\lambda \in [0, \infty[$ *and* $\mu \vee \lambda > 0$.
Case (a): *utility function* $u(c) = c^\gamma/\gamma$, $\gamma \in \Gamma$.
Suppose that Conditions A *and* B *hold, and that*

$$(7.1) \qquad r < \alpha < r + (1 - \gamma)\sigma^2.$$

Then there is a C^2 *solution* ψ *to the free boundary problem* (5.2)–(5.4) *with* $0 < x_0 < x_T < \infty$, *and the policy* (c^*, L^*, U^*) *described in Theorem 4.2 is optimal in the class* $\mathfrak{U}'$ $(\gamma \in (0, 1))$ *or* $\mathfrak{U}''$ $(\gamma < 0)$. *In particular,* L^*, U^* *are the local times of the wealth* *equation* (4.1) *at the boundaries of the no-transaction region NT. Thus the optimal strategy is minimal trading to keep the proportion of wealth held in stock between* $\pi_1^* := (1 + x_T)^{-1}$ *and* $\pi_2^* := (1 + x_0)^{-1}$.

Case (b): *utility function* $u(c) = \log c$.

Suppose that $\delta > 0$, *that Condition* B *holds, and that* $r < \alpha < r + \sigma^2$ (*i.e.* (7.1) *holds with* $\gamma = 0$). *Then there is a* C^2 *solution to the free boundary problem* (5.7)–(5.9) *with* $0 < x_0 < x_T < \infty$ *and the policy* (c^*, L^*, U^*) *described in Theorem* 4.3 *is optimal in* $\mathfrak{U}''$.

If condition (7.1) is not met then the situation is similar to that described for the Merton problem in Remark 2.2: If $\alpha > r + (1 - \gamma)\sigma^2$ then leverage is optimal and the no-transaction region is a wedge in $\mathscr{S}_\mu' \cap \{x < 0\}$, whereas if $\alpha < r$ shortselling is optimal. If $\alpha = r$ then cashing out all stock holdings is optimal, as shown in Theorem 4.7. The case $\alpha = r + (1 - \gamma)\sigma^2$ is unsolved, but we conjecture that it involves a wedge with vertical upper barrier, with a discontinuity in the second derivative of the value function at this barrier. If Condition A does not hold then arbitrarily high utility can be attained.

We now turn to computation of the optimal policy. This is best done in terms of the transformed coordinates introduced in the proof of Theorem 5.1. Recall from (5.11), (5.12) that, for $u(c) = c^\gamma/\gamma$, if $\psi(x), x_0, x_T$ is the solution of the free boundary problem (5.3)–(5.5) then there are functions $f(x), h(x)$ which satisfy the system of differential equations

$$f' = \frac{1}{\beta_3 x}(R(f) - h) \quad h' = \frac{\gamma}{1-\gamma}\frac{h}{\beta_3 x f}(h - Q(f)), \tag{7.2}$$

$$f(x_0) = \frac{x_0}{x_0 + 1 - \mu} =: f_0, \quad h(x_0) = Q(f_0), \tag{7.3}$$

$$f(x_T) = \frac{x_T}{x_T + 1 + \lambda} =: f_T, \quad h(x_T) = Q(f_T). \tag{7.4}$$

Now from (5.14) ψ is given by

$$\psi(x) = \frac{1}{\gamma}p^\gamma(x)(x + q(x))^\gamma,$$

where p, q are defined in terms of x, f, h by

$$p(x) = \left(\frac{\gamma}{1-\gamma}h(x)\right)^{-(1-\gamma)/\gamma}, \quad q(x) = x\left(\frac{1}{f(x)} - 1\right).$$

We then see that

$$\psi(x) = \frac{1}{\gamma}\left(\frac{\gamma}{1-\gamma}h(x)\right)^{-(1-\gamma)} x^\gamma f^{-\gamma}. \tag{7.5}$$

From (5.15) we have

$$\psi'(x) = x^{-1}\gamma\psi(x)f(x), \tag{7.6}$$

while from (4.8) we know that the optimal consumption policy $c^*(x, y)$ is given by

$$c^*(x, y) = y\left[\psi'\left(\frac{x}{y}\right)\right]^{-1/(1-\gamma)}$$

In view of (7.5), (7.6) we can calculate c^* directly in terms of the function $f(x), h(x)$:

$$c^*(x, y) = \frac{\gamma x h(x/y)}{(1-\gamma)f(x/y)}.$$

The problem therefore reduces to computing the solution to (7.2) with boundary conditions (7.3), (7.4), which say that both at x_0 and at x_T we have $(f, h) \in \mathfrak{Q} = \{(f, h)\colon\ h = Q(f)\}$. Figure 4 below shows some typical trajectories (one should appreciate that the "phase space" is actually 3-dimensional since (7.2) is nonautonomous). The minimum of Q occurs at $f = f_m = 1 - (\alpha - r)/(\sigma^2(1-\gamma)) \in (0, 1)$. Thus $f_0 \leqslant f_m$, $f_T \geqslant f_m$.

The algorithm for solving (7.2)–(7.4) is as follows.

1. Choose any x_T such that $f_T \in (f_m, 1)$, where $f_T := x_T/(x_T + 1 + \lambda)$. Define $h_T = Q(f_T)$.

2. Using numerical integration, solve (7.2) backwards (i.e. in the direction of decreasing x) until the trajectory re-crosses $\mathfrak{Q}$. Let x_0 be the value of x at which this happens ($x_0 = \sup\{x < x_T\colon (f(x), h(x)) \in \mathfrak{Q}\}$) and let $f_0 := f(x_0)$.

3. Define

$$m := x_0 + 1 - \frac{x_0}{f_0}. \tag{7.7}$$

We see from (7.7) that $f_0 = x_0/(x_0 + 1 - m)$, and hence, referring to (7.3), that (x_0, x_T) *determined in this way solves* (7.2)–(7.4) *for the given value of* λ *and with* $\mu = m$. We can regard Steps 1–3 above as a function which maps x_T to $m = m(x_T)$. The solution of (7.2)–(7.4) is completed by embedding 1–3 in a *one-dimensional search procedure* to find a value of x_T such that $m(x_T) = \mu$ (the prescribed proportional cost for sales). The argument given in the Appendix shows that this search will always be successful. The reason for integrating backwards rather than forwards in Step 2 is that this is the "stable" direction of (7.2): the solution integrated forwards is very sensitive to the initial condition f_0, whereas the backwards solution is much more robust. An exactly similar algorithm, based on equations (5.16), solves the problem for the utility function $u(c) = \log c$.

We plan to report more fully on the numerical results in a later publication, but Figure 3 shows some typical results. Our result says that the proportion of wealth held in stock should be kept between $\pi_1^* = 100(1 + x_T)^{-1}\%$ and $\pi_2^* = 100(1 + x_0)^{-1}\%$. The Merton proportion (no transaction costs) is $\pi^* = 100 \times 2(\alpha - r)/\sigma^2$. In the present case this is equal to 15.63%. We have taken $\mu = \lambda$ (equal transaction costs on sale and purchase) and plotted π_1^*, π_2^* against λ. The most noticeable feature of these curves is that the upper (sell) barrier is very insensitive to λ while the lower (buy) barrier decreases quite rapidly as λ increases. This is probably due to the asymmetry in the model: all consumption takes place from the bank, so stock must be sold (and transaction charges paid) before it can be realized for consumption. If the selling charge is high then this is unfortunate but unavoidable. On the other hand if the bulk of the investor's holdings are in cash then the potential gains from investing

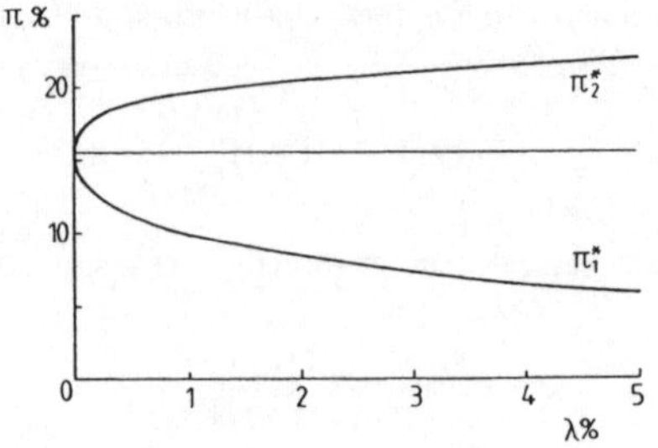

FIGURE 3. Dependence of π_1^*, π_2^* on λ (with $\mu = \lambda$). The Parameter Values are $\alpha = 0.12$, $r = 0.07$, $\sigma = 0.4$, $\delta = 0.1$, $\gamma = -1$.

in stock and then reselling at some later date may not be worthwhile if the associated costs are too high. Hence the decreasing value for π_1^*.

In [4], Constantinides considers exactly the same problem as in this paper and obtains approximate results by restricting the class of consumption policies $c(x, y)$ to those satisfying

$$\frac{c(x, y)}{x} = \text{constant}. \tag{7.8}$$

His results are qualitatively similar to those displayed in Figure 3. We can use our numerical technique to check whether (7.8) is exactly or approximately satisfied for truly optimal policies. For $\gamma \neq 0$ the optimal consumption c^* is given by (4.9) and we see that for $(x, y) \in NT$

$$\frac{c^*(x, y)}{x} = \xi^{-1}[\psi'(\xi)]^{-1/(1-\gamma)} =: \tilde{c}(\xi), \qquad \xi := \frac{x}{y}.$$

In NT, ξ ranges over the interval $[x_0, x_T]$. Taking parameter values as above and $\lambda = \mu = 0.01$, we find that $x_0 = 0.406$, $x_T = 1.112$, $\tilde{c}(x_0) = 0.188$ and $\tilde{c}(x_T) = 0.105$. Thus the ratio in (7.8) actually varies over a range of nearly two to one. We have not, however, investigated how much *utility* is lost by imposing the restriction (7.8).

Finally, let us consider possible extensions of this work. Of course, the most interesting extension would be to the case of $m > 1$ risky assets, but unfortunately this is essentially impossible except perhaps for $m = 2$ or 3. As Magill and Constantinides [17] point out, m risky assets imply 3^m possible transaction regions and, for example, $3^{10} \approx 60000$. Although the coordinate transformation introduced in §5 generalizes to higher dimensions, it is not clear how to locate the boundaries even when $m = 2$. The only readily solvable case is that in which transactions *between risky assets* are costless. The risky assets can then be combined via a mutual fund theorem [17] and the problem reduces to the single risky asset case considered here. See Magill [16]. Another important question is *nonconstant model parameters* (interest rates, return on assets, volatility). It is unlikely that our problem could ever be solved at the level of generality of, say, Karatzas *et al.* [11], where these parameters are taken as general stochastic processes. However, it might be solvable if the randomness of the parameters were modelled in specific ways, for example as finite state Markov processes. This is an interesting area for further research.

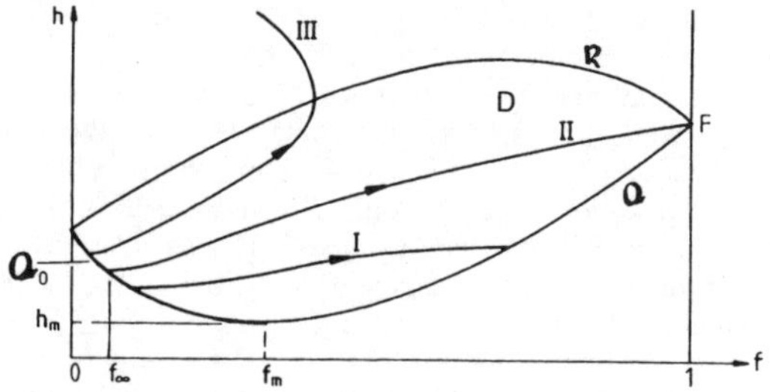

FIGURE 4. (f, h)-Plane for $\gamma \in (0, 1)$, $f_m < \frac{1}{2}$.

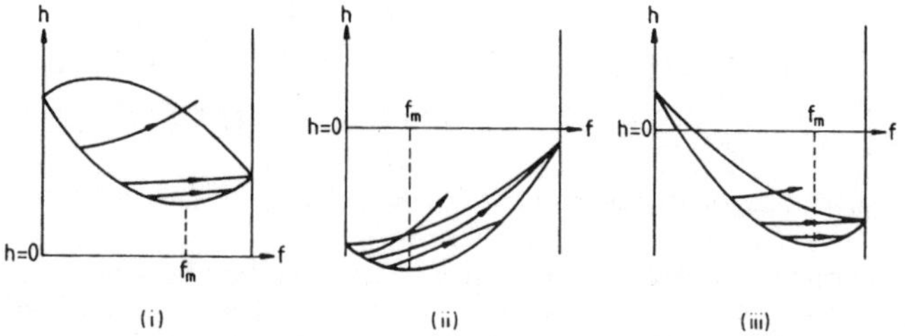

FIGURE 5. (f, h) plane for (i) $\gamma \in (0, 1)$, $f_m > \frac{1}{2}$, (ii) $\gamma < 0$, $f_m < \frac{1}{2}$, (iii) $\gamma < 0$, $f_m > \frac{1}{2}$. When $\gamma = 0$ the pictures are similar, but parabola $\mathfrak{R}$ becomes a straight line.

Acknowledgements. We would like to thank V. E. Beneš, I. Karatzas, P. Varaiya and R. J. Williams for helpful discussions and advice, and the two referees for their detailed attention and many valuable remarks. We would also like to thank D. Abeysekera for her unstinting help in the preparation of the manuscript.

Appendix. In this Appendix we examine the solution trajectories $(x, f(x), h(x)) \in \mathbb{R}^3$ of the nonautonomous first-order system defined by equation (5.11):

$$(5.11) \qquad f'(x) = \frac{1}{\beta_3 x}\left[R(f(x)) - h(x)\right],$$

$$h'(x) = \frac{\gamma}{1-\gamma}\frac{h}{\beta_3 x f(x)}\left[h(x) - Q(f(x))\right].$$

We show that for each $\mu < 1$ and $\lambda > -\mu$, these equations have a solution satisfying (5.12)(i)–(v).[6] This will follow from the sequence of lemmas presented below. The proofs of these lemmas are collected together at the end of the Appendix.

Denote by $\mathfrak{Q}$ and $\mathfrak{R}$ respectively the graphs in $\mathbb{R}^2$ of the functions Q and R for $f \in [0, 1]$, and define $\mathfrak{Q}_0 := \{(f, h): 0 < f < f_m\}$ where $f_m := 1 - (\alpha - r)/(1 - \gamma)\sigma^2$ is the value of f at which $Q(f)$ attains its minimum. We also define $\tilde{\mathfrak{Q}} = \mathbb{R} \times \mathfrak{Q}$, $\tilde{\mathfrak{Q}}_0 = \mathbb{R} \times \mathfrak{Q}_0$ and $\tilde{\mathfrak{R}} = \mathbb{R} \times \mathfrak{R}$. $\tilde{\mathfrak{Q}}$ and $\tilde{\mathfrak{R}}$ enclose a region $\tilde{D}$ in (x, f, h) space and we denote by D the projection of $\tilde{D}$ onto the (f, h)-plane (see Figures 4 and 5). The

[6] We only need to prove existence because the uniqueness of the optimal payoff functions (3.2) will follow immediately.

only "stationary point" $F := (1, Q(1)) = (1, R(1)) = (1, (\delta/\gamma) - r)$ corresponds to a straight line trajectory $\bar{F} = (x, 1, Q(1)) \subset \bar{\mathfrak{Q}} \cap \bar{\mathfrak{R}}$.[7]

Fix $\mu < 1$ and consider the solution of (5.11) starting at $(x_0, f(x_0), h(x_0)) = (x_0, f_0, h_0) \in \bar{\mathfrak{Q}}_0$ with $x_0 := X_\mu(f_0) := (1-\mu)f_0/(1-f_0)$. We note that $f'(x_0) > 0$ and $h'(x_0) = 0$, and that $f', h' > 0$ inside $\bar{D}$. Thus, the trajectory moves monotonically in each variable across $\bar{D}$ and can only (I) exit through $\bar{\mathfrak{Q}}$, (II) exit through $\bar{\mathfrak{R}}$ or (III) tend to $\bar{F}$. We call such trajectories types I, II, III respectively.

Suppose for a moment that (I) holds. Denote by x_T, f_T, h_T the exit values of x, f, h, and define $l = l(f_0) := (x_T/f_T) - x_T - 1$. Since $Q(f_m) = (\delta/\gamma) - r - (\alpha - r)^2/2(1-\gamma)\sigma^2$, Condition A implies that $h > 0$ for all $(f, h) \in D$ when $\gamma > 0$. When $\gamma < 0$, at each point (f, h) on our trajectory we have $h < h_T < Q(1) = (\delta/\gamma) - r < 0$. Thus $\gamma h > 0$ in either case, and properties (5.13)(i)–(v) are all satisfied with $\lambda = l$. *We therefore need to show that for each $\lambda > -\mu$ there is a type I trajectory with $l = \lambda$.*

Consider first the extreme case $f_0 = f_m$. We have the following result.

Lemma A.1. *Fix $\mu < 1$, as before. Set $f_0 = f_m$, $h_0 = Q(f_0)$ and $x_0 = X_\mu(f_0) > 0$. Then $h''(x_0) = 0$, $h'''(x_0) < 0$.*

This shows that the trajectory of (5.11) does not enter the interior of D, and hence that $x_T = x_0$, $f_T = f_m$, $h_T = Q(f_m)$ and $l = -\mu$.[8]

It remains to show that $l(f_0)$ ranges continuously up to infinity as we decrease the starting value f_0 of the type I trajectory keeping (x_0, f_0, h_0) on $\bar{\mathfrak{Q}}_0$ and maintaining the relationship $x_0 = X_\mu(f_0)$. We shall discover the behaviour of $l(f_0)$ for $f_0 < f_m$ by investigating the function $q(x) = x(1 - f(x))/f(x)$ introduced in the proof of Theorem 5.1, and noting that $q(x_0) = 1 - \mu$, and $q(x_T) = 1 + l$. We shall also use (without proof) the fact that solutions to (5.11) are line integrals which are continuous functions of the initial values. The following lemma is of crucial importance. It shows that the projections onto D of trajectories with distinct starting points in $\bar{\mathfrak{Q}}_0$ do not intersect.

Lemma A.2. *Let $(x, f_1(x), h_1(x))$ and $(x, f_2(x), h_2(x))$ be two solution trajectories of (5.11) starting at $(f_{i0}, h_{i0}) \in \mathfrak{Q}_0$, $x_{i0} = X_\mu(f_{i0})$, $i = 1, 2$. Define $\mathfrak{G}_i' = \{(f_i(x), h_i(x)) : x \geqslant x_{i0}\}$ and $\mathfrak{G}_i = \mathfrak{G}_i' \cap D$, $i = 1, 2$. Suppose that $f_{10} > 0$ and $f_{20} > 0$, $Q(f_{10}) \leqslant Q(1)$ and $Q(f_{20}) \leqslant Q(1)$, and $h_{20} > h_{10}$ (so $f_{20} < f_{10}$). Suppose $(f, h_1) \in \mathfrak{G}_1$ and $(f, h_2) \in \mathfrak{G}_2$ for $f \in [0, 1]$. Then $h_2 > h_1$.*

Corollary. *Let $(x, f_1(x), h_1(x))$ and $(x, f_2(x), h_2(x))$ be as above, and suppose that $(x, f_2(x), h_2(x))$ is a type* I *trajectory. Then $(x, f_1(x), h_1(x))$ is also of type* I. *Thus the terminal value $f_T \in (f_m, 1)$ is a monotonic decreasing function of f_0.*

Next, define $f_\infty := \inf\{f_0 : (x_T, f(x_T), h(x_T)) \in \bar{\mathfrak{Q}}\}$. In view of the above results, all trajectories with starting points f_0 such that $f_m > f_0 > f_\infty$ are of type I. We need the following condition:

Condition B. $f_\infty > 0$.

If $f_m > \frac{1}{2}$, $0 \leqslant \gamma < 1$, then Condition B automatically holds, since the trajectory with $h(x_0) = Q(1)$ is necessarily of type II (see Figure 5(i) and (iii)). Numerical work convinces us that $f_\infty > 0$ in the remaining cases, but we are unable at present to give a proof.

[7] The $\mu = 1$ case.

[8] When $\lambda = \mu = 0$, this corresponds to the solution of the Merton problem, and indeed we find that $x_0 = f_m/(1 - f_m)$, corresponding to the Merton proportion π^* of (2.6), namely $\pi^* = 1/(\pi_0 + 1) = (\alpha - r)/(1 - \gamma)\sigma^2$.

The next lemma completes the argument by establishing that for any specified $\lambda > -\mu$, there is a (type I) trajectory for which $q(\lambda_T) = 1 + \lambda$.

LEMMA A.3. *Suppose Condition* B *holds. Then as f_0 decreases from f_m to f_∞,*
(i) $q(x_T)$ increases from $1 - \mu$ to ∞, and
(ii) x_T increases from $(1 - \mu)((1 - f_m)/f_m)$ to ∞.

PROOF OF LEMMA A.1. The two cases are:
(a) $\gamma \in \Gamma$. Then

$$\frac{d}{dx}(\beta_3 xfh')\Big|_{x=x_0} = \frac{d}{dx}\left(\frac{\gamma}{1-\gamma}h[h - Q(f)]\right)\Big|_{x=x_0}$$

$$= \frac{\gamma}{1-\gamma}h'[h - Q(f)] + \frac{\gamma}{1-\gamma}h[h' - Q'f']\Big|_{x=x_0} = 0.$$

Also,

$$\frac{d}{dx}(\beta_3 xfh')\Big|_{x=x_0} = h' \cdot \frac{d}{dx}(\beta_3 xf) + \beta_3 xfh''\Big|_{x=x_0} = 0.$$

But $f(x_0) \neq 0$, so $h''(x_0) = 0$.
Next,

$$\frac{d^2}{dx^2}(\beta_3 xfh')\Big|_{x=x_0} = \beta_3((2f' + xf'')h' + 2(f + xf')h'' + xfh''')|_{x=x_0}$$

$$= h'''(x_0)\beta_3 x_0 f_0.$$

Another expression for this derivative is

$$\frac{d}{dx}\left(\frac{\gamma}{1-\gamma}h'[h - Q(f)]\right) + \frac{\gamma}{1-\gamma}h[h' - Q'(f')]\Big)\Big|_{x=x_0}$$

$$= \frac{\gamma}{1-\gamma}(h''[h - Q] + 2h'[h' - Q'f'] + h[h'' - Q''f'^2 + Q'f''])|_{x=x_0}$$

$$= \frac{-\gamma}{1-\gamma}h(x_0)\cdot 2\beta_3(1-\gamma)\left(\frac{R(f(x_0)) - h(x_0)}{\beta_3 x_0}\right)^2 < 0,$$

showing that $h'''(x_0) < 0$.
(b) $\gamma = 0$. In this case,

$$\frac{d}{dx}(\beta_3 xfh')\Big|_{x=x_0} = \delta\frac{d}{dx}(h - Q_1(f))\Big|_{x=x_0} = \delta(h' - Q_1'f')|_{x=x_0}$$

$$= \beta_3 x_0 f_0 h''(x_0).$$

So $h''(x_0) = 0$. Further,

$$\frac{d^2}{dx^2}(\beta_3 xfh')\bigg|_{x=x_0} = \beta_3((2f' + xf'')h' + 2(f + xf')h'' + xfh''')|_{x=x_0}$$

$$= h'''(x_0)\beta_3 x_0 f_0$$

$$= \delta(h'' - Q_1''f'^2 - Q_1'f'')|_{x=x_0}$$

$$= -2\delta\beta_3\left(\frac{R_1(f(x_0)) - h(x_0)}{\beta_3 x_0}\right)^2 < 0,$$

showing that $h'''(x_0) < 0$. This completes the proof.

Proof of Lemma A.2. Consider two trajectories evaluated at common $f_1 = f_2 = f$. When $\gamma \in \Gamma$, we have

$$\frac{dh}{df} = \frac{\gamma}{1-\gamma}\frac{h}{f}\left(\frac{h - Q(f)}{R(f) - h}\right).$$

Thus if h_1, h_2, lie in D (see Figure 5(i)), then

$$\frac{d}{df}(h_2 - h_1) = \frac{1}{1-\gamma}\frac{1}{f}\left(\gamma h_2\left(\frac{h_2 - Q(f)}{R(f) - h_2}\right) - \gamma h_1\left(\frac{h_1 - Q(f)}{R(f) - h_1}\right)\right).$$

When $\gamma = 0$, the corresponding expressions are:

$$\frac{dh}{df} = \frac{\delta}{f}\left(\frac{h - Q_1(f)}{R_1(f) - h}\right),$$

$$\frac{d}{df}(h_2 - h_1) = \frac{\delta}{f}\left(\left(\frac{h_2 - Q_1(f)}{R_1(f) - h_2}\right) - \left(\frac{h_1 - Q_1(f)}{R_1(f) - h_1}\right)\right).$$

In either case, if $h_2 > h_1$, then $d(h_2 - h_1)/df > 0$. Since h_2 increases in D, and $h_{20} > h_{10}$ then $h_2 > h_1$ for all f, as claimed.

Proof of Lemma A.3. (i) Consider the case $\gamma \in \Gamma$ first. We saw that $q(x_T) = 1 - \mu$ when $f_0 = f_m$. Take two trajectories with $h_2 > h_1$, as before. Now q_2 increases since $q' = [h - Q(f)]/\beta_3 f^2 \geqslant 0$. So, initially $q_2 > q_1 = 1 - \mu$. With a common f as in Lemma A.2, the corresponding values of x are x_1, x_2 given by:

$$f = \frac{x_1}{x_1 + q_1(x_1)} = \frac{x_2}{x_2 + q(x_2)},$$

$$\frac{q_1(x_1)}{x_1} = \frac{q_2(x_2)}{x_2} \quad \text{i.e.} \quad \frac{q_2(x_2)}{q_1(x_1)} = \frac{x_2}{x_1}.$$

Then

$$\frac{d}{df}(q_2 - q_1) = \frac{1}{f^2}\left(x_2\left(\frac{h_2 - Q(f)}{R(f) - h_2}\right) - x_1\left(\frac{h_1 - Q(f)}{R(f) - h_1}\right)\right) > 0$$

$$= \frac{x_1}{f^2}\left(\frac{q_1}{f^2}\left(\frac{h_2 - Q(f)}{R(f) - h_2}\right) - \left(\frac{h_1 - Q(f)}{R(f) - h_1}\right)\right) > 0$$

whenever $q_2 > q_1$ $(x_1 > 0)$.

In case $\gamma = 0$, the expressions are the same, with Q, R replaced by Q_1, R_1. In both cases, $q_2 > q_1$ for all (common) f. Finally, since q_2 increases, we have $q_2(x_{2T}) > q_1(x_{1T})$, showing that $q(x_T)$ increases as f_0 decreases.

To see that $q(x_T) \to \infty$ as f_0 decreases to f_∞, use the fact that q is a continuous function of f_0 and x and Lemma A.4 below which establishes that $q(x) \to \infty$ along the type III trajectory with $f_0 = f_\infty$.

(ii) Since $q_2/q_1 = x_2/x_1 > 1$, we have $x_2 > x_1$ for all f, and since $x_2(f)$ is increasing, we have that $x_{2T} > x_{1T}$. That is, x_T increases as f_0 decreases. When $f_0 = f_m$, we have $f_T = f_0$ and $x_T = x_0 = (1 - \mu)(1 - f_m)/f_m$, since $f_m = f_0 = x_0/(x_0 + 1 - \mu)$. Finally, since $f_T = x_T/(x_T + q(x_T))$ and $q(x_T)$ is increasing and positive, it follows x_T increases to infinity as f_T increases to 1, proving (ii).

In the proof of Lemma 3 we needed the following fact concerning the behaviour of the special (type III) trajectory with $f_0 = f_\infty$, $f_T = 1$ (see Figures 4, 5).[9]

LEMMA A.4. *Along the type* III *(asymptotic) trajectory*, $q(x) \to \infty$ *as* $x \to \infty$.

PROOF. (a) For $\gamma \in \Gamma$,

$$\frac{q'}{q} = \frac{1}{x}\left(\frac{h - Q}{R - Q}\right).$$

We know that $h \to Q(1)$, $f \to 1$ as $x \to \infty$. By L'Hôpital's rule,

$$\lim_{x\to\infty}\left(\frac{h - Q}{R - Q}\right) = \lim_{x\to\infty}\left(\frac{h' - Q'f'}{(R' - Q')f'}\right) \in [0, 1].$$

Write $a = h - Q$, $b = R - h$. Then

$$\lim_{x\to\infty}\left(\frac{a}{a+b}\right)$$

$$= \lim\left(\frac{\frac{\gamma}{1-\gamma}\cdot\frac{h}{\beta_3 xf}\cdot[h - Q(f)] - [-\beta_2 + 2\beta_3(1-\gamma)f]\frac{1}{\beta_3 x}[R - h]}{\beta_3(1 - 2f)\cdot\frac{1}{\beta_3 x}\cdot[R - h]}\right)$$

$$= \frac{-\gamma}{1-\gamma}\cdot\frac{Q(1)}{\beta_3}\lim\left(\frac{a}{b}\right) + \frac{-\beta_2 + 2\beta_3(1-\gamma)}{\beta_3}$$

$$= \lim\left(\frac{a/b}{(a/b) + 1}\right) = K, \text{ say.}$$

[9] This corresponds to a no-transaction region in which the lower barrier lies on the x-axis, i.e. the cost of buying into the stock is prohibitive.

So,

$$\beta_3 K = 2\beta_3(1-\gamma) - \beta_2 - \frac{\gamma}{1-\gamma}\cdot Q(1)\frac{K}{1-K},$$

and $K \in [0,1]$, i.e.

$$H(K) := \beta_3 K^2 + \left(-\beta_3 - 2\beta_3(1-\gamma) + \beta_2 - \frac{\gamma}{1-\gamma}\cdot Q(1)\right)K + 2\beta_3(1-\gamma) - \beta_2$$

$$= 0$$

$$= \frac{\sigma^2}{2}K^2 + \left(\frac{-\sigma^2}{2} - (\alpha - r) - \frac{\gamma}{1-\gamma}\left(\frac{\delta}{\gamma} - r\right)\right)K + \alpha - r.$$

Since

$$H(0) = \alpha - r > 0 \quad \textit{and} \quad H(1) = -\gamma/(1-\gamma)(\delta/\gamma - r) < 0,$$

it follows that the roots satisfy $0 < K_1 < 1 < K_2$. So

$$K = K_1 = \frac{1}{\sigma^2}\left(\frac{1}{2}\sigma^2 + \alpha - r + \frac{\gamma}{1-\gamma}\left(\frac{\delta}{\gamma} - r\right)\right.$$

$$\left. - \sqrt{\left(\frac{1}{2}\sigma^2 + \alpha - r + \frac{\gamma}{1-\gamma}\left(\frac{\delta}{\gamma} - r\right)\right)^2 - 2\sigma^2(\alpha - r)}\right).$$

(b) When $\gamma = 0$,

$$\frac{q'}{q} = \frac{1}{x}\left(\frac{h - Q_1}{R_1 - Q_1}\right).$$

Writing

$$\overline{K} = \lim_{x\to\infty}\left(\frac{h - Q_1}{R_1 - Q_1}\right),$$

the corresponding quadratic is

$$H_1(\overline{K}) = \tfrac{1}{2}\sigma^2\overline{K}^2 + \left[-\tfrac{1}{2}\sigma^2 - \delta - (\alpha - r)\right]\overline{K} - \alpha - r = 0,$$

$$H_1(0) = \alpha - r > 0, \quad H_1(1) = -\delta < 0.$$

So, $0 < \overline{K}_1 < 1 < \overline{K}_2$, and

$$\overline{K} = \overline{K}_1 = \frac{1}{\sigma^2}\left(\frac{1}{2}\sigma^2 + \delta + (\alpha - r) - \sqrt{\left(\frac{1}{2}\sigma^2 + \delta \pm (\alpha - r)\right)^2 - 2\sigma^2(\alpha - r)}\right).$$

Then, for large x, q is asymptotic to x^K (respectively $x^{\overline{K}}$). So, $q \to \infty$ as $x \to \infty$ along the special trajectory, as claimed.

References

[1] Anderson, R. F. and Orey, S. (1976). Small Random Perturbations of Dynamical Systems with Reflecting Boundary. *Nagoya Math J.* **60** 189–216.

[2] Beneš, V. E., Shepp, L. A. and Witsenhausen, H. S. (1980). Some Solvable Stochastic Control Problems. *Stochastics* **4** 134–160.

[3] Bensoussan, A. and Lions, J. L. (1984). *Impulse Control and Quasi-variational Inequalities*. Gauthier-Villars, Paris.

[4] Constantinides, G. M. (1986). Capital Market Equilibrium with Transaction Costs, *J. Political Economy* **94** 842–862.

[5] Davis, M. H. A. (1988). Local Time on the Stock Exchange. in *Stochastic Calculus in Application*. J. R. Norris (Ed.), Pitman Research Notes in Mathematics 197, Longman, London.

[6] Doléans-Dade, C. (1976). On the Existence and Unicity of Solutions of Stochastic Integral Equations. *Z. Wahrsch. Verw. Gebiete* **36** 93–101.

[7] Duffie, D. and Sun, T. S. Transaction Costs and Portfolio Choice in a Discrete-Continuous Time Setting. *J. Economic Dynamics and Control*, to appear.

[8] Fleming, W. H. and Rishel, R. W. (1975). *Deterministic and Stochastic Optimal Control*. Springer-Verlag, New York.

[9] Harrison, J. M. (1985). *Brownian Motion and Stochastic Flow Systems*. Wiley, New York.

[10] ______ and Taylor, A. J. (1978). Optimal Control of a Brownian Storage System. *Stochastic Process. Appl.* **6**.

[11] Karatzas, I., Lehoczky, J. P. and Shreve, S. E. (1987). Optimal Portfolio and Consumption Decisions for a "Small Investor" on a Finite Horizon. *SIAM J. Control Opt.* **25** 1557–1586.

[12] ______, ______, Sethi, S. P. and Shreve, S. E. (1986). Explicit Solution of a General Consumption/Investment Problem. *Math. Oper. Res.* **11** 261–294.

[13] ______ and Shreve, S. E. (1986). Equivalent Models for Finite Fuel Stochastic Control. *Stochastics* **18** 245–276.

[14] ______ and ______ (1984). (1985). Connections between Optimal Stopping and Singular Stochastic Control. I, II. *SIAM J. Control Optim.* **22** 856–877 and **23** 433–451.

[15] Leland, H. E. (1985). Option Pricing and Replication with Transactions Costs, *J. Finance* **40** 1283–1301.

[16] Magill, M. J. P. (1976). The Preferability of Investment through a Mutual Fund. *J. Economic Theory* **13** 264–271.

[17] ______ and Constantinides, G. M. (1976). Portfolio Selection with Transaction Costs. *J. Economic Theory* **13** 245–263.

[18] Merton, R. C. (1971). Optimum Consumption and Portfolio Rules in a Continuous-Time Model, *J. Economic Theory* **3** 373–413.

[19] Stroock, D. W. and Varadhan, S. R. S. (1971). Diffusion Processes with Boundary Conditions. *Comm. Pure Appl. Math.* **24** 147–225.

[20] Taksar, M., Klass, M. J. and Assaf, D. (1988). A Diffusion Model for Optimal Portfolio Selection in the Presence of Brokerage Fees. *Math. Oper. Res.* **13** 277–294.

[21] Tanaka, H. (1979). Stochastic Differential Equations with Reflecting Boundary Conditions in Convex Regions. *Hiroshima Math. J.* **9** 163–177.

[22] Varadhan, S. R. S. and Williams, R. J. (1985). Brownian Motion in a Wedge with Oblique Reflection. *Comm. Pure Appl. Math.* **38** 405–443.

DAVIS: DEPARTMENT OF ELECTRICAL ENGINEERING, IMPERIAL COLLEGE, LONDON SW7 2BT, UNITED KINGDOM

NORMAN: COUNTY NATWEST, LONDON, UNITED KINGDOM

Part III
Equilibrium Models

[11]

Econometrica, Vol. 41, No. 5, (September, 1973)

AN INTERTEMPORAL CAPITAL ASSET PRICING MODEL[1]

BY ROBERT C. MERTON

An intertemporal model for the capital market is deduced from the portfolio selection behavior by an arbitrary number of investors who act so as to maximize the expected utility of lifetime consumption and who can trade continuously in time. Explicit demand functions for assets are derived, and it is shown that, unlike the one-period model, current demands are affected by the possibility of uncertain changes in future investment opportunities. After aggregating demands and requiring market clearing, the equilibrium relationships among expected returns are derived, and contrary to the classical capital asset pricing model, expected returns on risky assets may differ from the riskless rate even when they have no systematic or market risk.

1. INTRODUCTION

ONE OF THE MORE important developments in modern capital market theory is the Sharpe-Lintner-Mossin mean-variance equilibrium model of exchange, commonly called the capital asset pricing model.[2] Although the model has been the basis for more than one hundred academic papers and has had significant impact on the non-academic financial community,[3] it is still subject to theoretical and empirical criticism. Because the model assumes that investors choose their portfolios according to the Markowitz [21] mean-variance criterion, it is subject to all the theoretical objections to this criterion, of which there are many.[4] It has also been criticized for the additional assumptions required,[5] especially homogeneous expectations and the single-period nature of the model. The proponents of the model who agree with the theoretical objections, but who argue that the capital market operates "as if" these assumptions were satisfied, are themselves not beyond criticism. While the model predicts that the expected excess return from holding an asset is proportional to the covariance of its return with the market

[1] This paper is a substantial revision of parts of [24] presented in various forms at the NBER Conference on Decision Rules and Uncertainty, Massachusetts Institute of Technology, February, 1971, and at the Wells Fargo Conference on Capital Market Theory, San Francisco, July, 1971. I am grateful to the participants for helpful comments. I thank Myron Scholes and Fischer Black for many useful discussions, and Robert K. Merton for editorial assistance. Aid from the National Science Foundation is gratefully acknowledged.

[2] See Sharpe [38 and 39], Lintner [19 and 20], and Mossin [29]. While more general and elegant than the capital asset pricing model in many ways, the general equilibrium model of Arrow [1] and Debreu [8, Ch. 7] has not had the same impact, principally because of its empirical intractability and the rather restrictive assumption that there exist as many securities as states of nature (see Stiglitz [41]). The "growth optimum" model of Hakansson [15] can be formulated as an equilibrium model although it is consistent with expected utility maximization only if all investors have logarithmic utility functions (see Samuelson [36] and Merton and Samuelson [27]). However, Roll [32] has shown that the model fits the data about as well as the capital asset pricing model.

[3] For academic references, see Sharpe [39] and the Jensen [17] survey article. For a summary of the model's impact on the financial community, see [42].

[4] See Borch [4], Feldstein [12], and Hakansson [15]. For a list of the conditions necessary for the validity of mean-variance, see Samuelson [34 and 35].

[5] See Sharpe [39, pp. 77–78] for a list of the assumptions required.

portfolio (its "beta"), the careful empirical work of Black, Jensen, and Scholes [3] has demonstrated that this is not the case. In particular, they found that "low beta" assets earn a higher return on average and "high beta" assets earn a lower return on average than is forecast by the model.[6] Nonetheless, the model is still used because it is an equilibrium model which provides a strong specification of the relationship among asset yields that is easily interpreted, and the empirical evidence suggests that it does explain a significant fraction of the variation in asset returns.

This paper develops an equilibrium model of the capital market which (i) has the simplicity and empirical tractability of the capital asset pricing model; (ii) is consistent with expected utility maximization and the limited liability of assets; and (iii) provides a specification of the relationship among yields that is more consistent with empirical evidence. Such a model cannot be constructed without costs. The assumptions, principally homogeneous expectations, which it holds in common with the classical model, make the new model subject to some of the same criticisms.

The capital asset pricing model is a static (single-period) model although it is generally treated as if it holds intertemporally. Fama [9] has provided some justification for this assumption by showing that, if preferences and future investment opportunity sets are not state-dependent, then intertemporal portfolio maximization can be treated as if the investor had a single-period utility function. However, these assumptions are rather restrictive as will be seen in later analysis.[7] Merton [25] has shown in a number of examples that portfolio behavior for an intertemporal maximizer will be significantly different when he faces a changing investment opportunity set instead of a constant one.

The model presented here is based on consumer-investor behavior as described in [25], and for the assumptions to be reasonable ones, it must be intertemporal. Far from a liability, the intertemporal nature of the model allows it to capture effects which would never appear in a static model, and it is precisely these effects which cause the significant differences in specification of the equilibrium relationship among asset yields that obtain in the new model and the classical model.

2. CAPITAL MARKET STRUCTURE

It is assumed that the capital market is structured as follows.

ASSUMPTION 1: *All assets have limited liability.*

ASSUMPTION 2: *There are no transactions costs, taxes, or problems with indivisibilities of assets.*

[6] Friend and Blume [14] also found that the empirical capital market line was "too flat." Their explanation was that the borrowing-lending assumption of the model is violated. Black [2] provides an alternative explanation based on the assumption of no riskless asset. Other less important, stylized facts in conflict with the model are that investors do not hold the same relative proportions of risky assets, and short sales occur in spite of unfavorable institutional requirements.

[7] Fama recognizes the restrictive nature of the assumptions as evidenced by discussion in Fama and Miller [11].

ASSUMPTION 3: *There are a sufficient number of investors with comparable wealth levels so that each investor believes that he can buy and sell as much of an asset as he wants at the market price.*

ASSUMPTION 4: *The capital market is always in equilibrium (i.e., there is no trading at non-equilibrium prices).*

ASSUMPTION 5: *There exists an exchange market for borrowing and lending at the same rate of interest.*

ASSUMPTION 6: *Short-sales of all assets, with full use of the proceeds, is allowed.*

ASSUMPTION 7: *Trading in assets takes place continually in time.*

ASSUMPTIONS 1–6 are the standard assumptions of a perfect market, and their merits have been discussed extensively in the literature. Although Assumption 7 is not standard, it almost follows directly from Assumption 2. If there are no costs to transacting and assets can be exchanged on any scale, then investors would prefer to be able to revise their portfolios at any time (whether they actually do so or not). In reality, transactions costs and indivisibilities do exist, and one reason given for finite trading-interval (discrete-time) models is to give implicit, if not explicit, recognition to these costs. However, this method of avoiding the problem of transactions costs is not satisfactory since a proper solution would almost certainly show that the trading intervals are stochastic and of non-constant length. Further, the portfolio demands and the resulting equilibrium relationships will be a function of the specific trading interval that is chosen.[8] An investor making a portfolio decision which is irrevocable ("frozen") for ten years, will choose quite differently than the one who has the option (even at a cost) to revise his portfolio daily. The essential issue is the market structure and not investors' tastes, and for well-developed capital markets, the time interval between successive market openings is sufficiently small to make the continuous-time assumption a good approximation.[9]

3. ASSET VALUE AND RATE OF RETURN DYNAMICS

Having described the structure of the capital market, we now develop the dynamics of the returns on assets traded in the market. It is sufficient for his decision

[8] A simple example from the expectations theory of the term structure will illustrate the point. It is well known (see, e.g., Stiglitz [40]) that bonds cannot be priced to equate expected returns over *all* holding periods. Hence, one must select a "fundamental" period (usually one "trading" period, our h) to equate expected returns. Clearly, the prices which satisfy this relationship will be a function of h. Similarly, the demand functions of investors will depend on h. We have chosen for our interval the smallest h possible. For processes which are well defined for every h, it can be shown that the limit of every discrete-time solution as h tends to zero, will be the continuous solutions derived here (see Samuelson [35]).

[9] What is "small" depends on the particular process being modeled. For the orders of magnitude typically found for the moments (mean, variance, skewness, etc.) of annual returns on common stocks, daily intervals ($h = 1/270$) are small. The essential test is: for what h does the distribution of returns become sufficiently "compact" in the Samuelson [35] sense?

making that the consumer-investor know at each point in time: (i) the transition probabilities for returns on each asset over the next trading interval (the *investment opportunity set*); and (ii) the transition probabilities for returns on assets in future periods (i.e., knowledge of the stochastic processes of the changes in the investment opportunity set). Unlike a single-period maximizer who, by definition, does not consider events beyond the present period, the intertemporal maximizer in selecting his portfolio takes into account the relationship between current period returns and returns that will be available in the future. For example, suppose that the current return on a particular asset is negatively correlated with changes in yields ("capitalization" rates). Then, by holding this asset, the investor expects a higher return on the asset if, ex post, yield opportunities next period are lower than were expected.

A brief description of the supply side of the asset market will be helpful in understanding the relationship between current returns on assets and changes in the investment opportunity set.

An asset is defined as a production technology which is a probability distribution for cash flow (valued in consumption units) and physical depreciation, as a function of the amount of capital, $K(t)$ (measured in physical units, e.g., number of machines), employed at time t. The price per unit capital in terms of the consumption good is $P_k(t)$, and the value of an asset at time t, $V(t)$, equals $P_k(t)K(t)$. The return on the asset over a period of length h will be the cash flow, X, plus the value of undepreciated capital, $(1 - \lambda)P_k(t + h)K(t)$ (where λ is the rate of physical depreciation of capital), minus the initial value of the asset, $V(t)$. The total change in the value of the asset outstanding, $V(t + h) - V(t)$, is equal to the sum of the return on the asset plus the value of gross new investment in excess of cash flow, $P_k(t + h)[K(t + h) - (1 - \lambda)K(t)] - X$.

Each firm in the model is assumed to invest in a single asset and to issue one class of securities, called equity.[10] Hence, the terms "firm" and "asset" can be used interchangeably. Let $N(t)$ be the number of shares of the firm outstanding and let $P(t)$ be the price per share, where $N(t)$ and $P(t)$ are defined by the difference equations,

$$(1) \qquad P(t + h) \equiv [X + (1 - \lambda)P_k(t + h)K(t)]/N(t)$$

and

$$(2) \qquad N(t + h) \equiv N(t) + [P_k(t + h)[K(t + h) - (1 - \lambda)K(t)] - X]/P(t + h),$$

subject to the initial conditions $P(0) = P$, $N(0) = N$, and $V(0) = N(0)P(0)$. If we assume that all dividend payments to shareholders are accomplished by share

[10] It is assumed that there are no economies or diseconomies to the "packaging" of assets (i.e., no "synergism"). Hence, any "real" firm holding more than one type of asset will be priced as if it held a portfolio of the "firms" in the text. Similarly, it is assumed that all financial leveraging and other capital structure differences are carried out by investors (possibly through financial intermediaries).

repurchase, then from (1) and (2), $[P(t+h) - P(t)]/P(t)$ is the rate of return on the asset over the period, in units of the consumption good.[11]

Since movements from equilibrium to equilibrium through time involve both price and quantity adjustment, a complete analysis would require a description of both the rate of return and change in asset value dynamics. To do so would require a specification of firm behavior in determining the supply of shares, which in turn would require knowledge of the real asset structure (i.e., technology; whether capital is "putty" or "clay"; etc.). In particular, the current returns on firms with large amounts (relative to current cash flow) of non-shiftable capital with low rates of depreciation will tend to be strongly affected by shifts in capitalization rates because, in the short run, most of the adjustment to the new equilibrium will be done by prices.

Since the present paper examines only investor behavior to derive the demands for assets and the relative yield requirements in equilibrium,[12] only the rate of return dynamics will be examined explicitly. Hence, certain variables, taken as exogeneous in the model, would be endogeneous to a full-equilibrium system.

From the assumption of continuous trading (Assumption 7), it is assumed that the returns and the changes in the opportunity set can be described by continuous-time stochastic processes. However, it will clarify the analysis to describe the processes for discrete trading intervals of length h, and then, to consider the limit as h tends to zero.

We assume the following:

ASSUMPTION 8: *The vector set of stochastic processes describing the opportunity set and its changes, is a time-homogeneous*[13] *Markov process.*

ASSUMPTION 9: *Only local changes in the state variables of the process are allowed.*

ASSUMPTION 10: *For each asset in the opportunity set at each point in time t, the expected rate of return per unit time, defined by*

$$\alpha \equiv E_t[(P(t+h) - P(t))/P(t)]/h,$$

[11] In an intertemporal model, it is necessary to define two quantities, such as number of shares and price per share, to distinguish between the two ways in which a firm's value can change. The return part, (1), reflects new additions to wealth, while (2) reflects a reallocation of capital among alternative assets. The former is important to the investor in selecting his portfolio while the latter is important in (determining) maintaining equilibrium through time. The definition of price per share used here (except for cash dividends) corresponds to the way open-ended, mutual funds determine asset value per share, and seems to reflect accurately the way the term is normally used in a portfolio context.

[12] While the analysis is not an equilibrium one in the strict sense because we do not develop the supply side, the derived model is as much an equilibrium model as the "exchange" model of Mossin [29]. Because his is a one-period model, he could take supplies as fixed. To assume this over time is nonsense.

[13] While it is not necessary to assume that the processes are independent of calendar time, nothing of content is lost by it. However, when a state variable is declared as constant in the text, we really mean non-stochastic. Thus, the term "constant" is used to describe variables which are deterministic functions of time.

and the variance of the return per unit time, defined by

$$\sigma^2 \equiv E_t[([P(t+h) - P(t)]/P(t) - \alpha h)^2]/h,$$

exist, are finite with $\sigma^2 > 0$, and are (right) continuous functions of h, where "E_t" is the conditional expectation operator, conditional on the levels of the state variables at time t. In the limit as h tends to zero, α is called the instantaneous expected return and σ^2 the instantaneous variance of the return.

Assumption 8 is not very restrictive since it is not required that the stochastic processes describing returns be Markov by themselves, but only that by the "expansion of the state" (supplementary variables) technique [7, p. 262] to include (a finite number of) other variables describing the changes in the transition probabilities, the entire (expanded) set be Markov. This generalized use of the Markov assumption for the returns is important because one would expect that the required returns will depend on other variables besides the price per share (e.g., the relative supplies of assets).

Assumption 9 is the discrete-time analog to the continuous-time assumption of continuity in the state variables (i.e., if $X(t+h)$ is the random state variable, then, with probability one, $\lim_{h\to 0}[X(t+h) - X(t)] = 0$). In words, it says that over small time intervals, price changes (returns) and changes in the opportunity set are small. This restriction is non-trivial since the implied "smoothness" rules out Pareto-Levy or Poisson-type jump processes.[14]

Assumption 10 ensures that, for small time intervals, the uncertainty neither "washes out" (i.e., $\sigma^2 = 0$) nor dominates the analysis (i.e., $\sigma^2 = \infty$). Actually, Assumption 10 follows from Assumptions 8 and 9 (see [**13**, p. 321]).

If we let $\{X(t)\}$ stand for the vector stochastic process, then Assumptions 8–10 imply that, in the limit as h tends to zero, $X(t)$ is a diffusion process with continuous state-space changes and that the transition probabilities will satisfy a (multi-dimensional) Fokker-Planck or Kolmogorov partial differential equation.

Although these partial differential equations are sufficient for study of the transition probabilities, it is useful to write down the explicit return dynamics in stochastic difference equation form and then, by taking limits, in stochastic differential equation form. From the previous analysis, we can write the returns dynamics as

$$\frac{P(t+h) - P(t)}{P(t)} = \alpha h + \sigma y(t)\sqrt{h}, \tag{3}$$

where, by construction, $E_t(y) = 0$ and $E_t(y^2) = 1$, and $y(t)$ is a purely random process; that is, $y(t)$ and $y(t+s)$, for $s > 0$, are identically distributed and mutually

[14] While a similar analysis can be performed for Poisson-type processes (see Kushner [**18**] and Merton [**25**]) and for the subordinated processes of Press [**30**] and Clark [**6**], most of the results derived under the continuity assumption will not obtain in these cases.

independent.[15] If we define the stochastic process, $z(t)$, by

$$z(t + h) = z(t) + y(t)\sqrt{h}, \tag{4}$$

then $z(t)$ is a stochastic process with independent increments. If it is further assumed that $y(t)$ is Gaussian distributed,[16] then the limit as h tends to zero of $z(t + h) - z(t)$ describes a Wiener process or Brownian motion. In the formalism of stochastic differential equations,

$$dz \equiv y(t)\sqrt{dt}. \tag{5}$$

In a similar fashion, we can take the limit of (3) to derive the stochastic differential equation for the instantaneous return on the ith asset as

$$\frac{dP_i}{P_i} = \alpha_i\, dt + \sigma_i\, dz_i. \tag{6}$$

Processes such as (6) are called Itô processes and while they are continuous, they are not differentiable.[17]

From (6), a sufficient set of statistics for the opportunity set at a given point in time is $\{\alpha_i, \sigma_i, \rho_{ij}\}$ where ρ_{ij} is the instantaneous correlation coefficient between the Wiener processes dz_i and dz_j. The vector of return dynamics as described in (6) will be Markov only if α_i, σ_i, and ρ_{ij} were, at most, functions of the P's. In general, one would not expect this to be the case since, at each point in time, equilibrium clearing conditions will define a set of implicit functions between equilibrium market values, $V_i(t) = N_i(t)P_i(t)$, and the α_i, σ_i, and ρ_{ij}. Hence, one would expect the changes in required expected returns to be stochastically related to changes in market values, and dependence on P solely would obtain only if changes in N (changes in supplies) were non-stochastic. Therefore, to close the system, we append the dynamics for the changes in the opportunity set over time: namely,

$$\begin{aligned} d\alpha_i &= a_i\, dt + b_i\, dq_i, \\ d\sigma_i &= f_i\, dt + g_i\, dx_i, \end{aligned} \tag{7}$$

where we do assume that (6) and (7), together, form a Markov system,[18] with dq_i and dx_i standard Wiener processes.

[15] It is sufficient to assume that the $y(t)$ are uncorrelated and that the higher order moments are $o(1/\sqrt{h})$. This assumption is consistent with a weak form of the efficient markets hypothesis of Samuelson [**33**] and Fama [**10**]. See Merton and Samuelson [**27**] for further discussion.

[16] While the Gaussian assumption is not necessary for the analysis, the generality gained by not making the assumption is more apparent than real, since it can be shown that all continuous diffusion processes can be described as functions of Brownian motion (see Feller [**13**, p. 326] and Itô and McKean [**16**]).

[17] See Merton [**25**] for a discussion of Itô processes in a portfolio context. For a general discussion of stochastic differential equations of the Itô type, see Itô and McKean [**16**], McKean [**22**], and Kushner [**18**].

[18] It is assumed that the dynamics of α and σ reflect the changes in the supply of shares as well as other factors such as new technical developments. The particular derivation of the dz_i in the text implies that the ρ_{ij} are constants. However, the analysis could be generalized by appending an additional set of dynamics to include changes in the ρ_{ij}.

Under the assumptions of continuous trading and the continuous Markov structure of the stochastic processes, it has been shown that the instantaneous, first two moments of the distributions are sufficient statistics.[19] Further, by the existence and boundedness of α and σ, P equal to zero is a natural absorbing barrier ensuring limited liability of all assets.

For the rest of the paper, it is assumed that there are n distinct[20] risky assets and one "instantaneously risk-less" asset. "Instantaneously risk-less" means that, at each instant of time, each investor knows with certainty that he can earn rate of return $r(t)$ over the next instant by holding the asset (i.e., $\sigma_{n+1} = 0$ and $\alpha_{n+1} \equiv r(t)$). However, the future values of $r(t)$ are not known with certainty (i.e., $b_{n+1} \neq 0$ in (7)). We interpret this asset as the exchange asset and $r(t)$ as the instantaneous private sector borrowing (and lending) rate. Alternatively, the asset could represent (very) short government bonds.

4. PREFERENCE STRUCTURE AND BUDGET EQUATION DYNAMICS

We assume that there are K consumer-investors with preference structures as described in [**25**]: namely, the kth consumer acts so as to

$$\text{(8)} \qquad \max E_0\left[\int_0^{T^k} U^k[c^k(s), s]\, ds + B^k[W^k(T^k), T^k]\right],$$

where "E_0" is the conditional expectation operator, conditional on the current value of his wealth, $W^k(0) = W^k$ are the state variables of the investment opportunity set, and T^k is the distribution for his age of death (which is assumed to be independent of investment outcomes). His instantaneous consumption flow at age t is $c^k(t)$.[21] U^k is a strictly concave von Neumann-Morgenstern utility function for consumption and B^k is a strictly concave "bequest" or utility-of-terminal wealth function.

Dropping the superscripts (except where required for clarity), we can write the accumulation equation for the kth investor as[22]

$$\text{(9)} \qquad dW = \sum_1^{n+1} w_i W\, dP_i/P_i + (y - c)\, dt,$$

where $w_i \equiv N_i P_i / W$ is the fraction of his wealth invested in the ith asset, N_i is the number of shares of the ith asset he owns, and y is his wage income. Substituting

[19] Since these are sufficient statistics, if there are $n + 1$ assets and n is finite, then our assumption of a finite vector for X is satisfied.

[20] "Distinct" means that none of the assets' returns can be written as an (instantaneous) linear combination of the other assets' returns. Hence, the instantaneous variance-covariance matrix of returns, $\Omega = [\sigma_{ij}]$, is non-singular.

[21] Because the paper is primarily interested in finding equilibrium conditions for the asset markets, the model assumes a single consumption good. The model could be generalized by making c^k a vector and introducing as state variables the relative prices. While the analysis would be similar to the one-good case, there would be systematic effects on the portfolio demands reflecting hedging behavior against unfavorable shifts in relative consumption goods prices (i.e., in the consumption opportunity set).

[22] See Merton [**25**] for a derivation of (9).

for dP_i/P_i from (6), we can re-write (9) as

$$(10)\qquad dW = \left[\sum_1^n w_i(\alpha_i - r) + r\right] W\,dt + \sum_1^n w_i W \sigma_i\,dz_i + (y - c)\,dt,$$

where his choice for $w_1, w_2, \ldots, w_n$ is unconstrained because w_{n+1} can always be chosen to satisfy the budget constraint $\Sigma_1^{n+1} w_i = 1$.

From the budget constraint, $W = \Sigma_1^{n+1} N_i P_i$, and the accumulation equation (9), we have that

$$(11)\qquad (y - c)\,dt = \sum_1^{n+1} dN_i(P_i + dP_i),$$

i.e., the net value of new shares purchased must equal the value of savings from wage income.

5. THE EQUATIONS OF OPTIMALITY: THE DEMAND FUNCTIONS FOR ASSETS

For computational simplicity, we will assume that investors derive all their income from capital gains sources (i.e., $y \equiv 0$),[23] and for notational simplicity, we introduce the state-variable vector, X, whose m elements, x_i, denote the current levels of P, α, and σ. The dynamics for X are written as the vector Itô process,

$$(12)\qquad dX = F(X)\,dt + G(X)\,dQ,$$

where F is the vector $[f_1, f_2, \ldots, f_m]$, G is a diagonal matrix with diagonal elements $[g_1, g_2, \ldots, g_m]$, dQ is the vector Wiener process $[dq_1, dq_2, \ldots, dq_m]$, η_{ij} is the instantaneous correlation coefficient between dq_i and dz_j, and v_{ij} is the instantaneous correlation coefficient between dq_i and dq_j.

I have shown elsewhere[24] that the necessary optimality conditions for an investor who acts according to (8) in choosing his consumption-investment program are that, at each point in time,

$$(13)\qquad 0 = \max_{\{c,w\}}\left[U(c,t) + J_t + J_W\left[\left(\sum_1^n w_i(\alpha_i - r) + r\right)W - c\right] + \sum_1^m J_i f_i + \tfrac{1}{2} J_{WW} \sum_1^n \sum_1^n w_i w_j \sigma_{ij} W^2 + \sum_1^m \sum_1^n J_{iW} w_j W g_i \sigma_j \eta_{ij} + \frac{1}{2}\sum_1^m \sum_1^m J_{ij} g_i g_j v_{ij}\right],$$

[23] The analysis would be the same with wage income, provided that investors can issue shares against future income, since we can always redefine wealth as including capitalized future wage income. However, since institutionally this cannot be done, the introduction of wage income will cause systematic effects on the portfolio and consumption decisions.

[24] See Merton [23 and 25]. $J(W, t, X) \equiv \max E_t\{\int_t^T U(c, s)\,ds + B[W(T), T]\}$ and is called the "derived" utility of wealth function. Substituting from (14) and (15) to eliminate w_i and c in (13) makes (13) a partial differential equation for J, subject to the boundary condition $J(W, T, X) = B(W, T)$. Having solved for J, we then substitute for J and its derivatives in (14) and (15) to find the optimal rules (w_i, c).

subject to $J(W, T, X) = B(W, T)$, where subscripts on the "derived" utility of wealth function, J, denote partial derivatives. The σ_{ij} are the instantaneous covariances between the returns on the ith and jth assets ($\equiv \sigma_i \sigma_j \rho_{ij}$).

The $n + 1$ first-order conditions derived from (13) are

$$(14) \qquad 0 = U_c(c, t) - J_W(W, t, X),$$

and

$$(15) \qquad 0 = J_W(\alpha_i - r) + J_{WW} \sum_1^n w_j W \sigma_{ij} + \sum_1^m J_{jW} g_j \sigma_i \eta_{ji} \qquad (i = 1, 2, \ldots, n),$$

where $c = c(W, t, X)$ and $w_i = w_i(W, t, X)$ are the optimum consumption and portfolio rules as functions of the state variables. Equation (14) is the usual intertemporal envelope condition to equate the marginal utility of current consumption to the marginal utility of wealth (future consumption). The manifest characteristic of (15) is its linearity in the portfolio demands; hence, we can solve explicitly for these functions by matrix inversion,

$$(16) \qquad w_i W = A \sum_1^n v_{ij}(\alpha_j - r) + \sum_1^m \sum_1^n H_k \sigma_j g_k \eta_{jk} v_{ij} \qquad (i = 1, 2, \ldots, n),$$

where the v_{ij} are the elements of the inverse of the instantaneous variance-covariance matrix of returns, $\Omega = [\sigma_{ij}]$, $A \equiv -J_W/J_{WW}$, and $H_k \equiv -J_{kW}/J_{WW}$.

Some insight in interpreting (16) can be gained by expressing A and H_k in terms of the utility and consumption functions: namely, by the implicit function theorem applied to (14),

$$(17) \qquad A = -U_c \Big/ \left(U_{cc} \frac{\partial c}{\partial W} \right) > 0,$$

and

$$(18) \qquad H_k = -\frac{\partial c}{\partial x_k} \Big/ \frac{\partial c}{\partial W} \lesseqgtr 0.$$

From (17) and (18), we can interpret the demand function (16) as having two components. The first term, $A \Sigma_1^n v_{ij}(\alpha_j - r)$, is the usual demand function for a risky asset by a single-period mean-variance maximizer, where A is proportional to the reciprocal of the investor's absolute risk aversion.[25] The second term, $\Sigma_1^m \Sigma_1^n H_k \sigma_j g_k \eta_{jk} v_{ij}$, reflects his demand for the asset as a vehicle to hedge against "unfavorable" shifts in the investment opportunity set. An "unfavorable" shift in the opportunity set variable x_k is defined as a change in x_k such that (future) consumption will fall for a given level of (future) wealth. An example of an unfavorable shift would be if $\partial c/\partial x_k < 0$ and x_k increased.

It can be shown, by differentiating (16) with respect to η_{ij}, that all risk-averse utility maximizers will attempt to hedge against such shifts in the sense that if $\partial c/\partial x_k < (>) 0$, then, ceteris paribus, they will demand more of the ith asset, the

[25] See Merton [**26**, equation (36)].

more positively (negatively) correlated its return is with changes in x_k. Thus, if the ex post opportunity set is less favorable than was anticipated, the investor will expect to be compensated by a higher level of wealth through the positive correlation of the returns. Similarly, if ex post returns are lower, he will expect a more favorable investment environment.

Although this behavior implies a type of intertemporal consumption "smoothing," it is not the traditional type of maintenance of a constant level of consumption, but rather it reflects an attempt to minimize the (unanticipated) variability in consumption over time. A simple example will illustrate the point. Assume a single risky asset, a riskless asset with return r, and X a scalar (e.g., $X = r$). Further, require that $\alpha = r$. Standard portfolio analysis would show that a risk-averse investor would invest all his wealth in the riskless asset (i.e., $w = 0$). Consider the (instantaneous) variance of his consumption which, by Itô's Lemma,[26] can be written as $[c_x^2 g^2 + c_W^2 w^2 W^2 \sigma^2 + 2c_x c_W w W g \sigma \eta]$, where subscripts denote partial derivatives of the (optimal) consumption function. Simple differentiation will show that this variance is minimized at $wW = -c_x \eta g/\sigma c_W$, which is exactly the demand given by (16), and for $c_x < 0$ and $\eta > 0$, $w > 0$. Thus, an intertemporal investor who currently faces a five per cent interest rate and a possible interest rate of either two or ten per cent next period will have portfolio demands different from a single-period maximizer in the same environment or an intertemporal maximizer facing a constant interest rate of five per cent over time.

While we have derived explicit expressions for the portfolio demands and given some interpretation of their meaning, further analysis at this level of generality is difficult. While some further results could be gained by restricting the class of utility functions (see Merton [**25**, p. 402]), a more fruitful approach is to add some additional (simplifying) assumptions to restrict the structure of the opportunity set.

6. CONSTANT INVESTMENT OPPORTUNITY SET

The simplest form of the model occurs when the investment opportunity set is constant through time (i.e., α, r, and Ω are constants), and from (6), the distributions for price per share will be log-normal for all assets. This form of the model is examined in detail in Merton [**25**, p. 384–88], and hence, the main results are presented without proof.

In this case, the demand for the ith asset by the kth investor, (16), reduces to

$$w_i^k W^k = A^k \sum_1^n v_{ij}(\alpha_j - r) \qquad (i = 1, 2, \ldots, n), \tag{19}$$

which is the same demand that a one-period[27] risk-averse mean-variance investor would have. If all investors agree on the investment opportunity set

[26] Itô's Lemma is the analog to the Fundamental Theorem of the calculus for Itô processes. See Merton [**25**, p. 375] for a brief description and McKean [**22**, p. 32] for a formal proof.

[27] Of course, since "one period" is an instant, a meaningful interpretation is that investors behave myopically.

(homogeneous expectations), then the ratio of the demands for risky assets will be independent of preferences, and the same for all investors. Further, we have the following theorem.

THEOREM 1:[28] *Given n risky assets whose returns are log-normally distributed and a riskless asset, then (i) there exists a unique pair of efficient portfolios ("mutual funds") one containing only the riskless asset and the other only risky assets, such that, independent of preferences, wealth distribution, or time horizon, all investors will be indifferent between choosing portfolios from among the original n + 1 assets or from these two funds; (ii) the distribution of the return on the risky fund is log-normal; (iii) the proportion of the risky fund's assets invested in the kth asset is*

$$\sum_1^n v_{kj}(\alpha_j - r) \Big/ \sum_1^n \sum_1^n v_{ij}(\alpha_i - r) \qquad (k = 1, 2, \ldots, n).$$

Theorem 1 is the continuous-time version of the Markowitz-Tobin separation theorem and the holdings of the risky fund correspond to the optimal combination of risky assets (see Sharpe [39, p. 69]).

Using the condition that the market portfolio is efficient in equilibrium, it can be shown (see Merton [26]) that, for this version of the model, the equilibrium returns will satisfy

$$(20) \qquad \alpha_i - r = \beta_i(\alpha_M - r) \qquad (i = 1, 2, \ldots, n),$$

where $\beta_i \equiv \sigma_{iM}/\sigma_M^2$, σ_{iM} is the covariance of the return on the ith asset with the return on the market portfolio, and α_M is the expected return on the market portfolio. Equation (20) is the continuous-time analog to the security market line of the classical capital asset pricing model.

Hence, the additional assumption of a constant investment opportunity set is a sufficient condition for investors to behave as if they were single-period maximizers and for the equilibrium return relationship specified by the capital asset pricing model to obtain. Except for some singular cases, this assumption is also necessary.

7. GENERALIZED SEPARATION: A THREE-FUND THEOREM

Unfortunately, the assumption of a constant investment opportunity set is not consistent with the facts, since there exists at least one element of the opportunity set which is directly observable: namely, the interest rate, and it is definitely

[28] Theorem 1 is stated and proved in a more general form, including the possibility of no riskless asset, in Merton [25, p. 384]. The uniqueness of the two funds is ensured by the requirement that one fund hold only the riskless asset and the other only risky assets, and that both funds be efficient. Otherwise, the funds are unique only up to a non-singular, linear transformation. A further requirement is that

$$r < \sum_1^n \sum_1^n v_{ij}\alpha_j \Big/ \sum_1^n \sum_1^n v_{ij}.$$

However, since this is a necessary condition for equilibrium, it is assumed to be satisfied. See Merton [26] for a complete discussion of this point.

changing stochastically over time. The simplest form of the model consistent with this observation occurs if it is assumed that a single state variable is sufficient to describe changes in the opportunity set. We further assume that this variable is the interest rate (i.e., $\alpha_i = \alpha_i(r)$ and $\sigma_i = \sigma_i(r)$).

The interest rate has always been an important variable in portfolio theory, general capital theory, and to practitioners. It is observable, satisfies the condition of being stochastic over time, and while it is surely not the sole determinant of yields on other assets,[28] it is an important factor. Hence, one should interpret the effects of a changing interest rate in the forthcoming analysis in the way economists have generally done in the past: namely, as a single (instrumental) variable representation of shifts in the investment opportunity set. For example, $\partial c/\partial r$ is the change in consumption due to a change in the opportunity set for a fixed level of wealth.

This assumed, we can write the kth investor's demand function for the ith asset, (16), as

$$d_i^k = A^k \sum_1^n v_{ij}(\alpha_j - r) + H^k \sum_1^n v_{ij}\sigma_{jr} \qquad (i = 1, 2, \ldots, n), \tag{21}$$

where $d_i^k \equiv w_i^k W^k$; $H^k \equiv -(\partial c^k/\partial r)/(\partial c^k/\partial W^k)$, and σ_{jr} is the (instantaneous) covariance between the return on the jth asset and changes in the interest rate $(\equiv \rho_{jr}\sigma_j g)$. By inspection of (21), the ratio of the demands for risky assets is a function of preferences, and hence, the standard separation theorem does not obtain. However, generalized separation (see [5]) does obtain. In particular, it will be shown that all investors' optimal portfolios can be represented as a linear combination of three mutual funds (portfolios).

Although not necessary for the theorem, it will throw light on the analysis to assume there exists an asset (by convention, the nth one) whose return is perfectly negatively correlated with changes in r, i.e., $\rho_{nr} = -1$. One such asset might be riskless (in terms of default), long-term bonds.[30] In this case, we can re-write the covariance term σ_{jr} as

$$\begin{aligned} \sigma_{jr} &= \rho_{jr}\sigma_j g, \\ &= -g(\rho_{jn}\sigma_j\sigma_n)/\sigma_n, \quad \text{because } \rho_{jr} = -\rho_{jn}, \\ &= -g\sigma_{jn}/\sigma_n, \end{aligned} \tag{22}$$

where g is the standard deviation of the change in r. From (22), we can write the second term in the demand function (21), $\Sigma_1^n v_{ij}\sigma_{jr}$, as $-g(\Sigma_1^n v_{ij}\sigma_{jn})/\sigma_n$ which equals zero for $i \neq n$ and equals $(-g/\sigma_n)$ for $i = n$, because the v_{ij} are the elements of the inverse of the variance-covariance matrix of returns.[31] Hence, we can

[29] The reader should not interpret this statement as implying a causal relationship between interest rates and yields. All that is questioned is whether there exists an implicit functional relationship between the interest rate and other yields.

[30] We only interpret this asset as a long-term bond as a conceptual device. Although long-term bonds will be highly correlated with short rate changes, it is quite likely that they are not perfectly correlated.

[31] I am indebted to Fischer Black for pointing out this simplification.

re-write (21) in the simplified form,

$$d_i^k = A^k \sum_1^n v_{ij}(\alpha_j - r) \qquad (i = 1, 2, \ldots, n-1), \tag{23}$$

$$d_n^k = A^k \sum_1^n v_{nj}(\alpha_j - r) - gH^k/\sigma_n.$$

THEOREM 2 ("*Three Fund*" *Theorem*): *Given n risky assets and a riskless asset satisfying the conditions of this section, then there exist three portfolios ("mutual funds") constructed from these assets, such that* (i) *all risk-averse investors, who behave according to* (8), *will be indifferent between choosing portfolios from among the original n* + 1 *assets or from these three funds*; (ii) *the proportions of each fund's portfolio invested in the individual assets are purely "technological"* (*i.e., depend only on the variables in the investment opportunity set for individual assets and not on investor preferences*); *and* (iii) *the investor's demands for the funds do not require knowledge of the investment opportunity set for the individual assets nor of the asset proportions held by the funds.*

PROOF: Let the first fund hold the same proportions as the risky fund in Theorem 1: namely, $\delta_k = \Sigma_1^n v_{kj}(\alpha_j - r)/\Sigma_1^n\Sigma_1^n v_{ij}(\alpha_j - r)$, for $k = 1, 2, \ldots, n$. Let the second fund hold only the nth asset and the third fund only the riskless asset. Let λ_i^k be the fraction of the kth investor's wealth invested in the ith fund, $i = 1, 2, 3$ $(\Sigma_1^3 \lambda_i^k = 1)$. To prove (i), we must show that there exists an allocation $(\lambda_1^k, \lambda_2^k)$ which exactly replicates the demand functions, (23), i.e., that

$$\lambda_1^k \delta_i = (A^k/W^k) \sum_1^n v_{ij}(\alpha_j - r) \qquad (i = 1, 2, \ldots, n-1), \tag{24}$$

$$\lambda_1^k \delta_n + \lambda_2^k = (A^k/W^k) \sum_1^n v_{nj}(\alpha_j - r) - gH^k/\sigma_n W^k.$$

From the definition of δ_i, the allocation $\lambda_1^k = (A^k/W^k)\Sigma_1^n\Sigma_1^n v_{ij}(\alpha_j - r)$ and $\lambda_2^k = -gH^k/\sigma_n W^k$ satisfied (24). Part (ii) follows from the choice for the three funds. To prove (iii), we must show that investors will select this allocation, given only the knowledge of the (aggregated) investment opportunity set, i.e., given $(\alpha, \alpha_n, r, \sigma, \sigma_n, \rho, g)$ where α and σ^2 is the expected return and variance on the first fund's portfolio and ρ is its covariance with the return on the second fund. From the definition of δ_i, it is straightforward to show that $(\alpha - r)/\sigma^2 = \Sigma_1^n \Sigma_1^n v_{ij}(\alpha_i - r)$ and $\rho = \sigma(\alpha_n - r)/\sigma_n(\alpha - r)$. The demand functions for the funds will be of the same form as (23) with $n = 2$, and the proportions derived from these equations are λ_1^k and λ_2^k where λ_1^k can be re-written as $A^k(\alpha - r)/\sigma^2 W^k$. *Q.E.D.*

Theorem 2 is a decentralization theorem which states that if investors believe that professional portfolio managers' estimates of the distribution of returns are at least as good as any the investor might form, then the investment decision can be separated into two parts by the establishment of three financial intermediaries (mutual funds) to hold all individual assets and to issue shares of their own for purchase by individual investors. Funds one and three provide the "service" to investors of an (instantaneously) efficient, risk-return frontier while fund two allows investors to hedge against unfavorable intertemporal shifts in the frontier. Note that the demand for the second fund by the kth investor, $\lambda_2^k W^k$, will be $\gtreqless 0$, depending on whether $\partial c^k/\partial r$ is $\gtreqless 0$, which is consistent with the hedging behavior discussed in the general case of Section 5.

8. THE EQUILIBRIUM YIELD RELATIONSHIP AMONG ASSETS

Given the demand functions (23), we now derive the equilibrium market clearing conditions for the model of Section 7, and from these, derive the equilibrium relationship between the expected return on an individual asset and the expected return on the market.

From (23), the aggregate demand functions, $D_i = \Sigma_1^K d_i^k$, can be written as

$$(25)\qquad D_i = A\sum_1^n v_{ij}(\alpha_j - r) \qquad (i = 1, 2, \ldots, n-1),$$

$$D_n = A\sum_1^n v_{nj}(\alpha_j - r) - Hg/\sigma_n,$$

where $A \equiv \Sigma_1^K A^k$ and $H \equiv \Sigma_1^K H^k$. If N_i is the number of shares supplied by the ith firm and if it is assumed that the asset market is *always* in equilibrium, then

$$(26)\qquad N_i = \sum_1^K N_i^k,$$

$$dN_i = \sum_1^K dN_i^k \qquad (i = 1, 2, \ldots, n+1).$$

Furthermore, $\Sigma_1^{n+1} N_i P_i = \Sigma_1^{n+1} D_i \equiv M$, where M is the (equilibrium) value of all assets, the market.

The equilibrium dynamics for market value can be written as

$$(27)\qquad dM = \sum_1^{n+1} N_i\, dP_i + \sum_1^{n+1} dN_i(P_i + dP_i)$$

$$= \sum_1^K dW^k$$

$$= \sum_1^{n+1} D_i\, dP_i/P_i + \sum_1^K (y^i - c^i)\, dt.$$

Hence, changes in the value of the market come about by capital gains on current shares outstanding (the first term) and by expansion of the total number of shares outstanding (the second term). To separate the two effects, we use the same technique employed to solve this problem for the individual firm: namely, let P_M be the price per "share" of the market portfolio and let N be the number of shares where $NP_M \equiv M$. Then, $dM = N\, dP_M + dN(P_M + dP_M)$, and P_M and N are defined by the stochastic differential equations

$$(28)\qquad N\,dP_M \equiv \sum_1^{n+1} N_i\,dP_i,$$

$$dN(P_M + dP_M) \equiv \sum_1^{n+1} dN_i(P_i + dP_i),$$

where, by construction, dP_M/P_M is the rate of return on the market (portfolio).
Substituting from (27) into (28) and using (11), we have

$$(29)\qquad dN(P_M + dP_M) = \sum_1^{K} (y^i - c^i)\,dt,$$

$$N\,dP_M = \sum_1^{n+1} D_i\,dP_i/P_i.$$

If $w_i \equiv N_iP_i/M = D_i/M$, the percentage contribution of the ith firm to total market value, then, from (6) and (29), the rate of return on the market can be written as

$$(30)\qquad \frac{dP_M}{P_M} = \left[\sum_1^n w_j(\alpha_j - r) + r\right]dt + \sum_1^n w_j\sigma_j\,dz_j.$$

Substituting w_iM for D_i in (25), we can solve for the equilibrium expected returns on the individual assets:

$$(31)\qquad \alpha_i - r = (M/A)\sum_1^n w_j\sigma_{ij} + (Hg/A\sigma_n)\sigma_{in} \qquad (i = 1, 2, \ldots, n).$$

As with any asset, we can define $\alpha_M(\equiv \Sigma_1^n w_j(\alpha_j - r) + r)$, $\sigma_{iM}(\equiv \Sigma_1^n w_j\sigma_{ij})$, and $\sigma_M^2(\equiv \Sigma_1^n w_j\sigma_{jM})$ as the (instantaneous) expected return, covariance, and variance of the market portfolio. Then (31) can be re-written as

$$(32)\qquad \alpha_i - r = (M/A)\sigma_{iM} + (Hg/A\sigma_n)\sigma_{in} \qquad (i = 1, 2, \ldots, n),$$

and multiplying (32) by w_i and summing, we have

$$(33)\qquad \alpha_M - r = (M/A)\sigma_M^2 + (Hg/A\sigma_n)\sigma_{Mn}.$$

Noting that the nth asset satisfies (32), we can use it together with (33) to re-write (32) as

$$(34)\qquad \alpha_i - r = \frac{\sigma_i[\rho_{iM} - \rho_{in}\rho_{nM}]}{\sigma_M(1 - \rho_{nM}^2)}(\alpha_M - r) + \frac{\sigma_i[\rho_{in} - \rho_{iM}\rho_{nM}]}{\sigma_n(1 - \rho_{Mn}^2)}(\alpha_n - r)$$

$$(i = 1, 2, \ldots, n - 1).$$

Equation (34) states that, in equilibrium, investors are compensated in terms of expected return, for bearing market (systematic) risk, and for bearing the risk of unfavorable (from the point of view of the aggregate) shifts in the investment opportunity set; and it is a natural generalization of the security market line of the classical capital asset pricing model. Note that if a security has no market risk (i.e., $\beta_i = 0 = \rho_{iM}$), its expected return will not be equal to the riskless rate as forecast by the usual model.

Under what conditions will the security market plane equation (34) reduce to the (continuous-time) classical security market line, equation (20)? From inspection of the demand equations (21), appropriately aggregated, the conditions are

$$\text{(35a)} \qquad H = \sum_{1}^{K} -(\partial c^k/\partial r)/(\partial c^k/\partial W^k) \equiv 0$$

or

$$\text{(35b)} \qquad \sigma_{ir} \equiv 0 \qquad (i = 1, 2, \ldots, n).$$

There is no obvious reason to believe that (35a) should hold unless $\partial c^k/\partial r \equiv 0$ for each investor, and the only additive utility function for which this is so is the Bernoulli logarithmic one.[32] Condition (35b) could obtain in two ways: $g \equiv 0$, i.e., the interest rate is non-stochastic, which is not so; or $\rho_{ir} \equiv 0$, i.e., all assets' returns are uncorrelated with changes in the interest rate. While this condition is possible, it would not be a true equilibrium state.

Suppose that by a quirk of nature, $\rho_{ir} \equiv 0$ for all available real assets. Then, since the nth asset does not exist, (34) reduces to (20). Consider constructing a "man-made" security (e.g., a long-term bond) which is perfectly negatively correlated with changes in the interest rates, and hence, by assumption, not correlated with any other asset or the market (i.e., $\beta_n = 0$). Since $D_n = 0$, we have, from (25), that $(\alpha_n - r) = Hg\sigma_n \neq 0$, if $g \neq 0$ and $H \neq 0$. Thus, even though security n has a zero beta, investors will pay a premium (relative to the riskless rate) to other investors for creating this security.

An implication of this analysis for the theory of the term structure of interest rates, is that long-term, riskless bonds will not satisfy the expectations hypothesis ($\alpha_n = r$), even if they have no market risk. The premium charged is not a liquidity premium, and it will be either positive or negative depending on the sign of H. These results are consistent with the "habitat" theory (see [**28**]), if one interprets habitat as a stronger (or weaker) preference to hedge against changes in future investment opportunities.

9. EMPIRICAL EVIDENCE

Although the model has not been formally tested, we can do some preliminary analysis using the findings of Black, Jensen, and Scholes (BJS) [3] and some later, unpublished work of Scholes [37]. As mentioned earlier, they found that portfolios constructed to have zero covariance with the market (i.e., $\beta = 0$) had average returns that significantly exceeded the riskless rate which suggests that there is (at least) another factor besides the market that systematically affects the returns on securities. They call this second factor the "beta factor" because an individual security's covariance with it is a function of the security's beta. In particular,

[32] Hence (20) would be the correct specification for the equilibrium relationships among expected returns in the "growth optimum" model even when the investment opportunity set is not constant through time.

high-beta ($\beta > 1$) stocks had negative correlation and low-beta ($\beta < 1$) stocks had positive correlation. We can summarize the BJS specification and empirical findings as follows:

(36) $$\alpha_i - r = \beta_i(\alpha_M - r) + \gamma_i(\alpha_0 - r),$$

where α_0 is the expected return on the "zero-beta" portfolio, and

(37a) $$\alpha_0 > r;$$

(37b) $$\gamma_i = \gamma_i(\beta_i) \quad \text{with} \quad \gamma_i(1) = 0, \quad \text{and} \quad \partial\gamma_i/\partial\beta_i < 0.$$

While the finding of a second factor is consistent with the a priori specification of our model, it cannot be said that their specific findings are in agreement with the model without some further specification of the effect of a shift in r on the investment opportunity set. However, if a shift in r is an instrumental variable for a shift in capitalization rates generally, then an argument can be made that the two are in agreement.

The plan is to show that qualitative characteristics of the coefficient $(\rho_{in} - \rho_{iM}\rho_{nM})\sigma_i/\sigma_n(1 - \rho_{nM}^2)$ in (34) as a function of β_i would be the same as γ_i in (37b), and that the empirical characteristics of the zero-beta portfolio are similar to those of a portfolio of long term bonds.

If we take the classical security market line, $\alpha_i = r + \beta_i\lambda$, where $\lambda \equiv (\alpha_M - r)$, as a reasonable approximation to the relationship among capitalization rates, α_i, then we can compute the logarithmic elasticity of α_i with respect to r as a function of β_i, to be

(38) $$\psi(\beta_i) \equiv r(1 + \beta_i\lambda')/(r + \beta_i\lambda),$$

where $\lambda' \equiv \partial\lambda/\partial r$, the change in the slope of the security market line with a change in r. From (27) we have that this elasticity is almost certainly a monotone decreasing function of β_i since $\psi'(\beta_i) \equiv \partial\psi/\partial\beta_i < 0$ if $\psi(1) < 1$.[33]

If we write the value of firm i as $V_i \equiv \bar{X}_i/\alpha_i$ where $\bar{X}_i$ is the "long-run" expected earnings and α_i, the rate at which they are capitalized, then the percentage change in firm value due to a change in r can be written as

(39) $$\left(\frac{dV_i}{V_i}\right)_r \equiv \left[\frac{\partial\bar{X}_i}{\partial r}\bigg/\bar{X}_i - \frac{\partial\alpha_i}{\partial r}\bigg/\alpha_i\right] dr.$$

If we neglect, as second-order, the effect of a shift in r on expected future earnings, then the residual effect on return due to a change in r, after taking out the common market factor, will be a systematic function of β_i:

(40) $$\begin{aligned} d\varepsilon(\beta_i) &\equiv \left(\frac{dV_i}{V_i}\right)_r - \beta_i\left(\frac{dV_M}{V_M}\right)_r \\ &= -\psi(\beta_i)\frac{dr}{r} + \beta_i\psi(1)\frac{dr}{r} \\ &= -\phi(\beta_i)\frac{dr}{r} \end{aligned}$$

[33] $\psi(1) \geqslant 1$ would imply that $\lambda'/\lambda \geqslant 1/r$ which, for typical values of r, would imply a very large, positive increase in the slope of the security market line. It is contended that such a shift would be highly unlikely.

where $\phi(\beta_i) \equiv \psi(\beta_i) - \beta_i\psi(1)$ satisfies $\phi(1) = 0$ and $\phi'(\beta_i) < 0$. From (40), the correlation coefficient between $d\varepsilon$ and dr, $\rho_{\varepsilon r}$, will satisfy

$$\rho_{\varepsilon r} \gtreqless 0 \quad \text{as} \quad \beta_i \lesseqgtr 1. \tag{41}$$

From the definition of $d\varepsilon$ in (40), $\rho_{\varepsilon r}$ is the partial correlation coefficient, $\rho_{ir} - \rho_{iM}\rho_{rM}$. By definition the nth asset in (34) is perfectly negatively correlated with changes in r. Hence (41) can be rewritten as

$$\rho_{in} - \rho_{iM}\rho_{nM} \lesseqgtr 0 \quad \text{as} \quad \beta_i \lesseqgtr 1. \tag{42}$$

Hence the coefficient of $(\alpha_n - r)$ in (34) could be expected to have the same properties as γ_i in (36) and (37b).

It still remains to be determined whether the zero-beta portfolio is a proxy for our long-term bond portfolio. Since there are no strong theoretical grounds for $(\alpha_n - r)$ to be positive[34] and since the zero-beta portfolio is an empirical construct, we resort to an indirect empirical argument based on the findings of BJS and Scholes.

Since Scholes found the correlation between the market portfolio and the bond portfolio, ρ_{Mn}, to be close to zero and the correlation between the zero-beta portfolio and the bond portfolio to be significantly positive, it then follows from (36) that one would expect to find $(\alpha_n - r)$ significantly positive.

While the analysis of this section can only be called preliminary, the model specification of Section 7 does seem to be more consistent with the data than the capital asset pricing model.[35]

10. CONCLUSION

An intertemporal model of the capital market has been developed which is consistent with both the expected utility maxim and the limited liability of assets. It was shown that the equilibrium relationships among expected returns specified by the classical capital asset pricing model will obtain only under very special additional assumptions. Whether the special form of the general model presented in Sections 7–9 will explain the empirical discrepancies found in the BJS study is an empirical question as yet unanswered. However, whether it does or not, the main purposes were to illustrate how testable specifications can be generated from the model and to induce those who do it best to pursue further empirical testing.

The model is robust in the sense that it can be extended in an obvious way to include effects other than shifts in the investment opportunity set. Two important factors not considered are wage income and many consumption goods whose relative prices are changing over time. In a more complete model the three-fund

[34] One could argue that $\alpha_n > r$ on the grounds that current consumption is a normal good and, hence, $\partial c/\partial r < 0$ for most people. Also, the existence of wage income would tend to force $\alpha_n > r$. Finally, in a number of studies of the term structure, investigators have found positive premiums on long-term bonds, implying that $\alpha_n > r$.

[35] M. Scholes is in the process of testing the model of Section 7. D. Rie [31] has also examined the effect of capitalization rate changes on the classical capital asset pricing model.

theorem of Section 7 will generalize to an m-fund theorem. Although there was no discussion of the supply side, given a micro theory of the firm, (1), (2), and (29) could be used to close the model.

Massachusetts Institute of Technology

Manuscript received February, 1972; revision received July, 1972.

REFERENCES

[1] ARROW, K. J.: "The Role of Securities in the Optimal Allocation of Risk Bearing," *Review of Economic Studies*, 31 (1964), 91–96.

[2] BLACK, F.: "Capital Market Equilibrium with Restricted Borrowing," *Journal of Business*, 45 (1972), 444–455.

[3] BLACK, F., M. C. JENSEN, AND M. SCHOLES: "The Capital Asset Pricing Model: Some Empirical Tests," in *Studies in the Theory of Capital Markets*, M. C. Jensen, ed. New York: Praeger Publishers, 1972.

[4] BORCH, K.: "A Note on Uncertainty and Indifference Curves," *Review of Economic Studies*, 36 (1969), 1–4.

[5] CASS, D., AND J. E. STIGLITZ: "The Structure of Investor Preferences and Asset Returns, and Separability in Portfolio Allocation: A Contribution to the Pure Theory of Mutual Funds," *Journal of Economic Theory*, 2 (1970), 122–160.

[6] CLARK, P. K.: "A Subordinated Stochastic Process Model with Finite Variance for Speculative Prices," *Econometrica*, 41 (1973), 135–155.

[7] COX, D. A., AND H. D. MILLER: *The Theory of Stochastic Processes*. New York: John Wiley, 1968.

[8] DEBREU, G.: *Theory of Value: An Axiomatic Analysis of Economic Equilibrium*. New York: John Wiley, 1959.

[9] FAMA, E. F.: "Multiperiod Consumption-Investment Decisions," *American Economic Review*, 60 (1970), 163–174.

[10] ———: "Efficient Capital Markets: A Review of Theory and Empirical Work," *Journal of Finance*, 25 (1970), 383–417.

[11] FAMA, E. F., AND M. H. MILLER: *The Theory of Finance*. New York: Holt, Rhinehart, Winston, 1972.

[12] FELDSTEIN, M. S.: "Mean-Variance Analysis in the Theory of Liquidity Preference and Portfolio Selection," *Review of Economic Studies*, 36 (1969), 5–12.

[13] FELLER, W.: *An Introduction to Probability Theory and Its Applications*. Volume 2. New York: John Wiley, 1966.

[14] FRIEND, I., AND M. BLUME: "Measurement of Portfolio Performance under Uncertainty," *American Economic Review*, 60 (1970), 561–575.

[15] HAKANSSON, N. H.: "Capital Growth and the Mean-Variance Approach to Portfolio Selection," *Journal of Financial and Quantitative Analysis*, 6 (1971), 517–557.

[16] ITÔ, K., AND H. P. MCKEAN, JR.: *Diffusion Processes and Their Sample Paths*. New York: Academic Press, 1964.

[17] JENSEN, M. C.: "Capital Markets: Theory and Evidence," *Bell Journal of Economics and Management Science*, 2 (1972), 357–398.

[18] KUSHNER, H. J.: *Stochastic Stability and Control*. New York: Academic Press, 1967.

[19] LINTNER, J.: "The Valuation of Risk Assets and the Selection of Risky Investments in Stock Portfolios and Capital Budgets," *Review of Economics and Statistics*, 47 (1965), 13–37.

[20] ———: "Security Prices, Risk and Maximal Gains from Diversification," *Journal of Finance*, 20 (1965), 587–615.

[21] MARKOWITZ, H.: *Portfolio Selection: Efficient Diversification of Investment*. New York: John Wiley, 1959.

[22] MCKEAN, H. P., JR.: *Stochastic Integrals*. New York: Academic Press, 1969.

[23] MERTON, R. C.: "Lifetime Portfolio Selection under Uncertainty: The Continuous-Time Case," *Review of Economics and Statistics*, 51 (1969), 247–257.

[24] ———: "A Dynamic General Equilibrium Model of the Asset Market and Its Application to the Pricing of the Capital Structure of the Firm," Working Paper 497-70, Sloan School of Management, Massachusetts Institute of Technology, December, 1970.

[25] ———: "Optimum Consumption and Portfolio Rules in a Continuous-time Model," *Journal of Economic Theory*, 3 (1971), 373–413.
[26] ———: "An Analytic Derivation of the Efficient Portfolio Frontier," *Journal of Financial and Quantitative Analysis*, 7 (1972), 1851–1872.
[27] MERTON, R. C., AND P. A. SAMUELSON: "Fallacy of the Asymptotic Log-Normal Approximation in Portfolio Decision Making Over Many Periods," Working Paper 623-72, Sloan School of Management, Massachusetts Institute of Technology, 1972.
[28] MODIGLIANI, F., AND C. R. SUTCH: "Innovations in Interest Rate Policy," *American Economic Review*, 56 (1966), 178–197.
[29] MOSSIN, J.: "Equilibrium in a Capital Asset Market," *Econometrica*, 34 (1966), 768–783.
[30] PRESS, S. J.: "A Compound Events Model for Security Prices," *Journal of Business*, 40 (1967), 317–335.
[31] RIE, D.: "Single Parameter Risk Measures and Multiple Sources of Risk: A Re-Examination of the Data Based on Changes in Determinants of Price Over Time." Working Paper # 14-72, Rodney L. White Center for Financial Research, Wharton School of Finance and Commerce, University of Pennsylvania.
[32] ROLL, R.: "Some Preliminary Evidence on the 'Growth Optimum' Model," Working Paper 3-71-2, Graduate School of Industrial Administration, Carnegie-Mellon University, July, 1971.
[33] SAMUELSON, P. A.: "Proof that Properly Anticipated Prices Fluctuate Randomly," *Industrial Management Review*, 6 (1965), 41–49.
[34] ———: "General Proof that Diversification Pays," *Journal of Financial and Quantitative Analysis*, 2 (1967).
[35] ———: "The Fundamental Approximation Theorem of Portfolio Analysis in Terms of Means, Variances, and Higher Moments," *Review of Economic Studies*, 37 (1970), 537–542.
[36] ———: "The 'Fallacy' of Maximizing the Geometric Mean in Long Sequences of Investing or Gambling," *Proceedings of the National Academy of Sciences*, 68 (1971).
[37] SCHOLES, M.: "The Relationship Between the Returns on Bonds and the Returns on Common Stocks." Mimeograph, Massachusetts Institute of Technology, November, 1971.
[38] SHARPE, W. F.: "Capital Asset Prices: A Theory of Market Equilibrium under Conditions of Risk," *Journal of Finance*, 19 (1964), 425–442.
[39] ———: *Portfolio Theory and Capital Markets*. New York: McGraw-Hill, 1970.
[40] STIGLITZ, J. E.: "A Consumption-Oriented Theory of the Demand for Financial Assets and the Term-Structure of Interest Rates," *Review of Economic Studies*, 37 (1970), 321–351.
[41] ———: "Some Aspects of the Pure Theory of Corporate Finance, Bankruptcies, and Take-Overs," *Bell Journal of Economics and Management Science*, 2 (1972), 458–482.
[42] WELLES, C.: "The Beta Revolution: Learning to Live with Risk," *Institutional Investor* (1971).

[12]

Journal of Financial Economics 7 (1979) 265–296. © North-Holland Publishing Company

AN INTERTEMPORAL ASSET PRICING MODEL WITH STOCHASTIC CONSUMPTION AND INVESTMENT OPPORTUNITIES

Douglas T. BREEDEN*

Stanford University, Stanford, CA 94305, USA

Received October 1978, revised version received July 1979

This paper derives a single-beta asset pricing model in a multi-good, continuous-time model with uncertain consumption-goods prices and uncertain investment opportunities. When no riskless asset exists, a zero-beta pricing model is derived. Asset betas are measured relative to changes in the aggregate real consumption rate, rather than relative to the market. In a single-good model, an individual's asset portfolio results in an optimal consumption rate that has the maximum possible correlation with changes in aggregate consumption. If the capital markets are unconstrained Pareto-optimal, then changes in all individuals' optimal consumption rates are shown to be perfectly correlated.

1. Introduction

The capital asset pricing model (CAPM) of Sharpe (1964) and Lintner (1965) is an important theory of the structure of equilibrium expected returns on securities in the capital markets. Empirical tests of the model have had mixed results, in that security returns do appear to be positively related to their respective measured market 'betas', but not in the precise manner implied by the CAPM.[1] By relaxing the assumptions involved in the derivation of the CAPM, the model has been extended to more general economies, usually at the expense of simplicity in the structure of equilibrium expected returns. This paper further develops the intertemporal extension of the CAPM that was initiated by Merton (1973) in a continuous-time model.

Merton's intertemporal CAPM with stochastic investment opportunities states that the expected excess return on any asset is given by a 'multi-beta' version of the CAPM with the number of betas being equal to one plus the number of state variables needed to describe the relevant characteristics of

*I am grateful for the helpful comments of Sudipto Bhattacharya, George Constantanides, Eugene Fama, Nils Hakansson, Jon Ingersoll, John Long (the referee), Merton Miller, Stephen Ross, Myron Scholes, and especially Robert Litzenberger. Of course, they are not responsible for any remaining errors.

[1]See Jensen (1972) for a survey of many of these results.

the investment opportunity set. Since all of those state variables are not easily identified, this intertemporal extension, while quite important from a theoretical standpoint, is not very tractable for empirical testing, nor is it very useful for financial decision-making. This paper utilizes the *same* continuous-time economic framework as that used by Merton, likewise permitting stochastic investment opportunities. However, it is shown that Merton's multi-beta pricing equation can be collapsed into a single-beta equation, where the instantaneous expected excess return on any security is proportional to its 'beta' (or covariance) with respect to aggregate consumption alone. In this paper, it is also demonstrated that this result extends to a multi-good world, with an asset's beta measured relative to aggregate real consumption. The fact that this model involves a single beta relative to a specific variable, rather than many betas measured relative to unspecified variables, may make it easier to test and to implement, given certain stationarity assumptions on the joint distributions of rates of return and aggregate consumption.

Section 2 presents the continuous-time economic model with stochastic investment opportunities. General versions of the 'mutual fund' theorem of Merton (1973) and Long (1974) and of their multi-beta CAPM are briefly derived. The single-beta, single-good intertemporal CAPM as described above is derived and discussed in section 3. This derivation also generalizes a similar single-beta CAPM derived in a multi-period state preference model by Breeden and Litzenberger (1978). They derived the same pricing equation, but only for assets with cash flows that are jointly lognormally distributed with aggregate consumption. Neither consumption nor asset prices need be lognormally distributed here, but they are assumed to follow diffusion processes. A simple example is presented in section 4 to illustrate the point that the relation of an asset's return with aggregate consumption precisely measures its relevant risk, whereas the return's relation to aggregate wealth is not an adequate measure of an asset's risk.

Section 5 demonstrates that there are intertemporal analogs to the single-period results that state that all individuals' wealths will be perfectly correlated and that each individual's portfolio beta is proportional to his Pratt (1964) – Arrow (1965) measure of relative risk tolerance. In particular, it is proven that changes in all individuals' optimal consumption rates are perfectly correlated at each instant, and each individual's optimal instantaneous standard deviation of changes in consumption is proportional to his relative risk tolerance, if the capital markets permit an unconstrained Pareto-optimal allocation of consumption. For general capital markets, it is shown that each individual's optimal portfolio is such that changes in the individual's optimal consumption rate have the maximum possible correlation with changes in the aggregate consumption rate.

Section 6 presents a derivation of a 'zero-beta' intertemporal CAPM for an economy with no riskless asset. The expected return on the zero-beta portfolio is obtained from a portfolio with returns that are uncorrelated with changes in aggregate consumption. This pricing model is an intertemporal analog to the single-period zero-beta model of Lintner (1969), Black (1972), and Vasicek (1971).

A multi-good extension of the intertemporal CAPM is presented in section 7. Long (1974) has extended Merton's multi-beta model to the multi-good case in a discrete-time economy, but this extension resulted in a pricing equation with even more terms. The focus of this section of the paper is on the derivation of a single-beta CAPM in the multi-good world. It is shown that equilibrium expected excess real returns on assets are proportional to the assets' betas with respect to aggregate *real* consumption, where aggregate real consumption is computed for an instantaneously additive price index with aggregate expenditure fractions on the various goods as weights. This result also extends the single-risk-measure asset pricing equation of Grauer and Litzenberger (1979) from a multi-good economy with strong 'homothetic' restrictions on consumption preferences to an economy with general and diverse consumption preferences. The continuous-time framework permits their covariance of an asset's return with the marginal utility of aggregate consumption to be written as a function of the asset's consumption-beta.

2. The economic model

The continuous-time model of this paper is very similar to the models utilized by Merton (1971, 1973), Lucas (1978), and Cox, Ingersoll and Ross (CIR) (1977). Therefore, in the interest of brevity, common facets of this model will only be sketched, with the unfamiliar reader being referred to those earlier developments of the model. Readers familiar with these continuous-time models may skip this section without losing the thrust of the paper.

Initially, it is assumed that there is a single good that may be consumed by individuals or invested via firms; a multi-good extension is presented in section 7. Individuals are assumed to behave as price takers in perfectly competitive, but possibly incomplete capital markets that are frictionless. They may trade continuously and may short-sell any assets with full use of the proceeds. Trading takes place only at equilibrium prices. Also, it is assumed that all investors have identical probability beliefs for states of the world. Individuals hold wealth in the form of risky asset shares or in an instantaneously riskless asset; the case where no riskless asset exists is presented in section 6. W^k is individual k's wealth and $\boldsymbol{w}^k$ is his $A \times 1$ vector of fractions of wealth invested in the various risky assets. (Throughout this paper, vectors will appear as bold italic and multi-column matrices will appear as bold roman.) Letting $\boldsymbol{1}$ be a vector of ones, $w_0^k = 1 - \boldsymbol{1}'\boldsymbol{w}^k$ is individual k's fraction of wealth invested in the riskless asset. Each individual k has a stochastic number of labor units, y^k, that yield a continuous wage income rate of ly^k.[2]

It is assumed that there exists an $N \times 1$ vector of state variables, $\boldsymbol{\theta}$ that (with time) describes the state of the world. For example, asset prices, dividend yields, and income rates may be written as $\boldsymbol{P}(\boldsymbol{\theta}, t)$, $\boldsymbol{\delta}(\boldsymbol{\theta}, t)$, and $l(\boldsymbol{\theta}, t)y^k(\boldsymbol{\theta}, t)$, respectively. Assuming that the state vector $\boldsymbol{\theta}$ follows a continuous-time vector Markov process of the Ito type, the following stochastic differential equations may be written as

$$\mathrm{d}\boldsymbol{\theta} = \boldsymbol{\mu}_\theta(\boldsymbol{\theta}, t)\,\mathrm{d}t + \boldsymbol{\sigma}_\theta(\boldsymbol{\theta}, t)\,\mathrm{d}\mathbf{z}_\theta, \tag{1}$$

$$\frac{\mathrm{d}P_a}{P_a} = [\mu_a(\boldsymbol{\theta}, t) - \delta_a(\boldsymbol{\theta}, t)]\,\mathrm{d}t + \sigma_a(\boldsymbol{\theta}, t)\,\mathrm{d}z_a \quad \text{for each asset } a, \tag{2}$$

$$\mathrm{d}y^k = \mu_{yk}(\boldsymbol{\theta}, t)\,\mathrm{d}t + \sigma_{yk}(\boldsymbol{\theta}, t)\,\mathrm{d}z_{yk} \quad \text{for each individual } k, \tag{3}$$

where the drift and diffusion coefficients in (2) and (3) may be obtained from those in (1) by Ito's Lemma.[3] Throughout, $\mu_j(\boldsymbol{\theta}, t)$ represents the expected rate of change in variable j at time t, when the state vector is $\boldsymbol{\theta}$ at that time. Similarly, $\sigma_j(\boldsymbol{\theta}, t)$ represents the standard deviation of that rate of change, which depends upon time and the state vector; $\boldsymbol{\sigma}_\theta$ is the diagonal matrix of the instantaneous standard deviations of the state variables. The $\mathbf{z}_\theta$ variables are correlated Weiner processes, having zero means, unit variances per unit of time, and variance–covariance matrix and correlation matrix $\mathbf{V}_{\theta\theta}$, which may depend upon $\boldsymbol{\theta}$ and t.

Although there are a number of technical conditions that functions of Ito processes must meet for the application of Ito's Lemma [and for the representations of (2) and (3) to be rigorous], the economic restrictions on the movement of asset prices and incomes are not severe. Asset prices, dividends and incomes must follow continuous sample paths, but their levels, their mean rates of change and their variances and covariances may be stochastic, depending upon the evolution of the state vector over time. Thus,

[2]The labor–leisure choice is not examined in this paper. The formal model of sections 2–6 treats an individual's labor units supplied as stochastic and possibly correlated with all other economic variables, but there is no disutility for labor supplied. The multi-good model of section 7 could be adapted to handle the labor–leisure choice.

[3]For discussions of stochastic differential equations and of Ito's Lemma, see Merton (1978), Arnold (1974, sec. 5.3–5.5), Gihman and Skorohod (1972, part II, ch. 2, sec. 6), Kushner (1967, sec. 1.4), or McKean (1969, ch. 2). For discussions of the optimal control of these stochastic processes, see Arnold (1974, sec. 13.1–13.2) or Kushner (1967, ch. 6). For less technical discussions of these processes and theorems and for applications of them in economic models, see Merton (1971, 1973), Garman (1976), and Cox, Ingersoll and Ross (1977).

in Merton's (1973) terminology, the 'investment opportunity set' may be stochastic here. The state variables need not be restricted in number, nor do they need to be specified for the purposes of this paper. Restrictions on their number would restrict the dimensionality of the price system, as noted by Rosenberg and Ohlson (1976).

For the derivations that follow, it is not necessary to explicitly examine firms' production decisions and the supply of asset shares, provided that the assumptions made are consistent with optimal behavior of firms in a general equilibrium model. To be consistent with general equilibrium, prices must be recognized to be endogenously determined through the equilibrium of supply and demand. The model presented is consistent with endogenously determined prices if, as assumed, all random shocks to the economy are captured as elements of the state vector, $\boldsymbol{\theta}$. These random shocks may affect both the supplies and demands for shares. However, assuming that both supply and demand functions are functions of the state variables (shocks) that follow Ito processes, the equilibrium prices that arise will also follow Ito processes that are representable as in (2). This statement follows from Ito's Lemma, subject to the qualification that the supply and demand functions be sufficiently smooth for Ito's Lemma to apply.[4] Thus, the economic model of (1)–(3) is consistent with endogenously-determined prices.

As an example of a supply side that can be imbedded in this model without changing any of the analysis, consider the following economy. The output of the economy is produced by F different productive units (firms) under conditions of uncertainty about current investment productivity and about future investment technology. Firms buy stocks of the good and rent labor units of the good for use in their production processes. The current stock of the good that firm f owns is x_f, and the current amount of labor employed by it is y_f. The $F \times 1$ vectors of capital investment and labor employment by the various firms are denoted $\boldsymbol{x}$ and $\boldsymbol{y}$, respectively, and the current wage rate is l. Changes in the amount of the good that a firm has are caused by its production, less its wage payments and dividends, d_f, and plus any new capital infusions, η_f, from sales of stock (negative η_f represents stock repurchases). It is assumed that such changes in the stock of the good that productive units have may be described by a system of stochastic differential equations of the Ito type,

$$\mathrm{d}\boldsymbol{x} = [\boldsymbol{\mu}_x(\boldsymbol{x}, \boldsymbol{y}, \boldsymbol{e}, t) - l\boldsymbol{y} - \boldsymbol{d} + \boldsymbol{\eta}]\,\mathrm{d}t + \boldsymbol{\sigma}_x(\boldsymbol{x}, \boldsymbol{y}, \boldsymbol{e}, t)\,\mathrm{d}\boldsymbol{z}_x, \tag{4}$$

and

$$\mathrm{d}\boldsymbol{e} = \boldsymbol{\mu}_e(\boldsymbol{e}, t)\,\mathrm{d}t + \boldsymbol{\sigma}_e(\boldsymbol{e}, t)\,\mathrm{d}\boldsymbol{z}_e, \tag{5}$$

[4]See footnote 3.

where $\boldsymbol{e}$ is an $E \times 1$ vector of indices that describe the productivity of current technology, and $\boldsymbol{z}_x$ and $\boldsymbol{z}_e$ are vectors of correlated Wiener processes. The vector of expected production rates is $\boldsymbol{\mu}_x$, and $\boldsymbol{\sigma}_x$ is the diagonal matrix of instantaneous standard deviations of the various production rates. Both expected and random components of a firm's production may depend upon the capital and labor employed and upon the current level of technology. As indicated by (5), technological change is assumed to be random, with the productivity indices following a vector Markov process. Although it is not done here, it is also possible (with more notation) to model expenditures on research and development that would affect the rates of technological change in the various production processes.

In the example, each firm may issue a number of different securities, such as debt and equity, that contractually partition its cash flows over time among investors in the firm. Each firm is assumed to maximize the value of its securities, net of input costs. For slightly greater generality, it is also assumed that individuals may issue or purchase a number of contractually defined securities ('side bets') that have zero net supplies. Options and forward contracts are permissible in this class of financial assets.

In a rational expectations equilibrium, asset prices in this economy are functions of the consumption preferences of individuals and time, which are non-stochastic, and the following stochastic variables: (1) the current productivities of the production processes, (2) the current supplies of capital and labor, and (3) the current distribution of income and wealth among individuals. Since all of these stochastic variables follow Ito processes in this model, and since they jointly comprise a Markov system, the initial representation of prices, dividends and income rates as functions of a Markov vector of state variables and time, as given by eqs. (1)–(3), is consistent with the existence of a production sector as sketched and with the endogenous determination of asset prices. Changes in the state vector, $\boldsymbol{\theta}$, for this economy are the results of stochastic production and stochastic technological change, which are the underlying exogenous variables of this example. Any other economies with supply side structures that are consistent with (1)–(3), given the preference and the other assumptions, are also governed by the theorems and pricing relations of this paper.

It is possible, with certain preference and/or probabilistic assumptions, that fluctuations in some of the elements of the state vector $\boldsymbol{\theta}$ do not affect any individual's expected utility of lifetime consumption, given the individual's wealth. For example, certain elements of the state vector may affect the distribution of payoffs between two assets in such a way that the total payoff to the two is unaffected. If all individuals hold identical fractions of the two assets, then their expected utilities are unaffected by fluctuations in those state variables, assuming that the state variables have no other effects. To distinguish between state variables that do affect at least one individual's expected utility, given the person's wealth, it is convenient to define another state vector, $\boldsymbol{s}$, that contains those state variables that do affect at least one individual's expected utility, given his wealth. This $S \times 1$ vector of variables is a subset of the comprehensive state vector, $\boldsymbol{\theta}$, and is assumed to follow a vector Markov process. Summarizing, each individual's expected utility of (remaining) lifetime consumption may be written as a function of his wealth, the vector of relevant state variables, and time, $J^k = J^k(W^k, \boldsymbol{s}, t)$, where

$$\mathrm{d}\boldsymbol{s} = \boldsymbol{\mu}_s(\boldsymbol{s}, t)\,\mathrm{d}t + \boldsymbol{\sigma}_s\,\mathrm{d}\boldsymbol{z}_s. \tag{1'}$$

As all of the subsequent analysis and theorems are in terms of only these state variables, $\boldsymbol{s}$, they are referred to throughout the paper as the 'state vector' or as the 'vector of state variables'.

Each individual k is assumed to maximize the expected value at each instant in time of a time-additive and state-independent von Neumann–Morgenstern utility function for lifetime consumption,

$$E_t\left\{\int_t^{t^k} U^k(c^k(\tau),\tau)\,\mathrm{d}\tau + B^k[W^k(t^k), t^k, \boldsymbol{s}(t^k)]\right\}, \tag{6}$$

where t^k is individual k's time of death, and U^k and B^k are his strictly quasiconcave utility and bequest functions of consumption, c^k, and terminal wealth, $W^k(t^k)$, respectively.[5] E_t is the expectation operator at time t, conditional upon the state of the world at that time.

At each instant, individual k chooses an optimal rate of consumption, c^k, and an optimal portfolio of risky assets, $\boldsymbol{w}^k W^k$. Given these choices, Merton (1971) has shown that the individual's wealth will follow the stochastic differential equation,

$$\mathrm{d}W^k = [\boldsymbol{w}^{k'}(\boldsymbol{\mu}_a - \boldsymbol{r}) + r]W^k\,\mathrm{d}t + (ly^k - c^k)\,\mathrm{d}t + W^k\boldsymbol{w}^{k'}\boldsymbol{\sigma}_a(\mathrm{d}\boldsymbol{z}_a), \tag{7}$$

where r is the instantaneously risk-free interest rate, $\boldsymbol{r} = r \cdot \boldsymbol{1}$, $\boldsymbol{\mu}_a$ is the $A \times 1$ vector of expected total (capital gains and dividends) rates of return on assets, and $\boldsymbol{\sigma}_a$ is the $A \times A$ diagonal matrix of assets' instantaneous standard deviations. Thus, $\boldsymbol{\mu}_a$, $\boldsymbol{\sigma}_a$, and $\mathrm{d}\boldsymbol{z}_a$ are all as presented in (2).

Let $J^k(W^k, \boldsymbol{s}, t)$ be the maximum expected utility of lifetime consumption in (6) that is obtainable with wealth W^k and opportunities $\boldsymbol{s}$ at time t. Under certain conditions, if there exists a well-behaved function $J^k(W^k, \boldsymbol{s}, t)$ and controls $c^k(W^k, \boldsymbol{s}, t)$ and $\boldsymbol{w}^k(W^k, \boldsymbol{s}, t)$ that solve the following problem subject

[5]Under certain conditions, individuals' lifetimes may be uncertain. See Merton (1973) or Richard (1975). See the Richard paper for an analysis of optimal life insurance rules in a continuous-time model.

to the constraint of (7), then the consumption and portfolio decisions are optimal (with superscript k suppressed),[6]

$$0=\max_{\{c,w\}}\left\{U(c,t)+(J_W \mathbf{J}_s' J_t)\begin{pmatrix}[w'(\boldsymbol{\mu}_a-r)+r]W+ly-c\\ \boldsymbol{\mu}_s\\ 1\end{pmatrix}\right.$$
$$\left.+\frac{1}{2}\begin{pmatrix}V_{WW} & \mathbf{V}_{Ws}\\ \mathbf{V}_{sW} & \mathbf{V}_{ss}\end{pmatrix}\Box\begin{pmatrix}J_{WW} & \mathbf{J}_{Ws}\\ \mathbf{J}_{sW} & \mathbf{J}_{ss}\end{pmatrix}\right\}, \tag{8}$$

where subscripts of the J function represent partial derivatives with respect to wealth (J_W) and the various state variables ($\mathbf{J}_s$). The matrix of V's is a partitioning of the variance–covariance matrix of the individual's wealth and the state variables. The box multiply sign implies that corresponding elements of the two matrices are multiplied, then summed. Note that the individual's variance rate for wealth is $V^k_{WW}=(W^k)^2\mathbf{w}^{k\prime}\mathbf{V}_{aa}\mathbf{w}^k$, and his vector of covariances of wealth with the state variables is $\mathbf{V}^k_{Ws}=W^k\mathbf{w}^{k\prime}\mathbf{V}_{as}$, where $\mathbf{V}_{aa}$ is the $A\times A$ variance–covariance matrix of asset returns, and $\mathbf{V}_{as}$ is the $A\times S$ matrix of covariances of asset returns with state variables.

First-order conditions for an interior maximum in (8) may be stated as

$$U^k_c(c^k,t)=J^k_W(W^k,s,t), \tag{9}$$

and

$$\mathbf{w}^k W^k=(-J^k_W/J^k_{WW})\mathbf{V}_{aa}^{-1}(\boldsymbol{\mu}_a-\mathbf{r})-\mathbf{V}_{aa}^{-1}\mathbf{V}_{as}(\mathbf{J}^k_{sW}/J^k_{WW}). \tag{10}$$

These conditions give the individual's optimal risky asset portfolio, (10), and state that the marginal utility of another unit of consumption must equal the indirect marginal utility of wealth for an optimal policy.

The following portfolio allocation theorem is obtained directly from individuals' portfolio demands as given by (10). Its proof is in appendix 1.

Theorem 1. $S+2$ Funds. All individuals in this economy, regardless of preferences, may obtain their optimal portfolio positions by investing in at most $S+2$ funds. These funds may be chosen to be: (1) *the instantaneously riskless asset,* (2) *the S portfolios having the highest correlations, respectively, with the S state variables summarizing investment and income opportunities, and* (3) *the market portfolio.*

Of course, any $S+2$ funds that span the same vector space would also suffice.

[6]See footnote 3 for references for this result and the conditions under which it is valid.

To see that Merton's (1973) 'multi-beta' asset pricing model obtains in this economy when betas are measured with respect to aggregate wealth and the returns of assets that hedge against changes in the various state variables, aggregate individuals' portfolio demands in (10) and substitute in equilibrium expected excess returns for the market portfolio, $(\mu_M - r)$, and for assets perfectly correlated with the state variables, $(\boldsymbol{\mu}_s - \boldsymbol{r})$, assuming that such assets exist. Doing this, Merton's model is obtained,[7]

$$\boldsymbol{\mu}_a - \boldsymbol{r} = \boldsymbol{\beta}_{a,Ms}\begin{pmatrix}\mu_M - r\\ \boldsymbol{\mu}_s^* - \boldsymbol{r}\end{pmatrix}, \tag{11}$$

where $\boldsymbol{\beta}_{a,Ms}$ is the $A \times (S+1)$ matrix of 'multiple-regression' betas for all assets on the market and on the assets perfectly correlated with the state variables. This type of multi-beta equation was also derived in a discrete-time model by Long (1974). As both Merton and Long noted, the Sharpe–Lintner CAPM will not generally hold in these intertemporal economic models – expected excess returns are not proportional to market betas in these models with stochastic investment opportunities.

As shown by Garman (1976) and by Cox, Ingersoll and Ross (1977), each asset's price in this economy is a solution to a second-order partial differential equation in its price. This 'fundamental valuation equation' may be obtained for any asset by using Ito's Lemma to find its expected

[7]When assets with returns that are perfectly correlated with the state variables do not exist, a multi-beta CAPM as in (11) holds with one modification: expected excess returns for the S portfolios in (11) are those of the S portfolios with the maximum correlations with the S state variables, respectively, which have portfolio weights that are proportional to the columns of $\mathbf{V}_{aa}^{-1}\mathbf{V}_{as}$. Similarly, the S non-market betas required for each asset for (11) may be measured relative to the returns on these S most highly correlated portfolios. Briefly, the proof is as follows. From Appendix 1, (A.1),

$$\mathbf{w}^M = k_1 \mathbf{V}_{aa}^{-1}(\boldsymbol{\mu}_a - \boldsymbol{r}) + \mathbf{w}_{s'}\mathbf{k}_2,$$

where $\mathbf{w}_{s'}$ is the $A \times S$ matrix of S portfolios with the maximum correlation of returns with the various state variables, respectively. Pre-multiplying this equation by $\mathbf{V}_{aa}$ gives

$$\boldsymbol{\mu}_a - \boldsymbol{r} = V_{aM}(1/k_1) + \mathbf{V}_{as'}(-k_2/k_1) = \mathbf{V}_{a,Ms'}\begin{pmatrix}1/k_1\\ -k_2/k_1\end{pmatrix},$$

$$\begin{pmatrix}\mu_M - r\\ \boldsymbol{\mu}_{s'} - \boldsymbol{r}\end{pmatrix} = \mathbf{V}_{Ms',Ms'}\begin{pmatrix}1/k_1\\ -\mathbf{k}_2/k_1\end{pmatrix},$$

where $\mathbf{V}_{Ms',Ms'}$ is the $(S+1)\times(S+1)$ variance–covariance matrix for the market and the most correlated portfolios' returns. Substituting this result into the previous equation gives

$$\boldsymbol{\mu}_a - \boldsymbol{r} = \mathbf{V}_{a,Ms'}\mathbf{V}_{Ms'Ms'}^{-1}\begin{pmatrix}\mu_M - r\\ \boldsymbol{\mu}_{s'} - \boldsymbol{r}\end{pmatrix} = \boldsymbol{\beta}_{a,Ms'}\begin{pmatrix}\mu_M - r\\ \boldsymbol{\mu}_{s'} - \boldsymbol{r}\end{pmatrix},$$

which is the result stated.

instantaneous return from the function $P(\theta, t)$ and then by equating this drift rate to the equilibrium drift rates implied by the multi-beta model of (11). An interpretation of the general mathematical solution to the valuation equation is given in the CIR paper, but useful closed-form solutions are known only for a few assets, and then only under highly restrictive preference and state assumptions. In particular, CIR assume logarithmic utility functions and a single state variable to derive their closed-form solution for the term structure of interest rates. In this paper, no restrictions on state variables are imposed, and only the relatively weak preference assumption of (6) is made. Consequently, the goal here is to simplify the expression relating asset risks and returns, rather than to solve for an explicit pricing function, $P(\theta, t)$. The next section demonstrates that the multi-beta intertemporal CAPM of (11) can be collapsed into a single-beta intertemporal CAPM, with no additional assumptions.

3. A 'single-beta' intertemporal asset pricing model

Up to this point, the consumption–investment analysis is virtually the same as in Merton's (1973) continuous-time development, but with slightly more discussion of the supply side. An individual's portfolio holdings are found in terms of his indirect utility function for wealth, $J^k(W^k, s, t)$, and equilibrium expected asset returns are correspondingly found in terms of aggregate wealth and the returns on assets that are perfectly correlated with changes in the various state variables, if they exist. This paper focuses upon the individual's direct utility function for consumption, $U^k(c^k, t)$, in the analysis of equilibrium expected returns on assets. The two approaches are intimately linked by the optimality condition that the marginal utility of consumption equals the marginal utility of wealth.

To restate the optimal portfolio demands in terms of the individual k's optimal consumption function, $c^k(W^k, s, t)$, note from (9) that: $J^k_W = U^k_c$, which implies that $\mathbf{J}^k_{Ws} = U^k_{cc}\mathbf{c}^k_s$ and $J^k_{WW} = U^k_{cc}c^k_W$, where subscripts of U, J and c denote partial derivatives. Define T^k to be individual k's absolute risk tolerance: $T^k = -U^k_c/U^k_{cc}$. Then the optimal portfolio may be written as

$$\mathbf{w}^k W^k = (T^k/c^k_W)\mathbf{V}_{aa}^{-1}(\boldsymbol{\mu}_a - \mathbf{r}) - \mathbf{V}_{aa}^{-1}\mathbf{V}_{as}(\mathbf{c}^k_s/c^k_W), \tag{12}$$

where $\boldsymbol{\mu}_a - \mathbf{r}$ is the vector of instantaneous expected excess returns on assets, $\mathbf{V}_{aa}$ is their variance–covariance matrix, and $\mathbf{V}_{as}$ is the $A \times S$ matrix of covariances of asset returns with changes in the state variables.

Pre-multiplying (12) by $c^k_W\mathbf{V}_{aa}$ and rearranging terms gives

$$T^k(\boldsymbol{\mu}_a - \mathbf{r}) = \mathbf{V}_{aW_k}c^k_W + \mathbf{V}_{as}\mathbf{c}^k_s, \tag{13}$$

where V_{aW_k} is the vector of covariances of asset returns with k's wealth change. Since k's optimal consumption is a function, $c^k(W^k, s, t)$, of his wealth, the state variables and time, Ito's Lemma implies that the local covariances of asset returns with changes in k's consumption rate are given by

$$V_{ac_k} = V_{aW_k} c_W^k + \mathbf{V}_{as} c_s^k, \tag{14}$$

which is the right-hand side of (13). Intuitively, (14) can also be seen by noting that the random change in k's consumption rate is locally linear in the random changes in k's wealth and the state variables, with the weights in the linear relation being the partial derivatives of k's consumption with respect to wealth and the state variables. Thus, the local covariance of asset j's return with k's change in consumption is

$$\begin{aligned} \operatorname{cov}(\tilde{r}_j, \mathrm{d}\tilde{c}^k) &= \operatorname{cov}\left(\tilde{r}_j, c_W^k(\mathrm{d}\tilde{W}^k) + \sum_i c_{s_i}^k(\mathrm{d}\tilde{s}_i)\right) \\ &= c_W^k \operatorname{cov}(\tilde{r}_j, \mathrm{d}\tilde{W}^k) + \sum_i c_{s_i}^k \operatorname{cov}(\tilde{r}_j, \mathrm{d}\tilde{s}_i), \end{aligned} \tag{15}$$

which is what is stated by (14).

By substituting (14) into (13), it is seen that each individual will choose an optimal portfolio in such a way that the local covariance of each asset's return with changes in his optimal consumption is proportional to the asset's expected excess return,

$$V_{ac_k} = T^k(\mu_a - r). \tag{16}$$

This relation holds for each individual k and can be aggregated by summing over all individuals in (16). Using the aggregate relation, defining the aggregate consumption rate to be C, and defining a measure of aggregate risk tolerance to be $T^M = \sum_k T^k$, it follows that the expected excess returns on assets in equilibrium will be proportional to their covariances with changes in aggregate consumption,

$$\mu_a - r = (T^M)^{-1} V_{aC}. \tag{17}$$

By dividing both the random consumption change and aggregate risk tolerance by current aggregate consumption, (17) may be expressed in terms of aggregate relative risk tolerance and return covariances with changes in the logarithm of consumption (percentage rates of change of consumption),

$$\mu_a - r = (T^M/C)^{-1} V_{a,\ln C}. \tag{17'}$$

For any portfolio M with weights w^M, pre-multiplying (17′) by those weights gives

$$(\mu_M - r)/\sigma_{M,\ln C} = (T^M/C)^{-1}, \tag{18}$$

and

$$\begin{aligned}\mu_a - r &= (V_{a,\ln C}/\sigma_{m,\ln C})(\mu_M - r)\\ &= (\beta_{aC}/\beta_{MC})(\mu_M - r),\end{aligned} \tag{19}$$

where β_{aC} and β_{MC} are the 'consumption-betas' of asset returns and of portfolio M's return. The consumption-beta for any asset j's return is defined to be

$$\beta_{jC} = \operatorname{cov}(\tilde{r}_j, \mathrm{d}\ln\tilde{C})/\operatorname{var}(\mathrm{d}\ln\tilde{C}). \tag{20}$$

If there exists a security whose return is perfectly correlated with changes in aggregate consumption over the next instant, then the risk–return relation of (19) can be written in terms of assets' betas measured relative to that security's return, β_C, and the expected excess return on this security, $\mu_C^* - r$,[8]

$$\mu_a - r = \beta_C(\mu_C^* - r). \tag{21}$$

Portfolio M may be any measure of the market portfolio or any other portfolio. Eq. (19) states that the ratio of expected excess returns on any two assets or portfolios in equilibrium will be equal to the ratio of their betas measured relative to aggregate consumption. Thus, the relevant risk of a security's return may be summarized by a single beta with respect to consumption – a considerable simplification over the Merton multi-beta derivation, at no loss of generality in assumptions.

The intertemporal asset pricing relation of (19) or (21) holds at each instant in time, but does not necessarily hold for returns and betas that are measured over finite periods of time. Breeden and Litzenberger (1978) have shown that assumptions of identical constant relative risk aversion utility functions for individuals and lognormally distributed consumption are sufficient to derive (19) for returns and consumption-betas measured over finite time periods.

There are two ways to understand the economic intuition of this result:

[8]In general, even if there does not exist a portfolio whose return is perfectly correlated with aggregate consumption, the consumption-betas in (19), (20), and (21) may be equivalently derived as the betas measured relative to the returns on the asset portfolio that has the most highly correlated returns with changes in aggregate consumption. The proof is a univariate version of footnote 7, working from (17) and the fact that the most correlated portfolio has weights proportional to $\mathbf{V}_{aa}^{-1}V_{aC}$.

the first focuses upon the marginal rates of substitution between consumption today and consumption in the future, whereas the second interpretation focuses upon the level of wealth and the productivity of investments at future dates and states. Both explanations are briefly presented here. Although capital market completeness was not necessary for the ICAPM of (19), the first explanation is cast in the simplified framework of complete markets.[9]

Any asset may be described for valuation purposes by its total payoff, price and dividend, in the various possible states of the world in the next instant (a period in discrete time). The value in equilibrium of a $1 payoff in a particular state of the world at a future date is equal to the state's probability multiplied by the ratio of the marginal utility of consumption at the future state to the marginal utility of consumption in the current period. That is,

$$\lambda_{t_1 s_1} = \pi_{t_1 s_1}(U_c^k(c_{t_1 s_1}^k, t_1)/U_c^k(c_t^k, t)) \quad \text{for all } k, \tag{22}$$

where $\lambda_{t_1 s_1}$ is k's shadow price at time t of $1 received at time t_1 if state s_1 occurs, $\pi_{t_1 s_1}$ is the probability of that state, $c_{t_1 s_1}^k$ is k's optimal consumption if that state occurs, and c_t^k is k's current consumption. The value of any asset having a dividend, $d_{t+1,s}$, and price, $P_{t+1,s}$, at time $t+1$ in different states of the world is

$$P_t = \sum_s (d_{t+1,s} + P_{t+1,s})\lambda_{t+1,s}, \tag{23}$$

which must be the same for all individuals behaving optimally. Thus, the price per unit of probability for these elementary state-contingent claims varies among states only as planned consumption varies among states. The relation is inverse between planned consumption and the price/probability ratio for the state, due to the diminishing marginal utility of consumption. Therefore, holding the expected payoff on an asset constant, the value of the asset will be negatively related to its covariance with the individual's consumption. As seen from (22), for each date in this economy, if the capital markets are Pareto-optimal, the larger $\lambda_{t_1 s_1}/\pi_{t_1 s_1}$ is, the smaller each individual's consumption is in state s_1.[10] Since each individual's planned consumption in various states is positively and monotonically related to aggregate planned consumption, it can also be said that, holding the

[9]Theorem 3 of section 6 characterizes the relation of individuals' optimal consumption rates to the aggregate consumption rate for the general case of incomplete capital markets. Following that theorem, additional discussion of the pricing results of (19) and (21) is presented.

[10]For a detailed analysis of optimal consumption allocations in a multi-period state preference framework, see Breeden and Litzenberger (1978).

expected payoff on an asset constant, the value of the asset will be negatively related to its covariance with aggregate consumption. This implies relatively large (small) equilibrium expected returns on assets with relatively large (small) covariances with aggregate consumption, as is indicated by (19).

The key to this analysis is the relation between low levels of aggregate consumption and highly-valued state payoffs via the relation between value and marginal rates of substitution of consumption. The reason that payoff covariances with more distant levels of aggregate consumption (or their present value, aggregate wealth) do not appear explicitly in the pricing equation is that they are already reflected in the levels of equilibrium asset prices that will occur in alternative states at the next instant. That is, the asset's value in the next period appropriately reflects the covariances of its more distant payoffs with more distant levels of aggregate consumption.

The alternative, equivalent explanation is presented somewhat less rigorously, but may be more intuitive in light of the development of the finance literature. Holding expected payoffs constant between two assets, one asset's payoff probability distribution is preferred to the other's, if it tends to pay more highly in states where another dollar to invest gives large benefits (high marginal utility) and tends to pay relatively less in states where another dollar invested gives small benefits (low marginal utility). Whether an additional dollar invested is more or less beneficial depends upon: (1) the wealth of the economy in that state, via the diminishing marginal utility of wealth (future consumption), and (2) the physical productivity of investments in the state, that is, the marginal rate of transformation of goods today into goods in the future. The diminishing marginal utility of wealth was the driving force for the single-period CAPM and its portfolio diversification theorem. In the intertemporal model, as Merton (1973) has shown, changing investment opportunities create what he terms 'hedging demands' for assets, with their concomitant implications for equilibrium expected returns on assets.

An asset's covariance with aggregate consumption is all that is necessary for asset pricing, because aggregate consumption is perfectly negatively correlated with the marginal utility of an additional dollar of wealth invested through the optimality condition: $U_c(c,t)=J_W(W,s,t)$. Holding investment opportunities constant, if wealth is relatively high in a state, then the value per dollar of payoffs in that state is low. Optimal consumption is relatively high in that state. Holding wealth constant, if investment opportunities are relatively good in a state, then the present value of a dollar payoff in that state is high, as it can be invested quite profitably. In this case, optimal consumption is relatively low for individuals. *Always*, when the value of an additional dollar payoff in a state is high, consumption is low in that state, and when the value of additional investment is low, optimal consumption is high. This is *not* always true for wealth, when investment opportunities are uncertain. It is quite possible that there are states of the world where wealth is high and, yet, the marginal utility of a dollar is high due to the excellent investment opportunities in the state. Similarly, it is quite possible that there are states where wealth is low and, yet, the marginal utility of a dollar is low due to poor investment opportunities. Given preferences, wealth is not a sufficient statistic for the marginal utility of a dollar – consumption is.[11] For optimum consumption and portfolio choices, an individual's marginal utility of wealth or consumption is a monotonically decreasing function of consumption. For this reason, holding the expected payoff on an asset constant, its present value is a decreasing function of its covariance with aggregate consumption. Consequently, the higher that an asset's beta with respect to consumption is, the higher its equilibrium expected rate of return.

Note that this analysis is consistent with the derivations of the market-oriented CAPM by Sharpe (1964) and Lintner (1965) in a single-period context, and by Merton (1973) and Long (1974) in an intertemporal model. In the single-period model, all wealth is consumed at the end of the period, so investment opportunities are irrelevant. In Merton's model, investment opportunities are required to be constant for the derivation of the single-beta CAPM; thus, wealth is a sufficient statistic for marginal utility in that model. Merton and Long's multi-beta pricing models are derived with stochastic investment opportunities, as in this paper; the foregoing analysis demonstrates that wealth is not a sufficient statistic for marginal utility in their models.

4. An example

A simple example more graphically illustrates the main point. Consider a 3-date economy with many identical individuals and a single good called wheat. The current stock of wheat is the entire wealth of the economy. At each date, the amount of wheat to be consumed and the (residual) amount to be invested must be determined; wheat invested produces more wheat that will be available for future consumption. Assume that the optimal consumption/investment decision has already been made for date 1 and that the amount of wheat available for consumption and investment at date 2 will either be 200 bushels/person or 231 bushels/person, depending upon the state of the world. Furthermore, assume that the physical productivity of wheat invested at date 2 for consumption at date 3 may either be 0% or 20%, depending upon the state of the world. This 're-investment rate' will be

[11] The fact that consumption is a sufficient statistic for an individual's marginal utility is due to the assumption that individuals have time-additive and state-independent preferences for consumption.

known for certain at date 2, but is unknown at date 1. Constant returns to scale are assumed.

At date 2, each individual chooses consumption, c_2, and investment, $W_2 - c_2$, which results in consumption at date 3 of $c_3 = (W_2 - c_2)(1 + r_2)$, where r_2 is the physical productivity of investment at date 2. Each individual's utility function is $u(c_2, c_3) = c_2^{0.5} + c_3^{0.5}$. It may be verified that the optimal consumption at date 2 is $c_2 = W_2/(2 + r)$. At date 2 there are four possible states of the world, representing the different possible combinations of wealth and productivity, W_2 and r, respectively. Consumption and the marginal utility of another bushel of wheat at date 2 for either consumption or investment will depend upon the state of the world as shown in table 1.

It is seen from table 1 that marginal utility tends to be negatively related to wealth, but not perfectly. In particular, note that wealth in state 4 is greater than that in state 1, but marginal utility in state 4 is higher than that in state 1. This is true because the difference in physical productivity between the two states has offset the decline in marginal utility caused by the wealth differential. Since marginal utilities at time 2 are essential in the determination of prices of assets at time 1 from their state-contingent payoffs, covariances with wealth are inadequate risk measures, even in a mean-variance model.

Table 1

Consumption, wealth, and marginal utility: An example.

State	Wealth	Physical productivity	Optimal consumption	Marginal utility
1	220	0%	110	0.0476
2	220	20%	100	0.0500
3	231	0%	115.5	0.0465
4	231	20%	105	0.0488

From table 1, it is seen that consumption is perfectly negatively related to marginal utility, as it must be with state-independent preferences. As a consequence, in the locally mean-variance, continuous-time model, covariance with consumption is the relevant risk measure for the pricing of assets.

5. Properties of individuals' optimal consumption functions

In the single-period portfolio theory of Markowitz (1952), Sharpe (1964), Lintner (1965) and Mossin (1966), two important results were obtained: (1) all individuals hold the same risky asset portfolio or, alternatively stated, all individuals' rates of return on wealth are perfectly positively correlated, and (2) each individual's optimal portfolio beta or portfolio standard deviation is proportional to his Pratt (1964) – Arrow (1965) measure of relative risk tolerance. Clearly, from the portfolio theory of section 2, neither of these results holds in the intertemporal choice model with stochastic investment opportunities. This section presents two analogous results that do obtain in the intertemporal model, if the capital markets permit an unconstrained Pareto-optimal allocation: (1) at any instant, the changes in all individuals' optimal consumption rates are perfectly positively correlated, and (2) at each instant, every individual's instantaneous standard deviation of changes in his consumption rate is proportional to his Pratt–Arrow measure of relative risk tolerance.[12]

The first result, which was discussed in section 3, is stated more precisely by the following theorem:

Theorem 2. Optimal Consumption Paths. Given the continuous-time economic model and the assumption that the capital markets permit an unconstrained Pareto-optimal allocation of consumption, at every instant in time, the change in each individual's optimal consumption rate is perfectly positively correlated with the change in every other individual's optimal consumption rate and with the change in the aggregate consumption rate for the economy.

Proof. The assumption of Pareto-optimal capital markets implies that the state-contingent allocation of consumption is the same as when there exists, at each instant in time, the market portfolio, a riskless asset, and a set of portfolios whose returns are perfectly correlated with the various state variables that affect individuals' optimal consumption rates, $c^k(W^k, s, t)$.[13] As shown in section 2, individuals would need only to trade in those assets to achieve their optimal portfolios. Letting $\boldsymbol{\mu}$ and $\mathbf{V}$ represent the $(S+1)\times 1$ drift vector and the $(S+1)\times(S+1)$ incremental covariance matrix for the market portfolio and those S portfolios' rates of return, respectively, it is shown in appendix 2 that the instantaneous covariance between individual k's changes in consumption and individual j's is

$$\operatorname{cov}(c^k, c^j) = T^k T^j (\boldsymbol{\mu} - \boldsymbol{r})' \, \mathbf{V}^{-1} (\boldsymbol{\mu} - \boldsymbol{r}). \tag{24}$$

From (24) letting $\gamma = (\boldsymbol{\mu} - \boldsymbol{r})' \mathbf{V}^{-1} (\boldsymbol{\mu} - \boldsymbol{r})$, the correlation between k's and j's

[12]The relative risk tolerance referred to is calculated from the individual's (direct) utility function for consumption; it is not necessarily equal to the individual's risk tolerance measured by his (indirect) utility function for wealth. The 'direct' measure does not depend upon the state of the world, given the individual's consumption, whereas the 'indirect' measure in general does depend upon the state vector, given wealth.

[13]For a proof, see Breeden (1977, ch. 5).

changes in consumption is (where 'std' represents an instantaneous standard deviation)

$$\operatorname{corr}(c^k, c^j) = \frac{\operatorname{cov}(c^k, c^j)}{\operatorname{std}(c^k)\operatorname{std}(c^j)} = \frac{T^k T^j \gamma}{\sqrt{(T^k)^2\gamma}\sqrt{(T^j)^2\gamma}} = 1. \tag{25}$$

Similarly, by aggregating in (24) each individual's correlation of consumption with the aggregate is seen to be unity. Q.E.D.

Theorem 2 could have been anticipated by noting that Breeden and Litzenberger (1978) proved that an individual's optimal consumption at any date in the multiperiod economy may be expressed as a function of only aggregate consumption at that date. They utilized an assumption of partial homogeneity in beliefs and they assumed that individuals' preferences for consumption were time-additive and state-independent, as is assumed in section 2, eq. (6). With homogeneous beliefs as assumed here, the functional relationship between each individual's consumption rate and the aggregate consumption rate is strictly monotonic and increasing. Given their results, Ito's Lemma provides Theorem 2 in the continuous-time economy, since by Ito's Lemma any random variable that follows an Ito process is (locally) perfectly positively correlated with any positive, strictly monotonic function of it.

To see that risk tolerance (or, inversely, risk aversion) is reflected proportionally in each individual's standard deviation of changes in his optimal consumption path, note that from (24): $\operatorname{std}(c^k) = T^k\sqrt{\gamma}$ and that $\operatorname{std}(c^k)/\operatorname{std}(C) = T^k/T^M$. Similarly, in terms of standard deviations of growth *rates*, $\operatorname{std}(\ln c^k)/\operatorname{std}(\ln C) = T^{*k}/T^{*M}$, where $T^{*k} = T^k/c^k$ is k's relative risk tolerance and $T^{*M} = T^M/C$ is an aggregate measure of relative risk tolerance. The implication is intuitive: those who are very risk averse will choose consumption paths with low variability, compared to those chosen by individuals who are less risk averse. Of course, in the limiting case of an individual with infinite risk aversion, the individual would choose complete insurance against any fluctuation in his consumption path. His wealth would be variable in such a way as to offset any impact of changing investment opportunities on his optimal consumption. In general, those who are more or less risk averse than average can be identified by empirically observing the standard deviations of individuals' consumption rates. They cannot be identified merely from their asset portfolios, as was implied by single-period portfolio theory.

In general capital markets, it may or may not be possible to achieve an unconstrained Pareto-optimal allocation of consumption with portfolios of available securities. For example, this situation may occur if there does not exist a portfolio of assets with a return that perfectly 'hedges' (in Merton's terminology) against changes in one of the state variables. When an unconstrained Pareto-optimal allocation is not possible, one assumption of Theorem 2 is violated and changes in individuals' optimal consumption rates are not necessarily perfectly correlated with each other or with changes in the aggregate consumption rate. In a general capital market, the following theorem holds:

Theorem 3. Consumption Allocations in General Capital Markets. Given a continuous-time economic model with general capital markets, at every instant in time, the optimal portfolio for each individual results in changes in the individual's optimal consumption rate that have the maximum possible correlation with changes in the aggregate consumption rate.

Proof. Individual k's optimal portfolio given in (12) maximizes the covariance of k's changes in consumption with changes in aggregate consumption for a given variance of k's changes in consumption. That is: $w^k W^k$ solves

$$\max_{w} c_W^k w' V_{aC} + c_s' V_{sC} + \lambda \left[(c_W^k w' c_s^{k'}) \begin{pmatrix} \mathbf{V}_{aa} \mathbf{V}_{as} \\ \mathbf{V}_{sa} \mathbf{V}_{ss} \end{pmatrix} \begin{pmatrix} c_W^k w \\ c_s^k \end{pmatrix} - \operatorname{var}(\mathrm{d}c^k) \right].$$

By maximizing k's covariance of consumption changes with changes in aggregate consumption, for given variances of k's consumption changes and aggregate consumption changes, the correlation coefficient between the individual's consumption and aggregate consumption is maximized. Q.E.D.

This result provides an explanation for the fact that the derivation of the intertemporal CAPM does not require Pareto-optimal capital markets, i.e., the fact that perfect hedges against changes in all of the state variables are not necessary for the derivation. Since each individual's optimal portfolio maximizes the correlation of his consumption with aggregate consumption, fluctuations in each individual's consumption and marginal utility that are uncorrelated with aggregate consumption are also uncorrelated with the returns on all assets. Thus, an asset's risk premium, which is determined by the covariance of its return with individuals' marginal utilities of consumption, is unaffected by the fluctuations in individuals' consumption rates that are unrelated to aggregate consumption, because those fluctuations are also unrelated to all asset returns. The reason that asset betas with respect to only aggregate consumption are in the intertemporal CAPM is that the assets available have betas equal to zero when measured relative to the components of individuals' consumption risks that are uncorrelated with aggregate consumption.

6. Asset pricing with no riskless asset

This section derives for an economy with no riskless asset a 'zero-beta' intertemporal CAPM that corresponds to the zero-beta CAPM derived by Lintner (1969), Black (1972) and Vasicek (1971) in a single-period model. The differences between the models are: (1) an asset's beta is measured relative to aggregate consumption, rather than relative to aggregate wealth, and (2) the zero-beta portfolio, whose expected return replaces that of the riskless return in (19), is a portfolio with returns uncorrelated with aggregate consumption, rather than a portfolio with returns uncorrelated with the market portfolio's return.

The only formal modification to the individual's optimization problem [eqs. (6)–(8), section 2] is that the expected rate of return on invested wealth, which was $\boldsymbol{w}'\boldsymbol{\mu}_a+(1-\boldsymbol{1}'\boldsymbol{w})r$, is now simply a weighted average of risky asset returns, $\boldsymbol{w}'\boldsymbol{\mu}_a$. The wealth constraint is now that the risky asset portfolio weights sum to unity, which may be enforced by the use of a Lagrange multiplier in (8). The first-order condition that the marginal utility of consumption equals the marginal utility of wealth is unchanged; however, the optimal risky asset portfolio of (10) now becomes

$$w^k W^k = (-J^k_w/J^k_{WW})\mathbf{V}_{aa}^{-1}\boldsymbol{\mu}_a + (\lambda^k/W^k J^k_{WW})\mathbf{V}_{aa}^{-1}\boldsymbol{1} - \mathbf{V}_{aa}^{-1}\mathbf{V}_{as}(\boldsymbol{J}^k_{sW}/J^k_{WW}), \tag{10'}$$

where λ^k is individual k's Lagrange multiplier for his budget constraint.

By an extension of the proof in appendix 1 for the $(S+2)$-fund theorem of section 2, it is seen that an $(S+2)$-fund theorem holds in this economy with no riskless asset. The funds may be chosen to be (1) the S portfolios having the highest correlations, respectively, with the S state variables summarizing investment opportunities, (2) the market portfolio, and (3) the zero consumption-beta portfolio of the risky assets that has minimum variance.

Substituting partial derivatives of individual k's direct utility function for consumption and k's optimal consumption function for the partials of the indirect utility function in (10'), and proceeding as in eqs. (12)–(16) in section 3, gives

$$V_{ac_k} = T^k\boldsymbol{\mu}_a + (\lambda^k\boldsymbol{1}/W^k U^k_{cc}). \tag{16'}$$

Aggregating (16′) over all individuals gives

$$\boldsymbol{V}_{aC} = T^M \boldsymbol{\mu}_a + v\boldsymbol{1}, \tag{17''}$$

where

$$v = \sum_k \lambda^k / W^k U_{cc}^k.$$

For any portfolio z with returns that are uncorrelated with aggregate consumption, from (17″) above,

$$v = -T^M \mu_z. \tag{17'''}$$

Substituting this into (17″) gives

$$(\mu_M - \mu_z)/\sigma_{MC} = (T^M)^{-1}, \tag{18'}$$

and

$$\boldsymbol{\mu}_a - \mu_z \boldsymbol{1} = (\boldsymbol{\beta}_{aC}/\beta_{MC})(\mu_M - \mu_z). \tag{19'}$$

Thus, if there is no riskless asset in the single-good continuous-time model, then the equilibrium expected return on an asset is equal to the expected return on a portfolio with returns uncorrelated with aggregate consumption plus a risk premium proportional to the asset's consumption-beta. Both the mutual fund theorem of section 2 and the intertemporal CAPM of section 3 hold with no riskless asset when 'the riskless asset' in those results is replaced by 'the zero consumption-beta portfolio that has minimum variance'.[14]

The next section examines asset pricing in the multi-good continuous-time model, when a nominally riskless asset is assumed to exist.

7. Asset pricing with many consumption-goods

The derivations of the consumption, portfolio and pricing results thus far have been in the context of a rather general *single-good* economy. This section discusses some modifications of the results that would occur in a multi-good economy. The major focus will be on conditions that permit the derivation of a 'single-beta' intertemporal capital asset pricing model with stochastic investment *and* consumption opportunities (similar to that of section 3, which had only stochastic investment opportunities).

[14]The choice of a zero-beta, minimum-variance portfolio is intuitive, but not unique. For example, in the mutual fund theorem of section 2, the unconstrained minimum variance portfolio can also replace the riskless asset under the assumptions of this section. Also, the zero-beta intertemporal CAPM can be written in terms of the expected return on any zero consumption-beta portfolio.

Let there be Q goods in the economy and let $q^k(t)$ be individual k's $Q \times 1$ vector of the rates at which quantities are consumed of the various goods at time t. Each individual is assumed to maximize the expected utility of a time-additive utility function as in (6), but with $U^k(c^k, t)$ being replaced by $u^k(q^k, t)$. The vector of consumption-goods prices is P_c, and individual k's rate of nominal expenditures is $c^k = P_c' q^k$. Individual k's indirect utility function for consumption expenditures is now defined as

$$U^k(c^k, P_c', t) = \max_{\{P_c' q^k = c^k\}} u^k(q^k, t). \tag{26}$$

The analysis of section 2 is virtually unchanged in the multi-good model; first-order conditions (9) and (10) still hold when the state vector s is assumed to include as a subset P_c and its probability distribution. The $(S+2)$-fund theorem obtains with instantaneous-maturity commodity futures contracts being perfect hedges for changes in consumption-goods prices. Similarly, the multi-beta asset-pricing model given by (11) holds in this model, with expected excess returns on those futures contracts (if they exist) being a subset of $(\mu_s^* - r)$.[15]

Although, in the multi-good case, the form of the demand equations for assets is unchanged from section 2's eq. (10), section 3's translation of those demands in terms of the individual's optimal consumption function is somewhat different in the multi-good case. The difference arises from the fact that the utility of a given level of consumption expenditure now depends upon relative prices, P_c. Mathematically, in section 2, $U_c^k(c^k, t) = J_W^k(W^k, s, t)$ implied that $U_{cc}^k c_s^k = J_{Ws}^k$, but in the multi-good case we have: $U_c^k(c^k, P_c(s), t) = J_W^k(W^k, s, t)$ implies that $U_{cc}^k c_P^k + U_{cP}^k = J_{WP}^k$ by the implicit function theorem. Thus, individual k's asset demand functions, written in terms of his optimal consumption function, are [from (10) and above, assuming the first Q state variables are the logarithms of consumption-goods prices]

$$w^k W^k = (T^k / c_W^k) \mathbf{V}_{aa}^{-1} (\mu_a - r) - \mathbf{V}_{aa}^{-1} \mathbf{V}_{as} (c_s^k / c_W^k)$$
$$- \mathbf{V}_{aa}^{-1} \mathbf{V}_{as} \begin{pmatrix} U_{\ln P, c}^k / U_{cc}^k c_W^k \\ 0 \end{pmatrix}. \tag{27}$$

The last term in (27) represents long or short components of asset demands for the portfolios that are most highly correlated with the prices of consumption-goods; this term arises from the dependence of the individual's

[15] Since futures contracts require no investment and, therefore, rates of return are undefined, the expected excess return on a contract in this context should be viewed as the expected rate of return to a portfolio of the futures contract and an instantaneously riskless bond that has face value equal to the price of the futures contract.

indirect marginal utility for nominal expenditure on consumption-goods prices.

Let $\boldsymbol{\alpha}^k$ be the $Q \times 1$ vector of individual k's budget shares, i.e., $\alpha_j^k = P_j q_j^k / c^k$, and let $\boldsymbol{m}^k$ be individual k's vector of incremental ('marginal') budget shares, i.e., $m_j^k = P_j(\partial q_j^k / \partial c^k)$. The vector $\boldsymbol{m}^k$ is the set of fractions of an additional dollar of total expenditure that would be spent on the various consumption-goods. The new term in (27) due to the multi-good model may be expressed in terms of the average and marginal vectors of budget shares as shown in appendix 3, giving asset demands

$$\boldsymbol{w}^k W^k = (T^k / c_W^k)\mathbf{V}_{aa}^{-1}(\boldsymbol{\mu}_a - \boldsymbol{r}) - \mathbf{V}_{aa}^{-1}\mathbf{V}_{as}(\boldsymbol{c}_s^k / c_W^k)$$
$$+ \mathbf{V}_{aa}^{-1}\mathbf{V}_{as}\begin{pmatrix} c^k \boldsymbol{\alpha}^k / c_W^k - (T^k / c_W^k)\boldsymbol{m}^k \\ \boldsymbol{0} \end{pmatrix}. \tag{28}$$

Multiplying (28) by $(\mathbf{V}_{aa} c_W^k)$ and rearranging terms gives

$$T^k\left[\boldsymbol{\mu}_a - \boldsymbol{r} - \mathbf{V}_{as}\begin{pmatrix} \boldsymbol{m}^k \\ \boldsymbol{0} \end{pmatrix}\right] = \boldsymbol{V}_{aW_k} c_W^k + \mathbf{V}_{as}\boldsymbol{c}_s^k - \mathbf{V}_{as}\begin{pmatrix} \boldsymbol{\alpha}^k c^k \\ \boldsymbol{0} \end{pmatrix}$$
$$= \boldsymbol{V}_{ac_k} - \mathbf{V}_{as}\begin{pmatrix} \boldsymbol{\alpha}^k c^k \\ \boldsymbol{0} \end{pmatrix}, \tag{29}$$

where the second line recognizes that $c^k = c^k(W^k, s, t)$ and Ito's Lemma implies that $\boldsymbol{V}_{aW_k} c_W^k + \mathbf{V}_{as}\boldsymbol{c}_s^k = \boldsymbol{V}_{ac_k}$.

Aggregating the optimality condition in (29) for all individuals gives a similar relation in terms of aggregate consumption and aggregate vectors of average budget shares and marginal budget shares,

$$\boldsymbol{\mu}_a - \boldsymbol{r} - \mathbf{V}_{as}\begin{pmatrix} \boldsymbol{m} \\ \boldsymbol{0} \end{pmatrix} = (T^M / C)^{-1}\left[\boldsymbol{V}_{a,\ln C} - \mathbf{V}_{as}\begin{pmatrix} \boldsymbol{\alpha} \\ \boldsymbol{0} \end{pmatrix}\right], \tag{30}$$

where

$$\boldsymbol{\alpha} = \left(\sum_k \boldsymbol{\alpha}^k c^k\right) \Big/ C \quad \text{and} \quad \boldsymbol{m} = \left(\sum_k \boldsymbol{m}^k T^k\right) \Big/ T^M.$$

The calculation of the economy-wide vector of average budget shares, $\boldsymbol{\alpha}$, requires only data on the aggregate dollars spent on the various goods; no other preference information is required. These shares are the fractions of aggregate expenditure that are spent on the various consumption-goods. These budget shares are, in principal, the weights used in the computation of the price deflator for consumption expenditures in the National Income and Product Accounts.[16]

[16]See the *Survey of Current Business* of the U.S. Department of Commerce.

The vector of aggregate marginal budget shares, $\boldsymbol{m}$, is the set of fractions of an additional dollar of aggregate expenditure (allocated optimally among individuals) that would be spent on the various consumption goods, holding prices constant. The reason that this statement can be made, without explicit reference to the risk tolerances of individuals, is that the optimal allocation among individuals of an individual dollar of aggregate nominal expenditure is according to individuals' risk tolerances relative to aggregate risk tolerance, (T^k/T^M). Thus, the aggregate marginal budget shares for goods may be written as

$$m_j = \sum_k (\partial c^k/\partial C) P_j (\partial q_j^k/\partial c^k) = P_j(\partial q_j/\partial C). \tag{31}$$

Note that the aggregate marginal budget share for each good can be computed as the product of (1) the aggregate average budget share for the good and (2) the aggregate expenditure elasticity of demand for the good, $(\partial \ln q_j)/(\partial \ln C)$.

It is useful for the subsequent analysis to define the local percentage changes in two price indices – one based upon average budget shares for the economy and one based upon the marginal budget shares for the economy,[17]

$$\mathrm{d}I/I \equiv \sum_j \alpha_j(\mathrm{d}P_j/P_j), \qquad \mathrm{d}I_m/I_m \equiv \sum_j m_j(\mathrm{d}P_j/P_j). \tag{32}$$

The two terms in eq. (30) that involve $\boldsymbol{m}$ and $\boldsymbol{\alpha}$ can be rewritten in terms of these price indices, giving

$$\boldsymbol{\mu}_a - \boldsymbol{r} - \boldsymbol{V}_{aI_m} = (T^M/C)^{-1}[\boldsymbol{V}_{a,\ln C} - \boldsymbol{V}_{aI}], \tag{33}$$

where $\boldsymbol{V}_{aI_m}$ and $\boldsymbol{V}_{aI}$ are the vectors of the covariances of asset returns with the local percentage changes in the price indices.

Since it can be shown that a feasible (but not necessarily optimal) allocation exists such that everyone in the economy has a consumption

[17]A globally valid price index that is invariant to the level of nominal expenditure exists for an individual if and only if his indifference curves are 'homothetic'. This implies unitary demand elasticities for all goods. When they are not unitary, the individual's budget shares depend upon his level of nominal expenditure, making the weights in his price index vary with the level of expenditure. A survey of price index results is provided by Samuelson and Swamy (1974). Identical and homothetic consumption preferences for all individuals are typically assumed to justify the use of aggregate budget shares to compute a price index for the economy. The price indices used in this paper do not require that individuals be identical, nor that they have homothetic preferences. The continuity of the continuous-time framework and the weaker requirement that the price indices be locally (not globally) valid permits the greater generality of consumption preferences of this paper. For a paper that utilizes preference restrictions that give a globally valid price index, see Grauer and Litzenberger (1979).

allocation that is preferable to his current allocation if and only if the percentage change in aggregate nominal expenditure exceeds the percentage change in the average budget share price index, I, aggregate *real* consumption is defined as $C^* = C/I$.[18] Given this definition, note that the vector of covariances of real asset returns with aggregate real consumption is

$$V_{a^*C^*} = V_{a,\ln C} - V_{aI} - \dot{V}_{IC^*}\mathbf{1}, \tag{34}$$

where $\dot{V}_{IC^*}$ is the covariance of the aggregate average-weighted price index with aggregate real consumption. Defining an asset's 'real consumption-beta', β_j^*, as the local covariance of its real return with percentage changes in aggregate real consumption, divided by the variance rate of changes in aggregate real consumption, then (33) can be re-written in terms of assets' real consumption-betas,

$$\boldsymbol{\mu}_a - r - \dot{V}_{aI_m} = (T^M/C\sigma_{C^*}^2)^{-1}[\boldsymbol{\beta}_a^* - \beta_r^*\mathbf{1}], \tag{35}$$

where β_r^* is the real consumption-beta of the nominally riskless asset.

The left-hand side of (35) can be interpreted as the differences of the expected real returns on assets from the expected real return on the nominally riskless asset, where these expected real returns are evaluated relative to the price index with aggregate marginal budget shares. To see this, first note that the instantaneous expected percentage rate of change of an asset's real price, P_a/I, is given by Ito's Lemma as the expected nominal return on the asset, minus the expected rate of inflation measured by the index, and minus the covariance of the asset's nominal return with inflation. The covariance term is explained by the fact that an asset with high nominal payoffs when prices are low and low nominal payoffs when prices are high buys more real goods on average than an asset with positive covariance of its nominal returns with inflation, assuming that expected nominal payoffs are the same for both assets. Since the covariance of the nominal return on the nominally riskless asset with inflation is zero, the LHS of (35) is the difference between the expected real returns on assets, $\boldsymbol{\mu}_a^*$, and the expected real return on the nominally riskless asset, μ_r^*. It can be easily verified that for any three assets i, j and k,

$$(\mu_i^* - \mu_j^*)/(\beta_i^* - \beta_j^*) = (\mu_k^* - \mu_j^*)/(\beta_k^* - \beta_j^*) \quad \text{for all } i, j, k. \tag{36}$$

Letting z represent a portfolio with real returns that are uncorrelated with

[18]For a proof of the result stated, see Breeden (1977, ch. 3).

changes in aggregate real consumption, it is seen that a multi-good, zero-beta intertemporal CAPM obtains

$$\mu_i^* - \mu_z^* = (\beta_i^*/\beta_k^*)(\mu_k^* - \mu_z^*). \tag{37}$$

The use of the price index based upon aggregate marginal shares for calculation of expected real returns, while using the price index with aggregate average shares as weights for calculation of real consumption-betas, requires some intuitive explanation. Before proceeding with an explanation, note that there is no difference between the indices if aggregate expenditure elasticities of demand for goods are all unity. This aggregate 'homothetic' case involves strong preference assumptions and is not assumed to hold. As in the single-good economy, asset prices are determined from their payoffs and from individuals' marginal utilities of a dollar of consumption expenditure in the various states of the world. The marginal utility of a dollar to an individual depends upon: (1) the quantities of goods consumed, via diminishing marginal utilities for the consumption of goods, and (2) the quantities of goods that a dollar can buy. By the definition of the marginal budget share vector, an additional dollar is spent on goods in the proportions given by the marginal vector; thus, the price index with marginal weights evaluates the quantities of goods that another dollar purchases. As Samuelson and Swamy (1974) observed, real consumption is a quantity index. As a quantity index, the larger real consumption is, the smaller the marginal utility of goods consumed is. The role of the price index with average budget shares as weights in risk measurement arises from its use in the computation of aggregate real consumption, which is inversely related to the marginal utilities of consumption-goods.

To this point, a real riskless asset is not assumed to exist, nor are futures contracts that can create a real riskless return assumed to exist. If a real riskless asset or portfolio is assumed to exist and have a real return of r^*, then the expected return on a zero real consumption-beta portfolio in the pricing eq. (37) can be replaced by r^*,

$$\mu_i^* - r^* = (\beta_i^*/\beta_k^*)(\mu_k^* - r^*). \tag{38}$$

This is an intertemporal asset pricing model developed in a multi-good world with stochastic consumption and investment opportunities.

The results obtained here may be compared to those obtained in the explicitly multi-commodity economies of Long (1974) and Grauer and Litzenberger (1979). Long makes no restrictions on preferences for goods, but assumes joint normality of consumption-goods prices. The effect of many goods in his model is to extend the number of betas that must be calculated to find the expected excess return on any asset from the expected excess returns on futures contracts and on portfolios that hedge against investment opportunity set changes. The derivation in this paper of instantaneous expected excess returns in terms of a single beta for each asset is a contribution to the literature.

Grauer and Litzenberger work with a multi-commodity, two-period state preference model and derive asset prices with particular attention to the prices of commodity futures contracts. They make no assumptions about the probability distribution of states of the world, but they assume that the capital markets are Pareto-optimal and that each individual has 'homothetic' preferences for consumption-goods, i.e., that all income elasticities of demand are unity for all goods, for each individual. They derive an asset's risk premium from its return covariance with a single variable, the social marginal utility of wealth. This variable is a function of aggregate wealth deflated by a price index that is assumed to be the same for all individuals. The derivation in this paper of a single-beta measure of risk in a multi-commodity world is similar to theirs, but knowledge of the social marginal utility function is not needed for the beta computation of this paper. The difference between their focus upon wealth and the present focus on consumption is a product of their two-period world, which does not require an analysis of changing investment opportunities. Finally, the preference assumptions needed for the existence of a price index in a discrete-time model are not needed for the local statements of the continuous-time model.

8. Conclusion

An intertemporal capital asset pricing model has been derived in an economic environment permitting both stochastic consumption-goods prices and stochastic portfolio opportunities. The paper is an extension and generalization of Merton's (1973) continuous-time model, deriving equivalent pricing equations that are simpler in form and are potentially empirically testable.

The use of aggregate consumption in empirical tests, rather than the market portfolio that has been used, has both virtues and difficulties. Difficulties with consumption numbers that are available include: (1) instantaneous consumption rates are not measured; rather, weekly, monthly, quarterly, or annual integrals of these rates are measured,[19] (2) only the part of the measured consumption of goods that gives current utility should be included, which excludes a large fraction of current purchases of durables, and (3) the actual data that are available contain considerable measurement error, whereas the prices and numbers of shares used in the market portfolio

[19]With power utility functions and lognormal consumption, this is not a problem, since the pricing model holds with betas and returns measured over any interval. See Breeden and Litzenberger (1978) for a proof of this result.

computations are measured with very little error. The principal virtue of aggregate consumption measures, in comparison with the market proxies used, is that the consumption measures available cover a greater fraction of the true consumption variable than the fraction that the market portfolio measures cover of the true market portfolio (mainly because of the lack of coverage of human capital, real estate, and consumer durables in market measures). Note also that proposed capital expenditure projects typically have cash flows that are more significantly related to aggregate consumption, than to the market portfolio. This may make the distinction of projects with different risk levels more precise and more intuitive, thereby facilitating the use of asset pricing theory in capital budgeting.

In the continuous-time model, areas that need additional theoretical development include the role of firms and their optimal investment and capital structure decisions, and the impact of transaction costs, information costs, and diverse beliefs upon optimal consumption–investment decisions and upon the structure of asset returns.

Appendix 1: Proof of Theorem 1

By aggregating the optimal portfolio demands of all individuals given by (10) the market portfolio must be

$$w^M M = \sum_k w^k W^k = T_W^M \mathbf{V}_{aa}^{-1}(\boldsymbol{\mu}_a - r) + \mathbf{V}_{aa}^{-1}\mathbf{V}_{as}\boldsymbol{H}_s^M, \tag{A.1}$$

where

$$T_W^k = -J_W^k / J_{WW}^k \quad \text{and} \quad \boldsymbol{H}_s^k = -J_{Ws}^k / J_{WW}^k,$$

and where

$$T_W^M = \sum_k T_W^k \quad \text{and} \quad \boldsymbol{H}_s^M = \sum_k \boldsymbol{H}_s^k.$$

Substituting (A.1) into (10) allows the individual's portfolio demands to be written as

$$w^k W^k = (T_W^k / T_W^M) M (w^M) + \mathbf{V}_{aa}^{-1}\mathbf{V}_{as}(\boldsymbol{H}_s^k - \boldsymbol{H}_s^M T_W^k / T_W^M). \tag{A.2}$$

This proves that all individuals may obtain their optimal portfolio positions by trading in $(S+2)$ 'mutual funds', with one of them being the market portfolio, one being the riskless asset, and S of them being given by $\mathbf{V}_{aa}^{-1}\mathbf{V}_{as}$.

Next, note that column j of $\mathbf{V}_{aa}^{-1}\mathbf{V}_{as}$, i.e., $\mathbf{V}_{aa}^{-1}V_{as_j}$, is the solution to the following problem (up to a factor of proportionality):

$$\frac{1}{2\lambda}\mathbf{V}_{aa}^{-1}V_{as_j} \quad \text{solves} \quad \max_{w_j} \{w_j' V_{as_j} + \lambda(\sigma^2 - w_j' \mathbf{V}_{aa} w_j)\}. \tag{A.3}$$

In (A.3), by maximizing covariance of the portfolio with s_j for a given level of variance, we effectively find the portfolio of assets that maximizes the correlation coefficient of its returns with changes in state variable j. Given this, the theorem is proven from (A.2) and the fact that wealth not in risky assets is placed in the nominally riskless asset. Q.E.D.

Appendix 2

Since $c^k = c^k(W^k, s, t)$ and $c^j = c^j(W^j, s, t)$, Ito's Lemma implies that the covariance of c^k and c^j is

$$\operatorname{cov}(c^k, c^j) = (c^k_W \, 0 \, \mathbf{c}^{k'}_s) \begin{pmatrix} V_{W_k W_k} & V_{W_k W_j} & \mathbf{V}_{W_k s} \\ V_{W_j W_k} & V_{W_j W_j} & \mathbf{V}_{W_j s} \\ \mathbf{V}_{s W_k} & \mathbf{V}_{s W_j} & \mathbf{V}_{ss} \end{pmatrix} \begin{pmatrix} 0 \\ c^j_W \\ \mathbf{c}^j_s \end{pmatrix}, \tag{A.4}$$

$$= \mathbf{c}^{k'}_s \mathbf{V}_{s W_j} c^j_W + \mathbf{c}^{k'}_s \mathbf{V}_{ss} \mathbf{c}^j_s + c^k_W \mathbf{V}_{W_k s} \mathbf{c}^j_s + c^k_W V_{W_k W_j} c^j_W,$$

where subscripted V's represent covariance matrices with appropriate dimensions and subscripted c's represent partial derivatives or gradients of those consumption functions.

First, the assumption is that

$$\mathbf{V}_{aa} = \begin{pmatrix} V_{MM} & \mathbf{V}_{Ms} \\ \mathbf{V}_{sM} & \mathbf{V}_{ss} \end{pmatrix} \equiv \mathbf{V}, \tag{A.5}$$

and

$$\boldsymbol{\mu}_a - \mathbf{r} = \begin{pmatrix} \mu_M - r \\ \boldsymbol{\mu}^*_s - \mathbf{r} \end{pmatrix} \equiv \boldsymbol{\mu} - \mathbf{r}. \tag{A.6}$$

Define an $S \times (S+1)$ matrix $\mathbf{L}$ to be

$$\mathbf{L} = (\mathbf{0} \quad \mathbf{I}), \tag{A.7}$$

where $\mathbf{0}$ is an $S \times 1$ vector of zeros and $\mathbf{I}$ is an $S \times S$ identity matrix. Note that

$$\mathbf{L}(\boldsymbol{\mu} - \mathbf{r}) = \boldsymbol{\mu}^*_s - \mathbf{r}, \tag{A.8}$$

and

$$\mathbf{L}\mathbf{V} = \mathbf{V}_{s,Ms} \equiv (\mathbf{V}_{sM} \quad \mathbf{V}_{ss}). \tag{A.9}$$

From individuals' optimal asset demands, (12), it is seen that

$$c_W^k \mathbf{w}^k W^k = \mathbf{V}^{-1}[T^k(\boldsymbol{\mu}-\boldsymbol{r}) - \mathbf{VL}'\boldsymbol{c}_s^k], \tag{A.10}$$

which implies that

$$\begin{aligned} c_W^k V_{sW_k} &= \mathbf{LV}[c_W^k \mathbf{w}^k W^k] \\ &= T^k\mathbf{L}(\boldsymbol{\mu}-\boldsymbol{r}) - \mathbf{LVL}'\boldsymbol{c}_s^k. \end{aligned} \tag{A.11}$$

Next, evaluate the last term of (A.4),

$$\begin{aligned} c_W^k V_{W_k W_j} c_W^j &= c_W^k W^k \mathbf{w}^{k\prime} \mathbf{V} \mathbf{w}^j W^j c_W^j \\ &= [T^k(\boldsymbol{\mu}-\boldsymbol{r})' - \boldsymbol{c}_s^{k\prime}\mathbf{LV}]\mathbf{V}^{-1}[T^j(\boldsymbol{\mu}-\boldsymbol{r}) - \mathbf{VL}'\boldsymbol{c}_s^j] \\ &= T^kT^j(\boldsymbol{\mu}-\boldsymbol{r})'\mathbf{V}^{-1}(\boldsymbol{\mu}-\boldsymbol{r}) - T^k(\boldsymbol{\mu}-\boldsymbol{r})'\mathbf{L}'\boldsymbol{c}_s^j \\ &\quad - T^j\boldsymbol{c}_s^{k\prime}\mathbf{L}(\boldsymbol{\mu}-\boldsymbol{r}) + \boldsymbol{c}_s^{k\prime}\mathbf{LVL}'\boldsymbol{c}_s^j. \end{aligned} \tag{A.12}$$

Substituting the results of (A.11) and (A.12) into (A.4) gives the covariance of changes in individual k's optimal consumption rate with changes in j's optimal consumption rate,

$$\begin{aligned} \operatorname{cov}(c^k, c^j) &= \boldsymbol{c}_s^{k\prime}[T^j\mathbf{L}(\boldsymbol{\mu}-\boldsymbol{r}) - \mathbf{LVL}'\boldsymbol{c}_s^j] + \boldsymbol{c}_s^{k\prime}\mathbf{LVL}'\boldsymbol{c}_s^j \\ &\quad + [T^k(\boldsymbol{\mu}-\boldsymbol{r})'\mathbf{L}' - \boldsymbol{c}_s^{k\prime}\mathbf{LVL}']\boldsymbol{c}_s^j \\ &\quad + T^kT^j\gamma - T^k(\boldsymbol{\mu}-\boldsymbol{r})'\mathbf{L}'\boldsymbol{c}_s^j \\ &\quad - T^j\boldsymbol{c}_s^{k\prime}\mathbf{L}(\boldsymbol{\mu}-\boldsymbol{r}) + \boldsymbol{c}_s^{k\prime}\mathbf{LVL}'\boldsymbol{c}_s^j \\ &= T^kT^j\gamma, \end{aligned} \tag{A.13}$$

where $\gamma = (\boldsymbol{\mu}-\boldsymbol{r})'V^{-1}(\boldsymbol{\mu}-\boldsymbol{r})$. Eq. (A.13) is eq. (24) of the text, as was to be shown.

Appendix 3

The definition of the consumer's indirect utility function is

$$U(c, t, \boldsymbol{P}_c) = \max_{\boldsymbol{P}_c'\boldsymbol{q}=c} u(\boldsymbol{q}, t) = \max_{\boldsymbol{q}} \{u(\boldsymbol{q}, t) + \lambda(c - \boldsymbol{P}_c\boldsymbol{q})\} \tag{A.14}$$

and the first order conditions for a maximum imply that

$$\boldsymbol{u}_q = \lambda\boldsymbol{P}_c, \qquad \boldsymbol{U}_p = -\lambda\boldsymbol{q}, \tag{A.15}$$

and the shadow price $\lambda = U_c$.

By differentiating the optimality conditions in (A.15),

$$-U_{\ln P_j, c}/U_{cc} = (U_c/U_{cc})P_j(\partial q_j/\partial c) + P_j q_j = -Tm_j + c\alpha_j. \tag{A.16}$$

Substitute (A.16) into (21), and (22) is obtained.

References

Arnold, L., 1974, Stochastic differential equations: Theory and applications (Wiley, New York).

Arrow, K.J., 1964, The role of securities in the optimal allocation of risk-bearing, Review of Economic Studies, 91–96.

Arrow, K.J., 1965, The theory of risk aversion, in: Aspects of the theory of risk-bearing (Helsinki).

Black, F., 1972, Capital market equilibrium with restricted borrowing, Journal of Business 45, no. 3, July.

Breeden, D.T., 1977, Changing consumption and investment opportunities and the valuation of securities, Ph.D. dissertation (Stanford University, Stanford, CA).

Breeden, D.T. and R.H. Litzenberger, 1978, Prices of state-contingent claims implicit in option prices, Journal of Business, Oct.

Cox, J.C., J.E. Ingersoll and S.A. Ross, 1977, A theory of the term structure of interest rates, Econometrica, forthcoming.

Cox, J.C. and S.A. Ross, 1977, Some models of capital asset pricing with rational anticipations, Mimeo., Sept.

Debreu, G., 1959, The theory of value (Wiley, New York).

Fama, E.F., 1970, Multiperiod consumption–investment decisions, American Economic Review, March, 163–174.

Garman, M., 1976, A general theory of asset valuation under diffusion state processes, Working paper no. 50 (Graduate School of Business, University of California, Berkeley, CA).

Gihman, I.I. and A.V. Skorohod, 1972, Stochastic differential equations (Springer-Verlag, New York).

Grauer, F.L.A. and R.H. Litzenberger, 1979, The pricing of commodity futures contracts, nominal bonds and other risky assets under commodity price uncertainty, Journal of Finance, March, 69–84.

Hakansson, N.H., 1970, Optimal investment and consumption strategies under risk for a class of utility functions, Econometrica, 587–607.

Hakansson, N.H., 1977, Efficient paths toward efficient capital markets in large and small countries, in: H. Levy and M. Sarnat, eds., Financial decision making under uncertainty (Academic Press, New York).

Hakansson, N.H., 1978, Welfare aspects of options and supershares, Journal of Finance, June, 759–776.

Harrison, J.M. and D.M. Kreps, 1978, Martingales and the valuation of redundant assets, Research paper no. 444, May (Stanford University, Stanford, CA).

Jensen, M.C., 1972, Capital markets: Theory and evidence, Bell Journal of Economics and Management Science, Autumn, 357–398.

Kushner, H.J., 1967, Stochastic stability and control (Academic Press, New York).

Lintner, J., 1965, Valuation of risk assets and the selection of risky investments in stock portfolios and capital budgets, Review of Economics and Statistics, 13–37.

Lintner, John, 1969, Aggregation of investors' diverse judgements and preferences in purely competitive security markets, Journal of Financial and Quantitative Analysis, Dec.

Long, J.B., 1974, Stock prices, inflation, and the term structure of interest rates, Journal of Financial Economics, 131–170.

Lucas, R.E., 1978, Asset prices in an exchange economy, Econometrica 46, Nov., 1429–1445.
Markowitz, H., 1952, Portfolio selection, Journal of Finance, March.
McKean, H.P., 1969, Stochastic integrals (Academic Press, New York).
Merton, R.C., 1971, Optimum consumption and portfolio rules in a continuous-time model, Journal of Economic Theory, 373–413.
Merton, R.C., 1973, An intertemporal capital asset pricing model, Econometrica 41, 867–887.
Merton, R.C., 1978, On the mathematics and economic assumptions of continuous-time models, M.I.T. Working paper no. 981–78, March (Massachusetts Institute of Technology, Cambridge, MA).
Mossin, J., 1966, Equilibrium in a capital asset market, Econometrica, Oct.
Mossin, J., 1973, Theory of financial markets (Prentice–Hall, Englewood Cliffs, NJ).
Muth, J.F., 1961, Rational expectations and the theory of price movements, Econometrica.
Pratt, J., 1964, Risk aversion in the small and in the large, Econometrica 32.
Pye, G., 1972, Lifetime portfolio selection with age dependent risk aversion, in: G. Szego and K. Shell, Mathematical methods in investment and finance (North-Holland, Amsterdam) 49–64.
Richard, S.F., 1975, Optimal consumption, portfolio and life insurance rules for an uncertain lived individual in a continuous time model, Journal of Financial Economics 2, 187–203.
Roll, R., 1977, A critique of the asset pricing theory's tests; Part I: On past and potential testability of the theory, Journal of Financial Economics 4, March, 129–176.
Rosenberg, B. and J.A. Ohlson, 1976, The stationary distribution of returns and portfolio separation in capital markets: A fundamental contradiction, Journal of Financial and Quantitative Analysis, Sept.
Ross, S.A., 1976, The arbitrage theory of capital asset pricing, Journal of Economic Theory 3, Dec., 343–362.
Ross, S.A., 1978, The current status of the capital asset pricing model, Journal of Finance, June, 885–901.
Rubinstein, M., 1974, An aggregation theorem for securities markets, Journal of Financial Economics 1, 225–244.
Rubinstein, M., 1976, The valuation of uncertain income streams and the pricing of options, Bell Journal of Economics and Management Science 7, no. 2, 407–425.
Samuelson, P.A. and S. Swamy, 1974, Invariant economic index numbers and canonical duality: Survey and synthesis, American Economic Review 64, Sept., 566–593.
Sharpe, W.F., 1964, Capital asset prices: A theory of market equilibrium under conditions of risk, Journal of Finance, 429–442.
Stapleton, R.C. and M.G. Subrahmanyam, 1978, A multiperiod equilibrium asset pricing model, Econometrica 46, Sept., 1077–1096.
U.S. Department of Commerce, 1966, The national income and product accounts of the United States 1929–1965 (Washington, DC).
Vasicek, Oldrich, 1971, Capital market pricing model with no riskless asset, Unpublished manuscript, March (Wells Fargo Bank).

[13]

Econometrica, Vol. 53, No. 2 (March, 1985)

AN INTERTEMPORAL GENERAL EQUILIBRIUM MODEL OF ASSET PRICES[1]

BY JOHN C. COX, JONATHAN E. INGERSOLL, JR., AND STEPHEN A. ROSS

This paper develops a continuous time general equilibrium model of a simple but complete economy and uses it to examine the behavior of asset prices. In this model, asset prices and their stochastic properties are determined endogenously. One principal result is a partial differential equation which asset prices must satisfy. The solution of this equation gives the equilibrium price of any asset in terms of the underlying real variables in the economy.

1. INTRODUCTION

IN THIS PAPER, we develop a general equilibrium asset pricing model for use in applied research. An important feature of the model is its integration of real and financial markets. Among other things, the model endogenously determines the stochastic process followed by the equilibrium price of any financial asset and shows how this process depends on the underlying real variables. The model is fully consistent with rational expectations and maximizing behavior on the part of all agents.

Our framework is general enough to include many of the fundamental forces affecting asset markets, yet it is tractable enough to be specialized easily to produce specific testable results. Furthermore, the model can be extended in a number of straightforward ways. Consequently, it is well suited to a wide variety of applications. For example, in a companion paper, Cox, Ingersoll, and Ross [7], we use the model to develop a theory of the term structure of interest rates.

Many studies have been concerned with various aspects of asset pricing under uncertainty. The most relevant to our work are the important papers on intertemporal asset pricing by Merton [19] and Lucas [16]. Working in a continuous time framework, Merton derives a relationship among the equilibrium expected rates of return on assets. He shows that when investment opportunities are changing randomly over time this relationship will include effects which have no analogue in a static one period model. Lucas considers an economy with homogeneous individuals and a single consumption good which is produced by a number of processes. The random output of these processes is exogenously determined and perishable. Assets are defined as claims to all or a part of the output of a process, and the equilibrium determines the asset prices.

Our theory draws on some elements of both of these papers. Like Merton, we formulate our model in continuous time and make full use of the analytical tractability that this affords. The economic structure of our model is somewhat similar to that of Lucas. However, we include both endogenous production and

[1] This paper is an extended version of the first half of an earlier working paper titled "A Theory of the Term Structure of Interest Rates." We are grateful for the helpful comments and suggestions of many of our colleagues, both at our own institutions and others. This research was partially supported by the Dean Witter Foundation, the Center for Research in Security Prices, and the National Science Foundation.

random technological change. Since we allow for randomly changing investment opportunities, the intertemporal effects noted by Merton apply to our model and play an important role in our results.

In independent work, Brock [**4, 5**] and Prescott and Mehra [**22**] have also developed intertemporal models of asset pricing. The general approach of their papers is similar to ours, but the methods used and the issues addressed are quite different. Other related work includes papers by Breeden [**3**], Constantinides [**6**], Donaldson and Mehra [**9**], Huang [**14**], Richard and Sundaresan [**24**], Rubinstein [**26**], and Stapleton and Subrahmanyam [**28**].

Our paper is organized in the following way. In Section 2, we develop the model and characterize the equilibrium interest rate and equilibrium rates of return on assets. Section 3 presents our fundamental valuation equation and interprets its solution in a number of ways. Section 4 shows the relationship of our model to the Arrow-Debreu model and discusses the role of firms. In Section 5, we provide some concluding remarks and discuss several possible generalizations of our results.

2. AN EQUILIBRIUM VALUATION MODEL

This section will develop a model of general equilibrium in a simple economic setting. The following assumptions characterize our economy.

ASSUMPTION A1: *There is a single physical good which may be allocated to consumption or investment. All values are expressed in terms of units of this good.*

ASSUMPTION A2: *Production possibilities consist of a set of n linear activities.*[2] *The transformation of an investment of a vector η of amounts of the good in the n production processes is governed by a system of stochastic differential equations of the form:*[3,4]

$$d\eta(t) = I_\eta \alpha(Y, t)\, dt + I_\eta G(Y, t)\, dw(t), \tag{1}$$

[2] We consider a pure capital growth model by assuming that labor is unnecessary in production (or that there is a permanent labor surplus state). This provides a more streamlined setting for the issues which we wish to stress. There is no essential difficulty in expanding the analysis to include labor inputs and nonlinear technologies.

[3] In describing the probabilistic structure of the economy, we will be implicitly referring to an underlying probability space $(\Omega, \mathcal{B}, \mathcal{P})$. Here Ω is a set, $\mathcal{B}$ is a σ-algebra of subsets of Ω, and $\mathcal{P}$ is a probability measure on $\mathcal{B}$. Let $[t, t']$ be a time interval and M be a separable complete metric space. By a stochastic process z, we mean a function from $[t, t'] \times \Omega$ into M such that z is measurable with respect to $\mathcal{B}$ and the σ-algebra of Borel subsets of M. We will take M to be R^n, n-dimensional Euclidean space. A stochastic process is said to be continuous if its possible realizations, or sample paths, are continuous with probability one. A real valued process w on $[t, t']$ is a Wiener process if: (i) w is a continuous process with independent increments, (ii) $w(s) - w(t)$ has a normal distribution with mean zero and variance $s - t$. A process is an n-dimensional Wiener process if its components are independent one-dimensional Wiener processes.

[4] Stochastic differential equations used in this paper are to be understood in the following way. Let $x(t)$ be an m-dimensional stochastic process which satisfies the system of stochastic differential equations

$$dx = a(x, t)\, dt + B(x, t)\, dw(t),$$

where $w(t)$ is an $(n+k)$ dimensional Wiener process in R^{n+k}, Y is a k-dimensional vector of state variables whose movement will be described shortly, I_η is an $n\times n$ diagonal matrix valued function of η whose ith diagonal element is the ith component of η, $\alpha(Y,t)=[\alpha_i(Y,t)]$ is a bounded n-dimensional vector valued function of Y and t, and $G(Y,t)=[g_{ij}(Y,t)]$ is a bounded $n\times(n+k)$ matrix valued function of Y and t. The covariance matrix of physical rates of return on the production processes, GG', is positive definite.[5]

System (1) specifies the growth of an initial investment when the output of each process is continually reinvested in that same process. It thus provides a complete description of the available production opportunities. It does not imply that individuals or firms will necessarily reinvest in this way. The production processes have stochastic constant returns to scale in the sense that the distribution of the rate of return on an investment in any process is independent of the scale of the investment.[6]

ASSUMPTION A3: *The movement of the k-dimensional vector of state variables, Y, is determined by a system of stochastic differential equations of the form*:

$$dY(t)=\mu(Y,t)\,dt+S(Y,t)\,dw(t), \tag{2}$$

---

where $a(x,t)$ is an $m\times 1$ vector valued function and $B(x,t)$ is an $m\times n$ matrix valued function, and $w(t)$ is an n-dimensional Wiener process. A solution of this system with initial position $x(t)$ is a solution of the system of integral equations

$$x(s)=x(t)+\int_t^s a(x(u),u)\,du+\int_t^s B(x(u),u)\,dw(u),$$

where the latter integral is defined in the sense of Ito.

We assume, in reference to (1), (2), and (3), that a and B are measurable on $[t,t']\times R^m$ and satisfy the following growth and Lipschitz conditions:

(i) There exists a constant k_1 such that for all (x,s) in $[t,t']\times R^m$,

$$|a(x,s)|\leq k_1(1+|x|) \quad\text{and}\quad |B(x,s)|\leq k_1(1+|x|).$$

(ii) For any bounded $Q\subset R^m$ there exists a constant k_2, possibly depending on Q and s, such that for all $x, y\in Q$ and $t\leq s\leq t'$,

$$|a(x,s)-a(y,s)|\leq k_2|x-y|,$$

$$|B(x,s)-B(y,s)|\leq k_2|x-y|.$$

Detailed information on all of these topics can be found in Fleming and Rishel [**10**], Friedman [**11**], and Gihman and Skorohod [**12**].

[5] When discussing stochastic differential equations as given in footnote 4, we will refer to $a(x(t),t)$ as the vector of expected returns (or changes) of x and $B(x(t),t)B'(x(t),t)$ as the covariance matrix of returns (or changes) of x. Similarly, if I_x is a diagonal matrix with the ith component of x as its ith diagonal element, then $I_x^{-1}a$ is the vector of expected rates of return (or rates of change or percentage changes) of x and $I_x^{-1}BB'I_x^{-1}$ is the covariance matrix of rates of return (or rates of change or percentage changes) of x.

[6] This formulation allows for quite general probabilistic behavior by the capital stock. However, since the stochastic differential equations are driven by Wiener processes, sudden discontinuous changes in the capital stock are precluded. Note that the incremental return on an investment in any production process can be negative, thus reflecting random physical depreciation.

where $\mu(Y,t)=[\mu_i(Y,t)]$ *is a k-dimensional vector and* $S(Y,t)=[s_{ij}(Y,t)]$ *is a* $k\times(n+k)$ *dimensional matrix. The covariance matrix of changes in the state variables,* SS'*, is nonnegative definite. We will assume that* Y *has no accessible boundaries. Note that* (2) *need not be a linear homogeneous system, and that both* Y *and the joint process* (η, Y) *are Markov.*

This framework includes both uncertain production and random technological change. The probability distribution of current output depends on the current level of the state variables Y, which are themselves changing randomly over time. The development of Y will thus determine the production opportunities which will be available to the economy in the future. In general, opportunities may worsen as well as improve.

Unless GS' is a null matrix, changes in the state variables will be contemporaneously correlated with the incremental returns on the production processes. Indeed, when S is identically equal to G, they are perfectly correlated and the value of Y at any time will be completely determined by the previous returns on the production processes. Consequently, our description of technological change can easily represent situations in which the random shocks to any individual production process are correlated over time.[7]

Y may also include state variables which do not affect production opportunities but are nevertheless of interest to individuals. We postpone further discussion of these variables until a suitable context is developed later in the paper.

ASSUMPTION A4: *There is free entry to all production processes. Individuals can invest in physical production indirectly through firms or directly, in effect creating their own firms. We will adopt the second interpretation, with some remarks about the first. Individuals and firms are competitive and act as price takers in all markets.*

ASSUMPTION A5: *There is a market for instantaneous borrowing and lending at an interest rate r. The market clearing rate, as a function of underlying variables, is determined as part of the competitive equilibrium of the economy.*

ASSUMPTION A6: *There are markets for a variety of contingent claims to amounts of the good. These are securities which are issued and purchased by individuals and firms. The specification of each claim includes a full description of all payoffs which may be received from that claim. These payoffs may depend on the values of the state variables and on aggregate wealth. The values of the claims will in general depend on all variables necessary to describe the state of the economy. We can write the stochastic differential equation governing the movement of the value of claim i,* F^i*, as*

$$dF^i=(F^i\beta_i-\delta_i)\,dt+F^ih_i\,dw(t) \tag{3}$$

[7] As a simple example, suppose $k=n$, $\alpha=-Y$, $\mu=-Y$, and $S=G$, where G is a constant diagonal matrix. Then Y is an n-dimensional first-order autoregressive process and (1) can be rewritten as $d\eta(t)=I_\eta\, dY(t)$.

where h_i is a $1\times(n+k)$ vector valued function. In (3) the total mean return on claim i, $\beta_i F^i$, is defined as the payout received, δ_i, plus the mean price change, $\beta_i F^i - \delta_i$. The variance of the rate of return on claim i is $h_i h_i'$. Ito's formula implies a specific relationship of β_i and h_i to the partial derivatives of the value of the claim and the instantaneous means and covariances of the variables on which it depends, but for the moment, (3) should be considered as providing only a notation for entities which will be examined in detail later.[8] *It does not imply that the movement of a price is being specified exogenously. The equilibrium β_i and r are stochastic processes which are to be determined endogenously.*

Assumption A7: *There are a fixed number of individuals, identical in their endowments and preferences. All individuals agree that the production opportunities and state variables are as described. Each individual seeks to maximize an objective function of the form:*[9,10]

$$E\int_t^{t'} U[C(s), Y(s), s]\,ds. \tag{4}$$

In (4), E is an expectation operator conditional on current endowment and the state of the economy, $C(s)$ is the consumption flow at time s, and U is a von Neumann-Morgenstern utility function. We assume that U is increasing, strictly concave, twice differentiable, and satisfies the condition $|U(C(s), Y(s), s)| \le k_1(1+C(s)+|Y(s)|)^{k_2}$ for some positive constants k_1 and k_2.

Assumption A8: *Physical investment and trading in claims take place continuously in time with no adjustment or transactions costs. Trading takes place only at equilibrium prices.*

We will begin our analysis of this economy by considering the individual's allocation problem. In the presence of contingent claims, the individual portfolio selection problem will in general not have a unique solution. Consequently, it is convenient to choose a basis for the set of investment opportunities, including both production processes and contingent claims. A basis is defined as the set

[8] Let $dx = a(x,t)\,dt + B(x,t)\,dw(t)$, let $a_i(x,t)$ be the ith element of a, and let $b_{ij}(x,t)$ be the i, jth element of B. Ito's formula can be stated in the following way. If $f(x,t)$ is a continuous function with continuous partial derivatives f_t, f_x, f_{xx} on $[t,t']\times R^m$ then

$$df(x(t),t) = \left[f_t(x,t) + \sum_{i=1}^{m} f_{x_i}(x,t)a_i(x,t) + \tfrac{1}{2}\sum_{j,k=1}^{m} f_{x_k x_j}(x,t)\sum_{i=1}^{m} b_{ki}(x,t)b_{ji}(x,t)\right]dt$$
$$+\sum_{i=1}^{n}\sum_{j=1}^{m} f_{x_j}(x,t)b_{ji}(x,t)\,dw_i(t).$$

[9] We adopt a finite-horizon formulation to allow consideration of the effects of horizon length on contingent claim values. A bequest function assigning utility to terminal wealth could easily be added. The infinite-horizon case proceeds along the same lines with appropriate technical modifications.

[10] It should be stressed that the role of the state variables in our subsequent propositions is in no way due solely to their presence in the direct utility function, U. The only simplifications that would result from a state independent direct utility function are noted in equations (28), (29), and (30).

of production processes and a set of contingent claims, with row vectors h_i, as in (3), forming the matrix H, such that for any other contingent claim j, h_j can be written as a linear combination of the rows of G and H. Equation (3) will now be interpreted as referring to the claims in the basis. The explicit construction of the basis over time is not of importance as long as its dimension remains unchanged, which we assume to be the case. Any creation or expiration of contingent claims which causes a change in the dimension of the basis will cause a change in the hedging opportunities available to an individual. For simplicity we assume that the basis consists of the n production activities and k contingent claims.

It is sufficient for both individual choice and equilibrium valuation to determine the unique allocation resulting when the opportunity set is restricted to the basis. Any allocation involving nonbasis claims could be replicated by a controlled portfolio of claims in the basis.[11] Since any of these choices would give the individual the same portfolio behavior over time and the same consumption path, he would be indifferent among them. In this scheme of things there is no reason for nonbasis contingent claims to exist, but there is no reason for them not to exist either, and we may assume that in general there will be an infinite number of them, each of which must be consistently priced in equilibrium.[12]

After defining the opportunity set in this way, an individual will allocate his wealth among the $(n+k)$ basis opportunities, and the $(n+k+1)$st opportunity, riskless borrowing or lending. Make the following definitions: W is the individual's current total wealth, $a_i W$ is the amount of wealth invested in the ith production process, and $b_i W$ is the amount of wealth invested in the ith contingent claim. The individual wishes to choose the controls aW, bW, and C which will maximize his expected lifetime utility subject to the budget constraint:[13]

$$
\begin{aligned}
(5)\qquad dW &= \left[\sum_{i=1}^{n} a_i W(\alpha_i - r) + \sum_{i=1}^{k} b_i W(\beta_i - r) + rW - C\right] dt \\
&\quad + \sum_{i=1}^{n} a_i W\left(\sum_{j=1}^{n+k} g_{ij}\, dw_j\right) + \sum_{i=1}^{k} b_i W\left(\sum_{j=1}^{n+k} h_{ij}\, dw_j\right) \\
&\equiv W\mu(W)\, dt + W \sum_{j=1}^{n+k} q_j\, dw_j .
\end{aligned}
$$

We now make an assumption of a purely technical nature which enables us to apply standard results from stochastic control theory to this problem.

[11] For further details, see Merton [**20**], which contains a complete description of this concept. It is implicit in the earlier work of Black and Scholes [**2**] and Merton [**18**]. See also Harrison and Kreps [**13**].

[12] This would be the case, for example, for bonds with a continuum of maturity dates or options with a continuum of exercise prices. One could then describe individual holdings in terms of a measure on the admissible set, thus allowing finite holdings at points as well as over intervals.

[13] For a detailed explanation of the form of the budget constraint, see Merton [**17**].

ASSUMPTION A9: *In maximizing* (4), *the individual limits his attention to a class of admissible feedback controls, V. An admissible feedback control, v, is a Borel measurable function on* $[t, t') \times R^{n+k+1}$ *satisfying the growth and Lipschitz conditions given in footnote* 4. *Furthermore, admissible disequilibrium* β *and* r *are bounded and satisfy the Lipschitz conditions given in footnote* 4.

Measurability implies the natural restriction that the control chosen at any time must depend only on information available at that time.

Define

$$K(v(t), W(t), Y(t), t) = \underset{W,Y,t}{E} \int_t^{t'} U(v(s), Y(s), s)\, ds \tag{6}$$

where $v(t)$ is an admissible feedback control, and let $L^v(t)K$ be the differential generator of K associated with this control,

$$\begin{aligned} L^v(t)K = \mu(W)WK_W + \sum_{i=1}^{k} \mu_i K_{Y_i} + \tfrac{1}{2}W^2 K_{WW} \sum_{i=1}^{n+k} q_i^2 \\ + \sum_{i=1}^{k} WK_{WY_i} \sum_{j=1}^{n+k} q_j s_{ij} + \tfrac{1}{2} \sum_{i=1}^{k}\sum_{j=1}^{k} K_{Y_iY_j} \sum_{m=1}^{n+k} s_{im}s_{jm}. \end{aligned} \tag{7}$$

We can now state the following basic optimality condition for the individual's control problem:

LEMMA 1: *Let* $J(W, Y, t)$ *be a solution of the Bellman equation*

$$\max_{v \in V} [L^v(t)J + U(v, Y, t)] + J_t = 0 \tag{8}$$

for $(t, W, Y) \in \mathcal{D} \equiv [t, t') \times (0, \infty) \times R^k$, *with boundary conditions*

$$J(0, Y, t) = \underset{Y,t}{E} \int_t^{t'} U(0, Y(s), s)\, ds \quad \text{and} \quad J(W, Y, t') = 0, \tag{9}$$

such that J, its first partial derivatives with respect to t, W, Y, and its second partial derivatives with respect to W, Y are continuous on $\mathcal{D}$, *J is continuous on* $\bar{\mathcal{D}}$, *the closure of* $\mathcal{D}$, *and* $|J(W, Y, t)| \leq k_1 |W, Y|^{k_2}$ *for some constants* k_1 *and* k_2. *Then*: (i) $J(W, Y, t) \geq K(v, W, Y, t)$ *for any admissible feedback control v and initial position W, Y*; (ii) *if* $\hat{v}$ *is an admissible feedback control such that*

$$L^{\hat{v}}(t)J + U(\hat{v}, Y, t) = \max_{v \in V} [L^v(t)J + U(v, Y, t)] \tag{10}$$

for all $(t, W, Y) \in \mathcal{D}$, *then* $J(W, Y, t) = K(\hat{v}, W, Y, t)$ *for all* $(t, W, Y) \in \mathcal{D}$ *and* $\hat{v}$ *is optimal.*

PROOF: See Fleming and Rishel [**10**, p. 159].

Our interest is in characterizations of equilibrium, so to avoid further technicalities we now assume:[14]

ASSUMPTION A10: *There exists a unique function J and control $\hat{v}$ satisfying the Bellman equation and the stated regularity condition.*

The following lemma verifies that J, the indirect utility function, inherits some of the qualitative properties of the direct utility function, U.

LEMMA 2: *J is an increasing, strictly concave function of W.*

PROOF: Suppose an individual has current wealth $W_2 > W_1$. Since the feasible set V is convex, he could choose $\hat{C}(W_1)+\hat{C}(W_2-W_1)$, $\hat{a}(W_1)W_1+\hat{a}(W_2-W_1)(W_2-W_1)$, $\hat{b}(W_1)W_1+\hat{b}(W_2-W_1)(W_2-W_1)$. Hence $J(W_2)\geq K(\hat{v}(W_1)+\hat{v}(W_2-W_1), W_2)>K(\hat{v}(W_1), W_1)=J(W_1)$, and J is an increasing function of W. Now suppose the individual has current wealth $\lambda W_1+(1-\lambda)W_2$. Since he could certainly choose the control $\lambda\hat{C}(W_1)+(1-\lambda)\hat{C}(W_2)$, $\lambda\hat{a}(W_1)W_1+(1-\lambda)\hat{a}(W_2)$, $\lambda\hat{b}(W_1)W_1+(1-\lambda)\hat{b}(W_2)W_2$, we have

$$\begin{aligned} J(\lambda W_1+(1-\lambda)W_2) &\geq K(\lambda\hat{v}(W_1)+(1-\lambda)\hat{v}(W_2), \lambda W_1+(1-\lambda)W_2) \\ &> \lambda K(\hat{v}(W_1), W_1)+(1-\lambda)K(\hat{v}(W_2), W_2) \\ &= \lambda J(W_1)+(1-\lambda)J(W_2). \end{aligned}$$

Hence, J is a strictly concave function of W. *Q.E.D.*

The portfolio proportions a_i represent investment in physical production processes, so they must be nonnegative. Similarly, negative consumption has no meaning. With these constraints, necessary and sufficient conditions for the maximization of $\psi \equiv L^v J + U$ as a function of C, a, b are

(11a) $\psi_C = U_C - J_W \leq 0,$

(11b) $C\psi_C = 0,$

(11c) $\psi_a = [\alpha - r1]WJ_W + [GG'a + GH'b]W^2 J_{WW} + GS'WJ_{WY} \leq 0,$

(11d) $a'\psi_a = 0,$

(11e) $\psi_b = [\beta - r1]WJ_W + [HG'a + HH'b]W^2 J_{WW} + HS'WJ_{WY} = 0,$

where β is a $(k\times 1)$ vector whose ith element is β_i, J_{WY} is a $(k\times 1)$ vector whose ith element is J_{WY_i}, and 1 is a $(k\times 1)$ unit vector.

By solving (11) for $\hat{C}$, $\hat{a}$, $\hat{b}$ in terms of W, Y, t, and partial derivatives of J and substituting back into (8) we obtain a partial differential equation for J. By substituting the solution for J from this equation back into $\hat{C}$, $\hat{a}$, $\hat{b}$ we obtain

[14] For some results on the existence of solutions to equations of this type see [**10**]. It can also be shown that in our context any sufficiently smooth indirect utility function must satisfy (8).

them as functions of only W, Y, and t. W and J are, respectively, the current wealth and indirect utility function of the representative individual.

The individual chooses $\hat{C}$, $\hat{a}$, $\hat{b}$ taking r, α, and β as given. Equilibrium in the economy determines the market clearing interest rate, the equilibrium expected returns on the contingent claims, the total production plan, and the total consumption plan. In aggregate the net supply of contingent claims and riskless lending must be zero. Formally, we have the following definition:

DEFINITION: An equilibrium is defined as a set of stochastic processes $(r, \beta; a, C)$ satisfying (11) and the market clearing conditions $\sum a_i = 1$ and $b_i = 0$ for all i.

As will soon be apparent, this is equivalent to defining equilibrium in terms of a set of stochastic processes $(r, F; a, C)$. The existence and uniqueness of an equilibrium, and its characterization by the fundamental equation of dynamic programming, are in effect assumed in Assumption A10. In this homogeneous society, an equilibrium is clearly Pareto optimal since for any (r, β) all individuals have the opportunity of attaining the optimum of a corresponding planning problem with no borrowing or lending and no contingent claims.

Suppose now that investment is done through competitive value-maximizing firms. Assume for simplicity that each firm invests in only one process, and let an industry be the collection of all firms using a process. With free entry and stochastic constant returns to scale, there will be no incentive for firms to enter or leave the industry if and only if the returns on the shares of each firm (the terms on which it can acquire capital) are identical to the technologically determined physical returns on that process. The equilibrium scale of each industry would then be determined by the supply of investment, which would be the same as the equilibrium with direct investment by individuals. In other words, in this simple economy the solution to the planning problem will be equivalent to the competitive equilibrium.

Let us now turn to the determination of the equilibrium values of a, r, and β. It is evident that the equilibrium solution for these in terms of J is partially separable. With $b=0$, (11c, d) determines a and r. With a and r determined, (11e) is a linear system in β. This does not imply, however, that consumption and investment decisions are separable, since J must be determined jointly. As this separability suggests, we can gain insight into the equilibrium by examining two related problems: (i) the planning problem with the same physical production opportunities but with no borrowing and lending and no contingent claims, and (ii) the analogous problem with borrowing and lending but no contingent claims.

Consider the optimal physical investment policy, a^*, optimal consumption policy C^*, and the corresponding indirect utility function, J^*, of an individual facing the planning problem (i). The portfolio allocation component can be written as a quadratic programming problem:

$$\max_{a} a'\gamma + a'Da \tag{12}$$

subject to:

$$a'1 = 1,$$

$$a \geqslant 0,$$

where γ is $\alpha WJ^*_W + GS'WJ^*_{WY}$, D is $\frac{1}{2}GG'W^2J^*_{WW}$, and 1 is a unit vector. Since a^* is optimal, then by the Kuhn-Tucker theorem, there exists a λ^* such that

$$\text{(13)} \qquad \gamma - \lambda^* 1 + 2Da^* \leqslant 0,$$

$$a^{*\prime}\gamma - \lambda^* a^{*\prime}1 + 2a^{*\prime}Da^* = 0.$$

Consider now problem (ii), with borrowing or lending at r^*, and with indirect utility function J^{**}. Inspection shows that if $J^{**} = J^*$ and $r^* = \lambda^*/WJ^*_W$, then (r^*, a^*, C^*) is the equilibrium for problem (ii). This equilibrium interest rate r^* is proportional to the Lagrangian multiplier associated with the constraint $1'a = 1$. Hence, in equilibrium in our economy $J = J^* = J^{**}$, $\hat{a} = a^*$, $\hat{C} = C^*$, and $r = r^*$.

We will first discuss some properties of the equilibrium interest rate, and then turn to the equilibrium rates of return on contingent claims. The equilibrium interest rate can be written explicitly as

$$\text{(14)} \qquad r(W, Y, t) = \lambda^*/WJ_W = a^{*\prime}\alpha + a^{*\prime}GG'a^*W\left(\frac{J_{WW}}{J_W}\right) + a^{*\prime}GS'\left(\frac{J_{WY}}{J_W}\right)$$

$$= a^{*\prime}\alpha - \left(\frac{-J_{WW}}{J_W}\right)\left(\frac{\operatorname{var} W}{W}\right) - \sum_{i=1}^{k}\left(\frac{-J_{WY_i}}{J_W}\right)\left(\frac{\operatorname{cov} W, Y_i}{W}\right),$$

where $(\operatorname{cov} W, Y_i)$ stands for the covariance of changes in optimally invested wealth with changes in the state variable Y_i, and similarly for $(\operatorname{var} W)$ and $(\operatorname{cov} Y_i, Y_j)$.[15]

$a^{*\prime}\alpha$ is the expected rate of return on optimally invested wealth. The equilibrium interest rate r may be either less or greater than $a^{*\prime}\alpha$, even though all individuals are risk averse to gambles on consumption paths. Although investment in the production processes exposes an individual to uncertainty about the output received, it may also allow him to hedge against the risk of less favorable changes in technology. An individual investing only in locally riskless lending would be unprotected against this latter risk. In general, either effect may dominate.[16]

The following theorem provides a more intuitive interpretation of the equilibrium interest rate. We first make one further technical assumption which will be needed only in the proof of Theorem 1.

[15] If a locally riskless production process exists, then its return would be a lower bound for the interest rate. The interest rate would be at this lower bound whenever the locally riskless process is used in equilibrium. It is easy to verify that (14) still holds.

[16] The presence of risk aversion suggests that the certainty equivalent rate of return on physical investment, $\bar{r}$, should exceed the interest rate. Consider a single locally riskless production process whose return is such that individuals would receive the same utility for investing their wealth in this process as they would from optimally investing it in the original n processes. The rate of return on this process is by definition $\bar{r}$. Inspection of (10) shows that

$$\bar{r}(W, Y, t) = r(W, Y, t) + \frac{1}{2}\left(\frac{-J_{WW}}{J_W}\right)\left(\frac{\operatorname{var} W}{W}\right).$$

ASSUMPTION A11: *J_{WW}, J_{WY_i}, $J_{Y_iY_j}$, J_t, a_i^*, and C^* have one continuous derivative with respect to W on $\mathcal{D}$.*

THEOREM 1: *In equilibrium we have*

$$(15)\qquad \begin{aligned} r &= -(\textit{expected rate of change in the marginal utility of wealth}) \\ &= (\textit{expected rate of return on wealth}) \\ &\quad + (\textit{covariance of the rate of return on wealth with the} \\ &\quad\quad \textit{rate of change in the marginal utility of wealth}). \end{aligned}$$

PROOF: By Ito's formula, J_W will satisfy the stochastic differential equation

$$(16)\qquad dJ_W = (J_{Wt} + LJ_W)\,dt + [J_{WW}a^{*\prime}GW + J'_{WY}S]\,dw(t),$$

where L is the differential generator defined in (7). Hence, the expected rate of change in marginal utility is $(J_{Wt} + LJ_W)/J_W$. By differentiating (8) with respect to W, using (11), and rearranging, we find that

$$(17)\qquad \begin{aligned} r &= \left[a^{*\prime}\alpha - \left(\frac{-J_{WW}}{J_W}\right)\left(\frac{\text{var } W}{W}\right) - \sum_{i=1}^{k}\left(\frac{-J_{WY_i}}{J_W}\right)\left(\frac{\text{cov } W, Y_i}{W}\right)\right] \\ &= -\left[\tfrac{1}{2}(\text{var } W)J_{WWW} + \sum_{i=1}^{k}(\text{cov } W, Y_i)J_{WWY_i}\right. \\ &\quad + \tfrac{1}{2}\sum_{i=1}^{k}\sum_{j=1}^{k}(\text{cov } Y_i, Y_j)J_{WY_iY_j} + [a^{*\prime}\alpha W - C^*(W, Y, t)]J_{WW} \\ &\quad \left. + \sum_{i=1}^{k}\mu_i(Y)J_{WY_i} + J_{Wt}\right]\Big/ J_W = -(J_{Wt} + LJ_W)/J_W, \end{aligned}$$

which proves the first part. Recall that

$$dW = [a^{*\prime}\alpha W - C^*]\,dt + a^{*\prime}GW\,dw(t)$$

and

$$(18)\qquad dY = \mu\,dt + S\,dw(t).$$

We then find that the covariance of the rate of return on wealth with the rate of change in the marginal utility of wealth, $(\text{cov } W, J_W)/WJ_W$, is

$$(19)\qquad \begin{aligned} \left(\frac{\text{cov } W, J_W}{WJ_W}\right) &= \left(\frac{1}{J_W}\right)[J_{WW}a^{*\prime}GW + J'_{WY}S][a^{*\prime}G]' \\ &= -\left[\left(\frac{-J_{WW}}{J_W}\right)\left(\frac{\text{var } W}{W}\right) + \sum_{i=1}^{k}\left(\frac{-J_{WY_i}}{J_W}\right)\left(\frac{\text{cov } W, Y_i}{W}\right)\right]. \end{aligned}$$

The expected rate of return on wealth is $a^{*\prime}\alpha$. Combining these and comparing with (14) confirms the second part. *Q.E.D.*

When $U(C(s), Y(s), s) = e^{-\rho s}U(C(s), Y(s))$, then the first expression on the right hand side of (15) can be written as ρ minus the expected rate of change in the undiscounted marginal utility of wealth. These interpretations of course reduce to standard results when there is no uncertainty.

We now turn to the equilibrium expected return on contingent claims. Our second theorem gives these equilibrium expected returns in terms of the underlying fundamental variables.

THEOREM 2: *The equilibrium expected return on any contingent claim, say the ith, is given by*

$$(\beta_i - r)F^i = [\phi_W \quad \phi_{Y_1} \quad \cdots \quad \phi_{Y_k}][F^i_W \quad F^i_{Y_1} \quad \cdots \quad F^i_{Y_k}]', \tag{20}$$

where

$$\phi_W = \left[\left(\frac{-J_{WW}}{J_W}\right)(\text{var } W) + \sum_{i=1}^{k}\left(\frac{-J_{WY_i}}{J_W}\right)(\text{cov } W, Y_i)\right],$$

$$\phi_{Y_i} = \left[\left(\frac{-J_{WW}}{J_W}\right)(\text{cov } W, Y_i) + \sum_{j=1}^{k}\left(\frac{-J_{WY_j}}{J_W}\right)(\text{cov } Y_i, Y_j)\right].$$

PROOF: Substituting a^* and r into (11e) gives

$$\beta(W, Y, t) = (a^{*\prime}\alpha)1 + \left(\frac{1}{J_W}\right)[(a^{*\prime}GS'J_{WY})1 - HS'J_{WY}] + \left(\frac{WJ_{WW}}{J_W}\right)[(a^{*\prime}GG'a^*)1 - HG'a^*]. \tag{21}$$

By using Ito's formula to give H explicitly and then rearranging terms, the expected return on any contingent claim in the basis, say the ith, can be rewritten as

$$\beta_i F^i = rF^i + F^i_W\left[\left(\frac{-J_{WW}}{J_W}\right)(\text{var } W) + \sum_{i=1}^{k}\left(\frac{-J_{WY_i}}{J_W}\right)(\text{cov } W, Y_i)\right] + \sum_{i=1}^{k} F^i_{Y_i}\left[\left(\frac{-J_{WW}}{J_W}\right)(\text{cov } W, Y_i) + \sum_{j=1}^{k}\left(\frac{-J_{WY_j}}{J_W}\right)(\text{cov } Y_i, Y_j)\right], \tag{22}$$

which can be abbreviated as

$$(\beta_i - r)F^i \equiv [\phi_W \quad \phi_{Y_1} \quad \cdots \quad \phi_{Y_k}][F^i_W \quad F^i_{Y_1} \quad \cdots \quad F^i_{Y_k}]'. \tag{23}$$

The equilibrium expected rates of return of contingent claims not in the basis are uniquely determined by the equilibrium expected rates of return of those in the basis. Recall that it is possible to construct a controlled portfolio from basis assets which would exactly duplicate the payout pattern of any non-basis contingent claim, $\bar{F}$. In equilibrium the initial value and expected rate of return on $\bar{F}$ must be equal to that of the controlled portfolio. Let θ_i be the number of units of F^i held in the controlled portfolio. Let F^1 be optimally invested wealth and let F^{k+2} be a unit investment in locally riskless lending, so $F^{k+2} \equiv 1$. Thus we have $\bar{F}=\sum_{i=1}^{k+2}\theta_i F^i$ and $\bar{\beta}\bar{F}=\sum_{i=1}^{k+2}\theta_i\beta_i F^i$. Combining these and using $\beta_{k+2}=r$ gives

$$(\bar{\beta}-r)\bar{F}=[(\beta_1-r)F^1\ (\beta_2-r)F^2\cdots(\beta_{k+1}-r)F^{k+1}][\theta_1\ \theta_2\cdots\theta_{k+1}]' \tag{24}$$

$$=[\phi_W\quad \phi_{Y_1}\cdots\phi_{Y_k}]\begin{bmatrix}F_W^1 & \cdots & F_W^{k+1}\\ F_Y^1 & \cdots & F_{Y_1}^{k+1}\\ \vdots & & \vdots\\ F_{Y_k}^1 & \cdots & F_{Y_k}^{k+1}\end{bmatrix}\begin{bmatrix}\theta_1\\ \theta_2\\ \vdots\\ \theta_{k+1}\end{bmatrix},$$

with the second line following from (23). By again using Ito's formula we can write θ explicitly as

$$\begin{bmatrix}\theta_1\\ \theta_2\\ \vdots\\ \theta_{k+1}\end{bmatrix}=\begin{bmatrix}F_W^1 & \cdots & F_W^{k+1}\\ F_{Y_1}^1 & \cdots & F_{Y_1}^{k+1}\\ \vdots & & \vdots\\ F_{Y_k}^1 & \cdots & F_{Y_k}^{k+1}\end{bmatrix}^{-1}\begin{bmatrix}\bar{F}_W\\ \bar{F}_{Y_1}\\ \vdots\\ \bar{F}_{Y_k}\end{bmatrix}. \tag{25}$$

Combining (24) and (25) gives

$$(\bar{\beta}-r)\bar{F}=[\phi_W\quad \phi_{Y_1}\quad\cdots\quad\phi_{Y_k}][\bar{F}_W\quad \bar{F}_{Y_1}\quad\cdots\quad\bar{F}_{Y_k}]', \tag{26}$$

which confirms that (20) holds for all contingent claims. *Q.E.D.*

The equilibrium expected return for any contingent claim can thus be written as the riskfree return plus a linear combination of the first partials of the asset price with respect to W and Y. While these derivatives depend on the contractual provisions of the asset, the coefficients of the linear combination do not, and are the same for all contingent claims.

The coefficients of the linear combination in (20) can be given in terms of equilibrium expected rates of return on particular securities or portfolios. From (14), we see that $\phi_W=(a^{*\prime}\alpha-r)W$, the expected excess return (over the risk free return) on optimally invested wealth. The coefficient of ϕ_{Y_j} is the excess expected return on a security constructed so that its value is always equal to Y_j. Equation (31) below can be used to give the contractual terms required in this construction. ϕ_{Y_j} could also be expressed as a function of the expected rate of return on any other security or portfolio whose value depends only on Y_j.

In [**25**], Ross shows that if security returns are generated by a linear factor model, then under quite general conditions, the equilibrium excess expected rate of return of any security can be written as a linear combination of the factor risk premiums. The risk premium of the jth factor is defined as the excess expected rate of return on a security or portfolio which has only the risk of the jth factor. Although our underlying model is much more fully developed, the coefficients ϕ_W and ϕ_{Y_j} are Ross factor risk premiums and can be interpreted in this way.

The proof of the second part of Theorem 1 established that ϕ_W is the negative of the covariance of the change in wealth with the rate of change in the marginal utility of wealth. A similar argument shows that ϕ_{Y_i} is the negative of the covariance of the change in the ith state variable with the rate of change in the marginal utility of wealth. By using Ito's formula to write out (3) explicitly, as in the proof of Theorem 2, it then follows that

$$(27) \qquad \beta_i - r = -(\text{cov } F^i, J_W)/F^i J_W.$$

That is, the excess expected rate of return on the ith contingent claim is equal to the negative of the covariance of its rate of return with the rate of change in the marginal utility of wealth. Just as we would expect, individuals are willing to accept a lower expected rate of return on securities which tend to pay off more highly when marginal utility is higher. Hence, in equilibrium such securities will have a lower total risk premium.

If the direct utility function U does not depend on the state variables Y, and if both U and the optimal consumption function C^* possess the required derivatives, then it follows from applying Ito's formula to the marginal utility of consumption $U_C(C^*)$ that

$$(28) \qquad dU_C = [LU_C + U_{Ct}]\,dt + U_{CC}[C^*_W a^{*\prime} GW + C^*_Y S]\,dw(t),$$

where C^*_W is the partial derivative of C^* with respect to W and C^*_Y is a $(1 \times k)$ vector whose ith element is $C^*_{Y_i}$, the partial derivative of C^* with respect to Y_i. If in addition optimal consumption is always positive, then $U_C(C^*)$ always equals J_W. By differentiating (11a) to obtain $J_{WW} = U_{CC}C^*_W$ and $J_{WY_i} = U_{CC}C^*_{Y_i}$ and using (28), we can rewrite the factor risk premiums as

$$(29) \qquad \phi_W = \left(\frac{-U_{CC}(C^*)}{U_C(C^*)}\right)(\text{cov } C^*, W),$$

$$\phi_Y = \left(\frac{-U_{CC}(C^*)}{U_C(C^*)}\right)(\text{cov } C^*, Y),$$

where (cov C^*, W) denotes the covariance of changes in consumption with changes in wealth and (cov C^*, Y) is defined in a similar way. It then follows that

$$(30) \qquad (\beta_i - r)F^i = \left(\frac{-U_{CC}(C^*)}{U_C(C^*)}\right)(\text{cov } C^*, F^i),$$

so the expected excess return on any security is proportional to its covariance with optimal consumption.[17]

Two final observations on Theorem 2 deserve mention. Notice, first, that as preferences tend to risk neutrality over consumption paths all of the factor risk premiums do not vanish. Individuals who are risk neutral over consumption paths would not be neutral to uncertainty about changes in technology, and the factor risk premiums would reflect their desire to hedge away this uncertainty.[18] Second, we could rewrite (20) so that the equilibrium expected rate of return on any contingent claim, or on any active production process, is stated in terms of the equilibrium expected rate of return on other claims or portfolios. In this way

[17] For related observations in other contexts, see Breeden [3] and Brock [4, 5].

[18] We are grateful to Fischer Black for this observation.

one can write an expression for relative rates of return which does not explicitly involve preferences.[19]

3. THE FUNDAMENTAL VALUATION EQUATION AND ITS INTERPRETATION

We can now use the developments of the previous section to give one of the main results of the paper. This is the fundamental valuation equation for contingent claims, stated in the following theorem.

THEOREM 3: *The price of any contingent claim satisfies the partial differential equation*

$$
\begin{aligned}
(31)\qquad & \tfrac{1}{2}(\operatorname{var} W)F_{WW}+\sum_{i=1}^{k}(\operatorname{cov} W, Y_i)F_{WY_i}+\tfrac{1}{2}\sum_{i=1}^{k}\sum_{j=1}^{k}(\operatorname{cov} Y_i, Y_j)F_{Y_iY_j}\\
&+[r(W, Y, t)W-C^*(W, Y, t)]F_W\\
&+\sum_{i=1}^{k}F_{Y_i}\left[\mu_i-\left(\frac{-J_{WW}}{J_W}\right)(\operatorname{cov} W, Y_i)-\sum_{j=1}^{k}\left(\frac{-J_{WY_j}}{J_W}\right)(\operatorname{cov} Y_i, Y_j)\right]\\
&+F_t-r(W, Y, t)F+\delta(W, Y, t)=0,
\end{aligned}
$$

where $r(W, Y, t)$ *is given from equation* (14) *as*

$$r(W, Y, t)=a^{*\prime}\alpha-\left(\frac{-J_{WW}}{J_W}\right)\left(\frac{\operatorname{var} W}{W}\right)-\sum_{i=1}^{k}\left(\frac{-J_{WY_i}}{J_W}\right)\left(\frac{\operatorname{cov} W, Y_i}{W}\right).$$

PROOF: Ito's formula tells us that the drift of $F(W, Y, t)$ is given by

$$
\begin{aligned}
(32)\qquad \beta F-\delta=&\tfrac{1}{2}(\operatorname{var} W)F_{WW}+\sum_{i=1}^{k}(\operatorname{cov} W, Y_i)F_{WY_i}\\
&+\tfrac{1}{2}\sum_{i=1}^{k}\sum_{j=1}^{k}(\operatorname{cov} Y_i, Y_j)F_{Y_iY_j}\\
&+(a^{*\prime}\alpha W-C^*(W, Y, t))F_W+\sum_{i=1}^{k}\mu_iF_{Y_i}+F_t.
\end{aligned}
$$

On the other hand, Theorem 2 tells us that in equilibrium, the expected return on F must be

$$
\begin{aligned}
(33)\qquad \beta F=&rF+F_W\left[\left(\frac{-J_{WW}}{J_W}\right)(\operatorname{var} W)+\sum_{i=1}^{k}\left(\frac{-J_{WY_i}}{J_W}\right)(\operatorname{cov} W, Y_i)\right]\\
&+\sum_{i=1}^{k}F_{Y_i}\left[\left(\frac{-J_{WW}}{J_W}\right)(\operatorname{cov} W, Y_i)+\sum_{j=1}^{k}\left(\frac{-J_{WY_j}}{J_W}\right)(\operatorname{cov} Y_i, Y_j)\right].
\end{aligned}
$$

Combining (32) and (33) gives (31). *Q.E.D.*

[19] In other contexts, relationships of this kind are given in the static capital asset pricing models of Sharpe [**27**], Lintner [**15**], and Mossin [**21**], in the generalization of these models in Merton [**19**], in the consumption-based model of Breeden [**3**], and in the arbitrage model of Ross [**25**].

The valuation equation (31) holds for any contingent claim. The form of δ and the appropriate terminal and boundary conditions are particular for each claim and are given by the contractual provisions. In general, F is defined on $[t, T)\times Z$, where $Z\subset(0,\infty)\times R^k$ is an open set and ∂Z is its boundary. Let $\hat{\partial} Z$ be the closed subset of ∂Z such that $(W(\tau), Y(\tau))\in\hat{\partial} Z$ for all $(W(t), Y(t))$, where τ is the time of first passage from Z. That is, $\hat{\partial} Z$ is the set of all accessible boundary points. So (31) holds for all $(s, W(s), Y(s))\in[t, T)\times Z$, with the contractual provisions determining the boundary information[20]

$$
(34)\qquad
\begin{aligned}
&F(W(T), Y(T), T)=\Theta(W(T), Y(T)), && W(T), Y(T)\in Z,\\
&F(W(\tau), Y(\tau), \tau)=\Psi(W(\tau), Y(\tau), \tau), && W(\tau), Y(\tau)\in\hat{\partial} Z.
\end{aligned}
$$

In other words, the contingent claim F entitles its owner to receive three types of payments: (i) if the underlying variables do not leave a certain region before the maturity date T, a payment of Θ is received at the maturity date, (ii) if the underlying variables do leave the region before T, at time τ, a payment of Ψ is received at that time, and (iii) a payout flow of δ is received until time T or time τ, whichever is sooner. The boundaries of the region may be specified in the contract or may be chosen by the owner to maximize the value of the claim. All of our results will apply in either case. This formulation thus includes most securities of practical interest.

The existence and uniqueness of a solution to the fundamental valuation equation can be established under some additional regularity conditions.[21] To interpret the solution, consider the following two systems of stochastic differential equations: System I,

$$
(35a)\qquad
\begin{aligned}
&dW(t)=[a^{*\prime}\alpha W-C^*]\,dt+a^{*\prime}GW\,dw(t),\\
&dY(t)=\mu(Y,t)\,dt+S(Y,t)\,dw(t);
\end{aligned}
$$

and System II,

$$
(35b)\qquad
\begin{aligned}
&dW(t)=[a^{*\prime}\alpha W-\phi_W-C^*]\,dt+a^{*\prime}GW\,dw(t),\\
&dY(t)=[\mu(Y,t)-[\phi_{Y_1}\ \cdots\ \phi_{Y_k}]']\,dt+S(Y,t)\,dw(t),
\end{aligned}
$$

[20] It is important to distinguish between boundary conditions for the contingent claims F and those for the indirect utility function J. The results of the preceding section are unaffected by the boundary conditions which are imposed on any particular claim. However, if Y has accessible boundaries, then conditions will have to be imposed on J at these boundaries. Also, if these boundaries are contained in Z, then the value of F will not necessarily be given by the terms of the contract, and additional conditions on F at these boundaries may have to be determined from further economic considerations. For example, if Y_i can reach an instantaneously reflecting barrièr at d, then the absence of arbitrage opportunities will normally require $F_{Y_i}(W,\dots Y_{i-1}, d, Y_{i+1}\dots, t)=0$.

[21] To establish the existence and uniqueness of a solution to (31), we make some additional technical assumptions and continue them throughout the paper. Let Z be bounded and $(0, Y)\notin\bar{Z}$, the closure of Z. Let every point of $\hat{\partial} Z$ have a barrier, where a barrier $f_y(x)$ at the point $y\in\partial Z$ is a continuous nonnegative function in $\bar{Z}$ that vanishes only at the point y and for which $Lf_y(x)\leq -1$. Also assume: (i) δ is uniformly Hölder continuous on $(W, Y, s)\in\bar{Z}\times[t, T]$, (ii) Θ is continuous on $\bar{Z}$, (iii) Ψ is continuous on $\hat{\partial} Z\times[t, T]$, and (iv) $\Psi(W(T), Y(T), T)=\Theta(W(T), Y(T), T)$ if $(W(T), Y(T))\in\hat{\partial} Z$. Previous assumptions imply that the coefficients of F and LF are uniformly Lipschitz continuous in $(W, Y, s)\in\bar{Z}$. Then from Friedman [11, p. 138], there exists a unique solution to (31) with boundary conditions (34).

where the processes solving (I) and (II) are defined on the same probability space and start from the same initial position. System (I) describes the actual movement of $W(t)$, $Y(t)$ until the first passage to $W=0$, while System (II) describes the movement of a similar process when the drifts are altered by the factor risk premiums. Assume that the coefficients are extended from $(0,\infty)\times R^k$ into R^{k+1} in any arbitrary way such that the regularity conditions of footnote 4 are satisfied and positive values of W are inaccessible from a nonpositive initial position. Our interest will be limited to the behavior of I and II in Z. Each of the processes j, $j=1, 2$, induces a probability Π_j on (C_T^{k+1}, Q_T), where C_T^{k+1} is the space of continuous functions $f(s)$ from $[t, T]$ into R^{k+1} and Q_T is the σ-algebra generated by the sets $(f(s)\in B)$, where B is any Borel set in R^{k+1} and $s\in[t, T]$.

Systems I and II can be used to give probabilistic interpretations of the solution to the valuation equation (31). These are contained in the following two lemmas.

LEMMA 3: *The unique solution to* (31) *with boundary conditions* (34) *is given by*

$$F(W,Y,t,T)=\underset{W,Y,t}{E}\Bigg[\Theta(W(T),Y(T))\times\left[\exp\left(-\int_t^T\beta(W(u),Y(u),u)\,du\right)\right]I(\tau\geq T)$$
$$+\Psi(W(\tau),Y(\tau),\tau)\times\left[\exp\left(-\int_t^\tau\beta(W(u),Y(u),u)\,du\right)\right]I(\tau<T)$$
$$+\int_t^{\tau\wedge T}\delta(W(s),Y(s),s)\times\left[\exp\left(-\int_t^s\beta(W(u),Y(u),u)\,du\right)\right]ds\Bigg], \tag{36}$$

where E denotes expectation with respect to System I, $I(\cdot)$ *is an indicator function, and* τ *is the time of first passage to* $\hat{\partial}Z$.

PROOF: Recall that $LF+F_t+\delta=\beta F$ by Ito's formula and the definition of β, and then use Theorem 5.2 of Friedman [**11**, p. 147].

The expression in (36) clarifies the intuitive idea of discounting with respect to a randomly varying rate of return. However, it does not provide a constructive way of finding F unless the equilibrium expected rate of return, β, of that security is known explicitly in advance. In contrast, the next lemma requires only the interest rate and the factor risk premiums for a constructive solution, and these are common to all securities.

LEMMA 4: *The unique solution to* (31) *with boundary conditions* (34) *is also given by*

$$F(W, Y, t, T) = \hat{E}_{W,Y,t}\Bigg[\Theta(W(T), Y(T)) \times\left[\exp\left(-\int_t^T r(W(u), Y(u), u)\,du\right)\right] I(\tau \geq T) + \Psi(W(\tau), Y(\tau), \tau) \times\left[\exp\left(-\int_t^\tau r(W(u), Y(u), u)\,du\right)\right] I(\tau < T) + \int_t^{\tau \wedge T} \delta(W(s), Y(s), s) \times\left[\exp\left(-\int_t^s r(W(u), Y(u), u)\,du\right)\right] ds\Bigg], \tag{37}$$

where $\hat{E}$ *denotes expectation with respect to System II, and* $I(\cdot)$ *and* τ *are as defined in* (36).

PROOF: Apply Theorem 5.2 of Friedman [**11**, p. 147] to equation (31).

Equation (37) says that the equilibrium price of a claim is given by its expected discounted value, with discounting done at the risk free rate, when the expectation is taken with respect to a risk-adjusted process for wealth and the state variables. The risk adjustment is accomplished by reducing the drift of each underlying variable by the corresponding factor risk premium.

4. THE RELATIONSHIP TO THE ARROW-DEBREU MODEL AND THE ROLE OF FIRMS

The model presented here is consistent with the framework of Arrow [**1**] and Debreu [**8**], and the following theorem verifies that the solution of (31) can be interpreted in terms of marginal-utility-weighted expected values. In the course of its proof, we recall the definition of L from (7) and define χ as the $(k+1)\times 1$ vector

$$\chi' \equiv \left[\left(\frac{-J_{WW}}{J_W}\right)\left(\frac{-J_{WY_1}}{J_W}\right)\cdots\left(\frac{-J_{WY_k}}{J_W}\right)\right]$$

and Σ as the $(k+1)\times(n+k)$ matrix

$$\Sigma \equiv \begin{bmatrix} a^{*\prime}GW \\ \cdot\ \dot{S}\ \cdot \end{bmatrix}.$$

Assume that $E_{W,Y,t} \exp(\lambda |\chi'(s)\Sigma(s)|^2) \leq d$, for some $\lambda > 0$, $d > 0$, and all s, $t \leq s \leq T$.

THEOREM 4: *The price of any contingent claim is given by*

$$(38)\qquad F(W, Y, t, T) = \underset{W,Y,t}{E}\Bigg[\Theta(W(T), Y(T)) \times\left(\frac{J_W(W(T), Y(T), T)}{J_W(W(t), Y(t), t)}\right) I(\tau \geq T) + \Psi(W(\tau), Y(\tau), \tau)\left(\frac{J_W(W(\tau), Y(\tau), \tau)}{J_W(W(t), Y(t), t)}\right) I(\tau < T) + \int_t^{\tau\wedge T} \delta(W(s), Y(s), s)\left(\frac{J_W(W(s), Y(s), s)}{J_W(W(t), Y(t), t)}\right) ds\Bigg],$$

where, again, E *denotes expectation with respect to System I, and* $I(\cdot)$ *and* τ *are as defined in* (36).

PROOF: By Ito's formula,

$$\left(\frac{J_W(W(s), Y(s), s)}{J_W(W(t), Y(t), t)}\right) = \exp\left[\log J_W(W(s), Y(s), s) - \log J_W(W(t), Y(t), t)\right] = \exp\left[\int_t^s \left(L(\log J_W(u)) + \frac{\partial(\log J_W(u))}{\partial t}\right) du + \int_t^s (-\chi'\Sigma)\, dw(u)\right].$$

Now

$$L \log J_W = \left(\frac{1}{J_W}\right) LJ_W - \tfrac{1}{2}(\text{var } W)\left(\frac{-J_{WW}}{J_W}\right)^2 - \sum_{i=1}^{k} (\text{cov } W, Y_i)\left(\frac{-J_{WY_i}}{J_W}\right)\left(\frac{-J_{WW}}{J_W}\right) - \tfrac{1}{2}\sum_{i=1}^{k}\sum_{j=1}^{k} (\text{cov } Y_i, Y_j)\left(\frac{-J_{WY_i}}{J_W}\right)\left(\frac{-J_{WY_j}}{J_W}\right)$$
$$= \left(\frac{1}{J_W}\right) LJ_W - \tfrac{1}{2}\chi'\Sigma\Sigma'\chi = \left(\frac{1}{J_W}\right) LJ_W - \tfrac{1}{2}|\chi'\Sigma|^2.$$

Furthermore, from Theorem 1,

$$\left(\frac{1}{J_W}\right)(LJ_W + J_{Wt}) = -r(W, Y, t).$$

Thus the expression

$$\left(\frac{J_W(W(s), Y(s), s)}{J_W(W(t), Y(t), t)}\right)$$

can be written as

$$(39)\quad \left(\frac{J_W(W(s), Y(s), s)}{J_W(W(t), Y(t), t)}\right) = \left[\exp\left(-\int_t^s r(W(u), Y(u), u)\, du\right)\right] \times \left[\exp\left(\int_t^s (-\chi'\Sigma)\, dw(u) - \tfrac{1}{2}\int_t^s |\chi'\Sigma|^2\, du\right)\right].$$

It then follows directly from Girsanov's theorem as stated in Friedman [**11**, p. 169] that (38) is the same as (37), which was shown to be the solution to (31). *Q.E.D.*

In the context of Arrow and Debreu, $C_{t'}^{k+1}$ is the state space. The state-space pricing system is a measure π, nonnegative but not generally a probability, on $(C_{t'}^{k+1}, Q_{t'})$. π is absolutely continuous with respect to the actual system probability π_1, and the Radon–Nikodym derivative of π with respect to π_1 is $d\pi/d\pi_1 = J_W(s)/J_W(t)$.

Equations (38) and (39) say that the value of any payment is equal to the expectation of the product of its random amount, a time-discount factor, and a risk-adjustment factor. The time-discount factor represents the accumulated effect of locally anticipated percentage changes in the marginal utility of wealth. The risk-adjustment factor in turn captures the accumulated effect of locally unanticipated percentage changes in the marginal utility of wealth, and is thus a martingale. This is suggestive of procedures which make separate sequential adjustments for time and uncertainty, but it does not imply this, since in general neither term can be brought outside the expectation. Another way to state the results is that if values are measured in utility terms, as quantities times the planning price J_W, then all contingent claims are priced so that their expected rate of return over any holding period is equal to zero.

A similar interpretation applies when investment is made through value-maximizing firms. We can without loss of generality consider firms which confine their investment to a single production process. As mentioned earlier, such firms will have an incentive to expand or contract their investments in each process unless the aggregate allocation corresponds to that with direct investment by individuals.

To see this in the context of the valuation equation, consider an aggregate allocation with the proportion of physical wealth invested in each process given by the vector $\bar{a}$. The shares of the firms can be valued in the same way as other contingent claims. However, their net supply will be positive rather than zero. The expected rate of return on the shares of firms in the ith industry, β_i, would then be given by the hypothetical value of α_i which would solve (11c) and (11d) with $a = \bar{a}$. The strict concavity of J implies that this β_i will differ from the actual technologically determined α_i whenever $\bar{a}$ differs from a^*.

The amount of the good held by a firm continually reinvesting its output in the ith process could then be taken as an additional state variable having an expected rate of return of α_i. By applying the valuation equation to this firm, we find that its market value is equal to the physical amount of the good it holds plus the value of a continual payout stream of $\alpha_i - \beta_i$. The market value of a firm will thus differ from the physical amount of the good that it holds whenever $\alpha_i \neq \beta_i$. Consequently, all firms will be in equilibrium, with no incentive to expand or contract their investments, only when $\bar{a} = a^*$.

5. CONCLUDING COMMENTS

In this paper, we have developed a general equilibrium model of a simple but complete economy and used it to study asset prices. One of our principal results was a partial differential equation which asset prices must satisfy. The solution of this equation determines the equilibrium price of a given asset in terms of the underlying real variables in the economy. By combining this solution with probabilistic information about the underlying variables, one can answer a wide variety of questions about the stochastic structure of asset prices.

We have intentionally kept our model as streamlined as possible in order to concentrate on the most important issues. A number of additional features could be added in a straightforward way. For example, we could introduce multiple goods or nonlinear production technologies. As another example, we could examine how the tradeoff between labor and leisure would affect asset prices by including labor in the production function and leisure in the direct utility function.

A further generalization follows from the fact that we are free to introduce state variables which do not affect production opportunities but are nevertheless of interest to individuals. There is no reason why the movement of these additional state variables could not be influenced by individual consumption decisions. Consequently, we could define the state variables as particular functions of past consumption. For example, if we specified $dY_j(t) = C(t)\,dt$, then the change in Y_j over any period would be the integral of consumption over that period. Further flexibility could be obtained by including a state-dependent utility of terminal wealth function, $B(W(t'), Y(t'))$. As a simple example, the specification $U(C(s), Y(s)) = 0$, $B(W(t'), Y(t')) = \gamma Y_j(t')$, and $dY_j(t) = [\gamma \log C(t)]Y_j(t)\,dt$, with γ a constant less than one, would correspond to the multiplicative utility functions studied in Pye [**23**]. In this way, we could introduce many types of intertemporal dependencies in preferences while still maintaining the tractability of our basic model.

Massachusetts Institute of Technology
and
Yale University

Manuscript received September, 1978; revision received October, 1984.

REFERENCES

[1] ARROW, K. J.: "The Role of Securities in the Optimal Allocation of Risk Bearing," *Review of Economic Studies*, 31(1964), 91-96.

[2] BLACK, F., AND M. SCHOLES: "The Pricing of Options and Corporate Liabilities," *Journal of Political Economy*, 81(1973), 637-654.

[3] BREEDEN, D. T.: "An Intertemporal Asset Pricing Model with Stochastic Consumption and Investment Opportunities," *Journal of Financial Economics*, 7(1979), 265-296.

[4] BROCK, W. A.: "An Integration of Stochastic Growth Theory and the Theory of Finance, Part 1: The Growth Model," in *General Equilibrium, Growth, and Trade*, ed. by J. R. Green and J. A. Scheinkman. New York: Academic Press, 1979.

[5] ———: "Asset Prices in a Production Economy," in *The Economics of Information and Uncertainty*, ed. by J. J. McCall. Chicago: University of Chicago Press, 1982.

[6] CONSTANTINIDES, G. M.: "Admissible Uncertainty in the Intertemporal Asset Pricing Model," *Journal of Financial Economics*, 8(1980), 71-86.

[7] COX, J. C., J. E. INGERSOLL, JR., AND S. A. ROSS: "A Theory of the Term Structure of Interest Rates," *Econometrica*, 53(1985), 385-407.

[8] DEBREU, G.: *The Theory of Value*. New York: John Wiley, 1959.

[9] DONALDSON, J. B., AND R. MEHRA: "Comparative Dynamics of an Equilibrium Intertemporal Asset Pricing Model," *Review of Economic Studies*, 51(1984), 491-508.

[10] FLEMING, W. H., AND R. W. RISHEL: *Deterministic and Stochastic Optimal Control*. New York: Springer-Verlag, 1975.

[11] FRIEDMAN, A.: *Stochastic Differential Equations and Applications*, Volume 1. New York: Academic Press, 1975.

[12] GIHMAN, I. I., AND A. V. SKOROHOD: *Stochastic Differential Equations*. New York: Springer-Verlag, 1972.

[13] HARRISON, J. M., AND D. M. KREPS: "Martingales and Arbitrage in Multiperiod Securities Markets," *Journal of Economic Theory*, 20(1979), 381-408.

[14] HUANG, C.: "Information Structure and Equilibrium Asset Prices," *Journal of Economic Theory*, forthcoming.

[15] LINTNER, J.: "The Valuation of Risky Assets and the Selection of Risky Investments in Stock Portfolios and Capital Budgets," *Review of Economics and Statistics*, 47(1965), 13-37.

[16] LUCAS, R. E., JR.: "Asset Prices in an Exchange Economy," *Econometrica*, 46(1978), 1426-1446.

[17] MERTON, R. C.: "Optimum Consumption and Portfolio Rules in a Continuous Time Model," *Journal of Economic Theory*, 3(1971), 373-413.

[18] ———: "Rational Theory of Option Pricing," *Bell Journal of Economics and Management Science*, 4(1973), 141-183.

[19] ———: "An Intertemporal Capital Asset Pricing Model," *Econometrica*, 41(1973), 867-887.

[20] ———: "On the Pricing of Contingent Claims and the Modigliani-Miller Theorem," *Journal of Financial Economics*, 5(1977), 241-249.

[21] MOSSIN, J.: "Equilibrium in a Capital Asset Market," *Econometrica*, 34(1966), 768-783.

[22] PRESCOTT, E. C., AND R. MEHRA, "Recursive Competitive Equilibrium: The Case of Homogeneous Households," *Econometrica*, 48(1980), 1365-1379.

[23] PYE, G.: "Lifetime Portfolio Selection in Continuous Time for a Multiplicative Class of Utility Functions," *American Economic Review*, 63(1973), 1013-1016.

[24] RICHARD, S. F., AND M. SUNDARESAN: "A Continuous Time Equilibrium Model of Forward Prices and Futures Prices in a Multigood Economy," *Journal of Financial Economics*, 9(1981), 347-371.

[25] ROSS, S. A.: "The Arbitrage Theory of Capital Asset Pricing," *Journal of Economic Theory*, 13(1976), 341-360.

[26] RUBINSTEIN, M. E.: "The Valuation of Uncertain Income Streams and the Pricing of Options," *Bell Journal of Economics*, 7(1976), 407-425.

[27] SHARPE, W. F.: "Capital Asset Prices: A Theory of Market Equilibrium under Conditions of Risk," *Journal of Finance*, 19(1964), 425-442.

[28] STAPLETON, R. C., AND M. G. SUBRAHMANYAM: "A Multiperiod Equilibrium Asset Pricing Model," *Econometrica*, 46(1978), 1077-1096.

[14]

Journal of Financial Economics 16 (1986) 3–39. North-Holland

CONSUMPTION, PRODUCTION, INFLATION AND INTEREST RATES
A Synthesis*

Douglas T. BREEDEN

Duke University, Durham, NC 27706, USA

Received January 1984, final version received October 1985

This paper uses discrete-time and continuous-time models to derive equilibrium relations among real and nominal interest rates and the expected growth, variance and covariance parameters of optimally chosen paths for aggregate real consumption and aggregate production. Simple, intuitive and fairly general relations are obtained which apply to most of the models of financial economics of the past 20 years. The single-good analysis generalizes and provides a synthesis of many prior works, whereas the multi-good analysis provides more original results. Consistent business cycle movements are examined for interest rates, inflation and consumption and production aggregates.

1. Introduction

In a single-good, continuous-time model, Cox, Ingersoll and Ross (1985) – hereafter also referred to as CIR – derived a relation of the instantaneous interest rate to the mean and covariance structure of returns in production processes. Rubinstein (1976, 1981) in a discrete-time model, and Garman (1977) and Cox and Ross (1977) derived relations of the parameters of optimal consumption paths to interest rates.[1] This paper provides a synthesis of the relations among interest rates and optimally chosen consumption and production paths in an economy with uncertainty and inflation. The economic analysis of interest rates and optimal production policies significantly extends and generalizes the Cox, Ingersoll and Ross (1985) analysis. Additionally, the paper utilizes consumption aggregation results that are not in those earlier papers. Simple, intuitive and fairly general relations of interest rates to consumption and production aggregates are obtained. Properties of an optimal

*This work was conducted in part during the 1981–1982 academic year when I was a Batterymarch Fellow. I am very grateful for this financial support. Of course, Batterymarch Financial Management may not agree with the analysis or conclusions expressed here. I also wish to thank seminar participants at several schools, and particularly Wayne Ferson, Michael Gibbons, Robert Litzenberger, John Long, Mark Rubinstein and Rene Stulz for their helpful comments. Of course, I am responsible for all remaining errors.

[1] Of course, much economic analysis of consumption, production and interest rates in certainty models precedes those works and certainly precedes this. See Hirshleifer (1970, particularly pp. 116–117) for an excellent discussion of the general equilibrium relationships in a certainty model.

0304-405X/86/$3.50©1986, Elsevier Science Publishers B.V. (North-Holland)

aggregate consumption function are derived and used to explain how the consumption and production results are consistent.

The paper utilizes two standard economic models to examine consumption, production, inflation and interest rates. The principal results can be seen in both models. In section 2, a discrete-time, multi-period state preference model is first used to develop the relations of consumption growth and of production opportunities to the term structure of interest rates in a single-good economy. Section 3 discusses consistent movements in these variables during a business cycle. In section 4, following CIR, the continuous-time model is used to examine the production and interest rates relation in some detail. Section 5 provides the corresponding continuous-time relation of consumption and interest rates, and section 6 provides a synthesis of the consumption and production results in a single-good economy.

Sections 7 and 8 derive nominally riskless and real riskless interest rates in a multi-good economy; they are much more complex than in a single-good economy. These complexities are likely to be economically significant for analyses of nominal interest rates, since it is generally assumed that movements in anticipated inflation are of the same order of magnitude as the movements of the 'real' interest rate. In much of the multi-good analysis, individuals are assumed to have time-additive, but otherwise general preferences for bundles of consumption goods. Individuals' vectors of budget shares are not assumed to be identical, which virtually ensures that they will measure inflation differently. In the multi-good economies examined, Divisia's price indices are used to show four significant points: (1) the positive relation between the interest rate and the expected growth of aggregate real consumption is essentially unchanged from the similar single-good relation; (2) the relevant inflation rate for the 'Fisher' effect is measured by goods' percentage price changes multiplied by their respective aggregate marginal (not average) expenditure shares and summed; (3) the equilibrium nominal interest rate should include a risk premium or discount proportional to the negative of the covariance of inflation with real consumption; and (4) the negative relation of interest rates to the variance of aggregate real consumption does not unambiguously follow from the decreasing absolute risk aversion assumption. However, note that in an economy with Cobb–Douglas preferences, the negative relation of interest rates to consumption uncertainty does hold, as is shown. A variant of the Fisher equation is a special case of the model.

Section 9 concludes the paper with a few comments on the limitations and possible future extensions of the theory.

2. A state preference model of consumption, production and interest rates

The time–state preference model originated with Arrow (1953) and Debreu (1959), and was significantly elucidated by Hirshleifer (1970). Some of the more recent asset pricing papers that used the time–state preference approach are those by Fama (1970), Beja (1971), Rubinstein (1974, 1976a, b, 1981), Kraus and Litzenberger (1975), Hakansson (1977), Banz and Miller (1978), Breeden and Litzenberger (1978), Grauer and Litzenberger (1979), Bhattacharya (1981), and Constantinides (1982). Other significant discrete-time, multi-period valuation models that could easily be rephrased in terms of state–preference are those by Long (1974), Dieffenbach (1975), Brennan (1979), Lucas (1978), and Long and Plosser (1983).

The continuous-time economic model of consumption and portfolio choice was pioneered by Merton (1971, 1973) and extended to a production economy by Cox, Ingersoll and Ross (1985). Other well-known continuous-time asset pricing models include papers by Garman (1977), Cox and Ross (1977), Breeden (1979), and Stulz (1981), as well as the entire literature on option pricing that was begun by Black and Scholes' (1973) seminal work. Since almost all of the general (not arbitrage-based) discrete- and continuous-time asset pricing models assume time-additive utility functions and homogeneous beliefs (the crucial assumptions), the equilibrium interest rate derivations that follow should characterize these models.

In both the time–state preference model and the continuous-time model, the following assumptions are made: (A.1) The economy has a single physical good. (This assumption is relaxed in sections 7 and 8.) Since individuals' preferences are based entirely upon the consumption of this single good, the interest rate analysis of sections 2–6 should be interpreted as applying to 'real' rates. (A.2) In the time–state preference economies examined, there are N risky production processes that have non-increasing returns to scale. In the continuous-time economy of section 4, the stronger assumption of (A.2′) stochastically constant returns to scale is made (as in the CIR paper). Individuals allocate their wealths to production processes and to state-contingent financial claims. (A.3) Individuals have homogeneous probability beliefs for future states of the world, with the time 0 probability for the occurence of state θ at time t defined as $\pi_{t\theta}$. (A.4) Each individual $\{k\}$ maximizes the expected value of a time-additive and state-independent von Neumann–Morgenstern utility function for lifetime consumption, i.e.,

$$\max_{\{c_{t\theta}^k\}} \sum_t \sum_{\theta \in S(t)} \pi_{t\theta} \cdot u^k\left(c_{t\theta}^k, t\right), \tag{1}$$

where $c_{t\theta}^k$ is k's consumption of the good at time t if state θ occurs. It is assumed that $u^k(c_t^k, t)$ is monotonically increasing and strictly concave in consumption, displays decreasing absolute risk aversion (which implies that $u_{ccc}^k > 0$), and has marginal utility that approaches infinity as consumption approaches zero. Finally, (A.5) it is assumed that the capital markets are sufficiently complete to permit an unconstrained Pareto-optimal allocation of time–state contingent consumption claims.

With a Pareto-optimal allocation, the shadow price for one unit of the good to be received in time–state $t\theta$ is the same for all individuals; let it be $\phi_{t\theta}$. The standard first-order condition is that $\phi_{t\theta}$ equals the marginal rate of substitution of consumption today for consumption in time–state $t\theta$:

$$\phi_{t\theta} = \frac{\pi_{t\theta} u'^k\left(c^k_{t\theta}, t\right)}{u'^k_0\left(c^k_0, t_0\right)}, \quad \forall k. \tag{2}$$

Note that ranking states at time t in order of their price-to-probability ratios, $\{\phi_{t\theta}/\pi_{t\theta}\}$, gives an exactly inverse ranking of every individual's optimal consumption in the various possible states at time t. Thus, each individual's optimal consumption function may be written in 'reduced form' as a strictly monotonic function of only aggregate consumption, $C_{t\theta}$, and time, $c^k_{t\theta} = c^k(C_{t\theta}, t)$, as shown by Breeden and Litzenberger (1978). Letting $u'(C_{t\theta}, t) = u'^k_t(c^k(C_{t\theta}, t), t)$ for some k, the value of any asset with time–state contingent payoffs $\{X_{t\theta}\}$ equals in equilibrium

$$V_0\{X_{t\theta}\} = \sum_t \sum_{\theta \in S(t)} \phi_{t\theta} X_{t\theta} = \sum_t \frac{\mathrm{E}_0[\tilde{X}_t u'(\tilde{C}_t, t)]}{u'(C_0, t_0)}. \tag{3}$$

With Pareto-optimal capital markets, this valuation equation holds at every instant, with the relevant probabilities being those conditional upon all information available at the time and state of valuation. Thus, the value of any asset at any time and state may be written in terms of only its payoffs' (conditional) joint probability distributions with aggregate consumption.

From (3), the value at time t of a riskless unit discount bond maturing at T, $B(t,T)$, and the associated continuously-compounded interest rate for the period, $r(t,T)$, are[2]

$$B(t,T) = \mathrm{e}^{-r(t,T)(T-t)} = \frac{\mathrm{E}_t[u'(\tilde{C}_T, T)]}{u'(C_t, t)}, \qquad \forall t, \quad T > t. \tag{4}$$

Let subscripts of the u' function be partial derivatives, and let $m_{(n)}(t,T)$ be the nth central moment for $\ln C_T$ as seen at time t. For $n = 3$, this gives the skewness of $\ln C_T$, $n = 4$ gives its kurtosis, and so on. Expanding (4) in a

[2] Rubinstein (1976b) derived (4) with the assumption that all individuals have isoelastic utility functions with the same power. This derivation shows that the relation of bond prices to the probability distribution for aggregate consumption does not require such strong preference assumptions.

Taylor series about the current time and the current level of the log of aggregate consumption, $\{t, \ln C_t\}$ gives the following term structure approximation:

$$r(t,T) = [-u'_t/u'] + [-u'_{\ln C}/u']\mu_{\ln C}(t,T)$$
$$- \left[\tfrac{1}{2}(u'_{\ln C, \ln C}/u')\right]\sigma^2_{\ln C}(t,T)$$
$$- \sum_{n=3}^{\infty} (1/n!)\left[u'_{(n)}/u'\right] m_{(n)}(t,T) + \text{higher-order terms}, \tag{5}$$

where

$$\mu_{\ln C}(t,T) = \frac{\mathrm{E}_t(\ln \tilde{C}_T) - \ln C_t}{T-t} \quad \text{and} \quad \sigma^2_{\ln C}(t,T) = \frac{\mathrm{var}_t(\ln \tilde{C}_T)}{T-t}.$$

The bond price equation and the term structure approximation are worthy of further discussion. They say that the entire term structure of interest rates at every point in time may be written in terms of just (1) time, (2) the current level of aggregate consumption, and (3) the probability distributions for aggregate consumption at the maturity dates of the bonds examined. Utility functions are quite general and diverse within the time-additive class, and no assumptions about the stochastic processes for production have been made. Thus, the model applies to most of the general asset pricing models in the finance literature of the 1970s.

Other items that might have been in the bond pricing equation, but are not, include aggregate wealth, the distribution of wealth, the composition of consumption, past consumption levels, and the parameters of the production possibility frontier. Of course, the fact that these variables do not explicitly appear is the result of the endogenous nature of aggregate consumption. Aggregate consumption reflects aggregate wealth and its distribution, as well as production possibilities. Similarly, the probability distribution for future levels of aggregate consumption reflects both initial wealth and the production possibility set.

With the much stronger assumption [see Rubinstein (1974)] that (A.6) individuals' preferences give an aggregate utility function of

$$u(C_t, t) = \mathrm{e}^{-\rho t} C_t^{1-\gamma}, \tag{1'}$$

which has constant relative risk aversion equal to γ, and (A.7) aggregate consumption at time T is lognormally distributed as seen at time t, the term structure equation becomes much simpler:[3,4]

$$r(t,T) = \rho + \gamma\mu_{\ln C}(t,T) - (\gamma^2/2)\sigma^2_{\ln C}(t,T). \tag{6}$$

While the CRRA and lognormal assumptions made for (6) are probably not bad first approximations for preferences and for probability distributions, they are almost surely inconsistent as an exact model of a stochastic term structure.[5] However, section 6 shows that in a continuous-time model, such a relation describes the instantaneous riskless rate for general preferences and general probability distributions (generated by diffusion processes).

The intuitive basis for the positive relation of interest rates to time preference is well-known. The higher the measure of pure time preference [ρ in eq. (6), $-u'_t/u'$ in eq. (5)], the greater the relative preference for goods today. Thus, the higher the rate of time preference, the higher the interest rate must be to induce individuals to defer consumption and buy a bond.

The positive relation of the riskless rate to expected consumption growth is also easily understood. The price of any discount bond is equal to the expected marginal utility of consumption at the maturity date, divided by the marginal utility of consumption today. With the maintained assumptions that each individual has decreasing marginal utility and decreasing absolute risk aversion, the relation of future marginal utility to (uncertain) future consumption can be graphed as in fig. 1. Holding current consumption constant and shifting the probability distribution of future consumption towards higher levels decreases expected future marginal utility, which decreases the bond price and increases the interest rate. Therefore, the riskless rate is positively related to the expected change in the log of consumption, $\mu_{\ln C}$.

[3] To derive (6), substitute marginal utilities for (1′) into (4) to get:

$$B(t,T) = e^{-r(t,T)(T-t)} = e^{-\rho(T-t)}E_t\left[(\tilde{C}_T/C_t)^{-\gamma}\right]. \tag{4'}$$

Next, if $\tilde{C}_T/C_t$ is lognormal with the log's mean equal to $(T-t)\mu_{\ln C}$ and its variance equal to $(T-t)\sigma^2_{\ln C}$, then $(\tilde{C}_T/C_t)^{-\gamma}$ is lognormal with its log's mean of $-(T-t)\gamma\mu_{\ln C}$ and its variance equal to $(T-t)\gamma^2\sigma^2_{\ln C}$. Substituting these into (4′), using the fact that $E(e^{\tilde{x}}) = \exp[\mu + \sigma^2/2]$ when $\tilde{x}$ is normal, and taking logs of both sides gives (6).

[4] The CRRA–lognormal term structure of (6) was derived independently by Garman (1977, p. 39) and Breeden (1977, ch. 7). This combination of CRRA and lognormal consumption assumptions is presented solely as an example that permits an exact identification of coefficients in the more general term structure of (5). Consumption is clearly an endogenous function of wealth, the production opportunity set, and time, and its probability distribution ideally should be derived from preferences and the joint probability distribution of those more fundamental variables.

[5] An exact continuous-time model with CRRA preferences and consumption endogenously determined to be lognormally distributed implies a constant term structure of interest rates. I thank John Cox and Chi-Fu Huang for pointing this out to me. However, the approximation of (5) is quite general and is consistent with a stochastic term structure, and (6) may be viewed as a mean–variance version of it. Furthermore, section 5's quite general derivation of the instantaneous rate in terms of instantaneous parameters for aggregate consumption yields the same equation as (6).

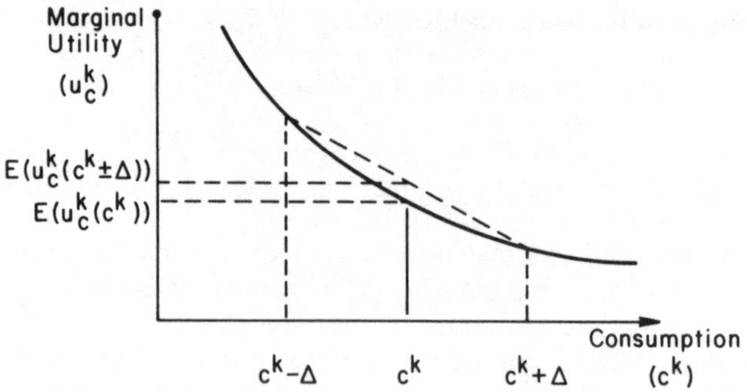

Fig. 1. This figure shows that increases in consumption variance increase expected marginal utility. It compares the expected marginal utility of an individual who consumes c^k for sure to the expected marginal utility of an individual who consumes either $c^k+\Delta$ or $c^k-\Delta$ with equal probability.

To see the negative relation of interest rates to the variance of consumption, consider the effects of a mean-preserving spread of the distribution for consumption at the maturity date (again holding current consumption constant). This is illustrated in fig. 1 by taking probability from the expected future consumption level, $\bar{c}^k$, and splitting it into increased probabilities for levels $\bar{c}^k+\Delta$ and $\bar{c}^k-\Delta$. Due to the decreasing absolute risk aversion assumption, $u_{ccc}^k > 0$ for each individual k, so the increased variance for consumption increases expected marginal utility in the future. This is consistent only with a higher bond price and a lower interest rate. Intuitively, the greater the uncertainty about consumption that will be optimal at time T, the greater the value of the certain payoff provided by a bond maturing at that time, *ceteris paribus*.

Now consider the production side of the economy. For an optimal policy, k's marginal utility for wealth at any time and state equals her marginal utility for consumption in the same state and time, $u_c^k(c^k(Q^k, s, t), t)$, where s is a vector of variables that describe the state of production opportunities and Q^k is k's wealth. Corresponding to the result that each individual's optimal consumption is a monotonic function of only aggregate consumption, we have the following theorem on optimal wealth allocations in a production economy:[6]

Theorem. Optimal Allocations With Production. If (A1) each individual has a time-additive, state-independent utility function for lifetime consumption and (A2) individuals agree upon the (conditional) probabilities of states at every point in time, then any unconstrained Pareto-optimal allocation of resources to production processes and of time–state contingent consumption claims is such

[6] For related theorems, see Constantinides (1982) and Breeden (1984).

that, at each date, all states with the same level of aggregate supply of the good and the same investment opportunities have the same allocation of wealth to individuals in the corresponding competitive economy. With diminishing marginal utility for wealth, this implies that individual k's optimal amount of the good at time t may be written as a strictly positive monotonic function of only the aggregate *amount of wealth at that time, given the state vector for production opportunities and time, i.e.,* $Q_t^k = F^k(Q, s, t)$, *with* $F_Q^k > 0$.

An outline of the proof of this theorem is in appendix 1.

An important implication of this theorem is that neither the past path of production, nor the past path of the state vector for production opportunities should affect an optimal allocation, given the current production opportunity set and the current aggregate supply of the good. This theorem also implies that if the allocation is Pareto-optimal, the distribution of wealth to individuals is not needed as a descriptor of the system at every point in time. Given knowledge of the initial wealth distribution, preferences and probability beliefs, all future optimal distributions of wealth are fully determined by aggregate wealth and the state of production opportunities.

Let individual k's expected utility for lifetime consumption be given by $J^k(Q^k(Q, s, t), s, t)$. From the optimality condition that the marginal utility of wealth equals the marginal utility of consumption, production-oriented valuation equations obtain which are similar to the consumption-oriented equations (3) and (4). Defining $J'(Q, s, t) = J_Q^k(Q^k(Q, s, t), s, t)$ for some k, and substituting the envelope condition into (3) and (4) gives

$$V_0\{X_{t\theta}\} = \sum_t \frac{\mathrm{E}_0[\tilde{X}_t J'(\tilde{Q}_t, \tilde{s}_t, t)]}{J'(Q_0, s_0, t_0)}, \tag{7}$$

$$B(t, T) = \mathrm{e}^{-r(t,T)(T-t)} = \frac{\mathrm{E}_t[J'(\tilde{Q}_T, \tilde{s}_T, T)]}{J'(Q_t, s_t, t)}, \qquad \forall t, \quad T > t. \tag{8}$$

As (8) reflects the sacrifice of $B(t, T)$ at t for a riskless return of unity at T, it arises from equilibrium in the markets for 'riskless intertemporal exchanges'. An equation reflecting an 'intratemporal equilibrium' in the markets for risk and return is obtained as follows. In equilibrium, consider investing at time t one more unit in a risky portfolio or in an active production process that pays $\tilde{x}_T$ at time T per unit invested. That is, $x_{Ts} = \partial X_{Ts}/\partial X_t$, so $\tilde{x}_T$ is the marginal return on investment. In equilibrium, one unit must be the value at t of this, so $1 = \mathrm{E}_t[\tilde{x}_T \tilde{J}_T']/J_t'$, from (7). Combining this with (8), the price of a riskless bond maturing at T may be written as

$$B(t, T) = \mathrm{E}_t[J'(\tilde{Q}_T, \tilde{s}_T, T)]/\mathrm{E}_t[\tilde{x}_T J'(\tilde{Q}_T, \tilde{s}_T, T)]. \tag{9}$$

Thus, this equilibrium condition represents indifference (at the margin) between the returns received at T from additional risky investment and the returns at T from the riskless investment. It is in this sense that (9) represents equilibrium at t in the market for intratemporal risks resolved at T.

In a manner similar to that used for consumption, first-order Taylor series approximations for the term structure can be obtained from (8) and (9). The expansion of (9) gives the following:[7]

$$r(t,T) = \mu_x(t,T) - [\partial \ln J'/\partial \ln Q]\sigma_{x,\ln Q}(t,T) + [\partial \ln J'/\partial s]V_{xs}(t,T) + \text{terms with higher-order co-moments of } x \text{ with } \{\ln \tilde{Q}, \tilde{s}\}, \tag{10}$$

where

$$\mu_x(t,T) = \ln[\mathrm{E}_t(\tilde{x}_T)]/(T-t),$$

$$\sigma_{x,\ln Q}(t,T) = \mathrm{cov}(\ln \tilde{x}_T, \ln \tilde{Q}_T)/(T-t),$$

$$V_{xs}(t,T) = \mathrm{cov}(\ln \tilde{x}_T, \tilde{s}_T)/(T-t).$$

This production-oriented equation suggests some interesting possible term structures. Consider that at any point in time there are productive investments that are being made that result in output and profits at various dates in the future. Some investments take one year before production is forthcoming, some take two years, and so on. Some investments can be brought into production more quickly, but at higher cost. For all active processes in which current investment is being made, (10) must hold. Holding constant the covariances of production with wealth and the state variables, the term structure of interest rates is seen to mirror the 'term structure of expected returns on investments'.[8] Since the cost of production is usually assumed to

[7]There are two more obvious Taylor series approximations that are not presented in the paper – an approximation of (8) for the term structure, and of (3) for an arbitrary asset. The approximation of (8) gives a term structure that could be analyzed much like what follows. The approximation of (3) gives a multi-moment consumption-oriented CAPM.

[8]Note that since these are simultaneous relationships, one could just as correctly say that the optimal marginal returns on investments adjust to the term structure of interest rates. However, with the constant returns to scale technology examined later in section 4, the text's statement is more consistent. Note also that Fama and Gibbons (1982) found empirical evidence supporting this theoretical relation of real interest rates to expected returns from production. They found that increases in the *ex ante* real rate were associated with increased subsequent capital investment, presumably induced by increased expected returns on investment. Similarly, they found that real returns on capital were positively correlated with the *ex ante* real rate.

decrease (and profitability increase) as production time increases, the term structure should have an upward slope under normal circumstances. In that case, short-term interest rates would be lower than long-term interest rates in equilibrium, due to the lower returns from their principal competitors – short-term productive investments.[9] However, if (at the optimum) expected profitability is higher for active short-term investments than for active long-term investments, this term structure can also give a downward-sloping term structure. Again, the import of the theory is that the term structure of interest rates mirrors the term structure of (marginal) expected returns on productive investments.

The interpretations of the uncertainty terms in this term structure are similar to those for the instantaneous rate, which will be examined in detail in the next section. However, there is one difference that should be noted. The covariance of the investment's return with aggregate wealth at time T is a portion of the risk adjustment for the investment, as it is in the instantaneous case. The difference is that, in the instantaneous case, the stochastic properties of the aggregate supply of the good are completely determined by the instant's production uncertainty; over discrete intervals, the probability distribution for aggregate wealth reflects consumption withdrawals in the interim, and they are endogenous functions of wealth, the state vector and time throughout the interval. One would still expect that an investment that has a positive correlation with aggregate output at each instant would have a positive correlation with aggregate wealth over a discrete interval, so the basic intuition does not change. But if consumption withdrawals were positively related to aggregate output, the wealth variable in (10) is a smoothed version of the returns to a rolled-over portfolio of investments in the economy's technologies.

3. Fluctuations of interest rates during a business cycle

While it is recognized again that consumption, production and interest rates are all endogenous variables, the term structure equations derived can be used to place restrictions on their equilibrium joint stochastic processes. For exam-

[9] In an insightful paper, Hirshleifer (1971) arrived at similar results, but for different reasons. Hirshleifer examined the term structure effects of the relative illiquidity of long-term point-input point-output production processes. Rolled-over investments in short-term production processes allow intermediate reallocations of goods between investment and consumption ('flexibility'); long-term production processes have little or no such flexibility. Intermediate reallocations may be optimal due to the arrival of new information about production possibilities or the distribution of future endowments. Thus, if the probability distributions of long-term and short-term investment returns were identical, individuals would prefer short-term investments. Hirshleifer shows that, in equilibrium, marginal investments in long-term activities must provide higher expected returns than provided on similar short-term activities, which is consistent with an upward-sloping term structure. With decreasing returns to scale, this could be achieved by relatively larger investments in short-term processes (giving them lower marginal products) than in long-term processes. Hirshleifer's model is compatible with this model, so his results must also occur here, given his assumptions.

ple, if one has information that real interest rates are higher now than in the past, a rational prediction (given the assumptions of the model) is that real consumption growth will be higher in the future than in the past, or that it will be less variable. It is in this spirit that the following discusses consistent movements in interest rates over a business cycle. Implicit in this discussion is the assumption that economists and individuals do have changing predictions about real consumption growth, and that those are rationally coordinated with their portfolio decisions.

The real term structure given by the CRRA–lognormal model or by the more general term structure approximation, (6) and (5) respectively, may have a variety of interesting shapes, depending upon the expected growth rate of aggregate consumption, as well as the uncertainty of that growth. In particular, the CRRA–lognormal term structure will be flat and will remain flat over time if the aggregate consumption process is a geometric Brownian motion, even if aggregate consumption is wildly variable. Actually, with CRRA utility, this result does not require the assumption of lognormality, as can be seen by examining the pricing equation for bonds for the special case where u' is a pure power of aggregate consumption. All that is required is that the probability distribution of $\tilde{C}_{t+\Delta}/C_t$ not change over time.

From (6), the T-period real riskless rate will be positively and linearly related to the T-period expected growth rate of aggregate consumption, whereas it will be negatively and linearly related to the T-period average variance rate for real consumption. For a maturing economy with the expectation of a gradually declining rate of growth of real aggregate consumption, the real term structure should tend to be downward-sloping, *ceteris paribus*. However, if the average variance rate of real aggregate consumption, $\sigma_C^2(t, T)$, were a decreasing function of $T-t$, the time to maturity of the associated discount bond, then the term structure would tend to be upward-sloping, *ceteris paribus*. There is some indirect evidence that, *ex post*, the one-year variance rate of aggregate real consumption has declined in the United States since about the year 1900, while average per capita real growth has not changed dramatically over the past 100 years (splitting the 100 years into two 50-year subperiods).[10] If this trend were expected, *ex ante*, then the term structure at that time should have been rising. If this trend were expected to continue, then the term structure should presently tend to be upward-sloping.

Even if one-year variance rates for aggregate consumption are constant over time, it is possible that the (unconditional) multi-period average variance rates in eqs. (5) and (6), $\mathrm{var}(\ln \tilde{C}_t)/(T-t)$, are decreasing in time to maturity, $T-t$. For example, this would occur if one-year (conditional) expected growth rates for aggregate consumption increase from one period to the next when current

[10]See Roberts (1977) for the evidence on declining variability. The evidence on the average per-capita real growth rate was provided by my research assistant, Ehud Ronn, using Kuznets' data for the early years.

consumption unexpectedly declines.[11] Intuitively stated, this is an economy that has negative autocorrelation in one-year real consumption growth rates, but stable one-year variances. Such an economy should tend to have an upward-sloping term structure.

If both the T-period mean growth rate and the T-period average variance rate decline with increasing time to maturity, T, at a given time, then the real term structure may either be rising or falling or be humped, depending upon the parameter values in (6). In that case, the mean effect offsets the variance effect on the term structure. Thus, the term structure equation given is quite flexible in terms of the shapes that may obtain; however, it is not so flexible as to be entirely useless. It predicts the signs of the partial effects of two parameters of aggregate consumption's probability distribution at any future date, one of which is the subject of numerous economists' forecasts (the mean), and the other of which (the variance) may be amenable to estimation.

Holding the maturity structure of average variance rates constant, the cyclical behavior of real rates may be examined by considering cyclical changes in expected economic growth rates. If the expectation is that economic growth will be rapid for a couple of years and then decline, then real interest rates should be 'high' for short-maturity discount bonds and relatively 'low' for long-term bonds. Thus, if the economy is thought to be entering a short-term rapid growth phase (coming out of a recession), real short-term interest rates should be high and the real term structure downward-sloping (or not rising as much as usual). Conversely, when the economy is believed to be entering a period of decline or of very slow growth relative to its long-term expected growth, the real term structure should tend to be rising.[12]

[11] This scenario is plausible for an economy with cyclical fluctuations about a long-term stationary trend. However, Mishkin (1981) found the *ex post* real rate to be unrelated to the gap between potential GNP and actual GNP; a positive relation would be expected with the long-term stationary economy posited. Additionally, Nelson and Plosser (1982) could not find evidence of a tendency for real GNP per capita to return to a deterministic path. Their conclusion is that (from their Abstract) 'macroeconomic models that focus on monetary disturbances as a source of purely transitory fluctuations may never be successful in explaining a large fraction of output variation, and that stochastic variation due to real factors is an essential element of any model of macroeconomic fluctuations'. Thus, Nelson and Plosser's evidence is against this particular hypothetical case. However, since the models derived here are much more general than this one example, their work does not contradict the general relations derived here of real consumption growth and real returns on investment to real interest rates.

[12] Note that movements in the term structure for inflation could reasonably offset these movements in the real term structure, resulting in shifts in the nominal term structure that are opposite to the cyclical predictions of this model. Consider an economy with negatively correlated growth rates in consumption. Furthermore, assume that at times when consumption has grown rapidly, the expected inflation rate is quite high. At a time when expected real short-term consumption growth is quite low relative to anticipated long-term consumption growth, short-term real interest rates should be low, and the real term structure rising. However, at that time, inflation might be very high and be expected to fall with the decreasing growth of the economy. The downward-sloping inflation structure, combined with the upward-sloping real term structure can give a nominal term structure that is either rising, falling or humped. Empirical research by

The term structure equations indicate that the hypothesis that the short-term real rate of interest is constant is rather implausible, as the expected real growth rate of aggregate consumption for small T may fluctuate considerably over a business cycle. Certainly the average of economists' forecasts of real consumption growth varies considerably over time, as does its dispersion. Furthermore, implied standard deviations of stocks' returns (from option prices) vary considerably through time, which at least suggests changes in the general level of economic uncertainty. The hypothesis that the long-term real rate of interest is constant (or at most a function of time) is more plausible, as long-term expected real growth rates and variance rates may be much more stable.

4. A continuous-time model of production and interest rates

The continuous-time model with constant-returns-to-scale production is essentially that of Cox, Ingersoll and Ross (1985), so its principal features will only be outlined. At time t, individual k's wealth is Q^k units of the good. From that wealth, at each instant, k chooses: (1) a consumption rate, c^k, (2) an optimal vector of investments in N risky production processes, $\boldsymbol{q}^k$, (3) an amount to be lent risklessly (borrowed if negative), q_0^k, and (4) a portfolio of investments in risky financial assets, $\boldsymbol{w}^k$. Individual k's resource constraint is $\sum_i q_i^k + q_0^k + \sum_j w_j^k = Q^k$. Individuals again are assumed to have time-additive preferences, maximizing an integral version of (1). However, the slightly more specialized assumption that $u^k(c^k, t) = \mathrm{e}^{-\rho t} U^k(c^k)$ is used in this section.

It is assumed that holdings of financial assets may be long or short for anyone, but that aggregate supplies of financial assets are all zeroes (since production is done only by individuals). With constant returns to scale and the unlimited borrowing assumption, individuals can do what firms could do. Thus, the financial assets are 'side bets' in this economy. Market clearing conditions at each point in time are $\sum_k \boldsymbol{w}^k = \boldsymbol{0}$ and $\sum_k Q^k = Q$. The vector of aggregate amounts invested in the various production processes is $\boldsymbol{q}^M = \sum_k \boldsymbol{q}^k$.

Each individual has the same production opportunity set, with the output from production process i being governed by a stochastic differential equation of the following type:

$$\mathrm{d}q_i^k = q_i^k \mu_{qi}(s, t)\,\mathrm{d}t + q_i^k \sigma_{qi}(s, t)\,\mathrm{d}z_{qi}, \tag{11}$$

where s is an $S \times 1$ vector of state variables that follow a vector Markov process with drift and diffusion parameters $\boldsymbol{\mu}_s(s, t)$ and $\boldsymbol{\sigma}_s(s, t)$, respectively.

Mishkin (1981) shows a strong negative correlation of the real rate with expected inflation, which results in low real rates typically when nominal rates are 'high'. Quoting Mishkin (1981, p. 173): 'When nominal rates are high, it is more likely that we are in a period of 'easy money' with low real rates than the contrary as has frequently been assumed.'

From (11), both uncertain production rates and random technological change are modeled, the former through the $\mathrm{d}z_q$ term, and the latter through the impact of stochastic fluctuations in the state variables on the means and uncertainties of the various production processes. It will be argued that the role of the financial assets in this model is to allocate the risks of changes in production technologies.

Financial asset j has a price P_j and pays no dividends. Financial assets' prices are endogenous functions of wealth, the state vector and time, moving stochastically through time as Ito processes. [See Huang (1983) for a rigorous model of information and asset prices in a continuous-time economy.] The $A \times 1$ vector of instantaneous expected returns on risky assets is $\boldsymbol{\mu}_a(Q, \boldsymbol{s}, t)$, with incremental covariance matrix $\mathbf{V}_{aa}$, covariances with production rates given by the $A \times N$ matrix $\mathbf{V}_{aq}$, and covariances with the state vector in the $A \times S$ matrix, $\mathbf{V}_{as}$. All of these covariance matrices may depend upon the state vector.

First-order conditions for the optimal production inputs and the optimal asset portfolio imply [see CIR (1985, eq. 10) and Huang (1983)]:

$$\begin{bmatrix} \boldsymbol{q}^k \\ \boldsymbol{w}^k \end{bmatrix} = T^k \begin{bmatrix} \mathbf{V}_{qq} & \mathbf{V}_{qa} \\ \mathbf{V}_{aq} & \mathbf{V}_{aa} \end{bmatrix}^{-1} \begin{bmatrix} \boldsymbol{\mu}_q - \boldsymbol{r} \\ \boldsymbol{\mu}_a - \boldsymbol{r} \end{bmatrix} + \begin{bmatrix} \mathbf{V}_{qq} & \mathbf{V}_{qa} \\ \mathbf{V}_{aq} & \mathbf{V}_{aa} \end{bmatrix}^{-1} \begin{bmatrix} \mathbf{V}_{qs} \\ \mathbf{V}_{as} \end{bmatrix} \boldsymbol{H}_s^k \qquad (12)$$

$$= T^k \mathbf{V}^{-1}(\boldsymbol{\mu} - \boldsymbol{r}) + \mathbf{V}^{-1}\mathbf{V}_{qa,s}\boldsymbol{H}_s^k, \qquad (12')$$

where $\mathbf{V}$ and $\boldsymbol{\mu}$ are defined as the covariance matrix and expected return vector for the augmented vector of physical productivities and returns on financial assets. The variables T^k and $\boldsymbol{H}_s^k$ are absolute risk tolerance and Merton's (1973) 'hedging' demands, $T^k = -J_Q^k/J_{QQ}^k$ and $\boldsymbol{H}_s^k = -\boldsymbol{J}_{Qs}^k/J_{QQ}^k$. Risk tolerance based upon the direct utility function is defined as $T_c^k = -u_c^k/u_{cc}^k$. Relative risk tolerances are written with the same notation, but with asterisks attached.

Note that individuals differ in their production and investment policies only as they differ in risk tolerance and in hedging preferences. This is due to the combination of assumptions that all have the same production and investment opportunities and that those opportunities all exhibit stochastically constant returns to scale. Furthermore, since this model is formally identical to that of Merton (1973) and Breeden (1979), the expected excess return on any risk production process or asset is given by a 'multibeta' CAPM (with betas measured relative to the market and to the S state variables) and also by a consumption-oriented CAPM. However, since the pricing of risky assets is not the focus of this paper, these results will not be further discussed.

Aggregate investments in the various production processes and financial assets are given by summing individuals' investments, given in (12). Noting that aggregate financial investments are all zeroes, this gives

$$\begin{bmatrix} \boldsymbol{q}^M \\ \boldsymbol{0} \end{bmatrix} = T^M \mathbf{V}^{-1}(\boldsymbol{\mu} - \boldsymbol{r}) + \mathbf{V}^{-1}\mathbf{V}_{qa,s}\boldsymbol{H}_s^M, \tag{13}$$

where

$$T^M = \sum_k T^k \quad \text{and} \quad \boldsymbol{H}_s^M = \sum_k \boldsymbol{H}_s^k.$$

Let $\boldsymbol{q}_M^* = \boldsymbol{q}^M/Q$ be the aggregate fractions invested in the production processes, and let $T^{*M} = T^M/Q$ be an aggregate measure of relative risk tolerance. Multiplying (13) by $(\boldsymbol{q}^{M'}\ \boldsymbol{0})\mathbf{V}/Q^2$ gives an important relation:

$$\begin{aligned} \boldsymbol{q}_M^{*\prime}\mathbf{V}_{qq}\boldsymbol{q}_M^* &= T^{*M}\boldsymbol{q}_M^{*\prime}(\boldsymbol{\mu}_q - \boldsymbol{r}) + \boldsymbol{q}_M^*\mathbf{V}_{qs}\boldsymbol{H}_s^M/Q \\ &= \sigma_Q^2 = T^{*M}(\mu_Q - r) + \boldsymbol{V}_{Qs}\boldsymbol{H}_s^M/Q, \end{aligned} \tag{14}$$

where σ_Q^2 is the variance of optimal aggregate production (as a fraction of the amount invested), μ_Q is the expected return on the market portfolio of productive investments, and $\boldsymbol{V}_{Qs}$ is the vector of covariances of aggregate production with the state variables.

Rearranging terms in (14) gives the instantaneous riskless rate in terms of the expected growth rate, the variance rate, and the covariances with state variables for aggregate production:

$$r = \mu_Q - \left(1/T^{*M}\right)\sigma_Q^2 + \boldsymbol{V}_{Qs}\left(\boldsymbol{H}_s^M/T^M\right). \tag{15}$$

This was derived by CIR (1985, eq. 14) for an economy with identical individuals. This equation is also the same as the mean–variance part of the term structure approximation in the state preference model's eq. (10).

Before going into a fairly detailed analysis of this relation (and a similar consumption relation), a couple of significant points should be emphasized. First, the riskless rate is positively related to expected aggregate productivity and is negatively related to the variance of productivity, *ceteris paribus*. Second, a truly dynamic analysis is consistent with (15), since all of the terms in it are, in general, stochastic. The model used in the derivation assumed that means, variances and covariances of production returns with each other and with the state vector are functions of time and a stochastic state vector. Of course, the risk aversion and hedging parameters are derived from individuals' indirect utility functions, so they also are stochastic unless stronger preference assumptions are made. For example, logarithmic utility functions for consumption imply that $\boldsymbol{H}_s^M = \boldsymbol{0}$ and that $T^{*M} = 1$, as noted by Merton (1973).

To further examine the relation of the interest rate to production technology, the production plans of different individuals, as well as the 'hedging' term, $\boldsymbol{H}_s^M$, must be analyzed. Let $\boldsymbol{\varepsilon}_s^k$ be individual k's vector of compensating variations in wealth as a percentage of wealth that are required to offset changes in the state variables and keep expected lifetime utility constant. That is, $\boldsymbol{\varepsilon}_s^k = -\boldsymbol{J}_s^k/(J_Q^k Q^k)$. If, for example, there is a state variable s_j that represents technological development by having high values when expected productivity is high, and low values when productivity is low, the percentage compensating variation in wealth for an increase in s_j is negative, i.e., $\varepsilon_{sj} < 0$. For the remainder of this section, assume that (A.8) these percentage compensating variations are invariant with respect to individual k's wealth. Given this assumption, Breeden (1984) has shown that $\boldsymbol{H}_s^k$ and $\boldsymbol{\varepsilon}_s^k$ are related as follows:

$$\boldsymbol{H}_s^k = Q^k[1 - T^{*k}]\boldsymbol{\varepsilon}_s^k. \tag{16}$$

Substituting (16) into (15), the riskless rate may be written as

$$r = \mu_Q - (Q/T^M)\sigma_Q^2 + (1/T^M)\mathbf{V}_{Qs}\left[\sum_k (1 - T^{*k})\boldsymbol{\varepsilon}_s^k Q^k/Q\right], \tag{17}$$

and k's optimal allocation of investment to production processes is [from (12)]

$$\begin{bmatrix} \boldsymbol{q}^M \\ \boldsymbol{0} \end{bmatrix} = T^M \mathbf{V}^{-1}(\boldsymbol{\mu} - \boldsymbol{r}) + \mathbf{V}^{-1}\mathbf{V}_{qa,s}\boldsymbol{\varepsilon}_s^k(1 - T^{*k})Q^k. \tag{18}$$

From (18), if all individuals have logarithmic utility functions, then $T^{*k} = 1$ and all individuals invest the same wealth fractions in the various production processes. No trading in risky financial assets takes place in this case. In this case, the riskless rate is equal to the expected return on optimal risky investment, less its variance.[13]

Since ε_{sj}^k is k's percentage compensating variation in wealth for an increase in state variable s_j, $\boldsymbol{\varepsilon}_s^{k\prime}(\mathrm{d}\boldsymbol{s})$ is the net percentage compensating variation in wealth for the random fluctuations in the entire state vector. Given this, $\mathbf{V}_{qa,Ik} = -\mathbf{V}_{qa,s}\boldsymbol{\varepsilon}_s^k$ is the vector of covariances of the various activities' outputs and financial assets' returns with the net change in the value of investment technology to k.

The optimal production plan for k can be interpreted with the same insights as in the multi-period portfolio theory of Merton (1973) and Breeden (1984). The first term in (18) is the locally mean–variance efficient combination of productive investments and financial assets, and the second term adjusts the

[13]Both of these logarithmic utility results were obtained by Kraus and Litzenberger (1975) and Rubinstein (1976a) in exchange economies, and by CIR in the production model.

production plan to either hedge or 'reverse hedge' against technological changes. If k's relative risk aversion exceeds one, then $1 - T^{*k} > 0$ and k will tend to adjust his production plan to hedge against unfavorable technological changes. If k's relative risk aversion is less than one, then k will reverse hedge by allocating more to production processes whose outputs are positively correlated with changes in production technology.[14] Thus, those who are relatively risk-tolerant will tend to invest more in production processes that have positively autocorrelated returns than in processes that have mean-reverting cash flows. Those who are very risk-averse will tend to invest more in mean-reverting processes and less in positively autocorrelated processes.

The equilibrium interest rate is also affected by the nature of production autocorrelations in a way that depends upon individuals' risk aversion functions. If the economy is populated by individuals who exhibit normal hedging behavior (which seems most reasonable), then $1 - T^{*k} > 0$ in (18) and the riskless rate will be negatively related to the degree of autocorrelation of output, holding the mean and variance of the aggregate production rate constant. Intuitively, the high-risk aspect of production processes with positive autocorrelation would make individuals reluctant to invest in them; individuals would be more willing to lend risklessly to others who are more risk-tolerant, thereby lowering the riskless interest rate. If production processes have negative autocorrelation, their multi-period returns are more stable than with no autocorrelation. Thus, relatively risk-averse individuals would wish to lend less and invest more in negatively autocorrelated processes, resulting in a higher equilibrium riskless rate.

With an economy of individuals who are more risk-tolerant than the logarithm, the effects of autocorrelation on the riskless rate are correctly predicted by focusing upon the effects of production autocorrelations on mean multi-period returns (rather than upon the variance). Positive production autocorrelations lead to higher multi-period returns on average than those with no autocorrelation. Individuals who are relatively risk-tolerant will attempt to borrow and invest more in such processes, which results in a higher riskless rate than without autocorrelation. Thus, an economy that is not very risk-averse has a riskless rate that is positively related to the degree of autocorrelation in production processes.

As noted, the allocation of inputs to production processes will, in general, be different for each individual. However, if there exist financial assets that perfectly hedge against technological changes, then separation of production mixes from preferences occurs. If the first financial asset were perfectly correlated with the first state variable, then a multiple regression of the first

[14] Breeden (1984) showed that this reverse hedging policy increases the mean lifetime consumption stream. Since relative risk tolerance is a marginal rate of substitution of mean for variance, it is not too surprising that some individuals will choose high mean and high variance, while others will choose low mean and low variance, depending upon their mrs functions.

state variable on all productivities and all financial assets would give zero investments in all of them, except for the first financial asset (which is the perfect hedge). Similarly, assuming that there are exactly S financial assets, each of which is perfectly correlated with a state variable, implies that the matrix of hedge portfolios simplifies to[15]

$$\mathbf{V}^{-1}\mathbf{V}_{qa,s}=\begin{bmatrix} \mathbf{0} \\ \mathbf{I} \end{bmatrix}.$$

Given this and (12′), with these financial assets as hedges, all individuals have the same mix of production inputs, regardless of preferences and covariances of productivities with the state variables.

There are a couple of points to note about this result. One is that the risk exposure of an individual to technological changes can, with these assumptions, be perfectly controlled by investments solely in financial assets. Still, the aggregate Pareto-optimal investments in production processes should reflect their covariances with technological change and individuals' preferences regarding those technological changes. They do, but now they are reflected in all individuals' production plans in the same way through the $\mathbf{V}^{-1}(\boldsymbol{\mu}-\boldsymbol{r})$ term in (12). This is true since $\mathbf{V}$ includes the covariances of productivities with assets' returns, which are assumed to reflect technological changes. The expected excess returns on assets are the market's equilibrium prices for the risks of technological change (as given by a consumption-oriented CAPM). If financial assets do not perfectly reflect those technological changes, then the final $\boldsymbol{H}_s^k$ term in (12) does affect production decisions, as those decisions may then help achieve an optimal exposure to technological risks in ways not possible with financial assets alone.

5. Consumption and interest rates in the continuous-time model

Cox, Ingersoll and Ross (1985, theorem 1) have shown that each individual optimally sets the negative of the expected rate of change in the marginal utility of wealth equal to the instantaneous riskless rate. Letting $\mu_{J'}^k$ and $\mu_{u'}^k$ be k's drift parameters for the marginal utility of wealth and consumption, this implies (along with the envelope condition)

$$r=-\mu_{J'}^k/J'^k=-\mu_{u'}^k/u'^k, \quad \forall k. \tag{19}$$

This result is a limiting case, $T\rightarrow t$, of the state preference valuation [eq. (4)] for an instantaneous-maturity bond, since that formula holds for each individ-

[15]In this case, the allocation is Pareto-optimal [Breeden (1984)] and there is local unanimity among investors for production plans. Production and consumption separation occurs as in Hirshleifer (1970, ch. 3).

ual. Intuitively, the higher the riskless rate, the more individuals should defer consumption; this results in a higher optimal growth rate for consumption and a larger expected decline in marginal utility.

Using Ito's Lemma, the marginal utility of consumption for k, $u_c^k(c^k, t)$, has a drift that may be found from k's instantaneous expected consumption change, μ_c^k, and its variance, σ_{ck}^2,

$$\mu_{u'}^k = u_{ct}^k + u_{cc}^k \mu_c^k + \tfrac{1}{2} u_{ccc}^k \sigma_{ck}^2. \tag{20}$$

Substituting (20) into (19), and using the fact that $-u_{ct}^k/u_c^k = \rho^k$ with the time-separable preferences assumed, gives

$$r = \rho^k + \left[-u_{cc}^k/u_c^k\right]\mu_c^k - \tfrac{1}{2}\left[u_{ccc}^k/u_c^k\right]\sigma_{ck}^2, \quad \forall k. \tag{21}$$

Note that this corresponds precisely to the first-order terms in the term structure approximation derived in a discrete-time, state preference model in section 2, eq. (5). The riskless rate is positively related to time preference and to the expected growth rate for consumption and is negatively related to the variance of that growth. Equivalently, as Cox and Ross (1977) and Garman (1977) pointed out, each individual adjusts her expected instantaneous growth rate of consumption to correspond to the difference between the riskless rate and her pure rate of time preference, holding the variance of consumption constant. With the diffusion model's assumptions, consumption is locally normal and, thus, higher-order moments of consumption do not appear in the local return relations. Note that the preferences for which this holds are quite general within the time-additive class.

To derive an aggregate version of this relation in continuous time, let us make use of the assumption that the allocation of time–state consumption claims is Pareto-optimal (A.5); were it not, there would be incentives for individuals to create new claims so as to improve the allocation. As noted in section 2, with an optimal allocation, each individual's optimal consumption rate may be written in 'reduced form' as a function of aggregate consumption and time, i.e., $c^k(Q^k, s, t) = c^k(C, t)$, $\forall k$. Given this, and again defining $u'(C, t) = u_c'^k(c^k(C, t), t)$ for some k, the riskless rate may be written in terms of the expected growth rate and variance rate of aggregate consumption:

$$r = [-u_t'/u'] + [-u_C'/u']\mu_C - \tfrac{1}{2}[u_{CC}'/u']\sigma_C^2. \tag{22}$$

Again, this is an instantaneous version of the general term structure relation to aggregate consumption's distribution, eq. (5). The terms of this were discussed in section 2. However, it is important to note that (22) is an exact relation of the instantaneous riskless interest rate to consumption's growth parameters, and it holds for an economy of individuals with general and diverse time-additive preferences. The drawback of this derivation, relative to the term structure derived in the state preference model, is that this continuous-time version does not (by itself) say anything about interest rates for finite-maturity bonds, whereas the state preference model applies to the entire term structure.

6. Consumption, production, and interest rates: A synthesis

Given a relation of optimal aggregate consumption and interest rates from sections 2 and 5, and a relation of optimal aggregate production and interest rates from sections 2 and 4, a synthesis will be presented. The synthesis is presented for the continuous-time model, since the relations derived in that model are exact equations that can be rigorously analyzed without Taylor series approximations. However, since it was shown that the discrete- and continuous-time models give results that are closely related (as they should be), a similar discrete-time synthesis could be presented.

To simplify the synthesis without losing the main points of economic interest, the preference assumption (A.6) is made, which is that individuals' utility functions aggregate to a power utility function that has pure time preference of ρ and relative risk aversion of γ. No assumption is made about the probability distribution for aggregate consumption, except that it follows an Ito process. With the preference assumption, the principal continuous-time equations for the interest rate in terms of production and consumption parameters, eqs. (17) and (22), are

$$r = \mu_Q - \gamma\sigma_Q^2 + V_{\ln Q, s}\left[\sum_k (\gamma - 1)\varepsilon_s^k Q^k/Q\right], \tag{17'}$$

$$r = \rho + \gamma\mu_{\ln C} - (\gamma^2/2)\sigma_{\ln C}^2. \tag{22'}$$

The riskless rate has been related to expected growth and to the variance of both production and consumption rates. For a minimum level of understanding, a shift in expected productivities should be traced through the optimal consumption function to ascertain that these shifts affect the consumption and production sides of the interest rate equations by the same amounts. A comparison of the coefficients for mean consumption growth and for mean production growth provides little comfort, since the coefficient of the expected return from production in (17′) is one, whereas the coefficient of expected consumption growth in (22′) is a measure of relative risk aversion, which may be much different from one. Similarly, changes in uncertainty in the economy do not obviously affect the variance component of the consumption relation by the same amount as in the production relation. The variance of consumption has a coefficient of $(-\gamma^2/2)$, whereas the production variance rate has a coefficient that is a measure of relative risk aversion, and production's covariances with state variables have coefficients related to hedging preferences.

Thus, simple statements that a 1% increase in the expected return from production (or its variance) results in a 1% increase in expected consumption growth (or its variance) cannot, in general, be made consistent with the interest relations derived. The exception to this statement is the case of logarithmic utility [examined by Kraus and Litzenberger (1975), Rubinstein (1976a), and CIR (1985)], for which coefficients of expected production, production variance, consumption growth and consumption variance are all ones, and the production covariances have zeroes as coefficients in (22′). Since the assumption of logarithmic utility for all individuals is very restrictive, the simple 1–1 intuition must be generalized if we are to provide a true synthesis of the consumption and production relations.

Again, let the state vector $\boldsymbol{s}$ positively reflect technological change through the productivity functions $\boldsymbol{\mu}_q(\boldsymbol{s}, t)$. Consider an increase in the productivities of a number of production processes, i.e., $\mathrm{d}\boldsymbol{s} > \boldsymbol{0}$. For discussion, the increase in aggregate productivity, μ_Q, is assumed to be 1%, the variance of aggregate productivity, σ_Q^2, is assumed to remain constant, and the covariances of aggregate production with the state variables are all assumed not to change. Thus, from (17′), the interest rate rises by 1% with the 1% rise in the expected return in production. If the variance of the rate of growth of consumption does not change, the 1% increase in the interest rate must result in an increase in the expected growth rate of consumption equal to the 1%, divided by the aggregate relative risk aversion of the economy, γ. For example, if relative risk aversion (RRA) equals 2, then the change in expected consumption growth must be 0.5%, whereas if RRA is 0.5, then expected consumption growth must increase by 2% for the 1% productivity increase.

The question now is: How may it be shown that the response of the optimal expected growth rate of consumption to the hypothesized 1% change in expected productivity is inversely related to relative risk aversion? With a Pareto-optimal allocation in this economy, aggregate consumption may be written as a function of aggregate supplies, the state vector, and time, i.e., $C(t) = C(Q, \boldsymbol{s}, t)$. Applying Ito's Lemma to this consumption function gives the expected growth rate and variance rate for aggregate consumption in terms of parameters for production and the state variables:

$$\mu_C = C_Q\left[\mu_Q Q - C\right] + \boldsymbol{C}_s \boldsymbol{\mu}_s + C_t + \tfrac{1}{2}\begin{bmatrix} C_{QQ} & \boldsymbol{C}_{Qs} \\ \boldsymbol{C}_{sQ} & \boldsymbol{C}_{ss} \end{bmatrix} \square \begin{bmatrix} Q^2\sigma_Q^2 & \boldsymbol{V}_{Qs} \\ \boldsymbol{V}_{sQ} & \boldsymbol{V}_{ss} \end{bmatrix},$$

(23)

$$\sigma_C^2 = (C_Q\ \boldsymbol{C}_s)\begin{bmatrix} \sigma_Q^2 Q^2 & \boldsymbol{V}_{Qs} \\ \boldsymbol{V}_{sQ} & \boldsymbol{V}_{ss} \end{bmatrix}\begin{bmatrix} C_Q \\ \boldsymbol{C}_s \end{bmatrix}.$$

From (23), the principal effects of the productivity improvement on expected consumption growth are two: first, the change in productivity per unit of investment, μ_Q, and second, the change in the aggregate consumption rate that is due to the change in the state vector. Holding current supplies and current consumption constant, higher expected productivity implies higher future consumption and, therefore, a higher growth rate of consumption. Holding current supplies and expected productivity constant, as the current consumption rate is increased, productive investment is decreased and, hence, future consumption and the consumption growth rate is decreased. Next we show that the higher risk aversion is, the greater the increase in current consumption is with the hypothesized increase in productivity. By showing that current consumption responds more positively to productivity improvements the higher is risk aversion, we will have shown that the optimal expected consumption growth rate change is negatively related to risk aversion, as was to be shown.

With a Pareto-optimal allocation, the envelope condition for individual k may be written in functional form as

$$u_c^k(c^k(C(Q,s,t),t),t) = J_Q^k(Q^k(Q,s,t),s,t), \tag{24}$$

as was discussed. Implicitly differentiating (24) with respect to s gives

$$u_{cc}^k[\partial c^k/\partial C]C_s = J_{QQ}^k[\partial Q^k/\partial s] + J_{Qs}^k, \quad \forall k. \tag{25}$$

Dividing (25) by (24), noting that Breeden (1979) has shown that

$$\partial c^k/\partial C = [-u_c^k/u_{cc}^k]/T_c^M = T_c^k/T_c^M,$$

and then multiplying by $T^k = -J_Q^k/J_{QQ}^k$ gives

$$[-C_s/T_c^M]T^k = (\partial Q^k/\partial s) + H_s^k, \quad \forall k. \tag{26}$$

Summing this across individuals and noting that $\sum_k(\partial Q^k/\partial s) = 0$ gives

$$C_s = -H_s^M[T_c^M/T^M]. \tag{27}$$

Combining (27) and (16) gives

$$C_s = [T_c^M/T^M]\sum_k[Q^k(\gamma-1)(-\varepsilon_s^k)/\gamma]. \tag{28}$$

Remembering that $\{T_c^M, T^M, \gamma, -\varepsilon_s^k\}$ are all positive for the economy, it is seen from (28) that aggregate consumption responds positively to productivity increases ($C_s > 0$) if relative risk aversion is greater than one. If individuals are more risk-tolerant than the log utility case, then aggregate consumption decreases as productivity improves; this leads to higher expected future consumption and, thus, to a higher expected growth rate for consumption than in the more risk-averse case. Thus, the fact that the coefficient of the expected consumption growth rate in (22′) is relative risk aversion, whereas the coefficient of expected productivity is unity, is due to the dependence of current consumption's response upon aggregate relative risk aversion.

The optimality of the relation of RRA to consumption's response to productivity changes can be seen from a multi-period mean–variance perspective, much like the production analysis of section 4. By having a policy of reducing consumption and increasing investment when production opportunities improve, one produces a consumption stream with a higher lifetime mean and a higher lifetime variance than would be generated by the opposite policy. Thus, since RRA just describes investors' marginal rates of substitution of mean for variance, it is not surprising that relatively risk-tolerant investors would follow that policy. In contrast, relatively risk-averse investors would increase consumption as production opportunities improve, thereby generating a low mean–low variance lifetime consumption path. As the analysis shows, the equilibrium interest rate response to productivity changes thereby depends upon the level of risk aversion in the economy.

7. A multi-good model of interest rates, expected real growth and inflation

In the multi-good, continuous-time economy, let $\boldsymbol{c}_t^k$ be k's vector of consumption rates of the various goods at time t. Define the indirect utility function, U_t^k, for nominal expenditure at time t by individual k, e_t^k, as a function of the spot commodity price vector, $\boldsymbol{P}$, in the usual way:[16]

$$U_t^k\left(e_t^k, \boldsymbol{P}_t\right) = \max_{\{\boldsymbol{c}_t^k\}} \left\{ u_t^k\left(\boldsymbol{c}_t^k\right)\right\} \quad \text{s.t.} \quad \boldsymbol{P}'\boldsymbol{c}^k = e^k. \tag{29}$$

At the optimum, first-order conditions imply that

$$\boldsymbol{u}_c^k = U_e^k \boldsymbol{P} \quad \text{and} \quad -\boldsymbol{U}_p^k = U_e^k \boldsymbol{c}^k. \tag{30}$$

[16] Money is not modeled in this economy. However, if money were modeled in such a way that it entered the utility function like any other good, the analysis would not change. Stochastic properties of changes in the supply of money no doubt affect the covariances of goods' prices with aggregate real consumption; given this, monetary policy will affect the risk premium that the nominally riskless asset requires (see section 8). For such a model in a discrete-time economy, see Grauer and Litzenberger (1980).

From (30), at the optimum the percentage compensating variation in expenditure for a 1% change in a good's price is the good's budget share, i.e.,

$$\frac{-U_{pj}^k P_j}{U_e^k e^k} = \left.\frac{\partial \ln e^k}{\partial \ln p_j}\right|_{U^k} = \frac{P_j c_j^k}{e^k} = \alpha_j^k, \quad \forall j, \tag{31}$$

where α_j^k is k's budget share for good j. These are standard results.

An additional result that is later useful is the following, which arises from differentiating (30) with respect to expenditure:

$$\boldsymbol{U}_{pe}^k = -U_e^k\left[\partial \boldsymbol{c}^k/\partial e^k\right] - U_{ee}^k \boldsymbol{c}^k, \tag{32}$$

or

$$\mathbf{I}_P \boldsymbol{U}_{pe}^k = U_{ee}^k\left[T^k \boldsymbol{m}^k - e^k \boldsymbol{\alpha}^k\right], \tag{33}$$

where $\mathbf{I}_P$ is the diagonal matrix of goods prices, T_e^k is k's absolute risk tolerance for expenditure, $\boldsymbol{\alpha}^k$ is k's vector of budget shares, and $\boldsymbol{m}^k$ is k's vector of 'marginal budget shares'. That is, m_j^k is the fraction of an additional dollar of expenditure that would be spent by k on good j. The marginal and average budget share vectors are related by expenditure elasticities of demand, η_j^k, as follows: $m_j^k = \alpha_j^k \eta_j^k$. With this structure, the local validity of the Divisia price index is straightforward, as is shown in appendix 2.

In a multi-good economy, the price of a nominally riskless, T-period discount bond is equal in equilibrium to the expected marginal rate of substitution of nominal expenditure at time T for current nominal expenditure,

$$B_{t,T} = \mathrm{e}^{-r(t,T)(T-t)} = \frac{\mathrm{E}\left\{\mathrm{e}^{-\rho(T-t)} U_e^k\left(e_T^k, \boldsymbol{P}_T\right)\right\}}{U_e^k\left(e_t^k, \boldsymbol{P}_t\right)}, \tag{34}$$

which is identical in structure to the single-good relation. The Cox, Ingersoll and Ross (1985) proof that the instantaneous-maturity nominally riskless rate equals the negative of the expected rate of change of the marginal utility of wealth did not depend upon their assumption that there was only a single good. That fact, combined with the multi-good optimality condition that the marginal utility of nominal expenditure equals the marginal utility of wealth, permits us to express the riskless rate as the negative of the expected rate of change of $U_e^k(e^k, \boldsymbol{P}, t)$. Using Ito's Lemma to determine that expected rate of change, the instantaneously riskless nominal interest rate may be written as

$$r=\rho^k-\left(U^k_{ee}/U^k_e\right)\mu_{ek}-\boldsymbol{U}^k_{eP}\mathbf{I}_P\boldsymbol{\mu}_P-\left(U^k_{eee}/2U^k_e\right)\sigma^2_{ek}$$

$$-\left(\boldsymbol{U}^k_{eeP'}/U^k_e\right)\mathbf{I}_P\boldsymbol{V}_{Pe}-\left(1/2U^k_e\right)\left[\mathbf{U}^k_{ePP}\square\mathbf{I}_P\mathbf{V}_{PP}\mathbf{I}_P\right],\quad\forall k. \tag{35}$$

In (35), μ_{ek} and σ^2_{ek} are the drift and variance rates for k's nominal expenditure rate, $\boldsymbol{V}_{Pe}$ is the vector of covariances of k's expenditure with consumption-goods' percentage price changes, and $\mathbf{V}_{PP}$ is the variance–covariance matrix of goods' percentage price changes.

Aggregation of the drift components of individuals' expenditure rates and budget share vectors in (35) is straightforward, but aggregation of the variance terms is not. To see this, multiply (35) by T^k_e, sum across individuals, divide by $T^m_e=\sum_k T^k_e$, and substitute (33) for $\boldsymbol{U}^k_{eP}$ to get

$$r=\sum_k\left(T^k_e/T^m_e\right)\rho^k+\left(1/T^m_e\right)\mu_E+\left(1/T^m_e\right)\sum_k\left[T^k_e\boldsymbol{m}^k-e^k\boldsymbol{\alpha}^k\right]'\boldsymbol{\mu}_P$$

$$+\left[\left(1/2T^m_e\right)\left[\sum_k\left(u^k_{eee}/U^k_{ee}\right)\sigma^2_{ek}\right]+\left(1/T^m_e\right)\left[\sum_k\left(\boldsymbol{U}^k_{eeP'}U^k_{ee}\right)\mathbf{I}_P\boldsymbol{V}_{Pe}\right]\right.$$

$$\left.+\left(1/2T^m_e\right)\left[\sum_k\left(\mathbf{U}_{ePP}/U^k_{ee}\right)\square\left(\mathbf{I}_P\mathbf{V}_{PP}\mathbf{I}_P\right]\right]\right]. \tag{36}$$

The first term of (36) is just a risk tolerance weighted average of individuals' pure rates of time preference, which will be denoted ρ^m. The second term reflects the expected growth of aggregate nominal expenditure, the third term picks up two offsetting inflation effects, and the final bracketed expression, which will be denoted $F(\mathbf{V})$, is a function of preferences and the variances and covariances of expenditures and prices.

The expected inflation effects aggregate cleanly. First, since $\boldsymbol{\alpha}^k$ is k's vector of budget shares, $\sum_k\boldsymbol{\alpha}^k e^k=\boldsymbol{\alpha}^m E$, where E is aggregate nominal expenditure and $\boldsymbol{\alpha}^m$ are the fractions of aggregate expenditure spent on the various goods in the economy. Next, it has been shown [Breeden (1979)] that one dollar additional aggregate expenditure is optimally allocated (holding prices constant) to individuals in proportion to their risk tolerances, i.e., T^k_e/T^m_e goes to individual k. Since individual k spends an additional dollar on goods in the marginal proportions $\boldsymbol{m}^k$, $\sum_k(T^k_e/T^m_e)\boldsymbol{m}^k$ gives the aggregate marginal budget share vector, $\boldsymbol{m}^m$. That is, $\boldsymbol{m}^m$ represents the incremental aggregate expenditures on the various goods that occur when one dollar additional aggregate nominal expenditure is optimally allocated across individuals and then optimally spent on goods by the individuals. Goods that have aggregate expenditure elasticities in excess of one will have marginal expenditure shares that exceed their average expenditure shares, whereas those with low expenditure elasticities will have $m_j^m < \alpha_j^m$. Finally, the products $\boldsymbol{m}^{m\prime}\boldsymbol{\mu}_P$ and $\boldsymbol{\alpha}^{m\prime}\boldsymbol{\mu}_P$ represent the expected inflation rate with aggregate marginal budget shares and aggregate average budget shares, respectively.

Given these arguments and definitions, the instantaneous nominally riskless interest rate may be written as

$$r = \rho^m + (E/T_e^m)\left[(\mu_E/E) - \boldsymbol{\alpha}^{m\prime}\boldsymbol{\mu}_P\right] + \boldsymbol{m}^{m\prime}\boldsymbol{\mu}_P + F(\mathbf{V}). \tag{37}$$

This expression for the riskless rate is intuitive in light of the single-good analyses. The aggregate pure rate of time preference is the first term. The expected percentage growth rate of aggregate real consumption is positively related to the riskless rate, multiplied by an aggregate measure of relative risk aversion. Appendix 2 demonstrated that the percentage change in aggregate nominal expenditure, less an inflation rate computed with aggregate budget shares as weights, is an apt aggregate quantity index, so the second term in (37) is analogous to the single-good economy's growth term.

The 'Fisher effect' term in the nominally risk-free rate is interesting, in that it is an inflation rate measured with aggregate marginal expenditure shares. Thus, while the Personal Consumption Expenditure Deflator is appropriate for measuring real consumption growth (since it uses aggregate value weights), it is theoretically inappropriate as an 'add-on inflation premium'. If homotheticity assumptions are made, the marginal and average aggregate inflation rates are identical, but that is an unlikely case.

A simple, heuristic explanation for the marginally weighted inflation rate is the following. Interest rates reflect optimal consumption–savings decisions by equating bond prices to all individuals' optimal expected marginal rates of substitution of future dollars for current dollars. At the margin, the evaluation of dollars now versus future dollars is an evaluation of the bundle of goods sacrificed at the margin today for an increment to the future bundle. The effects of price level changes on optimal marginal rates of substitution should be weighted in proportion to the quantities sacrificed and the future quantities gained, which are the marginal consumption bundles. Note that since the time period is infinitesimal in the period covered by (37), and since the Ito assumption makes the marginal bundles continuous, the relevant current and future marginal bundles are the same for (37). For discrete horizons, a similar marginal analysis could be done, but the marginal bundle today would not be the same as the marginal bundle at future dates.

In the discussion thus far, the variance and covariance terms have all been lumped into $F(\mathbf{V})$. Before these terms are explored, note that under certainty these terms are zeroes and this analysis is complete. Also note that in a model with logarithmic utility and homothetic indifference curves, the $(E/T_e^m)\boldsymbol{\alpha}^m$ and the $\boldsymbol{m}^m$ terms cancel, leaving only the growth of aggregate nominal expenditure from the middle term of (37). That case corresponds to the uncertain inflation model examined by Cox, Ingersoll and Ross (1985, sect. V).

8. Interest rates and consumption uncertainty with inflation

With no restrictions on individuals' preferences for goods, the analysis of the relation between the nominally riskless interest rate and goods' price level *uncertainties* [eq. (37)] is extremely complex. Although some qualitative features of that general relation will be noted later, a simple and clean (negative) relation of the riskless interest rate and the variance of aggregate real consumption is not easily derived. These difficulties arise due to the changing average and marginal consumption bundles in the general case, which affect the coefficients of the variance and covariance terms in the riskless rate relation. Another way to see the problem is through eq. (33), which shows the marginal utility may be either upward- or downward-sloping in commodities' prices. Thus, marginal utility is not monotonically related to real consumption for general utility [there are offsetting price and quantity effects in (33)]. The mean preserving spread approach that worked with a single good in the comparative statics on variance gives ambiguous results in the general case.

To circumvent these problems and proceed with the analysis of the effects of uncertainty, this section assumes that individuals have Cobb–Douglas (power) utility functions for goods. These utility functions are well-known to have unitary income elasticities of demand for all goods, unitary own-price elasticities of demand, and zero cross-price elasticities of demand. Optimal budget shares are non-stochastic, which permits computation of an invariant price index. Many authors have used this assumption in multi-good analyses, despite its lack of generality.[17] The specific assumption is that k's instantaneous utility for the goods bundle $\boldsymbol{c}^k$ is

$$u^k(\boldsymbol{c}^k, t) = \mathrm{e}^{-\rho t}\left[\prod_{i=1}^{N} c_i^{\alpha(i,k)}\right]^{1-\gamma}, \tag{38}$$

where $\sum_i \alpha(i,k) = 1$. For an expenditure rate of e^k and a price vector $\boldsymbol{P}$ the individual's optimal consumption rates [which maximize (38)] are

$$c_i^k = \alpha_i^k e^k / P_i \quad \text{or} \quad \alpha_i^k = P_i c_i^k / e^k, \quad \forall i. \tag{39}$$

These demand functions are well-known and have the properties noted earlier.

[17] Grauer and Litzenberger (1979), Long and Plosser (1983), and Cox, Ingersoll and Ross (1985) all used the Cobb–Douglas formulation, with LP and CIR also using a logarithmic utility assumption.

Given these optimal demand functions, k's indirect utility function for nominal expenditure and price vector $\boldsymbol{P}$ is

$$U^k(e^k, P, t) = \mathrm{e}^{-\rho t}\left[\prod_{i=1}^{N}\left(\alpha_i^k e^k/P_i\right)^{\alpha(i,k)}\right]^{1-\gamma} = A\,\mathrm{e}^{-\rho t}\left[e^k/I^k\right]^{1-\gamma}, \tag{40}$$

where

$$I^k = \prod_{i=1}^{N} P_i^{\alpha(i)/\Sigma\alpha(j)} \quad \text{and} \quad A = \left[\prod_{i=1}^{N}\alpha^{\alpha(i,k)}\right]^{1-\gamma} \tag{40'}$$

The individual's consumer price index, I^k, does not depend upon the level of expenditure, which is mathematically useful, but not economically plausible. It has constant elasticities with respect to commodities' prices, which are a result of the optimality of constant budget shares across states of the world. Utility is monotonically increasing and strictly concave in real expenditure, $e^{*k} = e^k/I^k$, and relative risk aversion for fluctuations in real expenditure is the constant γ.

At the optimum, the nominally riskless interest rate is minus the expected rate of growth of the marginal utility of a dollar. For analytical convenience, let that marginal utility function be denoted by $u'(\ln\tilde{e}, \ln\tilde{I}, t)$, where the individual superscripts are suppressed. From (40), letting subscripts of u' denote partial derivatives, we have

$$u' = A(1-\gamma)\,\mathrm{e}^{-\rho t}\mathrm{e}^{-\gamma\ln e}\mathrm{e}^{(\gamma-1)\ln I}. \tag{41}$$

The nominal rate is $r = -\mu_{u'}/u'$, which Ito's Lemma for u' gives as[18]

$$\begin{aligned} r = {} & \rho + \gamma\mu_{\ln e} - (\gamma-1)\mu_{\ln I} \\ & - \tfrac{1}{2}\left[\gamma^2\sigma_{\ln e}^2 + 2\gamma(1-\gamma)\sigma_{\ln e,\ln I} + (\gamma-1)^2\sigma_{\ln I}^2\right]. \end{aligned} \tag{42}$$

This is just eq. (40) for the special case of Cobb–Douglas utility functions. This equation can be re-arranged to a much more intuitive form:

$$r - \mu_I/I + \sigma_{\ln I}^2 = \rho + \gamma\mu_{\ln e^*} - (\gamma^2/2)\sigma_{\ln e^*}^2 + \gamma\sigma_{-\ln I,\ln e^*}, \tag{43}$$

[18]Partial derivatives in log form are simple:

$$u'_{\ln e} = -\gamma u', \quad u'_{\ln e,\ln e} = \gamma^2 u', \quad u'_{\ln I} = (\gamma-1)u',$$
$$u'_{\ln I,\ln I} = (\gamma-1)^2 u', \quad u'_{\ln e,\ln I} = \gamma(1-\gamma)u'.$$

where

$$\mu_I/I = \mu_{\ln I} + \sigma^2_{\ln I}/2,$$

$$\mu_{\ln e^*} = \mu_{\ln e} - \mu_{\ln I},$$

$$\sigma^2_{\ln e^*} = \operatorname{var}(\ln(e/I)) = \sigma^2_{\ln e} - 2\sigma_{\ln e,\ln I} + \sigma^2_{\ln I}.$$

Fischer (1974) showed that the LHS of (43) is the expected real return on the nominally riskless bond. Thus, this says that, in equilibrium, the expected real return on the nominally riskless assets equals (1) the rate of pure time preference, plus (2) the expected growth rate of real expenditure, multiplied by relative risk aversion, minus (3) the variance of real expenditure, multiplied by RRA squared, and plus (4) the risk premium for the nominally riskless bond, which is proportional to the covariance of the real return on the nominal bond with real expenditure (as in the consumption-oriented CAPM).

Consider this expression for the nominal rate in relation to that of eq. (37), which was derived with very general consumption preferences. The drift terms in the general case were easy to explain, so the Cobb–Douglas assumption is unnecessary for understanding those terms. The variance term in (37) is seen to include at least two effects – the negative relation of the riskless rate to the uncertainty of real expenditure and the positive or negative risk adjustment for the real consumption beta of the nominally riskless asset. In general, the variance term in (37) also has terms that reflect uncertain changes in budget shares (and inflation measures) as prices and expenditure fluctuate, as well as changes in relative risk aversion. These terms are all zeroes with the Cobb–Douglas preferences of this section.

In this economy, a real riskless asset maturing at time t for individual k is one that pays k's price index at that time, $\tilde{I}^k_t = \prod_i \tilde{P}_i^{\alpha(i,k)}(t)$. Such an asset has a real payoff of one dollar at time t in all events. From Ito's Lemma, the stochastic component of the nominal return on this real riskless asset when it is at maturity is the following linear combination of commodity prices' stochastic components:

$$\sum_i \left(\partial I^k/\partial P_i\right)\sigma_{P_i}\,\mathrm{d}z_{P_i} = \sum_i I_k\alpha_i^k\sigma_{P_i}\,\mathrm{d}z_{P_i}/P_i = \sum_i I^k\alpha_i^k\sigma_{\ln P_i}\,\mathrm{d}z_{P_i}. \quad (44)$$

Given this, the equilibrium expected nominal return on the real riskless asset can be found from the return on the nominally riskless asset (43) and from the first-order conditions for an optimal portfolio [eq. (12′)]. Letting w^{*k} be individual k's augmented vector of investments in both productive processes and financial assets, the optimal portfolio is

$$w^{*k}Q^k = \left[-J^k_Q/J^k_{QQ}\right]\mathbf{V}^{-1}(\boldsymbol{\mu} - \boldsymbol{r}) - \mathbf{V}^{-1}\mathbf{V}_{qa,s}\left[J^k_{sQ}/J^k_{QQ}\right], \quad \forall k. \quad (12')$$

Multiplying this by $J^k_{QQ}\mathbf{V}$ and re-arranging terms gives

$$\begin{aligned}\boldsymbol{\mu}-\boldsymbol{r}&=\left(-1/J^k_Q\right)\left[\mathbf{V}_{qa,Q}J^k_{QQ}+\mathbf{V}_{qa,s}J^k_{sQ}\right]\\&=\operatorname{cov}\left(\tilde{\boldsymbol{r}}_a,\ -\mathrm{d}\tilde{J}^k_Q/J^k_Q\right)=\operatorname{cov}\left(\tilde{\boldsymbol{r}}_a,\ -\mathrm{d}\tilde{U}^k_e/U^k_e\right),\quad\forall k,\end{aligned}\tag{45}$$

where $\tilde{\boldsymbol{r}}_a$ is the vector of realized nominal returns on risky investments. This is the familiar result that the equilibrium expected nominal excess returns on all assets are equal in equilibrium to the negatives of their covariances with the rate of change of marginal utility. Furthermore, since for an optimal policy the marginal utility of nominal expenditure equals the marginal utility of nominal wealth, (45) may be rewritten with J^k_Q replaced by U^k_e or U'^k.

Let μ_r be the expected instantaneous nominal return on the real riskless asset, and let r_r be its realized value. Given the Cobb–Douglas preference assumption, Ito's Lemma and (41) and (44) may be substituted into (45) to give μ_r:

$$\begin{aligned}\mu_r-r&=\operatorname{cov}\left[\tilde{r}_r,\quad-(1/u')\{u'_{\ln e}(\mathrm{d}\ln\tilde{e})+u'_{\ln I}(\mathrm{d}\ln\tilde{I})\}\right]\\&=\operatorname{cov}\left[\boldsymbol{\alpha}^k(\mathrm{d}\ln\tilde{\boldsymbol{P}}),\quad\gamma(\mathrm{d}\ln\tilde{e})+(1-\gamma)(\mathrm{d}\ln\tilde{I})\right]\\&=\sigma^2_{\ln I}+\gamma\sigma_{\ln I,\ln e^*}.\end{aligned}\tag{46}$$

Combining (46) with (44), the equilibrium expected nominal return on the real riskless asset is

$$\mu_r-\mu_I/I=\rho+\gamma\mu_{\ln e^*}-\left(\gamma^2/2\right)\sigma^2_{\ln e^*}.\tag{47}$$

As in the single-good case, the real riskless rate is positively related to pure time preference, and to the expected rate of growth of real expenditure, and is negatively related to the variance of real expenditure.

Note, however, that the real riskless rate is not observed, so the return on a nominally riskless bond is used in empirical tests. For that, (43) applies, which includes a risk premium for the real consumption risk of the nominally riskless asset. Since inflation is typically believed to be related to the growth rate of real consumption, the risk premium of the nominally riskless asset may be non-trivial. The relation of inflation to the real growth of the economy may be nonstationary, as can be easily illustrated. If a Phillips curve relates inflation and unemployment (pre-1973?), then inflation is likely to be high when real consumption is high, resulting in a negative real consumption beta for the nominally riskless assets (Treasury bills). This negative beta implies a lower equilibrium real return on Treasury bills than on purchasing power bonds. In contrast, recent experience [see Fama (1982)] has been that inflation is negatively related to real movements in the economy. If that were expected, then the real consumption betas for nominally riskless assets are positive, which results in equilibrium real returns on them that are in excess of those on purchasing power bonds.

9. Conclusion

This paper derived fairly general relations of consumption, production and interest rates in both a discrete-time state preference economy and in a continuous-time economy, using time-additive preferences throughout. Riskless interest rates were shown to be positively related to the expected growth rate of aggregate consumption, with a coefficient that is a measure of aggregate relative risk aversion. Rates were negatively related to the variance rate of aggregate consumption. In a separate equation, riskless rates were positively related to the expected productivity for optimal aggregate investments, with a coefficient of unity. They were negatively related to the variance of optimal aggregate production. The riskless interest rate was shown to be related to the autocorrelation (if any) in production, with the coefficient being related to the degree of relative risk aversion. Some of these results have been derived in less general models by other authors [notably Rubinstein (1976, 1981) and Cox, Ingersoll and Ross (1985)]. The focus in this paper was upon generalizing and explaining these results in simple economic terms and showing how optimal behavior leads to two separate interest rate relations to give the same term structure (since they must hold simultaneously in equilibrium).

Uncertainty in the economy arose from uncertain production and random technological change. The modeling included no stationarity assumptions for most results, so the uncertainty representation was quite general. Thus, consistent dynamic analysis of the term structure under uncertainty is well justified for these equations. A non-exhaustive discussion was presented of possible rational movements of interest rates during a business cycle.

There are two important extensions that are left for subsequent research. First, preferences exhibiting time complementarity in the utility of consumption were not permitted. Modeling of non-additive preferences will significantly affect marginal rates of substitution of consumption at one date for consumption at another date. Therefore, relaxation of the time-additive assumption could have a significant effect on the sizes of some of the effects (although the general relations derived here should remain intact). See Hansen and Singleton (1983), Dunn and Singleton (1983), and Ronn (1983) for results with particular forms of non-additive preferences.

A second important area for future research is on dropping the assumption (in the continuous-time model) that production plans are fully adjustable at each instant. In the continuous-time economy, there is no formal modeling of the 'time to build', as in Kydland and Prescott's (1982) work. Since the discrete approximations to the term structure (section 2) can handle time-to-build analyses, and since the results of that section are similar to those in the remainder of the paper, the basic relations should remain intact with more formal modeling of time to build. A virtue of this paper, in contrast to the early works in the non-separable utility and time-to-build areas (which are just developing), is that the general aggregation problem has been attacked with some success. Simple and intuitive relations of aggregate production, aggregate consumption and interest rates were derived.

Appendix 1

Outline of the Proof of Theorem 1: With appropriate convexity assumptions [see Debreu (1959, ch. 6)], there is a correspondence between the production plans and consumption allocations that a central planner would choose and those of a competitive equilibrium with complete capital markets. Characteristics of the central planner's optimal choices also apply to a competitive equilibrium with complete (or Pareto-optimal) capital markets. With assumptions (A.1) and (A.2), each individual's optimal consumption at each date is a function of only aggregate consumption and time. The probability distribution for aggregate consumption completely describes the probability distributions for all individuals' consumptions and, as a result, fully describes each individual's expected utility and marginal utility levels. Thus, if the (conditional) probability distribution for optimal aggregate consumption at all future dates is the same at time t in states θ_1 and θ_2, then each individual's expected utility of lifetime consumption is the same in those two states, and the probability distribution of marginal rates of substitution across dates is the same as seen in the two states. These results are useful in the proof.

For a discrete-time economy with a final date of T, consider the problem moving backwards from T. At any date t, let $S(t)=\{\theta_{1t},\theta_{2t},\dots,\theta_{n(t)t}\}$ be the set of fully descriptive (Arrow–Debreu) states that are possible, where the θ_{jt} are all scalars. The joint probability distribution of all future returns from investments in production processes in any state θ_{1t} is fully described by the vector $\boldsymbol{s}_t(\theta_t)$. Since at T the entire amount of the good will be consumed, all states at $T-1$ that have the same total amount of the good, $Q(\theta,T-1)$, and the same production opportunity set, $\boldsymbol{s}(\theta,T-1)$, have the same objective function and feasible set and, hence, the same optimal production and consumption plans. In particular, they have the same probability distribution at $T-1$ for everyone's consumption at T. From this argument, everyone's expected utility of (remaining) lifetime consumption as seen at $T-1$ depends only upon aggregate supplies at that time and the production opportunity set, $\boldsymbol{s}$, i.e., $J^k(T-1,\theta)=J^k(Q(\theta),\boldsymbol{s}(\theta),T-1)$.

Next, consider the situation at $T-2$. If two states at $T-2$ have the same production opportunity set, then the joint distribution for $\{Q(T-1)|$

$\boldsymbol{q}(T-2), \boldsymbol{s}(T-2)\}$ must be the same in both states [where $\boldsymbol{q}(T-2)$ is the vector of inputs at $T-2$ to the various production processes]. Note that the production opportunity set describes not only current production possibilities, but also future production possibilities and the joint distribution of current and future possibilities. As at $T-1$, if the planner has the same aggregate supplies and production possibilities in two states, then the planner faces the same objective and is subject to the same constraints on probability distributions for lifetime consumption that can be given to individuals. Thus, assuming uniqueness of the solution to this problem, individuals' expected utilities at $T-2$ for lifetime consumption are functions of only $Q(T-2)$ and $s(T-2)$. This argument can be iterated back to the initial date, deriving k's expected utility as a function of only aggregate supplies, the production opportunity set, and time.

Consider the roles played by the two assumptions. With heterogeneous beliefs, allocations depend upon the distribution of beliefs, as well as on technology and supplies. If individuals have utility functions that are not time-additive, then past and future consumption will affect the expected utility and expected marginal utility of current consumption. Thus, even with the same aggregate wealth and production opportunities in two states at the same date, the optimal consumption and production plans may vary.

In our model, current optimal consumption and the probability distribution for future consumption depends only upon $\{Q(t), s(t), t\}$. The last step is to show that the optimal wealth allocation in the competitive equilibrium is also completely determined by $\{Q, s, t\}$. Let $S(Q, s, t)$ be the set of states at t that have aggregate supply Q and opportunity set s. From the budget constraint, k's wealth at time τ in state ξ is

$$
\begin{aligned}
W_{\tau\xi}^{k} &= \sum_{t>\tau}\sum_{\theta\in S(t)} c^{k}(Q_{t\theta}, s_{t\theta}, t)\,\phi_{t\theta|\tau\xi} \\
&= \sum_{t>\tau}\sum_{\theta\in S(t)} c^{k}(Q_{t\theta}, s_{t\theta}, t)\left[\pi_{t\theta|\tau\xi}u'^{k}(Q_{t\theta}, s_{t\theta}, t)/u'^{k}(Q_{\tau\xi}, s_{\tau\xi}, \tau)\right] \\
&= \sum_{t>\tau}\sum_{S\{Q,s,t\}} c^{k}(Q, s, t)\left[\pi_{\{Q,s,t\}|\tau\xi}u'^{k}(Q, s, t)/u'^{k}(Q_{\xi}, s_{\xi}, \tau)\right] \\
&\quad \times \sum_{\theta\in S(Q,s,t)} \pi_{t\theta|Q,s,t} \\
&= \sum_{t>\tau}\sum_{S\{Q,s,t\}} c^{k}(Q, s, t)\left[\pi_{\{Q,s,t\}|\tau\xi}u'^{k}(Q, s, t)/u'^{k}(Q_{\tau\xi}, s_{\tau\xi}, \tau)\right].
\end{aligned}
$$

Since the last expression is the same for all states at τ that have the same aggregate supply and opportunity set, $W_{\tau\xi}^{k} = f\{Q, s, t\}$. Q.E.D.

Appendix 2

One well-known price index problem is that the mix of goods consumed varies with the level of expenditure, so the measurement of inflation also varies with expenditure. A second problem is aggregation of individuals' real consumptions, or alternatively, with the construction of a meaningful index of inflation for the economy. Even if all expenditure elasticities are assumed to be unity, different individuals will have different vectors of budget shares and, hence, different price indices. Is there any meaning to aggregate real consumption and a price index with aggregate budget shares?

With both nominal expenditure and consumption-goods prices following Ito processes, Ito's Lemma implies that the current utility of consumption, $u^k(e^k, \boldsymbol{P})$, has the stochastic differential

$$\mathrm{d}u^k = \left[u_t^k + u_e^k \mu_{ek} + \boldsymbol{u}_P^k \boldsymbol{\mu}_P + \tfrac{1}{2} \begin{bmatrix} u_{ee}^k & \boldsymbol{u}_{eP}^k \\ \boldsymbol{u}_{Pe}^k & \mathbf{u}_{PP}^k \end{bmatrix} \square \begin{bmatrix} \sigma_{ek}^2 & V_{eP}^k \\ V_{Pe}^k & \mathbf{V}_{PP} \end{bmatrix} \right] \mathrm{d}t$$

$$+ u_e^k \sigma_{ek} \mathrm{d}z_{ek} + \boldsymbol{u}_P^k \boldsymbol{\sigma}_P \mathrm{d}\boldsymbol{z}_P. \tag{A.1}$$

Letting the unexpected local changes in nominal expenditure and prices be denoted by $\widetilde{\mathrm{d}e^k}$ and $\widetilde{\mathrm{d}\boldsymbol{P}}$, the unexpected change in instantaneous utility is

$$\widetilde{\mathrm{d}u}^k = u_e^k \left[\widetilde{\mathrm{d}e}^k + \left(\boldsymbol{u}_P^{k\prime} / u_e^k \right) \left(\widetilde{\mathrm{d}\boldsymbol{P}} \right) \right]$$

$$= u_e^k \left[\left(\widetilde{\mathrm{d}e}^k / e^k \right) - \boldsymbol{\alpha}^{k\prime} \left(\mathbf{I}_P^{-1} \widetilde{\mathrm{d}\boldsymbol{P}} \right) \right] e^k. \tag{A.2}$$

Divisia's computation of real consumption's percentage change is the percentage change in k's nominal expenditure, less a budget share weighted average of the percentage changes in goods prices. This is precisely the bracketed term in (A.2). Thus, k's utility of current consumption in alternate $\{e^k, \boldsymbol{P}\}$ states is one-to-one with the Divisia measure of percentage change in k's real consumption. Individual k has a higher utility of current consumption if and only if k's real consumption grows, given inflation measured by a value-weighted price index (similar to the PCE deflator). Note that this did not require unitary expenditure elasticities.

A more interesting result is that computed changes in *aggregate* real consumption have economic content, even with diversity and non-homotheticity of consumption preferences across individuals. To see this, define as a reference state that state where each individual's expenditure is as expected and where the commodity price vector is at its expected level. Define the computed percentage change in aggregate real consumption as the percentage change in aggregate nominal expenditure, $E=\sum_k e^k$, less an inflation rate computed with the aggregate expenditure shares of goods as weights, $\boldsymbol{\alpha}^m = \sum_k e^k \boldsymbol{\alpha}^k / E$:

$$\mathrm{d}E^* = \mathrm{d}E - E\boldsymbol{\alpha}^{m\prime}\left[\mathbf{I}_P^{-1}\mathrm{d}\boldsymbol{P}\right]. \tag{A.3}$$

Let $\overline{\mathrm{d}E}$ and $\overline{\mathrm{d}\boldsymbol{P}}$ be the expected changes in aggregate expenditure and goods prices. Consider now a state where aggregate real expenditure grows at a rate g percent more than its expected growth, i.e.,

$$\mathrm{d}E_s - E\boldsymbol{\alpha}^{m\prime}\left[\mathbf{I}_P^{-1}\mathrm{d}\boldsymbol{P}_s\right] = \overline{\mathrm{d}E} - E\boldsymbol{\alpha}^{m\prime}\left[\mathbf{I}_P^{-1}\overline{\mathrm{d}\boldsymbol{P}}\right] + gE\,\mathrm{d}t. \tag{A.4}$$

In such a state, goods can be allocated so that each individual has higher real consumption (as she computes it) than in the reference state. One such allocation gives each individual the following:

$$\mathrm{d}e_s^k - e^k\boldsymbol{\alpha}^k\left[\mathbf{I}_P^{-1}\mathrm{d}\boldsymbol{P}_s\right] = \overline{\mathrm{d}e}^k - e^k\boldsymbol{\alpha}^k\left[\mathbf{I}_P^{-1}\overline{\mathrm{d}\boldsymbol{P}}\right] + ge^k\,\mathrm{d}t. \tag{A.5}$$

Aggregating (A.5) across individuals gives (A.4), which shows that the allocation is feasible. Thus, if aggregate real consumption grows at a greater rate than expected, then there exists a Pareto-superior allocation of consumption goods, relative to the expected allocation.

It is also necessary that aggregate real consumption be above the expected for there to exist a Pareto-superior allocation relative to the expected allocation. To see this, assume the contrary, i.e., that there is a Pareto-superior allocation in a state s that has lower than expected growth of aggregate real consumption. For each individual to view his allocation as superior to the expected, (A.2) implies

$$\mathrm{d}e_s^k - e^k\boldsymbol{\alpha}^{k\prime}\left[\mathbf{I}_P^{-1}\mathrm{d}\boldsymbol{P}_s\right] > \overline{\mathrm{d}e}^k - e^k\boldsymbol{\alpha}^{k\prime}\left[\mathbf{I}_P^{-1}\overline{\mathrm{d}\boldsymbol{P}}\right], \quad \forall k. \tag{A.6}$$

However, aggregation of this across individuals implies that the growth of aggregate real consumption exceeds its expected growth, if all individuals prefer the state s allocation. This contradicts the hypothesis and demonstrates the necessity result.

Restated, the result is that local aggregate real consumption changes are valid local measures of changes in an economic quantity index for the economy. The larger the change in aggregate real consumption, the larger the feasible change in each individual's quantity index. This is true locally even with diverse and non-homothetic consumption preferences, which helps to explain why eq. (37) holds quite generally for the nominally riskless rate.

References

Arrow, Kenneth J., 1964, The role of securities in the optimal allocation of risk-bearing, Review of Economic Studies 31, 91–96.

Banz, Rolf W. and Merton H. Miller, 1978, Prices for state-contingent claims: Some estimates and applications, Journal of Business 51, 653–672.

Beja, Avraham, 1971, The structure of the cost of capital under uncertainty, Review of Economic Studies 38, 359–376.

Bhattacharya, Sudipto, 1981, Notes on multiperiod valuation and the pricing of options, Journal of Finance 36, 163–180.

Black, Fischer and Myron S. Scholes, 1973, The pricing of options and corporate liabilities, Journal of Political Economy 81, 637–654.

Breeden, Douglas T., 1977, Changes in consumption and investment opportunities and the valuation of securities, Unpublished doctoral dissertation (Graduate School of Business, Stanford University, Stanford, CA).

Breedon, Douglas T., 1979, An intertemporal asset pricing model with stochastic consumption and investment opportunities, Journal of Financial Economics 7, 265–296.

Breeden, Douglas T., 1984, Futures markets and commodity options: Hedging and optimality in incomplete markets, Journal of Economic Theory 32, 275–300.

Breeden, Douglas T. and Robert H. Litzenberger, 1978, Prices of state-contingent claims implicit in option prices, Journal of Business 51, 621–651.

Brennan, Michael J., 1979, The pricing of contingent claims in discrete time models, Journal of Finance 34, 53–68.

Constantanides, George M., 1982, Intertemporal asset pricing with heterogeneous consumers and without demand aggregation, Journal of Business 55, 253–267.

Cox, John C., Jonathan E. Ingersoll and Stephen A. Ross, 1985, A theory of the term structure of interest rates, Econometrica 53, 385–407.

Cox, John C. and Stephen A. Ross, 1977, Some models of capital asset pricing with rational anticipations, Unpublished working paper (School of Organization and Management, Yale University, New Haven, CT).

Debreu, Gerard, 1959, Theory of value (Wiley, New York).

Dieffenbach, Bruce C., 1975, A quantitative theory of risk premiums on securities with an application to the term structure of interest rates, Econometrica 43, 431–454.

Dunn, Kenneth B. and Kenneth J. Singleton, 1986, Modeling the term structure of interest rates under nonseparable utility and durability of goods, Journal of Financial Economics 16, forthcoming.

Fama, Eugene F., 1970, Multiperiod consumption–investment decisions, American Economic Review 60, 163–174.

Fama, Eugene F., 1975, Short-term interest rates as predictors of inflation, American Economic Review 65, 269–282.

Fama, Eugene F. and Michael R. Gibbons, 1982, Inflation, real returns and capital investment, Journal of Monetary Economics 9, 297–323.

Ferson, Wayne E., 1983, Expected real interest rates and aggregate consumption: Empirical tests, Journal of Financial and Quantitative Analysis 18, 477–498.

Fischer, Stanley, 1975, The demand for index bonds, Journal of Political Economy 83, 509–534.

Garman, Mark, 1977, A general theory of asset pricing under diffusion state processes, Working paper no. 50 (Research Program in Finance, University of California, Berkeley, CA).

Grauer, Frederick and Robert Litzenberger, 1979, The pricing of commodity futures contracts, nominal bonds and other risky assets under commodity price uncertainty, Journal of Finance 34, 69–83.

Grauer, Frederick and Robert Litzenberger, 1980, Monetary rules and the nominal rate of interest under uncertainty, Journal of Monetary Economics 6, 277–288.

Grossman, Sanford J. and Robert J. Shiller, 1982, Consumption correlatedness and risk measurement in economies with non-traded assets and heterogeneous information, Journal of Financial Economics 10, 195–210.

Hall, Robert E., 1978, Stochastic implications of the life cycle-permanent income hypothesis: Theory and evidence, Journal of Political Economy 86, 971–987.

Hansen, Lars P. and Kenneth J. Singleton, 1983, Stochastic consumption, risk aversion, and the temporal behavior of asset returns, Journal of Political Economy 91, 249–265.

Hirshleifer, Jack, 1970, Investment, interest and capital (Prentice-Hall, Englewood Cliffs, NJ).

Hirshleifer, Jack, 1971, Liquidity, uncertainty, and the accumulation of information, Working paper no. 168 (Western Management Science Institute, University of California, Los Angeles, CA).

Huang, Chi-Fu, 1983, Essays of financial economics, Unpublished doctoral dissertation (Graduate School of Business, Stanford University, Stanford, CA).

Kraus, Alan and Robert H. Litzenberger, 1975, Market equilibrium in a state preference model with logarithmic utility, Journal of Finance 30, 1213–1228.

Kydland, Finn E. and Edward C. Prescott, 1982, Time to build and aggregate fluctuations, Econometrica 50, 1345–1370.

Long, John B., 1975, Stock prices, inflation, and the term structure of interest rates, Journal of Financial Economics 2, 131–170.

Long, John B. and Charles I. Plosser, 1982, Real business cycles, Journal of Political Economy 91, 39–69.

Lucas, Robert E., 1978, Asset prices in an exchange economy, Econometrica 46, 1429–1445.

Marsh, Terry, 1980, Asset pricing model specification and the term structure evidence, Working paper no. 1420–83 (Sloan School of Management, Massachusetts Institute of Technology, Cambridge, MA).

Marsh, Terry A. and Eric A. Rosenfeld, 1982, Stochastic processes for interest rates and equilibrium bond prices, Journal of Finance 38, 635–646.

Merton, Robert C., 1973, An intertemporal capital asset pricing model, Econometrica 41, 867–887.

Mishkin, Frederic S., 1981, The real interest rate: An empirical investigation, Carnegie–Rochester Conference Series on Public Policy 15, 151–200.

Mishkin, Frederic S., 1981, Monetary policy and long-term interest rates, Journal of Monetary Economics 7, 29–55.

Nelson, Charles R. and Charles I. Plosser, 1982, Trends and random walks in macroeconomic time series: Some evidence and implications, Journal of Monetary Economics 10, 139–162.

Richard, Scott F., 1978, An arbitrage model of the term structure of interest rates, Journal of Financial Economics 6, 33–58.

Roberts, Harry, 1977, Nonparametric diagnostic checks for nonconstant scatter, Unpublished working paper (Graduate School of Business, University of Chicago, Chicago, IL).

Ronn, Ehud I., 1983, Essays in finance: 1. The effect of time complementarity, and 2. The variability of stocks and bonds, Unpublished doctoral dissertation (Graduate School of Business, Stanford University, Stanford, CA).

Rubinstein, Mark, 1974, An aggregation theorem for securities markets, Journal of Financial Economics 1, 225–244.

Rubinstein, Mark, 1976a, The strong case for the generalized logarithmic utility model as the premier model of financial markets, Journal of Finance 31, 551–571.

Rubinstein, Mark, 1976b, The valuation of uncertain income streams and the pricing of options, Bell Journal of Economics and Management Science 7, 407–425.

Rubinstein, Mark, 1981, A discrete-time synthesis of financial theory, in: Research in finance, Vol. 3 (JAI Press, Greenwich, CT) 53–102.

Stulz, Rene M., 1981, A model of international asset pricing, Journal of Financial Economics 9, 383–406.

Sundaresan, Mahadevan, 1984, Consumption and equilibrium interest rates in stochastic production economies, Journal of Finance 39, 77–92.

[15]

On Equilibrium Asset Price Processes

Hua He
Hayne Leland
University of California, Berkeley

In this article we derive necessary and sufficient conditions that must be satisfied by equilibrium asset price processes in a pure exchange economy. We examine a world in which asset prices follow a diffusion process, asset markets are dynamically complete, all investors maximize their (state-independent) expected utility of consumption at some future date, and investors have nonrandom exogenous income. We show that it is necessary and sufficient that the coefficients of an equilibrium diffusion price process satisfy a partial differential equation and a boundary condition. We also examine how the dynamics of asset prices are related to the shape of the representative investor's utility function through the boundary condition. For example, in a constant-volatility economy, the expected instantaneous return of the market portfolio is mean reverting if and only if the relative risk aversion of the representative investor is decreasing in terminal wealth.

In this article we derive necessary and sufficient conditions that must be satisfied by equilibrium asset price processes in a pure exchange economy. We

This article is a revised version of an earlier one, entitled "Equilibrium Asset Price Processes". We thank seminar participants at HEC, UC Berkeley, UCLA, University of Minnesota, and the University of Pennsylvania-Wharton for helpful comments. We are also grateful to the referee (S. Maheswaran) and editor Phil Dybvig for many helpful comments and suggestions, and thank executive editor Chester Spatt for editorial suggestions. Financial support from the Batterymarch Fellowship Program (for Hua He) and the Berkeley Program in Finance is gratefully acknowledged. Address proofs and reprint requests to Hua He, Haas School of Business, University of California at Berkeley, Berkeley, CA 94720.

The Review of Financial Studies 1993 Volume 6, number 3, pp. 593–617
© 1993 The Review of Financial Studies 0893-9454/93/$1.50

examine a world in which asset prices follow a diffusion process, asset markets are dynamically complete, all investors maximize their (state-independent) expected utility of consumption at some future date, and investors have nonrandom exogenous income. The assumption of dynamically complete markets allows us to work in a representative investor framework [see Constantinides (1982)].

We show that for a diffusion process to be an equilibrium asset price process of the market, it is necessary and sufficient that the coefficients of the diffusion process satisfy a partial differential equation and a boundary condition. The partial differential equation is derived from the fact that the representative investor optimally holds the market portfolio and therefore follows a path-independent strategy. We also examine how the dynamics of asset prices are related to the shape of the representative investor's utility function through the boundary condition. For example, in a constant-volatility economy, the expected instantaneous return of the market portfolio is mean reverting if and only if the relative-risk aversion of the representative investor is decreasing in terminal wealth.

Our assumptions of diffusion processes for asset prices and state-independent utility functions for investors are common in the finance literature: see Merton (1971, 1973) and Breeden (1979).[1] Economies with dynamically complete markets have also been widely studied, as illustrated in Black and Scholes (1973). The assumption of nonrandom exogenous income is special but later will be weakened.

The results of this article supplement those of the international capital asset pricing models (ICAPM) developed by Merton (1973) and extended by Breeden (1979). These models assume that asset prices and a vector of exogenously specified state variables follow a multidimensional diffusion process. With this assumption, equilibrium conditions are then imposed that restrict the expected instantaneous returns of individual assets relative to the expected instantaneous return of the market portfolio. Since the ICAPM emphasizes only the relative pricing between individual assets and the market portfolio, these models have not provided a full characterization of the asset price processes consistent with a market equilibrium.[2] With our (additional) assumptions of the economy, we are able to provide a complete characterization of equilibrium price processes.[3]

[1] Huang (1987) provides a theoretical foundation for the system of equilibrium prices and state variables to form a diffusion process in a pure exchange economy. The sufficient conditions involve certain properties of investors' utility functions, the aggregate endowment process, and the dividend processes of the traded assets.

[2] Rubinstein (1976), Breeden and Litzenberger (1979), and Brennan (1979) have shown that a lognormal process for the market portfolio is consistent with a representative investor having constant relative-risk aversion. Gennotte and Marsh (1993) extend the analysis to allow random volatility of the dividend process; the price process no longer remains lognormal.

Our article is closely related to Bick (1990), who also presents a set of necessary and sufficient conditions for a diffusion price process to be supported by an economy similar to ours. But, our approach is quite different from, and simpler than that of, Bick. In order to verify that a given process is an equilibrium process, Bick's approach involves computing the conditional expectations of the marginal utility of consuming the terminal value of assets at the final date, which could be very difficult to calculate if the conditional density function does not have an analytical form. However, in the special case where asset prices are time-homogeneous diffusions, Bick simplifies his conditions so that computing conditional expectations is no longer required. Our necessary and sufficient conditions in this special case are the same as Bick's.

Our article is also related to Wang (1991), who studies equilibrium conditions for asset price processes in an economy similar to ours, except that Wang allows intermediate consumption. Wang's approach relies upon the existence of a solution to a certain differential equation, an approach that is also different from ours. While Wang derives a set of sufficient conditions for a given price process to be an equilibrium process, these conditions are much stronger than necessary. Therefore, a complete characterization of equilibrium price process is not provided. However, we can apply our approach to Wang's economy to get conditions that are both necessary and sufficient.

The rest of the article is organized as follows. Section 1 formulates a continuous-time securities market–pure exchange economy in a single representative investor setting. Section 2 derives the necessary and sufficient conditions for a diffusion price process of the market to be an equilibrium in our economy. Examples are also provided to illustrate these conditions. In Section 3 we examine an economy in which the volatility of asset returns is a constant. Section 4 contains some concluding remarks.

1. Formulation

Consider a continuous-time dynamically complete securities market–pure exchange economy in which there is a single representative investor who has a finite lifetime horizon $[0, T]$. There is one risky stock and one riskless bond available for trading at any time between 0 and T. The risky stock can be viewed as the market portfolio, the total supply of which is normalized to one share. The riskless bond

[1] Had we allowed arbitrary state-dependent utility functions or arbitrary exogenous income processes, then arbitrary arbitrage-free price systems could be supported by competitive equilibrium [see Kreps (1981)].

is viewed as a financial asset, which is in zero net supply.[4] We assume that the price process for the stock S is a diffusion process and can be described by the stochastic differential equation

$$\frac{dS(t)}{S(t)} = \mu(S(t), t)\, dt + \sigma(S(t), t)\, dw(t), \qquad t \in [0, T], \tag{1}$$

where μ and σ are twice continuously differentiable with respect to S and continuously differentiable with respect to t, and w is a standard Brownian motion defined on a complete probability space $(\Omega, P, \mathcal{F})$.[5] It is assumed that $\sigma > 0$ almost surely and that the stock price is strictly positive with probability 1. Thus, each $\omega \in \Omega$ specifies a complete history of the Brownian motion as well as the stock price. We assume that the stock pays no dividends. To avoid the potential difficulty of classifying boundary behavior, we further assume that S can take values on the entire positive real line and S cannot be negative. For simplicity, the equilibrium interest rate for the bond is taken to a constant, r.[6] The representative investor is assumed to have access only to the information contained in the historical prices, which can be modeled by the σ-field generated by $\mathcal{F}_t = \sigma\{S(s); 0 \leq s \leq t\}$ for $t \in [0, T]$ with $\mathcal{F} = \mathcal{F}_T$.

We assume that there exists an equivalent martingale measure or a risk-neutral probability Q for the stock-price process considered in (1).[7] This equivalent martingale measure is defined as

$$Q(A) \equiv \int_A \xi(\omega, T) P(d\omega) \qquad \forall\, A \in \mathcal{F}, \tag{2}$$

[4] See Remark 1(C) for the case with a positive net supply of the riskless bond.

[5] Implicit in this is the assumption that a solution to the stochastic differential equation (1) exists. The assumption that the equilibrium price process for the stock is a diffusion process can be derived from a set of more primitive assumptions. For example, one can view the stock as a claim to an endowment or crop to be received at the final date T, where the endowment is taken to be a numeraire good. The size of the endowment or crop follows a diffusion process

$$dz(t) = \alpha(z(t), t)\, dt + \beta(z(t), t)\, dw(t).$$

If we assume that $z(t)$ is observable to the investor at time t and that the investor has a von Neumann–Morgenstern, state-independent utility function, then the equilibrium stock-price process must be a function of z and t and, consequently, should have the form as assumed here. See Huang (1987) for more details. Wang (1991) works directly with the condition that the equilibrium price should be a function of z and provides sufficient conditions for this function to become an equilibrium price.

[6] Since there is no intermediate consumption in our model, the riskless interest rate cannot be determined in equilibrium and is therefore specified exogenously.

[7] See Harrison and Kreps (1979) for the former and Cox and Ross (1976) for the latter.

where

$$\xi(\omega, t) = \exp\left\{\int_0^t -\frac{\mu(S(s), s) - r}{\sigma(S(s), s)}\, dw(s) - \frac{1}{2}\int_0^t \left(\frac{\mu(S(s), s) - r}{\sigma(S(s), s)}\right)^2 ds\right\}. \tag{3}$$

The $\xi(\omega, t)e^{-rt}$ can also be interpreted as the Arrow–Debreu state price (at time 0) per unit of probability for one unit consumption good to be received at state ω and time t. We will sometimes call $\{\xi(t)\}$ state prices without mentioning interest rate discounting and per unit of probabilty. Under the equivalent martingale measure Q, the stock-price dynamics becomes

$$\frac{dS(t)}{S(t)} = r\, dt + \sigma(S(t), t)\, dw^*(t),$$

where $w^*(t) \equiv w(t) + \int_0^t (\mu(s) - r)/\sigma(s)\, ds$ is a standard Brownian motion under Q. Given our current setup, the equivalent martingale measure must be unique [see Harrison and Kreps (1979)].

We consider a representative investor who consumes only at the final date[8] and whose preferences for consumption at the final date can be represented by the expected utility of a von Neumann–Morgenstern, state-independent utility function $\mathbf{E}U(W(T))$, where $W(T)$ denotes the wealth at the final date, and U is twice continuously differentiable, increasing, and concave. For now, we assume that the representative investor does not receive any exogenous income,[9] is endowed with one unit of the stock at time 0, and is allowed to allocate the wealth between the stock and the bond so that he maximizes the expected utility of consuming the final wealth at the final date. That is, he solves the dynamic consumption and investment problem

$$\sup_A \mathbf{E}U(W(T))$$

$$\text{s.t.} \quad dW(t) = (rW(t) + A(t)(\mu(S(t), t) - r))\, dt + A(t)\sigma(S(t), t)\, dw(t), \qquad t \in [0, T],$$

$$W(t) \geq 0, \qquad t \in [0, T], \tag{4}$$

where $A(t)$ denotes the dollar amount invested in the stock at time t. The first constraint in (4) is the dynamic budget constraint determining the evolution of the wealth process. The second constraint in (4) is the nonnegative wealth constraint, which rules out the pos-

[8] We will discuss the effect of intermediate consumption in Section 2.

[9] We will relax this assumption in Section 2.

sibility of creating something out of nothing [see Dybvig and Huang (1988)]. A dynamic investment strategy is said to be an equilibrium investment strategy if it requires that the investor optimally invest all the wealth in the risky stock at each moment in time and consume the terminal value of the stock at the final date. In this case, the stock-price process considered in (1) is said to be an equilibrium in our economy.

Our definition of equilibrium is stronger than what we usually mean by competitive equilibrium. Specifically, we have assumed that U is state-independent, the representative investor does not receive exogenous income, and consumption occurs at the final date T. Thus, the class of asset price processes considered here is only a subclass of equilibrium asset price processes consistent with competitive equilibrium.

2. Characterization of Equilibrium Price Processes

In this section we characterize equilibrium asset price processes for the economy specified in the previous section. The main idea of our analysis is to exploit the condition that in equilibrium the representative investor follows a path-independent strategy (i.e., holding the market portfolio). We derive necessary and sufficient conditions for a given price process to be an equilibrium in our economy. We also provide examples that show how our results can be used to identify equilibrium asset prices.

Let A be the investment function that solves the investor's dynamic consumption and investment problem, and let $J(W, S, t)$ be the value of the optimal objective function or the *indirect utility function*, given that the wealth and the stock price at time t are W and S, respectively. Assume that J is twice continuously differentiable with respect to W and S and continuously differentiable with respect to t for $W > 0$, $S > 0$, and $t \in (0, T)$. Then, following Merton (1971, 1973), J must satisfy the Bellman equation

$$0 = \max_{A} \Big\{J_t + (rW + A(\mu - r))J_W + \mu S J_S$$

$$\tfrac{1}{2}\sigma^2 A^2 J_{WW} + \sigma^2 SAJ_{WS} + \tfrac{1}{2}\sigma^2 S^2 J_{SS}\Big\}, \tag{5}$$

for all $W > 0, S > 0$, and $t \in (0, T)$, and the boundary conditions

$$\lim_{t \uparrow T} J(W, S, t) = U(W) \qquad \text{and} \qquad \lim_{W \downarrow 0} J(W, S, t) = U(0),$$

where all subscripts denote partial derivatives. Note that the second boundary condition reflects the nonnegativity constraints on wealth. The first-order condition implies that

Equilibrium Price Processes

$$A(W, S, t) = -\frac{\mu(S, t) - r}{\sigma(S, t)^2}\frac{J_W(W, S, t)}{J_{WW}(W, S, t)} - S\frac{J_{WS}(W, S, t)}{J_{WW}(W, S, t)}, \quad (6)$$

where the first term on the right-hand-side is an instantaneous mean-variance efficient portfolio, and the second term represents the hedging demands against adverse changes in the consumption–investment opportunity set. In equilibrium, we have

$$A(S(t), S(t), t) = S(t),$$

because there is only one unit of the stock available for trading. We should restrict our attention only to those price processes and utility functions so that J are continuously differentiable with respect to W and S up to the fourth order and that J, J_W, J_{WW}, and J_{WS} are continuously differentiable with respect to t. This allows us to work with many derivatives of the indirect utility function. Differentiating (5) with respect to W gives

$$0 = J_{Wt} + rJ_W + (rW + A(\mu - r))J_{WW} + \mu S J_{WS}$$
$$+ \tfrac{1}{2}\sigma^2 A^2 J_{WWW} + A\sigma^2 S J_{WWS} + \tfrac{1}{2}\sigma^2 S^2 J_{WSS},$$

where we have used (6) to simplify terms. This equation implies that the drift of dJ_W is $-rJ_W$. The diffusion term of dJ_W is $J_{WW}\sigma A + J_{WS}\sigma S$, which equals $-((\mu - r)/\sigma)J_W$ by (6). We conclude that

$$dJ_W(W(t), S(t), t)$$
$$= -rJ_W\, dt - \frac{\mu(S(t), t) - r}{\sigma(S(t), t)} J_W(W(t), S(t), t)\, dw(t).$$

Solving this stochastic differential equation gives

$$J_W(W(t), S(t), t)$$
$$= J_W(0)e^{-rt}\exp\left\{\int_0^t -\frac{\mu(S(s), s) - r}{\sigma(S(s), s)}\, dw(s) - \frac{1}{2}\int_0^t \left(\frac{\mu(S(s), s) - r}{\sigma(S(s), s)}\right)^2 ds\right\}$$
$$= J_W(0)\xi(t)e^{-rt},$$

where $J_W(0) = J_W(W(0), S(0), 0)$ and $\xi(t)$ is defined in (3). Since in equilibrium the representative investor holds one share of the risky stock, we have $W(t) = S(t)$ and

$$J_W(S(t),S(t),t) = J_W(S(0),S(0),0)\xi(t)e^{-rt}.$$

The previous equilibrium condition implies that the Arrow–Debreu state price at time t, $\xi(t)$, must be path independent (i.e., independent of the past history of stock prices) for all t. Since the state-price process at time t, $\xi(t)$, depends in general on the historical stock prices through the integral of $(\mu - r)/\sigma$ with respect to dw, path independence clearly puts stringent conditions on μ and σ. The equilibrium condition also implies that $U'(S(T)) = J_w(0)\xi(T)e^{-rT}$, which requires in equilibrium that holding the total supply of the risky stock be optimal and that the state price at time T and the stock price be inversely related.

The following theorem explores the foregoing discussion and provides necessary and sufficient conditions for the stock-price process to satisfy in equilibrium in our economy.

Theorem 1. *The necessary and sufficient conditions for $\{S_t, t \in [0, T]\}$ defined in (1) to be in equilibrium in our economy with a single representative investor consuming at a fixed final date are as follows:*

(i) (μ, σ) satisfies the partial differential equation

$$\tfrac{1}{2}\sigma^2 S^2 f_{SS} + \mu S f_S + f_t + \sigma\sigma_S S(S f_s + f^2 - f) = 0, \qquad (7)$$

where $f(S, t) = (\mu(S, t) - r)/\sigma(S, t)^2$.

(ii) There exists an increasing and concave utility function U such that f satisfies the boundary condition

$$f(S, T) = -SU''(S)/U'(S). \qquad (8)$$

Remark 1. (A) If we let $\mathcal{L}$ be the differential generator associated with S—that is, $\mathcal{L}(f) \equiv \frac{1}{2}\sigma^2 S^2 f_{SS} + \mu S f_S$—then (7) can be rewritten as

$$\mathcal{L}f + f_t + \sigma\sigma_S S(Sf_S + f^2 - f) = 0.$$

(B) Condition (ii) is essentially equivalent to the condition that $\mu(S, T) \geq r$. To verify the existence of U that satisfies (8), it is sufficient to require that $f(S, T) \geq 0$ for all $S > 0$ and that $f(x, T)/x$ is integrable on any closed interval in $(0, \infty)$ or, equivalently, $f(e^x, T)$ is integrable on any closed interval in $(-\infty, +\infty)$. The utility function that satisfies (8) is determined by

$$U'(S) = \gamma \exp\left(-\int_{S_0}^{S} \frac{f(x, T)}{x}\, dx\right), \qquad S > 0,$$

or

$$U'(S) = \gamma \exp\left(-\int_{\ln S_0}^{\ln S} f(e^x, T)\, dx\right), \qquad S > 0,$$

where γ and S_0 are positive constants. Integrating both sides with respect to S yields the utility function U that satisfies (8).

(C) If the total supply of the riskless bond is strictly positive, say $\bar{B} > 0$, then we have

$$J_w(S(t) + \bar{B}e^{rt}, S(t), t) = J_w(S(0) + \bar{B}, S(0), 0)\xi(t)e^{-rt}.$$

Obviously, f shall satisfy the same partial differential equation (7) with the boundary condition

$$f(S, T) = -SU''(S + \bar{B}e^{rT})/U'(S + \bar{B}e^{rT}).$$

Proof. We prove the necessity here, while leaving the proof for the sufficiency to the Appendix. Define $h(S(t), t) = \ln J_w(S(t), S(t), t) - \ln J_w(S(0), S(0), 0)$. Since $J_w(t) = J_w(0)\xi(t)e^{-rt}$ in equilibrium, we have $h(S(t), t) = \ln \xi(t) - rt$. Hence, the drift and diffusion terms of dh must be the same as those of $d(\ln \xi(t) - rt)$. Applying Itô's lemma, we obtain

$$\tfrac{1}{2}\sigma^2 S^2 h_{SS} + \mu S h_S + h_t = -\tfrac{1}{2}((\mu - r)/\sigma)^2 - r,$$

$$\sigma S h_S = -(\mu - r)/\sigma,$$

or, equivalently,

$$Sh_S = -f, \tag{9}$$

$$\tfrac{1}{2}\sigma^2 S^2 h_{SS} - \tfrac{1}{2}\sigma^2 f^2 + rf + r + h_t = 0. \tag{10}$$

Now, differentiating (9) with respect to S and t, we get $h_{SS}S + h_S = -f_S$, and $Sh_{St} = -f_t$. Hence, $S^2 h_{SS} = -Sf_S + f$, and (10) becomes

$$\tfrac{1}{2}\sigma^2(-Sf_S + f) - \tfrac{1}{2}\sigma^2 f^2 + rf + r + h_t = 0. \tag{11}$$

Next, differentiating (11) with respect to S and substituting $Sh_{St} = -f_t$ into the resulting equation, we get (7). Finally, the boundary condition for f is obviously satisfied if we set $t = T$ in (6). ■

The partial differential equation (7) is an equilibrium condition imposed on the coefficients of the stock-price process. The argument that is crucial to the derivation of this equation is the observation that h is a function of $S(t)$ and t but not of the history of S. Thus, (7) is equivalent to that the state-price process at time t, $\xi(t)$, is path independent for all t. Consequently, (7) guarantees that for any investor with a state-independent utility function, he will follow a path-independent investment strategy. Cox and Leland (1982) have shown that any optimal investment strategy must be path independent if the stock-price process follows a lognormal process. Our result extends that of Cox and Leland to a more general class of diffusion processes. The boundary condition (8) ensures that holding the total supply of the risky stock is optimal for an investor with a utility function U.

Theorem 1 provides a complete characterization of equilibrium asset price processes within the family of diffusion processes. We obtain this characterization by exploiting the equilibrium condition that the representative investor optimally holds the total supply of the risky stock. Note that this characterization cannot be derived directly from the ICAPM. Consequently, our equilibrium conditions are stronger than those derived in the ICAPM.

If we are given a pair of diffusion coefficients (μ, σ), then we can easily check whether it satisfies the necessary conditions of Theorem 1. If any of these necessary conditions is violated, then we can immediately conclude that S can never be an equilibrium in our economy.

Theorem 1 also suggests that for a given volatility function σ and a given utility function U the expected instantaneous excess-return function normalized by the volatility function, f, is determined by a nonlinear partial differential equation subject to a boundary condition at $t = T$. Under some standard regularity conditions, the boundary value problem defined by (7) and (8) has a unique solution [see Friedman (1969)]. Thus, for given σ and U, one can derive f by solving the partial differential equation (7), which can then be used to find the expected instantaneous return function μ. Clearly, the expected instantaneous return function depends on the shape of the utility function in an important way through the boundary condition. Of course, in order for a price process to be an equilibrium process, we still have to make sure that S is strictly positive.

Similarly, for a given expected instantaneous return function μ, we can rewrite (7) as

$$\frac{1}{2}S^2 f_{SS} + Sff_S + \frac{rf^2}{\mu - r} + \frac{1}{\mu - r}ff_t + \frac{S}{2}\left(\frac{\mu_S}{\mu - r} - \frac{f_S}{f}\right)(Sf_S + f^2 - f) = 0. \tag{12}$$

Thus, we can alternatively solve (12) for f and thereby find the volatility function σ. In this case, we have to make sure that $\sigma^2 = (\mu - r)/f$ is strictly positive. In summary, if we specify either the volatility function or the expected instantaneous return function, then the expected instantaneous return function or the volatility function can be determined by (7) or (12) and by the corresponding boundary condition. Theorem 1 suggests that for any given utility function, there exists a fairly large class of the expected instantaneous return and volatility functions that are consistent with our definition of equilibrium. Equation (7) or (12) can be used to find systematically all of the equilibrium expected instantaneous return and volatility functions.

Bick (1990) has obtained a characterization of equilibrium or ***viable*** price processes for the same class of diffusion processes studied in this article. For a given pair of diffusion coefficients (μ, σ), Bick constructs the utility function in the same manner as we did in Remark 1 and shows that the price process S is consistent with an equilibrium if and only if

$$S(t) = E[U'(S(T))S(T) \mid \mathcal{F}_t]/E[U'(S(T)) \mid \mathcal{F}_t],$$

where $\mathcal{F}_t$ denotes the information set generated from the historical stock prices. Therefore, in order to verify whether S is consistent with an equilibrium, we must compute conditional expectations. Since the conditional density functions are difficult to calculate in general, the necessary conditions derived in Propositions 1 and 2 of Bick (1990) can hardly be verified for general diffusion processes. In contrast, the necessary conditions derived in Theorem 1 are easy to verify for any arbitrarily given diffusion process. Bick's (1990) condition (P2) in Proposition 2 states that in equilibrium, for any $0 \le t_1 < \ldots < t_n \le T$ and $S_0, S_1, \ldots, S_n > 0$,

$$k(t_0, S_0; t_1, S_1)k(t_1, S_1; t_2, S_2) \ldots k(t_{n-1}, S_{n-1}; t_n, S_n) = k(t_0, S_0; t_n, S_n),$$

where $k(t, x; s, y) = p(t, x; s, y)/q(t, x; s, y)$, and p and q are the transition density functions under probability measures P and Q, respectively. This condition is essentially equivalent to that ξ is path independent as $dQ/dP = \xi(T)$.

Our approach is also quite different from that of Wang, who works directly with a dividend process and derives equilibrium conditions on the function that maps from the value of current dividend to the asset price. However, Wang's general characterization of the equilibrium price contains an unknown utility function that makes it difficult to verify. By working directly with the dynamics of the equilibrium asset price process, we derive explicit conditions that are easy to verify.

We now focus on an important subclass of diffusion processes that are of particular interest to financial economists, namely the class of time-homogeneous diffusion processes,

$$\frac{dS(t)}{S(t)} = a(S(t))\, dt + b(S(t))\, dw(t), \tag{13}$$

where $a \ge 0$ and b are functions of S. To check whether such a process is consistent with an equilibrium, one can verify whether f satisfies (7). Since in this special case f is independent of t, or $f_t = 0$, (7) is equivalent to

$$\frac{d}{dS}(\sigma^2[Sf_S + f^2 - f]) = 0.$$

That is, there exists a constant K such that $\sigma^2[Sf_S + f^2 - f] = K$. This is the same condition that Bick (1990) obtains in Proposition 3 for time-homogeneous diffusions. We summarize the necessary conditions for this special case in the following corollary.

Corollary 1. The necessary and sufficient conditions for $\{St_t, t \in [0, T]\}$ defined in (13) to be consistent with an equilibrium are as follows:

(i) There exists a constant K such that

$$\sigma^2[Sf_S + f^2 - f] = K, \tag{14}$$

where $f(S) = (\mu(S) - r)/\sigma^2(S)$.

(ii) There exists an increasing and concave utility function U such that $f(S) = -SU''(S)/U'(S)$.

To illustrate the use of Theorem 1 and Corollary 1, we consider one example. More examples with time-homogeneous processes can be found in Bick (1990).

Example 1. Assume $r = 0$. Consider the class of diffusion processes defined by

$$\frac{dS(t)}{S(t)} = a(S(t))\, dt + b\, dw(t),$$

where b is a constant and a is a function of S. We have $\mu = a(S)$, $\sigma = b$, and $f = a(S)/b^2$. Thus,

$$\sigma^2(Sf_S + f^2 - f) = Sa_S + a^2/b^2 - a.$$

For the right-hand side of the equation to be a constant, it is necessary that

$$a(S) = \alpha\frac{AS^{2\alpha} - 1}{AS^{2\alpha} + 1} + \frac{1}{2}b^2$$

or

$$a(S) = \alpha\tan(AS^{-\alpha}) + \tfrac{1}{2}b^2$$

for some $\alpha > 0$ and $A > 0$. Since we require $a > 0$, the second class of solutions is not useful. For the first class of solutions, we require $\alpha \leq \frac{1}{2}b^2$.

It is important to point out that when we restrict the price processes to the class of time-homogeneous diffusion processes, the volatility function can be determined from the utility function. We can do this because f is now completely determined by the utility function U; that is, $f = -SU''/U'$ and

$$\sigma^2 = K/(Sf_S + f^2 - f).$$

Since K is a constant, the sign of $Sf_S + f^2 - f$ must be constant for all $S > 0$. This clearly puts further restrictions on the utility function. Specifically, it requires that the sign of $-(d/dS)\ (U''(S)/U'(S)) + (U''(S)/U'(S))^2$ be constant for all $S > 0$, as shown in Bick (1990) as well. For example, if $U(S) = \ln S + S^{1-\alpha}/(1-\alpha)$, then

$$-\frac{d}{dS}\left(\frac{U''(S)}{U'(S)}\right) + \left(\frac{U''(S)}{U'(S)}\right)^2 = (\alpha - 1)\left(\frac{\alpha}{S^{2\alpha+2}} - \frac{\alpha - 2}{S^{\alpha+3}}\right).$$

For $\alpha > 2$, the right-hand side of this equation can change signs. Hence, there does not exist a time-homogeneous diffusion process that is consistent with our definition of equilibrium under such a utility function. Later, we demonstrate that there exists a non-time-homogeneous diffusion process for this utility function that is consistent with our definition of equilibrium. Thus, in some cases, if one wants to identify the equilibrium price process for a given utility function, one may have to search among processes that are not time homogeneous. In summary, Theorem 1 has provided a general approach that characterizes the equilibrium asset price processes.

There are a number of ways in which we can extend our result. First, we can allow intermediate consumption in our pure exchange economy (with no production). As it turns out, intermediate consumption does not have any significant effect on the characterization of equilibrium price processes as long as we specify the dividend process as a function of the current stock price and time. Let $D(t) = D(S(t), t)$ be the dividend process, and let S satisfy

$$dS(t) = (\mu(S(t), t)S(t) - D(S(t), t))\,dt + \sigma(S(t), t)S(t)\,dw(t).$$

If S can be supported by utility functions (u, U), where $u(x, t)$ and $U(x)$ are increasing and concave in x, u is the utility function for intermediate consumption and U for final wealth, then in equilibrium

$$u'(D(S(t), t)) = J_W(S(t), S(t), t) = J_W(S(0), S(0), 0)\xi(t)e^{-rt}.$$

Defining h as in the proof of Theorem 1, we have

$$\tfrac{1}{2}\sigma^2 S^2 h_{SS} + (\mu S - D)h_S + h_t = -\tfrac{1}{2}((\mu - r)/\sigma)^2 - r,$$

$$\sigma S h_S = -(\mu - r)/\sigma.$$

Eliminating h in the same way as before, we can show that (μ, σ) must satisfy the partial differential equation

$$\mathcal{L}f + f_t + (D/S)_S Sf + \sigma\sigma_S S(Sf_S + f^2 - f) = 0,$$

where $\mathcal{L}f = \frac{1}{2}\sigma^2 S^2 f_S + (\mu S - D)f_S$. The boundary condition is the same as in (8). When there is intermediate consumption, we should also have

$$u'(D(S(t), t)) = J_w(0)\xi(t)e^{-rt}.$$

Apply Itô's lemma, we find that the utility function for intermediate consumption must satisfy

$$-\frac{u''(D(S(t), t), t)}{u'(D(S(t), t), t)} S(t) D_S(S(t), t) = \frac{\mu(S(t), t) - r}{\sigma^2(S(t), t)}.$$

Since u is concave, we require that $\mu(S, t) \geq r$ for all $S > 0$ and $t \in [0, T]$ if the dividend rate is increasing in the level of stock price. The above equation also suggests how one should be able to back out u by integration for given μ, σ, and D.

Second, we point out that the class of diffusion processes we examined here presumes that all relevant information to future returns is fully reflected in the current price.[10] However, we can enlarge the class of equilibrium price processes to include Itô processes that have the form

$$\frac{dS(t)}{S(t)} = \mu(\omega, t)\ dt + \sigma(S(t), t)\ dw(t),$$

where ω is the entire stock-price history rather than just the current stock price. We will show that in this case the equilibrium condition implies that μ must depend only on the current stock price and not on the past history of stock prices. Therefore, even if we allow the expected return to depend on the entire history of the stock price, the equilibrium price process must follow a diffusion as assumed in (7) as long as the volatility of return depends only on the current stock price.

This observation is useful, since empirically it is very difficult to estimate the drift term, and yet it is fairly easy to estimate the diffusion term by using finely sampled observations. If one can empirically determine that the diffusion term depends only on the current price and time, then one can claim that stock price must follow a diffusion process.

To demonstrate our claim, we recall the first-order equilibrium condition

$$U'(S(T)) = \lambda\xi(T)e^{-rT},$$

where ξ is now defined similarly as in (3), except that $\mu(S(t), t)$ is replaced by $\mu(\omega, t)$. Thus,

$$\frac{1}{U'(S(T))} = \frac{e^{rT}}{\lambda}\xi(T)^{-1}.$$

[10] Recent studies have suggested that other economic variables may help predict the future return distribution; see, for example, Harvey (1989).

Now, consider processes S and ξ under the equivalent martingale measure Q. Since $w^*(t) = w(t) + (\mu(t) - r)/\sigma(t)$ is a standard Brownian motion under Q, we have

$$\frac{dS(t)}{S(t)} = r\,dt + \sigma(S(t), t)\,dw^*(t),$$

$$d\xi(t)^{-1} = \frac{\mu(\omega, t) - r}{\sigma(S(t), t)}\xi(t)^{-1}\,dw^*(t).$$

Thus, S is a diffusion process under Q, while ξ^{-1} is a martingale under Q. Invoking conditional expectation under Q, we get

$$E_Q\left[\frac{1}{U'(S(T))} \;\middle|\; S(T) = S\right] = \frac{e^{rT}}{\lambda}\xi(t)^{-1},$$

where the left-hand side must be a function of S and t only, since S is a diffusion process under Q. Define

$$h(S, t) \equiv -\ln\left(E_Q\left[\frac{1}{U'(S(T))} \;\middle|\; S(T) = S\right]\right) + rT - \ln\lambda.$$

Then $\ln \xi(t) = h(S(t), t)$. Assuming h is twice continuously differentiable with respect to S and continuously differentiable with respect to t, we have, by Itô's lemma,

$$\mu(\omega, t) = r - \sigma(S(t), t)^2 S(t) h_S(S(t), t).$$

We conclude that μ is a function of S and t. Consequently, S is a diffusion process.

Third, we have so far assumed that the representative investor does not receive any exogenous income. This is not necessary. Our results hold as long as the exogenous income (to be distributed at the final date) is a function of the current stock price (but not the history of stock prices). In particular, our results hold if the exogenous income is nonrandom, because with such an exogenous income distribution the representative investor's marginal utility or shadow prices is still path independent.

Finally, we mention briefly that we can extend our characterization of equilibrium asset price processes to the case when there is more than one risky stock. The basic technique should be the same as in the case with a single stock, that is, to exploit the condition that the state-price process ξ be path independent in equilibrium. For example, in the case of two risky stocks, suppose that

$$dS_1 = \mu_1 S_1\,dt + \sigma_1 S_1\,dw_1,$$

$$dS_2 = \mu_2 S_2\,dt + \sigma_2 S_2(\rho\,dw_1 + \sqrt{1 - \rho^2}\,dw_2),$$

where μ_i, σ_i, and ρ are functions of S_1, S_2, and t. As in the one-dimensional case, define

$$\begin{pmatrix} f \\ g \end{pmatrix} = (\sigma\sigma^{\mathsf{T}})^{-1}(\mu - r\mathbf{1}),$$

where

$$\mu = \begin{pmatrix} \mu_1 \\ \mu_2 \end{pmatrix}, \qquad \mathbf{1} = \begin{pmatrix} 1 \\ 1 \end{pmatrix}, \qquad \sigma = \begin{pmatrix} \sigma_1 & 0 \\ \sigma_2\rho & \sigma_2\sqrt{1-\rho^2} \end{pmatrix}.$$

Then, in equilibrium, we have

$$S_2 f_2 = S_1 g_1, \tag{15}$$

$$\begin{aligned} &\mathcal{L}f + f_t + \tfrac{1}{2}S_1(\sigma_1^2)_{S_1}(S_1 f_1 + f^2 - f) \\ &\quad + \tfrac{1}{2}S_1(\sigma_2^2)_{S_1}(S_2 g_2 + g^2 - g) + S_1(\rho\sigma_1\sigma_2)_{S_1}(fg + S_2 f_2) = 0, \end{aligned} \tag{16}$$

$$\begin{aligned} &\mathcal{L}g + g_t + \tfrac{1}{2}S_2(\sigma_1^2)_{S_2}(S_1 f_1 + f^2 - f) \\ &\quad + \tfrac{1}{2}S_2(\sigma_2^2)_{S_2}(S_2 g_2 + g^2 - g) + S_2(\rho\sigma_1\sigma_2)_{S_2}(fg + S_1 g_1) = 0, \end{aligned} \tag{17}$$

where $\mathcal{L}$ is the differential generator associated with processes S_1 and S_2. The boundary conditions are

$$f(S_1, S_2, T) = -S_1 U''(S_1 + S_2)/U'(S_1 + S_2), \tag{18}$$

$$g(S_1, S_2, T) = -S_2 U''(S_1 + S_2)/U'(S_1 + S_2), \tag{19}$$

for some increasing and concave utility function U and for all $S_1 \geq 0$ and $S_2 \geq 0$. We refer the reader to He and Leland (1992) for a more detailed derivation.

If we require that S be a time-homogeneous diffusion, then (16) and (17) are equivalent to

$$\frac{\sigma_1^2}{2}[S_1 f_1 + f^2 - f] + \rho\sigma_1\sigma_2[S_2 f_2 + fg] + \frac{\sigma_2^2}{2}[S_2 g_2 + g^2 - g] = K \tag{20}$$

for some constant K. This is clearly a generalization of Corollary 1.

3. Asset Price Processes with Constant Volatility

In this section we consider the Black and Scholes economy in which the equilibrium volatility function of stock return is a constant [see Black and Scholes (1973)]. This is an important class of processes, since most stock option pricing models used in practice assume constant volatility. It would be interesting from a theoretical point of view to investigate the dynamics, and in particular the risk premia, of equilibrium price processes when the volatility of stock return is held constant.

If we assume σ is a constant, we can simplify the partial differential equation (7). We summarize our result in the following proposition.

Proposition 1. If the volatility function σ is constant, then a necessary and sufficient condition for $\{S_t, t \in [0, T]\}$ to be an equilibrium in our economy is that the expected instantaneous return μ satisfies the partial differential equation[11]

$$\tfrac{1}{2}\sigma^2 S^2 \mu_{SS} + S\mu\mu_S + \mu_t = 0 \tag{21}$$

with the boundary condition

$$\mu(S, T) = r - \sigma^2 S U''(S)/U'(S) \tag{22}$$

for some increasing and concave utility function U.

Remark 2. (i) Equation (21) implies that $\{\mu(S(t), t), t \in [0, T]\}$ is a local martingale under P. With some additional regularity conditions, μ is a martingale under P. That is, the expected instantaneous returns in the future, given the current stock price, will equal the current expected instantaneous return.

(ii) Similar results hold in the case with multiple stocks. For example, in the case with two stocks, if σ_1, σ_2, and ρ are constants, then (16) and (17) become

$$\mathcal{L}f + f_t = 0, \qquad \mathcal{L}g + g_t = 0; \tag{23}$$

that is, f and g are martingales. This implies that μ_1 and μ_2 are martingales as well, since they are linear combinations of f and g.

Proposition 1 suggests that for any given utility function, it is always possible to find a diffusion process with a constant volatility so that it is an equilibrium process in our economy. To derive the equilibrium expected instantaneous return function for a given level of volatility and a given utility function, we provide two lemmas. The first lemma gives a solution to a heat equation that satisfies a given boundary condition. The proof of this lemma is omitted, since it can be found in standard textbooks. The second lemma utilizes the solution to the heat equation to get a solution to the partial differential equation (PDE) (21) satisfying the boundary condition (22).

[11] After we completed the first version of this article, we became aware of the work of Hodges and Carverhill (1991, revised March 1992), who independently uncovered the same PDE for the equilibrium process of the market in a Black-Scholes economy. Their result is only limited to this special case with a constant volatility.

Lemma 1. Let ϕ be the solution to the heat equation

$$\phi_t = \tfrac{1}{2}\sigma^2\phi_{xx} \tag{24}$$

with boundary condition

$$\phi(x, 0) = 1/U'(e^x)' \tag{25}$$

where $1/U'(e^x)$ is continuous and bounded above by Ae^{Bx} for some positive constants A and B. Then we have

$$\phi(x, t) = \frac{1}{\sqrt{2\pi}}\int_{-\infty}^{+\infty}\frac{1}{U'(e^{x+\sigma\sqrt{t}z})}e^{-z^2/2}\,dz.$$

To find the solution to the PDE (21), we consider the transformation $V(x, t) = \mu(e^x, T - t) - r$. Since $V_x = \mu_S e^x$, $V_{xx} = \mu_{SS}e^{2x} + \mu_S e^x$, and $V_t = -\mu_t$, (21) becomes

$$\tfrac{1}{2}\sigma^2 V_{xx} + VV_x = V_t + (\tfrac{1}{2}\sigma^2 - r)V_x, \tag{26}$$

and the boundary condition becomes

$$V(x, 0) = -\sigma^2 e^x U''(e^x)/U'(e^x). \tag{27}$$

Next, consider the transformation $W(x, t) = -V(x + (\frac{1}{2}\sigma^2 - r)t, t)$. Then (26) becomes

$$\tfrac{1}{2}\sigma^2 W_{xx} = W_t + WW_x \tag{28}$$

with boundary condition

$$W(x, 0) = \sigma^2 e^x U''(e^x)/U'(e^x). \tag{29}$$

Equation (28) is called Burgers' equation [see Kevorkian (1990, p. 31)]. Its solution can be obtained by using the Cole–Hopf transformation: $W(x, t) = -\sigma^2\phi_x(x, t)/\phi(x, t)$, where ϕ is a solution to the heat equation

$$\phi_t = \tfrac{1}{2}\sigma^2\phi_{xx}.$$

The boundary condition for ϕ can be determined by the boundary condition for W, which gives

$$\sigma^2\frac{\phi_x(x, 0)}{\phi(x, 0)} = -\frac{\sigma^2 e^x U''(e^x)}{U'(e^x)},$$

or, equivalently,

$$\phi(x, 0) = 1/U'(e^x).$$

It is now immediate that

$$\mu(S, t) = r - W\left(\ln S - \left(\tfrac{1}{2}\sigma^2 - r\right)(T - t), T - t\right)$$
$$= r + \sigma^2 \frac{\phi_x\left(\ln S - \left(\tfrac{1}{2}\sigma^2 - r\right)(T - t), T - t\right)}{\phi\left(\ln S - \left(\tfrac{1}{2}\sigma^2 - r\right)(T - t), T - t\right)}$$

is the solution to the PDE (21) satisfying the boundary condition (22). We summarize our disucssion in the following lemma.

Lemma 2. Let ϕ be the solution to the heat equation (24) satisfying the boundary condition (25). Then

$$\mu(S, t) \equiv r + \sigma^2 \frac{\phi_x\left(\ln S - \left(\tfrac{1}{2}\sigma^2 - r\right)(T - t), T - t\right)}{\phi\left(\ln S - \left(\tfrac{1}{2}\sigma^2 - r\right)(T - t), T - t\right)}$$

is a solution to the partial differential equation (21) satisfying the boundary condition (22).

We have now obtained the general solution for the expected instantaneous return function corresponding to a given utility function and a constant volatility. Given that our solution of the expected instantaneous return function depends on the length of lifetime horizon, it would be interesting to investigate the dynamic behavior of stock prices for very large T or when T goes to infinity. This is similar to the approach used in the standard turnpike theory for intertemporal consumption and portfolio policies. To illustrate our results, we consider two more examples.

Example 2. Assume $r = 0$. Consider the HARA class of utility functions

$$-U'(S)/U''(S) = A + BS,$$

where A, $B \geq 0$. By integration, we have $U'(S) = K(A + BS)^{-1/B}$, where $K > 0$ is a constant. For simplicity, we take $K = 1$. Hence,

$$\phi(x, t) = \frac{1}{\sqrt{2\pi}} \int_{-\infty}^{+\infty} (A + Be^{x+\sigma\sqrt{t}z})^{1/B} e^{-z^2/2}\, dz.$$

If $B = 1$, $\phi(x, t) = e^x e^{\sigma^2 t/2} + A$. According to Lemma 2, we conclude that

$$\mu(S, t) = \sigma^2(S/(S + A)).$$

Thus, S is a time-homogeneous diffusion process. If $B = \frac{1}{2}$, then $\phi(x, t) = A^2 + Ae^{x+\sigma^2 t/2} + \frac{1}{4}e^{2x+2\sigma^2 t}$. Hence,

$$\mu(S, t) = \sigma^2 S \frac{A + \frac{1}{2}Se^{\sigma^2(T-t)}}{A^2 + AS + \frac{1}{4}S^2 e^{\sigma^2(T-t)}}.$$

Clearly, S is not a time-homogeneous diffusion process. If we let $T \to +\infty$, we get $\mu = 2\sigma^2$. Thus, if the lifetime horizon is sufficiently long, S behaves approximately like a geometric Brownian motion. Moreover, the constant A has no real effect on the price process.

Example 3. Assume $r = 0$. Consider a utility function $U(S) = \ln S + S^{1-\alpha}/(1-\alpha)$, where $\alpha > 0$. We saw in Section 2 that there is no time-homogeneous diffusion process that is consistent with an equilibrium with this utility function. Since $U'(S) = S^{-1} + S^{-\alpha}$, we find

$$\phi(x, t) = \frac{1}{\sqrt{2\pi}} \int_{-\infty}^{+\infty} \frac{1}{e^{-x-\sigma\sqrt{t}z} + e^{-\alpha x-\alpha\sigma\sqrt{t}z}} e^{-z^2/2}\, dz,$$

$$\phi_x(x, t) = \frac{1}{\sqrt{2\pi}} \int_{-\infty}^{+\infty} \frac{e^{-x-\sigma\sqrt{t}z} + \alpha e^{-\alpha x-\alpha\sigma\sqrt{t}z}}{(e^{-x-\sigma\sqrt{t}z} + e^{-\alpha x-\alpha\sigma\sqrt{t}z})^2} e^{-z^2/2}\, dz.$$

According to Lemma 2, we have

$$\mu(S, t) = \sigma^2 \frac{\phi_x\left(\ln S - \frac{1}{2}\sigma^2(T-t)\ T-t\right)}{\phi\left(\ln S - \frac{1}{2}\sigma^2(T-t)\ T-t\right)}.$$

Clearly, S is not a time-homogeneous diffusion process. If we let T go to infinity, then μ converges to σ^2 if $\alpha \le 1$ and to $\sigma^2\alpha$ if $\alpha > 1$. Thus, if the lifetime horizon is sufficiently long, the equilibrium price will behave approximately like a geometric Brownian motion. Note that when $0 < \alpha < 1$, $\ln S$ dominates $S^{1-\alpha}/(1-\alpha)$, so the equilibrium price is determined by the log utility. When $\alpha > 1$, $S^{1-\alpha}/(1-\alpha)$ dominates $\ln S$, and therefore the equilibrium price is determined by $S^{1-\alpha}/(1-\alpha)$.

The following proposition establishes an important property of the expected instantaneous return function when the utility function of the representative investor exhibits increasing or decreasing relative-risk aversion. We need to impose some regularity conditions for this proposition.

Condition R

1. *There exists a constant $K > 0$ such that for all $x, y > 0$ and $t \in [0, t]$,*

$$|x\mu(x, t) - y\mu(y, t)| \le K|x-y|, \qquad |x\mu(x, t)| \le K(1+x),$$

and there exist constants $L > 0$ and $m > 0$ such that for all $x > 0$ and $t \in [0, T]$,

$$\left|\frac{\partial}{\partial x}(x\mu(x, t))\right| + \left|\frac{\partial^2}{\partial x^2}(x\mu(x, t))\right| \le L(1+x^m).$$

2. *$xU''(x)|U'(x)$ is twice continuously differentiable for $x > 0$ and its derivatives satisfy a polynomial growth condition, where U is the utility function for the representative investor.*

Proposition 2. Suppose Condition R is satisfied. Let μ be the equilibrium expected instantaneous return function such that it satisfies the conditions in Proposition 1 with a constant σ. Then, for every $t \in [0, T]$, $\mu(x, t)$ is increasing (decreasing) in x if and only if the relative risk aversion $-xU''(x)/U'(x)$ is increasing (decreasing) in x.

Proof. The necessary part of this proposition is obvious. We only prove the sufficient part. First, we note that given the regularity conditions imposed on μ and the fact that μ satisfies the necessary conditions in Proposition 1, the Feyman–Kac representation implies that μ is a martingale under P [see, for example, Karatzas and Shreve (1988, Theorem 5.7.6)]. Thus, we can express μ as

$$\mu(x, t) = \mathbf{E}[\mu(S(T), T) \mid S(t) = x].$$

Now, let us fix t and x and denote the price process on $[t, T]$ with $S(t) = x$ by $\{S^x(\tau); \tau \in [t, T]\}$. Applying Theorem 5.5 of Friedman (1975) or Theorem 1, Chapter 2, of Gilman and Skorohod (1972), we claim that S^x is differentiable with respect to x, the initial data S^x. Furthermore, let D^x denote the derivative of S^x with respect to x defined on $[t, T]$. Then D^x satisfies

$$dD^x(\tau) = (\mu(S^x(\tau), \tau) + S^x(\tau)\mu_S(S^x(\tau), \tau))D^x(\tau)\, d\tau + \sigma D^x(\tau)\, dw(\tau),$$

with $D^x(t) = 1$. Since $|\mu(S, t) + S\mu_S(S, t)|$ is continuous and bounded above by a polynomial function, $\int_t^T |\mu(S^x(\tau), \tau) + S^x(\tau)\mu_S(S^x(\tau), \tau)|\, d\tau < \infty$, P-a.s. It then follows that

$$D^x(s) = \exp\left\{\int_t^s \left(\mu(S^x(\tau), \tau) + S^x(\tau)\mu_S(S^x(\tau), \tau) - \frac{1}{2}\sigma^2\right) d\tau \right.$$
$$\left. + \sigma(w(s) - w(t))\right\} > 0.$$

Following again Theorem 5.5 of Friedman (1975), we obtain

$$\begin{aligned}\mu_S(x, t) &= \mathbf{E}_t[\mu_S(S^x(T), T) D^x(T)] \\ &= \sigma^2 \mathbf{E}_t\left[\frac{\partial}{\partial y}\left(-\frac{yU''(y)}{U'(y)}\right)\bigg|_{y=S^x(T)} D^x(T)\right].\end{aligned}$$

Since $D^x(T) > 0$, we conclude that $\mu_S(S, t)$ is increasing (decreasing) in S for $t \in [0, T]$ if the relative-risk aversion is increasing (decreasing) in terminal wealth. ∎

The Review of Financial Studies / v 6 n 3 1993

Now, consider the dynamics for the log price,

$$d \ln S(t) = (\mu(S(t), t) - \tfrac{1}{2}\sigma^2)\, dt + \sigma\, dw(t).$$

When μ is decreasing in the level of the stock price, the log-price process always exhibits "mean reversion" in the sense that the return of the stock price moves in the opposite direction to the level of the stock price. Proposition 2 demonstrates that mean reversion is naturally associated with preferences that exhibit decreasing relative-risk aversion, when the volatility of stock return is constant. Similarly, "mean aversion" processes are naturally associated with preferences that exhibit increasing relative-risk aversion.

4. Concluding Remarks

We have provided an approach to characterize equilibrium asset price processes within the family of diffusion processes in a specialized pure exchange economy. In our economy, we assume that the securities markets are dynamically complete, all investors have a state-independent utility function and receive no exogenous income, and all investors consume at some fixed future date. We derive our characterization by exploiting the equilibrium condition that the representative investor optimally holds the total supply of risky assets and therefore follows a path-independent strategy. Consequently, our equilibrium conditions include, but are stronger than, those derived in the intertemporal capital asset pricing models.

Market completeness has played an important role in our analysis. It allows us to formulate the model by using a representative investor framework. It also permits us to determine the unique Arrow–Debreu state prices. It would therefore be interesting to see how our approach can be generalized to an incomplete markets setting.

The assumptions that investors receive no exogenous income and that their preferences can be represented by a von Neumann–Morgenstern, state-independent utility function are also crucial ones. For example, if we had allowed state-dependent utility functions or random exogenous income, then any arbitrage-free asset price process could be supported by an equilibrium. Given that there is a growing interest in non-time-additive utility functions, such as utility functions that exhibit habit formation, it would be interesting to extend our analysis for such utility functions.

Appendix

Proof of Theorem 1. We prove the sufficiency of Theorem 1. To do so, we transform the representative investor's dynamic consumption and investment problem into a static utility maximization problem:

$$\sup_{W(T)\geq 0} \mathbf{E}U(W(T)),$$

$$\mathbf{E}[\xi(T)W(T)e^{-rT}] \leq W_0, \qquad \text{(A1)}$$

In other words, the dynamic budget constraint in (4) is replaced by a static budget constraint [see Cox and Huang (1989)]. The first-order condition for the static problem is that there exists a scalar $\lambda > 0$ so that

$$U'(W(T)) \begin{cases} = \lambda\xi(T)e^{-rT}, & \text{if } W(T) > 0, \\ \leq \lambda\xi(T)e^{-rT}, & \text{if } W(T) = 0. \end{cases}$$

Since in equilibrium the representative investor holds one unit of the stock and consumes the final value of the stock at the final date, we have $W(T) = S(T)$ in equilibrium. Because we have assumed that $S(T) > 0$, a.s., the first-order condition should always hold in equality.

As we discussed earlier, the utility function that supports this equilibrium satisfies

$$\frac{U'(S)}{U'(S_0)} = \exp\left(-\int_{S_0}^{S} \frac{f(x, T)}{x}\, dx\right),$$

where $S_0 = S(0)$. Define $g(S, t) = -\int_{S_0}^{S} f(x, t)/x\, dx$. It is now sufficient to show that $g(S(T), T) = \ln \xi(T) + c$ for some constant c. To do so, we apply Itô's lemma to g:

$$\begin{aligned} dg(S, t) &= -\frac{f}{S}(\mu S\, dt + \sigma S\, dw) - \left(\frac{f_S}{S} - \frac{f}{S^2}\right)\frac{\sigma^2 S^2}{2}\, dt \\ &\quad - \left(\int_{S_0}^{S} \frac{f_t(x, t)}{x}\, dx\right) dt \\ &= -\frac{\mu - r}{\sigma}\, dw - \frac{1}{2}\left(\frac{\mu - r}{\sigma}\right)^2 dt + rf\, dt \\ &\quad - \left(\frac{\sigma^2}{2}(f^2 + Sf_S - f) + \int_{S_0}^{S} \frac{f_t(x, t)}{x}\, dx\right) dt \\ &= d\ln\xi(t) - \left(rf + \frac{\sigma^2}{2}(f^2 + Sf_S - f) + \int_{S_0}^{S} \frac{f_t(x, t)}{x}\, dx\right) dt. \qquad \text{(A2)} \end{aligned}$$

Now, define

$$I(S, t) = rf + (\sigma^2/2)(f^2 + Sf_S - f).$$

Since $I(S, t) = I(S_0, t) + \int_{S_0}^{S} I_S(x, t)\, dx$ and f satisfies the PDE (7), we have

$$I(S,t) = I(S_0,t) + \int_{S_0}^{S} \Bigg(rf_S(x,t) + \sigma(x,t)\sigma_S(x,t) \times (f^2(x,t) + xf_S(x,t) - f(x,t)) + \frac{\sigma(x,t)^2}{2}(2f(x,t)f_S(x,t) + xf_{SS}(x,t)) \Bigg) dx$$

$$= I(S_0,t) - \int_{S_0}^{S} \frac{f_t(x,t)}{x}\, dx.$$

Substituting $I(S, t)$ into (A2), we get

$$dg(S(t), t) = d \ln \xi(t) - I(S_0, t)\, dt.$$

Integrating both sides, we find

$$g(S(T), T) = \ln \xi(T) - \int_0^T I(S_0, t)\, dt.$$

This completes our proof. ■

References

Bick, A., 1990, "On Viable Diffusion Price Processes of the Market Portfolio," *Journal of Finance*, 45, 673–689.

Black, F., and M. Scholes, 1973, "The Pricing of Options and Corporate Liabilities," *Journal of Political Economy*, 81, 637–659.

Breeden, D., 1979, "An Intertemporal Asset Pricing Model with Stochastic Consumption and Investment Opportunities," *Journal of Financial Economics*, 7, 265–296.

Breeden, D., and R. Litzenberger, 1979, "Prices of State-Contingent Claims Implicit in Option Prices," *Journal of Business*, 51, 621–651.

Brennan, M., 1979, "The Pricing of Contingent Claims in Discrete Time Models," *Journal of Finance*, 34, 53–68.

Constantinides, G., 1982, "Intertemporal Asset Pricing with Heterogenous Consumers and without Demand Aggregation," *Journal of Business*, 55, 253–267.

Cox, J., and C. Huang, 1989, "Optimal Consumption and Portfolio Policies When Asset Prices Follow a Diffusion Process," *Journal of Economic Theory*, 49, 33–83.

Cox, J., J. Ingersoll, and S. Ross, 1985, "An Intertemporal General Equilibrium Model of Asset Prices," *Econometrica*, 53, 363–384.

Cox, J., and H. Leland, 1982, "On Dynamic Investment Strategies," *Proceedings of Seminar on the Analysis of Security Prices*, Center for Research in Security Prices (CRSP), Graduate School of Business, University of Chicago, 139–173.

Dybvig, P., and C. Huang, 1988, "Nonnegative Wealth, Absence of Arbitrage, and Feasible Consumption Plans," *Review of Financial Studies*, 1, 377–401.

Friedman, A., 1975, *Stochastic Differential Equations and Applications*, Academic Press, New York.

Friedman, A., 1976, *Partial Differential Equations*, Krieger, New York.

Gennotte, G., and T. Marsh, 1993, "Variations in Economic Uncertainty and Risk Premiums on Capital Assets"; forthcoming in *European Economic Review.*

Gilman, I., and A. Skorohod, 1972, *Stochastic Differential Equations,* Springer-Verlag, New York.

Harrison, M., and D. Kreps, 1979, "Martingale and Multiperiod Securities Markets," *Journal of Economic Theory,* 20, 381–408.

Hansen, L., 1982, "Large Sample Properties of Generalized Method of Moments Estimators," *Econometrica,* 50, 1029–1054.

Harvey, C., 1989, "Time-Varying Conditional Covariances in Tests of Asset Pricing Models," *Journal of Financial Economics,* 24, 289–317.

He, H., and H. Leland, 1992, "Equilibrium Asset Price Processes," working paper, University of California at Berkeley.

Hodges, S., and A. Carverhill, 1991, "The Characterization of Economic Equilibria Which Support Black-Scholes Option Pricing," Financial Options Research Centre, University of Warwick, forthcoming in *Economic Journal.*

Huang, C., 1987, "An Intertemporal General Equilibrium Asset Pricing Model: The Case of Diffusion Information," *Econometrica,* 55, 117–142.

Karatzas, I., and S. Shreve, 1988, *Brownian Motion and Stochastic Calculus,* Springer-Verlag, New York.

Kevorkian, J., 1990, *Partial Differential Equations: Analytical Solution Techniques,* Wadsworth, Belmont, CA.

Kreps, D., 1981, "Arbitrage and Equilibrium in Economies with Infinitely Many Commodities," *Journal of Mathematical Economics,* 8, 15–35.

Merton, R., 1971, "Optimal Consumption and Portfolio Rules in a Continuous Time Model," *Journal of Economic Theory,* 3, 373–413.

Merton, R., 1973, "An Intertemporal Capital Asset Pricing Model," *Econometrica,* 41, 867–887.

Rubinstein, M., 1976, "The Valuation of Uncertain Income Streams and the Pricing of Options," *Bell Journal of Economics,* 7, 407–425.

Wang, S., 1991, "The Integrability Problem of Asset Prices"; forthcoming in *Journal of Economic Theory.*

Part IV
Derivative Pricing

[16]

Journal of Financial Economics 5 (1977) 241–249. © North-Holland Publishing Company

ON THE PRICING OF CONTINGENT CLAIMS AND THE MODIGLIANI–MILLER THEOREM*

Robert C. MERTON

Sloan School of Management, M.I.T., Cambridge, MA 02139, U.S.A.

Received July 1977, revised version received August 1977

A general formula is derived for the price of a security whose value under specified conditions is a known function of the value of another security. Although the formula can be derived using the arbitrage technique of Black and Scholes, the alternative approach of continuous-time portfolio strategies is used instead. This alternative derivation allows the resolution of some controversies surrounding the Black and Scholes methodology. Specifically, it is demonstrated that the derived pricing formula must be continuous with continuous first derivatives, and that there is not a 'pre-selection bias' in the choice of independent variables used in the formula. Finally, the alternative derivation provides a direct proof of the Modigliani–Miller theorem even when there is a positive probability of bankruptcy.

1. Introduction

The theory of portfolio selection in continuous-time has as its foundation two assumptions: (1) the capital markets are assumed to be open at all times, and therefore, economic agents have the opportunity to trade continuously and (2) the stochastic processes generating the state variables can be described by diffusion processes with continuous sample paths.[1] If these assumptions are accepted, then the continuous-time model can be used to derive equilibrium security prices.[2] The pricing formulas derived by this method will in general require as minimum inputs estimates of the price of risk, the covariance of the security's cash flows with the market, and the expected cash flows. These numbers are difficult to estimate. However, it is not always necessary to have these numbers to price a security.

*The paper is a substantial revision of parts of Merton (1976) presented in seminars at Yale and Brown Universities in April 1976 and at the EIASM Workshop in Management Science, Bergamo, Italy in October 1976. I thank the participants for their helpful comments. Aid from the National Science Foundation is gratefully acknowledged. My thanks to the referee for editorial suggestions.

[1]For references to the mathematics of diffusion processes and their applications in economics, see the bibliographies in Merton (1971) and (1973b).

[2]See Merton (1973a) and (1975).

In a seminal paper, Black and Scholes (1973) used the continuous-time analysis to derive a formula for pricing common stock call options.[3] Although their derivation uses the same assumptions and analytical tools used in the continuous-time portfolio analysis, the resulting formula expressed in terms of the price of the underlying stock does not require as inputs expected returns, expected cash flows, the price of risk, or the covariance of the returns with the market. In effect, all these variables are implicit in the stock's price. Because expected returns and market covariances are not part of the inputs, the Black–Scholes evaluation formula is robust with respect to a reasonable amount of heterogeneity of expectations among investors, and because the required inputs are for the most part observable, the formula is testable. All of this has created substantial interest in extending their analysis to the evaluation of other types of securities.

The essential reason that the Black–Scholes pricing formula requires so little information as inputs is that the call option is a security whose value on a specified future date is uniquely determined by the price of another security (the stock). As such, a call option is an example of a *contingent claim*. While call options are very specialized financial instruments, Black and Scholes and others[4] recognized that the same analysis could be applied to the pricing of corporate liabilities generally where such liabilities were viewed as claims whose values were contingent on the value of the firm. Moreover, whenever a security's return structure is such that it can be described as a contingent claim, the same technique is applicable.

In section 2 of this paper, I derive a general formula for the price of a security whose value under specified conditions is a known function of the value of another security. Although the formula can be derived using the arbitrage technique employed by Merton (1974) to derive the price of risky debt, an alternative approach is used to demonstrate that the resulting formula will obtain even if institutional restrictions prohibit arbitrage.

Because the formula is often used to evaluate corporate liabilities as a function of the value of the firm, it is important to know conditions under which the value of the firm will not be affected by the form of its capital structure. In section 3, the Modigliani–Miller Theorem (1958) that the value of the firm is invariant to its capital structure is extended to the case where there is a positive probability of bankruptcy.

[3]A call option gives its owner the right to buy a specified number of shares of a given stock at a specified price (the 'exercise price') on or before a specified date (the 'expiration date').

[4]The literature based on the Black–Scholes analysis has expanded so rapidly that rather than attempt to list individual published articles and works-in-progress, I refer the reader to a survey article by Smith (1976).

2. A general derivation of a contingent claim price

To develop the contingent-claim pricing model, I make the following assumptions:

(A.1) *'Frictionless markets'*

There are no transactions costs or taxes. Trading takes place continuously in time. Borrowing and shortselling are allowed without restriction. The borrowing rate equals the lending rate.

(A.2) *Riskless asset*

There is a riskless asset whose rate of return per unit time is known and constant over time. Denote this return rate by r.

(A.3) *Asset #1*

There is a risky asset whose value at any point in time is denoted by $V(t)$. The dynamics of the stochastic process generating $V(\ )$ over time is assumed to be describable by a diffusion process with a formal stochastic differential equation representation of

$$\mathrm{d}V = [\alpha V - D_1(V, t)]\mathrm{d}t + \sigma V \mathrm{d}Z,$$

where α = instantaneous expected rate of return on the asset per unit time; σ^2 = instantaneous variance per unit time of the rate of return; $D_1(V, t)$ = instantaneous payout to the owners of the asset per unit time; $\mathrm{d}Z \equiv$ standard Wiener process; α can be generated by a stochastic process of a quite general type, and σ^2 is restricted to be at most a function of V and t.

(A.4) *Asset #2*

There is a second risky asset whose value at any date t is denoted by $W(t)$ with the following properties: For $0 \leq t < T$, its owners will receive an instantaneous payout per unit time, $D_2(V, t)$. For any $t(0 \leq t < T)$, if $V(t) = \overline{V}(t)$, then the value of the second asset is given by: $W(t) = f[\overline{V}(t), t]$, where f is a known function. For any $t(0 \leq t < T)$, if $V(t) = \underline{V}(t)$, then the value of the second asset is given by $[\underline{V}(t) < \overline{V}(t)]$: $W(t) = g[\underline{V}(t), t]$, where g is a known function. For $t = T$, the value of the second asset is given by: $W(T) = h[V(T)]$. Asset #2 will be called a contingent claim, contingent on the value of Asset #1.

(A.5) *Investor preferences and expectations*

It is assumed that investors prefer more to less. It is assumed that investors agree upon σ^2, but it is *not* assumed that they necessarily agree on α.

(A.6) *Other*

There can be as many or as few other assets or securities as one likes. Market prices need not be general equilibrium prices. The constant interest rate and most of the 'frictionless' market assumptions are not essential to the development of the model but are chosen for expositional convenience. The critical assumptions are continuous-trading opportunities and the dynamics description for Asset #1.

If it is assumed that the value of Asset #2 can be written as a twice-continuously differentiable function of the price of Asset #1 and time, then the pricing formula for Asset #2 can be derived by the same procedure used in Merton (1974, pp. 451–453) to derive the value of risky debt. If $W(t) = F[V(t), t]$ for $0 \leq t \leq T$ and for $\underline{V}(t) \leq V(t) \leq \overline{V}(t)$, then to avoid arbitrage, F must satisfy the linear partial differential equation

$$0 = \tfrac{1}{2}\sigma^2 V^2 F_{11} + [rV - D_1]F_1 - rF + F_2 + D_2, \tag{1}$$

where subscripts on F denote partial derivatives with respect to its two explicit arguments, V and t. Inspection of (1) shows that in addition to V and t, F will depend on σ^2 and r. However, F does *not* depend on the expected return on Asset #1, α, and it does *not* depend on the characteristics of other assets available in the economy. Moreover, investors' preferences do not enter the equation either.

To solve (1), boundary conditions must be specified. From (A.4), we have that

$$F[\overline{V}(t), t] = f[\overline{V}(t), t], \tag{2a}$$

$$F[\underline{V}(t), t] = g[\underline{V}(t), t], \tag{2b}$$

$$F[V, T] = h[V]. \tag{2c}$$

While the functions f, g, and h are required to solve for F, they are generally deducible from the terms of the specific contingent claim being priced. For example, the original case examined by Black and Scholes is a common stock call option with an exercise price of E dollars and an expiration date of T. If V is the value of the underlying stock, then the boundary conditions can be written as

$$F/V \leq 1 \quad \text{as} \quad V \to \infty, \tag{3a}$$

$$F[0, t] = 0, \tag{3b}$$

$$F[V, T] = \text{Max}\,[0, V - E], \tag{3c}$$

where (3a) is a regularity condition which replaces the usual boundary condition when $\overline{V}(t) = \infty$. Both (3a) and (3b) follow from limited liability and from the easy-to-prove condition that the underlying stock is always more valuable than the option. (3c) follows from the terms of the call option which establish the exact price relationship between the stock and option on the expiration date.[5]

Hence, (1) together with (2a)–(2c) provide the general equation for pricing contingent claims. Moreover, if the contingent claim is priced according to (1) and (2), then it follows that there is no opportunity for intertemporal arbitrage. I.e., the relative prices (W, V, r) are intertemporally consistent.

Suppose there exists a twice-continuously differentiable solution to (1) and (2). Because the derivation of (1) used the *assumption* that the pricing function satisfies this condition, it is possible that some other solution exists which does not satisfy this differentiability condition. Indeed, in discussing the Black–Scholes solution to the call option case, Smith[6] points out that there are an infinite number of continuous solutions to eqs. (1) and (3) which have discontinuous derivatives at only one interior point although the Black–Scholes solution is the only solution with continuous derivatives. He goes on to state 'the economics of the option pricing problem would suggest that the solution be continuous, but there is no obvious argument that it be differentiable everywhere'.

The following alternative derivation is a direct proof that if a twice-continuously differential solution to (1) and (2) exists, then to rule out arbitrage, it must be the pricing function.

Let F be the formal twice-continuously differentiable solution to eq. (1) with boundary conditions (2). Consider the continuous-time portfolio strategy where the investor allocates the fraction $w(t)$ of his portfolio to Asset #1 and $[1-w(t)]$ to the riskless asset. Moreover, let the investor make net 'withdrawals' per unit time (for example, for consumption) of $C(t)$. If $C(t)$ and $w(t)$ are right-continuous functions and $P(t)$ denotes the value of the investor's portfolio, then I have shown elsewhere[7] that the dynamics for the value of the portfolio, P, will satisfy the stochastic differential equation

$$\mathrm{d}P = \{[w(\alpha-r)+r]P-C\}\mathrm{d}t+w\sigma P\mathrm{d}Z. \tag{4}$$

Suppose we pick the particular portfolio strategy with

$$w(t) = F_1[V, t]V(t)/P(t), \tag{5}$$

where F_1 is the partial derivative of F with respect to V, and the 'consumption'

[5]In some cases, either $\bar{V}(t)$ or $\underline{V}(t)$ must be determined simultaneously with the solution of eq. (1) for F. Two examples are the American call and put options on a dividend-paying stock with the potential for early exercise. In such cases, there is usually an additional boundary condition imposed on the derivative of F which allows just enough 'over-specification' to determine $\bar{V}$. See Merton (1973b, pp. 173–174) for discussion. The structural definition of Asset #2 can be easily adjusted to include these cases.

[6]See Smith (1976, p. 23, footnote 21).

[7]See Merton (1971, p. 379).

strategy,

$$C(t) = D_2(V, t). \tag{6}$$

By construction, F_1 is continuously-differentiable, and hence is a right-continuous function. Substituting from (5) and (6) into (4), we have that

$$\mathrm{d}P = F_1\mathrm{d}V + \{F_1(D_1 - rV) + rP - D_2\}\mathrm{d}t, \tag{7}$$

where $\mathrm{d}V$ is given in (A.3).

Since F is twice-continuously differentiable, we can use Ito's Lemma[8] to express the stochastic process for F as

$$\mathrm{d}F = [\tfrac{1}{2}\sigma^2 V^2 F_{11} + (\alpha V - D_1)F_1 + F_2]\mathrm{d}t + F_1\sigma V\mathrm{d}Z. \tag{8}$$

But F satisfies eq. (1). Hence, we can rewrite (8) as

$$\mathrm{d}F = F_1\mathrm{d}V + \{F_1(D_1 - rV) + rF - D_2\}\mathrm{d}t. \tag{9}$$

Let $Q(t) \equiv P(t) - F[V(t), t]$. Then, from (7) and (9), we have that

$$\begin{aligned} \mathrm{d}Q &= \mathrm{d}P - \mathrm{d}F \\ &= r(P - F)\mathrm{d}t \\ &= rQ\mathrm{d}t. \end{aligned} \tag{10}$$

But, (10) is a non-stochastic differential equation with solution

$$Q(t) = Q(0)\mathrm{e}^{rt}, \tag{11}$$

for any time t and where $Q(0) \equiv P(0) - F[V(0), 0]$. Suppose the initial amount invested in the portfolio, $P(0)$, is chosen equal to $F[V(0), 0]$. Then from (11) we have that

$$P(t) = F[V(t), t]. \tag{12}$$

By construction, the value of Asset #2, $W(t)$, will equal F at the boundaries $\underline{V}(t)$ and $\overline{V}(t)$ and at the termination date T. Hence, from (12), the constructed portfolio's value, $P(t)$, will equal $W(t)$ at the boundaries. Moreover, the interim 'payments' or withdrawals available to the portfolio strategy, $D_2[V(t), t]$, are identical to the interim payments made to Asset #2.

[8]See Merton (1971) for a discussion of Itô's Lemma and stochastic differential equations.

Therefore, if $W(t) > P(t)$, then the investor could short-sell Asset #2; proceed with the prescribed portfolio strategy including all interim payments; and be guaranteed a positive return on zero investment. I.e., there would be an arbitrage opportunity. If $W(t) < P(t)$, then the investor could essentially 'short-sell' the prescribed portfolio strategy; use the proceeds to buy Asset #2; and again be guaranteed a positive return on zero investment. If institutional restrictions prohibit arbitrage,[9] then a similar argument can be applied using the principle that no security should be priced so as to 'dominate' another security.[10] Hence, $W(t)$ must equal $F[V(t), t]$.

While this method of proof may appear to be very close to the original derivation, unlike the original derivation, it does not *assume* that the dynamics of Asset #2 can be described by an Ito process, and therefore, it does not assume that Asset #2 has a smooth pricing function. Indeed, the portfolio stategy described by (5) and (6) involves only combinations of Asset #1 and the riskless asset, and therefore, does not even require that Asset #2 exists! The connection between the portfolio strategy and Asset #2 is that if Asset #2 exists, then the price of Asset #2 must equal $F[V(t), t]$, or else, there will be an opportunity for intertemporal arbitrage.

Not only does this alternative derivation provide the 'obvious argument' why such pricing functions must be differentiable everywhere, but it also can be used to resolve other issues that have been raised about results derived using this type of analysis. In the next section, two of the more important issues are resolved.

3. On the Modigliani–Miller theorem with bankruptcy

In an earlier paper (1974, p. 460), I proved that in the absence of bankruptcy costs and corporate taxes, the Modigliani–Miller theorem (1958) obtains even in the presence of bankruptcy. In a comment on this earlier paper, Long (1974) has asserted that my method of proof was 'logically incoherent'. Rather than debate over the original proof's validity, the method of derivation used in the previous section provides an immediate alternative proof.

Let there be a firm with two corporate liabilities: (1) a single homogeneous debt issue and (2) equity. The debt issue is promised a continuous coupon payment per unit time, C, which continues until either the maturity date of the bond, T, or until the total assets of the firm reach zero. The firm is prohibited by the debt indenture from issuing additional debt or paying dividends. At the maturity date, there is a promised principal payment of B to the debtholders. In the event the payment is not made, the firm is defaulted to the debtholders, and the equityholders receive nothing. If $S(t)$ denotes the value of the firm's equity and

[9] One example would be restrictions on short-sales.

[10] See Merton (1973b, p. 143) and Smith (1976, p. 7) for a discussion of 'dominance' in this context.

$D(t)$ the value of the firm's debt, then the value of the (levered) firm, $V_L(t)$, is identically equal to $S(t)+D(t)$. Moreover, in the event that the total assets of the firm reach zero, $V_L(t) = S(t) = D(t) = 0$ by limited liability. Also, by limited liability, $D(t)/V_L(t) \leq 1$.

Consider a second firm with initial assets and an investment policy identical to those of the levered firm. However, the second firm is all-equity financed with total value equal to $V(t)$. To ensure the identical investment policy including scale, it follows from the well-known accounting identity that the net payout policy of the second firm must be the same as for the first firm. Hence, let the second firm have a dividend policy that pays dividends of C per unit time until either date T or until the value of its total assets reach zero (i.e., $V = 0$). Let the dynamics of the firm's value be as posited in (A.3) where $D_1(V, t) = C$ for $V > 0$ and $D_1 = 0$ for $V = 0$.

Let $F[V, t]$ be the formal twice-continuously differentiable solution to eq. (1) subject to the boundary conditions: $F[0, t] = 0$; $F[V, t]/V \leq 1$; and $F[V(T), T] = \text{Min}\,[V(T), B]$. Consider the dynamic portfolio strategy of investing in the all-equity firm and the riskless asset according to the 'rules' (5) and (6) of section 2 where $C(t)$ is taken equal to C. If the total initial amount invested in the portfolio, $P(0)$, is equal to $F[V(0), 0]$, then from (12), $P(t) = F[V(t), t]$.

Because both the levered firm and the all-equity firm have identical investment policies including scale, it follows that $V(t) = 0$ if and only if $V_L(t) = 0$. And it also follows that on the maturity date T, $V_L(T) = V(T)$.

By the indenture conditions on the levered firm's debt, $D(T) = \text{Min}\,[V_L(T), B]$. But since $V(T) = V_L(T)$ and $P(T) = F[V(T), T]$, it follows that $P(T) = D(T)$. Moreover, since $V_L(t) = 0$ if and only if $V(t) = 0$, it follows that $P(t) = F[0, t] = D(t) = 0$ in that event.

Thus, by following the prescribed portfolio strategy, one would receive interim payments exactly equal to those on the debt of the levered firm. Moreover, on a specified future date, T, the value of the portfolio will equal the value of the debt. Hence, to avoid arbitrage or dominance, $P(t) = D(t)$.

The proof for equity follows along similar lines. Let $f[V, t]$ be the formal solution to eq. (1) subject to the boundary conditions: $f[0, t] = , f[V, t]/V \leq 1$; and $f[V(T), T] = \text{Max}\,[0, V(T)-B]$. Consider the dynamic portfolio strategy of investing in the all-equity firm and the riskless asset according to the 'rules' (5) and (6) of section 2 where $C(t)$ is now taken equal to zero. If the total initial amount invested in this portfolio, $p(0)$, is equal to $f[V(0), 0]$, then from (12), $p(t) = f[V(t), t]$.

As with debt, if $V(t) = 0$, then $p(t) = S(t) = 0$, and at the maturity date, $p(T) = \text{Max}\,[0, V(T)-B] = S(T)$.

Thus, by following this prescribed portfolio strategy, one would receive the same interim payments as those on the equity of the levered firm. On the maturity date, the value of the portfolio will equal the value of the levered firm's equity. Therefore, to avoid arbitrage or dominance, $p(t) = S(t)$.

If one were to combine both portfolio strategies, then the resulting interim payments would be C per unit time with a value at the maturity date of $V(T)$. I.e., both strategies together are the same as holding the equity of the unlevered firm. Hence, $f[V(t), t]+F[V(t), t] = V(t)$. But it was shown that $f[V(t), t]+F[V(t), t] = S(t)+D(t) \equiv V_L(t)$. Therefore, $V_L(t) = V(t)$, and the proof is completed.

While the proof was presented in the traditional context of a firm with a single debt issue, the proof goes through in essentially the same fashion for multiple debt issues or for 'hybrid securities' such as convertible bonds, preferred stock, or warrants.[11]

In his comment on my earlier paper Long (1974, p. 485) claims that the original derivation builds into the model that risky debt can only depend on the 'prespecified explanatory variables'. His point is that in fact, bond prices could depend on 'the price of beer'; 'the value of the market portfolio'; or 'the rate of inflation', but by assuming that the bond price depends only on the value of the firm, the market rate of interest, the volatility of the market value of the firm, and time until maturity, the derived model price rules out such additional dependencies. The derivation in section 2 did not assume that the value of Asset #2 depends only on these prespecified variables. The assumptions used are only the stated ones (A.1)–(A.6). Hence, given the current values of Asset #1, the only way that the price of beer, the market portfolio, or the rate of inflation can affect the price of Asset #2 is if they affect σ^2, r, or the boundary conditions. While it could be argued that *in fact*, σ^2 and r may depend on these other variables, such an argument would simply be a criticism of assumptions (A.2) and (A.3), and not of the derivation itself.

[11]In more complicated bond indentures, the restrictions may be in terms of accounting variables rather than market values. In such cases, the analysis requires that these accounting variables can be written as functions of the market values.

References

Black, F. and M. Scholes, 1973, The pricing of options and corporate liabilities, Journal of Political Economy 81, 637–659.

Long, J.B., 1974, Discussion, Journal of Finance 29, 485–488.

Merton, R.C., 1971, Optimum consumption and portfolio rules in a continuous-time model, Journal of Economic Theory 3, 373–413.

Merton, R.C., 1973a, An intertemporal capital asset pricing model, Econometrica 41, 867–887.

Merton, R.C., 1973b, Theory of rational option pricing, Bell Journal of Economics and Management Science 4, 141–183.

Merton, R.C., 1974, On the pricing of corporate debt: The risk structure of interest rates, Journal of Finance 29, 449–470.

Merton, R.C., 1975, Theory of finance from the perspective of continuous time, Journal of Financial and Quantitative Analysis, 659–674.

Merton, R.C., 1976, Continuous-time portfolio theory and the pricing of contingent claims, Working Paper no. 881–76 (Sloan School of Management, M.I.T., Cambridge, MA).

Miller, M. and F. Modigliani, 1958, The cost of capital, corporation finance and the theory of investment, American Economic Review 48.

Smith, C.W., Jr., 1976, Option pricing: A review, Journal of Financial Economics 3, 3–51.

[17]

Journal of Financial Economics 5 (1977) 251–258. © North-Holland Publishing Company

AN ANALYTIC VALUATION FORMULA FOR UNPROTECTED AMERICAN CALL OPTIONS ON STOCKS WITH KNOWN DIVIDENDS

Richard ROLL*

Graduate School of Management, University of California, Los Angeles, CA 90024, U.S.A.

Received April 1977, revised version received September 1977

Sometimes it pays to exercise an American-type call option prematurely, just prior to a cash emission by the underlying security. Such an option can be expressed as a combination of three European-type options whose valuation formulae are known.

The unprotected American call written against a dividend-paying stock is the predominant actively-traded option. On the C.B.O.E., call options have no contracted 'protection' against the stock price decline that occurs when a dividend is paid. Thus, there is an important deficiency in option pricing theory in terms of its empirical applicability. All known valuation formulae assume an absence of dividends [Black–Scholes (1973)], or a continuous dividend generating process [Merton (1973), Geske (1975)], or else require numerical solution [Schwartz (1977)]. Furthermore, the original Black–Scholes formula is known to give biased predictions of market prices [see Black (1975, p. 64)]; and the bias is widely believed to be related at least partly to the dividend problem.

This note amends the theory by presenting a simple revised formula that could apply to many empirical situations and that can be extended to more complex situations with ease.

The notation is the standard proposed by Smith (1976):

$c(S,T,X)$, the market value of a European call option,
$C(S,T,X)$, the market value of an American call option,
S, the current stock price, net of escrowed dividend (S_τ is the stock price after τ periods),
T, the time until expiration,
X, the exercise price,
r, the riskless (and constant) rate of interest, continuously compounded,
σ^2, the variance rate of the return on S.

*Many useful comments and suggestions by Charles Davidson, Robert Geske, David Mayers and Stephen Ross are gratefully acknowledged.

Assuming that the stock pays no dividend and that its price follows a lognormal diffusion process, Black and Scholes used an arbitrage argument in a no-tax world to obtain their well-known analytic formula for c (which depends only on S, T, X, σ^2, and r). Other work has relaxed the diffusion process assumption [Cox and Ross (1976), Merton (1976), and Rubinstein (1977)], the constant riskless rate assumption [Merton (1973)], and the tax assumption [Ingersoll (1976, pp. 109–112)]. Smith (1976) gives a lucid review of some of this work.

When the stock pays no dividends, Merton has shown that the American and European call options have equal value because the American option will never be exercised before maturity. When dividends are paid, however, the American call can be worth more than the European because there is a non-zero probability of early exercise.

Let the stock's dividend history be described by the following additional assumptions:

D, a dividend of known size, will be paid to each shareholder with certainty.

t is the known time until the ex-dividend instant ($t < T$). At t, the stock has just gone ex-dividend.

α is the known decline in the stock price at the ex-dividend instant as a proportion of the dividend.

No other dividend will be paid before T has elapsed.

If the dividend is certain, the total market value of the stock *cum* dividend cannot follow a lognormal process; for there would then be some chance that the dividend could not be paid. This difficulty is easily and sensibly resolved by defining the 'stock price', S, as the total market price, P, less the discounted escrowed dividend; i.e., for any $\tau < t$, $S_\tau = P_\tau - \alpha D e^{-r(t-\tau)}$ and for $\tau \geq t$, $S_\tau = P_\tau$. Note that the variance rate σ^2 applies to the process described by S.

At the instant before the stock goes ex-dividend, the American option holder observes that his option would be worth $c(S_t, T-t, X)$ an instant later if he allows it to remain unexercised. (Just after the ex-dividend date, the American and European options have equal value since no additional dividends will be paid before expiration.) If he exercises just before t, however, he will receive $S_t + \alpha D - X$. But we know from the Black–Scholes formula that c is bounded from below and is asymptotic to the lower bound for increasing stock price; i.e.,

$$\lim_{S\to\infty} c(S, T-t, X) = S_t - Xe^{-r(T-t)}.$$

Thus, if $\alpha D > X[1 - e^{-r(T-t)}]$, there exists some finite ex-dividend stock price above which the American option will be exercised just before t. Early exercise is more likely the larger the dividend, the higher the stock price relative to the exercise price (the more 'deeply-in-the-money' the option), and the shorter the time period between expiration and dividend payment dates.[1] Generally speaking whether or not an American call option will be exercised just an instant before the stock goes ex-dividend depends on the value of a European option just an instant after. Fig. 1 illustrates this with the well known chart of option price versus stock price at time *t*.

An example of these circumstances occurred in October 1976 when General Motors declared a three-dollar dividend to be paid to stockholders of record on November 4. The in-the-money option maturing in January ($X = \$60$, $T = 2$ months), was quoted for sale at near $P-X$ for a week before the ex-dividend date. On the ex-dividend day, the option closed at $S-X+75¢$. This seemed to imply an option price decline of $16\frac{1}{2}\%$ in one day (accompanying the decline in

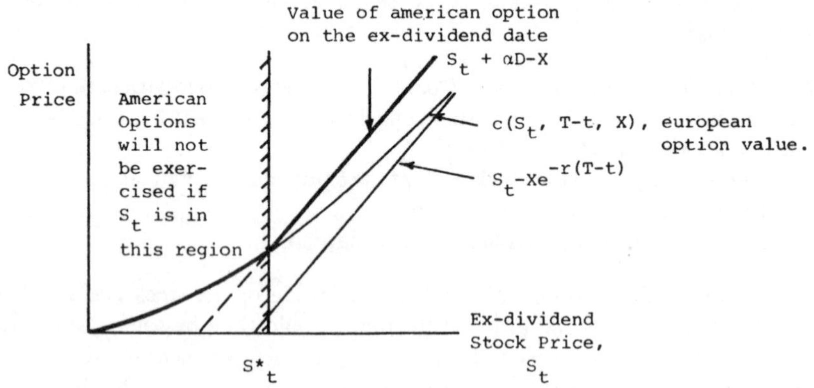

Fig. 1. American option value at the ex-dividend time.

P of about three dollars). The option price sequence was rational only if all of the outstanding options were exercised on November 3, new options having been written with the same exercise price and maturity date the next day. Only prices of newly-written options could have been quoted then. Notice that such large 'price declines' are easily forecastable but that they do not represent extraordinary profit opportunities for option writers.

Anytime *before* the ex-dividend date, the American option should reflect the probability that it will be exercised early. In fact, there is one very simple circumstance in which the unprotected option valuation formula can be given directly. The option may be so deeply in the money that the probability is nil that it won't be exercised early. Formally:

[1]For an alternative proof of the early exercise of an American call, see Smith (1976, pp. 13–14).

Proposition I. As $\text{Prob}(c_t < S_t + \alpha D - X) \to 1$, then an unprotected American option approaches the Black–Scholes valuation but with the ex-dividend date used in place of the option's contracted expiration date.[2]

The argument is rather obvious: Since the option is almost sure to be exercised an instant before t, t becomes its effective maturity. No dividend is paid before t so the Black–Scholes European formula applies, but over an interval shorter than the maturity stated on the option contract. Usually the probability will not be one, no matter how deeply-in-the-money an option may be.[3] In many practical situations, however, the probability may be so close to one that Proposition I gives a valuation whose error is within the bounds of transaction costs. Notice that this valuation formula would apply even with an uncertain dividend, provided that the dividend were known to be 'large' relative to $c - S + X$.

When Proposition I does not apply, similar reasoning can yield more general (but more complicated) results. We know the ex-dividend stock price above which the original American option will be exercised. It is the solution S_t^* to

$$c(S_t^*, T-t, X) = S_t^* + \alpha D - X. \tag{1}$$

This is the critical ingredient in the more general result. Note that S_t^* is different for each option whose contractual features are different.

Since the stock price S_t^* that separates the exercise and non-exercise regions on the ex-dividend date is known in advance,[4] a combination of hypothetical options can be constructed which match perfectly the contingencies faced by the original American option holder. Formally:

Proposition II. The value of an unprotected American call option with exercise price X, whose stock makes a single, certain dividend payment D after t periods and before the option's contracted expiration (which occurs after T periods) is the sum of the values of:

(a) a European call option on the stock with an exercise price of X and maturity T,

(b) plus a European call option on the stock with exercise price $S_t^* + \alpha D$ and maturity $t - \varepsilon$ ($\varepsilon > 0$, $\varepsilon \simeq 0$).

(c) minus a European call option on the option described under (a) with maturity of $t - \varepsilon$ and exercise price of $S_t^* + \alpha D - X$.

[2]This valuation was suggested first by Black (1975, pp. 41, 61) as the lower bound on the value of an unprotected American call.

[3]Except for option contracts with unusually small exercise prices or for liquidating dividends.

[4]Provided, of course, that the variance rate of the stock's return and the riskless rate of interest are known and constant. Schwartz (1977) mentioned this point and used the value of S^* in a numerical solution algorithm.

At the instant after the ex-dividend date, the cash receipts and net position are as follows.

For $S_t > S_t^*$,		For $S_t < S_t^*$,
Cash receipts are		Portfolio positions are
From	(a) 0	From (a) Open
	(b) $S_t+\alpha D-S_t^*-\alpha D$	(b) Expired
	(c) $S_t^*+\alpha D-X$	(c) Expired
Total	$S_t+\alpha D-X$ in cash	Option on S until T with exercise price X

If the ex-dividend stock price is above S_t^*, options (b) and (c) are exercised. This provides a net cash flow of $S_t+\alpha D-X$ and leaves the investor with no open options [option (a) being taken by the exercise of (c)]. If the ex-dividend price is below S_t^*, however, options (b) and (c) are allowed to expire unexercised and (a) remains alive. No cash is transferred at the ex-dividend date in this case.

In order to calculate the value of the American option, we merely need to value the sum of its three components. Component (b) is no problem since the Black–Scholes formula applies directly. As for component (a), the Black–Scholes formula also applies because the stock price drop on the ex-dividend date is known in advance.[5]

Component (c) presents the most difficult valuation problem. Fortunately, the recent work of Geske (1976) provides a solution as his compound option formula can be applied directly. The details are given in the appendix and examples of the resulting formula are plotted in fig. 2.

Caveats and generalizations

The present modification to the Black–Scholes formula does not explain all the empirical facts. For example, the modified American call value curve always lies below the original Black–Scholes curve, as fig. 2 shows, and this makes the Black–Scholes bias worse for deep out-of-the-money options. Geske (1976) is able to explain the upward price bias of out-of-the-money options by noting that the stock of a levered firm is itself an option on the firm's assets. Perhaps a combination of these two formulations would explain better the prices of unprotected American calls on dividend-paying, levered firms. Then again, there are other candidates for explanatory variables such as transaction costs, non-lognormal processes ruling the stock price, and uncertainty in dividends. In

[5]As demonstrated by Rubinstein (1977, pp. 419–420), the value of a *European* option can also be obtained under the more general condition that the dividend *yield* is a non-stochastic function of time.

this last regard, the stock price decline (α) on the ex-dividend date might be important. This decline is related to the capital gains/ordinary tax differential on personal income and to the 85 percent exclusion from corporate taxes of dividends. Conceivably, if the present modified formula were accurate, it could be used to estimate α for the next ex-dividend date, once the dividend is announced, and the marginal shareholder tax rate could thereby be deduced. (However, the slack in prices caused by trading costs would work against the accuracy of such an estimate.)

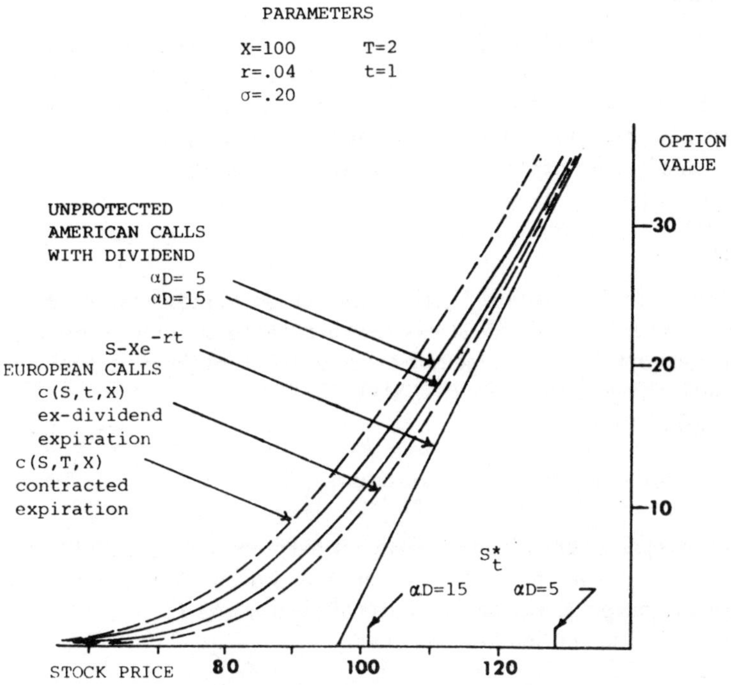

Fig. 2. Unprotected American call options with known dividends.

The basic solution can easily be generalized to cases where more than one future known cash payment will be made within the option's term. Two or more *known* successive dividends are rare for common stocks; but the generalization might apply to call options on corporate bonds or to prepayment options on standard mortgages (since the periodic cash payments are known throughout the lives of these contracts). To sketch the generalization, imagine a stock that has promised N successive known dividends. Between the $(N-1)$st and the Nth dividends, the American option on the stock would be valued by the formula in this paper. Before the $(N-1)$st dividend, a three part portfolio of options could again be constructed such that the contingencies were perfectly matched. This portfolio would consist of:

(a) a modified American option, valued by the formula in this paper, with the same parameters (X,T, plus the date and size of the Nth dividend),
(b) plus a European call on the stock with an exercise price of $S^{**}+\alpha D$ and maturity $t_{N-1}-\varepsilon$ [where S^{**} is the stock price above which the American option would be exercised at t_{N-1}, the date of the $(N-1)$st dividend],
(c) minus a European option on the option in (a) with maturity $t_{N-1}-\varepsilon$ and exercise price of $S^{**}+\alpha D-X$.

Of course, the resulting formulae would be more complex because there would now be an option (c) of an option of an option. For N payments, the final formulae would include an N-fold option of options. Conceptually, however, the generalization is straightforward. The only difficulty in obtaining the exact analytic formula seems to be the tedious algebra.

Appendix

According to Proposition II, the value of an unprotected American call option facing a known dividend payment is equal to the sum of three separate hypothetical options. This appendix presents details of the individual valuation expressions and gives the aggregate value.

Define the function q by

$$q(s,\tau,x) \equiv [\ln(s/x)+(r+\sigma^2/2)\tau]/\sigma\sqrt{\tau}.$$

Define $N(q)$ as the univariate standard normal probability distribution function (i.e., Prob $(y \leq q)$ where y is unit normal), and define $N(q,p)$ as the bivariate standard normal p.d.f. with correlation coefficient $+\sqrt{(t/T)}$.

Define S_t^* as the solution to

$$S_t^* N[q(S_t^*,T-t,X)]-X\mathrm{e}^{-r(T-t)}\,N[q(S_t^*,T-t,X)-\sigma\sqrt{(T-t)}]$$

$$-S_t^*-\alpha D+X = 0.$$

The values of components (a) and (b) in Proposition II are then given by the Black–Scholes formulae,

$$c_{\mathrm{a}} = SN[q(S,T,X)]-N[q(S,T,X)-\sigma\sqrt{T}]\mathrm{e}^{-rT}X,$$

and

$$c_{\mathrm{b}} = SN[q(S,t,S_t^*+\alpha D)]-(S_t^*+\alpha D)\,N[q(S,t,S_t^*+\alpha D)-\sigma\sqrt{t}]\mathrm{e}^{-rt},$$

and the value of component (c) is given by the Geske formula

$$c_c = SN[q(S,t,S_t^*), q(S,T,X)] - XN[q(S,t,S_t^*) - \sigma\sqrt{t}, q(S,T,X) - \sigma\sqrt{T}]e^{-rT} - (S_t^* + \alpha D - X)\, N[q(S,t,S_t^*) - \sigma\sqrt{t}]e^{-rt}.$$

The unprotected American call option would then have the value

$$c_a + c_b - c_c.$$

References

Black, F., 1975, Fact and fantasy in the use of options, Financial Analysts Journal 31, 36–41, 61–72.
Black, F. and M. Scholes, 1973, The pricing of options and corporate liabilities, Journal of Political Economy 81, 637–654.
Cox, J.C. and S. Ross, 1976, The valuation of options for alternative stochastic processes, Journal of Financial Economics 3, 145–166.
Geske, R., 1975, The pricing of options with stochastic dividend yield, Working Paper (University of California, Berkeley, CA).
Geske, R., 1976, The valuation of compound options, Working Paper (University of California, Berkeley, CA).
Ingersoll, J.E., Jr., 1976, A theoretical and empirical investigation of the dual purpose funds, Journal of Financial Economics 3, 83–123.
Merton, R.C., 1976, Option pricing when underlaying stock returns are discontinuous, Journal of Financial Economics 3, 125–144.
Merton, R.C., 1973, The theory of rational option pricing, Bell Journal of Economics and Management Science 4, 141–183.
Rubinstein, M., 1977, The valuation of uncertain income streams and the pricing of options, Bell Journal of Economics 7, 407–425.
Schwartz, E.S., 1977, The valuation of warrants: Implementing a new approach, Journal of Financial Economics 4, 79–93.
Smith, C.W., Jr., 1976, Option pricing: A review, Journal of Financial Economics 3, 3–51.

[18]

THE JOURNAL OF FINANCE · VOL. XXXIII, NO. 1 · MARCH 1978

THE VALUE OF AN OPTION TO EXCHANGE ONE ASSET FOR ANOTHER

WILLIAM MARGRABE*

I. INTRODUCTION

SOME COMMON FINANCIAL ARRANGEMENTS are equivalent to options to exchange one risky asset for another: the investment adviser's performance incentive fee, the general margin account, the exchange offer, and the standby commitment. Yet the literature does not discuss the theory of such an option.[1] In this paper, I develop an equation for the value of the option to exchange one risky asset for another. My theory grows out of the brilliant Black-Scholes (1973) solution to the longstanding call option pricing problem—which assumes that the price of a riskless discount bond grew exponentially at the riskless interest rate—and Merton's (1973) extension—in which the discount bond's value is stochastic until maturity.

In section II, I develop the pricing equation for a European-type option to exchange one asset for another. In section III, I show that such an option is worth more alive than dead, which implies that its owner will not exercise it until the last possible moment. Thus, the formula for the European option is also valid for its American counterpart. Since such an option is not only a call, but also a put, the formula is a closed-form expression for the value of a special sort of American put option. I derive the put-call parity theorem for American options of this sort. Section IV contains applications of the model to financial arrangements commonplace in the real world: the investment adviser's performance incentive fee, the general margin account, the exchange offer, and the standby commitment. In the last section, I summarize the findings.

II. THE MATHEMATICAL PROBLEM AND SOLUTION

Since this problem and its solution are extensions of the Black-Scholes work, I will use their notation and assumptions as much as possible. The capital market is perfect, of course. Let x_1 and x_2 be the prices of assets one and two. Assume there are no dividends: all returns come from capital gains. The rate of return on each asset is given by

$$dx_i = x_i[\alpha_i dt + v_i dz_i] \qquad (i = 1,2),$$

* Lecturer, Department of Finance, The Wharton School, University of Pennsylvania. The author thanks Stephen Ross, Jeffrey Jaffe, and Randolph Westerfield for helpful discussions; Sudipto Bhattacharya, a referee for this *Journal*, for useful comments; and the Rodney L. White Center for Financial Research for assistance in preparing the manuscript.

1. The Black-Scholes (1973) breakthrough spawned a burgeoning literature on the theory of option pricing—with applications. Smith (1976) comprehensively reviews these articles.

where dz_i is a Wiener process. That is, the rate of return is an "Ito process."[2] The correlation between the Wiener processes dz_1 and dz_2 is ρ_{12}. Further assume that α_i and v_i are constants.

We want the equation for the value $w(x_1,x_2,t)$ of a European-type option which can be exercised only at t^*, when it will yield $x_1 - x_2$ if exercised or nothing if not exercised. This option is simultaneously a call option on asset one with exercise price x_2 and a put option on asset two with exercise price x_1. Of course, the owner exercises his option if and only if this brings him a positive return. This implies the initial condition

$$w(x_1,x_2,t^*) = \max(0, x_1 - x_2). \tag{1}$$

The option is worth at least zero, and no more than x_1, if assets one and two are worth at least zero:

$$0 \leqslant w(x_1,x_2,t) \leqslant x_1. \tag{2}$$

The option buyer can hedge his position by selling $w_1 \equiv \partial w/\partial x_1$ units of asset one short and buying $-w_2 \equiv -\partial w/\partial x_2$ units of asset two. The pricing formula $w(\cdot)$ must be linear homogeneous in x_1 and x_2,[3] so the hedger's investment will be

$$w - w_1 x_1 - w_2 x_2 = 0, \tag{3}$$

by Euler's Theorem.

That investment equals zero may seem puzzling. But in this hedge, to eliminate risk we eliminate the entire return. Thus, the value of the hedged position must be nil.

The return on this investment over a short interval is nil:

$$dw - w_1 dx_1 - w_2 dx_2 = 0. \tag{4}$$

Black and Scholes (1973, p. 642) eliminate all risk, but not all the return. They convert a long position in the stock and a short position in the option into a riskless

2. See McKean (1969) for a discussion of the theory of Ito processes and Merton (1973a) and Fischer (1975) for applications.

3. First, consider the distribution of returns on an option to exchange asset two for asset one. This distribution of returns sells for $w(x_1,x_2,t)$.

Second, the distribution of returns on λ options to exchange asset two for asset one sells for $\lambda w(x_1,x_2,t)$ in a perfect market (where all participants are price takers).

Third, consider the distribution of returns of the option to exchange asset two for asset one, when both assets sell for λ times what they sold for in the first case. Denote this market value by $w(\lambda x_2, \lambda x_2, t)$.

The distribution of returns in the third case is identical to that given in the second case, given the Ito processes (described in paragraph one of section II) which generate prices x_1 and x_2. Thus, the returns in the second case must sell for the same as those in the third case:

$$\lambda w(x_1,x_2,t) = w(\lambda x_1, \lambda x_2, t).$$

Thus $w(\cdot)$ is linear homogeneous in x_1 and x_2. See also Merton (1973c, p. 149) on this point.

investment.[4] From the stochastic calculus,[5] the return on the option is

$$dw = w_1 dx_1 + w_2 dx_2 + w_3 dt + \tfrac{1}{2}\left[w_{11}v_1^2x_1^2 + 2w_{12}v_1v_2\rho_{12}x_1x_2 + w_{22}v_2^2x_2^2\right]dt, \tag{5}$$

where $w_3 = \partial w/\partial t$.

Equations (3) and (5) imply

$$w_3 + \tfrac{1}{2}\left[w_{11}v_1^2x_1^2 + 2w_{12}v_1v_2\rho_{12}x_1x_2 + w_{22}v_2^2x_2^2\right] = 0. \tag{6}$$

The function $w(x_1, x_2, t)$ is the solution to the differential equation (6), subject to the boundary conditions (2) and the initial condition (1):

$$w(x_1, x_2, t) = x_1 N(d_1) - x_2 N(d_2)$$
$$d_1 = \frac{\ln(x_1/x_2) + \frac{1}{2}v^2(t^* - t)}{v\sqrt{t^* - t}} \tag{7}$$
$$d_2 = d_1 - v\sqrt{t^* - t}\,.$$

Here, $N(\cdot)$ is the cumulative standard normal density function and $v^2 = v_1^2 - 2v_1v_2\rho_{12} + v_2^2$ is the variance of $(x_1/x_2)^{-1}d(x_1/x_2)$. ($v^2 = v_1^2$ if $v_2 = 0$, the Black-Scholes case.)

Equations (7) satisfy (6), (2), and (1), and are unique. The easiest way to prove this is to transform the problem at hand into the Black-Scholes problem. Let asset two be the numeraire.[6] Then the price of asset two in terms of itself is unity. The price of asset one is $x \equiv x_1/x_2$. The option sells for

$$w(x_1, x_2, t)/x_1 = w(x_1/x_2, 1, t).$$

The interest rate on a riskless loan denominated in units of asset two is zero in a perfect market. A lender of one unit of asset two demands one unit of asset two back as repayment of principle. He charges no interest on the loan, because asset

4. We can create a long (short) position in either underlying asset out of a short (long) position in the other asset and an appropriate position in the option to exchange the assets. According to equation (3):

$$x_1 = (w - w_2x_2)/w_1$$

and

$$x_2 = (w - w_1x_1)/w_2.$$

5. See McKean (1969). Merton (1973c, sec. 6) develops the same differential equation en route to his alternative derivation of the Black-Scholes model.

6. Stephen Ross suggested this lucid approach, which emphasizes the Black-Scholes heritage of this problem and its solution, and which lets us avoid much tedious mathematics. The student who wants to see all the mathematics can follow Merton's (1973c, sec. 6) solution to an isomorphic problem.

two's appreciation over the loan period is equilibrium compensation for the investment and risk.

Taking asset two as numeraire, the option to exchange asset two for asset one is a call option on asset one, with exercise price equal to unity and interest rate equal to zero. This is a special case of the Black-Scholes problem. Thus,

$$w(x_1,x_2,t)/x_2 = w(x,t)$$
$$\equiv (x_1/x_2)N(d_1) - 1\cdot e^{0(t-t^*)}N(d_2),$$

where $w(x,t)$ is the Black-Scholes formula. Equations (7) follow immediately.

The Black-Scholes model is also a special case of (7), where $x_2 = ce^{r(t-t^*)}$. The Merton (1973) model, which allows a stochastic interest rate, is also a special case, where $x_2 = cP(t^* - t)$, $P(t^* - t)$ is the stochastic value of a default-free discount bond maturing at t^*, and $P(0) = 1$. Thus, in Merton's model as in the Black-Scholes model, $x_2 = c$ at $t = t^*$.

III. Some Extensions

Equations (7) also give the value for American options, if x_1 and x_2 are equilibrium asset prices. The proof is simple. Consider two portfolios:

A: purchase a European option to exchange asset one for asset two;
B: purchase asset one and sell two short.

The values of the portfolios at any time t are

A: $w(x_1,x_2,t)$
B: $x_1 - x_2$.

The returns at t^* are

A: $\max(0, x_1^* - x_2^*)$
B: $x_1^* - x_2^*$.

The return on Portfolio A dominates that on B, so A must sell for at least as much as B:

$$w(x_1,x_2,t) \geqslant x_1 - x_2.$$

Thus, the value of a European option exceeds what you would get if you exercised a similar American option. So you will not exercise the American option early, and its value $W(x_1,x_2,t)$ will be exactly the same as that of a similar Eurorean option: $W(x_1,x_2,t) = w(x_1,x_2,t)$.

Recall that the option to exchange two assets can be viewed as a call on x_1 or a put on x_2, and that such an option is worth more alive than dead for $t < t^*$. This does not contradict Merton's (1973) conclusion that it may pay to exercise the ordinary American put option early. The exercise price for the ordinary American put is constant, not an asset price.

For the moment, assume as Black and Scholes did that the interest rate is known and constant. Then $ce^{r(t-t^*)}$ is the value of a default-free discount bond paying c at t^*. We know that an American option (whether a put or a call) with such an exercise price is worth more alive than dead. Then, equation (7) gives the formula for an American option (put or call) whose exercise price grows exponentially at the riskless interest rate and equals c at t^*.

Now, let $E(t)$ be the deterministic exercise price of the option, a function of time. Stipulate that $E(t^*)=c$. Any American call option with an exercise price $E(t) \geq ce^{r(t-t^*)}$ for $t<t^*$, must be worth the same as a European call option with exercise price c.[7] We know that an American call option with exercise price $E(t)=ce^{r(t-t^*)}$ is worth the same as the similar European option. Increasing the exercise price cannot increase the call option's value. Nor can increasing the exercise price decrease the option's value. The European call option has, in effect, an infinite exercise price until t^*. Yet, this option sells for as much as the American call option with exercise price growing exponentially at the instantaneous interest rate.

Similarly, an American put option with exercise price growing exponentially at the market interest rate until it reaches c at t^* will sell for the same as a European put option with exercise price c at t^*. If the American put option's exercise price is always less than or equal to $ce^{r(t-t^*)}$, then that American option is worth the same as a similar European option.

The preceding arguments imply a parity theorem[8] for European- and American-type put and call options whose common exercise price is the price of some asset. Consider two portfolios. The first portfolio contains an American call option on asset one with exercise price equal to the price of asset two, a short position in an American put on asset one with the same exercise price as the call, and asset two. The second portfolio contains asset one. We know that an American option is worth more alive than dead, if its exercise price is an asset price. So the American options are worth the same as European options and will not be exercised before the expiration date t^*. The holder of portfolio one will exchange asset two for asset one at t^*, in any event. Thus, portfolios one and two will have the same value at t^*. They must be worth the same at any time $t<t^*$, or arbitrage would occur. Hence, the usual put-call parity theorem holds for these options to exchange two assets. The reader can confirm that

$$w(x_1,x_2,t)-w(x_2,x_1,t)+x_2=x_1$$

and

$$W(x_1,x_2,t)-W(x_2,x_1,t)+x_2=x_1.$$

IV. Applications

The performance incentive fee, the margin account, the exchange offer, and the standby commitment are common arrangements which are also options to exchange one risky asset for another.

7. Merton (1973c, p. 155) proves a similar theorem for discrete changes in the exercise price.

8. Stoll (1969) states the theorem. Merton (1973b) shows that the theorem does not hold for ordinary American options.

A. *The Performance Incentive Fee*

Modigliani and Pogue (1975) opened the discussion of performance incentive fees of the form

$$\text{Fee} = \delta(R_1 - R_2) \tag{8}$$

for portfolio managers, where R_1 is the rate of return on the managed portfolio, R_2 is the rate of return on the standard against which performance is measured, and δ is a number of dollars. The number δ will usually fall between zero and the total that investors have invested in the managed portfolio. Margrabe (1976) proves that such a fee is worth nothing when entered into, in Sharpe-Lintner equilibrium.

This fee arrangement is valuable to the adviser if he can default on his obligation under the arrangement. The adviser could declare personal bankruptcy in case the fee were so negative that his net worth was negative. Or an investment adviser might form a corporation to handle his business and collect the fee. He would have the protection of limited liability in case the fee were negative. In such cases, the portfolio management fee is equivalent to an option. We can compute its value using equations (7).

For example, suppose the management corporation receives $10 million from its clients and invests it all. Management has no other assets. Management collects 10% of any superior performance of the managed portfolio over the standard and promises to pay its clients 10% of any inferior performance. (That is, $\delta = 1$ million.) Management plans to default if the managed portfolio does worse than the standard, and its clients know this. The fee arrangement lasts for six months. The monthly standard deviation of rate of return is 5% for the managed portfolio and 5% for the standard. The rates of return on the two portfolios are uncorrelated. Under these assumptions, the management corporation's option would be worth $690 thousand, and management would have to pay its investors for it to get their business.[9]

If management put up collateral to ensure its compliance with the fee agreement, it would be less likely to default and its option would be worth less. Equations (7) would still give the option value, though the calculations would be more tedious.

In order to prohibit abuse, the management contract may specify that the management cannot change the nature of the managed portfolio, without compensating the investors for the change. Management would never unilaterally end the contract, because its option is always worth more alive than dead. Investors may find it desirable to withdraw their funds early, if that is allowed. But, this would void the manager's option, so he would either rule out this possibility by contract or refuse to pay anything for the performance incentive fee.

B. *The Margin Account*

Suppose an investor buys securities worth x_1 on margin. (He borrows a fraction of the securities' cost from his broker, securing the loan with the portfolio of securities.) When the sum c of the principal amount and accrued interest is payable, he can either repay his debt and claim the collateral or default. If the

9. Evaluate equations (7) for $x_1 = x_2 = \$10$ million, $t^* - t = 6$, $v_1 = v_2 = .05$, and $\rho_{12} = 0$.

margin loan is his only liability and the collateral includes all his assets, he has an option on the collateral, where the striking price is c. Below, I discuss mainly this simple case.

One may not think of this as an option, because its life is so brief. When the securities markets are open, the broker monitors the value of the collateral for the margin loan. He may ask for more collateral if its value shrinks (this is the margin call). If the investor fails to put up more collateral immediately, the broker may sell off some of the collateral and reduce the investor's debit balance, until the remaining debit balance is adequately secured. If the collateral is dangerously small, the broker may sell some of it without notifying the investor.

If the broker measures the value of the collateral every t^*-t months, he has issued an option with a life of t^*-t. In this application t^*-t can grow arbitrarily small, at the broker's discretion. As t^*-t approaches zero, the option value approaches the net asset value of the account, x_1-c.

At the market's daily close the margin trader has a European option which expires when the markets reopen. He ordinarily exercises this option by borrowing the exercise price from the broker if the collateral is adequate. He may have to meet a margin call if the collateral is poor. He might let the option expire if the collateral were inadequate.

Sometimes the option lasts longer than the eighteen hours from the New York Stock Exchanges's daily close at 4:00 p.m. until the 10:00 a.m. reopening. When a holiday interrupts the business week, the option is for 42 hours. Over a normal weekend the option is for 66 hours. Over a three-day weekend the option is for 90 hours.

An investor might not exercise his option under exactly the circumstances implied by my analysis. I assume the investor holds all his non-human capital in his margin account. If the investor has other assets and liabilities, he may default when his net worth is negative. An investor might not default even if his net worth, as usually measured, was negative, if he thought the stigma of personal bankruptcy was horrible enough or would cause him sufficient future inconvenience.

If the margin trader sells a risky security short, his option is to exchange his risky short position for his risky long position. Equations (7) can tell us what this option is worth.

For example, consider two closed-end funds with the same systematic and nonsystematic risk ($\rho_{12}=1$ and $v_1=v_2=.05$, for monthly rates of return). An investor wants to finance the purchase of \$100,000 worth of shares in the first fund with a short sale of shares in the second.[10] The broker arranging this transaction will find it less risky than making a margin loan. In fact, the investor's option is worthless. In equilibrium the broker will demand less compensation for this sort of transaction than he would for selling securities on margin.

For other values of ρ_{12}, v_1 and v_2, the broker may find a short sale riskier. Suppose in the above example $\rho_{12}=-1$. Then the short sale and purchase would together be twice as risky as either one alone ($v=2v_1=2v_2$). The margin trader would be willing to pay some \$1433 for this option over a three-day weekend and the broker would not sell it for less.

10. Here we assume away regulations on short sales.

C. *The Exchange Offer*[11]

An exchange offer of shares in one unlevered corporation for shares in another presents shareholders in the offeree corporation with an option to exchange one type of share for another. For simplicity, let the price of a share in firm one, z_1, equal the price of a share in firm two, z_2. Firm one has N shares; firm two has n. Suppose firm one, the much larger firm, announces it will trade one of its shares for one of firm two's.[12] The offer, firm and uncontested by firm two's management, expires at t^*.

Further, assume this offer conveys no information about the prospects of either firm. Then the offer may increase the price of shares in the second firm, because these shareholders now have an option to exchange their shares for something else. This option is worth at least zero.

We can compute the *increase in* the value of a share in firm two, after the exchange offer is made, but before it expires: substitute the value of what a shareholder in firm two gets if he exercises his option,

$$x_1 = [(N-n)z_1 + nz_2]/N,$$

and the value of what he gives up,

$$x_2 = z_2$$

into equations (7). As usual, this option's value depends on the characteristics of the joint distribution of x_1 and x_2 and on the length of time until the option expires.

Under these circumstances, the management of firm one is acting against the best interest of its shareholders. Any gain to shareholders of firm two is a loss to shareholders in firm one, which grants the option. For, firm one is giving up this option in return for nothing. In a perfect market, a cash tender offer would be a similarly unwise move. (This says more about the stringent assumptions in this paper than about managerial irrationality.)

Management of the offering firm could charge shareholders of the offeree firm a premium for the right to tender a share of the offeree's stock. It would compensate the shareholders of the offering firm for the option they give up. This right would be valuable and might even trade apart from the stock to be tendered.

D. *The Standby Commitment*

The standby commitment is a put option on a forward contract in mortgage notes.[13] The buyer gets the option to sell a bundle of mortgage notes at a predetermined price. He must exercise his option on or before the notification date, some month(s) before the delivery date: if he exercises his option, he sells his

11. Ron Masulis suggested this application of the model.

12. Firm one will sell n/N of its (homogeneous) assets, use the proceeds to repurchase n shares, and trade the n shares for n shares in firm two.

13. Several types of standbyes exist. This section refers to the easiest type to analyze. The Federal National Mortgage Association offers types which do not fit this model. In this section we assume away problems associated with coupons on the mortgage notes. One can handle them as one handles dividend payments on stock.

mortgages in the forward market. Thus, the option is on a forward sale of mortgage notes. The commitment fee is the option premium.

We want to find the value at t of an option expiring at t^* on a forward contract calling for delivery at some later date t^{**}. Buyer will exercise his option at t^* (he won't exercise it earlier) if the value at t^* of his profit at t^{**} is positive. Define C as the striking price. $P(t)=P(t^{**},t)$ is the price at t of a riskless, discount bond maturing at t^{**}. Let $X(t)$ be the spot price for the underlying mortgage notes. Thus buyer will exercise his option if $CP(t^*)-X(t^*)>0$, and the option value at t^* is

$$\max[0, PC-X].$$

Assume that percentage changes in the spot price X are an Ito process with constant drift α_x and dispersion V_x: $dX/X=\alpha_x dt+V_x dz_x$. As Merton (1973c) proposes, assume the riskless discount bond will be worth unity when it matures. Until then changes in its prices are given by the stochastic differential

$$dP/P=\alpha_p dt+v_p dz_p.$$

Let $x_1=PC$ and $x_2=X$, both asset prices. Then for all $t\leqslant t^*$ this option is worth

$$\begin{aligned} &w(x_1,x_2,t)\\ &=w(PC,X,t)\\ &=PCN(d_1)-XN(d_2), \end{aligned}$$

where

$$d_1=\left[\ln(PC/X)+v^2(t^*-t)\div 2\right]\div v\sqrt{t^*-t}\ ,$$

$$d_2=d_1-v\sqrt{t^*-t}\ ,$$

and

$$v^2=v_p^2-2v_pv_x\rho_{px}+v_x^2.$$

V. Summary

In this paper I develop an equation for the value of an option to exchange one asset for another within a stated period. The formula applies to American options, as well as European ones; to puts, as well as calls. Thus, I found a closed-form expression for this sort of American put option and a put-call parity theorem for such American options.

One can apply the equation to options that investors create when they enter into certain common financial arrangements. The investment adviser, who receives a fee which depends at least in part on how well his managed portfolio does relative to some standard, has an option to refuse the fee and declare bankruptcy if the fee is extremely negative. The short-seller has the option to similarly escape his obligations, at the expense of his broker. The offeree in an exchange offer may have the opportunity to exchange one company's securities for those of another. The buyer of a standby commitment has the (put) option to trade mortgage notes for dollars in the forward market. In each case the value of the option depends not only on the current values of the assets which might be exchanged, but also on the variance-covariance matrix for the rates of return on the two assets, and on the life of the option.

REFERENCES

1. Fischer Black. "The Pricing of Commodity Contracts," *Journal of Financial Economics*, Volume 3 (January/March 1976).
2. ———. "The Pricing of Complex Options and Corporate Liabilities," Graduate School of Business, University of Chicago, 1975.
3. ——— and Myron Scholes. "The Pricing of Options and Corporate Liabilities," *Journal of Political Economy*, Volume 81 (May/June 1973), pp. 637–654.
4. Ruel Vance Churchill. *Fourier Series and Boundary Value Problems*, 2nd ed. New York, McGraw-Hill, 1963.
5. Stanley Fischer. "The Demand for Index Bonds," *Journal of Political Economy*, Volume 83 (June 1975), pp. 509–534.
6. Jonathan E. Ingersoll, Jr. "A Theoretical and Empirical Investigation of the Dual Purpose Funds," *Journal of Financial Economics*, Volume 3 (January/March 1976), pp. 83–123.
7. Fritz John. *Partial Differential Equations*, 2nd ed. New York, Springer Verlag, 1975.
8. William Margrabe. "Alternative Investment Performance Fee Arangements and Implications for SEC Regulatory Policy: A Comment," *Bell Journal of Economics*, Volume 7 (Autumn 1976), pp. 716–718.
9. H. P. McKean, Jr., *Stochastic Integrals*, New York, Academic Press, 1969.
10. Robert C. Merton. "An Intertemporal Capital Asset Pricing Model," *Econometrica*, Volume 41 (September 1973a), pp. 867–887.
11. ———. "The Relationship between Put and Call Option Prices: Comment," *Journal of Finance*, Volume 28 (March 1973b), pp. 183–184.
12. ———. "The Theory of Rational Option Pricing," *The Bell Journal of Economics and Management Science*, Volume 4 (Spring 1973c), pp. 141–183.
13. Franco Modigliani and Gerald A. Pogue. "Alternative Investment Performance Fee Arrangements and Implications for SEC Regulatory Policy," *Bell Journal of Economics*, Volume 6 (Spring 1975), pp. 127–160.
14. Clifford W. Smith, Jr. "Option Pricing: A Review," *Journal of Financial Economics*, Volume 3 (January/March 1976), pp. 3–51.
15. Hans R. Stoll. "The Relationship between Put and Call Option Prices," *Journal of Finance*, Volume 24 (December 1969), pp. 802–824.

[19]

THE JOURNAL OF FINANCE • VOL. XXXIV, NO. 5 • DECEMBER 1979

Path Dependent Options: "Buy at the Low, Sell at the High"

M. BARRY GOLDMAN, HOWARD B. SOSIN and MARY ANN GATTO

I. Introduction

IT IS WELL KNOWN that the valuation of European puts and calls with fixed exercise prices is solely dependent on the distribution of the terminal price of the underlying stock. This paper examines the properties of European options with exercise prices that are functions of the realized sample path of the stock. In particular, the commonplace shareholder desire to "buy at the low" and sell at the high" can be satisfied with a combination of a call on the stock with an exercise price equal to $\min_{0\leq\tau\leq T} S(\tau)$ and a put with exercise price equal to $\max_{0\leq\tau\leq T} S(\tau)$ where S is the stock price and T is the term of the option.[1]

Strictly speaking, the creation of these new options in a *frictionless* context would not expand the investor's opportunity set. However, in a *realistic* market setting such new options might very well acquire substantial popularity. The appeal would be threefold: (1) the options would guarantee the investor's fantasy of buying at the low and selling at the high, (2) the options would, in some loose intuitive sense, minimize regret, and (3) the options would allow investors with special information on the range (but possibly without special information on the terminal stock price) to directly take advantage of such information.

In this paper we analyze the hedging, pricing, and economic properties of these options. Wherever possible we compare and contrast these options with their traditional counterparts. In section two we establish that these options can be hedged and that closed-form valuation equations exist. Particular emphasis here centers on the hedgeability of these options when the stock is at an extremum (i.e., equal to its current maximum or minimum). In section three, by analysis and simulation, we establish the properties of these options and contrast them with those of their traditional counterparts. In particular we examine: (1) the functional dependence of these options with respect to two state variables—stock price and time to expiration, and (2) the pricing of these options relative to the stock and traditional options at the time of inception. Due to the ungainliness of the general pricing relations developed in section two, we found it convenient throughout section three to provide detailed analyses and explicit derivations of the properties of these options for the particularly intuitive case where the logarithm of the adjusted geometric mean return of the stock is zero. We then illustrate by simulation that, qualitatively, the results of our specific example carry over to the general case. We conclude in section four with a general discussion of path-dependent options.

[1] Another example of a path-dependent option that has been examined in the pricing of an American put. See Parkinson [7] for details.

Throughout the paper we will adhere to the following notation

Timing conventions:

O:	All options are assumed to be written at time zero,
T:	The expiration date of all options,
τ:	The current date,
t:	$T - \tau$, the time to expiration.

Remaining notation:

$S(\tau)$:	Stock price at time τ, (occasionally abbreviated to S),
X:	Exercise price,
r:	Risk free rate of interest,
σ^2:	Variance per unit time of log of stock price return,[2]
$C[S(\tau), X, t]$:	Value of an ordinary European call,
$P[S(\tau), X, t]$:	Value of an ordinary European put,
$M(\tau)$:	$\max_{0 \leq \delta \leq \tau} S(\delta)$, (occasionally abbreviated to M),
$Q(\tau)$:	$\min_{0 \leq \delta \leq \tau} S(\delta)$, (occasionally abbreviated to Q),
$C_{\min}[S(\tau), Q(\tau), t]$:	Value of a European option to buy the stock at its realized minimum, when the current stock price is $S(\tau)$, the realized minimum to date is $Q(\tau)$, and the time remaining on the option is t,
$P_{\max}[S(\tau), M(\tau), t]$:	Value of a European option to sell the stock at its realized maximum, when the current stock price is $S(\tau)$, the realized maximum to date is $M(\tau)$, and the time remaining on the option is t,
$N\{\cdot\}, N'\{\cdot\}$:	Standard normal cumulative distribution and density functions,
d_1:	$\dfrac{[\ln(S/X) + (r + \sigma^2/2)t]}{\sigma\sqrt{t}}$,
d_2:	$\dfrac{[\ln(S/X) + (r - \sigma^2/2)t]}{\sigma\sqrt{t}}$,
E:	Expectation operator,
dy:	Limit of a Wiener process, and
α:	Drift term of the rate of the return on the stock.

II. Hedging and Valuation

In order to hedge a position, the writer of any option must find a way to invest the proceeds from the sale of the option in an initial portfolio and to then alter the composition of this portfolio as is required to guarantee that in all states of nature (i.e., with probability one) the terminal value of the portfolio is adequate to meet his terminal obligation. This portfolio strategy is termed a *perfect hedge* and has the following properties: (1) the value of the terminal portfolio is *exactly* equal to the terminal obligation, and (2) the hedging policy is *self-financing*-each portfolio revision undertaken is exactly financed by the proceeds from the sale of the previous position.

[2] By "return" we denote $(S_{t+\Delta t}/S_t)$; The proportional gain or loss, $(S_{t+\Delta t} - S_t)/S_t$, we call "rate of return".

Recent work by Black and Scholes [1] and Merton [6] has established that in a perfect (i.e., frictionless) market, when the natural logarithm of the underlying stock price follows a Wiener process with drift (i.e., $dS/S = \alpha \cdot dt + \sigma \cdot dy$) so that $d(\ln S) = (\alpha - \sigma^2/2)\, dt + \sigma \cdot dy$, the payoff of a European put or call with a fixed exercise price can be identically duplicated by a portfolio consisting of shares of stock and units of riskless bond. Thus, this portfolio meets the criteria established for a perfect hedge. Cox and Ross [3] have illustrated and Harrison and Kreps [5] have proved that if a contingent claim can be perfectly hedge it can be priced as if it existed in a risk-neutral world. This result implies that the instantaneous rate of return (α) of the underlying stock is of no consequence to the pricing of the option and in fact it may be assumed equal to the riskless rate (r). The drift of the logarithm of the stock price becomes effectively $(r - \sigma^2/2)$ per unit time, and after making this substitution, the option will be priced at its discounted expected terminal value.

Together these authors have illustrated that in equilibrium, to prevent riskless arbitrage, ordinary European puts and calls will have the following closed-form valuation equations:

$$C[S, X, t] = S \cdot N\{d_1\} - e^{-rt} X \cdot N\{d_2\} \tag{1}$$

$$P[S, X, t] = C[S, X, t] - S + X \cdot e^{-rt} \tag{2}$$

In this section we illustrate that puts on the maximum (P_{max}) and calls on the minimum (C_{min}) can be perfectly hedged and that closed-form valuation equations can be derived. The major insight in this section concerns the hedgeability of these options when the stock is at an extremum (i.e., at its current maximum or minimum). We begin this section by deriving the hedging portfolio when $r = \sigma^2/2$ (i.e., the logarithm of the underlying stock has zero effective drift). Here a hedging portfolio for writers of these options may be deduced as is illustrated in the following theorem.

THEOREM 1: *When* $r = \sigma^2/2$,

$$P_{max}[S(\tau), M(\tau), t] = P[S(\tau), M(\tau), t] + C[S(\tau), M(\tau), t] \tag{3}$$

and

$$C_{min}[S(\tau), Q(\tau), t] = P[S(\tau), Q(\tau), t] + C[S(\tau), Q(\tau), t]. \tag{4}$$

Proof: For the proof of this result we refer the reader to the derivation of the general pricing relations as summarized in relations (10) and (11) (i.e., letting $r = \sigma^2/2$ and using the definitions of puts and call affirms the equivalence of P_{max} and C_{min} to straddles).

Note that at $\tau = 0$, $S(0) = M(0) = Q(0)$. Thus, the theorem implies that an initial hedging portfolio for P_{max} (for C_{min}) is an ordinary put plus an ordinary call (i.e., a straddle) both with an exercise price equal to the initial stock price and term to maturity equal to the term to maturity of $P_{max}(C_{min})$. By examination, theorem 1 also implies that as long as the stock never rises above (falls below) its initial value, the composition of the hedging portfolio is unaltered. Clearly, if, over the life of the option, the stock price never rises above (falls below) its initial value, the initial straddle would exactly satisfy the writer's terminal obligation. For P_{max}, $M(T) = S(0)$ (for C_{min}, $Q(T) = S(0)$), the call (put) in the straddle would be valueless but the put (call) in the straddle would be just what was required to meet the terminal obligation. When the stock price is equal to its old maximum (minimum) (i.e., the stock is at an extremum) and then achieves a new maximum (minimum), theorem 1 implies that the old portfolio—the straddle with exercise price equal to the old maximum (minimum)—should be sold and a new porfolio established—a straddle with exercise price equal to the new maximum (minimum). Theorem 2 establishes that this is a self-financing portfolio strategy.

THEOREM 2: *If* $r = \sigma^2$ *and* $X = S$ *then*

$$P[S + ds, S, t] + C[S + ds, S, t] = P[S + ds, S + ds, t] + C[S + ds, S + ds, t] \quad (5)$$

and hence this is a self-financing portfolio strategy.

Proof: Taking a Taylor Series Expansion of the LHS of relation (5) around $X = S$ (holding the stock price and the term to expiration constant) yields:

$$P[S + ds, X, t] + C[S + ds, X, t] = P[S + ds, X + ds, t] + C[S + ds, X + ds, t] - \left(\frac{\partial P[S + ds, X + ds, t]}{\partial X} + \frac{\partial C[S + ds, X + ds, t]}{\partial X}\right) ds + o(ds)$$

where $o(ds) \equiv$ terms of higher order than ds. These may be ignored since the derivations of $P[\cdot]$ and $C[\cdot]$ are bounded. Using the Black-Scholes formulae (relations (1) and (2)) to evaluate the terms in $(\cdot)$ yields

$$-(-2e^{-rt}N\{d_2\} + e^{-rt}) = 0$$

since, $N\{d_2\} = ½$ when $r = \sigma^2/2$ and $S = X$. Q.E.D.

Another way to state the result of theorem 2 is that when $r = \sigma^2/2$ and

$$S(\tau) = M(\tau)(\text{or } S(\tau) = Q(\tau)), \frac{\partial P_{\max}}{\partial M} = 0 \left(\frac{\partial C_{\min}}{\partial Q} = 0\right).$$

Thus, in contrast to ordinary puts (calls) where increases (decreases) in the exercise price always increase the value of the option, for these special options, when the stock is at its current maximum (minimum) infinitesimal changes in the maximum (minimum) are valueless.

Hedging: The General Case

Theorem 3 below illustrates that the results of theorem 2 concerning changes in the value of $P_{\max}$ (or $C_{\min}$)caused by changes in the maximum (minimum) when the stock price is equal to its current maximum (minimum) hold in general. However, before presenting the proof, we will first motivate the result. To this end it is useful to present a simplifying concept.

The Joint Distribution of M(T) and S(T): A Red Herring

If these options are hedgeable, then after making the Cox-Ross transformation (i.e., substituting the risk-free rate of interest for the logarithm of the stock's expected return and assuming that these securities are priced in a risk neutral world) we know that P_{max} will be priced equal to the probability weighted, conditional (over non-negative payouts) expected value of the realized maximum over the life of the option minus the terminal stock price, discounted back to the present; C_{min} will be priced equal to the probability weighted, conditional expected value of the terminal stock price minus the realized minimum, discounted back to the present:

$$P_{max}[S(\tau), M(\tau), t] = e^{-rt}E\,|_{m \geqslant S}[M(T) - S(T)]Prob(M \geqslant S) \tag{6}$$

$$C_{min}[S(\tau), Q(\tau), t] = e^{-rt}E\,|_{Q \leqslant S}[S(T) - Q(T)]Prob(Q \leqslant S) \tag{7}$$

where E is a conditional expectation operator.

A casual examination of (6) and (7) seems to indicate that knowledge of the conditional joint distribution of the maximum (minimum) and the terminal value of a Wiener process with drift (conditioned on the current price, the curent maximum (minimum) to date and the length of time remaining to expiration) is required. However, since these options are always exercised we know that $Prob(M \geqslant S) = 1$, and $Prob(Q \leqslant S) = 1$, hence we can use the distributive property of expectation. Since $e^{-rt}E[S(T)] = S(\tau)$, relations (6) and (7) may be rewritten as

$$P_{max}[S(\tau), M(\tau), t] = e^{-rt}E[M(T)] - S(\tau) \tag{6$'$}$$

$$C_{min}[S(\tau), Q(\tau), t] = S(\tau) - e^{-rt}E[Q(T)]. \tag{7$'$}$$

Thus, knowledge of the joint distribution is unnecessary; all that is required is knowledge of the conditional distribution of the maximum (minimum). The importance of this observation is that in order to value P_{max} it is sufficient to value a security that pays off the realized maximum (call it V_{max}) and to then subtract the current stock price; to value C_{min} it is sufficient to subtract from the current stock price the value of a security that pays off the realized minimum (call it V_{min}). Hence

$$P_{max}[S(\tau), M(\tau), t] = V_{max}[S(\tau), M(\tau), t] - S(\tau) \tag{8}$$

$$C_{min}[S(\tau), Q(\tau), t] = S(\tau) - V_{min}[S(\tau), Q(\tau), t]. \tag{9}$$

Further, in order to prove that P_{max} and C_{min} are hedgeable it suffices to prove that V_{max} and V_{min} are hedgeable since we know that the $S(T)$ can be hedged with $S(\tau)$.

It is intuitive that for $P_{max}(C_{min})$ when $S(\tau) < M(\tau)$, $(S(\tau) > Q(\tau))$ instantaneous changes in its value can only be effected by changes in the stock price and changes in time. That is, the assumed Wiener process for the stock insures that over the infinitesimal horizon the stock price will not rise above (fall below) its current maximum (minimum). Thus, when the stock price is not equal to its current maximum (minimum) potential changes in the maximum (minimum) can be ignored (i.e., $dM = 0$, or $dQ = 0$). However, when $S(\tau) = M(\tau)$, $(S(\tau) = Q(\tau))$ it might appear that infinitesimal changes in the value of the maximum (minimum) would cause changes in the value of $V_{max}(V_{min})$. This result, if it were true, has the disturbing implication that when the stock price is at an extremum there would appear to be two hedging ratios: one if the stock price rises, and one if the stock price falls. Two hedging ratios at a point in time would imply that a portfolio of stock and bonds would not span these options.

Theorem 3 establishes that when $S(\tau) = M(\tau)$, the distribution of $M(T)$, (i.e., the distribution of the maximum for the entire interval) is unaffected by marginal changes in the current maximum. Since V_{max} is only dependent upon the distribution of $M(T)$, this theorem establishes that $\left.\frac{\partial V_{max}}{\partial M(\tau)}\right|_{M(\tau)=S(\tau)} = 0$. Although not presented, it is also true that $\left.\frac{\partial V_{min}}{\partial Q(\tau)}\right|_{Q(\tau)=S(\tau)} = 0$.

THEOREM 3: *When $S(\tau) = M(\tau)$, holding S constant, all of the moments of $M(T)$ are unaffected by marginal changes in $M(\tau)$. Thus when $S(\tau) = M(\tau)$ the distribution of $M(T)$ and hence the value of P_{max} is unaffected by marginal changes in the maximum.*

Proof: See Appendix 2.

The intuition behind this result is that when $S(\tau) < M(\tau)$ there is always a positive probability that $M(\tau)$ will be the final maximum (i.e., $M(\tau) = M(T)$) and hence marginal increases in $M(\tau)$ will have value. However, in the limit as $S(\tau) \to M(\tau)$ if the stock follows a Wiener process then the probability that $M(\tau) = M(T)$ approaches zero. At $M(\tau) = S(\tau)$ infinitesimal increases in $M(\tau)$ will be of no value. Thus the value of marginal changes in $M(\tau)$ may be thought of as being proportional to the probability that $M(\tau)$ will be the terminal maximum.

The General Pricing Relations

Equations (10) and (11) present the pricing relations for V_{max} and V_{min} obtained by making the Cox-Ross transformation and then computing the discounted expected value of the terminal maximum and minimum. (Remember $P_{max} = V_{max} - S$, $C_{min} = S - V_{min}$).

$$V_{max}[S(\tau), M(\tau), t] = M(\tau)e^{-rt}\left[N\left\{\frac{a - \mu t}{\sigma\sqrt{t}}\right\} - \frac{\sigma^2}{2r}e^{2\mu a/\sigma^2}N\left\{\frac{-a - \mu t}{\sigma\sqrt{t}}\right\}\right] + S(\tau)\left[1 + \frac{\sigma^2}{2r}\right]\left[1 - N\left\{\frac{a - (\mu + \sigma^2)t}{\sigma\sqrt{t}}\right\}\right] \tag{10}$$

$$V_{min}[S(\tau), Q(\tau), t] = Q(\tau)e^{-rt}\left[N\left\{\frac{b + \mu t}{\sigma\sqrt{t}}\right\} - \frac{\sigma^2}{2r}e^{-2\mu b/\sigma^2}N\left\{\frac{-b + \mu t}{\sigma\sqrt{t}}\right\}\right] + S(\tau)\left[1 + \frac{\sigma^2}{2r}\right]N\left\{\frac{-b - (\mu + \sigma^2)t}{\sigma\sqrt{t}}\right\} \tag{11}$$

where:

$$a \equiv \ln[M(\tau)/S(\tau)] \geqslant 0,$$

$$b \equiv \ln[S(\tau)/Q(\tau)] \geqslant 0, \quad \text{and}$$

$$\mu \equiv r - \sigma^2/2.$$

Casual observation reveals that these relations meet their respective terminal conditions. That is,

$$V_{max}[S(T), M(T), 0] = M(T)$$
$$V_{max}[0, M(\tau), t] = M(\tau)e^{-rt}$$

and,

$$V_{min}[S(T), Q(T), 0] = Q(T)$$
$$V_{min}[0, 0, t] = 0.$$

To establish that relations (10) and (11) are self-financing it is necessary to examine the evolution of V_{max} and V_{min} through time. By hypothesis (i.e., since the logarithm of the underlying stock follows a Wiener process with drift) $V = V_{max}[S(\tau), M(\tau), t]$ is a smooth function of S and t. Dependence on $M(\tau)$ will be suppressed since theorem 3 established that $\left.\frac{\partial V_{max}}{\partial M}\right|_{M=S} = 0$ and since dM is zero otherwise[3]. Ito's Lemma implies that

$$dV = V_1 dS + V_3\, dt + \tfrac{1}{2}\, V_{11}(dS)^2 \tag{12}$$

where:

$$(dS)^2 = -S^2\sigma^2\, dt,$$
$$dS = \alpha \cdot S \cdot dt + \sigma \cdot S \cdot dy, \quad \text{and}$$
$$\alpha \equiv \text{drift term.}$$

The only stochastic term (dS) may be hedged out by combining V with a short position in stock equal to $V_1 S$ dollars (where $V_1 = \partial V/\partial S$). The coefficient of dy will be zero hence the portfolio is riskless and must satisfy the following relation:

$$dV - V_1 dS = (V - V_1 S)r \cdot d\tau. \tag{13}$$

The LHS is the return on the option, short the stock. The term in parentheses on the RHS is the value of the portfolio remaining after shorting the stock. Noting that $d\tau = -dt$ and substituting (12) into (13) yields

$$V_3\, dt - \tfrac{1}{2}\, V_{11} S^2\sigma^2\, dt = -(V - V_1 S)r \cdot dt.$$

Rearranging and canceling defines a differential equation for the value of V_{max}.

$$(V - V_1 S)r + V_3 - \tfrac{1}{2}\, V_{11} S^2\sigma^2 = 0. \tag{14}$$

It is important to note that not only is relation (14) the differential equation for V_{max} but in addition it is the basic differential equation for *all* contingent claims written on a stock whose rates of return follow a Wiener process. In particular it is the differential equation for V_{min}, P_{max}, C_{min} and for ordinary puts and calls. Of course each option will have its own boundary conditions.

[3] This fact guarantees the arbitrage. However, (12) is exact only when $S \neq M$ and must be modified at the boundary $S = M$ since the second partials w.r.t. M do not disappear on the boundary. This is a mathematical curiosity and does not affect the solution technique. See Appendix 1 for details.

Careful differentiation of (10) and (11) reveals that they satisfy relation (14). Thus, relations (10) and (11) meet the criteria for a perfect hedge and will be the equilibrium valuation equations for V_{max} and V_{min}.

III. Properties of P_{max} and C_{min}

In this section we briefly explore some of the properties of these path-dependent options. In the first two subsections we describe these options as a function of the state variables S and t and compare the prices of these options with the prices of traditional options and the price of the underlying stock. As a benchmark, whenever illuminating, we briefly review the behavior of traditional puts and calls before proceeding to analyze the properties of P_{max} and C_{min}. In Table I, we contrast the inception values of these options for three alternative relations between r and T^2, and four alternative terms.

Table 1

Option Prices at Inception
($S=M=Q=X=100¢$, $r=0.06$)

$T = 0.2$ years,

	$r = 2\sigma^2$	$r = \sigma^2/2$	$r = \sigma^2/4$
Put	2.51¢	5.56	8.09
Call	3.70	6.75	9.28
P_{max}	5.72	12.31	18.02
C_{min}	6.62	12.31	16.82

$T = 0.5$ years

Put	3.48	8.20	12.12
Call	6.43	11.15	15.08
P_{max}	8.62	19.35	28.88
C_{min}	10.84	19.35	25.92

$T = 1.0$ years

Put	4.19	10.64	16.01
Call	10.01	16.46	21.84
P_{max}	11.51	27.10	41.33
C_{min}	15.88	27.10	35.50

$T = 5.0$ years

Put	4.14	15.11	24.47
Call	30.06	41.03	50.39
P_{max}	19.79	56.14	93.27
C_{min}	39.22	56.14	67.35

Options as Functions of the State Variables S and t: Properties of Traditional Puts and Calls

It is well known (see Merton [6]) that ordinary calls are convex-increasing functions of the stock price and increasing functions of the time to expiration. Calls have the following boundary conditions:

$$C[S, X, 0] = \max[S - X, 0],\ C[S, X, \infty] = S, \quad \text{and} \quad C[0, X, t] = 0.$$

Less often exhibited are the properties of ordinary European puts. Puts are convex-decreasing functions of the stock price. All "in-the-money" puts ($S < X$) are first decreasing functions of the time to expiration (i.e., at $t = 0$, $\partial P/\partial t|_{S>X} = -rX$). Puts sufficiently in-the-money are decreasing-convex functions of the time to expiration. Puts only slightly in-the-money first decrease, then increase and finally decrease as a function of the time of expiration. Out-of-the-money puts, ($S > X$) first increase (although at $t = 0$, $\left.\frac{\partial P}{\partial t}\right|_{S>X} = 0$) and then decrease as a function of t. The boundary conditions for a put are:

$$P[S, X, 0] = \max[0, X - S],\ P[0, X, t] = Xe^{-rt}, \quad \text{and} \quad P[S, X, \infty] = 0.$$

Graphs for ordinary puts and calls are presented in panel a of Figures 1–4. Since the case where $r = \sigma^2/2$ plays an important role in the analysis, and since the qualitative results are unaffected, we have chosen to plot ordinary puts and calls assuming this risk specification.

Properties of $P_{\max}$

Panels *b–d* of Figure 1 present pictures of $P_{\max}$ as a function of S for three alternative relations between the riskless rate of interest and the variance of the stock. For the case where $r = \sigma^2/2$ (Panel *b*), theorem 1 has established that $P_{\max}$ is equivalent to a straddle with exercise price equal to the current maximum. The composition of this straddle is an in-the-money put plus an out-of-the-money call (i.e., the exercise price for both options is M and by construction $M > S$). The following theorem proves that for $r = \sigma^2/2$ and M normalized to unity, $P_{\max}$ as a function of S first behaves like an in-the-money put and then like an ordinary call. That is, $P_{\max}$ is convex in S-first decreasing and then increasing.

THEOREM 4: *When $r = \sigma^2/2$, $P_{\max}$ is convex in S for $t < \infty$. $P_{\max}$ as a function of S first decreases, reaches a unique minimum and then increases. Its unique minimum occurs at $-\ln(S/M) = \sigma^2 t$.*

Proof: see Appendix 2.

The intuition behind the behavior of $P_{\max}$ is that for $S(\tau)$ sufficiently below $M(\tau)$, not enough time (probabilistically) remains to establish a new maximum and to then establish a larger $M(T) - S(T)$. Thus increases in $S(\tau)$ lead to a smaller expected $M(T) - S(T)$. However, for $S(\tau)$ sufficiently close to $M(\tau)$ enough time remains to establish a new maximum and to then establish a larger expected $M(T) - S(T)$. In other words, at inception and at all other times when $M(\tau) = S(\tau)$ and throughout the life of the option whenever $M(\tau) - S(\tau)$ is

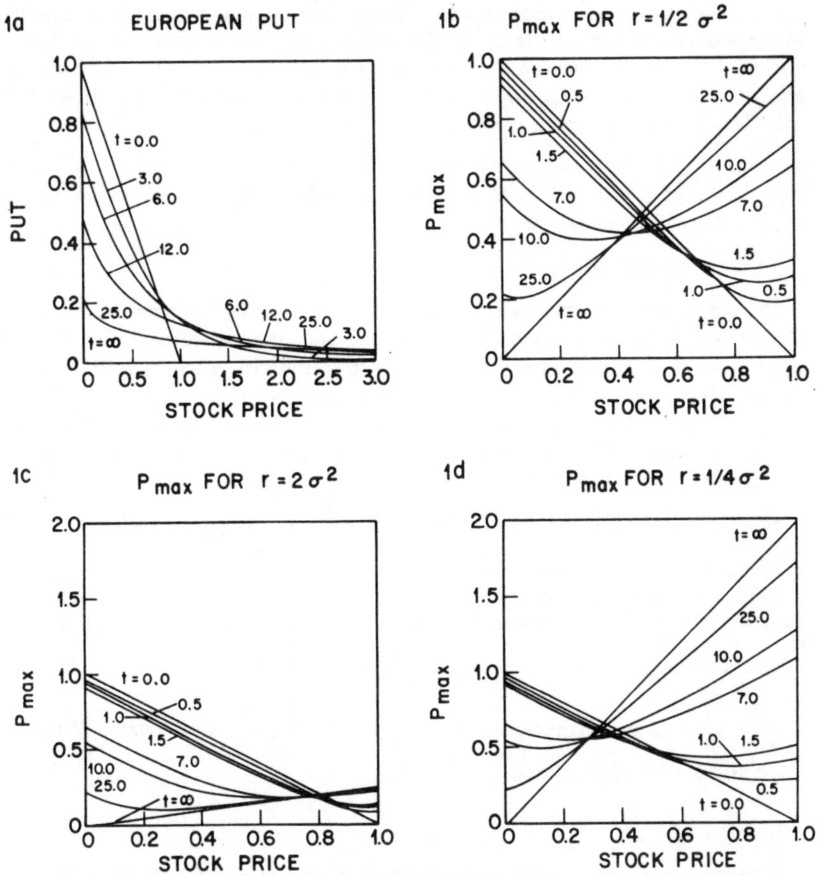

Figure 1. *Price of options to sell as a function of stock price for alternative times to maturity (t) assuming m = 1*

sufficiently small the purchaser of the option first hopes that the stock will go up (as he would if he held a call) and establish a new high. He then hopes that the stock will go down (as he would if he held a put). Analogously, when t is sufficiently small (i.e., a new maximum is unlikely) P_{max} behaves as an ordinary put (i.e., a decreasing function of S) and when t is sufficiently large (i.e., a new maximum is likely) P_{max} behaves as an ordinary call (i.e., an increasing function of S).

Qualitatively, the convexity of P_{max} for the case of $r \neq \sigma^2/2$ is exhibited in panels c and d of Figure 1. Analytical confirmation of convexity is straightforward. Using the notation of Theorem 3:

$$\frac{\partial^2 P_{max}}{\partial S^2} = e^{-rt}\left[\frac{\partial^2 L(1)}{\partial S^2}\right] - \frac{\partial^2 S}{\partial S^2} = e^{-rt}\left[\frac{M^2(\tau)}{S^3(\tau)}\right]\frac{dH(\bar{Z})}{d\bar{Z}}\bigg|_{\bar{Z}=M/S} > 0.$$

From before we know that as a function of t the value of a call is maximized with $t = \infty$ and that a sufficiently in-the-money put is maximized with $t = 0$. The next theorem establishes the somewhat surprising result that for $r = \sigma^2/2$ and $M \equiv 1$, as a function of t, for any S, the value of P_{max} is *uniquely* maximized with either $t = 0$ or $t = \infty$ except for $S = ½$ where $P_{max}[½, 0] = P_{max}[½, \infty]$.

THEOREM 5: *Let* $r = \sigma^2/2$, $\gamma = \sigma^2 t$ *and* $M \equiv 1$. *If* $S \leqslant ½$, $P_{max}[S, \gamma]$ *will be maximized at* $\gamma = 0$. *If* $S \geqslant ½$, $P_{max}[S, \gamma]$ *will be maximized at* $\gamma = \infty$. (*Note*: $P_{max}[½, 0] = P_{max}[½, \infty] = ½$).

Proof: See Appendix 2.

Theorems 4 and 5 established that for $r = \sigma^2/2$ and M normalized to unity, P_{max} first acts like a put and then a call and that the critical value of S below which zero time is preferred and above which infinite time is preferred occurs at the intersection of $P_{max}[S, 0] = 1 - S$ with $P_{max}[S, \infty] = S$ or at $S = ½$. Panels *c* and *d* illustrate that the qualitative properties of theorems 4 and 5 hold for arbitrary relations between r and σ^2. The critical point determining whether zero or infinite time is preferred will now occur at the intersection of $P_{max}[S, 0] = 1 - S$ and $P_{max}[S, \infty] = (\sigma^2/2r) \cdot S$ or at $S = \left[\dfrac{2r}{\sigma^2 + 2r}\right]$. Thus the riskier the stock the earlier the critical value of S.

Panels *b–d* of Figure 2 graph P_{max} as a function of t first for $r = \sigma^2/2$ and then for $r = 2\sigma^2$ and $r = \sigma^2/4$. These figures reinforce the results of theorems 4 and 5 for it is clear that for $S > \left[\dfrac{2r}{2r + \sigma^2}\right]$, P_{max} is maximized at $t = \infty$; for $S < \left[\dfrac{2r}{2r + \sigma^2}\right]$, P_{max} is maximized at $t = 0$ and for $S = \left[\dfrac{2r}{2r + \sigma^2}\right]$ the value of P_{max} at $t = 0$ and $t = \infty$ are identical.

Properties of C_{min}

When $r = \sigma^2/2$, C_{min} has been characterized as a straddle with exercise price equal to the current minimum. The straddle consists of an out-of-the-money put plus an in-the-money call. By an argument similar to that used for P_{max}, C_{min} is a convex function of S. However, in contrast to P_{max}, C_{min} is a strictly increasing function of S and hence acts only like a call. That is,

$$\frac{\partial C_{min}}{\partial S} = N\left\{\frac{\ln(S/Q) + (r + \sigma^2/2)t}{\sigma\sqrt{t}}\right\} + \left[N\left\{\frac{\ln(S/Q) + (r + \sigma^2/2)t}{\sigma\sqrt{t}}\right\} - 1\right] \geqslant 0 \quad (16)$$

since $S \geqslant Q$ by construction. Since $\dfrac{\partial C}{\partial S} > 0$ and $\dfrac{\partial P}{\partial S} < 0$, relation (16) illustrates that (regardless of the relation between r and σ^2) changes in the value of an in-the-money call (the first term on the RHS) dominates changes in the value of an

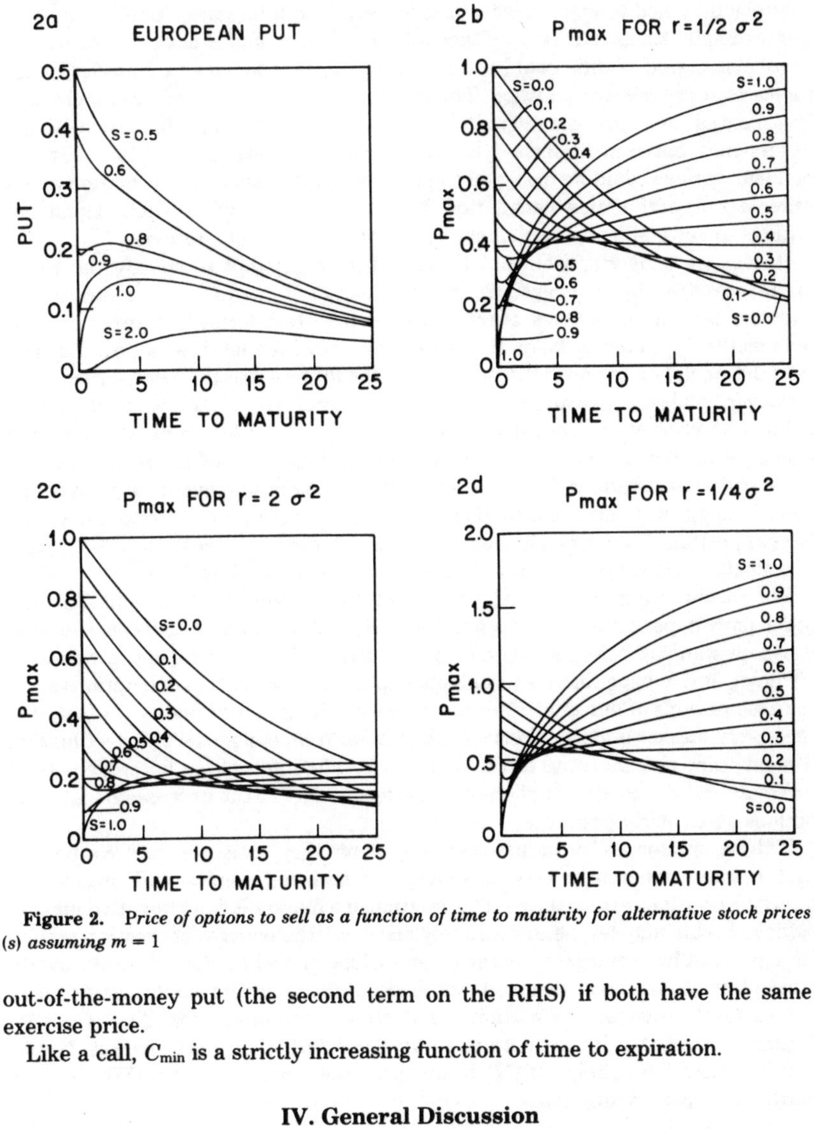

Figure 2. *Price of options to sell as a function of time to maturity for alternative stock prices (s) assuming m = 1*

out-of-the-money put (the second term on the RHS) if both have the same exercise price.

Like a call, C_{min} is a strictly increasing function of time to expiration.

IV. General Discussion

Hitherto, we have focused our attention upon the mathematical aspects of some path dependent options, to wit, the existence of pricing formulae and the qualitative properties of such formulae. Let us now speak more loosely about the possible application of this knowledge.

The financial community expends considerable resources in attempts to better predict the path of stock prices. Yet a few capital market instruments are designed to take direct advantage of such information. Obviously, path dependent options could be designed to exploit these real or perceived informational opportunities. For example an analyst with "special" knowledge of a stock's range over a particular period of time could use P_{max} and C_{min} to achieve a tidy profit [Range forecasts are regularly published. The value of such forecasts could be empirically investigated by using strategies of P_{max} and C_{min} that are functions of the discrepancy between published forecasts and naive forecasts]. Other path dependent options could be designed to profitably utilize special information about other aspects of the price distribution. Thus technicians could use path dependent options to automatically implement the classical technical strategies.

Recent work by Harrison and Kreps [5] is an attempt to specify the set of options that can be arbitraged. A modificiation of V_{max} which can be arbitraged and has certain advantages over V_{max} is forthwith described: A program that obtains the V_{max} payout holds the stock long until the high is attained and then sells the stock holding onto the proceeds in the form of non-interest bearing cash. However, a clever investor would prefer to switch from a stock position to a riskless bond position (that does pay interest). Further, the time of the switch would be a function of both the price path and the rate of interest. Thus, we could define new options that pay (ex-post) the maximum payouts obtainable by going long stock (bonds) and then at some intermediate time substituting a bond (stock) position for the stock (bond) position. A further discussion of such path dependent options may be found in Goldman-Sosin and Shepp [4].

Our casual empiricism makes compelling the demand for P_{max} and C_{min} and other path dependent options since they allow *direct* and *effective* speculation based on standard forecasts of share price distributions. Of course the valuation formulae of this paper are only guidelines to the true values of such options since the assumptions of our model are but a rough description of reality. In fact, it is these very market imperfections (the deviations from our model's perfect market context) that give meaning to the new assets. The information heterogeneity of investors and the costliness of creating perfect hedges of the new assets make the options particularly desirable.

If these options are desirable then why don't they already exist? We believe that markets inherently take advantage of scale economies and attempt to internalize various externalities. The creation of a market is frought with danger—sufficient scale may not be immediately achieved, the benefits of creation may in large part not be captureable by the creators, legal impediments may prove overly burdensome to the creators etc. Accordingly, a desirable and viable security may not currently exist in the market. The test of a security's viability is not its existence but rather its capacity to survive in a fully developed market. Notice that the new flourishing CBOE bears little resemblance to the OTC options market of the preceding era.

Appendix 1[4]

Technically, (12) should be:

$$dV = V_1\,dS + V_3\,dt + V_2\,dM + \tfrac{1}{2}V_{11}(dS)^2 + V_{12}\,dS\,dM + \tfrac{1}{2}V_{22}(dM)^2 + o(dl) \quad (12')$$

[4] We thank Mr. William Boyce for his persistence in the clarification of this issue.

When $S < M$, $dM = 0$ and all partial derivative terms taken with respect to M disappear—hence, yielding (12). However, when $M = S$ and $dS > 0$, V_{12} and V_{22} do not disappear ($V_2 = 0$ by Theorem 3). Accordingly, when $M = S$ (12′) becomes:

$$dV = V_1\,dS + V_3\,dt + \tfrac{1}{4}\,V_{11}(dS)^2 + o(dt) \qquad (12'')$$

To derive (12″) from (12′), set V_2 equal to zero (by Theorem 3). Theorem 3 implies that when $S = M$ and $dS > 0$:

(a) $0 = dV_2 \equiv V_{21}\,dS + V_{22}\,dM$

(b) $0 = dV_1 \equiv V_{11}\,dS + V_{12}\,dM$

Putting (a) and (b) together, when $S = M$ yields:

(c) $-V_{12} = V_{11} = V_{22}$

Notice that relation (c), although obtained assuming $dS > 0$, is in fact independent of dS since the values of the second-order partial derivatives are independent of dS.

For our dynamical system, by the properties of stochastic differential equations, when $S = M$: $dS > 0 => dM = dS$, $dS \leq 0 => dM = 0$, and

(d) $(dS)^2 \approx \tfrac{1}{2}\,(dM\,dS) \approx \tfrac{1}{2}\,(dM)^2$

(c) and (d) require that when $S = M$

$$\tfrac{1}{2}\,V_{11}(dS)^2 + V_{12}\,dS\,dM + \tfrac{1}{2}\,V_{22}(dM)^2 + o(dt) = \tfrac{1}{4}\,V_{11}(dS)^2 + o(dt)$$

and hence (12″).

The switch from (12′) to (12″) is a mathematical curiosity which has no bearing on our solution technique since in all contingencies we can short V_1 shares of stock to form the riskless hedge (note that $V_1 + V_2 = V_1$ *iff* $S = M$).

Appendix 2

Proof of theorem 3: We know that $M(T) = \max[M(\tau), M(\tau, T)]$ where $M(\tau, T)$ is the maximum realized over the interval from τ to T. We want to examine the moments of $(M(T)|\,\tau, S(\tau), M(\tau))$ in the limit as $S(\tau) \to M(\tau)$. Let $\tilde{Z} = \tilde{M}(\tau, T)/S(\tau)$ and

$$\tilde{\lambda} = \begin{cases} M(\tau)/S(\tau) & \text{for } \tilde{M}(\tau, T) < M(T) \\ \tilde{M}(\tau, T)/S(\tau)(\equiv \tilde{Z}) & \text{otherwise.} \end{cases}$$

Note that $\tilde{Z}$ is like a return and since S follows a random walk, the distribution of $\tilde{Z}$ is independent of the level of $S(\tau)$. Let $\tilde{Z}$ have a distribution function $H(Z)$. Also note that $M(T) = S(\tau)\tilde{\lambda}$.

The nth raw moment of $M(T)$ may be written as

$$L(n) = \int_{S(\tau)}^{\infty} [M(T)]^n\, dG[M(T)]$$

where $G(\cdot)$ is the CDF of $M(T)$. By substitution this becomes

$$L(n) = \int_1^\infty [S(\tau)\tilde{\lambda}]^n \, dF(\tilde{\lambda}).$$

Using the definition of λ this may be decomposed into

$$L(n) = \left[[M(\tau)]^n \int_1^{M(\tau)/S(\tau)} dH(\tilde{Z}) \right] + \left[[S(\tau)]^n \int_{M(\tau)/S(\tau)}^\infty \tilde{Z}^n \, dH(\tilde{Z}) \right].$$

Differentiation of $L(n)$ with respect to $M(\tau)$ yields

$$\frac{\partial L(n)}{\partial M(\tau)} = n[M(\tau)]^{n-1} \int_1^{M(\tau)/S(\tau)} dH(\tilde{Z})$$

Finally, $\lim_{S(\tau)\to M(\tau)} \dfrac{\partial L(n)}{\partial M(\tau)} = 0$ since the assumed Wiener process guarantees that there is no probability mass associated with the point $M(\tau)/S(\tau)$.

Q.E.D.

Proof of theorem 4: P_{max} has been characterized as the sum of a put (which is convex-decreasing in S) and a call (which is convex-increasing in S). The sum of two convex functions is convex and hence P_{max} is convex. The uniqueness of the minimum is also a result of convexity.

To establish the minimum, let $\gamma \equiv \sigma^2 t$ and normalized $M = 1$ (remember by construction $S \leqslant M = 1$). Then, $P_{max}[S, \gamma] = P[S, \gamma] + C[S, \gamma]$ for $S \leqslant 1, \dfrac{\partial P_{max}}{\partial S} = 2N\left\{\dfrac{\ln(S) + \gamma}{\sqrt{\gamma}}\right\} - 1, \left.\dfrac{\partial P_{max}}{\partial S}\right|_{\gamma=0} = -1$, hence P_{max} decreases initially. $\left.\dfrac{\partial P_{max}}{\partial S}\right|_{\gamma=\infty} = 1$, hence P_{max} eventually increases. $\dfrac{\partial P_{max}}{\partial S} = 0$ *iff* $N\{\cdot\} = ½$ or $-\ln(S) = \gamma$.

Q.E.D.

Proof of theorem 5:

From theorem 4, $[-1 \leqslant \partial P_{max}/\partial S \leqslant 1]$. Further, $\partial P_{max}/\partial S\,|_{\gamma=0} = -1$ and $P[S, 0] = 1 - S$; $\partial P_{max}/\partial S\,|_{\gamma=\infty} = 1$ and $P[S, \infty] = S$. Thus, if $P_{max}[½, \gamma] < ½ \;\forall\; \gamma$ other than $\gamma = 0$, $\gamma = \infty$ the proof is established. To see this, consider Figure A which plots

FIGURE A

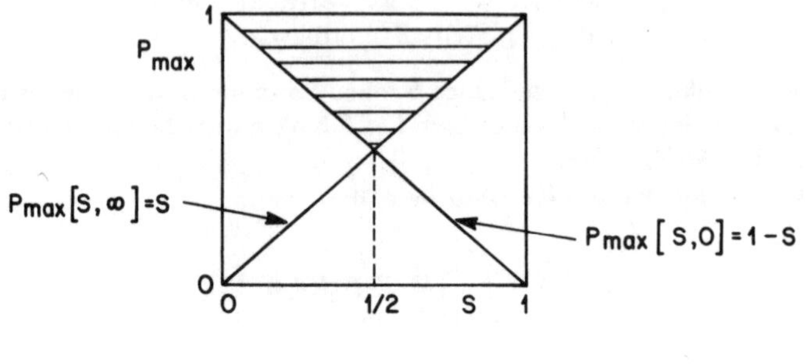

$P_{max}[S, 0]$ and $P_{max}[S, \infty]$. Given the bounds on $\partial P_{max}/\partial S$, if $P[\frac{1}{2}, \gamma] < \frac{1}{2}\ \forall\ \gamma$ other than $\gamma = 0$ and $\gamma = \infty$, then it will be impossible for any P_{max} as a function of S to "invade" the shaded region. Hence the value of either $P_{max}[S, 0]$ or $P_{max}[S, \infty]$ will dominate.

We will now prove that $\left.\frac{\partial P_{max}}{\partial \gamma}\right|_{S=1/2}$ first decreases and then increases as a function of γ.

$$L = \partial P_{max}/\partial\gamma\Big|_{S=1/2} = \frac{1}{2}e^{-\gamma/2}\left[\frac{2}{\sqrt{\gamma}}N'\left\{\frac{-\theta}{\sqrt{\gamma}}\right\} + 2N\left\{\frac{-\theta}{\sqrt{\gamma}}\right\} - 1\right]$$

$$= \frac{1}{2}e^{-\gamma/2}\left[\frac{2}{\sqrt{\gamma}}N'\left\{\frac{-\theta}{\sqrt{\gamma}}\right\} + N\left\{\frac{-\theta}{\sqrt{\gamma}}\right\} - N\left\{\frac{\theta}{\sqrt{\gamma}}\right\}\right] \tag{15}$$

where $\theta = \ln 2$. Notice that at $\gamma = 0$, $L = -1$ and at $\gamma = \infty$, $L = 0$. We now show that γ sufficiently large implies $L > 0$. Clearly $L > 0$ if $[\cdot]$ in relation (15) is positive. For the normal density, $\frac{2\theta}{\sqrt{\gamma}}N'\{0\} > N\left\{\frac{\theta}{\sqrt{\gamma}}\right\} - N\left\{\frac{-\theta}{\sqrt{\gamma}}\right\}$. Hence $[\cdot] > 0$ if $\frac{2}{\sqrt{\gamma}}N'\left\{\frac{-\theta}{\sqrt{\gamma}}\right\} \geqslant \frac{2\theta}{\sqrt{\gamma}}N'\{0\}$ or whenever $N'\{0\}/N'\left\{\frac{-\theta}{\sqrt{\gamma}}\right\} = e^{\theta^2/2\gamma} \leqslant \frac{1}{\theta} \cong 1.44$. Thus we know that L initially decreases with γ and that for γ sufficiently large L is an increasing function of γ.

Now consider $\gamma \geqslant \frac{\theta^2}{1-\theta}$. $e^{\theta^2/2\gamma}$ will be maximized at the smallest γ, or at $\gamma = \frac{\theta^2}{1-\theta}$. At $\gamma = \frac{\theta^2}{1-\theta}$, $e^{\theta^2/2\gamma} = e^{(1-\theta)/2} \cong e^{.154} \cong 1.18 < \frac{1}{\theta} \cong 1.44$. Thus $L > 0$ if $\gamma \geqslant \frac{\theta^2}{1-\theta}$. Consider $0 \leqslant \gamma < \frac{\theta^2}{1-\theta}$. At $\gamma = 0$, $L < 0$ and $[\cdot] < 0$, $\frac{\partial[\cdot]}{\partial\gamma} = N'\left\{\frac{-\theta}{\sqrt{\gamma}}\right\}\gamma^{-3/2}\left[-1 + \frac{\theta^2}{\gamma} + \theta\right]$, which implies, $\frac{\partial[\cdot]}{\partial\gamma} > 0$ if $\gamma < \frac{\theta^2}{1-\theta}$. Thus $= \left.\frac{\partial P_{max}}{\partial S}\right|_{S=1/2}$ can change signs only once during interval $0 \leqslant \gamma \leqslant \frac{\theta^2}{1-\theta}$. Thus L starts out negative at $\gamma = 0$, and is positive at $\gamma = \frac{\theta^2}{1-\theta}$ and remains positive thereafter.

Q.E.D.

REFERENCES

1. F. Black, and M. Scholes. "The Pricing of Options and Corporate Liabilities." *Journal of Political Economy* (1973).
2. D. Cox, and H. Miller. *Theory of Stochastic Processes* (Methuen & Co., LTD., London: 1965).
3. J. Cox, and S. Ross. "The Pricing of Options for Jump Processes." Rodney L. White, Center for Financial Research, Working Paper 2-75 (University of Penn., Philadelphia, Penn.).
4. M. Goldman, H. Sosin, and L. Shepp. "On Contingent Claims that Insure Optimal Stock Market Investment." *Journal of Finance* (1979).

5. M. Harrision, and D. Kreps. "Martingales and the Pricing of Contingent Claims." Memorandum, Stanford University.
6. R. Merton, "Theory of Rational Option Pricing." *Bell Journal of Economics and Management Scient* (1973).
7. M. Parkinson, "Optional Pricing: The American Put." *Journal of Business* (Jan., 1977).
8. L. Shepp, "The Joint Density of the Maximum and its Location for a Wiener Process with Drift." *Journal of Applied Probability* (1979).
9. C. Smith, "Option Pricing." *Journal of Financial Economics* (1976).

[20]

Mathematical Finance, Vol. 3, No. 2 (April 1993), 149–159

OPTION AND FUTURES EVALUATION WITH DETERMINISTIC VOLATILITIES[1]

FARSHID JAMSHIDIAN

Fuji International Finance PLC, 7-11 Finsbury Circus, London, England

Several risk-neutral expectation formulae are derived in a general multifactor setting. Specializing to deterministic covariances of returns, they lead to formulae for forward and future prices as well as formulae for options on forward and futures contracts. The results are applicable to currencies, bonds, commodities with stochastic convenience yield, and stock indices. For currencies, a no-arbitrage relation between domestic and foreign economies is formulated and applied to evaluate quanto futures and options.

Merton (1973) extended the Black-Scholes (1973) European spot option formula to stochastic interest rates under the assumption of deterministic bond price volatilities. In a somewhat more general multifactor setting, but retaining the assumption of deterministic volatilities and covariances, we extend Merton's formula to options on futures contracts. This also extends the Black (1976) commodity model.[2]

Using the Cox, Ingersoll, and Ross (1981) characterization of futures and forward prices, we see that when the covariance of the spot and zero-coupon bond returns is deterministic, the forward price simply equals the futures price times the exponential of the integral of this covariance. To apply the forward option formula to futures options, the relevant variable is the forward price of the futures contract. Like the relation between forward and futures prices, it admits a simple formula under the assumption of deterministic covariances. These formulae, as well as others for forward and futures prices in terms of the spot price, are immediate consequences of certain general expectation formulae of independent interest which are derived by simple applications of the risk-neutral valuation methodology.

There are several ways to express forward and futures prices in terms of the spot price. The appropriate choice depends on the underlying security. This is emphasized by different treatments of foreign currencies as opposed to commodities with stochastic convenience yield. In the former case, risk-neutral valuations in the domestic and foreign economies are related by a no-arbitrage condition which is applied to evaluate quanto futures and options. It turns out that the "risk-neutral Brownian motion" of the domestic economy differs from that of the foreign economy by the volatility of the spot exchange rate, while the "forward-risk-adjusted Brownian motion" of the domestic economy differs from that of the foreign economy by the volatility of the forward exchange rate. Options on the ratio of two assets are also discussed.

[1]This paper expands a 1990 version entitled "Option and Futures Evaluation with Stochastic Interest Rate and Spot Yield."

[2]For a special case, a similar extension is obtained independently by Amin and Jarrow (1991) using different methods. Interest-rate models with deterministic bond price volatilities, together with a specific example, first appeared in Merton (1970), where it was also pointed out that they entail normally distributed and hence possibly negative interest rates. Merton's example was later generalized in Vasicek (1977). The probability of negative interest rates is often negligible, and because of their analytical tractability, these models have been of considerable interest. A detailed analysis of Gaussian interest rate models and additional references can be found in Jamshidian (1991).

We work in a multifactor continuous-time setting in which security prices and the instantaneous interest rate $r(t)$ are Itô processes with respect to an n-dimensional (column vector) Brownian motion $\tilde{z}(t)$ on an interval of time $[0, \tau]$ (or a subinterval of it). For any Itô process $X(t) > 0$, we write $dX(t)/X(t) = \tilde{\mu}_X(t)\,dt + \sigma_X(t)\,d\tilde{z}(t)$, with $\sigma_X(t)$ a row vector. We assume the absence of arbitrage opportunities as in Harrison and Pliska (1981). More specifically, we assume that there is an n-dimensional (column vector) Itô process $\lambda(t)$, known as the market price of risk, such that the cash price $C(t)$ of any asset which has no cash flows on an interval of time (e.g., a zero-dividend stock, a zero-coupon bond, or a European option) satisfies $\tilde{\mu}_C(t) = r(t) + \sigma_C(t)\lambda(t)$ on that interval. Assuming $\tilde{E}[\exp(\frac{1}{2}\int_0^\tau |\lambda(t)|^2\,dt)] < \infty$, there exists by Girsonov's theorem an equivalent measure, known as the equivalent martingale measure or the risk-neutral measure, under which the process $z(t) = \tilde{z}(t) + \int_0^t \lambda(s)\,ds$, referred to here as the risk-neutral Brownian motion, is a Brownian motion on $[0, \tau]$. The expectation operator with respect to the risk-neutral measure is denoted by $E[\cdot]$ and referred to as the risk-neutral expectation. For an Itô process $X(t) > 0$, we write $dX(t)/X(t) = \mu_X(t)\,dt + \sigma_X(t)\,dz(t)$ and refer to $\mu_X = \tilde{\mu}_X - \sigma_X\lambda$ as the risk-neutral drift.

If $C(t) > 0$ is the cash price of a traded asset with no cash flows, then it follows from this setup that $\mu_C(t) = r(t)$. This (together with the condition $E[\exp(\frac{1}{2}\int_0^\tau |\sigma_C(t)|^2\,dt)] < \infty$) implies the risk-neutral valuation formula that for all $t \le T$,

$$C(t) = E_t\left[\exp\left(-\int_t^T r(s)\,ds\right) C(T)\right]. \tag{1.1}$$

In particular, the price at time t of the T-maturity zero-coupon bond ($t \le T$) is given by

$$P_T(t) \equiv E_t\left[\exp\left(-\int_t^T r(s)\,ds\right)\right]. \tag{1.2}$$

Cox, Ingersoll, and Ross (1981) have shown that the price at time t of a futures contract with delivery date T ($t \le T$) on a security with price process $S(t)$ is given by

$$F_T(t) \equiv E_t[S(T)], \tag{1.3}$$

while the T-delivery forward price is given by (e.g., as in their equation (48) or (23))

$$f_T(t) \equiv E_t[\exp\left(-\int_t^T r(s)\,ds\right) S(T)]/P_T(t). \tag{1.4}$$

Note $F_T(T) = f_T(T) = S(T)$, and if $r(t)$ is deterministic, then $f_T(t) = F_T(t)$ for all $t \le T$.

The above setup and formulae are well known and constitute the starting point of our discussion. The proofs of the following propositions are provided in Appendix A.[3]

[3] All positive Itô processes $X(t)$ in this paper are assumed from now on to satisfy $E[\exp(\frac{1}{2}\int_0^\tau |\sigma_X(t)|^2\,dt)] < \infty$. The notation $\mathrm{cov}_t[dX/X, dY/Y] = \sigma_X(t)\sigma_Y(t)'\,dt$ is employed to denote the instantaneous covariance of returns between $X(t)$ and $Y(t)$ (i.e., the quadratic covariation of $\log(X(t))$ and $\log(Y(t))$). All times and maturities will be presumed to be less than or equal to τ.

PROPOSITION 1.1. *In general, for any positive spot price process $S(t)$ and all $t \le T$,*

$$f_T(t) = E_t\left[S(T)\exp\left(\int_t^T \mathrm{cov}_s\left[\frac{df_T}{f_T}, \frac{dP_T}{P_t}\right]\right)\right]. \tag{1.5}$$

In particular, if $\mathrm{cov}_t[df_T(t)/f_T(t), dP_T(t)/P_T(t)]$ *is deterministic, then* $\sigma_{f_T} = \sigma_{F_T}$, and

$$f_T(t) = F_T(t)\exp\left(\int_t^T \mathrm{cov}_s\left[\frac{df_T}{f_T}, \frac{dP_T}{P_T}\right]\right). \tag{1.6}$$

If a call option with expiration T and strike price K on an s-delivery forward contract ($T \le s$) is exercised at time T, then the payoff $f_s(T) - K$ is realized not at time T but at time s. Consequently, the value of this option at expiration T is $\max(0, P_s(T)(f_s(T) - K))$, and therefore by (1.1) its value at time t ($t \le T \le s$) is[4]

$$c(t; s, T, K) \equiv E_t\left[\exp\left(-\int_t^T r(u)\,du\right)\max(0, P_s(T)(f_s(T) - K))\right]. \tag{1.7}$$

PROPOSITION 1.2. *If $\sigma_{f_s}(t)$ is deterministic, then*

$$c(t; s, T, K) = P_s(t)[f_s(t)\Phi(h_+) - K\Phi(h_-)], \tag{1.8}$$

where $\Phi(h)$ denotes the standard normal distribution function and

$$h_\pm \equiv \frac{(\log f_s(t)/K)}{\nu} \pm \frac{\nu}{2}, \qquad \nu^2 \equiv \int_t^T \mathrm{var}_u\left[\frac{df_s(u)}{f_s(u)}\right]. \tag{1.9}$$

The T-expiration option on the spot security is the special case of an option on the forward contract with $s = T$. Proposition 1.2 is thus applicable to an option on futures provided that the spot is regarded as the futures on the original security. For this purpose, we must first calculate the forward price of the futures contract (i.e., the price set today for entering an s-delivery futures contract at option expiration T) given by

$$F(t; s, T) \equiv E_t\left[\exp\left(-\int_t^T r(u)\,du\right)F_s(T)\right]/P_T(t). \tag{1.10}$$

[4] American and European options on forward contracts are the same. Indeed, for European forward options, by put/call parity, call $-$ put $= P_s(t)[f_s(t) - K]$. It follows that call $> P_s(t)[f_s(t) - K]$. But the latter is the payoff of the forward call option if it is exercised at time t. Thus, it is suboptimal to exercise early a forward call (or put) option. For American options on futures, the following simplification occurs when $\sigma_{F_T}(t)$ and $r(t)$ are deterministic, or more generally when they are respectively functions $\sigma(F, t)$ and $r(F, t)$ of the futures price $F_T(t)$ and time t. Then, the price $C(t)$ of any contingent claim whose payoff depends only on the futures price will be a function $C(F, t)$ of $F_T(t)$ and t, and by Itô's lemma, $C(F, t)$ satisfies $\partial C/\partial t + \frac{1}{2}\sigma^2(F, t)F^2\partial^2 C/\partial F^2 - r(F, t)C = 0$. American call (put) options satisfy this partial differential equation below (above) the optimal exercise boundary. Thus in this case, American options on futures can be evaluated numerically by solving a *one* state-variable partial differential equation (together with the usual boundary conditions) regardless of the number of factors n.

PROPOSITION 1.3. *(a) If* $\mathrm{cov}_t[dF_s(t)/F_s(t), dP_T(t)/P_T(t)]$ *is deterministic, then*

$$F(t;\, s,\, T) = F_s(t) \exp\left(-\int_t^T \mathrm{cov}_u\left[\frac{dF_s}{F_s}, \frac{dP_T}{P_T}\right]\right). \tag{1.11}$$

(b) If $\sigma_{F_s}(t)$ *and* $\sigma_{P_T}(t)$ *are deterministic, then the price of a European call option with expiration T and strike price K on the s-delivery futures contract (having payoff* $\max(0, F_s(T) - K)$*) is given by*

$$C(t;\, s,\, T,\, K) = P_T(t)[F(t;\, s,\, T)\Phi(h_+) - K\Phi(h_-)], \tag{1.12}$$

$$h_\pm \equiv \frac{(\log F(t;\, s,\, T)/K)}{\nu} \pm \frac{\nu}{2}, \qquad \nu^2 \equiv \int_t^T \mathrm{var}_u\left[\frac{dF_s(u)}{F_s(u)}\right]. \tag{1.13}$$

In order to express forward and futures prices in terms of the spot price $S(t)$, we define the "spot yield" $y(t) = r(t) - \mu_S(t)$, so that

$$\frac{dS}{S} = (r - y)\, dt + \sigma_S\, dz. \tag{1.14}$$

For zero-coupon bonds and European options, $y(t) = 0$. If the spot security is a futures contract on another asset, then $y(t) = r(t)$. If the spot is a currency, then $y(t)$ is the foreign interest rate. In general, for all $t \le T$, $S(t) = E_t[\exp(\int_t^T (y(s) - r(s))\, ds))S(T)]$. Therefore, if $y(t)$ is deterministic, then by (1.4), $f_T(t) = S(t)\exp(-\int_t^T y(s)\, ds)/P_T(t)$. If the spot is an equity index with a continuous and stochastic dividend yield, or if it is a commodity with a stochastic convenience yield, then an appropriate quantity to consider is

$$Q_T(t) \equiv E_t\left[\exp\left(-\int_t^T y(s)\, ds\right)\right]. \tag{1.15}$$

In general, $Q_T(t)$ does not represent a security price. (But when $y(t) = r(t)$, $Q_T(t) = P_T(t)$.) Nevertheless, if the stochastic process for $y(t)$ is specified, $Q_T(t)$ is in principle calculable. For example, Gibson and Schwartz (1990) assume that $y(t)$ follows a mean-reverting process similar to the Vasicek (1977) interest-rate process. Vasicek's zero-coupon bond pricing formula thus provides a similar formula for $Q_T(t)$ in the Gibson-Schwartz oil model.

PROPOSITION 1.4. *(a) If* $\mathrm{cov}_t[dS(t)/S(t), dQ_T(t)/Q_T(t)]$ *is deterministic, then* $\sigma_{f_T}(t) = \sigma_S(t) + \sigma_{Q_T}(t) - \sigma_{P_T}(t)$, *and*

$$f_T(t) = \frac{S(t)Q_T(t)}{P_T(t)} \exp\left(\int_t^T \mathrm{cov}_s\left[\frac{dS}{S}, \frac{dQ_T}{Q_T}\right]\right). \tag{1.16}$$

(b) If $\mathrm{cov}_t[dS/S - dP_T/P_T, dQ_T/Q_T - dP_T/P_T]$ *is deterministic, then* $\sigma_{F_T}(t) = \sigma_S(t) + \sigma_{Q_T}(t) - \sigma_{P_T}(t)$, *and*

$$F_T(t) = \frac{S(t)Q_T(t)}{P_T(t)} \exp\left(\int_t^T \operatorname{cov}_s\left[\frac{dS}{S} - \frac{dP_T}{P_T}, \frac{dQ_T}{Q_T} - \frac{dP_T}{P_T}\right]\right). \tag{1.17}$$

Note that (1.16) and (1.17) are consistent with (1.6). For some applications to commodities with stochastic convenience yield, it is desirable to alternatively express the "term structure of futures prices" in terms of the spot price $S(t)$, the initial "futures price curve" $F_T(0)$, and the "initial futures volatility curve" $\sigma_{F_T}(0)$. Jamshidian (1990) has shown that

$$\sigma_{F_T}(t) = \sigma_S(t)\frac{\sigma_{F_T}(0)}{\sigma_{F_t}(0)} \tag{1.18}$$

for all $t \leq T$ if and only if

$$F_T(t) = F_T(0)\left(\frac{S(t)}{F_t(0)}\right)^{\alpha_t^T} \exp\left(\frac{1}{2}\alpha_t^T(1 - \alpha_t^T)\int_0^t \sigma_{F_T}{}^2(s)\, ds\right) \tag{1.19}$$

for all $t \leq T$, where $\alpha_t^T \equiv \sigma_{F_T}(0)/\sigma_{F_t}(0)$. These "quasi-Gaussian" properties hold when $\log(S(t))$ is Gaussian in the risk-neutral measure (in which case $\sigma_S(t)$ is deterministic).

Suppose the spot is the exchange rate, i.e., $S(t)$ equals the price of one unit of the foreign currency. A forward exchange-rate contract can be replicated by issuing (shorting) a domestic zero-coupon bond, exchanging the proceeds into the foreign currency at the prevailing spot rate, and purchasing a foreign zero-coupon bond with it. Therefore,

$$f_T(t) = S(t)\hat{Q}_T(t)/P_T(t), \tag{1.20}$$

where

$$\hat{Q}_T(t) \equiv \hat{E}_t\left[\exp\left(-\int_t^T y(s)\, ds\right)\right] \tag{1.21}$$

denotes the price in units of the foreign currency of the T-maturity foreign zero-coupon bond. Here, $\hat{E}[\cdot]$ denotes the risk-neutral expectation operator of the foreign economy. As discussed in Appendix B, it is related to the risk-neutral expectation operator $E[\cdot]$ of the domestic economy as follows. For all Itô processes $X(t)$ and all $t \leq T$,

$$\hat{E}_t[X(T)] = E_t\left[\exp\left(\int_t^T (y(s) - r(s))\, ds\right)S(T)X(T)\right]/S(t). \tag{1.22}$$

Appendix B also shows that the risk-neutral Brownian motion $\hat{z}(t)$ of the foreign economy is related to that of the domestic economy by $d\hat{z} = dz - \sigma_S^t\, dt$. Let us now apply these results to "quanto" futures and options, which are essentially contracts on a foreign asset with payoff fixed beforehand at a given exchange rate. For example, U.S. dollar denominated futures on the Japanese stock index Nikkei 225 are traded in the Chicago Mercantile Exchange. If $X(t)$ is the yen level of Nikkei 225 (currently around 15,000 yen), then the value of this quanto futures contract at expiration T is $X(T)$ dollars. Nikkei 225 futures also trade in the Osaka stock exchange in yen. (Actually, the value of one point of the Osaka (the MERC) contract is 1000 yen (respectively, 5 dollars).) With $S(t)$ denoting the exchange rate and $\hat{E}[\cdot]$ as before, the following proposition relates the level $F_T(t)$ of the Chicago quanto futures contract to the level $\hat{F}_T(t)$ of Osaka futures contract.

PROPOSITION 1.5. *Let $X(t) > 0$ be an Itô process. Set $\hat{F}_T(t) = \hat{E}_t[X(T)]$ and $F_T(t) = E_t[X(T)]$. Then*

$$F_T(t) = \hat{E}_t\left[X(T)\exp\left(-\int_t^T \mathrm{cov}_s\left[\frac{dS}{S}, \frac{dF_T}{F_T}\right]\right)\right]. \tag{1.23}$$

In particular, if $\mathrm{cov}_t[dS/S, dF_T/F_T]$ is deterministic, then $\sigma_{F_T} = \sigma_{\hat{F}T}$ and

$$F_T(t) = \hat{F}_T(t)\exp\left(-\int_t^T \mathrm{cov}_s\left[\frac{dS}{S}, \frac{d\hat{F}_T}{\hat{F}_T}\right]\right). \tag{1.24}$$

There also exist a variety of over-the-counter "quanto options," often embedded in fixed income securities. For example, a quanto call option on the Nikkei 225 has payoff $\max(X(T) - K, 0)$ dollars, where $X(T)$ is the yen level of Nikkei 225 at expiration. The following proposition expresses the dollar quanto forward price $f_T(t)$ in terms of the actual yen forward price $\hat{f}_T(t)$. Proposition 1.2 then yields the price of a European quanto option, and Proposition 1.4(a) (applied to the Japanese economy) can be used to express the result in terms of the yen spot Nikkei price $X(t)$ if desired.[5]

PROPOSITION 1.6. *Let $X(t) > 0$ be an Itô process. Set $f_T(t) = E_t[\exp(-\int_t^T r(s)\cdot ds)X(T)]/P_T(t)$ and $\hat{f}_T(t) = \hat{E}_t[\exp(-\int_t^T y(s)\,ds)X(T)]/\hat{Q}_T(t)$. If $\mathrm{cov}_t[dS/S + d\hat{Q}_T/\hat{Q}_T - dP_T/P_T, df_T/f_T]$ is deterministic, then $\sigma_{f_T} = \sigma_{\hat{f}_T}$, and*

$$f_T(t) = \hat{f}_T(t)\exp\left(-\int_t^T \mathrm{cov}_s\left[\frac{dS}{S} + \frac{d\hat{Q}_T}{\hat{Q}_T} - \frac{d\mathbf{P}_T}{\mathbf{P}_T}, \frac{d\hat{f}_T}{\hat{f}_T}\right]\right). \tag{1.25}$$

Thus, the quanto futures price differs from the actual futures price by the covariance of the spot exchange rate with the futures price, while the quanto forward price differs from the actual forward price by the covariance of the forward exchange rate with the forward price.

Recently, options on the ratio of two assets have appeared over-the-counter, e.g., on the ratio of S&P 500 with S&P 100. To evaluate such an option, by Proposition 1.2 it is again sufficient to calculate the forward price of the ratio, which is given in

[5] Reiner (1992) has independently obtained the quanto option formula for the special case of deterministic interest rates and dividend yields. Quanto futures and option prices are sensitive to changes in the exchange rate, despite the fact that the exchange rate does not appear in formulae (1.24) and (1.25). To calculate the hedge ratio with respect to the spot exchange rate $S(t)$, one should multiply and divide these formulae by $S(t)$, thereby expressing quanto futures and forward prices as the product of two "domestically traded assets." The partial derivatives of quanto futures and forward prices with respect to the spot exchange rate thus turn out to be, respectively, the right-hand sides of (1.24) and (1.25) divided by $S(t)$.

PROPOSITION 1.7. *For any Itô process* $X(t) > 0$ *set* $f_T^X(t) = E_t[\exp(-\int_t^T r(s) \cdot ds)X(T)]/P_T(t)$. *If* $\mathrm{cov}_t[df_T^Y/f_T^Y, df_T^Y/f_T^Y - df_T^X/f_T^X)$ *is deterministic, then*

$$f_T^{X/Y}(t) = \frac{f_T^X(t)}{f_T^Y(t)} \exp\left(\int_t^T \mathrm{cov}_s\left[\frac{df_T^Y}{f_T^Y}, \frac{df_T^Y}{f_T^Y} - \frac{df_T^X}{f_T^X}\right]\right). \tag{1.26}$$

APPENDIX A

The key tool in all the derivations is Itô's product and division rules. Let $X(t) > 0$ and $Y(t) > 0$ be Itô processes. Then by Itô's product rule

$$\mu_{XY} = \mu_X + \mu_Y + \sigma_X \sigma_Y^t, \qquad \sigma_{XY} = \sigma_X + \sigma_Y; \tag{1.27}$$

and by Itô's division rule,

$$\mu_{X/Y} = \mu_X - \mu_Y + \sigma_Y(\sigma_Y - \sigma_X)^t, \qquad \sigma_{X/Y} = \sigma_X - \sigma_Y. \tag{1.28}$$

LEMMA A.1. *(a) For any Itô process* $X(t) > 0$ *satisfying* $E_t[\exp(\frac{1}{2}\int_t^T |\sigma_X(s)|^2\, ds)] < \infty$, *and all* $t \leq T$,

$$X(t) = E_t\left[\exp\left(-\int_t^T \mu_X(s)\, ds\right) X(T)\right]. \tag{1.29}$$

(b) If $X(t) > 0$, $Z(t) > 0$, *and* $\mu(t)$ *are Itô processes such that for some* $T > 0$, $X(t) = E_t[\exp(-\int_t^T \mu(s)\, ds)Z(T)]$ *for all* $t \leq T$, *then* $\mu_X(t) = \mu(t)$ *for all* $t \leq T$.

Proof. (a) Set $Y(t) = X(t)\exp(-\int_0^t \mu(s)\, ds)$. Then $dY/Y = dX/X - \mu_X\, dt = \sigma_X\, dz$. Hence, $Y(t)$ is a martingale in the risk-neutral measure (provided $\mathrm{E}_t[\exp(\frac{1}{2}\int_t^T \sigma_X^2(s)\, ds)] < \infty$.) Thus $Y(t) = E_t[Y(T)]$. Substituting for Y gives (1.29).

(b) Noting $Z(T) = X(T)$, the assumption implies that $Y(t) \equiv X(t)\exp(-\int_0^t \mu(s)\, ds)$ satisfies $Y(t) = E_t[Y(T)]$, and is hence a martingale. Thus, $0 = \mu_Y = \mu_X - \mu$. □

Proof of Proposition 1.1. Set $C(t) = \mathrm{E}_t[\exp(-\int_t^T r(s)\, ds)S(T)]$. By Lemma A.1(b), $\mu_C(t) = r(t)$. Since $f_T(t) = C(t)/P_T(t)$, it follows from Itô's division rule that

$$\mu_{f_T} = \mu_C - \mu_{P_T} + \sigma_{P_T}(\sigma_{P_T} - \sigma_C)^t = -\sigma_{P_T}\sigma_{f_T}^t. \tag{1.30}$$

Equation (1.5) now follows from Lemma A.1(a). □

REMARK. Applying Itô's division rule and Lemma A.1(a) to $X(t) \equiv F_T(t)/f_T(t)$, one also has

$$F_T(t) = f_T(t)E_t\left[\exp\left(\int_t^T \mathrm{cov}_s\left[\frac{df_T}{f_T}, \frac{dF_T}{F_T} - \frac{df_T}{f_T} - \frac{dP_T}{P_T}\right]\right)\right].$$

To prove Propositions 1.2, 1.6, and 1.7, we utilize the concept of forward-risk adjustment from Jamshidian (1987). For a fixed $T > 0$, assuming that $E[\exp(\frac{1}{2}\int_0^T |\sigma_{P_T}(t)|^2\, dt)] < \infty$, there exists by Girsonov's theorem an equivalent measure under which the process

$$z^T(t) \equiv z(t) - \int_0^t \sigma_{P_T}(s)' \, ds \qquad (t \leq T) \tag{1.31}$$

is a Brownian motion. We refer to this measure as the *T-maturity forward-risk-adjusted (FRA) measure* and denote the associated expectation operator by $E^T[\cdot]$. Thus, for all Itô processes $X(t)$ and all $0 \leq t \leq T \leq s$,

$$E_t^s[X(T)] = E_t\left[\exp\left(-\frac{1}{2}\int_t^T |\sigma_{P_s}(u)|^2\, du + \int_t^T \sigma_{P_s}(u)\, dz(u)\right) X(T)\right]$$

$$= E_t\left[\exp\left(-\int_t^T r(u)\, du\right) P_s(T)\, X(T)\right] / P_s(t).$$

In particular, $f_T(t) = E_t^T[S(T)]$, and consequently $f_T(t)$ is a martingale in the T-maturity FRA measure. This is also indicated by (1.30) which (for $X(t) > 0$) implies $df_T(t)/f_T(t) = \sigma_{f_T}(t) dz^T(t)$.[6]

Proof of Proposition 1.2. Since $c(t;\, s,\, T,\, K)/P_s(t)$ is the forward option price, it is a martingale in the s-maturity FRA measure. Thus in general,

$$c(t;\, s,\, T,\, K) = P_s(t) E_t^s[\max(0,\, f_s(T) - K)]. \tag{1.32}$$

Now if $\sigma_{f_s}(t)$ is deterministic, then $\log(f_s(t))$ is a Gaussian process in the s-maturity FRA measure, and hence, conditioned on time t, $f_s(T)$ is log-normally distributed in the s-maturity FRA measure with mean $f_s(t)$ and

$$\text{var}_t^s[\log f_s(T)] = \int_t^T |\sigma_{f_s}(u)|^2\, du = \nu^2. \tag{1.33}$$

The desired result follows from a standard formula for the expectation in (1.32). □

[6] Like forward prices, forward interest rates $r_T(t) \equiv -\partial \log(P_T(t))/\partial T$ are martingales in the FRA measure, and $r_T(t) = E_t^T[r(T)]$. Since $\partial(P_s(T)/P_s(t))/\partial s = (r_s(t) - r_s(T))P_s(T)/P_s(t)$, differentiating the identity

$$E_t^s[X(T)] = E_t[\exp(-\textstyle\int_t^T r(u)\, du) P_s(T) X(T)]/P_s(t)$$

gives $\partial E_t^s[X(T)]/\partial s = -\text{cov}_t^s[r_s(T), X(T)]$. This in turn implies that

$$\frac{\partial E_t^T[X(T)]}{\partial T} = E_t^T[\nu_X(T)] - \text{cov}_t^T[r(T), X(T)], \qquad \text{where } dX = \nu_X\, dt + \delta_X\, dz.$$

It is possible to prove Proposition 1.2 without recourse to forward risk adjustment. However, one then additionally needs to assume that $\sigma_{P_s}(t)$ is deterministic. Forward risk adjustment is also useful for other contingent claims and more complex interest-rate processes. See Jamshidian (1991).

Proof of Proposition 1.3. Equation (1.11) is a direct consequence of the fact that in general

$$F_s(t)P_T(t) = E_t\left[\exp\left(-\int_t^T (r(u) + \sigma_{P_T}(u)\sigma_{F_s}(u)^t)\, du\right) F_s(T)\right]. \tag{1.34}$$

This follows from Lemma A.1(a) because $P_T(T) = 1$ and by Itô's product rule the (risk-neutral) drift of $F_s(t)P_T(t)$ is the integrand in (1.34). Part (b) is now a direct consequence of Proposition 1.2. (Note the volatility vectors of $F(t;\, s,\, T)$ and $F_s(t)$ are the same by (1.11).) □

Proof of Proposition 1.4. Equation (1.16) is a direct consequence of (1.4) and the fact that in general

$$S(t)Q_T(t) = E_t\left[\exp\left(-\int_t^T (r(s) + \sigma_{Q_T}(s)\sigma_S(s)^t)\, ds\right) S(T)\right]. \tag{1.35}$$

This follows from Lemma A.1(a) because $Q_T(T) = 1$ and by Itô's product rule the drift of $S(t)Q_T(t)$ is the integrand in (1.35). Equation (1.17) is a direct consequence of (1.3) and the fact that in general

$$\frac{S(t)Q_T(t)}{P_T(t)} = E_t\left[\exp\left(\int_t^T (\sigma_{P_T} - \sigma_{Q_T})(\sigma_S - \sigma_{P_T})^t\, ds\right) S(T)\right]. \tag{1.36}$$

This follows from Lemma A.1(a) because $P_T(T) = Q_T(T) = 1$ and by Itô's product and division rules the drift of $S(t)Q_T(t)/P_T(t)$ is the negative of the integrand in (1.36). □

Proof of Proposition 1.5. Recall, $d\hat{z}(t) = dz(t) - \sigma_S(t)^t\, dt$. Therefore, setting $F(t) = F_T(t)$, we have $dF/F = \sigma_F\, dz = \sigma_F\sigma_S^t\, dt + \sigma_F\, d\hat{z}$. Equation (1.23) now follows from Lemma A.1(a) applied to $F(t)$ in the foreign risk-neutral measure and by using that $F(T) = X(T)$. □

Proof of Proposition 1.6. Recall the definition of forward-risk-adjusted (FRA) measure and use a similar notation with a hat for the FRA measure of the foreign economy. Then,

$$d\hat{z}^T = d\hat{z} - \sigma_{\hat{Q}_T}^t\, dt = dz - (\sigma_S + \sigma_{\hat{Q}_T})^t\, dt = dz^T - (\sigma_S + \sigma_{\hat{Q}_T} - \sigma_{P_T})^t\, dt.$$

Setting $f(t) = f_T(t) = E_t^T[X(T)]$, we get $df/f = \sigma_f\, dz^T = \sigma_f(\sigma_S + \sigma_{\hat{Q}_T} - \sigma_{P_T})^t\, dt + \sigma_f\, d\hat{z}^T$. Applying Lemma A.1(a) to $f(t)$ in the foreign FRA measure while noting $f(T) = X(T)$ gives

$$f_T(t) = \hat{E}_t^T\left[X(T)\exp\left(-\int_t^T \text{cov}_s\left[\frac{dS}{S} + \frac{d\hat{Q}_T}{\hat{Q}_T} - \frac{dP_T}{P_T}, \frac{df_T}{f_T}\right]\right)\right].$$

Since $\hat{f}_T(t) = \hat{E}_t^T[X(T)]$, (1.25) follows if the above covariance is deterministic. □

Proof of Proposition 1.7. By Itô's division rule, the drift in the T-maturity FRA measure of $f_T^X(t)/f_T^Y(t)$ equals $\sigma_{f_T^Y}(\sigma_{f_T^Y} - \sigma_{f_T^X})^t$. Hence, Lemma A.1(a) applies in the FRA measure implies

$$\frac{f_T^X(t)}{f_T^Y(t)} = E_t^T\left[\frac{X(T)}{Y(T)} \exp\left(-\int_t^T \sigma_{f_T^Y}(\sigma_{f_T^Y} - \sigma_{f_T^X})^t\, ds\right)\right].$$

Since $f_T^{X/Y}(t) = E_t^T[X(T)/Y(T)]$, (1.26) follows if the above covariance is deterministic. □

APPENDIX B

Absence of arbitrage clearly implies that the forward price in units of the foreign currency of an asset times the forward exchange rate must equal the forward asset price in units of the domestic currency. In other words, if $X(T)$ is the forward payoff in units of the foreign currency, then one has

$$E_t\left[\exp\left(-\int_t^T r(s)\, ds\right) S(T)X(T)\right] / P_T(t)$$
$$= \frac{S(t)\hat{Q}_T(t)}{P_T(t)} \hat{E}_t\left[\exp\left(-\int_t^T y(s)\, ds\right) X(T)\right] / \hat{Q}_T(t).$$

(Note, in terms of the forward-risk-adjusted notation of Appendix A, this relation is more succinctly expressed as $E_t^T[S(T)X(T)] = E_t^T[S(T)]\hat{E}_t^T[X(T)]$.) Replacing $X(T)$ by $\exp(\int_0^T y(s)\, ds)X(T)$ gives (1.22). As an alternative argument, let $\hat{C}(t)$ denote the price in units of the foreign currency of a cash asset with no cash flows. Then $C(t) \equiv S(t)\hat{C}(t)$ is the price in units of the domestic currency of this asset. We know $C(t)$ and $\hat{C}(t)$ must satisfy (1.1) in, respectively, the domestic and the foreign economy. Hence,

$$E_t\left[\exp\left(-\int_t^T r(s)\, ds\right) S(T)C(T)\right] = S(t)\hat{E}_t\left[\exp\left(-\int_t^T y(s)\, ds\right) C(T)\right],$$

which is similar to the previously derived relation. Next, we claim that the vector process $\hat{z}(t)$ defined by $d\hat{z}(t) = dz(t) - \sigma_S(t)^t\, dt$ is a risk-neutral Brownian motion for the foreign economy. Indeed, with $C(t)$ and $\hat{C}(t)$ as above, we know that $\mu_C = r$. On the other hand, by Itô's product rule, $\mu_C = r - y + \mu_{\hat{C}} + \sigma_S\sigma_{\hat{C}}^t$. Hence, $\mu_{\hat{C}} = y - \sigma_S\sigma_{\hat{C}}^t$, which shows that $d\hat{C}/\hat{C} = y\, dt + \sigma_{\hat{C}}\, d\hat{z}$, as claimed. The relation $d\hat{z} = dz - \sigma_S^t\, dt$ implies

$$\text{(1.37)} \qquad \hat{E}_t[X(T)] = E_t\left[\exp\left(\int_t^T -\frac{1}{2}|\sigma_S(s)|^2\, ds + \sigma_S(s)\, dz(s)\right) X(T)\right],$$

which again gives (1.22) because

$$S(T) = S(t)\exp\left[\int_t^T \left(r(s) - y(s) - \frac{1}{2}|\sigma_S(s)|^2\right) ds + \sigma_S(s)\, dz(s)\right].$$

As a consequence, let $\hat{S}(t) = 1/S(t)$ denote the exchange rate from the foreign economy viewpoint. Then, using Itô's division rule we see that, as expected,

$$\frac{d\hat{S}}{\hat{S}} = (y - r + |\sigma_S|^2)\,dt - \sigma_S\,dz = (y - r)\,dt + \sigma_{\hat{S}}\,d\hat{z}.$$

As another consequence, $\mu_{\hat{Q}_T} = y - \sigma_{\hat{Q}_T}\sigma_{\hat{S}}^t$. Since $\hat{Q}_T(T) = 1$, it follows from Lemma A.1 that

$$\hat{Q}_T(t) = E_t\left[\exp\left(\int_t^T (\sigma_{\hat{Q}_T}(s)\sigma_S(s)^t - y(s))\,ds\right)\right].$$

In particular, for a deterministic covariance, $\hat{Q}_T(t) = Q_T(t)\exp(\int_t^T \mathrm{cov}_s[dS/S,\, dQ_T/Q_T])$.

REFERENCES

AMIN, K., and R. JARROW (1991): "Pricing Foreign Currency Options under Stochastic Interest Rates," *Int. J. Money Finance*, 10 (3), 310–324.

BLACK, F. (1976): "The Pricing of Commodity Contracts," *J. Financial Econ.*, 3, 167–179.

BLACK, F., and M. SCHOLES (1973): "The Pricing of Options and Corporate Liabilities," *J. Political Econ.*, 81, 637–154.

COX, J., J. INGERSOLL, and S. ROSS (1981): "The Relation between Forward and Futures Prices," *J. Financial Econ.*, 9, 321–346.

GIBSON, R., and E. SCHWARTZ (1990): "Stochastic Convenience Yield and the Pricing of Oil Contingent Claims," *J. Finance*, 45, 959–976.

HARRISON, R. J., and S. PLISKA (1981): "Martingales and Stochastic Integrals in the Theory of Continuous Trading," *Stoch. Process. Appl.*, 11, 215–260.

JAMSHIDIAN, F. (1987): "Pricing of Contingent Claims in the One-Factor Term Structure Model," Working Paper.

JAMSHIDIAN, F. (1990): "Commodity Option Evaluation in the Gaussian Futures Term Structure Model," *Rev. Futures Markets*, 10, 324–346.

JAMSHIDIAN, F. (1991): "Bond and Option Evaluation in the Gaussian Interest Rate Model," *Res. Finance*, 9, 131–170.

MERTON, R. (1970): "A Dynamic General Equilibrium Model of the Asset Market and Its Application to the Pricing of the Capital Structure of the Firm," working paper.

MERTON, R. (1973): "The Theory of Rational Option Pricing," *Bell J. Econ. Management Sci.*, 4, 141–183.

REINER, E. (1992): "Quanto Mechanics," *Risk*, 5 (3).

VASICEK, O. A. (1977): "An Equilibrium Characterization of the Term Structure," *J. Financial Econ.*, 5, 177–188.

[21]

J. Appl. Prob. 32, 443–458 (1995)
Printed in Israel
© *Applied Probability Trust* 1995

CHANGES OF NUMÉRAIRE, CHANGES OF PROBABILITY MEASURE AND OPTION PRICING

HÉLYETTE GEMAN,* *ESSEC, Cergy-Pontoise*
NICOLE EL KAROUI,** *Université Paris VI*
JEAN-CHARLES ROCHET,*** *GREMAQ, Université Toulouse I*

Abstract

The use of the risk-neutral probability measure has proved to be very powerful for computing the prices of contingent claims in the context of complete markets, or the prices of redundant securities when the assumption of complete markets is relaxed. We show here that many other probability measures can be defined in the same way to solve different asset-pricing problems, in particular option pricing. Moreover, these probability measure changes are in fact associated with numéraire changes; this feature, besides providing a financial interpretation, permits efficient selection of the numéraire appropriate for the pricing of a given contingent claim and also permits exhibition of the hedging portfolio, which is in many respects more important than the valuation itself.

The key theorem of general numéraire change is illustrated by many examples, among which the extension to a stochastic interest rates framework of the Margrabe formula, Geske formula, etc.

PROBABILITY MEASURE CHANGES; MARTINGALES; PRICES RELATIVE TO A NUMÉRAIRE; HEDGING PORTFOLIO; FORWARD VOLATILITY

AMS 1991 SUBJECT CLASSIFICATION: PRIMARY 90A09
SECONDARY 60G35

1. Introduction

One of the most popular technical tools for computing asset prices is the so-called 'risk-adjusted probability measure'. Elaborating on an initial idea of Arrow, Ross (1978) and Harrison and Kreps (1979) have shown that the absence of arbitrage opportunities implies the existence of a probability measure Q, such that the current price of any basic security is equal to the Q-expectation of its discounted future payments. In particular, between two payment dates, the discounted price of any security is a Q-martingale. When markets are complete, i.e. when enough non-redundant securities are being traded, Q is unique.

Received 20 July 1993; revision received 4 January 1994.

* Postal address: Finance Department, ESSEC, Avenue Bernard Hirsch, BP105, 95021 Cergy-Pontoise Cedex, France.

** Postal address: GREMAQ, IDEI, Université Toulouse 1, Plane Anatole France, 31042 Toulouse, France.

*** Postal address: Laboratoire de Probabilités, Université Paris VI, 4 Place Jussieu, Tour 56–66, 75252 Paris Cedex 05, France.

By using a very simple technical argument (Theorem 1, Section 2) we prove that many other probability measures can be defined in a similar way, and prove equally useful in various kinds of option pricing problems. More specifically, if $X(t)$ is the price process of a non-dividend-paying security (at least in the relevant time period), our main theorem states the existence of a probability measure Q_X such that the price of any security S relative to the numèraire X is a Q_X-martingale. A very general numéraire change formula is then provided and different applications to exchange options and options on options in a stochastic interest rates environment, options on bonds, etc. illustrate the efficiency of the right choice of numéraire. Some of the results in the paper may be found more or less explicitly in the existing literature. Our goal is to emphasize the generality and the efficiency of the numéraire change methodology.

2. The model and the crucial theorem

We consider a stochastic intertemporal economy, where uncertainty is represented by a probability space $(\Omega, \mathcal{F}, P)$. The only role of the probability P is in fact to define the negligible sets. Most of our applications will be taken in a continuous-time framework, within a bounded time interval $[0, T]$ but our basic argument is also valid for a discrete-time economy.

We will not completely specify the underlying assumptions on the economy. The flow of information accruing to all the agents in the economy is represented by a filtration $(\mathcal{F}_t)t \in [0, T]$, satisfying 'the usual hypotheses', i.e. the filtration $(\mathcal{F}_t)_{0 \leq t \leq \infty}$ is right continuous and $\mathcal{F}_0$ contains all the P-null sets of $\mathcal{F}$.

In the following, the word 'asset' represents a general financial instrument. We distinguish two classes of assets. One class consists of the basic securities, which are traded on the markets and are the components of the portfolio defined below. The other class of assets to be considered is the class of derivative securities, also called contingent claims, for which the key issues are the valuation and hedging. All asset price processes are continuous $\mathcal{F}_t$-semimartingales. The prices $S_1(t), \cdots, S_n(t)$ of the basic securities are observed on the financial markets and almost surely strictly positive for all t; more generally, unless otherwise specified, the price of any asset is almost surely positive.

The fundamental concept in the pricing or hedging of contingent claims is the self-financing replicating portfolio, and these self-financing portfolios consequently deserve particular attention (buy and hold portfolios are the simplest example of self-financing portfolios since there is no trade). More generally, these portfolios track the target changes over time with no addition of money.

The financial value $V(t)$ of a portfolio which includes the quantities $w_1(t), \cdots, w_n(t)$ of the assets $1, 2, \cdots, n$ is given by

$$V(t) = \sum_{k=1}^{n} w_k(t) S_k(t) \quad \text{and} \quad V(t) \geqq 0 \quad \text{for all } t \tag{1}$$

where the processes $(w_1(t))_{t \geq 0}, \cdots, (w_n(t))_{t \geq 0}$ are adapted, i.e. the quantities $w_1(t), \cdots, w_n(t)$ are chosen according to the information available at time t. The vector process $(w_1(t)), \cdots, (w_n(t))_{t \geq 0}$ is called the portfolio strategy.

Definition 1. The portfolio is called self-financing if the vector stochastic integral $\int_0^T \sum_{k=1}^n w_k(t)dS_k(t)$ exists and

$$dV(t) = \sum_{k=1}^{n} w_k(t)dS_k(t). \tag{2}$$

Remark. To understand the intuition behind Equation (2), let us take the example of a simple strategy, i.e. a strategy rebalanced only at fixed dates $0 = t_0 < t_1 < \cdots < t_n$ and that we suppose left continuous. The self-financing equation can then be written as

$$V(t_j) - V(t_{j-1}) = \sum_{k=1}^{n} w_k(t_{j-1}^{+})[S_k(t_j) - S_k(t_{j-1})].$$

By definition,

$$V(t_j) = \sum_{k=1}^{n} w_k(t_j)S_k(t_j).$$

The self-financing condition is $V(t_j) = V(t_j^+)$ for all j or in other terms,

$$\sum_{k=1}^{n} w_k(t_j)S_k(t_j) = \sum_{k=1}^{n} w_k(t_j^+)S_k(t_j). \tag{3}$$

Using (3) at time t_{j-1} and remembering that $w_k(t_j) = w_k(t_{j-1}^+)$, the self-financing condition can also be written as

$$V(t_j) - V(t_{j-1}) = \int_{]t_{j-1},t_j]} \sum_{k=1}^{n} w_k(u)dS_k(u).$$

More generally, the change of the portfolio value between any dates $t < t'$ is

$$V(t') - V(t) = \int_t^{t'} \sum_{k=1}^{n} w_k(u)dS_k(u).$$

For non-elementary strategies, this will be the definition of self-financing strategies. We have not emphasized so far the fact that there was an implicit numéraire behind the prices $S_1, S_2, \cdots, S_n$; it is the numéraire relevant for domestic transactions at time t and obviously plays a particular role. Our objective is to show that other quantities may be chosen as numéraires and that, for a given problem, there is a 'best' numéraire.

Definition 2. A numéraire is a price process $X(t)$ almost surely strictly positive for each $t \in [0, T]$.

Proposition 1. Self-financing portfolios remain self-financing after a numéraire change.

Proof. This property is straightforward from a financial viewpoint. Mathematically, it is also clear that Equation (3) still holds after a numéraire change. Let X be a new numéraire. From Itô's lemma, we derive

$$d\left(\frac{S_k(t)}{X(t)}\right) = S_k(t)d\left(\frac{1}{X(t)}\right) + \frac{1}{X(t)}dS_k(t) + d\langle S_k, 1/X\rangle_t$$

where $d\langle S_k, 1/X\rangle$ denotes the instantaneous covariance between the semimartingales S_k and $1/X$. In the same manner

$$d\left(\frac{V(t)}{X(t)}\right) = V(t)d\left(\frac{1}{X(t)}\right) + \frac{1}{X(t)}dV(t) + d\langle V, 1/X\rangle_t.$$

The self-financing condition

$$dV(t) = \sum_{k=1}^{n} w_k(t)dS_k(t) \quad \text{and} \quad V(t) = \sum_{k=1}^{n} w_k(t)S_k(t)$$

implies that

$$\begin{aligned} d\left(\frac{V(t)}{X(t)}\right) &= \sum_{k=1}^{n} w_k(t)\left\{S_k(t)d\left(\frac{1}{X(t)}\right) + \frac{1}{X(t)}dS_k(1) + d\langle S_k, 1/X\rangle_t\right\} \\ &= \sum_{k=1}^{n} w_k(t)d\left(\frac{S_k(t)}{X(t)}\right) \end{aligned}$$

and the portfolio expressed in the new numéraire remains self-financing.

Corollary and Definition 3

(a) A contingent claim (i.e. a random cash-flow H paid at time T) is called attainable if there exists a self-financing portfolio whose terminal value equals $H(T)$.

(b) If a contingent claim is attainable in a given numéraire, it is also attainable in any other numéraire and the replicating strategy is the same.

This property is immediately derived from Proposition 1.

The pricing methodology developed in the paper follows Harrison and Kreps (1979) and Harrison and Pliska (1981) in the no arbitrage assumption: for every self-financing portfolio V belonging to a particular class of portfolios, $V(0) = 0$ and $V(T) \geqq 0$ almost surely imply $V(T) = 0$.

If Ω is finite as well as the set of transaction dates, there is no restriction on the class of portfolios and the no arbitrage assumption is equivalent to the existence of a 'risk-neutral probability measure' (see Harrison and Kreps (1979), Harrison and Pliska (1981)). In our setting, as observed by Duffie and Huang (1985), this equivalence no longer holds and some requirements have to be put on the portfolios: the natural one involves square integrability conditions of the weights of the portfolio with respect to the instantaneous variance–covariance matrix of the basic assets. Delbaen and Schachermayer (1992) introduce a weaker formulation of the no arbitrage assumption, the no free lunch with vanishing risk (NFLVR), which only requires portfolios bounded below. The NFLVR condition is necessary and sufficient to exhibit a (local) martingale measure.

The former condition is clearly not invariant in a numéraire change. The latter one is if the lower bound is zero, hence the condition $V(t) \geqq 0$ for all t that we introduced earlier and which will remain valid throughout the paper unless otherwise specified. More precisely, our no arbitrage assumption will be expressed in the following manner.

Assumption 1. There exists a non-dividend-paying asset $n(t)$ and a probability π equivalent to the initial probability P such that for any basic security S_k without intermediate payments, the price of S_k relative to n, i.e. $S_k(t)/n(t)$ is a local martingale with respect to π.

By convention, we will take $n(0) = 1$.

Observations

• Portfolios themselves expressed in this numéraire will be, by definition, π-local martingales.

• Moreover, if they are positive for all t, portfolios are supermartingales, i.e.

$$\frac{V(t)}{n(t)} \geq E_\pi\left[\frac{V(T)}{n(T)} \,\middle|\, \mathscr{F}_t\right] \quad \text{almost surely.}$$

• If the terminal value $V(T)/n(T)$ is square integrable, i.e. $E_\pi[(V(T)/n(T))^2]$ is finite, then the portfolio value is a π-martingale and

$$\frac{V(t)}{n(t)} = E_\pi\left[\frac{V(T)}{n(T)} \,\middle|\, \mathscr{F}_t\right].$$

• The consequence is that if a contingent claim H is attainable and its terminal value in the numéraire n is π-square integrable, then all replicating portfolios have the same value at any intermediary date t. This value is the price at time t of the contingent claim.

• In the general case (relaxing the assumption of square integrability), all replicating (positive) portfolios do not necessarily have the same value at any date t (see Dudley (1977), developed in Karatzas and Shreve (1988)) for the non-unicity of these portfolios but all these values are bounded below by $E_\pi[H(T)/n(T) \mid \mathscr{F}_t]$.

Moreover, if there exists one replicating portfolio whose value at any time t is equal to this expectation, this value will be called the price (or *fair price*) of the contingent claim (with respect to (n, π)) and the corresponding portfolio called the hedging portfolio. Keeping the same numéraire n, if there exists another probability π' satisfying the same replicability property, then

$$E_{\pi'}\left[\frac{H(T)}{n(T)} \,\middle|\, \mathscr{F}_t\right] = E_\pi\left[\frac{H(T)}{n(T)} \,\middle|\, \mathscr{F}_t\right].$$

Hence, the fair price does not depend on the choice of the 'risk-neutral' probability measure π (as long as this price exists); this remark is very important for the main purpose of this paper, namely the choice of the optimal numéraire when pricing and hedging a given contingent claim.

We now give an example of a situation where all contingent claims have a fair price. Suppose that the prices $S_1(t), S_2(t), \cdots, S_n(t)$ of the basic securities expressed in the numéraire n are stochastic integrals with respect to q Brownian motions $W_1, \cdots, W_q$ and that the filtration $\mathscr{F}_t$ is generated by these Brownian motions. Since $S_1, S_2, \cdots, S_n$ are local martingales, their dynamics under π are driven by the stochastic differential equations

$$\frac{dS_i}{S_i} = \sum_{j=1}^{q} \sigma_{ij} dW_j, \qquad i = 1, \cdots, n.$$

If we assume that the matrix $\Sigma = [\sigma_{ij}]$ is invertible (which obviously implies $q = n$), then the martingale representation allows us to express any conditional expectation as a stochastic integral with respect to the basic asset prices, hence as a portfolio.

The same property holds if the number n of basic securities is greater than the number of Brownian motions (and rank $\Sigma = q$).

Theorem 1. Let $X(t)$ be a non-dividend paying numéraire such that $X(t)$ is a π-martingale. Then there exists a probability measure Q_X defined by its Radon–Nikodym derivative with respect to π

$$\frac{dQ_X}{d\pi} \bigg| \mathcal{F}_T = \frac{X(T)}{X(0)n(T)}$$

such that

(i) the basic securities prices are Q_X-local martingales,

(ii) if a contingent claim H has a fair price under (n, π), then it has a fair price under (X, Q_X) and the hedging portfolio is the same.

Proof

(i) If we denote by $\tilde{S} = (S(t)/X(t))$ the relative price of a security S with respect to the numéraire X, the conditional expectations formula gives

$$E_\pi\left(\frac{dQ_X}{d\pi}\tilde{S}(T) \mid \mathcal{F}_t\right) = E_{Q_X}[\tilde{S}(T) \mid \mathcal{F}_t] E_\pi\left[\frac{dQ_X}{d\pi} \bigg| \mathcal{F}_t\right].$$

By Assumption 1, we have

$$\frac{S(t)}{n(t)X(0)} = E_\pi\left[\frac{dQ_X}{d\pi}\tilde{S}(T) \mid \mathcal{F}_t\right]$$

and similarly

$$\frac{X(t)}{n(t)X(0)} = E_\pi\left[\frac{dQ_X}{d\pi} \bigg| \mathcal{F}_t\right].$$

This gives the martingale property $\tilde{S}(t)$ under Q_X, and consequently for any portfolio.

(ii) If H has a fair price under (n, π), $E_\pi[H(T)/n(T) \mid \mathcal{F}_t]$ is a self-financing portfolio. Since

$$E_{Q_X}\left[\frac{H(T)}{X(T)} \bigg| \mathcal{F}_t\right] = E_\pi\left[\frac{H(T)}{n(T)} \bigg| \mathcal{F}_t\right] \bigg/ \frac{X(t)}{n(t)}$$

and we observed earlier that the property of being a self-financing portfolio is invariant through a numéraire change, $E_{Q_X}[H(T)/n(T) \mid \mathcal{F}_t]$ is also a self-financing theorem and Theorem 1 holds.

From now on, we will concentrate on the changes of numéraire techniques.

Corollary 2. If X and Y are two arbitrary securities, the general numéraire change formula can be written at any time $t < T$ as

$$X(0)E_{Q_X}[Y(T)\Phi \mid \mathscr{F}_t] = Y(0)E_{Q_Y}[X(T)\Phi \mid \mathscr{F}_t]$$

where Φ is any random cash flow $\mathscr{F}_T$-measurable.

Proof. The formula can be immediately derived from Theorem 1, which entails

$$\left.\frac{dQ_X}{dQ_Y}\right|_{\mathscr{F}_T} = \frac{dQ_X}{d\pi}\frac{1}{dQ_Y/d\pi} = \frac{X(T)}{X(0)n(T)} \cdot \frac{1}{Y(T)/Y(0)n(T)} = \frac{X(T)/Y(T)}{X(0)/Y(0)}.$$

We will show later on in the paper how the choice of an appropriate numéraire permits us to simplify pricing and hedging problems.

We start by giving two examples of such numéraire changes already encountered in the literature. We want to emphasize the fact that in both cases, the important message is the financial suitability of the chosen numéraire to a given problem; the probability changes that follow are useful technically but also convey an economic interpretation.

Example 1: *The money market account as a numéraire.* It is natural to take as a first example of numéraire the riskless asset (assuming it exists). More precisely, we define $\beta(t)$ (also called the accumulation factor) as the value at date t of a fund created by investing one dollar at time 0 on the money market and continuously reinvested at the (instantaneously riskless) instantaneous interest rate $r(t)$. The interest rate process is denoted by $(r_t)_{t \geq 0}$. At this point we need a technical assumption.

Assumption 2. For almost all ω, $t \to r_t(\omega)$ is strictly positive and continuous and r_t is an $\mathscr{F}_t$-measurable process on $(\Omega, \mathscr{F}, \boldsymbol{P})$. Under this assumption, it is clear that

$$\beta(t) = \exp \int_0^t r(s)ds.$$

Then the relative price $\tilde{S}(t)$ of a security with respect to the numéraire β is simply its discounted price

$$\tilde{S}(t) = \left[\exp - \int_0^t r(s)ds\right] S(t).$$

The probability measure Q_β is the usual 'risk-neutral' probability measure Q defined by

$$\frac{dQ}{d\pi} = \frac{1}{n(T)} \exp \int_0^T r(s)ds.$$

'Historically' (see Harrison and Pliska (1981)), $Q = \pi$ was the first 'risk-neutral' probability measure (associated with the numéraire β) expressing that discounted asset prices are Q-martingales.

Example 2: *Zero-coupon bonds as numéraires.* A zero-coupon bond imposes itself as the numéraire when one looks at the price at time t of an asset giving right to a single cash-flow at a well-defined future time T. Keeping in mind the general martingale property of Theorem 1, the right numéraire to introduce, whether interest rates are stochastic or not, is the zero-coupon bond maturing at time T. Let us make explicit the corresponding probability measure change.

The price process of the bond will be denoted either by $B(t, T)$ or by $B_T(t)$,

$$B_T(t) = E_Q\left[\exp - \int_t^T r(s)ds \mid \mathcal{F}_t\right]$$

where Q is the probability defined in Example 1.

Corollary 2 of Theorem 1 gives

$$\frac{dQ_T}{dQ} = \frac{1}{\beta(T)} \frac{\beta(0)}{B(0, T)} = \frac{1}{B(0, T)} \exp - \left[\int_0^T r(s)dt\right].$$

The relative price $S(t)/B(t, T)$ is precisely the forward price $F_S(t)$ of the security S and from Theorem 1 we get

$$F_S(t) = E_{Q_T}\left[\frac{S(T)}{B(T, T)} \,\middle|\, \mathcal{F}_t\right].$$

In other words, the forward price, relative to time T, of a security which pays no dividend up to time T is equal to the expectation of the value at time T of this security under the 'forward neutral' probability.

The financial intuition of this result can be found in Bick (1988) and Merton (1973); the mathematical treatment was developed in the general case of stochastic interest rates by Geman (1989) and in a Gaussian interest rate framework by Jamshidian (1989). Even if this change of numéraire depends on time T and is not as universal as the 'accumulating factor' presented in Example 1, it turns out to be the right numéraire when evaluating a future random cash-flow in a stochastic interest rates environment. Besides its applications to option pricing presented in the next section, this numéraire change gives remarkable results in the pricing of floating-rate notes and of interest rate swaps, as shown in El Karoui and Geman (1991), (1994).

3. Applications to options

In this section we focus on finding interesting expressions for option prices rather than discussing their existence. Consequently, we will suppose that all options considered in the following are attainable assets. We gave earlier an example of a situation where this property holds; we must observe, though, that in many situations weaker assumptions suffice. The best example is the classical Black and Scholes framework where no assumption of completeness is necessary since it is easy to replicate the conditional expectation of the terminal pay-off by a portfolio of the riskless asset and the risky asset, hence to derive a fair price for the European call.

3.1. *A general formula.* Let us consider a call written on a security whose price dynamics $S(t)$ does not require any other specification than the fact of being a positive semimartingale.

Theorem 2. Under Assumptions 1 and 2, and denoting by T and K respectively its maturity and exercise price, the price at time 0 of the call can be written as

$$\frac{C(0)}{B(0,T)} = E_{Q_T}\left[\left(\frac{S(T)}{B(T,T)} - K\right)^+\right]$$

or

$$C(0) = S(0)Q_S(A) - KB(0,T)Q_T(A)$$

where $A = \{\omega \mid S(T,\omega) > KB(T,T)\}$.

The first expression of $C(0)$ is immediately derived from Theorem 1 used in the context of Example 2. We will prove the second one:

$$\frac{C(0)}{B(0,T)} = E_{Q_T}[(S(T) - K)^+] = E_{Q_T}\left(\frac{S(T)}{B(T,T)}\, \mathbf{1}_A\right) - KQ_T(A).$$

From the general numéraire change formula (Corollary 2 of Theorem 1), we get

$$E_{Q_T}\left(\frac{S(T)}{B(T,T)}\, \mathbf{1}_A\right) = \frac{S(0)}{B(0,T)} E_{Q_S}(\mathbf{1}_A).$$

We thus obtain the second expression of $C(0)$.

Corollary 3. In the same way, the option of exchanging asset 2 against asset 1 at time T gives right to the cash-flow $[S_1(T) - KS_2(T)]^+$ with $K = 1$ and its price $C(0)$ at time 0 is such that

$$\frac{C(0)}{S_2(0)} = E_{Q_{S_2}}\left\{\left[\frac{S_1(T)}{S_2(T)} - K\right]^+\right\}$$

or

$$C(0) = S_1(0)Q_{S_1}(A) - KS_2(0)Q_{S_1}(A)$$

where $A = \{\omega \in \Omega \mid S_1(T,\omega) \geqq KS_2(T,\omega)\}$.

This formula holds even when risky asset volatilities and interest rates are stochastic.

Corollary 4. More generally, an option which gives right to the payment at time T of the quantity $(\Sigma_{k=1}^n \lambda_k X_k(T))^+$, where $\lambda_1, \cdots, \lambda_n$ are any real numbers, $X_1, \cdots, X_n$ are risky assets and possibly $X_1(T) = K$ (the usual strike price of the option), has a value at time 0 which can be written as

$$C(0) = \sum_{k=1}^{n} \lambda_k X_k(0) Q_{X_k}(A).$$

Obviously, this is the situation encountered with options on bonds.

3.2. *Applications of Theorem* 2

(a) *A reexamination of the Black and Scholes' formula.* We will make the usual assumptions of the Black and Scholes' model, except that we will allow interest rates and risky asset volatility to be stochastic. Theorem 2 entails the following call price:

$$C(0) = S(0)Q_S(A) - KB(0, T)Q_T(A).$$

The asset involved in the second term is in fact the forward price of S,

$$F^S(t) = \frac{S(t)}{B(t, T)},$$

which is a positive martingale under Q_T and can therefore be written as a stochastic integral of a Brownian process:

$$\frac{dF^S(t)}{F^S(t)} = \sigma_{F_S}(t)dW_t^{F_S}$$

where $(\sigma_{F_S})^2 = (1/dt)\mathrm{Var}(dF^S/F^S)$.

Assuming that σ_{F_S} is deterministic, $Q_T(A)$ is equal to $\Pr(u \geqq 0)$, where u is a Gaussian variable with mean $\ln(S(0)/KB(0, T)) - \frac{1}{2}\sigma_{F_S}T$ and variance $\sigma_{F_S}T$. Consequently, $Q_T(A) = N(d_2)$ with

$$d_2 = \frac{1}{\sigma_{F_S}\sqrt{T}}\left\{\ln\frac{S(0)}{KB(0, T)} - \tfrac{1}{2}\sigma_{F_S}T\right\}.$$

The first term in the Theorem 2 formula involves the asset

$$\frac{B(t, T)}{S(t)} = \frac{1}{F^S(t)} = Z^T(t).$$

Whether stochastic or not, the volatility of Z^T under Q_S is the same as the volatility of F^S under Q_T (with possibly different Brownian processes). Assuming these volatilities deterministic,

$$Q_S(A) = Q_S\left(Z^T(T) \leqq \frac{1}{K}\right) = Q_S\left(Z(0)\exp\left(\sigma_{F_S}W_T - \frac{\sigma_{F_S}}{2}T\right) \leqq \frac{1}{K}\right)$$

$$Q_S(A) = Q_S\left(\sigma_{F_S}W_T - \frac{\sigma_{F_S}}{2}T \leqq \ln\frac{1}{KZ(0)}\right)$$

$$= N\left[\frac{1}{\sigma_{F_S}\sqrt{T}}\ln\frac{S(0)}{KB((0, T))} + \frac{1}{2}\sigma_{F_S}\sqrt{T}\right] = N(d_1).$$

In fact we obtain the Merton formula, and, if we define r by $B(0, T) = e^{-rT}$, it becomes the Black and Scholes' formula.

We have thus shown that these two formulae hold under the sole hypothesis of a volatility for the forward contract $S(t)/B(t, T)$, without any necessary specification on the asset price or interest rates.

Obviously, in the Black and Scholes' framework, interest rates are assumed constant and the hypothesis of a deterministic volatility of the forward contract is equivalent to the hypothesis of a deterministic volatility of the stock price.

(b) *Application to the exchange option.* In this case, there is no 'forward contract' of S_1 with respect to S_2. Consequently we need to specify the movement of the two asset prices under the risk neutral probability:

$$\frac{dX_1}{X_1} = rdt + \sigma_1 dW_1, \qquad \frac{dX_2}{X_2} = rdt + \sigma_2 dW_2$$

where σ_1 and σ_2 are not supposed deterministic and $\langle dW_1, dW_2 \rangle = rdt$.

Consequently, the volatility of X_1/X_2 is equal to $\sqrt{\sigma_1^2 + \sigma_2^2 - 2\rho\sigma_1\sigma_2}$ and, for the same reasons as earlier, we see that Margrabe's formula (1978) holds under the sole hypothesis of a deterministic volatility for X_1/X_2, without summing non-stochastic interest rates.

We observe that the same methodology could be applied to the pricing of equity-linked foreign exchange options also called quanto options (see Reiner (1992)).

(c) *Application to hedging.* From the calculations conducted in (a), we see that in the general situation of stochastic interest rates, the right way of hedging should not be read in the Black and Scholes' formula but in the Merton formula

$$C(0) = S(0)N(d_1) - KB(0, T)N(d_2).$$

From this, we can derive very symmetrically the quantity $N(d_1)$ to invest in the risky asset and the quantity $N(d_2)$ to invest in K zero-coupon bonds maturing at time T.

Practitioners who use these weights to hedge the option with the underlying asset and money market instruments implicitly assume non-stochastic interest rates. Moreover, it is clear that if interest rates are stochastic, what is usually denominated as the 'implied volatility' of the asset is in fact the implied volatility of the forward contract.

If interest rates are stochastic and if one wants to hedge the option with the underlying asset and short-term bills, it is necessary to assume that the same Brownian motion perturbates the movement of the risky asset and the one of the zero-coupon bond maturing at time T, namely that under the risk neutral probability, we have the following dynamics:

$$\frac{dS}{S} = rdt + \sigma_1 dW, \qquad \frac{dB^T}{B^T} = rdt + \sigma_2 dW$$

from which we derive

$$\frac{dB^T}{B^T} = r\left(1 - \frac{\sigma_2}{\sigma_1}\right) dt + \frac{\sigma_2}{\sigma_1}\frac{dS}{S}.$$

Consequently, we see that the quantity to hold short in the risky asset in order to hedge the option is not $N(d_1)$ but in fact

$$\frac{\partial C}{\partial S}+\frac{\sigma_2}{\sigma_1}\frac{B(t,T)}{S(t)}\frac{\partial C}{\partial B},$$

i.e.

$$N(d_1)-K\frac{\sigma_2}{\sigma_1}\frac{B(t,T)}{S(t)}N(d_2).$$

The number of risky stocks involved in the self-financing portfolio replicating the European call is not $N(d_1)$, but the partial derivative of the Black and Scholes price with respect to the underlying stock and well-known as the delta of the call.

The classical 'Δ hedging' is correct under stochastic interest rates only if the hedging portfolio involves, besides the risky stock, the zero-coupon bond maturing at time T.

(d) *Application to compound options.* We now extend the pricing formula given by Geske (1979) for a compound option but without assuming deterministic interest rates. This involves, besides the risky stock, the zero-coupon. Let $C_1(t, S)$ be the price at date t of a European call option on the stock, with strike price K_1 and exercise data T_1; $C_2(t, S)$ be the price at date t of a European call option on C_1, with strike price K_2 and $T_2 < T_1$; $A_1 = \{\omega \in \Omega \mid S(T_1, \omega) \geqq K_1\}$ be the exercise set of option C_1; and $A_2 = \{\omega \in \Omega \mid S(T_2, \omega) \geqq S^*\}$ be the exercise set of option C_2, where S^* is defined implicitly by $C_1(T_2, S^*) = K_2$.

In the same spirit as earlier, we write

$$C_2(0) = B(0, T_2)E_{Q_{T_2}}\{[C_1(T_2, S(T_2)) - K_2]^+\}$$

$$C_2(0) = -K_2B(0, T_2)Q_{T_2}(A_2) + B(0, T_2)E_{Q_{T_2}}[C_1(T_2, S(T_2))\mathbf{1}_{A_2}].$$

Making explicit $C_1(T_2, S(T_2))$, we get

$$B(0, T_2)E_{Q_{T_2}}[C_1(T_2, S(T_2)\mathbf{1}_{A_2}]$$

$$= B(0, T_2)E_{Q_{T_2}}[\mathbf{1}_{A_2}B(T_2, T_1)E_{Q_{T_1}}\{(S(T_1) - K_1)^+\} \mid \mathscr{F}_{T_2}].$$

Taking in Corollary 1 the asset X as the zero-coupon bond maturing at time T_1, Y as the zero-coupon bond maturing at time T_2 and $T = T_2$, we rewrite this expression as

$$B(0, T_1)E_{Q_{T_1}}[\mathbf{1}_{A_2}E_{Q_{T_1}}\{(S(T_1) - K_1)^+ \mid \mathscr{F}_{T_2}\}]$$

or

$$B(0, T_1)E_{Q_{T_1}}[\mathbf{1}_{A_2}S(T_1)\mathbf{1}_{A_1}] - K_1B(0, T_1)Q_{T_1}(A_1 \cap A_2).$$

Using again the change of numéraire formula, we obtain

$$B(0, T_1)E_{Q_{T_1}}[S(T_1)\mathbf{1}_{A_1 \cap A_2}] = S(0)Q_S(A_1 \cap A_2).$$

Regrouping the different terms, we write the price of the compound option as

$$C_2(0) = S(0)Q_S(A_1 \cap A_2) - K_1B(0, T_1)Q_{T_1}(A_1 \cap A_2) - K_2B(0, T_2)Q_{T_2}(A_2).$$

This formula does not assume interest rates and stock price volatility to be non-stochastic.

If we make the assumption of a deterministic stock price volatility, we can prove by the same arguments as in Section 2.2 that

$$Q_{T_2}(A_2) = N(\delta_2) = N\left(\frac{1}{\sigma\sqrt{T_2}} \ln \frac{S(0)}{S^*B(0, T_2)} - \frac{1}{2}\sigma\sqrt{T_2}\right),$$

$$Q_{T_1}(A_1 \cap A_2) = N(\delta_1, \delta_2)$$

where

$$\delta_1 = \frac{1}{\sigma\sqrt{T_1}} \ln \frac{S(0)}{K_1 B(0, T_1)} - \frac{1}{2}\sigma\sqrt{T_1}$$

and $N(\cdot,\cdot)$ is the cumulative function of a centred bivariate Gaussian distribution with covariance matrix

$$\begin{bmatrix} 1 & \sqrt{\dfrac{T_2}{T_1}} \\ \sqrt{\dfrac{T_2}{T_1}} & 1 \end{bmatrix},$$

$$Q_S(A_1 \cap A_2) = N(\delta_1 + \sigma\sqrt{T_1}, \delta_2 + \sigma\sqrt{T_2}).$$

Regrouping the different terms, we obtain Geske's formula for stochastic interest rates

$$\begin{aligned} C_2(0) = {} & S(0)N(\delta_1 + \sigma\sqrt{T_1}, \delta_2 + \sigma\sqrt{T_2}) \\ & - K_1 B(0, T_1)N(\delta_1, \delta_2) - K_2 B(0, T_2)N(\delta_2). \end{aligned}$$

4. Options on bonds

This section concerns European calls on default-free bonds.

4.1. *Options on zero-coupon bonds*. Theorem 2 entails the following formula for the price of a call maturing at date T_0 written on zero-coupon bonds maturing at date T_1

$$C(0) = B(0, T_1)Q_{T_1}(A) - KB(0, T_0)Q_{T_0}(A)$$

where K is the exercise price and A the exercise set.

(a) In the same manner as Heath et al. (1987), we will assume the following dynamics of the term structure of interest rates

$$\frac{dB(t, T)}{B(t, T)} = r(t)dt + \sigma(t, T)dW_t$$

where $\sigma(t, T)$ is decreasing in t and $\sigma(T, T) = 0$.

Assuming $\sigma(t, T)$ deterministic, the same arguments as in Example 1 of Section 3 provide a formula of the Black–Scholes type

$$C(0) = B(0, T_1)N(d_1) - KB(0, T_0)N(d_2)$$

where

$$d_2 = \frac{1}{2}\sigma\sqrt{T_0} + \frac{1}{\sigma\sqrt{T_0}} \ln \frac{B(0, T_1)}{KB(0, T_0)}$$

$$d_1 = d_2 - \sigma\sqrt{T_0}$$

and σ is the volatility of the forward price $B(t, T_1)/B(t, T_0)$ of the zero-coupon bond.

(b) Another explicit formula was obtained by Cox et al. (1985) in the context of stochastic volatilities, but with a one-state variable description of the term structure of interest rates. The (risk-adjusted) dynamics of the short rate is defined by

$$dr(t) = a(b - r(t))dt + \sigma dW_t \quad \text{where } a, b \text{ and } \sigma \text{ are positive constants.}$$

From that dynamics, it follows that the short rate is distributed under Q (respectively Q_{T_0}, Q_{T_1}) as a non-central χ^2 process with parameter of non-centrality q (respectively q_0, q_1). Cox et al. show that the call is exercised if and only if $r(T_0)$ is less than a critical level d_0; they obtain an explicit formula for a call on a zero-coupon bond, which can be written in our notation as

$$C(0) = B(0, T_1)\chi^2(d_1, n_1, q_1) - KB(0, T_0)\chi^2(d_0, n, q_0)$$

where $\chi^2(\cdot, n, q)$ is the non-centred χ^2 distribution with n degrees of freedom and parameter of non-centrality q; n, q_0, q_1, d_0 and d_1 are parameters depending on a, b, σ and the characteristics of the call. It is interesting to notice that the assumption of a deterministic volatility of interest rates is not necessary to obtain a formula à la Black and Scholes. The result holds because the spot rate driven by the dynamics

$$dr = a(b - r)dt + \sigma\sqrt{r}dW$$

follows a χ^2 distribution and that under the 'forward neutral' probability associated to any date T, this is still true (with a change in the drift of dr); consequently, the probabilities of exercise under the different probabilities are expressed in terms of non-centred χ^2 distributions.

4.2. *Options on coupon bonds*. Let us suppose that the underlying asset is a general default-free bond, characterized by the sequence $F_1, F_2, \cdots, F_n$ of fixed payments it generates at times $T_1, \cdots, T_n$. Under the assumptions and notation of Section 3, its price at date t ($t < T_1 < \cdots < T_n$) is given by $P(t) = \Sigma_{i=1}^n F_i B(t, T_i)$, where

$$B(t, T) = E_Q\left[\exp - \int_t^T r(s)ds / F_t\right].$$

We consider a call written on the bond, with exercise price K and maturity $T_0 < T_1$.

The probability of exercise will involve the distribution of n variables, namely the prices of the n zero-coupon bonds $B(0, T_1), \cdots, B(0, T_n)$. To obtain a formula of the Black and Scholes type, it is necessary that these n prices depend on only one state-variable, for instance the spot rate.

In the Gaussian case with one source of randomness (as in Section 3, 1(a)), this is equivalent to assuming a Markovian spot rate, or in other words, a deterministic volatility $\sigma(t, T)$ which has the form

$$\sigma(t, T) = [h(T) - h(t)]g(t).$$

Jamshidian (1989) and El Karoui and Rochet (1989) obtain under these hypotheses a quasi-explicit formula for the call price

$$C(0) = \sum_{i=1}^{n} F_i B(0, T_i) N(d_i) - KB(0, T_0) N(d_0)$$

where $d_i = d_0 + \mu_i$,

$$\mu_i^2 = \int_0^{T_0} [\sigma(s, T_i) - \sigma(s, T_0)]^2 ds$$

and d_0 is defined implicitly by

$$\sum_{i=1}^{n} F_i B(0, T_i) \exp\{-\tfrac{1}{2}\mu_i^2 + d_0 \mu_i\} = KB(0, T_0).$$

5. Conclusion

The paper has shown that a change of numéraire does not change the self-financing portfolios, and hence does not change the hedging or replicating portfolios either. An immediate consequence in option pricing is that, depending on whether the option under analysis is written on a stock, on a bond, is an exchange option or a compound option, the choice of the appropriate numéraire will provide the easiest calculations and the relevant hedging portfolio.

Acknowledgements

Helpful comments from Robert Geske on an earlier version of this paper are gratefully acknowledged. All remaining errors are ours.

References

BALL, C. A. AND TOROUS, W. N. (1983) Bond price dynamics and options. *J. Financial and Quantitative Anal.* **18**(4).

BICK, A. (1988) Producing derivative assets with forward contracts. *J. Financial and Quantitative Anal.* **23**(2).

BLACK, F. AND SCHOLES, M. (1973) The pricing of options and corporate liabilities. *J. Political Econ.* **81**, 637–654.

COX, J. C., INGERSOLL, J. E. AND ROSS, S. A. (1985) A theory of the term structure of interest rates. *Econometrica* **53**, 407.

COX, J. C., ROSS, S. AND RUBINSTEIN, M. (1979) Option pricing: a simplified approach. *J. Financial Econ.* **3**, 145–166.

DELBAEN, F. AND SCHACHERMAYER, W. (1992) A general version of the fundamental theorem of asset pricing. *Conference INRIA-NSF on Mathematical Finance*, Paris.

DUDLEY, R. M. (1977) Wiener functionals as Itô integrals. *Ann. Prob.* **5**, 140–141.

DUFFIE, D. AND HUANG, C. F. (1985) Implementing Arrow–Debreu equilibrium by continuous trading of few long-lived securities. *Econometrica* **53**, 1337–1356.

EL KAROUI, N. AND ROCHET, J. C. (1989) A pricing formula for options on coupon-bonds. Working Paper, GREMAQ.

EL KAROUI, N. AND GEMAN H. (1991) A stochastic approach to the pricing of FRNs. *RISK* **4**(3).

EL KAROUI, N. AND GEMAN, H. (1994) A probabilistic approach to the valuation of floating rate notes with an application to interest rate swaps. *Adv. Options and Futures Res.* **7**, 47–64.

GEMAN, H. (1989) The importance of the forward neutral probability in a stochastic approach of interest rates. Working Paper, ESSEC.

GESKE, R. (1979) The valuation of compound-options. *J. Financial Econ.* **7**, 63–81.

HARRISON, J. M. AND KREPS, D. (1979) Martingale and arbitrage in multiperiods securities markets. *J. Econ. Theory* **20**, 381–408.

HARRISON, J. M. AND PLISKA, S. R. (1981) Martingales and stochastic integrals in the theory of continuous trading. *Stoch. Proc. Appl.* **11**, 215–260.

HEATH, D., JARROW, R. AND MORTON, A. (1987) Bond pricing and the term structure of interest rates. Working paper, Cornell University.

JAMSHIDIAN, F. (1989) An exact bond option formula. *J. Finance* **44**, 205–209.

KARATZAS, I. AND SHREVE, S. E. (1988) *Brownian Motion and Stochastic Calculus*. Springer-Verlag, Berlin.

MARGRABE, W. (1978) The value of an option to exchange one asset for another. *J. Finance* **33**.

MERTON, R. C. (1973) Theory of rational pricing. *Bell J. Econ. Mangement Sci.* **4**, 141–183.

REINER, E. (1992) Quanto Mechanics. *RISK* **5**(3).

ROSS, S. A. (1978) A simple approach to the valuation of risky streams. *J. Business* **51**, 453–475.

STRICKER, C. (1990) Arbitrage et lois de martingale. *Ann. Inst. H. Poincaré* **26**(3).

Part V
Term Structure and Other Applications

[22]

THE JOURNAL OF FINANCE · VOL. XXXI, NO. 2 · MAY 1976

VALUING CORPORATE SECURITIES: SOME EFFECTS OF BOND INDENTURE PROVISIONS

FISCHER BLACK AND JOHN C. COX*

I. THE VALUATION OF CORPORATE SECURITIES

IN A RECENT PAPER Black and Scholes [3] presented an explicit equilibrium model for valuing options. In this paper they indicated that a similar analysis could potentially be applied to all corporate securities. In other papers, both Merton [8] and Ross [11] noted the broad applicability of option pricing arguments. At the same time Black and Scholes also pointed out that actual security indentures have a variety of conditions that would bring new features and complications into the valuation process.

Our objective in this paper is to make some general statements on this valuation process and then turn to an analysis of certain types of bond indenture provisions which are often found in practice. Specifically, we will look at the effects of safety covenants, subordination arrangements, and restrictions on the financing of interest and dividend payments.

Throughout the paper we will make the following assumptions:

a1) Every individual acts as if he can buy or sell as much of any security as he wishes without affecting the market price.

a2) There exists a riskless asset paying a known constant interest rate r.

a3) Individuals may take short positions in any security, including the riskless asset, and receive the proceeds of the sale. Restitution is required for payouts made to securities held short.

a4) Trading takes place continuously.

a5) There are no taxes, indivisibilities, bankruptcy costs, transaction costs, or agency costs.

a6) The value of the firm follows a diffusion process with instantaneous variance proportional to the square of the value.

This last assumption is quite important and needs some amplification. Until very recently this was the standard framework for discussions of contingent claim pricing. Increasing evidence, however, indicates that it may not be completely appropriate.[1] The instantaneous variance may be some other function of the firm

* Sloan School of Management, Massachusetts Institute of Technology, and Graduate School of Business, Stanford University, respectively. We would like to thank Robert Merton, Stephen Ross, and Mark Rubinstein for many helpful discussions. We are also grateful to Andrew Christie and Johannes Mouritsen for technical assistance. This research was partially supported by a grant from the Dean Witter Foundation to Stanford University, and by the Center for Research in Security Prices, sponsored by Merrill Lynch, Pierce, Fenner, and Smith, Inc., at the University of Chicago.

1. See Black [1].

value, and possibly dependent on time as well.[2] It may also depend on other random variables. Furthermore, discontinuities associated with jump processes may be important.[3] Nevertheless, this assumption provides a useful setting for the points we want to make and facilitates comparison with earlier results.

With these assumptions, the standard hedging or capital asset pricing arguments lead to a valuation equation. For the process we are considering here, it is derived in its most general form in Merton [9] as

$$\tfrac{1}{2}\sigma^2 V^2 f_{vv} + (rV - p(V,t))f_v - rf + f_t + p'(V,t) = 0 \tag{1}$$

where f is a generic label for any of the firm's securities, V is the value of the firm, t denotes time, σ^2 is the instantaneous variance of the return on the firm, $p(V,t)$ is the net total payout made, or inflow received, by the firm, and $p'(V,t)$ is the payout received or payment made by security f.

Suppose the firm has outstanding only equity and a single bond issue with a promised final payment of P. At the maturity date of the bonds, T, the stockholders will pay off the bondholders if they can. If they cannot, the ownership of the firm passes to the bondholders. So at time T, the bonds will have the value $\min(V,P)$ and the stock will have the value $\max(V-P,0)$.

Now this formulation already implicity contains several assumptions about the bond indenture. The fact that σ^2, $p(V,t)$ and $p'(V,t)$, and P were assumed known (and finite) implies that the bond contract renders them determinate by placing limiting restrictions on, respectively, the firm's investment, payout, and further financing policies.

Furthermore, it assumes that the fortunes of the firm may cause its value to rise to an arbitrarily high level or dwindle to nearly nothing without any sort of reorganization occurring in the firm's financial arrangements. More generally, there may be both lower and upper boundaries at which the firm's securities must take on specific values. The boundaries may be given exogenously by the contract specifications or determined endogenously as part of an optimal decision problem.

The indenture agreements which we will consider serve as examples of a specified or induced lower boundary at which the firm will be reorganized. An example of an upper boundary is a call provision on a bond.[4] Also, the final payment at the maturity date may be a quite arbitrary function of the value of the firm at that time, $\xi(V(T))$.

It will be helpful to look at this problem in a way discussed in Cox and Ross [5, 6].[5] The valuation equation (1) does not involve preferences, so a solution derived for any specific set of preferences must hold in general. In particular, the

2. See Cox and Ross [6] for a discussion of some models of this type.

3. Processes with discontinuous sample paths are examined in Cox and Ross [5, 6] and Merton [10].

4. Call provisions on bonds have recently been examined by Brennan and Schwartz [4] and Ingersoll [7]. All of our results could be extended to include such upper boundaries as well.

5. For a related discussion, see Black and Scholes [2].

relative value of contingent claims in terms of the value of underlying assets must be consistent with risk neutrality.[6]

If we know the distribution of the underlying assets in a risk-neutral world, then we can readily solve a number of valuation problems.[7] We can in our problem think of each security as having four sources of value: its value at the maturity date if the firm is not reorganized before then, its value if the firm is reorganized at the lower boundary, its value if the firm is reorganized at the upper boundary, and the value of the payouts it will potentially receive. Although the first three sources are mutually exclusive, they are all possible outcomes given our current position, so they each contribute to current value. The contribution to the total value of a claim of any of its component sources will in a risk neutral world simply be the discounted expected value of that component.

For any claim f, let $h_i(V(t),t)$, $i=1,\dots,4$, denote respectively the four components referred to above, so $f(V(t),t)=\sum_{i=1}^{4}h_i(V(t),t)$. Let $g_1(\tau)(g_2(\tau))$ be the value of f, as given by the contract, if the firm is reorganized at the lower (upper) boundary $C_1(\tau)(C_2(\tau))$ at time τ. Denote the distribution in a risk neutral world of the value of the firm at time $\tau, V(\tau)$, conditional on its value at the current time $t, V(t), C_1(t)<V(t)<C_2(t)$, as $\Phi(V(\tau),\tau\,|\,V(t),t)$. Then taking the indicated expectations we can write

$$h_1(V(t),t)=e^{-r(T-t)}\int_{\kappa(T)}\xi(V(T))\,d\Phi(V(T),T\,|\,V(t),t) \tag{2}$$

and

$$h_4(V(t),t)=\int_t^T e^{-r(s-t)}\left[\int_{\kappa(s)}p'(V(s),s)\,d\Phi(V(s),s\,|\,V(t),t)\right]ds, \tag{3}$$

where $\kappa(\cdot)$ denotes the interval $(C_1(\cdot),C_2(\cdot))$.

The contribution of the potential value at the reorganization boundaries is somewhat different. Formerly we knew the time of receipt of each potential payment but not the amount which would actually be received. Here the amount to be received at each boundary is a known function specified by the contract, but the time of receipt is a random variable. However, its distribution is just that of the first passage time to the boundary, and the approach taken by Cox and Ross can still be applied.

6. The ability to form a perfectly hedged portfolio is a sufficient condition for the derivation of a valuation equation free of preferences. Note that this does not say that the value of the underlying assets in terms of the values of other assets is independent of preferences.

7. In a risk neutral world the instantaneous mean total return must be rV, so the instantaneous mean of the price component must be $rV-p(V,t)$. For a diffusion process, this, together with the instanteous variance and behavior at accessible boundaries, completely specifies the processes. The value of the assets of the firm would in general have only a lower barrier, an absorbing one at the origin. However, our interest is in probabilities for paths of firm value which have not previously reached one of the reorganization boundaries. A convenient way to introduce this is by considering the distribution with the boundaries taken as artificial absorbing barriers, and we will adopt this convention.

Let $\Psi_1(t^* | V(t), t)$ be the distribution of the first passage time t^* to the lower boundary, and let $\Psi_2(t^* | V(t), t)$ denote the corresponding distribution for the upper boundary. Then

$$h_{i+1}(V(t),t) = \int_t^T e^{-r(t^*-t)} g_i(t^*) d\Psi_i(t^* | V(t),t), \qquad i=1,2. \tag{4}$$

This development also disposes of uniqueness problems, since economically inadmissible solutions to the valuation equation are automatically avoided by the probabilistic approach. However, it cannot be applied directly to situations where the boundaries must be determined endogenously as part of an optimal stopping problem.

Actual payouts by firms, of course, occur in lumps at discrete intervals. In many situations it is more convenient and perfectly acceptable to represent these payouts as a continual flow. Many other times, however, it is preferable to explicitly recognize the discrete nature of things. This is particularly true in optimal stopping problems when the structure of the problem dictates that decisions will be made only at these discrete points. An example in terms of options would be an American call on a stock paying discrete dividends. Restrictions on the financing of coupon payments to debt, which we will discuss later, provides an example in terms of corporate liabilities. To solve these problems we could work recursively, with the terminal condition at each stage determined by the solution to the previous stage. Start at the last payment date. If a decision is made to stop at this point, the claimholder receives a payoff given by the terms of the contract. If he does not stop, his payoff is the value of a claim with one more period to go, given that the value of the firm is its current value minus the payment. This value is determined by the payment to be received at the maturity date. The claimholder can then determine his optimal decision rule. With the optimal decision rule specified, we can find the value of the claim as a function of firm value at the last decision point. At the next-to-last decision point we would face an identical problem except that the value function we just found would take the place of the function giving the payment to be received at the maturity date. By working backward we can find the value of the claim at any time. Note that this gives only an approximate solution when the optimal decision points are actually continuous in time. However, we could always get a better approximation by adding more discrete decision points, even though no payouts are being made at these additional points.

Throughout the paper we will make use of the relationship between the equilibrium expected return on any of the individual securities of the firm, ν, and the (exogenously determined) equilibrium expected return on the total firm, μ. As given in Black and Scholes [3] and Merton [9], this is $\nu - r = (Vf_v/f)(\mu - r)$. Furthermore, since the process followed by any individual security is a transformation of that governing the total value of the firm, its instantaneous variance will be $\sigma^2 V^2 [f_v]^2$. Thus we can write the ratio of the instantaneous standard deviation of the rate of return on any individual security to that of the firm as Vf_v/f. Another way to say this is that in equilibrium the excess expected return per unit of risk must be the same for all of the firm's securities. The elasticity Vf_v/f thus conveys the essential information about relative risk and expected return. In subsequent use of the term elasticity, we will always be referring to this function.

II. Bonds with Safety Covenants

In this section we will consider the effects of safety covenants on the value and behavior of the firm's securities. Safety covenants are contractual provisions which give the bondholders the right to bankrupt or force a reorganization of the firm if it is doing poorly according to some standard. One standard for this may be the omission of interest payments on the debt. However, if the stockholders are allowed to sell the assets of the firm to meet the interest payments, then this restriction is not very effective. In this situation a natural form for a safety covenant is the following: if the value of the firm falls to a specified level, which may change over time, then the bondholders are entitled to force the firm into bankruptcy and obtain the ownership of the assets. In this form of agreement, interest payments to the debt do not play a critical role, so we will assume that the firm has outstanding only a single issue of discount bonds. We will, however, assume that the contractual provisions allow the stockholders to receive a continuous dividend payment, aV, proportional to the value of the firm. With a continuous time analysis, it is quite reasonable for the time dependence of the safety covenant to take an exponential form, so we will let the specified bankruptcy level, $C_1(t)$, be $Ce^{-\gamma(T-t)}$.

The relevant form of the valuation equation (1) for the bonds, B, will be

$$\tfrac{1}{2}\sigma^2V^2B_{vv}+(r-a)VB_v-rB+B_t=0 \tag{5}$$

with boundary conditions

$$B(V,T)=\min(V,P)$$

$$B(Ce^{-\gamma(T-t)},t)=Ce^{-\gamma(T-t)}.$$

Similarly, the value of the stock, S, must satisfy

$$\tfrac{1}{2}\sigma^2V^2S_{vv}+(r-a)VS_v-rS+S_t+aV=0 \tag{6}$$

with boundary conditions

$$S(V,T)=\max(V-P,0)$$

$$S(Ce^{-\gamma(T-t)},t)=0.$$

To apply the probabilistic approach to valuation we need $\Phi(V(\tau),\tau\,|\,V(t),t)$, the distribution in a risk neutral world of the value of the firm at time τ, $V(\tau)$, conditional on its value at the current time t, $V(t)=V$. Under our assumptions, this will be the distribution of a lognormal process with an (artificial) absorbing barrier at the reorganization boundary $C_1(\tau)=Ce^{-\gamma(T-\tau)}$. The probability that $V(\tau)\geqslant K$

and has not reached the reorganization boundary in the meantime is given by

$$N\left(\frac{\ln V-\ln K+(r-a-\frac{1}{2}\sigma^2)(\tau-t)}{\sqrt{\sigma^2(\tau-t)}}\right)$$

$$-\left(\frac{V}{Ce^{-\gamma(T-t)}}\right)^{1-(2(r-a-\gamma)/\sigma^2)}N\left(\frac{2\ln Ce^{-\gamma(T-t)}-\ln V-\ln K+(r-a-\frac{1}{2}\sigma^2)(\tau-t)}{\sqrt{\sigma^2(\tau-t)}}\right), \tag{7}$$

where $N(\cdot)$ is the unit normal distribution function. Setting $K=Ce^{-\gamma(T-\tau)}$ gives the probability in a risk neutral world that the firm has not been reorganized before time τ. This is the complementary first passage time distribution. That is, if t^* is the first passage time to the boundary, the probability that $t^* \geqslant \tau$ is obtained from (7) by letting $K=Ce^{-\gamma(T-\tau)}$.

By using these distributions to find the expected discounted value of the payments, we can obtain the valuation formula for B as

$$B(V,t)=Pe^{-r(T-t)}[N(z_1)-y^{2\theta-2}N(z_2)]+Ve^{-a(T-t)}[N(z_3)+y^{2\theta}N(z_4)$$
$$+y^{\theta+\zeta}e^{a(T-t)}N(z_5)+y^{\theta-\zeta}e^{a(T-t)}N(z_6)-y^{\theta-\eta}N(z_7)-y^{\theta-\eta}N(z_8)], \tag{8}$$

where

$$y=Ce^{-\gamma(T-t)}/V$$

$$\theta=(r-a-\gamma+\tfrac{1}{2}\sigma^2)/\sigma^2$$

$$\delta=(r-a-\gamma-\tfrac{1}{2}\sigma^2)^2+2\sigma^2(r-\gamma)$$

$$\zeta=\sqrt{\delta}\,/\sigma^2$$

$$\eta=\sqrt{\delta-2\sigma^2 a}\,/\sigma^2$$

$$z_1=[\ln V-\ln P+(r-a-\tfrac{1}{2}\sigma^2)(T-t)]/\sqrt{\sigma^2(T-t)}$$

$$z_2=[\ln V-\ln P+2\ln y+(r-a-\tfrac{1}{2}\sigma^2)(T-t)]/\sqrt{\sigma^2(T-t)}$$

$$z_3=[\ln P-\ln V-(r-a+\tfrac{1}{2}\sigma^2)(T-t)]/\sqrt{\sigma^2(T-t)}$$

$$z_4=[\ln V-\ln P+2\ln y+(r-a+\tfrac{1}{2}\sigma^2)(T-t)]/\sqrt{\sigma^2(T-t)}$$

$$z_5=[\ln y+\zeta\sigma^2(T-t)]/\sqrt{\sigma^2(T-t)}$$

$$z_6=[\ln y-\zeta\sigma^2(T-t)]/\sqrt{\sigma^2(T-t)}$$

$$z_7=[\ln y+\eta\sigma^2(T-t)]/\sqrt{\sigma^2(T-t)}$$

$$z_8=[\ln y-\eta\sigma^2(T-t)]/\sqrt{\sigma^2(T-t)}\ .$$

This formula holds for all $Ce^{-\gamma(T-t)} \leq Pe^{r(T-t)}$. An interesting choice is $Ce^{-\gamma(T-t)} = \rho Pe^{-r(T-t)}$, with $0 \leq \rho \leq 1$, so that the reorganization value specified in the safety covenant is a constant fraction of the present value of the promised final payment. For clarity in making comparisons, we will use only this form below.

Merton [9] has extensively studied in this setting the properties of discount bonds when there are no safety covenants and no dividends. Rather than repeat parts of his analysis, we will focus on properties which are particular to the existence of safety covenants. The most basic properties, such as the fact that B is an increasing function of V and t and a decreasing function of σ^2, r, and a remain the same.

It is easy to verify that B is an increasing function of ρ. Contrary to what is sometimes claimed, premature bankruptcy is not in itself detrimental for the bondholders. It is in their interests to have a contract which will force bankruptcy as quickly as possible. If bankruptcy occurs, the total ownership of the firm will pass to the bondholders, and this is the best they can achieve in any circumstances. A second look shows that B is a convex function of ρ, going to $Pe^{-r(T-t)}$, the riskless value, as ρ goes to one. The elasticity of B is a decreasing concave function of ρ, going to zero as ρ goes to one, so a higher bankruptcy level always makes the debt safer. The elasticity of the stock is an increasing convex function of ρ.

Safety covenants provide a floor value for the bond which limits the gains to stockholders from somehow circumventing the other indenture restrictions. For example, as either σ^2 or a goes to infinity, the value of the bonds goes to $\rho Pe^{-r(T-t)}$ rather than zero. Similarly, if we compare the riskiness of bonds of firms differing only in investment policy or dividend policy, we find important differences for large values of a and σ^2. If $\rho = 0$, the elasticity is an increasing concave function of a, going to one as a goes to infinity. If $\rho > 0$, the elasticity has an initial increasing concave segment, but then reaches a maximum, followed successively by decreasing concave and convex segments going to zero as a goes to infinity. The behavior of the elasticity with respect to the variance is for small values of σ^2 qualitatively the same as the case with no safety covenant, but as σ^2 becomes large, it approaches zero rather than one-half.

The behavior of the elasticities with respect to the value of the firm is also interesting and is shown in Figure 1. When the stock is entitled to receive dividends, as the value of the firm declines, we find that the riskiness and expected return of the stock first increases, then decreases, and finally increases again as the value approaches the bankruptcy boundary. Intuitively we could think of this in the following way. For values of V near the boundary it is quite likely that the stockholders will lose everything and their claim is accordingly quite risky. As V increases, we reach a stage where bankruptcy is no longer imminent, but it is most unlikely that anything will be left for the stockholders at the maturity date. The value of the stock derives almost solely from the value of the dividends it is entitled to receive, and these are proportional to the value of the firm and hence have unitary elasticity. As V increases further, the major part of the stock's value becomes due to the uncertain amount it may receive at the maturity date, and hence the riskiness increases. Finally, as V reaches a very high level, it becomes virtually certain that the bonds will be redeemed in full and the stock becomes

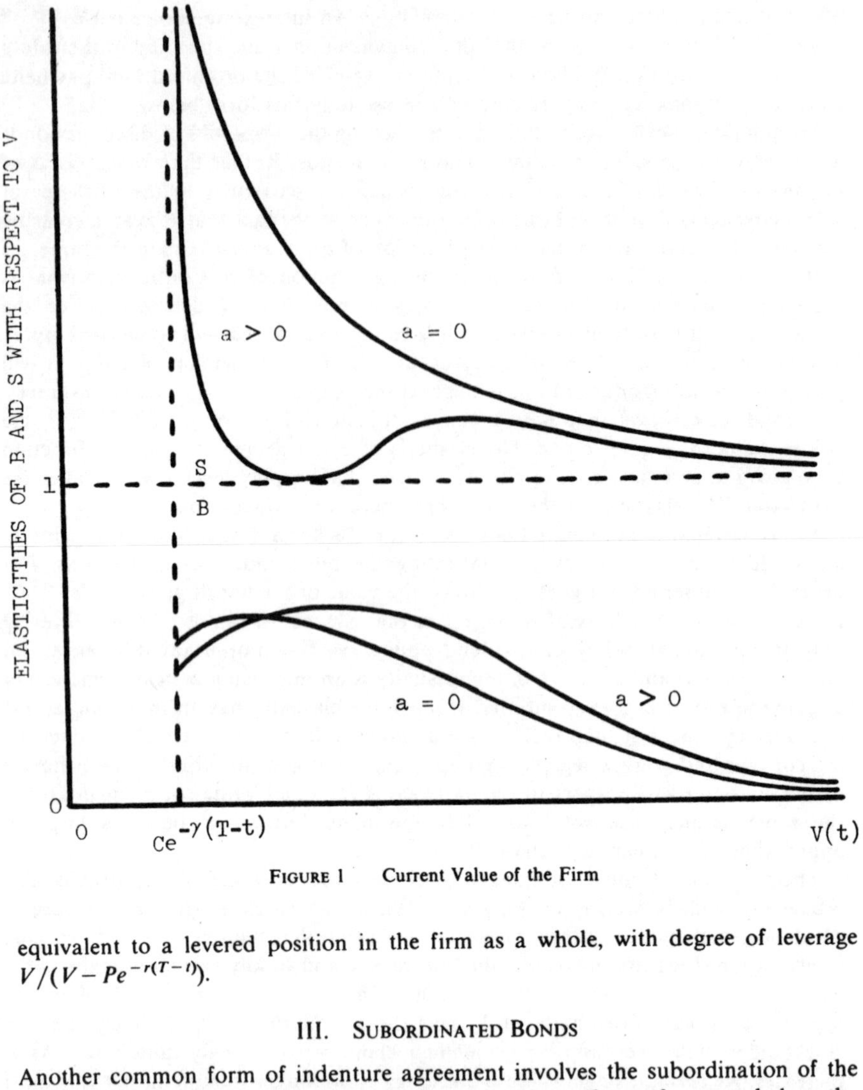

Figure 1 Current Value of the Firm

equivalent to a levered position in the firm as a whole, with degree of leverage $V/(V-Pe^{-r(T-t)})$.

III. Subordinated Bonds

Another common form of indenture agreement involves the subordination of the claims of one class of debt holders, the junior bonds, to those of a second class, the senior bonds. At the maturity date of the bonds, payments can be made to the junior debt holders only if the full promised payment to the senior debt holders has been made. Suppose that both classes of bonds are discount bonds, and let the promised payments to senior and junior debt be, respectively, P and Q. Then at the maturity date the value of each of the firm's securities will be as shown in Table 1.

This problem could be solved separately by the methods used earlier, but this is unnecessary since we can write the solution in terms of (8). To see this, note that

TABLE 1

VALUES OF CLAIMS AT MATURITY

Claim	$V<P$	$P<V<P+Q$	$V>P+Q$
Senior Bonds	V	P	P
Junior Bonds	0	$V-P$	Q
Stock	0	0	$V-P-Q$

the value of the senior bond (or stock) is the same as the corresponding security of an identical firm with a single bond issue having a promised payment of P (or $(P+Q)$). Let $B(V,t;P,\rho Pe^{-r(T-t)})$ denote the formula given in (8) for a single bond issue with promised payment P and a safety covenant boundary given by $\rho Pe^{-r(T-t)}$. Then the value of the junior debt, J, can be written as

$$\begin{aligned} J(V,t) &= B(V,t;P+Q,\rho Pe^{-r(T-t)}) - B(V,t;P,\rho Pe^{-r(T-t)}), \qquad \rho<1 \\ &= B(V,t;P+Q,\rho Pe^{-r(T-t)}) - Pe^{-r(T-t)}, \qquad 1 \leqslant \rho \leqslant \frac{P+Q}{P} \\ &= Qe^{-r(T-t)}, \qquad \rho > \frac{P+Q}{P}. \end{aligned} \tag{9}$$

The discussion in the first section suggested that the values of junior and senior discount bonds, and correspondingly of options with different exercise prices, could be given a geometric interpretation. Consider the case with no payouts and no safety covenants. Depict graphically the distribution function $\Phi(V(T),T\,|\,V(t),t)$. Then as shown in Figure 2, the values of the firm's securities can be interpreted as areas above the distribution function, when these areas are multiplied by the discount factor $e^{-r(T-t)}$.

To see this, consider, for example, the senior bonds. Since

$$\int_0^P V(T)\,d\Phi = \int_0^P [1-\Phi(V(T))]\,dV(T) - P[1-\Phi(P)],$$

then

$$\int_0^\infty \min(V(T),P)\,d\Phi = \int_0^P [1-\Phi(V(T))]\,dV(T),$$

which is represented by the indicated area.

Subordination does indeed achieve its anticipated effect of giving the senior bonds a larger value than they would have if they were the corresponding fraction

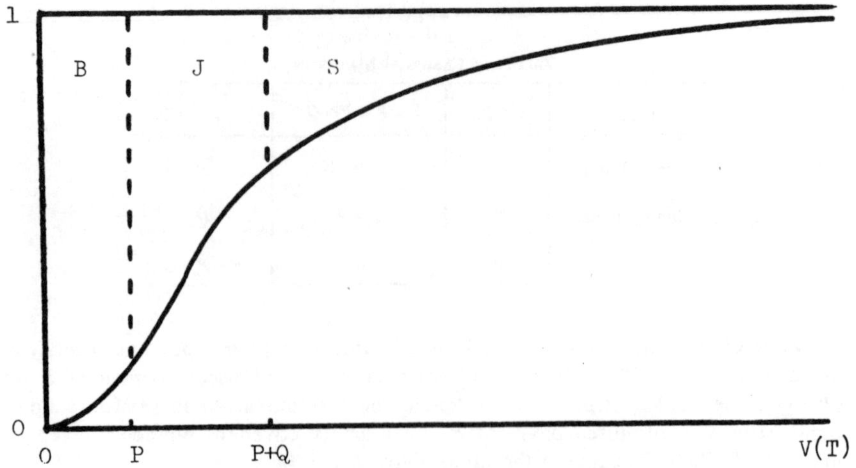

FIGURE 2 Security Values as Areas Above the Distribution Function

of an undifferentiated bond issue. That is, the value of the senior bonds will be greater than $P/(P+Q)$ times the value of a single issue with promised payment $P+Q$. This follows directly from the concavity of discount bonds in the final payment.

The effects of a safety covenant on the subordinated debt are just as we would expect. J is initially a decreasing convex function of ρ, reaching a minimum when $\rho=1$. For $\rho>1$, it is an increasing convex function, reaching a maximum when $\rho=P+Q$. For values of $\rho<1$, the benefits of the safety covenant accrue entirely to the senior bondholders and are partly at the expense of the junior bondholders as well as the stockholders. As ρ increases, the junior bondholders begin to receive benefits as well, and finally the entire expense falls upon the stockholders. In the remainder of this section we will let $\rho=0$.

Further analysis shows that the subordinated debt has many characteristics which are quite different from those normally associated with bonds. While senior bonds are always a concave function of V, the junior bonds are initially a convex function of V, becoming a concave function for larger values of V. The inflection point, V^*, occurs at

$$V=[P(P+Q)]^{1/2}\exp[-(r-a+\tfrac{1}{2}\sigma^2)(T-t)]. \tag{10}$$

Again unlike the senior debt, the value of the junior debt can be an increasing function of σ^2. Analysis of the function shows J is an increasing (decreasing) function of σ^2 for V less than (greater than) V^*. This means that the bondholders as a group may under some circumstances have conflicting interests with respect to changes in the total riskiness of the firm's investment policy. To fully protect the value of their claims, the senior bondholders must insist on the sole right to approve investment policy changes which will increase the business risk of the firm.

As we might now expect, J can be an increasing function of time to maturity. Unlike the senior debt, it is possible for the junior debt to be worthless at maturity, and if such a development is imminent, the junior bondholders would find it in their interests to try to extend the maturity date of the entire bond issue. Although it is possible for the value of the junior bonds to be either a decreasing or increasing function of the interest rate, it is always a decreasing function of the dividend rate.

Turning now to the characteristics of risk and expected return, we find that the junior bonds behave partly like a senior bond and partly like a stock. We normally think of a bond as being less risky than the assets of the firm, that is, having an elasticity of less than one, and of the stock as being more risky than the assets. However, we find that the elasticity, ϵ, of J is a decreasing convex function of V which goes to zero as V goes to infinity and to infinity as V goes to zero. Further inspection shows that

$$\epsilon \gtreqless 1 \quad \text{as} \quad PN(z_1;P) \gtreqless (P+Q)N(z_1;P+Q). \tag{11}$$

The behavior of the elasticity with respect to time until maturity for the relevant firm and parameter values is shown in Figure 3.

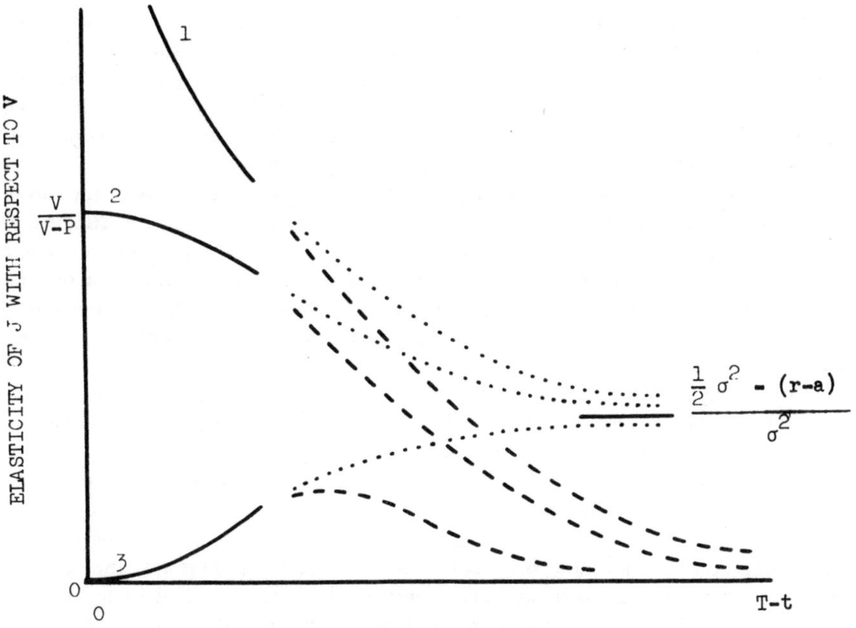

FIGURE 3 Time Until Maturity
$1 = V < P$, $2 = P < V < P+Q$, $3 = P+Q < V$
$\cdots\cdots = (r-a) < \frac{1}{2}\sigma^2$, $---- = (r-a) > \frac{1}{2}\sigma^2$

IV. Restrictions on the Financing of Interest and Dividend Payments

Suppose now that the firm has interest paying bonds outstanding. In this section we will see that it is quite important how the stockholders are allowed to raise the money to make the payments to the bondholders. Previous studies of interest paying bonds have assumed that the stockholders are allowed to sell the assets of the firm to make these payments. Many bonds have contractual provisions which limit the extent to which this can be done. To focus on the effects of these restrictions, suppose that the sale of assets for this purpose is in fact completely forbidden. Interest payments, and any dividend payments, must be financed by issuing new securities. To protect the value of their claim the bondholders must also require that the new securities be equity or subordinated bonds.

For concreteness suppose the bonds have a promised final payment of P and make periodic interest payments of $c = Pe^{rt'}$, where t' is the interval between payments. If an interest payment is not made, the firm is in default and the promised payment P becomes due immediately. The bonds would then be worth $\min(V, P+c)$. Since this is the maximum value the bonds can possibly have, the bondholders would always be glad to see a payment missed, and correspondingly the stockholders would always want to make the payment if there is any way they possibly can. However, they may not be able to. This would happen whenever the value of the equity after the payment is made, if it is made, would be less than the value of the payment. Even if the present stockholders offered an equity issue which would dilute their own interest to virtually nothing, they would still find no takers for it. All of this can occur when the assets of the firm still have substantial value. It provides one explanation, along with the safety covenants discussed earlier, of the observed fact that many firms end up in bankruptcy and reorganization even though their total value may be quite significant.

Under these conditions the use of junior debt, and the exact terms of the junior debt, have important implications. Suppose that because of legal restrictions or diffusion of ownership the junior bondholders are forced to play a purely passive role. They cannot at some later date agree to a change in their contract or take an active part in the firm. To protect themselves in these circumstances, the junior bondholders must require that any subsequent debt issues be subordinated to their own.

However, issuing any junior debt at all in this situation would actually help the senior bondholders and hurt the stockholders. This is because it would then be more likely that a payment will be missed and the bondholders will take over the firm. To see this, consider the value of the claims after a payment has been made. In an attempt to raise the money to in fact make that payment the stockholders were formerly able to offer up for sale the total value of the firm less the value of the senior bonds, while now they can offer only the total value less the value of both the senior and junior bonds. The senior bondholders would be better off, and assuming that the junior debt was sold at a fair price, the difference would have to come out of the pockets of the stockholders.

If it is possible for the junior debtholders to subsequently voluntarily change their status, things will be different. They may find it in their interests to permit the issue of additional unsubordinated debt rather than allow a payment to be missed. In fact, the disadvantages of junior debt could be completely circumvented by a contract of the following kind. Suppose that in the junior debt indenture it is specified that if the stockholders find that they cannot make a payment by issuing new equity, they will sign their entire equity interest over to the junior bondholders. The junior bondholders could then immediately reorganize the firm as one having only equity and senior bonds. If such an arrangement is possible, there would then be no disadvantage to issuing junior debt, since the firm would in effect switch back to equity at exactly the moment the debt would have been a disadvantage.

We have stated the discussion in terms of extreme cases in order to highlight the issues. Often there may be only partial restrictions on the sale of assets, such as those allowing the sale of assets added by current earnings, or the junior bondholders may be able to partly change their status. While these considerations would have a quantitative impact, the qualitative results would not be affected.

The relevant form of equation (1) for our problem is

$$\tfrac{1}{2}\sigma^2V^2F_{vv}+rVF_v-rF+F_t+\sum_{j=1}^{n}c_j\delta(t-t_j)=0 \tag{12}$$

where c_j is the jth interest payment, t_j is the time at which the jth interest payment is made, n is the total number of interest payments, and $\delta(\cdot)$ is the Dirac delta function. The first derivative term does not involve the outflow of interest or dividend payments because they are exactly offset by the inflow of new financing. The standard terminal condition and the stopping condition described above complete the specification of the problem.

The solution can be obtained by the recursive technique discussed in the first section. For example, consider the situation immediately before the last payment is due. Let $s(V,t_n)$ be the value of the firm's stock if the payment is made. This is the solution to the standard problem with terminal condition $\max(V-P,0)$. Then the minimum value of the firm at which the payment can be made, $\bar{V}$, is the root of $s(V,t_n)=c$. The value of the stock just before the payments is made, $\bar{s}(V,t_n)$, will be $s(V,t_n)-c$ if $V\geqslant\bar{V}$ and zero if $V<\bar{V}$. The value of the bonds will be $V-\bar{s}(V,t_n)$. For the situation just before the next-to-last payment is due, we apply the same analysis with $\bar{s}(V,t_n)$ replacing $\max(V-P,0)$. By working recursively in this way, we can obtain a complete solution to the problem, but in general no closed form expression will be available.

To obtain a better perspective on the behavior of F, consider the case of a perpetual bond with continual interest payments of c per unit time. Equation (1) now has the form

$$\tfrac{1}{2}\sigma^2V^2F_{vv}+rVF_v-rF+c=0. \tag{13}$$

From our earlier discussion we know that there will be some point at which no more equity can be sold and the bondholders will take over the firm. To find this point, think of things in the following way. In equilibrium new equity financing must sell at a fair price, so it makes no difference whether we think of it as being purchased by new investors or by the original stockholders. So we can think of this as a situation where the stockholders will make payments into the firm to cover the interest payments to the bondholders, but at any time they have the right to stop making payments and either turn the firm over to the bondholders or pay them c/r. It is clear that the critical value of the firm at which they will do this, $\bar{V}$, is independent of the current value of the firm and will be chosen by the stockholders to minimize the value of the bonds and hence maximize the value of their own claim.

While a solution could be obtained and interpreted by the probabilistic approach discussed earlier, in the perpetual case it may be clearer to proceed formally with the ordinary differential equation (13). The solution to (13) can be written as the sum of a particular solution to the full inhomogeneous equation and the general solution to the corresponding homogeneous equation. A particular solution is c/r. Combining this with the corresponding general solution gives

$$F(V)=\frac{c}{r}+K_1V+K_2V^{-\alpha}, \tag{14}$$

where $\alpha=2r/\sigma^2$ and K_1 and K_2 are arbitrary constants to be determined by the boundary conditions. As the value of the firm goes to infinity, the bonds must approach their riskless value and further increases in value must accrue solely to the stockholders, so $F_v(\infty)=0$ and hence $K_1=0$.

The lower boundary condition then gives

$$K_2\bar{V}^{-\alpha}+\frac{c}{r}=\min\left(\bar{V},\frac{c}{r}\right), \tag{15}$$

so $K_2=\bar{V}^{\alpha+1}-(c/r)\bar{V}^{\alpha}$ if $\bar{V}<c/r$ and $K_2=0$ if $\bar{V}\geqslant c/r$. Choosing $\bar{V}\geqslant c/r$ gives the bonds their maximum possible value, so the optimal $\bar{V}$ must be an interior point and the value of the bonds will be

$$F(V)=\frac{c}{r}+\left(\bar{V}^{\alpha+1}-\frac{c}{r}\bar{V}^{\alpha}\right)V^{-\alpha}. \tag{16}$$

Solving the first order condition for minimizing $F(V)$ gives $\bar{V}=(\alpha/\alpha+1)c/r$. Substitution and rearranging then gives

$$F(V)=\frac{c}{r}-\left[\left(\frac{\alpha}{\alpha+1}\right)^{\alpha}-\left(\frac{\alpha}{\alpha+1}\right)^{\alpha+1}\right]\left(\frac{c}{r}\right)^{\alpha+1}V^{-\alpha}. \tag{17}$$

For comparison consider now the corresponding case where the assets of the firm can be sold to make interest and dividend payments. The valuation equation for the bonds, G, will take the form

$$\tfrac{1}{2}\sigma^2V^2G_{vv}+[(r-a)V-(c+d)]G_v-rG+c=0 \tag{18}$$

where c again represents the continuous interest payments to the bonds and the stock is entitled to receive dividend payments of $aV+d$. The upper boundary condition will again be $F_v(\infty)=0$ and the lower boundary condition is now $F(0)=0$. The solution is

$$G(V)=\frac{c}{r}\left[1-\frac{\Gamma\left(k-\frac{2(r-a)}{\sigma^2}+2\right)\left(\frac{2(c+d)}{\sigma^2 V}\right)^k}{\Gamma\left(2k-\frac{2(r-a)}{\sigma^2}+2\right)}\right.$$

$$\left.\times M\left(k,2k-\frac{2(r-a)}{\sigma^2}+2,-\frac{2(c+d)}{\sigma^2 V}\right)\right], \tag{19}$$

where $M(\cdot,\cdot,\cdot)$ is the confluent hypergeometric function, $\Gamma(\cdot)$ is the gamma function, and k is the positive root of

$$\sigma^2k^2+[\sigma^2-2(r-a)]k-2r=0.\text{[8]} \tag{20}$$

When $a=0$, $k=(2r/\sigma^2)=\alpha$, so with $d=0$ this reduces to formula (42) in Merton [9]. In this case (19) can be written in the more convenient form

$$G(V)=\frac{c}{r}[1-\Gamma(\alpha,Z)]+\left(\frac{cV}{c+d}\right)\Gamma(\alpha+1,Z), \tag{21}$$

where $Z=(2(c+d)/\sigma^2V)$ and $\Gamma(n,x)$ is the gamma distribution function with parameter n, $\Gamma(n,x)=\int_0^x e^{-s}s^{n-1}ds/\Gamma(n)$.[9]

8. Let $Z=(2(c+d)/\sigma^2V)$ and $G(V)=Z^ke^{-z}h(Z)$. This reduces the homogeneous part of the equation to

$$Zh_{zz}+[(\beta+k)-Z]h_z-\beta h=0,$$

where $\beta=k-(2(r-a)/\sigma^2)+2$. This is Kummer's equation, with general solution

$$K_1M(\beta,\beta+k,Z)+K_2Z^{1-\beta-k}M(1-k,2-\beta-k,Z).$$

Using the boundary conditions and well-known properties of the confluent hypergeometric function gives (19).

9. The solution in this form was shown to us by John Barry. It has also been independently derived by Jonathan Ingersoll. That it is equivalent to the solution given by Merton can be seen by noting that

$$M(A,A+1,-Z)=AZ^{-A}\Gamma(A)\Gamma(A,Z)$$

and

$$\begin{aligned}M(A,A+2,-Z)&=(A+1)M(A,A+1,-Z)-AM(A+1,A+2,-Z)\\&=\Gamma(A+2)Z^{-A}\Gamma(A,Z)\\&\quad-A\Gamma(A+2)Z^{-(A+1)}\Gamma(A+1,Z).\end{aligned}$$

Analysis of the solutions shows that F is always greater than G, so the financing restrictions do increase the value of the bonds. When V is large, F is less sensitive to changes in V than is G, and it is less risky in the sense of having a lower elasticity, but when V is small the relationships are reversed. The premium due to the restrictions achieves its maximum at $\overline{V}$ and is a decreasing convex function of V. For the case with financing restrictions, we find that the value at which the stockholders would abandon the firm is a linear increasing function of c and a decreasing convex function of σ^2 and r.

We would suspect that the premium of F over G is due partly to the increase in asset value from the inflow of new financing and partly from the implicit safety covenant which places the firm in the hands of the bondholders at some positive value. To get some idea of the different effects, consider a bond, H, which allows the sale of assets but which has a safety covenant giving the bondholders control of the firm at $\overline{V}$. It is easy to verify that

$$H(V)=\frac{c}{r}+\lambda\left[G(V)-\frac{c}{r}\right], \tag{22}$$

where

$$\lambda=\left[\frac{\overline{V}-\frac{c}{r}}{G(\overline{V})-\frac{c}{r}}\right].$$

Inspection shows that $F \geqslant H > G$. At $\overline{V}$, F and H have the same value by construction. As V increases the spread between them at first widens and then narrows to zero as the value of each claim approaches that of riskless debt, c/r. The sensitivity and riskiness of F compared to H is qualitatively the the same as its comparison to G.

Further examination of the functions shows that both F and G are increasing concave functions of V and c. They are both decreasing functions of σ^2, having an initial concave segment followed by a convex segment. Similarly, both elasticities are increasing functions of V, c, and σ^2.

V. Conclusion

In this paper we first discussed some general issues in the valuation of contingent claims. We outlined some solution methods which could be applied even when the problem possesses inherent discreteness and discussed an intuitive way of interpreting the solutions. We then investigated the effects of three specific provisions often found in bond indentures. These were safety covenants, subordination arrangements, and restrictions on the financing of interest and dividend payments. We found that these provisions do indeed increase the value of bonds, and that they may have a quite significant effect on the behavior of the firm's securities.

The most important qualifications to our results involve the assumptions about the absence of bankruptcy costs and about the probabilistic process governing the value of the firm. Most of our general results should hold for other stochastic processes, but of course the specific formulas and quantitative impact would be different. It should be noted that if the value of the firm follows a jump process, the value of a safety covenant may be drastically altered since the value of the firm could then reach points below the bankruptcy level without first passing through it.

The introduction of bankruptcy costs might have a more important effect. This would depend on the specific form of the bankruptcy costs and also on the influence of other factors, such as taxes, which would have to be introduced into the analysis to justify the existence of debt in a world with positive bankruptcy costs. However, their impact on our analysis should not be exaggerated. We are considering bankruptcy as simply the transfer of the entire ownership of the firm to the bondholders. The physical activities of the firm need not be affected. The bondholders may not want to actively run the company, but probably the stockholders did not either. The bondholders could retain the old managers or hire new ones, or they could refinance the firm and sell all or part of their holdings. Certain legal costs may be involved in the act of bankruptcy, but if contracts are carefully specified in the first place with an eye toward minimizing these costs, then their importance may be significantly reduced.

REFERENCES

1. Fischer Black. "Forecasting Variance of Stock Prices for Options Trading and Other Purposes," Seminar on the Analysis of Security Prices, University of Chicago, November, 1975.
2. ——— and Myron Scholes. "A Theoretical Valuation Formula for Options, Warrants, and Other Securities," Financial Note No. 16B, Associates in Finance, October, 1970.
3. ——— and ———. "The Pricing of Options and Corporate Liabilities," *Journal of Political Economy*, Vol. 81, No. 3, May-June, 1973.
4. Michael J. Brennan and Eduardo S. Schwartz. "Convertible Bonds: Valuation and Optimal Strategies for Call and Conversion," Working Paper No. 336, University of British Columbia, October, 1975.
5. John C. Cox and Stephen A. Ross. "The Pricing of Options for Jump Processes," Rodney L. White Center Working Paper 2-75, University of Pennsylvania, April, 1975.
6. ——— and ———. "The Valuation of Options for Alternative Stochastic Processes," *Journal of Financial Economics*, Vol. 3, Nos. 1–2, January-March, 1976.
7. Jonathan E. Ingersoll, Jr. "A Contingent Claims Evaluation of Convertible Bonds and the Optimal Policies for Call and Conversion," Ph.D. dissertation, Massachusetts Institute of Technology, February, 1976.
8. Robert C. Merton. "The Theory of Rational Option Pricing," *Bell Journal of Economics and Management Science*, Vol. 4, No. 1, Spring, 1973.
9. ———. "On the Pricing of Corporate Debt: The Risk Structure of Interest Rates," *Journal of Finance*, Vol. 29, No. 2, May, 1974.
10. ———. "Option Pricing When Underlying Stock Returns are Discontinuous," *Journal of Financial Economics*, Vol. 3, Nos. 1–2, January-March, 1976.
11. Stephen A. Ross. "Options and Efficiency," *Quarterly Journal of Economics*, Vol. 90, No. 1, February, 1976.

[23]

THE JOURNAL OF FINANCE • VOL. XLIX, NO. 4 • SEPTEMBER 1994

Corporate Debt Value, Bond Covenants, and Optimal Capital Structure

HAYNE E. LELAND*

ABSTRACT

This article examines corporate debt values and capital structure in a unified analytical framework. It derives *closed-form* results for the value of long-term risky debt and yield spreads, and for optimal capital structure, when firm asset value follows a diffusion process with constant volatility. Debt values and optimal leverage are explicitly linked to firm risk, taxes, bankruptcy costs, risk-free interest rates, payout rates, and bond covenants. The results elucidate the different behavior of junk bonds versus investment-grade bonds, and aspects of asset substitution, debt repurchase, and debt renegotiation.

THE VALUE OF CORPORATE debt and capital structure are interlinked variables. Debt values (and therefore yield spreads) cannot be determined without knowing the firm's capital structure, which affects the potential for default and bankruptcy. But capital structure cannot be optimized without knowing the effect of leverage on debt value.

This article examines corporate debt values and optimal capital structure in a unified analytical framework. It derives *closed-form* results relating the value of long-term corporate debt and optimal capital structure to firm risk, taxes, bankruptcy costs, bond covenants, and other parameters when firm asset value follows a diffusion process with constant volatility.

Traditional capital structure theory, pioneered by Modigliani and Miller (1958), holds that taxes are an important determinant of optimal capital structure.[1] As leverage increases, the tax advantage of debt eventually will be offset by an increased cost of debt, reflecting the greater likelihood of financial distress.[2] While identifying some prime determinants of optimal capital

*Haas School of Business, University of California, Berkeley. The author thanks Ronald Anderson, Fischer Black, Arnoud Boot, Michael Brennan, Philip Dybvig, Julian Franks, Robert Gertner, William Perraudin, Matthew Spiegel, Suresh Sundaresan, Ivo Welch, and especially Rob Heinkel and Klaus Toft for helpful comments. The referee and the editor, René Stulz, provided many valuable suggestions.

[1] Personal as well as corporate taxes will affect the tax benefits to leverage (Miller (1977)). Disagreement remains as to the precise value of net tax benefits.

[2] The costs of financial distress include bankruptcy costs and agency problems associated with risky debt. See, for example, Altman (1984), Asquith, Gertner, and Sharfstein (1991), Harris and Raviv (1991), Jensen and Meckling (1976), Myers and Majluf (1984), Titman and Wessels (1988), and Warner (1977).

structure, this theory has been less useful in practice because it provides qualitative guidance only.[3]

Brennan and Schwartz (1978) provide the first quantitative examination of optimal leverage. They utilize numerical techniques to determine optimal leverage when a firm's unlevered value follows a diffusion process with constant volatility.[4] Although an important beginning, the Brennan and Schwartz analysis has three limitations.

First and most importantly, their numerical approach precludes general closed-form solutions for the value of risky debt and optimal leverage. Numerical examples suggest some possible comparative static results but cannot claim generality.

Second, their analysis focuses on the special case in which bankruptcy is triggered when the firm's asset value falls to the debt's principal value. This provision approximates debt with a positive net-worth covenant. But it is by no means the only—or even the typical—situation.[5] We shall show that alternative bankruptcy-triggering conditions, including endogenously determined ones, lead to very different debt values and optimal capital structure.

Finally, Brennan and Schwartz (1978) consider changes in financial structure that last only until the bonds mature. A maturity date is required for their numerical algorithm; permanent capital structure changes are not explicitly analyzed.[6]

This article considers two possible bankruptcy determinants. The first is when bankruptcy is triggered (endogenously) by the inability of the firm to raise sufficient equity capital to meet its current debt obligations. The second is the Brennan and Schwartz case with a positive net-worth covenant. Debt with such a covenant will be termed *protected debt*.

We can derive closed-form results by examining corporate securities that depend on underlying firm value but are otherwise time independent. Yet debt securities generally have a specified maturity date and therefore have time-dependent cash flows and values. Time independence nonetheless can be justified, perhaps as an approximation, in at least two ways. First, if debt has sufficiently long maturity, the return of principal effectively has no value and

[3] Baxter (1967), Kraus and Litzenberger (1973), and Scott (1976) offer general analyses balancing tax advantages with the costs of financial distress, but their results have not provided directly usable formulas to determine optimal capital structure. For an alternative view on the determinants of capital structure, see Myers (1984).

[4] Kim (1978) also presents numerical examples of optimal capital structure, based on a mean-variance model. His model is less parsimonious, as knowledge of the joint distribution of market and firm returns is required.

[5] Minimum net-worth requirements are not uncommon in short-term debt contracts, but are rare in long-term debt instruments (also see Smith and Warner (1979)). In a later and more complex model, Brennan and Schwartz (1984) offer some examples with alternative bankruptcy conditions.

[6] Brennan and Schwartz do look at some examples when T becomes large. The relative insensitivity of these examples to T, as T exceeds 25 years, suggests that our limiting closed-form results for infinite maturity debt will be good approximations for debt with long but finite maturity.

can be ignored.[7] Very long time horizons for fixed obligations are not new, either in theory or in practice. The original Modigliani and Miller (1958) argument assumes debt with infinite maturity. Merton (1974) and Black and Cox (1976) look at infinite maturity debt in an explicitly dynamic model. Since 1752 the Bank of England has, on occasion, issued Consols, bonds promising a fixed coupon with no final maturity date. And preferred stock typically pays a fixed dividend without time limit.

An alternative time-independent environment is when, at each moment, the debt matures but is rolled over at a fixed interest rate (or fixed premium to a reference risk-free rate) unless terminated because of failure to meet a minimum value, such as a positive net-worth covenant. As we discuss later, this environment bears resemblance to some revolving credit agreements.

Time independence permits the derivation of closed-form solutions for risky debt value, given capital structure. These results extend those of Merton (1974) and Black and Cox (1976) to include taxes, bankruptcy costs, and protective covenants (if any). They are then used to derive closed-form solutions for optimal capital structure.[8] The analysis addresses the following questions:

- How do yield spreads on corporate debt depend on leverage, firm risk, taxes, payouts, protective covenants, and bankruptcy costs?
- Do high-risk ("junk") bond values behave in qualitatively different ways than investment-grade bond values?
- What is the optimal amount of leverage, and how does this depend on risk-free interest rates, firm risk, taxes, protective covenants, and bankruptcy costs?

[7] For 30-year debt, the final repayment of principal represents 1.5 percent of debt value when the interest rate is 15 percent, and 5.7 percent of value when the interest rate is 10 percent. Recently, a number of firms have issued 50-year debt, and one firm (Disney) has issued 100-year debt.

[8] Recently I have become aware of important related work by Anderson and Sundaresan (1992), Longstaff and Schwartz (1992), and Mella and Perraudin (1993). Anderson and Sundaresan (1992) focus on risky debt in a binomial framework. Using numerical examples, they examine the choice of debtors to discontinue coupon payments prior to bankruptcy and show that this may explain the sizable default premiums found in bond prices (see Jones, Mason, and Rosenfeld (1984), and Sarig and Warga (1989)). They do not examine optimal capital structure.

Longstaff and Schwartz (1992) derive solutions for risky debt values with finite maturity and with stochastic risk-free interest rates. Their key assumption is that bankruptcy is triggered whenever firm value, V, falls to an exogenously given level, K, (our V_B), which is time independent. This is a strong assumption for finite maturity debt, whose debt service payments are time dependent. Equation (14) below shows that V_B depends on the risk-free interest rate, suggesting that an endogenously determined K should depend upon the (stochastic) interest rate. Longstaff and Schwartz (1992) do not consider optimal capital structure.

Mella and Perraudin's approach more closely parallels this article, with endogenously determined bankruptcy levels. However, firm value is driven by a random product selling price whose drift as well as volatility must be specified, as must the firm's cost structure. (See also Fries, Miller, and Perraudin (1993)). Like Anderson and Sundaresan (1992), the article considers an endogenous decision to continue service debt.

- How does a positive net-worth covenant affect the potential for agency problems between bondholders and stockholders?
- When can debt renegotiation be expected prior to bankruptcy, and can renegotiation achieve results that debt repurchase cannot?

The model follows Modigliani and Miller (1958), Merton (1974), and Brennan and Schwartz (1978) in assuming (i) that the activities of the firm are unchanged by financial structure, and (ii) that capital structure decisions, once made, are not subsequently changed.

Much of the recent literature in corporate finance examines possible variants to assumption (i): see, for example, the survey by Harris and Raviv (1991). A particularly important variant is the "asset substitution" problem, where shareholders of highly leveraged firms may transfer value to themselves from bondholders by choosing riskier activities. If the appropriate functional form were known, feedback from capital structure to volatility could be captured in an extension of our model, at the likely cost of losing closed-form results.[9] But a simpler model that ignores such potential feedback still serves some important purposes:

1) Taxes and bankruptcy costs will importantly condition optimal capital structure even if asset substitution can occur; knowing these relationships in a basic model will provide useful insights for more complex situations.
2) The potential magnitude of the asset substitution problem can be identified by knowing how sensitive debt and equity values are to the risk of the activities chosen.
3) Bond covenants may directly limit opportunities for firms to alter the risk of their activities. In other cases, bond covenants may indirectly limit asset substitution by reducing potential conflicts of interest between stockholders and bondholders. Section VII below shows that a positive net worth requirement can eliminate the firm's incentive to increase risk.

Our second major assumption is that the face value of debt, once issued, remains static through time. This is not as unreasonable as it might appear. In Section VIII, we show that additional debt issuance will hurt current debtholders; it is typically proscribed by bond covenants. We further show that marginal debt reductions via repurchases will hurt current stockholders. These considerations may preclude continuous changes in the outstanding amount of debt, even if refinancing costs are zero.

[9] Mello and Parsons (1992), using a numerical approach similar to Brennan and Schwartz (1978) but including operating decisions of a (mining) firm, contrast decisions that maximize equity value with those that maximize the total value of the firm. They associate the difference in resulting values with agency costs and present an example showing the effect of these costs on optimal leverage. Mauer and Triantis (1993) also use the Brennan and Schwartz (1978) approach to examine the interaction of investment decisions and corporate financing policies.

However, large (discontinuous) debt repurchases via tender offers *may* under certain circumstances benefit both stock and bondholders, if refinancing costs are not excessive. A dynamic model of capital structure capturing these possibilities is desirable but considerably more difficult. First steps in this direction have been made in important work by Kane, Marcus, and McDonald (1984) and Fischer, Heinkel, and Zechner (1989). Their analyses pose several difficulties, which we avoid by adopting the static assumption shared with earlier authors.[10]

The structure of the article is as follows. Section I develops a simple dynamic model of a levered firm, and derives values for time-independent securities. Sections II and III consider debt value and optimal leverage when bankruptcy is determined endogenously. Sections IV and V consider debt value and optimal leverage when bankruptcy is triggered by a positive net-worth covenant. Section VI considers some alternative assumptions about tax deductibility, cash payouts by the firm, and the absolute priority of payments in bankruptcy. Section VII addresses agency problems and asset substitution, while Section VIII considers aspects of debt repurchase and renegotiation. Section IX concludes.

I. A Model of Time-Independent Security Values

Consider a firm whose activities have value V which follows a diffusion process with constant volatility of rate of return:

$$dV/V = \mu(V,t)dt + \sigma dW, \tag{1}$$

where W is a standard Brownian motion. We shall refer to V as the "asset value" of the firm.[11] The stochastic process of V is assumed to be unaffected by the financial structure of the firm. Thus any net cash outflows associated with the choice of leverage (e.g., coupons after tax benefits) must be financed by selling additional equity.[12]

Following Modigliani and Miller (1957), Merton (1974), Black and Cox (1976), and Brennan and Schwartz (1978), we assume that a riskless asset

[10] In Fischer, Heinkel, and Zechner (1989), the value of an unlevered firm (their A) cannot be exogenous, since it depends on the optimally levered firm value less costs of readjustment (see their p. 25). Since closed-form solutions are not available for the restructuring boundaries, they do not offer closed-form equations for risky debt value and optimal capital structure.

[11] We leave unanswered the delicate question of whether V, which could be associated with the value of an unlevered firm, is a traded asset. An alternative approach is to note that if equity, E, is a traded security, its process could be used to *define* a process, V, through equation (13) below, using Ito's Lemma. Our assumption that V has constant volatility will restrict the permissible process of E.

[12] This is consistent with bond covenants that restrict firms from selling assets. Brennan and Schwartz (1978) also make this assumption, although Merton (1974) does not. In Section VI.B, we consider how our results are affected by relaxing this assumption.

exists that pays a constant rate of interest r. This permits us to focus on the *risk structure* of interest rates directly.[13]

Now consider any claim on the firm that continuously pays a nonnegative coupon, C, per instant of time when the firm is solvent. Denote the value of such a claim by $F(V,t)$. When the firm finances the net cost of the coupon by issuing additional equity, it is well known (e.g., Black and Cox (1976)) that any such asset's value must satisfy the partial differential equation

$$(1/2)\sigma^2 V^2 F_{VV}(V,t) + rVF_V(V,t) - rF(V,t) + F_t(V,t) + C = 0 \quad (2)$$

with boundary conditions determined by payments at maturity, and by payments in bankruptcy should this happen prior to maturity.[14] In general, there exist no closed-form solutions to equation (2) for arbitrary boundary conditions. Hence Brennan and Schwartz (1978) resort to computer analysis of some examples. However, when securities have no explicit time dependence, the term $F_t(V,t) = 0$ and equation (2) becomes an ordinary differential equation with $F(V)$ satisfying

$$(1/2)\sigma^2 V^2 F_{VV}(V) + rVF_V(V) - rF(V) + C = 0. \quad (3)$$

Equation (3) has the general solution

$$F(V) = A_0 + A_1 V + A_2 V^{-X}, \quad (4)$$

where

$$X = 2r/\sigma^2 \quad (5)$$

and the constants A_0, A_1, and A_2 are determined by boundary conditions. *Any* time-independent claim with an equity-financed constant payout $C \geq 0$ must have this functional form. We turn now to examining specific securities.

Debt promises a perpetual coupon payment, C, whose level remains constant unless the firm declares bankruptcy. The value of debt can be expressed as $D(V;C)$. For simplicity, however, we will suppress the coupon as an argument and simply write debt value as $D(V)$. Let V_B denote the level of asset value at which bankruptcy is declared. (Note that we again suppress the argument C.) If bankruptcy occurs, a fraction $0 \leq \alpha \leq 1$ of value will be

[13] Extensions of numerical bond valuation to include interest rate risk are provided in Brennan and Schwartz (1980) and Kim, Ramaswamy, and Sundaresan (1993). They find that the yield spreads between corporate and Treasury bonds are quite insensitive to interest rate uncertainty.

[14] More generally, if net payouts by the firm not financed by further equity issuance are denoted $P(V,t)$, and $C(V,t)$ represents the payout flow to security F, then

$$(1/2)\sigma^2(V,t)V^2F_{VV}(V,t) + [rV - P(V,t)]F_V(V,t) - rF(V,t) + F_t(V,t) + C(V,t) = 0.$$

Note that $\sigma^2(V,t)$ could be of the form $\sigma^2[C(V,t),V,t]$, reflecting possible asset substitution.

Equation (2) requires that V, or an asset perfectly correlated (locally) with V, such as equity, be traded. See also footnote 11.

lost to bankruptcy costs, leaving debtholders with value $(1-\alpha)V_B$ and stockholders with nothing.[15]

Later we show how the bankruptcy value, V_B, is determined, given alternative debt covenants. For the moment regard it as fixed. Since the value of debt is of the form in equation (4), we must determine the constants A_0, A_1, and A_2. Boundary conditions are:

$$\text{At } V = V_B, \qquad D(V) = (1-\alpha)V_B \tag{6i}$$

$$\text{As } V \to \infty, \qquad D(V) \to C/r. \tag{6ii}$$

Condition (6ii) holds because bankruptcy becomes irrelevant as V becomes large, and the value of debt approaches the value of the capitalized coupon (and therefore the value of risk-free debt).

From equation (4), it is immediately apparent using equation (6ii) that $A_1 = 0$. Because $V^{-X} \to 0$ as $V \to \infty$, this with equation (6ii) implies that $A_0 = C/r$. Finally, $A_2 = [(1-\alpha)V_B - C/r]V_B^X$, using equation (6i). Thus

$$D(V) = C/r + [(1-\alpha)V_B - C/r][V/V_B]^{-X}. \tag{7}$$

Equation (7) can also be written as $D(V) = [1 - p_B](C/r) + p_B[(1-\alpha)V_B]$, where $p_B \equiv (V/V_B)^{-X}$ has the interpretation of the present value of \$1 contingent on future bankruptcy (i.e., V falling to V_B).[16]

Equation (7) represents a straightforward extension of Black and Cox (1976) to include bankruptcy costs.[17] But we shall see later that taxes affect the value, V_B, when bankruptcy is determined endogenously. Both taxes and bankruptcy costs are important determinants of debt value in this case.

Debt issuance affects the total value of the firm in two ways. First, it reduces firm value because of possible bankruptcy costs. Second, it increases firm value due to the tax deductibility of the interest payments, C. The value of both these effects will depend upon the level of firm value, V, and are time independent. Therefore they can be valued as if they were time-independent securities.

First, consider a security that pays no coupon, but has value equal to the bankruptcy costs αV_B at $V = V_B$. This security has current value, denoted

[15] We focus on bankruptcy costs that are proportional to asset value when bankruptcy is declared. Alternatives such as constant bankruptcy costs could readily be explored within the framework developed. Deviations from absolute priority (in which bondholders do not receive all remaining value) can also be incorporated in the boundary conditions; we do so in Section VI.C. Franks and Torous (1989) and Eberhart, Moore, and Roenfeldt (1990) document deviations from the absolute priority rule.

[16] More exactly,

$$p_B = \int_0^\infty \exp(-rt) f(t; V, V_B)\, dt,$$

where $f(t; V, V_B)$ is the density of the first passage time from V to V_B, when the process for V has drift equal to the risk-free interest rate, r.

[17] Merton (1974) derives a different formula for the case where $\alpha = 0$. This is because he assumes the firm liquidates assets to pay coupons.

$BC(V)$, that reflects the market value of a claim to αV_B should bankruptcy occur. Because its returns are time independent, it too must satisfy equation (4) with boundary conditions

$$\text{At } V = V_B, \qquad BC(V) = \alpha V_B \tag{8i}$$

$$\text{As } V \to \infty, \qquad BC(V) \to 0 \tag{8ii}$$

In this case equation (4) has solution

$$BC(V) = \alpha V_B (V/V_B)^{-X}. \tag{9}$$

BC is a decreasing, strictly convex function of V. Again, note the reinterpretation of equation (9) as $BC = p_B[\alpha V_B]$: the current value of bankruptcy costs is their magnitude if bankruptcy occurs, times the present value of \$1 conditional on future bankruptcy. Subsequent expressions will have similar interpretations.

Now consider the value of tax benefits associated with debt financing. These benefits resemble a security that pays a constant coupon equal to the tax-sheltering value of interest payments (τC) as long as the firm is solvent and pays nothing in bankruptcy. This security's value, $TB(V)$, equals the value of the tax benefit of debt. It too is time independent and therefore must satisfy equation (4) with boundary conditions

$$\text{At } V = V_B, \qquad TB(V) = 0 \tag{10i}$$

$$\text{As } V \to \infty, \qquad TB(V) = \tau C/r. \tag{10ii}$$

Equation (10i) reflects the loss of the tax benefits if the firm declares bankruptcy. Equation (10ii) reflects the fact that, as bankruptcy becomes increasingly unlikely in the relevant future, the value of tax benefits approaches the capitalized value of the tax benefit flow, τC. Using equation (4) and the boundary conditions above gives

$$TB(V) = \tau C/r - (\tau C/r)(V/V_B)^{-X}. \tag{11}$$

Tax benefits are an increasing, strictly concave function of V.

Note that the value of tax benefits, equation (11), presumes that the firm *always* benefits fully (in amount τC) from the tax deductibility of coupon payments when it is solvent. But under U.S. tax codes, to benefit fully the firm must have earnings before interest and taxes (EBIT) that is at least as large as the coupon payment, C.[18] An alternative approach, in which EBIT is related to asset value, V, and tax benefits may be lost when the firm is solvent (but close to bankruptcy), is considered in Section VI.A.

[18] The losses associated with interest payments exceeding EBIT may be carried forward, but lose time value, and may lose all value if the firm goes bankrupt. (Reorganizations under Chapter 11 of the Bankruptcy Code may carry forward some tax benefits. This could be modeled by a boundary condition, equation (10i), with a positive value.)

The total value of the firm, $v(V)$, reflects three terms: the firm's asset value, plus the value of the tax deduction of coupon payments, less the value of bankruptcy costs:

$$v(V) = V + TB(V) - BC(V)$$
$$= V + (\tau C/r)\left[1 - (V/V_B)^{-X}\right] - \alpha V_B (V/V_B)^{-X}. \quad (12)$$

Note that v is strictly concave in asset value, V, when $C > 0$ and either $\alpha > 0$ or $\tau > 0$. Note also that if $\alpha > 0$ and $\tau > 0$, then $v(V) < V$ as $V \to V_B$, and $v(V) > V$ as $V \to \infty$. This coupled with concavity implies that v is (proportionately) more volatile than V at low values of V and is less volatile at high values.

The value of equity is the total value of the firm less the value of debt:

$$E(V) = v(V) - D(V)$$
$$= V - (1 - \tau)C/r + [(1 - \tau)C/r - V_B][V/V_B]^{-X}. \quad (13)$$

We see from equation (14) below that when V_B is endogenously determined, $[(1 - \tau)C/r - V_B] > 0$, implying that $E(V)$ is a convex function of V. This reflects the "option-like" nature of equity, even when debt has an infinite horizon. When V_B is determined by a positive net worth requirement, however, we show in Section V that equity may be a *concave* function of V. This has important ramifications for agency problems associated with asset substitution, which are examined in Section VII. Finally, Ito's Lemma can be used to show that the volatility of equity's rate of return declines as V (and therefore E) rises. Stock option pricing models would need to reflect this nonconstant volatility, as well as the possibility that E reaches zero with positive probability.

Equations (7) and (13) indicate the importance of V_B in determining the values of debt and equity. In the following sections, we consider alternative bankruptcy-triggering scenarios.

II. Debt with No Protective Covenants: The Endogenous Bankruptcy Case

If the firm is not otherwise constrained by covenants, bankruptcy will occur only when the firm cannot meet the required (instantaneous) coupon payment by issuing additional equity: that is, when equity value falls to zero.[19] However, *any* level of asset value, V_B, that triggers bankruptcy will imply

[19] In continuous time, the coupon (Cdt) paid over the infinitesimal interval, dt, is itself infinitesimal. Therefore the value of equity simply needs to be positive to avoid bankruptcy over the next instant. In discrete time, where the time between periods, δt, is of a fixed size, the value of equity at each period must exceed the coupon ($C\delta t$) to be paid that period.

It is sometimes assumed that bankruptcy is triggered by a cashflow shortage. This can be criticized, because, if equity value remains, a firm will always be motivated and able to issue additional equity to cover the shortage, rather than declare bankruptcy. Positive equity value rather than positive cashflow seems to be the essential element when bankruptcy is endogenously determined.

that the value of equity is zero at that asset value, given the absolute priority rule.

When V_B can be chosen by the firm (rather than imposed by a covenant such as positive net-worth requirement), it can be seen from equation (12) that total firm value, v, will be maximized by setting V_B as low as possible. Limited liability of equity, however, prevents V_B from being arbitrarily small: $E(V)$ must be nonnegative for all values of $V \geq V_B$. From equation (13), $E(V)$ is strictly convex in V when $V_B < (1-\tau)C/r$. Thus the lowest possible value for V_B consistent with positive equity value for all $V > V_B$ is such that $dE/dV|_{V=V_B} = 0$: a "smooth-pasting" or "low contact" condition at $V = V_B$. (This choice of bankruptcy level can also be shown to maximize the value of equity at any level of V: $dE/dV_B = 0$[20]). Differentiating equation (13) with respect to V, setting this expression equal to zero with $V = V_B$, and solving for V_B gives

$$V_B = [(1-\tau)C/r][X/(1+X)] = (1-\tau)C/(r+0.5\sigma^2), \tag{14}$$

where the second line uses equation (5). Since $V_B < (1-\tau)C/r$, equity is indeed convex in V.

Observe that the asset value, V_B, at which bankruptcy occurs

a) is proportional to the coupon, C;
b) is independent of the current asset value, V;
c) decreases as the corporate tax rate, τ, increases;
d) is independent of bankruptcy costs, α;
e) decreases as the risk-free interest rate, r, rises; and
f) decreases with increases in the riskiness of the firm, σ^2.

The results above also describe the behavior of total firm value at bankruptcy, $v_B \equiv v[V_B] = (1-\alpha)V_B$, except that v_B falls as bankruptcy cost, α, increases. The fact that asset value, V, does not affect v_B means that the bankruptcy level of total firm market value can be estimated from the coupon, C, (plus parameters r, σ_2, α, and τ), without needing to know the firm's current asset value.[21]

Substituting equation (14) into equations (7), (12), and (13) gives

$$D(V) = (C/r)\left[1 - (C/V)^X k\right] \tag{15}$$

$$v(V) = V + (\tau C/r)\left[1 - (C/V)^X h\right] \tag{16}$$

$$E(V) = V - (1-\tau)(C/r)\left[1 - (C/V)^X m\right] \tag{17}$$

[20] See also Merton (1973; footnote 60). The equivalence of the two conditions suggests that the endogenously set V_B is incentive compatible in the following sense. Ex ante (before debt issuance), stockholders will wish to maximize firm value subject to the limited liability of equity. The ex ante optimal V_B achieves this by satisfying the smooth-pasting condition. Ex post, equity holders will have no incentive to declare bankruptcy at a different V, since V_B also satisfies the ex post optimal condition for maximizing equity value.

[21] Knowledge of the market value of equity, E, and debt, D, in addition to C, combined with equations (7), (13), and (14), permits calculation of a unique V and α given r, τ, and σ. Alternatively, α and σ can be recovered, given r, τ, and V.

where

$$m = [(1-\tau)X/r(1+X)]^X/(1+X)$$
$$h = [1+X+\alpha(1-\tau)X/\tau]m$$
$$k = [1+X-(1-\alpha)(1-\tau)X]m.$$

The interest rate paid by risky debt, $R(C/V)$, can be derived directly from dividing C by $D(V)$, giving

$$R(C/V) = C/D(V) = rK(C/V), \tag{18}$$

where

$$K(C/V) = \left[1-(C/V)^X k\right]^{-1}.$$

The interest rate depends positively on the *ratio* of the coupon, C, to firm asset value, V. Note $K(C/V)$ has the interpretation of a risk-adjustment factor (multiplying the risk-free rate) that the firm must pay to compensate bondholders for the risks assumed. The yield spread is $R(C/V)-r = r(C/V)^X k/[1-(C/V)^X k]$.

The values above are derived for an arbitrary level of the coupon, C. Section III examines the *optimal* choice of coupon (and leverage) for unprotected debt. But first, we examine the behavior of unprotected debt values and yield premiums for an arbitrary coupon level.

A. The Comparative Statics of Debt Value (D(V))

Equation (15) extends Black and Cox's (1976) results to include the effects of taxes and bankruptcy on debt value. Row 1 of Table I summarizes the comparative statics of debt value. Not surprisingly, larger bankruptcy costs decrease the value of debt. Less obvious is that an increase in the corporate tax rate will raise debt value, through lowering the bankruptcy level, V_B.[22]

More surprising still are the results when taxes or bankruptcy costs are positive and firm asset value, V, nears the bankruptcy level, V_B. Table I indicates that the effects of increases in the coupon, firm riskiness, and the risk-free rate become reversed from what is expected. An increase in coupon can *lower* debt value. An increase in firm risk can *raise* debt value, as can an increase in the risk-free rate. Thus *the behavior of "junk" bonds (or "fallen angels") differs significantly from the behavior of investment-grade bonds when bankruptcy costs and/or taxes are positive.*[23]

To understand these results, first consider the presence of positive bankruptcy costs. If V is close to V_B, the value of debt will be very sensitive to such costs. Lowering V_B will raise the value of debt since bankruptcy costs

[22] These comparative static results presume that other parameters (including V) remain at their current level, the usual ceteris paribus assumption. Note, however, that a change in the corporate tax rate might affect V as well.

[23] The ratios of V/V_B (or C/V) at which the various behaviors are reversed are not identical. Of course, these ratios may not correspond to Wall Street's definition of "junk" bonds.

Table I

Comparative Statics of Financial Variables: Unprotected Debt

This table describes properties of the equations describing debt value, D, the interest, R, paid on debt, the yield spread of the debt over the risk-free rate $(R - r)$, the total firm value, v, and the value of equity, E, when debt is *not* protected by a positive net-worth covenant. V is the firm's asset value, V_B is the endogeneously determined value at which bankruptcy is declared, C is the coupon paid on debt, σ^2 is the variance of the asset return, r is the risk-free interest rate, α is the fraction of asset value lost if bankruptcy occurs, and τ is the corporate tax rate.

			Limit As		Sign of Change in Instrument for an Increase in:					
Variable	Homogeneity	Shape	$V \to \infty$	$V \to V_B$	C	σ^2	r	α	τ	V
D	Degree 1 in V, C	Concave in V, C	C/r	$\frac{C(1-\alpha)(1-\tau)}{(r+0.5\sigma^2)}$	> 0; $< 0^*$ as $V \to V_B$	< 0; $> 0^*$ as $V \to V_B$	< 0; $> 0^*$ as $V \to V_B$	< 0	> 0	> 0
R	Degree 0 in V, C	Convex in V/C	r	$\frac{(r+0.5\sigma^2)}{(1-\alpha)(1-\tau)}$	> 0	> 0; $< 0^*$ as $V \to V_B$	> 0; $< 0^*$ as $V \to V_B$	> 0	< 0	< 0
$R - r$	Degree 0 in V, C	Convex in V/C	0	$[0.5\sigma^2 + r(\alpha + \tau - \alpha\tau)]/[(1-\alpha)(1-\tau)]$	> 0	> 0; $< 0^*$ as $V \to V_B$	< 0	> 0	< 0	< 0
v	Degree 1 in V, C	Concave in V, C	$V + \tau C/r$	$\frac{C(1-\alpha)(1-\tau)}{(r+0.5\sigma^2)}$	> 0; $< 0^*$ as $V \to V_B$	< 0; $> 0^*$ as $V \to V_B$	< 0; $> 0^*$ as $V \to V_B$	< 0	> 0	> 0
E	Degree 1 in V, C	Convex in V, C	$V - (1-\tau)C/r$	0	< 0	> 0	> 0	0	> 0	> 0

*Sign reversal as $V \to V_B$ only if α and/or $\tau > 0$.

will be less imminent. From equation (14), higher asset volatility, higher risk-free interest rates, or lower coupon, C, will all serve to lower V_B. For values of V close to V_B, this positive effect on $D(V)$ will dominate. Even if there are no direct bankruptcy costs, the event of bankruptcy causes the value of the tax shield to be lost when $\tau > 0$, and the previous conclusions continue to hold.

The fact that $D(V)$ is eventually decreasing as the coupon rises implies that debt value reaches a maximum, $D_{max}(V)$, for a finite coupon, $C_{max}(V)$. We can naturally think of D_{max} as the *debt capacity* of the firm. Differentiating equation (15) with respect to C, setting the resulting equation equal to zero and solving for C gives

$$C_{max}(V) = V[(1+X)k]^{-1/X} \tag{19}$$

Substituting this into equation (15) and simplifying gives

$$D_{max}(V) = V[Xk^{-1/X}(1+X)^{-(1+1/X)}]/r. \tag{20}$$

The debt capacity of a firm is proportional to asset value, V, and falls with increases in firm risk, σ^2, and bankruptcy costs, α. Debt capacity rises with increases in the corporate tax rate, τ, and the risk-free rate, r.

Figures 1 and 2 show the relationship between debt value and the coupon

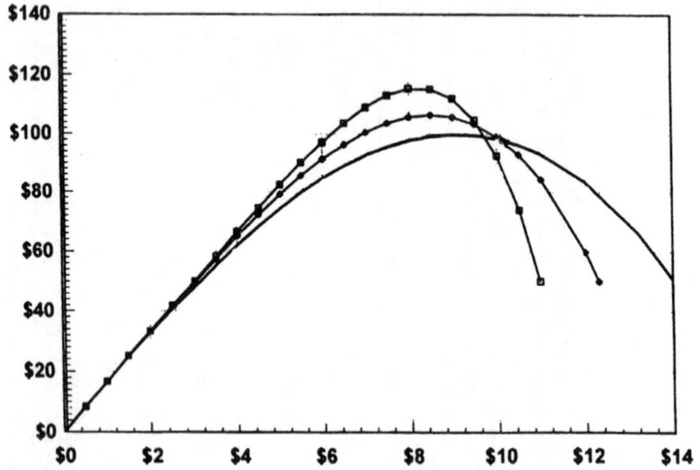

Figure 1. Debt value as a function of the coupon, when debt is unprotected. The lines plot the value of unprotected debt, D, at varying coupon levels C, for three levels of asset volatility, σ: 15 percent (*open square*), 20 percent (*filled diamond*), and 25 percent (*solid line*). It is assumed that the risk-free interest rate $r = 6.0\%$, bankruptcy costs are 50 percent ($\alpha = 0.5$), and the corporate tax rate is 35 percent ($\tau = 0.35$).

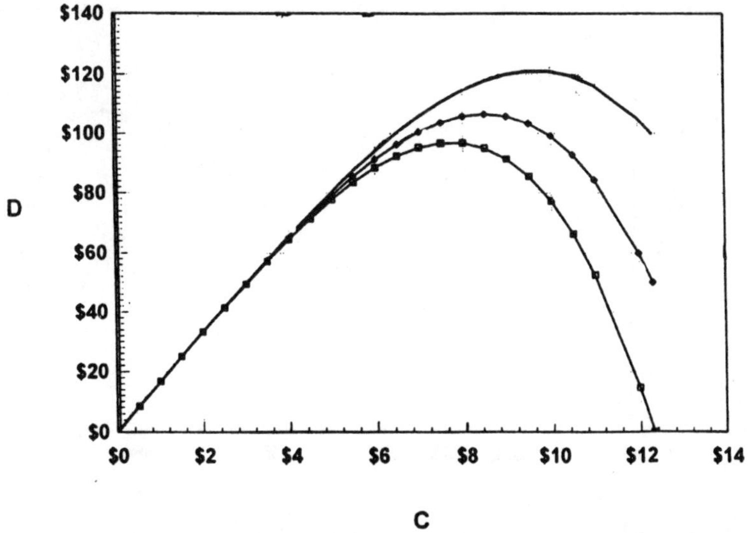

Figure 2. Debt value as a function of the coupon, when debt is unprotected. The lines plot the value of unprotected debt, D, at varying coupon levels, C, for three levels of bankruptcy costs: 0 (*solid line*), 50 percent (*filled diamond*), and 100 percent (*open square*) ($\alpha = 0, 0.5$, and 1, respectively). It is assumed that the risk-free interest rate $r = 6.0$ percent and the corporate tax rate is 35 percent ($\tau = 0.35$).

for varying firm volatility and bankruptcy costs, when $V = \$100$ and $r = 6$ percent. Our normalization implies that the coupon level (in dollars) also represents the coupon *rate* as a percentage of asset value, V. Note that at high coupon levels, the debt of riskier firms has higher value than that of less risky firms. The peak of each curve indicates the maximum debt capacity, D_{max}, with corresponding leverage level. Figure 3 repeats Figure 1, but with leverage, $[D/v]$, rather than coupon level on the x-axis. The reversals seen in Figure 1 do not appear in Figure 3. This is because leverage itself depends on the value of debt.

B. Yield Spreads: The Risk Structure of Interest Rates

Rows 2 and 3 of Table I indicate the behavior of risky interest rates and yield spreads. Increasing the coupon, C, always raises the yield spread. An increase in bankruptcy costs, α, also raises the spread, although a rise in the corporate tax rate will lower the spread because debt value will rise. Related to our earlier discussion, we observe the surprising result that *junk bond yield spreads may actually decline when firm riskiness increases.* Of course, this holds only for junk bonds: the yield spread on investment-grade debt will increase when firm risk rises. Also note that junk bond interest rates may

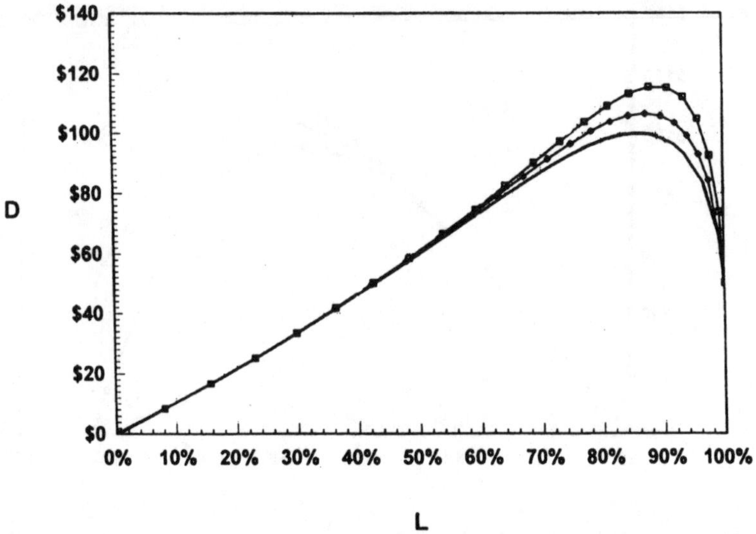

Figure 3. Debt value as a function of the leverage, when debt is unprotected. The lines plot the value of unprotected debt, D, at varying leverage ratios, L, for three levels of asset volatility, σ: 15 percent (*open square*), 20 percent (*filled diamond*), and 25 percent (*solid line*). It is assumed that the risk-free interest rate $r = 6.0\%$, bankruptcy costs are 50 percent ($\alpha = 0.5$), and the corporate tax rate is 35 percent ($\tau = 0.35$).

actually fall when the risk-free rate increases. Figures 4 and 5 plot yield spreads against coupon level and leverage, respectively, as asset value risk changes.

Observe that $R(C/V) \to (r + 0.5\sigma^2)$ as $V \to V_B$ when $\alpha = \tau = 0$. That is, long-term risky debt will never have a yield exceeding the risk-free rate by more than $0.5\sigma^2$ if there are no bankruptcy costs or tax benefits to debt.[24] Observing a yield spread greater than this on corporate long-term debt implies the presence of bankruptcy costs, taxes, or both.[25]

C. The Comparative Statics of Firm Value ($v(V)$) and Equity Value ($E(V)$)

Row 4 of Table I indicates the comparative statics of total firm value. Again observe the perverse behavior of total firm value for firms with junk debt. In the presence of bankruptcy costs and/or corporate taxes, total firm value

[24]A firm whose asset value has an annual standard deviation of 20 percent, for example, would have debt whose yield spread *never* exceeds two percent. It has been argued that the tax advantage to debt may be nil (Miller (1977)). For arguments that bankruptcy costs may be small, see Warner (1977) (who focuses on direct costs only) and Haugen and Senbet (1988).

[25]When the firm has several debt issues, junior debt could have higher rates. But the weighted average cost of debt will be limited to $r + 0.5\sigma^2$ in this case.

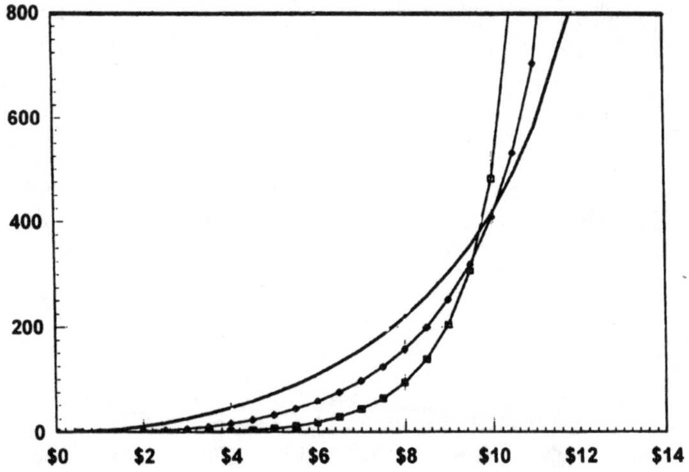

Figure 4. Yield spreads on unprotected debt as a function of the coupon. The lines plot the yield spread, *YS* (in basis points/year), the amount the firm's debt yield exceeds the risk-free rate, as a function of the coupon, *C*, for varying levels of asset volatility, σ: 15 percent (*open square*), 20 percent (*filled diamond*), and 25 percent (*solid line*). It is assumed that the risk-free interest rate $r = 6.0$ percent, bankruptcy costs are 50 percent ($\alpha = 0.5$), and the corporate tax rate is 35 percent ($\tau = 0.35$).

may rise as firm riskiness increases. Rising risk-free rates may also lead total firm value to increase. The values of firms with investment-grade debt will not exhibit such behavior. Figure 6 and Figure 7 illustrate total firm value, v, as a function of the coupon level C and the leverage D/v, respectively. Optimal leverage is the ratio at which each curve reaches its peak.

Row 5 of Table I indicates the behavior of equity value. Unlike debt, there are no reversals of comparative static results when V is close to V_B. The fact that bankruptcy costs do not affect equity value is perhaps surprising, but it reflects the fact that, given the coupon, C, debtholders bear all bankruptcy costs. In Section III we show that the *optimal* coupon and debt-equity ratio do depend upon α, and that initial equity holders ultimately are hurt by greater bankruptcy costs.

III. Optimal Leverage with Unprotected Debt

Consider now the coupon rate, C, which maximizes the total value, v, of the firm, given current asset value, V. Differentiating equation (16) with respect to C, setting the derivative equal to zero and solving for the optimal coupon,

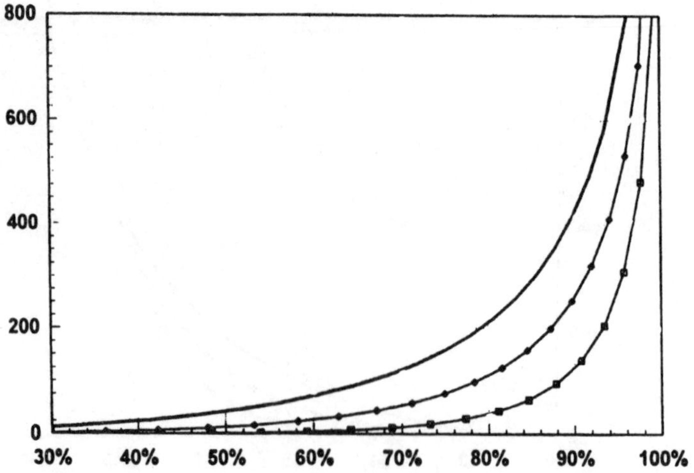

Figure 5. Yield spreads on unprotected debt as a function of the leverage. The lines plot the yield spread, *YS* (in basis points/year), the amount the firm's debt yield exceeds the risk-free rate, as a function of the leverage, L, for varying levels of asset volatility, σ: 15 percent (*open square*), 20 percent (*filled diamond*), and 25 percent (*solid line*). It is assumed that the risk-free interest rate $r = 6.0$ percent, bankruptcy costs are 50 percent ($\alpha = 0.5$), and the corporate tax rate is 35 percent ($\tau = 0.35$).

C^*, as a function of asset value, V, gives:

$$C^*(V) = V[(1+X)h]^{-1/X} \tag{21}$$

Note that $h > k$, implying $C^*(V) < C_{max}(V)$. Substituting $C^*(V)$ into equations (15), (16), (18), and (14) gives

$$D^*(V) = V[(1+X)h]^{-1/X}\{1 - k[(1+X)h]^{-1}\}/r \tag{22}$$

$$v^*(V) = V\{1 + (\tau/r)[(1+X)h]^{-1/X}[X/(1+X)]\} \tag{23}$$

$$R^* = r[(1+X)h]/[(1+X)h - k] \tag{24}$$

$$V_B^*(V) = V(m/h)^{1/X} \tag{25}$$

Table II indicates the comparative statics of these variables plus optimal leverage $L^* = D^*/v^*$ and equity $E^* = v^* - D^*$. While most results are consistent with what is expected, a few merit comment.

The optimal coupon C^* is a U-shaped function of firm riskiness, as illustrated in Figure 8. Firms with little business risk, or very large risk, will optimally commit to pay sizable coupons. Firms with intermediate levels of risk will promise smaller coupons. However, the optimal leverage ratios of riskier firms will always be less than those of less risky firms, as can be seen

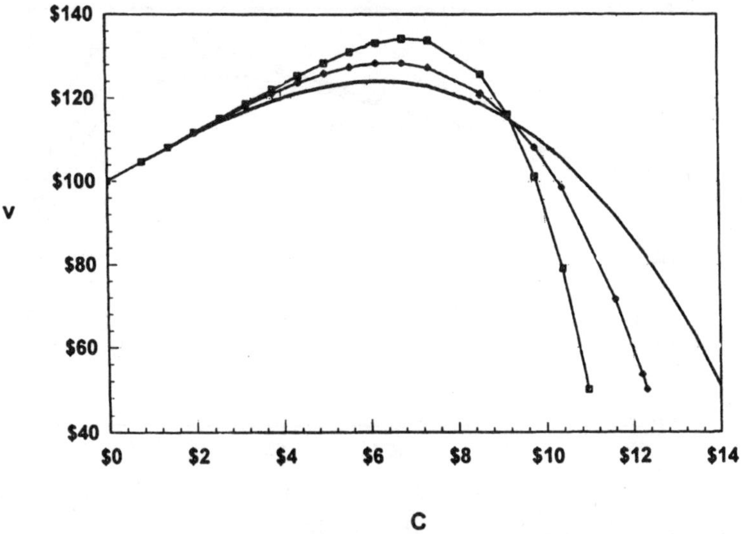

Figure 6. Total firm value as function of the coupon, when debt is unprotected. The lines plot total firm value, v, at varying coupon levels, C, for three levels of asset volatility, σ: 15 percent (*open square*), 20 percent (*filled diamond*), and 25 percent (*solid line*). It is assumed that the risk-free interest rate $r = 6.0$ percent, bankruptcy costs are 50 percent ($\alpha = 0.5$), and the corporate tax rate is 35 percent ($\tau = 0.35$).

by observing the maximal firm values in Figure 7. The potential gains in moving from no leverage to optimal leverage (where $v = v^*$) are considerable. For reasonable parameter levels, optimizing financial structure can increase firm value by as much as 25 to 40 percent over a firm with no leverage.

Our results confirm Brennan and Schwartz's (1978) observation that optimal leverage is less than 100 percent even when bankruptcy costs are zero. Too high leverage risks bankruptcy—and while there are no bankruptcy costs, the tax deductibility of coupon payments is lost.

Leverage of about 75 to 95 percent is optimal for firms with low-to-moderate levels of asset value risk and moderate bankruptcy costs.[26] Even firms with high risks and high bankruptcy costs should have leverage on the order of 50 to 60 percent, when the effective tax rate is 35 percent. Optimal

[26] It is of interest that many of the leveraged buyouts of the 1980s created capital structures that had 95 percent leverage or more. And targets were often firms with relatively stable value (low σ^2). Our analysis indicates these firms will reap maximal benefits from increased leverage. Subsequent leverage reduction by many of these firms could in part be explained by the substantial fall in interest rates, which reduces the optimal leverage ratio.

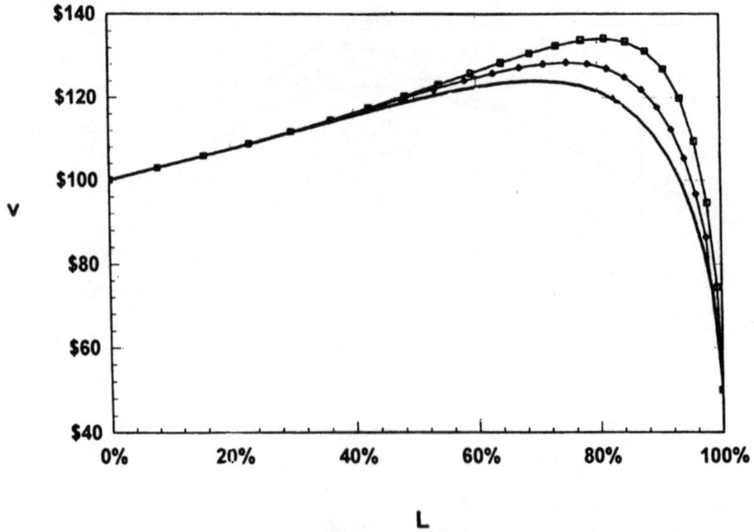

Figure 7. Total firm value as function of the leverage, when debt is unprotected. The lines plot total firm value, v, at varying levels of leverage L, for three levels of asset volatility, σ: 15 percent (*open square*), 20 percent (*filled diamond*), and 25 percent (*solid line*). It is assumed that the risk-free interest rate $r = 6.0$ percent, bankruptcy costs are 50 percent ($\alpha = 0.5$), and the corporate tax rate is 35 percent ($\tau = 0.35$).

leverage ratios drop by 5 to 25 percent when the effective tax rate is 15 percent, with the more pronounced falls at high volatility levels.[27] Variations of our assumptions that lead to lower optimal leverage ratios are discussed in Section VI.

The behavior of the yield spread at the optimal leverage ratio exhibits one surprise. Increased bankruptcy costs might be thought to increase interest rates. Indeed they do—but only if the coupon is fixed. As bankruptcy costs rise, the optimal coupon C^* falls. The probability of bankruptcy is then less and the yield spread decreases. Figure 9 illustrates yield spreads at the optimal leverage as a function of bankruptcy costs, α, and asset risk, σ.

Higher risk-free interest rates might also be expected to reduce the optimal amount of borrowing, but they do not: the added tax shield when interest rates are high more than offsets the greater costs of borrowing. This could be destabilizing, since supply would normally be expected to decrease as interest

[27] Following Miller (1977), if the effective personal tax rate on stock returns (reflecting tax deferment) were 20 percent, the tax rate on bond income were 40 percent, and the corporate tax rate 35 percent, the effective tax advantage of debt is $[1 - (1 - 0.35)(1 - 0.20)/(1 - 0.40)] = 0.133$, or slightly less than 15 percent.

Table II

Comparative Statics of Financial Variables at the Optimal Leverage Ratio: Unprotected Debt

This table describes the behavior of the coupon, C^*, that maximizes firm value, and the debt, D^*, leverage, L^*, interest rate, R^*, yield spread, $R^* - r$, total firm value, v^*, equity value, E^*, and bankruptcy value, V_B^*, at the optimal coupon level, for unprotected debt. (V is the firm's asset value, σ^2 is the variance of the asset return, r is the risk-free interest rate, α is the fraction of asset value lost if bankruptcy occurs, and τ is the corporate tax rate.

		Sign of Change in Variable for an Increase in:			
Variable	Shape	σ^2	r	α	τ
C^*	Linear in V	< 0, σ^2 small; > 0, σ^2 large	> 0	< 0	> 0
D^*	Linear in V	< 0	> 0	< 0	> 0
L^*	Invariant to V	< 0	> 0	< 0	> 0
R^*	Invariant to V	> 0	> 0	< 0	> 0
$R^* - r$	Invariant to V	> 0	< 0	< 0	> 0
v^*	Linear in V	< 0	> 0	< 0	> 0
E^*	Linear in V	> 0	< 0	> 0	< 0[a]
V_B^*	Linear in V	< 0	> 0	< 0	> 0[a]

[a]No effect if $\alpha = 0$.

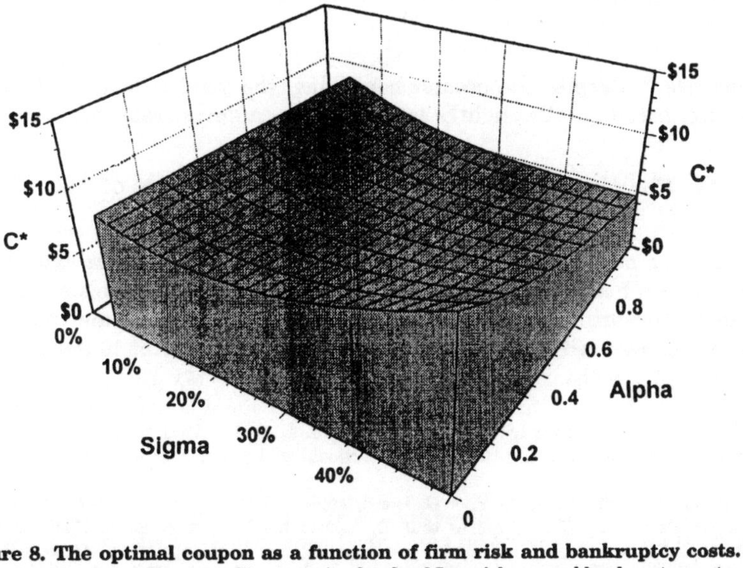

Figure 8. The optimal coupon as a function of firm risk and bankruptcy costs. The surface plots the optimal coupon, C^*, at varying levels of firm risk, σ, and bankruptcy costs, α. It is assumed that the risk-free interest rate $r = 6.0$ percent and the corporate tax rate is 35 percent ($\tau = 0.35$).

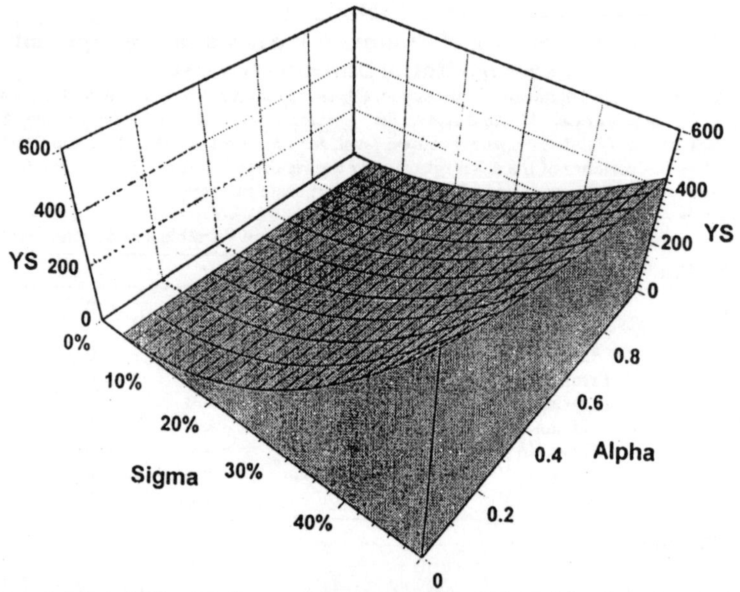

Figure 9. The yield spread as a function of firm risk and bankruptcy costs. The surface plots the yield spread, *YS*, the difference between the yield on the firm's debt (at the optimal coupon, C^*) and the risk-free interest rate, r, for varying levels of firm risk, σ, and bankruptcy costs, α. It is assumed that the risk-free interest rate $r = 6.0$ percent and the corporate tax rate is 35 percent ($\tau = 0.35$).

rates rise.[28] Despite the greater borrowing, the yield spread at the optimal leverage actually falls slightly as the risk-free interest rate increases.

IV. Positive Net-Worth Covenants and the Value of Protected Debt

Consider now the case in which debt remains outstanding without time limit unless bankruptcy is triggered by the value of the firm's assets falling beneath the principal value of debt, denoted P. We presume the principal value coincides with the market value of the debt when it is issued, denoted D_0. Thus $V_B = D_0$.[29]

[28] Note that an increase in r might well cause a decline in V. If so, it is possible that the desired amount of borrowing (which is proportional to V) could decline even though optimal leverage rises.

[29] It must be verified that the $V_B = D_0$ is consistent with the value of equity remaining positive at all levels $V \geq V_B$. This requires that D_0 exceed the level in equation (14) satisfying the smooth-pasting conditions. In fact, this is always the case at the optimal protected debt coupon level, and is satisfied at all but extremely high initial coupon levels. We limit our examination of protected debt to coupon levels for which the minimum net-worth requirement (rather than equation (14)) is the determinant of V_B.

Are there contractual arrangements in which this is a realistic description of bankruptcy? One possibility would be long-term debt as examined previously, with a protective covenant stipulating that the asset value of the firm always exceed the principal value of the debt: a positive net-worth requirement. Such covenants are not common in long-term bond contracts, however.

An alternative contractual arrangement approximating this case would be a continuously renewable line of credit, in which the borrowing amount and interest rate are fixed at inception.[30] At each instant the debt will be extended ("rolled over" at a fixed interest rate) if and only if the firm has sufficient asset value, V, to repay the loan's principal, P; otherwise bankruptcy occurs.[31] Thus the roll-over process proxies for a positive net-worth requirement. With this latter interpretation, the differences between the unprotected debt analyzed above and protected debt analyzed below *may capture many of the differences between long-term debt and (rolled over) short-term financing.*

From equation (7) with $V_B = D_0$, we can write the value of protected debt as a function of the value of assets, V_0, at the time the debt is initiated:

$$D_0(V_0) = C/r + [(1 - \alpha)D_0(V_0) - C/r][V_0/D_0(V_0)]^{-X} \tag{26}$$

Except when $\alpha = 0$, closed-form solutions for the function $D_0(V_0)$ satisfying equation (26) have not been found. However, we can easily solve this equation numerically to determine the value, D_0, of the debt, given initial values, V_0 and C (as before we suppress the argument C). Note that the function $D_0(V_0)$ is homogeneous of degree one in V_0 and C. Also note that equation (26) gives the value of protected debt only at the initial asset value, V_0. Equation (7) with $V_B = D_0(V_0)$ gives protected debt value as a function of asset value, V.

Figures 10 and 11 illustrate the behavior of protected debt value as the coupon and leverage change, for $V = V_0 = 100$. They should be compared with Figures 1 and 3. We observe that the surprising behavior of unprotected "junk" debt does not hold for protected debt, even when the debt exhibits considerable risk. Unlike the unprotected case, the value of debt increases with the coupon at all levels of C. And increased firm risk or a higher risk-free interest rate always lowers debt value. This is because the bankruptcy-triggering value, V_B, is determined exogenously rather than endogenously.

[30] We assume the firm will never choose to borrow less than the stipulated credit line amount. The fact that most credit lines are tied to a floating rate is not important here, since the risk-free rate is assumed to be constant. It is important that the interest rate paid by the firm be independent of the firm's asset value V (providing $V \geq V_B$) after the initial agreement is reached.

[31] Many lines of credit have a "paydown" provision, requiring that the amount borrowed must be reduced to zero at least once per year. A firm will fail to meet this provision if its (market) value of assets is less than the loan principal. Also note that Merton (1974) requires $V \geq P$ at maturity to avoid default on a pure-discount bond: the firm must have positive net worth at maturity or bankruptcy occurs.

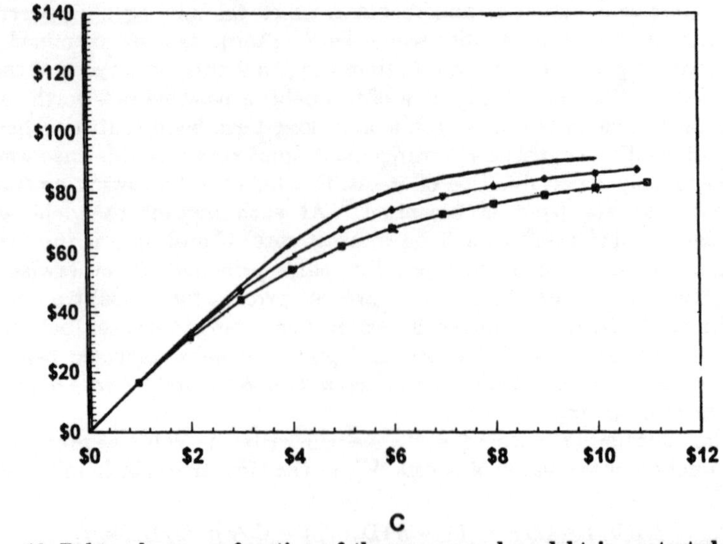

Figure 10. Debt value as a function of the coupon, when debt is protected by a minimum net-worth requirement. The lines plot the value of protected debt, D, at varying coupon levels, C, for three levels of asset volatility, σ: 15 percent (*solid line*), 20 percent (*filled diamond*), and 25 percent (*open square*). It is assumed that the risk-free interest rate $r = 6.0$ percent, bankruptcy costs are 50 percent ($\alpha = 0.5$), and the corporate tax rate is 35 percent ($\tau = 0.35$).

When there are no bankruptcy costs ($\alpha = 0$),

a) Protected debt is riskless and pays the risk-free rate, r.
b) For any C, the value of the tax shield with protected debt is less than the tax shield with unprotected debt.
c) For any C, the bankruptcy-triggering value of assets, V_B, for protected debt exceeds the V_B for unprotected debt.

Protected debt is riskless when $\alpha = 0$ because the firm's asset value is constantly monitored. Should asset value fall to the principal value, bankruptcy is declared and, because there are no bankruptcy costs, debtholders receive their full principal value. In this case, for a given coupon, C, the value of protected debt always exceeds that of unprotected debt. Further, $V_B = P = D_0(V_0) = C/r$. This exceeds the bankruptcy-triggering value, equation (14), of assets for unprotected debt, and implies smaller tax benefits from equation (11).

When bankruptcy costs are positive ($\alpha > 0$), the results change markedly. For a given coupon, C, protected debt may have a lesser value than unprotected debt (and therefore may pay a higher interest rate). This follows because bankruptcy will occur more frequently when debt is protected, because V_B is higher in the protected case, and bankruptcy costs will be

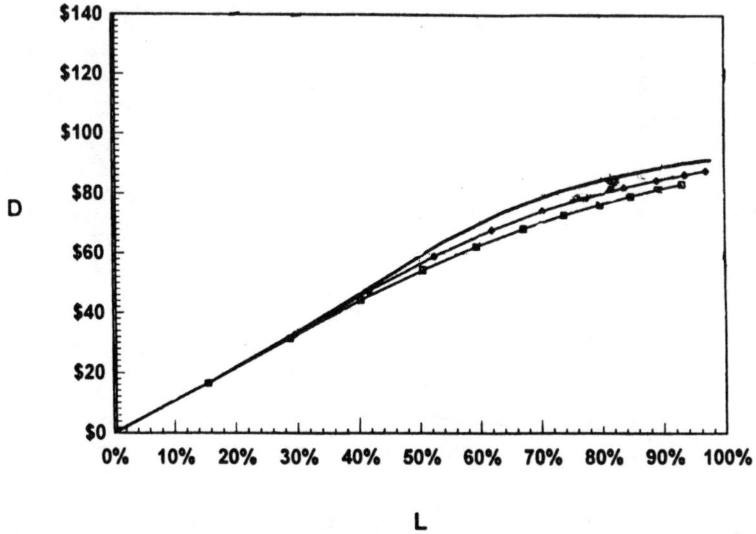

Figure 11. Debt value as a function of the leverage, when debt is protected by a minimum net-worth requirement. The lines plot the value of protected debt, D, at varying leverage ratios, L, for three levels of asset volatility, σ: 15 percent (*solid line*), 20 percent (*filled diamond*), and 25 percent (*open square*). It is assumed that the risk-free interest rate $r = 6.0$ percent, bankruptcy costs are 50 percent ($\alpha = 0.5$), and the corporate tax rate is 35 percent ($\tau = 0.35$).

incurred when $\alpha > 0$. Figure 12, when compared with Figure 5, shows yield spreads to be substantially higher for protected debt when $\alpha = 0.5$, except at extreme leverage ratios.

V. Optimal Leverage with Protected Debt

We now use a simple search procedure to find the coupon, C^*, that maximizes the total value, v, of the firm with protected debt. Figure 13, compared with Figure 7, illustrates that maximal firm value occurs at lower leverage when debt is protected.

For a reasonable range of parameters, we find that

a) Optimal leverage for protected debt is substantially less than for unprotected debt.
b) The interest rate paid at the optimum leverage is less for protected debt, even when bankruptcy costs are positive ($\alpha > 0$).
c) The maximum value of the firm (and therefore the benefit from leverage) is less when protected debt is used.

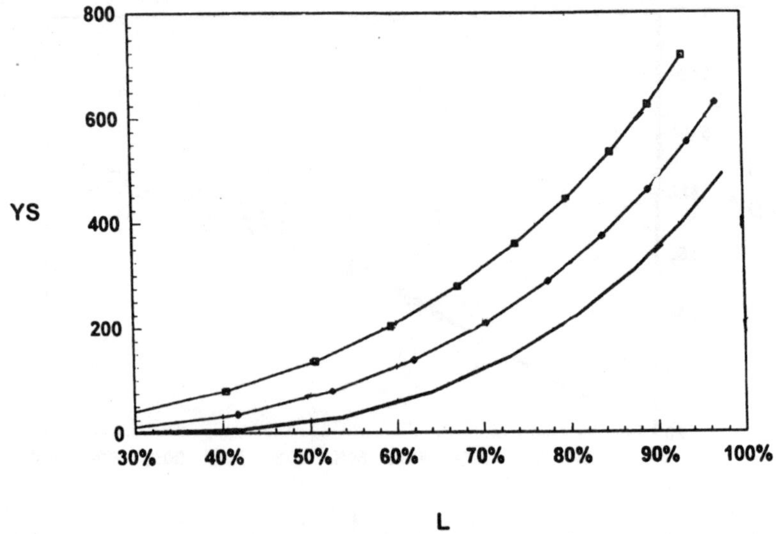

Figure 12. Yield spreads on protected debt as a function of the leverage. The lines plot the yield spread, *YS* (in basis points/year), the amount the firm's debt yield exceeds the risk-free rate, as a function of the leverage, L, for varying levels of asset volatility, σ: 15 percent (*solid line*), 20 percent (*filled diamond*), and 25 percent (*open square*). It is assumed that the risk-free interest rate $r = 6.0$ percent, bankruptcy costs are 50 percent ($\alpha = 0.5$), and the corporate tax rate is 35% ($\tau = 0.35$).

d) The maximal benefits of unprotected over protected debt increase as:

- Corporate taxes increase
- Interest rates are higher
- Bankruptcy costs are lower

A closer examination of numerical results reveals that *the optimal bankruptcy level V_B^* is the same for both protected and unprotected debt*, when bankruptcy costs are zero. We know, however, the closed-form solution for unprotected debt's optimal bankruptcy level, V_B, from equation (25). Since $D_0 = V_B$, this in turn suggests a closed-form solution for the optimal value of protected debt and related values when bankruptcy costs are zero and $V = V_0$:

$$D_0^*(V_0) = V_B^*(V_0) = V_0(m/h)^{1/X} \tag{27}$$

Because protected debt is risk free when $\alpha = 0$, it also follows that

$$C^*(V_0) = rD_0^*(V_0) = rV_B^*(V_0) = rV_0(m/h)^{1/X} \tag{28}$$

$$v^*(V_0) = V_0 + [\tau C^*(V_0)/r]\{1 - [C^*(V_0)/V_0]^X h\} \tag{29}$$

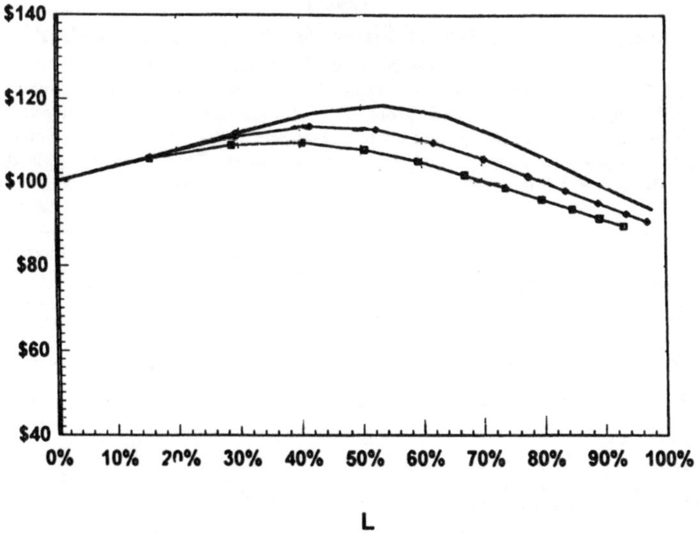

Figure 13. Total firm value as function of the leverage, when debt is protected. The lines plot total firm value, v, at varying levels of leverage, L, for three levels of asset volatility, σ: 15 percent (*solid line*), 20 percent (*filled diamond*), and 25 percent (*open square*). It is assumed that the risk-free interest rate $r = 6.0$ percent, bankruptcy costs are 50 percent ($\alpha = 0.5$), and the corporate tax rate is 35 percent ($\tau = 0.35$).

Recall that equations (27) to (29) hold only for the protected debt case with no bankruptcy costs. We have not been able to find closed-form solutions when $\alpha > 0$. Equation (28) implies that $[(1 - \tau)(C^*/r) - V_B^*] = -\tau C^*/r < 0$, when $\alpha = 0$. From equation (13), this implies that *equity is a strictly concave function of* V. By continuity, equity will be concave when α is close to zero. And in the numerical example considered in Section VI, equity is strictly concave in V for all α.

The observed comparative statics of optimal protected debt value (and related values) are given in Table III. There are some important differences with the comparative statics of optimal unprotected debt value. The debt yield and the yield spread at the optimum rise rather than fall as bankruptcy costs rise. The yield spread also increases as the risk-free interest rate rises, although the magnitude is small. The optimal leverage ratio, (D^*/v^*), *declines* as the corporate tax rate increases, when bankruptcy costs are low. Optimal debt, D^*, increases with τ, but (unlike the unprotected debt case) increases less rapidly than v^*.

VI. Discussion and Variations: Debt Value and Capital Structure

Our analysis has determined optimal leverage ratios and associated yield spreads in a variety of environments, for both long-term unprotected debt

Table III

Comparative Statics of Financial Variables at the Optimal Leverage Ratio: Protected Debt

This table describes the behavior of the coupon, C^*, that maximizes firm value, and the debt, D^*, leverage, L^*, interest rate, R^*, yield spread, $R^* - r$, total firm value, v^*, equity value, E^*, and bankruptcy value, V_B^*, at the optimal coupon level, for debt protected by a positive net-worth covenant. V is the firm's asset value, σ^2 is the variance of asset returns, r is the risk-free interest rate, α is the fraction of asset value lost if bankruptcy occurs, and τ is the corporate tax rate.

		Sign of Change in Variable for an Increase in:			
Variable	Shape	σ^2	r	α	τ
C^*	Linear in V	< 0[b]	> 0	< 0	> 0[a]
D^*	Linear in V	< 0	> 0	< 0	> 0[a]
L^*	Invariant to V	< 0	> 0	< 0	< 0, α small[b]; > 0, α large
R^*	Invariant to V	> 0[a]	> 0	> 0[b]	> 0[a]
$R^* - r$	Invariant to V	> 0[a]	> 0[b]	> 0[b]	> 0[a]
v^*	Linear in V	< 0	> 0	< 0	> 0
E^*	Linear in V	> 0	< 0	> 0	> 0, α small[b]; < 0, α large
V_B^*	Linear in V	< 0	> 0	< 0	> 0[a]

[a]No effect if $\alpha = 0$.
[b]Represents different behavior from unprotected debt.

and protected (or continuously rolled-over) debt. It is of interest to compare these results with typical leverage ratios and yield spreads in the United States. Leverage in companies with highly rated debt is generally less than 40 percent. Yields of investment-grade corporate bonds have exceeded Treasury bond yields by a minimum of 15 basis points (bps), and a maximum of 215 bps from 1926 to 1986. The average yield spread over this period was 77 bps.[32] These spreads reflect finite-maturity debt and also reflect the fact that corporate debt typically is callable. Call provisions may add about 25 bps to the annual cost of corporate debt.[33] Subtracting 25 bps from the average yield spread of 77 bps to eliminate the impact of call provisions gives an adjusted historical yield spread of about 52 bps.

We examine a base case where the volatility of the firm's assets is 20 percent, the corporate tax rate is 35 percent, the risk-free rate is 6 percent, and bankruptcy costs are 50 percent. In this case, optimal leverage with unprotected debt is 75 percent and the yield spread is 75 bps. The optimally

[32]As reported by Kim, Ramaswamy, and Sundaresan (1993); see also Sarig and Warga (1989).

[33]Kim, Ramaswamy, and Sundaresan (1993) estimate a call premium of 22 bps using a numerical example.

levered firm's equity is volatile, with a 57 percent annual standard deviation. Reducing the effective tax rate would reduce optimal leverage and the yield spread. For example, with an effective tax rate of 15 percent, optimal leverage is 59 percent, and the yield spread is 35 bps. Equity volatility is lower, but still substantial.

It is clear that, based on our assumptions thus far, the analysis of unprotected debt suggests optimal leverage considerably in excess of current practice. This could be construed as a criticism of current management rather than the model. Managers may be loath to pay out "free cash flow" (see Jensen (1986)); the wave of leveraged buyouts in the late 1980s suggests that firm value may be raised by using greater leverage (see Kaplan (1989) and Leland (1989)). However, the model's predicted yield spreads seem low given the suggested high leverage.

Optimal leverage ratios and yield spreads for protected debt are more consistent with historical ratios. In the base case, optimal leverage is 45 percent and the yield spread is 45 bps. Equity has a 34 percent annual standard deviation, which is a bit higher than the historical average equity risk of a single firm of about 30 percent.

We now consider how variations in the assumptions may affect the nature of optimal leverage and yield spreads, in both the unprotected and protected cases.

A. No Tax Shelter for Interest Payments When Value Falls

We have assumed that the deductibility of interest payments generates tax savings at all values above the bankruptcy level. But as firm asset value drops, it is quite possible that profits will be less than the coupon payout and tax savings will not be fully realized (or will be substantially postponed). If lesser tax benefits are available, the optimal leverage ratio declines.

In Appendix A, we extend the analysis to allow for no tax benefits whenever $V < V_T$, where V_T is an exogenously specified level of firm asset value.[34] In the base case considered above, optimal leverage falls from 75 to 70 percent, and the yield spread at the optimal leverage rises from 75 to 87 bps, when $V_T = 90$, i.e., 90 percent of the current asset value.

A possible criticism of the above approach is that V_T does not depend upon the amount of debt the firm has issued. Consider an alternative scenario in which higher profit is needed if higher coupon payments are to be fully deductible. For example, assume that the rate of EBIT is related to asset value as follows:

$$\text{EBIT} = (V - 60)/6. \tag{30}$$

Thus gross profit before interest drops to zero when V falls to 60 and represents one-sixth of asset value in excess of 60. Further, assume that

[34] We do not allow tax loss carryforwards in this analysis, since they would introduce a form of time (and path) dependence. Thus, we may overstate the loss of tax shields: the "truth" perhaps lies somewhere between the previous results and the results of this analysis.

coupon payments, C, can be deducted from profit (for tax purposes) only if EBIT $- C \geq 0$. (We ignore partial deductibility.) It then follows that

$$V_T = 60 + 6C. \tag{31}$$

In contrast with the previous scenario, greater debt now has a greater likelihood of losing its tax benefits.[35] Optimal leverage falls to 65 percent. The yield spread falls to 61 bps, reflecting the lesser leverage. Equity volatility remains high at 51 percent. In the case of protected debt, the loss of tax deductibility has a much smaller effect on optimal leverage and yield spread. As expected, the loss of tax deductibility reduces the maximum value of the firm in all cases.

B. Net Cash Payouts by the Firm

Following Brennan and Schwartz (1978) and others, we have focused on the case where the firm has no net cash outflows resulting from payments to bondholders or stockholders. We now change this assumption.[36] Net cash outflows may occur because dividends are paid to shareholders, and/or because after-tax coupon expenses are being paid, without fully offsetting equity financing. In this latter case, assets are being liquidated and the scale of the firm's activities is clearly affected by the extent of debt financing.

To keep matters analytically tractable, we consider only cash outflows that are proportional to firm asset value, where the proportion, d, may depend on the coupon paid on debt. Equation (3) is replaced by

$$(1/2)\sigma^2 V^2 F_{VV}(V) + (r - d)VF_V(V) - rF(V) + C = 0, \tag{32}$$

with general solution

$$F(V, t) = A_0 + A_1 V^{-Y} + A_2 V^{-X}, \tag{33}$$

where

$$X = \left\{(r - d - 0.5\sigma^2) + \left[(r - d - 0.5\sigma^2)^2 + 2\sigma^2 r\right]^{1/2}\right\}/\sigma^2 \tag{34}$$

$$Y = \left\{(r - d - 0.5\sigma^2) - \left[(r - d - 0.5\sigma^2)^2 + 2\sigma^2 r\right]^{1/2}\right\}/\sigma^2. \tag{35}$$

Boundary conditions remain unchanged, implying $A_1 = 0$ as before since $Y \leq -1$. Therefore, solutions for all security values will have exactly the same functional form as before, but with the exponent, X, given by equation (34) rather than equation (5).

When $d = 0.01$, a one-percent payout on asset value (equivalent to approximately a 3 percent dividend on equity value, given the leverage of the base

[35] In the base case the optimal coupon falls to \$5.08, implying V_T is about 90, as above.

[36] The reader may wonder how equity value could be positive if the firm never pays dividends. But our earlier assumption is *not* that firms never pay dividends—rather, there is no net cash outflow: any cash dividends must be financed by issuing new equity. Like Black and Scholes (1973), our model is a partial equilibrium one, and simply assumes the process for V.

case), the optimal leverage falls from 75 to 74 percent, and the yield spread rises from 75 to 86 bps. But what if payouts also depend upon the coupon being paid to debtholders? Consider the case where the proportional payout is sufficient to cover the after-tax cost of debt when it is initially offered.[37] Normalizing the initial value of V to 100 implies a payout $d = (1 - \tau)C/100$, or $0.0065C$ in the above example. Any dividend payout would be in addition to this amount. For the base case above, we search over coupon levels, C, that maximize v, subject to the constraint that $d = 0.0065C + 0.01$. This reduces optimal leverage from 75 to 64 percent and increases the yield spread at the optimum from 75 to 124 bps. The volatility of equity falls from 57 to 42 percent. In the case of protected debt, optimal leverage falls from 45 to 36 percent, the yield spread increases from 45 to 49 bps, and the volatility of equity falls from 34 to 29 percent.

The maximum firm value drops from \$128.4 to \$122.0 with unprotected debt, and from \$113.3 to \$110.0 with protected debt. This decrease in maximal value reflects the fact that bankruptcy is more likely with cash payouts, with a resulting loss of tax benefits. Therefore, ex ante, *shareholders (as well as bondholders) benefit from a covenant that prevents the firm from selling assets to meet coupon payments*. It is not surprising that many debt instruments have such a preventive covenant. But if such a covenant cannot be written (or cannot be enforced), shareholders will benefit (at bondholders' expense) from the firm selling assets to pay coupons *after* the debt has been issued. Recognizing this incentive, debtholders will pay less for debt and the optimal leverage will fall as indicated above.

C. Absolute Priority Not Respected

We have assumed that debtholders receive all assets (after costs) if bankruptcy occurs, and stockholders none: the "absolute priority" rule. Now consider a simple alternative, where debtholders receive some fraction $(1 - b)$ of remaining assets, $(1 - \alpha)V_B$, while equity holders receive $b(1 - \alpha)V_B$.[38] This will affect debt value in two ways: debtholders will receive less value if bankruptcy occurs, and bankruptcy will occur at a different level V_B.

It can readily be shown that equation (7) will be replaced by

$$D(V) = C/r + [(1 - b)(1 - \alpha)V_B - C/r][V/V_B]^{-X}, \tag{36}$$

[37] Note that as value falls, the proportional payout will no longer completely cover the after-tax coupon—some equity financing becomes necessary. This may not be unreasonable, since bondholders will become increasingly sensitive to liquidation of assets as firm value approaches the bankruptcy level.

[38] Franks and Torous (1989) estimate that deviations in favor of equity holders in Chapter 11 reorganizations are only 2.3 percent of the value of the reorganized firm. Eberhart, Moore, and Roenfeldt (1990) estimate average equity deviations of 7.8 percent for their sample of Chapter 11 firms. We choose a 10 percent deviation as an upper bound for this effect.

and equation (14) will be replaced by

$$V_B = (1 - \tau)C/[r(1 - b + \alpha b)][X/(1 + X)]. \qquad (37)$$

For the base case with unprotected debt, deviations from absolute priority of 10 percent ($b = 0.1$) cause the optimal leverage ratio to fall from 75 to 72 percent. The yield spread remains at 75 bps. The effect of deviations from absolute priority are also minor when debt is protected: leverage remains unchanged at 45 percent, while the yield spread rises from 45 to 51 bps.

D. All of the Above

As a final exercise, consider the base case where, in addition, (i) dividends equal 3 percent of equity value; (ii) after-tax coupon payments are *not* initially financed with additional equity; (iii) coupon payments are not tax deductible when $V < V_T = 60 + 6C$; and (iv) there is a 10 percent deviation from absolute priority ($b = 0.1$). When these conditions hold simultaneously, the optimal leverage with unprotected debt falls to 47 percent and the yield spread is 69 bps. The annual standard deviation of equity is 36 percent. For protected debt, the optimal leverage falls to 32 percent, the yield spread is 52 bps and the standard deviation of equity is 29 percent. These last numbers seem quite in line with historical yield spreads, leverage ratios, and equity risks.

VII. Protected versus Unprotected Debt: Potential Agency Problems

Our results suggest that optimal leverage ratios are lower when debt is protected, and that the maximal gains to leverage are less. This raises a key question: why should firms issue protected debt? The answer may lie with agency problems created by debt, and asset substitution in particular. Jensen and Meckling (1976) argue that equity holders would prefer to make the firm's activities riskier, ceteris paribus, so as to increase equity value at the expense of debt value. The expected cost to debtholders will be passed back to equity holders in a rational expectations equilibrium, through lower prices on newly issued debt.

Higher firm asset risk tends to benefit equity holders when equity is a strictly convex function of firm asset value, V. And equity is strictly convex in V when debt is unprotected. In Section V, however, it was shown that equity may be a strictly *concave* function of V when debt has a positive net-worth covenant. With protected debt, stockholders may *not* have an incentive to increase firm risk at debtholders' expense.

To illustrate our point, consider the base case above with different levels of asset volatility. If debt is unprotected, the optimal coupon is \$6.50, firm value is \$128.4, and V_B is \$52.8. If debt is protected, the optimal coupon is \$3.26, firm value is \$113.3, and V_B is \$50.6. Assume that, ex post, managers can raise the risk of the firm's assets from the current annual standard deviation

Table IV

Values of Protected and Unprotected Debt and Equity for Different Levels of Risk

This table gives the values of debt and equity for both unprotected and protected debt, when the coupon (in each case) is chosen to maximize total firm value given a 20 percent asset volatility, but asset volatility may be increased by management to higher levels.

	Unprotected Debt		Protected Debt	
Asset Volatility (%)	Debt Value ($)	Equity Value ($)	Debt Value ($)	Equity Value ($)
20	96.3	32.1	50.6	62.7
40	70.4	45.9	36.9	55.5
60	52.6	59.1	31.2	52.5

of 20 percent—with no change in current asset value V. Will they be motivated to engage in such "asset substitution"? Using equations (7) and (13), and recalling from equation (14) that V_B will change when debt is unprotected but not when debt is protected, gives the results reported in Table IV.

Debtholders are hurt by higher risk. In the case of unprotected debt, equity value is enhanced by greater risk. Without covenants to prevent such a change, it will always be in the interest of equityholders to increase risk. *But the opposite is true when debt is protected by a positive net worth covenant*: in this case, increasing risk lowers equity value as well as debt value.[39]

In the absence of protective covenants, investors recognize that shareholders will wish to raise asset volatility to the maximum (60 percent). They will pay only $52.6 for the debt, and total firm value will be $111.7. If the firm offers protected debt, investors recognize that shareholders will have no interest in increasing firm risk, and total firm value will be $113.30. The firm maximizes value by issuing protected rather than unprotected debt. (Even if the firm initially chose to issue the amount of unprotected debt optimal for a 60 percent volatility, the total firm value would be $112.1—less than the maximal value with protected debt.)

A reevaluation of the belief that asset substitution is always advantageous for equity holders seems warranted. It is true for unprotected debt, but it is false in the case examined here, when debt is protected by a positive net-worth covenant. Both debt and equity are concave functions of asset value

[39] The difference in behavior as σ changes reflects the convexity (concavity) of equity in V when debt is unprotected (protected). In addition, V_B changes in the unprotected case as σ changes. This latter effect explains the curious result in Section II.A, that (for V close to V_B) an increase in firm risk can raise unprotected debt value. Thus, there is yet a further anomaly with unprotected debt: at the brink of bankruptcy (and only there), both debtholders and stockholders wish to increase firm risk!

in this case.[40] The greater incentive compatibility of protected debt may well explain its prevalence (or the prevalence of short-term financing), despite the fact that, ceteris paribus, it exploits the tax advantage of debt less effectively.

VIII. Restructuring via Debt Repurchase or Debt Renegotiation: Some Preliminary Thoughts

The preceding analysis has assumed that the coupon, C, of the debt issue is fixed through time. In the absence of transactions costs, restructuring by continuous readjustments of C would seem to be desirable to maximize total firm value as V fluctuates. However, we shall see that continuous readjustments of C by debt repurchase (issuance) may be blocked by stockholders (debtholders).[41] *Debt renegotiation* may be required to maximize total firm value in these cases.

To prove this contention, first consider the firm selling a small amount of additional debt, thereby increasing the current debt service by dC. This will change the total value of debt by

$$dD = (\partial D/\partial C)dC. \tag{38}$$

But this total value change will be shared by current and new debtholders. New debtholders will hold a fraction dC/C of the total debt value, leaving current debtholders with value

$$(D + dD)(1 - dC/C) = D + dD - (D/C)dC, \tag{39}$$

(ignoring terms of $O(dC^2)$). The change from D, the current debtholders' value before the debt issuance, is

$$[(\partial D/\partial C) - (D/C)]dC < 0 \quad \text{for } dC > 0, \tag{40}$$

with the inequality resulting from the concavity of D in C and the fact that $D = 0$ when $C = 0$. This "dilution" result holds for arbitrary initial V and C, implying current *debtholders will always resist increasing the total coupon payments through additional debt issuance*, even though such sales may increase the value of equity and the firm. This resistance is frequently codified in debt covenants that restrict additional debt issuance at greater or equal seniority.[42]

[40] This, of course, is consistent with the earlier result, equation (12), where total firm value, v, is concave in V. Concavity of v follows from the concavity of tax benefits and convexity of bankruptcy costs (which are subtracted).

[41] We consider debt issuance/repurchase for capital restructuring only. Any funds raised by debt issuance will be used to retire equity, and vice-versa. Debt raised for new investment, or retired by asset sales, are asset-changing decisions that are not considered here.

[42] Our analysis assumes a single class of debt, implying that newly issued debt has the same seniority in the event of bankruptcy. Even if the newly issued debt is junior to the current debt, it will reduce the value of the current debt by raising V_B. A full analysis of multiple classes of debt securities is beyond the scope of the present article.

A related result on debt repurchase is perhaps more surprising: current shareholders will always resist *decreasing* the coupon, C, by repurchasing current debt (in small amounts) on the open market. To prove this, consider a small decrease, $dC < 0$, and its effect on current shareholders. The total value of equity will change by

$$dE = (\partial E/\partial C)dC \tag{41}$$

The cost of retiring debt will equal the value of the fraction of debt retired, or $-D(dC/C)$. This cost must be financed with newly issued equity, whose value is included in the change in total equity value above. Current shareholders will therefore have equity value

$$E + dE + D(dC/C), \tag{42}$$

implying a change in value to current shareholders of

$$[(\partial E/\partial C) + (D/C)]dC, \tag{43}$$

using equation (41). For unprotected debt, it follows from equations (15) and (17) that $[(\partial E/\partial C) + (D/C)] > 0$, implying that the change in equity value to the original shareholders is negative when $dC < 0$. This result holds for arbitrary initial V and C. Therefore, it will never be optimal for the firm's shareholders to restructure by retiring unprotected debt via small open market repurchases financed by new equity.[43] In Appendix B, we show that the result also holds for small repurchases of protected debt, when the coupon is near its optimal level.

To illustrate the arguments above, consider the base case with unprotected debt. With $V = \$100$, the optimal coupon is \$6.50 and $V_B = \$52.80$. Assume this coupon level has been chosen by the firm. Now let V drop from \$100 to \$90. Using equations (7) and (13) to compute the current values of debt and equity gives: $D = \$91.79$, $E = \$23.14$, and $v = \$114.93$. The firm's total value can now be increased by reducing debt. The firm should cut its coupon by 10 percent to \$5.85, since C^* is proportional to V, which has fallen from \$100 to \$90. This would increase the total firm value from \$114.93 to \$115.60.

But consider the firm repurchasing 10 percent of its debt to achieve the new optimal leverage. The coupon is reduced from \$6.50 to \$5.85, and V_B falls by 10 percent to \$47.52. The firm must pay (at least) \$9.18 to retire 10 percent of the bonds whose value is \$91.79 prior to repurchase.[44] It will raise this amount by issuing additional stock worth \$9.18. Again using equations (7) and (13) to compute debt and equity values with the lower coupon gives: $D = \$86.65$, and $E = \$28.95$.

[43] This debt repurchase result holds even if there are multiple classes of debt. Stockholders might benefit from retiring debt via asset sales, but this would violate the assumption that the asset value, V, is independent of the firm's capital structure.

[44] Note that debt becomes more valuable per unit, as the coupon is reduced. We are assuming here that the entire amount of repurchase can be effected at the lowest (i.e., current) price. Any higher price would magnify the losses to equity holders.

Debtholders are clearly better off, having received payments of \$9.18 to retire 10 percent of their holdings, plus retaining holdings worth \$86.65. The original equity holders have had their stock diluted: \$9.18 of stock—the amount raised to pay the debtholders—now belongs to new shareholders, leaving the original shareholders with stock worth \$28.95 − \$9.18 = \$19.77. This is less than the \$23.14 value of their shares prior to repurchase. Although the total value of the firm would be increased by the restructuring, *equity holders cannot benefit from the repurchase, and will want to block such refinancing*. This problem results from an externality: when debt is reduced, its "quality" is improved. Investors who continue to hold the firm's debt receive a windfall gain from the debt repurchase.

The example shows that restructuring through debt repurchases or sales may not be possible, although such changes could increase total firm value. To capture such potential increases, changes in the terms of the debtholders' securities (or "side payments") will be required. These types of restructurings will be labeled *debt renegotiation*. In our example, replacing current debt with convertible debt may be used to achieve the optimal coupon level. By agreeing to exchange the current debt for debt with coupon \$5.85 (worth \$86.65), plus a convertibility privilege into stock worth (say) \$5.50, debtholders receive a security worth \$92.15. This exceeds the \$91.79 value of the current debt paying a \$6.50 coupon, so bondholders will benefit. Stockholders will also benefit by the rise in the equity value of \$5.81 (\$28.95 − \$23.14) less the \$5.50 value of the convertibility option given bondholders.

Renegotiation of unprotected debt is particularly simple when bankruptcy is imminent (V is close to V_B), and $C > C_{max}(V)$. In this case, a small reduction in the coupon will increase the value of both debt and equity—with no further compensation to bondholders (such as the convertibility privilege) being required. The firm may be able to reduce its coupon payment all the way to $C^*(V)$ with no additional payments to bondholders if the value of debt $D^*(V)$ at the optimal coupon is greater than the value of debt $D(V)$ when the renegotiation begins. This assumes stockholders can credibly make a "take-it-or-leave-it" offer to bondholders. Note that the firm may wait until the brink of bankruptcy before renegotiating, since this will minimize $D(V)$.

IX. Conclusion

By assuming a debt structure with time-independent payouts, we have been able to develop closed-form solutions for the value of debt and for optimal capital structure. This permits a detailed analysis of the behavior of bond prices and optimal debt-equity ratios as firm asset value, risk, taxes, interest rates, bond covenants, payout rates, and bankruptcy costs change.

The analysis examines two types of bonds: those that are protected by a positive net-worth covenant, and those that are not. The distinction is critical in determining when bankruptcy is triggered, which in turn affects bond values and optimal leverage. To be rolled over, short-term financing typically requires that the firm maintain positive net worth. Therefore short-term financing seems to correspond to our model of protected debt. Long-term debt, in contrast, rarely has positive net-worth covenants; it seems closer to our model of unprotected debt.

Our results indicate that protected debt values and unprotected "investment grade" debt values behave very much as expected. Unprotected "junk" bonds exhibit quite different behavior. For example, an increase in firm risk will increase debt value, as will a decrease in the coupon. Such behavior is not exhibited by protected "junk" bonds.

Two curious aspects of optimal leverage are observed. First, a rise in the risk-free interest rate (increasing the cost of debt financing) leads to a *greater* optimal debt level. Higher interest rates generate greater tax benefits, which in turn dictate more debt despite its higher cost. Second, the optimal debt for firms with higher bankruptcy costs may carry a *lower* interest rate than for firms with lower bankruptcy costs. This is because firms will choose significantly lower optimal leverage when bankruptcy costs are substantial, making debt less risky. This result does not hold for protected debt: higher bankruptcy costs imply higher interest rates at the optimal leverage.

Optimal leverage, yield ratios, and equity risk are well within historical norms for protected debt. But optimal leverage seems high (and/or yield spreads seem low) for unprotected debt. Variants of the basic assumptions, discussed in Section VI, are needed for unprotected debt to fall within historical norms. The most important modification is dropping the requirement that payouts to bondholders be externally financed.

Issuing debt without protective net-worth covenants yields greater tax benefits and would seem to dominate issuing protected debt. However, this conclusion may be reversed if firms have the ability to increase the riskiness of their activities through "asset substitution." Increasing risk will transfer value from bondholders to stockholders when debt is unprotected, leading cautious bondholders to demand higher interest rates even when the firm currently has low risk. But such costs typically are not incurred when firms issue protected debt: stockholders will *not* gain by increasing firm risk when debt is protected by a positive net-worth covenant, and bondholders will not need to demand higher interest rates in anticipation of riskier firm activities. Protected debt may be the preferred form of financing in these situations, despite having lower potential tax benefits.

Our results offer some preliminary insights on debt repurchases and on debt renegotiations. The former cannot be used to adjust leverage continuously to its optimal level: bondholders will block further debt issuance, and shareholders will block (marginal) debt reductions. Debt renegotiation can achieve simultaneous increases in debt and equity value. But the costly nature of renegotiation suggests it would be suboptimal to do so continuously (see Fischer, Heinkel, and Zechner (1989)). Our analysis shows that it may be desirable for shareholders to wait until the brink of bankruptcy before renegotiating. When bankruptcy is neared, a reduction in coupon payments to the optimal level may benefit both stockholders and bondholders, without additional side payments.

Although we have not emphasized equity values, our analysis also provides some interesting insights. Equity return volatility will be stochastic, changing with the level of firm asset value, V. This (and the possibility of bankruptcy) has important ramifications for option pricing.[45]

The model can be extended in several further dimensions. Multiple classes of long-term debt can be analyzed, recognizing that payments to the various classes of debtholders when bankruptcy occurs are determined by seniority. More difficult extensions will include finite-lived debt, dynamic restructuring, and a stochastic term structure of risk-free interest rates.

Appendix A

We assume in this case that instantaneous tax benefits = 0 whenever $V \leq V_T$. There are no carryforwards. Differential equation (3) with $C = 0$ has solution:

$$TB(V) = \mathrm{A}_1 V + \mathrm{A}_2 V^{-X}, \qquad V_B < V \leq V_T. \tag{44}$$

Differential equation (3) with instantaneous tax benefit τC realized has solution:

$$TB(V) = (\tau C/r) + B_2 V^{-X}, \qquad V \geq V_T. \tag{45}$$

$TB(V)$ must satisfy:

$$TB[V_B] = \mathrm{A}_1 V_B + \mathrm{A}_2 V_B^{-X} = 0 \tag{46}$$

$$TB(V_T) = \mathrm{A}_1 V_T + \mathrm{A}_2 V_T^{-X} = (\tau C/r) + B_2 V_T^{-X} \tag{47}$$

$$TB'(V_T) = \mathrm{A}_1 - X\mathrm{A}_2 V_T^{-X-1} = -XB_2 V_T^{-X-1} \tag{48}$$

Solutions:

$$\mathrm{A}_1 = (\tau C/r)(X/(X+1))(1/V_T) \tag{49}$$

$$\mathrm{A}_2 = -(\tau C/r)(X/(X+1))(V_B^{X+1}/V_T) \tag{50}$$

$$B_2 = -(\tau C/r)(X/(X+1))(1/V_T)(V_B^{X+1} + (1/X)V_T^{X+1}) \tag{51}$$

Substituting for tax benefits from equation (44) into equation (13) for equity gives, for $V \leq V_T$,

$$E = v - D = V + \mathrm{A}_1 V + \mathrm{A}_2 V^{-X} - C/r - [V_B - (C/r)](V/V_B)^{-X}. \tag{52}$$

To find V_B, we again set $dE/dV|_{V=V_B} = 0$:

$$dE/dV = 1 + \mathrm{A}_1 - X\mathrm{A}_2 V^{-X-1} + X[V_B - (C/r)](V/V_B)^{-X-1}(1/V_B) = 0. \tag{53}$$

[45] Preliminary work on this question has been done by Klaus Toft (1993).

Evaluating equation (53) at $V = V_B$:

$$1 + A_1 - XA_2 V_B^{-X-1} + X - (C/r)(X/V_B) = 0. \quad (54)$$

Substituting for A_1 and A_2 gives

$$V_B = CV_T X/[rV_T(1 + X) + \tau CX]. \quad (55)$$

D can be computed from equation (7); and

$$v = V + (\tau C/r) + B_2 V^{-X} - \alpha V_B (V/V_B)^{-X}, \quad V > V_T. \quad (56)$$

Note we can rewrite the expression for V_B as

$$V_B = \underline{V}_B V_T/[(1 - \tau)V_T + \tau \underline{V}_B] > \underline{V}_B \quad (57)$$

with the last inequality holding since $V_T > \underline{V}_B$, where $\underline{V}_B$ satisfies equation (14).

Appendix B

Parallel to the discussion following equation (43), we know that shareholders will reject a buyback of debt (i.e., $dC < 0$) if $[(\partial E/\partial C) + (D/C)] > 0$. Since $E = v - D$,

$$[(\partial E/\partial C) + (D/C)] = \{\partial v/\partial C - [(\partial D/\partial C) - (D/C)]\}. \quad (58)$$

Define V^* as the firm asset value at which the current coupon would be optimal for protected debt, i.e., for which $\partial v(V^*)/\partial C = 0$. From equation (40), it follows that $[(\partial D/\partial C) - (D/C)]$ will be strictly negative, and therefore equation (58) will be strictly positive when $\partial v/\partial C = 0$. Continuity implies that there exists a neighborhood of values, V, around the value V^*, for which equation (58) is strictly positive. For all $V < V^*$ in this neighborhood, firm value, v, would be increased by lowering the coupon, since the optimal coupon is decreasing in V. But because equation (58) is positive in this neighborhood, current stockholders' equity value will fall when $dC < 0$ and shareholders will resist reducing the coupon to its optimal level.

REFERENCES

Altman, E., 1984, A further empirical investigation of the bankruptcy cost question, *Journal of Finance* 39, 1067–1090.

Anderson, R., and S. Sundaresan, 1992, Design and valuation of debt contracts, Working paper, Universite Catholique de Louvain.

Asquith, P., R. Gertner, and D. Scharfstein, 1991, Anatomy of financial distress: An examination of junk bond issuers, Working paper, University of Chicago.

Baxter, N., 1967, Leverage, risk of ruin, and the cost of capital, *Journal of Finance* 22, 395–403.

Black, F., and J. Cox, 1976, Valuing corporate securities: Some effects of bond indenture provisions, *Journal of Finance* 31, 351–367.

Black, F., and M. Scholes, 1973, The pricing of options and corporate liabilities, *Journal of Political Economy* 81, 637–654.

Brennan, M., and E. Schwartz, 1978, Corporate income taxes, valuation, and the problem of optimal capital structure, *Journal of Business* 51, 103–114.

———, 1980, Analyzing convertible bonds, *Journal of Financial and Quantitative Analysis* 15, 907–932.

———, 1984, Optimal financial policy and firm valuation, *Journal of Finance* 39, 593–607.

Eberhart, A., W. Moore, and R. Roenfeldt, 1990, Security pricing and deviations from the absolute priority rule in bankruptcy proceedings, *Journal of Finance* 45, 1457–1469.

Fischer, E., R. Heinkel, and J. Zechner, 1989, Dynamic capital structure choice: Theory and tests, *Journal of Finance* 44, 19–40.

Franks, J., and W. Torous, 1989, An empirical investigation of firms in reorganization, *Journal of Finance* 44, 747–779.

Fries, S., M. H. Miller, and W. Perraudin, 1993, Pricing bond default premia in a competitive industry equilibrium with costs of entry and exit, Working paper, University of Cambridge.

Harris, M., and A. Raviv, 1991, The theory of capital structure, *Journal of Finance* 44, 297–355.

Haugen, R., and L. Senbet, 1978, The insignificance of bankruptcy costs to the theory of optimal capital structure, *Journal of Finance* 33, 383–392.

Jensen, M., and W. Meckling, 1976, Theory of the firm: Managerial behavior, agency costs, and ownership structure, *Journal of Financial Economics* 4, 305–360.

Jensen, M., 1986, The agency costs of free cash flow: Corporate finance and takeovers, *American Economic Review* 76, 323–329.

Jones, E., S. Mason, and E. Rosenfeld, 1984, Contingent claims analysis of corporate capital structures: An empirical investigation, *Journal of Finance* 39, 611–625.

Kane, A., A. Marcus, and R. McDonald, 1984, How big is the tax advantage to debt?, *Journal of Finance* 39, 841–852.

Kaplan, S., 1989, Management buyouts: Evidence on taxes as a source of value, *Journal of Finance* 44, 611–632.

Kim, E. H., 1978, A mean-variance theory of optimal capital structure and corporate debt capacity, *Journal of Finance* 33, 45–64.

Kim, I., K. Ramaswamy, and S. Sundaresan, 1993, Does default risk in coupons affect the valuation of corporate bonds?: A contingent claims model, *Financial Management* 22, 117–131.

Kraus, A., and R. Litzenberger, 1973, A state-preference model of optimal financial leverage, *Journal of Finance* 28, 911–922.

Leland, H., 1989, LBOs and taxes: No one to blame but ourselves?, *California Management Review* 32, 19–28.

Longstaff, F., and E. Schwartz, 1992, Valuing risky debt: A new approach, Working paper, University of California, Los Angeles.

Mauer, D., and A. Triantis, 1993, Interactions of investment decisions and corporate financing policies, Working paper, University of Wisconsin.

Mella, P., and W. Perraudin, 1993, Strategic debt service, Working paper, University of Cambridge.

Mello, A., and J. Parsons, 1992, The agency costs of debt, *Journal of Finance* 47, 1887–1904.

Merton, R., 1973, A rational theory of option pricing, *Bell Journal of Economics and Management Science* 4, 141–183.

———, 1974, On the pricing of corporate debt: The risk structure of interest rates, *Journal of Finance* 29, 449–469.

Miller, M., 1977, Debt and taxes, *Journal of Finance* 32, 261–275.

Modigliani, F., and M. Miller, 1958, The cost of capital, corporation finance and the theory of investment, *American Economic Review* 48, 267–297.

Myers, S., 1984, The capital structure puzzle, *Journal of Finance* 39, 575–592.

———, and N. Majluf, 1984, Corporate financing and investment decisions when firms have information that investors do not have, *Journal of Financial Economics* 5, 187–221.

Sarig, O., and A. Warga, 1989, Some empirical estimates of the risk structure of interest rates, *Journal of Finance* 44, 1351–1360.

Scott, J., 1976, A theory of optimal capital structure, *Bell Journal of Economics and Management Science* 7, 33–54.

Smith, C., and J. Warner, 1979, On financial contracting: An analysis of bond covenants, *Journal of Financial Economics* 7, 117–161.

Titman, S., and R. Wessels, 1988, The determinants of capital structure choice, *Journal of Finance* 43, 1–20.

Toft, K., 1993, Options on leveraged equity with default risk, Working paper, Haas School of Business, University of California, Berkeley.

Warner, J., 1977, Bankruptcy costs: Some evidence, *Journal of Finance* 32, 337–347.

[24]

Econometrica, Vol. 53, No. 2 (March, 1985)

A THEORY OF THE TERM STRUCTURE OF INTEREST RATES[1]

BY JOHN C. COX, JONATHAN E. INGERSOLL, JR., AND STEPHEN A. ROSS

This paper uses an intertemporal general equilibrium asset pricing model to study the term structure of interest rates. In this model, anticipations, risk aversion, investment alternatives, and preferences about the timing of consumption all play a role in determining bond prices. Many of the factors traditionally mentioned as influencing the term structure are thus included in a way which is fully consistent with maximizing behavior and rational expectations. The model leads to specific formulas for bond prices which are well suited for empirical testing.

1. INTRODUCTION

THE TERM STRUCTURE of interest rates measures the relationship among the yields on default-free securities that differ only in their term to maturity. The determinants of this relationship have long been a topic of concern for economists. By offering a complete schedule of interest rates across time, the term structure embodies the market's anticipations of future events. An explanation of the term structure gives us a way to extract this information and to predict how changes in the underlying variables will affect the yield curve.

In a world of certainty, equilibrium forward rates must coincide with future spot rates, but when uncertainty about future rates is introduced the analysis becomes much more complex. By and large, previous theories of the term structure have taken the certainty model as their starting point and have proceeded by examining stochastic generalizations of the certainty equilibrium relationships. The literature in the area is voluminous, and a comprehensive survey would warrant a paper in itself. It is common, however, to identify much of the previous work in the area as belonging to one of four strands of thought.

First, there are various versions of the expectations hypothesis. These place predominant emphasis on the expected values of future spot rates or holding-period returns. In its simplest form, the expectations hypothesis postulates that bonds are priced so that the implied forward rates are equal to the expected spot rates. Generally, this approach is characterized by the following propositions: (a) the return on holding a long-term bond to maturity is equal to the expected return on repeated investment in a series of the short-term bonds, or (b) the expected rate of return over the next holding period is the same for bonds of all maturities.

The liquidity preference hypothesis, advanced by Hicks [**16**], concurs with the importance of expected future spot rates, but places more weight on the effects of the risk preferences of market participants. It asserts that risk aversion will cause forward rates to be systematically greater than expected spot rates, usually

[1] This paper is an extended version of the second half of an earlier working paper with the same title. We are grateful for the helpful comments and suggestions of many of our colleagues, both at our own institutions and others. This research was partially supported by the Dean Witter Foundation, the Center for Research in Security Prices, and the National Science Foundation.

by an amount increasing with maturity. This term premium is the increment required to induce investors to hold longer-term ("riskier") securities.

Third, there is the market segmentation hypothesis of Culbertson [7] and others, which offers a different explanation of term premiums. Here it is asserted that individuals have strong maturity preferences and that bonds of different maturities trade in separate and distinct markets. The demand and supply of bonds of a particular maturity are supposedly little affected by the prices of bonds of neighboring maturities. Of course, there is now no reason for the term premiums to be positive or to be increasing functions of maturity. Without attempting a detailed critique of this position, it is clear that there is a limit to how far one can go in maintaining that bonds of close maturities will not be close substitutes. The possibility of substitution is an important part of the theory which we develop.

In their preferred habitat theory, Modigliani and Sutch [**25**] use some arguments similar to those of the market segmentation theory. However, they recognize its limitations and combine it with aspects of the other theories. They intended their approach as a plausible rationale for term premiums which does not restrict them in sign or monotonicity, rather than as a necessary causal explanation.[2]

While the focus of such modern and eclectic analyses of the term structure on explaining and testing the term premiums is desirable, there are two difficulties with this approach. First, we need a better understanding of the determinants of the term premiums. The previous theories are basically only hypotheses which say little more than that forward rates should or need not equal expected spot rates. Second, all of the theories are couched in ex ante terms and they must be linked with ex post realizations to be testable.

The attempts to deal with these two elements constitute the fourth strand of work on the term structure. Roll [**29, 30**], for example, has built and tested a mean-variance model which treated bonds symmetrically with other assets and used a condition of market efficiency to relate ex ante and ex post concepts.[3] If rationality requires that ex post realizations not differ systematically from ex ante views, then statistical tests can be made on ex ante propositions by using ex post data.

We consider the problem of determining the term structure as being a problem in general equilibrium theory, and our approach contains elements of all of the previous theories. Anticipations of future events are important, as are risk preferences and the characteristics of other investment alternatives. Also, individuals can have specific preferences about the timing of their consumption, and thus have, in that sense, a preferred habitat. Our model thus permits detailed predictions about how changes in a wide range of underlying variables will affect the term structure.

[2] We thank Franco Modigliani for mentioning this point.

[3] Stiglitz [**35**] emphasizes the portfolio theory aspects involved with bonds of different maturities, as do Dieffenbach [**9**], Long [**18**], and Rubinstein [**31**], who incorporate the characteristics of other assets as well. Modigliani and Shiller [**24**] and Sargent [**33**] have stressed the importance of rational anticipations.

The plan of our paper is as follows. Section 2 summarizes the equilibrium model developed in Cox, Ingersoll, and Ross [6] and specializes it for studying the term structure. In Section 3, we derive and analyze a model which leads to a single factor description of the term structure. Section 4 shows how this model can be applied to other related securities such as options on bonds. In Section 5, we compare our general equilibrium approach with an alternative approach based purely on arbitrage. In Section 6, we consider some more general term structure models and show how the market prices of bonds can be used as instrumental variables in empirical tests of the theory. Section 7 presents some models which include the effects of random inflation. In Section 8, we give some brief concluding comments.

2. THE UNDERLYING EQUILIBRIUM MODEL

In this section, we briefly review and specialize the general equilibrium model of Cox, Ingersoll, and Ross [6]. The model is a complete intertemporal description of a continuous time competitive economy. We recall that in this economy there is a single good and all values are measured in terms of units of this good. Production opportunities consist of a set of n linear activities. The vector of expected rates of return on these activities is α, and the covariance matrix of the rates of return is GG'. The components of α and G are functions of a k-dimensional vector Y which represents the state of the technology and is itself changing randomly over time. The development of Y thus determines the production opportunities that will be available to the economy in the future. The vector of expected changes in Y is μ and the covariance matrix of the changes is SS'.

The economy is composed of identical individuals, each of whom seeks to maximize an objective function of the form

$$E\int_t^{t'} U(C(s), Y(s), s)\, ds, \tag{1}$$

where $C(s)$ is the consumption flow at time s, U is a Von Neumann-Morgenstern utility function, and t' is the terminal date. In performing this maximization, each individual chooses his optimal consumption C^*, the optimal proportion a^* of wealth W to be invested in each of the production processes, and the optimal proportion b^* of wealth to be invested in each of the contingent claims. These contingent claims are endogenously created securities whose payoffs are functions of W and Y. The remaining wealth to be invested in borrowing or lending at the interest rate r is then determined by the budget constraint. The indirect utility function J is determined by the solution to the maximization problem.

In equilibrium in this homogeneous society, the interest rate and the expected rates of return on the contingent claims must adjust until all wealth is invested in the physical production processes. This investment can be done either directly by individuals or indirectly by firms. Consequently, the equilibrium value of J is given by the solution to a planning problem with only the physical production processes available. For future reference, we note that the optimality conditions for the proportions invested will then have the form

$$\Psi \equiv \alpha W J_W + GG'a^* W^2 J_{WW} + GS' W J_{WY} - \lambda^* 1 \leq 0 \tag{2}$$

and $a^{*\prime}\Psi = 0$, where subscripts on J denote partial derivatives, J_{WY} is a $(k \times 1)$ vector whose ith element is J_{WY_i}, 1 is a $(k \times 1)$ unit vector, and λ^* is a Lagrangian multiplier. With J explicitly determined, the similar optimality conditions for the problem with contingent claims and borrowing and lending can be combined with the market clearing conditions to give the equilibrium interest rate and expected rates of return on contingent claims.

We now cite two principal results from [6] which we will need frequently in this paper. First, the equilibrium interest rate can be written explicitly as

$$\begin{aligned} r(W, Y, t) &= \frac{\lambda^*}{W J_W} = a^{*\prime}\alpha + a^{*\prime}GG'a^* W\left(\frac{J_{WW}}{J_W}\right) + a^{*\prime}GS'\left(\frac{J_{WY}}{J_W}\right) \\ &= a^{*\prime}\alpha - \left(\frac{-J_{WW}}{J_W}\right)\left(\frac{\text{var } W}{W}\right) - \sum_{i=1}^{k}\left(\frac{-J_{WY_i}}{J_W}\right)\left(\frac{\text{cov } W, Y_i}{W}\right), \end{aligned} \tag{3}$$

where (cov W, Y_i) is the covariance of the changes in optimally invested wealth with the changes in the state variable Y_i, with (var W) and (cov Y_i, Y_j) defined in an analogous way; note that $a^{*\prime}\alpha$ is the expected rate of return on optimally invested wealth. Second, the equilibrium value of any contingent claim, F, must satisfy the following differential equation:

$$\begin{aligned} &\tfrac{1}{2}a^{*\prime}GG'a^* W^2 F_{WW} + a^{*\prime}GS' W F_{WY} + \tfrac{1}{2}\operatorname{tr}(SS'F_{YY}) \\ &\quad + (a^{*\prime}\alpha W - C^*)F_W + \mu' F_Y + F_t + \delta - rF \\ &= \phi_W F_W + \phi_Y F_Y, \end{aligned} \tag{4}$$

where $\delta(W, Y, t)$ is the payout flow received by the security and

$$\begin{aligned} \phi_W &= (a^{*\prime}\alpha - r)W, \\ \phi_Y &= \left(\frac{-J_{WW}}{J_W}\right)a^{*\prime}GS' W + \left(\frac{-J_{WY}}{J_W}\right)' SS'. \end{aligned} \tag{5}$$

In (4) subscripts on F denote partial derivatives; F_Y and F_{WY} are $(k \times 1)$ vectors and F_{YY} is a $(k \times k)$ matrix. The left hand side of (4) gives the excess expected return on the security over and above the risk free return, while the right hand side gives the risk premium that the security must command in equilibrium. For future reference, we note that (4) can be written in the alternative form:

$$\begin{aligned} &\tfrac{1}{2}(\text{var } W)F_{WW} + \sum_{i=1}^{k}(\text{cov } W, Y_i)F_{WY_i} + \tfrac{1}{2}\sum_{i=1}^{k}\sum_{j=1}^{k}(\text{cov } Y_i, Y_j)F_{Y_iY_j} \\ &\quad + [rW - C^*]F_W + \sum_{i=1}^{k}\left[\mu_i - \left(\frac{-J_{WW}}{J_W}\right)(\text{cov } W, Y_i)\right. \\ &\quad \left. - \sum_{j=1}^{k}\left(\frac{-J_{WY_j}}{J_W}\right)(\text{cov } Y_i, Y_j)\right]F_{Y_i} + F_t - rF + \delta = 0. \end{aligned} \tag{6}$$

To apply these formulas to the problem of the term structure of interest rates, we specialize the preference structure first to the case of constant relative risk aversion utility functions and then further to the logarithmic utility function. In particular, we let $U(C(s), Y(s), s)$ be independent of the state variable Y and have the form

$$U(C(s), s) = e^{-\rho s}\left[\frac{C(s)^{\gamma}-1}{\gamma}\right], \tag{7}$$

where ρ is a constant discount factor.

It is easy to show that in this case the indirect utility function takes the form:[4]

$$J(W, Y, t) = f(Y, t)U(W, t) + g(Y, t). \tag{8}$$

This special form brings about two important simplifications. First, the coefficient of relative risk aversion of the indirect utility function is constant, independent of both wealth and the state variables:

$$\frac{-WJ_{WW}}{J_W} = 1-\gamma. \tag{9}$$

Second, the elasticity of the marginal utility of wealth with respect to each of the state variables does not depend on wealth, and we have

$$\frac{-J_{WY}}{J_W} = \frac{-f_Y}{f}. \tag{10}$$

Furthermore, it is straightforward to verify that the optimal portfolio proportions a^* will depend on Y but not on W. Consequently, the vector of factor risk premiums, ϕ_Y, reduces to $(1-\gamma)a^{*\prime}GS' + (f_Y/f)SS'$, which depends only on Y. In addition, it can be seen from (3) that the equilibrium interest rate also depends only on Y.

The logarithmic utility function corresponds to the special case of $\gamma = 0$. For this case, it can be shown that $f(Y, t) = [1 - \exp[-\rho(t'-t)]]/\rho$. The state-dependence of the indirect utility function thus enters only through $g(Y, t)$. As a result, ϕ_Y reduces further to $a^{*\prime}GS$. In addition, the particular form of the indirect utility function allows us to solve (2) explicitly for a^* as

$$a^* = (GG')^{-1}\alpha + \left(\frac{1 - 1'(GG')^{-1}\alpha}{1'(GG')^{-1}1}\right)(GG')^{-1}1 \tag{11}$$

when all production processes are active, with an analogous solution holding when some processes are inactive.

In the remainder of the paper, we will be valuing securities whose contractual terms do not depend explicitly on wealth. Since with constant relative risk aversion neither the interest rate r nor the factor risk premiums ϕ_Y depend on wealth, for such securities the partial derivatives F_W, F_{WW}, and F_{WY} are all equal to zero and the corresponding terms drop out of the valuation equation (4).

[4] This type of separability has been shown in other contexts by Hakansson [**15**], Merton [**22**], and Samuelson [**32**].

By combining these specializations, we find that the valuation equation (4) then reduces to

$$\frac{1}{2}\operatorname{tr}(SS'F_{YY})+[\mu'-a^{*\prime}GS']F_Y+F_t+\delta-rF=0. \tag{12}$$

Equation (12) will be the central valuation equation for this paper. We will use it together with various specifications about technological change to examine the implied term structure of interest rates.

3. A SINGLE FACTOR MODEL OF THE TERM STRUCTURE

In our first model of the term structure of interest rates, we assume that the state of technology can be represented by a single sufficient statistic or state variable. This is our most basic model, and we will examine it in some detail. This will serve to illustrate how a similarly detailed analysis can be conducted for the more complicated models that follow in Sections 5 and 6.

We make the following assumptions:

ASSUMPTION 1: *The change in production opportunities over time is described by a single state variable,* $Y(\equiv Y_1)$.

ASSUMPTION 2: *The means and variances of the rates of return on the production processes are proportional to Y.*[5] *In this way, neither the means nor the variances will dominate the portfolio decision for large values of Y. The state variable Y can be thought of as determining the rate of evolution of the capital stock in the following sense. If we compare a situation where* $Y=\bar{Y}$, *a constant, with a situation in which* $Y=2\bar{Y}$, *then the first situation has the same distribution of rate of return on a fixed investment in any process over a two-year period that the second situation has over a one-year period. We assume that the elements of* α *and G are such that the elements of* a^* *given by* (11) *are positive, so that all processes are always active, and that* $1'(GG')^{-1}\alpha$ *is greater than one.*[6]

ASSUMPTION 3: *The development of the state variable Y is given by the stochastic differential equation*

$$dY(t)=[\xi Y+\zeta]\,dt+\upsilon\sqrt{Y}\,dw(t), \tag{13}$$

where ξ *and* ζ *are constants, with* $\zeta\geqslant 0$, *and* υ *is a* $1\times(n+k)$ *vector, each of whose components is the constant* υ_0.

[5] Although our assumptions in this section do not satisfy all of the technical growth restrictions placed on the utility function and the coefficients of the production function in [6], they do in combination lead to a well-posed problem having an optimal solution with many useful properties. The optimal consumption function is $C^*(W,Y,t)=[\rho/(1-\exp(-\rho(t'-t))]W$ and the indirect utility function has the form $J(W,Y,t)=a(t)\log W+b(t)Y+c(t)$, where $a(t)$, $b(t)$, and $c(t)$ are explicitly determinable functions of time.

[6] The condition $1'(GG')^{-1}\alpha>1$, together with (13) and (14), insures that the interest rate will always be nonnegative. If $1'(GG')^{-1}\alpha<1$, the interest rate will always be nonpositive.

This structure makes it convenient to introduce the notation $\alpha \equiv \hat{\alpha} Y$, $GG' \equiv \Omega Y$, and $GS' \equiv \Sigma Y$, where the elements of $\hat{\alpha}$, Ω, and Σ are constants.

With these assumptions about technological change and our earlier assumptions about preferences, we can use (3) to write the equilibrium interest rate as

$$(14) \qquad r(Y) = \left(\frac{1'\Omega^{-1}\hat{\alpha} - 1}{1'\Omega^{-1}1} \right) Y.$$

The interest rate thus follows a diffusion process with

$$(15) \qquad \text{drift } r = \left(\frac{1'\Omega^{-1}\hat{\alpha} - 1}{1'\Omega^{-1}1} \right) (\xi Y + \zeta) \equiv \kappa(\theta - r),$$

$$\text{var } r = \left(\frac{1'\Omega^{-1}\hat{\alpha} - 1}{1'\Omega^{-1}1} \right)^2 \upsilon\upsilon' Y \equiv \sigma^2 r,$$

where κ, θ, and σ^2 are constants, with $\kappa\theta \geqslant 0$ and $\sigma^2 > 0$. It is convenient to define a new one-dimensional Wiener process, $z_1(t)$, such that:

$$(16) \qquad \sigma\sqrt{r}\, dz_1(t) \equiv \upsilon\sqrt{Y}\, dw(t);$$

this is permissible since each component of $w(t)$ is a Wiener process. The interest rate dynamics can then be expressed as:

$$(17) \qquad dr = \kappa(\theta - r)\, dt + \sigma\sqrt{r}\, dz_1.$$

For κ, $\theta > 0$, this corresponds to a continuous time first-order autoregressive process where the randomly moving interest rate is elastically pulled toward a central location or long-term value, θ. The parameter κ determines the speed of adjustment.[7]

An examination of the boundary classification criteria shows that r can reach zero if $\sigma^2 > 2\kappa\theta$. If $2\kappa\theta \geqslant \sigma^2$, the upward drift is sufficiently large to make the origin inaccessible.[8] In either case, the singularity of the diffusion coefficient at the origin implies that an initially nonnegative interest rate can never subsequently become negative.

The interest rate behavior implied by this structure thus has the following empirically relevant properties: (i) Negative interest rates are precluded. (ii) If the interest rate reaches zero, it can subsequently become positive. (iii) The absolute variance of the interest rate increases when the interest rate itself increases. (iv) There is a steady state distribution for the interest rate.

The probability density of the interest rate at time s, conditional on its value at the current time, t, is given by:

$$(18) \qquad f(r(s), s; r(t), t) = c\, e^{-u-v} \left(\frac{v}{u} \right)^{q/2} I_q(2(uv)^{1/2}),$$

[7] The discrete time equivalent of this model was tested by Wood [**38**], although, being concerned only with expectations, he left the error term unspecified.

[8] See Feller [**12**].

where

$$c \equiv \frac{2\kappa}{\sigma^2(1-e^{-\kappa(s-t)})},$$

$$u \equiv cr(t)\, e^{-\kappa(s-t)},$$

$$v \equiv cr(s),$$

$$q \equiv \frac{2\kappa\theta}{\sigma^2} - 1,$$

and $I_q(\cdot)$ is the modified Bessel function of the first kind of order q. The distribution function is the noncentral chi-square, $\chi^2[2cr(s); 2q+2, 2u]$, with $2q+2$ degrees of freedom and parameter of noncentrality $2u$ proportional to the current spot rate.[9]

Straightforward calculations give the expected value and variance of $r(s)$ as:

$$E(r(s)|r(t)) = r(t)\, e^{-\kappa(s-t)} + \theta(1-e^{-\kappa(s-t)}),$$

$$\text{(19)} \qquad \operatorname{var}(r(s)|r(t)) = r(t)\left(\frac{\sigma^2}{\kappa}\right)(e^{-\kappa(s-t)} - e^{-2\kappa(s-t)}) + \theta\left(\frac{\sigma^2}{2\kappa}\right)(1-e^{-\kappa(s-t)})^2.$$

The properties of the distribution of the future interest rates are those expected. As κ approaches infinity, the mean goes to θ and the variance to zero, while as κ approaches zero, the conditional mean goes to the current interest rate and the variance to $\sigma^2 r(t)\cdot(s-t)$.

If the interest rate does display mean reversion ($\kappa, \theta > 0$), then as s becomes large its distribution will approach a gamma distribution. The steady state density function is:

$$\text{(20)} \qquad f[r(\infty), \infty; r(t), t] = \frac{\omega^\nu}{\Gamma(\nu)} r^{\nu-1}\, e^{-\omega r},$$

where $\omega \equiv 2\kappa/\sigma^2$ and $\nu \equiv 2\kappa\theta/\sigma^2$. The steady state mean and variance are θ and $\sigma^2\theta/2\kappa$, respectively.

Consider now the problem of valuing a default-free discount bond promising to pay one unit at time T.[10] The prices of these bonds for all T will completely determine the term structure. Under our assumptions, the factor risk premium in (12) is

$$\text{(21)} \qquad \left[\hat{\alpha}'\Omega^{-1}\Sigma + \left(\frac{1-1'\Omega^{-1}\hat{\alpha}}{1'\Omega^{-1}1}\right)1'\Omega^{-1}\Sigma\right] Y \equiv \lambda Y.$$

[9] Processes similar to (17) have been extensively studied by Feller. The Laplace transform of (18) is given in Feller [**12**]. See Johnson and Kotz [**17**] for a description of the noncentral chi-square distribution. Oliver [**27**] contains properties of the modified Bessel function.

[10] A number of contractual provisions are sufficient to preclude default risk and make the value of a bond independent of the wealth of its seller. For example, the terms of the bond could specify that the seller must repurchase the bond at the price schedule given by (23) whenever his wealth falls to a designated level.

By using (15) and (21), we can write the fundamental equation for the price of a discount bond, P, most conveniently as

$$\tag{22} \tfrac{1}{2}\sigma^2 rP_{rr} + \kappa(\theta - r)P_r + P_t - \lambda rP_r - rP = 0,$$

with the boundary condition $P(r, T, T) = 1$. The first three terms in (22) are, from Ito's formula, the expected price change for the bond. Thus, the expected rate of return on the bond is $r + (\lambda rP_r/P)$. The instantaneous return premium on a bond is proportional to its interest elasticity. The factor λr is the covariance of changes in the interest rate with percentage changes in optimally invested wealth (the "market portfolio"). Since $P_r < 0$, positive premiums will arise if this covariance is negative ($\lambda < 0$).

We may note from (22) that bond prices depend on only one random variable, the spot interest rate, which serves as an instrumental variable for the underlying technological uncertainty. While the proposition that current (and future) interest rates play an important, and to a first approximation, predominant role in determining the term structure would meet with general approval, we have seen that this will be precisely true only under special conditions.[11]

By taking the relevant expectation (see Cox, Ingersoll, and Ross [**6**]), we obtain the bond prices as:

$$P(r, t, T) = A(t, T)\, e^{-B(t,T)r},$$

where

$$A(t, T) \equiv \left[\frac{2\gamma\, e^{[(\kappa+\lambda+\gamma)(T-t)]/2}}{(\gamma+\kappa+\lambda)(e^{\gamma(T-t)}-1)+2\gamma}\right]^{2\kappa\theta/\sigma^2},$$

$$\tag{23} B(t, T) \equiv \frac{2(e^{\gamma(T-t)}-1)}{(\gamma+\kappa+\lambda)(e^{\gamma(T-t)}-1)+2\gamma},$$

$$\gamma \equiv ((\kappa+\lambda)^2 + 2\sigma^2)^{1/2}.$$

The bond price is a decreasing convex function of the interest rate and an increasing (decreasing) function of time (maturity). The parameters of the interest rate process have the following effects. The bond price is a decreasing convex function of the mean interest rate level θ and an increasing concave (decreasing convex) function of the speed of adjustment parameter κ if the interest rate is greater (less) than θ. Both of these results are immediately obvious from their effects on expected future interest rates. Bond prices are an increasing concave function of the "market" risk parameter λ. Intuitively, this is mainly because higher values of λ indicate a greater covariance of the interest rate with wealth. Thus, with large λ it is more likely that bond prices will be higher when wealth is low and, hence, has greater marginal utility. The bond price is an increasing

[11] In our framework, the most important circumstances sufficient for bond prices to depend only on the spot interest rate are: (i) individuals have constant relative risk aversion, uncertainty in the technology can be described by a single variable, and the interest rate is a monotonic function of this variable, or (ii) changes in the technology are nonstochastic and the interest rate is a monotonic function of wealth.

concave function of the interest rate variance σ^2. Here several effects are involved. The most important is that a larger σ^2 value indicates more uncertainty about future real production opportunities, and thus more uncertainty about future consumption. In such a world, risk-averse investors would value the guaranteed claim in a bond more highly.

The dynamics of bond prices are given by the stochastic differential equation:

$$dP = r[1 - \lambda B(t, T)]P\,dt - B(t, T)P\sigma\sqrt{r}\,dz_1. \tag{24}$$

For this single state variable model, the returns on bonds are perfectly negatively correlated with changes in the interest rate. The returns are less variable when the interest rate is low. Indeed, they become certain if a zero interest rate is reached, since interest rate changes are then certain. As we would intuitively expect, other things remaining equal, the variability of returns decreases as the bond approaches maturity. In fact, letting t approach T and denoting $T-t$ as Δt, we find that the expected rate of return is $r\Delta t + O(\Delta t^2)$ and the variance of the rate of return is $O(\Delta t^2)$ rather than $O(\Delta t)$, as would be the case for the returns on an investment in the production processes over a small interval. It is in this sense that the return on very short-term bonds becomes certain.

Bonds are commonly quoted in terms of yields rather than prices. For the discount bonds we are now considering, the yield-to-maturity, $R(r, t, T)$, is defined by $\exp[-(T-t)R(r, t, T)] \equiv P(r, t, T)$. Thus, we have:

$$R(r, t, T) = [rB(t, T) - \log A(t, T)]/(T-t). \tag{25}$$

As maturity nears, the yield-to-maturity approaches the current interest rate independently of any of the parameters. As we consider longer and longer maturities, the yield approaches a limit which is independent of the current interest rate:

$$R(r, t, \infty) = \frac{2\kappa\theta}{\gamma + \kappa + \lambda}. \tag{26}$$

When the spot rate is below this long-term yield, the term structure is uniformly rising. With an interest rate in excess of $\kappa\theta/(\kappa+\lambda)$, the term structure is falling. For intermediate values of the interest rate, the yield curve is humped.

Other comparative statics for the yield curve are easily obtained from those of the bond pricing function. An increase in the current interest rate increases yields for all maturities, but the effect is greater for shorter maturities. Similarly, an increase in the steady state mean θ increases all yields, but here the effect is greater for longer maturities. The yields to maturity decrease as σ^2 or λ increases, while the effect of a change in κ may be of either sign depending on the current interest rate.

There has always been considerable concern with unbiased predictions of future interest rates. In the present situation, we could work directly with equation (19), which gives expected values of future interest rates in terms of the current rate and the parameters κ and θ. However, in the rational expectations model we have constructed, all of the information that is currently known about the future movement of interest rates is impounded in current bond prices and the term structure. If the model is correct, then any single parameter can be determined from the term structure and the values of the other parameters.

This approach is particularly important when the model is extended to allow a time-dependent drift term, $\theta(t)$. We can then use information contained in the term structure to obtain $\theta(t)$ and expected future spot rates without having to place prior restrictions on its functional form.

Now, the future expected spot rate given by (19) is altered to:

$$(27) \qquad E(r(T)|r(t)) = r(t)\, e^{-\kappa(T-t)} + \kappa \int_t^T \theta(s)\, e^{-\kappa(T-s)}\, ds.$$

The bond pricing formula (30), in turn, is modified to:

$$(28) \qquad P(r, t, T) = \hat{A}(t, T)\, e^{-B(t,T)r},$$

where

$$(29) \qquad \hat{A}(t, T) = \exp\left(-\kappa \int_t^T \theta(s) B(s, T)\, ds\right),$$

which reduces to (23) when $\theta(s)$ is constant.

Assuming, for illustration, that the other process parameters are known, we can then use the term structure to determine unbiased forecasts of future interest rates. By (28), $\hat{A}(t, T)$ is an observable function of T, given the term structure and the known form of $B(t, T)$, and standard techniques can be invoked to invert (29) and obtain an expression for $\theta(t)$ in terms of $\hat{A}(t, T)$ and $B(t, T)$. Equation (27) can now be used to obtain predictions of the expected values of future spot rates implicit in the current term structure.

Note that these are not the same values that would be given by the traditional expectations assumption that the expected values of future spot rates are contained in the term structure in the form of implicit forward rates. In a continuous-time model, the forward rate $\hat{r}(T)$ is given by $-P_T/P$. Then, by differentiating (28):

$$(30) \qquad \hat{r}(T) = -P_T(r, t, T)/P(r, t, T)$$
$$= rB_T(t, T) + \kappa \int_t^T \theta(s) B_T(s, T)\, ds.$$

Comparing (27) and (30), we see they have the same general form. However, the traditional forward rate predictor applies the improper weights $B_T(s, T) \neq e^{-\kappa(T-s)}$, resulting in a biased prediction.

A number of alternative specifications of time dependence may also be included with only minor changes in the model. One particularly tractable example leads to an interest rate of $\bar{r}(t) + g(t)$, where $\bar{r}(t)$ is given by (17) and $g(t)$ is a function which provides a positive lower bound for the interest rate. The essential point in all such cases is that in the rational expectations model, the current term structure embodies the information required to evaluate the market's probability distribution of the future course of interest rates. Furthermore, the term structure can be inverted to find these expectations.

Other single variable specifications of technological change will in turn imply other stochastic properties for the interest rate. It is easy to verify that in our model if α and GG' are proportional to some function $h(Y, t)$, then the interest rate will also be proportional to $h(Y, t)$. By a suitable choice of $h(Y, t)$, $\mu(Y, t)$, and $S(Y, t)$, a wide range of a priori properties of interest rate movements can be included within the context of a completely consistent model.

4. VALUING ASSETS WITH GENERAL INTEREST RATE DEPENDENT PAYOFFS

Our valuation framework can easily be applied to other securities whose payoffs depend on interest rates, such as options on bonds and futures on bonds. This flexibility enables the model to make predictions about the pricing patterns that should prevail simultaneously across several financial markets. Consequently, applications to other securities may permit richer and more powerful empirical tests than could be done with the bond market alone.

As an example of valuing other kinds of interest rate securities, consider options on bonds. Denote the value at time t of a call option on a discount bond of maturity date s, with exercise price K and expiration date T as $C(r, t, T; s, K)$.[12] The option price will follow the basic valuation equation with terminal condition:

$$(31) \qquad C(r, t, T; s, K) = \max\,[P(r, T, s) - K, 0].$$

It is understood that $s \geqslant T \geqslant t$, and K is restricted to be less than $A(T, s)$, the maximum possible bond price at time T, since otherwise the option would never be exercised and would be worthless. By again taking the relevant expectations, we arrive at the following formula for the option price:

$$(32) \qquad C(r, t, T; s, K)$$
$$= P(r, t, s)\chi^2\left(2r^*[\phi + \psi + B(T, s)]; \frac{4\kappa\theta}{\sigma^2}, \frac{2\phi^2 r e^{\gamma(T-t)}}{\phi + \psi + B(T, s)}\right)$$
$$-KP(r, t, T)\chi^2\left(2r^*[\phi + \psi]; \frac{4\kappa\theta}{\sigma^2}, \frac{2\phi^2 r e^{\gamma(T-t)}}{\phi + \psi}\right),$$

where

$$\gamma \equiv ((\kappa + \lambda)^2 + 2\sigma^2)^{1/2},$$

$$\phi \equiv \frac{2\gamma}{\sigma^2(e^{\gamma(T-t)} - 1)},$$

$$\psi \equiv (\kappa + \lambda + \gamma)/\sigma^2,$$

$$r^* \equiv \left[\log\left(\frac{A(T, s)}{K}\right)\right] / B(T, s),$$

[12] Since the underlying security, a discount bond, makes no payments during the life of the option, the analysis of Merton [23] implies that premature exercise is never optimal, and, hence, American and European calls have the same value.

and $\chi^2(\cdot)$ is the previously introduced noncentral chi-square distribution function. r^* is the critical interest rate below which exercise will occur; i.e., $K = P(r^*, T, s)$.

The call option is an increasing function of maturity (when the expiration date on which the underlying bond matures remains fixed). Call options on stocks are increasing functions of the interest rate, partly because such an increase reduces the present value of the exercise price. However, here an increase in the interest rate will also depress the price of the underlying bond. Numerical analysis indicates that the latter effect is stronger and that the option value is a decreasing convex function of the interest rate. The remaining comparative statics are indeterminate.

5. A COMPARISON WITH BOND PRICING BY ARBITRAGE METHODS

In this section, we briefly compare our methodology to some alternative ways to model bond pricing in continuous time. It is useful to do this now rather than later because the model of Section 3 provides an ideal standard for comparison.

Our approach begins with a detailed description of the underlying economy. This allows us to specify the following ingredients of bond pricing: (a) the variables on which the bond price depends, (b) the stochastic properties of the underlying variables which are endogenously determined, and (c) the exact form of the factor risk premiums. In [**21**], Merton shows that if one begins instead by imposing assumptions directly about (a) and (b), then Ito's formula can be used to state the excess expected return on a bond in the same form as the left-hand side of (4). If the functional form of the right-hand side of (4) were known, then one could obtain a bond pricing equation. For example, if one arbitrarily assumed that bond prices depend only on the spot interest rate r, that the interest rate follows the process given by (17), and that the excess expected return on a bond with maturity date T is $Y(r, t, T)$, then one would obtain

(33) $$\tfrac{1}{2}\sigma^2 r P_{rr} + \kappa(\theta - r)P_r + P_t - rP = Y(r, t, T).$$

If there is some underlying equilibrium which will support the assumptions (a) and (b), then there must be some function Y for which bond prices are given by (33). However, as Merton notes, this derivation in itself provides no way to determine Y or to relate it to the underlying real variables.

An arbitrage approach to bond pricing was developed in a series of papers by Brennan and Schwartz [**3**], Dothan [**10**], Garman [**14**], Richard [**28**], and Vasicek [**37**]. Arguments similar to those employed in the proof of Theorem 2 of Cox, Ingersoll, and Ross [**6**] are used to show that if there are no arbitrage opportunities, Y must have the form

(34) $$Y(r, t, T) = \psi(r, t)P_r(r, t, T),$$

where ψ is a function depending only on calendar time and not on the maturity date of the bond. This places definite restrictions on the form of the excess expected return; not all functions Y will satisfy both (33) and (34).

There are some potential problems, however, in going one step further and using the arbitrage approach to determine a complete and specific model of the term structure. The approach itself provides no way of guaranteeing that there is some underlying equilibrium for which assumptions (a) and (b) are consistent. Setting this problem aside, another difficulty arises from the fact that the arbitrage approach does not imply that every choice of ψ in (34) will lead to bond prices which do not admit arbitrage opportunities. Indeed, closing the model by assuming a specific functional form for ψ can lead to internal inconsistencies.

As an example of the potential problem, consider (33) with Y as shown in (34). This gives the valuation equation

$$(35)\quad \tfrac{1}{2}\sigma^2 rP_{rr} + \kappa(\theta - r)P_r + P_t - rP = \psi(r, t)P_r,$$

which is identical to (22) apart from a specification of the function ψ. We could now close the model by assuming that ψ is linear in the spot rate, $\psi(r, t) = \psi_0 + \lambda r$. The solution to (35) is then

$$(36)\quad P(r, t, T) = [A(t, T)]^{(\kappa\theta - \psi_0)/\kappa\theta} \exp[-rB(t, T)],$$

and the dynamic behavior of the bond price is given by

$$(37)\quad dP = [r - (\psi_0 + \lambda r)B(t, T)]P\,dt - B(t, T)\sigma\sqrt{r}P\,dz_1.$$

The linear form assumed for the risk premium seems quite reasonable and would appear to be a good choice for empirical work, but it in fact produces a model that is not viable. This is most easily seen when $r = 0$. In this case, the bond's return over the next instant is riskless; nevertheless, it is appreciating in price at the rate $-\psi_0 B(t, T)$, which is different from the prevailing zero rate of interest.[13] We thus have a model that guarantees arbitrage opportunities rather than precluding them. The difficulty, of course, is that there is no underlying equilibrium which would support the assumed premiums.

The equilibrium approach developed here thus has two important advantages over alternative methods of bond pricing in continuous time. First, it automatically insures that the model can be completely specified without losing internal consistency. Second, it provides a way to predict how changes in the underlying real economic variables will affect the term structure.

6. MULTIFACTOR TERM STRUCTURE MODELS AND THE USE OF PRICES AS INSTRUMENTAL VARIABLES

In Section 3, we specialized the general equilibrium framework of Cox, Ingersoll, and Ross [6] to develop a complete model of bond pricing. We purposely chose a simple specialization in order to illustrate the detailed information that such a model can produce. In the model, the prices of bonds of all maturities depended on a single random explanatory factor, the spot interest rate. Although the resulting term structure could assume several alternative shapes, it is inherent

[13] As stated earlier, the origin is accessible only if $\sigma^2 > 2\kappa\theta$. Somewhat more complex arguments can be used to demonstrate that the model is not viable even if the origin is inaccessible.

in a single factor model that price changes in bonds of all maturities are perfectly correlated. Such a model also implies that bond prices do not depend on the path followed by the spot rate in reaching its current level. For some applications, these properties may be too restrictive. However, more general specifications of technological opportunities will in turn imply more general bond pricing models. The resulting multifactor term structures will have more flexibility than the single factor model, but they will inevitably also be more cumbersome and more difficult to analyze.

To illustrate the possibilities, we consider two straightforward generalizations of our previous model. Suppose that in our description of technological change in (13) and (15), the central tendency parameter θ is itself allowed to vary randomly according to the equation

$$d\theta = \nu(Y-\theta)\,dt, \tag{38}$$

where ν is a positive constant. That is, we let $\theta \equiv Y_2$ and $\mu_2 = \nu(Y_1 - Y_2)$. The value of θ at any time will thus be an exponentially weighted integral of past values of Y. It can then be verified that the interest rate r is again given by (14) and that the bond price P will have the form

$$P(r, \theta, t, T) = \exp[-rf(t, T) - \theta g(t, T)], \tag{39}$$

where f and g are explicitly determinable functions of time. In this case, both the yields-to-maturity of discount bonds and the expected values of future spot rates are linear functions of current and past spot rates.[14]

As a second generalization, suppose that the production coefficients α and GG' are proportional to the sum of two independent random variables, Y_1 and Y_2, each of which follows an equation of the form (13). Then it can be shown that the spot interest rate r will be proportional to the sum of Y_1 and Y_2 and that bond prices will again have the exponential form

$$P(r, Y_2, t, T) = f(t, T)\exp[-rg(t, T) - Y_2 h(t, T)], \tag{40}$$

where f, g, and h are other explicitly determinable functions of time. In this model, price changes in bonds of all maturities are no longer perfectly correlated.

Each of these generalizations gives a two factor model of the term structure, and the resulting yield curves can assume a wide variety of shapes. Further multifactor generalizations can be constructed along the same lines.

In each of the models considered in this section, one of the explanatory variables is not directly observable. Multifactor generalizations will typically inherit this drawback to an even greater degree. Consequently, it may be very convenient for empirical applications to use some of the endogenously determined prices as instrumental variables to eliminate the variables that cannot be directly observed. In certain instances, it will be possible to do so. Let us choose the spot rate, r,

[14] Studies which have expressed expected future spot rates as linear combinations of current and past spot rates include Bierwag and Grove [**2**], Cagan [**4**], De Leeuw [**8**], Duesenberry [**11**], Malkiel [**19**], Meiselman [**20**], Modigliani and Shiller [**24**], Modigliani and Sutch [**25**], Van Horne [**36**], and Wood [**38**]. Cox, Ingersoll, and Ross [**5**] examine this issue in a diffusion setting.

and a vector of long interest rates, l, as instrumental variables. In general, each of these interest rates will be functions of W (unless the common utility function is isoelastic) and all the state variables. If it is possible to invert this system globally and express the latter as twice differentiable functions of r and l, then r and l can be used as instrumental variables in a manner consistent with the general equilibrium framework.

For the purposes of illustration, suppose that there are two state variables, Y_1 and Y_2, and that utility is isoelastic so that the level of wealth is immaterial. Then, for instrumental variables r and l, a scalar, direct but involved calculations show that the valuation equation (4) may be rewritten as:

$$\text{(41)}\qquad \tfrac{1}{2}(\operatorname{var} r)F_{rr}+(\operatorname{cov} r, l)F_{rl}+\tfrac{1}{2}(\operatorname{var} l)F_{ll}+[\mu_r-\lambda_r(r,l)]F_r$$
$$+[\mu_l-\lambda_l(r,l)]F_l-rF+F_t+\delta=0.$$

The functions λ_r and λ_l serve the role of the factor risk premiums in (5). They are related to the factor risk premiums, ϕ_Y, by:

$$\lambda_r(r,l)=\left[\psi_1\frac{\partial g}{\partial l}-\psi_2\frac{\partial f}{\partial l}\right]\Big/\Delta,$$

$$\lambda_l(r,l)=\left[\psi_2\frac{\partial f}{\partial r}-\psi_1\frac{\partial g}{\partial r}\right]\Big/\Delta,$$

where

$$\text{(42)}\qquad Y_1\equiv f(r,l,t),\qquad Y_2\equiv g(r,l,t),$$
$$\phi_{Y_1}(Y_1,Y_2,t)\equiv\psi_1(r,l,t),\qquad \phi_{Y_2}(Y_1,Y_2,t)\equiv\psi_2(r,l,t),$$

and

$$\Delta\equiv\frac{\partial f}{\partial r}\frac{\partial g}{\partial l}-\frac{\partial f}{\partial l}\frac{\partial g}{\partial r}.$$

Thus far we have not used the fact that l is an interest rate, and the transformation of (4) to (41) can be performed for an arbitrary instrumental variable if the inversion is possible. The advantage of choosing an interest rate instrument is that the second risk factor premium λ_l and the drift μ_l can be eliminated from (41) as follows.

Let Q denote the value of the particular bond for which l is the continuously compounded yield-to-maturity. Denote the payment flow from the bond, including both coupons and return of principal, by $c(t)$. In general, this flow will be zero most of the time, with impulses representing an infinite flow rate when payments are made. Since by definition $Q\equiv\int_t^T c(s)\exp[-l(s-t)]\,ds$, we can write:

$$\text{(43)}\qquad Q\equiv\Lambda_0(l),\quad Q_l=\Lambda_1(l),$$
$$Q_{ll}=\Lambda_2(l),\quad Q_t=-c(t)+l\Lambda_0(l)=-\delta+l\Lambda_0(l),$$
$$Q_r=Q_{rr}=Q_{rl}=0,$$

where

$$\Lambda_n \equiv \int_t^T (t-s)^n c(s)\, e^{-l(s-t)}\, ds,$$

and the integral is to be interpreted in the Stieltjes sense. If (43) is substituted into (41), we then obtain:

$$\text{(44)} \qquad \mu_l - \lambda_l(r, l) = \frac{(r-l)\Lambda_0(l) - \frac{1}{2}(\operatorname{var} l)\Lambda_2(l)}{\Lambda_1(l)},$$

and the unobservable factor risk premium may be replaced by the observable function in (44). If Q is a consol bond with coupons paid continuously at the rate c, then $\Lambda_0 = c/l$, $\Lambda_1 = -c/l^2$, $\Lambda_2 = 2c/l^3$, and (44) may be written as:[15]

$$\text{(45)} \qquad \mu_l - \lambda_l(r, l) = \frac{(\operatorname{var} l)}{l} + l(l-r).$$

These representations may be a useful starting point for empirical work. However, it is important to remember that they cannot be fully justified without considering the characteristics of the underlying economy. In the next section, we examine some additional multiple state variable models, all of which could be reexpressed in this form.

7. UNCERTAIN INFLATION AND THE PRICING OF NOMINAL BONDS

The model presented here deals with a real economy in which money would serve no purpose. To provide a valid role for money, we would have to introduce additional features which would lead far afield of our original intent. However, for a world in which changes in the money supply have no real effects, we can introduce some aspects of money and inflation in an artificial way by imagining that one of the state variables represents a price level and that some contracts have payoffs whose real value depends on this price level. That is, they are specified in nominal terms. None of this requires any changes in the general theory.

Suppose that we let the price level, p, be the kth state variable. Since we assume that this variable has no effect on the underlying real equilibrium, the functions α, μ, G, S, and J will not depend on p. Of course, this would not preclude changes in p from being statistically correlated with changes in real wealth and the other state variables. Under these circumstances, the real value of a claim whose payoff is specified in nominal terms still satisfies equation (4). All that needs to be done is to express the nominal payoff in real terms for the boundary conditions. Alternatively, the valuation equation (4) will also still hold if p is a differentiable function of W, Y, and t.[16]

[15] See Brennan and Schwartz [3] for this representation.

[16] If one wished to make real money balances an argument in the direct utility function U, it would be straightforward to do so in our model. A utility-maximizing money supply policy would depend only on the state variables, real wealth, and time, so the induced price level would depend only on these variables as well.

We can illustrate some of these points in the context of the model of Section 3. Let us take a second state variable to be the price level, $p(\equiv Y_2)$, and consider how to value a contract which will at time T pay with certainty an amount $1/p(T)$. Call this a nominal unit discount bond, and denote its value at time t in real terms as $N(r, p, t, T)$. Suppose that the price level p moves according to

$$(46) \qquad dp = \mu(p)\,dt + \sigma(p)\,dw_{n+2}(t)$$

and that it is uncorrelated with W and Y_1. Assume also that the coefficients in (45) are such that $E[p^{-1}(s)]$ exists for all finite s.

We would then have the valuation equation for N

$$(47) \qquad \tfrac{1}{2}\sigma^2 r N_{rr} + \tfrac{1}{2}\sigma^2(p) N_{pp} + [\kappa\theta - (\kappa+\lambda)r]N_r + \mu(p)N_p + N_t - rN = 0$$

with terminal condition $N(r, p, T, T) = 1/p(T)$. It can be directly verified that the solution is

$$(48) \qquad N(r, p, t, T) = P(r, t, T) \underset{p(t),t}{E}[1/p(T)]$$

where P is the price of a real discount bond given in (23).

In this formulation, the expected inflation rate changes only with the price level. For the commonly assumed case of lognormally distributed prices, however, $\mu(p) = \mu_p p$, $\sigma(p) = \sigma_p p$, and

$$(49) \qquad N(r, p, t, T) = e^{-(\mu_p - \sigma_p^2)(T-t)} P(r, t, T)/p(t),$$

so in this case the price of a nominal bond in nominal terms, $\hat{N} \equiv p(t)N$, would be independent of the current price level. With lognormally distributed prices, the expected inflation rate is constant, although of course realized inflation will not be.

As a somewhat more general example, we can separate the expected inflation rate factor from the price level factor and identify it with a third state variable. Again no change in the general theory is necessary. Label the expected inflation rate as y. We propose two alternative models for the behavior of the inflation rate: (i) Model 1,

$$(50) \qquad dy = \kappa_1 y(\theta_1 - y)\,dt + \sigma_1 y^{3/2}\,dz_3;$$

(ii) Model 2,

$$(51) \qquad dy = \kappa_2(\theta_2 - y)\,dt + \sigma_2 y^{1/2}\,dz_3$$

with the stochastic differential equation governing the movement of the price level being in each case

$$(52) \qquad dp = yp\,dt + \sigma_p p y^{1/2}\,dz_2$$

with $(\text{cov}\ y, p) \equiv \rho\sigma_1\sigma_p y^2 p$ in Model 1, $(\text{cov}\ y, p) \equiv \rho\sigma_1\sigma_p yp$ in Model 2, and $\sigma_p < 1$. Here, as in (17), we have for convenience defined $z_2(t)$ and $z_3(t)$ as the appropriate linear combinations of $w_{n+2}(t)$ and $w_{n+3}(t)$.

Model 1 may well be the better choice empirically, since informal evidence suggests that the relative (percentage) variance of the expected inflation rate increases as its level increases. Model 1 has this property, while Model 2 does not. However, the solution to Model 2 is more tractable, so we will record both for possible empirical use. In both models the expected inflation rate is pulled toward a long-run equilibrium level. Both models also allow for correlation between changes in the inflation rate and changes in the price level, thus allowing for positive or negative extrapolative forces in the movement of the price level.

The valuation equation for the real value of a nominal bond, specialized for our example with Model 1, will then be

$$\tag{53} \begin{aligned} &\tfrac{1}{2}\sigma^2 rN_{rr} + \tfrac{1}{2}\sigma_1^2 y^3 N_{yy} + \rho\sigma_1\sigma_p y^2 pN_{yp} + \tfrac{1}{2}\sigma_p^2 p^2 yN_{pp} + [\kappa\theta - (\kappa+\lambda)r]N_r \\ &\quad + \kappa_1 y(\theta_1 - y)N_y + ypN_p + N_t - rN = 0 \end{aligned}$$

with $N(r, y, p, T, T) = 1/p(T)$. The solution to equation (53) is

$$N(r, y, p, t, T) = \frac{\Gamma(\nu-\delta)}{\Gamma(\nu)}\left[\frac{c(t)}{y}\right]^{\delta} M\left(\delta, \nu, -\frac{c(t)}{y}\right) P(r, t, T)/p(t),$$

where

$$c(t) \equiv \frac{2\kappa_1\theta_1}{\sigma_1^2(e^{\kappa_1\theta_1(T-t)} - 1)},$$

$$\tag{54} \begin{aligned} &\delta \equiv [[(\kappa_1 + \rho\sigma_1\sigma_p + \tfrac{1}{2}\sigma_1^2)^2 + 2(1-\sigma_p^2)\sigma_1^2]^{1/2} - (\kappa_1 + \rho\sigma_1\sigma_p + \tfrac{1}{2}\sigma_1^2)]/\sigma_1^2, \\ &\nu \equiv 2[(1+\delta)\sigma_1^2 + \kappa_1 + \rho\sigma_1\sigma_p]/\sigma_1^2, \end{aligned}$$

$M(\cdot, \cdot, \cdot)$ is the confluent hypergeometric function, and $\Gamma(\cdot)$ is the gamma function.[17]

Proceeding in the same way with Model 2, we obtain the valuation equation:

$$\tag{55} \begin{aligned} &\tfrac{1}{2}\sigma^2 rN_{rr} + \tfrac{1}{2}\sigma_2^2 yN_{yy} + \rho\sigma_2\sigma_p ypN_{yp} + \tfrac{1}{2}\sigma_p^2 yp^2 N_{pp} + [\kappa\theta - (\kappa+\lambda)r]N_r \\ &\quad + \kappa_2[\theta_2 - y]N_y + ypN_p + N_t - rN = 0 \end{aligned}$$

with $N(r, y, p, T, T) = 1/p(T)$. The corresponding valuation formula is:

$$\tag{56} \begin{aligned} &N(r, y, p, t, T) \\ &= \left(\frac{2\xi e^{[(\kappa_2+\rho\sigma_2\sigma_p+\xi)(T-t)]/2}}{(\xi+\kappa_2+\rho\sigma_2\sigma_p)(e^{\xi(T-t)}-1)+2\xi}\right)^{2\kappa_2\theta_2/\sigma_2^2} \\ &\quad \times \exp\left(\frac{-2(e^{\xi(T-t)}-1)(1-\sigma_p^2)y}{(\xi+\kappa_2+\rho\sigma_2\sigma_p)(e^{\xi(T-t)}-1)+2\xi}\right) P(r, t, T)/p(t), \end{aligned}$$

where

$$\xi \equiv [(\kappa_2 + \rho\sigma_2\sigma_p)^2 + 2\sigma_2^2(1-\sigma_p^2)]^{1/2}.$$

[17] Slater [34] gives properties of the confluent hypergeometric function.

The term structure of interest rates implied by (54) and (56) can assume a wide variety of shapes, depending on the relative values of the variables and parameters. More complex models incorporating more detailed effects can be built along the same lines.

Throughout our paper, we have used specializations of the fundamental valuation equation (6). This equation determines the real value of a contingent claim as a function of real wealth and the state variables. For some empirical purposes, it may be convenient to have a corresponding valuation equation in which all values are expressed in nominal terms.

In our setting, this is given by the following proposition. In this proposition, we let nominal wealth be $X \equiv pW$, the indirect utility function in terms of nominal wealth be $V(X, Y, t) \equiv J(X/p, Y, t) \equiv J(W, Y, t)$, and the nominal value of a claim in terms of nominal wealth be $H(X, Y, t) \equiv pF(X/p, Y, t) \equiv pF(W, Y, t)$. As before, we let p be the kth element of Y.

PROPOSITION: *The nominal value of a contingent claim in terms of nominal wealth, $H(X, Y, t)$, satisfies the partial differential equation*

$$\begin{aligned} (57)\qquad & \tfrac{1}{2}(\operatorname{var} X)H_{XX} + \sum_{i=1}^{k} (\operatorname{cov} X, Y_i)H_{XY_i} + \tfrac{1}{2}\sum_{i=1}^{k}\sum_{j=1}^{k} (\operatorname{cov} Y_i, Y_j)H_{Y_iY_j} \\ & + (\iota X - pC^*)H_x + \sum_{i=1}^{k}\left[\mu_i - \left(\frac{-V_{XX}}{V_X}\right)(\operatorname{cov} X, Y_i)\right. \\ & \left. - \sum_{j=1}^{k}\left(\frac{-V_{XY_j}}{V_X}\right)(\operatorname{cov} Y_i, Y_j)\right]H_{Y_i} + H_t + p\delta - \iota H = 0, \end{aligned}$$

where the nominal interest rate, ι, is given by

$$(58)\qquad \iota = \alpha_X - \left(\frac{-V_{XY}}{V_X}\right)\left(\frac{\operatorname{var} X}{X}\right) - \sum_{i=1}^{k}\left(\frac{-V_{XY_i}}{V_X}\right)\left(\frac{\operatorname{cov} X, Y_i}{X}\right)$$

and α_X is the expected rate of return on nominal wealth,

$$(59)\qquad \alpha_X = a^{*\prime}\alpha + \left(\frac{\mu_p}{p}\right) + \left(\frac{\operatorname{cov} p, X}{pX}\right) - \left(\frac{\operatorname{var} p}{p^2}\right).$$

PROOF: Ito's multiplication rule implies that

$$(\operatorname{var} W) = (1/p^2)(\operatorname{var} X) - (2X/p^3)(\operatorname{cov} X, p) + (X^2/p^4)(\operatorname{var} p),$$

$$(\operatorname{cov} W, p) = (1/p)(\operatorname{cov} X, p) - (X/p^2)(\operatorname{var} p),$$

$$(\operatorname{cov} W, Y) = (1/p)(\operatorname{cov} X, Y) - (X/p^2)(\operatorname{cov} p, Y),$$

and

$$\alpha_X = a^{*\prime}\alpha + (\mu_p/p) + (1/pX)(\operatorname{cov} X, p) - (1/p^2)(\operatorname{var} p).$$

With

$$J(W, Y, t) \equiv J(X/p, Y, t) \equiv V(X, Y, t),$$

we have

$$(J_{WW}/J_W) = p(V_{XX}/V_X),$$
$$(J_{WY_i}/J_W) = (V_{XY_i}/V_X), \qquad \text{and}$$
$$(V_{Xp}/V_X) = -(1/p) - (X/p)(V_{XX}/V_X).$$

Equation (57) follows by writing the derivatives of $F(W, Y, t)$ in terms of those of $H(X, Y, t)$ and substituting all of the above into (6). The nominal interest rate can then be identified as the nominal payout flow necessary to keep the nominal value of a security identically equal to one, which is ι as given in (58).

Q.E.D.

A comparison of (57) and (58) with (6) and (3) shows that the interest rate equation and the fundamental valuation equation have exactly the same form when all variables are expressed in nominal terms as when all variables are expressed in real terms. By using the arguments given in the proof of the proposition, the nominal interest rate can be expressed in terms of real wealth as

$$\text{(60)} \qquad \iota = r + \left(\frac{1}{p}\right)\left[\mu_p - \left(\frac{-J_{WW}}{J_W}\right)(\text{cov } W, p) - \sum_{i=1}^{k}\left(\frac{-J_{WY_i}}{J_W}\right)(\text{cov } Y_i, p) - \left(\frac{\text{var } p}{p}\right)\right],$$

where r, the real interest rate, is as given by equation (3). The term (μ_p/p) is the expected rate of inflation. The remaining terms may in general have either sign, so the nominal interest rate may be either greater or less than the sum of the real interest rate and the expected inflation rate.[18]

8. CONCLUDING COMMENTS

In this paper, we have applied a rational asset pricing model to study the term structure of interest rates. In this model, the current prices and stochastic properties of all contingent claims, including bonds, are derived endogenously. Anticipations, risk aversion, investment alternatives, and preferences about the timing of consumption all play a role in determining the term structure. The model thus includes the main factors traditionally mentioned in a way which is consistent with maximizing behavior and rational expectations.

By exploring specific examples, we have obtained simple closed form solutions for bond prices which depend on observable economic variables and can be tested. The combination of equilibrium intertemporal asset pricing principles and appropriate modelling of the underlying stochastic processes provides a powerful tool for deriving consistent and potentially refutable theories. This is the first

[18] For a related discussion, see Fischer [**13**].

such exercise along these lines, and the methods developed should have many applications beyond those which we considered here.

In a separate paper, Cox, Ingersoll, and Ross [**5**], we use our approach to examine some aspects of what may be called traditional theories of the term structure. There we show that some forms of the classical expectations hypothesis are consistent with our simple equilibrium model and more complex ones, while other forms in general are not. We also show the relationship between some continuous time equilibrium models and traditional theories which express expected future spot rates as linear combinations of past spot rates.

Massachusetts Institute of Technology
and
Yale University

Manuscript received September, 1978; revision received October, 1984.

REFERENCES

[1] BEJA, A.: "State Preference and the Riskless Interest Rate: A Markov Model of Capital Markets," *Review of Economic Studies*, 46(1979), 435–446.

[2] BIERWAG, G. O., AND M. A. GROVE: "A Model of the Term Structure of Interest Rates," *Review of Economics and Statistics*, 49(1967), 50–62.

[3] BRENNAN, M. J., AND E. S. SCHWARTZ: "A Continuous Time Approach to the Pricing of Bonds," *Journal of Banking and Finance*, 3(1979), 133–155.

[4] CAGAN, P.: "The Monetary Dynamics of Hyperinflation," in *Studies in the Quantity Theory of Money*, ed. by M. Friedman. Chicago: University of Chicago Press, 1956.

[5] COX, J. C., J. E. INGERSOLL, JR., AND S. A. ROSS: "A Re-examination of Traditional Hypotheses about the Term Structure of Interest Rates, *Journal of Finance*, 36(1981), 769–799.

[6] ———: "An Intertemporal General Equilibrium Model of Asset Prices," *Econometrica*, 53 (1985), 363–384.

[7] CULBERTSON, J. M.: "The Term Structure of Interest Rates," *Quarterly Journal of Economics*, 71(1957), 485–517.

[8] DE LEEUW, F.: "A Model of Financial Behavior," in *The Brookings Quarterly Econometric Model of the United States*, ed. by J. S. Duesenberry et al. Chicago: Rand McNally, 1965.

[9] DIEFFENBACH, B. C.: "A Quantitative Theory of Risk Premiums on Securities with an Application to the Term Structure of Interest Rates," *Econometrica*, 43(1975), 431–454.

[10] DOTHAN, L. U.: "On the Term Structure of Interest Rates," *Journal of Financial Economics*, 6(1978), 59–69.

[11] DUESENBERRY, J. A.: *Business Cycles and Economic Growth.* New York: McGraw-Hill, 1958.

[12] FELLER, W.: "Two Singular Diffusion Problems," *Annals of Mathematics*, 54(1951), 173–182.

[13] FISCHER, S.: "The Demand for Index Bonds," *Journal of Political Economy*, 83(1975), 509–534.

[14] GERMAN, M. B.: "A General Theory of Asset Valuation Under Diffusion Processes," University of California, Berkeley, Institute of Business and Economic Research, Working Paper No. 50, 1977.

[15] HAKANSSON, N. H.: "Optimal Investment and Consumption Strategies under Risk for a Class of Utility Functions," *Econometrica*, 38(1970), 587–607.

[16] HICKS, J. R.: *Value and Capital*, 2nd edition. London: Oxford University Press, 1946.

[17] JOHNSON, N. L., AND S. KOTZ: *Distributions in Statistics: Continuous Univariate Distributions—2.* Boston: Houghton Miffin Company, 1970.

[18] LONG, J. B.: "Stock Prices, Inflation, and the Term Structure of Interest Rates," *Journal of Financial Economics*, 1(1974), 131–170.

[19] MALKIEL, B. G.: *The Term Structure of Interest Rates: Excpectations and Behavior Patterns.* Princeton, New Jersey: Princeton University Press, 1966.

[20] MEISELMAN, D.: *The Term Structure of Interest Rates.* Englewood Cliffs, New Jersey: Prentice Hall, 1962.

[21] MERTON, R. C.: "A Dynamic General Equilibrium Model of the Asset Market and Its Application to the Pricing of the Capital Structure of the Firm," Massachusetts Institute of Technology, Sloan School of Management, Working Paper No. 497-70, 1970.

[22] ———: "Optimum Consumption and Portfolio Rules in a Continuous Time Model," *Journal of Economic Theory,* 3(1971), 373-413.

[23] ———: "Theory of Rational Option Pricing," *Bell Journal of Economics and Management Science,* 4(1973), 141-183.

[24] MODIGLIANI, F., AND R. J. SHILLER: "Inflation, Rational Expectations and the Term Structure of Interest Rates," *Economica,* 40 N.S. (1973), 12-43.

[25] MODIGLIANI, F., AND R. SUTCH: "Innovations in Interest Rate Policy," *American Economic Review,* 56(1966), 178-197.

[26] NELSON, C. R.: *The Term Structure of Interest Rates.* New York: Basic Books, Inc., 1972.

[27] OLIVER, F. W. J.: "Bessel Functions of Integer Order," *Handbook of Mathematical Functions,* ed. by M. A. Abramowitz and I. A. Stegun. New York: Dover, 1965.

[28] RICHARD, S. F.: "An Arbitrage Model of the Term Structure of Interest Rates," *Journal of Financial Economics,* 6(1978), 33-57.

[29] ROLL, R.: *The Behavior of Interest Rates.* New York: Basic Books, Inc., 1970.

[30] ———: "Investment Diversification and Bond Maturity," *Journal of Finance,* 26(1971), 51-66.

[31] RUBINSTEIN, M. E.: "The Valuation of Uncertain Income Streams and the Pricing of Options," *Bell Journal of Economics,* 7(1976), 407-425.

[32] SAMUELSON, P. A.: "Lifetime Portfolio Selection by Dynamic Stochastic Programming," *Review of Economics and Statistics,* 51(1969), 239-246.

[33] SARGENT, T. J.: "Rational Expectations and the Term Structure of Interest Rates," *Journal of Money, Credit, and Banking,* 4(1972), 74-97.

[34] SLATER, L. J.: "Confluent Hypergeometric Functions," in *Handbook of Mathematical Functions,* ed. by M. Abramowitz and I. A. Stegun. New York: Dover, 1965.

[35] STIGLITZ, J. E.: "A Consumption-Oriented Theory of Demand for Financial Assets and the Term Structure of Interest Rates," *Review of Economic Studies,* 37(1970), 321-351.

[36] VAN HORNE, J. C.: "Interest-Rate Risk and the Term Structure of Interest Rates," *Journal of Political Economy,* 73(1965), 344-351.

[37] VASICEK, O. A.: "An Equilibrium Characterization of the Term Structure," *Journal of Financial Economics,* 5(1977), 177-188.

[38] WOOD, J. H.: "The Expectations Hypothesis, the Yield Curve and Monetary Policy," *Quarterly Journal of Economics,* 78(1964), 457-470.

[25]

Michael J. Brennan
Eduardo S. Schwartz
University of British Columbia

Evaluating Natural Resource Investments*

The evaluation of mining and other natural resource projects is made particularly difficult by the high degree of uncertainty attaching to output prices. It is shown that the techniques of continuous time arbitrage and stochastic control theory may be used not only to value such projects but also to determine the optimal policies for developing, managing, and abandoning them. The approach may be adapted to a wide variety of contexts outside the natural resource sector where uncertainty about future project revenues is a paramount concern.

Notwithstanding impressive advances in the theory of finance over the past 2 decades, practical procedures for capital budgeting have evolved only slowly. The standard technique, which has remained unchanged in essentials since it was originally proposed (see Dean 1951; Bierman and Smidt 1960), derives from a simple adaptation of the Fisher (1907) model of valuation under certainty: under this technique, expected cash flows from an investment project are discounted at a rate deemed appropriate to their risk, and the resulting present value is compared with the cost of the project. This standard textbook technique reflects modern theoretical developments only insofar as estimates of the discount rate may be obtained from crude application of single period asset pricing theory (but see Brennan 1973; Bogue and Roll 1974; Turnbull 1977; Constantinides 1978).

The inadequacy of this approach to capital budgeting is widely acknowledged, although not widely discussed. Its obvious deficiency is its

* Research support from the Corporate Finance Division of the Department of Finance, Ottawa, is gratefully acknowledged. We especially thank the referee whose insightful comments have enabled us to eliminate several errors and to improve the presentation. We also thank Robert Pyndyck, Rene Stulz, Suresh Sundaresan, Merton Miller, and participants at seminars in London, Stockholm, Stanford, and Los Angeles.

(*Journal of Business,* 1985, vol. 58, no. 2)
© 1985 by The University of Chicago. All rights reserved.
0021-9398/85/5802-0004$01.50

total neglect of the stochastic nature of output prices and of possible managerial responses to price variations. While price uncertainty is unimportant in applications for which the relevant prices are reasonably predictable, it is of paramount importance in many natural resource industries, where price swings of 25%–40% per year are not uncommon.[1] Under such conditions the practice of replacing distributions of future prices by their expected values is likely to cause errors in the calculation both of expected cash flows and of appropriate discount rates and thereby to lead to suboptimal investment decisions.

The model for the evaluation of investment projects presented in this paper treats output prices as stochastic. While this makes it particularly suitable for analyzing natural resource investment projects, where uncertain prices are a particular concern, the model may be applied in other contexts also. The model also takes explicit account of managerial control over the output rate, which is assumed to be variable in response to the output price; moreover, the possibility that a project may be closed down or even abandoned if output prices fall far enough is also considered. Variation in risk and the discount rate due both to depletion of the resource and to stochastic variation in the output price are explicitly taken into account in deriving the equilibrium condition underlying the valuation model.

Two essentially distinct approaches may be taken to the general problem of valuing the uncertain cash flow stream generated by an investment project. First, the market equilibrium approach requires both complete specification of the stochastic properties of the cash flow stream and an underlying model of capital equilibrium whose parameters are known.[2] A general limitation of this approach is that it is difficult to devise adequately powerful tests of the model of market equilibrium and to obtain refined estimates of the model parameters. In the present instance, the market equilibrium approach is further hampered by the difficulty of determining the stochastic properties of the cash flow stream that depend on the stochastic process of the output price: as we have already remarked, it is often very difficult to estimate the expected rate of change in commodity prices. Therefore in this paper we resort to a second approach, which yields the value of one security relative to the value of a portfolio of other traded securities.

Our approach is to find a self-financing portfolio whose cash flows replicate those which are to be valued.[3] The present value of the cash

1. Bodie and Rosansky (1980) report that the standard deviation of annual changes in futures prices over the period 1950–76 was 25.6% for silver, 47.2% for copper, and 25.2% for platinum.

2. See, e.g., the framework developed by Cox, Ingersoll, and Ross (1978); this was used by Brennan and Schwartz (1982*a*, 1982*b*) to analyze the valuation of regulated public utilities.

3. A self-financing portfolio has the property that its value at any time is exactly equal to the value of the investment and cash flow distributions required at that time. See

flow stream is then equal to the current value of this replicating portfolio. When a replicating self-financing portfolio can be constructed, our approach offers several advantages over the market equilibrium approach; not only does it obviate the need for a discount rate derived from an inadequately supported model of market equilibrium but, most important in the current context, it eliminates the need for estimates of the expected rate of change of the underlying cash flow and therefore of the output price.

Construction of the requisite replicating self-financing portfolio rests on the assumption that the convenience yield on the output commodity can be written as a function of the output price alone and that the interest rate is nonstochastic. These assumptions suffice to yield a deterministic relation between the spot and futures price of the commodity, and the cash flows from the project can then be replicated by a self-financing portfolio of riskless bills and futures contracts.

Specific limitations of the valuation model include the assumptions that the resource to be exploited is homogeneous and of a known amount, that costs are known, and that interest rates are nonstochastic. Any one of these assumptions may be relaxed at the expense of adding one further dimension to the state space on which the model is defined: as a practical matter it would be difficult to obtain tractable results if more than one of these assumptions were relaxed at a time. While the model as presented here presupposes the existence of a futures market in the output commodity, it would be straightforward to derive an analogous model in a general equilibrium context similar to that employed by Brennan and Schwartz (1982*a*, 1982*b*).

To allow for dependence of the output rate on the stochastic output price the capital budgeting decision is modeled as a problem of stochastic optimal control. Stochastic optimal control theory has been applied to the investment decision in a general context by Constantinides (1978), and in the specific context of a regulated public utility by Brennan and Schwartz (1982*a*, 1982*b*). Dothan and Williams (1980) have also analyzed the capital-budgeting decision within a similar framework. Pindyck (1980), like us, applies stochastic optimal control to the problem of the optimal exploitation of an exhaustible resource under uncertainty. In some respects Pindyck's analysis is more general than ours: in particular, he allows the level of reserves of the resource to vary stochastically and to be influenced by exploration activities. On the other hand, by confining his attention to risk-neutral firms he neglects the issues of risk and valuation that are the focus of the capital-budgeting decision and of this paper. Other writers who have recognized the importance of the option whether or not to exploit a natural

Harrison and Kreps (1979). The notion of a replicating self-financing portfolio is closely related to the option-pricing models of Black and Scholes (1973) and Merton (1973).

resource, which is inherent in the ownership of the resource, include Tourinho (1979); Brock, Rothschild, and Stiglitz (1982); and Paddock, Siegel, and Smith (1982). These writers have not however analyzed the present value of the decision to exploit a given resource or the optimal operating policy for a given facility, as we do, and Brock et al. do not exploit the arbitrage implications of a replicating self-financing portfolio.

Miller and Upton (1985) develop and test empirically a model for the valuation of natural resources based on the Hotelling model. Although it is close in spirit to our model, in that the spot price of the commodity is a sufficient statistic for the value of the mine, unlike ours their model assumes no upper limit on the output rate and ignores the possibility of closing and reopening the mine in response to current market conditions. As they point out this may be a good approximation when output prices exceed extraction costs by a wide margin, just as the value of a stock option approaches its intrinsic value when it is deep in the money.

The general type of model presented here lends itself to use in a number of related contexts—most obviously, to corporations considering when, whether, and how, to develop a given resource; to financial analysts concerned with the valuation of such corporations; and to policymakers concerned with the social costs of layoffs in cyclical industries and with policies to avert them. The model is well suited to analysis of the effects of alternative taxation, royalty, and subsidy policies on investment, employment, and unemployment in the natural resource sector.

Section I develops a general model for valuing the cash flows from a natural resource investment. A specialized version of the general model is presented in Section II. Under the assumption of an inexhaustible resource the model allows for only a single feasible operating rate when the project is operating but includes the possibility of costs of closing and reopening the project. Section III discusses a numerical example based on the general model. Section IV considers the problem, previously raised by Tourinho (1979), of the optimal timing of natural resource investments. Section V discusses briefly the application of the model to the analysis of fixed price long term purchase contracts for natural resources.

I. The General Valuation Model

The first step in analyzing an investment project is to determine the present value of the future cash flows it will generate and to compare this present value with the required investment. If the present value exceeds the investment a further decision is whether to proceed with the project immediately or to wait. We shall postpone consideration of this second, dynamic aspect of the capital-budgeting decision until Section III and in this and the following section will restrict our attention to the problem of determining the present value of the cash flows from a project. In this section we develop a general model, a specialization of which is considered in Section II.

To focus discussion we will suppose that the project under consideration is a mine that will produce a single homogeneous commodity, whose spot price, S, is determined competitively and is assumed to follow the exogenously given continuous stochastic process

$$\frac{dS}{S} = \mu\, dt + \sigma\, dz, \tag{1}$$

where dz is the increment to a standard Gauss-Wiener process; σ, the instantaneous standard deviation of the spot price, is assumed to be known; and μ, the local trend in the price, may be stochastic.

As a preliminary to developing the valuation model it will prove useful to consider the relation between spot and futures prices and the convenience yield on the commodity. The convenience yield is the flow of services that accrues to an owner of the physical commodity but not to the owner of a contract for future delivery of the commodity (see Kaldor 1939; Working 1948; Brennan 1958; Telser 1958). Most obviously, the owner of the physical commodity is able to choose where it will be stored and when to liquidate the inventory. Recognizing the time lost and the costs incurred in transporting a commodity from one location to another, the convenience yield may be thought of as the value of being able to profit from temporary local shortages of the commodity through ownership of the physical commodity. The profit may arise either from local price variations or from the ability to maintain a production process as a result of ownership of an inventory of raw material.[4]

The convenience yield will depend on the identity of the individual holding the inventory and in equilibrium inventories will be held by individuals for whom the marginal convenience yield net of any physical storage costs is highest. We assume that a positive amount of the commodity is always held in inventory, and note that competition among potential storers will ensure that the net convenience yield of the marginal unit of inventory will be the same across all individuals who hold positive inventories. This marginal (net) convenience yield can be expected to be inversely proportional to the amount of the commodity held in inventory. Moreover, when stocks of the physical commodity are high, not only will the marginal convenience yield tend to be low, but so also will be the spot price S, and conversely when

4. Cootner (1967, p. 65) defines the convenience yield of inventory as "the present value of an increased income stream expected as a result of conveniently large inventories." This contrasts with our definition of the convenience yield as a flow.

stocks of the physical commodity are low. We make the simplifying assumption that the marginal net convenience yield of the commodity can be written as a function of the current spot price and time, $C(S, t)$. Detailed modeling of the behavior of the convenience yield is beyond the scope of this paper, and in the interest of tractability we shall sometimes assume simply that the convenience yield is proportional to the current spot price.

Our assumption that the convenience yield is a function only of the current spot price, together with the further assumption which we maintain throughout the paper, that the interest rate is a constant, ρ, suffices to yield a determinate relation between the spot and futures prices of the commodity. Thus let $F(S, \tau)$ represent the futures price at time t for delivery of one unit of the commodity at time T where $\tau = T - t$. The instantaneous change in the futures prices is given from Ito's lemma by

$$dF = (-F_\tau + \tfrac{1}{2}F_{SS}\,\sigma^2S^2)\,dt + F_S\,dS. \tag{2}$$

Then consider the instantaneous rate of return earned by an individual who purchases one unit of the commodity and goes short $(F_S)^{-1}$ futures contracts. Since entering the futures contract involves no receipt or outlay of funds, his instantaneous return per dollar of investment including the marginal net convenience yield, using (2), is

$$\begin{aligned}\frac{dS}{S} + \frac{C(S)dt}{S} &- (SF_S)^{-1}dF \\ &= (SF_S)^{-1}[F_SC(S) - \tfrac{1}{2}F_{SS}\,\sigma^2S^2 + F_\tau]\,dt.\end{aligned} \tag{3}$$

Since this return to nonstochastic and since $C(S)$ is defined as the (net) convenience yield of the marginal unit of inventory, it follows that the return must be equal to the riskless return $\rho\, dt$. Setting the right hand side of (3) equal to $\rho\, dt$, we obtain the partial differential equation

$$\tfrac{1}{2}F_{SS}\,\sigma^2S^2 + F_S(\rho S - C) - F_\tau = 0. \tag{4}$$

Thus the futures price is given by the solution to (4) subject to the boundary condition

$$F(S, 0) = S. \tag{5}$$

This establishes that the futures price is a function of the current spot price and the time to maturity. Moreover, the parameters of the convenience yield function may be estimated directly from the relation between spot and futures prices. If the convenience yield is proportional to the spot price,

$$C(S, t) = cS, \tag{6}$$

then following Ross (1978) the futures price is given by

$$F(S, \tau) = Se^{(\rho - c)\tau}, \tag{7}$$

independent of the stochastic process of the spot price. For more general specifications of the convenience yield it is necessary to solve (4) and (5) directly.

Finally, using (4) in expression (2), the instantaneous change in the futures price may be expressed in terms of the convenience yield and the instantaneous change in the spot price as

$$dF = F_S[S(\mu - \rho) + C]dt + F_S S\sigma\, dz. \tag{8}$$

We are now in a position to derive the partial differential equation that must be satisfied by the value of the mine and to characterize the optimal output policy of the mine.

The output rate of the mine, q, is assumed to be costlessly variable between the upper and lower bounds $\overline{q}$ and $\underline{q}$.[5] The output rate can be reduced below $\underline{q}$ only by closing the mine, and it is costly both to close the mine and to open it again. For this reason the value of the mine will depend on whether it is currently open or closed. The value of the mine will also depend on the current commodity price, S; the physical inventory in the mine, Q; calendar time, t; and the mine operating policy, ϕ. We write the value of the mine as

$$H \equiv H(S, Q, t; j, \quad \phi). \tag{9}$$

The indicator variable j takes the value one if the mine is open and zero if it is closed. The operating policy is described by the function determining the output rate when the mine is open $q(S, Q, t)$, and three critical commodity output prices: $S_1(Q, t)$ is the output price at which the mine is closed down or abandoned if it was previously open; $S_2(Q, t)$ is the price at which the mine is opened up if it was previously closed; $S_0\ (Q, t)$ is the price at which the mine is abandoned if it is already closed. The distinction between closure and abandonment is that a closed mine incurs fixed maintenance costs but may be opened up again. An abandoned mine incurs no costs but is assumed to be permanently abandoned. It is assumed that abandonment involves no costs.

Applying Ito's lemma to (9), the instantaneous change in the value of the mine is given by

$$dH = H_S\, dS + H_Q\, dQ + H_t\, dt + \tfrac{1}{2}H_{SS}(dS)^2, \tag{10}$$

5. These bounds may depend on the amount of inventory remaining in the mine and time.

where the instantaneous change in the mine inventory is determined by the output rate

$$dQ = -q\,dt. \tag{11}$$

The after-tax cash flow, or continuous dividend rate, from the mine is

$$q(S - A) - M(1 - j) - \lambda_j H - T, \tag{12}$$

where

$A(q, Q, t)$ is the average cash cost rate of producing at the rate q at time t when the mine inventory is Q;

$M(t)$ is the after-tax fixed-cost rate of maintaining the mine at time t when it is closed;

$\lambda_j (j = 0, 1)$ is proportional rate of tax on the value of the mine when it is closed and open; and

$T(q,Q,S,t)$ is the total income tax and royalties levied on the mine when it is operating. While alternative forms are possible we shall assume that the tax function is

$$T(q, Q, S,t) = t_1 qS + \max\{t_2 q[S(1 - t_1) - A],0\}, \tag{13}$$

where

t_1 is the royalty rate and t_2 is the income tax rate.[6]

The parameters λ_0 and λ_1 are interpreted most simply as property tax rates. However an alternative interpretation may be apposite in some contexts: they may represent the intensities of Poisson processes governing the event of uncompensated expropriation of the owners of the mine. Then the expected loss rate from expropriation is $\lambda_j H$ and expression (12) represents the cash flow net of the expected cost of expropriation. Under this interpretation the arbitrage strategy outlined below is not entirely risk free; however, we shall assume that there is no risk premium associated with the possibility of expropriation.

To derive the differential equation governing the value of the mine under the output policy ϕ consider the return to a portfolio consisting of a long position in the mine and a short position in (H_S/F_S) futures contracts. The return on the mine is given by (10)–(12) and the change in the futures price is given by (8). Combining these and using (1), the return on this portfolio is

$$\begin{aligned} &\tfrac{1}{2}\sigma^2 S^2 H_{SS} - qH_Q + H_t + q(S - A) \\ &\qquad - M(1 - j) - T - \lambda_j H + (\rho S - C)H_s. \end{aligned} \tag{14}$$

6. For simplicity we have ignored depreciation tax allowances.

Ignoring the possibility of expropriation, this return is nonstochastic, and to avoid riskless arbitrage opportunities it must be equal to the riskless return on the value of the investment. Setting expression (14) equal to the riskless return ρH, the value of the mine must satisfy the partial differential equation

$$\tfrac{1}{2}\sigma^2 S^2 H_{SS} + (\rho S - C)H_S - qH_Q + H_t + q(S - A) - M(1 - j) - T - (\rho + \lambda_j) H = 0 \quad (j = 0, 1). \tag{15}$$

The mine value satisfies (15) for any operating policy $\phi \equiv \{q, S_0, S_1, S_2\}$. Under the value maximizing operating policy $\phi^* = \{q^*, S_0^*, S_1^*, S_2^*\}$, the values of the mine when open, $V(S, Q, t)$, and when closed, $W(S, Q, t)$ are given by

$$V(S, Q, t) \equiv \max_{\phi} H(S, Q, t;\ 1, \phi) \tag{16}$$

$$W(S, Q, t) \equiv \max_{\phi} H(S, Q, t;\ 0, \phi). \tag{17}$$

The value-maximizing output and the value of the mine under the value-maximizing policy satisfy the two equations

$$\max_{q \in (\underline{q}, \bar{q})} [\tfrac{1}{2}\sigma^2 S^2 V_{SS} + (\rho S - C)V_S - qV_Q + V_t + q(S - A) - T - (\rho + \lambda_1)V] = 0, \tag{18}$$

$$\tfrac{1}{2}\sigma^2 S^2 W_{SS} + (\rho S - C)W_S + W_t - M - (\rho + \lambda_0)W = 0 \tag{19}$$

(see Merton 1971, theorem 1; Fleming and Rishel 1975, chap. 6; Cox, Ingersoll, and Ross 1978, lemma 1).

Since the policies regarding opening, closing, and abandoning the mine are known to investors, we have

$$W(S_0^*, Q, t) = 0 \tag{20}$$

$$V(S_1^*, Q, t) = \max[W(S_1^*, Q, t) - K_1(Q, t), 0] \tag{21}$$

$$W(S_2^*, Q, t) = V(S_2^*, Q, t) - K_2(Q, t) \tag{22}$$

where $K_1(\cdot)$ and $K_2(\cdot)$ are the cost of closing and opening the mine respectively. Assuming that the value of an exhausted mine is zero we also have the boundary condition

$$W(S, 0, t) = V(S, 0, t) = 0. \tag{23}$$

Finally, since S_0^*, S_1^*, S_2^* are chosen to maximize the value of the mine it follows from the Merton-Samuelson high-contact condition (Samuelson 1965; Merton 1973) that

$$W_S(S_0^*, Q, t) = 0; \tag{24}$$

$$V_S(S_1^*, Q, t) = \begin{cases} W_S(S_1^*, Q, t) & \text{if } W(S_1^*, Q, t) - K_1(Q, t) \geq 0, \\ 0 & \text{if } W(S_1^*, Q, t) - K_1(Q, t) < 0; \end{cases} \tag{25}$$

$$W_S(S_2^*, Q, t) = V_S(S_2^*, Q, t). \tag{26}$$

The value of the mine depends on calendar time only because the costs A, M, K_1, and K_2 and the convenience yield C depend on time. If there is a constant rate of inflation π in all of these and if $C(S, t)$ may be written as κS, then equations (18)–(26) may be simplified as follows: Define the deflated variables

$$a(q, Q) = A(q, Q, t)\, e^{-\pi t},$$

$$f = M(t)\, e^{-\pi t},$$

$$k_1(Q) = K_1(Q, t)\, e^{-\pi t},\ k_2(Q) = K_2(Q, t)\, e^{-\pi t},$$

$$s = Se^{-\pi t},$$

$$v(s, Q) = V(S, Q, t)\, e^{-\pi t},$$

$$w(s, Q) = W(S, Q, t)\, e^{-\pi t}.$$

Then it may be verified that the deflated value of the mine satisfies

$$\max_{q \in (\underline{q}, \bar{q})} [\tfrac{1}{2} \sigma^2 s^2 v_{ss} + (r - \kappa) s v_s - q v_Q + q(s - a) - \tau - (r + \lambda_1) v] = 0, \tag{27}$$

$$\tfrac{1}{2} \sigma^2 s^2 w_{ss} + (r - \kappa) s w_s - f - (r + \lambda_0) w = 0, \tag{28}$$

where $r = \rho - \pi$ is the real interest rate,

$$\tau = t_1 q s + \max\{t_2 q[s(1 - t_1) - a], 0\}; \tag{29}$$

$$w(s_0^*, Q) = 0; \tag{30}$$

$$v(s_1^*, Q) = \max[w(s_1^*, Q) - k_1(Q), 0]; \tag{31}$$

$$w(s_2^*, Q) = v(s_2^*, Q) - k_2(Q); \tag{32}$$

$$w(s, 0) = v(s, 0) = 0; \tag{33}$$

$$w_s(s_0^*, Q) = 0; \tag{34}$$

$$v_s(s_1^*, Q) = \begin{cases} w_s(s_1^*, Q) & \text{if } w(s_1^*, Q, t) - k_1(Q, t) \geq 0, \\ 0 \text{ if } w(s_1^*, Q, t) - k_1(Q, t) < 0; \end{cases} \tag{35}$$

$$w_s(s_2^*, Q) = v_s(s_2^*, Q). \tag{36}$$

Equations (27)–(36) constitute the general model for the value of a mine. They suffice to determine not only the (deflated) value of the mine when open and closed, but also the optimal policies for opening, closing, and abandoning the mine and for setting the output rates. In general there exists no analytic solution to the valuation model, though it is straightforward to solve it numerically. In the next section we present a simplified version of the model.

II. The Infinite Resource Case

To obtain a model that is analytically tractable we assume that the physical inventory of the commodity in the mine, Q, is infinite. This infinite resource assumption enables us to replace the partial differential equations (27) and (28) for the value of the mine with ordinary differential equations, since the mine inventory, Q, is no longer a relevant state variable. To facilitate the analysis further we assume that the tax system allows for full loss offset so that (29) becomes

$$\tau(q, s) = t_1 qs + t_2 q[s(1 - t_1) - a]. \tag{29'}$$

Finally, we assume that the mine has only two possible operating rates, q^* when it is open, and zero when it is closed; furthermore, because it is costly to open or close the mine, costs must be incurred in moving from one output rate to the other.[7]

Under the foregoing assumptions the (deflated) value of the mine when it is open and operating at the rate q^* satisfies the ordinary differential equation

$$\tfrac{1}{2}\sigma^2 s^2 v_{ss} + (r - \kappa)sv_s + ms - n - (r + \lambda)v = 0, \tag{37}$$

where $m = q^*(1 - t_1)(1 - t_2)$, and $n = q^*a(1 - t_2)$.

If we assume that f, the periodic maintenance cost for a closed mine, is equal to zero, then the value of the mine when closed satisfies the corresponding differential equation

$$\tfrac{1}{2}\sigma^2 s^2 w_{ss} + (r - \kappa)sw_s - (r + \lambda)w = 0. \tag{38}$$

The boundary conditions are obtained by ignoring Q in (31), (32), (35), and (36) and by setting $w(0) = 0$.[8]

The complete solutions to equations (37) and (38) are

$$w(s) = \beta_1 s^{\gamma_1} + \beta_2 s^{\gamma_2}, \tag{39}$$

$$v(s) = \beta_3 s^{\gamma_1} + \beta_4 s^{\gamma_2} + \frac{ms}{\lambda + \kappa} - \frac{n}{r + \lambda}, \tag{40}$$

7. The App. develops the model under the neoclassical assumption of a continuously variable output rate with convex costs.

8. In the absence of maintenance costs it is never optimal to abandon a closed mine so long as there is a possibility that it will be optimal to reopen it. Hence $w(0) = 0$ and $w(s) > 0$ for $s > 0$.

where the β's are constants to be determined by the boundary conditions and

$$\gamma_1 = \alpha_1 + \alpha_2, \quad \gamma_2 = \alpha_1 - \alpha_2,$$

$$\alpha_1 = \tfrac{1}{2} - \frac{r - \kappa}{\sigma^2}, \quad \alpha_2 = \left[\alpha_1^2 + \frac{2(r + \lambda)}{\sigma^2}\right]^{1/2}.$$

If we assume that $(r + \lambda) > 0$,[9] then $\beta_2 = 0$ since γ_2 is negative and $w(s)$ must remain finite as s approaches zero. Similarly, since $\gamma_1 > 1$, $\beta_3 = 0$ if we impose the requirement that v/s remain finite as $s \to \infty$. Thus the value of the mine when closed is given by $w(s) = \beta_1 s^{\gamma_1}$, and the value when open is

$$v(s) = \beta_4 s^{\gamma_2} + \frac{ms}{\lambda + \kappa} - \frac{n}{r + \lambda}. \tag{41}$$

If the possibility of closing the mine when output prices are low is ignored, the value of the mine is given by the last two terms in (41); thus the first term represents the value of the closure option.

The remaining constants β_1 and β_4, as well as the optimal policy for closing and opening the mine represented by the output prices s_1^* and s_2^*, are determined by conditions (31), (32), (35), and (36), which imply that

$$\beta_1 = \frac{d\, s_2^*(\gamma_2 - 1) + b\gamma_2}{(\gamma_2 - \gamma_1)\, s_2^{*\gamma_1}}, \quad \beta_4 = \frac{d\, s_2^*(\gamma_1 - 1) + b\gamma_1}{(\gamma_2 - \gamma_1)\, s_1^{*\gamma_2}},$$

$$s_2^* = \gamma_2(e - bx^{\gamma_1})/(x^{\gamma_1} - x)\, d\, (\gamma_2 - 1),$$

$$\frac{s_1^*}{s_2^*} = x,$$

where $e = k_1 - n/(r + \lambda)$, $b = -k_2 - n/(r + \lambda)$, $d = m/(\lambda + \kappa)$, and x, the ratio of the commodity prices at which the mine is closed and opened, is the solution to the nonlinear equation

$$\frac{(x^{\gamma_2} - x)(\gamma_1 - 1)}{\gamma_1(e - bx^{\gamma_2})} = \frac{(x^{\gamma_1} - x)(\gamma_2 - 1)}{\gamma_2(e - bx^{\gamma_1})}. \tag{42}$$

The solution is illustrated in figure 1. In this figure the dotted line represents the present value of the cash flows from the mine assuming that it can never be shut down; this is obtained by setting $\beta_4 = 0$ in equation (42). Since $\gamma_2 < 0$, the value of the closure option diminishes and approaches zero for high output prices. For very low output prices the mine is worth more when it is closed than when it is open and making losses because of the cost of closure. However, for higher output prices the mine is worth more when open, and at the commodity

9. This is necessary for the present value of the future costs to be finite.

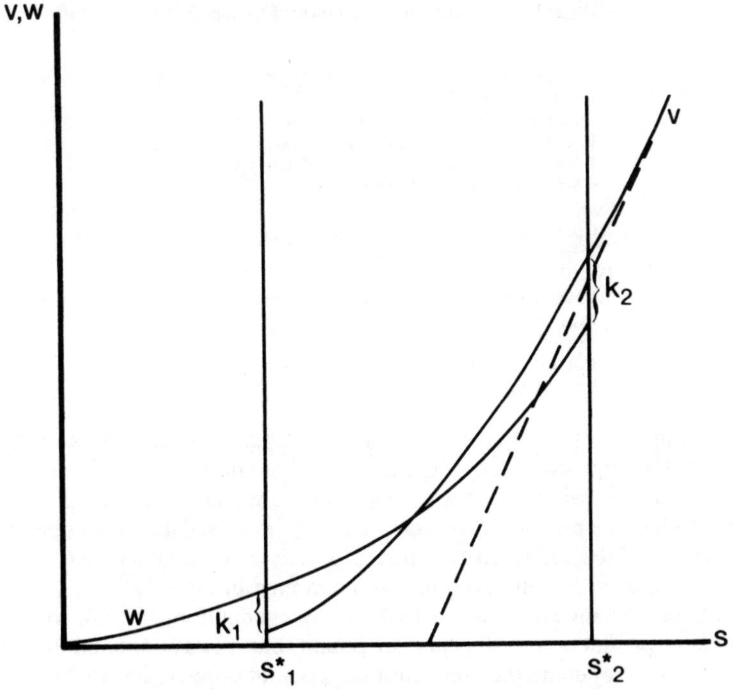

FIG. 1.—Mine value when open (v) and closed (w) as a function of the commodity price (s); k_1: cost of closing mine; k_2: cost of opening mine.

price s_2^* it is worth just enough more to warrant the outlay k_2 to open it. It is clear from the figure and can be demonstrated analytically that as the costs of opening and closing the mine approach zero, s_1^* and s_2^* approach the same value and the mine value schedule becomes a single curve. On the other hand, as the cost of mine closure becomes very large the closure option becomes worthless, and in the limit the value schedule for the open mine approaches the dotted line. Changes in the cost of mine closure, brought about for example by government regulation, will alter the optimal policy for closing the mine, s_1^*: however, they will also affect the original decision to invest in the mine by changing the present value of the future cash flows. Such effects, or those induced by changes in the tax regime, are readily analyzed in the context of this simplified model or the general model of the previous section.

III. An Example

To illustrate the nature of our solution we consider a mine example based on the stylized facts for copper. In this example there is a finite

TABLE 1 Data for a Hypothetical Copper Mine

Mine:	
	Output rate (q^*): 10 million pounds/year
	Inventory (Q): 150 million pounds
	Initial average cost of production $a(q^*, Q)$: \$0.50/pound
	Initial cost of opening and closing (k_1, k_2): \$200,000
	Initial maintenance costs (f): \$500,000/year
	Cost inflation rate (π): 8%/year
Copper:	
	Convenience yield (κ): 1%/year
	Price variance (σ^2): 8%/year
Taxes:	
	Real estate (λ_1, λ_2): 2%/year
	Income (t_2): 50%
	Royalty (t_1): 0%
	Interest rate (ρ): 10%/year

mine inventory so that the stochastic optimal control problem represented by equations (27)–(36) must be solved numerically. To simplify matters somewhat we assume that there is a single feasible operating rate when the mine is open. The mine may be closed down or opened at a cost of \$200,000 in current prices; it may also be abandoned. Other data required for this example are contained in table 1.[10]

Given an inventory equal to 15 years production, we find that the cost of production is 50 cents per pound, but it is not optimal to incur the cost of opening the mine until the price of copper rises to 76 cents. On the other hand, if the mine is already open and operating, it is not optimal to close it down until the copper price drops to 44 cents. Finally, the mine should be abandoned if the price drops below 20 cents. Obviously these critical prices depend on the assumed costs of opening, closing, and maintaining the mine: they also depend upon the remaining inventory in the mine. The greater the inventory in the mine the greater is the incentive to extract the copper immediately, since the opportunity cost of immediate extraction falls as the expected life of the mine increases. Thus the greater the inventory the lower is the price at which the mine is opened and closed and, since the mine value is a nondecreasing function of the inventory, the lower the price at which it is abandoned.

Table 2 summarizes the results when the mine has a 15-year inventory. Columns 1 and 3 give the present values of the future cash flows from the mine, assuming that it is open and closed, respectively, for different copper prices. These are the relevant values for the investment decision. Column 4 gives the value of the mine assuming that it

10. The variance rate and convenience yield used in table 1 compare with a variance rate for COMEX monthly settlement prices for copper of 7.8% per year for 1971–82 and an average convenience yield of 0.7% per year computed from annual data on the May contract for the same period, using eq. (7).

TABLE 2 Value of Copper Mine for Different Copper Prices

Copper Price ($/pound) (1)	Mine Value ($ million) Open (2)	Mine Value ($ million) Closed (3)	Value of Fixed-Output-Rate Mine ($ million) (4)	Value of Closure Option ($ million) (5)	Risk (6)	Value of Mine under Certainty, $\sigma^2 = 0$ ($ million) (7)
.30	(1.25)*	1.45	.38	1.07		0
.40	(4.15)*	4.35	3.12	1.23		0
.50	7.95	8.11	7.22	.89	.75	1.85†
.60	12.52	12.49	12.01	.51	.66	7.84†
.70	17.56	17.38	17.19	.37	.59	13.87†
.80	22.88	(22.68)†	22.61	.27	.54	19.91†
.90	28.38	(28.18)†	28.18	.20	.50	25.94†
1.00	34.01	(33.81)†	33.85	.16	.47	31.98†

* Optimal to close mine
† Optimal to open mine

cannot be closed down but must be operated at the rate of 10 million pounds per year until the inventory is exhausted in 15 years. The difference between column 4 and the greater of the values shown in columns 2 and 3 represents the value of the option to close down or abandon the mine if the price of copper falls far enough. The value of this closure option is shown in column 5: it amounts to 12% of the value of the fixed-output-rate mine when the copper price is equal to the variable cost of 50 cents per pound; of course this would represent a much higher proportion of the *net* present value of an investment in the mine.

Column 6 of the table reports the instantaneous risk of the mine at different copper prices. This is the instantaneous standard deviation of the mine value, defined as $(v_s/v)\sigma s$ when the mine is open and $(w_s/w)\sigma s$ when the mine is closed. As we would expect, the risk of the mine decreases as the copper price and hence the operating margin increases. Since the copper price is stochastic, so also is the risk of the mine and the instantaneous rate of return required by investors, pointing to the dangers of assuming a single discount rate in a present value analysis.

Ownership of a mine that is not currently operating involves three distinct types of decision possibilities or options: first, the decision to begin operations; second, the decision to close the mine when it is currently operating (and possibly to reopen it later), which we have referred to as the closure option; and third, the decision to abandon the mine early, before the inventory is exhausted.

The decision to begin operations depends in our model on the current spot price of the commodity and the mine inventory. When there is no uncertainty, so that the time path of the commodity price is deterministic, the optimal decision rule for beginning operations can be expressed in calendar time (and the mine inventory). This certainty case, which has been analyzed extensively under the rubric of the "timing option" (see, e.g., Solow 1974), corresponds to column 7, of table 2: this gives the value of the closed mine under the assumption of certainty, which may be contrasted with the uncertainty case of column 3. For our parameter values it is never optimal under certainty to close or abandon the mine, once it is open, before the inventory is exhausted,[11] so that the closure and early abandonment options are worthless. When the commodity price is in the neighborhood of the production costs the elimination of uncertainty reduces the value of the mine dramatically. Of course this depends on the particular values of the convenience yield and other parameters.

IV. The Investment Decision

Thus far, only the valuation of the cash flows from an investment project has been considered. The investment decision itself requires that a comparison be made between the present value of the project cash flows and the initial investment needed for the project. Continuing with the example of a mine, $V(S, Q^*, t)$ represents the (nominal) value at time t of a completed operating mine with inventory Q^* when the current output price is S; $V(\cdot)$ is equal to the present value of the cash flows that will be realized from the mine under the optimal operating policy. Similarly, let $I(S, Q^*, t)$ represent the investment required to construct an operating mine with inventory Q^* on a particular property: the amount of this initial investment may obviously depend on calendar time and upon the size of the mine as represented by Q^*, and S is included as an argument for the sake of generality. Then, assuming that construction lags can be neglected, the net present value (NPV) at time t of constructing the mine immediately is given by

$$\text{NPV}(S, Q^*, t) = V(S, Q^*, t) - I(S, Q^*, t). \tag{43}$$

However, once the possibility of postponing an investment decision is recognized, it is clear that it is not in general optimal to proceed with construction simply because the net present value of construction is positive: there is a "timing option" and it may pay to wait in the expectation that the net present value of construction will increase. This dynamic aspect of the investment decision is closely related to the problem of determining the optimal strategy for exercising an option on a share of common stock: the right to make the investment decision and to appropriate the resulting net present value is the ownership right in the undeveloped mine property, and the value of this ownership right corresponds to the value of the stock option.

Define $X(S, Q^*, t)$ as the value of the ownership right to an unde-

11. Because the commodity price is increasing faster than the production costs.

veloped mine with inventory Q^* at time t when the current output price is S. The stochastic process for $X(\cdot)$ is obtained from Ito's lemma, using the assumption about the stochastic process for S embodied in expression (1). Then the arbitrage argument used to derive the differential equation (15) for the value of a completed mine may be repeated to show that $X(\cdot)$ must satisfy the partial differential equation

$$\tfrac{1}{2}\,\sigma^2 S^2 X_{ss} + (\rho S - C)X_s + X_t - (\rho + \lambda)X = 0, \qquad (44)$$

where, as before, λ represents either the rate of tax on the value of the property or the intensity of a Poisson process governing the event of expropriation.[12]

Since the origin is an absorbing state for the commodity price, S, we have the boundary condition

$$X(0, Q^*, t) = 0, \qquad (45)$$

and if the ownership rights are in the form of a lease which expires at time T, then

$$X(S, Q^*, T) = 0. \qquad (46)$$

Assuming that the size of the mine inventory, Q^*, is predetermined by technical and geological factors, the optimal strategy for investment can be characterized in terms of a time dependent schedule of output prices $S^I(t)$ such that

$$X(S^I, Q^*, t) = V(S^I, Q^*, t) - I(S^I, Q^*, t), \qquad (47)$$

$$X_S(S^I, Q^*, t) = V_S(S^I, Q^*, t) - I_S(S^I, Q^*, t). \qquad (48)$$

Equation (47) states simply that the value of the property is equal to the net present value of the investment at the time it is made. Equation (48) is the Merton-Samuelson high-contact or envelope condition for a maximizing choice of S^I.

If the amount of the accessible inventory in the mine, Q^*, depends on the amount of the initial investment instead of being determined exogenously, then we have the additional value-maximizing condition to determine the size of the initial mine inventory, Q^*:

$$V_Q(S^I, Q^*, t) = I_Q(S^I, Q^*, t). \qquad (49)$$

Thus the optimal investment strategy is obtained by solving the partial differential equation (44) for the value of the ownership right, subject to boundary conditions (45)–(49). The optimal time to invest is determined by the series of critical output prices $S^I(t)$ described by (47) and (48); the optimal amount to invest is determined by the first order condition (49). Note that the boundary conditions for this problem

12. An alternative assumption is that all costs inflate at the common rate π; this would convert (44) into an *ordinary* differential eq. for the deflated mine value $x = Xe^{-\pi t}$.

involve $V(S, Q, t)$, the present value of the cash flows from a completed mine. Thus solving the cash flow valuation problem is a prerequisite for the investment decision analysis described in this section.

V. Long-Term Supply Contracts

It is not uncommon for the outputs of natural resource investments to be sold under long-term contracts that fix the price of the commodity but leave the purchase rate at least partially to the discretion of the purchaser. Where they exist, such contracts must be taken into account in valuing ongoing projects. Therefore in this section we show briefly how these contracts may be valued and the equilibrium contract price determined.

Let $Y(S, t;\; p, T)$ denote the value at time t of a particular contract to purchase the commodity up to time T at the contract price p, when the current spot price of the commodity is S. The contract is assumed to permit the purchaser to vary the price rate, q, between the lower and upper bounds $\underline{q}$ and $\bar{q}$. Since the commodity is by assumption available for purchase at the prevailing spot price S, ownership of the contract yields an instantaneous benefit or cash flow $q(S - p)$.

Using Ito's lemma and the stochastic process for S, the instantaneous change in the value of the contract is given by

$$dY = (\tfrac{1}{2}\sigma^2 S^2 Y_{ss} + Y_t)dt + Y_s\, dS. \tag{50}$$

Then an arbitrage argument analogous to that presented in Section I implies that the value of the contract must satisfy the partial differential equation:

$$\max_{q \in (\underline{q}, \bar{q})} [\tfrac{1}{2}\sigma^2 S^2 Y_{ss} + (\rho S - C)Y_s + Y_t + q(S - p) - \rho Y] = 0. \tag{51}$$

The value of the contract at maturity, $t = T$, is equal to zero, so that

$$Y(S, T;\; p, T) = 0. \tag{52}$$

In addition, the origin is an absorbing state for the spot price S. This implies that if $S = 0$, the holder of the contract must incur certain losses at the rate $\underline{q}p$ up to the maturity of the contract, so that

$$Y(0, t;\; p, T) = \frac{-p\underline{q}}{\rho}[1 - e^{-\rho(T-t)}]. \tag{53}$$

Finally, for sufficiently high values of S, the value of the right to vary the purchase rate approaches zero and the value of the contract approaches that of a series of forward contracts to purchase at the rate $\bar{q}$

at the fixed price p. Noting that forward and futures prices are equivalent when the interest rate is nonstochastic (see Cox et al. 1981; Jarrow and Oldfield 1981; Richard and Sundaresan 1981), this implies that

$$\lim_{S \to \infty} \frac{\partial Y(S, t;\ p, T)}{\partial S} = \frac{\partial}{\partial S} \int_0^{T-t} \bar{q}\, F(S, \tau)\, d\tau, \tag{54}$$

where $F(S, \tau)$ is the futures price for delivery in τ periods as defined previously.

The equilibrium contract price (or price schedule) is that which makes the value of the contract at inception equal to zero, given the prevailing spot price, S, and maturity, T. Writing the equilibrium contract price as $p^*(S, T)$, we have

$$Y[S, 0; p^*(S, T), T] = 0 \tag{55}$$

In general there does not exist a closed-form solution for $Y(\cdot)$ or $p^*(\cdot)$. However, if the convenience yield can be written as $C(s) = \kappa S$, then closed-form solutions may be obtained in two special cases.

First, if the purchaser has no discretion over the purchase rate, so that $\bar{q} = \underline{q} = q^*$, then the contract is equivalent to a series of forward contracts with value given by[13]

$$Y(S, t;\ p, T) = q^* \left\{ \frac{S}{\kappa} [1 - e^{-\kappa(T-t)}] - \frac{p}{\rho} [1 - e^{-\rho(T-t)}] \right\}. \tag{56}$$

This implies that the equilibrium contract price is

$$p^*(S, T) = \frac{\rho S}{\kappa} \left(\frac{1 - e^{-\kappa T}}{1 - e^{-\rho T}} \right). \tag{57}$$

Second, if the contract has an infinite maturity, the value of the contract is equal to the sum of the values of two assets we have already valued: a perpetual contract to purchase the commodity at the fixed rate $\underline{q}$ and a mine with infinite inventory, an average cost of production p, feasible production rates $\bar{q} - \underline{q}$, and with no taxes, maintenance costs, or costs of opening and closing. The former may be valued using equation (56) and the latter is a special case of Section II.[14] It can then be shown that

$$Y(S, t;\ p, \infty) = \begin{cases} \beta_1 S^{\gamma_1} + \underline{q} \left(\dfrac{S}{\kappa} - \dfrac{p}{\rho} \right), & S < p \\[2ex] \beta_4 S^{\gamma_2} = \bar{q} \left(\dfrac{S}{\kappa} - \dfrac{p}{\rho} \right), & S \geq p, \end{cases} \tag{58}$$

13. We thank the referee for this point.

14. As the referee remarks, this contract is equivalent to a perpetuity of European options on the commodity.

where

$$\beta_1 = \frac{1}{2\alpha_2\kappa}\left[1 - \gamma_2\left(\frac{\rho - \kappa}{\rho}\right)\right] q^d p^{1-\gamma_1},$$

$$\beta_4 = \frac{1}{2\alpha_2\kappa}\left[1 - \frac{\gamma_1}{\rho}(\rho - \kappa)\right] q^d p^{1-\gamma_2},$$

$$q^d = \bar{q} - \underline{q},$$

and γ_1, γ_2, and α_2 are as defined following equation (40). The equilibrium price $p^*(S, \tau)$ is found from the nonlinear equation obtained by setting either of the expressions (58) equal to zero.

VI. Conclusion

We have shown in the paper how assets whose cash flows depend on highly variable output prices may be valued and how the optimal policies for managing them may be determined by exploiting the properties of replicating self-financing portfolios. The explicit analysis rests on the assumption that such portfolios may be formed by trading in futures contracts in the output commodity, but the general approach can also be developed in a general equilibrium context if the relevant futures markets do not exist.

In addition to providing a rich set of empirical predictions for empirical research, this framework should be useful for the analysis of capital-budgeting decisions in a wide variety of situations in which the distribution of future cash flows is not given exogenously but must be determined by future management decisions.

Appendix

In contrast to the assumption of Section II that there are only two feasible output rates, zero and q^*, and that it is costly to shift from one to the other, we assume in this case that the output rate is continuously and costlessly variable between zero and $\bar{q}$; in keeping with this assumption, costs of opening and closing the mine are neglected and this renders the distinction between an open and a closed mine otiose.

We assume that no costs are incurred if the output rate is zero and that for positive output rates the total cost per unit time of the output rate q is $c(q) = q \cdot a(q) = a_0 + a_1 q + a_2 q^2$, where $a_1, a_2 > 0$; this represents a (linearly) increasing marginal cost schedule.

Using these assumptions in equation (27), the optimal output policy and the value of the mine satisfy

$$\tfrac{1}{2}\sigma^2 s^2 v_{ss} + (r - \kappa)vs + (1 - t_2)\max_{q\in(0,\bar{q})}[(1 - t_1)qs - a_0 - a_1 q - a_2 q^2, 0] - (r + \lambda)v = 0. \tag{A1}$$

Carrying out the maximization we find that the optimal output policy is

$$q^*(s) = \begin{cases} \bar{q} & s > \bar{s} \\ \dfrac{(1 - t_1)\, s - a_1}{2a_2} & \bar{s} > s > s^* \\ 0 & s \leq s^*, \end{cases}$$

where $s^* = (a_1 + 2\sqrt{a_0 a_2})/(1 - t_1)$ and $\bar{s} = (a_1 + 2a_2\bar{q})/(1 - t_1)$. Thus the optimal output policy maximizes the instantaneous profit rate; since the profit rate is zero when the output rate is zero, the output rate is positive whenever the net-of-royalty output price exceeds the minimum average cost of production.

The after-tax cash flow from the mine under the optimal output policy, $p(s)$, is given by

$$p(s) = \begin{cases} (1 - t_2)[(1 - t_1)\bar{q}s - a_0 - a_1\bar{q} - a_2\bar{q}^2] & s > \bar{s}, \\ (1 - t_2)\dfrac{(1 - t_1)(s - a_1)^2}{4a_2 - a_0} & \bar{s} > s > s^*, \\ 0 & s \leq s^*. \end{cases}$$

When $p(s)$ is substituted for the maximand in equation (A1), the complete solutions for the three regions are

$$v(s) = \beta_1 s^{\gamma_1} + \beta_2 s^{\gamma_2} \qquad s \leq s^*, \tag{A2}$$

$$v(s) = \beta_3 s^{\gamma_1} + \beta_4 s^{\gamma_2} + \delta(s) \qquad \bar{s} > s > s^*, \tag{A3}$$

$$v(s) = \beta_5 s^{\gamma_1} + \beta_6 s^{\gamma_2} + \frac{ms}{\lambda + \kappa} - \frac{n}{r + \lambda} \qquad s > \bar{s}, \tag{A4}$$

where

$$\delta(s) = \frac{(1 - t_2)}{r + \lambda}\left[\frac{a_1^2}{4a_2} - a_0\right] - \left[\frac{a_1(1 - t_1)(1 - t_2)}{2a_2(\lambda + c)}\right]s,$$
$$+ \left[\frac{(1 - t_1)^2 (1 - t_2)}{4a_2(\lambda + 2c - \sigma^2 - r)}\right]s^2,$$
$$m = \bar{q}(1 - t_1)(1 - t_2),$$
$$n = (1 - t_2)(a_0 + a_1\bar{q} + a_2\bar{q}^2).$$

Variables γ_1 and γ_2 are as defined following equation (40), and the coefficients β_i ($i = 1, \ldots, 6$) are constants determined as follows. As in the case of Section II the requirements that v and v/s remain finite for very small and very large s, respectively, imply that $\beta_2 = \beta_5 = 0$. The remaining four constants are obtained by solving the four linear equations yielded by imposing the condition that the valuation schedule $v(s)$ be continuous and have a finite second derivative at s^* and $\bar{s}$:

$$\beta_1 s^{*\gamma_1} = \beta_3 s^{*\gamma_1} + \beta_4 s^{*\gamma_2} + \delta(s^*), \tag{A5}$$

$$\gamma_1\beta_1 s^{*\gamma_1 - 1} = \gamma_1\beta_3 s^{*\gamma_1 - 1} + \gamma_2\beta_4 s^{*\gamma_2 - 1} + \delta'(s^*), \tag{A6}$$

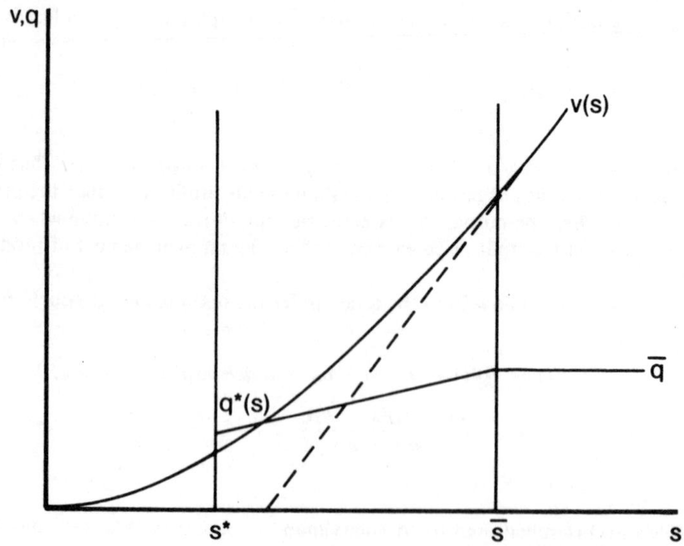

FIG. 2.—Case ii: Mine value (v) and optimal output as a function of the output price (s).

$$\beta_3\bar{s}^{\gamma_1} + \beta_4\bar{s}^{\gamma_2} + \delta(\bar{s}) = \beta_6\bar{s}^{\gamma_2} + \frac{m\bar{s}}{\lambda + \kappa} - \frac{n}{r + \lambda}, \tag{A7}$$

$$\gamma_1\beta_3\bar{s}^{\gamma_1 - 1} + \gamma_2\beta_4\bar{s}^{\gamma_2 - 1} + \delta'(\bar{s}) = \gamma_2\beta_6\bar{s}^{\gamma_2 - 1} + \frac{m}{\lambda + \kappa}. \tag{A8}$$

Thus the value of the mine is given by the solution to equations (A2)–(A8) with $\beta_2 = \beta_5 = 0$. Since the equation system (A5)–(A8) is linear it is a straightforward if tedious task to obtain an explicit valuation expression which may be used for comparative statics. The valuation schedule and the optimal output policy are illustrated in figure 2. In this figure the dotted line corresponds to the value of the mine if it is required to operate perpetually at its maximum rate $\bar{q}$: thus the difference between the $v(s)$ schedule and this line represents the value of the option to vary the output rate in response to changing output prices.

References

Bierman, H., and Smidt, S. 1960. *The Capital Budgeting Decision*. New York: Macmillan.

Black, F., and Scholes, M. 1973. The pricing of options and corporate liabilities. *Journal of Political Economy* 81 (May–June): 637–54.

Bodie, Z., and Rosansky, V. I. 1980. Risk and return in commodity futures. *Financial Analysts Journal* 36 (May–June): 27–40.

Bogue M. C., and Roll, R. 1974. Capital budgeting of risky projects with imperfect markets for physical capital. *Journal of Finance* 29 (May): 601–13.

Brennan, M. J. 1958. The supply of storage. *American Economic Review* 48 (March): 50–72.

Brennan, M. J. 1973. An approach to the valuation of uncertain income streams. *Journal of Finance* 28 (July): 661–73.

Brennan, M. J., and Schwartz, E. S. 1982*a*. Consistent regulatory policy under uncertainty. *Bell Journal of Economics* 13 (Autumn): 506–21.

Brennan, M. J., and Schwartz, E. S. 1982*b*. Regulation and corporate investment policy. *Journal of Finance* 37 (May): 289–300.

Brock, W. A.; Rothschild, M.; and Stiglitz, J. E. 1982. Stochastic capital theory. Financial Research Center Memorandum no. 40. Princeton, N.J.: Princeton University, April.

Constantinides, G. M. 1978. Market risk adjustment in project valuation. *Journal of Finance* 33 (May): 603–16.

Cootner, P. 1967. Speculation and hedging. *Food Research Institute Studies* 7 (Suppl.): 65–106.

Cox, J. C.; Ingersoll, J. E.; and Ross, S. A. 1978. A theory of the term structure of interest rates. Research Paper no. 468. Stanford, Calif.: Stanford University.

Cox, J. C.; Ingersoll, J. E.; and Ross, S. A. 1981. The relation between forward prices and futures prices. *Journal of Financial Economics* 9 (December): 321–46.

Dean, Joel 1951. *Capital Budgeting; Top Management Policy on Plant Equipment and Product Development*. New York: Columbia University.

Dothan, U., and Williams, J. 1980. Term-risk structures and the valuation of projects. *Journal of Financial and Quantitative Analysis* 15 (November): 875–906.

Fama, E. F. 1977. Risk-adjusted discount rates and capital budgeting under uncertainty. *Journal of Financial Economics* 5 (August): 3–24.

Fisher, Irving. 1907. *The Rate of Interest: Its Nature, Determination and Relation to Economic Phenomena*. New York: Macmillan.

Fleming, W. H., and Rishel, R. W. 1975. *Deterministic and Stochastic Optimal Control*. New York: Springer-Verlag.

Harrison, J. M., and Kreps, D. M. 1979. Martingales and arbitrage in multiperiod securities markets. *Journal of Economic Theory* 20:381–408.

Jarrow, R. A., and Oldfield, G. S. 1981. Forward contracts and futures contracts. *Journal of Financial Economics* 9 (December): 373–82.

Kaldor, N. 1939. Speculation and economic stability. *Review of Economic Studies* 7:1–27.

Merton, R. C. 1971. Optimum consumption and portfolio rules in a continuous time model. *Journal of Economic Theory* 3 (December): 373–413.

Merton, R. 1973. The theory of rational option pricing. *Bell Journal of Economic and Management Science* 4 (Spring): 141–83.

Miller, M. H., and Upton, C. W. 1985. A test of the Hotelling valuation principle. *Journal of Political Economy* 93 (February): in press.

Myers, S. C., and Turnbull, S. M. 1977. Capital budgeting and the capital asset pricing model: Good news and bad news. *Journal of Finance* 32 (May): 321–32.

Paddock, J. L.; Siegel, D. R.; and Smith, J. L. 1982. Option valuation of claims on physical assets: The case of off-shore petroleum leases. Unpublished manuscript. Evanston, Ill.: Northwestern University.

Pindyck, R. S. 1980. Uncertainty and exhaustible resource markets. *Journal of Political Economy* 88 (December): 1203–25.

Richard, S. F., and Sundaresan, M. 1981. A continuous time equilibrium model of forward prices and futures prices in a multigood economy. *Journal of Financial Economics* 9 (December): 347–72.

Ross, S. A. 1978. A simple approach to the valuation of risky streams. *Journal of Business* 51 (July): 453–75.

Samuelson, P. A. 1965. Rational theory of warrant pricing. *Industrial Management Review* 6 (Spring): 3–31.

Solow, R. M. 1974. The economics of resources or the resources of economics. *American Economic Review* 64 (May): 1–14.

Telser, L. G. 1958. Futures trading and the storage of cotton and wheat. In A. E. Peck, ed., *Selected Writings on Future Markets*. Chicago, 1977.

Tourinho, O. A. F. 1979. The option value of reserves of natural resources. Unpublished manuscript. Berkeley: University of California.

Working, H. 1948. The theory of price of storage. *Journal of Farm Economics* 30:1–28. Reprinted in *Selected Writings of Holbrook Working*. Chicago: Chicago Board of Trade, 1977.

Name Index